Rand Morimoto, Ph.D., MCITP, MVP
Michael Noel, MVP, MCITP
Guy Yardeni, MCITP, CISSP, MVP
Omar Droubi, MCSE, MCTS
Andrew Abbate, MCITP
Chris Amaris, MCITP, MCTS, CISSP
Technical Edit by Tyson Kopczynski, CISSP, GCIH

Windows Server® 2012

UNLEASHED

SAMS | 800 East 96th Street, Indianapolis, Indiana 46240 USA

Windows Server® 2012 Unleashed

ISBN-13: 978-0-672-33622-5
ISBN-10: 0-672-33622-7

Library of Congress Cataloging-in-Publication Data is on file.

Printed in the United States of America
Third Printing June 2013

Trademarks

Warning and Disclaimer

Bulk Sales

Sams Publishing offers excellent discounts on this book when ordered in quantity for bulk purchases or special sales. For more information, please contact

U.S. Corporate and Government Sales
1-800-382-3419
corpsales@pearsontechgroup.com

For sales outside of the U.S., please contact

International Sales
international@pearsoned.com

Editor-in-Chief
Greg Wiegand

Executive Editor
Neil Rowe

Development Editor
Mark Renfrow

Managing Editor
Kristy Hart

Project Editor
Andrew Beaster

Copy Editor
Keith Cline

Indexer
Brad Herriman

Proofreader
Jess DeGabriele

Technical Editor
Tyson Kopczynski

Publishing Coordinator
Cindy Teeters

Interior Designer
Gary Adair

Cover Designer
Anne Jones

Compositor
Nonie Ratcliff

Contributing Writers
Colin Spence
Yasu SabaLin
Aman Ayaz
Peter Handley

Table of Contents

Contents at a Glance

About the Authors

Rand Morimoto, Ph.D., MVP, MCITP, CISSP, has been in the computer industry for more than 30 years and has authored, coauthored, or been a contributing writer for dozens of books on Windows, Security, Exchange, BizTalk, and Remote and Mobile Computing. Rand is the president of Convergent Computing, an IT-consulting firm in the San Francisco Bay area that has been one of the key early adopter program partners with Microsoft, implementing the latest Microsoft technologies, including Microsoft Windows Server 2008 R2, System Center 2012, Windows 7, Exchange Server 2013, Windows Server 2012, and SharePoint 2010 in production environments more than 18 months before the initial product releases.

Michael Noel, MCITP, MVP, is an internationally recognized technology expert, best-selling author, and well-known public speaker on a broad range of IT topics. He authored multiple major industry books that have been translated into more than a dozen languages worldwide. Michael has presented at over one hundred technical and business conferences in more than fifty countries around the world and on all seven continents, including the first ever IT conference in Antarctica. Currently a partner at Convergent Computing (www.cco.com) in the San Francisco Bay area, Michael's writing and extensive public-speaking experience across all seven continents leverage his real-world expertise in helping organizations realize business value from Information Technology infrastructure.

Guy Yardeni, MCITP, CISSP, MVP, is an accomplished infrastructure architect, author, and overall geek-for-hire. Guy has been working in the IT industry for more than 15 years and has extensive experience designing, implementing, and supporting enterprise technology solutions. Guy is an expert at connecting business requirements to technology solutions and driving to successful completion the technical details of the effort while maintaining overall goals and vision. Guy maintains a widely read technical blog at www.rdpfiles.com and is a Windows MVP.

Omar Droubi, MCSE, MCTS, has maintained a successful career and delivered quality work as a senior Information Technology professional for more than 20 years by keeping current with the latest technological developments and trends. As a writer, he has coauthored several Sams Publishing best-selling books, including *Microsoft Windows Server 2003 Unleashed, Windows Server 2008 Unleashed,* and *Windows Server 2008 R2 Unleashed*. Omar has also been a contributing writer and technical reviewer on several Microsoft Exchange Server books and publications. He has been deeply involved in testing, designing, and prototyping Windows 8 and Windows Server 2012 for the past several years and plans to assist organizations in getting the most out of the latest features included in the products.

Andrew Abbate enjoys the position of principal consultant and partner at Convergent Computing. With nearly 20 years of experience in IT, Andrew's area of expertise is understanding a business's needs and translating that to process and technologies to solve real problems. Having worked with companies from the Fortune Ten to companies of 10,

Andrew has a unique perspective on IT and a grasp on "big picture" consulting. Andrew has also written eight industry books on varying technologies ranging from Windows to Security to Unified Communications.

Chris Amaris, MCITP, MCTS, CISSP/ISSAP, CHS III, is the chief technology officer and cofounder of Convergent Computing. He has more than 20 years experience consulting for Fortune 500 companies, leading companies in the technology selection, design, planning, and implementation of complex information technology projects. Chris has worked with Microsoft System Center products such as Operations Manager and Configuration Manager since their original releases in 2000 and 1994. He specializes in messaging, security, performance tuning, systems management, and migration. Receiving his first Microsoft technologies certification in 1993, Chris is a current Microsoft Certified IT Professional (MCITP) with multiple Microsoft Certified Technology Specialist (MCTS) certifications in System Center technologies, a Certified Information Systems Security Professional (CISSP) with an Information System Security Architecture Professional (ISSAP) concentration, Certified Homeland Security (CHS III), a Novell CNE, a Banyan CBE, and a Certified Project Manager. Chris is also an author, writer, and technical editor for a number of IT books, including *System Center 2012 Unleashed, Network Security for Government and Corporate Executives, Exchange 2010 Unleashed,* and *Microsoft Windows Server 2008 R2 Unleashed.*

Dedication

I dedicate this book to the two eldest kids, Noble and Kelly; may you lead the way for yourselves and your siblings with the finest examples of hard work, dedication, and determination in all you do!

—Rand Morimoto, Ph.D., MVP, MCITP, CISSP

This book is dedicated to my brother David. Your fun-loving and resourceful attitude is an inspiration to the rest of us.

—Michael Noel, MCSE+I, CISSP, MCSA, MVP

I dedicate this book to my wonderful wife, Allison, who puts up with the insanity of writing these books and to my two daughters, Maya Aviv and Zoe Carmel, who are the motivation and inspiration for the work.

—Guy Yardeni, MCSE, MCITP, CISSP

I dedicate this book to the one who constantly reminds me to save my work and lock my workstation, Jamil K. Droubi (aka Little Hacker).

—Omar Droubi, MCSE, MCTS

This book is dedicated to my girlfriend Erika Halstead and the rest of "Team Petting Zoo." Thanks for being OK with weekends where I had to disappear to write. I couldn't have done it without your support... .

—Andrew Abbate, MCITP

I dedicate this book to my wife, Sophia, light of my life. And to my children, Michelle, Megan, Zoe, Zachary, and Ian, who give meaning to my life and work.

—Chris Amaris, MCITP, MCTS, CISSP/ISSAP, CHS III

I dedicate this book to my son, Morgan, and his wonderful mother, Maiko. Despite a massive earthquake, nuclear meltdowns, and the general craziness that followed, you have both provided me with a central focus of stability from which I have drawn upon to hold it all together.

—Tyson Kopczynski, CISSP, GCIH

Acknowledgments

Rand Morimoto, Ph.D., MVP, MCITP, CISSP A note of thanks to the Windows 8 (Server 2012) TAP and product teams for all your support to our early adopter clients in your making a solid product! After a couple years of slugging through the features and functions, by the time Windows Server 2012 shipped to the public, it was truly enterprise ready—so great to see!

I want to thank the team at Sams Publishing for continuing to support our writing efforts and turning this book around and out to print in record time! Thank you, Neil, Mark, Andy, Keith, and all the folks behind the scenes in making this happen!

I also wanted to thank the consultants at Convergent Computing and our early adopter clients who fiddle with these new technologies really early on and then take the leap of faith in putting the products into production to experience (and at times feel the pain) as we work through best practices. The early adopter experiences give us the knowledge and experience we need to share with all who use this book as their guide in their production environments based on the lessons learned.

To Kelly, Noble, Chip, and Eduardo: Two down, one more book to go before the year is up! Remember to work hard at everything you do; as you've found so far, you can accomplish a lot when you put your mind to things!

Michael Noel, MCITP, MVP It's now been a decade since I first got involved in the business of writing computer books, and indeed the *Windows Unleashed* series was the first series I wrote those many years ago. I can tell you one thing: These volumes are the result of a great deal of blood, sweat, and tears, and I am extremely fortunate to have had the backing of a great team at Sams Publishing over the years, especially my good friend and editor, Neil Rowe, but also including the rest of the fantastic group of people who work behind the scenes to make books like this a reality.

On that note, this book offers a great debt of gratitude to lead author, Rand Morimoto, whom I've had the pleasure of working with for more than a decade now. At the same time, I'm grateful for the help of the other authors and contributing writers who get involved, particularly several of my coworkers at CCO—great work, everyone!

I'd also like to thank the many people who have attended my conferences and events over the past years, all around the world. I find it fascinating that we all live different lives in different cultures but are tied together with the same technical challenges that all IT workers worldwide face.

And last but not least, a huge thanks to my wonderful family for putting up with all of the book writing, public speaking, and late nights working in the lab. My wonderful wife, Marina; my beautiful daughter, Julia; my parents, George and Mary; and my most amazing in-laws, Val and Liza. I love all of you dearly!

Guy Yardeni, MCITP, CISSP I want to first and foremost thank Rand for the opportunity to join another book team and for the ridiculous amount of work he puts in to keep a group of authors moving ahead and focused on target.

I also want to thank Microsoft's TAP team for providing the information and support that makes writing these books a much easier and more enjoyable process. To the folks at Sams publishing, especially Neil and Cindy for their efforts and assistance in making the project happen and making sure we get paid.

And another thanks to my family because they bear the brunt of my stress and craziness during the writing process. I couldn't have done this without you.

Omar Droubi I would like to thank and acknowledge many of my customers, business associates, friends, and family for the support and inspiration they give me. I would also like to thank Rand Morimoto, Sams Publishing, and the other coauthors and contributing writers of this book and my previous books. I would like to acknowledge my brother, Hadi Droubi; my wife, Colby; and Khalil and Jamil for all the family love and support. To Sherre England, Raul Alcaraz, Rick Hernandez, thanks for helping me build my business and complete my writing assignments.

Andrew Abbate, MCITP I think this is book #8 for me, and I continue to be amazed at the amount of work that goes into these things. Sometimes I think that we, as authors, have the easy part. We get to just sit back and talk about the same geekery that we'd be talking about anyway. It's the team of editors and reviewers and techies at Sams that turn our ramblings into an amazing product; as always, I'd like to thank them for another opportunity to get our ideas and words out to such a wide audience. I'd also like to thanks all the clients I've worked with over the years, as a fair amount of the knowledge and experience that go into these books came from them. I'm truly blessed to work in an industry where I can both learn and teach every day.

Chris Amaris, MCSE, MVP, CISSP Writing these books is a lot like eating really spicy food. You think it sounds like fun when the idea comes up, you wonder what you were thinking in the middle of it, and you think "Yeah, I did it!" when it is all over. I want to thank Rand Morimoto for once again letting me back in the game at a Scoville rating of 100,000.

I would also like to thank Sophia for handling all the myriad of family tasks such as driving to math classes, games, and practices and cooking dinners while I scrambled to meet deadlines. I could not do it without you.

We Want to Hear from You!

As the reader of this book, *you* are our most important critic and commentator. We value your opinion and want to know what we're doing right, what we could do better, what areas you'd like to see us publish in, and any other words of wisdom you're willing to pass our way.

You can email or write me directly to let me know what you did or didn't like about this book—as well as what we can do to make our books stronger.

Please note that I cannot help you with technical problems related to the topic of this book, and that due to the high volume of mail I receive, I might not be able to reply to every message.

When you write, please be sure to include this book's title and author as well as your name and phone or email address. I will carefully review your comments and share them with the author and editors who worked on the book.

E-mail: feedback@samspublishing.com

Mail: Neil Rowe
xecutive Editor
Sams Publishing
800 East 96th Street
Indianapolis, IN 46240 USA

Reader Services

Visit our website and register this book at informit.com/register for convenient access to any updates, downloads, or errata that might be available for this book.

Introduction

Every couple of years, Microsoft releases a new version of Windows Server, and if you don't keep tabs on the differences between versions, entire new feature sets become available without you being aware. One thing that we have seen lately is that the newer versions of Windows improve performance, reliability, and scalability, partly because of the new features of Windows and partly because of advances in hardware systems and technologies. Sure enough, with Windows Server 2012, server hardware has increased in capacity. So, just by the nature of the equipment Windows is being installed on, the systems can host a lot more applications, support more users per system, and just overall do more than earlier versions of Windows.

This is where Windows Server 2012 comes in to play, where it takes advantage of the hardware. We've had the opportunity to write a book on every version of Windows Server over the past 2 decades, and when we set out to write this book, we wanted to once again provide you, the reader, with a lot of really valuable information. Instead of just marketing fluff that talks about features and functions, we wanted to really dig down into the product and share with you best practices on planning, preparing, implementing, migrating, and supporting a Windows Server 2012 environment.

Even though Windows Server 2012 released midway through 2012, we've been fortunate enough to work with Windows Server 2012 and Windows 8 Client for more than 2 years in priority early-adopter programs. The thing about being involved with a product so early on is that our first experiences with these products were without any documentation, Help files that provided guidance, or any shared experiences from others. We had to learn Windows Server 2012 from experience, usually the hard way, but that has given us a distinct advantage of knowing the product forward and backward better than anyone could ever imagine. And we started to implement Windows Server 2012 in production environments for a select group of our enterprise customers over 18 months before the product release—where organizations were depending on the server operating system to run key areas of their business.

So the pages of this book are filled with years of experience with Windows Server 2012, live production environment best practices, and fully updated with Release to Manufacturing (RTM) code specifics that will hopefully help you design, plan, prototype, implement, migrate, administer, and support your Windows Server 2012 environment.

This book is organized into 11 parts, each part focusing on core Windows Server 2012 areas, with several chapters making up each part. The parts of the book are as follows:

- **Part I: Windows Server 2012 Overview**—This part provides an introduction to Windows Server 2012 to give not only a general technology overview but also to note what is truly new in Windows Server 2012 that made it compelling enough for organizations to implement the technology in beta in production environments. We also cover basic planning, prototype testing, and migration techniques, and provide a full chapter on the installation of Windows Server 2012 and the GUI-less Windows Server Core.

- **Part II: Windows Server 2012 Active Directory**—This part covers Active Directory planning and design. If you have already designed and implemented your Active Directory, you will likely not read through this section of the book in detail. However, you might want to look through the notes and tips throughout the chapters and the best practices at the end of each chapter because we highlight some of the tips and tricks new to Windows Server 2012 that differ from earlier versions of Windows. You might find that limitations or restrictions you faced when designing and implementing Active Directory 2003 and 2008 have now been updated. Topics such as federated forests, lightweight directory services, and identity lifecycle management capabilities might be of interest.
- **Part III: Networking Services**—This part covers domain name system (DNS), Dynamic Host Configuration Protocol (DHCP), domain controllers, IPv6, IP Address Management (IPAM), and Internet Information Services (IIS) from the perspective of planning, integrating, migrating, and coexisting. Again, just like in Part II, you might find the notes, tips, and best practices to have valuable information on features that are new in Windows Server 2012; you might find yourself perusing these chapters to understand what's new and different that you can leverage after a migration to Windows Server 2012.
- **Part IV: Security**—Security is on everyone's mind these days, so it was a major enhancement to Windows Server 2012. We actually dedicated three chapters of the book to security, breaking the information into server-level security such as public key infrastructure (PKI) certificate services; transport-level security such as IP Security (IPsec) and Network Address Translation-Traversal (NAT-T); and security policies, Network Access Protection (NAP), and Network Policy Server (NPS) as updated in Windows Server 2012.
- **Part V: Migrating to Windows Server 2012**—This part is dedicated to the migrations from Windows 2003 and 2008 to Windows Server 2012. We provide a chapter specifically on tips, tricks, best practices, and lessons learned on the planning and migration process to Windows Server 2012. We also have a chapter on application-compatibility testing of applications currently running on earlier versions of Windows Server and how to test and migrate applications to a Windows Server 2012 platform.
- **Part VI: Windows Server 2012 Administration and Management**—After you get Windows Server 2012 in place, you end up spending the rest of your time managing and administering the new operating system platform. So, we've dedicated six chapters to administration and management. This section covers the administration and management of users, sites, organizational units, domains, and forests typical of a Windows Server 2012 environment. Although you can continue to perform tasks the way you did in earlier versions of Windows, because of significant changes in replication, background transaction processing, secured communications, group policy

management, and Windows PowerShell management tools, there are better ways to work with Windows Server 2012. The biggest change is the new Server Manager console where installation, configuration, and management tasks are centralized. These chapters drill down into specialty areas helpful to administrators of varying levels of responsibility. This part of the book also has a chapter on managing Windows Server 2012 using System Center Operations Manager 2012.

- **Part VII: Remote and Mobile Technologies**—Mobility is a key improvement in Windows Server 2012, so this part focuses on enhancements made to Routing and Remote Access Service (RRAS) and so significant improvements in Remote Desktop Services (formerly Terminal Services) and highlights improvements in DirectAccess. Instead of just providing a remote node connection, Windows Server 2012 provides true end-to-end secured anytime/anywhere access functionality. The chapters in this part highlight best practices on implementing and leveraging these technologies.
- **Part VIII: Desktop Administration**—Another major enhancement in Windows Server 2012 is the variety of new tools provided to support better desktop administration. So, this part focuses on desktop administration. The chapters in this part go in depth on client-specific group policies, the Group Policy Management Console, Active Directory Administrative Center, Windows PowerShell-based group policies, Windows Deployment Services (WDS), and desktop administration tools in Windows Server 2012.
- **Part IX: Fault-Tolerance Technologies**—Because networks have become the backbone for information and communications, Windows Server 2012 needed to be reliable and more manageable, and sure enough, Microsoft included several new enhancements in fault-tolerant technologies. The four chapters in this part address file system management and file-level fault tolerance in Distributed File System (DFS), clustering, network load balancing, and backup and restore procedures. When these new technologies are implemented in a networking environment, an organization can truly achieve enterprise-level reliability and recoverability.
- **Part X: Optimizing, Tuning, Debugging, and Problem Solving**—This part of the book covers performance optimization, capacity analysis, logging, and debugging to help optimize and solve problems in a Windows Server 2012 networking environment.
- **Part XI: Integrated Windows Application Services**—The last part of this book covers core application services integrated in Windows Server 2012, including updates to Windows SharePoint Services and Windows Media Services, and wrapping up with a big chapter on Hyper-V virtualization, which Microsoft has made huge improvements in terms of high availability, redundancy, site replication, guest session management, and the like.

It is our hope that the real-world experience we have had working with Windows Server 2012 and our commitment to relaying to you information that will be valuable in your planning, implementation, and migration to a Windows Server 2012 environment will help you get up-to-speed on the latest in the Windows Server operating system software.

CHAPTER 1

Windows Server 2012 Technology Primer

IN THIS CHAPTER

- Windows Server 2012 Defined
- When Is the Right Time to Migrate?
- Versions of Windows Server 2012
- Improvements for Continuous Availability
- Enhancements for Flexible Identity and Security
- Enabling Users to Work Anywhere
- Simplifying the Datacenter
- Addition of Migration Tools
- Improvements in Server Roles in Windows Server 2012
- Identifying Which Windows Server 2012 Service to Install or Migrate to First

With the release of Windows Server 2012, some questions immediately come to mind for IT professionals: "What's new?" "How do I leverage the new version of Windows in my business environment?" "How do I make the new stuff work?" The challenging part for IT professionals is that not only is Microsoft releasing a new operating system every couple years, but applications are being updated on a regular basis, and the influx of cloud-based technologies provide alternatives for organizations to choose their technology platform.

So, where's one to start?

The focus of this book is to identify what's new, what's the same, and what's the difference in Windows 2012 compared to earlier versions of Windows, and then drill down into tips, tricks, and best practices from early-adopter lessons learned for the planning, implementation, and support of old and new technologies built in to Windows Server 2012.

To start, Windows 2012 is built on the same base technology that Windows has been running on for years. Granted, Windows Server 2012 is now solely a 64-bit operating system, so there's no 32-bit version of the code, but much of the feature set adds enhancements in providing high availability, redundancy, high performance, and scalability for the enterprise.

With Windows Server 2012, Microsoft is shipping an entire platform based on a common codebase that includes Windows 8 for tablets and client systems through Windows Server 2012 for datacenters in enterprises. The similarities start with a common user interface with the new Windows

Metro style menu, but that's about where the similarities also end. Obviously, client systems are targeted toward the touchscreen interface and user apps, whereas Windows Server 2012 focuses on datacenter and cloud-based back-end infrastructure.

This chapter provides an overview of what's in Windows Server 2012, explains how IT professionals have leveraged the technologies to improve IT services for their organization, and acts as a guide for where to find more information about these core technology solutions in the various chapters of this book.

Windows Server 2012 Defined

Windows Server 2012 is the next generation of the Windows Server operating system. Upon initial boot, shown in Figure 1.1, Windows Server 2012 looks like any other version of Windows relative to having a taskbar at the bottom and a console screen displayed. In fact, on Windows Server 2012, rather than booting to a blank screen, Windows 2012 boots to the Server Manager console. From Server Manager, an IT professional can add server roles, configure server settings, and launch management tools, which are all things that are done by the Windows administrator.

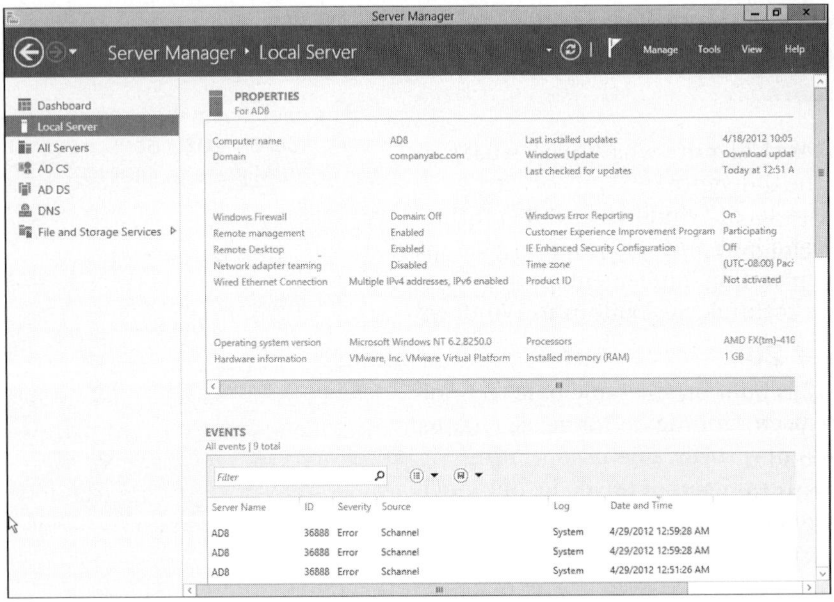

FIGURE 1.1 Windows Server 2012 desktop screen.

However, as mentioned, Windows Server 2012 has the Windows 8 "Metro" interface similar to what is shown in Figure 1.2, and as such, the Start button is no longer on the bottom left as it has been "forever." Instead, a "charm" at the bottom right of the screen pops up a series of quick launch buttons (including ones to search or configure settings on the system). Chapter 3, "Installing Windows Server 2012 and Server Core," and in Chapter 18, "Windows Server 2012 Administration," cover the Windows Metro style interface in more detail.

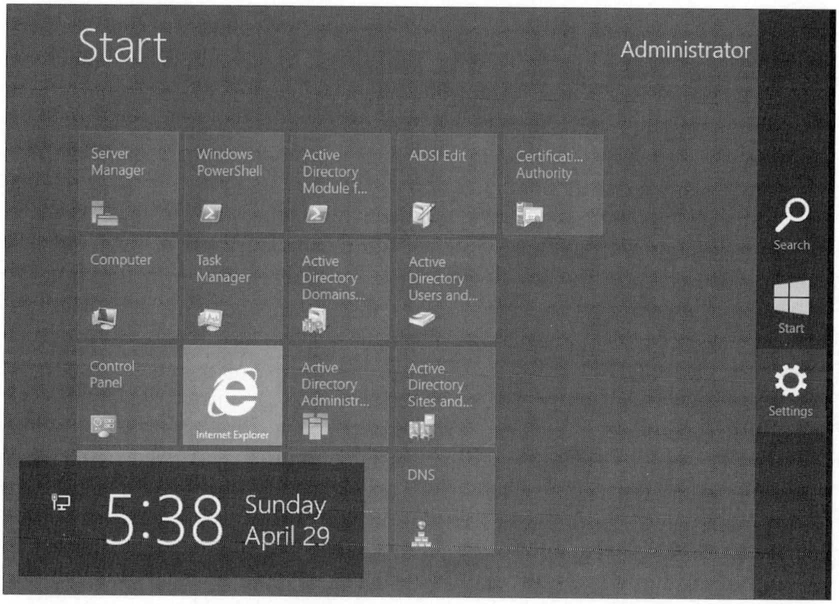

FIGURE 1.2 Windows Metro style interface in Windows 2012.

Under the surface, though, and covered through the pages of this chapter are the new server, datacenter, cloud-based technologies, and capabilities built in to Windows Server 2012.

Windows Server 2012 Under the Hood

Although there are a lot of new features and functions added in to Windows Server in the past couple revisions (2012 and 2008 R2) that make the headlines, one of the first places I like to start is around the things that don't make the headlines that are really core technology improvements from which many of the features are built from. These are technologies that make the new operating system faster, more reliable, and do more things—but they aren't features that you have to install or configure.

Self-Healing NTFS

One of the embedded technologies in Windows Server 2008 and extended into Windows Server 2012 is self-healing New Technology File System (NTFS). Effectively, the operating system has a worker thread that runs in the background, which makes corrections to the file system when NTFS detects a corrupt file or directory. In the past when there was a file system problem, you typically had to reboot the server for chkdsk to run and clean up file and directory corrupt errors.

This self-healing function is not something you will ever see running; however, it is an added capability under the hood in Windows Server 2012 that keeps the operating system running reliably and with fewer system problems.

Server Message Block 3.0

Introduced in Windows Server 2012 is Server Message Block 3.0, more commonly called SMB3 or SMB for short. SMB is a protocol that handles the transfer of files between systems. Effectively, SMB compresses file communications and, through a larger communications buffer, is able to reduce the number of round trips needed when transmitting data between systems.

For the old-timers reading this chapter, it is analogous to the difference between the **copy** command and the **xcopy** command in DOS. The **copy** command reads, writes, reads, writes information. The **xcopy** command reads, reads, reads information and then writes, writes, writes the information. Because more information is read into a buffer and transferred in bulk, the information is transmitted significantly faster.

Most users on a high-speed local-area network (LAN) won't notice the improvements when opening and saving files out of something like Microsoft Office against a Windows Server 2012 system; however, for users who might be copying up large image files or data sets between systems will find the information copying 10 to 30 times faster. The performance improvement is very noticeable in wide-area network (WAN) situations on networks with high latency. Because a typical transfer of files requires short read and write segments of data, a file could take minutes to transfer across a WAN that can transfer in seconds between SMB-connected systems because the round-trip chatter is drastically reduced.

For SMB3 to work effectively, the systems on both ends need to be Windows Server 2012, or Windows 8 systems. A Windows XP client to a Windows Server 2012 server will communicate over SMB 1.0 for backward compatibility and will not gain from this new technology. In addition, when talking to Windows 7 or Windows Server 2008 R2 machines they can only negotiate up to SMB 2.1.

Significant to Windows Server 2012 in regards to SMB is Microsoft's inclusion of SMB for clustering and replication technologies built in to the new operating system. It used to be that if you wanted to setup a clustered server environment, you needed a storage-area network (SAN) shared stored solution to failover clustered servers from one to another. With Windows Server 2012, clustering can be done simply with SMB. Two Hyper-V hosts can be set up, load on the Failover Clustering feature, set up a basic Windows 2012 file server, point the servers to an (SMB file share) of the file server, and build the cluster without a SAN.

SMB2 and the benefits of this embedded technology are discussed in more detail in Chapter 29, "System-Level Fault Tolerance (Clustering / Network Load Balancing)," and Chapter 37, "Deploying and Using Windows Virtualization," among other chapters on file system and storage.

Hyper-V

Hyper-V is a technology built in to the core of the operating system in Windows Server 2008 and expanded in Windows Server 2012 that greatly enhances the performance and capabilities of server virtualization in a Windows environment. In the past, virtual server software sat on top of the network operating system and each guest session was dependent on many shared components of the operating system.

Hyper-V provides a very thin layer between the hardware abstract layer of the system and the operating system that provides guest sessions in a virtualized environment to communicate directly with the hardware layer of the system. Without having the host operating system in the way, guest sessions can perform significantly faster than in the past, and guest sessions can operate independent of the host operating system in terms of better reliability from eliminating host operating system bottlenecks.

As mentioned in the previous section on Hyper-V and the ability to create a cluster with SMB file storage, there have been other very significant improvements in Hyper-V, including the ability to do site-to-site replication of Hyper-V guest sessions. Instead of purchasing expensive replication technologies, Hyper-V hosts can be pointed to one another for server to server replication. A number of other technologies have been greatly improved in Windows Server 2012.

Hyper-V and server virtualization is covered in more detail in Chapter 36.

Storage Spaces

Storage spaces represent a significant inclusion in Windows Server 2012, effectively the ability to group together storage space on multiple servers and having them displayed and accessible as a single storage share. Storage spaces work in the same way that RAID drive mirroring or RAID striping works, replicating or striping data across drives for higher availability. With storage spaces, however, the mirroring and striping can be done across systems. So, instead of having two drives mirrored in one server (with the server as a bottleneck or point of failure), the two drives can be in two separate servers, and the mirroring happens between the two servers. Or three drives can be split across three different servers and striped across the three servers providing both storage resilience as well as server resilience.

The concept of mirroring and striping storage spaces on small 50GB or 100GB levels doesn't register as a benefit for most IT people because mirroring 100GB drives is done all the time inside a server. But what if you want to create a 10TB video, media, and large-image storage repository, and that "server" that the 10TB disks are in fails? What will it take to restore 10TB from tape? Or what if you want to copy the 10TB to another server? It will take an extremely long time, which is why organizations buy external SAN storage, to put large amounts of data and then snapshot that large amount of data for redundancy.

But what if you create two servers or three servers or five servers with each 10TB or 5TB and mirror or stripe the storage across multiple servers? Now you have no single point of failure, the servers have data mirrored or striped, the servers are redundant, and you do this all at a fraction of the cost of a SAN or SAN plus snapshots.

Add in all of this the flexibility provided by SMB shares as an underlying technology for high-speed data clustering and site replication, and storage spaces start to make a lot of sense. Storage spaces, shown in Figure 1.3, are covered in Chapter 28, "File System Management and Fault Tolerance."

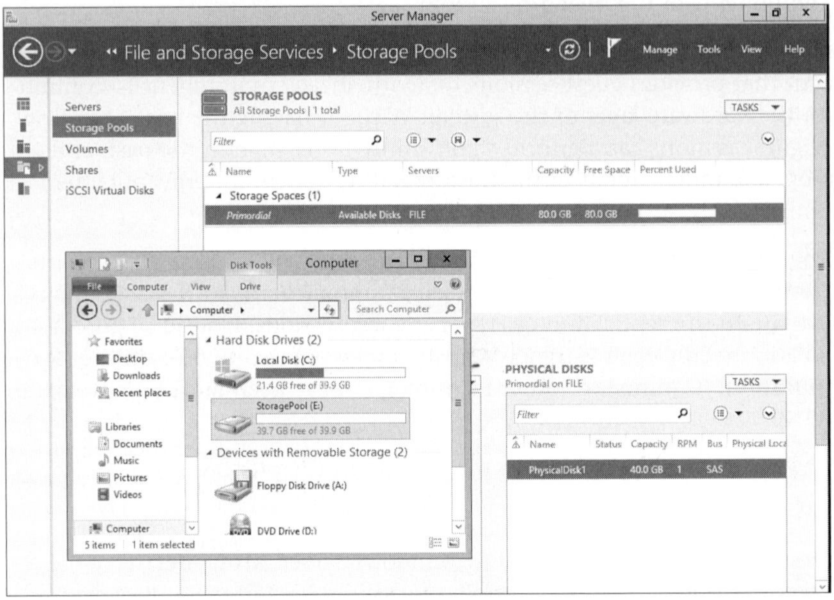

FIGURE 1.3 Storage Spaces in Windows Server 2012.

De-Dupe

De-dupe, or data de-duplication is built in to Windows Server 2012 and is the ability for basic Windows 2012 file system storage to be de-duplicated to decrease storage capacity demands. As an example, if a 10TB share of data has the same video 20 times with variations of the video from early draft cuts through near final and final versions, the video could take up a lot of disk space. Data de-duplication acknowledges the replication of bits on the disk, and instead of having the same data multiple times, it flags the data as duplicates and opens up space for the storage of other information.

In many cases, data de-duplication has saved 30% to upward of 70%, with averages being somewhere in the middle. Organizations with 10TB of space are often able to achieve 50% to 55% space reduction, and no longer have to purchase more storage as they reach 10TB that might be the limit of their current storage subsystem. This 50% savings could prevent the organization from buying more storage for another year or two, potentially a huge benefit to organizations today.

Data de-duplication is covered in Chapter 28.

Visual Changes in Windows Server 2012

The first thing you notice when Windows Server 2012 boots is that it boots to the Server Manager console that enables administration and management of the server or servers in the environment. If you press the Start or Windows key on a keyboard, the Windows Metro style menu pops up. This might seem to be a simple cosmetic change to standardize the current look and feel of the Windows operating systems with other "Windows 8" operating systems like those for tablets, laptops, and desktops. Interestingly, with the release of Windows Server 2012, Microsoft did away with the Classic view of Windows (the Start button is no longer on the lower left, where it has been for years), so there are a few things to get used to. So, the seasoned Windows administrator needs a bit of time to get used to Windows 2012, but then it's easy to find what you need.

Windows Server 2012 as an Application Server

As much as there have been significant improvements in Windows Server 2012 under the hood that greatly enhance the performance, reliability, and scalability of Windows Server 2012 in the enterprise, Windows servers have always been exceptional application servers hosting critical business applications for organizations. Windows Server 2012 continues the tradition of the operating system being an application server with common server roles being included in the operating system. When you are installing Windows Server 2012, the Server Manager Add Roles Wizard provides a list of server roles that you can add to a system, as shown in Figure 1.4.

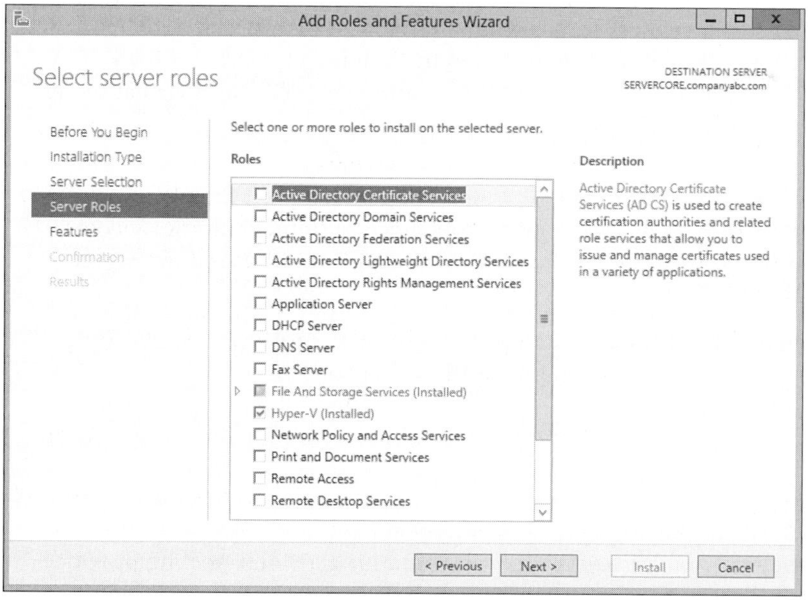

FIGURE 1.4 Server roles in Windows Server 2012.

The various server roles in Windows Server 2012 typically fall into three categories, as follows:

- **File and print services**—As a file and print server, Windows Server 2012 provides the basic services leveraged by users in the storage of data and the printing of information off the network. Several improvements have been made in Windows Server 2012 for file security (covered in Chapter 13, "Server-Level Security") and file server fault tolerance (covered in Chapter 28).
- **Domain services**—In enterprise environments running Windows networking, the organization is usually running Active Directory to provide centralized logon authentication. Active Directory continues to be a key component in Windows Server 2012, with several extensions to the basic internal forest concept of an organization to expanded federated forests that allow Active Directories to interconnect with one another. Several chapters in Part II, "Windows Server 2012 Active Directory," address Active Directory, federated forests, lightweight directories, and so on.
- **Application services**—Windows Server 2012 provides the basis for the installation of business applications such as Microsoft Exchange, Microsoft SharePoint server, SQL Server, and so on. These applications are initially made to be compatible with Windows Server 2012, and later are updated to leverage and take full advantage of the new technologies built in to the Windows Server 2012 operating system. Some of the applications that come with Windows Server 2012 include Remote Desktop Services for thin-client computing access (covered in Chapter 25, "Remote Desktop Services"), utility server services such as domain name system (DNS) and Dynamic Host Configuration Protocol (DHCP) (covered in Chapter 11, "DHCP / IPv6 / IPAM," and Chapter 10, "Domain Name System, WINS, and DNSSEC"), and virtual server hosting (covered in Chapter 36).

This book focuses on the Windows Server 2012 operating system and the planning, migration, security, administration, and support of the operating system. Windows Server 2012 is also the base network operating system on top of which all future Windows Server applications will be built.

However, Windows Server 2012 is more than just adding server roles and applications to the system' some significant improvements of the server roles have helped organizations decrease the number of servers needed in the datacenter. A couple of the server role enhancements are Multitenant Internet Information Service (IIS) and Cluster-Aware Updating (CAU).

Internet Information Services (IIS) Support for Multitenant

Most people when they hear *multitenant* think it is something a cloud hosting provider might use to provide web services to a number of organizations. However, multitenant IIS can also be used to decrease the number of servers of every organization around. Multitenant IIS is the ability to take multiple instances of IIS web services and consolidate them into a single Windows Server 2012 IIS server. Unlike IIS web services in the past, where most of the time you could not combine web services into a single host system, now with Windows Server 2012, a single host server can host 5, 10, 15, or 20 isolated instances of IIS.

The single IIS server can front end SharePoint Web, Exchange Outlook Web Access (OWA), the corporate intranet, a handful of web apps, and the like. The consolidation of IIS web instances is done with the separation of rights, privileges, and execution operations. Multitenant IIS helps organizations eliminate several if not dozens of web servers and decreases physical server and license counts for guest sessions running small/thin Windows web services.

Multitenant IIS is covered in Chapter 12, "Internet Information Services."

Cluster-Aware Updating

Cluster-Aware Updating, or CAU, is a feature that assists organizations in failing over cluster servers to other nodes of the cluster so that another cluster node can be patched or updated. This functionality is not new to organizations, but what is new is the ability for Windows Server 2012 clusters to have built in to them the technology to be patch update and cluster aware so that when a cluster needs to be updated the core operating systems knows to fail over and fail back the cluster nodes. CAU technology simplifies cluster updates by automating the process to keep clusters up-to-date.

Chapter 29 covers CAU in more detail.

Windows Server 2012 Active Directory

Although the release of each subsequent version of Windows Server provides a number of new server roles for application services, the latest releases of Windows Server 2008, Windows Server 2008 R2, and Windows Server 2012 also bring with them an update to Active Directory. Unlike the shift from Windows NT to Active Directory a decade ago that required a major restructuring of domain functions, Active Directory 2008 and Active Directory 2012 are more evolutionary than revolutionary. AD 2008 R2 added a handful of features that many organizations have yet to implement still, and AD 2012 will no doubt be the same. However, there are significant enhancements in AD 2008 and AD 2012 that are worth being aware of in case the organization has a need for such functionality (typically security or policy/manageability related):

The new features in Active Directory 2008 R2 and Active Directory 2012 are as follows:

- **Active Directory Recycle Bin**—The AD Recycle Bin was included in Active Directory 2008 and provides administrators an easy way to undelete objects in Active Directory. In the past, when an administrator inadvertently deleted an Active Directory object like a user, group, organizational unit container, or the like, the object was effectively gone, and the administrator would have to create the object from scratch, which would create a whole new series of security concerns for the new/unique object. The AD Recycle Bin now enables an administrator to simply run the recovery tool and undelete objects.

- **Global catalog cloning**—In earlier versions of Active Directory, the only way you could create a global catalog (GC) server was to build a new server and let the data from other GCs replicate to it over the wire. This was fine for a small or mid-size organization because the global catalog typically didn't have a whole lot of stuff inside of it, so it took a few minutes, maybe an hour, and everything was replicated. Even in large corporate enterprises, a GC server might take a few hours to replicate over a WAN link, but that is still well within typical acceptable tolerances. However, as cloud-based environments grow to include hundreds of thousands or millions of users, the replication time in multiple datacenters gets past typical tolerable limits. GC cloning in Windows Server 2012 allows an organization to take a GC, clone the information, and send the information to another site and recover the cloned server or information, and only changes (deltas) are replicated over the WAN.
- **Managed service accounts**—Applications in a network frequently use service accounts associated with the security to start a database, conduct data searches and indexing, or launch background tasks. However, when an organization changes the password of a service account, all servers with applications using the service account need to be updated with the new password, which is an administration nightmare. With Active Directory 2008 R2 mode supported both in AD 2008 and AD 2012, service accounts can be identified and then managed so that a password change to a service account will initiate a process of updating the service account changes to application servers throughout the organization.
- **Authentication mechanism assurance**—Another Active Directory 2008 R2 feature that is supported both on AD 2008 and AD 2012 is the enhancement of claims-based authentication in Active Directory. With authentication mechanism assurance, information in a token can be extracted whenever a user attempts to access a claims-aware application to determine authorization based on the user's logon method. This extension will be leveraged by future applications to improve claims-based authentication in the enterprise.
- **Offline domain join**—For desktop administrators who create system images, the challenge of creating images is that a system needs to be physically connected to the network before the system can be joined to the domain. With offline domain join, a system can be prejoined with a file created with a unique system credential written to a file. When a Windows client system or Windows Server system needs to be joined, rather than physically connecting the system to the network and joining the system to the domain, this exported file can be used offline to join the system to the Active Directory domain.

These are some of the capabilities built in to Active Directory 2012, something that organizations can choose to upgrade AD or wait until an application requires an updated version of Active Directory to be in place before the organization updates their directory system.

When Is the Right Time to Migrate?

Every time a new version of Windows ships, organizations wonder when the right time to migrate to the new operating system. It used to be that you waited until the first service pack shipped before installing any Microsoft product. However, Windows Server has been extremely solid in its release over the past decade; even the beta program for Windows Server 2012 didn't turn up any surprises. Early-adopter organizations were implementing Windows Server 2012 (known early on as Windows Server 8) in their production environments upward of 12 to 18 months prior to the product release.

So, the decision of when to implement Windows Server 2012 comes down to the same decision on migration to any new technology: Identify the value received by implementing Windows Server 2012, test the solution in a limited environment, and roll out Windows Server 2012 when you are comfortable that the product meets the needs of your organization.

This introductory chapter notes the many features and functions built in to Windows Server 2012 that have helped other organizations decide that Windows Server 2012 has significant value to them. Improvements in security, performance, and manageability provide benefits to organizations looking to minimize administration costs while providing more functionality to users.

The cost and effort to migrate to Windows Server 2012 vary based on the current state of an organization's networking environment, as well as the Windows Server 2012 features and functions the organization wants to implement. Some organizations begin their migration process to Windows Server 2012 by adding a Windows Server 2012 member server into an existing Windows 2003/2008 network. Others choose to migrate their Active Directory to Windows Server 2012 as their introduction to the new operating system.

Adding a Windows Server 2012 System to a Windows 2003/2008 Environment

Many organizations want to add in a specific Windows Server 2012 function such as Windows Server 2012 Remote Desktop Services (previously called Terminal Services), Hyper-V R2 virtualization, DirectAccess, or BranchCache. Such functions can be installed on Windows Server 2012 member servers in an existing Active Directory 2003 or Active Directory 2008 networking environment. This allows an organization to get Windows Server 2012 application capabilities fairly quickly and easily without having to do a full migration to Active Directory 2012. In most cases, a Windows Server 2012 member server can simply be added to an existing network without ever affecting the existing network. This addition provides extremely low network impact but enables an organization to prototype and test the new technology, pilot it for a handful of users, and slowly roll out the technology to the client base as part of a regular system replacement or upgrade process.

Some organizations have replaced all their member servers with Windows Server 2012 systems over a period of weeks or months as a preparatory step to eventually migrate to a Windows Server 2012 Active Directory structure.

Migrating from Windows 2003 and Windows 2008 Active Directory to Windows Server 2012 Active Directory

For organizations that are still running an Active Directory 2003 environment, migrating to Active Directory 2012 can provide access to several additional capabilities, of which some were mentioned earlier in this chapter, including Active Directory Recycle Bin, global catalog cloning, managed service accounts, PowerShell administration, and offline domain join.

Organizations that have already migrated to Active Directory 2008 or 2008 R2 already have most of the new functionality available in Active Directory and may determine whether a movement to AD/2012 will be of value. Effectively, Windows Server 2012 uses the same Active Directory organizational structure that was created with Windows 2003 and 2008, so forests, domain trees, domains, organizational units, sites, groups, and users all transfer directly into Windows Server 2012 Active Directory. If the organizational structure in Windows 2003 or 2008 meets the needs of the organization, the migration to Windows Server 2012 is essentially just the insertion of a Windows Server 2012 GC server into the existing Windows 2003 or 2008 Active Directory domain to perform a GC update to Windows Server 2012 Active Directory.

Of course, planning, system backup, and prototype testing (covered in Chapter 16, "Migrating from Active Directory 2008 / 2008 R2 to Active Directory 8") help minimize migration risks and errors and lead to a more successful migration process. However, the migration process from Windows 2003 and Windows Server 2008 to Windows Server 2012 is a relatively easy migration path for organizations to follow.

Versions of Windows Server 2012

Microsoft has greatly simplified the licensing and version options for Windows Server 2012. There are effectively only two versions of Windows Server 2012 now: the Standard edition and the Datacenter edition. Microsoft eliminated the Enterprise edition and the Web edition of the software, which effectively just enabled or disabled feature sets. In a virtualized world such as we're in, organizations really only choose the density of their virtualization, whether they are running physical (or lightly virtualized systems) or that they are heavily virtualizing their server environment. So, the two versions fulfill those requirements.

NOTE

Microsoft will be releasing two other versions of Windows Server 2012, but they are specialized versions of the operating system and not covered in this book. Windows Server 2012 Foundation Server is a version of the operating system that is targeted at installation on appliance systems, with functionality limited to specific tasks such as web services, or potentially just to run a custom Windows-based application. Windows Server 2012 also has a Hyper-V edition that will focus on providing a virtualization host (Hyper-V host) that does not entail the cost of licensing any guest sessions. These are specialized versions of Windows Server 2012 and are not the usual focus of businesses or organizations that are the general audience of this book.

When installing Windows Server 2012, beside choosing Standard or Datacenter editions, the installer of Windows will choose either the full graphical user interface (GUI) version of Windows Server or a the non-GUI version called Server Core.

Windows Server 2012 Standard Edition

The Windows Server 2012 Standard Edition is the recommended version of Windows Server for a physical server that won't usually be virtualizing guest sessions. The Standard edition provides a license for the physical system, and includes *all* the features and functions built in to Windows Server 2012.

Unlike in the past, where the Standard edition did not do clustering or had caps on the amount of memory supported by the system and the like, with Windows Server 2012, the Standard edition has all the same features/functions as the Datacenter edition, just supports fewer simultaneous virtualized guest sessions.

A basic Windows Server 2012 x64-bit Standard edition system supports all the server roles available in Windows Server 2012. It is a good version of the operating system for physical servers (high-performance database servers, standalone web servers, and the like).

It used to be you put utility servers (such as DNS or DHCP), file servers, print servers, media servers, and domain controllers on the Standard edition of Windows. In a highly virtualized environment, however, these servers are simply guest sessions of a larger Windows Datacenter edition host system. The good thing with the new licensing model for Windows is that you don't have to worry about capacity planning and starting off "small" with Standard edition and then having to completely rebuild the Standard edition servers with an Enterprise or Datacenter edition as your needs grow. The new licensing model simplifies implementation solely on the density of servers that'll be virtualized on a system.

NOTE

One of the first things an organization becomes aware of is that Windows Server 2012 comes in 64-bit (x64) versions *only*. 32-bit hardware and a 32-bit installation is not supported. The most recent version of the Windows Server operating system that supports 32-bit is Windows Server 2008.

Windows Server 2012 Datacenter Edition

Windows Server 2012 Datacenter edition is the most common license organizations buy these days because the Datacenter edition provides support for an unlimited number of virtual guest sessions on the server. So, in a highly virtualized environment where a server might be running 5, 6, 8, 10 guest sessions, the Datacenter license is a flat cost, and therefore it gets cheaper per guest session every time additional sessions are added to a server.

Unlike early editions of Windows Datacenter edition that only worked on proprietary hardware, the Datacenter edition of Windows Server 2012 is nothing more than a different way of licensing the software. The code is basically the same across the Standard edition and Datacenter editions. As noted about the Standard edition, there are no limitations in features in the Standard edition. All features and functions, including clustering, load balancing, certificate services, and so on, are included in the Standard edition and the Datacenter edition. So, only from a licensing standpoint does an organization end up being able to support more guest sessions with Datacenter than with Standard edition.

As noted in Chapter 34, "Capacity Analysis and Performance Optimization," an organization can scale out or scale up its server applications. *Scale out* refers to an application that performs better when it is distributed across multiple servers, whereas *scale up* refers to an application that performs better when more processors are added to a single system. Typical scale-out applications include web server services, electronic messaging systems, and file and print servers. In those cases, organizations are better off distributing the application server functions to multiple Windows Server 2012 systems. However, applications that scale up, such as e-commerce or data warehousing applications, benefit from having all the data and processing on a single server cluster. For these applications, centralization for scalability purposes provides the added benefit to the organization. In either case, though, with Windows Server 2012, the version of the license (Standard or Datacenter) has no impact on how the organization is forced to deploy the application; it is now up to the organization to decide the best application architecture fit.

Windows Server 2012 Server Core

Initially introduced in Windows Server 2008 and now supported also with Windows Server 2012 is a Server Core version of the operating system. Windows Server 2012 Server Core, shown in Figure 1.5, is a GUI-less version of the Windows Server 2012 operating system. When a system boots with Server Core installed on it, the system does not load up the normal Windows GUI. Instead, the Server Core system boots to a logon prompt, and from the logon prompt the system drops to a DOS command prompt. There is no Start button, no menu—no GUI at all.

Server Core is not sold as a separate edition, but rather as an install option that comes with the Standard and Datacenter editions of the operating system. So, when you purchase a license of Windows Server 2012, the DVD has both the normal GUI edition code plus a Windows Server 2012 Server Core version.

The operating system capabilities are limited to the edition of Server Core being installed, so a Windows Server 2012, Standard edition Server Core server has the same functionality as the GUI version of Windows Server 2012 Standard edition.

Server Core has been a great version of Windows for utility servers such as domain controllers, DHCP servers, DNS servers, IIS web servers, and Windows virtualization servers because the limited overhead provides more resources to the applications running on the server, and by removing the GUI and associated applications there is less of a security attack footprint on the Server Core system. Because most administrators don't play Solitaire or use Media Player on a domain controller, those are applications that don't need to be patched, updated, or maintained on the GUI-less version of Windows. With fewer applications to be patched, the system requires less maintenance and management to keep operational.

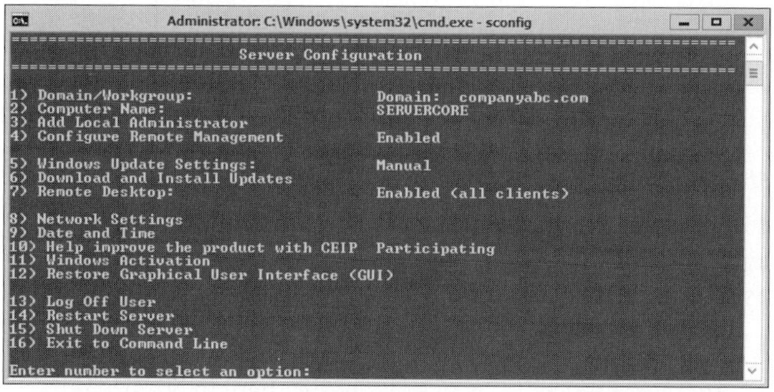

FIGURE 1.5 Windows Server 2012 Server Core.

NOTE

With the Server Manager remote administration capabilities of Windows Server 2012, covered in Chapter 20, "Windows Server 2012 Management and Maintenance Practices," administrators can now remotely manage a Server Core system from the Server Manager GUI interface on another server. This greatly enhances the management of Server Core hosts so that administrators can use a GUI console to manage the otherwise GUI-less version of Windows Server.

Those who have tried Server Core in early editions of Windows (2008 or 2008 R2) may have found the nongraphical experience with Server Core to not be pleasant or even usable. With SConfig on the Server Core system, server administrators can now have a graphical-like experience for configuring server name, IP address, joining the domain, and the like and do not have to remember long text strings for configurations. Additionally, the new Windows 2012 Server Manager console allows remote installation of server roles, features, and the like that greatly improves the experience of setting up Server Core.

In addition, Microsoft provides the ability for an organization to take a Server Core system, temporarily make the Server Core system into a GUI-version of Windows (to potentially install an application, drivers, and so on) and then drop the configuration back down to Server Core once installed. This provides the best solution for applications that may have previously not been supported in installing on Server Core to be installed in a GUI console, and then remove the GUI back down to a base Server Core system.

Improvements for Continuous Availability

Although clustering of servers has been around for a long time in Windows (dating back to Windows NT 4.0, when it was available, but really didn't work), clustering in Windows Server 2012 now not only works, but also provides a series of significant improvements. In Windows Server 2012, you can set up clustering without a lot of the complexity that was previously necessary to get high availability working in Windows; even the previous requirement of having a storage-area network (SAN) with cluster share volumes (CSV) is no longer. All these improvements in Windows Server 2012 make continuous availability a viable solution for enterprise-class high availability. Clustering is covered in detail in Chapter 29.

No Single Point of Failure in Clustering

Clustering, by definition, should provide redundancy and high availability of server systems. However, in earlier versions of Windows clustering, a "quorum drive" was required for the cluster systems to connect to as the point of validation for cluster operations. If at any point the quorum drive failed, the cluster would not be able to fail over from one system to another. Windows Server 2008 / 2008 R2 and Windows Server 2012 clustering removed this requirement of a static quorum drive. Two major technologies facilitate this elimination of a single or central point of failure: majority-based cluster membership verification and witness-based quorum validation.

The majority-based cluster membership enables the IT administrator to define what devices in the cluster get a vote to determine whether a cluster node is in a failed state and so needs to fail over to another node. Instead of assuming that the disk will always be available, as in the previous quorum disk model, now nodes of the cluster and shared storage devices participate in the new enhanced quorum model in Windows Server 2012. Effectively, Windows Server 2012 server clusters have better information to determine whether it is appropriate to fail over a cluster in the event of a system or device failure.

The witness-based quorum eliminates the single quorum disk from the cluster operation validation model. Instead, a completely separate node or file share can be set as the file share witness. In the case of a GeoCluster, where cluster nodes are in completely different locations, the ability to place the file share in a third site and even enable that file share to serve as the witness for multiple clusters becomes a benefit for organizations with distributed datacenters and also provides more resiliency in the cluster operation's components.

Stretched Clusters

Windows Server 2012 also supports the concept of stretched clusters to provide better server and site server redundancy. Effectively, Microsoft has eliminated the need to have cluster servers remain on the same subnet, as has been the case in Windows clustering in the past. Although organizations have used virtual local-area networks (VLANs) to stretch a subnet across multiple locations, this was not always easy to do, and, in many cases, was not the right thing to do technologically in IP networking design.

By allowing cluster nodes to reside on different subnets, plus with the addition of a configurable heartbeat timeout, clusters can now be set up in ways that match an organization's disaster failover and recovery strategy.

64-Node Clusters

Clustering provides redundancy of nodes in the cluster, but now with Windows Server 2012, an organization can have 64 nodes in the cluster, a significant improvement over the 16-node limit in earlier versions of Windows. With 64 nodes in a cluster, an organization can set up cluster nodes for high availability, for redundancy, and to serve as standby servers in the event of a server failure in the cluster. With potentially 64 nodes in the cluster, the organization can greatly improve high availability and continuous operations of the network systems.

Hyper-V Replication

Another new technology built-in to Windows Server 2012 is called Hyper-V Replication. Hyper-V Replication, shown in Figure 1.6, allows a cluster node to replicate Hyper-V guest sessions from one server to another server, typically across a WAN providing site redundancy. If a server in one site fails, the guest sessions in a site that has been replicated can be brought up in another site. This concept has been realized over the past couple years through the use of SAN snapshots, where data is replicated from one server to another using expensive storage hardware. However, with Hyper-V Replication, no SAN is required for data replication. In fact, all the technology needed to initiate Hyper-V Replication is a source Hyper-V host server and a destination Hyper-V host server. Just pointing the source to the destination server can begin the replication of Hyper-V guest sessions between hosts.

Because Hyper-V Replication does not require SAN snapshots or other fancy hardware, it makes the entry into site replication a low-cost and simple task. With Windows Server 2012, continuous availability now extends between sites; so, beyond local clustering and high availability, organizations can now do disaster recovery and business continuity with site-level guest session replication. Hyper-V Replication is covered in Chapter 36.

Cluster-Aware Updating

With clustering as a major component of many of the continuous availability technologies, the ability to patch and update the cluster nodes without interruption to network services becomes important for continuous availability. New in Windows Server 2012 is Cluster-Aware Updating (CAU), which enables, as part of the patching and updating process, a method for cluster nodes to have network services failed over, get patched and updated, and failed back to an operational state. The CAU process simplifies updates and minimizes system operations downtime during critical patches and update cycles. You can find more on CAU in Chapter 29.

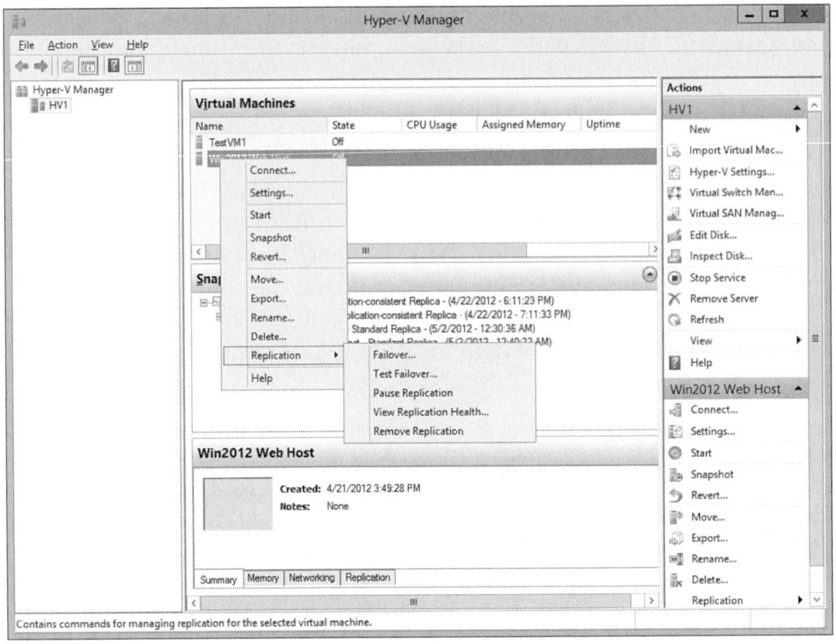

FIGURE 1.6 Hyper-V Replication between host systems.

DHCP Failover

Another technology important in continuous availability is the ability to do DHCP failover in Windows Server 2012. Normally when a DHCP server fails, another server takes on the responsibility of managing DHCP-issued addresses. With DHCP failover, a DHCP scope can be set to transfer to another DHCP server, maintaining DHCP lease tables and maintaining the issuance of addresses for an enterprise. DHCP failover is not as complex as setting up a cluster between DHCP servers, yet provides continuous availability of IP addressing that is tightly integrated with Active Directory and DNS.

Improved Support for SANs

Windows Server 2008 and Windows Server 2012 support for storage-area networks (SANs) by providing enhanced mechanisms for connecting to SANs and switching between SAN nodes. In the past, a connection to a SAN was a static connection, meaning that a server was connected to a SAN just as if the server were physically connected to a direct-attached storage system. However, the concept of a SAN is that if a SAN fails, the server should reconnect to a SAN device that is now online. This could not be easily done with Windows 2003 or earlier. SCSI bus resets were required to disconnect a server from one SAN device to another.

With Windows Server 2012, a server can be associated with a SAN with a persistent reservation to access a specific shared disk; however, if the SAN fails, the server session can be logically connected to another SAN target system without having to script device resets that have been complicated and disruptive in disaster recovery scenarios.

Enhancements for Flexible Identity and Security

In addition to the infrastructure updates in Windows Server 2012 are the security enhancements added to the operating system. As organizations struggle to secure their environments, employees can depend on information privacy, and content is protected for regulatory compliance reasons; so, having the tools to secure the environment is critical. Security enhancements in Windows Server 2012 include increased support for security standards, enhancements in the Windows security subsystem, options to leverage Windows 2012 Server Core, Dynamic Access Control for flexibility in role-based security, DNS Security Extensions (DNSSEC) and zone signing for network protection, transport security using IPsec/certificates, security and management policy enforcement, BitLocker for server security, and Rights Management Services (RMS) for data leakage protection.

Increased Support for Standards

Windows Server 2008 introduced several industry standards built in to the Windows operating system that have since been updated in Windows Server 2012. These changes continue a trend of the Windows operating system supporting industry standards rather than proprietary Microsoft standards. One of the key standards built in to Windows Server 2008 and Windows Server 2012 is IPv6.

Internet Protocol version 6 (IPv6) is the future Internet standard for TCP/IP addressing. Most organizations support IPv4. The current Internet numbering scheme is running out of address space, and so Internet communications of the future need to support IPv6, which provides a more robust address space.

In addition, IPv6 supports new standards in dynamic addressing and Internet Protocol Security (IPsec). IPv6 also supports the current IPv4 standards, and so dual addressing is possible. With Windows Server 2012 supporting IPv6, an organization can choose to implement a dual IPv6 and IPv4 standard to prepare for Internet communications support in the future. IPv6 is covered in detail in Chapter 11.

Enhancing the Windows Server 2012 Security Subsystem

Part IV of this book, "Security," is focused on security in the different core areas. Chapter 13 addresses core security subsystems of Windows Server 2012 with regard to server systems. This discussion includes the basics of server hardening, patching, and updating, but also extends into new server security areas added to Windows Server 2012, such as device control level security, wireless access security, and Active Directory Rights Management Services (AD RMS). Windows Server 2012 has continued the "secure by default" theme at Microsoft and no longer installs components such as Internet Information Services (IIS) by default. The good part about it is that components that are not core to the operation of a server are not installed on the system; however, it means every time you install software, you need to add basic components and features.

Server Core and Minimized User Interface

Windows 2012 Server Core was mentioned in the preceding section when the various installation operations of Windows 2012 were noted, and with Server Core and the minimized user interface, a lighter, more secure version of Windows Server can be implemented in the enterprise. Instead of having complex policies, practices, and systems to lock down servers and systems, just decreasing the attack surface with the minimized user interface on Windows Servers helps organizations improve security and decrease management overhead related to maintaining and supporting patches and updates on servers.

Dynamic Access Control

Dynamic Access Control in Windows Server 2012 is a great addition to file system security, something that has been a challenge for organizations for years. Dynamic Access Control provides central access policies, similar to what is shown in Figure 1.7, to files and folders across *all* Windows 2012 file servers in the enterprise. In the past, file permissions were done on a server-by-server (or file share-by-file share) basis. To find what rights a user had was nearly impossible because each server and each share had to be queried. File permissions were hard to set, hard to apply, and hard to manage.

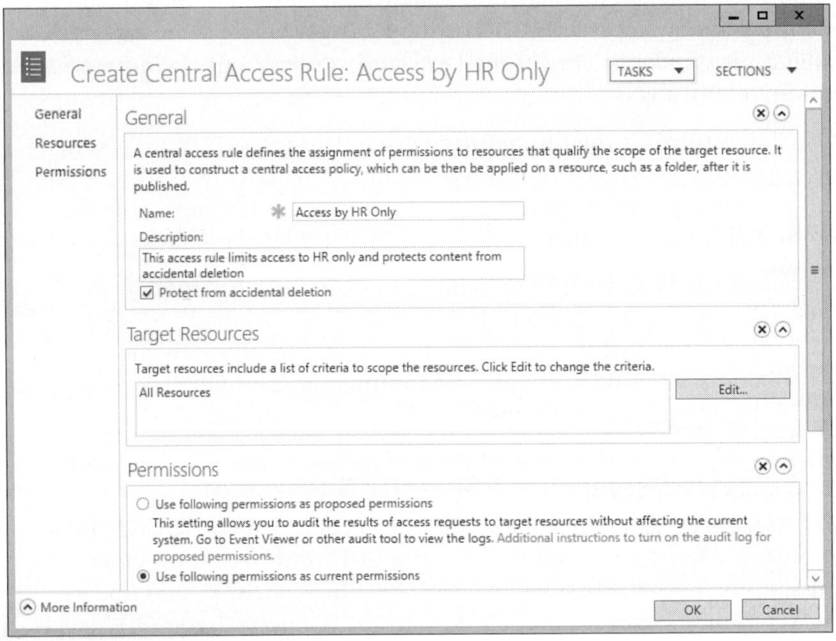

FIGURE 1.7 Central access rules in Dynamic Access Control.

Dynamic Access Control not only provides a centralized policy for enabling and disabling access per user or group, but Dynamic Access Control also enables you to tag and classify data, either manually or by doing keyword assessment and tag application. Tags can be applied through identification of keyword data looking for specific words (like confidential, financial statement, product codename x) or by content format (Social Security number format and so on).

Chapter 29 covers Dynamic Access Control in more detail.

DNSSEC—Zone Signing

Zone signing in DNSSEC provides better infrastructure security by depending on signed security for changes, updates, and other aspects of communications with DNS servers within a Windows Server 2012 environment. DNSSEC is critical for organizations looking to implement zone signing and better DNS management. So, with Microsoft's inclusion of DNSSEC in Windows Server 2012, organizations can meet their security needs accordingly. DNSSEC is covered in Chapter 10.

Transport Security Using IPSec and Certificate Services

Chapter 14, "Transport-Level Security," covers site-to-site and server-to-server security, addressed through the implementation of IPsec encryption. Not new to Windows, IPsec has finally gotten several new Group Policy management components added to aid in the implementation and management of IPsec in the enterprise. Also not new to Windows, but something that has become critical to organizations lately is Microsoft's offering around public key infrastructure (PKI), specifically certificate services. It seems like everything security related is somehow connected to certificates, whether that is file encryption, email encryption, remote mobile device certificate access, or transport security using IPsec. Everything needs a certificate, and the ability of an organization to easily create and manage certificates is the focus of Chapter 14.

Security Policies, Policy Management, and Policy Enforcement Tools

Completely new to Windows Server 2008, and updated in Windows Server 2012, and a major focus for organizations, are security policies and policy management related to security systems. It used to be we would just lock down systems, make sure they were secure by default, and use our best judgment and best effort to secure a network. However, with laws and regulations, and even human resource departments getting involved in information security, all IT security practices now rely on set security policies being defined so that IT can implement technologies to address the organization policies related to information security. This is covered in detail in Chapter 15, "Security Policies, Network Policy Server, and Network Access Protection."

Chapter 15 goes beyond the policies and common best practices related to policy management in an enterprise; it also examines the underlying technologies that help organizations turn security policies into IT-managed technology services. Tools such as the Network Policy Server in Windows Server 2012 allow policies to be defined, and the Network Policy Server enforces those policies, specifically related to remote logon access, access over wireless network connections, or the integration of Network Access Protection (NAP) in querying a device and making sure the device (desktop, laptop, or mobile device) has the latest patches, updates, and antivirus software as required by management to ensure a device is secure.

BitLocker for Server Security

BitLocker is a technology first introduced with Windows Vista that enables an organization to do a full partition encryption of all files, documents, and information stored on the encrypted partition. When BitLocker was first introduced in Windows Server 2008 as a server tool, it was hard to understand why a server would need to have its drive volume encrypted. It made sense that a laptop would be encrypted (in case of theft, so that no one could get access to the data on the laptop hard drive). BitLocker has proven to be beneficial for servers that are placed in remote locations such as in a simple wiring closet or under a cash register in the situation of a retail store as the point-of-sale system. Servers with sensitive data are prevalent in enterprise environments, and BitLocker benefits organizations for security.

So, BitLocker provides encryption of the volume of a Windows Server 2012 server. For organizations that are concerned that the server might be physically compromised by the theft of the server or a physical attack on the system, BitLocker is a great component to implement on the server system.

Windows Rights Management Services

Windows Rights Management Services (RMS) was available as a downloadable feature pack in Windows 2003 and is now included as an installable server role in Windows Server 2012. Windows RMS sets the framework for secured information sharing of data by encrypting content and setting a policy on the content that protects the file and the information stored in the file.

Organizations have been shifting to RMS rather than the old secured file folder primarily because users who should be saving sensitive information into a file folder frequently forget to save files in the folder, and thus sensitive information becomes public information. By encrypting the content of the file itself, even if a file with sensitive information is stored in the wrong place, the file cannot be opened, and the information in the file cannot be accessed without proper security credentials to access the file.

In addition, RMS allows the individual saving the file to set specific attributes regarding what the person would like to be secured about the file. For example, a secured file in RMS can be set to not be edited, meaning that a person receiving the file can read the file, but he or she cannot select content in the file, copy the content, or edit the content. This prevents individuals from taking a secured file, cutting and pasting the content into a different file, and then saving the new file without encryption or security.

RMS also provides attributes to enable the person creating a file to prevent others from printing the file. The file itself can have an expiration date, so that after a given period of time, the contents of the file expire and the entire file is inaccessible.

RMS is covered in Chapter 13.

Active Directory Unification for Various Directory Services

As noted earlier in this chapter, Active Directory in Windows Server 2012 hasn't changed to the point where organizations with solid AD structures have to make changes to their directory environment. Forests, domains, sites, organizational units, groups, and users all remain the same. There are several improvements made in Active Directory and the breadth of functionality provided by directory services in Windows Server 2012.

The changes made in Active Directory are captured in the name changes of directory services as well as the introduction of a read-only domain controller (RODC) service introduced in Windows Server 2008.

Active Directory Domain Services

In Windows Server 2008, Active Directory was renamed to Active Directory Domain Services (AD DS), and Windows Server 2012 continues with that new name. Active Directory Domain Services refers to what used to be just called Active Directory with the same architectural design and structure that Microsoft introduced with Windows 2000 and Windows 2003. In Windows Server 2012, administration is now done through the Active Directory Administrative Center, shown in Figure 1.8.

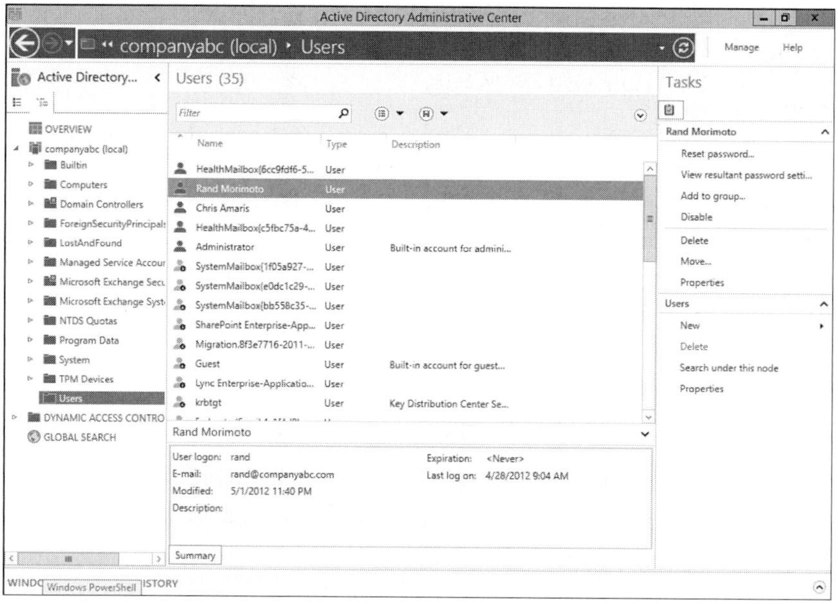

FIGURE 1.8 Active Directory Administrative Center.

The designation of *domain services* identifies this directory as the service that provides authentication and policy management internal to an organization where an organization's internal domain controls network services.

For the first time, AD DS can be stopped and started as any other true service. This facilitates AD DS maintenance without having to restart the domain controller in Directory Services Restore Mode (DSRM).

Active Directory Lightweight Directory Service

Another name change in the directory services components with Windows Server 2008 from Microsoft is the renaming of Active Directory in Application (ADAM) to Active Directory Lightweight Directory Services (AD LDS). ADAM has been a downloadable add-in to Windows 2003 Active Directory that provides a directory typically used in organizations for nonemployees who need access to network services. Rather than putting nonemployees into the Active Directory, these individuals—such as contractors, temporary workers, or even external contacts, such as outside legal counsel, marketing firms, and so on—have been put in ADAM and given rights to access network resources such as SharePoint file libraries, extranet content, or web services.

AD LDS is identical to ADAM in its functionality, and provides an organization with options for enabling or sharing resources with individuals outside of the organizational structure. With the name change, organizations that didn't quite know what ADAM was before have begun to leverage the Lightweight Directory Services function of Active Directory for not just resource sharing but also for a lookup directory resource for clients, patients, membership directories, and so on. AD LDS is covered in detail in Chapter 8, "Creating Federated Forests and Lightweight Directories."

Active Directory Federation Services

That leads to the third Active Directory service, called Active Directory Federation Services, or AD FS. AD FS was introduced with Windows 2003 R2 and continues to provide the linking, or federation, between multiple AD forests, or now with Windows Server 2012 AD FS, the ability to federate between multiple Active Directory Domain Services systems.

Effectively, for organizations that want to share information between AD DS environments, two or more AD DS systems can be connected together to share information. This has been used by organizations that have multiple subsidiaries with their own Active Directory implemented to exchange directory information between the two organizations. And AD FS has been used by business trading partners (suppliers and distributors) to interlink directories together to be able to have groups of users in both organizations easily share information, freely communicate, and easily collaborate between the two organizations.

Chapter 8 covers AD FS in detail.

Read-Only Domain Controllers

Another change in Active Directory in Windows Server 2008 that was continued in Windows 2012 was the addition of a read-only domain controller (RODC). The RODC is just like a global catalog server in Active Directory used to authenticate users and as a resource to look up objects in the directory; however, instead of being a read/write copy of the directory, an RODC maintains only a read-only copy of Active Directory and forwards all write and authentication requests to a read/write domain controller.

RODCs can also be configured to cache specified logon credentials. Cached credentials speed up authentication requests for the specified users. The cached credentials are stored in cache on the RODC system, not every object in the entire global catalog. If the RODC is shut down or powered off, the cache on the RODC is flushed, and the objects in cache are no longer available until the RODC connects back to a global catalog server on the network.

The RODC is a huge advancement in the area of security, being that a RODC cannot be compromised in the same manner that a global catalog server can be in the event of a physical theft of a domain server. Organizations that require the functionality of a global catalog server for user authentication that have the global catalog server in an area that is not completely secure, such as in a remote office, in a branch office location, or even in a retail store outlet, can instead put a RODC in the remote location.

Enabling Users to Work Anywhere

As organizations find their workforce becoming more and more mobile, Microsoft has made significant improvements to mobility in Windows Server 2012. New technologies provide a more seamless experience for users with laptops to move from office, to home, to Internet Wi-Fi hot spots and maintain connectivity to network resources. These improvements do require mobile users to run the latest Windows 8 client operating system (or sometimes, Windows 7 client is also supported with limitations) on their laptop system to gain access to these new services; however, once implemented, users find the functionality to greatly support easier access to network resources no matter where the user resides.

Technologies available in Windows Server 2012 for "work anywhere" scenarios include DirectAccess, RODCs for branch offices, BranchCache file access, Remote Desktop Services for thin-client access, and Windows to Go.

Windows Server 2012 DirectAccess

One of the significant remote-access enhancements in Windows Server 2008 R2 was the DirectAccess technology, which has been further enhanced in Windows Server 2012. DirectAccess enables remote users to access network resources such as file shares, SharePoint shares, and the like without having to launch a virtual private network (VPN) to gain access into the network.

DirectAccess is an amazing technology that combines sophisticated security technology and policy-based access technology to provide remote access to a network. However, organizations do find it challenging to get up to speed with all the technology components necessary to make DirectAccess work. So, although many organizations will seek to achieve DirectAccess capabilities, it might be months or a couple of years before all the technologies are in place for the organization to easily enable DirectAccess in their enterprise environment.

Technologies required to make DirectAccess work include the following:

- **PKI certificates / Kerberos**—DirectAccess supports both PKI certificates as well as Kerberos for identification of the remote device and the basis for encrypted communications from the remote device and the network. The simpler model is to use Kerberos because no additional certificate model has to be implemented to support DirectAccess. However, to be able to use Kerberos, the endpoint needs to be a Windows 8 client system or tablet. For backward compatibility to Windows 7 endpoints, PKI certificates are still supported.

- **Windows 7 and Windows 8 clients**—DirectAccess only works with clients that are running Windows 7 or Windows 8. The client component for encryption, encapsulation, and policy control depends on Windows 7 or Windows 8 to make all the components work together. The improvements in DirectAccess in Windows Server 2012 that include site-level redundancy as well as the simplification where Kerberos is used instead of PKI certificates comes only when Windows 8 clients are used. If the organization has Windows 7 clients as well, then DirectAccess can be configured to support DirectAccess for Windows 7 support, and DirectAccess for a simpler Windows 8 support.
- **IPsec**—The policy control used in DirectAccess leverages IPsec to identify the destination resources that a remote user should have access to. IPsec can be endpoint to endpoint (that is, from the client system all the way to the application server) or IPsec can be simplified from the client system to a DirectAccess proxy server where the actual endpoint application servers do not need to be IPsec enabled. In any case, IPsec is a part of the security and policy structure that ensures the remote client system is only accessing server resources that by policy the remote client should have access to as part of the DirectAccess session connection.
- **IPv6**—Lastly, DirectAccess uses IPv6 as the IP session identifier. Although most organizations have not yet implemented IPv6 and most on-ramps to the Internet are still IPv4, tunneling of IPv6 is fully supported in Windows 7 and Windows Server 2012 and can be used in the interim until IPv6 is fully adopted. For now, IPv6 is a requirement of DirectAccess and is used as part of the remote-access solution.

Windows Server 2012 has greatly enhanced the technology offerings that provide better redundancy and site-to-site mobility, effectively providing more than one DirectAccess gateway server without the need to purchase Unified Access Gateway (UAG), which was almost a requirement for high availability and redundancy of DirectAccess in Windows 2008 R2.

If a remote or branch office has limited IT support or at least the site needs to have the same functionality and reliability as the main corporate or business office, DirectAccess provides seamless access from end clients without the need to purchase expensive hardware and software; you don't have to purchase costly redundant hardware add-ins, either. With the Windows Server 2012 branch office resources, a remote location can have high security, high performance, access to data without significant latency, and operational capabilities, even if the remote site is dropped off the network because of a WAN or Internet connection problem. More on DirectAccess is covered in Chapter 24, "Server-to-Client Remote and Mobile Access," and you will find additional details on the new technologies built in to Windows Server 2012 that better support remote and branch offices in Chapter 32, "Optimizing Windows 2012 for Branch Office Communications."

RODCs for the Branch Office

As covered in the "Read-Only Domain Controllers" section earlier in this chapter, the RODC provides a copy of the Active Directory global catalog for logon authentication of select users and communications with the Active Directory tree without having the security exposure of a full global catalog server in the remote location. Many organizations concerned with distributed global catalog servers chose to not place a server in a remote location, but rather kept their global catalog and domain controllers centralized. What this meant for remote and branch offices was that all logon authentication had to go across the WAN or Internet connection, which could be very slow. And in the event of a WAN or Internet connection failure, the remote or branch office would be offline because users could not authenticate to the network and access network resources until the WAN or Internet connection was restored.

RODCs provide a way for organizations to distribute authentication and Active Directory access without increasing their security risk caused by the distribution of directory services.

BranchCache File Access

New to Windows Server 2008 R2 and further expanded in Windows Server 2012 is a role called BranchCache. BranchCache is a technology that provides users with better access to files across a WAN. Normally, if one user accesses a file, the file is transferred across the WAN for the user, and then when another user accesses the same file, the same file is again transferred across the WAN for the other user. BranchCache acknowledges that a file has been transferred across the WAN by a previous user, and instead of retrieving the file across the WAN, the file is accessed locally by the subsequent user.

BranchCache requires Windows 7 or Windows 8 on the client side and can be set up so that the file is effectively retrieved in a peer-to-peer manner from another Windows 7 or Windows 8 client that had previously accessed a file. Or, a Windows Server 2012 server with the BranchCache server role can be set up in the remote location where remotely accessed files are temporarily cached for other Windows 7 and Windows 8 client users to seamlessly access the files locally instead of being downloaded across the WAN.

BranchCache does not require the user to do anything differently. Users simply accesses files as they normally do (either off a Windows file system or from a SharePoint document library), and the combination of Windows 7 or Windows 8 client, and Windows Server 2012 does all the caching automatically. BranchCache has proven to improve access time on average 30% to 45% for remote users, thus increasing user experience and potentially user productivity by having faster access to information in remote locations.

Improvements for Thin-Client Remote Desktop Services

Windows Server 2012 has seen significant improvements in the Terminal Services (now called Remote Desktop Services [RDS]) capabilities for thin-client access for remote users and managed users in the enterprise. Third-party add-ons used to be required to make the basic Windows 2000 or 2003 Terminal Services functional, but Microsoft included those technologies in Windows Server 2008 and further enhanced them in Windows Server 2012. You can now access RDS using a standard port 443 Secure Sockets Layer (SSL) connection rather than the proprietary port 3389, and can publish just specific programs rather than the entire desktop. In addition, improvements now allow a client to have a larger remote-access screen, multiple screens, and to more easily print to remote print devices.

In addition, with a technology called RemoteFX that leverages the processing capability of a GPU-assisted video adapter in a RDS server, full-motion video and graphics can now be accelerated and support in Virtual Desktop Infrastructure (VDI) guest sessions and in RDS thin-client RDS guest sessions. RemoteFX makes rich desktop experiences that incorporate graphics and video fully realizable in shared-system environments. This is a significant improvement in supporting business needs in a shared environment, without compromising performance and capabilities.

These improvements in Windows Server 2012 RDS have made RDS one of the easiest components to add to an existing Active Directory 2003 or Active Directory 2008 environment to test out the new Windows Server 2012 capabilities. After all, the installation of a Windows Server 2012 RDS system is just the addition of a member server to the domain and can easily be removed at any time. Chapter 25 covers all of these new improvements in Windows Server 2012 RDS.

Improvements in Remote Desktop Client

Other improvements to Windows Server 2012 RDS include updates to the Remote Desktop Protocol (RDP) and Remote Desktop Client (RDC).

The latest versions of the RDC support the following:

- **Video support up to 4,096 x 2,048**—Users can use very large monitors across an RDP connection to view data off a Windows Server 2008 Terminal Services system. With Windows Server 2012 RDS, the latest support has been extended to support DirectX 9, 10, and 11 redirection.
- **Multimonitor support**—Users can also have multiple (up to 10) monitors supported off a single RDP connection. For applications like computer-aided design (CAD), graphical arts, and publishing, users can view graphical information on one screen and text information on another screen at the same time.
- **Secured connections**—The latest RDP clients now provides for a highly encrypted remote connection to an RDS system through the use of Windows Server 2012 security. Organizations that need to ensure their data is protected and that employee privacy is ensured can implement a highly secured encrypted connection between a Windows Server 2012 RDS system and the remote client.

RDS Web Access

Also new to Windows Server 2008 and extended in Windows Server 2012 RDS is a role called RDS Web Access. RDS Web Access allows a remote client to access an RDS session without having to launch the RDP client, but instead connect to a web page, similar to that shown in Figure 1.9, that then allows the user to log on and access his or her session off the web page. This simplifies the access method for users; where they can just set a browser favorite to link them to a URL that provides them Terminal Services access.

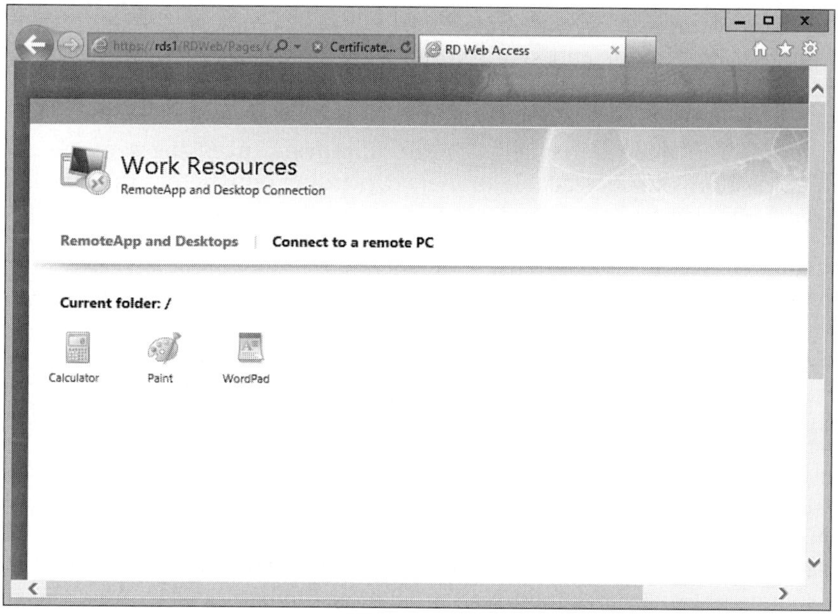

FIGURE 1.9 RDS Web Access.

RDS Gateway

RDS Gateway is an update to Windows Server 2012 RDS and provides the connectivity to an RDS session over a standard port 443 SSL connection. In early releases or RDS, users could only connect to Windows RDS using a proprietary port 3389 connection. Unfortunately, most organizations block nonstandard port connections for security purposes, and so if a user was connected to an Internet connection at a hotel, airport, coffee shop, or other location that blocked nonstandard ports, the user could not access Terminal Services.

Now with RDS Gateway, the remote user to the RDS Gateway connection goes over port 443, just like surfing a secured web page. Because of the use of SSL in web page access (anytime someone accesses a web page with https://), a user can now effectively access Windows Server 2012 RDS from any location.

RDS RemoteApps

Another server role added to Windows Server 2008 and updated in Windows Server 2012 is called RDS RemoteApps. RDS RemoteApps enables administrators to "publish" certain applications for users to access. These applications could be things like Microsoft Outlook,

Microsoft Word, the company's timesheet tracking software, or a customer relationship management (CRM) program. Instead of giving users full access to a full desktop session complete with a Start button and access to all applications on the session, an organization can just publish a handful of applications that it allows for access.

Leveraging group policies and Network Policy Server, along with RDS RemoteApps, the administrators of a network can publish different groups of applications for different users. So, some users might get just Outlook and Word, whereas other users get Outlook, Word, and the CRM application. Add in to the policy component the ability to leverage network location awareness (new to Windows Server 2012 and covered in the earlier section "Improvements in the Group Policy Management"), the administrators of the network can allow different applications to be available to users depending on whether the user is logging on to the network on the LAN or from a remote location.

Beyond just limiting users by policy to only the programs they should have access to, RDS RemoteApps minimizes the overhead for each user connection because the user no longer has a full desktop running, but only a handful of applications deemed necessary for the remote user's access.

Remote Desktop Virtualization Host for VDI

Lastly, a completely new role added to Windows Server 2008 and also greatly enhanced in Window Server 2012 is the Remote Desktop Virtualization Host (RDVH) role that provides Virtual Desktop Infrastructure (VDI) functionality. Instead of RDS that provides a one-to-many experience, where effectively a single server instance is shared across multiple users, VDI provides a one-to-one virtual guest session relationship between the server and remote client. When a VDI client user logs on to a guest session, a dedicated guest session is made available to the user with a separate client boot shell, separate memory pool allocated, and complete isolation of the guest session from other guest sessions on the host server.

Windows Server 2012 VDI provides two different VDI modes. One mode is a personalized desktop, and the other is a pooled desktop. The personalized desktop is a dedicated guest session that users have access to each and every time they log on to the VDI server. It is basically a dedicated guest session where the image the guest uses is the same every time. A pooled desktop is a guest session where the user settings (favorites, background, and application configuration settings) are saved and reloaded on logon to a standard template. Actual guest session resources are not permanently allocated but rather allocated and dedicated at the time of logon.

Chapter 25 covers RDVH for VDI in more detail.

Windows to Go

Windows to Go is a great addition to Windows Server 2012, where effectively Windows is installed on a USB drive and Windows can be booted from the thumb drive. By having a bootable thumb drive, organizations can allow users to use various desktop and laptop systems that may otherwise be installed and configured with a different operating system or configuration (for example, a home system) but booted to the thumb drive that has a secured version of an organization's operating system and applications. Windows to Go helps organizations maintain security of system configurations while allowing employees to retain personal laptop or desktop configurations.

Simplifying the Datacenter

After years of building, configuring, and upgrading servers in the datacenter, organizations really want to simplify the datacenter with fewer tools, fewer third-party add-ins, and more efficiency in operations. Windows Server 2012 provides a number of new tools and technologies that outright help organizations simplify IT. This section covers those technologies, including Server Manager, distributed administration, PowerShell, AD Administrative Center, Hyper-V SMB, storage spaces, data de-dupe, Group Policy management improvements, IP Address Management (IPAM), and the continuation of Performance and Reliability Monitoring tools, such as Best Practice Analyzer (BPA), Windows Deployment Services (WDS), and Distributed File System (DFS).

New Server Manager Tool

A tool that has been completely redone for Windows Server 2012 is the Server Manager console, shown in Figure 1.10. Server Manager consolidates all the server configuration tasks into a single unified management tool. Administrators can now configure server names and IP addresses (that used to be in Control Panel), add server roles and features (was in Server Manager), and launch administrator tools (was off the Start button) that are now all in the new Server Manager console.

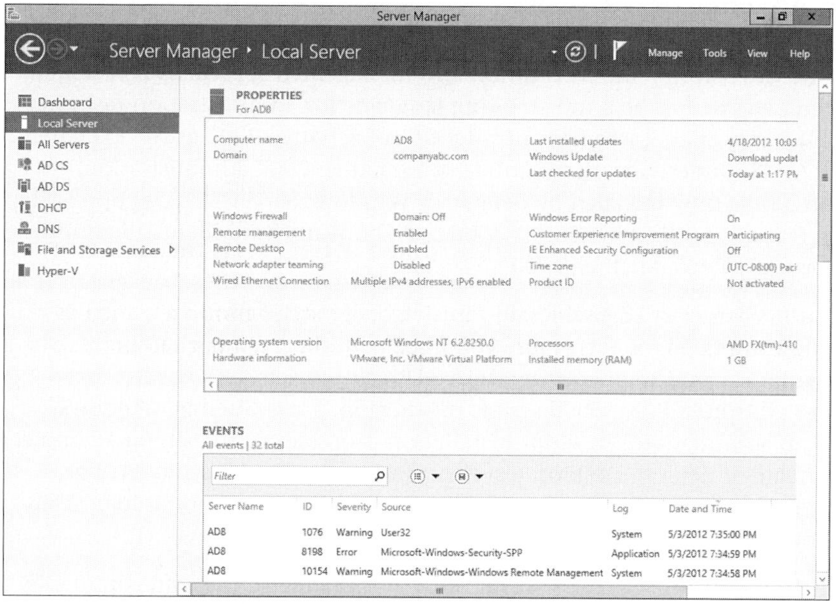

FIGURE 1.10 Server Manager.

Updated in Windows Server 2012 is the ability for an administrator to use the Server Manager tool to access not only the server resources on the current server system, but also to remotely access server resources through the Server Manager tool on remote server systems. This remote capability of Server Manager minimizes the need of the administrator to remotely log on to systems to manage them; it allows the administrator to sit at a single Server Manager console and gain access to other servers in the organization.

Improvements in Distributed Administration

For remote or branch offices that do have IT personnel in the remote locations, administration and management tasks have been challenging as related to the distribution of proper security rights. Either remote IT personnel were given full domain administrator rights when they should have only been given limited to rights specific to their site or administrators were not given any administrative rights because it was too difficult to apply a more limiting role.

Windows Server 2012 Active Directory has now defined a set of rights specific to branch office and remote site administrators. Very similar to site administrators back in the old Exchange Server 5.5 days—when an administrator could add users, contacts, and administer local Exchange servers—now network administrators in Active Directory can be delegated rights based on a branch or remote site role. This enables those administrators to make changes specific to their branch location. This, along with all the other tools in Windows Server 2012 specific to branch office and remote office locations, now provides better IT services to organizations with multiple offices in the enterprise.

PowerShell for Administrative Tasks

In the past couple versions of Windows Server, Microsoft has been adding in more and more support for the extension of administration and management based on PowerShell. PowerShell has been extended to be a full scripting language for administration tasks in Windows Server 2012. PowerShell was first introduced in Exchange 2007 as the Exchange Management Shell (EMS) underlying all functions of Exchange 2007 administration. PowerShell (version 3.0) is now installed by default in Windows Server 2012, as opposed to being an add-in feature in Windows Server 2008. As a built-in component, all administrative tasks are now fully PowerShell enabled.

PowerShell in Windows Server 2012 enables administrators to script processes, such as adding users, adding computers, or even more complicated tasks such as querying a database, extracting usernames, and then creating Active Directory users, and to provision Exchange mailboxes all from a PowerShell script. In addition, PowerShell in Windows Server 2012 allows an administrator to script installation processes so that if, for example, the administrator creates a Remote Desktop server or web server with specific settings, the administrator can use a PowerShell script and deploy additional servers all identically configured using the same script over and over.

And with PowerShell built in to Windows Server 2012, PowerShell scripts and commands can be run against remote servers. This enables an administrator to sit at one server and remotely execute scripts on other servers in the environment. Using secured server-to-server session communications, an administrator can configure a group of servers, manage a group of servers, and reboot a group of servers all from a series of PowerShell commands.

All future server products released from Microsoft will have the PowerShell foundation built in to the core Windows Server 2012 operating system, thus making it easier for products running on Windows Server 2012 to use the same administrative scripting language. PowerShell is covered in detail in Chapter 21, "Automating Tasks Using PowerShell Scripting."

Active Directory Administrative Center

Newly updated in Windows Server 2012 and built on PowerShell v3.0, the Active Directory Administrative Center is a customizable console that an organization can create for specific administrators in the organization. For example, an organization might have an administrator who only needs to reset passwords, or another administrator who only needs or manage print queues. Instead of giving the administrator access to the full Active Directory Users and Computers or Print Management consoles, an Active Directory Administrative console can be created with just a task or two specific to the administrator's responsibilities.

The console is built on PowerShell, so underlying the GUI consists of simple PowerShell scripts. Anything that can be done in PowerShell on a Windows Server 2012 server can be front-ended by the administration console. An example of the console is shown in Figure 1.11, and the tool is covered in detail in Chapter 18, "Windows Server 2012 Administration."

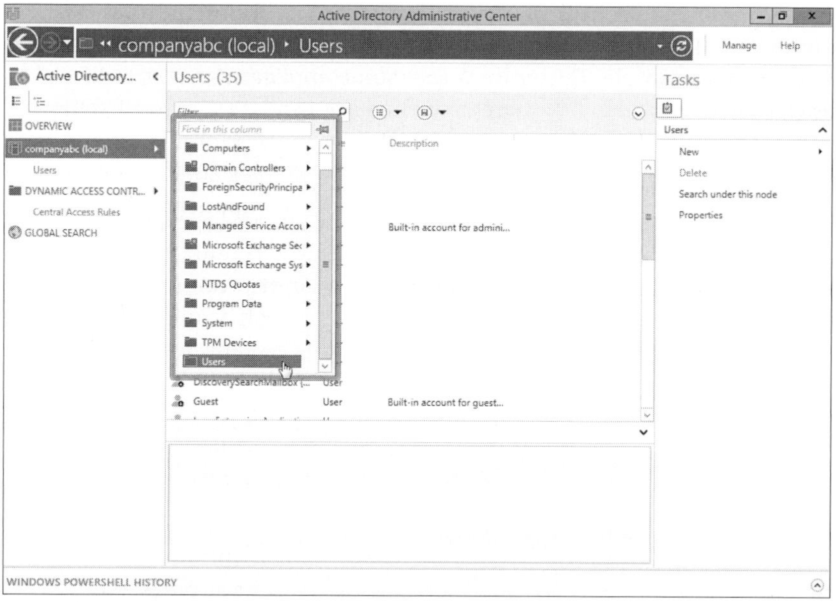

FIGURE 1.11 Active Directory Administrative Center.

Windows Server 2012 provides several new benefits that help organizations better administer their networking environment. These new features provide better file and data management, better performance monitoring and reliability tracking tools to identify system problems and proactively address issues, a new image deployment tool, and a whole new set of Group Policy objects that help administrators better manage users, computers, and other Active Directory objects.

Storage Spaces

The Storage Spaces feature is new to Windows Server 2012 and is the first time the basic file server file system has had a major update in Windows in years. The Storage Spaces feature makes it possible for the file share to span multiple drive shares and multiple servers. Unlike in the past, when a file share was data and directories on a single drive volume, now with Storage Spaces, the share can span across two, three, or more volumes yet still appear to be a single directory of files.

Organizations are using the Storage Spaces feature to not only simply add on more storage as an existing drive volume runs out of space, but also to mirror and stripe storage spaces for higher redundancy and reliable of storage. By mirroring multiple volumes, the storage space can be made redundant at the file system level. Of course, organizations can also mirror hard drives inside a server, so why are storage spaces any better? The real answer is that storage spaces can be mirrored and striped across multiple servers.

By having multiple servers with mirrored copies of the file system, the basic file server now has redundancy spanning multiple servers. If one server with the storage space goes offline, the other copy of the storage space continues to operate. Some IT professionals familiar with Windows server technologies will wonder how this differs from Distributed File System (DFS), which also enables you to mirror storage and replicate information across multiple servers. The big difference is that storage spaces appear as physical drives to the local server (for example, D>, or local E>). Some applications do not like a DFS share because it is seen as a network share, and thus not available for local share functionality.

The Storage Spaces feature provides yet another way for organizations to achieve higher availability and redundancy of information without the need to purchase expensive SANs or complicated shared-storage solutions. The Storage Spaces feature is built in to Windows Server 2012 and provides organizations a simple alternative to achieve many basic file storage requirements.

Improvements in Group Policy Management

In Windows Server 2012, the basic functions of Group Policy haven't changed, so the Group Policy Management Console is the same, but with more options and settings available.

The Group Policy Management Console is launched off the Server Manager console or just run as a separate tool, as shown in Figure 1.12. Group policies in the past few years in Windows Server provide more granular management of local machines, specifically having policies that push down to a client that are different for administrator and nonadministrator users.

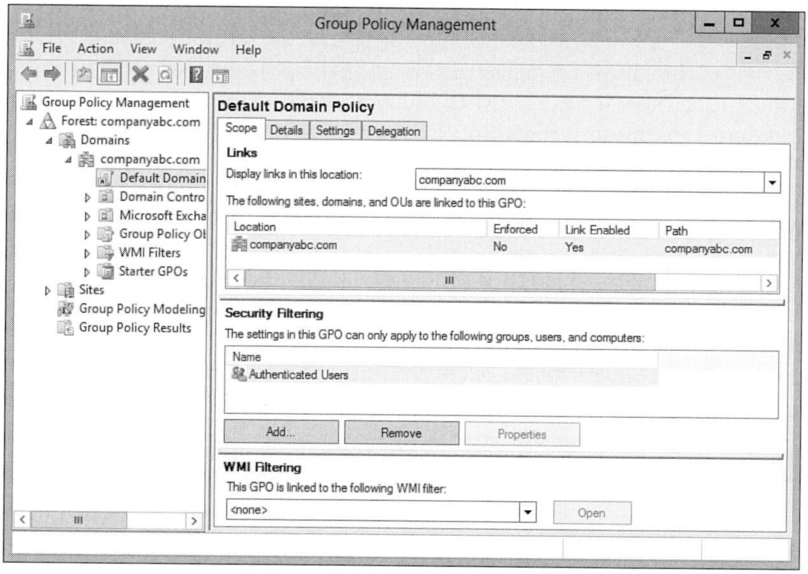

FIGURE 1.12 Group Policy Management Console.

In addition, starting with group policies in Active Directory 2008, applications have been able to query or register with a network-location awareness service within Group Policy Management, which provides the identity where a user or computer object resides. For example, a policy can be written that allows users to have access to applications and files if they are on a local network segment, but for security and privacy reasons blocks users from accessing the same content when they are on a remote segment. This addition to group policies adds a third dimension to policies so that administrators can not only define who and what someone has access to, but also limit their access based on where they are.

Group policies are covered in detail in Chapter 27, "Group Policy Management for Network Clients," as well as in Chapter 19, "Windows Server 2012 Group Policies and Policy Management."

NOTE

When running the Group Policy Management Console to manage a Windows Server 2012 Active Directory environment, you can run it on a Windows server or installed on a Windows client system. The Remote Server Administration Tools (RSAT) are available for installation on various Windows endpoints. Check the requirements to confirm the version of RSAT you want to install supports the operating system you want to manage from.

IP Address Management

New to Windows Server 2012 is the IP Address Management (IPAM) tool. IPAM enables an organization to organize, view, and report on utility systems on the network, specifically IP address mapping, DNS server configurations and assignment, DHCP server configurations and assignments, and the like.

A key area where organizations have found IPAM to be most useful is in the replacement of spreadsheets and databases mapping servers, routers, Internet connections, and the like with IP addresses, those manual IP address sheets that provide the mapping of devices and addresses. Through the use of tagging, devices and IP addresses can be tagged to note which city, campus building, server room, rack, and rack position a specific IP addresses and its corresponding server or device is connected to.

IPAM also provides an "at a glance" view of IP address blocks, IP address assignments, IP ranges and groups, and the like, similar to what is shown in Figure 1.13. A very helpful resource added to Windows Server 2012, IPAM is covered in detail in Chapter 11.

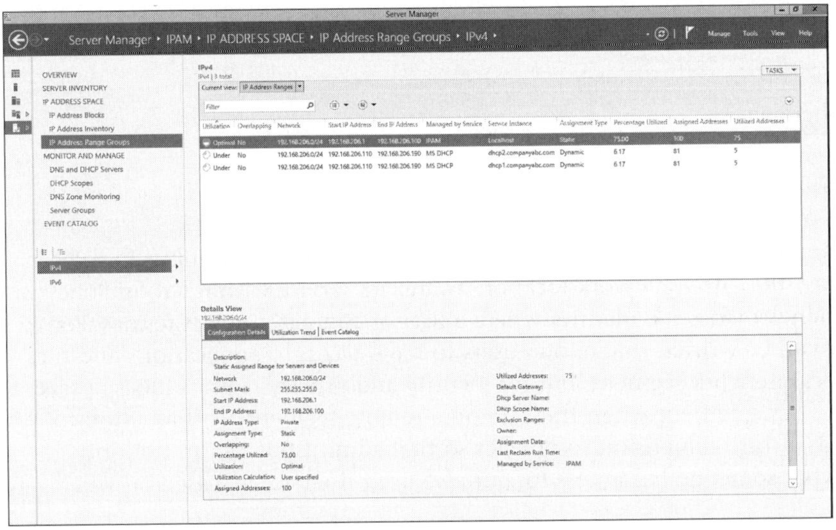

FIGURE 1.13 IPAM Console.

Managing Windows 2012 with Performance and Reliability Monitoring Tools

Windows Server 2012 continues to extend the support for viewing, identifying, reporting on, and assisting in the monitoring of the Windows-based environment. Windows performance and reliability monitoring tools help network administrators better understand the health and operations of Windows Server 2012 systems. Just as with the Group Policy Management Console, you can launch the Reliability and Performance Monitor from the Server Manager console. When you click Tools, Performance Monitor, the tool displays a screen similar to what is shown in Figure 1.14.

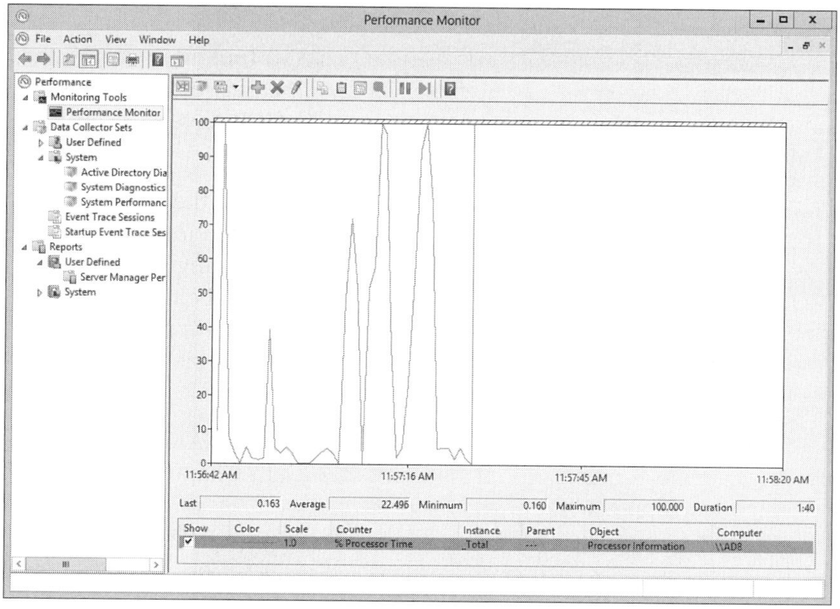

FIGURE 1.14 Performance Monitor console.

The new tool keeps track of system activity and resource usage and displays key counters and system status on screen. The Reliability Monitor diagnoses potential causes of server instability by noting the last time a server was rebooted, what patches or updates were applied, and when (chronologically) services have failed on the system so that system faults can potentially be traced back to specific system updates or changes that occurred prior to the problem.

Using this combination (in single console) of what used to be three or four tools back in Windows 2003, administrators can now look at system performance, operational tasks, and historical event information as they analyze a server problem or system instability. You can find more information about performance and reliability monitoring in Chapter 34.

Leveraging the Best Practice Analyzer

Included in Windows Server 2012 is a built-in Best Practice Analyzer (BPA), shown in Figure 1.15. Found in the Server Manager console tool, the BPA runs a series of tests against Active Directory roles, such as the Hyper-V role, the DNS role, and the RDS role, to assess whether the role has been installed and configured properly and to compare the installation with tested best practices.

BPA results might tell administrators they need to add more memory to a server, move a role to a separate server to improve role optimization, or shift a database to a different drive on the server to distribute disk performance demands on the system. You can find more information about BPA in Chapter 20.

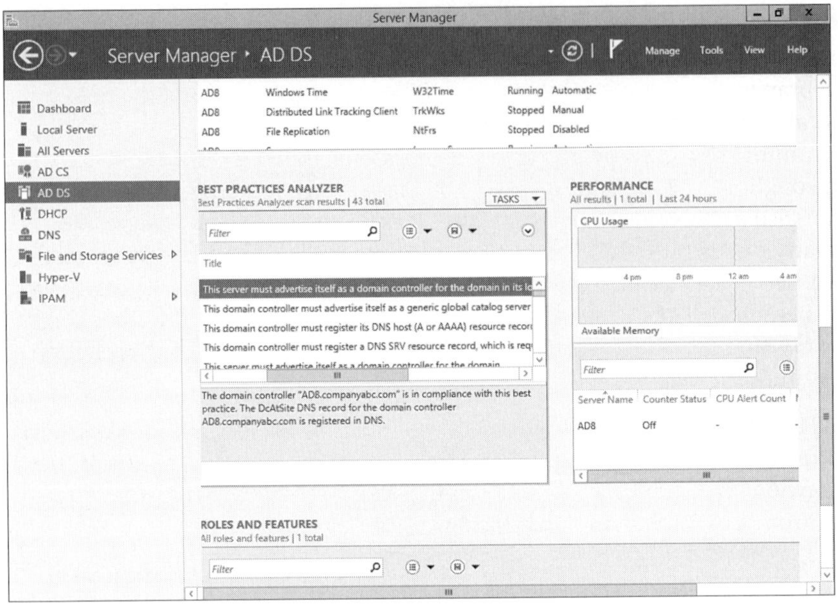

FIGURE 1.15 BPA in the Server Manager console.

Windows Deployment Services Integration

Windows Server 2008 introduced a new tool called Windows Deployment Services (WDS), which was formerly known as Remote Installation Services (RIS) in earlier versions of Windows Server. Unlike RIS, which was focused primarily on scripted installations and client images, WDS in Windows Server 2012 can distribute images of Windows 7 and Windows 8 clients or Windows Server 2008 and 2012 servers in a significantly more flexible and modifiable deployment process.

Like RIS, WDS allows a client system to initiate a Preboot Execution Environment (PXE), effectively "booting" to the WDS server to see a list of images that can be deployed on the system. Alternatively, an organization can create a Windows PE boot disc and have an image initiated from a CD or DVD.

With Windows Server 2008/2012 and Windows 7/8, the image can be created in Windows Imaging (WIM) format, which allows for the injection of patches, updates, or even new code to a WIM file without even booting the image file. This provides the organization with more than just static images that get pushed out like in RIS, but rather a tool that provides ongoing and manageable updates to image files.

WDS is covered in detail in Chapter 26, "Windows Server 2012 Administration Tools for Desktops."

Distributed File System Replication

Introduced in Windows 2000, improved in Windows 2003 and 2008, and now a core component of the branch office offerings in Windows Server 2012, Distributed File System Replication (DFSR) allows files to be replicated between servers, effectively providing duplicate information in multiple locations. In most organizations, files are distributed across multiple servers throughout the enterprise. Users access file shares that are geographically distributed, but can also access file shares sitting on several servers in a site within the organization. In many organizations, when file shares were originally created years ago, server performance, server disk capacity, and the workgroup nature of file and print server distribution created environments in which those organizations had a file share for every department and every site. So, files have typically been distributed throughout an entire organization across multiple servers.

Windows Server 2012 DFSR enables an organization to combine file shares to fewer servers and create a file directory tree not based on a server-by-server or share-by-share basis, but rather an enterprisewide directory tree. This allows an organization to have a single directory spanning files from multiple servers throughout the enterprise.

Because the DFSR directory is a logical directory that spans the entire organization with links back to physical data, the actual physical data can be moved without having to make changes to the way the users see the logical DFS directory. This enables an organization to add or delete servers, or move and consolidate information, however it works best within the organization.

For branch office locations, DFSR allows for data stored on a file server in a remote location to be trickled back to the home office for nightly backup. Instead of having the remote location responsible for data backup, or the requirement of an organization to have tape drives in each of its branch offices, any data saved on the branch office can be trickle replicated back to a share at the main office for backup and recovery.

If the main office has data that it wants to push out to all remote offices, whether that is template files, company policy documents, standard company materials, or even shared data that a workgroup of users needs to access and collaborate on, DFSR provides the ability to push out data to other servers on the network. Users with access rights to the data no longer have to go across a WAN connection to access common data. The information is pushed out to a server that is more local to the user, and the user accesses the local copy of the information. If any changes are made to remote or centralized copies of data, those changes are automatically redistributed back to all volumes storing a copy of the data.

One of the enhancements made in Windows Server 2008 and extended in Windows Server 2012 specific to DFSR is the ability for an administrator to set a DFS replica to be read-only. In the past, DFS replicas were all read/write replicas, and so a user in a remote location could accidentally overwrite files that would then replicate to all replicas in the environment. Administrators have compensated for this potential issue by setting file-level permissions across files and folders; however, for many remote branch offices, if the administrator could simply make the entire replica read-only, it would simplify the security task dramatically. Therefore, read-only replicas can now be set so that an entire server or branch of a DFS tree can be set to replicate to a remote server on a read-only basis.

DFSR is covered in detail in Chapter 28.

Addition of Migration Tools

Beyond the standard migration tools that help administrators migrate from one version of Active Directory to another, or to perform an in-place upgrade from one version of Windows to another, Microsoft provides migration tools to help administrators move entire server roles from one system to another. These new tools provide migration paths from physical servers to virtual servers, or from virtual servers to physical servers. Other tools allow for the migration of DHCP configuration and lease information from one server to another. These tools and the prescriptive guidance help administrators migrate servers more easily than ever before.

Operating System Migration Tools

Microsoft provides tools that help administrators migrate from older versions of the Windows Server operating system to Windows Server 2012. The supported migration paths are as follows:

- **Windows Server 2003, Windows Server 2008, Windows Server 2008 R2**—These operating systems can be migrated to Windows Server 2012 using the operating system migration tools and guidance documentation.
- **x86 and x64**—Servers can be migrated from x86 to x64 and from x64 to x64 with limitations. Because Windows Server 2012 is an x64 operating system only, there is no in-place upgrade support from x86 to x64, so the upgrade path is a server-to-server transition, not in-place. However, x64 to x64 in-place is supported as long as any applications sitting on the server can be upgraded from one x64 platform to the Windows Server 2012 x64 platform.
- **Full Server and Server Core**—Operating system migration from Full Server to Server Core and from Server Core to Full Server are supported typically as a server-to-server migration because in-place migrations between Full Server and Server Core have limitations. The GUI needs to be added or removed and, thus, applications are typically migrated rather than complete operating system migrations between the platforms.
- **Physical and virtual**—Virtualization of guest sessions is the de facto standard in data centers these days and the implementation of applications on virtual guest sessions is the norm. Therefore, organizations wanting to migrate from physical server configurations to virtual guest sessions can leverage the migration tools and guidance available in performing server and application migrations to virtual server roles.

Server Role Migrations

Included in Windows Server 2012 are tools and guidance that help administrators migrate server roles to Windows Server 2012 server systems. The supported migration paths are as follows:

- **Active Directory Domain Services**—The migration from Active Directory 2003 and Active Directory 2008 / 2008R2 to Active Directory 2012 is fully supported and covered in Chapter 16 of this book.
- **DNS and DHCP migrations**—New migration tools are available that help administrators migrate their DNS and DHCP servers from running on previous versions of Windows to servers running Windows Server 2012, and not only just the service configurations, but also DNS and DHCP data. In the past, the migration of DHCP to a new server usually meant the loss of DHCP lease information. With the new migration tools in Windows Server 2012, an administrator can now migrate the server configuration as well as the lease data, including lease expiration data, as part of the migration process. These migration tools are covered in Chapters 10 and 11 of this book.
- **File and print migrations**—Included in the migration tools for Windows Server 2012 are features that migrate file data, included file permissions, and the migration of print server configurations and settings from older servers to new Windows Server 2012 configurations. These migration tools help simplify the process of updating servers from old server systems to new systems with the least amount of impact on the organization and drastically simplify the process of migration for domain administrators.

Identifying Which Windows Server 2012 Service to Install or Migrate to First

With the release of Windows Server 2012, organizations need to create a plan to install or migrate to Windows Server 2012 in a logical manner. Covered so far in this chapter have been all the top features, functions, and technologies built in to Windows Server 2012 that organizations have found as key solution implemented in enterprises to improve technology-driven business processes.

Because Windows Server 2012 provides many different functions, each organization has to choose how to best implement Windows Server 2012 and the various networking features that meet its own needs. In small network environments with fewer than 20 to 30 users, an organization might choose to implement all the Windows Server 2012 features on a single server. However, in larger environments, multiple servers might be implemented to improve system performance, and to provide fault tolerance and redundancy; therefore, a more staged implementation of core services needs to be followed.

Windows Server 2012 Core to an Active Directory Environment

For an organization that does not have Windows Active Directory already in place, that is one place to start because AD DS is key to application and user authentication. For organizations that already have a fully operational Active Directory running on Windows 2003 or Windows 2008, upgrading to AD DS on Windows Server 2012 might be something that is addressed a little later in the upgrade cycle when AD DS 2012 functionality is needed. To get a lot of the Windows Server 2012 server functionality like 2012 DFS, SharePoint Services, Hyper-V virtualization, and so on, an organization can still run on an older Active Directory environment (typically Active Directory 2003 Native mode). However, the point is that Active Directory 2012 is not a prerequisite to get Windows Server 2012 server role functionality.

Because Active Directory is more than a simple list of users and passwords for authentication into a network, but rather a directory that Microsoft has embedded into the policy-based security, remote-access security, and certificate-based security enhancements in Windows Server 2012, AD DS 2012 implementation does occur earlier in the migration cycle for organizations wanting to implement many of the new Active Directory 2012 technologies, such as Active Directory Recycle Bin, Offline Domain Join, Managed Service Accounts, and the ability to use PowerShell cmdlets within a Group Policy object.

Windows Server 2012 extends the capabilities of the Active Directory by creating better management tools, provides for more robust directory replication across a global enterprise, and allows for better scalability and redundancy to improve directory operations. Windows Server 2012 effectively adds in more reliability, faster performance, and better management tools to a system that can be leveraged as a true enterprise directory provisioning, resource tracking, and resource management tool. Because of the importance of Active Directory to the Windows Server 2012 operating system, plus the breadth of capabilities that Active Directory can facilitate, six chapters in Part II of this book are dedicated to Active Directory.

Windows Server 2012 Running Built-In Application Server Functions

As much as many administrators think of Active Directory as one of the key areas to upgrade when a new release of the operating system becomes available, in reality Active Directory tends to not be the first thing updated. Instead, the real business drivers for migrating to Windows Server 2012 typically come from the built-in application server programs that are available on Windows Server 2012.

Windows Server 2012 comes with several programs and utilities to provide robust networking capabilities. In addition to the basic file and print capabilities covered earlier in this chapter, Windows Server 2012 can provide name resolution for the network and enable high availability through clustering and fault tolerance, connectivity for mobile users, web services functions, and dozens of other application server functions.

When convincing management that an upgrade to Windows Server 2012 is important, the IT professional needs to sift through the technologies built in to Windows Server 2012 and pick those services that help an organization use technology to achieve its business initiatives. When planning the implementation of Windows Server 2012, a network architect needs to consider which of the server services are desired, how they will be combined on servers, and how they will be made redundant across multiple servers for business continuity failover.

For a small organization, the choice to combine several server functions to a single system or to just a few systems is one of economics. However, an organization might distribute server services to multiple servers to improve performance (covered in Chapter 34), distribute administration (covered in Chapter 18), create server redundancy (covered in Chapter 29), create a disaster recovery strategy (covered in Chapter 31, "Recovering from a Disaster"), enable security (covered in Chapter 13), or to serve users in other remote site locations of the organization (covered in Chapter 32).

Built-in application server functions in Windows Server 2012 include the following:

- **Domain controller**—As in earlier versions of the Windows operating system, the domain controller enables users to authenticate to the domain for access to network resources.
- **Global catalog server**—The global catalog server is a domain controller that also stores a subset of AD DS objects from other domains in the forest. When an internal or external user with appropriate security rights wants to look at a list of Active Directory users in the forest, the global catalog server provides the list.
- **DNS server**—The domain name system (DNS) maintains a list of network servers and systems and their associated IP addresses, so a DNS server provides information about the devices connected to the network.
- **DHCP server**—The Dynamic Host Configuration Protocol (DHCP) assigns IPv4/IPv6 network addresses to devices on the network. Windows Server 2012 provides the service function to facilitate DHCP addresses to network devices.
- **Cluster server**—When fault tolerance is important to an organization, clustering provides failover from one system to another. Windows Server 2012 provides the ability to link systems together so that when one system fails, another system takes over.
- **Network Policy Server**—NPS is the Microsoft implementation of a Remote Authentication Dial-In User Service (RADIUS) server and proxy. NPS performs centralized connection authentication, authorization, and accounting for many types of network access, including wireless and virtual private network (VPN) connections. NPS routes authentication and accounting messages to other RADIUS servers. It also acts as a health evaluation server for Network Access Protection (NAP).
- **Remote Desktop server**—Instead of having a full desktop or laptop computer for each user on the network, organizations have the option of setting up simple, low-cost thin terminals for users to gain access to network resources. Windows Server 2012 RDS allows a single server to host network system access for dozens of users.
- **Remote-access server**—When a remote user has a desktop or laptop system and needs access to network services, Windows Server 2012 provides remote access services that allow the remote systems to establish a secure remote connection.

- **Web server**—As more and more technologies become web aware and are hosted on web servers, Windows Server 2012 provides the technology to host these applications for browser-based access.
- **Virtualization server**—Windows Server 2012 provides the core capabilities to do server virtualization, providing the capability for an organization to consolidate physical servers into fewer host server systems, thus decreasing the total cost of IT operations.
- **Distributed File System (DFS) server**—For the past decade, data files have been stored on file servers all around an organization. Windows Server 2012 provides DFSs that allow an organization to take control of distributed files into a common unified namespace.

These plus several other functions provide robust networking services that help organizations leverage the Windows Server 2012 technologies into solutions that solve business needs.

Utilizing Windows Server 2012 to Run Business Critical Server Applications

Although some of the newer, built-in server application functions in Windows Server 2012—such as Network Policy Server, server virtualization, RDS Web Access, and so on—provide key areas for organizations to select as initial areas to implement Windows Server 2012 technologies, other organizations might find add-in applications as being the key areas that drive an initial implementation of Windows Server 2012. Some of the add-in applications come from Microsoft, such as the Microsoft Exchange Server 2010 messaging system or Microsoft SQL Server 2012 database system. Other add-ins to Windows Server 2012 come from companies that provide human resource management applications, accounting software, document management tools, fax or voicemail add-ins, or other business/industry/user productivity capabilities.

In earlier Windows Server operating systems, the core operating system provided simple logon and network connectivity functions. With Windows Server 2012, however, the operating system includes many core capabilities built in to the Windows Server 2012 operating environment. With integrated fault tolerance, data recovery, server security, remote-access connectivity, web access technologies, and similar capabilities, organizations creating add-ins for Windows Server 2012 can focus on business functions and capabilities, not on core infrastructure reliability, security, and mobile access functionality. This offloading of the requirement of third-party add-in organizations to implement basic networking technologies into their applications enables these developers to focus on improving the business productivity and functionality of their applications. In addition, consolidating information routing, security, remote management, and so on into the core operating system provides a common method of communication, authentication, and access to users without having to load up special drivers, add-ins, or tools to support each and every new application.

Much of the shift from application-focused infrastructure components to core operating system-focused functionality was built in to Windows 2000 and then later enhanced in Windows 2003 and Windows Server 2008. There were many challenges to earlier versions of the Windows operating system; however, after being on the market for many years now, Windows Server add-ins have had several revisions to work through system functionality and component reliability between application and operating system. Fortunately, Windows Server 2012 uses the same application/operating system technology used in Windows 2008 and Windows Server 2008 R2, so applications written for Windows 2008 / 2008 R2 typically need just a simple service pack update to be able to run on Windows Server 2012, if anything at all.

Summary

This introductory chapter highlighted the new features, functions, migration tools, and management utilities in Windows Server 2012 that will help administrators take advantage of the capabilities of the new operating system. If Windows Server 2012 is seen as just a simple upgrade to Windows 2003/2008, an organization will not benefit from the operating system enhancements. When Windows Server 2012 is fully leveraged, an organization can improve services to its employees through the use of new tools and technologies built in to the operating system.

Because Windows Server 2012 can be a relatively simple migration from existing Windows 2003 and Windows 2008 Active Directory environments, and Windows Server 2012 application servers can be added to existing Active Directory 2003/2008 domains, the migration process really is one where the IT administrators need to prioritize which Windows Server 2012 services to install or migrate to first, and then plan and test the new technologies to make sure they improve IT services to the organization.

Best Practices

The following are best practices from this chapter:

- When implementing Windows Server 2012 for the first time, or migrating to Windows Server 2012 from an earlier version of Windows, first choose to implement the technologies in Windows Server 2012 that will provide the organization with the most value in terms of employee productivity enhancements, regulatory compliance, and security improvements.
- When considering adding a Windows Server 2012 server to an existing Windows 2003/2008 Active Directory environment, consider implementing things like RDS Web Access, SharePoint Services, or Windows virtualization, which have proven to be pretty easy to implement and provide a lot of value to organizations.
- To ultimately improve Windows security, tune and optimize Windows Server 2012 for a secured networking environment.

- Use RDS in Windows Server 2012 to provide users with access to local hard drives, as well as to redirect the audio from a centralized Terminal Server to a remote system.
- Use WDS to create client system images that can be quickly and easily rolled back through Group Policy.
- Windows Server 2012 virtualization can help organizations deploy clustering and add in disaster recovery data centers without having to add additional physical servers to the network.
- Remote and branch office locations greatly benefit from the use of RODCs, DFSR, BitLocker security, and distributed administration tools built in to Windows Server 2012.
- Using the new Windows Server 2012 Server Manager can simplify the task of a network administrator trying to access information residing on different servers and in different server roles in the environment.
- It is best to run the Group Policy Management Console on a Windows Server 2012 or Windows 7/8 system to have access to all the policy features available (compared with running GPMC on a Windows XP or Windows Server 2003 system).

CHAPTER 2

Planning, Prototyping, Migrating, and Deploying Windows Server 2012

IN THIS CHAPTER

The technical process to implement or to migrate to a Windows Server 2012 environment is similar to the migration processes that have been available for migrations to Windows 2003, 2008, and 2008 R2 in the past; however, the requirements and expectations of organizations have made it important for IT professionals to do better planning, preparation, and testing before merely shoving in a DVD and performing an upgrade. Organizations are extremely dependent on the reliability of their network systems and less tolerant to downtime such that the migration process needs to be planned and executed with great attention paid to minimizing user impact and system downtime.

This chapter examines how a structured multistep process for migrating to the Windows Server 2012 environment can enhance the success of the project. Consisting of discovery, design, testing, and implementation phases, this methodology can be scaled to meet the needs of the wide variety of organizations and businesses that use Microsoft technologies. The results of this methodology are three very important documents created to map out the implementation process: the design document, the migration document, and the migration plan.

The examples used in this chapter assume that the environments being migrated are primarily Windows 2008/2008 R2 based, but the concepts and process can certainly apply to other environments.

Determining the Scope of Your Project

As outlined in Chapter 1, "Windows Server 2012 Technology Primary," the Windows Server 2012 platform contains such a wealth of features that planning a migration to it can seem quite daunting at first. This chapter provides some guidance and best practices that can assist with the process and help organizations create a well-thought-out and structured implementation plan.

Rather than forging ahead with no plan or goals and simply building new servers, loading application software, and inserting it into an existing network environment, a more organized process controls the risks involved and defines in detail what the end state will look like.

The first steps involve getting a better sense of the scope of the project, in essence writing the executive summary of your design document. The scope should define from a high level what the project consists of and why the organization is devoting time, energy, and resources to its completion.

Creating this scope of work requires an understanding of the different goals of the organization as well as the pieces of the puzzle that need to fit together to meet the company's stated goals for the project. For Windows Server 2012, the primary pieces are servers that handle key network functionality, servers that handle and manage the data, servers that control or provide access to the information, and servers that handle specific applications.

Identifying the Business Goals and Objectives to Implement Windows Server 2012

It is important to establish a thorough understanding of the goals and objectives of a company that guide and direct the efforts of the different components of the organization, to help ensure the success of the Windows Server 2012 project. It might seem counterintuitive to start at this very high level and keep away from the bits- and bytes-level details, but time spent in this area will clarify the purposes of the project and start to generate productive discussions.

As an example of the value of setting high-level business goals and objectives, an organization can identify the desire for zero downtime on file access; this downtime could be facilitated through the implementation of the Distributed File System (DFS) technology or the Failover Clustering feature. Starting with broad goals and objectives will create an outline for a technical solution that will meet all the criteria the organization wants, at a lower cost, and with an easier-managed solution.

In every organization, a variety of different goals and objectives must be identified and met for a project to be considered successful. These goals and objectives represent a snapshot of the end state that the company or organization seeks to create. For a smaller company, this process might be completed in a few brainstorming sessions, whereas larger companies might require more extensive discussions and assistance from external resources or firms.

High-Level Business Goals

To start the organizational process, it is helpful to break up business goals and objectives into different levels or vantage points. Most organizations have high-level business goals, often referred to as the *vision of the company*, which are typically shaped by the key decision makers in the organization (such as the CEO, CFO, CIO, and so on); these goals are commonly called the *50,000-foot view*. Business unit or departmental goals (the *10,000-foot view*) are usually shaped by the key executives and managers in the organization (such as the VP of sales, HR director, site facilities manager, and so on). Most organizations also have well-defined *1,000-foot view* goals, which are usually tactical in nature and implemented by IT staff and technical specialists.

It is well worth the time to perform some research and ask the right questions to help ensure that the networking system implementation will be successful. To get specific information and clarification of the objectives of the different business units, make sure the goals of a technology implementation or upgrade are in line with these business goals.

Although most organizations have stated company visions and goals, and a quick visit to the company's website or intranet can provide this information, it is worth taking the time to gather more information on what the key stakeholders feel to be their primary objectives. Often, this task starts with asking the right questions of the right people and then opening discussion groups on the topic. Of course, it also matters who asks the questions because the answers will vary accordingly, and employees might be more forthcoming when speaking with external consultants as opposed to co-workers. Often, the publicly stated vision and goals are "the tip of the iceberg" and might even be in contrast to internal company goals, ambitions, or initiatives.

High-level business goals and visions can vary greatly among different organizations, but generally they bracket and guide the goals of the units that make up the company. For example, a corporation might be interested in offering the "best" product in its class, and this requires corresponding goals for the sales, engineering, marketing, finance, and manufacturing departments. Additional concepts to look for are whether the highest-level goals embrace change and new ideas and processes, or want to refine the existing practices and methods.

High-level business goals of a company can also change rapidly, whether in response to changing economic conditions or as affected by a new key stakeholder or leader in the company. So, it is also important to get a sense of the timeline involved for meeting these high-level goals.

NOTE

An example of some high-level business goals include a desire to have no downtime, access to the network from any of the organization's offices around the world, and secured communications when users access the network from home or a remote location.

Business Unit or Departmental Goals

When the vision or 50,000-foot view is defined, additional discussions should reveal the goals of the different departments and the executives who run them. Theoretically, they should "add up" to the highest-level goals, but the findings might be surprising. Whatever the case turns out to be, the results start to reveal the complexity of the organization and the primary concerns of the different stakeholders.

The high-level goals of the organization also start to paint the picture of which departments carry the most weight in the organization, and will most likely get budgets approved, which will assist in the design process. Logically, the goals of the IT department will play a very important role in an (OS) migration project, but the other key departments shouldn't be forgotten.

As an example of the business unit or departmental goals for an organization, an HR department might influence the decision for right-to-privacy access to core personnel records. Or a legal department might influence security access on information storage rights and storage retention.

If the department's goals do not align with the overall vision of the company, or do not take into account the needs of the key stakeholders, the result of the project might not be appreciated. Technology for technology's sake does not always fulfill the needs of the organization and in the long run is viewed as a wasteful expenditure of organizational funds.

In the process of clarifying these goals, the features of the OS and network applications that are most important to the different departments and executives should become apparent. It is safe to assume that access to company data in the form of documents or database information, to communications tools (such as email, faxing, and Internet access), and to vertical market software applications that the company relies on will affect the company's ability to meet its various business goals.

The sales department will most likely have goals that require a specific customer relationship management (CRM) application and access to key company data and communications tools. Likewise, the finance department will have applications that track specific accounts receivable (AR) and accounts payable (AP) information and that most likely tie into applications used by other departments. The IT department will have its key technologies that support the applications in use, store and maintain the company's data, and manage key servers and network devices.

It is also worth looking for the "holes" in the goals and objectives presented. Some of the less-glamorous objectives, such as a stable network, data-recovery abilities, or protection from the hostile outside world, are often neglected.

A by-product of these discussions will ideally be a sense of excitement over the possibilities presented by the new technologies that will be introduced, and will convey to the executives and key stakeholders that they are involved in helping to define and craft a solution that takes into account the varied needs of the company. Many executives look for this high-level strategy, thinking, and discussions to reveal the maturity of the planning and implementation process in action.

NOTE

An example of some departmental goals include a desire to have secured storage of human resource and personnel information, 30-minute response time to help desk questions during business hours, 24-hour support for sales executives when they are traveling, and easy lookup of files stored on servers throughout the organization.

Identifying the Technical Goals and Objectives to Implement Windows Server 2012

Although an OS upgrade to Windows Server 2012 might not initially seem integral to the highest-level company goals, its importance becomes clearer as the goals get close to the 1,000-foot view. When the business goals are sketched out, the technical goals should fall into place quite naturally.

At this point in the process, questions should focus on which components and capabilities of the network are most important and how they contribute to or hinder the goals expressed by the different units.

As with business goals, the technical goals of the project should be clarified on different levels (50,000 foot, 10,000 foot, 1,000 foot, and so on). At the highest level, the technical goals might be quite vague, such as "no downtime" or "access to data from anywhere." But as the goals are clarified on a departmental and individual level, they should become specific and measurable. For example, instead of identifying a goal as "no downtime," ferreting out the details might result in a more specific goal of "99.99% uptime during business hours, and no more than 4-hour downtime during nonbusiness hours scheduled at least 2 days in advance." Instead of stating a goal of "access to data from anywhere," a more specific goal of "high-speed remote logon from any corporate regional office around the world and dial-up or virtual private network (VPN) access from the home offices of the organization's senior managers" can more reasonably be attained.

Part of the art of defining technical goals and objectives also resides in limiting them. Data can be accessed in many different ways, and the complexity of the network environment can boggle even the veteran IT manager's mind. So, for example, instead of setting a goal of "remote access to all employees," a more focused goal such as "access to email for all employees, remote access to email and the accounting software for the finance department, and remote access to email and the CRM software for sales executives" is more actionable.

Departmental technical goals can include 10,000-foot items—for example, implementing a new software application or set of functions that require other network changes, such as an OS upgrade to Windows Server 2012. The marketing department might require some of the advanced features of the latest version of Microsoft Exchange, as well as enhanced website capabilities that necessitate the implementation of Windows Server 2012. Or, the sales department might require better remote access to the company's data through mobile devices and the Internet, and a solution was already chosen that requires Windows Server 2012 as the core OS platform.

Two key components should also be included in these discussions: budget and timeline. A huge amount of time in the design phase can be saved if these components are clarified (and agreed on) early in the process. Some projects have to happen "yesterday," whereas others can happen over a period of quarters or even years. In most cases, the budget will vary with the time frame involved because longer timelines enable organizations to train resources internally and migrate in a more gradual fashion. Even if a firm budget or timeline isn't available, order-of-magnitude ranges can be established. If $500,000 is too much, how about $250,000? $100,000? $50,000? If a year is too long, but the budget won't be available for 4 months, the time frame becomes better clarified.

Defining the Scope of the Work

By now, the list of goals and objectives might be getting quite long. But when the myriad business and technical objectives and the overall priorities start to become clear, the scope of work starts to take shape. A key question to ask at this point, to home in on the scope of the project, is whether the migration is primarily an OS upgrade or an application upgrade. Often the answer to this question seems clear at first but becomes more complex as the different goals of the business units are discussed, so the scope of work that is created might be quite different than it appeared at first.

Specifically, a decision needs to be made whether the entire OS needs to be upgraded or only a subset of it, and what other infrastructure components need to be changed or replaced. This section focuses on the server components, but later chapters focus on other hardware and software areas that should be reviewed.

Upgrading to the latest version of a key network application (CRM solution, document management system, or remote-access solution) might require an OS upgrade, but it might need to involve only a limited portion of the network (perhaps only one server). However, if this application needs to be accessed by every member of the organization, in several offices, and requires upgrades to data storage solutions, tape backup software, antivirus software, remote access, and connectivity among offices, a full OS upgrade might make more sense. An upgrade to Windows Server 2012 enterprisewide can allow centralization of resources, consolidation of servers, enhanced management tools, and other features that can make a larger project more attractive.

It is important to also examine how the business and technology goals fit into this plan. If one of the goals of the organization is 99.99% uptime during business hours, this might affect the migration process and limit changes to the network to weekends or after hours. Or, a goal that involves a dramatically short timeline might likewise affect the strategy and require a partial OS upgrade.

Questions raised at this point might require further discussion and even research. Later in this chapter, the section "The Discovery Phase: Understanding the Existing Environment" examines some areas that generally need review. But with a solid understanding of the different departmental and companywide goals for the project, you can sketch out a basic outline of the required configuration.

You need to get answers to these sample questions:

- How many servers need to be upgraded?
- Where do these servers reside?
- Are the servers physical or virtual?
- What OS are the servers running under?
- If virtualized, what type of virtual environment is in use (VMware, Hyper-V, Citrix)?
- What core business applications need to be upgraded?
- What additional applications and devices need to be upgraded or modified to support the new servers and applications?
- How will this affect the desktop configurations?

Based on the goals and objectives for the project and the answers to these types of questions, the high-level scope of the work begins to take shape. Here are some general rules to consider:

- Keep it as simple as possible.
- Break up the project into logical segments.
- Don't forget that the staff and user community will need to learn new skills to be productive.

Often, it makes sense to upgrade the OS first and then add directory services and file and print functionality; then you ensure the system is properly protected with a compatible backup solution, virus protection, and disaster recovery plan. When this foundation is in place, the applications can be migrated in a more gradual process. In other cases, the new application must be installed in advance of the OS upgrade, for testing purposes, or because of budget limitations or a tight timeline.

Implementing the latest version of Exchange is a good example; this implementation not only requires a core OS like Windows Server 2012, but also requires Active Directory Domain Services (ADDS) to be properly implemented. For an organization implementing Hyper-V, because Hyper-V does not require ADDS to set up virtual guest sessions, the organization can choose to implement just Windows Server 2012 as an application server and can delay the implementation of ADDS or other Windows Server 2012 components to a future date.

Note, however, that if the OS in use is too old or no longer supported by the manufacturer, the upgrade choices might be limited. You might simply have to implement a completely new collection of servers with compatible network applications and phase out the old ones.

Often, an application-focused upgrade introduces a limited number of new servers but also sets the stage for the eventual migration. This can be an effective way to implement the new technology in a faster method than an enterprisewide OS upgrade. A partial upgrade can also defer the costs of purchasing new server licenses, client access licenses, and other enterprisewide applications, including virus protection and tape backup. Ideally, the servers that are upgraded for the new applications should be designed to integrate into the OS after a full-fledged upgrade. In other words, ideally these servers will not need to be rebuilt later.

As discussed in Chapter 9, "Integrating AD in a UNIX Environment," Windows Server 2012 is designed for compatibility and coexistence with other OSs in addition to Windows 2008/2008 R2 servers. An important point to consider during the design process is whether it makes sense to upgrade the entire OS even though doing so might not be absolutely essential. There might be convincing arguments for a complete upgrade because management of a uniform environment can be easier to administer organizationwide, and an upgrade to Windows Server 2012 might solve a number of existing issues.

Again, the answers might not be obvious at this point in the design process. But by asking the questions and engaging in what-if discussions and speculations, you can identify the primary pieces of the puzzle. The next step is to determine how best to fit those pieces together.

Determining the Time Frame for Implementation or Migration

An equally important component of the migration is the time frame, and this component affects the path and process that need to be followed to create the desired results. Often, the goals for the project dictates the timeline, and the technology upgrade can drastically affect other critical business project dependencies. Other upgrades might not have strict timelines, and it is more important that the process be a smooth one than a quick one.

Depending on the scope of the project, a time frame of 2 to 4 months could be considered to be a short time frame, with 4 to 6 months offering a more comfortable window. Within these time constraints, several weeks are available for discovery and design, a similar amount of time is available for the testing process, and then the implementation can proceed.

A fundamental point to remember is that change brings with it a learning curve to both the user communities and the administrative staff. And the greater the amount of change that employees need to adjust to, the more support and training required to ensure their productivity when the new platform is rolled out. This holds especially true when the applications change along with the OS.

A safe strategy to take when sketching out the timeline is to start by setting a completion date and then working backward from it, to get a sense for the time available to each component of the process. As this chapter discusses, the project has several key phases—discovery, design, prototype, and implementation—and sufficient time should be allowed for each one of them. Although there are no hard-and-fast rules of how the time should be split up among each of these phases, each phase tends to take longer than its predecessor, and the discovery and design phases typically take as long, combined, as the testing phase (that is, discovery + design = prototype time frame).

The implementation phase will vary tremendously based on the scope of the project. For simpler projects, where the implementation consists only of a new server housing a new application, the implementation might be as simple as "flipping a switch" over a weekend (assuming the solution has been thoroughly tested in the lab environment). At the other end of the spectrum, a full OS upgrade, happening in several locations, with changes required on the desktop, can take a period of months or quarters.

Even when the deadline for the completion of the project is the infamous "by yesterday," time should be allocated for the design and planning process. If time and energy are not invested at this point, the prototype testing process might be missing the mark because it might not be clear exactly what is being tested, and the implementation might not be smooth or even successful. A good analogy here is that of the explorer who sets off on an adventure without planning what should go in her backpack or bringing a map along.

Slower, phased migrations typically occur when the existing environment is fairly mature and stable and the vertical applications are still fairly current and meet the company's needs.

Slower time frames should allow a period of weeks or months for the staff to fully understand the goals of the project and requirements of the key stakeholders, review the existing environment, and document the design. Time will also be available to choose the right partner for the project, train the internal resources who will assist in (or lead) the process, and prototype the solution in a safe lab environment. Assuming the testing is successful, a phased implementation can further limit the risks of the project, and the pilot phase of the implementation will allow the staff to learn lessons that smooth out the remaining phases.

Milestones should be set for the completion of the phases, even if they aren't essential to the project's success, to keep momentum going and to avoid the "never-ending project." Projects without periodic dates set as interim milestone points will almost certainly not meet an expected completion date. Projects that extend too far beyond the allotted time frame add costs and risks such as employee turnover, changing business conditions, and new revisions of hardware and software products.

Naturally, projects with shorter timelines bring their own challenges, and often compromises need to be made to successfully complete a large project in a limited amount of time. However, it is important not to abandon the basic principles of discovery, design, and testing. If these steps are skipped and an upgrade is kicked off without planning or a clear understanding of the desired results, the result will often be flawed. In fact, the result might never even be reached because "showstoppers" can suddenly appear in the middle of the project.

It is usually possible to meet a quick timeline (a number of weeks at the very least) and have the results make the stakeholders happy. The real key is to understand the risks involved in the tight time frame and define the scope of the project so that the risks are controlled. This might include putting off some of the functionality that is not essential or contracting outside assistance to speed up the process and leverage the experience of a firm that has performed similar upgrades many times.

Hardware and software procurement can also pose delays. So, for shorter time frames, they should be procured as soon as possible after the ideal configuration has been defined. Note that often the "latest and greatest" hardware—that is, the fastest processors and largest-capacity drives—might take longer to arrive than those a step down. The new equipment should still be tested, or burned in, and fine-tuned in a lab environment, but can often be moved right into production with the pilot implementation. For most medium-size and large organizations, it is recommended that a permanent lab be set up; this step is discussed in more depth in the section, "The Prototype Phase: Creating and Testing the Plan," later in this chapter.

Defining the Participants of the Design and Deployment Teams

Division of labor is a key component of the implementation process. Organizations should evaluate the capabilities of their internal staff and consider hiring an outside firm for assistance in the appropriate areas. If the organization understands and defines the roles that internal staff can play, and defines the areas where professional assistance is needed, the project will flow more smoothly.

The experience levels of the existing resources should be assessed and the bandwidth that they have available for learning new technologies or participating in a new project. If the staff is fully occupied on a daily basis supporting the user base, it is unlikely that they can "make more time" to design and plan the new implementation, even with outside assistance. The track record of the existing staff often reveals how the next project will turn out, and if there are existing half-finished or unsuccessful projects, they can interfere with a new project.

Although classroom-style training and manufacturer-sponsored training do not guarantee expertise, they do indicate the IT staff's willingness to learn and illustrate that they are willing to dedicate time to learning new technologies. A new implementation can be a great opportunity to test the commitment levels of the existing staff and to encourage them to update their skills.

Consider also how the changes to the environment will affect the complexity of the environment that will need to be supported. For example, an upgrade to Windows Server 2012 might enable a company to consolidate and reduce the number of servers on the network and replace "flaky" applications with more stable ones. An upgrade might also introduce brand-new tools that can add support duties in unfamiliar areas to the existing staff.

After the organization takes an inventory of resources at this level and determines roughly what percentage of the project can be handled internally, an external partner should be considered. Even a smaller organization faced with a relatively simple project of, say, installing a Windows Server 2012 server handling one new application can benefit from outside assistance. Some tight time frames necessitate delegating 90% of the tasks to outside resources, whereas other, more leisurely projects might require only 10% assistance levels.

A key distinction to make at this point is between the design resources and the deployment resources. The company or individuals in charge of the design work must have significant experience with the technologies to be implemented and be able to educate and lead the other members of the project team. For projects of moderate or greater complexity, these resources should be dedicated to the design process to ensure that the details are fully sketched out and that the solution designed is as well thought out as possible. Often, the design team has the challenging task of negotiating with the key stakeholders concerning the final design because not all the staff will get everything they want and wish for in the project. The deployment team can contain members of the design team, and these individuals should have training and hands-on experience with the technologies involved and will have more end-user interaction.

You want to look for certain prerequisites when choosing an independent consultant or solution provider organization as a partner. Without going into too much detail, the individual or firm should have proven experience with the exact technologies to be implemented, have a flexible approach to implementing the solution, and have specialized resources to handle the different components of the project. No one person can "do it all," especially if he gets sick or goes on vacation, so breadth and depth of experience should be considered. Obviously, the hourly fees charged are important, but the overall costs, if a firm is willing to commit to a cap or not to exceed a certain price, can be more important. In the current business environment, it makes sense to invest your time wisely in choosing a firm that is very good at what it does; otherwise, it might not be around in future months when your project reaches its critical phases.

Soft skills of the partner are also important because many projects are judged not only by whether the project is complete on time, on scope, and on budget, but also by the response of the stakeholders and user community. Communications skills, reliability, and willingness to educate and share knowledge along the way bring great value in the long run.

The Discovery Phase: Understanding the Existing Environment

Assuming that the previous steps have been taken, the high-level picture of the Windows Server 2012 upgrade should be clear by now. You should understand what the business and technology goals are from a 50,000-foot view business standpoint all the way down to the 1,000-foot staff level. The components of the upgrade, or the scope of the work, and priorities of these components should also be identified, as should the time constraints and who will be on the design and implementation teams.

The picture of the end state (or scope of work) and goals of the project should start becoming more clear. Before the final design is agreed on and documented, however, it is essential to review and evaluate the existing environment to ensure the network foundation in place will support the new Windows Server 2012 environment.

It is an important time to ensure the existing environment is configured the way you think it is and to identify existing areas of exposure or weakness in the network. The level of effort required varies greatly here, depending on the complexity and sheer scope of the network. Organizations with fewer than 200 users and a single or small number of locations that use off-the-shelf software applications and standard hardware products (for example, Hewlett-Packard, IBM, Cisco) usually have relatively simple configurations. In contrast, larger companies, with multiple locations and vertical-market custom software and hardware are more complex. Companies that have grown through the acquisition of other organizations might also have mystery devices on the network that play unknown roles.

Another important variable to define is the somewhat intangible element of network stability and performance. What is considered acceptable performance for one company might be unacceptable for another, depending on the importance of the infrastructure and type of business. Some organizations lose thousands of dollars of revenue per minute of downtime, whereas others can go back to paper for a day or more without noticeable impact.

The discovery work needs to involve the design team as well as internal resources. External partners can often produce more thorough results because they have extensive experience with network reviews and analysis and predicting the problems that can emerge midway through a project and become showstoppers. The discovery process usually starts with onsite interviews with the IT resources responsible for the different areas of the network and proceeds with hands-on review of the network configuration.

Developing standard questionnaires can prove helpful in collecting data on the various network device configurations and recording input on areas of concern of the network. Key end users can reveal needs that their managers or directors aren't aware of, especially in organizations with less-effective IT management or unstable infrastructures. Special attention should be paid to ferreting out the problem areas and technologies that have never worked right or have proven to be unstable.

For the most part, the bigger the project, the more thorough the discovery should be. For projects involving a complete OS upgrade, every affected device and application must be reviewed and evaluated to help determine its role in the new environment.

If network diagrams exist, review them to ensure they are up-to-date and contain enough information (such as server names, roles, applications managed, switches, routers, firewalls, and so on) to fully define the location and function of each infrastructure device.

If additional documentation exists on the detailed configuration of key infrastructure devices (for instance, as-built server documents with details on the server hardware and software configurations or details about router configurations or firewalls), they should be dusted off and reviewed. Information such as whether patches and fixes have been applied to servers and software applications becomes important in the design process. In some cases, the desktop configurations need to be inventoried if client changes are required. Software inventory tools can save many hours of work in these cases.

Certain documented company policies and procedures that are in place need to be reviewed. Some, such as disaster recovery plans or service-level agreements (SLAs), can be vital to the IT department's ability to meet the needs of the user community.

The discovery process can also shed light on constraints to the implementation process that were not considered previously, such as time restrictions that would affect the window of opportunity for change. These restrictions can include seasonal businesses as well as company budgeting cycles or even vacation schedules.

Ultimately, the amount of time spent in the discovery process will vary greatly, but the goals are the same: to really understand the technology infrastructure in place and the risks involved in the project, and to limit the surprises that might occur during the testing and implementation phases.

Understanding the Geographical Depth and Breadth

At the same time that data is being gathered and verified pertaining to what is in place and what it does, connectivity among devices should also be reviewed, to review the logical and the physical components of the network. This information might be available from existing diagrams and documentation or might need to be gathered in the field.

Important items questions to answer include the following: How are domain name system (DNS) and Dynamic Host Configuration Protocol (DHCP) being handled? Are there VPNs or VLANs in place? How are the routers configured? What protocols are in use? What types of circuits connect the offices: digital subscriber line (DSL), T1, fiber? What is the guaranteed throughput or the SLAs that are in place? Has connectivity failure been planned for through a partially or fully meshed environment?

Connections to the outside world and other organizations need to be reviewed and fully understood at the same level, especially with an eye toward the security features in place. The best security design in the world can be defeated by a modem plugged in a plain old telephone line and a disgruntled ex-employee.

Along the same lines, remote access needs, such as access to email, network file and print resources, and the support needs for PDAs and other mobile devices, should be reviewed.

Geographically diverse companies bring added challenges to the table. As much as possible, the same level of information should be gathered on all the sites that will be involved in and affected by the migration. Is the IT environment centralized, where one location manages the whole environment, or decentralized, where each office is its own fiefdom?

The distribution of personnel should be reviewed and clarified. How many support personnel are in each location, what key hardware and software are they tasked with supporting, and how many end users are there? Often, different offices have specific functions that require a different combination of support personnel. Some smaller, remote offices might have no dedicated staff at all, and this can make it difficult to gather updated information. Accordingly, is there expansion or contraction likely in the near future or office consolidations that will change the user distribution?

Problems and challenges that the wide-area network (WAN) design has presented in the past should be reviewed. How is directory information replicated between sites, and what domain design is in place? If the company already has Active Directory in place, is a single domain with a simple organizational unit (OU) structure in place, or are there multiple domains with a complex OU structure? Global Catalog placement should also be clarified.

How is the Internet accessed? Does each office have its own Internet connection, firewall, router, and so on, or is it accessed through one location?

The answers to these questions directly shape the design of the solution and affect the testing and rollout processes.

Managing Information Overload

Another area that can dramatically affect the design of the Windows Server 2012 solution to be implemented is the place where the company's data lives and how it is managed.

At this point, you should know what the key network software applications are, so it is worth having some numbers on the amount of data being managed and where it lives on the network (1 server? 10 servers?). The total number of individual user files should be reviewed, and if available, statistics on the growth of this data should be reviewed.

Database information is often critical to an organization, whether it pertains to the services and products the company offers to the outside world or enables the employees to perform their jobs. Databases also require regular maintenance to avoid corruption and optimize performance, so it is useful to know whether maintenance is happening on a regular basis.

Mail databases pose their own challenges. Older mail systems were usually quite limited in the size of their databases, and many organizations were forced to come up with interesting ways of handling large amounts of data. As email has grown in importance and become a primary tool for many companies, the inbox and personal folders have become the primary storage place for many email users. If the organization uses Microsoft Exchange for its email system, users might have personal stores or offline stores that might need to be taken into account.

How the data is backed up and stored should also be reviewed. Some organizations have extremely complex enterprise storage systems and use clustering, storage-area networks, and a distributed file system to ensure that data is always available to the user community. Sometimes, hierarchical storage processes are in place to move old data to optical media or even to tape.

An overall goal of this sleuthing is to determine where the data is, what file stores and databases are out there, how the data is maintained, and whether it is safe. It might also become clear that the data can be consolidated or needs to be better protected through clustering or fault-tolerant disk solutions. The costs to the company of data loss or temporary unavailability should also be discussed.

The Design Phase: Documenting the Vision and the Plan

With the completion of the discovery process and documentation of the results, it should now be clear what you have to work with in terms of the foundation on which the new solution will be implemented. Essentially, the research is all done, and now you need to make many decisions and document them.

By now, a dozen documents could be written; however, the most important document that needs to be created is the design document. This document is a log of the salient points of the discussions that have taken place to date; it should make clear why the project is being invested in, describe what the scope of the project is, and provide details of what the results will look like. A second document that needs to be created is the migration document, which provides the road map showing how this end state will be reached.

Often companies strive for an all-in-one document, but as explained in the next section, there are specific advantages to breaking up this information into two key components. A simple analogy is that you want to agree on what the floor plan for a house will look like (the design) and what the function of each room will be before deciding on how to build it (the migration/implementation).

Collaboration Sessions: Making the Design Decisions

The design team is most likely not ready to make all the decisions yet, even though quite a bit of homework has already been done. A more formal collaborative and educational process should follow to ensure that the end state of the project is defined in detail and that the design team members fully understand the new technologies to be introduced. The collaborative process involves interactive brainstorming and knowledge-sharing sessions, in which the stakeholders work with facilitators who have expertise with the technologies in question.

Ideally, a consultant with hands-on experience designing and implementing Windows Server 2012 will provide leadership through this process. Well-thought-out agendas can lead the design team through a logical process that educates them about the key decisions to be made and helps with the decisions.

Whiteboards can be used to illustrate the new physical layout of the Windows Server 2012 environment and to explain how the data will be managed and protected on the network. Notes should be taken on the decisions that are made in these sessions. If the sessions are effectively planned and executed, a relatively small number of collaboration sessions will provide the key decisions required for the implementation.

With effective leadership, these sessions can also help establish positive team dynamics and excitement for the project itself. Employees might feel negative about a major upgrade for a wide variety of reasons, but through contributing to the design, learning about the technologies to be implemented, and better understanding their own roles in the process, attitudes can change.

Through these sessions, the details of the end state should become crystal clear. Specifics can be discussed, such as how many servers are needed in which locations, which specific functions they will perform (file and print or application servers, firewalls, and so on), and which key software applications will be managed. Other design decisions and logistical concerns will come up and should be discussed, such as whether to use existing server and network infrastructure hardware or to buy new equipment. Decisions also need to be made concerning secondary applications to support the upgraded environment, such as tape backup software, antivirus solutions, firewall protection, and network management software.

Ideally, some of the details of the actual migration process will start to become clear. For instance, the members of the testing and deployment teams, the training they will require, and the level of involvement from outside resources can be discussed.

Organizing Information for a Structured Design Document

The complexity of the project will affect the size of the document and the effort required to create it. As mentioned previously, this document summarizes the goals and objectives that were gathered in the initial discovery phase and describes how the project's result will meet them. It should represent a detailed picture of the end state when the new technologies and devices have been implemented. The amount of detail can vary, but it should include key design decisions made in the discovery process and collaboration sessions.

The following is a sample table of contents and brief description of the design document:

- **Executive Summary**—Provides a brief discussion of the scope of the Windows Server 2012 implementation (the pieces of the puzzle).
- **Goals and Objectives**—Includes the 50,000-foot view business objectives, down to the 1,000-foot view staff level tasks that will be met by the project.
- **Background**—Provides a high-level summary of the current state of the network, focusing on problem areas, as clarified in the discovery process, as well as summary decisions made in the collaboration sessions.
- **Approach**—Outlines the high-level phases and tasks required to implement the solution (the details of each task as determined in the migration document).
- **End State**—Defines the details of the new technology configurations. For example, this section describes the number, placement, and functions of Windows Server 2012.
- **Budget Estimate**—Provides an estimate of basic costs involved in the project. Although a detailed cost estimate requires the creation of the migration document, experienced estimators can provide order of magnitude numbers at this point. Also, it should be clear what software and hardware are needed, so budgetary numbers can be provided.

The Executive Summary

The executive summary sets the stage and prepares the audience for what the document will contain, and it should be concise. It outlines, at the highest level, the scope of the work. Ideally, the executive summary also positions the document in the decision-making process and clarifies that approvals of the design are required to move forward.

The Goals and Objectives

The goals and objectives section should cover the high-level goals of the project and include the pertinent departmental goals. It's easy to go too far in the goals and objectives sections and get down to the 1,000-foot view level, but this can end up becoming very confusing, so this information might better be recorded in the migration document and the detailed project plan for the project.

The Background

The background section summarizes the results of the discovery process and the collaboration sessions, and can list specific design decisions that were made during the collaboration sessions. In addition, decisions made about what technologies or features not to include can be summarized here. This information should stay at a relatively high level, as well, and more details can be provided in the end state section of the design document. This information is extremely useful to have as a reference to come back to later in the project when the infamous question, "Who made that decision?" comes up.

The Approach

The approach section documents the implementation strategy agreed on to this point, and also serves to record decisions made in the discovery and design process about the timeline (end to end, and for each phase) and the team members participating in the different phases. This section should avoid going into too much detail because in many cases the end design might not yet be approved and might change after review. Also, the migration document should provide the detailed processes that will be followed.

The End State

The end state section spells out in detail the specifics of the Windows Server 2012 implementation, and the high-level decisions that were summarized in the background section should be fleshed out here. Essentially, the software to be installed on each server and the roles that Windows Server 2012 will play (Global Catalog servers, domain controllers, DNS services) are spelled out here, along with the future roles of existing legacy servers. Information on the OU structure, group structures, and replication sites should be included. Diagrams and tables can help explain the new concepts, and actually show what the solution will look like, where the key network devices will be located, and how the overall topology of the network will change. Often, besides a standard physical diagram of "what goes where," a logical diagram illustrating how devices communicate is needed.

The Budget Estimate

The budget section will not be exact but should provide order-of-magnitude prices for the different phases of the project. If an outside consulting firm is assisting with this document, it can draw from experience with similar projects with like-sized companies. Because no two projects are ever the same, there needs to be some flexibility in these estimates. Ranges for each phase should be provided.

Windows Server 2012 Design Decisions

As the previous section mentioned, the key Windows Server 2012 design decisions should be recorded in the design document. This is perhaps the most important section of the document because it defines how Windows Server 2012 will be configured and how it will interact with the network infrastructure.

Decisions should have been made about the hardware and software needed for the migration. They should take into account whether the existing hardware will be used in the migration, upgraded, left in place, or retired. This decision, in turn, determines the number of server software licenses required, which directly affects the cost of the project.

The level of redundancy and security the solution will provide should be detailed. Again, it is important to be specific when talking about data availability and discussing the situations that have been planned for in the design.

The server and other infrastructure hardware and software should be defined in this section. If upgrades are needed for existing hardware (more processors, RAM, hard drives, tape drives, and so on) or the existing software (upgrades from the existing OS, server applications, and vertical market applications), detail them here.

Other key technologies such as messaging applications or industry-specific applications are included here, in as much detail as appropriate.

Agreeing On the Design

The final step in the design document process actually takes place after the document has been created. When the document is considered complete, it should be presented to the project stakeholders and reviewed to ensure that it does, in fact, meet their requirements, that they understand the contents, and to see whether any additional concerns come up that were not addressed in the document.

Although it is unlikely that every goal of every stakeholder will be met (because some might conflict), this process clarifies which goals are the most important and can be met by the technologies to be implemented.

Specific decisions made in the design document that should be reviewed include any disparities between the wish lists the stakeholders had and what the final results of the project will be. Also, the timeline and high-level budget should be discussed and confirmed. If the design document outlines a budget of $500K for hardware and software, but the stakeholders cannot allocate more than $250K, the changes should be made at this point, rather than after the migration document is created. A smaller budget might require drastic changes to the design document because capabilities in the solution might need to be removed, which will have ripple effects throughout the project.

If the time frame outlined in the design document needs to be modified to meet the requirements of the stakeholders, this should be identified before expending the effort of creating the detailed implementation plan.

Remember as well that the design document can be used for different purposes. Some companies want the design document to serve as an educational document to inform not only what the end state will look like, but why it should be that way. Others just need to document the decisions made and come up with budgetary information.

Having this level of detail also makes it easier to get competitive bids on the costs to implement. Many organizations make the mistake of seeking bids for solutions before they even know what the solution will consist of.

The Migration Planning Phase: Documenting the Process for Migration

Before the migration document is created, the end state of the project has been documented in detail and agreed on by the key stakeholders in the organization. There should not be any question as to exactly what the next evolution of the network will be composed of and what functionality it will offer. In addition, an estimated budget for the hardware and software required and an estimated timeline for the project have been identified. In some cases, depending on the size and complexity of the project, and whether outside consulting assistance has been contracted, a budget has also been established for the implementation services.

So, now that the end state has been clearly defined, the migration document can be created to document the details of the steps required to reach the end state with minimal risk of negative impact to the network environment.

The migration plan should not contain any major surprises.

A key component of the migration document is the project plan, or migration plan, that provides a list of the tasks required to implement the solution. It is the road map from which the migration document is created. The migration document also provides a narrative, where needed, of the specifics of the tasks that the project plan does not provide, and provides other details as outlined next.

Time for the Project Plan

As mentioned previously, the primary stepping-stones needed to reach the endpoint have been sketched out in the discovery process and in collaboration sessions or design discussions that have taken place. The project plan in the migration document provides a tool to complement the design document, which graphically illustrates the process of building and testing the technologies required and outlines who is doing what during the project.

By using a product such as Microsoft Project, you can organize the steps in a logical, linear process. The high-level tasks should be established first. Typically, they are the phases or high-level tasks involved in the project, such as lab testing, pilot implementation, production implementation, and support. Then, the main components of these tasks can be filled in.

Dates and durations should be included in the project plan, using the basic concept of starting with the end date when everything needs to be up and running and then working backward. It is important to include key milestones, such as acquiring new software and hardware, sending administrative resources to training classes, and provisioning new data circuits. Slack time should also be included for unexpected events or stumbling blocks that might be encountered. Each phase of the project needs to be outlined and then expanded.

A good rule of thumb is not to try to list every task that needs to take place during the phase, but to have each line represent several hours or days of work. If too much detail is put into the project plan, it quickly becomes unmanageable. For the detailed information that does not necessarily need to be placed in the project plan (Gantt chart), the information can be detailed in the migration document. The migration document adds in technical and operational details that help clarify more specific project information.

NOTE

The terms *project plan* and *Gantt chart* are commonly interchanged in IT organizations and might have different meanings to different individuals. In this book, the term project plan refers to the chronological steps needed to successfully plan, prepare, and implement Windows Server 2012. The term Gantt chart is used to refer to the chronological steps, but also the inclusion of resource allocation, start and end dates, and cost distribution.

The plan should also assign resources to the tasks and start to define the teams that will work on the different components of the project. If an outside organization is going to assist in the process, it should be included at the appropriate points in the project. Microsoft Project offers an additional wealth of features to produce reports and graphical information from this plan; they prove extremely helpful when the work starts. Also, accurate budgetary information can be extracted, which can take into account overtime and after-hours rates and easily give what-if scenario information.

Speed Versus Risk

The project plan also enables you to test what-if scenarios. When the high-level tasks are defined, and the resources required to complete each task are also defined, you can easily plug in external contractors to certain tasks and see how the costs change. After-hours work might take place during working hours in certain places.

If the timeline still is not acceptable, tasks can be stacked so that multiple tasks occur at the same time, instead of one after the other. Microsoft Project also offers extensive tools for resource leveling to ensure that you have not accidentally committed a resource to (for example, 20 hours of work in 1 day).

The critical path of the project should also be defined. Certain key events need to take place for the project to proceed beyond a certain point. Ordering the hardware and having it arrive is one of these steps. Getting stakeholder approval on the lab environment and proving that key network applications can be supported might be another. Administrative and end-user training might need to happen to ensure that the resulting environment can be effectively supported.

You might also need to build contingency time into the project plan. Hardware can get delayed and take an extra week or two to arrive. Testing can take longer, especially with complex configurations and when customization of the OS is required or directory information needs to be modified.

Creating the Migration Document

The migration document can now narrate the process detailed in the project plan. The project plan does not need to be 100% complete, but the order of the steps and the strategies for testing and implementing will be identified. Generally, the migration document is similar to the structure of the design document (a reason why many organizations combine the two documents), but the design document relates the design decisions made and details the end state of the upgrade, whereas the migration document details the process and steps to be taken.

The following is a sample table of contents for the migration document:

- Executive Summary
- Goals and Objectives of the Migration Process
- Background
- Risks and Assumptions
- Roles and Responsibilities
- Timeline and Milestones
- Training Plan
- Migration Process
    - Hardware and Software Procurement Process
    - Prototype Proof-of-Concept Process
    - Server Configuration and Testing
    - Desktop Configuration and Testing
    - Documentation Required from Prototype
    - Pilot Phases Detailed
    - Migration/Upgrade Detailed
    - Support Phase Detailed
    - Support Documentation Detailed
- Budget Estimate
    - Labor Costs for Prototype Phase
    - Labor Costs for Pilot Phase
    - Labor Costs for Migration/Upgrade Phase
    - Labor Costs for Support Phase
    - Costs for Training
- Project Schedule

The Executive Summary Section

The executive summary should set the stage and prepare the audience for what the document contains, and it should be concise. It should outline, at the highest level, the scope of the work. Ideally, the executive summary also positions the document in the decision-making process and clarifies that approvals of the design are required to move forward.

The Goals and Objectives Section

The goals and objectives section might seem redundant because the design documents documented the objectives in great detail, but it is important to consider which specific goals and objectives are important to the success of the migration project that might not have been included in the design document. For example, although the design document outlined what the final server configuration will look like, it might not have outlined the tools needed to migrate key user data or the order that the company offices will be migrated. So, the goals and objectives in the migration document will be very process specific.

The Background Section

A summary of the migration-specific decisions should be provided to answer questions such as "Why are we doing it that way?" because there are always a number of ways to implement new messaging technologies, such as using built-in tools or using third-party tools. Because a number of conversations will have taken place during the planning phase to compare the merits of one method versus another, it is worth summarizing them early in the document for anyone who was not involved in those conversations.

The Risks and Assumptions Section

Risks pertaining to the phases of the migration should be detailed and are usually more specific than in the design document. For example, a risk of the prototype phase might be that the hardware available will not perform adequately and needs to be upgraded. Faxing, virus protection, or backup software might not meet the requirements of the design document and therefore needs to be upgraded. Custom-designed messaging applications or Windows add-ons might turn out not to be Windows Server 2012 compatible.

The Roles and Responsibilities Section

The roles and responsibilities section identifies in detail the teams that will do the work. If an outside company will be performing portions of the work, which tasks it will be responsible for and which ones internal resources will take ownership of should be documented.

The Timeline and Milestones Section

Specific target dates can be listed and should be available directly from the project schedule already created. This summary can be very helpful to executives and managers, whereas the Gantt chart contains too much information. Constraints that were identified in the discovery process need to be kept in mind here because there might be important dates (such as the end of the fiscal year), seasonal demands on the company that black out certain date ranges, and key company events or holidays. Again, be aware of other large projects going on in your environment that might impact your timeline. There is no point trying to deploy new servers on the same weekend that the data center will be powered off for facility upgrades.

The Training Plan Section

It is useful during the planning of any upgrade to examine the skill sets of the people who will be performing the upgrade and managing the new environment to see whether any gaps need to be filled with training. Often, training happens during the prototype testing process in a hands-on fashion for the project team, with the alternate choice being classroom-style training, often provided by an outside company. Also ask yourself whether end users require training to use new client-side tools. Also pay attention to how the new environment will integrate into existing systems such as backup or monitoring. Determine if those groups need any training specific to interacting with Windows Server 2012 components.

The Migration Process Section

The project schedule Gantt chart line items should be included and expanded on so that it is clear to the resources doing the work what is expected of them. The information does not need to be on the level of step-by-step instructions, but it should clarify the process and results expected from each task. For example, the Gantt chart might indicate that a Windows Server 2012 server needs to be configured, and in the migration document, information would be added about which server roles need to be installed, how the hard drives are to be configured, and which additional applications (virus protection, tape backup, faxing, network management) need to be installed.

If the Gantt chart lists a task of, for example, "Configure and test Windows client access," the migration document gives a similar level of detail: Which image should be used to configure the base workstation configuration, which additional applications and version of Windows should be loaded, how is the workstation to be locked down, and what testing process should be followed (is it scripted or will an end user from the department do the testing)?

Documentation also should be described in more detail. The Gantt chart might simply list "Create as-built documents," with *as-built* defined as "document containing key server configuration information and screenshots so that a knowledgeable resource can rebuild the system from scratch."

Sign-off conditions for the prototype phase are important and should be included. Who needs to sign off on the results of the prototype phase to indicate that the goals were all met and that the design agreed on is ready to be created in the production environment?

Similar levels of information are included for the pilot phase and the all-important migration itself. During the pilot phase, all the upgraded functionality usually needs to be tested, including remote access, file encryption access, and access to shared folders. Be aware that pilot testing might require external coordination. For example, if you are testing remote access through a VPN connection, you might need to acquire an additional external IP address and arrange to have an address record created in DNS to allow your external testers to reach it without having to disturb your existing remote access systems.

The migration plan should also account for support tasks that need to occur after the Windows Server 2012 infrastructure is fully in place. If you are using an outside consulting firm for assistance in the design and implementation, make sure that they will leave staff onsite for a period of time immediately after the upgrade to be available to support user issues or to troubleshoot any technical issues that crop up.

If documentation is specified as part of the support phase, such as Windows maintenance documents, disaster recovery plans, or procedural guides, expectations for these documents should be included to help the technical writers make sure the documents are satisfactory.

The Budget Section

With regard to the budget information, although a great amount of thought and planning has gone into the design and migration documents, as well as the project plan, there are still variables. No matter how detailed these documents are, the later phases of the project might change based on the results of the earlier phases. For instance, the prototype testing might go flawlessly, but during the pilot implementation, performing data migration simply takes longer than anticipated; this extra time requires modifications to the amount of time required and the associated costs. Note that changes in the opposite direction can happen, as well, if tasks can occur more quickly than anticipated. Often, the implementation costs can be reduced by keeping an eye on ways to improve the process during the prototype and pilot phases.

The Project Schedule Section

Whereas the project plan provides the high-level details of the steps, or tasks, required in each phase, the approach sections of the migration document can go into more detail about the details of each step of the project plan, as needed. Certain very complex tasks are represented with one line on the project plan, such as "Configure Windows Server 2012 #1" and might take several pages to describe in sufficient detail in the migration document.

Data availability testing and disaster recovery testing should be discussed. In the design document, you might have decided that clustering and that a particular tape backup program will be used, but the migration plan should outline exactly which scenarios should be tested in the prototype lab environment.

Documents to be provided during the migration should be defined so that it is clear what they will contain.

The Prototype Phase: Creating and Testing the Plan

The main goal of the prototype phase is to create a lab environment in which the key elements of the design as defined in the design document can be configured and tested. Based on the results of the prototype, you can determine whether any changes are needed to the implementation and support phases as outlined in the migration document.

The prototype phase is also a training phase, in which the members of the deployment team get a chance to get their hands dirty with the new hardware and software technologies to be implemented. If an external consulting firm is assisting with the prototype testing, knowledge transfer should occur and be expected during this process. Even if the deployment team has attended classroom training, the prototype process is an environment that will more closely reflect the end state of the network that needs to be supported, and will involve technologies and processes not typically covered in classroom-style training. The deployment team can also benefit from the real-world experience of the consultants if they are assisting in this phase.

This environment should be isolated from the production network so that problems created by or encountered in the process don't affect the user community.

The design details of testing applications, confirming hardware performance, testing fault-tolerant failover, and the like should be verified in a safe lab environment. If changes are needed to the design document, make them now.

How Do You Build the Lab?

Although the details of the project determine the specifics of exactly what will be in the prototype lab, certain common elements are required. The migration document should clearly outline the components of the lab and which applications and processes should be tested. A typical environment consists of the primary Windows Server 2012 server required for the implementation and network switches, sample workstations, and printers from the production environment. Connectivity to the outside world should be available for testing purposes.

A key decision to make is whether the lab will be implemented into the environment or stay as a lab. Some companies proceed from the prototype phase to the pilot phase with the same equipment, whereas others prefer to keep a lab set up for future use. The advantages of having a lab environment for a Windows Server 2012 environment are many, and include testing OS and application updates, upgrades and patches, and having hardware available for replacement of failed components in the production environment.

Real data and applications should be installed and tested. Data can be copied from live production servers, or data from tape can be restored to the test server. Applications should be installed on the servers according to a manufacturer's installation instructions; however, compatibility validation with Windows Server 2012 should be conducted as outlined in Chapter 17, "Compatibility Testing."

After the software applications have been installed, representative users from the different company departments could be brought into the lab to put the applications through their paces. These users will be best able to do what they normally do in the lab environment to ensure that their requirements will be met by the new configuration. Areas that do not meet their expectations should be recorded and identified as either *showstoppers* that need to be addressed immediately or issues that will not harm the implementation plan.

Results of the Lab Testing Environment

In addition to the valuable learning that takes place, a number of other things come out of the lab testing process. If time permits, and there is room in the budget, a variety of documents can be produced to facilitate the pilot and implementation process. Another key result of the lab is hard evidence of the accuracy and completeness of the design and migration documents.

Some of the documents that can be created assist the deployment team during the migration process. One key document is the as-built document, which provides a snapshot of the key configuration details of the primary servers that have been configured and tested. Whereas the design document outlines many of the key configuration details, the as-built document contains actual screenshots of the server configurations and the output from the Windows Server 2012 Computer Management administrative tool that provides important details such as physical and logical disk configuration, system memory and processor information, services installed and in use on the system, and so on.

Another important document is the disaster recovery (DR) document. This document outlines exactly which types of failures were tested and the process for rectifying these situations. Keep in mind that a complete DR plan should include offsite data and application access, so the DR document that comes out of the prototype phase will, in most cases, be more of a hardware failure document that discusses how to replace failed components, such as hard drives or power supplies, and how to restore the server configuration from tape backup or restore datasets.

If you need to implement multiple servers in the pilot and implementation phases, you can document checklists for the step-by-step processes in the prototype phase. Remember that creating step-by-step documents takes a great deal of time (and paper), and a change in process requires drastic changes to these documents. Typically, creating a step-by-step "recipe" for server builds is not worth the time unless lower-level resources need to build a large number in a short period of time.

When the testing is complete, revisit the migration plan to ensure that the timeline and milestones are still accurate. Ideally, there should be no major surprises during the prototype phase, but adjustments might be needed to the migration plan to ensure the success of the project.

Depending on the time frame for the pilot and implementation phases, the hardware and software required for the full implementation might be ordered at this point. Because the cost of server hardware has decreased over the past several years, many companies "over-spec" the hardware they think they need, and they might determine during the prototype phase that lesser amounts of RAM or fewer processors will still exceed the needs of the technologies to be implemented, so the hardware requirements might change.

The Pilot Phase: Validating the Plan to a Limited Number of Users

Now that the prototype phase has been completed, the deployment team will be raring to go and have hands-on experience with all the new technologies to be implemented. The process documented in the migration document and migration plan will have been tested in the lab environment as completely as practical, and documentation detailing the steps to be followed during the pilot implementation will be at hand.

Although the pilot process varies in complexity based on the extent of the changes to be made to the network infrastructure, the process should be well documented at this point.

It is important to identify the first group of users who will be moved to the new Windows Server 2012 environment. Users with a higher tolerance for pain are a better choice than the key stakeholders, for the most part.

NOTE

In many organizations, the CEO, CIO, VP of sales, or other key executives might want to be part of the initial pilot rollout; however, we suggest not making these individuals part of the initial rollout. These individuals usually have the most complex user configuration with the lowest tolerance for interruption of network services. Users in the production environment with simpler needs can be used for the initial pilot. If necessary, create a prepilot phase so that the senior executives can be part of the official pilot phase, but do not make the challenges of pilot testing more difficult by starting with users who have the most complex needs.

A rollback strategy should be clarified, just in case.

Test the disaster recovery and redundancy capabilities thoroughly at this point with live data but a small user group to ensure everything works as advertised.

Migration processes can be fine-tuned during this process, and time estimates can be nailed down.

The First Server in the Pilot

The pilot phase is begun when the first Windows Server 2012 server accessed by users is implemented in the production environment. Depending on the scope of the migration project, this first server might be a simple application server running Remote Desktop Services or SharePoint, or the first server might be an Active Directory domain controller.

Just as in the prototype phase, the testing to be conducted in the pilot phase is to verify successful access to the server or application services the system provides. One of the best ways to validate functionality is to take the test sequences used in the prototype phase and repeat the test steps in the pilot production environment.

The major difference between the prototype and pilot phases is interconnectivity and enterprisewide compatibility. In many lab-based prototype phases, the testing is isolated to clean system configurations or homogeneous system configurations; however, in a pilot production environment, the new technology is integrated with old technology. It is the validation that the new setup works with existing users, servers, and systems, and software that is the added focus of the production pilot phase.

Rolling Out the Pilot Phase

The pilot phase is usually rolled out in subphases, with each subphase growing in number of users affected, uses of system technology by the pilot users, and the distribution of users throughout the organization.

Number of Pilot Users

The whole purpose of the pilot phase is to slowly roll out users throughout the organization to validate that prototype and test assumptions were accurate and that they can be successful in the production environment. An initial group of 5 to 10 pilot users (usually members of the IT department overseeing and managing the migration) are first to be migrated. These users test basic functionality.

After successful basic testing, the pilot users group can grow to 1%, then to 3%, on to 5%, and finally to 10% of the user base in the organization. This phased rollout helps the migration team test compatibility, connectivity, and communications with existing systems, while working with a manageable group of users that will not overwhelm the help desk services in place during the pilot and migration process.

The pilot phase is also a time when help desk and migration support personnel build the knowledge base of problems that occur during the migration process so that if or when problems occur again (possibly in the full rollout phase of the product) lessons have been learned and workarounds already created to resolve stumbling blocks.

Application Complexity of Pilot Users

In addition to expanding the scope of the pilot phase by sheer number, selecting users who have different application usage requirements can provide a level of complexity across software platforms. Application compatibility and operation are critical to the end-user experience during the migration process. Often, users do not mind if something runs a little slower during the migration process or that a new process takes a while to learn; however, users get upset if the applications they require and depend on each day to get their job done lock up while they use the application, data is lost because of system instability, or the application just does not work. So, testing applications is critical in the early pilot phase of the project.

Role Complexity of Pilot Users

Pilot users should also be drawn from various roles throughout an organization. In many migrations, all pilot users are tested from a single department using just a single set of applications, and it is not until the full migration process that a feature or function that is critical to everyone in the organization (except the pilot group users' department) does not work. An example might be a specific financial trading application, a proprietary health-care tracking application or a critical sales force automation remote access tool that causes the entire project to come to a halt far into the full rollout phase.

Geographical Diversity of Pilot Users

The pilot group should eventually include members geographically distributed throughout the organization. It is important to start the pilot phase with a set of users who are local to the IT or help desk operation so that initial pilot support can be done in person or directly with the initial pilot group. Before the pilot is considered complete, however, users from remote sites should be tested to ensure their user experience to the new networking environment has not been negatively affected.

Fixing Problems in the Pilot Phase

No matter how much planning and testing are conducted in the earlier phases of the project, problems always crop up in the pilot phase of the project. It is important to have the prototype lab still intact so that any outstanding problems can be re-created in the lab, tested, and resolved to be tested in the pilot production phase again.

Documenting the Results of the Pilot

After the pilot, it is important to document the results. Even with the extensive discovery and design work, as well as the prototype lab testing and pilot phases that have taken place, problems might reoccur in the postpilot phases, and any documented information on how problems were resolved or configurations made to resolve problems in the pilot phase help simplify the resolution in future phases. If you take some extra time to give attention to the pilot users, you can fine-tune the solution to ensure the full implementation is a success.

The Migration/Implementation Phase: Conducting the Migration or Installation

By this point in the project, more than 10% of the organization's users should have been rolled out and tested in the pilot phase, applications thoroughly tested, help desk and support personnel trained, and common problem resolution clearly documented so that the organization can proceed with the migration and installation throughout the rest of the organization.

Verifying End-User Satisfaction

A critical task that can be conducted at this point in the project is to conduct a checkpoint for end-user satisfaction, making sure that users are getting their systems, applications, or functionality upgraded; questions are answered; problems are resolved; and, most important, users are being made aware of the benefits and improvements of the new environment.

Not only does this phase of the project focus on the sheer rollout of the technology, but it is also the key public relations and communications phase of the project. Make sure the user community gets the training and support it needs throughout the process.

Plan on issues arising that will need support for several days after each department or user group is upgraded.

Do not forget the special users with unique requirements and remote users; they will require additional support.

Supporting the New Windows Server 2012 Environment

Before the last users are rolled into the new networking environment, besides planning the project-completion party, you need to allocate time to ensure the ongoing support and maintenance of the new environment is being conducted. This step not only includes doing regular backups of the new servers (covered in detail in Chapter 30, "Backing Up the Windows Server 2012 Environment"), but also includes planning for regular maintenance (Chapter 20, "Windows Server 2012 Management and Maintenance Practices"), monitoring (Chapter 23, "Integrating System Center Operations Manager 2012 with Windows Server 2012"), and tuning and optimization (Chapter 34, "Capacity Analysis and Performance Optimization") of the new Windows Server 2012 environment.

Now is the time to begin planning for some of the wish-list items that did not make sense to include in the initial migration—for example, a new antiviral solution, knowledge-management solutions, enhanced security, and so on.

If you have a lab still in place, use it for testing patches and software updates.

Summary

One analogy used in this chapter is that of building a house. Although this analogy does not stand up to intense scrutiny, the similarities are helpful. When an organization is planning a Windows Server 2012 implementation, it is important to first understand the goals for the implementation, and not only the 50,000-foot high-level goals, but also the 10,000-foot departmental and 1,000-foot IT staff goals. Then, it is important to more fully understand the environment that will serve as the foundation for the upgrade. Whether this work is performed by external resources or by internal resources, a great deal is learned about what is really in place and where there might be areas of risk or exposure. Collaboration sessions with experienced and effective leadership can then educate the stakeholders and deployment resources about the technologies to be implemented and guide the group through the key decisions that need to be made. Now all this information needs to be documented in the design document so that the details are clear, and some initial estimates for the resources required, timeline, and budget can be set. This document serves as a blueprint of sorts, and defines in detail what the "house" will look like when it is built. When all the stakeholders agree that this is exactly what they want to see, and the timeline and budget are in line, the migration document can be produced.

The migration document includes a detailed project plan that provides the tasks that need to take place to produce the results detailed in the design document. The project plan should not go into step-by-step detail describing how to build each server, but should stick to summary tasks from 4 hours to a day or more in duration. The migration document then provides a narrative of the project plan and supplies additional information pertaining to goals, resources, risks, deliverables, and budgetary information accurate in the 10% to 20% range.

Based on these documents, the organization can now proceed with building the solution in a lab environment and testing the proposed design with actual company data and resources involved. The results of the testing might require modifications to the migration document and prepares the deployment team for live implementation. Ideally, a pilot phase with a limited, noncritical group of users will occur to fine-tune the live implementation process and put in place key technologies and Windows Server 2012. Now the remainder of the implementation process should proceed with a minimum of surprises, and the result will meet the expectations set in the design phase and verified during the prototype and pilot phases.

Even the support phase has been considered, and during this phase, the "icing on the cake" can be applied as appropriate.

Although this process might seem complex, it can be molded to fit all different sizes of projects and will yield better results.

Best Practices

The following are best practices from this chapter:

- Use a migration methodology consisting of discovery, design, testing, and implementation phases to meet the needs of your organization.
- Fully understand the business and technical goals and objectives of the upgrade and the breadth and scope of benefits the implementation will provide before implementing a new application or upgrade.
- Create a scope of work detailing the Windows Server 2012 network functionality, data management, information access, and application hosting.
- Define high-level organizational goals.
- Define departmental goals.
- Determine which components and capabilities of the network are most important and how they contribute to or hinder the goals expressed by the different units.
- Clearly define the technical goals of the project on different levels (50,000-foot, 10,000-foot, 1,000-foot, and so on).

The Discovery Phase

- Review and evaluate the existing environment to ensure the network foundation in place will support the new Windows Server 2012 environment.
- Make sure the existing environment is configured the way you think it is, and identify existing areas of exposure or weakness in the network.
- Define the current network stability and performance measurements and operation.
- Use external partners to produce more thorough results due to their extensive experience with network reviews and analysis and predict the problems that can emerge midway through a project and become showstoppers.
- Start the discovery process with onsite interviews.
- Review and evaluate every affected device and application to help determine its role in the new environment.

- Maintain and protect database information that is critical to an organization on a regular basis.
- Determine where data resides, what file stores and databases are out there, how the data is maintained, and whether it is safe.

The Design Phase

- Create a design document that includes the salient points of the discussion, the reasons the project is being invested in, the scope of the project, and the details of what the results will look like.
- Create a migration document providing the road map showing how the end state will be reached.
- Use a consultant with hands-on experience designing and implementing Windows Server 2012 to provide leadership through this process.
- Determine what hardware and software will be needed for the migration.
- To more accurately calculate project costs, determine how many server software licenses are required.
- Detail the level of redundancy and security that is required and that the solution will ultimately provide.
- Present the design and migration documents to the project stakeholders for review.

The Migration Planning Phase

- Create a migration document containing the details of the steps required to reach the end state with minimal risk or negative impact to the network environment.
- Create a project plan that provides a list of the tasks, resources, and durations required to implement the solution.

The Prototype Phase

- Create a lab environment in which the key elements of the design as defined in the design document can be configured and tested.
- Isolate the lab environment from the production network so that any problems created or encountered in the process do not affect the user community.
- Thoroughly test all applications.

The Pilot Phase

- Identify the first group of users who will be moved to the new Windows Server 2012 environment. Users with a higher tolerance for pain are a better choice than the key stakeholders, for the most part.
- Clarify a rollback strategy, just in case unexpected problems occur.
- Test the disaster recovery and redundancy capabilities thoroughly.
- Fine-tune the migration processes and nail down time estimates.

The Migration/Implementation Phase

- Verify that applications have been thoroughly tested, help desk and support personnel have been trained, and common problem resolution is clearly documented.
- Conduct a checkpoint for end-user satisfaction.
- Allocate time to ensure that ongoing support and maintenance of the new environment are being conducted before the last users are rolled into the new networking environment.
- Plan a project-completion party.

CHAPTER 3

Installing Windows Server 2012 and Server Core

IN THIS CHAPTER

This chapter describes the step-by-step process to install a clean version of the Windows Server 2012 operating system, upgrade an existing system to Windows Server 2012, and, finally, install a Windows Server 2012 Server Core edition.

Even though the installation process is intuitive and has been simplified, an administrator must make several key decisions to ensure that the completed installation will meet the needs of the organization. For example, is it beneficial to upgrade an existing system to Windows Server 2012, or is it preferred to conduct a clean install from scratch? What are the ramifications of these alternatives? Will I lose my existing settings, programs, and configurations? This chapter covers the required planning tasks to address administrator questions and concerns.

In addition, this chapter focuses on how to install and manage the Server Core edition of Windows Server 2012.

Planning for a Server Installation

Before you begin the actual installation of Windows Server 2012, you must make several decisions concerning prerequisite tasks. How well you plan these steps will determine how successful your installation is because many of these decisions cannot be changed after the installation is complete.

Minimum Hardware Requirements

Whether you are installing Windows Server 2012 in a lab or production environment, you need to ensure that the hardware chosen meets the minimum system requirements.

In most situations, the minimum hardware requirements presented will not suffice. Therefore, Table 3.1 provides not only the minimum requirements, but also the recommended and maximum system requirements for the hardware components.

TABLE 3.1 Windows Server 2012 System Requirements

Component	Minimum Requirement	Recommended	Maximum
Processor	1.4GHZ 64-bit	2GHZ or faster dual core	Not applicable
Memory	512MB RAM	2GB RAM or greater	32GB RAM Standard Edition4TB RAM Datacenter Edition
Disk space	32GB	40GB Full installation or 10GB Server Core installation	Not applicable

NOTE

When designing and selecting the system specifications for a new server solution, even the optimal system requirements recommendations from Microsoft might not suffice. It is a best practice to assess the server specifications of the planned server role while taking the load during the time of deployment and future growth into consideration. For example, a Windows Server 2012 system running the Exchange Server 2010 Mailbox Server role or a SQL Server 2012 providing enterprise business intelligence solutions will require much more than 2GB of RAM to run adequately. Therefore, size the system accordingly and test the load before going live into production.

CAUTION

Windows Server 2012 supports *only* 64-bit processor architectures. A server running 32-bit processors is *not* supported.

Choosing the Appropriate Windows Edition

There are only two editions in the Windows Server 2012 family of operating systems. Microsoft is opting to simplify the product line, and as a result, Windows Server 2012 will be available in Standard and Datacenter Editions. There is no longer a feature difference between the editions, only a difference in support for hardware and guest virtual machines (VMs).

Each edition supports a Server Core version. For a full list of Windows Server 2012 features and functionality, see Chapter 1, "Windows Server 2012 Technology Primer," which covers the editions in depth.

Choosing a New Installation or an Upgrade

If you have an existing Windows environment, you might need to perform a new installation or upgrade an existing server. There are benefits to each of these options. The next two sections outline the benefits for each.

Should You Perform a New Installation?

The primary benefit of a new installation is that by installing the operating system from scratch you are starting with a known good server. You can avoid migrating problems that might have existed on your previous server—whether due to corrupt software, incorrect configuration settings, or improperly installed applications. Keep in mind, however, that you also lose all configuration settings from your previous installation. In addition, required applications on the legacy server need to be reinstalled after the installation of the new operating system is complete. Make sure you document your server configuration information, have all the appropriate software you plan on reinstalling, and back up any data that you want to keep.

When performing a new installation, you can install on a new hard drive (or partition). Typically, most new installations are installed on a new or freshly formatted hard drive. Doing so removes any old software and gives you the cleanest installation.

Should You Upgrade an Existing Server?

Upgrading, in contrast, replaces your current Windows files but keeps existing users, settings, groups, rights, and permissions intact. In this scenario, you don't have to reinstall applications or restore data. Before choosing this option, keep in mind that you should test your applications for compatibility before migration. Just because they worked on earlier versions of Windows does not mean they will work on Windows Server 2012.

As always, before performing any type of server maintenance such as a Windows Server 2012 installation, perform a complete backup of any applications and data that you want to preserve. Do not forget to include the system state when backing up the legacy Windows operating system. It is required when performing a restore if you want to maintain the existing Windows settings.

To upgrade to Windows Server 2012, you must be running the most recent server level operating system, Windows Server 2008 R2. Upgrades from older operating systems are not supported. Table 3.2 lists edition upgrades.

TABLE 3.2 Windows Server 2012 Upgrade Paths

Previous Operating System Edition	Upgrade to Windows Server 2012 Edition
Windows Server 2008/2008 R2 Standard	Standard, Datacenter
Windows Server 2008/2008 R2 Enterprise	Datacenter
Windows Server 2008/2008 R2 Datacenter	Datacenter

NOTE

If you need to preserve settings and upgrade a legacy operating system such as Windows 2003 or Windows 2008 Server, you should first upgrade the system should to Windows Server 2008 R2 and then to Windows Server 2012. Typically, this is not the recommended approach because the hardware is usually outdated; however, the multiple upgrade approach is doable.

NOTE

Although direct upgrades from a GUI version of the server to a core installation is still not supported, with Windows Server 2012, you can easily upgrade to a GUI version and then convert to a core installation or vice versa.

Determining the Type of Server to Install

One of the first decisions you have to make when installing Windows Server 2012 is whether you will be using a Server Core installation or a server with GUI installation. Server Core installations were introduced with the release of the Windows Server 2008 family of operating systems and consist of only a minimal installation footprint. On a Server Core installation, the traditional GUI tools are not available, and there is also limited managed code support.

Windows Server 2012 supports more roles on a Server Core installation than any earlier version of the operating system. Roles that are supported with a Server Core installation include Active Directory Domain Services, Active Directory Lightweight Directory Services (AD LDS), DHCP Server, DNS Server, File Services, Print Server, Hyper-V, and Web Server (IIS). Windows Server 2012 adds support for the Windows Software Update Services and Remote Access roles along with support for running SQL Server 2012 on a core installation.

Even more important, Windows Server 2012 can be switched from a Server Core installation to a GUI installation with a single command and a reboot. A third installation state exists and is comprised of a minimal GUI installation with some GUI features, such as Internet Explorer, Windows Explorer, and the desktop, removed. The third state, called the Minimal Server Interface, can be converted to a full GUI server by installing the Server Graphical Shell feature.

Preparing Configuration Information

After the installation of Windows Server 2012, you have the opportunity to configure the core settings required for server operation. Taking the time to gather the information described in the following sections before starting your installation will likely make your installation go faster, smoother, and easier.

NOTE

Although items such as the server name and IP address are required for a server to function, values are automatically generated during installation. Specific system settings are manually entered after the installation is complete, unless an unattended installation with an answer file is used.

Selecting the Computer Name

Each computer on a network must have a name that is unique within that network. Many companies have a standard naming convention for their servers and workstations. If not, you can use the following information as a guideline for creating your own.

Although the computer name can contain up to 63 characters, workstations and servers that are pre-Windows 2000 recognize only the first 15 characters.

It is widely considered a best practice to use only Internet standard characters in your computer name. This includes the letters A–Z (uppercase and lowercase), the numbers 0–9, and the hyphen (-).

Although it's true that implementing the Microsoft domain name system (DNS) service in your environment could allow you to use some non-Internet standard characters (such as Unicode characters and the underscore), keep in mind that this is likely to cause problems with any non-Microsoft DNS servers on your network. Think carefully and test thoroughly before straying from the standard Internet characters noted in the preceding paragraph.

Name of the Workgroup or Domain

In addition to the server name, you need to determine the name of the workgroup or domain that the server will be joining. You can either enter the name of an existing Windows domain or workgroup to join or create a new workgroup by entering in a new name.

Users new to Microsoft networking might ask, "What is the difference between a workgroup and a domain?" Simply put, a domain is a collection of computers and supporting hardware that shares the same security database using Active Directory. Grouping the equipment in this manner allows you to set up centralized security and administration. Conversely, a workgroup has no centralized security or administration. Each server or workstation is configured independently and locally for all security and administration settings.

Network Protocol and IP Address of the Server

When installing Windows Server 2012, you must install and configure a network protocol that will allow it to communicate with other machines on the network.

Currently, the most commonly used protocol is called TCP/IP version 4, which stands for Transmission Control Protocol/Internet Protocol. This protocol allows computers throughout the Internet to communicate. After you install TCP/IP, you need to configure an IP address for the server. You can choose one of the following three methods to assign an IP address:

- **Automatic Private IP Addressing (APIPA)**—APIPA can be used if you have a small network that does not have a Dynamic Host Configuration Protocol (DHCP) server, which is used for dynamic IP addresses. A unique IP address is assigned to the network adapter using the link-local IP address space. The address always starts with 169.254 and is in the format 169.254.x.x. Note that if APIPA is in use, and a DHCP server is brought up on the network, the computer will detect this and will use the address that is assigned by the DHCP server instead.
- **Dynamic IP address**—A dynamic IP address is assigned by a DHCP server. This allows a server to assign IP addresses and configuration information to clients. Some examples of the information that is distributed include IP address, subnet mask, default gateway, DNS server address, and the DNS domain. As the dynamic portion of the name suggests, this address is assigned to the computer for a configurable length of time, known as a lease. Before the lease expires, the workstation must again request an IP address from the DHCP server. It might or might not get the same address that it had previously. Although servers and workstations can both be configured to use this method of addressing, it is generally used for workstations rather than servers.
- **Static IP address**—Using a static IP address is the most common decision for a server configuration. By static, we mean the server or workstation will not leverage DHCP; the IP address and settings are configured manually. The address will not change unless you change the configuration of the server. This point is important because clients and resources that need to access the server must know the address to be able to connect to it. If the IP address changed regularly, connecting to it would be difficult.

NOTE

Windows Server 2012 includes the latest TCP/IP protocol suite known as the Next Generation TCP/IP stack. The legacy protocol stack was designed in the early 1990s and has been modified to accommodate future growth of computers networked together. The new TCP/IP stack is known as Internet Protocol version 6 (IPv6).

Backing Up Files

Whether you are performing a new installation on a previously used server or upgrading an existing server, you should perform a complete backup of the data and operating system before you begin your new installation. This way, you have a fallback plan if the installation fails or the server does not perform the way you anticipated.

When performing a new installation on a previously used server, you overwrite any data that was stored there. In this scenario, you have to use your backup tape to restore any data that you want to recover.

Conversely, if you are going to upgrade an existing server, a known good backup will enable you to recover to your previous state if the upgrade does not go as planned.

NOTE

Many people back up their servers but never confirm that the data can be read from the backup media. When the time comes to recover their data, they find that the data is unusable or unreadable, or that they do not know the proper procedures for restoring their server. You should perform backup/recovery procedures on a regular basis in a lab environment to make sure that your equipment is working properly, that you are comfortable with performing the process, and that the recovery actually works.

Installing a Clean Version of Windows Server 2012 Operating System

The setup GUI for Windows Server 2012 is very similar to the installation process for Windows Server 2008 and Windows Server 2008 R2. After the installation software loads into memory, the configuration setup pages have a consistent look and feel. Each step outlined in the following sections also has integrated links to relevant Help topics. Many of the choices and options that were historically part of the pre-installation setup process in Windows 2000/2003 are now relegated to post-install configuration after the base OS installation has completed. Therefore, the steps required during initial installation are minimized, allowing for a faster installation and more streamlined initial process, consolidating operations pertaining to settings specific to the final role of the server to the post-installation phase.

The following sections outline the elements that must be entered during a clean installation of Windows Server 2012.

Customizing the Language, Time, Currency, and Keyboard Preferences

The first element when installing Windows Server 2012 is to choose the language to install on the server. Usually, the language selected is English; however, the language selections vary based on a region. Examples of languages include English, Arabic, French, Dutch, Spanish, and many more. The next element to be specified is the time and currency format. This setting dictates how the server will handle currencies, dates, and times, including daylight savings. The final element is the keyboard or input method. Specify the country code, such as US, Canada, or China, and click Next to begin the installation.

The Install Now Page

The next page in the installation process prompts you with an action to Install Now. Click Install Now to commence the Windows Server 2012 installation. In addition, this screen provides access to the new Windows Server 2012 repair console via the Repair Your Server link.

The repair console includes a link to a group of troubleshooting tools:

- **System Image Recovery**—Initiates a wizard-driven process to restore the system from a previously created system image

- **Command prompt**—A conventional command prompt including access to useful tools such as diskpart, bcdedit and xcopy. This command prompt can be a useful tool for troubleshooting installation problems and even problems with existing servers that won't boot.

Selecting the Type of Operating System to Install

The next page in the installation process is Select the Operating System You Want to Install. One of the first items that needs to be addressed on every new installation of Windows Server 2012 is which edition and type of operating system will be installed. The options include a Full installation or a Server Core installation. A Full installation is a traditional installation of Windows and includes all the user interfaces and supports all the server roles. As mentioned earlier, a Server Core installation is a scaled-down installation of Windows Server 2012 with the intent to reduce the attack surface and management.

Thanks to the new ability of a Windows Server 2012 server to transition quickly from a Full installation to a Server Core installation, the operating system type can be changed at a later time.

In addition to the server type, the operating system edition must also be selected. Here, again, Windows Server 2012 simplifies the choices with two editions: Standard and Datacenter. There are no longer any feature differences between the editions, only a difference in hardware and virtual systems supported.

Accepting the Terms of the Windows Server 2012 License

The License Terms page is presented next. Review the license terms and check the I Accept the License Terms check box if you comply with these terms. Click Next to continue.

Selecting the Type of Windows Server 2012 Installation

On the Which Type of Installation Do You Want page, you can either select to upgrade an existing Windows server or install a clean copy of Windows. Because this is a clean installation and a legacy operating system does not exist, the upgrade selection will present a message to this effect and prevent the installation from proceeding. Therefore, in this scenario, select Custom: Install Windows Only (Advanced) to perform a clean installation of Windows Server 2012. Click Next to continue, as shown in Figure 3.1.

Selecting the Location for the Installation

On the next page, the Install Windows Wizard asks where you want to install Windows. You need to specify where you want to install the OS and then click Next to continue, as illustrated in Figure 3.2. At this point, you can supply additional disk drivers, or add, delete, extend, or format partitions in preparation for the install. Once any required operations are done, select the partition for the new operating system installation and click Next.

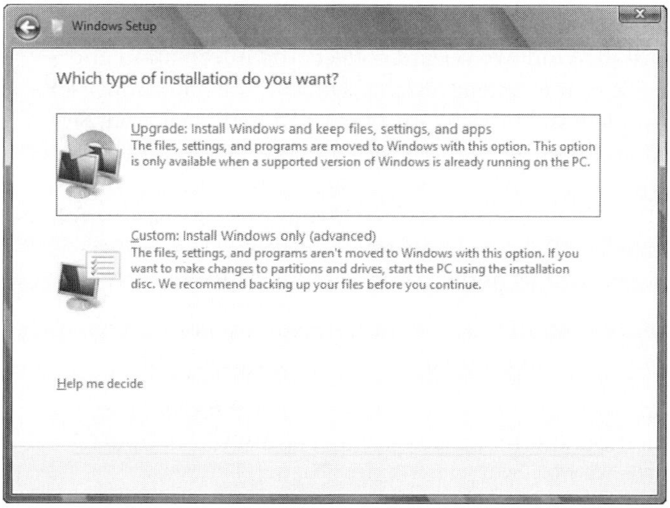

FIGURE 3.1 Specifying whether to upgrade or install a clean copy of Windows.

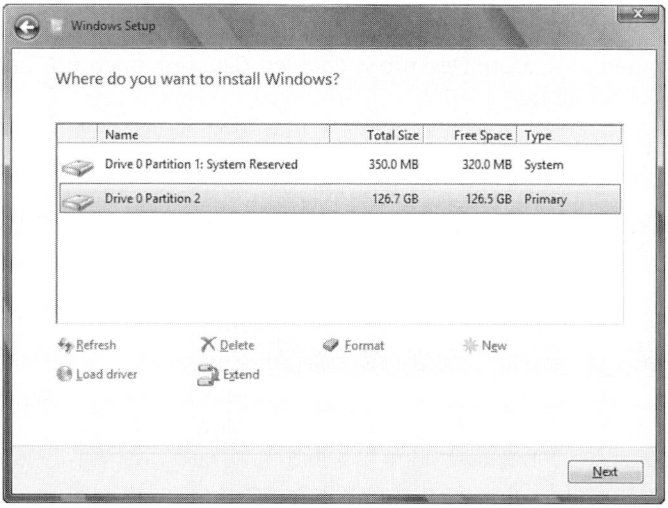

FIGURE 3.2 Specifying the location for the installation.

NOTE

As with the previous two versions of the operating system, there is no choice as to the file system on the partition. Windows Server 2012 automatically uses the new ReFS file system for all created partitions. ReFS is an improved and updated version of the NTFS file system. You can find more information about ReFS in Chapter 28, "File System Management and Fault Tolerance."

Finalizing the Installation and Customizing the Configuration

After the Windows Server 2012 Install Windows Wizard collects the information and installs the Windows operating system, the system restarts. The administrator must set a password before logging on to complete the installation process. When logged on, Server Manager is automatically invoked and presents the Dashboard view, which provides a quick-start series of steps to getting started with the server. By selecting the first link, Configure This Local Server, the Local Server view is activated and presents basic information about the server as well as links to common core configuration tasks, as shown in Figure 3.3. These tasks are commonly used to initially configure the server:

- **Computer Name/Workgroup**—Both links allow the configuration of the computer name and workgroup or domain membership as well as primary DNS suffix.
- **Last Installed Updates/Windows Update/Last Checked for Updated**—These sections display the configuration and recent activity for the Windows Update client. All three links open the Windows Update control panel.
- **Windows Firewall**—Shows the state of the firewall. The link opens the Windows Firewall control panel.
- **Remote Management**—Shows whether Remote Management is enabled. The link allows the option to be configured.
- **Remote Desktop**—Shows whether Remote Desktop is enabled. The link open the System control panel to the Remote tab.
- **Network Adapter Teaming**—Shows whether NIC teaming is enabled. The link opens the NIC teaming configuration console
- **Wired Ethernet Connection**—Shows the status of the network connection. The link opens the Network Connections control panel

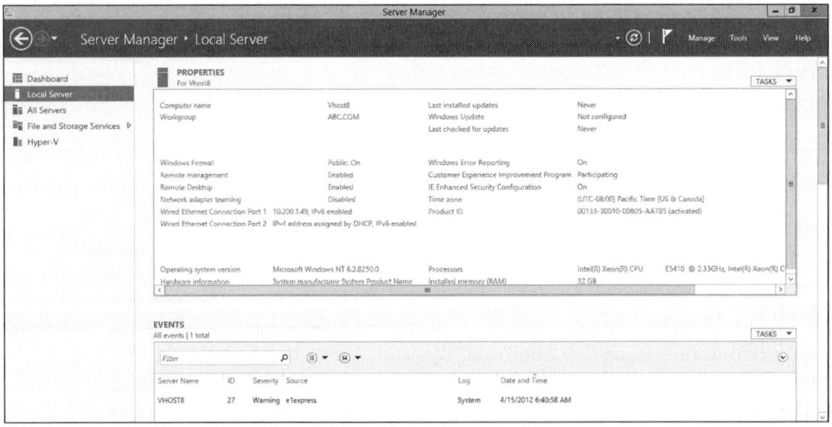

FIGURE 3.3 The Local Server view.

- **Windows Error Reporting/Customer Experience Improvement Program—** Shows participation setting for each program. The link allows participation to be configured.
- **IE Enhanced Security Configuration—**Shows the state of the IE protection mechanism. The link opens the configuration dialog for the mechanism.
- **Time Zone—**Shows the current time zone. The link opens the Date/Time control panel.
- **Product ID—**Shows the configured product ID. The link opens the Windows Activation Wizard.

Selecting the Administrator Password

The first configuration task to perform after installing Windows Server 2012 is to set an administrator password. This must be done before you can log on the first time. The installation process automatically creates the default administrator account called, surprisingly enough, Administrator. This account has local administrative privileges and enables you to manage all local configuration settings for the server. For security reasons, it is a good idea to rename the account after the installation.

Enter and confirm the selected administrator password. As in earlier Windows operating systems, the password is case sensitive and can contain up to 127 characters. As a best practice, always use a strong password for high-privilege accounts such as this one. A strong password should be at least eight characters long and include a combination of uppercase and lowercase letters, numbers, and non-alphanumeric characters.

Choose your password carefully to ensure the security of the system. You can change both the administrator account name and password in the Change Password dialog box, which can be opened the Ctrl+Alt+Del menu.

Providing the Computer Name and Domain

Once the administrator password has been set, initial configuration tasks can be executed using the Local Server view in Server Manager, starting with the computer name and domain or workgroup membership.

Use the current computer name and workgroup name links to open the System Properties dialog and click the Change button to specify a new computer name and to change your workgroup name or join a domain. If you are joining an existing domain, you need the logon name and password for an account with appropriate domain permissions. Alternatively, you can have the administrator of the domain add your computer name into the domain so that your server can connect. If you do not know the name of the domain that the server will be a member of, or if you do not have the administrative rights to join the server to the domain, you can still change the computer name and you can always join the server to a domain later.

Enabling Automatic Updating and Feedback

Next, the link next to the Windows Update label can is used to configure how your system maintains its health and security by automatically downloading and installing software updates.

Although you can select the default configuration that will install updates automatically by clicking the Turn On Automatic Updates button, server administrators click use the Let Me Choose My Settings link to open the advanced configuration dialog and select the desired options.

Options for deployment of important updates include the ability to not check for updates, only check for updates and notify the administrator, to check and download updates before prompting the administrator to install the patches, and the final option (the default option) is to automatically install updates. Servers are usually configured using the second or third options to strike a balance between timely patch deployment and administrative control.

Additional options include the ability to include recommended updates in the automated process and, if the automatic updates option was selected, the option to configure the maintenance window for automated installation.

When patching enterprise environments, it is a best practice to control software updates via a patching solution, such as System Center Configuration Manager 2012 or Windows Server Update Services (WSUS).

Downloading and Installing Updates

Even though you might have selected the option in the previous steps to automatically configure server updates, it is still possible to download and install updates manually by clicking the links next to Last Installed Updates and Last Checked for Updated. When these are clicked, the server connects to the Microsoft Windows Update site. Before configuring roles or features or making your server available to users on the network, it is a best practice to install the latest updates and patches from Microsoft. If your environment uses an automated tool such as WSUS, tested and approved patches might already be installed by your update and patching infrastructure if the system was joined to the domain and is configured to do so.

NOTE

When selecting the install links for the very first time, if updates are not being installed automatically, you are prompted with the option to turn on automatic updates. In addition, it is possible to click the Find Out More link to obtain updates for other Microsoft products installed on the server.

Configuring Windows Firewall

By default, Windows Firewall is turned on when the base OS is first installed. Although the firewall only protects the server from inbound and outbound access (as opposed to compromises from within the OS, such as a virus or other malware), this is usually adequate protection on a newly built machine until the system is patched and loaded with antivirus software or any other protective systems.

Unless you configure exceptions to the firewall, users cannot access resources or services on the server. Exceptions to this are roles and features installed using Server Manager or PowerShell. Many roles and features automatically create the required exceptions for their own workload, enabling you to leave the firewall on while allowing access to specific functions on the server, if desired. With Windows Server 2012, it is possible to configure incoming and outgoing firewall rules on each network connection using the Windows Firewall with Advanced Security console available from the tools menu in Server Manager.

Enabling Remote Management and Remote Desktop

The links for Remote Management and Remote Desktop provide a quick way to configure the server for remote administration. Remote Management allows remote connections to the server using tools such as Server Manager, PowerShell, and Windows Management Instrumentation (WMI).

By enabling Remote Desktop, you can connect to the server using a remote desktop (or Remote Desktop Protocol [RDP]) session. An important security option is configured when the component is enabled. The two choices for allowing Remote Desktop access are Allow Connections from Computers Running Any Version of Remote Desktop (Less Secure) and Allow Connections from Computers Running Remote Desktop with Network Level Authentication (More Secure).

Using Remote Desktop to manage systems greatly eases administration of servers but does open another door into each system; therefore, consider restricting access via Remote Desktop to users who have a need to access those systems. Access to RDP sessions is controlled using the membership of the Remote Desktop Users group.

Configuring Networking

Windows Server 2012 introduces network interface card (NIC) teaming as part of the operating system. Click the Network Adapter Teaming link to open the NIC Teaming configuration dialog, from where you can create and manage teams on local and remote servers.

Links for each network connection are available to configure network settings. By default, Windows Server 2012, as with earlier versions of Windows, installs Client for Microsoft Networks, File and Printer Sharing for Microsoft Networks, and TCP/IPv4. In addition, Windows Server 2012 installs Microsoft Network Monitor 3 Driver, QoS Packet Scheduler, Internet Protocol version 6 (TCP/IPv6), Link-Layer Topology Discovery Mapper I/O Driver, and Link-Layer Topology Discovery Responder.

The client, service, and protocols that are installed by default will meet most companies' needs and require little manual configuration. You will, however, likely want to change the TCP/IPv4 and TCP/IPv6 settings and assign a static address for the server.

For more details on configuring TCP/IP and the new protocol stack, review the chapters in Part III of this book, "Networking Services."

Sending Feedback to Microsoft

Two core configuration options configure the ability to participate in Microsoft programs designed to improve Windows Server product. Although it is easy to dismiss these features, the tools do provide you an easy way to submit your experience with Microsoft products with very little or no effort. Anonymous information gathered from users shapes Microsoft products and technologies, so if you don't have corporate policies that prohibit sharing technical information outside of your organization, give some thought to participating. If selected, the following options can be configured:

- **Windows Error Reporting**—Windows Error Reporting, by default, prompts you to send detailed information to Microsoft when errors occur on your server. You can turn this function off or configure it to automatically send the error information to Microsoft. You can further configure whether detailed or summary reports are sent. Reports contain information that is most useful for diagnosing and solving the problem that has occurred.

- **Customer Experience Improvement Program**—The Customer Experience Improvement Program (CEIP) gathers anonymous information and periodically sends it to Microsoft. CEIP reports generally include information about the features and general tasks performed by a user as well as any problems encountered when using the Microsoft product.

Configuring Browser Security

Internet Explorer Enhanced Security Configuration (IE ESC) is a default application configuration on servers that greatly reduces the potential for the server to be infected with malware when browsing the web. This is accomplished by disabling many components and interfaces in Internet Explorer, which makes the browser experience more secure and extremely limited. Because the best practice is to avoid browsing websites directly on a server, this is a welcome protection layer that should be maintained.

Certain server workloads, most typically Remote Desktop Services, might require disabling IE ESC for users. Even in those environments, it is still recommended to keep the setting enabled for administrators as a security precaution.

Setting the Time Zone

The Time Zone link is used to open the Date and Time dialog box. On the Date and Time tab, set the time zone where the server will operate by clicking the Change Date and Time button. In addition, click the Change Time Zone button to configure the time zone for the server. The next tab, Additional Clocks, as displayed in Figure 3.4, should be utilized if there is a need to display the time in another time zone. Up to two clocks can be configured on this tab.

Activate Windows

The last link, labeled Product ID, opens the Windows Activation Wizard. As with other Microsoft operating systems, Windows Server 2012 must be activated within a set number of days. In the Windows Activation dialog box, enter the product key, which will be validated once complete. Click Activate to complete the activation.

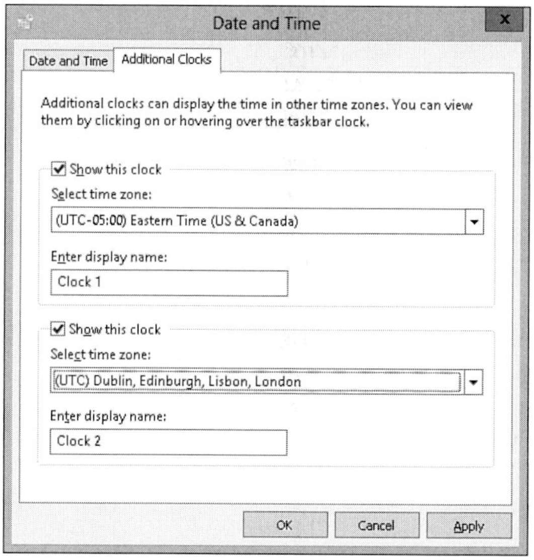

FIGURE 3.4 Configuring additional clocks.

Adding Roles

Once the basic configuration steps are completed, you can install server roles from the Manage menu, such as Active Directory Domain Services, Active Directory Rights Management Services, DNS Server, and much more to your server. The process also adds dependent services and components as needed (alerting you along the way). This ensures that as you are setting up your system, all the necessary components are installed—alleviating the need to use multiple tools to install, secure, and manage a given server role—and that the roles are set up securely, meaning that only the required components and configurations are implemented and nothing more. Although it's critical to understand dependencies for whatever role or function the server might hold, getting the system set up quickly, efficiently, and accurately is always paramount, and these setup tools help accomplish just that.

Adding Features

Features are added from the same wizard as roles, using the Manage menu. Features are secondary to roles but contain powerful and useful tools that can be installed on the server. Features such as RPC over HTTP Proxy (for Exchange), Multipath I/O, .NET Framework 3.5 features, Background Intelligent Transfer Service (BITS), and SMTP Server can be installed and configured. Backup and other management tools can also be installed using this tool.

Upgrading to Windows Server 2012

When upgrading an existing server to Windows Server 2012, all configuration settings, files, and programs are retained from the previous installation. However, there are still several important required tasks that you perform before the upgrade, as discussed in the following sections.

NOTE

When upgrading a system to Windows Server 2012, you need to have at least 1237MB of free space on the system partition; otherwise, the upgrade will come to a halt.

Backing Up the Server

When making a major change on a server, something could go wrong. A complete backup of your operating system and data, including the system state, can make the difference between confidently telling the boss you had a setback and so you conducted a rollback or trying to find a way to tell your boss a complete disaster has taken place.

Verifying System Compatibility

In the past, you could check system compatibility before starting an upgrade. Now, it is a best practice to use the Microsoft Application Compatibility Toolkit to verify Windows Server 2012 compatibility before an installation. The tool can be accessed from the following Microsoft link: http://technet.microsoft.com/en-us/windows/aa905066.aspx.

Running the Windows Memory Diagnostics Tool

As a prerequisite task, it is also beneficial to test the physical memory in the server before conducting the upgrade. Do the test by running the Windows Memory Diagnostics tool. The tool can be executed by booting into the Advance Boot Options on your server using the F8 button or by opening the system recovery options using boot media.

Ensuring the Drivers Are Digitally Signed

Microsoft started certifying drivers for plug-and-play devices during the release of Windows 2000 Server to stabilize the operating system. When installing drivers, an administrator had the opportunity to choose from digitally signed drivers or unsigned drivers. Digitally signed drivers ensure stability; however, it was also possible to install unsigned drivers. The unsigned drivers were not blessed or certified by Microsoft.

When upgrading to Windows Server 2012, an error message is displayed when unsigned drivers are detected. In addition, the unsigned driver will not be loaded when the operating system is upgraded and finally rebooted. Based on these issues, it is a best practice to obtain only digitally signed drivers, upgrade unsigned drivers, or disable the signature requirement for a driver if you cannot boot your computer after the upgrade.

The following procedures should be used to disable the signature requirement on Windows Server 2012:

1. Reboot the server and press Shift+F8 during startup.
2. Select Disable Driver Signature Enforcement.

3. Boot into Windows.
4. Uninstall the unsigned driver.

Performing Additional Tasks

It is also beneficial to perform the following additional tasks before proceeding with the installation upgrade. Disconnect UPS devices as they negatively affect installation when detecting devices on serial ports, disable antivirus software as it might affect this installation process, and obtain drivers for the mass storage devices from the manufacturers.

Performing the Upgrade

At this point, your data is backed up, you have verified compatibility with the new operating system, and you have read the release notes. It's time to upgrade, so complete the following steps:

1. Log on to the server and insert the Windows Server 2012 media. The Install Windows page should automatically launch; otherwise, click Setup.exe.
2. Click Install Now to begin the upgrade process.
3. On the Get important updates for Windows Setup page, first select the I Want to Help Make Windows Install Better option. By doing this, you will participate in the Windows Installation Customer Experience Improvement Program that allows Microsoft to collect information about the hardware configuration, installation settings, and errors received. This information helps Microsoft determine whether updates are needed and identify areas of improvement.
4. On the same page, select either Go Online to Get the Latest Updates for Setup (recommended) or Don't Get the Latest Updates for Setup, as shown in Figure 3.5.

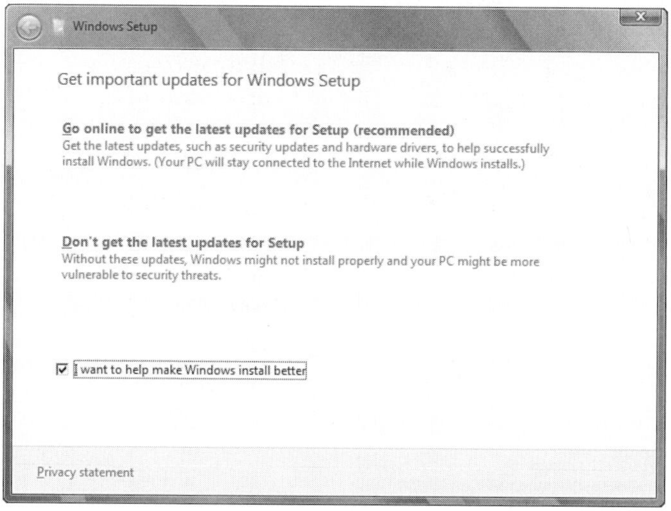

FIGURE 3.5 Getting important updates for the Windows Server 2012 installation.

NOTE

If the server is connected to the Internet, it is a best practice to select the first option. Obtaining the latest updates helps ensure a successful installation as the latest hardware drivers and Windows code are utilized.

5. On the Select the Operating System You Want to Install page, select the desired operating system, such as Windows Server 2012 Enterprise (Full Installation). Click Next to continue.

NOTE

Just as a reminder, as stated earlier in this chapter, you cannot upgrade a Windows Server 2008 R2 system full installation to Windows Server 2012 Server Core installation. If a Server Core installation is selected, the compatibility check later in the process will produce an error and require a different edition to be selected.

6. Review the license terms and select the I Accept the License Terms option, and then click Next.
7. On the Which Type of Installation Do You Want page, select the Upgrade option. Upgrading the system maintains existing files, settings, and programs.
8. The Compatibility report page is invoked, as illustrated in Figure 3.6. This screen includes a warning that it is a best practice to visit the following Microsoft link, http://go.microsoft.com/fwlink/?LinkID=85172, to ensure all programs are supported and can remain installed during the installation. It is recommended to uninstall any applications that are not supported. Click Next to continue.

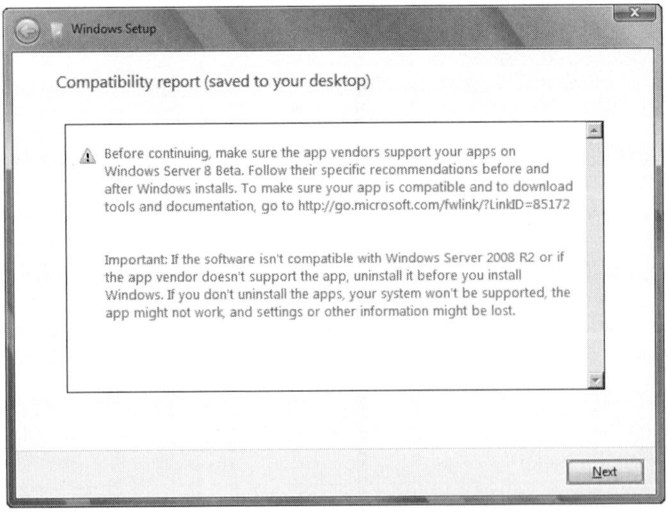

FIGURE 3.6 The Windows Setup compatibility report.

9. The upgrade process commences and the Upgrading Windows page displays status on the following items: Copying Windows files, Collecting files, settings and apps, Expanding Windows files, Installing features and updates, and Almost done moving files, settings and programs.

NOTE

During this process, Windows automatically reboots the machine a few times, completes the installation process, and prepares the server for its first use.

The process for completing the installation and conducting post-installation tasks is the same for an upgrade as a new installation except that some settings may have been preserved during the upgrade process. In addition, after the upgrade is complete, it is a best practice to use Server Manager to review the event-log events, verify that system services are operational, and ensure the upgraded server roles were, in fact, installed and configured correctly. In addition, the Best Practices Analyzer (BPA) section of the Local Server view can be used to execute a BPA scan to get additional information about recommended configurations, tasks, and best practices.

Understanding Server Core Installation

Windows Server Core, an installation option, was one of the most innovative and anticipated features of Windows Server 2008. The Windows Server Core installation provides a minimal environment for running a specific server role, including, but not limited to, a domain controller, web server, or DHCP server. In this situation, only a subset of the Windows Server 2012 binaries is utilized. The Server Core installation is so stripped that traditional installation components, such as a desktop shell, GUI, Windows Explorer, Microsoft Internet Explorer, and the Microsoft Management Console (MMC), are not included. Therefore, the server must be fully managed and configured via the command prompt or by using remote administration tools from another server.

By maintaining a minimized installation footprint, stripping out many typical components and only supporting specific roles, the Server Core installation reduces maintenance, attack surface, management, and disk space required to support the installation.

Supporting a Server Core installation, particularly for administrators who do not understand scripting commands and who heavily rely on the GUI tools to manage a server, is possible by enabling the ability to remotely manage the Server Core installation through the MMC and other remote consoles.

Windows Server 2012 includes the following new features and functionality for Server Core:

- **Support for additional roles**—Core installations now support more server roles than ever before. Newly added support for Remote Access (Routing and Remote Access Service [RRAS]), Windows Server Update Services (WSUS), and several role services for Remote Desktop Services, among others, now make core installations more versatile and useful.

- **Support for SQL Server**—Probably the most important new functionality is the support for SQL Server 2012 databases on a Server Core installation.
- **Easy migration between Core and GUI**—Using a single command, a Windows Server 2012 server can be migrated from a core installation to a GUI installation and vice versa.
- **Minimal server interface**—Graphical Management Tools, Desktop Experience, and Server Graphical Shell are now features that you can install or remove independently, resulting in a Minimal Server GUI installation, a new mode between a Server Core installation and a full GUI installation. This provides even more flexibility in balancing security, manageability, and functionality.

Installing Server Core

When installing Windows Server 2012 Server Core, the actual installation process is very similar to a regular server install, which was conducted in the earlier sections of this chapter. To recap, an administrator agrees to the licensing terms, supplies configuration responses, and the Windows Server 2012 Setup Windows Wizard copies the files and configures the server. However, unlike a traditional installation of Windows, when the installation is complete and you log on, there isn't a GUI to configure the server. The server can only be configured and managed via the command prompt.

The Server Core installation reboots your machine or virtual server a couple of times when device detection and the installation takes place. Eventually, the logon screen appears.

Follow these steps to complete a Windows Server 2012 Server Core installation:

1. Insert the Windows Server 2012 media and boot the system from media.
2. Specify the language to install, time and currency format, and keyboard or input method, and then click Next.
3. Click Install Now to begin the installation process.
4. On the Select the Operating System You Want to Install page, select the Windows Server 2012 Server Core. Click Next to continue.
5. Review the license terms and select the I Accept the License Terms option, and then click Next.
6. On the Which Type of Installation Do You Want Page, select Custom: Install Windows only (Advanced), as shown in Figure 3.7.
7. On the Where Do You Want to Install Windows page, select the disk where you plan to install the Windows system files. Alternatively, you can click the Drive options (advanced) to create, delete, extend, or format partitions. In addition, click Load Driver to install drivers for the Windows Server 2012 installation that are not available on the media.

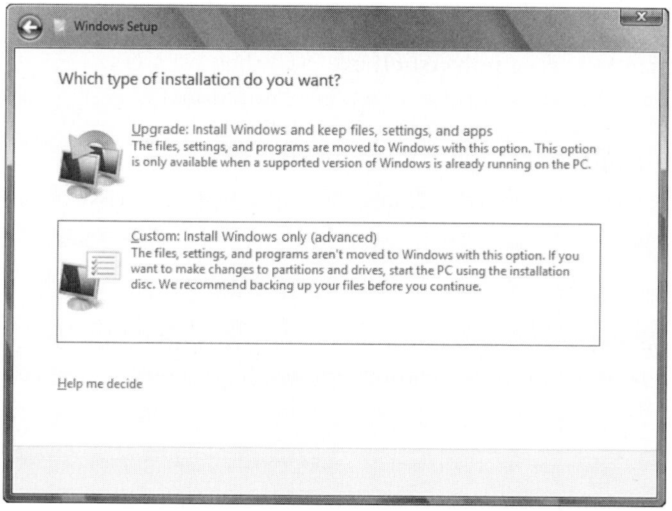

FIGURE 3.7 Selecting a custom installation.

NOTE

If the only drive available is Unallocated Space, Windows Server 2012 automatically creates a partition based on the largest size and format the partition with ReFS.

The installation process commences by copying the files, installing the Windows operating system, and configuring features. After this process is complete, the server automatically reboots itself and require the installer to change the administrator password for the system. Enter and confirm the administrator password to change the password and log on. You will now be presented with a command prompt window, the only GUI available in Server Core.

Managing and Configuring a Server Core Installation

The following sections cover general tasks associated with managing and configuring a Server Core system via the command prompt after the installation is complete. As an alternative, an administrator can use the SCONFIG utility to configure general settings.

Launching the Command Prompt in a Server Core Installation

Remember, the Start menu does not exist. Because of this, one of the most important tasks an administrator must understand when managing a Server Core installation is how to launch a PowerShell console session. The following steps will assist you:

1. Press Ctrl+Alt+Delete.
2. Select Start Task Manager.

3. On the Windows Task Manager screen, select File, New Task (Run).
4. In the Create New Task dialog box, type **powershell.exe**, and then click OK.

Changing the Server Core Administrator's Password

After the initial password has been set, the syntax to change the administrator password is as follows:

```
Net user administrator *
```

After the command has been executed, you are prompted to type a password for the user. Enter the password and then retype it for the confirmation process. It is a best practice to use a complex password when assigning passwords to the administrator account and the default password policy on the server will require complex passwords.

Changing the Server Core Machine Name

After the Server Core installation is complete, another common task is to change the machine name of the server. By default, Windows automatically generates and assigns a server name starting with *WIN* and followed by a string of characters. The syntax to change the Server Core machine name follows:

```
netdom renamecomputer <CurrentComputerName> /newname:<NewComputerName>
```

When executing this command, replace the *<CurrentComputerName>* argument with the existing hostname (which can be found using the `hostname` command) and the *<NewComputerName>* argument with the new machine name for the Server Core installation. Changing the server name from Win-123 to ABCDC2 is depicted in the following example:

```
netdom renamecomputer Win-123 /newname:ABCDC2
```

The same function can be performed using PowerShell with the following command:

```
Rename-computer -NewName ABCDC2
```

Assigning a Static IPV4 IP Address and DNS Settings

Another common Server Core management task is assigning an IP address, including the primary and secondary DNS settings. Before this task can be executed, you must run the following command to obtain and identify the names of the network interfaces installed on the server. This includes capturing the unique ID associated with each network interface. To display a list of network interfaces, including their respective unique IDs, run the following command:

```
netsh interface ipv4 show interfaces
```

NOTE

Netsh commands can usually be abbreviated to make typing easier once the administrator is familiar with the command. For example, the preceding command can also be executed by running the following:

```
Netsh int ipv4 sh int
```

The next step is to make a note of the network interface name and unique ID that you must change. The ID is located in the leftmost column and is referred to as Idx. This is depicted in the output of the `netsh interface ipv4 show interfaces` command, as displayed in Figure 3.8.

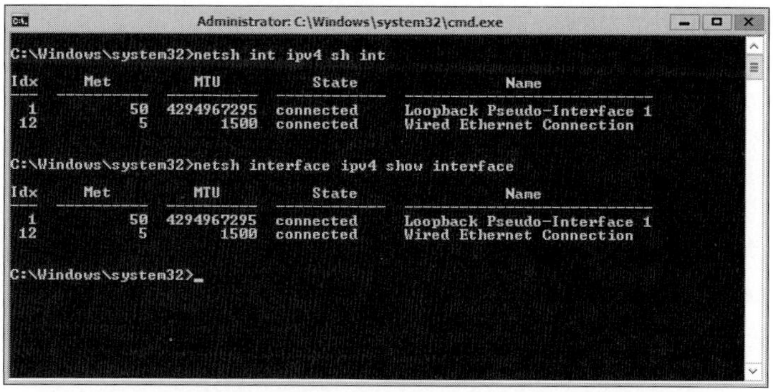

FIGURE 3.8 Reviewing the Idx ID for a network interface.

NOTE

If you plan to change the IP address settings on more than one interface, take note of all the interface names and Idx unique IDs.

Now that you have captured the names and IDs, use the following syntax to change the IP address for a desired interface:

```
netsh interface ipv4 set address name="<ID>" source=static address=<StaticIP>
mask=<SubnetMask> gateway=<DefaultGateway>
```

Replace the ID argument with the network interface name or ID. In addition, enter the static IP address, subnet mask, and default gateway in subsequent arguments, as follows:

```
netsh interface ipv4 set address name="1" source=static ad
dress=192.168.115.10 mask=255.255.255.0 gateway=192.168.115.1.
```

The final step when configuring the network interface is to enter a primary and secondary DNS entry for the interface. Do this by using the following syntax:

```
netsh interface ipv4 add dnsserver name="<ID>" address=<DNSIP> index=1
```

The same command is used and repeated when entering more than one DNS entry. However, increment the index each time. When finalized, run IP Config /all to verify the IP address settings.

The same function can be performed using PowerShell with the following commands:

```
Get-NETIPInterface
Set-NetIPAddress -InterfaceIndex 12 -IPv4Address 192.168.115.10 -PrefixLength 24
-DefaultGateway 192.168.115.1
Set-DNSClientServerAddress -InterfaceIndex 12 -ServerAddresses "DNSIP1","DNSIP2"
```

Adding the Server Core System to a Domain

The following script illustrates the basic syntax to add a Server Core system to a Windows domain:

```
Netdom join <computername> /domain:<domain> /OU:<ou path> /userd:<domain>\<username>
/passwordD:*
```

Input the domain name and the target OU. Supply the user account and password for an account that has permissions to add computers to the domain.

The same function can be performed using PowerShell with the following commands:

```
Add-Computer -domainname <domain> -OUPath "OU=OU,=Domain,DC=com"
```

Activating the Server Core System

Activating a Server Core system can be achieved in two easy steps. First, you enter a product key, and then you activate the server. The syntax to enter a product key is as follows:

```
slmgr.vbs -ipk<productkey>
```

After the product key has been successfully entered, you activate the server by typing in the following command.

```
slmgr.vbs -ato
```

Using SCONFIG to Configure a Server Core Installation

As mentioned previously, Windows Server 2012 includes a utility to make the initial configuration or a core installation easier. The SCONFIG utility, which has been available since Windows Server 2008 R2, is very easy to use and is usually the preferred configuration option if scripting is not required.

The utility can be executed by running sconfig.exe in the core installation command prompt and presents the set of options shown in Figure 3.9.

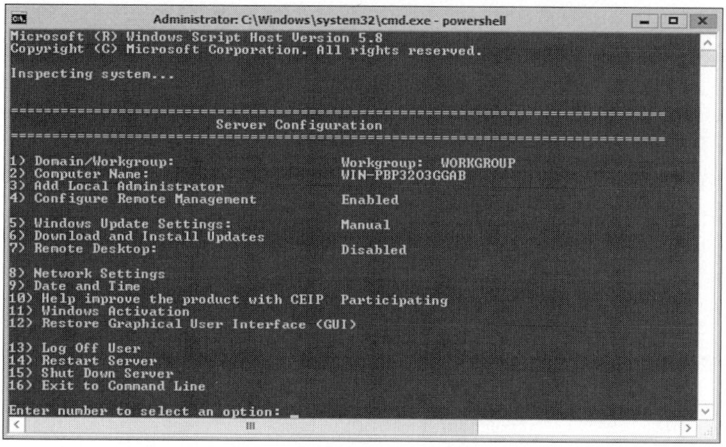

FIGURE 3.9 SCONFIG utility.

Server Core Roles and Feature Installations

The typical Windows server roles can be configured on a Server Core installation. The following server roles are currently supported on a Server Core installation:

- Active Directory Certificate Services
- Active Directory Domain Services (AD DS)
- Active Directory Lightweight Directory Services (AD LDS)
- Active Directory Rights Management Server
- DHCP Server
- DNS Server
- File and Storage Services
- Hyper-V
- Print and Document Services
- Remote Access Server
- Remote Desktop Services (partial support)
    - Connection Broker
    - Licensing
    - Virtualization Host only
- Volume Activation Services

- Web Server (IIS)
- Windows Deployment Services
- Windows Software Update Services

The following are some of the features that are also supported on a Server Core installation:

- .NET Framework 4.5
- BITS Compact Server
- BitLocker Drive Encryption
- BranchCache
- Failover Clustering
- Group Policy Management
- IP Address Management (IPAM) Server
- Multipath I/O
- Network Load Balancing
- Remote Server Administration Tools (partial)
- Simple Network Management Protocol (SNMP)
- Telnet Client
- Windows PowerShell 2.0
- Windows Server Backup

NOTE

The following command lists all the potential server roles and associated features:

```
Dism /online /get-features /format:table
```

The OCSetup command-line program familiar from earlier versions is still available (but deprecated) for setting up and configuring the server roles and features on a Server Core installation. You can configure the OCSetup command-line options using the following syntax:

```
ocsetup.exe [/?] [/h] [/help] component [/log:file] [/norestart] [/passive] [/quiet]
[/unattendfile:file] [/uninstall] [/x: parameter]
```

Table 3.3 describes each of the options that are available when using the OCSetup command-line program.

TABLE 3.3 Available Command Options for OCSetup

Parameter	Description
`/?, /h, /help`	Explains all the options available for OCSetup
`component`	Represents the name of the component you plan on installing, such as DNS, DHCP, Web Server (IIS), and more
`/log:file`	Specifies the log file location if you do not want to take advantage of the default location
`/norestart`	Does not reboot the computer after the installation
`/passive`	Suppresses unnecessary noise and only includes progress status
`/quiet`	Does not require user interaction
`/unattendfile:file`	Requires additional configurations
`/uninstall`	Removes server components
`/x: parameter`	Supplies additional configuration parameters

Using Powershell to Install a Server Role on a Server Core Installation

In addition to OCSetup, Powershell can be used to install roles and features, as follows:

1. Run PowerShell by executing powershell.exe in the command prompt.
2. Run `import-module servermanager` to enable Server Manager features within the PowerShell session.
3. Use `Get-WindowsFeature` to identify installed and available roles and features.
4. Use `Add-WindowsFeature` to add the required role or feature. Table 3.4 outlines an example of common server role installations using `Add-WindowsFeature`.

TABLE 3.4 Server Role Installation Command Lines with PowerShell

Server Role	Command
DNS Server role	`Add-WindowsFeature DNS`
DHCP Server role	`Add-WindowsFeature DHCP`
File Server role	`Add-WindowsFeature File-Services`
Print Server role	`Add-WindowsFeature Print-Server`
Active Directory Lightweight Directory Server role	`Add-WindowsFeature ADLDS`
Windows Server Update Services role	`Add-WindowsFeature UpdateServices`
Web Server (IIS) role	`Add-WindowsFeature Web-Server`
Remote Access role	`Add-WindowsFeature RemoteAccess`
Hyper-V role	`Add-WindowsFeature Hyper-V`

The previous sections are a prelude to some of the common Server Core command-line arguments for installing and configuring elements on a Windows Server 2012 Server Core installation. For a full list of command-line arguments, visit the Microsoft website and conduct a search for Windows Server 2012 Server Core.

Installing the Active Directory Domain Services Role

Installation of AD DS is more complex and vital to the operation of the environment and therefore deserves more detailed attention. Installation of the role using `Add-WindowsFeature AD-domain-services` will install the required binaries but not configure the server as a domain controller.

In earlier versions, the recommended tool for that is the dcpromo utility. The problem is that dcpromo normally starts a wizard with a GUI that is not supported on Server Core. As a result, the dcpromo utility on server core is a command-line utility that requires input by supplying the operation parameters or by using an answer file.

The dcpromo utility can accept more than 30 different operation parameters. Although this might seem like a dizzying array of options, few command lines will use all of them. Refer to the TechNet dcpromo command reference at http://technet.microsoft.com/en-us/library/cc732887(WS.10).aspx for a complete list and explanation of each parameter. You can use this reference to build the correct dcpromo command line or create an unattend file suitable for your core domain controller.

As with many other aspects of the operating system, Windows Server 2012 provides PowerShell support to perform that same function. Promoting a domain controller using PowerShell is very convenient and is based on the ADDSDeployment module, which includes the following commands:

- **Install-ADDSForest**
- **Install-ADDSDomain**
- **Install-ADDSDomainController**

These commands are available by first loading the appropriate module using `Import-Module ADDSDeployment`. Then, all that's required is using the correct command from above depending on whether the goal is to deploy a new forest, add a domain to an existing forest, or add a domain controller to an existing domain. All the commands accept the required parameters, which you can discover by using the `Get-Help` cmdlet.

For example, use the following command to get the syntax for the `Install-ADDSForest` cmdlet:

```
Get-Help Install-ADDSForest
```

Then, using the following syntax to install a new Windows 2012 forest with a root domain called abc.com:

```
Install-ADDSForest -ForestMode "Win8" -DomainMode "Win8" -DomainName "abc.com"
-DomainNetBIOSName "ABC" -DatabasePath "C:\Windows\NTDS" -LogPath "C:\Windows\NTDS"
-SYSVOLPath "C:\Windows\SYSVOL" -InstallDNS:$true -CreateDNSDelegation:$false
-RebootOnCompletion:$true -Force:$true
```

You will be prompted for the safe mode boot password, and the forest will be created. The server reboots upon completion as specified in the command.

Performing an Unattended Windows Server 2012 Installation

In many large enterprise environments, it is necessary to automate the installation of Windows Server 2012. This is because there might be a large number of servers within the organization and installing or upgrading each server manually is not a practical or efficient way of utilizing resources or capital expenditures. Windows Deployment Services is a great tool offered by Microsoft to automate the installation process of Windows Server 2012 when trying to achieve economies of scale.

For more information about Windows Deployment Services and performing an unattended installation of Windows Server 2012, see Chapter 26, "Windows Server 2012 Administration Tools for Desktops."

Summary

The Windows Server 2012 installation process and deployment tools bear similarities to those found in earlier versions of Windows. However, feature and performance enhancements have improved the installation experience—whether you are installing a single system by hand or deploying thousands of systems across your corporate environment with Windows Deployment Services.

The new Windows Server Core supported roles and features such as RRAS, WSUS, and even SQL Server have been a much anticipated feature set for the Windows Server 2012 family of operating systems. Server Core installations can further meet today's administrator and organization needs by providing a way to use the Windows Server 2012 operating system with the fewest number of binaries, in the most highly secured fashion, and while also reducing management overhead.

Best Practices

The following are best practices from this chapter:

- Verify that Windows Server 2012 supports your hardware, devices, and drivers.
- Stick to using the recommended or optimal hardware and software requirements.
- Make sure you document your server configuration information and perform a backup of any data that you want to keep.

- Use the Windows Server 2012 Server Manager Local Server view to conduct post-installation tasks.
- Utilize Windows Server Core installations when the highest level of security is warranted.
- Use a consistent naming convention to name the servers and client machines.
- Use only Internet standard characters in your computer name. This includes the letters A–Z (uppercase and lowercase), the numbers 0–9, and the hyphen (-).
- Periodically verify that system backups can be used to recover a system in a lab environment.
- As soon as you complete the installation, rename the administrator account and assign a strong password, for the sake of security.
- Automate installation by using Windows Deployment Services or System Center Configuration Manager 2012.
- Choose and install Windows Server 2012 roles and features to a server to take advantage of new capabilities built in to Windows Server 2012.

CHAPTER 4

Active Directory Domain Services Primer

IN THIS CHAPTER

Microsoft's Active Directory technologies have come a long way since their original release with Windows 2000 Server. From a single product referred to simply as Active Directory, or AD, Windows Server 2012 now encompasses a total of five separate Active Directory technologies. Each of these technologies is similar—they all exist to supply directory services and to serve as a platform for future integration of Microsoft technologies. The additional four Active Directory services roles in Windows Server 2012 are Active Directory Lightweight Directory Services (AD LDS), Active Directory Federation Services (AD FS), Active Directory Certificate Services (AD CS), and Active Directory Rights Management Services (AD RMS).

The focus of this chapter is on the traditional Active Directory service, Active Directory Domain Services (AD DS), and touches on the information needed to understand what AD DS is and how it has become the most common enterprise directory platform in use today. This chapter initially focuses on describing a history of directory services in general. It then proceeds to give a primer on AD DS itself as a technology. Finally, specific changes made to Active Directory technologies in general are outlined at the end of the chapter, including all new improvements introduced in the Windows Server 2012 version of AD DS. The additional Active Directory services outside of AD DS are covered in subsequent chapters, primarily in Chapter 8, "Creating Federated Forests and Lightweight Directories."

The Evolution of Directory Services

Directory services have existed in one form or another since the early days of computing to provide basic lookup and authentication functionality for enterprise network implementations. A directory service provides detailed information about a user or object in a network, much in the same way that a phone book is used to look up a telephone number for a provided name. For example, a user object in a directory service can store the phone number, email address, department name, and as many other attributes as an administrator desires.

Directory services are commonly referred to as the white pages of a network. They provide user and object definition and administration. Early electronic directories were developed soon after the invention of the digital computer and were used for user authentication and to control access to resources. With the growth of the Internet and the increase in the use of computers for collaboration, the use of directories expanded to include basic contact information about users. Examples of early directories included MVS PROFS (IBM), Grapevine's Registration Database, and WHOIS.

Application-specific directory services soon arose to address the specific addressing and contact-lookup needs of each product. These directories were accessible only via proprietary access methods and were limited in scope. Applications utilizing these types of directories were programs such as Novell GroupWise Directory, Lotus Notes, and the UNIX sendmail /etc/aliases file.

The further development of large-scale enterprise directory services was spearheaded by Novell with the release of Novell Directory Services (NDS) in the early 1990s. It was adopted by NetWare organizations and eventually was expanded to include support for mixed NetWare/NT environments. The flat, unwieldy structure of NT domains and the lack of synchronization and collaboration between the two environments led many organizations to adopt NDS as a directory service implementation. It was these specific deficiencies in NT that Microsoft addressed with the introduction of AD DS.

The development of the Lightweight Directory Access Protocol (LDAP) corresponded with the growth of the Internet and a need for greater collaboration and standardization. This nonproprietary method of accessing and modifying directory information that fully utilized TCP/IP was determined to be robust and functional, and new directory services implementations were written to utilize this protocol. AD DS itself was specifically designed to conform to the LDAP standard.

Reviewing the Original Microsoft Directory Systems

Exchange Server 5.5 ran its own directory service as part of its email environment. In fact, AD DS took many of its key design components from the original Exchange directory service. For example, the AD DS database uses the same Jet database format as Exchange 5.5 and the site replication topology is similar in many ways.

Several other Microsoft applications ran their own directory services, namely Internet Information Server and Site Server. However, each directory service was separate from the others, and integration was not very tight between the different implementations.

Outlining the Key Features of Active Directory Domain Services

Five key components are central to AD DS's functionality. As compatibility with Internet standards has become required for new directory services, the existing implementations have adjusted and focused on these areas:

- **TCP/IP compatibility**—Unlike some of the original proprietary protocols such as IPX/SPX and NetBEUI, the Transmission Control Protocol/Internet Protocol (TCP/IP) was designed to be cross-platform. The subsequent adoption of TCP/IP as an Internet standard for computer communications has propelled it to the forefront of the protocol world and essentially made it a requirement for enterprise operating systems. AD DS and Windows Server 2012 utilize the TCP/IP protocol stack as their primary method of communications.
- **Lightweight Directory Access Protocol support**—LDAP has emerged as the standard Internet directory protocol and is used to update and query data within the directory. AD DS directly supports LDAP.
- **Domain name system (DNS) support**—DNS was created out of a need to translate simplified names that can be understood by humans (such as www.cco.com) into an IP address that is understood by a computer (such as 12.222.165.154). The AD DS structure supports and effectively requires DNS to function properly.
- **Security support**—Internet standards-based security support is vital to the smooth functioning of an environment that is essentially connected to millions of computers around the world. Lack of strong security is an invitation to be hacked, and Windows Server 2012 and AD DS have taken security to greater levels. Support for IP Security (IPsec), Kerberos, certificate authorities, and Secure Sockets Layer (SSL) encryption is built in to Windows Server 2012 and AD DS.
- **Ease of administration**—Although often overlooked in powerful directory services implementations, the ease in which the environment is administered and configured directly affects the overall costs associated with its use. AD DS and Windows Server 2012 are specifically designed for ease of use to lessen the learning curve associated with the use of a new environment. Windows Server 2012 also enhanced AD DS administration with the introduction of the Active Directory Administration Center, Active Directory Web Services, and an Active Directory module for Windows PowerShell command-line administration which has been greatly improved from the one originally included in Windows Server 2008 and Windows Server 2008 R2. PowerShell support in Windows Server 2012 AD DS now allows for better troubleshooting and fully automated provisioning of domain controllers and entire forests from the command line. In addition, Windows Server 2012 also allows for better domain controller virtualization support, a concept that is explored more fully in this section of the book.

Understanding the Development of AD DS

Introduced with Windows 2000 Server as a replacement to Windows NT 4.0 domains, AD DS (then known simply as AD in Windows 2000) was later greatly improved in the 2003,

2003 R2, 2008, 2008 R2, and now the 2012 versions. AD DS has achieved wide industry recognition and acceptance and has proven itself in reliability, scalability, and performance. The introduction of AD DS served to address some limitations in the legacy NT 4.0 domain structure design and also allowed for future Microsoft and third-party products to tie into a common interface.

Detailing Microsoft's Adoption of Internet Standards

Since the early development of Windows 2000/2003/2003 R2/2008/2008 R2 and continuing with Windows Server 2012, Microsoft has strived to make all its products Internet compatible and friendly. Standards that before had been options or previously incompatible were subsequently woven into the software as primary methods of communication and operability. All applications and operating systems became TCP/IP compliant, and proprietary protocols such as NetBEUI were phased out.

With the introduction of Windows Server 2012, the Internet readiness of the Microsoft environment reaches new levels of functionality, with enhancements such as the ability to join virtual domain controller templates to a forest; the ability to restore deleted objects using the Active Directory Recycle Bin, offline domain join, and Managed Service Accounts; the ability to use multiple password policies per domain; read-only domain controller (RODC) support, the ability to start/stop AD on a domain controller (DC), and the ability to audit changes made to AD objects.

AD DS Structure

The logical structure of AD DS enables it to scale from small offices to large, multinational organizations. Administrative granularity is built in to allow delegation of control to groups or specific users. No longer is the assigning of administrative rights an all-or-nothing scenario.

AD DS loosely follows an X.500 directory model, but takes on several characteristics of its own. Many of us are already getting used to the forests and trees of AD DS, and some limitations that existed before in previous versions of AD DS have been lifted. To understand AD DS, we must first take a good look at its core structural components.

Understanding the AD DS Domain

An AD DS domain, traditionally represented by a triangle, as shown in Figure 4.1, is the initial logical boundary of AD DS. In a standalone sense, an AD DS domain acts very much like the legacy Windows NT 4.0 domain structure that it replaced. Users and computers are all stored and managed from within the boundaries of the domain. However, several major changes have been made to the structure of the domain and how it relates to other domains within the AD DS structure.

Domains in AD DS serve as administrative security boundaries for objects and contain their own security policies. It is important to keep in mind that domains are a logical organization of objects and can easily span multiple physical locations. Consequently, it is no longer necessary to set up multiple domains for different remote offices or sites as replication concerns and security concerns are more properly addressed with the use of AD DS sites or RODCs, which are described in greater detail in the following sections.

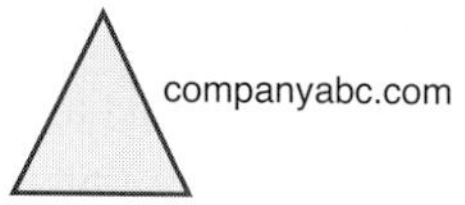

FIGURE 4.1 Examining a sample domain in AD DS.

Describing AD DS Domain Trees

An AD DS tree consists of multiple domains connected by two-way transitive trusts. Each domain in an AD DS tree shares a common schema and global catalog. In Figure 4.2, the root domain of the AD DS tree is companyabc.com and the subdomains are asia.companyabc.com and europe.companyabc.com.

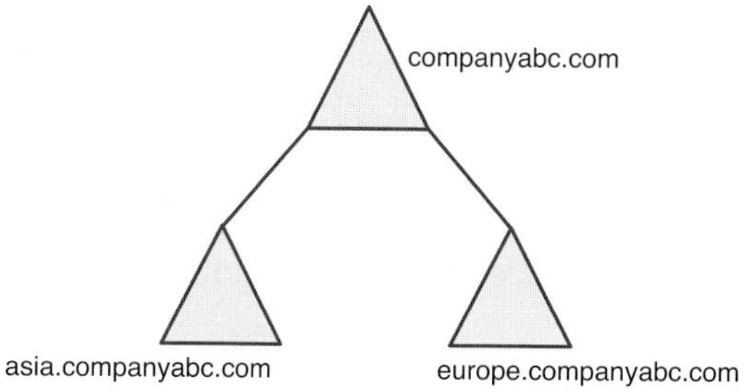

FIGURE 4.2 A Windows Server 2012 AD DS tree with subdomains.

The transitive trust relationship is automatic. The transitive trust relationship means that because the Asia domain trusts the root companyabc domain, and the Europe domain trusts the companyabc domain, the Asia domain trusts the Europe domain as well. The trusts flow through the domain structure.

NOTE

Although trusts are transitive in an AD DS environment, that does not mean that permissions are fully accessible to all users or even to administrators between domains. The trust only provides a pathway from one domain to another. By default, no access rights are granted from one transitive domain to another. The administrator of a domain must issue rights for users or administrators in another domain to access resources within their domain.

All domains within a tree share the same namespace (in this example, companyabc.com), but have security mechanisms in place to segregate access from other domains. In other words, an administrator in the Europe domain could have relative control over his entire domain, without users from the Asia or companyabc domains having privileges to resources. Conversely, the administrators in Europe can allow groups of users from other domains access if they so want. The administration is granular and configurable.

Incidentally, just because you can create subdomains within a forest, such as the ones shown in Figure 4.2, does not meant that it makes sense to do so. Many environments are better served with a single domain for all of their worldwide resources, and after you make the decision to create subdomains, it is not easy to change your mind and move resources later. You can find more information about this in Chapter 5, "Designing a Windows Server 2012 Active Directory."

Describing Forests in AD DS

Forests are a group of interconnected domain trees. Implicit trusts connect the roots of each tree together into a common forest.

The overlying characteristics that tie together all domains and domain trees into a common forest are the existence of a common schema and a common global catalog. However, domains and domain trees in a forest do not need to share a common namespace. For example, the domains microsoft.internal and technet.internal could theoretically be part of the same forest but maintain their own separate namespaces.

Forests are the main organizational security boundary for AD DS, and it is assumed that all domain administrators within a forest are trusted to some degree. If a domain administrator is not trusted, that domain administrator should be placed in a separate forest.

Understanding the AD DS Authentication Modes

Windows NT 4.0 used a system of authentication known as NT LAN Manager (NTLM). This form of authentication sent the encrypted password across the network in the form of a hash. The problem with this method of authentication was that anyone could monitor the network for passing hashes, collect them, and then use third-party decryption tools that effectively decrypt the password using dictionary and brute-force techniques.

All versions of Windows Server beyond Windows 2000 use a form of authentication known as Kerberos, which is described in greater detail later in this chapter. In essence, Kerberos does not send password information over the network and is inherently more secure than NTLM.

Outlining Functional Levels in Windows Server 2012 AD DS

Just as Windows 2000 and Windows 2003 had their own functional levels that ensured down-level compatibility with legacy domain versions, Windows Server 2012 has its own functional levels that are used to maintain compatibility.

By default, a fresh installation of Active Directory on Windows Server 2012 DCs automatically puts you into Windows Server 2012 domain and forest functional levels. If you install Windows Server 2012 DCs into an existing legacy domain, however, you are allowed to choose which functional level you want to start the forest in. If an existing forest is in place, you can bring it to Windows Server 2012 functional level as follows:

1. Ensure that all DCs in the forest are upgraded to Windows Server 2012 or replaced with new Windows Server 2012 DCs.
2. Open Active Directory Domains and Trusts from the Tools menu in Server Manager on a DC.
3. In the left scope pane, right-click the domain name, and then click Raise Domain Functional Level.
4. In the Raise Domain Functional Level box, select Windows Server 2012, and then click Raise.
5. Click OK, and then click OK again to complete the task.
6. Repeat steps 1–5 for all domains in the forest.
7. Perform the same steps on the forest root, except this time choose Raise Forest Functional Level and follow the prompts.

When all domains and the forest level have been raised to Windows Server 2012 functionality, the forest can take advantage of the latest AD DS functionality. Remember, before you accomplish this task in a mixed-mode environment, Windows Server 2012 essentially operates in a downgraded mode of compatibility.

Outlining AD DS Components

The main components of AD DS were designed to be highly configurable and secure. AD DS and all it contains are physically located in a database file but are composed of a wide assortment of objects and their attributes. Many of these characteristics are familiar to those acquainted with other directory services products, but there are some new additions as well.

Understanding AD DS X.500 Roots

AD DS loosely follows, but does not exactly conform to, the X.500 directory services information model. In a nutshell, X.500 defines a directory service through a distributed approach defined by a directory information tree (DIT). This logically divides a directory service structure into the now familiar servername.subdomainname.domainname.com layout. In X.500, directory information is stored across the hierarchical layout in what are called directory system agents (DSAs). Microsoft designed AD DS around many of the basic principles of the X.500 definition, but AD DS itself is not compatible with X.500 implementations, as X.500 follows an OSI model that is inefficient under the TCP/IP implementation that AD DS follows.

Conceptualizing the AD DS Schema

The AD DS schema is a set of definitions for all object types in the directory and their related attributes. The schema determines the way that all user, computer, and other object data are stored in AD DS and configured to be standard across the entire AD DS structure. Secured by the use of discretionary access control lists (DACLs), the schema controls the possible attributes to each object within AD DS. In a nutshell, the schema is the basic definition of the directory itself and is central to the functionality of a domain environment. Care should be taken to delegate schema control to a highly selective group of administrators because schema modification affects the entire AD DS environment.

Schema Objects

Objects within the AD DS structure such as users, printers, computers, and sites are defined in the schema as objects. Each object has a list of attributes that define it and that can be used to search for that object. For example, a user object for the employee named Weyland Wong will have a `FirstName` attribute of Weyland and a `LastName` attribute of Wong. In addition, there might be other attributes assigned, such as departmental name, email address, and an entire range of possibilities. Users looking up information in AD DS can make queries based on this information (for example, searching for all users in the Sales department).

Extending the Schema

One of the major advantages to the AD DS structure is the ability to directly modify and extend the schema to provide for custom attributes. A common attribute extension occurs with the installation of Microsoft Exchange Server, which extends the schema, significantly from the default size. An upgrade from Windows 2003 or 2008 AD to Windows Server 2012 AD DS also extends the schema to include attributes specific to Windows Server 2012. Many third-party products have their own schema extensions as well, each providing for different types of directory information to be displayed. It should be noted that schema extensions should only be performed when absolutely required, however, as an improper schema extension can wreak havoc on an AD DS environment.

Performing Schema Modifications with the AD DS Service Interfaces

An interesting way to actually view the nuts and bolts of the AD DS schema is by using the AD Service Interfaces (ADSI) utility. This utility was developed to simplify access to the AD DS and can also view any compatible foreign LDAP directory. The ADSIEdit utility, shown in Figure 4.3, enables an administrator to view, delete, and modify schema attributes. Great care should be taken before schema modifications are undertaken because problems in the schema can be difficult to fix.

Defining the Lightweight Directory Access Protocol

The Directory Service Protocol that is used by AD DS is compliant with the Internet-standard Lightweight Directory Access Protocol as defined by RFC 2251. LDAP allows queries and updates to take place in AD DS. Objects in an LDAP-compliant directory must be uniquely identified by a naming path to the object. These naming paths take two forms: distinguished names and relative distinguished names.

Distinguished Names in AD

The distinguished name of an object in AD DS is represented by the entire naming path that the object occupies in AD DS. For example, the user named Joel Oleson can be represented by the following distinguished name:

```
CN=Joel Oleson,OU=SLC,DC=Companyabc,DC=com
```

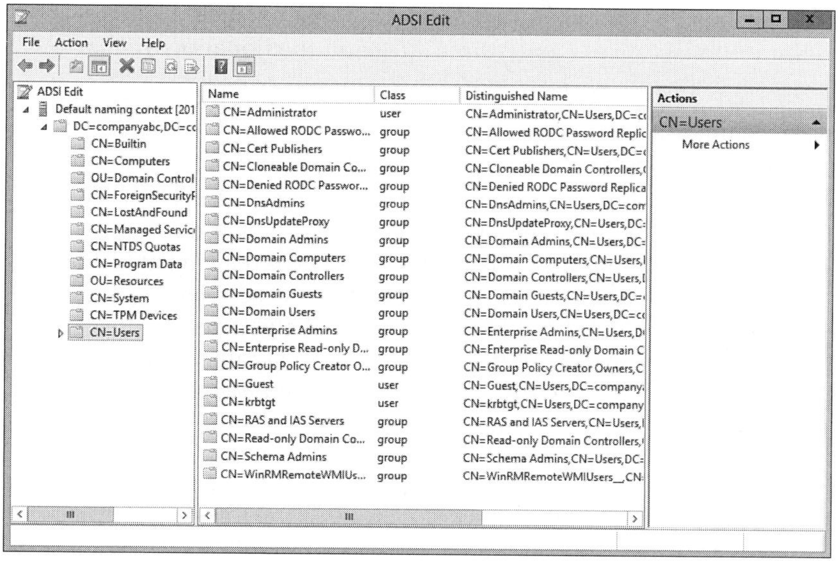

FIGURE 4.3 Using the ADSIEdit tool to view schema attributes in AD DS.

The CN component of the distinguished name is the common name, which defines an object within the directory. The OU portion is the organizational unit in which the object belongs. The DC components define the DNS name of the Active Directory domain.

Relative Distinguished Names

The relative distinguished name of an object is basically a truncated distinguished name that defines the object's place within a set container. For example, take a look at the following object:

```
OU=SLC,DC=companyabc,DC=com
```

This object would have a relative distinguished name of `OU=SLC`. The relative distinguished name in this case defines itself as an organizational unit within its current domain container.

Detailing Multimaster Replication with AD DS Domain Controllers

AD DS uses domain controllers (DCs) to authenticate users. These DCs use the concept of multiple DCs that each contains a master read/write copy of domain information. Changes that are made on any DC within the environment are replicated to all other DCs in what is known as multimaster replication.

Understanding Global Catalog and Global Catalog Servers

The global catalog is an index of the AD DS database that contains a partial copy of its contents. All objects within the AD DS tree are referenced within the global catalog, which allows users to search for objects located in other domains. Not every attribute of each object is replicated to the global catalogs, only those attributes that are commonly used in search operations, such as first name, last name, and so on.

Global catalog servers, commonly referred to as GCs or GC/DCs, are AD DS DCs that contain a copy of the global catalog. It is wise to either locate a minimum of one global catalog server in each physical location or use RODCs in remote sites because the global catalog must be referenced often by clients and the traffic across slower wide-area network (WAN) links would limit this traffic. In addition, technologies such as Microsoft Exchange Server need fast access to global catalog servers for all user transactions, making it very important to have a global catalog server nearby. Note that Exchange cannot make use of RODCs or read-only global catalog (ROGC) servers.

Often, a larger organization will use multiple DCs and multiple global catalog servers in each large location, which distributes load, provides redundancy, and locates resources where they are needed. Choosing the right blend of global catalog servers and DCs is vital to the proper functionality of your AD DS environment.

Defining the Operations Master Roles

Most DC functionality in Windows 2000/2003/2008 and Windows Server 2012 was designed to be distributed, multimaster based. This effectively eliminated the single point of failure that was present with Windows NT primary domain controllers (PDCs). However, five functions still require the use of a single server because their functionality makes it impossible to follow a distributed approach. These operations master (OM) roles (previously referred to as FSMO roles) are as follows:

- **Schema master**—There is only one writable master copy of the AD DS schema in a single AD DS forest. It was deliberately designed this way to limit access to the schema and to minimize potential replication conflicts. There can be only one schema master in the entire AD DS forest.
- **Domain naming master**—The domain naming master is responsible for the addition of domains into the AD DS forest. This OM role must be placed on a global catalog server because it must have a record of all domains and objects to perform its function. There can be only one domain naming master in a forest.
- **PDC emulator**—This role used to exist to emulate the legacy Windows NT 4.0 PDC for down-level clients. With Windows Server 2012, the PDC emulator still performs certain roles, such as acting as the primary time sync server for the domain. There is one PDC emulator FSMO role per AD DS domain.
- **RID master**—All objects within AD DS that can be assigned permissions are uniquely identified through the use of a security identifier (SID). Each SID is composed of a domain SID, which is the same for each object in a single domain, and a relative identifier (RID), which is unique for each object within that domain. When assigning SIDs, a DC must be able to assign a corresponding RID from a pool that it obtains from the RID master. When that pool is exhausted, it requests another pool from the RID master. If the RID master is down, you might not be able to create new

objects in your domain if a specific DC runs out of its allocated pool of RIDs. There is one RID master per AD DS domain.

- **Infrastructure master**—The infrastructure master manages references to domain objects not within its own domain. In other words, a DC in one domain contains a list of all objects within its own domain plus a list of references to other objects in other domains in the forest. If a referenced object changes, the infrastructure master handles this change. Because it deals with only referenced objects and not copies of the object itself, the infrastructure master must not reside on a global catalog server in multiple domain environments. The only exceptions to this are if every DC in your domain is a global catalog server or if you are in a single-domain environment. In the first case, there is no need to reference objects in other domains because full copies are available. In the second case, the infrastructure master role is not used because all copies of objects are local to the domain.

Transfer of an OM role to another DC can be performed as part of regular maintenance, or in the case of a disaster recovery situation where an OM server is brought offline, the OM can be seized to be brought back online. This is true for conditions where the schema master, domain naming master, or RID master either needs to be moved to another system (transfer) or has gone down and no backup is available (seized). The transfer and seizure of an OM role is done through the use of a command-line tool called `Ntdsutil`, shown in Figure 4.4. Keep in mind that you should use this utility only in emergency situations and should never bring the old OM server that has had its role seized back online into the domain (at the risk of some serious system conflicts). You can read more about this tool in Chapter 7, "Active Directory Infrastructure."

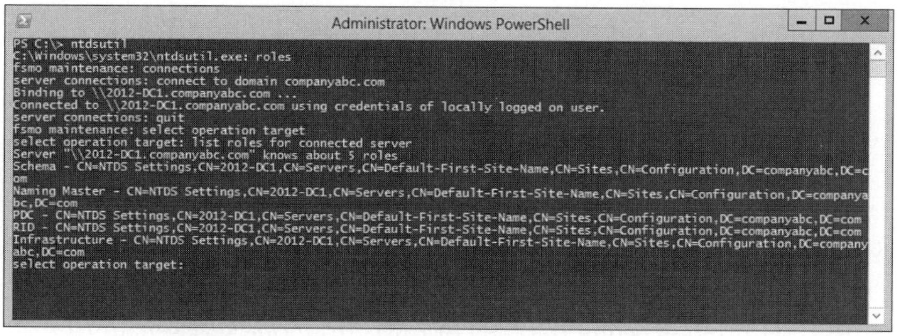

FIGURE 4.4 The `Ntdsutil` utility for AD DS management.

Understanding Domain Trusts

Domain trusts across forests used to require individual, explicitly defined trusts for each domain. This created an exponential trust relationship, which was difficult, to say the least, to manage. Windows Server 2003 and later versions took the trust relationship to a new level of functionality, with transitive trusts supplying automatic paths "up and down the forest tree." These trusts are implicitly easier to understand and troubleshoot, and have greatly improved the manageability of Windows networks.

Conceptualizing Transitive Trusts

Two-way transitive trusts are automatically established upon the creation of a subdomain or with the addition of a domain tree into an AD DS forest. Transitive trusts are normally two-way, with each domain trusting the other domain. In other words, users in each domain can access resources such as printers or servers in the other domain if they are explicitly given rights in those domains. Bear in mind that just because two domains have a trust relationship does not mean that users from one domain can automatically access all the resources in the other domain; it is simply the first step in accessing those resources. The proper permissions still need to be applied.

Understanding Explicit Trusts

Explicit trusts are those that are set up manually, similar to the way that Windows NT trusts were constructed. A trust can be set up to join two unrelated domain trees into the same forest, for example. Explicit trusts are one-way, but two explicit trusts can be established to create a two-way trust. In Figure 4.5, an explicit trust has been established between the companyabc domain and the companyxyz domain to join them into the same forest structure.

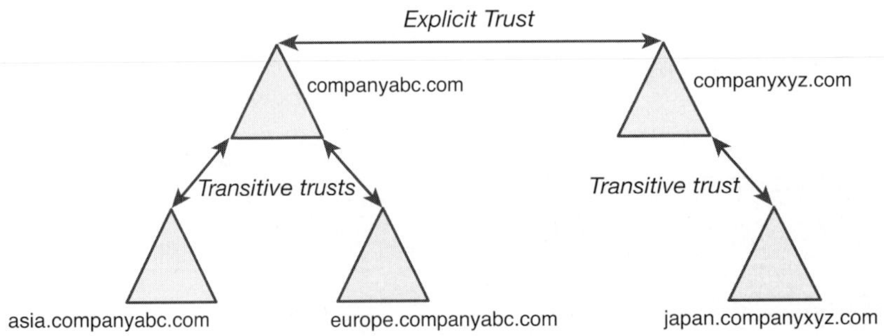

FIGURE 4.5 Explicit trust between two domain trees.

When an explicit trust is set up to expedite the flow of trusts from one subdomain to another, it is known as a shortcut trust. Shortcut trusts simply allow authentication verifications to be processed faster, as opposed to having to move up and down a domain tree. In Figure 4.6, even though a transitive trust exists between the asia.companyabc.com and the europe.companyabc.com domains, a shortcut trust has been created to minimize authentication time for access between the two subdomains of this organization.

Another possible use for explicit trusts is to allow connectivity between an AD DS forest and an external domain. These types of explicitly defined trusts are known as external trusts, and they allow different forests to share information without actually merging schema information or global catalogs.

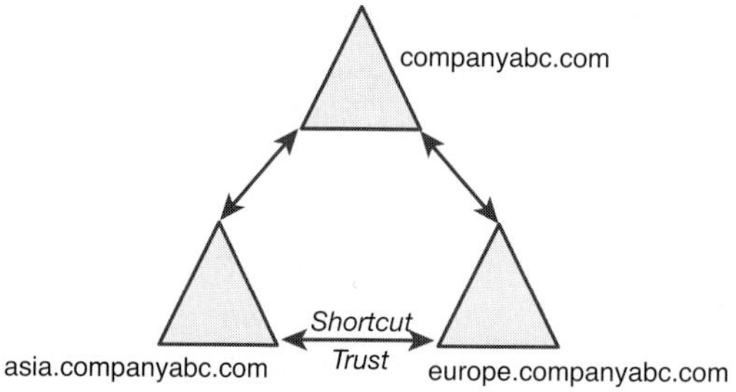

FIGURE 4.6 Shortcut trust between two subdomains in a forest.

Defining Organizational Units

As defined in the RFC for the LDAP standard, organizational units (OUs) are containers that logically store directory information and provide a method of addressing AD DS through LDAP. In AD DS, OUs are the primary method for organizing user, computer, and other object information into a more easily understandable layout. As shown in Figure 4.7, the organization has a root organizational unit where three nested organizational units (marketing, IT, and research) have been placed. This nesting enables the organization to distribute users across multiple containers for easier viewing and administration of network resources.

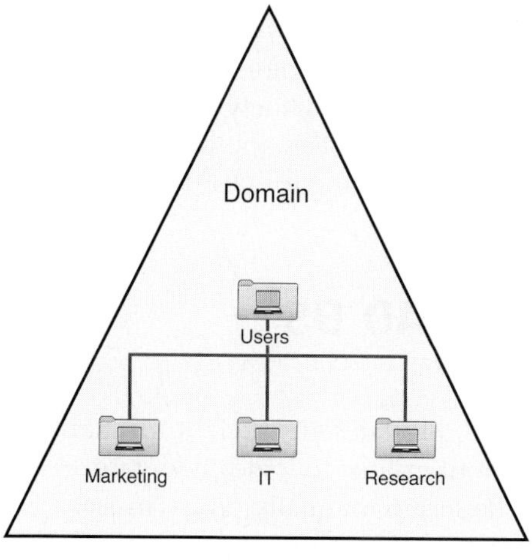

FIGURE 4.7 An organizational unit structure provides a graphical view of network resource distribution.

As you can see, OUs can be further subdivided into resource OUs for easy organization and delegation of administration. Far-flung offices could have their own OUs for local administration as well. It is important to understand, however, that an OU should usually be created when the organization has a specific need to delegate administration to another set of administrators. If the same person or group of people administer the entire domain, there is no need to increase the complexity of the environment by adding OUs. In fact, too many OUs can affect group policies, logons, and other factors. Chapter 6, "Designing Organizational Unit and Group Structure," gives a detailed rundown of the design considerations encountered with organizational units.

Determining Domain Usage Versus OU Usage

As previously mentioned, some administrators try to apply the AD DS domain structure to political boundaries within the organization. The dry-erase markers come out and, very soon, well-meaning managers get involved, organizing the AD DS structure based on political boundaries. Subdomains start to become multiple layers deep, with each department taking its own subdomain. The AD DS structure allows for this type of administrative granularity without division into multiple domains. In fact, the rule of thumb when designing domains is to start with a single domain and add additional domains only when necessary. In a nutshell, the type of administrative control required by many organizations can be realized by division of groups into separate OUs rather than into separate domains.

OUs can, therefore, be structured to allow for separate departments to have various levels of administrative control over their own users. For example, a secretary in the Engineering department can be delegated control of resetting passwords for users within his own OU. Another advantage of OU use in these situations is that users can be easily dragged and dropped from one OU to another. For example, if users are moved from one department to another, moving them into their new department's OU is extremely simple.

It is important to keep in mind that OU structure can be modified when an administrator feels fit to make structural changes, within certain constraints (namely after mapping out any group policies and administrative permissions that have been applied to the OU structure). This gives AD DS the added advantage of being forgiving for OU design flaws because changes can be made at any time.

Outlining the Role of Groups in an AD DS Environment

The AD DS group structure, although not new in AD DS, provides an efficient mechanism for managing security on large numbers of users. Without groups to logically organize users, permissions on each object in a network must be set up manually on a per-user basis. This means that if an entire department needs access to a printer, each user must be manually entered into the permissions list of that printer. These tasks make administration of security daunting.

The concept of groups was therefore devised to ease administration. If a large department needs access to that same printer, the department's group need only be supplied the necessary permissions. This greatly eases security-based administration and has the added advantage of providing for ease of transition if specific users leave the company or are transferred to a different department. For example, suppose an administrator is in charge of printing and her user account is a member of a group named Printer Admins, which has full administrative privilege to the printers. Now, if this user transfers to become an email administrator, for example, reassigning permissions to a new print administrator is as simple as adding that new user to the Printer Admins group. This capability greatly simplifies these types of situations.

Groups in AD DS work in the way that previous group structures, particularly in Windows NT, have worked, but with a few modifications to their design. Groups are divided into two categories: group type and group scope. There are two group types in AD DS: security and distribution. Essentially, a security group can be used to apply permissions to objects for the members of the group. A distribution group, however, cannot be used for permissions but is used instead to send mail to members of the group. Group scope in AD DS is likewise divided into several components, as follows:

- **Machine local groups**—Machine local groups, also known as simply local groups, can theoretically contain members from any trusted location. Users and groups in the local domain, as well as in other trusted domains and forests, can be included in this type of group. However, it is important to note that local groups allow resources to be accessed only on the machine where they are located, which greatly reduces their usability.
- **Domain local groups**—Domain local groups are essentially the same thing as local groups in Windows NT, and are used to administer resources located only on their own domain. They can contain users and groups from any other trusted domain. Most typically, these types of groups are used to grant access to resources for groups in different domains.
- **Global groups**—Global groups are on the opposite side from domain local groups. They can contain users only in the domain in which they exist but are used to grant access to resources in other trusted domains. These types of groups are best used to supply security membership to user accounts that share a similar function, such as the sales global group.
- **Universal groups**—Universal groups can contain users and groups from any domain in the forest and can grant access to any resource in the forest. Along with this added power come a few caveats. First, universal groups are available only in Native mode domains. Second, all members of each universal group are stored in the global catalog, increasing the replication load. It is important to note, however, that universal group membership replication has been noticeably streamlined and optimized in Windows Server 2012 because the membership is incrementally replicated.

TYPES OF GROUPS

Although groups are covered in more detail in Chapter 6, the type of group used (domain local, global, or universal) has significant impact on replication of group objects for large, multidomain organizations and on organizations with sites connected through slow links.

For a single-domain organization with high-speed connections to all sites, domain local, global, and universal groups are effectively the same because the organization has only one domain and replication occurs at high speeds to all DCs.

However, in a multidomain environment, by default, only the group name of a global group replicates between domains, not the membership names. Therefore, if a user in one domain wants to view the member list of a global group in another domain, the user's request will have to query across a WAN to the other domain to view the membership of the global group.

Universal groups, however, do replicate group membership information between domains, so a user query of a universal group membership list will be immediately available in the user's local domain. However, because universal group membership replicates between domains, if a list of group members is not needed to replicate between domains, traffic can be minimized by simply making the group a global group.

Choosing Between OUs and Groups

Whereas OUs are primarily used to segregate administrative function, groups are useful for logical organization of security functions. Translated, OUs are created if there is a need for a department or physical location to have some certain type of administrative control over its own environment. For example, an organization with offices in Japan could organize its Japanese users into a separate OU and give a local administrator password-change and account-creation privileges for that OU. Groups, however, can be used to organize users to more easily apply security permissions. For example, you can create a group named Japanese Office Users that contains all the users from the office in Japan. Security permissions can then be established on objects in AD DS using that group. They could, for example, be given privileges to folders in the main corporate location, something that could not be done at the OU level.

To summarize, the basic differences between OUs and groups is that groups can be used when applying security to objects, whereas OUs exist when certain administrative functionality needs to be delegated. Chapter 6 gives a more thorough explanation of groups and OU design.

Understanding AD DS Replication

Replication in AD DS is a critical function that is necessary to fulfill the functionality of a multimaster environment. The ability to make changes on any DC in a forest and then have those changes replicate to the other DCs is key. Consequently, a robust method of distributing this information was a major consideration for the development team at Microsoft. AD DS replication is independent of the forest, tree, or domain structure, and it is this flexibility that is central to AD's success.

Sites, Site Links, and Site Link Bridgeheads

For purposes of replication, AD DS logically organizes groups of servers into a concept known as sites. Generally speaking, a single site should be composed of servers that are connected to each other via high-speed connections. The links that are established to connect two or more locations connected potentially through slower-speed connections are known as site links. Sites are created with site links connecting the locations together to enable the administrator to specify the bandwidth used to replicate information between sites.

Instead of having information replicated immediately between servers within a high-speed connected site, the administrator can specify to replicate information between two sites only once per night or at a time when network demands are low, allowing more bandwidth availability to replicate AD DS information.

Servers that funnel intersite replication through themselves are known as site link bridgeheads.

Figure 4.8 shows a potential Windows Server 2012 AD DS site structure. Site links exist between offices, and a DC in each site acts as the site link bridgehead. The site structure is completely modifiable and should roughly follow the WAN structure of an organization. By default, only a single site is created in AD DS, and administrators must manually create additional sites to be able to optimize replication. You can find more information about these concepts in Chapter 7.

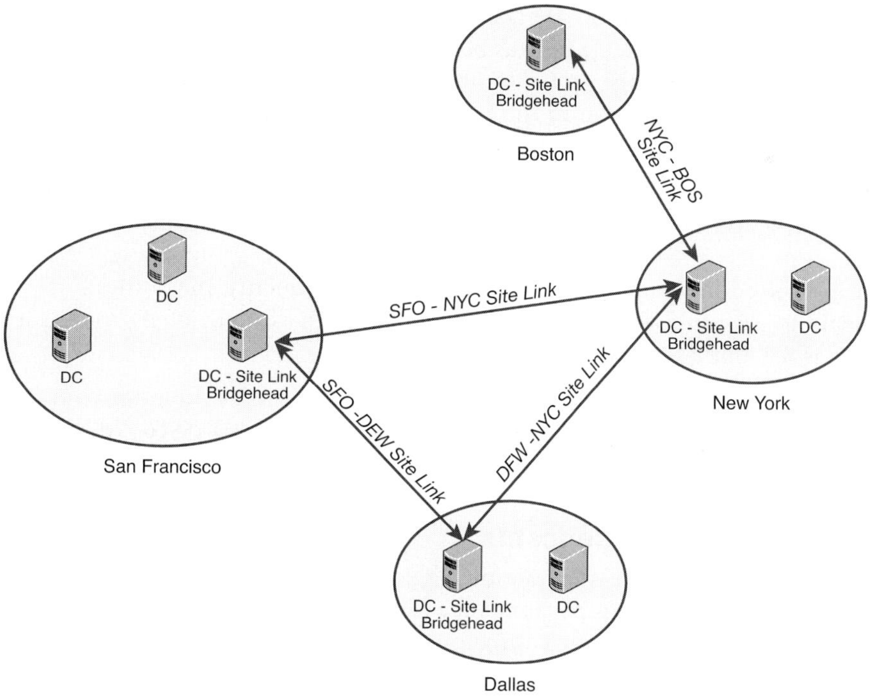

FIGURE 4.8 A potential AD DS Site Structure

Understanding Originating Writes

Replication of objects between DCs is accomplished through the use of a property known as originating writes. As changes are made to an object, this property is incrementally increased in value. A DC compares its own version of this value with the one received during a replication request. If it is lower, the change is applied; if not, it is discarded. This simple approach to replication is also extremely reliable and efficient and allows for effective object synchronization. For more information about replication, including a detailed analysis of originating writes and its other key components, see Chapter 7.

Using New PowerShell Replication Commandlets in Windows Server 2012

Windows Server 2012 introduces new PowerShell commandlets that are meant to act as a replacement for legacy tools such as repadmin, which were previously used to control AD DS replication. These commandlets, described in detail in Chapter 7, allow for fully automated replication administration and the creation of automated scripts for managing replication between DCs.

Outlining the Role of DNS in AD DS

When Microsoft began development on AD DS, full compatibility with the domain name system (DNS) was a critical priority. AD DS was built from the ground up, not just to be fully compatible with DNS but also to be so integrated with it that one cannot exist without the other. Microsoft's direction in this case did not just happen by chance, but because of the central role that DNS plays in Internet name resolution and Microsoft's desire to make its product lines embrace the Internet.

While fully conforming to the standards established for DNS, AD DS can expand on the standard feature set of DNS and offer some new capabilities such as AD-integrated DNS, which greatly eases the administration required for DNS environments. In addition, AD DS can easily adapt to exist in a foreign DNS environment, such as UNIX BIND, as long as the BIND version is 8.2.x or later.

Given the importance of DNS in Windows Server 2012 AD DS, a thorough understanding of DNS is a must. Chapter 10, "Domain Name System, WINS, and DNSSLC," discusses DNS in Windows Server 2012 in detail.

Examining DNS Namespace Concepts

A DNS namespace, simply defined, is the bounded logical area formed by a DNS name and its subdomains. For example, europe.companyabc.com, asia.companyabc.com, and companyabc.com are all part of the same contiguous DNS namespace. A DNS namespace in AD DS can be published on the Internet, such as microsoft.com or cco.com, or it can be hidden from public exposure, depending on the strategy and security needs of its implementers.

- **External (published) namespaces**—A DNS name that can be resolved from anywhere on the Internet is known as a published or external namespace. This type of namespace was previously common for organizations that wanted the full convenience of having their commonly used Internet domain name represent their AD DS structure. Best practices have evolved to make this model less attractive, however, as security becomes a concern and DNS must be set up as "split brain" because it is generally ill-advised to have internal AD DNS zones accessible from the Internet.

- **Internal (hidden) namespaces**—For many organizations, publication of their internal domain structure is too high a security risk. These organizations can easily define their AD DS with an internal namespace that is not readable from the Internet. For example, a company might have an external DNS namespace of cco.com but decide that its AD DS structure will correspond to cco.internal or any namespace it wants. Bear in mind that any combination will work for internal namespaces because there is no limitation on using .com, .net, .gov, and so on when dealing with a namespace that is not published. For all intents and purposes, you could name your domain ilovemydomain.verymuch if you want (although it's not recommended, of course). For practical reasons, however, the .internal namespace has been specifically reserved for private name addressing, and using it is a best practice approach in many cases.

NOTE

If deciding to use a domain namespace that theoretically could be bought and used on the Internet either now or in the future, it is wise to purchase the rights to that domain name to prevent potential conflicts with name resolution in the future. For example, if you choose the internal namespace companyabc.com, you might want to first verify that it is not taken and buy it if possible. If you find the domain name is already owned by another company, you might choose a different domain name for your AD DS namespace. Even though your domain might not be published on the Internet, home or laptop users who need dial-in or VPN access to your domain might experience conflicts because they would be incorrectly routed to the wrong DNS name on the Internet instead of to your company's namespace.

Dynamic DNS

Dynamic DNS (DDNS) was developed as an answer to the problem of DNS tables having to be manually updated when changes were made. DDNS in Windows Server 2012 automatically updates the DNS table based on registrations, and can work in conjunction with Dynamic Host Configuration Protocol (DHCP) to automatically process DNS changes as clients are added and removed from the network infrastructure. DDNS is not required for AD DS to function properly, but it makes administration much easier than previous manual methods.

Comparing Standard DNS Zones and AD-Integrated DNS Zones

Standard DNS essentially stores all name records in a text file and keeps it updated via dynamic updates. If you are accustomed to using UNIX BIND DNS or other standard forms of DNS, this is essentially what standard DNS is in Windows Server 2012.

AD DS expands on other implementations of DNS by allowing administrators to integrate DNS into AD DS. By doing this, the DNS zones themselves exist as objects in the AD DS, which allows for automatic zone transfers to be accomplished. DNS replication traffic piggybacks off AD DS traffic, and the DNS records are stored as objects in the directory. In the Windows Server 2012 implementation of AD DS, AD-integrated DNS zones are optimized by being stored in the application partition, thus reducing replication traffic and improving performance. For more information about DNS, see Chapter 10.

Understanding How AD DS DNS Works with Foreign DNS

Often, some local administrators might be hesitant to deploy AD DS because of their desire to maintain their own foreign DNS implementation, usually UNIX BIND. If this is the case, it is possible for Windows Server 2012 DNS to coexist in this type of environment, as long as the DNS supports dynamic updates and SRV records (BIND 8.2.x or later). These situations occur more often than not, as political situations within IT departments are often divided into pro-Microsoft and pro-UNIX groups, each of which has its own ideology and plans. The ability of Windows Server 2012 to coexist peacefully in these types of environments is, therefore, key.

Outlining AD DS Security

The security built around Active Directory was designed to protect valuable network assets. Development of Windows Server 2012 security has also been affected by the Trustworthy Computing initiative by Microsoft, which changed the primary focus of Microsoft products to security. In a nutshell, Microsoft is more focused than ever before on the security of its products, and all new features must pass a security litmus test before they can be released. This initiative has affected the development of Windows Server 2012 and is evident in the security features.

Understanding Kerberos Authentication

Kerberos was originally designed at MIT as a secure method of authenticating users without actually sending a user password across the network, encrypted or not. Being able to send a password this way greatly reduces the threat of password theft because malicious users can no longer seize a copy of the password as it crosses the network and run brute-force attacks on the information to decrypt it.

The actual functionality of Kerberos is complicated, but essentially what happens is the computer sends an information packet to the client that requires authentication. This packet contains a "riddle" of sorts that can be answered only by the user's proper credentials. The user applies the "answer" to the riddle and sends it back to the server. If the proper password was applied to the answer, the user is authenticated. Although used in Windows Server 2012, this form of authentication is not proprietary to Microsoft and is available as an Internet standard. For a greater understanding of Kerberos security, see Chapter 13, "Server-Level Security."

Taking Additional Security Precautions

AD DS implementations are, in essence, as secure as the Windows Server 2012 environment in which they run. The security of the AD DS structure can be increased through the utilization of additional security precautions, such as secured server-to-server communications using IPsec or the use of smart cards or other encryption techniques. In addition, the user environment can be secured through the use of group policies that can set parameter changes such as user password restrictions, domain security, and logon access privileges.

Outlining AD DS Changes in Windows Server 2012

Improvements in the functionality and reliability of AD DS are of key importance to the development team at Microsoft. It is, therefore, no small surprise that Windows Server 2012 introduces improvements in AD DS. From the ability to create DCs from virtual machine templates, to the ability to have multiple password policies in a domain to improvements in DC deployment with the RODC role, the changes made to the structure of AD DS warrant a closer look.

Windows Server 2008 itself introduced multiple changes to AD DS functionality above and beyond the Windows Server 2003 and Windows Server 2003 R2 Active Directory versions. Windows Server 2012 then introduced additional features and functionalities above those introduced with the RTM version of Windows Server 2008 and the later Windows Server 2008 R2 version. The Windows Server 2012 enhancements include the following:

- **Improved virtualization support**—The ability to create DCs based on virtual machine templates is a huge change in Windows Server 2012. At the same time, Microsoft also added safeguards into AD DS that protects DCs from mistakes made with virtual machine snapshotting that would cause major issues in the past. This concept is discussed in step-by-step detail in Chapter 7.
- **Dynamic access control**—Dynamic access control creates a new central access policy (CAP) model that allows for file classification information to be used in authorization decisions. This allows for business intent to be more readily apparent when examining the security that is set on file servers. This model is supported on Windows Server 2012 DCs, assuming the file servers also are running Windows Server 2012 as well.
- **Kerberos security improvements**—Microsoft added the industry standard Flexible Authentication Secure Tunneling (FAST) feature to Kerberos to reduce the likelihood of Kerberos errors being spoofed by hacking attacks. This is often referred to as Kerberos armoring.
- **Better fine-grained password policy control and AD Recycle Bin interfaces**—Microsoft has now made it much easier to implement either fine-grained password policy controls or the AD Recycle Bin, both features that were previously difficult to implement.

- **Active Directory deployment improvements**—Features such as Active Directory Based Activation (AD BA) allow for server licenses to be more easily activated, while improvements to off-premises domain join functionality have been added. ADPrep functionality has been added into the deployment tools, and the entire process to join a DC to a domain or create a new forest can now be done from PowerShell.
- **Active Directory Federation Services (AD FS) improvements**—AD FS 2.1 is now included natively in Windows Server, and supports AD DS claims directly, allowing for the population of SAML tokens with user and device claims taken directly from the Kerberos ticket.
- **Group Managed Service Accounts (gMSA)**—Group Managed Service Accounts allows for managed service accounts to be used by services that need to share a single security principal, such as clusters.
- **Enhanced PowerShell support**—A whole host of new PowerShell commandlets for Windows Server 2012 AD DS has been designed, allowing for nearly all operations to be automated from the command line.

These features are in addition to the features introduced in Windows Server 2008 R2, which included the following:

- **Active Directory Recycle Bin**—Enables you to restore deleted AD DS objects.
- **Offline domain join**—Allows for prestaging of the act of joining a workstation to the AD DS domain.
- **Managed Service Accounts**—Provides a mechanism for controlling and managing AD DS service accounts.
- **Authentication mechanism assurance**—Enables administrators to grant access to resources differently based on whether a user logs in with a smart card or multifactor authentication source or whether the user logs in via traditional techniques.
- **Enhanced administrative tools**—This includes newly designed and powerful utilities such as Active Directory Web Services, Active Directory Administrative Center, Active Directory Best Practice Analyzer, a new AD DS Management Pack, and an Active Directory Module for Windows PowerShell

The previous version of AD DS, introduced in Windows Server 2008, included the following key features that are still available with Windows Server 2012. If you are upgrading from any of the Windows Server 2003 versions of Active Directory or Windows 2000 Active Directory, all of these new features will be made available:

- **Ability to create multiple fine-grained password policies per domain**—Lifts the restrictions of a single password policy per domain.
- **Ability to restart AD DS on a domain controller**—Allows for maintenance of an AD DS database without shutting the machine down.

- **Enhanced AD DS auditing capabilities**—Provides useful and detailed item-level auditing capabilities in AD DS without an overwhelming number of logs generated.

Restoring Deleted AD DS Objects Using the Active Directory Recycle Bin

The AD Recycle Bin was supported in the Windows Server 2008 R2 version of AD DS, but was extremely complicated to implement, and the administrative tools provided were not easy to use. In Windows Server 2012, the AD Recycle Bin functionality is now built in to the Active Directory Administration Center (ADAC) and need only be enabled to start using the functionality. A few prerequisites must be satisfied, however, before the AD Recycle Bin can be enabled:

- The AD DS forest and domain must be at least at Windows Server 2008 R2 functional level (or at Windows Server 2012 functional level).
- Membership in the Enterprise Administrators group is required to enable the AD Recycle Bin.
- The process of enabling the AD Recycle Bin is nonreversible.

Enabling the AD Recycle Bin

To enable the Active Directory Recycle Bin, follow these steps:

1. Right-click Windows PowerShell, and then select Run as Administrator.
2. From the PowerShell prompt, type in **dsac.exe** to start the ADAC.
3. Click Manage - Add Navigation Nodes, and then select the target domain and click OK.
4. Next, select the target domain and then under Tasks, click Enable Recycle Bin, and then click OK and OK twice to accept the changes, as shown in Figure 4.9. Click F5 to refresh ADAC.
5. To validate that the Recycle Bin is enabled, go to the CN=Partitions container, using an editor such as ADSIEdit. In the details pane, find the msDS-EnabledFeature attribute and confirm that the value includes the Recycle Bin DN that you typed above.

Alternatively, you can enable the AD Recycle Bin by using the following PowerShell command. Replace companyabc.com and DC=companyabc,DC=com with the appropriate name of the domain where the AD Recycle bin will be enabled.

```
Enable-ADOptionalFeature -Identity 'CN=Recycle Bin Feature,CN=Optional Features,
CN=Directory Service,CN=Windows
NT,CN=Services,CN=Configuration,DC=companyabc,DC=com' -Scope ForestOrConfiguration
Set -Target 'companyabc.com'
```

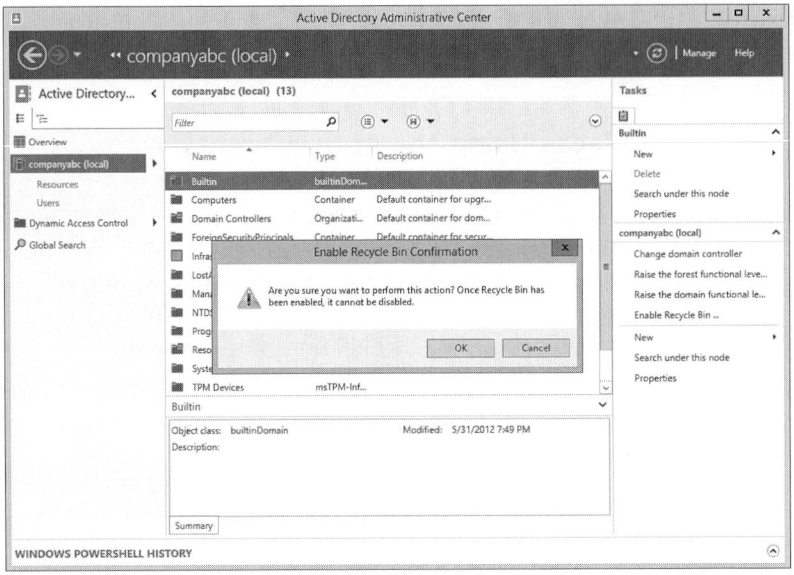

FIGURE 4.9 Enabling the AD Recycle Bin.

Recovering Deleted Items Using the AD Recycle Bin

Deleted objects can be restored directly from ADAC, by looking in the Deleted Objects folder, which should be displayed in the root of the domain. Just right-click the object and select Restore, as shown in Figure 4.10.

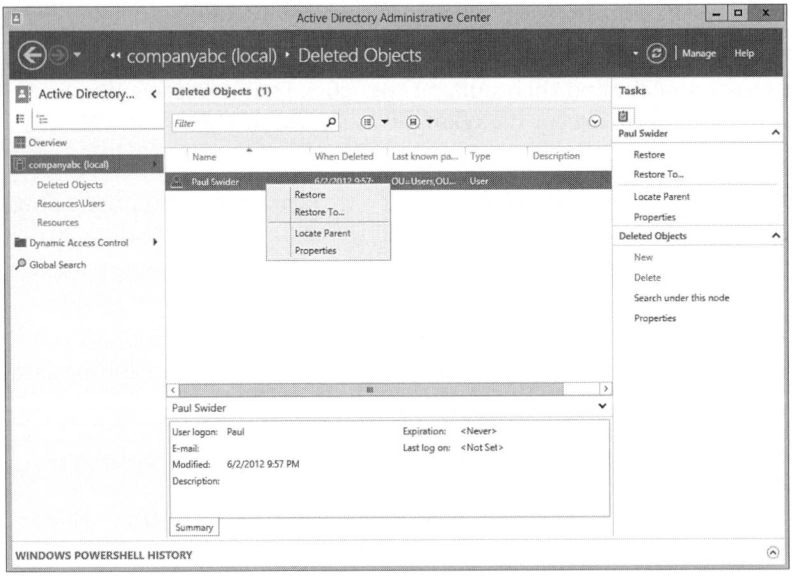

FIGURE 4.10 Restoring a deleted AD object from the AD Recycle Bin.

Restarting AD DS on a Domain Controller

Windows Server 2008 originally introduced new capabilities to start or stop directory services running on a DC without having to shut it down. This enables administrators to perform maintenance or recovery on the Active Directory database without having to reboot into Directory Services Restore Mode. This feature is also present in Windows Server 2012 DCs.

In addition to allowing for maintenance and recovery, turning off the DC functionality on an AD DC essentially turns that DC into a member server, allowing for a server to be quickly brought out of DC mode if necessary. In addition, with RODCs, Microsoft has removed the need for local administrators on the DC to have Domain Admin rights as well, which improves overall security in places where administration of the DC server is required but full Domain Admin rights are not needed.

To take a Windows Server 2012 DC offline, follow these steps:

1. Open up the Services MMC (Start, All Programs, Administrative Tools, Services).
2. From the Services MMC, select the Active Directory Domain Services service, as shown in Figure 4.11. Right-click it and choose Stop.
3. When prompted that stopping AD DS will stop other associated services such as DNS, DFS, Kerberos, and Intersite Messaging, choose Yes to continue.
4. To restart AD DS, right-click the AD DS service and choose Start.

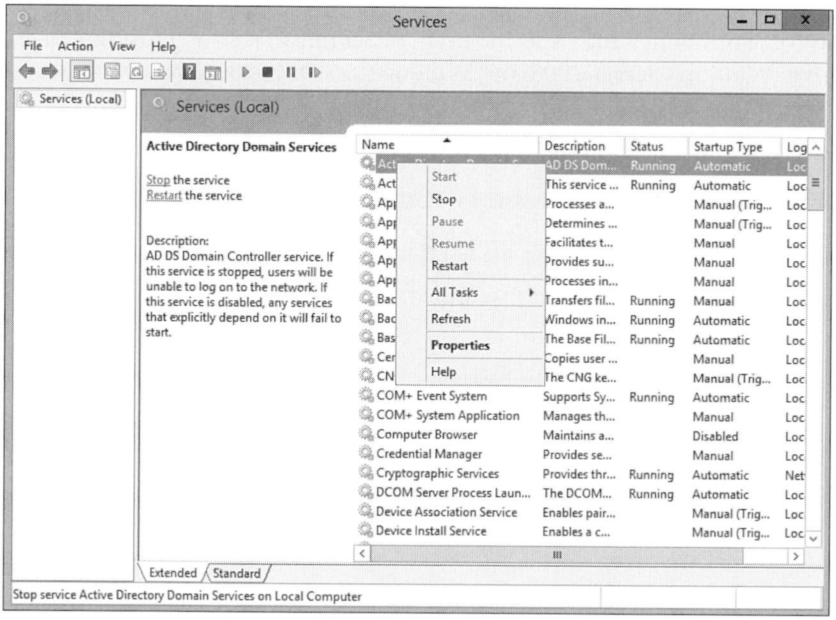

FIGURE 4.11 Restarting AD DS on a Domain Controller

Implementing Multiple Password Policies per Domain

Another Windows Server 2008 addition to AD DS is the ability to implement granular password policies across a single domain. Previously, this was only an option with third-party password-change utilities installed on the DCs in a forest. With Windows Server 2008, Windows Server 2008 R2, or Windows Server 2012, administrators can define which users have more complex password policies and which will be able to use more lenient policies.

You need to understand a few key points about this technology before implementing it, as follows:

- Domain mode must be set to Windows Server 2008, Windows Server 2008 R2, or Windows Server 2012 level.
- Fine-grained password policies always win over a domain password policy.
- Password policies can be applied to groups, but they must be global security groups.
- Fine-grained password policies applied to a user always win over settings applied to a group.
- The Password Settings objects (PSOs) are stored in the Password Settings Container in AD (that is, CN=Password Settings Container,CN=System,DC=companyabc, DC=com).
- Only one set of password policies can apply to a user. If multiple password policies are applied, the policy with the lower-number precedence wins.

To create a custom password policy for a specific user, a PSO must be created using ADAC, an improvement over Windows Server 2008 and Windows Server 2008 R2, which required creation of the PSOs using ADSIEdit.

To create a new PSO, open ADAC and follow these steps:

1. Navigate to domain root - System - Passwords Settings Container.
2. Under Tasks, select New - Password Settings.
3. Enter the information into the dialog box, shown in Figure 4.12, using Table 4.1 as a reference.
4. Click OK to finalize the creation of the PSO.

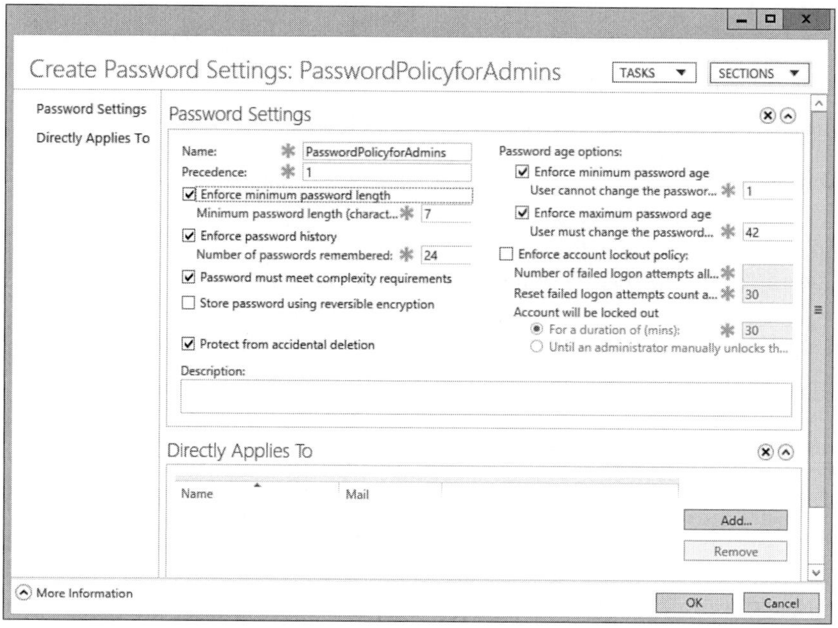

FIGURE 4.12 Creating a PSO.

TABLE 4.1 PSO Attributes

Attribute	Description	Sample Value
Name	The unique name of the password policy.	PasswordPolicy forAdmins
Precedence	The priority of the policy. Lower number "wins." Leave space on both sides of the number to reprioritize if necessary.	10
Enforce password history: Number of passwords remembered	The number of passwords "remembered" by the system.	24
Password must meet complexity requirements	The policy that sets whether password complexity is enabled. Password complexity enforces whether users should be forced to include a combination of numbers, uppercase letters, lowercase letters, and special characters as part of their password. Enabling complexity forces them to include at least three of the four types in their passwords.	Checked
Enforce minimum password length	The policy setting that enforces the minimum password character length.	8

Attribute	Description	Sample Value
Enforce minimum password age: User cannot change the password within (days)	The minimum number of days that must be waited before resetting the password to something different. This disallows users from simply "cycling through" password changes to keep the same password. Expressed in a format of Days:Hours:Minutes:Seconds. For example, 3:00:00:00 equals 3 days.	1
Enforce maximum password age: User must change the password within (days)	The maximum number of days that a password is valid for. Expressed in a format of Days:Hours:Minutes:Seconds.	42
Enforce account lockout policy: Number of failed logon attempts allowed:	The number of invalid password attempts that can be made before locking out the account.	5
Reset failed logon attempts count after (mins)	The length of time (expressed in minutes) before the invalid password attempt counter is reset.	30
Accounts will be locked out	The length of time (expressed in an account remains locked out.	30
Directly Applies To:	The user or group of users to which the PSO applies.	Group or User Account selected from AD that the PSO applies to
msDS-PasswordReversible ÂEncryptionEnabled	The policy used for specific circumstances where a user's password needs to be able to be decrypted. Normally set to False. Not available in the GUI, but can be set with ADSIEdit.	False

Auditing Changes Made to AD Objects

Another important change to Active Directory that can be enabled in a Windows Server 2008 or Windows Server 2012 functional domain is the concept of auditing changes made to Active Directory objects. Previously, it was difficult to tell when changes were made, and AD-specific auditing logs were not available. Windows Server 2008/2012 enables administrators to determine when AD objects were modified, moved, or deleted.

To enable AD object auditing on a Windows Server 2012 DC, follow these steps:

1. From Server Manager, click Tools, Group Policy Management
2. Navigate to *forest name*, Domains, *domain name*, Domain Controllers, Default Domain Controllers Policy.
3. Right-click the Default Domain Controllers Policy and click Edit.

4. In the GPO window, navigate to Preferences, Computer Configuration, Windows Settings, Security Settings, Local Policies, Audit Policy.
5. Under the Audit Policy setting, right-click Audit Directory Service Access and click Properties.
6. Check the Define These Policy Settings check box, and then check the Success and Failure check boxes, as shown in Figure 4.13.
7. Click OK to save the settings.

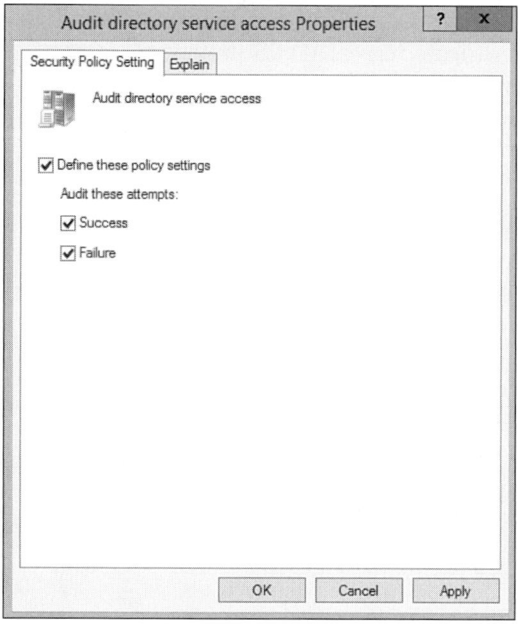

FIGURE 4.13 Enabling AD DS object auditing.

Global AD DS auditing on all DCs will subsequently be turned on. Audit event IDs will be displayed as Event ID 5136, 5137, 5138, or 5139, depending on whether the operation is a modify, create, undelete, or move, respectively.

Reviewing Additional Active Directory Services

Five separate technologies in Windows Server 2012 contain the Active Directory moniker in their title. Some of the technologies previously existed as separate products, but they have all come under the global AD umbrella. These technologies are as follows:

- **Active Directory Lightweight Directory Services (AD LDS)**—AD LDS, previously referred to as Active Directory in Application Mode (ADAM), is a smaller-scale directory service that can be used by applications that require a separate directory. It can be used in situations when a separate directory is needed but the overhead and cost of setting up a separate AD DS forest is not warranted. You can find detailed information about AD LDS in Chapter 8 "Creating Federated Forests and Lightweight Directories."

- **Active Directory Federation Services (AD FS)**—AD FS in Windows Server 2012 is an improvement over the older standalone versions of the ADFS product previously offered by Microsoft. AD FS 2.1, included in Windows Server 2012 provides for Single Sign-On technology to allow for a user logon to be passed to multiple web applications within a single session. You can find more information about AD FS in Chapter 8.
- **Active Directory Certificate Services (AD CS)**—AD CS is a newly formed term that refers to the new version of Windows Certificate Server. AD CS provides for the ability to create a public key infrastructure (PKI) environment and assign PKI certificates to AD users and machines. These certificates can be used for encryption of traffic, content, or logon credentials. You can find more information about deploying AD CS in Chapter 14, "Transport-Level Security."
- **Active Directory Rights Management Services (AD RMS)**—AD RMS is the evolution of the older Windows Rights Management Server technology. AD RMS is a service that protects confidential information from data leakage by controlling what can be done to that data. For example, restrictions can be placed on documents, disallowing them from being printed or programmatically accessed (such as by cutting/pasting of content). Chapter 13 covers this Active Directory technology in more detail.

Examining Additional Windows Server 2012 AD DS Improvements

In addition to the changes listed in the preceding sections, AD DS in Windows Server 2012 supports the following new features:

- **Read-only domain controller (RODC) support**—Windows Server 2012 includes the ability to deploy DCs with read-only copies of the domain. This is useful for remote branch office scenarios where security might not be tight. This scenario is covered in detail in Chapter 7.
- **Group Policy central store**—Administrative templates for group policies are stored in the SYSVOL on the PDC emulator in Windows Server 2012, resulting in reduced replication and reduced SYSVOL size.
- **DFS-R replication of the SYSVOL**—A Windows Server 2008 RTM/R2 functional domain uses the improved Distributed File System Replication (DFS-R) technology rather than the older, problematic File Replication Service (FRS) to replicate the SYSVOL.
- **Active Directory database mounting tool**—The Active Directory database mounting tool (DSAMain.exe) enables administrators to view snapshots of data within an AD DS or AD LDS database. This can be used to compare data within databases, which can prove useful when performing AD DS data restores.

- **GlobalNames DNS zone**—Windows Server 2012 DNS allows for creation of the concept of the GlobalNames DNS zone. This type of DNS zone allows for a global namespace to be spread across multiple subdomains. For example, a client in the asia.companyabc.com subdomain would resolve the DNS name portal.asia.companyabc.com to the same IP address as a client in a different subdomain resolving portal.europe.companyabc.com. This can improve DNS resolution in multizone environments. You can read more about this technology in Chapter 10.

Reviewing Legacy Windows Server 2003 Active Directory Improvements

It is important to understand that AD DS is a product that has been in constant development since its release with Windows 2000. From humble beginnings, Active Directory as a product has developed and improved over the years. The first major set of improvements to AD was released with the Windows Server 2003 product. Many of the improvements made with Windows Server 2003 AD still exist today in Windows Server 2012 AD DS. Therefore, it is important to understand what functionality in AD was born from Windows Server 2003. The following key improvements were made in this time frame:

- **Windows Server 2003 Active Directory Domain Rename Tool**—Windows Server 2003 originally introduced the concept of domain rename, which has continued to be supported in Windows Server 2012. This enables administrators to prune, splice, and rename AD DS domains. Given the nature of corporations, with restructuring, acquisitions, and name changes occurring constantly, the ability of AD DS to be flexible in naming and structure is of utmost importance. The Active Directory Domain Rename Tool was devised to address this very need.

  Before AD DS domains can be renamed, several key prerequisites must be in place before the domain structure can be modified. First, and probably the most important, all DCs in the entire forest must be upgraded to Windows Server 2003 or 2008 in advance. In addition, the domains and the forest must be upgraded to at least Windows Server 2003 functional level. Finally, comprehensive backups of the environment should be performed before undertaking the rename.

  The domain rename process is complex and should never be considered as routine. After the process, each DC must be rebooted and each member computer across the entire forest must also be rebooted (twice). For a greater understanding of the Domain Rename Tool and process, see Chapter 5.

- **Cross-forest transitive trust capabilities**—Windows Server 2003 Active Directory introduced the capability to establish cross-forest transitive trusts between two disparate AD DS forests. This capability allows two companies to share resources more easily, without actually merging the forests. Note that both forests must be running at least at Windows Server 2003 functional levels for the transitive portion of this trust to function properly.

- **AD DS replication compression disable support**—Another feature introduced in Windows Server 2003 AD was the ability to turn off replication compression to increase DC performance. This would normally be an option only for organizations with very fast connections between all their DCs.
- **Schema attribute deactivation**—Developers who write applications for AD DS continue to have the ability, introduced in Windows Server 2003, to deactivate schema attributes, allowing custom-built applications to use custom attributes without fear of conflict. In addition, attributes can be deactivated to reduce replication traffic.
- **Incremental universal group membership replication**—Before Windows Server 2003, Windows 2000 Active Directory had a major drawback in the use of universal groups. Membership in those groups was stored in a single, multivalued attribute in AD DS. Essentially, what this meant was that any changes to membership in a universal group required a complete re-replication of all membership. In other words, if you had a universal group with 5,000 users, adding number 5,001 would require a major replication effort because all 5,001 users would be re-replicated across the forest. Windows Server 2003 and 2008 simplify this process and allow for incremental replication of universal group membership. In essence, only the 5,001st member is replicated in Windows Server 2003/2008.
- **AD-integrated DNS zones in application partitions**—Windows Server 2003 improved DNS replication by storing DNS zones in the application partition. This basically meant that fewer objects needed to be stored in AD, reducing replication concerns with DNS.
- **AD lingering objects removal**—Another major improvement originally introduced with Windows Server 2003 and still supported in 2008 is the ability to remove lingering objects from the directory that no longer exist.

Summary

Microsoft has worked to continue development of Active Directory Domain Services, which has become a common framework to tie together the various applications and frameworks. Along with the addition of new capabilities such as improved virtualization support, the AD Recycle Bin, fine-grained password policy support, RODCs, object auditing, and other enhancements, the newest version of Active Directory builds on its "road worthiness" and the real-world experience it gained with Windows 2000/2003/2008 to bring a robust, secure environment for networking services and functionality.

Best Practices

The following are best practices from this chapter:

- Design domains sparingly: Don't necessarily set up multiple domains for different remote offices or sites.

- Turn on the Active Directory Recycle Bin after upgrading to Windows Server 2012 forest-functional level to take advantage of the ability to do a full-fidelity restore of domain objects that have been deleted and to use the much improved interface provided with this version of AD DS.
- Purchase any external domain namespaces that you might want to use on the Internet.
- Use RODCs in remote sites where security is not as strong.
- Strongly consider using dynamic DNS in an AD DS domain environment.
- Turn on global AD DS auditing to better understand changes made to Active Directory objects.
- Consider using cross-forest transitive trusts between two disparate AD DS forests when merging the forests is not an option.
- Place the infrastructure master role on a DC that isn't also a global catalog, unless all DCs in the domain are global catalog servers or you are in a single domain environment.
- Properly plan fine-grained password policies to avoid conflicting policies being applied to users. Leave enough numeric space between the precedence numbers of individual PSOs so as to allow for new PSOs to be placed above and below the PSO in order of priority.
- Switch to Windows Server 2012 Functional mode as early as possible, to be able to take advantage of the numerous improvements, including AD Recycle Bin support, fine-grained password policies, Kerberos improvements, last interactive logon information, and the use of DFS-R for the SYSVOL replication.
- Use DC virtualization with Windows Server 2008 R2 to be able to quickly stage and deploy multiple DCs across a wide environment.
- Seriously consider deploying AD DS DCs on Server Core to reduce their security footprint. Use PowerShell to manage and control the DCs.
- Use global groups to contain users in the domain in which they exist but also to grant access to resources in other trusted domains.
- Use universal groups to contain users from any domain in the forest and to grant access to any resource in the forest.

CHAPTER 5

Designing a Windows Server 2012 Active Directory

IN THIS CHAPTER

- Understanding AD DS Domain Design
- Choosing a Domain Namespace
- Domain Design Features
- Choosing a Domain Structure
- Understanding the Single-Domain Model
- Understanding the Multiple-Domain Model
- Understanding the Multiple Trees in a Single-Forest Model
- Understanding the Federated-Forests Model
- Understanding the Empty-Root Domain Model
- Understanding the Placeholder Domain Model
- Understanding the Special-Purpose Domain Model
- Renaming an AD DS Domain

Proper design of a Windows Server 2012 Active Directory Domain Services (AD DS) structure is a critical component in the successful deployment of the technology. Mistakes made in the design portion of AD DS can prove to be costly and difficult to correct. Many assumptions about basic AD DS domain and functional structure have been made, and many of them have been incorrect or based on erroneous information. Solid understanding of these components is vital, however, and anyone looking at Windows Server 2012 should keep this point in mind

AD DS was specifically designed to be scalable. This means that, theoretically, organizations of every shape and size should be able to implement the technology. For obvious reasons, this means that the structure of the AD DS forest will vary from organization to organization.

This chapter focuses on best practices for AD DS design, including a discussion of the specific elements that compose AD DS, including feature upgrades added in this latest version, Windows Server 2012. Various domain design models for AD DS are presented and identified with specific real-world scenarios. The domain rename procedure is outlined, as well, to explain how the concept affects domain design decisions.

Understanding AD DS Domain Design

Before any domain design decisions can be made, it is important to have a good grasp of the AD DS domain structure and functionality. Some fairly major changes have been made in more recent Windows Server versions that require a reintroduction to the domain design process. In addition, real-world experience with AD domain design has changed some of the assumptions that were made previously.

Examining Domain Trusts

Windows Server 2012 AD DS domains can be linked to each other through the use of a concept known as trusts. A trust is essentially a mechanism that allows resources in one domain to be accessible by authenticated users from another domain. AD trusts take on many forms but typically fall into one of the four categories described in the following sections.

Transitive Trusts

Transitive trusts are automatic two-way trusts that exist between domains in the same forest in AD DS. These trusts connect resources between domains in AD DS and are different from explicit trusts in that the trusts flow through from one domain to the other. In other words, if Domain A trusts Domain B, and Domain B trusts Domain C, Domain A trusts Domain C. This flow greatly simplifies the trust relationships between Windows domains because it forgoes the need for multiple exponential trusts between each domain.

Explicit Trusts

An explicit trust is one that is set up manually between domains to provide for a specific path for authentication sharing between domains. This type of trust relationship can be one-way or two-way, depending on the needs of the environment. In other words, all trusts in legacy Windows NT 4.0 could have been defined as explicit trusts because they all are manually created and do not allow permissions to flow in the same way as transitive trusts do. The use of explicit trusts in AD DS allows designers to have more flexibility and to be able to establish trusts with external and down-level domains. All trusts between AD DS domains and other forest domains that aren't in Windows Server 2003, Windows Server 2003 R2, Windows Server 2008, Windows Server 2008 R2, or Windows Server 2012 forest functional level are explicit trusts.

Shortcut Trusts

A shortcut trust is essentially an explicit trust that creates a shortcut between any two domains in a domain structure. For example, if a domain tree has multiple subdomains that are many layers deep, a shortcut trust can exist between two domains deep within the tree, similar to the shortcut trust shown in Figure 5.1. This relationship allows for increased connectivity between those two domains and decreases the number of hops required for authentication requests. Normally, those requests would have to travel up the transitive trust tree and back down again, thus increasing overhead.

The example in Figure 5.1 shows how a shortcut trust could theoretically be used to reduce the overhead involved in sharing resources between the two sales subdomains in the companyabc.com tree. You can find more information about these trusts in the individual design model sections later in this chapter.

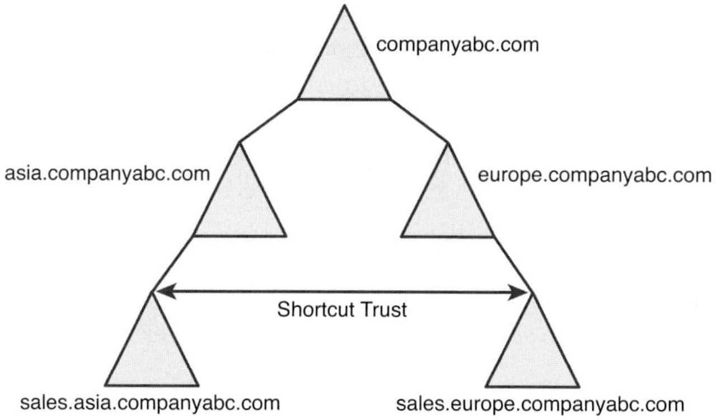

FIGURE 5.1 Shortcut trusts minimize hops between domains.

Cross-Forest Transitive Trusts

Cross-forest transitive trusts are essentially two-way transitive trusts that exist between two disparate AD DS forests. Although explicit trusts between separate AD domains in separate forests were possible in Windows 2000 Server, the cross-forest trusts in all versions of Windows Server beyond the 2003 release allow for two-way transitive trusts to exist between two separate forests. You can find more information about these trusts later in this chapter in the section "Understanding the Federated-Forests Model."

Choosing a Domain Namespace

The first step in the actual design of the AD DS structure is the decision on a common domain name system (DNS) namespace that AD DS will occupy. AD DS revolves around, and is inseparable from, DNS, and this decision is one of the most important ones to make. The namespace chosen can be as straightforward as microsoft.com, for example, or it can be more complex. Multiple factors must be considered, however, before this decision can be made. Is it better to register an AD namespace on the Internet and potentially expose it to intruders, or is it better to choose an unregistered internal namespace? Is it necessary to tie in multiple namespaces into the same forest? These and other questions must be answered before the design process can proceed.

Choosing an External (Published) Namespace

The simplest method of implementing an AD DS structure is through the use of a single, common DNS namespace that reflects the company's name and is registered on the Internet. Microsoft.com is an obvious example, and myriad other possibilities exist. Several advantages to a published namespace are that it is readily accessible from the Internet and there is less confusion on the end user's part in regard to the location on the network and on the Internet. For example, a user named Eric Harlan working for the CompanyABC Corporation will be represented in the network through the user principal name (UPN) as EricH@companyabc.com. This name can be set up to exactly match his email address, limiting confusion for the end user.

The limitations to this type of namespace strategy are primarily security based. Publishing your AD DS namespace leaves potential hackers with the name of your domain system and part of what is needed to compromise user accounts. Administering your firewall to block internal DNS queries also becomes less intuitive when the namespace is the same as the published Internet namespace for the organization. If the namespaces were separate, for example, a simple rule could be written to block any traffic to the internal domain structure. Another limitation arises if an organization currently employs multiple namespaces to identify itself and all those namespaces need to be joined into the same forest; in this case, a common namespace design is not an option. Mergers and acquisitions or even multiple business units within the same corporate parent can present these types of problems.

Choosing an Internal Namespace

If desired or required by your organization, the namespace that the AD DS structure inhabits can be internal, or not published to the Internet. Using internal namespaces adds a layer of complexity to your network because user UPNs are different from their email addresses. However, the increase in security that is realized from this design is also a factor that leads organizations to choose this route. Another factor that might influence your decision to choose an Internet namespace is that you are no longer limited to the InterNIC standard namespaces of .com, .net, .biz, .info, and so on. For example, many organizations use the .internal namespace, or some other namespace that is not used on the Internet.

Keep in mind that it is important to secure an internal namespace from registration anywhere on the Internet other than in your own network. In other words, if an organization registers internalnetwork.net, and another organization on the Internet registers the same domain name for its network, there could be naming conflicts with applications and other systems that perform DNS lookups against your forest. For example, if an application on a laptop usually attempts to access an internal namespace but then tries to access it remotely through an Internet service provider (ISP), the ISP's DNS will forward you to the registered DNS name on the Internet. In a nutshell, if you are going to design your domain with an unpublished namespace but use a standard such as .net or .org that someone else could theoretically register, it is best to register and reserve that domain but not point it anywhere. Another common tactic is to name your domain something that will never be published, such as a root with your company's stock ticker symbol (for example, network.msft), or by using the .internal suffix, which has been specifically reserved for internal use only.

Examining Domain Design Features

AD DS has evolved over the years and has added additional functionality with Windows Server 2003, Windows Server 2003 R2, Windows Server 2008, Windows Server 2008 R2, and finally Windows Server 2012. Some of these functionality improvements have changed some of the design concepts associated with Windows Server 2012. These functionality changes are as follows:

- **Active Directory Recycle Bin**—The ability to do a full-fidelity recovery of deleted objects in AD DS was introduced in Windows Server 2008 R2, but was greatly improved in this latest version of AD DS included with Windows Server 2012. By adding this critical functionality, there is less worry that accidental deletion of user accounts, groups, or even entire organizational units (OUs) will cause major havoc, and there is subsequently less reason to create multiple domains in a forest simply to spread the risk of domain object deletion. Note that this capability is available only when the forest functional level is raised to Windows Server 2008 R2 or later functional level and when it is subsequently turned on in a domain. You can read more about this in Chapter 4, "Active Directory Domain Services Primer."
- **Fine-grained password policies**—The ability to have multiple password policies within a single domain was originally released in Windows Server 2008 and is still supported with Windows Server 2012 (and is becoming much easier to use, as well). The addition of this functionality means that many organizations that previously implemented additional domains because of the restriction of a single password policy per domain might be able to collapse those domains. Note that this functionality is available only in Windows Server 2008, Windows Server 2008 R2, or Windows Server 2012 domain functional levels. For more information about using fine-grained password policies, see Chapter 4.
- **Domain rename function**—The capability to rename a domain in a Windows Server 2003/2008/2012 forest has opened up a new field of possibilities for the design and potential redesign of AD DS domain structures. Previously, stern caveats were issued about the inability to rename domains or change the overall structure of an AD DS forest. With the domain rename functionality present in AD DS implementation, these limitations are lifted, and designers can take heart in the fact that design changes can be made after implementation. Having this ability does not change the fact that it is still wise to plan out your domain design thoroughly, however. Not having to make changes to domain names or reposition domains in a forest is much easier than having to go through the domain rename process. Just knowing that such functionality exists, however, is a breath of fresh air for designers.
- **Cross-forest transitive trusts**—Introduced in Windows Server 2003, the concept of cross-forest transitive trusts lessens domain designer connectivity worries. In the past, some administrators balked at the limitations of collaboration within Windows 2000 Active Directory structures. The cross-forest transitive trust capability of AD DS negates those concerns because multiple AD DS forests can now be joined via cross-forest trusts that are transitive, rather than explicit, in nature. The combination of these forests is known in the Microsoft world as federated forests.
- **Domain controller virtualization support**—Microsoft has added the capability to create domain controllers (DCs) from virtual machine templates, greatly improving the time it takes to build a new DC. At the same time, they have made it possible to have virtual DCs recovered from snapshots without the worry of corruption or lingering object issues. All of these virtualization features are new for AD DS in

Windows Server 2012 and change the design options, allowing for much more advanced virtualization design options.

- **Server Core and PowerShell enhancements**—Windows Server 2012 is the first version that makes it preferable to deploy an AD DS DC running on Windows Server Core, because all DC functionality can now be performed using PowerShell, and Server Core greatly reduces the security footprint of the DCs.
- **Domain controller promotion from media**—The capability to promote remote servers to DCs via a CD image of the global catalog helps to limit replication traffic and the time associated with establishing remote domain controllers. Windows Server 2003/2008/2012 solves the issue of replication over the wide-area network (WAN) by providing you with the ability to save the global catalog to media (like a CD-ROM), ship it to a remote site, and, finally, run domain controller promotion and insert the data disk with the directory on it for restoration. Only the deltas, or changes made since media creation, are then replicated, saving time and bandwidth. The effect of this on domain design creation is reflected in reduced setup times, less network bandwidth consumption, and increased flexibility of global catalog domain controller placement.

Choosing a Domain Structure

There is a basic tenet to consider when designing the AD DS domain structure. Start simple, and then expand only if expansion is necessary to address a specific need. This concept is, by and large, the most important concept to remember when you're designing AD DS components. With regard to domain design, this means you should always start the design process with a single domain and then add on to your design if your organizational concerns dictate that you do so. Following this basic philosophy during the design process will reduce headaches down the road.

When you're designing the AD DS, you must contemplate a common framework for diagrams. In AD DS, for example, domains are often pictorially represented by triangles, as shown in Figure 5.2. So, when beginning your design, start with a single triangle.

In this example, the fictional company named CompanyABC has begun the process of domain design. Depending on its unique needs, CompanyABC might decide to expand upon that model or keep it simple. These decisions should be made with a detailed knowledge of the different domain design models and the environments in which they work best.

FIGURE 5.2 Domain diagram representation as a triangle.

Active Directory was designed to be a flexible, forgiving directory services implementation. This is even more true with Windows Server 2012 AD DS implementation. Consequently, multiple design models are available to choose from, depending on the individual needs of organizations. The major design models are as follows:

- Single-domain model
- Multiple-domain model
- Multiple trees in a single-forest model
- Federated-forests model
- Peer-root model
- Placeholder domain model
- Special-purpose domain model

In reality, not all AD structures fall within these categories; possibilities exist for numerous variations and mutations of AD structure. However, most domain structures either fit into these categories or are a hybrid model, possessing traits of two different models. Out of all these models, however, the single-domain model is the most common design model and also happens to be the easiest to deploy.

Understanding the Single-Domain Model

The most basic of all AD DS structures is the single-domain model; this type of domain structure comes with one major advantage over the other models: simplicity. A single security boundary defines the borders of the domain, and all objects are located within that boundary. The establishment of trust relationships between other domains is not necessary, and implementation of technologies such as group policies is made easier by the simple structure. More organizations than not can take advantage of this design because AD DS has been simplified and its capability to span multiple physical boundaries has been enhanced.

Choosing the Single-Domain Model

The single-domain model is ideal for many organizations and can be modified to fit many more. A single-domain structure possesses multiple advantages, first and foremost being simplicity. As any administrator or engineer who has done work in the trenches can confirm, often the simplest design works the best. Adding unnecessary complexity to the system's architecture introduces potential risk and makes troubleshooting these systems more difficult. Consequently, consolidating complex domain structures into a simpler single-domain AD DS structure can reduce the costs of administration and minimize headaches in the process.

Another advantage realized by the creation of a single domain is the attainment of centralized administration. Many organizations with a strong central IT structure want the capability to consolidate control over the entire IT and user structure. AD DS and, specifically, the single-domain model allows for a high level of administrative control and the ability to delegate tasks to lower sets of administrators. This has proven to be a strong draw to AD DS.

Not all AD DS structures can be composed of a single domain, however, and some factors might limit an organization's ability to adopt a single domain structure. If these factors affect your organization, you might need to begin expanding your domain model to include other domains in the forest and a different domain design. For example, the single security boundary formed by a single domain might not be exactly what your organization needs. Organizational units (OUs) can be used to delegate administration of security elements, but members of the Domain Admins group can still override permissions within different OUs. If the security lines within your organization need to follow exact boundaries, a single domain might not be for you. For example, if your HR department requires that no users from IT have access to resources within its environment, you will need to expand your domain structure to accommodate the additional security concerns.

Another disadvantage of the single-domain model is that a single domain in a forest necessitates that the computer with the role of schema master is located in that domain. This places the schema master within the domain that contains all the user accounts. Although access to the schema master can be strictly controlled through proper administration, your risk of schema exposure is greater when the schema master role resides in a user domain. For example, members of the Domain Administrators group could override the security of the Schema Administrators group and add their account to that group. If this design model poses problems for you as an organization, design models that separate the schema master into a placeholder domain can do the trick. The placeholder domain model is described in more detail later in this chapter in the section "Understanding the Placeholder Domain Model."

Exploring a Single-Domain Real-World Design Example

To illustrate a good example of an organization that would logically choose a single-domain model, let's consider fictional CompanyA. CompanyA is a 500-user organization with a central office located in Minneapolis. A few smaller branch offices are scattered throughout the Midwest, but all help desk administration is centralized at the company headquarters. CompanyA currently uses a single user domain and has multiple resource domains in various locations across the country.

The IT team in Minneapolis is designing an AD DS structure and wants to centralize administration at corporate headquarters. Branch offices should have the capability to change passwords and clear print jobs locally, but should have no other form of administrative privilege on the network.

During the AD DS design process, CompanyA started with a single AD DS forest, domain, and namespace named companya.net. OUs for each branch office were added to delegate password-change control and print administration to those offices.

Current legacy Windows 2000 AD and Windows Server 2003 forests and domain were consolidated into the AD DS structure, as shown in Figure 5.3. CompanyA could not justify the existence of additional domains because their security model was centralized, and it did not have any far-flung geographic locations with slow link speeds to the main office or any other similar constraints that required additional domains.

Delegation of password-change control and other local administrative functions was granted to individuals in each specific geographic OU, which gave those administrators permissions specific to only resources within their own group but maintained central administrative control in Minneapolis. A detailed discussion of organizational unit design is covered in Chapter 6, "Designing Organizational Unit and Group Structure."

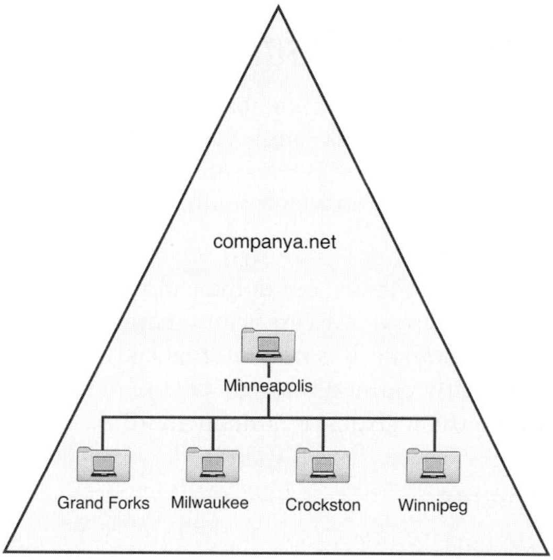

FIGURE 5.3 AD DS structure with organizational unit structure.

Several AD DS sites were created to control the frequency of replication. A site was positioned to correspond with each separate geographic area, creating a site structure similar to the one shown in Figure 5.4.

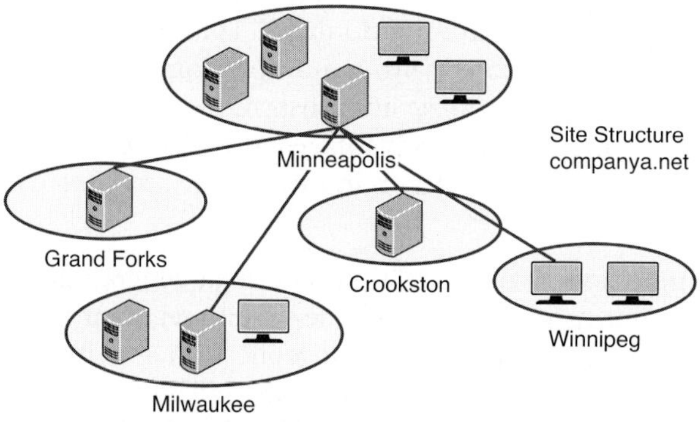

FIGURE 5.4 Site structure created by geographic locations.

Creating the separate sites helped to throttle replication traffic and reduce the load placed on the WAN links between the sites. For more details about site links and replication, see Chapter 7, "Active Directory Infrastructure."

This type of single-domain design is ideal for the type of organization described in this section and actually can be used for many other types of organizations, large and small. Because delegation of administration is now accomplished through the use of OUs and Group Policy objects, and the throttling of replication is accomplished through AD sites, the number of reasons for organizations to use multiple domains has been reduced.

Understanding the Multiple-Domain Model

For various reasons, organizations might need to add more than one domain to their environment but preserve the functionality that is inherent in a single forest. When this occurs, the addition of one or multiple domains into the forest is warranted. Domain addition should not be taken lightly, however, and proper consideration must be given to the particular characteristics of multiple-domain models.

By default, two-way transitive trusts exist between subdomains and domains in AD DS. Bear in mind, however, that this does not mean that resource access is automatically granted to members of other domains. A user in subdomain B is not automatically granted any rights in domain A; the rights need to be explicitly defined through the use of groups. Understanding this concept will help to determine the logistics of domain addition.

Deciding When to Add Additional Domains

As previously mentioned, it is advisable to begin your Windows Server 2012 AD DS design with a single domain and then add domains only when absolutely necessary. Adding child domains to an existing domain structure might become necessary if the following traits exist within an infrastructure:

- **Decentralized administration**—If different branches of an organization generally manage their own IT structure and there are no future plans to consolidate them into a centralized model, multiple interconnected domains might be ideal. Each domain acts as a security boundary for most types of activity and can be set up to disallow administration from escaping the boundaries of domains. This approach, however, exposes many of the limitations associated with a multiple domain environment. In other words, it is better to try to centralize administration before deploying AD DS because you will gain more of AD's advantages. It is also much better to organize administration along OU boundaries than by domains, so consider this option first.
- **Geographic limitations**—If extremely slow or unreliable links or great geographic distances separate different parts of your company, it might be wise to segment the user population into separate domains. This will help to limit replication activity between domains and also make it easier to provide support during business hours for distant time zones. Keep in mind that slow links by themselves do not necessitate the creation of multiple domains, because Windows Server 2012 AD DS uses the

concept of AD DS sites to throttle replication across slow links. The main reason that might exist for domain creation for geographic reasons is administrative flexibility. In other words, if there is a problem with the network in Japan, a Japanese administrator will have more power to administer the Asia domain and will not need to call the North American administrator in the middle of the night.

- **Unique DNS namespace considerations**—If two organizational entities want to use their Internet-registered namespace for AD DS but use a common forest, such as hotmail.com or microsoft.com, those domains must be added as separate domains. This type of domain model is described more fully in the "Understanding the Multiple Trees in a Single-Forest Model" section later in this chapter.
- **Enhanced security concerns**—Depending on the needs of your organization, separating the schema master role into a domain separate from your users might be applicable. In this case, the single-domain model would not be applicable, and a model such as the peer-root or placeholder domain would be more appropriate.

When contemplating additional domains, remember the mantra "Simplicity is best." However, if during the design process, the specific need arises to add domains, proper design is still warranted, or your environment will run the risk of becoming more inefficient than it could be.

Exploring a Multiple-Domain Real-World Design Example

The following example illustrates an organization that would have grounds to establish multiple domains. CompanyB is an engineering company based in York, Pennsylvania. Administration for all branch locations is currently centralized in the home office, and OUs and group policies are used for delegation of lower-level tasks. Recently, the company acquired two separate companies named Subsidiary A and Subsidiary B; each contains its own IT department and operates in separate geographic areas. CompanyB decided to implement AD DS as part of a Windows Server 2012 implementation and wanted to include the two acquired companies into a single common forest.

Because each acquired company possesses its own IT department and there was no agreement on the ownership of the Domain Admins accounts, CompanyB decided to deploy an AD DS structure with two subdomains for Subsidiary A and Subsidiary B, as shown in Figure 5.5.

This design model allowed for a certain degree of administrative freedom with the newly acquired subsidiaries but also allowed for a common forest and schema to be used and kept the domains within the same DNS namespace.

This design model has the particular advantage of being politically easier to implement than consolidation of existing domains. Branch offices and subsidiary companies can keep their own domain structure and security boundaries, and their IT teams can retain a greater deal of administrative autonomy.

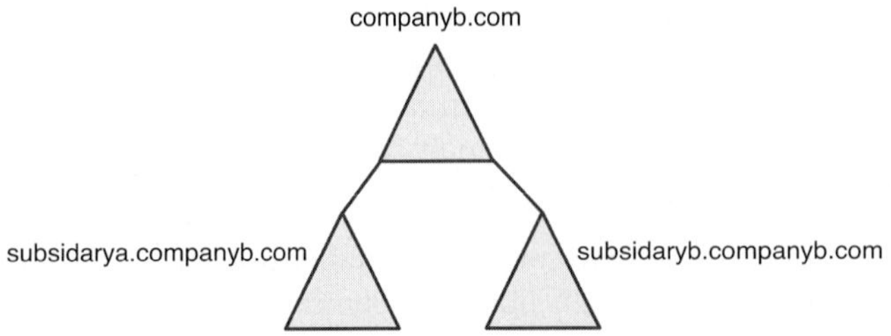

FIGURE 5.5 AD DS with two subdomains.

Be warned, however, that consolidation of a larger number of domains into fewer domains is a key feature of AD DS, so the addition of domains purely for political reasons adds complexity and potentially unnecessary infrastructure. It is, therefore, very important to consider the alternatives before deciding on this design model.

Understanding the Multiple Trees in a Single-Forest Model

Let's say that your organization wants to look at AD DS and wants to use an external namespace for your design. However, your environment currently uses multiple DNS namespaces and needs to integrate them into the same design. Contrary to popular misconception, integration of these namespaces into a single AD forest can be done through the use of multiple trees that exist in one forest. One of the most misunderstood characteristics of AD DS is the difference between a contiguous forest and a contiguous DNS namespace. Many people do not realize that multiple DNS namespaces can be integrated into a single AD DS forest as separate trees in the forest. For example, Figure 5.6 shows how Microsoft could theoretically organize several AD DS do mains that share the same forest but reside in different DNS namespaces.

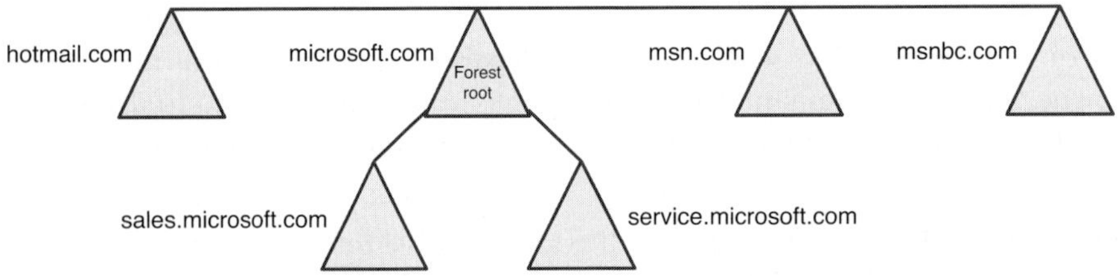

FIGURE 5.6 Sample AD DS forest with multiple unique trees within the same forest.

Only one domain in this design is the forest root, in this case microsoft.com, and only this domain controls access to the forest schema. All other domains, including subdomains of microsoft.com and the other domains that occupy different DNS structures, are members of the same forest. All trust relationships between the domains are transitive, and trusts flow from one domain to another.

Deploying a Multiple Tree Domain Model

If an organization currently operates multiple units under separate DNS namespaces, one option might be to consider a design such as this one. It is important to understand, however, that simply using multiple DNS namespaces does not automatically qualify you as a candidate for this domain design. For example, you could own five separate DNS namespaces and instead decide to create an AD DS structure based on a new namespace that is contiguous throughout your organization. Consolidating your AD DS under this single domain could simplify the logical structure of your environment while keeping your DNS namespaces separate from AD DS.

If your organization makes extensive use of its separate namespaces, you might want to consider a design like this. Each domain tree in the forest can then maintain a certain degree of autonomy, both perceived and real. Often, this type of design will seek to satisfy even the most paranoid of branch office administrators who demand complete control over their entire IT structure.

Exploring a Multiple-Tree Domain Real-World Design Example

To gain a greater understanding of the times an organization might use this particular design model, examine the following AD structure. CityA is a local county governmental organization with a loose-knit network of semi-independent city offices such as the police and fire departments that are spread out around the city. Each department currently uses a DNS namespace for name resolution to all hosts and user accounts local to itself, which provides different email addresses for users located in the fire department, police department, and other branches. The following namespaces are used within the city's infrastructure:

- citya.org
- firedeptcitya.org
- policeofcitya.org
- cityalibrary.org

The decision was made to merge the existing network environments into a single AD DS forest that will accommodate the existing departmental namespaces but maintain a common schema and forest root. To accomplish this, AD DS was established with citya.gov as the namespace for the root domain. The additional domains were added to the forest as separate trees but with a shared schema, as shown in Figure 5.7.

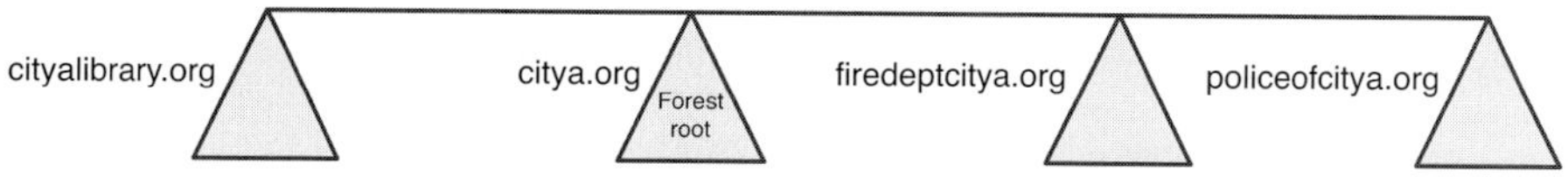

FIGURE 5.7 Examining a forest structure that includes multiple trees.

The individual departments were able to maintain control over their individual security and are disallowed from making changes in domains outside their control. The common forest schema and global catalog helped to increase collaboration between the varying organizations and allow for a certain amount of central administration.

This type of domain design is logically a bit messier but technically carries the same functionality as any other single forest design model. All the domains are set up with two-way transitive trusts to the root domain and share a common schema and global catalog. The difference lies in the fact that they all use separate DNS namespaces, a fact that must also be reflected in the zones that exist in DNS.

Understanding the Federated-Forests Model

A feature of Windows Server 2012's AD DS implementation is the concept of cross-forest transitive trusts. In essence, this allows you to establish transitive trusts between two forests with completely separate schemas that allow users between the forests to share information and to authenticate users.

The capability to perform cross-forest trusts and synchronization is not automatic, however, because the forest functionality of each forest must be brought up to at least Windows Server 2003 (or later) functional levels.

The federated-forest design model is ideal for two different situations. One is to unite two disparate AD DS structures in situations that arise from corporate acquisitions, mergers, and other forms of organizational restructuring. In these cases, two AD forests need to be linked to exchange information. For example, a corporate merger between two large organizations with fully populated AD DS forests could take advantage of this capability and link their two environments, as shown in Figure 5.8, without the need for complex domain migration tools.

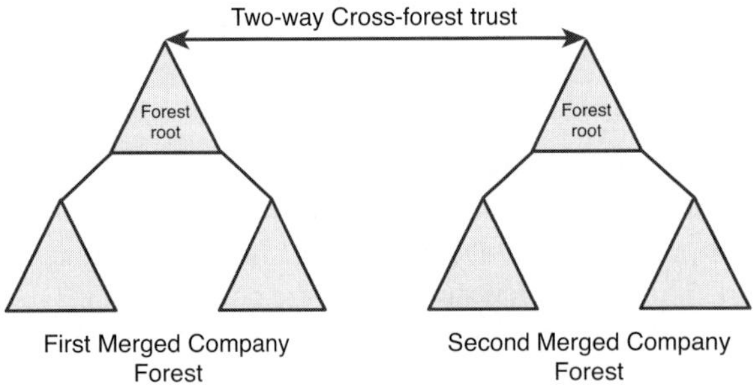

FIGURE 5.8 Cross-forest trust between two completely different organizations needing to share resources.

In this example, users in both forests now can access information in each other's forests through the two-way cross-forest trust set up between each forest's root.

The second type of scenario in which this form of forest design could be chosen is one in which absolute security and ownership of IT structure are required by different divisions or subsidiaries within an organization, but exchange of information is also required. For example, an aeronautics organization could set up two AD forests, one for the civilian branch of its operations and one for the military branch. This would effectively segregate the two environments, giving each department complete control over its environment. A one- or two-way cross-forest trust could then be set up to exchange and synchronize information between the two forests to facilitate communication exchange.

This type of design is sometimes precipitated by a need for the complete isolation of security between different branches of an organization. Since the release of Active Directory in Windows 2000, several interdomain security vulnerabilities have been uncovered that effectively set the true security boundary at the forest level. One in particular takes advantage of the SIDHistory attribute to allow a domain administrator in a trusted domain in the forest to mimic and effectively seize the Schema Admin or Enterprise Admin roles. With these vulnerabilities in mind, some organizations might choose separate forests, and simply set up trusts between the forests that are specifically designed to strip off the SIDHistory of a user.

In Figure 5.9, a one-way cross-forest transitive trust with SIDHistory-filtering enabled was set up between the civilian branch and the military branch of the sample aeronautics organization. In this example, this setup would allow only accounts from the military branch to be trusted in the civilian branch, in essence giving the military branch users the ability to access files in both forests. As with other types of trusts, cross-forest trusts are one-way by default. Unlike explicit trusts, however, cross-forest trusts are transitive. To set up two-way transitive trusts, you must establish two one-way trusts between the two forest roots.

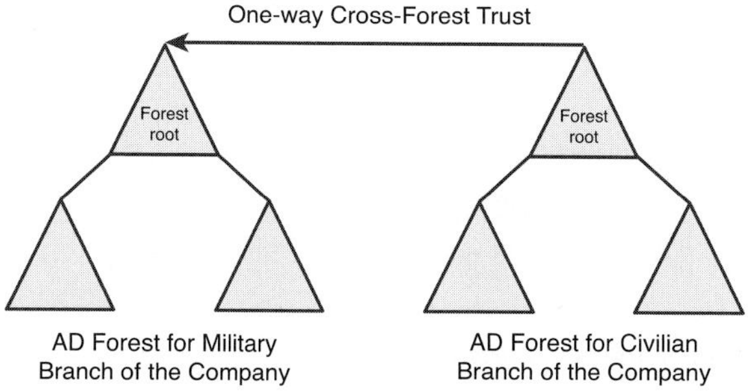

FIGURE 5.9 One-way cross-forest trust.

Choosing Federated Forests

The concept of federated forests greatly enhances the abilities of AD DS forests to exchange information with other environments. In addition, organizations that were reluctant to implement AD because of the lack of a solid security boundary between domains can now take heart in the capability of the federated-forest design to allow specific departments or areas to have complete control over their own forests, while allowing for the transfer of information between the domains.

Federated-Forests Real-World Design Example

To illustrate a good example of an organization that would choose a federated-forest design model, let's consider fictional ConglomerateA, which is a food distributor with multiple sites worldwide. It currently operates a Windows Server 2012 AD DS implementation across its entire organization. All computers are members of the forest with a namespace of companyb.net. A root domain exists for conglomeratea.net, but it is not populated because all users exist in one of three subdomains: asia, europe, and na.

ConglomerateA has recently entered into a joint venture with SupplierA and wants to facilitate the sharing of information between the two companies. SupplierA also currently operates in a Windows Server 2012 AD DS environment and keeps all user and computer accounts in an AD DS forest that is composed of two domains in the suppliera.com namespace and a separate tree with a DNS namespace of supplierabranch.org that reflects a certain function of one of its branches.

The decision was made to create a cross-forest trust between the two forests so that credentials from one forest are trusted by the other forest and information can be exchanged. The cross-forest trust was put into place between the root domains in each forest, as shown in Figure 5.10.

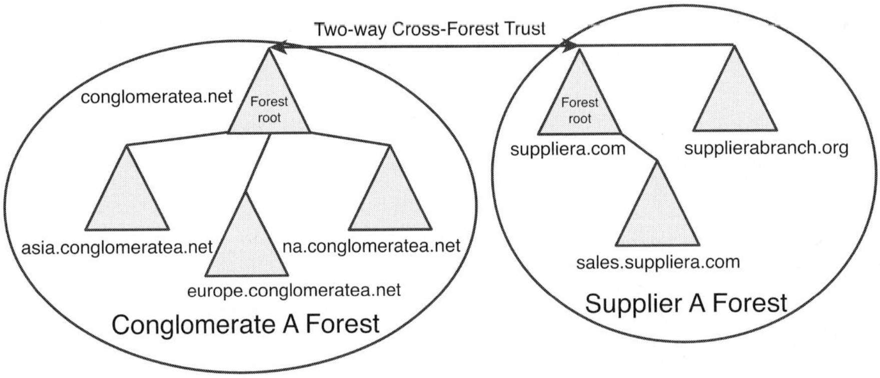

FIGURE 5.10 Cross-forest trust between root domains in each forest.

Remember, a trust does not automatically grant any permissions in other domains or forests; it simply allows for resources to be implicitly shared. Administrators from the trusting domain still need to manually grant access. In our example, administrators in both forests can decide what resources will be shared and can configure their environment as such.

Understanding the Empty-Root Domain Model

The schema is the most critical component of AD DS and should, therefore, be protected and guarded closely. Unauthorized access to the schema master domain controller for a forest can cause some serious problems and is probably the best way to corrupt the entire directory. Needless to say, segregation of the keys to the schema from the user base is a wise option to consider. From this concept was born the empty-root domain model, shown in Figure 5.11.

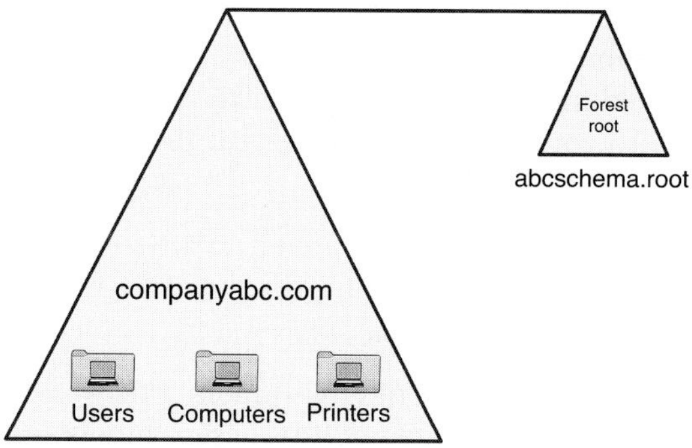

FIGURE 5.11 Empty-root domain model with an unpopulated forest root.

In short, the peer-root domain model makes use of an unpopulated forest root domain that exists solely to segregate the schema master function from the rest of the network.

In Figure 5.11, the companyabc.com domain is used for all user and computer accounts, whereas the abcschema.root domain is the peer-root domain that holds the schema master role for the company. Most users would not even be aware of the fact that this domain exists, which makes it even more secure.

The one major disadvantage to this design model lies in the hardware costs. Because a separate domain is necessary, at least one extra domain controller is needed as part of the design plan, and preferably two for redundancy issues. This domain controller for the empty-root domain will not need to be the speediest machine because it will not perform much work, but it should definitely be made redundant, because the forest-specific flexible single master operations (FSMO) roles will be handled by the machine.

NOTE

Instead of using a physical hardware system for the schema master, an organization could choose to use Windows Server 2012 Hyper-V virtualization and create virtual domain controllers for the empty root domain. This would help to reduce the costs of deploying the empty root model. This is especially the case with Windows Server 2012 domain controllers, which have built-in safeguards to protect them from lingering object problems when virtualized. Do be sure to treat these virtual machines with the same respect as you would any other domain controller, however, with regular maintenance and backups, because losing the forest root would be disastrous for the other domains in the forest.

Determining When to Choose the Empty-Root Model

Security needs vary from organization to organization. A company that performs top-secret work for the military is going to have drastically different security issues than a company that manufactures toys. Consequently, if the needs of your organization require a greater amount of security, the peer-root domain model might be the right one for you.

An additional advantage that this type of environment gives you is the flexibility to rename domains, add domains, and essentially move in and out of subdomains without the need to rename the forest. Although the Domain Rename Tool exists in Windows Server 2012, undertaking this task is still complicated, and using the peer-root model can help to simplify changes. In a merger, for example, if your peer root is named root.network and all your resource domains are located in companyabc.com in the same forest, it becomes much easier to add companya.net into your forest by joining it to the root.network domain.

The beauty of the peer-root domain model is that it can be incorporated into any one of the previously defined domain models. For example, a large grouping of trees with published namespaces can have a forest root with any name desired.

The example shown in Figure 5.12 demonstrates how this type of environment could conceivably be configured. The flexibility of AD DS is not limited by this design model because the options available for multiple configurations still exist.

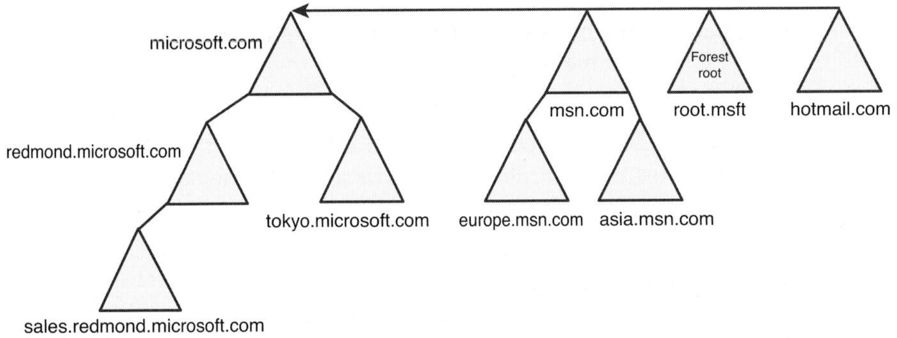

FIGURE 5.12 The empty-root domain model using different domain tree names throughout the forest.

Of course, many organizations often cannot justify the increased hardware costs, and this type of design model can prove to be more costly. Realistically, at least two domain controllers need to be established in the root domain to handle authentication requests and to provide for redundancy within the domain. Keeping these costs in mind, it is important to align your organization's security requirements with the cost-benefit ratio of this design model.

Exploring a Real-World Empty-Root Domain Design Example

CompanyD is a biomedical corporation centered in the San Francisco Bay area. Infrastructure security is highly important for the organization, and the company needs to ensure that directory information is safe and secure in the network environment. The IT organization is centralized, and most employees are located at the main headquarters building.

The administrators of CompanyD originally chose AD DS and Windows Server 2012 to provide for robust security for their environment and to take advantage of the increased functionality. However, management was concerned about limiting access to vital components of the directory service such as the schema. Further investigation into the varying domain design models for AD DS uncovered the peer-root domain model as a fully functional substitute to the single-domain model, but with the added schema security that they desired. This resulted in a forest structure similar to the one shown in Figure 5.13.

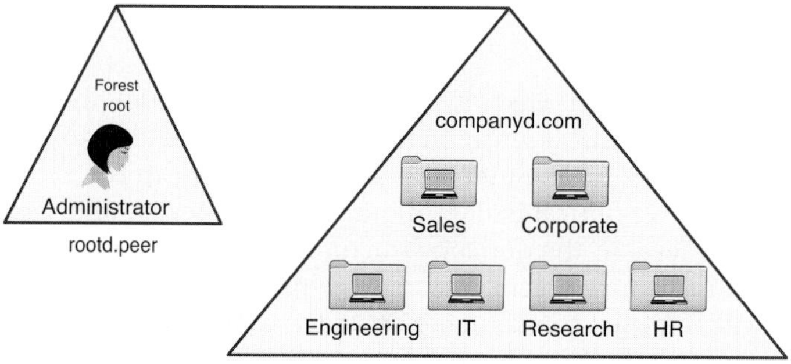

FIGURE 5.13 Peer-root domain with schema security for added protection and integrity.

OUs were created for each department and placed in the companyd.com domain. The only user account in the rootd.peer domain is the administrator account for the forest. Access to this account was limited to a choice group of high-level administrators. This helped to control access to the schema root for the security-conscious organization and provided for the simplicity of a single domain environment for its users.

Understanding the Placeholder Domain Model

The placeholder domain model, also known as the sterile-parent domain model, deserves special mention because of its combination of a single namespace/multiple-domain model and the peer-root model. Simply put, the placeholder domain model, shown in Figure 5.14, is composed of an unoccupied domain as the forest root, with multiple subdomains populated with user accounts and other objects.

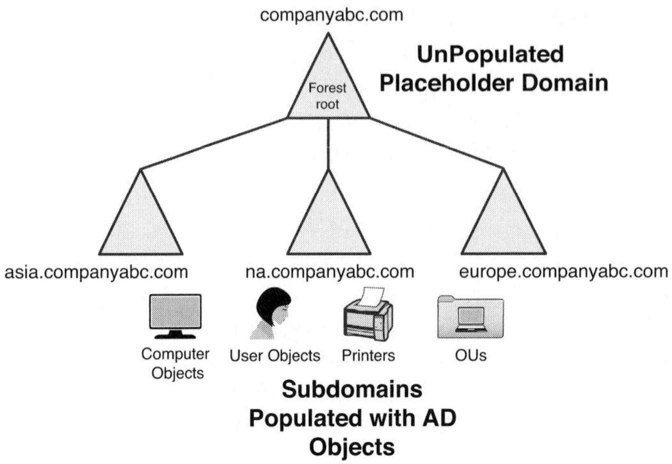

FIGURE 5.14 Unpopulated placeholder domain.

There are two distinct advantages to this design. First, as with the peer-root model, the schema is separate from the user domains, thus limiting their exposure and helping to protect the schema. Second, the namespace for the user accounts is consistent in the namespace, thus mitigating any potential political issues. In other words, because all users in all locations are at the same logical level in the domain structure, no one group will feel superior or inferior to another. This issue might seem trite, but the psychological nature of humans is finicky, and you might find that this design offers advantages for certain organizations.

Exploring a Placeholder Domain Real-World Design Example

CompanyE is an architectural firm with major offices located in New York, Chicago, Los Angeles, San Paulo, Rio de Janeiro, Berlin, Paris, London, Tokyo, Singapore, and Hong Kong. Administration is centralized in New York, but regional administration takes place in Rio de Janeiro, London, and Tokyo. The company has recently migrated to AD DS and has chosen to deploy a placeholder domain model for its organization that looks similar to Figure 5.15.

All users authenticate to geographically centric subdomains. In addition, the administrators in New York have segregated the schema master function into the placeholder domain, limiting its exposure and have limited access to this domain to a small group of high-level administrators. Each domain is logically oriented, as well, to give the impression of autonomy to each geographic unit.

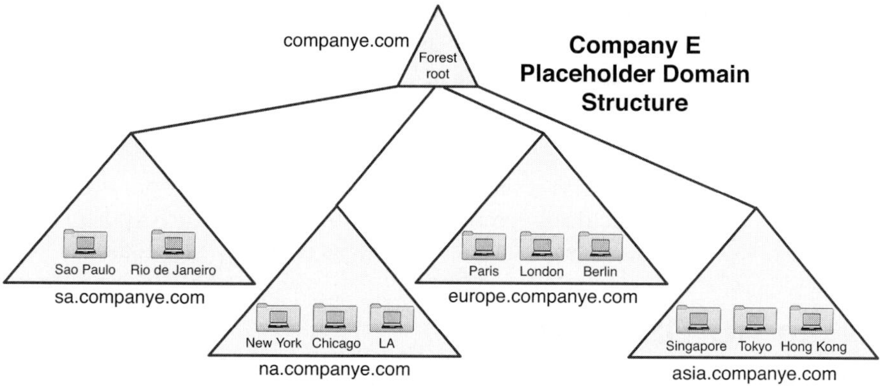

FIGURE 5.15 Complex AD DS placeholder domain structure.

Understanding the Special-Purpose Domain Model

A special-purpose domain or forest is one that is set up to serve a specific need. For example, your organization might set up a special-purpose domain to house outside contractors or temporary workers to limit their exposure to the main AD DS forest. In addition, trust relationships could be established between this domain or other domains to allow for resource access.

Generally, there has to be a good reason before additional domains are deployed in AD DS. Overhead is increased with each domain that is added to an environment, and your logical network structure begins to look convoluted. However, in some unique cases, a special-purpose domain might become necessary.

Another possible use for a separate special-purpose domain structure is to house a directory service-capable application that requires itself, for security or other reasons, to have exclusive access to the schema. In other words, if your HR department runs an application that stores confidential employee information in an application that uses an LDAP-compliant directory, such as AD DS, a domain could be set up for that application alone. A cross-forest trust relationship can be established to allow for the sharing of information between the two environments. This type of situation is rare because most of these applications make use of their own directory, but it is possible. Because the AD DS schema must be unique across the forest, this would preclude the use of a single forest if these applications require exclusive access or utilize common schema attributes. This concept, known as Active Directory Lightweight Domain Services (AD LDS), is further elaborated in Chapter 8, "Creating Federated Forests and Lightweight Directories."

Exploring a Special-Purpose Domain Real-World Design Example

CompanyE is a computer consulting firm headquartered in Morioka, Japan. Most consulting work is performed by full-time CompanyE employees; however, some outside contractors are brought in from time to time to help on projects. The company had already deployed AD DS for the internal organization, but was concerned about opening access to the forest for any nonemployees of the company. Consequently, a single domain AD DS implementation was created for the nonemployees to use. A cross-forest transitive trust was established between this domain and the internal forest, and access to resources such as file and print services were delegated and controlled by the central IT organization.

Users in the contractor domain can access resources in the main companye.com domain, but only those to which they are specifically granted access. In addition, the exposure that the main companye.com domain receives from nonemployees is greatly reduced.

Renaming an AD DS Domain

AD DS in Windows Server 2012 gives domain designers the flexibility to rename their domain namespace and/or splice domains in a forest to different locations within a forest. This capability gives AD DS great new functionality because design changes can be made because of corporate mergers or organizational changes.

Domain rename supports renaming either the AD DS namespace (for example, companyabc.com) or the NetBIOS (legacy NT) domain name or both. The procedure is a rather brute-force process, however, and should not be considered to be a routine operation.

The domain rename functionality in Windows Server 2012 is mainly a psychological factor because the prerequisites for deploying domain rename make it unlikely to be widely performed. Domain rename offers long-term answers to the previous barriers to AD DS adoption, which revolved around the fact that organizations did not want to be locked in to any decisions that could not be changed. Because a Windows 2000 AD namespace decision was irreversible, this effectively put many decision makers on edge, as they did not want to "paint themselves into a corner," so to speak. Domain rename removes this stipulation and makes AD DS adoption much more palatable to decision makers within an organization.

Domain Rename Limitations

Domain rename has several limitations. It is important to understand the following restrictions before considering a domain rename operation:

- **Cannot reduce the number of domains in a forest**—The Domain Rename Tool cannot be used to drop additional domains from a forest. For example, if a forest is composed of four domains, there must be four domains remaining after the procedure is complete. This type of domain consolidation role can be performed only through the use of other tools, such as the Active Directory Migration Tool.

- **The current root domain cannot be demoted**—Although the Domain Rename Tool can splice and transplant domains from one portion of an AD DS namespace to another, it cannot fundamentally change the root domain in a tree. A root domain can be renamed, however.

- **Cannot transfer current domain names in one cycle**—A production domain cannot be named the same as another production domain that exists in a forest. You need to run the domain rename procedure twice to achieve this type of desired functionality.

Outlining Domain Rename Prerequisites

In addition to the limitations of the Domain Rename Tool, specific prerequisites for domain rename must be met before a domain can be renamed, as follows:

- **The entire forest must be at least Windows Server 2003 functional level**—All domain controllers in the domain must be first upgraded or replaced with Windows Server 2003, 2003 R2, 2008, 2008 R2, or 2012 functional level and the forest functional level raised to at least Windows Server 2003 functional level or above.
- **New DNS zones must be created**—The DNS servers for a domain must have a zone added for the new domain namespace to which the domain will be renamed. The exception is if the domain rename procedure will be renaming only the NetBIOS domain.
- **Domain rename must run from a console server**—A member Windows Server 2012 computer (not a domain controller) must serve as the console server for the domain rename procedure. All domain rename operations are run from this one box.
- **Shortcut trust relationships might need to be created**—Any domains that will be "spliced" into a new location in the AD DS forest will need to have a shortcut trust established between itself and the parent domain where it will be transplanted.

Renaming a Domain

The domain rename procedure, from the back end, is not extremely complex. Most of the barriers to domain renaming, aside from the limitations and prerequisites listed in the preceding section, come in the form of the disruption to the forest that is caused by the reboots applied to all the computers in the forest.

After the prerequisites have been satisfied, the domain rename process can proceed. The entire domain rename process is accomplished through six basic steps. As previously mentioned, however, this routine is rather harsh on the network because it causes downtime to a network infrastructure and should not be considered to be a common operation.

Step 1: List Current Forest Description

The tool used for domain rename is known as Rendom. Rendom has several flags that are used in import and export operations. The first procedure run from the console server is **rendom /list**, which locates the domain controllers for a domain and parses all domain-naming information into an XML document named Domainlist.xml.

This XML document can easily be modified by any text editor such as Notepad and, as will become evident, is central to the domain rename procedure.

Step 2: Modify Forest Description with New Domain Names

The XML file generated by the **/list** flag must be modified with the new domain-naming information. For example, if CompanyABC is changing its name to CompanyXYZ, all references to companyabc in the XML list are changed to companyxyz. This includes the NetBIOS and DNS names.

Step 3: Upload Rename Script to DCs

After the XML document is updated with the new domain information, it can be uploaded to all domain controllers in a forest through the use of the **rendom /upload** command. This procedure copies the instructions and new domain information up to all domain controllers within a forest.

Step 4: Prepare DCs for Domain Rename

Domain rename is a thorough process because it is absolutely necessary that all domain controllers in a forest receive the update information. It is, therefore, necessary to run **rendom /prepare** to initiate a preparation process that checks to see whether every single domain controller listed in AD DS responds and signifies that it is ready for the migration. If every single domain controller does not respond, the prepare function fails and must be restarted. This precaution exists to keep domain controllers that are powered down, or not accessible across the network, from coming up at a later time and attempting to service clients on the old domain name.

Step 5: Execute Domain Rename Procedure

After all domain controllers respond positively to the prepare operation, you can initiate the actual domain rename by running the **rendom /execute** command from the console server. Before the **execute** command is run, there are actually no changes made to the production environment. However, as the command is run, all domain controllers execute the changes and automatically reboot. You then must establish a method of rebooting all member servers, workstations, and other client machines and then reboot them all twice to ensure that all services receive the domain-naming change.

Step 6: Post-Rename Tasks

The final step in the Rendom task is to run the **rendom /clean** operation, which will remove temporary files created on the domain controller and return the domain to a normal operating state.

In addition to the cleanup tasks, you need to effectively rename each domain controller, to change its primary DNS suffix. Each domain controller needs to go through this operation, which you run via the Netdom command-line utility. The following steps outline the renaming of a domain controller:

1. Open a command prompt window (by choosing Start, Run, and then type **cmd.exe**).
2. Enter **netdom computername OldServerName /add:NewServerName**.
3. Enter **netdom computername OldServerName /makeprimary:NewServerName**.

4. Restart the server.

5. Enter **netdom computername NewServerName /remove:OldServerName**.

You run all the preceding commands from the command line. Replace the generic designators OldServerName and NewServerName with the entire DNS name of the old server and the new server, such as server1.companyabc.com and server1.companyxyz.com.

Summary

With the advent of technologies such as domain rename, fine-grained password policies, domain controller virtualization improvements, and cross-forest trusts, mistakes in AD DS design have become more forgiving than they were in the past. However, it is still important to thoroughly examine the political and technical aspects of any organization to design an infrastructure that aligns with its needs. AD DS is very flexible in these regards and can be matched with the needs of almost any organization.

Best Practices

The following are best practices from this chapter:

- Fully understand the structure of AD DS before designing.
- Implement fine-grained password policies and the Active Directory Recycle Bin to reduce the need for additional domains.
- Secure any external namespace chosen by registering it so that it cannot be used anywhere on the Internet.
- Start a domain design by considering the single-domain model first.
- Consider using multiple domains for specific reasons only.
- Consider using the federated-forest design model when uniting two disparate AD DS structures.
- Control and optimize replication traffic by using sites.
- Upgrade any down-level clients to reduce administration and maintenance.
- Use domain rename sparingly, and only when faced with no other alternative.

CHAPTER 6

Designing Organizational Unit and Group Structure

IN THIS CHAPTER

The organization of users, computers, and other objects within the Windows Server 2012 Active Directory Domain Services (AD DS) structure gives administrators great flexibility and control over their environments. Both organizational unit (OU) and group structure design can be tailored to fit nearly any business need. There is, however, a great bit of confusion among administrators in the design and use of OUs and groups, particularly in the role-based administration model provided with Windows Server 2012. Often, OUs are indiscriminately used without reason, and group structure is ineffectual and confusing. With the proper preparation and advance knowledge of their use, however, a functional OU and group design can do wonders to simplify a Windows Server 2012 AD DS environment.

In addition to the lessons learned from OU and group use in previous versions of AD DS, Windows Server 2012 improved on functionality such as the Active Directory Recycle Bin, which reduces the risk of OU deletion, and Active Directory Web Services and an Active Directory Module for Windows PowerShell that makes it easier to administer OUs. In addition, AD DS builds on the improvements to OU structure and design introduced with the release of Windows Server 2008 such as OU deletion protection, universal group membership caching, and incremental group replication; other enhancements have increased the flexibility of OU and group design, and have given administrators greater tools to work with.

This chapter defines OUs and groups within Windows Server 2012 AD DS and describes how to integrate them into various AD DS designs. Specific step-by-step instructions and "best practice" design advice are given. In addition, functional OU and group design models are detailed and compared.

Defining Organizational Units in AD DS

An organizational unit is an administrative-level container, depicted in Figure 6.1, that is used to logically organize objects in AD DS. The concept of the organizational unit is derived from the Lightweight Directory Access Protocol (LDAP) standard upon which AD DS was built, although there are some conceptual differences between pure LDAP and AD DS.

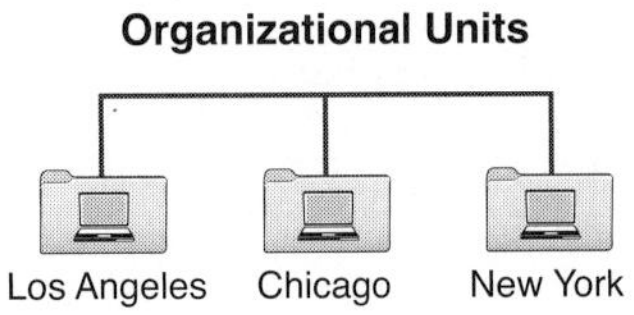

FIGURE 6.1 AD DS organizational unit structure.

Objects within Active Directory can be logically placed into OUs as defined by the administrator. Although all user objects are placed in the Users container by default and computer objects are placed in the Computers container, they can be moved at any time.

NOTE

The default Users and Computers folders in AD DS are not technically OUs. Rather, they are technically defined as Container class objects. It is important to understand this point because these Container class objects do not behave in the same way as OUs. To be able to properly uses services such as group policies, which depend on the functionality of OUs, it is recommended that you move your user and computer objects from their default container locations into an OU structure.

Each object in the AD DS structure can be referenced via LDAP queries that point to its specific location in the OU structure. You will often see objects referenced in this format when you're writing scripts to modify or create users in AD DS or simply running LDAP queries against AD DS. For example, in Figure 6.2, a user named Paul Swider in the Charleston sub-OU of the Locations OU would be represented by the following LDAP string:

```
CN=Paul Swider,OU=Charleston,OU=Locations,DC=companyabc,DC=com
```

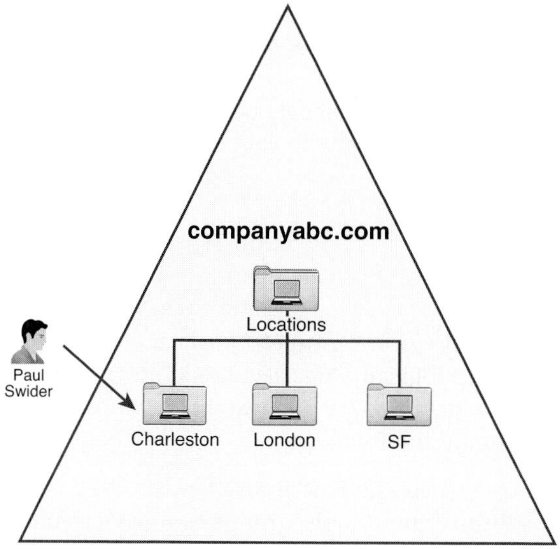

FIGURE 6.2 The LDAP structure of a user object in AD.

NOTE

OU structure can be nested, or include sub-OUs that are many layers deep. Keep in mind, however, that the more complex the OU structure, the more difficult it becomes to administer and the more time consuming directory queries become. It is recommended to not nest OUs more than 10 layers deep. However, it is wise to keep the complexity significantly shorter than that number to maintain the responsiveness of directory queries.

OUs primarily satisfy the need to delegate administration to separate groups of administrators. Although there are other possibilities for the use of OUs, this type of administration delegation is, in reality, the primary factor that exists for the creation of OUs in an AD environment. See the "Starting an OU Design" section of this chapter for more information about this concept.

THE NEED FOR ORGANIZATIONAL UNITS

Although there is a tendency to use OUs to structure the design of AD DS, OUs should not be created to just document the organizational chart of the company. The fact that the organization has a Sales department, a Manufacturing department, and a Marketing department doesn't suggest that there should be these three AD DS OUs. An administrator should create OUs if the departments will be administered separately or if policies will be applied differently to the various departments. However, if the departments will all be administered by the same IT team, and the policies being applied will also be the same, having multiple OUs is not necessary.

In addition, OUs are not exposed to the directory, meaning that if a user wants to send an email to the members of an OU, he would not see the OU structure or the members in the OU grouping.

To see members of an organizational structure, AD DS groups should be created. Groups are exposed to the directory and will be seen when a user wants to list members and groups in the organization.

Defining AD Groups

The idea of groups has been around in the Microsoft world for much longer than OUs have been. As with the OU concept, groups serve to logically organize users into an easily identifiable structure. However, some major differences exist in the way that groups function as opposed to OUs. Among these differences are the following:

- **Group membership is viewable by users**—Whereas OU visibility tends to be limited to administrators using special administrative tools, groups can be viewed by all users engaged in domain activities. For example, users who are setting security on a local share can apply permissions to security groups that have been set up on the domain level.
- **Membership in multiple groups**—OUs are similar to a file system's folder structure. In other words, a file can reside in only one folder or OU at a time. Group membership, however, is not exclusive. A user can become a member of any one of a number of groups, and her membership in that group can be changed at any time.
- **Groups as security principles**—Each security group in AD DS has a unique security identifier (SID) associated with it upon creation. OUs do not have associated access control entries (ACEs) and consequently cannot be applied to object-level security. This is one of the most significant differences because security groups allow users to grant or deny security access to resources based on group membership. Note, however, that the exception to this is distribution groups, which are not used for security.
- **Mail-enabled group functionality**—Through distribution groups and (with the latest version of Microsoft Exchange) mail-enabled security groups, users can send a single email to a group and have that email distributed to all the members of that group. The groups themselves become distribution lists, while at the same time being available for security-based applications. This concept is elaborated further in the "Designing Distribution Groups" section later in this chapter.

Outlining Group Types: Security or Distribution

Groups in Windows Server 2012 come in two flavors: security and distribution. In addition, groups can be organized into different scopes: machine local, domain local, global, and universal.

Security Groups

The type of group that administrators are most familiar with is the security group. This type of group is used to apply permissions to resources en masse so that large groups of users can be administered more easily. Security groups can be established for each department in an organization. For example, users in the Marketing department can be given membership in a Marketing security group, as shown in Figure 6.3. This group is then allowed to have permissions on specific directories in the environment.

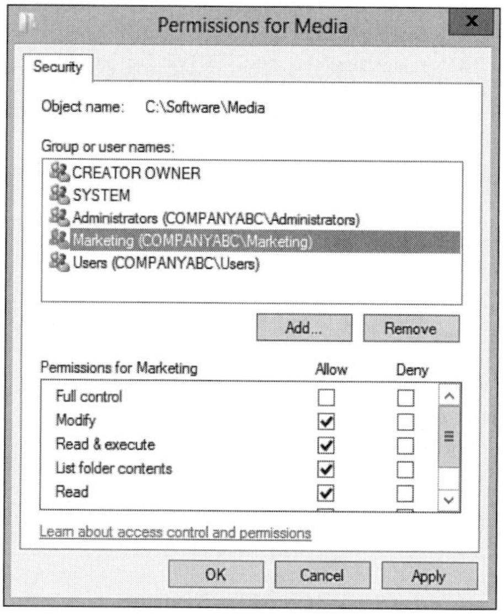

FIGURE 6.3 Examining security group permission sharing.

As previously mentioned, security groups have a unique security identifier (SID) associated with them, much in the same way that individual users in AD DS have an SID. The uniqueness of the SID is utilized to apply security to objects and resources in the domain. This concept also explains why you cannot simply delete and rename a group to have the same permissions that the old group previously maintained.

Distribution Groups

The concept of distribution groups in Windows Server 2012 was introduced in Windows 2000 Server along with its implementation of Active Directory. Essentially, a distribution group is a group whose members are able to receive Simple Mail Transfer Protocol (SMTP) mail messages that are sent to the group. Any application that can use AD DS for address book lookups (essentially LDAP lookups) can utilize this functionality in Windows Server 2012.

Distribution groups are often confused with mail-enabled groups, a concept in environments with Exchange 2000/2003/2007/2010/2013. In addition, in most cases distribution groups are not used in environments without Exchange Server because their functionality is limited to infrastructures that can support them.

NOTE

In environments with Exchange Server, distribution groups can be used to create email distribution lists that cannot be used to apply security. However, if separation of security and email functionality is not required, you can make security groups mail-enabled.

Mail-Enabled Groups

AD DS includes a concept called mail-enabled groups. These groups are essentially security groups that are referenced by an email address, and can be used to send SMTP messages to the members of the group. This type of group is primarily used with Exchange Server, but can also be used with foreign mail systems integrated with AD DS.

Most organizations will find that mail-enabled security groups satisfy most of their needs, both security-wise and email-wise. For example, a single group called Marketing that contains all users in that department could also be mail-enabled to allow Exchange users to send emails to everyone in the department.

Understanding Group Scope

There are four primary scopes of groups in AD DS. Each scope is used for different purposes, but they simply serve to ease administration and provide a way to view or perform functions on large groups of users at a time. The group scopes are as follows:

- Machine local groups
- Domain local groups
- Global groups
- Universal groups

Group scope can become one of the most confusing aspects of AD DS. However, if certain design criteria are applied to group membership and creation, the concept becomes more palatable.

Machine Local Groups

Machine local groups are essentially groups that are built in to the operating system and can be applied only to objects local to the machine in which they exist. In other words, they are the default local groups such as Power Users, Administrators, and the like created on a standalone system. Before networking simplified administration, local groups were used to control access to the resources on a server. The downside to this approach was that users needed to have a separate user account on each machine that they wanted to access. In a domain environment, using these groups for permissions is not recommended because the administrative overhead would be overwhelming.

Domain Local Groups

Domain local groups, a term that might seem contradictory at first, are domain-level groups that can be used to establish permissions on resources in the domain in which they reside. Essentially, domain local groups are the evolution of the old Windows NT local groups.

Domain local groups can contain members from anywhere in an AD DS forest or any trusted domain outside the forest. A domain local group can contain members from any of the following:

- Global groups
- User accounts
- Universal groups
- Other domain local groups

Domain local groups are primarily used for access to resources because different domain local groups are created for each resource and then other accounts/groups are added to them. This helps to readily determine which users and groups have access to a resource.

Global Groups

Global groups are the reincarnation of the legacy Windows NT global group, but with slightly different characteristics. These groups can contain the following types of objects:

- User accounts
- Global groups from their own domain

Global groups are primarily useful in sorting users into easily identifiable groupings and using them to apply permissions to resources. What separates global groups from universal groups, however, is that global groups stop their membership replication at the domain boundary, limiting replication outside the domain.

Universal Groups

The concept of universal groups was new with the release of Windows 2000 and are still useful in Windows Server 2012. Universal groups are just that: universal. They can contain objects from any trusted domain and can be used to apply permissions to any resource in the domain.

Although simply making all groups within a domain into universal groups might seem practical, the limiting factor has always been that membership in universal groups is replicated across the entire forest. To make matters worse, Windows 2000 AD DS universal group objects contained a single multi-entry attribute that defined membership. This meant that any time membership was changed in a universal group, the entire group membership was re-replicated across the forest. Consequently, universal groups were limited in functionality.

Windows Server 2003 introduced the concept of incremental universal group membership replication, which accomplishes replication of membership in universal groups on a member-by-member basis. This drastically reduced the replication effects that universal groups had on an environment and made the concept of universal groups more feasible for distributed environments. This functionality is available in any domain functional level at or beyond Windows Server 2003 functional level.

OU and Group Design

Understanding the concepts used with Windows Server 2012 design is only part of the battle. The application of those concepts into a best-practice design is the tricky part. You can take heart in the fact that of all the design elements in AD DS, OU and group structure is the most flexible and forgiving. Although care should be taken when moving objects between OUs that have group policies enabled, the operation is not visible to end users and has no effect. That said, care should be taken to ensure that group policies that might be in place on OUs are moved in before user or computer accounts move. Not taking this into account can lead to the application of unwanted group policies to various computer or user objects, often with adverse effects. Group membership is also readily changeable, although thought should be given to the deletion of security groups that are already in use.

NOTE

Because each group SID is unique, you must take care not to simply delete and re-create groups as you go. As with user accounts, even if you give a new group the same name as a deleted group and add the same users into it, permissions set on the old group will not be applied to the new group. If a group is deleted, it can be recovered, but only if the Active Directory Recycle Bin is enabled, as outlined in Chapter 4, "Active Directory Domain Services Primer."

While keeping these factors in mind and after successfully completing your forest and domain design (see Chapters 4, "Active Directory Domain Services Primer," and 5, "Designing a Windows Server 2012 Active Directory"), it's now time to start designing an OU and group structure.

Starting an OU Design

As with AD DS domain design, OU design should be kept simple and expanded only if a specific need makes the creation of an OU necessary. As you will see, compelling reasons to create of are generally limited to delegation of administration, in most cases.

As with domain design, it is important to establish a frame of reference and common design criteria when beginning design of the OU structure. Organizational units are often graphically represented by a folder that looks like the icon in Figure 6.4.

FIGURE 6.4 Organization Unit representation

Another common method of displaying OU structure is represented by simple text hierarchy, as shown in Figure 6.5.

Whichever method is chosen, it is important to establish a standard method of illustrating the OU design chosen for an organization.

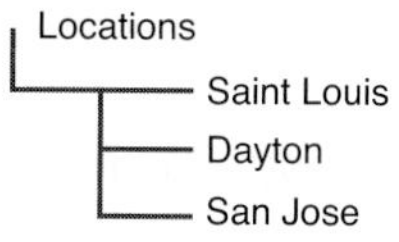

FIGURE 6.5 Simple text hierarchy for an OU structure.

The first step in the design process is to determine the best method of organizing users, computers, and other domain objects within an OU structure. It is, in a way, too easy to create OUs, and often domain designers create a complex structure of nested OUs, with three or more for every department. Although this approach will work, the fact is that it gives no technical advantages, and instead complicates LDAP directory queries and requires a large amount of administrative overhead. Consequently, it is better to start an OU design with a single OU and expand the number of OUs only if absolutely necessary.

Overuse of OUs in Domain Design

Administrators have heard conflicting reports for years about the use of OUs in AD DS. Books and resource guides and pure conjecture have fueled the confusion and befuddled many administrators over best practice for their OU structure.

The basic truth about OUs, however, is that you likely do not need as many as you think you need. Add an OU to a domain if a completely separate group needs special administrative access to a segment of users. If this condition does not exist, and a single group of people administers the entire environment, there is often no need to create more than one OU.

This is not to say that there might be other reasons to create OUs. Application of Group Policy, for example, is a potential candidate for OU creation. However, even this type of functionality is better accomplished through other means. It is a little-known fact that Group Policy can be applied to groups of users, thus limiting the need to create an OU for this express purpose. For more information about how to accomplish this, see the section "Group Policies and OU Design" later in this chapter.

OU Flexibility

Domain designers are in no way locked in to an OU structure. Users can be moved back and forth between OUs during normal business hours without affecting domain functionality (aside from Group Policy application, which should be verified first.) This fact also helps designers to easily correct any design flaws that might have been made to the OU structure.

OUs were introduced as part of Active Directory with the release of Windows 2000 and continued with later versions of Windows Server. Essentially, no real technical differences exist between the functionality of OUs in earlier versions of AD DS, but one important update was added with Windows Server 2008 and later versions. By default, Windows Server 2008 and later allow for OUs to be created with Delete Protection turned on, making it much more difficult for them to be accidently deleted. In addition, real-world experience with OU design has changed some of the major design assumptions that were previously made.

Using OUs to Delegate Administration

As previously mentioned, one of the most important reasons for creating an OU structure in AD DS is for the purpose of delegating administration to a separate administrator or administrative group. AD DS allows for this level of administrative granularity in a single domain. This concept is further illustrated in this section.

A group of users can be easily granted specific levels of administrative access to a subset of users. For example, a remote IT group can be granted standard user creation/deletion/password-change privileges to its own OU. The process of delegating this type of access is quite simple and involves the following steps:

1. In Active Directory Users and Computers, right-click the OU where you want to delegate permissions, and choose Delegate Control.
2. Click Next at the Welcome screen.
3. Click Add to select the group to which you want to give access.
4. Type in the name of the group, and click OK.
5. Click Next to continue.
6. Under Delegate the Following Common Tasks, choose the permissions you want (as in the example shown in Figure 6.6), and then click Next to continue.

   For example, select Create, Delete, and Manage User Accounts, and then click Next.
7. Click Finish to finalize the changes.

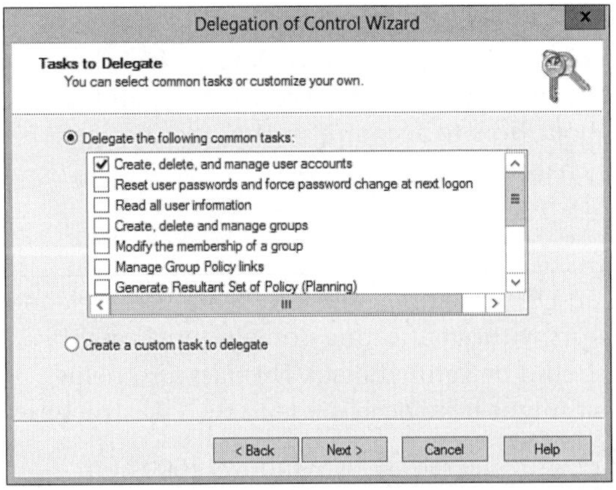

FIGURE 6.6 Choosing delegation of common tasks.

In fact, the Delegation of Control Wizard allows for an extremely specific degree of administrative granularity. If desired, an administrator can delegate a group of users to be able to modify only phone numbers or similar functionality for users in a specific OU. Custom tasks can be created and enabled on OUs to accomplish this and many other administrative tasks. For the most part, a very large percentage of all the types of administration that could possibly be required for delegation can work in this way. To use the phone administration example, follow these steps to set up custom delegation:

1. In Active Directory Users and Computers, right-click the OU where you want to delegate permissions, and choose Delegate Control.
2. Click Next at the Welcome screen.
3. Click Add to select the group to which you want to give access.
4. Type in the name of the group, and click OK.
5. Click Next to continue.
6. Select Create a Custom Task to Delegate, and click Next.
7. Under Delegate Control Of, choose Only the Following Objects in the Folder.
8. Check Users Objects and click Next.
9. Under Permissions, Property-Specific, check Read and Write Telephone Number, as shown in Figure 6.7, and then click Next.
10. Click Finish to finalize the changes.

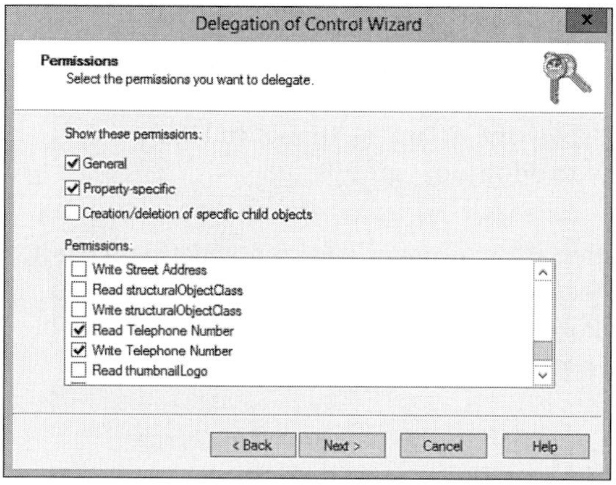

FIGURE 6.7 Selecting permissions to delegate.

The possible variations are enormous, but the concept is sound. AD DS's capability to delegate administrative functionality to this degree of granularity is one of the major advantages inherent in Windows Server 2012.

Group Policies and OU Design

Administrators create group policies to limit users from performing certain tasks or to automatically set up specific functionality. For example, a group policy can be established to display a legal disclosure to all users who attempt to log on to a system, or it can be set up to limit access to the command prompt. Group policies can be set on AD DS sites, domains, and OUs, but can also be configured to apply specifically to groups. This functionality increases the domain designer's flexibility to apply group policies.

As previously mentioned in this chapter, creating additional OUs simply to apply multiple group policies is not an efficient use of OU structure and can lead to overuse of OUs in general. Rather, you can achieve a more straightforward approach to group policies by applying them directly to groups of users. The following procedure illustrates how you can apply a specific group policy at the domain level but enact it only on a specific group:

1. Open the Group Policy Management Console (Server Manager, Tools, Group Policy Management).
2. Navigate to the OU where the group policy is linked, and then select the group policy that you want to apply to a group.
3. In the details pane, under Security Filtering, select the Authenticated Users group, click Remove, and then click OK to acknowledge removal.
4. In the details pane, under Security Filtering, click the Add button to select a group to which you want to apply the policy.
5. Type the name of the group into the text box, and click OK.
6. The Security Filtering settings should display the group, as shown in Figure 6.8. Repeat steps 4 and 5 to apply the policy to additional groups.

This concept of applying a specific group policy at the domain level but enacting it for a specific group can reduce the number of unnecessary OUs in an environment and help simplify administration. In addition, Group Policy enforcement becomes easier to troubleshoot as complex OU structures need not be scrutinized.

Understanding Group Design

As with organizational unit design, it is best to simplify your group structure to avoid unnecessary administrative overhead. Establishing a set policy on how to deal with groups and which groups can be created will help to manage large groups of users more effectively and help troubleshoot security more effectively.

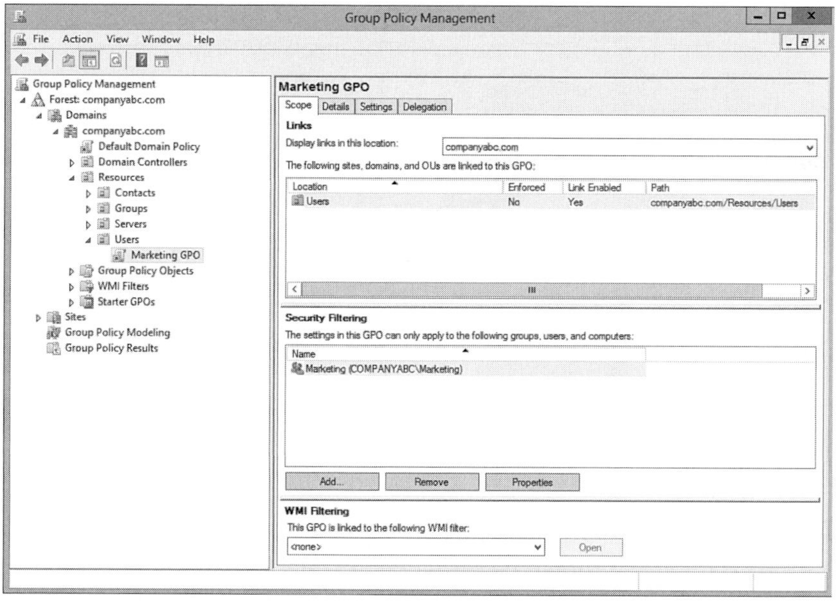

FIGURE 6.8 Adding Read and Apply Group Policy security properties.

Detailing Best Practice for Groups

In the days before Windows Server 2003 and Exchange Server 2007, it was common to use domain local groups to control access to resources and use global groups to organize similar groups of users. When this is done, the global groups created are then applied to the domain local groups as members, allowing those users permissions to those resources and limiting the effect that replication has on an environment.

To illustrate this type of use, consider the example shown in Figure 6.9. Users in the Marketing and Finance departments need access to the same shared printer on the network. Two global groups named Marketing and Finance, respectively, were created and all user accounts from each respective group were added. A single domain local group called Printer1 was created and granted sole access to the shared printer. The Marketing and Finance groups were then added as members of the Printer1 group. While this is still feasible, current best practice holds that universal groups can be used instead of domain local and global groups in an AD DS environment.

The concept of the universal group is also coming of age in Windows Server 2012. Now that the replication issue has been solved through incremental membership replication in Windows 2003, it is more likely that this form of group will be possible in an environment. When necessary, a universal group can take the place of global groups or can potentially include global groups as members. Universal groups are most useful in consolidating group membership across domain boundaries, and this should be their primary function if utilized in Windows Server 2012.

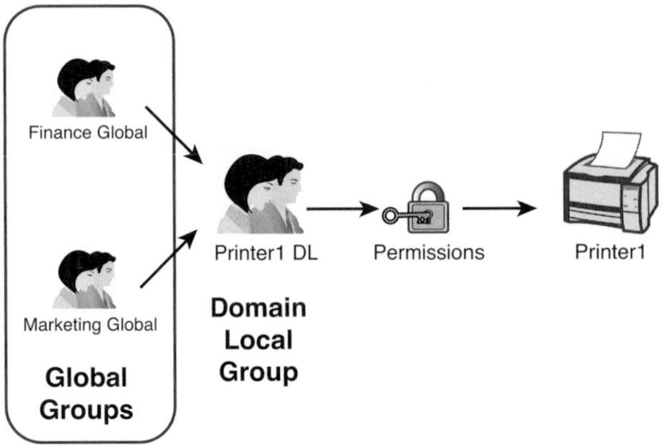

FIGURE 6.9 Best practice group design example.

Establishing Group Naming Standards

As with all objects in AD DS, a group should be easily identifiable so that there is less ambiguity for both end users and administrators. Consequently, it is important to establish some form of naming convention for all groups to have and to communicate those naming conventions to the administrators who will create those groups. Using such conventions will help to alleviate headaches involved with determining what a certain group is used for, who owns it, and similar issues.

Group Nesting

Groups can be nested, or included as members in other groups, to easily add multiple members of known groups as members of other groups. This added flexibility reduces the total number of groups necessary and helps to reduce administrative overhead.

Designing Distribution Groups

If required by your organization, distribution groups can be set up to allow for SMTP mail to be sent to multiple recipients. Bear in mind that these groups do not have SIDs associated with them and consequently cannot be used for security permission assignments. In reality, it is rare that distribution groups will be designed in an organization that is not running a version of Microsoft Exchange Server. However, understanding their role and potential is important in determining proper group design.

Exploring Sample Design Models

Although the possibilities for OU and group design are nearly unlimited, often the same designs unfold because business needs are similar for many organizations. Over time, three distinctive models that influence OU and group design have emerged. The first model is based on a business function design, where varying departments dictate the existence of OUs and groups. The second model is geographically based, where remote sites are granted separate OUs and groups.

A Business Function-Based Design

CompanyA is a clothing manufacturer based in St. Louis, Missouri. Facilities for the company are limited to a small group of locations in Dayton, Ohio, that are connected by T1 lines. A central IT department directly manages approximately 50% of the computer infrastructure within the company. The rest of the company is remotely managed by the following independent groups within the company:

- Sales
- Manufacturing
- Design
- Management

Detailing OU Design for a Business Function-Based Design

Although the culture of the company revolves around a decentralized business approach, the IT department wanted to consolidate into a single AD domain, while at the same time preserving the administrative autonomy that the various departments had with the old environment. The result was a single AD DS domain named companya.com that used five separate OUs, one for each department, similar to the structure shown in Figure 6.10.

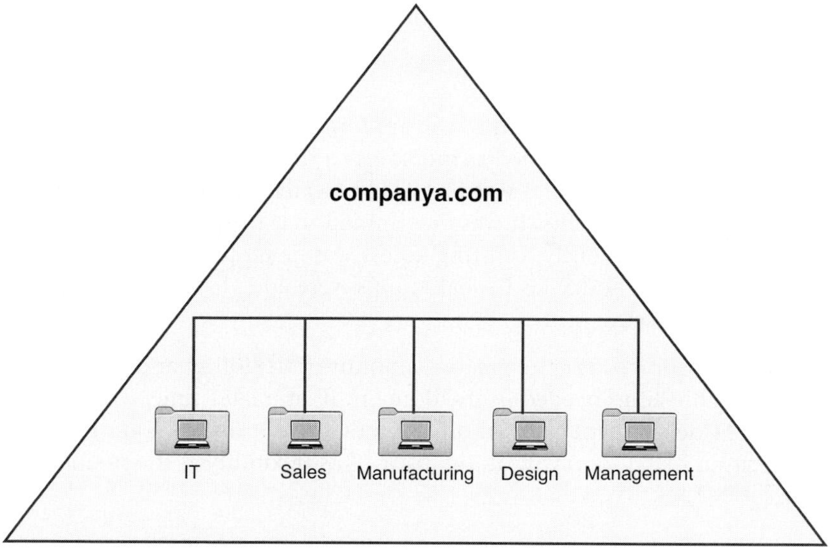

FIGURE 6.10 Organizational unit design.

To create this structure, resources were created in the single AD domain. Administrative rights were assigned to each OU by creating special global groups whose members included the local administrators for each department. These groups were then delegated password change, user creation/deletion, and other typical administrative capabilities on their respective department's OUs through use of the Delegation of Control Wizard (see the "Using OUs to Delegate Administration" section earlier in this chapter).

Detailing Group Design for a Business Function-Based Design

A group structure was created with five separate global groups that contained users from each department. The global groups were named as follows:

- IT Global
- Sales Global
- Manufacturing Global
- Design Global
- Management Global

Resources were assigned domain local groups that followed a standard naming scheme, such as that represented in the following examples:

- Printer1 DL
- FileServer3 DL
- VidConfServer1 DL
- Printer3 DL

Security rights for all resources were then given to the appropriate domain local groups that were set up. The global groups were added as members to those groups as appropriate. For example, the printer named Printer3 was physically located in an area between both the Design and the Sales departments. It was determined that this printer should be accessible from both groups. Consequently, printing access was given to the Printer3 DL group, and both the Design Global and Sales Global groups were added as members to the Printer3 DL group, as shown in Figure 6.11.

This type of resource security allowed for the greatest amount of flexibility and reduced the replication of group membership needed in the domain. If, at a later time, the decision is made to allow the IT department to print off Printer3 as well, simply adding the IT Global group into the Printer3 DL group will do the trick. This flexibility is the main goal of this type of design.

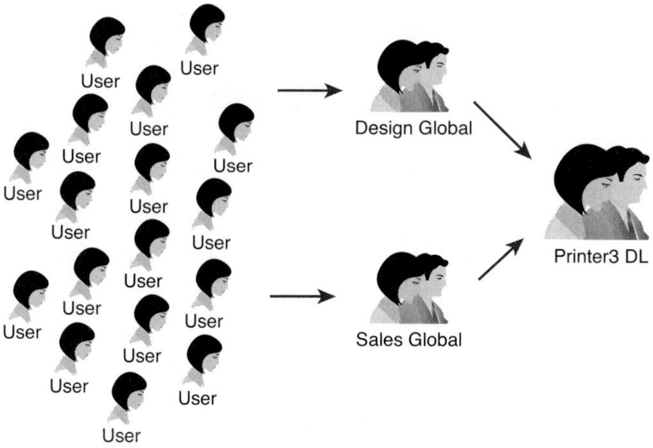

FIGURE 6.11 Nesting groups to assign permissions.

Understanding Geographically Based Design

As was the case with the business function-based design model, domain structures can easily be tailored to the needs of organizations with geographically dispersed locations, each with its own sets of administrators. It is important to understand that simply having sites in remote locations does not immediately warrant creation of an OU for each site. Some type of special local administration is required in those remote sites before OU creation should be considered.

Keeping this point in mind, consider the example of CompanyB. It is an international semiconductor producer that is centralized in Sacramento, California, but has worldwide remote branches in Malaysia, Costa Rica, Tokyo, Australia, Berlin, and Kiev, as shown in Figure 6.12.

Administration takes place on a continent-by-continent basis. In other words, Berlin and Kiev are both managed by the same team, and Tokyo and Malaysia use the same administrators. Australia administers its own users, as does Costa Rica.

Outlining OU Design for a Geographically Based Design

The AD designers at CompanyB determined that the local administrative requirements of the branch offices were best served through the creation of OUs for each administrative region. A Europe OU was created for users in Berlin and Kiev, and an Asia OU was created for Tokyo and Malaysia. The three other sites were given individual OUs, as shown in Figure 6.13.

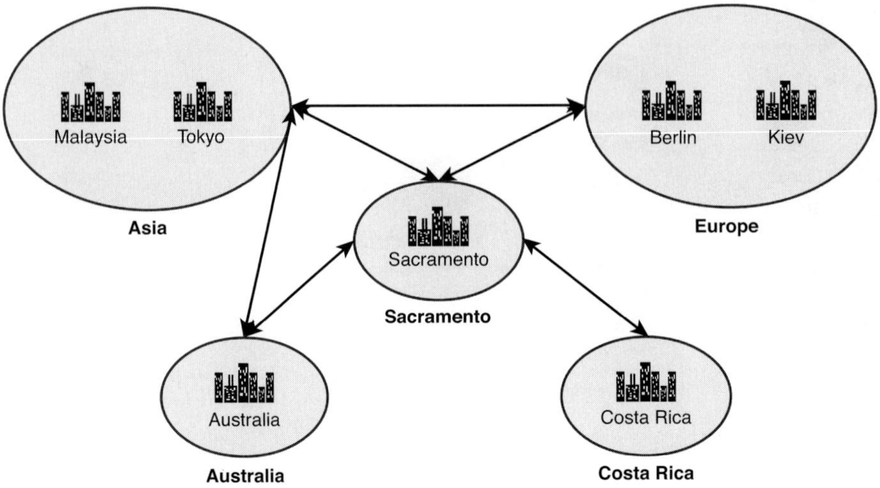

FIGURE 6.12 Sample administrative structure

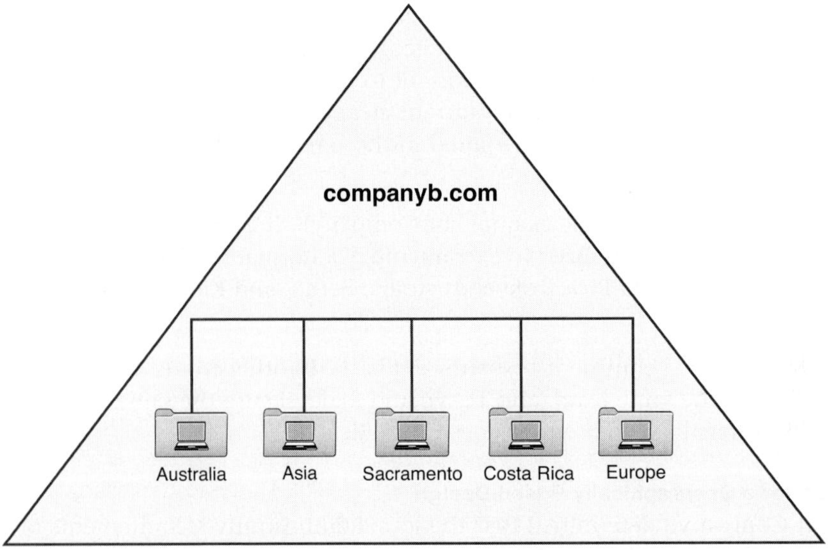

FIGURE 6.13 Redesign using OUs instead of domains.

Examining Group Design for a Geographically Based Design

Domain local groups were created to grant access to each OU on a resource basis. For example, a domain local group named Europe OU DL was created for application of security to the Europe OU. To apply this security, the Delegation of Control Wizard was run on each OU, and each corresponding domain local group was granted administrative access to its own respective OUs.

Membership in the domain local groups was only the first step for allowing CompanyB's administrators to manage their own environments. Global groups were created for each IT team, corresponding with their physical location. For example, Berlin IT Admins Global and Kiev IT Admins Global groups were created, and each IT admin user account for the remote locations was added as a member of its respective groups. The two global groups were then added as members of the Europe OU DL domain local group, as shown in Figure 6.14. The same process was applied to the other OUs in the organization. This solution allowed for the greatest degree of administrative flexibility when dealing with permissions set on the OUs.

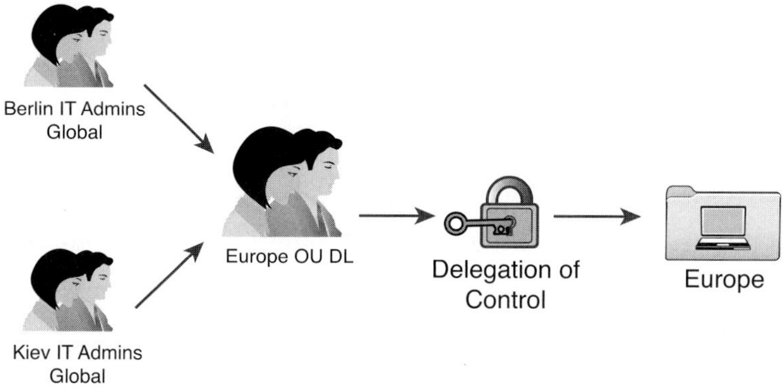

FIGURE 6.14 Nested delegation of control

Each administrative team was consequently granted a broad range of administrative powers over its own environment, allowing each team to create users, change passwords, and effectively administer its own environments without the need for broad, sweeping administrative powers over the entire domain.

The added advantage of this design is that it is completely flexible, and administrative control can be redelegated on-the-fly, so to speak. For example, if a branch office opens in Paris, and IT administrators in that location need to have equivalent administrative control over the Europe OU, a simple global group can be created and added as a member to the Europe OU DL domain local group. Removing permissions is subsequently straightforward. In addition, entire OU memberships can effectively be collapsed into a different OU structure, as required by the changing needs of different organizations.

Summary

Without some form of logical organization of users within your network environment, chaos reigns and administration grinds to a halt. Administrators need some way to lasso groups of users together into logically identifiable groupings so that changes, security privileges, and administration can be accomplished en masse. AD DS was specifically designed to be extremely scalable with regard to administrative functionality, and the flexibility of organizational unit and group design is a testament to this strength. Proper design of both

OU and group structure will go a long way toward helping gain control and reduce overhead in a domain environment.

Best Practices

The following are best practices from this chapter:

- Move your user and computer objects into an OU structure, as opposed to the default Users and Computers containers, because Group Policy objects cannot be applied to the container objects.
- Create critical OUs with Deletion Protection enabled, to avoid accidental deletion. Enable the Active Directory Recycle Bin to be able to recover OUs and their objects if they have been deleted.
- Keep the OU structure as simple as possible, and only expand on the design if there is a specific reason to do so.
- Do not nest OUs more than 10 layers deep when possible.
- Use the principles of role-based access control (RBAC) to control access to resources.
- Apply Group Policy to members of groups through Group Policy Security Filtering to avoid the creation of OUs simply for the sake of creating group policies.
- Use domain local groups to control access to resources, and use global groups to organize similar groups of users.
- Use distribution groups or mail-enabled security groups to create email distribution lists in environments with Exchange Server.
- Mail-enable security groups if separation of security and email functionality is not required. Alternately, use distribution groups if separation is required.
- Don't simply delete and re-create groups on-the-fly because each group SID is unique.
- Enable the Active Directory Recycle Bin functionality in ADAC.
- Don't use local groups for permissions in a domain environment.

CHAPTER 7

Active Directory Infrastructure

IN THIS CHAPTER

- ▶ Understanding AD DS Replication in Depth
- ▶ Understanding Active Directory Sites
- ▶ Planning Replication Topology
- ▶ Outlining Windows Server 2012 IPv6 Support
- ▶ Detailing Real-World Replication Designs
- ▶ Deploying Read-Only Domain Controllers

In an ideal world, all areas of your network would be connected with high-capacity links, and every server would communicate with each other without latency or congestion. Alas, no real networks work this way, and traffic concerns must be considered in all but the smallest, single-server Active Directory Domain Services (AD DS) structure. Windows Server 2012 expands upon the AD DS replication capabilities introduced with the original Active Directory implementation in Windows 2000 Server with a range of new features and functionality. Consequently, the introduction of these new capabilities greatly increases the capabilities of AD DS and also changes some of the fundamental design elements of Active Directory (AD) replication.

This chapter focuses on the definition of the components of Windows Server 2012 AD DS that make up its replication topology. It details design strategies for AD DS sites and provides real-world examples to illustrate the principles behind them. The concept of read-only domain controllers (RODCs) and how they can be deployed in remote sites is covered. In addition, Windows Server 2012 support for Internet Protocol version 6 (IPv6) is outlined and described.

Understanding AD DS Replication in Depth

Windows Server 2012 improvements in AD DS replication are directly drawn from lessons learned in Windows 2000, Windows Server 2003, Windows Server 2008, and Windows Server 2008 R2. Read-only domain controllers (RODCs) can be created in remote sites to reduce replication and increase security. Replication compression can now be disabled in well-connected sites, enabling designers to sacrifice bandwidth for processor utilization in domain controllers (DCs). In addition, concepts such as virtual DC cloning and DC promotion from media allow global catalog (GC) servers to be created from virtual hosts or media, which greatly increases DC placement flexibility. Other improvements, such as universal group caching on DCs, allow remote DCs to function as GC servers by caching frequently used universal group membership locally.

Many of these improvements to AD DS replication were introduced with Windows Server 2008 and, although there are few replication-specific improvements in Windows Server 2012, this latest version cements these new features and fixes design limitations that have thwarted replication plans in the past. Problems with replication design can potentially cripple a network, and it is, therefore, wise to put some serious thought into the proper layout and design of an effective replication scheme.

Understanding the Role of Replication in AD DS

All enterprise directory environments must include mechanisms to synchronize and update directory information across the entire directory structure. In Windows Server 2012 AD DS, this means that every DC must be updated with the most recent information so that users can log on, access resources, and interact with the directory accurately.

AD DS differs from many directory services implementations in that the replication of directory information is accomplished independently from the actual logical directory design. The concept of AD DS sites is completely independent from the logical structure of AD DS forests, trees, and domains. In fact, a single site in AD DS can actually host DCs from different domains or different trees within the same forest. This allows for the creation of a replication topology based on a wide-area network (WAN) structure, while the directory topology can mirror the organization's structure.

Outlining Multimaster Topology Concepts

AD DS was specifically written to allow for the creation, modification, and deletion of directory information from multiple DCs. This concept, known as multimaster replication, allows no one DC to be authoritative. If any DCs go out of service, any one of the rest of the writable DCs can make changes to directory information. Those changes are then replicated across the domain infrastructure. Of course, there needs to be some level of control on this type of replication so that only the most recent changes take precedence. This type of control is realized in AD DS through the concept of update sequence numbers (USNs).

Explaining Update Sequence Numbers

All enterprise directory services implementations require a mechanism to handle the incremental storage of changes made to directory objects. In other words, whenever a password is changed, that information must be accurately passed to all DCs in the domain. This mechanism must also be able to apply only those changes that occurred at the most recent intervals.

Many directory services implementations relied on exact time synchronization on all DCs to synchronize information. However, keeping the clocks of multiple servers in sync has been proven to be extremely difficult, and even slight variations in time could affect replication results.

Thus was born the concept of the update sequence number (USN). AD DS uses USNs to provide for accurate application of directory changes. A USN is a 64-bit number that is maintained by each DC in AD DS. The USN is sequentially advanced upon each change that is made to the directory on that specific server. Each additional DC also contains a copy of the last-known USN from its peers. Updates are subsequently made to be more straightforward. For example, when requesting a replication update from Server2, Server1 references its internal table for the most recent USN that it received from Server2 and requests only those changes that were made since that specific number. The simplicity of this design also ensures accuracy of replication across the domain environment.

The integrity of replication is ensured with USNs because the USN number is updated only upon confirmation that the change has been written to the specific DC. This way, if a server failure interrupts the replication cycle, the server in question will still seek an update based on its USN number, ensuring the integrity of the transaction.

Resolving Replication Collisions

The concept of USNs does not completely eliminate the role of proper time synchronization in AD DS. It is still important to maintain accurate time across a domain environment because of the possibility of replication collisions. A replication collision is an inaccuracy in replicated information that takes place because of changes that are enacted on the same object, but before that change has been replicated to all DCs. For example, if an administrator resets a user's password on Server1, and another administrator resets the same user's password on Server2 before Server1 has had a chance to replicate that change, a replication collision will occur. Replication collisions are resolved through the use of property version numbers.

7

Applying Property Version Numbers

Property version numbers are applied as an attribute to all objects within AD DS. These numbers are sequentially updated and time-stamped whenever a change is made to that object. If a replication collision occurs, the property version number with the latest time stamp will be enacted, and the older change will be discarded. In the example from the preceding section, the password change with the latest time stamp will be applied to the user.

This concept subsequently requires accurate time synchronization to be a priority for an AD DS domain—although it is not as critical as in other directory services implementations that rely on it for all replication activity.

WINDOWS TIME

Time is an important aspect in AD DS. Kerberos is the native authentication mechanism used by Windows AD DS and bases its ticketing system on an accurate time source. If two machines in the same domain differ by more than five minutes, authentication will break. Therefore, accurate time must be shared among domain members.

Windows Server 2012 uses the Windows Time Service and the domain hierarchy to maintain a consistent source of time among all the DCs throughout the domain.

One server, the primary domain controller (PDC) emulator, is responsible for getting accurate time from a manual trusted source, such as National Institute of Standards and Technology (NIST), time.windows.com, pool.ntp.org, or a GPS clock. This trusted source is known as stratum 0. The PDC emulator is stratum 1. Stratum 2 goes to all other DCs in the same site as the PDC emulator. The bridgehead server in remote sites is stratum 3 and all other DCs in the same remote site are stratum 4.

Member computers will try to get time from the lowest stratum DC in their own site. If that DC is not serving time, they use the next highest stratum.

Domain computers always honor this system, which explains why the clock resets to the domain time automatically, even if you change the local clock. Time normally syncs at startup and every 45 minutes thereafter for three consecutive, successful times, and then the interval check period is increased to 8 hours.

It is important that administrators configure and test the manually configured external time source on the PDC emulator.

Establishing Connection Objects

Connection objects are automatically generated by the AD DS Knowledge Consistency Checker (KCC) to act as pathways for replication communication. They can be manually established, as well, and essentially provide a replication path between one DC and another. If, for example, an organization wants to have all replication pushed to a primary domain controller (PDC) before it is disseminated elsewhere, direct connection objects can be established between the two DCs.

Creating a connection object is a straightforward process. After one is created, Windows Server 2012 does not attempt to automatically generate a new one across the same route unless that connection object is deleted. To manually set a connection object to replicate between DCs, follow these steps:

1. From Server Manager, click Tools, Active Directory Sites and Services.
2. Expand Sites*Sitename*\\Servers*Servername*\\NTDS Settings, where *Servername* is the source server for the connection object.
3. Right-click NTDS Settings and choose New Active Directory Domain Services Connection.
4. Select the target DC, and click OK.
5. Name the connection object, and click OK.

6. Right-click the newly created connection object, and select Properties to open a properties page for the object. You can then modify the connection object to fit any specific schedule, transport, and so on.

NOTE

The connection objects that appear as automatically generated were created by the KCC component of AD DS to provide for the most efficient replication pathways. You must, therefore, have a good reason to manually create these pathways because the automatically generated ones usually do the trick.

Understanding Replication Latency

Administrators who are not accustomed to AD DS replication topology might become confused when they make a change in AD and find that the change is not replicated immediately across their environment. For example, an administrator might reset a password on a user's account, only to have that user complain that the new password does not immediately work. The reason for these types of discrepancies simply lies in the fact that not all AD changes are replicated immediately. This concept is known as replication latency. Because the overhead required in replicating change information to all DCs immediately is large, the default schedule for replication is not as often as might be desired. Replication of critical information can be forced through the following procedure:

1. From Server Manager, click Tools, Active Directory Sites and Services.
2. Drill down to Sites*Sitename*\\Servers*Servername*\\ NTDS Settings, where *Servername* is the server that you are connected to and that the desired change should be replicated from.
3. Right-click each connection object and choose Replicate Now.

Alternatively, you can use PowerShell to force or manage replication. Microsoft has added a large number of PowerShell commands to this version of Windows Server, which enable you to get even more granular with replication, allowing you to synchronize a single object using the Sync-ADObject cmdlet. For a full list of Active Directory PowerShell cmdlets, type **get-command –module ActiveDirectory** at the PowerShell prompt.

Another useful tool that can be used to force replication is the repadmin command-line tool. This tool is installed as part of a default Windows Server 2012 DC install. After it is installed, you can use repadmin to force replication for the entire directory, specific portions of the directory, or to sync DCs across site boundaries. If the bandwidth is available, a batch file can be effectively written to force replication between DCs, effectively making the directory quiescent.

The default replication schedule can be modified to fit the needs of your organization. For example, you might decide to change the default schedule of 180 minutes to a schedule as low as every 15 minutes. To make this change, follow these steps:

1. From Server Manager, click Tools, Active Directory Sites and Services.
2. Drill down to Sites*Sitename*.
3. Right-click NTDS Site Settings and choose Properties.
4. Click Change Schedule.
5. Set the Schedule to Four Times per Hour, as shown in Figure 7.1.

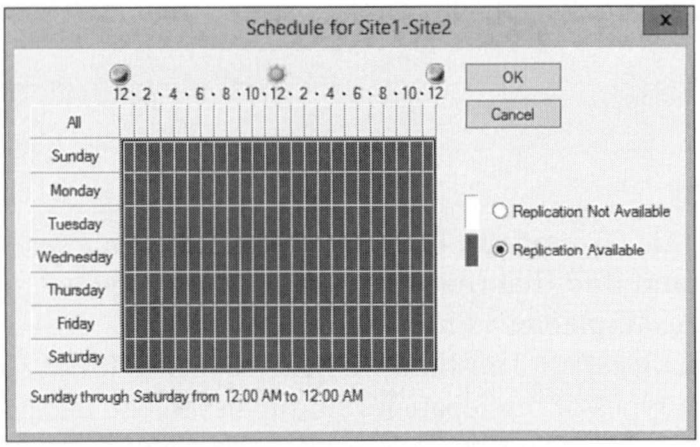

FIGURE 7.1 Setting the default site replication schedule.

6. Click OK to save any schedule changes, and then click OK again to close the NTDS Site Settings Properties page.

Of course, changing this schedule comes with some caveats, namely watching for increased frequency of network bandwidth consumption. You should match the trade-off of your organization's needs with the increased resource consumption levels required.

Understanding Active Directory Sites

The basic unit of AD DS replication is known as the site. Not to be confused with actual physical sites, the AD site is simply a group of highly connected computers and DCs. Each site is established to more effectively replicate directory information across the network. In a nutshell, DCs within a single site will, by default, replicate more often than those that exist in other sites. The concept of the site constitutes the centerpiece of replication design in AD DS.

NOTE

Intrasite replication is approximately 15 seconds when the forest functional level is set to Windows Server 2003 or higher. The intrasite replication is set to 5 minutes for Windows 2000 Server forest functional level.

Windows Server 2012 Site Improvements

Specific functionality that affects sites has evolved since the early days of Active Directory. Windows Server 2003 introduced numerous replication enhancements that directly affect the functionality of sites and allow for greater design flexibility with regard to site design. These changes continue to exist in Windows Server 2012 and have been further improved. These enhancements include the following:

- Read-only domain controllers (RODCs) and read-only global catalogs (ROGCs)
- AD DS optionally installed on Server Core
- GC universal group membership caching
- Media-based DC creation
- Linked-value replication
- ISTG algorithm improvements
- No GC full synchronization with schema changes
- Ability to disable replication packet compression
- Lingering object detection

In addition, Windows Server 2012 added the following new features to its replication engine:

- Deferred Index Creation
- Off-Premises Domain Join

These concepts are elaborated more fully in later sections of this chapter.

Associating Subnets with Sites

In most cases, a separate instance of a site in AD DS physically resides in a separate subnet for other sites. This idea stems from the fact that the site topology most often mimics, or should mimic, the physical network infrastructure of an environment.

In AD DS, sites are associated with their respective subnets to allow for the intelligent assignment of users to their respective DCs. For example, consider the design shown in Figure 7.2.

Server1 and Server2, both members of Site1, are both physically members of the 10.1.1.x subnet. Server3 and Server4 are both members of the 10.1.2.x subnet. Client1, which has a physical IP address of 10.1.2.145, will be automatically assigned Server3 and Server4 as its default DCs by AD DS because the subnets have been assigned to the sites in advance. Making this type of assignment is fairly straightforward. The following procedure details how to associate a subnet with a site. You can also create the subnet using the New-ADReplicationSubnet cmdlet in PowerShell.

1. From Server Manager, click Tools, Active Directory Sites and Services.
2. Drill down to Sites\Subnets.
3. Right-click Subnets and choose New Subnet.
4. Enter the network portion of the IP range that the site will encompass, such as what is shown in Figure 7.3. Select a site for the subnet, and click OK.

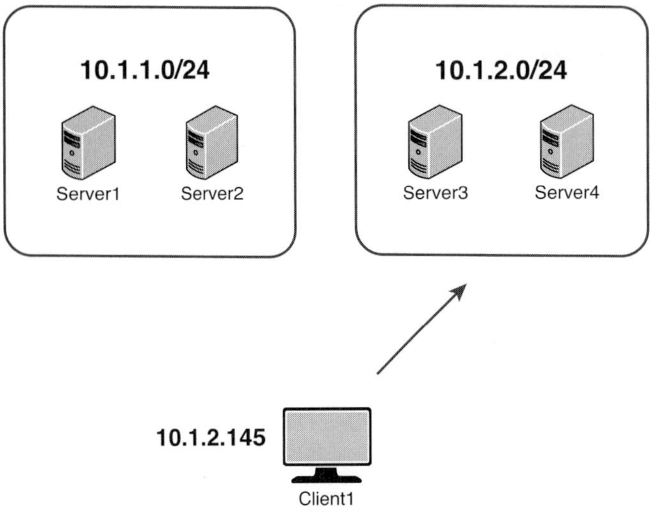

FIGURE 7.2 Client site assignment.

Creating Site Links

By default, the creation of two sites in AD DS does not automatically create a connection linking the two sites. This type of functionality must be manually created, in the form of a site link.

A site link is essentially a type of connection that joins together two sites and allows for replication traffic to flow from one site to another. Multiple site links can be set up and should normally follow the WAN lines that your organization follows. Multiple site links also ensure redundancy so that if one link goes down, replication traffic follows the second link.

Creation of site links is another straightforward process, although you should establish in advance which type of traffic will be utilized by your site link: SMTP or IP (refer to the "Choosing SMTP or IP Replication" section).

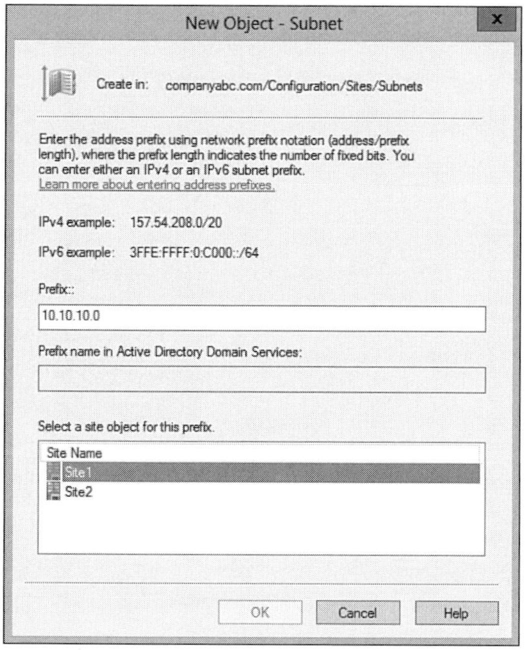

FIGURE 7.3 Associating a subnet with a site.

Site link replication schedules can be modified to fit the existing requirements of your organization. If, for example, the WAN link is saturated during the day, a schedule can be established to replicate information at night. This functionality allows you to easily adjust site links to the needs of any WAN link.

With the assumption that a default IP site link is required, the following steps will create a simple site link to connect Site1 to Site2. In addition, the replication schedule will be modified to allow replication traffic to occur only from 6:00 p.m. to 6:00 a.m. at one-hour intervals:

1. From Server Manager, click Tools, Active Directory Sites and Services.
2. Drill down to Sites\Inter-Site Transports\IP.
3. Right-click IP and choose New Site Link to open a properties page similar to the one shown in Figure 7.4.
4. Give a name to the site link that will easily identify what it is. In our example, we named it Site1-Site2.
5. Ensure that the sites you want to connect are located in the Sites in This Site Link box.

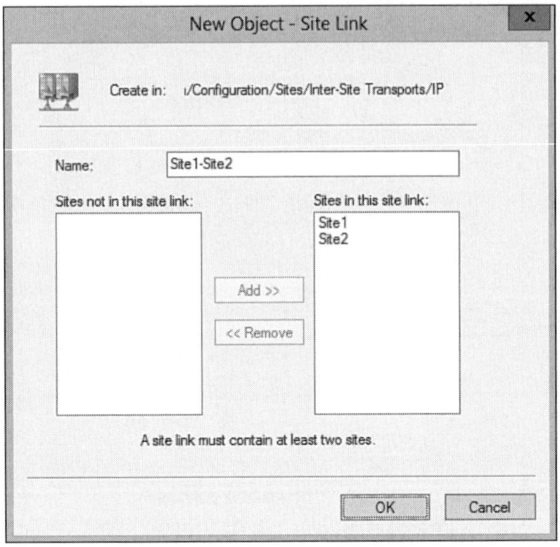

FIGURE 7.4 Site link creation properties page.

6. Click OK to create the site link.
7. Right-click the newly created site link and choose Properties.
8. Click Change Schedule.
9. Select the appropriate time for replication to occur.
10. Click OK twice to save all settings to the site link.

Turning Off Site Link Bridging

By default, all site links are bridged, which means that all DCs in every site can communicate directly with any other DC through any of a series of site links. Such a bridge has the advantage of introducing redundancy into an environment; for example, if Site A has a link with Site B, and Site B is linked to Site C, servers in Site C can communicate directly with Site A.

Sometimes it is preferable to turn off this type of replication. For example, your organization might require that certain DCs never communicate directly with other DCs. In this case, site bridging can be turned off through the following procedure:

1. From Server Manager, click Tools, Active Directory Sites and Services.
2. Navigate to Sites\Inter-Site Transports\IP (or SMTP, if appropriate).
3. Right-click the IP (or SMTP) folder and choose Properties.
4. Uncheck the Bridge All Site Links check box.
5. Click OK to save the changes.

NOTE

Turning off site link bridging will effectively make your DC replication dependent on the explicit site links you have established.

Understanding the Knowledge Consistency Checker and the Intersite Topology Generator

Every DC contains a role called the Knowledge Consistency Checker (KCC) that automatically generates the most efficient replication topology at a default interval of every 15 minutes. The KCC creates connection objects that link DCs into a common replication topology. The KCC has two components: an intrasite KCC, which deals with replication within the site, and an Intersite Topology Generator (ISTG), which establishes connection objects between sites (only one DC in each site holds the ISTG role at any given time).

In Windows Server 2003, the Active Directory design team vastly improved the algorithm used by the ISTG, which resulted in a several-fold increase in the number of sites that can effectively be managed in AD DS. The number of sites that can be effectively managed in AD DS now exceeds 5,000, particularly with Windows Server 2012 and 64-bit DCs.

Determining Site Cost

An AD replication mechanism allows designers and administrators to establish preferred routes for replication to follow. This mechanism is known as site cost, and every site link in AD DS has a cost associated with it. The concept of site cost, which might be familiar to many administrators, follows a fairly simple formula. The lowest-cost site link becomes the preferred site link for communications to a site. Higher-cost site links are established mainly for redundancy or to reduce traffic on a specific segment. In this way, administrators can "shape" the flow of traffic between and among sites. Figure 7.5 illustrates a sample AD site structure that utilizes different costs on specific site links.

In this example, traffic between the Sendai and Fukuoka sites follow the Sendai-Tokyo site link because the cost of that site link is 15. However, if there is a problem with that connection or it is saturated, replication traffic will be routed through the Sendai-Morioka and then through the Morioka-Tokyo and Tokyo-Fukuoka site links because the total cost (all site link costs added together) for this route is 17. This type of situation illustrates the advantage of using multiple routes in an AD DS site topology.

Utilizing Preferred Site Link Bridgeheads

Often, it becomes necessary to segregate all outgoing or incoming intersite traffic to a single DC, thus controlling the flow of traffic and offloading the special processor requirements that are required for this functionality. This concept gave rise to preferred site link bridgeheads, DCs in a site that are specifically assigned to be the end or starting point of a site link. The preferred bridgehead servers will subsequently be the handler for all traffic for that specific site link.

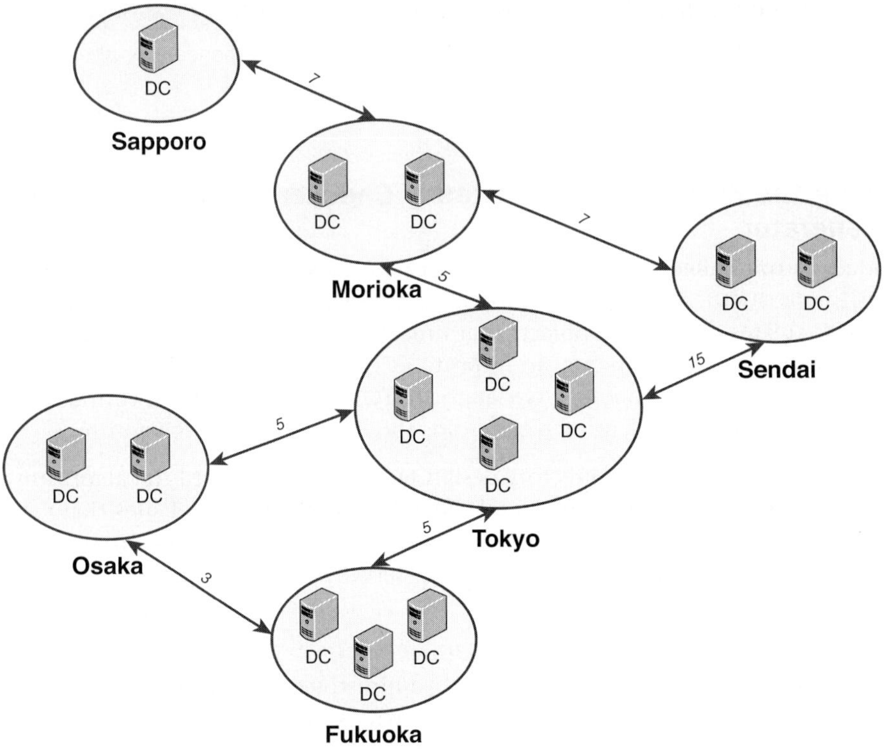

FIGURE 7.5 Understanding site costs.

Multiple site link bridgeheads can be easily defined in AD DS. The following example illustrates how this is accomplished. In these steps, Server2 is added as a preferred site link bridgehead for the site link named Site1-Site2:

1. From Server Manager, click Tools, Active Directory Sites and Services.
2. Drill down to Sites*Sitename*\Servers*Servername*, where *Servername* is the server you want to establish as a bridgehead server.
3. Right-click *Servername* and choose Properties.
4. Select the transport for which this server will be made a bridgehead and click Add.
5. Click OK to save the settings.

Preferred bridgehead servers bring with them both advantages and disadvantages. The advantage of designating a preferred bridgehead server is that in an environment where DCs with weaker processors need to be excluded as designated site bridgeheads or when a DC holds an Operations Master (OM) role, especially that of the PDC emulator, having a designated preferred bridgehead server can allow for controlled communications to a specific bridgehead server.

However, the problem with selecting a preferred bridgehead server is that the preferred server designation prevents the KCC from failing over to other DCs in the same site if the preferred bridgehead server goes offline. Effectively, the preferred bridgehead servers must remain up as general AD redundancy is now focused at a sole server, not to any surviving server in a site.

Typically, organizations choose to not implement preferred bridgehead servers, and only implement them when they have a specific need to designate a server in a site as a preferred bridgehead server.

Deploying AD DS DCs on Server Core

Windows Server 2012 has an installation option called Server Core that allows the operating system to be deployed with only those services that are absolutely required for the role that the server holds. For DCs, this includes only those services that are needed for a DC to operate. Server Core is configured to run at a command prompt, without a graphical user interface (GUI) to further reduce the security profile of the box.

Deploying dedicated DCs using Server Core is ideal in many situations where security is a strong requirement. By doing so, only the necessary functionality is deployed, and no auxiliary services are required.

Planning Replication Topology

Network traffic patterns are an important consideration when implementing AD DS, and a firm understanding of the "pipes" that exist in an organization's network is warranted. If all remote sites are connected by 30Mb WAN links, for example, there will be fewer replication concerns than if network traffic passes through a slow link.

With this point in mind, mapping out network topology is one of the first steps in creating a functional and reliable replication topology.

Mapping Site Design into Network Design

Site structure in Windows Server 2012 is completely independent from the domain, tree, and forest structure of the directory. This type of flexibility allows domain designers to structure domain environments without needing to consider replication constrictions. Consequently, domain designers can focus solely on the replication topology when designing their site structure, enabling them to create the most efficient replication environment.

Essentially, a site diagram in Windows Server 2012 should look similar to a WAN diagram of your environment. In fact, site topology in AD DS was specifically designed to be flexible and adhere to normal WAN traffic and layout. This concept helps to define where to create sites, site links, and preferred site link bridgeheads.

Figure 7.6 illustrates how a sample site structure in AD overlays easily onto a WAN diagram from the same organization. Consequently, it is a very good idea to involve the WAN personnel in a site design discussion. Because WAN environments also change in structure, WAN personnel will subsequently be more inclined to inform the operating system group of changes that could also affect the efficiency of your site design.

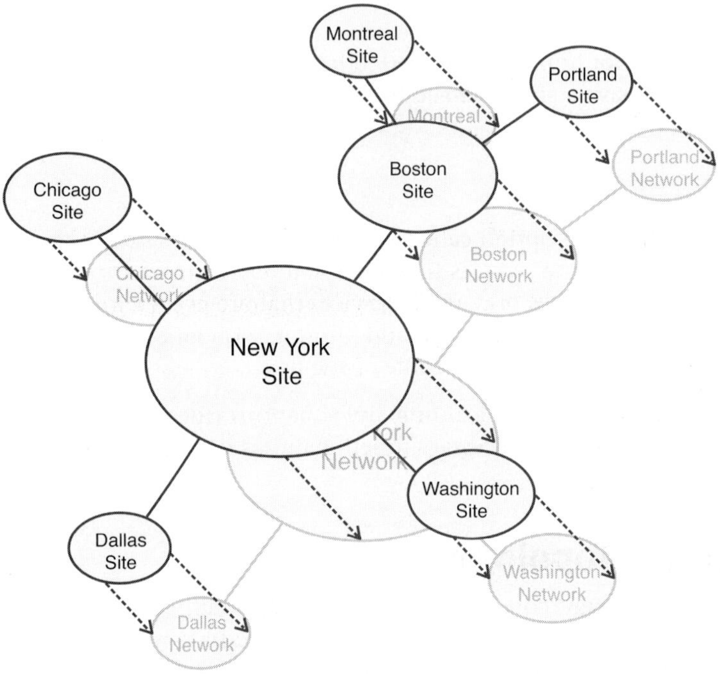

FIGURE 7.6 Site and WAN structure.

Establishing Sites

Each "island" of high connectivity should normally be broken into separate sites. This not only assists in DC replication, but also ensures that clients receive the closest DC and GC server to themselves.

NOTE

If your DNS records are inaccurate for a site, clients could be potentially redirected to a DC or GC server other than the one that is closest to them. Consequently, it is important to ensure that all your sites listed in DNS contain the appropriate server host records. This concept is explained more thoroughly in Chapter 10, "Domain Name System and IPv6."

Choosing Between One Site or Many Sites

In some cases, multiple LAN segments might be consolidated into a single site, given that the appropriate bandwidth exists between the two segments. This might be the case for a corporate campus, with various buildings that are associated with LAN "islands" but that are all joined by high-speed backbones. However, there might also be reasons to break these segments into sites themselves. Before the decision is made to consolidate sites or separate into individual sites, all factors must be taken into account.

Single-site design is simpler to configure and administer, but also introduces an increase in intersegment traffic because all computers in all buildings must traverse the network for domain authentication, lookups, and so on.

A multiple-site design addresses the problems of the intersegment traffic because all local client requests are handled by DCs or GC servers locally. However, the complexity of the environment is more significant and the resources required increase.

NOTE

It is no longer a firm recommendation that all sites contain at least one GC DC server. The introduction of the universal group caching capability and RODCs can reduce the number of GC servers in your environment and significantly reduce the amount of replication activity that occurs. This recommendation still stands, however, for sites with a local Exchange server because one or more local full GC servers are still critical for these environments.

The requirements of an organization with the resources available should be mapped to determine the best-case scenario for site design. Proper site layout helps to logically organize traffic, increase network responsiveness, and introduce redundancy into an environment.

Optimizing Subnet Site Associations

It is critical to establish the physical boundaries of your AD sites because this information utilizes the most efficient logon and directory requests from clients and helps to determine where new DCs should be located. Multiple subnets can be associated with a single site, and all potential subnets within an organization should be associated with their respective sites to realize the greatest benefit.

Determining Site Links and Site Link Costs

As previously mentioned, site links should normally be designed to overlay the WAN link structure of an organization. If multiple WAN routes exist throughout an organization, it is wise to establish multiple site links to correspond with those routes.

Organizations with a meshed WAN topology need not establish site links for every connection, however. Logically consolidating the potential traffic routes into a series of pathways is a more effective approach and helps to make your environment easier to understand and troubleshoot.

Choosing Replication Scheduling

Replication traffic can potentially consume all available bandwidth on small or saturated WAN links. By changing the site link replication schedule for off-hours, you can easily force this type of traffic to occur during times when the link is not utilized as heavily. Of course, the drawback to this approach is that changes made on one side of the site link would not be replicated until the replication schedule dictates. Weighing the needs of the WAN with the consistency needs of your directory is, therefore, important. Throttling the replication schedule is just another tool that can help to achieve these goals.

Choosing SMTP or IP Replication

By default, most connections between sites in AD DS utilize IP for replication because the default protocol used, Remote Procedure Call (RPC), is more efficient and faster. However, in some cases, it might be wiser to utilize SMTP-based replication. For example, if the physical links on which the replication traffic passes are not always on (or intermittent), Simple Mail Transport Protocol (SMTP) traffic might be more ideal because RPC has a much lower retry threshold.

A second common use for SMTP connections is in cases where replication needs to be encrypted so as to cross unsecured physical links, such as the Internet. SMTP can be encrypted through the use of a certificate authority (CA) so that an organization that requires replication across an unsecured connection can implement certificate-based encryption.

NOTE

SMTP replication cannot be used as the only method of replicating to a remote site. It can only be used as a supplemental replication transport because only certain aspects of domain replication are supported over SMTP. Subsequently, the use of SMTP replication as a transport is limited to scenarios where this form of replication is used in addition to RPC-based replication.

Windows Server 2012 Replication Enhancements

The introduction of Windows 2000 provided a strong replication topology that was adaptive to multiple environments and allowed for efficient, site-based dissemination of directory information. Real-world experience with the product has uncovered several areas in replication that required improvement. Windows Server 2012 addressed these areas by including replication enhancements in AD DS that can help to increase the value of an organization's investment in AD.

DC Promotion from Media

An ingenious mechanism in Windows Server 2012 that allows for the creation of a DC directly from media such as a burnt CD/DVD, USB drives, or tape. The upshot of this technique is that it is now possible to remotely build a DC or GC server across a slow WAN link by shipping the media to the remote site ahead of time, effectively eliminating the common practice of building a DC in the central site and then shipping it to a remote site after the fact.

The concept behind the media-based GC/DC replication is straightforward. A current, running DC backs up the directory through a normal backup process. The backup files are then copied to a backup media, such as a CD/DVD, USB drive, or tape, and shipped off to the remote destination. Upon their arrival, the DC promotion process can be run, and Advanced mode can be chosen from the wizard. In the Advanced mode of the wizard, the dialog box shown in Figure 7.7 allows for DC promotion to be performed against a local media source.

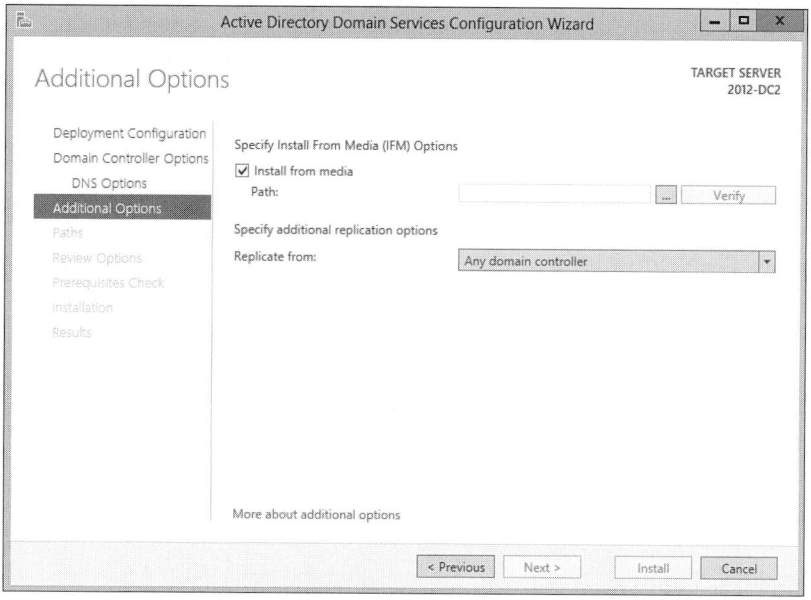

FIGURE 7.7 DC promotion from media.

After the wizard restores the directory information from the backup, an incremental update of the changes made since the media was created will be performed. Because of this, there still needs to be network connectivity throughout the DC promotion process, although the amount of replication required is significantly less. Because some DC promotion operations across slow WAN links have been known to take days and even weeks, this concept can dramatically help to deploy remote DCs.

NOTE

If the copy of the GC that has been backed up is older than the tombstone date for objects in the AD DS (by default, 60 days from when an object was last validated as being active), this type of DC promotion will fail. This built-in safety mechanism prevents the introduction of lingering objects and also ensures that the information is relatively up to date and no significant incremental replication is required.

Identifying Linked-Value Replication/Universal Group Membership Caching

Previously, all groups in AD DS had their membership listed as a multivalued attribute. This meant that any time the group membership was changed, the entire group membership needed to be re-replicated across the entire forest. Windows Server 2012 includes an incremental replication approach to these objects, known as linked-value replication. This approach significantly reduces replication traffic associated with AD DS.

Directly associated with this concept, Windows Server 2012 allows for the creation of DCs that cache universal group membership. This means that it no longer is necessary to place a GC server in each site. Any time a user utilizes a universal group; the membership of that group is cached on the local DC and is used when the next request comes for that group's membership. This also lessens the replication traffic that would occur if a GC was placed in remote sites.

One of the main sources of replication traffic was discovered to be group membership queries—hence, the focus on fixing this problem. In older versions of Active Directory, every time a client logged on, the client's universal group membership was queried, requiring a GC to be contacted. This significantly increased logon and query time for clients who did not have local GC servers. Consequently, many organizations stipulated that every site, no matter the size, must have a local GC server to ensure quick authentication and directory lookups. The downside of this was that replication across the directory was increased because every site received a copy of every item in the entire AD, even though only a small portion of those items was referenced by an average site.

Universal group caching solved this problem because only those groups that are commonly referenced by a site are stored locally, and requests for group replication are limited to the items in the cache. This helps to limit replication and keep domain logons speedy.

Universal group caching capability is established on a per-site basis as follows:

1. From Server Manager, click Tools, Active Directory Sites and Services.
2. Navigate to Sites*Sitename*.
3. Right-click NTDS Site Settings and choose Properties.
4. Check the Enable Universal Group Membership Caching check box, as shown in Figure 7.8.

   Optionally, you can specify which site to refresh the cache from.
5. Click OK to save the changes.

Removing Lingering Objects

Lingering objects, also known as zombies, are created when a DC is down for a period of time that is longer than the tombstone date for the deletion of items. When the DC is brought back online, it never receives the tombstone request and those objects always exist on the downed server. These objects could then be re-replicated to other DCs, arising from the dead as "zombies." Windows Server 2012 has a mechanism for detecting lingering objects, isolating them, and marking them for cleanup.

FIGURE 7.8 Enabling universal group caching in a site.

Disabling Replication Compression

By default, intersite AD replication is compressed so as to reduce the bandwidth consumption required. The drawback to this technique is that extra CPU cycles are required on the DCs to properly compress and decompress this data. Windows Server 2012 allows designers the flexibility to turn off this compression, if an organization is short on processor time and long on bandwidth, so to speak.

Understanding How AD Avoids Full Synchronization of Global Catalog with Schema Changes

In the original version of Active Directory, any schema modifications forced a complete resynchronization of the GC with all DCs across an enterprise. This made it extremely ominous to institute any type of schema modifications because replication modifications would increase significantly following schema modifications. Windows Server 2003 and later AD DS environments do not have this limitation, however, and schema modifications are incrementally updated in the GC.

Intersite Topology Generator Algorithm Improvements

The Intersite Topology Generator (ISTG) portion of the Knowledge Consistency Checker (KCC) has been updated to allow AD environments to scale to site structures of up to

5,000 sites. Previous limitations to the Windows 2000 ISTG essentially kept AD implementations effectively limited to 1,000 sites. This improvement, however, is available only when all DCs in your AD DS environment are at least Windows Server 2003 systems and the forest functional level has been raised to Windows Server 2003 or higher levels.

Windows Server 2012 IPv6 Support

When the original structure of the Internet was taking shape, an addressing scheme was formulated to scale to a large number of hosts. From this thinking came the original design of the Internet Protocol, which included theoretical support for around 4 billion addresses, or 2 ^ 32. The thinking at the time was that this would be more than enough addresses for all hosts on the Internet. This original design gave birth to the IP address structure that is common today, known as dotted-decimal format (such as 12.155.166.151). At the time, this address space filled the addressing needs of the Internet. However, it was quickly discovered that the range of addresses was inadequate, and stopgap measures such as Network Address Translation (NAT) were required to make more efficient use of the available addresses.

In addition to an inadequate supply of available addresses, the Internet Protocol version 4 (IPv4), as it is known, did not handle routing, IP Security (IPsec), and quality of service (QoS) support very efficiently. The need for a replacement to IPv4 was evident.

In the early 1990s, a new version of the Internet Protocol, known as Internet Protocol version 6 (IPv6), was formulated. This design had several functional advantages to IPv4, namely a much larger pool of addresses from which to choose by allowing for 2 ^ 128 theoretical IP addresses, or over 340 undecillion, which gives more than enough IP addresses for every square centimeter on the earth. This protocol is the future of Internet addressing, and it is vitally important that an operating system support it.

Windows Server 2012 comes with a version of IPv6 installed, and is fully supported as part of the operating system and enabled by default on all systems. It is subsequently important to better understand how IPv6 works in a Windows Server 2012 environment.

Defining the Structure of IPv6

To say that IPv6 is complicated is an understatement. Attempting to understand IPv4 has been difficult enough for network engineers; throw in hexadecimal 128-bit addresses and life becomes much more interesting. At a minimum, however, the basics of IPv6 must be understood as future networks will use the protocol more and more as time goes by.

IPv6 was written to solve many of the problems that persist on the modern Internet today. The most notable areas that IPv6 improved upon are the following:

- **Vastly improved address space**—The differences between the available addresses from IPv4 to IPv6 are literally exponential. Without taking into account loss because of subnetting and other factors, IPv4 could support up to 4,294,967,296 nodes. IPv6, on the other hand, supports up to 340,282,366,920,938,463,463,374,607,431,768 ,211,456 nodes. Even taking into account IP addresses reserved for overhead, IPv6 authors were obviously thinking ahead and wanted to make sure that they wouldn't run out of space again.

- **Improved network headers**—The header for IPv6 packets has been streamlined, standardized in size, and optimized. To illustrate, even though the address is four times as long as an IPv4 address, the header is only twice the size. In addition, by having a standardized header size, routers can more efficiently handle IPv6 traffic than they could with IPv4.
- **Native support for auto address configuration**—In environments where manual addressing of clients is not supported or desired, automatic configuration of IPv6 addresses on clients is natively built in to the protocol. This technology is the IPv6 equivalent to the Automatic Private Internet Protocol Addressing (APIPA) feature added to Windows for IPv4 addresses.
- **Integrated support for IPsec and QoS**—IPv6 contains native support for IPsec encryption technologies and QoS network traffic optimization approaches, improving their functionality and expanding their capabilities.

Understanding IPv6 Addressing

An IPv6 address, as previously mentioned, is 128 bits long, as compared with IPv4 32-bit addresses. The address itself uses hexadecimal format to shorten the nonbinary written form. Take, for example, the following 128-bit IPv6 address written in binary:

111111101000000000000000000000000000000000000000000000000000000000000
01000001100001010011111111111111111001000100011111100011111 1

The first step in creating the nonbinary form of the address is to divide the number in 16-bit values:

1111111010000000 0000000000000000

0000000000000000 0000000000000000

0000001000001100 0010100111111111

1111111001000100 0111111000111111

Each 16-bit value is then converted to hexadecimal format to produce the IPv6 address:

FE80:0000:0000:0000:020C:29FF:FE44:7E3F

Luckily, the authors of IPv6 included ways of writing IPv6 addresses in shorthand by allowing for the removal of 0 values that come before other values. For example, in the address listed previously, the 020C value becomes simply 20C when abbreviated. In addition to this form of shorthand, IPv6 allows continuous fields of 0s to be abbreviated by using a double colon. This can only occur once in an address, but can greatly simplify the overall address. The example used previously then become this:

FE80:::20C:29FF:FE44:7E3F

NOTE

It is futile to attempt to memorize IPv6 addresses, and converting hexadecimal to decimal format is often best accomplished via a calculator for most people. This has proven to be one of the disadvantages of IPv6 addressing for many administrators.

IPv6 addresses operate much in the same way as IPv4 addresses, with the larger network nodes indicated by the first string of values and the individual interfaces illustrated by the numbers on the right. By following the same principles as IPv4, a better understanding of IPv6 can be achieved.

Migrating to IPv6

The migration to IPv6 has been, and will continue to be, a slow and gradual process. In addition, support for IPv4 during and after a migration must still be considered for a considerable period of time. It is consequently important to understand the tools and techniques available to maintain both IPv4 and IPv6 infrastructure in place during a migration process.

Even though IPv6 is installed by default on Windows Server 2012, IPv4 support remains. This allows for a period of time in which both protocols are supported. After migrating completely to IPv6, however, connectivity to IPv4 nodes that exist outside of the network (on the Internet, for example) must still be maintained. This support can be accomplished through the deployment of IPv6 tunneling technologies.

Windows Server 2012 tunneling technology consists of two separate technologies. The first technology, the Intrasite Automatic Tunnel Addressing Protocol (ISATAP), allows for intrasite tunnels to be created between pools of IPv6 connectivity internally in an organization. The second technology is known as 6to4, which provides for automatic intersite tunnels between IPv6 nodes on disparate networks, such as across the Internet. Deploying one or both of these technologies is a must in the initial stages of IPv6 industry adoption.

Making the Leap to IPv6

Understanding a new protocol implementation is not at the top of most people's wish lists. In many cases, improvements such as improved routing, support for IPsec, no NAT requirements, and so on are not enough to convince organizations to make the change. The process of change is inevitable, however, as the number of available nodes on the IPv4 model decreases. Consequently, it's good to know that Windows Server 2012 is well prepared for the eventual adoption of IPv6.

Detailing Real-World Replication Designs

Site topology in Windows Server 2012 AD DS has been engineered in a way to be adaptable to network environments of all shapes and sizes. Because so many WAN topologies exist, a subsequently large number of site topologies can be designed to match the WAN environment. Despite the variations, several common site topologies are implemented, roughly following the two design models detailed in the following sections. These real-world models detail how the Windows Server 2012 AD site topology can be used effectively.

Viewing a Hub-and-Spoke Replication Design

CompanyA is a glass manufacturer with a central factory and headquarters located in Leuven, Belgium. Four smaller manufacturing facilities are located in Marseille, Brussels, Amsterdam, and Krakow. WAN traffic follows a typical hub-and-spoke pattern, as diagrammed in Figure 7.9.

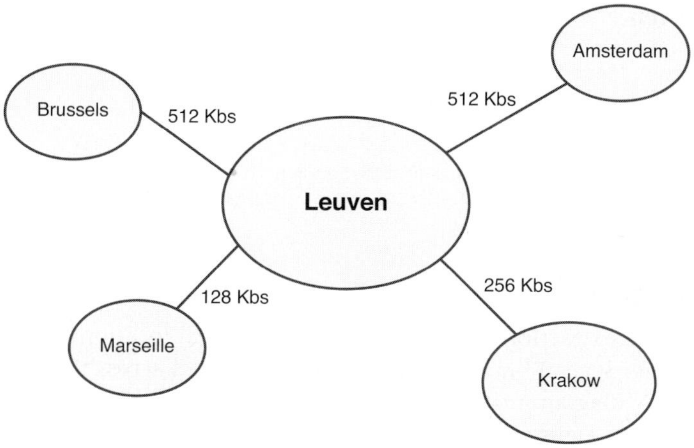

FIGURE 7.9 CompanyA WAN diagram.

CompanyA decided to deploy Windows Server 2012 to all its branch locations and allocated several DCs for each location. Sites in AD DS were designated for each major location within the company and given names to match their physical location. Site links were created to correspond with the WAN link locations, and their replication schedules were closely tied with WAN utilization levels on the links themselves. The result was a Windows Server 2012 AD DS site diagram that looks similar to Figure 7.10.

Both DCs in each site were designated as a preferred bridgehead server to lessen the replication load on the GC servers in the remote sites. However, the PDC emulator in the main site was left off the list of preferred bridgehead servers to lessen the load on that server. Site link bridging was kept activated because there was no specific need to turn off this functionality.

This design left CompanyA with a relatively simple but robust replication model that it can easily modify at a future time as WAN infrastructure changes.

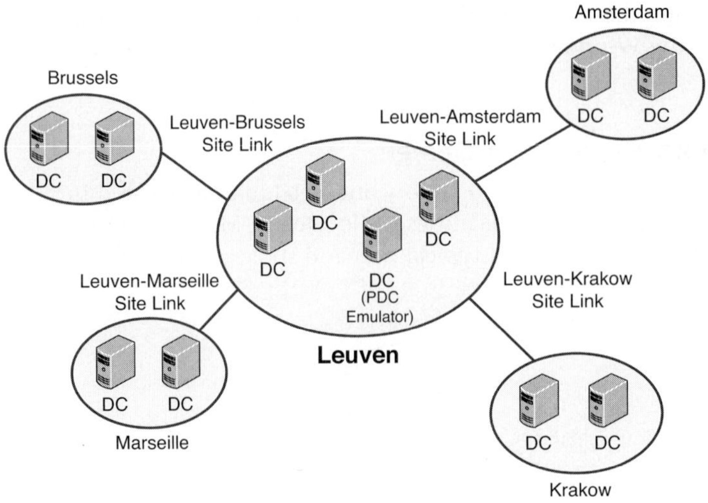

FIGURE 7.10 CompanyA site topology.

Decentralized Replication Design

CompanyB is a mining and mineral extraction corporation that has central locations in Duluth, Charleston, and Cheyenne. Several branch locations are distributed across the continental United States. Its WAN diagram utilizes multiple WAN links, with various connection speeds, as diagrammed in Figure 7.11.

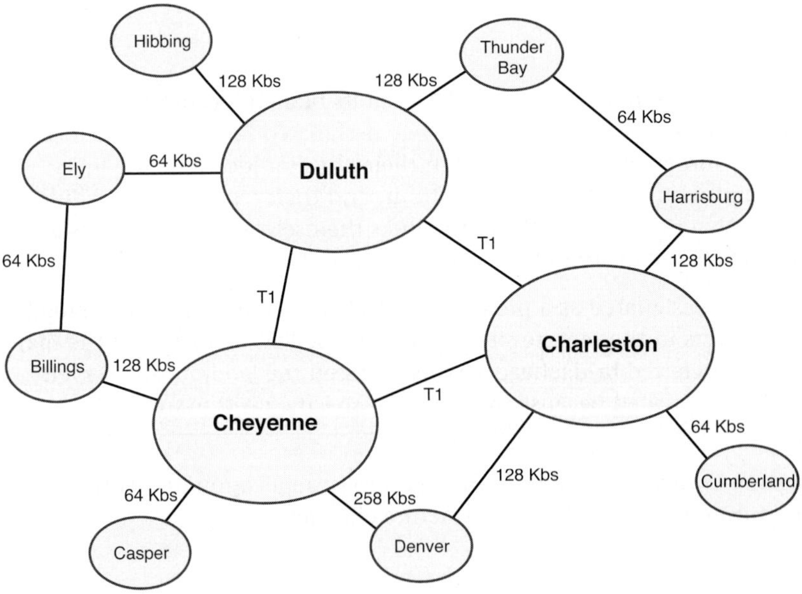

FIGURE 7.11 CompanyB WAN diagram.

CompanyB recently implemented Windows Server 2012 AD DS across its infrastructure. The three main locations consist of five AD DS DCs and two GC servers. The smaller sites use one or two DCs for each site, depending on the size. Each server setup in the remote sites was installed using the Install from Media option because the WAN links were not robust enough to handle the site traffic that a full DC promotion operation would involve.

A site link design scheme, like the one shown in Figure 7.12, was chosen to take into account the multiple routes that the WAN topology provides. This design scheme provides for a degree of redundancy, as well, because replication traffic could continue to succeed even if one of the major WAN links was down.

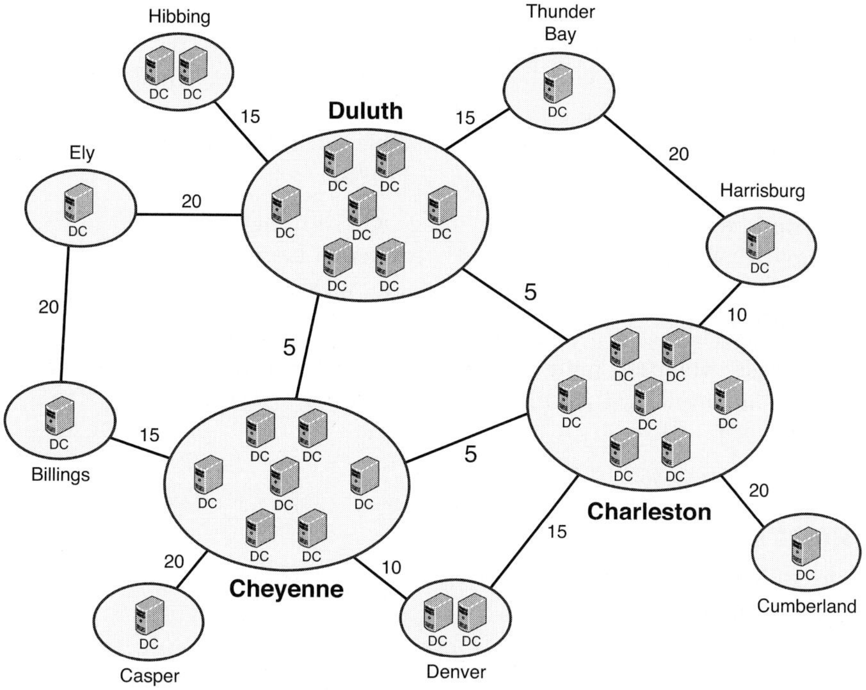

FIGURE 7.12 CompanyB site topology.

Each smaller site was designated to cache universal group membership because bandwidth was at a minimum and CompanyB wanted to reduce replication traffic to the lowest levels possible, while keeping user logons and directory access prompt. In addition, traffic on the site links to the smaller sites was scheduled to occur only at hour intervals in the evening so that it did not interfere with regular WAN traffic during business hours.

Each DC in the smaller sites was designated as a preferred bridgehead server. In the larger sites, three DCs with extra processor capacity were designated as the preferred bridgehead servers for their respective sites to off-load the extra processing load from the other DCs in those sites.

This design left CompanyB with a robust method of throttling replication traffic to its slower WAN links, but at the same time maintaining a distributed directory service environment that AD provides.

Deploying Read-Only Domain Controllers

A concept introduced in Windows Server 2008, and supported in Windows Server 2012 is the read-only domain controller (RODC) server role. RODCs, as their name implies, hold read-only copies of forest objects in their directory partitions. This role was created to fill the need of branch office or remote site locations, where physical security might not be optimal and storing a read/write copy of directory information is ill advised.

Understanding the Need for RODCs

Before Windows Server 2008, DCs could only be deployed with full read/write replicas of domain objects. Any change initiated at a DC would eventually replicate to all DCs in the forest. This would occur even if the change was undesirable, such as in the case of a security compromise.

In remote sites, physical security was an issue for these DCs. Although organizations didn't want to deploy DCs to these sites for security reasons, in many cases slow WAN links would dictate that the remote office would need a local DC, or run the risk of diminished performance in those sites.

In response to these issues, Microsoft built the concept of RODCs into Windows Server AD DS. They also built functionality in RODCs that allowed only specific passwords to be replicated to these RODCs. This greatly reduces the security risk of deploying DCs to remote sites.

Features of RODCs

Several key features of RODCs must be understood before they are deployed in an organization, including the following:

- RODCs can be installed on a server with Windows Server 2012 Server Core, to further reduce the security risk by reducing the number of services running on the server.
- RODCs can be configured as GC servers, which effectively makes them ROGCs.
- Domain and forest functional levels must be set to Windows Server 2003 or higher levels to install RODCs.
- Replication to RODCs is unidirectional; there is nothing to replicate back from the RODCs.
- RODCs that run the domain name system (DNS) service will maintain a read-only copy of DNS partitions, as well. Clients who need to write their records into DNS will be issued a referral to a writable DNS server. The record that they write will be quickly replicated back to the RODC.

Deploying an RODC

The process for deploying an RODC is similar to the process of deploying a regular DC. In both scenarios, the DC promotion wizard (or corresponding PowerShell commandlet) is used to initiate the process. To configure a server as an RODC, follow these steps:

1. Install the AD DS Role from Server Manager or from PowerShell (**Add-WindowsFeature –name ad-domain-services –IncludeManagementTools**).
2. Start the Active Directory Domain Services Configuration Wizard when prompted (or manually by clicking Notifications - Promote This Server to a DC.)
3. From the wizard welcome screen, select Add a DC to an existing domain, and type the domain into the Domain dialog box.
4. Enter credentials of a domain administrator after clicking the Change button, as shown in Figure 7.13, and then click Next to continue.

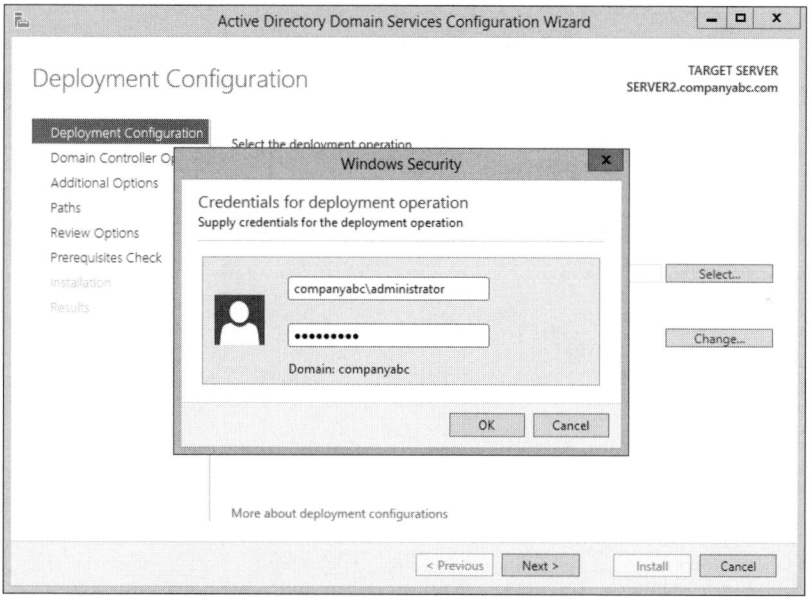

FIGURE 7.13 Installing an RODC.

5. Select a site to install the DC into from the list, and check Read Only DC check box, as shown in Figure 7.14. You can also define if the RODC is a GC server. Enter a Directory Services Restore Mode password, as well, and click Next to continue.
6. On the RODC Options page, shown in Figure 7.15, specify if the passwords of any specific accounts will be replicated to the RODC. Often, local users and passwords in the remote location could be added here to allow for them to be replicated and to improve logon times.

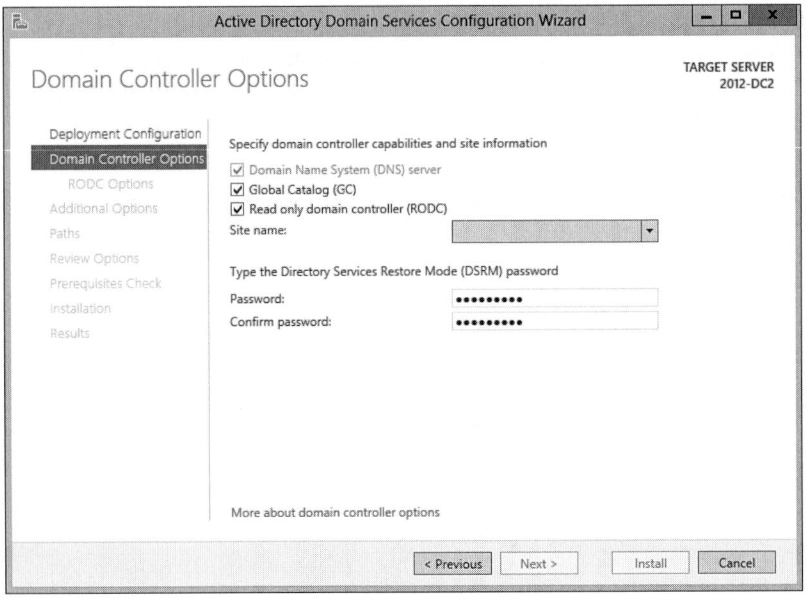

FIGURE 7.14 Choosing to make a server into an RODC.

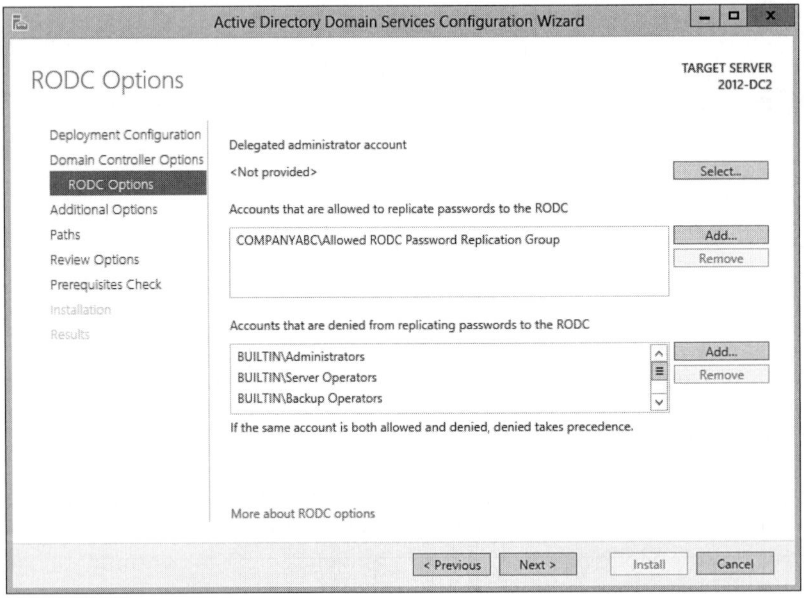

FIGURE 7.15 Setting local administrator rights on the RODC.

7. On the same page, specify any accounts or groups that will be local administrators on the box. Windows Server 2012 removes the requirement that local administrators of RODCs be Domain Admins, which gives greater flexibility for remote site administration of the server. Enter a group (preferred) or user account into the Group or User field, and click Next to continue.
8. On the Additional Options page, choose to replicate either from an existing DC or from local media. By storing the DC information about a burnt CD or other media and shipping it to the remote location, replication time can be greatly reduced. In this case, we are replicating from an existing DC, so select a DC to replicate from and then click Next to continue.
9. The next dialog box on database location, set the location for the SYSVOL, logs file, and database, and click Next to continue.
10. On the Review Options page, review the options chosen, and click Next to continue.
11. After the prerequisites check has completed, click Install to start the process. After several minutes to hours (depending on the size of your AD DS environment,) the DC promotion process will be complete, and the RODC will be ready to service requests within the site it is installed in.

Deploying a Clone Virtualized DC

One of the most interesting and useful improvements to AD DS in Windows Server 2012 is the ability to deploy virtual DCs from virtual machine templates. This greatly reduces the overall time it takes to deploy a new AD DS DC, particularly in those environments with a very large number of AD objects.

Prerequisites for Virtualized DC Cloning

- The DC running the PDC emulator role cannot be cloned
- The Hypervisor that performs the cloning must support VM-Generation ID (Windows Server 2012 Hyper-V currently supports this.)
- You must perform the steps as a member of the Domain Admins group, and the PowerShell commands listed must be run from an elevated command prompt (right-click and select Run as Administrator.)
- The PDC emulator role must run on a DC that is running Windows Server 2012.

Adding the Source Virtual DC to the Cloneable DC Group

The first step to cloning the DC is to add it to the Cloneable Domain Controllers group in Active Directory. This can be done in Active Directory Administrative Center (ADAC), as shown in Figure 7.16, or it can be inputted via the following PowerShell cmdlet (assuming a domain of companyabc.com):

```
Add-ADGroupMember -Identity "CN=Cloneable Domain
Controllers,CN=Users,DC=companyabc,DC=com" -Member "CN=2012-DC2,OU=Domain
Controllers,DC=companyabc,DC=com"
```

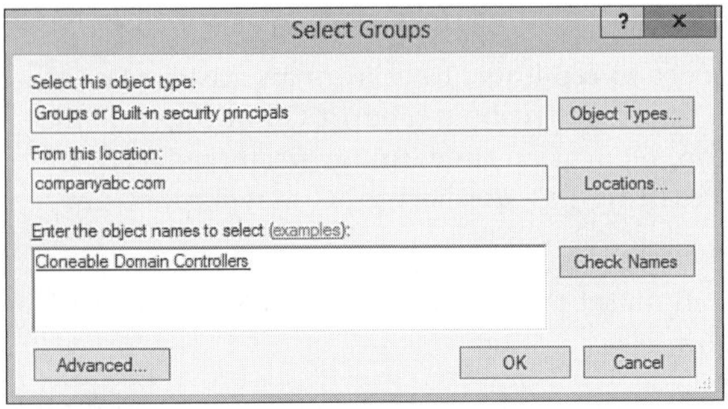

FIGURE 7.16 Adding the DC to the proper group in AD for virtualization cloning

Running the Excluded App List and New Clone Config File Cmdlets

The second set of steps required for cloning a DC are to run a series of PowerShell cmdlets that are required for cloning. The first returns a list of applications which must be excluded before cloning the DC. If you choose a standard AD DS installation with only DNS added, there should not be any extra applications in that list. Run the following PowerShell to determine whether any apps need to be excluded in advance:

```
Get-ADDCCloningExcludedApplicationList
```

After vetting the list for any apps to be excluded, you can then generate the ADDCClone configuration file. You can specify within the file the name of the DC, any static IP assignments, and DNS and WINS assignments, or you can just use the defaults (DHCP, generated name, and so on) by typing in the following, as shown in Figure 7.17:

```
New-ADDCCloneConfigFile
```

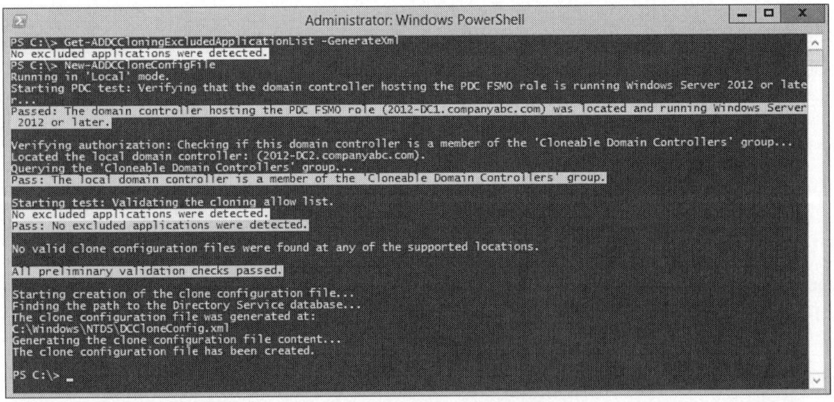

FIGURE 7.17 Creating the ADDC Clone Config File

Exporting and Importing the Source DC Virtual Machine

To create the clone, the source DC (remember that the source DC cannot be the PDC emulator) must be shut down and exported in Hyper-V. You can do this by just right-clicking the guest session in Hyper-V manager, choosing Export, and specifying an export directory, or you can do so via PowerShell with the following syntax (where 2012-DC2 is the name of the virtual DC session and Hyper-V is the name of the Hyper-V host):

```
Export-VM -Name 2012-DC2 -ComputerName HyperV -Path C:\Export
```

You can then import it via the GUI interface, as a new guest session; just be sure to choose to Copy the Virtual Machine (Create New Unique ID) option, as shown in Figure 7.18, and to choose a new location for the virtual hard drives, snapshots, and smart paging folder. In addition, after cloning, be sure to delete any snapshots. A PowerShell equivalent of the process requires the following syntax (or similar depending on your variables):

```
$path = Get-ChildItem "C:\Export\2010-DC2\2010-DC2\Virtual Machines"
$vm = Import-VM -Path $path.fullname -Copy -GenerateNewID
Rename-VM $vm VirtualDC2
Get-VMSnapshot VirtualDC2 | Remove-VMSnapshot -IncludeAllChildSnapshots
```

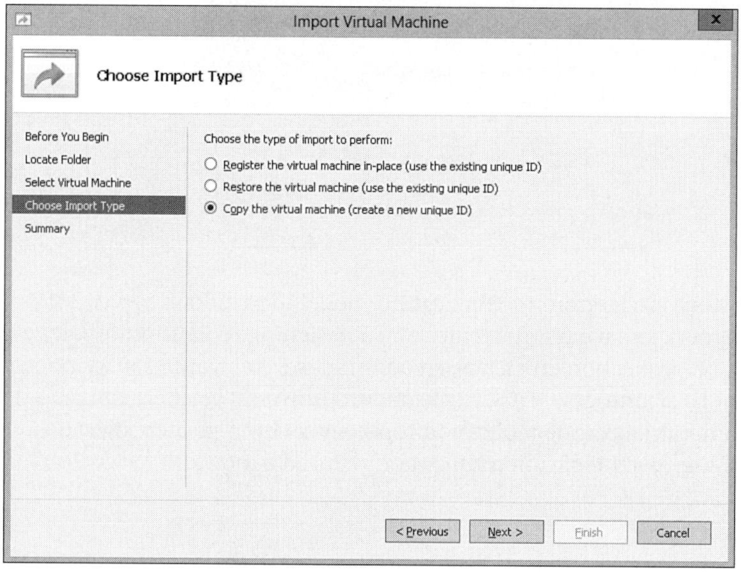

FIGURE 7.18 Cloning a DC using Hyper-V.

Restarting the Source DC and Bringing the Clone DC Online

You can import the DC multiple additional times to bring up more DCs, up to 16 at a time, but be sure to change the file locations where the VHDs, snapshots, and smart paging folder are located each time. When you are done creating replicas, bring the original source DC back online and verify it in AD DS. At this point, you need simply to bring the clone DC (or DCs, for multiple copies) back online, and the cloning process will then proceed automatically, as shown in Figure 7.19.

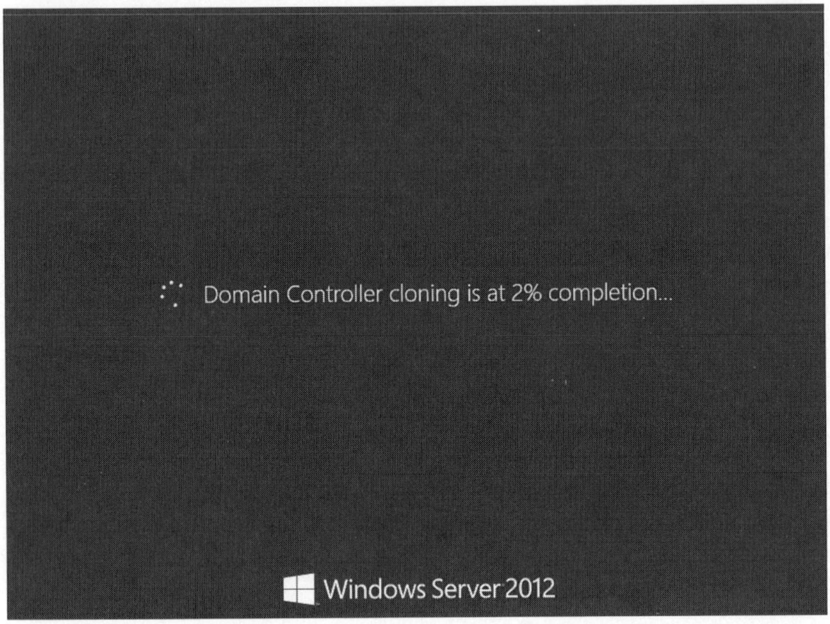

FIGURE 7.19 Finalizing the cloning of a DC using Hyper-V.

Summary

The separation of the directory model from the replication model in Windows Server 2012 AD DS allows domain designers to have full flexibility when designing replication topology and enables them to focus on replication efficiency. In addition, several features in Windows Server 2012, such as virtual DC cloning, RODCs, IPv6 support, universal group caching, and install from media DC promotion, give the replication topology an even greater edge and allow for the realization of improved replication times and reduced bandwidth.

Best Practices

The following are best practices from this chapter:

- Use RODCs to allow for local DC functionality in sites with lessened security.
- Consider using virtualized DC cloning to more quickly deploy virtualized DCs.
- Consider installing dedicated DCs using Server Core, to reduce the overall security profile that a server presents.

- Use the automatically generated connection objects that are created by the KCC, unless a specific reason exists to hard-code replication pathways.
- Ensure that all your sites listed in DNS contain the appropriate SRV records.
- Use the new PowerShell replication commandlets to troubleshoot and validate AD DS replication.
- Consider using IPv6 for environments consisting of Windows 7/Vista and Windows Server 2008/2012 and other IPv6-compliant devices.
- Use IPv6 tunneling mechanisms such as ISATAP and 6to4 to provide long-term compatibility between IPv4 and IPv6.
- Do not turn off site link bridging unless you want to make your DC replication dependent on the explicit site links that you have established.

CHAPTER 8

Creating Federated Forests and Lightweight Directories

IN THIS CHAPTER

- Keeping a Distributed Environment in Sync
- Active Directory Federation Services
- Microsoft Forefront Identity Manager
- Harnessing the Power and Potential of FIM

Windows Server 2012 not only contains the traditional directory services known as Active Directory Domain Services (AD DS), it also includes a version of directory services meant for specific applications and smaller, more lightweight applications. This directory services version is known as Active Directory Lightweight Directory Services (AD LDS).

Keeping information and identities synchronized across these directories can be a challenge, so Microsoft also included Active Directory Federation Services (AD FS) and supports a metadirectory synchronization tool known as Forefront Identity Manager (FIM) to help with federation. This chapter addresses the creation of federated forests and lightweight directories for enterprise directory and application use.

Keeping a Distributed Environment in Sync

When Microsoft originally developed Active Directory in Windows 2000 Server, it was designed to be the only directory an organization would ever need. The idea was that all services would be centralized within an organization's Active Directory environment and that applications would use it as their own directory.

As information technology developed, the exact opposite effect happened; a proliferation of directories within organizations occurred. Not only were multiple directories created within applications, but many organizations deployed multiple Active Directory forests for security reasons.

As Active Directory matured, Microsoft saw a need to tie these directories together into a single, federated metadirectory. In addition, they also saw an opportunity to supply applications with their own directories that were based on the AD model.

This chapter covers these technologies, examining how multiple AD DS forests can be unified into a single federated forest and how that structure can be synchronized with other foreign directory platforms. Microsoft's FIM, which provides for these capabilities, is covered in detail. In addition, AD LDS and AD FS are explained.

Active Directory Lightweight Directory Services

A feature of the Active Directory technologies in Windows Server 2012 is the Active Directory Lightweight Domain Services (AD LDS). AD LDS, previously known as Active Directory in Application Mode (ADAM), is a directory technology that is very similar to the full Active Directory Domain Services (AD DS), but has the capability to run separate instances of itself as unique services. AD LDS allows specialized applications to utilize AD LDS as their own directory service, negating the need for a new form of directory service for every critical application within an organization.

AD LDS uses the same replication engine as AD DS, follows the same X.500 structure, and is close enough to real AD DS functionality to allow it to be installed as a test bed for developers who design AD DS applications. Despite the similarities, however, AD LDS runs as a separate service from the operating system, with its own schema and structure.

The real value to an AD LDS implementation comes from its capability to utilize the security structure of the production domains while maintaining its own directory structure.

Understanding the Need for AD LDS

AD LDS functionality was developed in direct response to one of the main limitations in using Microsoft's AD DS: the fact that the directory was so intrinsically tied to the network operating system (NOS) that applications that did not require the extra NOS-related functionality of AD DS were restricted in their particular directory needs. AD LDS allows each application to have its own separate AD DS directory forest and allows for personalized modification of the directory, such as schema extensions, tailored replication (or lack of replication) needs, and other key directory needs.

One of the major advantages to AD LDS also lies in the fact that multiple instances of AD LDS can run on a single machine, each with its own unique name, port number, and separate binaries. In addition, AD LDS can run on any version of Windows Server 2012 or even on Windows 7 for development purposes. Each instance of AD LDS can use a separate, tailored schema.

AD LDS is nearly indistinguishable from a normal NOS instance of AD DS and consequently can be administered using the standard tools used for AD, such as ADSIEdit, LDP.exe, and the Microsoft Management Console (MMC) tools. In addition, user accounts can be created, unique replication topologies can be created, and all normal AD DS functionality can be performed on a tailored copy of an AD DS forest.

In short, AD LDS provides applications with the advantages of the AD DS environment, but without the NOS limitations that previously forced the implementation of multiple, cost-ineffective directories. Developers now can exploit the full functionality of Windows Server 2012 AD DS without limitation, while at the same time assuming the numerous advantages of integration into a common security structure.

Features of AD LDS

The following key points about AD LDS should be understood before installing it into an organization:

- Unlike AD DS, AD LDS does not support Global Catalogs, Group Policy, domains, forests, or domain trusts.
- AD LDS does not need to be installed on domain controllers. In fact, it is completely independent of the operating system, and more than one AD LDS entity can exist on each server.
- Management of AD LDS cannot be performed using the familiar AD DS tools such as Active Directory Users and Computers. Tools such as ADSIEdit or LDP.exe or a custom front end need to be used instead.

Installing AD LDS

Multiple AD LDS instances can be installed on the same server, or a single AD LDS instance can be replicated to multiple servers for redundancy. If installing the first AD LDS instance, follow these steps:

1. Open Server Manager by clicking the link on the taskbar.
2. Under Configure This Local Server, click Add Roles and Features.
3. On the Before You Begin page, review the notes provided, and click Next to continue.
4. Under Select Installation Type, select Role-Based or Feature-Based Installation and click Next.
5. Select the server from the server pool and click Next to continue.
6. From the list of server roles, shown in Figure 8.1, choose Active Directory Lightweight Directory Services by checking the box next to it, click Add Features when prompted, and then click Next to continue.
7. On the Select Features page, click Next to continue.
8. On the Introduction to Active Directory Lightweight Directory Services page, review the information provided, and click Next to continue.
9. Note the additional informational messages on the confirmation page, and then click the Install button.

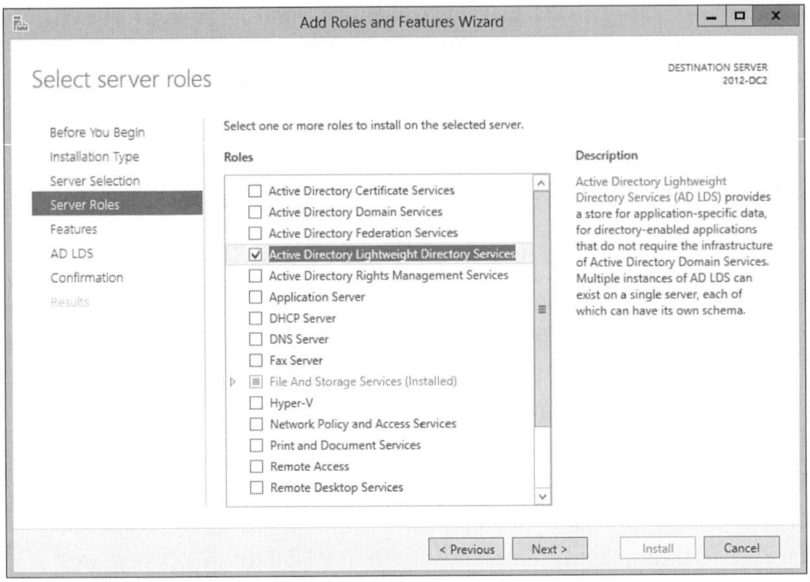

FIGURE 8.1 Installing the AD LDS role on a server.

10. Click Close when the Add Roles Wizard is complete.
11. Launch the Active Directory Lightweight Directory Services Setup Wizard from the Tools drop-down box in Server Manager.
12. Click Next at the Welcome screen.
13. From the dialog box shown in Figure 8.2, choose whether to create a new unique instance or a replica of an existing instance. In this example, we are creating a new instance from scratch. Click Next to continue.

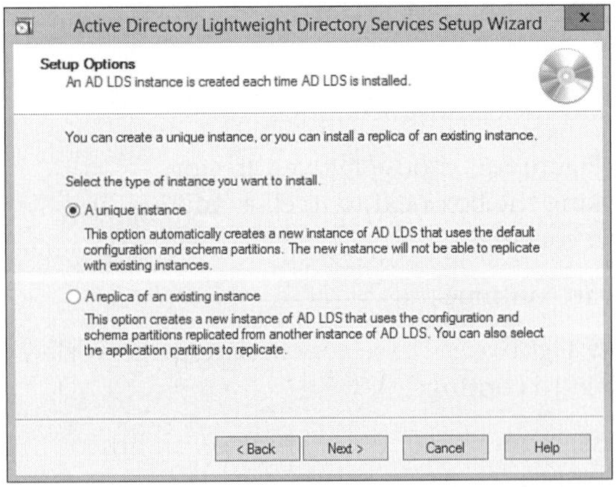

FIGURE 8.2 Installing AD LDS.

14. Type a name for the instance. This name should reflect what the AD LDS instance will be used for. Click Next to continue.

15. Enter the LDAP and LDAP port that will be used for this instance. If the default LDAP port of 389 or LDAPS port of 636 is already in use (for example, if the server is already running AD DS or if another instance of AD LDS is running), choose a unique port. In this example, we choose the default ports and click Next to continue.

16. On the Application Directory Partition page, shown in Figure 8.3, choose whether to create an Application Directory partition. If the application you will be installing creates its own partition, leave it as No. If it does not, and you need to create a partition manually to store objects in, enter it in distinguished name format (that is, `CN=PartitionName,DC=domain,DC=com`). Click Next to continue.

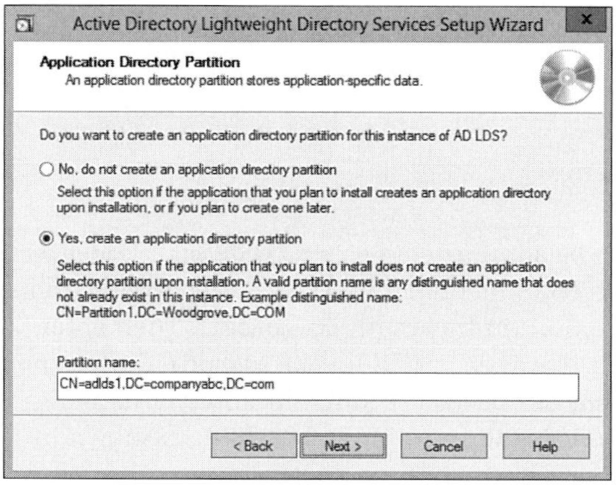

FIGURE 8.3 Configuring the Application Directory partition for AD LDS.

17. Select where to store the data and data recovery files for AD LDS on the File Locations page, and then click Next.

18. On the Service Account Selection page, select whether to use the network service account (the default) as the service account for this instance of AD LDS. Click Next to continue.

19. The subsequent page allows for a specific user or group to be defined as administrators for the AD LDS instance. A group account is recommended. After choosing This Account and adding the group, click Next to continue.

20. The Importing LDIF Files page, shown in Figure 8.4, allows for custom LDIF files to be imported. These LDIF files were created for specific scenarios that required AD LDS, such as when users will be created in AD LDS. In this example, we import the `MS-User.LDF` file, so we can create user class objects in the AD LDS instance. Check the boxes required and click Next to continue.

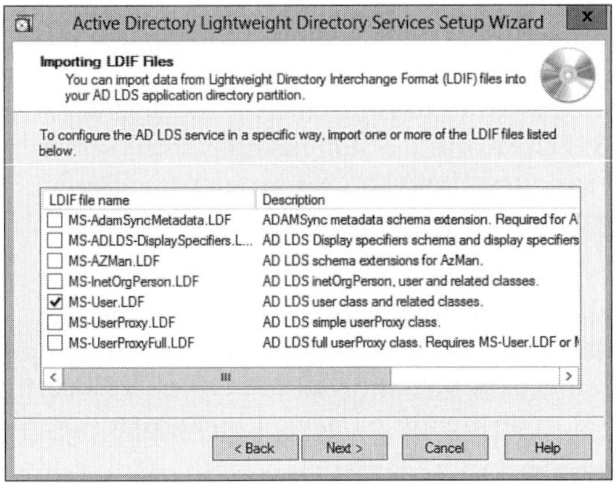

FIGURE 8.4 Importing LDIF files into the AD LDS instance.

21. On the summary page, review the selections and click Next to start the creation of the AD LDS instance.

22. Click Finish when the wizard is complete.

After being created, the AD LDS instance can be administered using ADSIEdit, a low-level directory tool available in the Administrative Tools menu. From ADSIEdit, choose Action, Connect To, and enter a name for the connection (in this example, `ADLDS1`). Then enter the naming context for the connection point that was created for the instance during the wizard (in our example, `CN=adlds1,DC=companyabc,DC=com`) and the local server name and custom port created for the computer (in this example, 2012-DC2:389), as shown in Figure 8.5.

FIGURE 8.5 Connecting to the AD LDS instance.

Although it is a much cruder tool to use than the full AD Users and Computers tool, ADSIEdit is very powerful, and full administration of the naming context for the AD LDS instance can be performed. In addition, some custom applications might have their own front end for AD LDS, allowing for eased administration of the instance.

Active Directory Federation Services

Active Directory Federation Services (AD FS) 2.1, included in Windows Server 2012, provides for Single Sign-On (SSO) capabilities across multiple platforms, including non-Microsoft environments. By managing web-based logon identities and tying them together, through Windows logon authentication, organizations can more easily manage customer access to web-based applications without compromising internal security infrastructure.

AD FS is managed from an MMC administrative tool, shown in Figure 8.6, and can be added as a server role in Windows Server 2012.

AD FS is not a replacement for technologies such as Forefront Identity Manager (FIM), a directory-sync product introduced later in this chapter. Instead of synchronizing identities across various directories as FIM does, AD FS manages logon attempts to web applications made from disparate directories. It is important to understand this concept as AD FS and FIM perform different roles in an organization's environment.

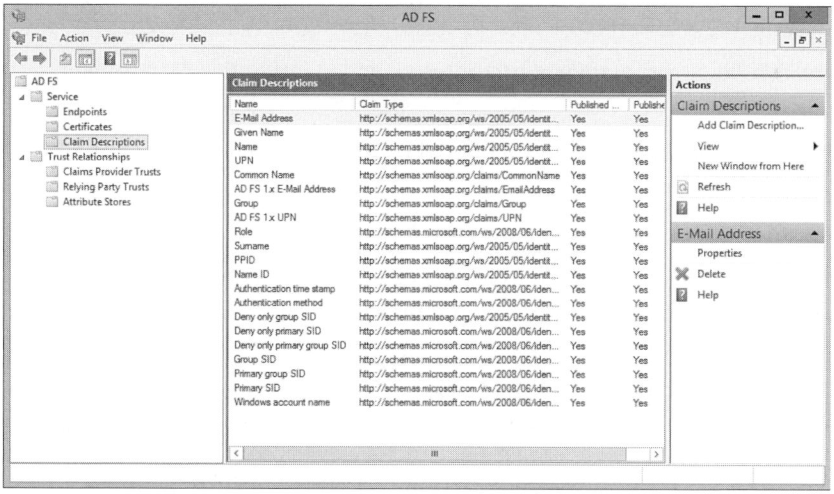

FIGURE 8.6 Viewing the AD FS MMC administrative tool.

Understanding the Key Components of AD FS

AD FS is composed of three different server components, as follows:

- **Federation server**—A federation server is the main AD FS component, which holds the Federation Service role. These servers route authentication requests between connected directories.
- **Federation proxy server**—A federation proxy server acts as a reverse proxy for AD FS authentication requests. This type of server normally resides in the demilitarized zone (DMZ) of a firewall, and is used to protect the back-end AD FS server from direct exposure to the untrusted Internet.
- **AD FS Web Agents**—The Web Agents component of AD FS hosts the claims-aware agent and the Windows token-based agent components that manage authentication cookies sent to web server applications.

Each one of these components can be individually installed in an AD FS structure, or they can be all installed on the same system.

Installing AD FS with Windows Server 2012

To install the AD FS role on a server, follow these steps:

1. Open Server Manager by clicking the link on the taskbar.
2. Under Configure This Local Server, click Add Roles and Features.
3. On the Before You Begin page, review the notes provided, and click Next to continue.
4. Under Select Installation Type, select Role-Based or Feature-Based Installation and click Next.
5. Select the server from the server pool, and click Next to continue.
6. From the list of server roles, choose Active Directory Federation Services by checking the box next to it, click Add Features when prompted, and then click Next to continue.
7. On the Introduction to Active Directory Federations Services page, review the information provided, and click Next to continue.
8. On the Select Role Services page, select which roles to install. After you have selected the appropriate check boxes, click Next to continue.
9. Click through the Web Server Role (IIS) dialog boxes (Next, Next) and accept the defaults.
10. Click Install to install the role. After installation, run the AD FS Configuration Wizard. (You can invoke it by clicking on Notifications – Run the AD FS Management snap-in – AD FS Federation Server Configuration Wizard.)

11. Select whether to create a new federation service or to add the server to an existing federation service and click Next.
12. Select whether to create a new federation server farm or a standalone federation server and click Next to continue. In this example, a standalone server is deployed.
13. Select whether to create a server authentication certificate or to choose an existing certificate installed on the server, as shown in Figure 8.7. Because Secure Sockets Layer (SSL) encryption is required for AD FS, a certificate from either a trusted internal certificate authority (CA) or an external trusted authority (most common scenario) must be used to install AD FS. Click Import if a certificate is available, but it must be installed locally on the server. After making your selection, click Next to continue.

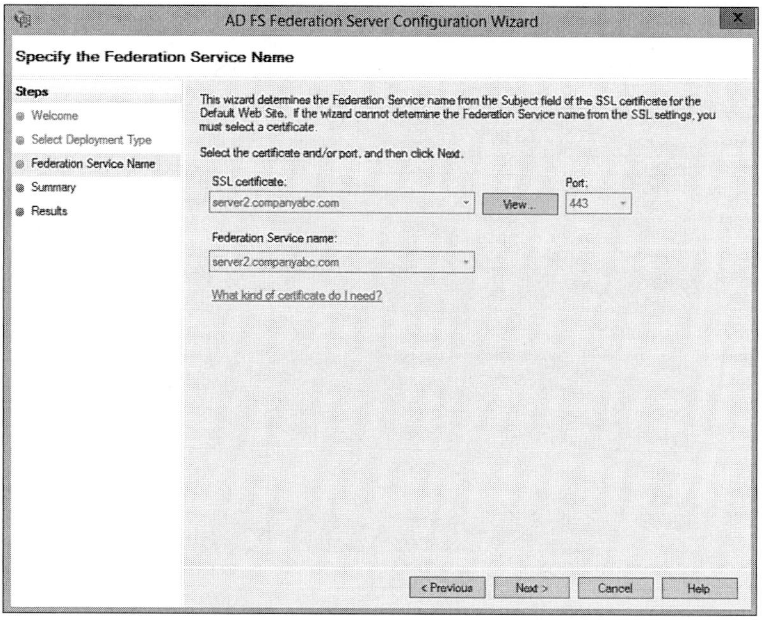

FIGURE 8.7 Selecting a certificate for AD FS.

14. Review the settings on the subsequent Ready to Apply Settings page and click Next to continue.
15. Click Close when the Add Roles Wizard is complete.

Working with AD FS

AD FS works by inputting information about connected partners, such as AD forests or AD LDS organizations, and inputting specific partner and application information. Each set of information can be inputted by running the various wizards installed by AD FS, as follows:

- **Add Claims Provider Trust Wizard**—This wizard, shown in Figure 8.8, allows for resource partners to be manually created or automatically imported by using an Extensible Markup Language (XML) file or by pointing to the published metadata the partner provides online. Resource partners contain information about the specific web-based applications that users can access.
- **Add Relying Party Trust Wizard**—This wizard adds the information about specific account partners, which consume claims in security tokens issued by AD FS.
- **Add Claim Description Wizard**—This wizard adds specific claims to AD FS so they can be used by specific applications.

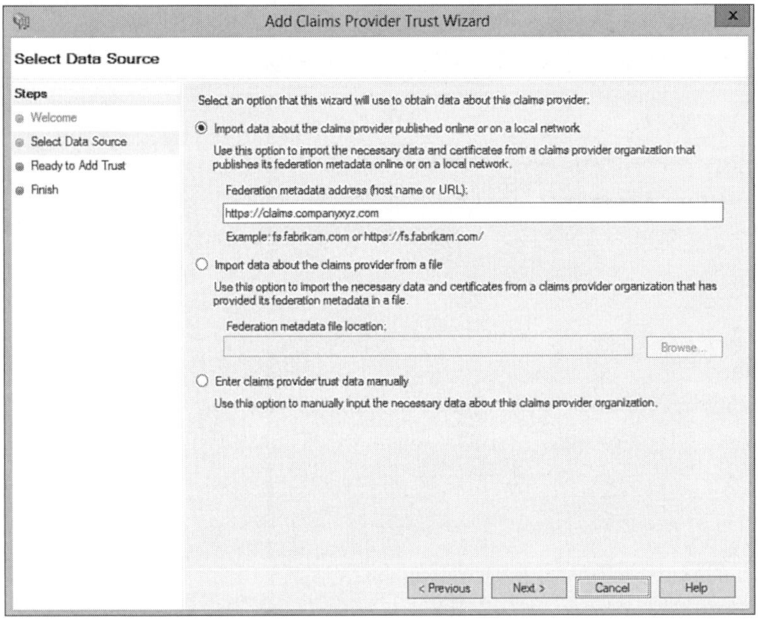

FIGURE 8.8 Selecting a trust policy for AD FS.

By entering in the information about the various web-based applications, and which directories and identities are to be granted access, AD FS can provide for seamless sign-on capabilities between various directories. It can be a valuable asset for an organization that wants to share corporate information with trusted partners, but without exposing their valuable internal assets to unnecessary exposure.

Synchronizing Directory Information with Forefront Identity Manager

Organizations today are faced with a proliferation of user identities across multiple directory platforms. They may have an AD DS user account, multiple NIS accounts, NDS,

Oracle, LDAP, or even more. Keeping these identities and passwords managed as well as synchronizing information between these accounts has proven to be a massive problem for these organizations.

In response to this problem, Microsoft originally developed Microsoft Metadirectory Services (MMS) to provide for identity synchronization between different directories. As the product improved, it was rereleased under the new name Microsoft Identity Integration Server (MIIS). For a third time, the tool was renamed, this time as Identity Lifecycle Manager (ILM) 2007. The latest and fourth rename of this tool is known as Forefront Identity Manager (FIM).

Understanding FIM

FIM enables a company to synchronize identity information across a wide variety of heterogeneous directory and identity stores. This enables customers to automate the process of updating identity information across heterogeneous platforms while maintaining the integrity and ownership of that data across the enterprise.

Password management capabilities enable end users or help desk staff to easily reset passwords across multiple systems from one easy-to-use web interface. End users and help desk staff no longer have to use multiple tools to change their passwords across multiple systems.

Understanding FIM Concepts

It is important to understand some key terms used with FIM before learning how you can use it to integrate various directories. Keep in mind that the following terms are used to describe FIM concepts but might also help give you a broader understanding of how metadirectories function in general:

- **Management agent (MA)**—A FIM MA is a tool used to communicate with a specific type of data source. For example, an Active Directory MA enables FIM to import or export data and perform tasks within Active Directory.
- **Connected data source**—A connected data source is simply just a data repository that contains identity information. A valid data source might be a SQL Database, text file, an LDAP Directory, and so on.
- **Connector namespace (CS)**—The connector namespace is the replicated information and container hierarchy extracted from or destined to the respective connected directory.
- **Metaverse namespace (MV)**—The metaverse namespace is the authoritative directory data created from the information gathered from each of the respective connector namespaces.
- **Metadirectory**—Within FIM, the metadirectory is made up of all the connector namespaces plus the authoritative metaverse namespace.

- **Attributes**—Attributes are the fields of information that are exported from or imported to directory entries. Common directory entry attributes are name, alias, email address, phone number, employee ID, or other information.

FIM can be used for many tasks, but is most commonly used for managing directory entry identity information. The intention here is to manage user accounts by synchronizing attributes, such as logon ID, first name, last name, telephone number, title, and department. For example, if a user named Jane Doe is promoted and her title is changed from manager to vice president, the title change could first be entered in the HR or Payroll databases; then through FIM MAs, the change could be replicated to other directories within the organization. This ensures that when someone looks up the title attribute for Jane Doe, it is the same in all the directories synchronized with FIM. This is a common and basic use of FIM referred to as identity management. Other common uses of FIM include account provisioning and group management.

NOTE

FIM is a versatile and powerful directory synchronization tool that can be used to simplify and automate some directory management tasks. Due to the nature of FIM, it can also be a very dangerous tool because MAs can have full access to the connected directories. Misconfiguration of FIM MAs could result in data loss, so careful planning and extensive lab testing should be performed before FIM is released to the production directories of any organization. In many cases, it might be prudent to contact Microsoft consulting services and certified Microsoft solution provider/partners to help an organization decide whether FIM is right for its environment, or even to design and facilitate the implementation.

Exploring FIM Account Provisioning

FIM enables administrators to easily provision and deprovision user accounts and identity information, such as distribution, email and security groups across systems, and platforms. Administrators can quickly create new accounts for employees based on events or changes in authoritative stores, such as the human resources system. In addition, as employees leave a company, they can be immediately deprovisioned from those same systems.

Account provisioning in FIM enables advanced configurations of directory MAs, along with special provisioning agents, to be used to automate account creation and deletion in several directories. For example, if a new user account is created in Active Directory, the Active Directory MA could tag this account. Then, when the respective MAs are run for other connected directories, a new user account could be automatically generated.

One enhancement of FIM over previous versions is that password synchronization is now supported for specific directories that manage passwords within the directory. FIM provides an application programming interface (API) accessed through the Windows Management Instrumentation (WMI). For connected directories that manage passwords in the directory's store, password management is activated when an MA is configured in Management Agent Designer. In addition to enabling password management for each MA,

Management Agent Designer returns a system nameattribute using the WMI interface for each connector space object.

Understanding the Role of Management Agents in FIM

An MA links a specific connected data source to the metadirectory. The MA is responsible for moving data from the connected data source and the metadirectory. When data in the metadirectory is modified, the MA can also export the data to the connected data source to keep the connected data source synchronized with the metadirectory. Generally, there is at least one MA for each connected directory.

NOTE

FIM includes integrated support for synchronization with additional directories such as SAP, Oracle, IBM, and Sun. In addition, it also introduced the ability for end users to reset their own passwords via a web management interface.

MAs contain rules that govern how an object's attributes are mapped, how connected directory objects are found in the metaverse, and when connected directory objects should be created or deleted.

These agents are used to configure how FIM will communicate and interact with the connected directories when the agent is run. When an MA is first created, all the configuration of that agent can be performed during that instance. The elements that can be configured include which type of directory objects will be replicated to the connector namespace, which attributes will be replicated, directory entry join and projection rules, attribute flow rules between the connector namespace and the metaverse namespace, plus more. If a necessary configuration is unknown during the MA creation, it can be revisited and modified later.

Managing Groups with FIM

Just as FIM can perform identity management for user accounts, it also can perform management tasks for groups. When a group is projected into the metaverse namespace, the group membership attribute can be replicated to other connected directories through their MAs. This enables a group membership change to occur in one directory and be replicated to other directories automatically.

Harnessing the Power and Potential of FIM

FIM is a very capable and powerful tool. With the right configuration and some fancy scripting, it can be configured to perform an incredible variety of automatic tasks. Today's environments are rife with directories, which increase the amount of administration required to create accounts, delete accounts, and update user information manually. FIM can greatly ease these requirements, improving administration and security, allowing for a user to manage multiple identities, such as what is illustrated in Figure 8.9. The next section focuses on some of the most valuable capabilities of FIM and how to use them effectively.

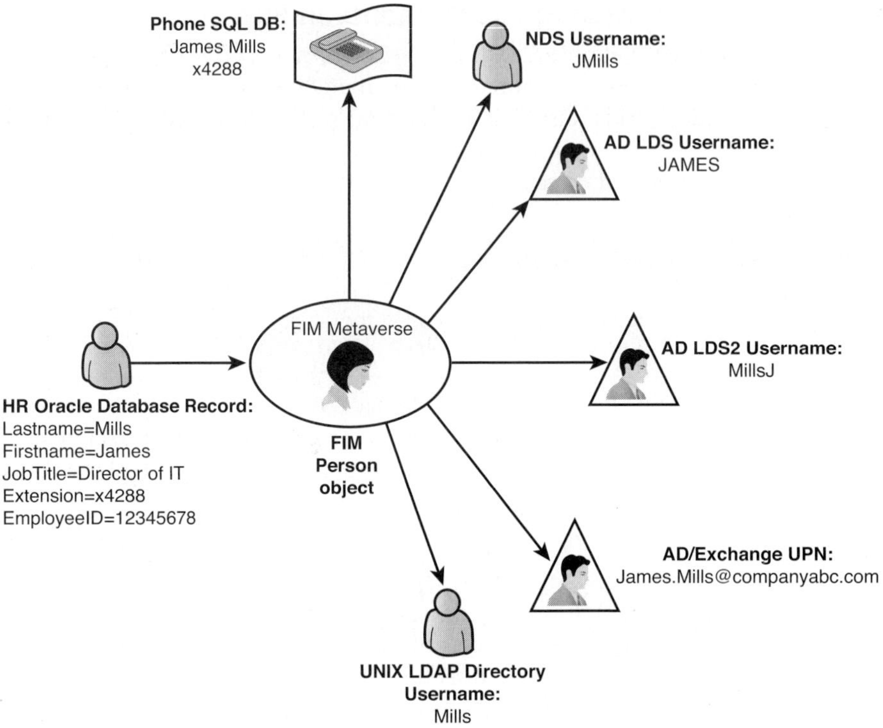

FIGURE 8.9 Synchronizing multiple identities with FIM.

Managing Identities with FIM

FIM can be used for the most basic and easiest configurations. For example, FIM can be used to synchronize identity information between accounts in different directories. Identity information could include names, email and physical addresses, titles, department affiliations, and much more. Generally speaking, identity information is the type of data commonly found in corporate phone books or intranets. To use FIM for identity management between Active Directory and an LDAP directory server, for example, follow these high-level steps:

1. Install the Synchronization Service component of FIM.
2. Create an MA for each of the directories, including an Active Directory management agent and an LDAP agent.
3. Configure the MAs to import directory object types into their respective connector namespaces.

4. Configure one of the MAs (for example, the Active Directory MA) to project the connector space directory objects and directory hierarchy into the metaverse namespace.

5. Within each of the management agents, a function can be configured called attribute flow to define which directory object attributes from each directory will be projected into the respective metaverse directory objects. Configure the attribute flow rules for each MA.

6. Configure the account-joining properties for directory objects. This is the most crucial step because it determines how the objects in each directory are related to one another within the metaverse namespace. To configure the account join, certain criteria such as an employee ID or first name and last name combination can be used. The key is to find the most unique combination to avoid problems when two objects with similar names are located (for example, if Active Directory contains two users named Toni Frankola).

7. After completely configuring the MAs and account joins, configure MA run profiles to tell the MA what to perform with the connected directory and connector namespace (for example, perform a full import or an export of data). The first time the MA is run, the connected directory information is imported to create the initial connector namespace.

8. After running the MAs once, they can be run a second time to propagate the authoritative metaverse data to the respective connector namespaces and out to the connected directories.

These steps can be used to simplify account maintenance tasks when several directories need to be managed simultaneously. In addition to performing identity management for user accounts, FIM can also be used to perform management tasks for groups. When a group is projected into the metaverse namespace, the group membership attribute can be replicated out to other connected directories through their management agents. This allows a group membership change to occur in one directory and be replicated to other directories automatically.

Provisioning and Deprovisioning Accounts with FIM

Account provisioning in FIM allows advanced configurations of directory MAs, along with special provisioning agents, to be used to automate account creation and deletion in several directories. For example, if a new user account is created in Active Directory, the Active Directory MA could tag this account. Then, when the respective MAs are run for other connected directories, a new user account can be automatically generated in those other accounts.

The provisioning and deprovisioning process in FIM can be an extremely useful tool in situations where automatic creation and deletion of user accounts is required. For example, a single user account can be created in an HR Oracle database, which can initiate a chain-event of account creations, as illustrated in Figure 8.9.

In addition to creating these accounts, all associated accounts can be automatically deleted through a deprovisioning process in FIM. By automating this process, administration of the multitude of user accounts in an organization can be simplified and the risk of accidentally leaving a user account enabled after an employee has been terminated can be minimized.

Summary

Active Directory as a platform provides for powerful tools to allow organizations to centralize and store information about users and other objects in an organization. The efficiencies built in to having a centralized directory platform are greatly diminished if multiple directory platforms, each with its own disparate users and attributes, are maintained. Tools from Microsoft, such as the Forefront Identity Manager (FIM) product, enable administrators to synchronize across these directories and to keep organizational information standardized across multiple platforms.

In addition to directory-sync technologies such as FIM, Microsoft offers support for products such as AD FS and AD LDS, thus allowing organizations to streamline identity logons and create personalized directories for applications. Through proper use of these technologies, organizations can take greater advantage of the knowledge that is traditionally distributed across multiple technologies.

Best Practices

The following are best practices from this chapter:

- Use FIM or another metadirectory management tool to keep disparate directories synchronized.
- Use AD LDS for applications that require custom schema changes, and keep the information in those AD LDS instances synchronized to a central AD DS farm with the use of FIM.
- Use AD FS 2.0 to provide for Single Sign-On to claims-aware applications on the Internet, such as those that use SAML 2.0 tokens.
- Use AD FS for Single Sign-On support across multiple platforms.
- Consider using FIM for automatic provisioning/provisioning of user accounts across multiple directories. By establishing a firm policy on deprovisioning accounts that are no longer active, greater overall security can be achieved.
- Consider deploying AD LDS on Windows Server 2012 Server Core to reduce the attack surface area of the server.

CHAPTER 9

Integrating AD in a UNIX Environment

IN THIS CHAPTER

In the past, Microsoft had a bad reputation for giving the impression that its technologies would be the only ones deployed at organizations. The toolsets available to coexist in cross-platform environments were often weak and were provided mostly as a direct means to migrate from those environments to Microsoft environments. The introduction of Windows Server 2012, however, coincides with the maturation of technologies from Microsoft that simplify and expand the ability to integrate with UNIX environments.

This chapter focuses on those technologies, and pays considerable attention to the Server for NFS role service in Windows Server 2012 and how it can be used to integrate UNIX clients together with file services running on Windows Server 2012.

Understanding and Using Windows Server 2012 UNIX Integration Components

Microsoft has a long history of not "playing well" with other technologies. With Windows Server 2012, Microsoft provides native support for Windows Server 2012 UNIX Integration, a series of technologies that was previously included in a product line called Windows Services for UNIX (SFU). With Windows Server 2012, several of the components of the old SFU product are included as integrated services in the Windows Server 2012 OS.

For many years, UNIX and Windows systems were viewed as separate, incompatible environments that were physically, technically, and ideologically different. Over the years, however, organizations found that supporting two completely separate topologies within their environments was inefficient and expensive; a great deal of redundant work was also required to maintain multiple sets of user accounts, passwords, environments, and so on.

Slowly, the means to interoperate between these environments was developed. At first, most of the interoperability tools were written to join UNIX with Windows, as evidenced by Samba, a method for Linux/UNIX platforms to be able to access Windows file shares. Microsoft tools always seemed a step behind that available elsewhere. With Windows Server 2012 UNIX Integration tools, Microsoft leapfrogs traditional solutions, like Samba, and becomes a leader for cross-platform integration. Cross-platform file access, the capability to run UNIX scripts on Windows, joint security credentials, and the like were presented as viable options and can now be considered as part of a migration to or interoperability scenario with Windows Server 2012.

The Development of Windows Server 2012 UNIX Integration Components

Windows Server 2012 UNIX Integration has made large strides in its development since the original attempts Microsoft made in this area. Originally released as a package of products called Services for UNIX (SFU), it received initial skepticism. Since then, the line of technologies has developed into a formidable integration and migration utility that allows for a great deal of inter-environmental flexibility. The first versions of the software, 1.x and 2.x, were limited in many ways, however. Subsequent updates to the software vastly improved its capabilities and further integrated it with the core operating system.

A watershed development in the development of SFU was the introduction of the 3.0 version of the software. This version enhanced support for UNIX through the addition or enhancement of nearly all components. Included was the Interix product, as well, an extension to the POSIX infrastructure of Windows to support UNIX scripting and applications natively on a Windows server.

Then, version 3.5 of SFU was released, which included several functionality improvements over Windows SFU 3.0. The following components and improvements were made in the 3.5 release:

- Greater support for Windows Server Active Directory (AD) authentication
- Improved utilities for international language support
- Threaded application support in Interix (separated into a separate application in Windows Server 2012 and named the Subsystem for UNIX-based Applications)
- Support for the Volume Shadow Copy Service of Windows Server 2012

Finally, we come to the Windows Server 2012 version of what was previously SFU, which was broken into several components that became embedded into the OS. No longer were the components a part of a separate package. Instead, the components were built in to the various server roles on the operating system for the first time.

The following is a list of improvements to the UNIX integration in the platform that were first included with Windows Server 2008 and are still provided in Windows Server 2012.

- AD lookup capabilities through the inclusion of Group ID (GID) and User ID (UID) fields in the AD schema
- Enhanced UNIX support with multiple versions supported, including Solaris v9, Red Hat Linux v9, IBM AIX version 5L 5.2, and Hewlett Packard HP-UX version 11i
- Ability for the Telnet Server component to accept both Windows and UNIX clients
- Removal of the User Mapping component and transfer of the functionality directly into the AD DS schema
- NFS server functionality expanded to Mac OS X and higher clients

Finally, some minor changes were added to the UNIX support in Windows Server 2008 R2 and now also supported in Windows Server 2012. These include the following, all related to the Services for NFS component:

- Net group support, which provides the ability to create and manage networkwide named groups of hosts.
- Unmapped UNIX user access: This functionality allows Network File System (NFS) data to be stored on Windows servers without first creating UNIX to Windows account mapping.
- RPCSEC_GSS support: Provides for native support of this RPC security feature. Windows Server 2012 does not provide support for the RPCSEC_GSS privacy security service, however.
- Windows Management Instrumentation (WMI) management support
- Kerberos authentication (Krb5 and Krb5i) on shares

Understanding the UNIX Interoperability Components in Windows Server 2012

Windows Server 2012 UNIX Integration is composed of several key components, each of which provides a specific integration task with different UNIX environments. Any or all of these components can be used as part of Windows Server 2012 UNIX Integration, as the installation of the suite can be customized, depending on an organization's needs. The major components of Windows Server 2012 UNIX Integration are as follows:

- Server for NFS
- Client for NFS
- Telnet Server (supports Windows and UNIX clients)
- Subsystem for UNIX-based Applications (SUA) (deprecated but still supported in this release)

Each component can be installed as part of a server role (Server for NFS) or as a feature (Client for NFS). For example, the Services for NFS component is installed as part of the File Services role in Windows Server 2012. Each component is described in more detail in the following sections.

Prerequisites for Windows Server 2012 UNIX Integration

Windows Server 2012 UNIX services interoperate with various flavors of UNIX, including, but not necessarily limited to the following:

- Sun Solaris 7.x, 8.x, 9.x, or 10
- Red Hat Linux 8.0 and later
- Hewlett-Packard HP-UX 11i
- IBM AIX 5L 5.2
- Apple Macintosh OS X

NOTE

Windows Server 2012 UNIX Integration is not limited to these versions of Sun Solaris, Red Hat Linux, HP-UX, IBM AIX, and Apple OS X. It actually performs quite well in various other similar versions and implementations of UNIX, Linux, and Mac OS X.

Installing Services for Network File System

The installation of Windows Server 2012 UNIX Integration for Windows Server 2012 is as simple as adding specific server roles to a server using the Add Roles Wizard. The individual components can be installed as part of different roles added to the server. For example, to add the Services for NFS role, simply add the File Services role to a server as follows:

1. From Server Manager, click Manage – Add Roles and Features.
2. Click Next at the Before You Begin screen.
3. Choose a Role-Based or Feature-Based Installation and click Next.
4. Select the server from the server pool where the component will be installed and click Next.
5. From the list of roles to install, expand File and Storage Services, check the box for File Services and the sub-box for Server for NFS shown in Figure 9.1, and then click Next to continue.
6. At the Features dialog box, click Next to continue.
7. Click Install to finish the installation.
8. Click Close when the wizard completes.

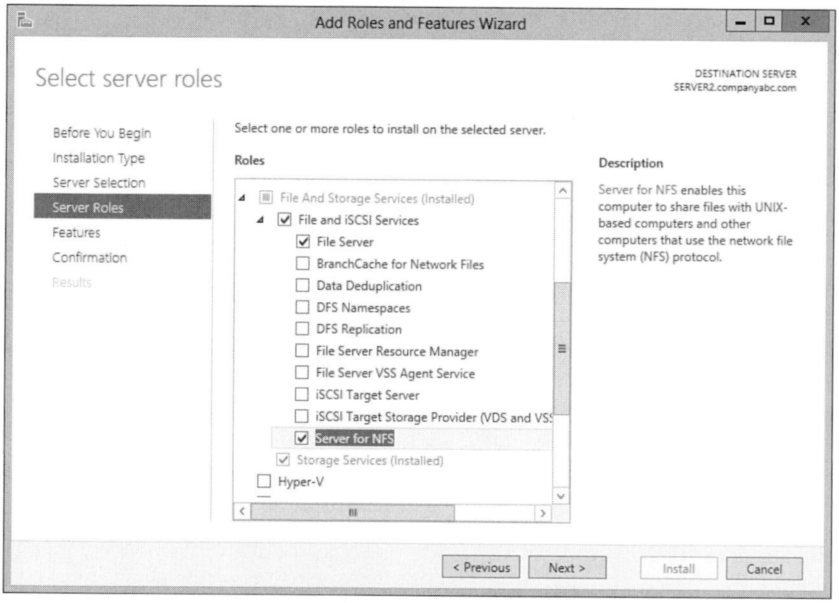

FIGURE 9.1 Installing Server for NFS.

NOTE

If the File Services role has already been installed, you can add the Server for NFS role by rerunning the wizard and selecting the subcomponent of the File Services role.

The Client for NFS role can also be added by checking the associated box in the Add Features screen. Both components make up the Services for NFS toolkit, which streamlines the sharing of information between UNIX and Windows Server 2012, allowing users from both environments to seamlessly access data from each separate environment, without the need for specialized client software. Utilizing the Services for NFS and NFS Client allows for this level of functionality and provides for a more integrated environment.

Using and Administering Services for NFS

The Services for NFS component acts as a UNIX-standard NFS server by providing disk space from any Windows-based computer on a network to NFS clients, translating their NFS requests to Windows Server Message Block (SMB)-based requests. No additional client software is necessary, and the Windows Server 2012 server acts and functions like a normal NFS-based UNIX server for these clients. This is a great way to bring a standardized share format to a heterogeneous network as UNIX and Apple clients might have difficulties using standard Windows file protocols such as Common Internet File System (CIFS).

After you install Services for NFS, you need to complete several tasks before accepting UNIX clients to the Windows file shares. These tasks include the following, covered in more detail in the following sections of this chapter:

- Configure AD DS lookup for UNIX GID and UID
- Configure the Server for NFS and Client for NFS components
- Create NFS shared network resources

Configuring Active Directory Lookup for UNIX GID and UID Information

So that NTFS permissions can be properly mapped to UNIX user accounts, integration with Active Directory Domain Services (AD DS) must be set up between AD DS and UNIX. This requires the proper schema extensions to be enabled in the domain. By default, Windows Server 2012 AD DS includes these schema extensions. If installing Services for NFS into a down-level schema version of AD, such as with Windows Server 2003, the schema must be extended first to Windows Server 2012 levels.

To enable AD DS lookup for Services for NFS, do the following:

1. Open Server Manager, select Tools and then select Services for Network File System.
2. Right-click the Services for NFS node in the node pane, and choose Properties.
3. In the Identity Mapping Source section, check the Active Directory Domain Name check box, and enter the name of the domain in which identity mapping will be enabled, as shown in Figure 9.2.
4. Click OK to save the changes.

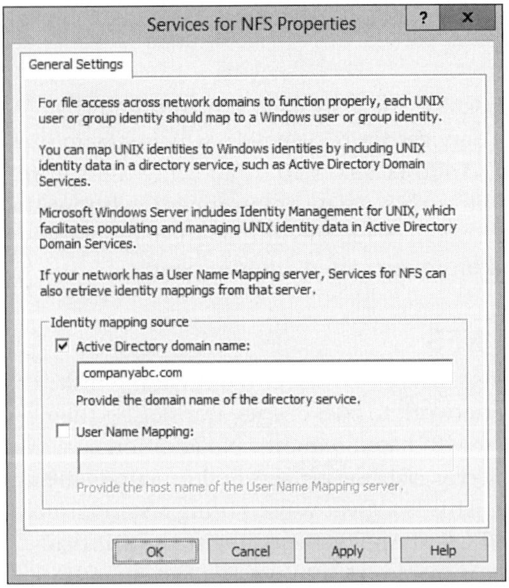

FIGURE 9.2 Enabling AD DS mapping for Services for NFS.

NOTE

Windows Server 2012 Services for NFS still supports the legacy User Name Mapping service, although installation of the User Name Mapping service itself cannot be done on a Windows Server 2012 server. It is preferable to use the AD DS integration, however, rather than the User Name Mapping service.

Configuring Client for NFS and Server for NFS Settings

After enabling the lookup method used for Services for NFS, you can configure the individual Server for NFS and Client for NFS settings by right-clicking the individual nodes and choosing Properties. This allows you to change default file permissions levels, TCP and UDP settings, mount types, new Windows Server 2012 Kerberos settings, and filename support levels. For example, in Figure 9.3, the screen for customizing Client for NFS settings is displayed.

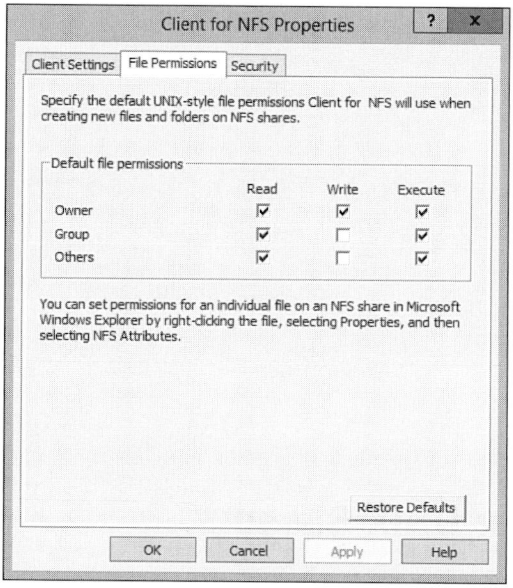

FIGURE 9.3 Customizing Client for NFS settings.

Creating NFS Shared Network Resources

Configuring a shared resource with Server for NFS requires opening the PowerShell window with elevated privileges and then creating the share using the `nfsshare` command-line utility. Type `nfsshare /?` for the exact syntax.

To create an NFS shared network resource using the GUI interface, follow these steps:

1. From Windows Explorer on the server, navigate to the folder that will be shared, right-click it, and choose Properties.

2. Select the NFS Sharing tab.
3. Click the Manage NFS Sharing button.
4. Check the Share This Folder check box, as shown in Figure 9.4. Configure if anonymous access will be allowed (not normally recommended) or configure any special permissions by clicking Permissions.
5. Click OK, and then click Close to save the changes.

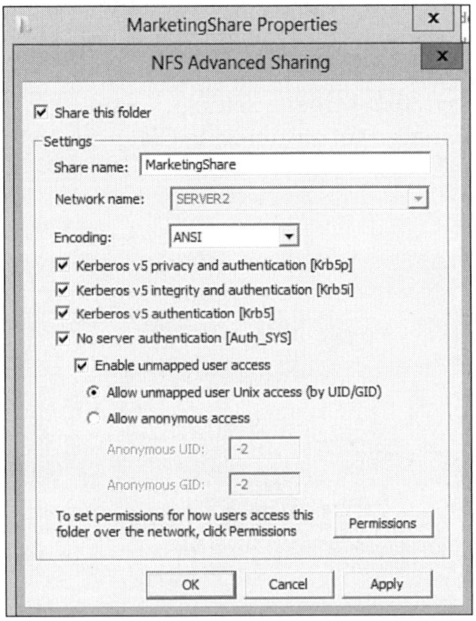

FIGURE 9.4 Creating a shared resource for NFS.

Reviewing the Subsystem for UNIX-Based Applications

The Subsystem for UNIX-based Applications (SUA), previously referred to as Interix, fills the gap between development on UNIX platforms and development in Windows. It was written to allow programmers familiar with UNIX to continue to use the most familiar programming tools and scripts, such as grep, tar, cut, awk, vi, and many others. In addition, with limited reprogramming efforts, applications that run on UNIX-based systems can be ported over to the Wintel platform.

NOTE

While the SUA is still supported as a feature in Windows Server 2012, it has been officially deprecated by Microsoft, so it is not recommended for installation for new coding efforts. Microsoft provides support to allow clients to transition off of the technology.

Installing the Subsystem for UNIX-Based Applications

The SUA component is available as a feature on Windows Server 2012. You can install it as follows:

1. From Server Manager, click Manage – Add Roles and Features.
2. Click Next at the Before You Begin screen.
3. Choose a Role-Based or Feature-Based Installation and click Next.
4. Select the server from the server pool where the component will be installed and click Next.
5. From the list of roles to install, click Next to continue (because the SUA component is not a role, but a feature).
6. Select the Subsystem for UNIX-based Applications from the Features list and click Next to continue.
7. Click Install, and then click Close when complete.

Subsystem for UNIX-Based Applications Scripting

Administrators familiar with UNIX environments will feel at home working with Interix because both the Korn and C shells are available, and both behave exactly as they would in UNIX. Windows Server 2012 UNIX Integration also supports the single-rooted file system through these shells, which negates the need to convert scripts to support drive letters. The single-rooted file system allows for a great deal of functionality, allowing scripts written for UNIX to more natively port over to a Windows environment.

Subsystem for UNIX-Based Application Tools and Programming Languages

SUA supports all common UNIX tools and utilities, with all the familiar commands such as grep, man, env, pr, nice, ps, kill, and many others. Each tool was built to respond exactly the way it is expected to behave in UNIX, and SUA users can build or import their own customizable tools using the same procedures that they would in a UNIX environment.

Administrative Improvements with Windows Server 2012

One of the main focuses of Windows Server 2012 UNIX Integration was the ability to gain a better measure of centralized control over multiple environments. Tools such as an enhanced Telnet server and client, ActivePerl 5.6 for scripting, and a centralized Microsoft Management Console (MMC) Admin console make the administration of the Windows Server 2012 UNIX Integration components easier than ever. Combined with the improved MMC interface and PowerShell support in Windows Server 2012, it is easier than ever to manage mixed environments from the Windows platform.

Performing Remote Administration with Telnet Server and Client

Windows Server 2012 UNIX Integration uses a single Telnet service to provide for Telnet functionality to both Windows and UNIX clients. This was a change over the way that it previously was, as two separate components were installed. This version of Windows Server 2012 Telnet Server supports NT LAN Manager (NTLM) authentication in addition to the basic logon that supports UNIX users.

To install the Telnet Server component follow these steps:

1. From Server Manager, click Manage – Add Roles and Features.
2. Click Next at the Before You Begin screen.
3. Choose a Role-Based or Feature-Based Installation and click Next.
4. Select the server from the server pool where the component will be installed and click Next.
5. Click through the role list without selecting anything (click Next.)
6. At the Features dialog box, check the box next to the Telnet Server role, as shown in Figure 9.5. Click Next to continue.
7. Review the settings and click Install.

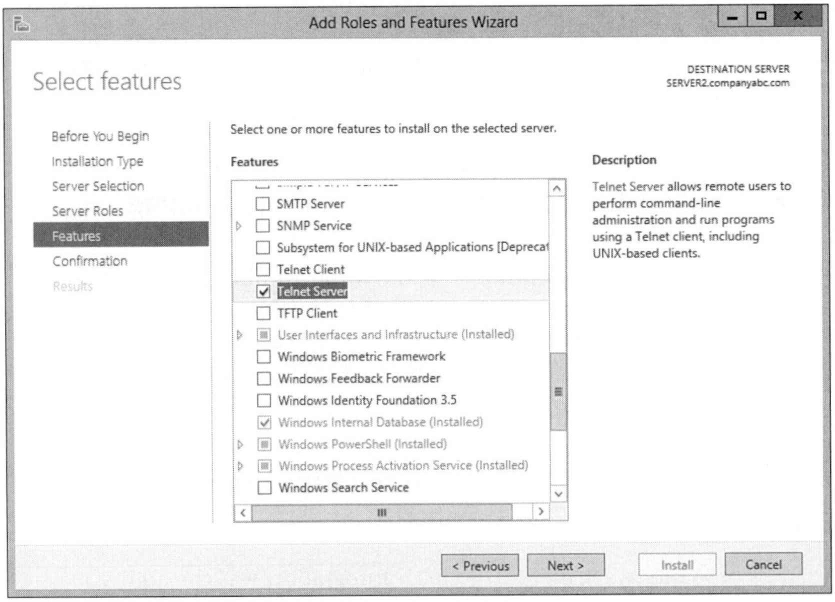

FIGURE 9.5 Installing the Telnet Server role for UNIX clients.

8. When the wizard is finished, click Close.

Summary

Integration of key Microsoft technology with non-Microsoft environments is no longer an afterthought with the maturation of the major products detailed in this chapter. No longer a separate product, integration with UNIX is built in to the OS with components such as Server for NFS, Client for NFS, and UNIX Telnet support. Proper utilization of Windows UNIX integration components can help to lower the total cost of ownership associated with maintaining multiple platform environments. In addition, these technologies bring closer the lofty ideal of bringing multiple directory environments under a single directory umbrella through the realization of Single Sign-On and other key functionality that integrates directories with Windows Server 2012.

Best Practices

The following are best practices from this chapter:

- Install the Services for NFS components to provide cross-platform access to File Services for both Windows and UNIX/Mac clients.
- Transition off of SUA when possible as Microsoft has deprecated this tool.
- Use the ForeFront Identity Manager (FIM) product for more advanced scenarios where automatic provisioning/deprovisioning of UNIX and AD DS accounts is required.

CHAPTER 10

Domain Name System, WINS, and DNSSEC

IN THIS CHAPTER

Name resolution is a key component in any network operating system (NOS) implementation. The capability of any one resource to locate other resources is the centerpiece of a functional network. Consequently, the name-resolution strategy chosen for a particular NOS must be robust and reliable, and it ideally will conform to industry standards.

Windows Server 2012 utilizes the domain name system (DNS) as its primary method of name resolution, and DNS is a vital component of any Active Directory implementation. Windows Server 2012's DNS implementation was designed to be compliant with the key Request For Comments (RFCs) that define the nature of how DNS should function. This makes it particularly beneficial for existing network implementations because it allows Windows Server 2012 to interoperate with other types of RFC-compliant DNS implementations.

IPv6 is rapidly gaining traction in the IT world and is an integral feature of the Windows Server 2012 operating system. Windows Server 2012 supports IPv4 fully in roles such as DNS, Dynamic Host Configuration Protocol (DHCP), and Internet Information Services (IIS). Windows Server 2012 even includes additional features such as the GlobalNames zone (GNZ) to support single-label names with IPv6.

The second type of name resolution, mapping legacy Microsoft NetBIOS names into IP addresses, is provided by Windows Internet Naming Service (WINS). Although it is technically possible (and ideal) to create a Windows Server 2012 environment free of NetBIOS name resolution, the truth is that divorcing a network from WINS dependency is very difficult, so it will likely remain an active part of network services in most organizations, at least for a few more years. You can find more information about WINS in the "Reviewing the Windows Internet Naming Service" section later in this chapter.

NOTE

When Windows Server 2008 DNS service was released, it introduced a new feature known as the GNZ. The GNZ provided single-label name resolution for large enterprise networks that do not deploy WINS and for which using DNS name suffixes to provide single-label name resolution was not practical. Windows 2012 supports the GNZ.

Windows 2012 introduces two major changes in the DNS services: an enhanced DNS Security Extensions (DNSSEC) and enhanced PowerShell support. Introduced to the platform in Windows 2008, DNSSEC in Windows 2012 now includes online signing and automated key management to allow signing of Active Directory integrated zones and easier management. PowerShell now has feature parity with the traditional DNSCMD.EXE tool, allowing administrators to switch to PowerShell for all DNS administration and automation.

This chapter details the key components of DNS in general and provides an overview of Windows Server 2012's specific implementation of DNS. A particular emphasis is placed on the role of DNS in Active Directory Domain Services (AD DS) and the way it fits in standard and nonstandard configurations. Step-by-step instructions outline how to install and configure specific DNS components on Windows Server 2012. In addition, troubleshooting DNS issues and specific Active Directory design scenarios help to give a hands-on approach to your understanding of DNS.

The Need for DNS

Computers and humans conceptualize in drastically different ways. In terms of understanding locations, humans are much better at grasping the concept of names rather than numbers. For example, most people think of cities by their names, not by their ZIP codes. Computers, however, work in binary, and subsequently prefer to work with numbers. For example, computers at the post office translate the city and address names into specific ZIP codes for that region, helping each letter reach its destination.

Name resolution for computer systems works in a similar way. A user-friendly name is translated into a computer-identifiable number. TCP/IP uses a number scheme that uniquely identifies each computer interface on a network by a series of numbers, such as 10.1.2.145, known as an IP address. Because most humans are not interested in memorizing several of these types of numbers, they must be easily resolvable into user-friendly names such as www.microsoft.com.

DNS, in its simplest form, provides for name resolution in a distributed fashion, with each server or set of servers controlling a specified zone and with entries for each resource called resource records (RRs) that indicate the location of a particular object.

A good analogy for DNS can be found in telephone books. Each city or metropolitan area (namespace) publishes a separate phone book (zone) that contains many listings (resource records) that map people's names to their phone numbers (IP addresses). This simple example illustrates the basic principle behind DNS. When you understand these basics, further drilling down into the specifics, especially with regard to Windows Server 2012's DNS, is possible.

History of DNS

The Internet, as originally implemented, utilized a simple text file called a HOSTS file that contained a simple list of all servers on the Internet and their corresponding IP addresses. This file was copied manually from the master server to multiple secondary HOSTS servers. As more and more servers were added to the Internet, however, updating this file became unmanageable, and a new system became necessary.

In 1983, in direct response to this problem, the RFCs for the DNS were drawn up, and this form of name resolution was implemented on a large scale across the Internet. Instead of a small number of static HOSTS files, DNS servers formed a hierarchical method of name resolution, in which servers resolved only a certain segment of hosts on the Internet and delegated requests that it did not manage. This allowed the number of records held in DNS to scale enormously, without a subsequently large performance decrease.

Microsoft developed its own implementation of DNS in Windows NT 4.0, which was based on the RFC standards on which DNS was founded. With the introduction of Windows 2000, Microsoft adopted DNS as the principle name-resolution strategy for Microsoft products. Older, legacy name-resolution systems such as WINS are slowly being phased out. Since that time, the DNS implementation used by Microsoft has evolved to include a number of key benefits that distinguish it from standard DNS implementations (for example, UNIX BIND). To understand these improvements, however, you first need a basic understanding of DNS functionality.

Establishing a Framework for DNS

DNS structure is closely tied to the structure of the Internet and often is confused with the Internet itself. The structure of DNS is highly useful, and the fact that it has thrived for so long is a tribute to its functionality. A closer examination of what constitutes DNS and how it is logically structured is important in understanding the bigger picture of how DNS fits into Windows Server 2012.

Explaining the DNS Hierarchy

DNS uses a hierarchical approach to name resolution in which resolution is passed up and down a hierarchy of domain names until a particular computer is located. Each level of the hierarchy is divided by dots (.), which symbolize the division. A fully qualified domain name (FQDN), such as server1.sales.companyabc.com, uniquely identifies a resource's space in the DNS hierarchy. Figure 10.1 shows how the fictional CompanyABC fits into the DNS hierarchy.

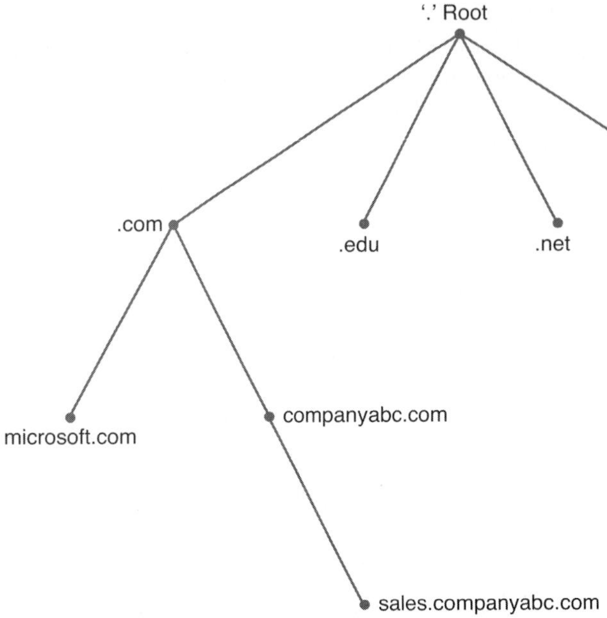

FIGURE 10.1 DNS hierarchy.

The top of the hierarchy is known as the root, and is represented by a single . (dot). Moving down the DNS hierarchy, the next layer in the model is made up of top-level domain (TLD) names, which are .com, .net, .gov, .fr, and similar domain namespaces that loosely define the particular category that a domain namespace fits into. The Internet Assigned Numbers Authority (IANA) oversees the global root zone management and management of the TLDs. The IANA is operated by the Internet Corporation for Assigned Names and Numbers (ICANN). The official list of all generic TLDs maintained by IANA is given in Table 10.1.

TABLE 10.1 List of Generic Top-Level Domain Names

TLD	Purpose
.aero	Air Travel Industry
.asia	Asia-Pacific Region
.biz	Businesses
.cat	Catalan Language
.com	Commercial
.coop	Cooperatives
.edu	Educational Institutions
.gov	U.S. Government
.info	Informational

TLD	Purpose
.int	International Organizations
.jobs	Companies (Job Postings)
.mil	U.S. Military
.mobi	Mobile Devices
.museum	Museums
.name	Individuals
.net	Network
.org	Organization
.pro	Professions
.tel	Internet Communications
.travel	Travel and Tourism Industry
.xxx	Adult Entertainment

For example, educational institutions are commonly given .edu extensions, and commercial businesses are given .com extensions. These extensions form the first set of branches to the DNS tree. The .biz, .com, .info, .name, .net, and .org are all open TLDs, meaning any individual or entity can register the domains. Other TLDs have restrictions based on the intended use.

In addition to the generic TLDs, the IANA maintains country-code TLDs. These country codes are the two-letter codes specified in International Organization for Standardization (ISO) 3166 standard. For example, .co is maintained for Colombia and .fr is maintained for France. Interestingly, all the country-code TLDs listed in ISO 3166 are maintained, but some are unused, such as the Saint Martin (.mf). There are also a handful of exceptions, such as the listing for United Kingdom, which is listed in the ISO 3166 standard as .gb, but .uk is used instead.

The second level in the DNS hierarchy commonly contains the business name of an organization, such as companyabc in Figure 10.1. This level is normally the first area in the DNS hierarchy where an organization has control over the records within the domain and where it can be authoritative.

Subdomains can easily be, and often are, created in the DNS hierarchy for various reasons. For example, sales.microsoft.com is a potential domain that could exist as a sublevel of the microsoft.com domain. The DNS hierarchy works in this way, with multiple levels possible.

The DNS Namespace

The bounded area that is defined by the DNS name is known as the DNS namespace. microsoft.com is a namespace, as is marketing.companyabc.com. Namespaces can be either public or private. Public namespaces are published on the Internet and are defined by a set of standards. All the .com, .net, .org, and similar namespaces are external, or public. An internal namespace is not published to the Internet, but is also not restricted by extension name. In other words, an internal, unpublished namespace can occupy any conceivable namespace, such as companyabc.local or companyabc.internal. Internal namespaces are most often used with Active Directory because they give increased security to a namespace. Because such namespaces are not published, they cannot be directly accessed from the Internet.

Getting Started with DNS on Windows Server 2012

To fully understand the capabilities that Windows Server 2012 offers for DNS, the product should be installed in a lab environment. This helps to conceptualize the various components of DNS that are presented in this chapter.

Installing DNS Using the Add Roles Wizard

Although you can install and configure DNS in various ways, the most straightforward and complete process involves invoking the Add Roles Wizard and the subsequent Configure a DNS Server Wizard. The process detailed in this section illustrates the installation of a standard zone. Multiple variations of the installation are possible, but this particular scenario is illustrated to show the basics of DNS installation.

NOTE

It is recommended that DNS servers be configured with static IPv4 addresses because if the IP address changes, clients might be unable to contact the DNS server.

Installation of DNS on Windows Server 2012 is straightforward, and no reboot is necessary. To install and configure the DNS role on a Windows Server 2012 computer, follow these steps:

1. Launch Server Manager from a Windows 2012 server with a full GUI.
2. Select the Dashboard section and click the Add Roles and Features link.
3. Click Next on the Before You Begin page.
4. Leave the default selection Role-Based or Feature-Based Installation and click Next.
5. Select the server from the server pool to add the DNS role to and click Next.
6. Select the DNS Server Role check box and click Next.

NOTE

When the DNS Role box is checked, the Add Roles and Features Wizard does a readiness check to ensure that the target server is ready for the DNS role. For example, if a static IP address is not set for the target server, a warning will pop up.

7. Click Next to skip the Features selection.
8. Click Next on the Introduction to DNS Server page.
9. Click Install on the Confirmation page to install the DNS role.
10. Click Close to exit the Add Roles and Features Wizard.

The DNS role can also be installed locally on a server core installation using PowerShell with the following command:

```
Install-WindowsFeature -Name DNS-Server-Full-Role
```

The DNS role has been installed on the Windows Server 2012 server, but has not been configured. To configure the role, complete the following steps:

1. Launch Server Manager from a Windows 2012 server with a full GUI.
2. Select the DNS section. The list of servers in the server pool with the DNS role installed will be shown.
3. Right-click the DNS server to configure and select DNS Manager.
4. Select the DNS server name to configure.
5. Select Action, Configure a DNS Server.
6. On the Welcome page for the Configure a DNS Server Wizard, click Next to continue.
7. Select Create Forward and Reverse Lookup Zones (Recommended for Large Networks), and then click Next.
8. Select Yes, Create a Forward Lookup Zone Now (Recommended), and then click Next.
9. Select the type of zone to be created—in this case, choose Primary Zone—and click Next. If the server is a writable domain controller, the Store the Zone in Active Directory check box is available.
10. If storing the zone in Active Directory, select the replication scope and click Next.
11. Type the FQDN of the zone in the Zone Name box, and then click Next.
12. At this point, if creating a non-AD-integrated zone, you can create a new zone text file or import one from an existing zone file. In this case, choose Create a New File with This File Name, and accept the default. Click Next to continue.
13. The subsequent page allows a zone to either accept or decline dynamic updates. For this example, leave dynamic updates disabled by selecting the Do Not Allow Dynamic Updates option button and clicking Next.

NOTE

Dynamic updates allow DNS clients to register and update their own resource records in the DNS zone. When enabling dynamic updates to be accepted by your DNS server, be sure you know the sources of dynamic updated information. If the sources are not reliable, you can potentially receive corrupt or invalid information from a dynamic update.

14. The next page allows for the creation of a reverse lookup zone. Here, select Yes, Create a Reverse Lookup Zone Now, and then click Next.
15. Select Primary Zone for the reverse lookup zone type, and then click Next.
16. If storing the zone in Active Directory, select the replication scope and click Next.
17. Accept the default IPv4 Reverse Lookup Zone, and then click Next.
18. Type in the network ID of the reverse lookup zone, and then click Next. (The network ID is usually the first set of octets from an IP address in the zone. If a Class A IP range of 10.1.0.0 with a subnet mask of 255.255.0.0 is in use on a network, you enter the values 10.1, as illustrated in Figure 10.2.)

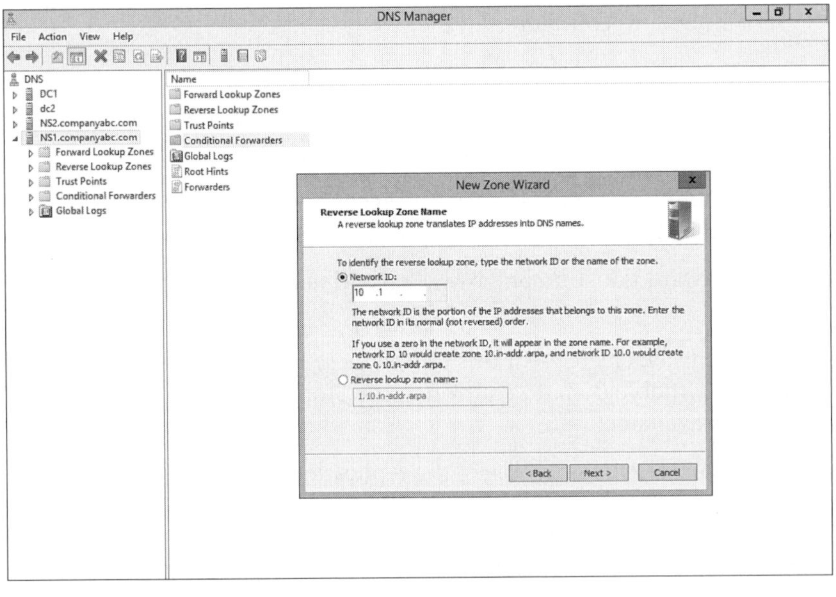

FIGURE 10.2 Reverse lookup zone creation.

19. Again, if creating a non-AD-integrated zone, you are offered the option to create a new zone file or to use an existing file. For this example, choose Create a New File with This File Name, and click Next to continue.

20. Again, you are presented the option for dynamic updates. For this example, leave dynamic updates disabled by selecting the Do Not Allow Dynamic Updates option button and clicking Next.

21. The next page deals with the setup of forwarders, which is described in more detail in the "Understanding DNS Zones" section later in this chapter. In this example, choose No, It Should Not Forward Queries, and click Next to continue.

22. The final window displays a summary of the changes that will be made and the zones that will be added to the DNS database. Click Finish to finalize the changes and create the zones.

NOTE

Depending on network connectivity, there might be a pop-up dialog box between the two clicks to finish the DNS changes in step 20. If you are not connected to a local-area network (LAN), an error dialog box is displayed regarding searching for root hints. Although the dialog box notes the root hint error, clicking OK will still configure DNS successfully.

Resource Records

In the DNS hierarchy, objects are identified through the use of resource records (RRs). These records are used for basic lookups of users and resources within the specified domain and are unique for the domain in which they are located. Because DNS is not a flat namespace, however, multiple identical RRs can exist at different levels in a DNS hierarchy. The distributed nature of the DNS hierarchy allows such levels.

Several key resource records exist in most DNS implementations, especially in those associated with Windows Server 2012 AD DS. A general familiarity with these specific types of RRs is required to gain a better understanding of DNS.

Start of Authority (SOA) Records

The Start of Authority (SOA) record in a DNS database indicates which server is authoritative for that particular zone. The server referenced by the SOA records is subsequently the server that is assumed to be the authoritative source of information about a particular zone and is in charge of processing zone updates. The SOA record contains information such as the Time-to-Live (TTL) interval, the contact person responsible for DNS, and other critical information, as illustrated in Figure 10.3.

An SOA record is automatically created when DNS is installed for AD DS in Windows Server 2012 and is populated with the default TTL, primary server, and other pertinent information for the zone. After installation, however, these values can be modified to fit the specific needs of an organization.

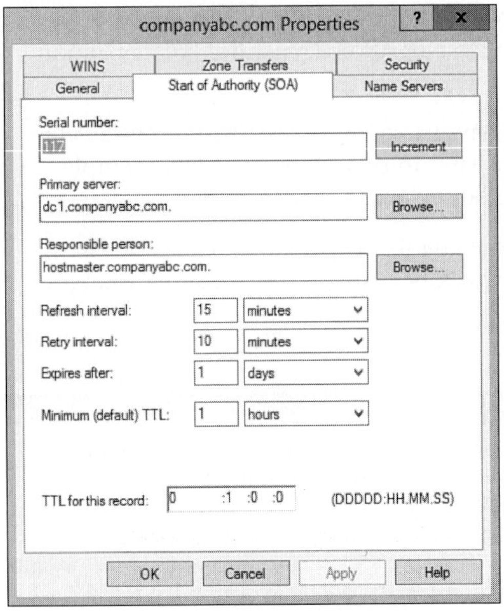

FIGURE 10.3 A sample SOA record.

Host (A) Records

The most common type of RR in DNS is the host record, also known as an A record. This type of RR simply contains the name of the host and its corresponding IP address, as illustrated in Figure 10.4.

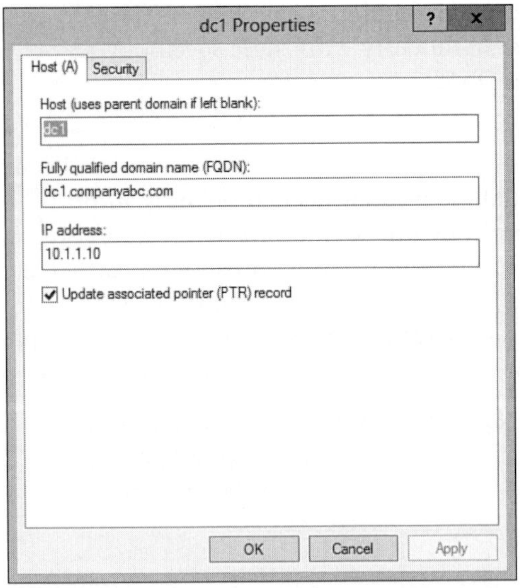

FIGURE 10.4 Sample host record.

The vast majority of RRs in DNS are A records because they are used to identify the IP addresses of most resources within a domain.

NOTE

Most resource records also contain advanced information about the record, which includes the TTL and, optionally, the record time stamp. To view or update this information, select Advanced from the View menu of the DNS Management console.

Name Server (NS) Records

Name Server (NS) records identify which computers in a DNS database are the name servers, essentially the DNS servers for a particular zone. Although there can be only one SOA record for a zone, there can be multiple NS records for the zone, which indicate to clients which machines are available to run DNS queries against for that zone.

NOTE

Name Server records, or NS records, do not actually contain the IP information of a particular resource. In fact, in most cases, only A records contain this information. NS records and other similar records simply point to a server's A record. For example, an NS record will simply point to dc1.companyabc.com, which will then direct the query to the dc1 A record in the companyabc.com zone.

Service (SRV) Records

Service (SRV) records are RRs that indicate which resources perform a particular service. Domain controllers in AD DS are referenced by SRV records that define specific services, such as the Global Catalog (GC), Lightweight Directory Access Protocol (LDAP), and Kerberos. SRV records are a relatively new addition to DNS, and did not exist in the original implementation of the standard. Each SRV record contains information about a particular functionality that a resource provides. For example, an LDAP server can add an SRV record, indicating that it can handle LDAP requests for a particular zone. SRV records can be very useful for AD DS because domain controllers can advertise that they handle Global Catalog requests, as illustrated in Figure 10.5.

NOTE

Because SRV records are a relatively new addition to DNS, they are not supported by several down-level DNS implementations, such as UNIX BIND 4.1.x and NT 4.0 DNS. It is, therefore, critical that the DNS environment that is used for Windows Server 2012's AD DS has the capability to create SRV records. For UNIX BIND servers, version 8.1.2 or later is recommended.

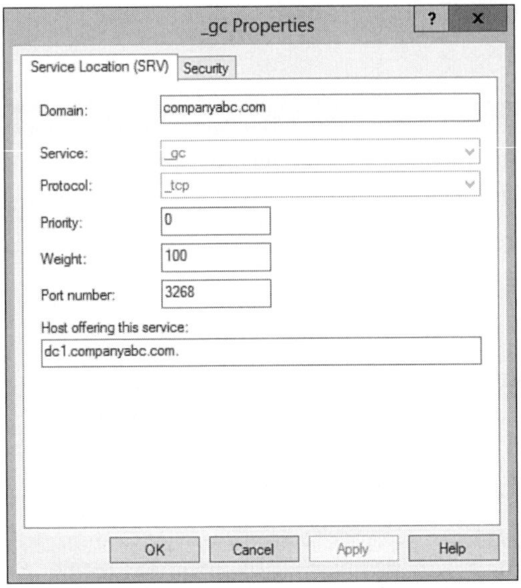

FIGURE 10.5 Sample SRV record for an AD GC entry.

Mail Exchanger (MX) Records

A Mail Exchanger (MX) record indicates which resources are available for Simple Mail Transfer Protocol (SMTP) mail reception. MX records can be set on a domain basis so that mail sent to a particular domain will be forwarded to the server or servers indicated by the MX record. For example, if an MX record is set for the domain companyabc.com, all mail sent to user@companyabc.com will be automatically directed to the server indicated by the MX record.

Pointer (PTR) Records

Reverse queries to DNS are accomplished through the use of Pointer (PTR) records. In other words, if a user wants to look up the name of a resource that is associated with a specific IP address, he would do a reverse lookup using that IP address. A DNS server would reply using a PTR record that would indicate the name associated with that IP address. PTR records are most commonly found in reverse lookup zones.

Canonical Name (CNAME) Records

A Canonical Name (CNAME) record represents a server alias, and allows any one of a number of servers to be referred to by multiple names in DNS. The record essentially redirects queries to the A record for that particular host. CNAME records are useful when migrating servers and for situations in which friendly names, such as mail.companyabc.com, are required to point to more complex server-naming conventions, such as sfoexch01.companyabc.com.

Other DNS Record Types

Other, less-common forms of records that might exist in DNS have specific purposes, and there might be cause to create them. The following is a sample list, but is by no means exhaustive:

- **AAAA**—Maps a standard IP address into a 128-bit IPv6 address. This type of record will become more prevalent as IPv6 is adopted. See Chapter 11 "DHCP / IPv6 / IPAM" for more details on IPv6.
- **ISDN**—Maps a specific DNS name to an ISDN telephone number.
- **KEY**—Stores a public key used for encryption for a particular domain.
- **RP**—Specifies the person responsible for a domain.
- **WKS**—Designates a particular well-known service.
- **MB**—Indicates which host contains a specific mailbox.

Understanding DNS Zones

A zone in DNS is a portion of a DNS namespace that is controlled by a particular DNS server or group of servers. The zone is the primary delegation mechanism in DNS and is used to establish boundaries over which a particular server can resolve requests. Any server that hosts a particular zone is said to be authoritative for that zone, with the exception of stub zones, which are defined later in this chapter in the "Stub Zones" section. Figure 10.6 illustrates how different portions of the DNS namespace can be divided into zones, each of which can be hosted on a DNS server or group of servers.

It is important to understand that any section or subsection of DNS can exist within a single zone. For example, an organization might decide to place an entire namespace of a domain, subdomains, and subsubdomains into a single zone. Or specific sections of that namespace can be divided up into separate zones. In fact, the entire Internet namespace can be envisioned as a single namespace with . as the root, which is divided into a multitude of different zones.

NOTE

A server that is installed with DNS but does not have any zones configured is known as a caching-only server. Establishing a caching-only server can be useful in some branch office situations because it can help to alleviate large amounts of client query traffic across the network and eliminate the need to replicate entire DNS zones to remote locations.

Forward Lookup Zones

A forward lookup zone is created to, as the name suggests, forward lookups to the DNS database. In other words, this type of zone resolves names to IP addresses and resource information. For example, if a user wants to reach dc1.companyabc.com and queries for its IP address through a forward lookup zone, DNS returns 172.16.1.11, the IP address for that resource.

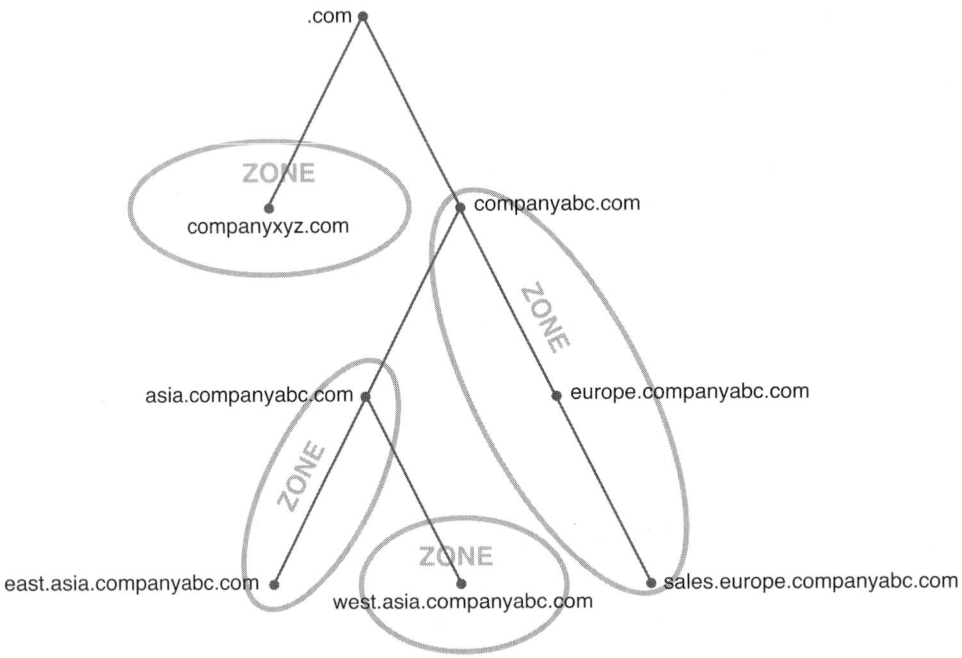

FIGURE 10.6 DNS zones.

NOTE

There is nothing to stop the assignment of multiple RRs to a single resource. In fact, this practice is common and useful in many situations. It might be practical to have a server respond to more than one name in specific circumstances. This type of functionality is normally accomplished through the creation of CNAME records, which create aliases for a particular resource.

Reverse Lookup Zones

A reverse lookup zone performs the exact opposite operation as a forward lookup zone. IP addresses are matched up with a common name in a reverse lookup zone. This is similar to knowing a phone number but not knowing the name associated with it. Reverse lookup zones are usually manually created and do not always exist in every implementation. Creating a new zone using the Configure a DNS Server Wizard, as in the example earlier in this chapter, can automatically create a reverse lookup zone. Reverse lookup zones are primarily populated with PTR records, which serve to point the reverse lookup query to the appropriate name.

Primary Zones

In traditional (non-Active Directory-integrated) DNS, a single server serves as the master DNS server for a zone, and all changes made to that particular zone are done on that particular server. A single DNS server can host multiple zones, and can be primary for one and secondary for another. If a zone is primary, however, all requested changes for that particular zone must be performed on the server that holds the master copy of the zone.

Secondary Zones

A secondary zone is established to provide redundancy and load balancing for the primary zone. Each copy of the DNS database is read-only, however, because all record keeping is done on the primary zone copy. A single DNS server can contain several zones that are primary and several that are secondary. The zone-creation process is similar to the one outlined in the preceding section on primary zones, but with the difference being that the zone is transferred from an existing primary server.

Stub Zones

The concept of stub zones is unique to Microsoft DNS. A stub zone is essentially a zone that contains no information about the members in a domain but simply serves to forward queries to a list of designated name servers for different domains. A stub zone subsequently contains only NS, SOA, and glue records. Glue records are essentially A records that work in conjunction with a particular NS record to resolve the IP address of a particular name server. A server that hosts a stub zone for a namespace is not authoritative for that zone.

As shown in Figure 10.7, the stub zone effectively serves as a placeholder for a zone that is authoritative on another server. It allows a server to forward queries that are made to a specific zone to the list of name servers in that zone.

You can easily create a stub zone in Windows Server 2012 after the need has been established for this particular type of functionality. To create a stub zone, follow these steps:

1. Launch Server Manager from a Windows 2012 server with a full GUI.
2. Select the DNS section. The list of servers in the server pool with the DNS role installed will be shown.
3. Right-click the DNS server to configure and select DNS Manager.
4. Select the DNS server name to configure.
5. Select the Forward Lookup Zones node.
6. Select Action, New Zone.
7. Click Next on the Welcome page.
8. Select Stub Zone from the list of zone types. Because this zone will not be AD integrated, uncheck the Store the Zone in Active Directory check box if it is checked, and then click Next to continue.

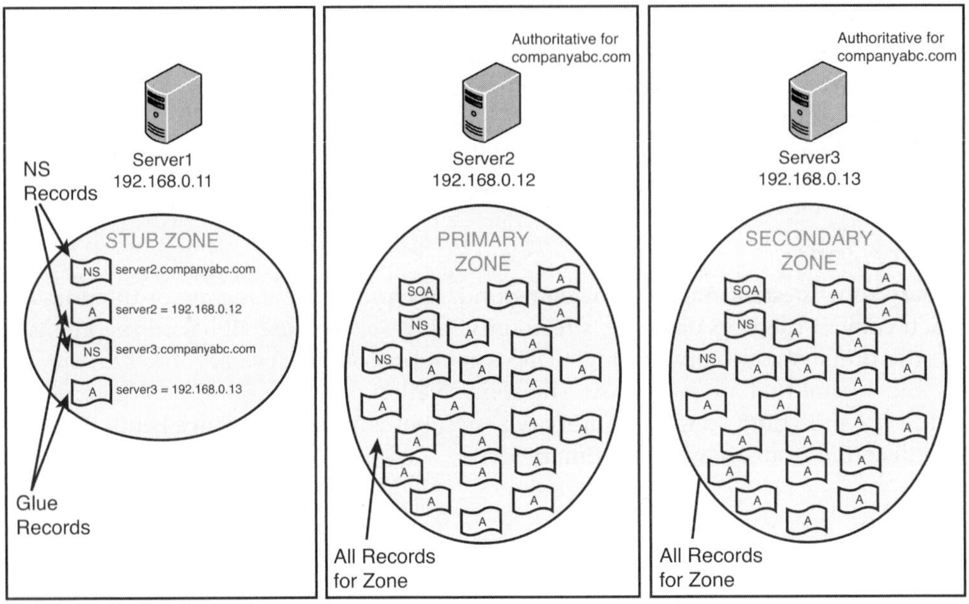

FIGURE 10.7 Stub zones.

9. Type in the name of the zone that will be created, and click Next to continue.
10. Select Create a New File with This File Name and accept the defaults, unless migrating from an existing zone file. Then click Next to continue.
11. Type in the IP address of the server or servers from which the zone records will be copied. Press Enter for each server entered, and they will be validated, as shown in Figure 10.8. Click Next to continue.
12. Click Finish on the Summary page to create the zone.

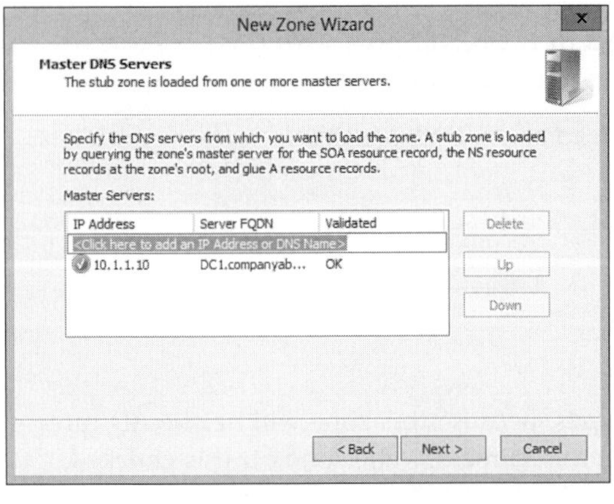

FIGURE 10.8 Entering stub master servers.

The newly created stub zone will hold only the SOA, NS, and glue records for the domain at which it is pointed.

Performing Zone Transfers

Copying the DNS database from one server to another is accomplished through a process known as a zone transfer. Zone transfers are required for any non-Active Directory-integrated zone that has more than one name server responsible for the contents of that zone. The mechanism for zone transfers varies, however, depending on the version of DNS. Zone transfers are always pulled by the secondary servers from the primary servers.

Primary DNS servers can be configured to notify secondary DNS servers of changes to a zone and to begin a zone transfer. They can also be configured to perform a zone transfer on a scheduled basis. To set up a secondary server to pull zone transfers from a forward lookup zone, follow this procedure:

1. Launch Server Manager from a Windows 2012 server with a full GUI.
2. Select the DNS section. The list of servers in the server pool with the DNS role installed will be shown.
3. Right-click the DNS server to configure and select DNS Manager.
4. Select the DNS server name to configure.
5. Select the Forward Lookup Zones node.
6. Right-click the name of the zone and choose Properties.
7. Choose the Zone Transfers tab.
8. Check Allow Zone Transfers and select Only to Servers Listed on the Name Servers Tab. This is normally the default setting.
9. Select the Name Servers tab.
10. Click Add, type in the FQDN of the server that will receive the updates, and click the Resolve button. The server will be validated, as shown in Figure 10.9. Because the server is not yet an authoritative server for the zone, the error message "The server with this IP address is not authoritative for the required zone" appears. This will be done in the next section. The error can be safely ignored. Click OK to save.
11. Click OK to save the changes.

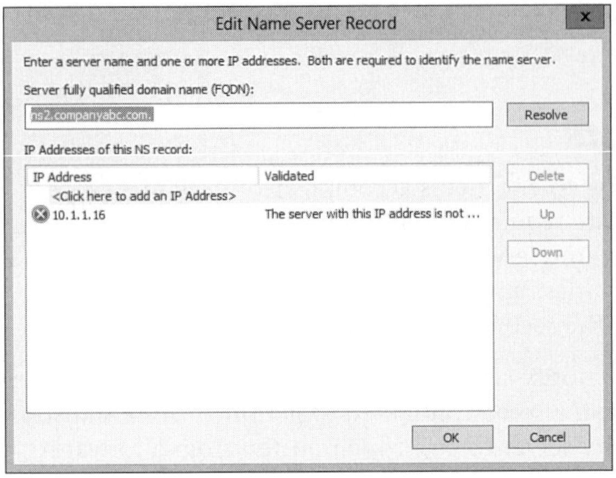

FIGURE 10.9 Setting up zone transfer servers.

Now that the primary zone on the primary DNS server has been configured to allow transfers, the secondary zone has to be configured on the secondary DNS server. To create the secondary zone and begin zone transfers, complete the following steps:

1. Launch Server Manager from a Windows 2012 server with a full GUI.
2. Select the DNS section. The list of servers in the server pool with the DNS role installed will be shown.
3. Right-click the DNS server to configure and select DNS Manager.
4. Select the DNS server name to configure.
5. Select the Forward Lookup Zones node.
6. Select Action, New Zone.
7. Click Next on the Welcome page.
8. Select Secondary Zone from the list of zone types. Secondary zones cannot be AD-integrated and the options will be grayed out. Click Next to continue.
9. Type in the name of the zone that will be created (this should match the primary zone name), and click Next to continue.

10. Type in the IP address or FQDN of the server or servers from which the zone records will be transferred. Press Enter for each server entered, and they will be validated. Click Next to continue.

NOTE

If there is an "No IPv6 address was found for the DNS name entered" error, highlight the error and click the Delete button to clear the entry.

11. Click Finish on the Summary page to create the zone.

After the last step, the zone will automatically transfer from the primary DNS server to the secondary DNS server.

Performing Full Zone Transfers

The standard method for zone transfers, which transfers the entire contents of a DNS zone from the primary server to the secondary server, is known as asynchronous zone transfer (AXFR), or full zone transfer. This type of zone transfer copies every item in the DNS database to the secondary server, regardless of whether the server already has some of the items in the database. Older implementations of DNS utilized AXFR exclusively, and it is still utilized for specific purposes today.

Initiating Incremental Zone Transfers

An incremental zone transfer (IXFR) is a process by which all incremental changes to a DNS database are replicated to the secondary DNS server. This saves bandwidth over AXFR replication changes because only the deltas, or changes made to the database since the last zone transfer, are replicated.

IXFR zone transfers are accomplished by referencing a serial number that is stored on the SOA of the DNS server that holds the primary zone. This number is incremented upon each change to a zone. If the server requesting the zone transfer has a serial number of 45, for example, and the primary zone server has a serial number of 55, only those changes made during the period of time between 45 and 55 will be incrementally sent to the requesting server via an IXFR transfer. However, if the difference in index numbers is too great, the information about the requesting server is assumed to be stale, and a full AXFR transfer will be initiated. For example, if a requesting server has an index of 25, and the primary zone server's index is 55, an AXFR zone transfer will be initiated, as illustrated in Figure 10.10.

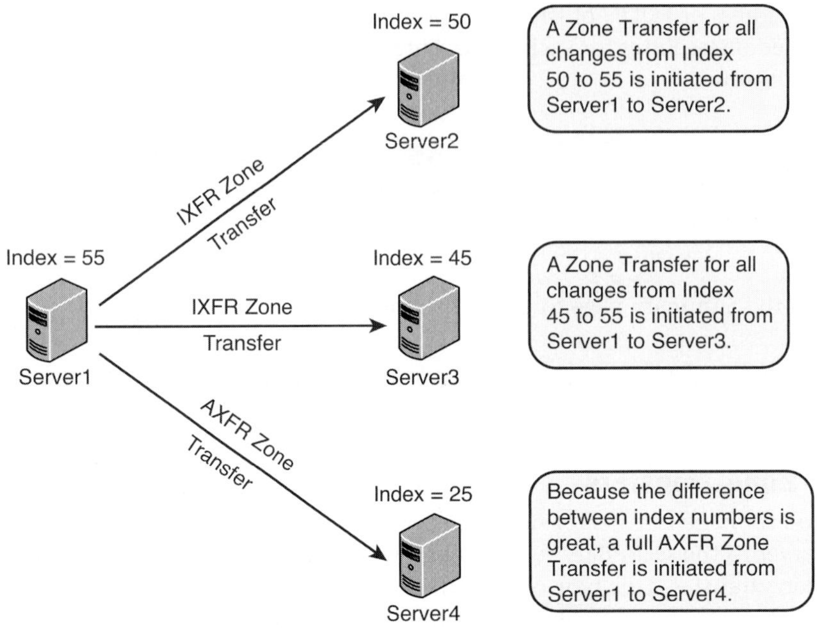

FIGURE 10.10 IXFR zone transfers.

Understanding DNS Queries

The primary function of DNS is to provide name resolution for requesting clients, so the query mechanism is subsequently one of the most important elements in the system. Two types of queries are commonly made to a DNS database: recursive and iterative.

Performing Recursive Queries

Recursive queries are most often performed by resolvers, or clients, that need a specific name resolved by a DNS server. Recursive queries are also accomplished by a DNS server if forwarders are configured to be used on a particular name server. A recursive query essentially asks whether a particular record can be resolved by a particular name server. The response to a recursive query is either negative or positive. Figure 10.11 shows a common recursive query scenario.

Performing Iterative Queries

Iterative queries ask a DNS server to either resolve the query or make a best-guess referral to a DNS server that might contain more accurate information about where the query can be resolved. Another iterative query is then performed to the referred server and so on until a result, positive or negative, is obtained.

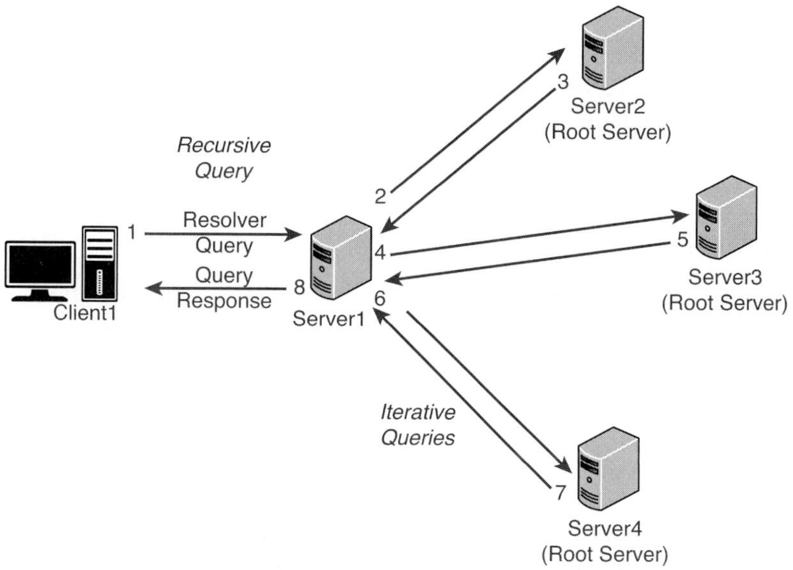

FIGURE 10.11 Recursive and iterative queries.

In the example shown in Figure 10.11, Client1 in CompanyABC opens a web browser and attempts to browse to the website for www.microsoft.com. A recursive query is initiated to the default name server; in this case, Server1 is contacted. Because Server1 is authoritative only for the companyabc.com namespace, and no entries exist for microsoft.com, the query is sent to an "upstream" DNS server that is listed in the root hints of the DNS server. That server, Server2, is not authoritative for microsoft.com but sends a referral back to Server1 for Server3, which is a name server for the .com namespace. Server3 knows that Server4 handles name-resolution requests for microsoft.com and sends that information back to Server1. A final iterative query is then sent from Server1 to Server4, and Server4 successfully resolves www to the proper IP address. Server1, with this information in hand, returns Client1's original recursive query with the proper IP address and Client1's browser successfully resolves www.microsoft.com.

This type of functionality lies at the heart of the distributed nature of DNS and allows DNS lookups to function as efficiently as they do.

Other DNS Components

Several other key components lie at the heart of DNS and are necessary for it to function properly. In addition, you need to fully understand the functionality of several key components of DNS that are utilized heavily by Microsoft DNS.

Dynamic DNS

Older versions of DNS relied on administrators manually updating all the records within a DNS database. Every time a resource was added or information about a resource was changed, the DNS database was updated manually, normally via a simple text editor, to reflect the changes. Dynamic DNS was developed as a direct response to the increasing administrative overhead that was required to keep DNS databases functional and up-to-date. With Dynamic DNS, clients can automatically update their own records in DNS, depending on the security settings of the zone.

It is important to note that only Windows 2000/XP and higher clients support dynamic updates and that down-level (NT/9x) clients must have DHCP configured properly for them to be updated in DNS. There are, however, security issues associated with this functionality that are detailed in subsequent sections of this chapter and are described further in Chapter 11.

The Time-to-Live Value

The TTL value for a RR is the amount of time (in seconds) that a resolver or name server will keep a cached DNS request before requesting it again from the original name server. This value helps to keep the information in the DNS database relevant. Setting TTL levels is essentially a balancing act between the need for updated information and the need to reduce DNS query traffic across the network.

In the example from the "Performing Iterative Queries" section, if Client1 already requested the IP address of www.microsoft.com, and the information was returned to the DNS server that showed the IP address, it would make sense that that IP address would not change often and could, therefore, be cached for future queries. The next time another client requests the same information, the local DNS server will give that client the IP address it received from the original Client1 query so long as the TTL has not expired. This helps to reduce network traffic and improve DNS query response time.

The TTL for a response is set by the name server that successfully resolves a query. In other words, you might have different TTLs set for items in a cache, based on where they were resolved and the TTL for the particular zone they originated from.

NOTE

The default TTL for manually created records in Windows Server 2012 DNS is one hour. Records created dynamically via Dynamic DNS have a 20-minute default TTL.

The TTL setting for a zone is modified via the SOA record. The procedure for doing this in Windows Server 2012 is as follows:

1. Launch Server Manager from a Windows 2012 server with a full GUI.
2. Select the DNS section. The list of servers in the server pool with the DNS role installed will be shown.
3. Right-click the DNS server to configure and select DNS Manager.

4. Select the DNS server name to configure.
5. Select the Forward Lookup Zones node.
6. Select the zone node.
7. Find the SOA record for the zone and double-click it.
8. Modify the Minimum (Default) TTL entry to match the TTL you want, as shown in Figure 10.12.
9. Click OK to accept the changes.

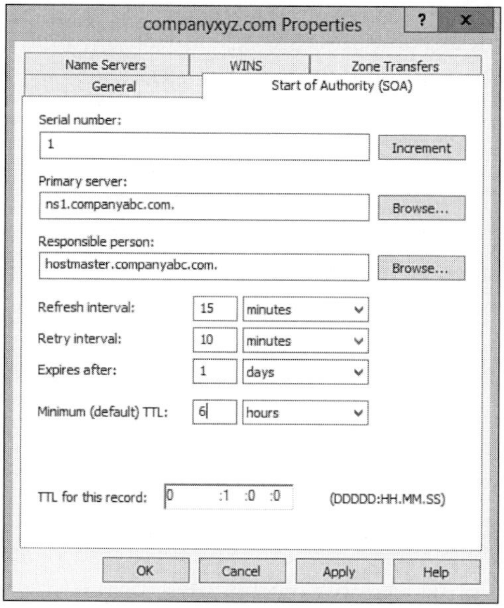

FIGURE 10.12 Changing the TTL.

Performing Secure Updates

One of the main problems with a Dynamic DNS implementation lies with the security of the update mechanism. If no security is enforced, nothing prevents malicious users from updating a record for a server, for example, to redirect it to another IP address. This is known as DNS poisoning. For this reason, dynamic updates are, by default, turned off on new standard zones that are created in Windows Server 2012. However, with AD-integrated DNS zones, a mechanism exists that allows clients to perform secure dynamic updates. Secure updates utilize Kerberos to authenticate computers and ensure that only those clients that created a record can subsequently update the same record.

If you're using DHCP to provide secure updates on behalf of DHCP clients, one important caveat is that DHCP servers should not be located on the domain controller, if possible, because of specific issues in regard to secure updates. The reason for this recommendation is that all DHCP servers are placed in a group known as DNSUpdateProxy. Any members of this group do not take ownership of items that are published in DNS. This group was created because DHCP servers can dynamically publish updates for clients automatically, and the clients would need to modify their entries themselves. Subsequently, the first client to access a newly created entry would take ownership of that entry. Because domain controllers create sensitive SRV records and the like, it is not wise to use a domain controller as a member of this group, and it is by extension not wise to have DHCP on domain controllers for this reason. If establishing DHCP on a domain controller is unavoidable, it is recommended to disable this functionality by not adding the server into this group.

Exploring Aging and Scavenging for DNS

DNS RRs often become stale, or no longer relevant, as computers are disconnected from the network or IP addresses are changed without first notifying the DNS server. The process of scavenging those records removes them from a database after their original owners do not update them. Scavenging is not turned on, by default, but this feature can be enabled in Windows Server 2012 by following these steps:

1. Launch Server Manager from a Windows 2012 server with a full GUI.
2. Select the DNS section. The list of servers in the server pool with the DNS role installed will be shown.
3. Right-click the DNS server to configure and select DNS Manager.
4. Select the DNS server name to configure.
5. Right-click the server name and choose Properties.
6. Select the Advanced tab.
7. Check the Enable Automatic Scavenging of Stale Records check box.
8. Select a scavenging period, as shown in Figure 10.13, and click OK to save your changes.

Scavenging makes a DNS database cleaner, but overly aggressive scavenging can also remove valid entries. Therefore, if you're using scavenging, it is wise to strike a balance between a clean database and a valid one.

Examining Root Hints

By default, a DNS installation includes a listing of Internet-level name servers that can be used for name resolution of the .com, .net, .uk, and like domain names on the Internet. When a DNS server cannot resolve a query locally in its cache or in local zones, it consults the Root Hints list, which indicates which servers to begin iterative queries with.

The Hints file should be updated on a regular basis to ensure that the servers listed are still relevant. This file is located in \%systemroot%\system32\DNS\cache.dns and can be updated on the Internet at the following address:

```
ftp://ftp. internic.net/domain/named.cache
```

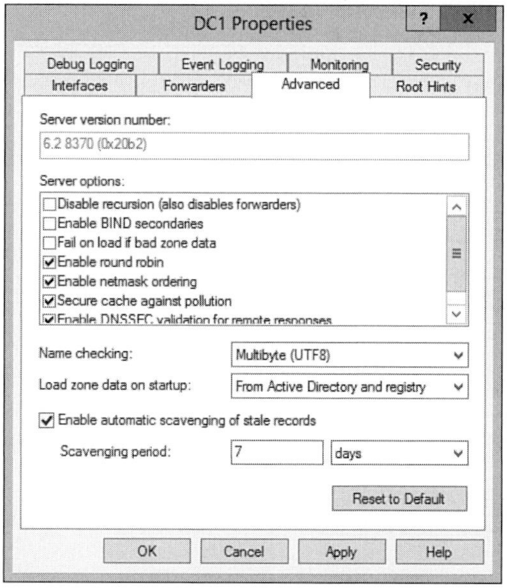

FIGURE 10.13 Turning on scavenging.

At the time of writing, the latest root hints file, or root name servers, was dated Jun 8, 2011. The contents are shown in Listing 10.1. You can see the root server names (for example, A.ROOT-SERVER.NET) and their A records (for example, 192.41.0.4).

LISTING 10.1 Root Hints File Contents

```
;       This file holds the information about root name servers needed to
;       initialize cache of Internet domain name servers
;       (e.g. reference this file in the "cache  .  <file>"
;       configuration file of BIND domain name servers).
;
;       This file is made available by InterNIC
;       under anonymous FTP as
;           file                /domain/named.cache
;           on server           FTP.INTERNIC.NET
;       -OR-                    RS.INTERNIC.NET
;
;       last update:    Jun 8, 2011
;       related version of root zone:   2011060800
;
; formerly NS.INTERNIC.NET
;
.                        3600000  IN  NS    A.ROOT-SERVERS.NET.
A.ROOT-SERVERS.NET.      3600000      A     198.41.0.4
```

```
A.ROOT-SERVERS.NET.      3600000      AAAA  2001:503:BA3E::2:30
;
; FORMERLY NS1.ISI.EDU
;
.                        3600000      NS    B.ROOT-SERVERS.NET.
B.ROOT-SERVERS.NET.      3600000      A     192.228.79.201
;
; FORMERLY C.PSI.NET
;
.                        3600000      NS    C.ROOT-SERVERS.NET.
C.ROOT-SERVERS.NET.      3600000      A     192.33.4.12
;
; FORMERLY TERP.UMD.EDU
;
.                        3600000      NS    D.ROOT-SERVERS.NET.
D.ROOT-SERVERS.NET.      3600000      A     128.8.10.90
D.ROOT-SERVERS.NET.      3600000      AAAA  2001:500:2D::D
;
; FORMERLY NS.NASA.GOV
;
.                        3600000      NS    E.ROOT-SERVERS.NET.
E.ROOT-SERVERS.NET.      3600000      A     192.203.230.10
;
; FORMERLY NS.ISC.ORG
;
.                        3600000      NS    F.ROOT-SERVERS.NET.
F.ROOT-SERVERS.NET.      3600000      A     192.5.5.241
F.ROOT-SERVERS.NET.      3600000      AAAA  2001:500:2F::F
;
; FORMERLY NS.NIC.DDN.MIL
;
.                        3600000      NS    G.ROOT-SERVERS.NET.
G.ROOT-SERVERS.NET.      3600000      A     192.112.36.4
;
; FORMERLY AOS.ARL.ARMY.MIL
;
.                        3600000      NS    H.ROOT-SERVERS.NET.
H.ROOT-SERVERS.NET.      3600000      A     128.63.2.53
H.ROOT-SERVERS.NET.      3600000      AAAA  2001:500:1::803F:235
;
; FORMERLY NIC.NORDU.NET
;
.                        3600000      NS    I.ROOT-SERVERS.NET.
I.ROOT-SERVERS.NET.      3600000      A     192.36.148.17
I.ROOT-SERVERS.NET.      3600000      AAAA  2001:7FE::53
;
```

```
; OPERATED BY VERISIGN, INC.
;
.                          3600000     NS    J.ROOT-SERVERS.NET.
J.ROOT-SERVERS.NET.        3600000     A     192.58.128.30
J.ROOT-SERVERS.NET.        3600000     AAAA  2001:503:C27::2:30
;
; OPERATED BY RIPE NCC
;
.                          3600000     NS    K.ROOT-SERVERS.NET.
K.ROOT-SERVERS.NET.        3600000     A     193.0.14.129
K.ROOT-SERVERS.NET.        3600000     AAAA  2001:7FD::1
;
; OPERATED BY ICANN
;
.                          3600000     NS    L.ROOT-SERVERS.NET.
L.ROOT-SERVERS.NET.        3600000     A     199.7.83.42
L.ROOT-SERVERS.NET.        3600000     AAAA  2001:500:3::42
;
; OPERATED BY WIDE
;
.                          3600000     NS    M.ROOT-SERVERS.NET.
M.ROOT-SERVERS.NET.        3600000     A     202.12.27.33
M.ROOT-SERVERS.NET.        3600000     AAAA  2001:DC3::35
; End of File
```

You can see the root hints for a Windows Server 2012 DNS server by doing the following:

1. Launch Server Manager from a Windows 2012 server with a full GUI.
2. Select the DNS section. The list of servers in the server pool with the DNS role installed will be shown.
3. Right-click the DNS server to configure and select DNS Manager.
4. Select the DNS server name to configure.
5. Right-click the server name and choose Properties.
6. Select the Root Hints tab.

The name servers should match those in the root hints file retrieved from the InterNIC FTP site.

Understanding the Role of Forwarders

Forwarders are name servers that handle all iterative queries for a name server. In other words, if a server cannot answer a query from a client resolver, servers that have forwarders simply forward the request to an upstream forwarder that will process the iterative queries to the Internet root name servers. Forwarders are often used in situations in which an organization uses the DNS servers of an Internet service provider (ISP) to handle all name-resolution traffic. Another common situation occurs when Active Directory's DNS servers handle all internal AD DNS resolution but forward outbound DNS requests to another DNS environment within an organization, such as a legacy UNIX BIND server.

In conditional forwarding, queries that are made to a specific domain or set of domains are sent to a specifically defined forwarder DNS server. This type of scenario is normally used to define routes that internal domain resolution traffic will follow. For example, if an organization controls the companyabc.com domain namespace and the companyxyz.com namespace, it might want queries between domains to be resolved on local DNS servers, as opposed to being sent out to the Internet just to be sent back again so that they are resolved internally.

Forward-only servers are never meant to do iterative queries, but rather to forward all requests that cannot be answered locally to a forwarder or set of forwarders. If those forwarders do not respond, a failure message is generated.

If you plan to use forwarders in a Windows Server 2012 DNS environment, you can establish them by following these steps:

1. Launch Server Manager from a Windows 2012 server with a full GUI.
2. Select the DNS section. The list of servers in the server pool with the DNS role installed will be shown.
3. Right-click the DNS server to configure and select DNS Manager.
4. Select the DNS server name to configure.
5. Right-click the server name and choose Properties.
6. Select the Forwarders tab.
7. Click Edit to create forwarders.
8. Type in the IP address or FQDN of the server or servers that will be forwarders. Press Enter for each server entered, and they will be validated. Click OK when you have finished.
9. If this server will be configured only to forward, and to otherwise fail if forwarding does not work, uncheck the Use Root Hints If No Forwarders Are Available check box.
10. Click OK to save the changes.

Using WINS for Lookups

In environments with a significant investment in WINS, the WINS database can be used in conjunction with DNS to provide for DNS name resolution. If a DNS query has exhausted all DNS methods of resolving a name, a WINS server can be queried to provide for resolution. This method creates WINS RRs in DNS that are established to support this approach.

To enable WINS to assist with DNS lookups, follow these steps:

1. Launch Server Manager from a Windows 2012 server with a full GUI.
2. Select the DNS section. The list of servers in the server pool with the DNS role installed will be shown.
3. Right-click the DNS server to configure and select DNS Manager.
4. Select the DNS server name to configure.
5. Expand the Forward Lookup Zones nodes.
6. Select the zone node.
7. Right-click the zone in question and choose Properties.
8. Choose the WINS tab.
9. Check the Use WINS Forward Lookup check box.
10. Enter the IP address of the WINS servers, click the Add button, and then click OK to save the changes.

Understanding the Evolution of Microsoft DNS

Windows Server 2012's implementation of AD DS expands upon the advanced feature set that Windows 2000 DNS introduced and was expanded again in Windows Server 2003 and Windows Server 2008. Several key functional improvements were added, but the overall design and functionality changes have not been significant enough to change any Windows 2008 design decisions that were previously made regarding DNS. The following sections describe the functionality introduced in Windows 2000/2003/2008 DNS that has been carried over to Windows Server 2012 DNS and helps to distinguish it from other DNS implementations.

Active Directory-Integrated Zones

The most dramatic change in Windows 2000's DNS implementation was the concept of directory-integrated DNS zones, known as AD-integrated zones. These zones were stored in Active Directory, as opposed to a text file as in standard DNS. When the Active Directory was replicated, the DNS zone was replicated as well. This also allowed for secure updates, using Kerberos authentication, as well as the concept of multimaster DNS, in which no one server is the master server and all DNS servers contain a writable copy of the zone.

Windows Server 2012, like Windows Server 2008, utilizes AD-integrated zones, but with one major change to the design: Instead of storing the zone information directly in the naming contexts of Active Directory, it is stored in the application partition to reduce replication overhead. You can find more information about this concept in the following sections.

Dynamic Updates

As previously mentioned, dynamic updates, using Dynamic DNS (DDNS), allow clients to automatically register, update, and unregister their own host records as they are connected to the network. This concept was a new feature introduced with Windows 2000 DNS and is carried over to Windows Server 2012.

Unicode Character Support

Introduced in Windows 2000 and supported in Windows Server 2012, Unicode support of extended character sets enables DNS to store records written in Unicode, or essentially multiple character sets from many different languages. This functionality essentially allows the DNS server to utilize and perform lookups on records that are written with nonstandard characters, such as underscores, foreign letters, and so on.

NOTE

Although Microsoft DNS supports Unicode characters, it is a best practice that you make any DNS implementation compliant with the standard DNS character set so that you can support zone transfers to and from non-Unicode-compliant DNS implementations, such as UNIX BIND servers. This character set includes a–z, A–Z, 0–9, and the hyphen (-) character.

DNS in Windows Server 2012

The Windows Server 2012 improvements on the basic BIND version of DNS help to further establish DNS as a reliable, robust name-resolution strategy for Microsoft and non-Microsoft environments. An overall knowledge of the increased functionality and the structural changes will help you to further understand the capabilities of DNS in Windows Server 2012.

Application Partition

Perhaps the most significant feature in Windows Server 2012 DNS implementation, Active Directory-integrated zones are stored in the application partition of the AD. For every domain in a forest, a separate application partition is created and is used to store all records that exist in each AD-integrated zone. Because the application partition is not included as part of the Global Catalog, DNS entries are no longer included as part of global catalog replication.

With the application partition concept, replication loads are now reduced while important zone information is delegated to areas of the network where they are needed.

Automatic Creation of DNS Zones

The Configure a DNS Server Wizard, as demonstrated in "Installing DNS Using the Add Roles Wizard" section, allows for the automatic creation of a DNS zone through a step-by-step wizard. This feature greatly eases the process of creating a zone, especially for Active Directory. The wizard can be invoked by right-clicking the server name in the DNS Manager and choosing Configure a DNS Server.

Fix to the "Island" Problem

Earlier versions of the Microsoft DNS had a well-documented issue that was known as the "island" problem, which was manifested by a DNS server that pointed to itself as a DNS server. If the IP address of that server changed, the DNS server updated its own entry in DNS, but then other DNS servers within the domain were unable to successfully retrieve updates from the original server because they were requesting from the old IP address. This effectively left the original DNS server in an island by itself, hence the term.

Microsoft DNS fixed this problem in Windows Server 2003 and above. Windows Server 2012 DNS first changes its host records on a sufficient number of other authoritative servers within DNS so that the IP changes made will be successfully replicated, thus eliminating this island problem. As a result, it is no longer necessary to point a root DNS server to another DNS server for updates, as was previously recommended as a method of resolving this issue.

Forest Root Zone for _msdcs

In Active Directory, all client logons and lookups are directed to local domain controllers and Global Catalog servers through references to the SRV records in DNS. These SRV records were stored in a subdomain to an Active Directory domain that is known as the _msdcs subdomain.

In Windows Server 2012, _msdcs is a separate zone in DNS, as shown in Figure 10.14. This zone, stored in the application partition, is replicated to every domain controller that is a DNS server. This listing of SRV records was moved mainly to satisfy the requirements of remote sites. In Windows 2000, these remote sites had to replicate the entire DNS database locally to access the _msdcs records, which led to increased replication time and reduced responsiveness. If you delegate the SRV records to their own zone, only this specific zone can be designated for replication to remote site DNS servers, saving replication throughput and increasing the response time for clients.

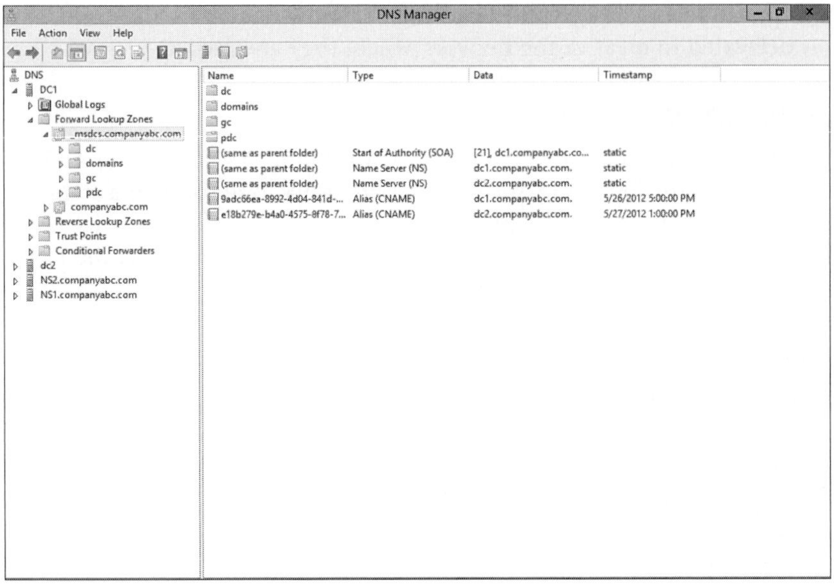

FIGURE 10.14 _msdcs zone.

DNS in an Active Directory Domain Services Environment

DNS is inseparable from Active Directory. In fact, the two are often confused for one another because of the similarities in their logical structures.

Active Directory uses a hierarchical X.500-based structure that was designed to map into the DNS hierarchy, hence the similarities. In addition, Active Directory utilizes DNS for all internal lookups, from client logons to Global Catalog lookups. Subsequently, strong consideration into how DNS integrates with Active Directory is required for those considering deploying or upgrading AD.

The Impact of DNS on AD DS

Problems with DNS can spell disaster for an Active Directory environment. Because all servers and clients are constantly performing lookups on one another, a break in name-resolution service can severely affect Active Directory functionality.

For this and other reasons, installing a redundant DNS infrastructure in any AD DS implementation is strongly recommended. Even smaller environments should consider duplication of the primary DNS zone, and nearly as much emphasis as is put into protecting the Global Catalog AD index should be put into protecting DNS.

Security considerations for the DNS database should not be taken for granted. Secure updates to AD-integrated zones are highly recommended, and keeping DHCP servers off a domain controller can also help to secure DNS (see previous sections of this chapter for more details on this concept). In addition, limiting administrative access to DNS will help to mitigate problems with unauthorized "monkeying around" with DNS.

AD DS in Non-Microsoft DNS Implementations

AD DS was specifically written to be able to coexist and, in fact, utilize a non-Microsoft DNS implementation as long as that implementation supports dynamic updates and SRV records. For example, AD functions in all versions of UNIX BIND 8.1.2 or higher. With this point in mind, however, it is still recommended that an organization with a significant investment in Microsoft technologies consider hosting Active Directory DNS on Windows Server 2012 systems because functionality and security enhancements provide for the best fit in these situations.

For environments that use older versions of DNS or are not able (or willing) to host Active Directory clients directly in their databases, Active Directory DNS can simply be delegated to a separate zone in which it can be authoritative. The Windows Server 2012 systems can simply set up forwarders to the foreign DNS implementations to provide for resolution of resources in the original zone.

Using Secondary Zones in an AD DS Environment

Certain situations in Active Directory require the use of secondary zones to handle specific name resolution. For example, in peer-root domain models, where two separate trees form different namespaces within the same forest, secondaries of each DNS root were required in Windows 2000 to maintain proper forestwide synchronization.

Because each tree in a peer-root model is composed of independent domains that might not have security privileges in the other domains, a mechanism will need to be in place to allow for lookups to occur between the two trees. The creation of secondary zones in each DNS environment will provide a solution to this scenario, as illustrated in Figure 10.15. Windows Server 2012 now has the option of replicating these separate trees to all DNS servers in the forest, reducing the need for secondary zones. Replicating secondary zones outside of a forest is still sometimes necessary, however. Conditional forwarding and stub zones can also be used in certain cases to achieve a similar result without the need for data replication.

SRV Records and Site Resolution

All AD DS clients use DNS for any type of domain-based lookups. Logons, for example, require lookups into the Active Directory for specific SRV records that indicate the location of domain controllers and Global Catalog servers. Windows Server 2012, as previously mentioned, divides the location of the SRV records into a separate zone, which is replicated to all domain controllers that have DNS installed on them.

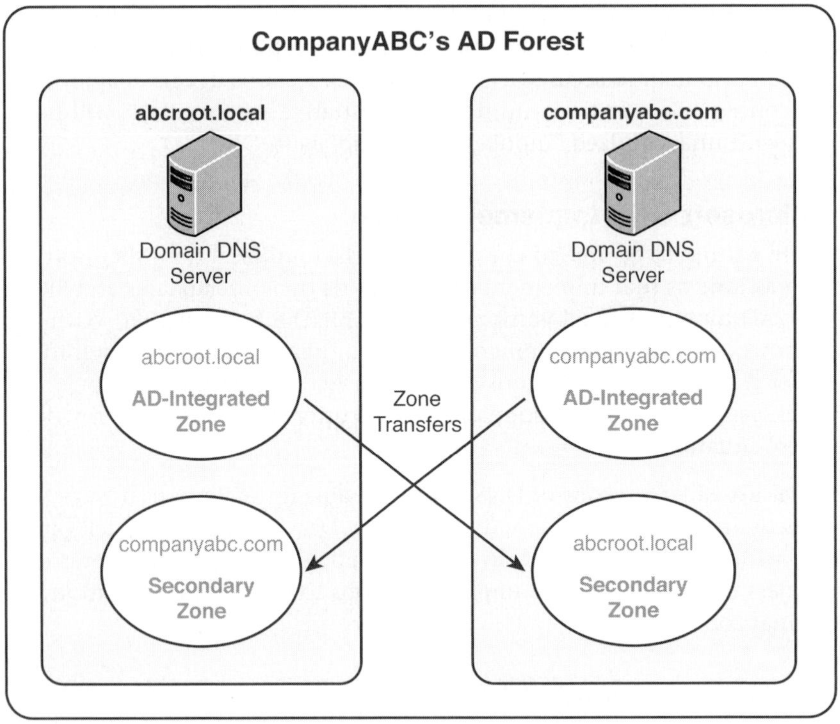

FIGURE 10.15 Peer-root domain DNS secondary zones.

Subdomains for each site are created in this zone; they indicate which resource is available in those specific sites, as shown in Figure 10.16. In a nutshell, if an SRV record in the specific site subdomain is incorrect, or another server from a different site is listed, all clients in that site are forced to authenticate in other sites. This concept is important because a common problem is that when Active Directory sites are created before they are populated with servers, an SRV record from the hub location is added to that site subdomain in DNS. When a new server is added to those sites, their SRV records join the other SRV records that were placed there when the site was created. These records are not automatically deleted, and they consequently direct clients to servers across slow wide-area network (WAN) links, often making logon times very slow.

In addition to the site containers, the root of these containers contains a list of all domain controllers in a specific domain. These lists are used for name resolution when a particular site server does not respond. If a site domain controller is down, clients randomly choose a domain controller in this site.

GlobalNames Zone

In some cases, using a fully qualified domain name (FQDN) is not convenient for the end users. This is especially true for novice users or in the case of very long domain names. A user entering the uniform resource locator (URL) http://intranet.convergentcomputing.

com is quite likely to make a mistake in the typing. The WINS name resolution provides relief from this, in that single-label names can be used instead. This allows the user to type the URL http://intranet and still reach the desired resource.

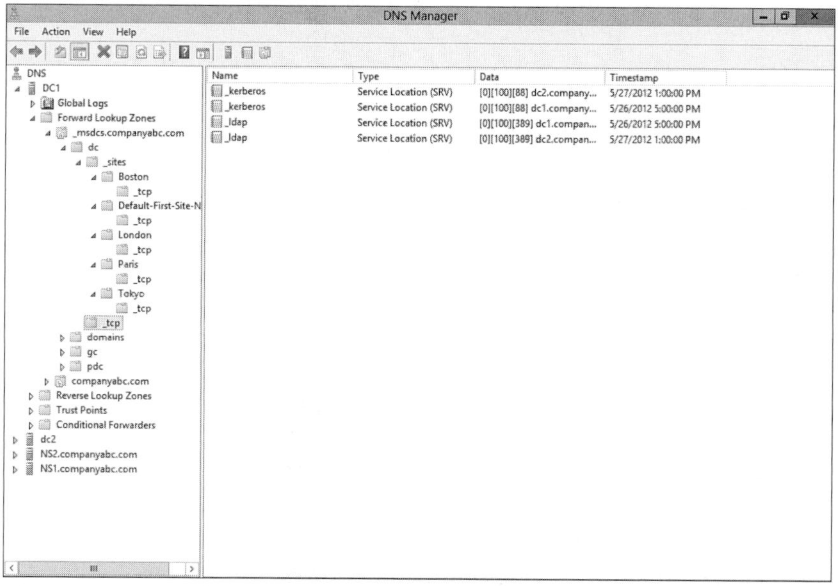

FIGURE 10.16 Site-level SRV records.

However, with the advent of IPv6, WINS will no longer be supported as the new addressing is deployed throughout the organization. There are also many advantages of DNS over WINS, including reducing administrative overhead, single name-resolution repository, security, and open standards.

Windows Server 2012 provides a feature that was introduced in Windows Server 2008 to address this problem, specifically the GlobalNames zone (GNZ). This zone provides single-label name resolution via a DNS zone, similar to WINS. The zone is a normal forward lookup zone, albeit with a special name (GlobalNames), and is used by the DNS server in a special way. If the DNS server is unable to resolve an address in its local zones, it will then resolve the single-label address against the GNZ.

The GNZ holds out the promise of finally doing away with WINS and NetBIOS naming.

To configure the GNZ, follow these steps:

1. Launch Server Manager from a Windows 2012 server with a full GUI.
2. Select the DNS section. The list of servers in the server pool with the DNS role installed will be shown.
3. Right-click the DNS server to configure and select DNS Manager.

4. Select the DNS server name to configure.
5. Select the Forward Lookup Zones node.
6. Select Action, New Zone.
7. Click Next on the Welcome page.
8. Select Primary Zone and make sure that the Store the Zone in Active Directory check box is checked. Click Next.
9. Select To All DNS Servers in This Forest, and then click Next.
10. Enter the Zone name GlobalNames and click Next.
11. Leave the default Dynamic Update setting and click Next.
12. Click Finish to create the zone.
13. Open a PowerShell command prompt and enter the command **Set-DnsServerGlobalNameZone -Enable $true**. This command must be run on each DNS server that is expected to resolve global names, regardless of if the zone is replicated to them already.

Now the GNZ is ready to respond to queries. For any server that needs to respond to single-label queries, enter a CNAME record in the GNZ with the appropriate FQDN for the resource. The DNS server will try the GNZ after trying other local zones.

NOTE

The global name-resolution status of a Windows Server 2012 server can be checked with the PowerShell command *Get-DnsServerGlobalNameZone*. If GNZ is enabled, the Enable will show as True.

Troubleshooting DNS

Much has been written about the complexity of DNS, and even more confusion and misconceptions have been written about it. In truth, however, DNS structure is logical, so you can easily troubleshoot it, if you use the proper tools and techniques. A good grasp of these tools and their functionality is a must for proper name-resolution troubleshooting with DNS.

Using the DNS Event Viewer to Diagnose Problems

As any good administrator knows, Event Viewer is the first place to look when troubleshooting. Windows Server 2012 makes it even more straightforward to use because DNS events compiled from Event Viewer are immediately accessible from the DNS Manager Console. Parsing this set of logs can help you troubleshoot DNS replication issues, query problems, and other issues.

For more advanced event log diagnosis, you can turn on Debug Logging on a per-server basis. It is recommended that this functionality be turned on only as required, however, as this can affect server performance and the log files can fill up fast. To enable Debug Logging, follow these steps:

1. Launch Server Manager from a Windows 2012 server with a full GUI.
2. Select the DNS section. The list of servers in the server pool with the DNS role installed will be shown.
3. Right-click the DNS server to configure and select DNS Manager.
4. Select the DNS server name to configure.
5. Right-click the server name and choose Properties.
6. Select the Debug Logging tab.
7. Check the Log Packets for Debugging check box.
8. Configure any additional settings as required, and click OK.

By default, the log file is named dns.log and is saved in The C:\Windows\System32\dns\ directory. Listing 10.2 shows the debug of the DNS server dc1.companyabc.com of a lookup of the record www.cco.com from the server at 10.1.2.13. You can see from the log that the request was forwarded to the DNS server at 12.222.165.144 and that the results were then sent to the requesting server at 10.1.1.1.

LISTING 10.2 DNS Log File

```
5/28/2012 6:48:32 PM 067C PACKET  000000BDAFD158A0 UDP Rcv 10.1.1.1        3b60
   Q [0001   D   NOERROR] A      (3)www(3)cco(3)com(0)
5/28/2012 6:48:32 PM 067C PACKET  000000BDB0216410 UDP Snd 12.222.165.144  ebfc
   Q [0000       NOERROR] A      (3)www(3)cco(3)com(0)
5/28/2012 6:48:32 PM 067C PACKET  000000BDB0D8FF80 UDP Rcv 12.222.165.144  ebfc
 R Q [8084 A  R  NOERROR] A      (3)www(3)cco(3)com(0)
5/28/2012 6:48:32 PM 067C PACKET  000000BDAFD158A0 UDP Snd 10.1.1.1        3b60
 R Q [8081   DR  NOERROR] A      (3)www(3)cco(3)com(0)
5/28/2012 6:48:58 PM 067C PACKET  000000BDB0A2B5B0 UDP Rcv 10.1.2.13       0006
   Q [0001   D   NOERROR] A      (3)www(3)cco(3)com(10)companyabc(3)com(0)
5/28/2012 6:48:58 PM 067C PACKET  000000BDB0A2B5B0 UDP Snd 10.1.2.13       0006
 R Q [8385 A DR NXDOMAIN] A      (3)www(3)cco(3)com(10)companyabc(3)com(0)
5/28/2012 6:48:58 PM 067C PACKET  000000BDB01CFCE0 UDP Rcv 10.1.2.13       0007
   Q [0001   D   NOERROR] AAAA   (3)www(3)cco(3)com(10)companyabc(3)com(0)
5/28/2012 6:48:58 PM 067C PACKET  000000BDB01CFCE0 UDP Snd 10.1.2.13       0007
 R Q [8385 A DR NXDOMAIN] AAAA   (3)www(3)cco(3)com(10)companyabc(3)com(0)
5/28/2012 6:48:58 PM 067C PACKET  000000BDB0D8FF80 UDP Rcv 10.1.2.13       0008
   Q [0001   D   NOERROR] A      (3)www(3)cco(3)com(0)
5/28/2012 6:48:58 PM 067C PACKET  000000BDAFD158A0 UDP Snd 128.8.10.90     d511
   Q [0000       NOERROR] A      (3)www(3)cco(3)com(0)
```

10

```
5/28/2012 6:48:59 PM 067C PACKET  000000BDAFD27B40 UDP Rcv 128.8.10.90     d511
 R Q [0080        NOERROR] A      (3)www(3)cco(3)com(0)
5/28/2012 6:48:59 PM 067C PACKET  000000BDAFD158A0 UDP Snd 192.55.83.30    9b01
   Q [0000        NOERROR] A      (3)www(3)cco(3)com(0)
5/28/2012 6:48:59 PM 067C PACKET  000000BDB09D48F0 UDP Rcv 192.55.83.30    9b01
 R Q [0080        NOERROR] A      (3)www(3)cco(3)com(0)
5/28/2012 6:48:59 PM 067C PACKET  000000BDAFD158A0 UDP Snd 12.222.165.144  c2da
   Q [0000        NOERROR] A      (3)www(3)cco(3)com(0)
5/28/2012 6:48:59 PM 067C PACKET  000000BDAF446E30 UDP Rcv 12.222.165.144  c2da
 R Q [8084 A  R  NOERROR] A      (3)www(3)cco(3)com(0)
5/28/2012 6:48:59 PM 067C PACKET  000000BDB0D8FF80 UDP Snd 10.1.2.13       0008
 R Q [8081   DR  NOERROR] A      (3)www(3)cco(3)com(0)
5/28/2012 6:48:59 PM 067C PACKET  000000BDB0A2B5B0 UDP Rcv 10.1.2.13       0009
   Q [0001   D   NOERROR] AAAA   (3)www(3)cco(3)com(0)
5/28/2012 6:48:59 PM 067C PACKET  000000BDB0D8FF80 UDP Snd 12.222.165.144  7b4a
   Q [0000        NOERROR] AAAA   (3)www(3)cco(3)com(0)
5/28/2012 6:48:59 PM 067C PACKET  000000BDB0F3BB90 UDP Rcv 12.222.165.144  7b4a
 R Q [8084 A  R  NOERROR] AAAA   (3)www(3)cco(3)com(0)
5/28/2012 6:48:59 PM 067C PACKET  000000BDB0A2B5B0 UDP Snd 10.1.2.13       0009
 R Q [8081   DR  NOERROR] AAAA   (3)www(3)cco(3)com(0)
```

The DNS log can be very detailed and tedious to read, but provides a wealth of information about exactly what the DNS server is doing. You can get even more detail by selecting the Details check box on the Debug Logging tab, which also enables you to see the data that was returned. Logging does add significantly to the load of the DNS server, so it should only be enabled when troubleshooting and disabled immediately afterwards.

Using Performance Monitor to Monitor DNS

Performance Monitor is a built-in, often-overlooked utility that allows for a great deal of insight into issues in a network. With regard to DNS, many critical DNS counters can be monitored relating to queries, zone transfers, memory utilization, and other important factors.

Client-Side Cache and HOST Resolution Problems

Windows 2000 and higher clients have a built-in client cache for name resolution that caches all information retrieved from name servers. When requesting lookups, the client resolver parses this cache first, before contacting the name server. Items remain in this cache until the TTL expires, the machine is rebooted, or the cache is flushed. In cases where erroneous information has been entered into the client cache, it can be flushed by typing **ipconfig /flushdns** at the command prompt.

By default, all clients have a file named HOSTS that provides for a simple line-by-line resolution of names to IP addresses. This file is normally located in \%Systemroot%\System32\Drivers\etc. Problems can occur when these manual entries conflict with DNS, and it is, therefore, wise to ensure that there are not conflicts with this HOSTS file and the DNS database when troubleshooting.

Using the Nslookup Command-Line Utility

The Nslookup command-line utility is perhaps the most useful tool for DNS client troubleshooting. Its functionality is basic, but the information obtained can do wonders for helping to understand DNS problems. Nslookup, in its most basic operation, contacts the default DNS server of a client and attempts to resolve a name that is inputted. For example, to test a lookup on www.companyabc.com, type **nslookup** www.companyabc.com at the command prompt. Different query types can also be input into Nslookup. For example, you can create simple queries to view the MX and SOA records associated with a specific domain by following these steps, which are illustrated in Figure 10.17:

1. Open a command prompt instance by choosing Start, All Programs, Accessories, Command Prompt.
2. Type **nslookup** and press Enter.
3. Type **set query=mx** and press Enter.
4. Type ***domainname*** and press Enter.
5. Type **set query=soa** and press Enter.
6. Type ***domainname*** and press Enter.

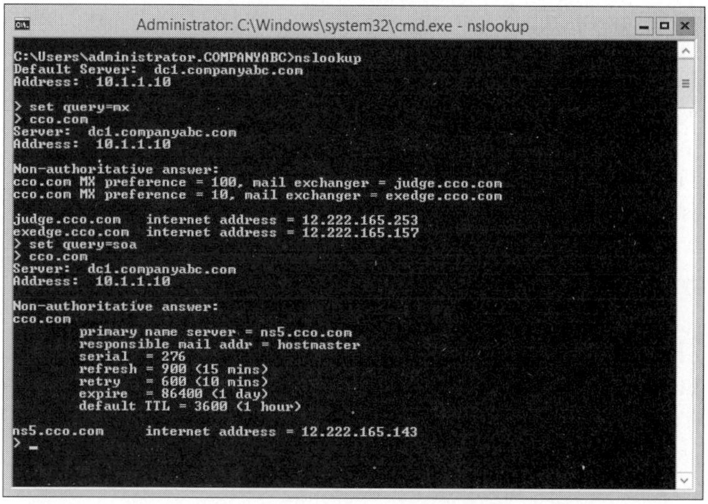

Administrator: C:\Windows\system32\cmd.exe - nslookup
C:\Users\administrator.COMPANYABC>nslookup
Default Server: dc1.companyabc.com
Address: 10.1.1.10
> set query=mx
> cco.com
Server: dc1.companyabc.com
Address: 10.1.1.10
Non-authoritative answer:
cco.com MX preference = 100, mail exchanger = judge.cco.com
cco.com MX preference = 10, mail exchanger = exedge.cco.com
judge.cco.com internet address = 12.222.165.253
exedge.cco.com internet address = 12.222.165.157
> set query=soa
> cco.com
Server: dc1.companyabc.com
Address: 10.1.1.10
Non-authoritative answer:
cco.com
primary name server = ns5.cco.com
responsible mail addr = hostmaster
serial = 276
refresh = 900 (15 mins)
retry = 600 (10 mins)
expire = 86400 (1 day)
default TTL = 3600 (1 hour)
ns5.cco.com internet address = 12.222.165.143
> _

FIGURE 10.17 Nslookup of an MX and an SOA record.

Nslookup's functionality is not limited to these simple lookups. Performing an **nslookup** /? lists the many functions it is capable of. Nslookup is a tool of choice for many name-resolution problems and is a must in any troubleshooter's arsenal.

Using the Ipconfig Command-Line Utility

Another important tool for DNS resolution problems is the Ipconfig utility, the same utility used for common TCP/IP issues. There are several key functions that Ipconfig offers with regard to DNS. These functions can be invoked from the command prompt with the right parameter, detailed as follows:

- **ipconfig /flushdns**—If you experience problems with the client-side cache, the cache itself can be "flushed" through the invocation of the **flushdns** flag. This removes all previously cached queries that a client might be storing and is particularly useful if a server name has just changed IP addresses and particular clients have trouble connecting to it.
- **ipconfig /registerdns**—The **registerdns** flag forces the client to dynamically reregister itself in DNS, if the particular zone supports dynamic updates.
- **ipconfig /displaydns**—An interesting but not well-known parameter is **displaydns**. This flag displays the contents of the client-side cache and is useful for troubleshooting specific issues with individual records.

Using the Tracert Command-Line Utility

The Tracert utility is a valuable resource that gives you an idea of the path that a DNS query takes when being sent over a network. By directing Tracert at www.microsoft.com, for example, you can get an idea of how many routers and DNS servers the packet is crossing. The way that Tracert works is simple, but actually quite interesting. A DNS query that has a TTL of 1 is sent out. Because all routers are supposed to drop the TTL by 1 on each packet that they process, this means that the first router will refuse to forward the packet and send that refusal back to the originator. The originating machine then increments the TTL by 1 and resends the packet. This time the packet will make it past the first router and get refused by the second. This process continues until the destination is met. Needless to say, using this command-line utility is a simple yet effective way of viewing the path that a DNS query takes as it crosses the Internet.

Using the DNSCmd Command-Line Utility

The DNSCmd utility is essentially a command-line version of the DNS Manager console. Installed as part of the Windows Server 2012 DNS Server role, this utility enables administrators to create zones, modify records, and perform other vital administrative functions via the command line. You can view the full functionality of this utility by typing **dnscmd** /? at the command line, as illustrated in Listing 10.3.

LISTING 10.3 DNSCMD Command Options

```
Usage: DnsCmd <ServerName> <Command> [<Command Parameters>]

<ServerName>:
  IP address or host name    -- remote or local DNS server
  .                          -- DNS server on local machine
```

```
<Command>:
  /Info                         -- Get server information
  /Config                       -- Reset server or zone configuration
  /EnumZones                    -- Enumerate zones
  /Statistics                   -- Query/clear server statistics data
  /ClearCache                   -- Clear DNS server cache
  /WriteBackFiles               -- Write back all zone or root-hint datafile(s)
  /StartScavenging              -- Initiates server scavenging
  /IpValidate                   -- Validate remote DNS servers
  /EnumKSPs                     -- Enumerate available key storage providers
  /ResetListenAddresses         -- Set server IP address(es) to serve DNS requests
  /ResetForwarders              -- Set DNS servers to forward recursive queries to
  /ZoneInfo                     -- View zone information
  /ZoneAdd                      -- Create a new zone on the DNS server
  /ZoneDelete                   -- Delete a zone from DNS server or DS
  /ZonePause                    -- Pause a zone
  /ZoneResume                   -- Resume a zone
  /ZoneReload                   -- Reload zone from its database (file or DS)
  /ZoneWriteBack                -- Write back zone to file
  /ZoneRefresh                  -- Force refresh of secondary zone from master
  /ZoneUpdateFromDs             -- Update a DS integrated zone by data from DS
  /ZonePrint                    -- Display all records in the zone
  /ZoneResetType                -- Change zone type
  /ZoneResetSecondaries         -- Reset secondary\notify information for a zone
  /ZoneResetScavengeServers     -- Reset scavenging servers for a zone
  /ZoneResetMasters             -- Reset secondary zone's master servers
  /ZoneExport                   -- Export a zone to file
  /ZoneChangeDirectoryPartition -- Move a zone to another directory partition
  /ZoneSeizeKeymasterRole       -- Seize the key master role for a zone
  /ZoneTransferKeymasterRole -- Transfer the key master role for a zone
  /ZoneEnumSKDs                 -- Enumerate the signing key descriptors for a zone
  /ZoneAddSKD                   -- Create a new signing key descriptor for a zone
  /ZoneDeleteSKD                -- Delete a signing key descriptor for a zone
  /ZoneModifySKD                -- Modify a signing key descriptor for a zone
  /ZoneValidateSigningParameters -- Validate DNSSEC online signing parameters for a
zone
  /ZoneSetSKDState              -- Set Active and/or Standby keys for a signing key
descriptor for a zone
  /ZoneGetSKDState              -- Retrieve dynamic state for a signing key descriptor
for a zone
  /ZonePerformKeyRollover       -- Trigger a key rollover in a signing key descriptor
for a zone
  /ZonePokeKeyRollover          -- Trigger a key rollover in a signing key descriptor
for a zone
  /ZoneSign                     -- Signs the zone using DNSSEC online signing param-
eters
```

```
  /ZoneUnsign                -- Removes DNSSEC signatures from a signed zone
  /ZoneResign                -- Regenerate DNSSEC signatures in a signed zone
  /EnumRecords               -- Enumerate records at a name
  /RecordAdd                 -- Create a record in zone or RootHints
  /RecordDelete              -- Delete a record from zone, RootHints or cache
  /NodeDelete                -- Delete all records at a name
  /AgeAllRecords             -- Force aging on node(s) in zone
  /TrustAnchorAdd            -- Create a new trust anchor zone on the DNS server
  /TrustAnchorDelete         -- Delete a trust anchor zone from DNS server or DS
  /EnumTrustAnchors          -- Display status information for trust anchors
  /TrustAnchorsResetType     -- Change zone type for a trust anchor zone
  /EnumDirectoryPartitions   -- Enumerate directory partitions
  /DirectoryPartitionInfo    -- Get info on a directory partition
  /CreateDirectoryPartition  -- Create a directory partition
  /DeleteDirectoryPartition  -- Delete a directory partition
  /EnlistDirectoryPartition  -- Add DNS server to partition replication scope
  /UnenlistDirectoryPartition -- Remove DNS server from replication scope
  /CreateBuiltinDirectoryPartitions -- Create built-in partitions
  /ExportSettings            -- Output settings to DnsSettings.txt in the DNS server
database directory
  /OfflineSign               -- Offline signing zone files, including key genera-
tion/deletion
  /EnumTrustPoints           -- Display active refresh information for all trust
points
  /ActiveRefreshAllTrustPoints -- Perform an active refresh on all trust points now
  /RetrieveRootTrustAnchors  -- Retrieve root trust anchors via HTTPS

<Command Parameters>:
  DnsCmd <CommandName> /? -- For help info on specific Command
```

In future versions of Windows, Microsoft might remove dnscmd.exe.

If you currently use dnscmd.exe to configure and manage the DNS server, Microsoft recommends that you transition to Windows PowerShell.

To view a list of commands for DNS server management, type **Get-Command -Module DnsServer** at the Windows PowerShell prompt. Additional information about Windows PowerShell commands for DNS is available at http://go.microsoft.com/fwlink/?LinkId=217627.

Managing DNS with PowerShell

The PowerShell cmdlets are essentially a command-line version of the DNS Manager console. Installed as part of the Windows Server 2012 DNS Server role, this PowerShell module enables administrators to create zones, modify records, and perform other vital administrative functions via the command line exactly as can be done with the traditional

DNSCmd tool. DNS configuration and management automation is greatly enhanced with Windows PowerShell, including the following:

- Feature parity with the user interface and DNSCmd.
- DNS Server role installation/removal using Windows PowerShell.
- Windows PowerShell client query with DNSSEC validation results.
- Server configuration is enabled for computers running older operating systems.

You can view the full functionality of this utility by typing **Get-Command -Module DnsServer** at the PowerShell command line, as shown in Listing 10.4.

LISTING 10.4 PowerShell DNS Cmdlets

```
CommandType     Name                                      ModuleName
-----------     ----                                      ----------
Alias           Export-DnsServerTrustAnchor               DnsServer
Function        Add-DnsServerConditionalForwarderZone     DnsServer
Function        Add-DnsServerDirectoryPartition           DnsServer
Function        Add-DnsServerForwarder                    DnsServer
Function        Add-DnsServerPrimaryZone                  DnsServer
Function        Add-DnsServerResourceRecord               DnsServer
Function        Add-DnsServerResourceRecordA              DnsServer
Function        Add-DnsServerResourceRecordAAAA           DnsServer
Function        Add-DnsServerResourceRecordCName          DnsServer
Function        Add-DnsServerResourceRecordDnsKey         DnsServer
Function        Add-DnsServerResourceRecordDS             DnsServer
Function        Add-DnsServerResourceRecordMX             DnsServer
Function        Add-DnsServerResourceRecordPtr            DnsServer
Function        Add-DnsServerRootHint                     DnsServer
Function        Add-DnsServerSecondaryZone                DnsServer
Function        Add-DnsServerSigningKey                   DnsServer
Function        Add-DnsServerStubZone                     DnsServer
Function        Add-DnsServerTrustAnchor                  DnsServer
Function        Add-DnsServerZoneDelegation               DnsServer
Function        Clear-DnsServerCache                      DnsServer
Function        Clear-DnsServerStatistics                 DnsServer
Function        ConvertTo-DnsServerPrimaryZone            DnsServer
Function        ConvertTo-DnsServerSecondaryZone          DnsServer
Function        Disable-DnsServerSigningKeyRollover       DnsServer
Function        Enable-DnsServerSigningKeyRollover        DnsServer
Function        Export-DnsServerDnsSecPublicKey           DnsServer
Function        Export-DnsServerZone                      DnsServer
Function        Get-DnsServer                             DnsServer
Function        Get-DnsServerCache                        DnsServer
Function        Get-DnsServerDiagnostics                  DnsServer
```

10

```
Function        Get-DnsServerDirectoryPartition               DnsServer
Function        Get-DnsServerDnsSecZoneSetting                DnsServer
Function        Get-DnsServerDsSetting                        DnsServer
Function        Get-DnsServerEDns                             DnsServer
Function        Get-DnsServerForwarder                        DnsServer
Function        Get-DnsServerGlobalNameZone                   DnsServer
Function        Get-DnsServerGlobalQueryBlockList             DnsServer
Function        Get-DnsServerRecursion                        DnsServer
Function        Get-DnsServerResourceRecord                   DnsServer
Function        Get-DnsServerRootHint                         DnsServer
Function        Get-DnsServerScavenging                       DnsServer
Function        Get-DnsServerSetting                          DnsServer
Function        Get-DnsServerSigningKey                       DnsServer
Function        Get-DnsServerStatistics                       DnsServer
Function        Get-DnsServerTrustAnchor                      DnsServer
Function        Get-DnsServerTrustPoint                       DnsServer
Function        Get-DnsServerZone                             DnsServer
Function        Get-DnsServerZoneAging                        DnsServer
Function        Get-DnsServerZoneDelegation                   DnsServer
Function        Import-DnsServerResourceRecordDS              DnsServer
Function        Import-DnsServerRootHint                      DnsServer
Function        Import-DnsServerTrustAnchor                   DnsServer
Function        Invoke-DnsServerSigningKeyRollover            DnsServer
Function        Invoke-DnsServerZoneSign                      DnsServer
Function        Invoke-DnsServerZoneUnsign                    DnsServer
Function        Register-DnsServerDirectoryPartition          DnsServer
Function        Remove-DnsServerDirectoryPartition            DnsServer
Function        Remove-DnsServerForwarder                     DnsServer
Function        Remove-DnsServerResourceRecord                DnsServer
Function        Remove-DnsServerRootHint                      DnsServer
Function        Remove-DnsServerSigningKey                    DnsServer
Function        Remove-DnsServerTrustAnchor                   DnsServer
Function        Remove-DnsServerZone                          DnsServer
Function        Remove-DnsServerZoneDelegation                DnsServer
Function        Reset-DnsServerZoneKeyMasterRole              DnsServer
Function        Restore-DnsServerPrimaryZone                  DnsServer
Function        Restore-DnsServerSecondaryZone                DnsServer
Function        Resume-DnsServerZone                          DnsServer
Function        Set-DnsServer                                 DnsServer
Function        Set-DnsServerCache                            DnsServer
Function        Set-DnsServerConditionalForwarderZone         DnsServer
Function        Set-DnsServerDiagnostics                      DnsServer
Function        Set-DnsServerDnsSecZoneSetting                DnsServer
Function        Set-DnsServerDsSetting                        DnsServer
Function        Set-DnsServerEDns                             DnsServer
Function        Set-DnsServerForwarder                        DnsServer
```

Function	Set-DnsServerGlobalNameZone	DnsServer
Function	Set-DnsServerGlobalQueryBlockList	DnsServer
Function	Set-DnsServerPrimaryZone	DnsServer
Function	Set-DnsServerRecursion	DnsServer
Function	Set-DnsServerResourceRecord	DnsServer
Function	Set-DnsServerResourceRecordAging	DnsServer
Function	Set-DnsServerRootHint	DnsServer
Function	Set-DnsServerScavenging	DnsServer
Function	Set-DnsServerSecondaryZone	DnsServer
Function	Set-DnsServerSetting	DnsServer
Function	Set-DnsServerSigningKey	DnsServer
Function	Set-DnsServerStubZone	DnsServer
Function	Set-DnsServerZoneAging	DnsServer
Function	Set-DnsServerZoneDelegation	DnsServer
Function	Show-DnsServerCache	DnsServer
Function	Show-DnsServerKeyStorageProvider	DnsServer
Function	Start-DnsServerScavenging	DnsServer
Function	Start-DnsServerZoneTransfer	DnsServer
Function	Suspend-DnsServerZone	DnsServer
Function	Sync-DnsServerZone	DnsServer
Function	Test-DnsServer	DnsServer
Function	Test-DnsServerDnsSecZoneSetting	DnsServer
Function	Unregister-DnsServerDirectoryPartition	DnsServer
Function	Update-DnsServerTrustPoint	DnsServer

The Set-DnsServerGlobalNameZone PowerShell cmdlet was used to enable the global names resolution earlier in the chapter.

Secure DNS with DNSSEC

Because DNS does not offer any form of security natively, it is vulnerable to spoofing, man-in-the-middle, and cache poisoning attacks. For this reason, it has become critical to develop a means for securing DNS. DNSSEC was developed to do just that.

There are a series of IETF RFCs that specify the DNSSEC extensions to DNS:

- **RFC 4033**—DNS Security Introduction and Requirements
- **RFC 4034**—Resource Records for the DNS Security Extensions
- **RFC 4035**—Protocol Modifications for the DNS Security Extensions
- **RFC 5155**—DNS Security (DNSSEC) Hashed Authenticated Denial of Existence
- **RFC 5702**—Use of SHA-2 Algorithms with RSA in DNSKEY and RRSIG Resource Records for DNSSEC
- **RFC 5011**—Automated Updates of DNS Security (DNSSEC) Trust Anchors

There are also several other supporting IETF RFCs. Together, these RFCs modify and extend the DNS protocol. The DNSSEC extensions provide the following:

- Origin authority
- Data integrity
- Authenticated denial of existence

In a nutshell, DNSSEC allows clients to know that the DNS information is coming from a valid server, wasn't changed, and that a given host exists or doesn't exist.

Windows Server 2008 and Windows 7 fully supported the DNSSEC RFCs 4033 through 4035. Windows Server 2012 extends DNSSEC and adds support for the DNSSEC RFCs 5011, 5155, and 5702.

Active Directory DNSSEC support is a critical new feature in Windows Server 2012, allowing secure DNS to be extended to Active Directory integrated DNS zones. Windows Server 2012 supports DNSSEC for Active Directory integrated DNS by supporting the following:

- Dynamic updates to zone records
- Multimaster DNS model for DNSSEC zones
- Use of AD for secure key and trust anchor distribution

Windows Server 2008 supported DNSSEC for AD-integrated zones, but did not support dynamic updates. This was a critical limiting factor in preventing rollout of DNSSEC to organizations because dynamic updates are a critical feature of AD-integrated zones and AD fault tolerance. Windows Server 2012 support for dynamic updates with DNSSEC allows AD-integrated zones to be fully utilized and organizations to realistically deploy DNSSEC.

Administration on DNSSEC in earlier versions of Windows Server was very manual, required a lot of steps, and required significant expertise. Windows Server 2012 simplifies the DNSSEC administration with the Zone Signing Wizard, allowing best practices defaults to be easily deployed and DNSSEC signed zones to be easily scaled out. Much of the administrative effort is automated, including the following:

- Automated re-signing on static and dynamic updates
- Automated key rollovers
- Automated signature refreshes
- Automated updates of secure delegations
- Automated distribution and updating of trust anchors

The ease of administration and automation brings DNSSEC in Windows Server 2012 to a production-ready capacity.

DNSSEC Components

The DNSSEC relies on signed zones, which is a zone whose records are signed as defined by RFC 4035. A signed zone contains one or more of the new DNSEC record types, which are DNSKEY, NSEC, RRSIG, and DS records. These records allow DNS data to be validated by resolvers.

Zone Signing Key (ZSK) is the encryption key used to sign the zone, essentially a public and private key combination stored in a certificate. The Key Signing Key (KSK) is the key used to sign the ZSK to validate it, essentially a public and private key combination as well.

The DNSKEY record is a DNSSEC record type used to store a public key. The KSK and the ZSK public keys are stored in the DNSKEY records to allow the zone signatures to be validated.

The Next Secure (NSEC) record is a DNSSEC record type used to prove the nonexistence of a DNS name. This allows DNS clients to be sure that if a record is not retrieved in a DNS lookup, the record does not exist in the DNSSEC zone.

The Resource Record Signature (RRSIG) record is used to hold the signature for a DNS record. For each A record, there will be a corresponding RRSIG record. For each NSEC record, there will also be a corresponding RRSIG record.

The Delegation Signer (DS) record is used to secure delegations to other DNS servers and confirm their validity. This prevents man-in-the-middle DNS servers from breaking the security chain during recursive lookups.

A nonvalidating security-aware stub resolver is a security-aware stub resolver that trusts one or more security-aware DNS servers to perform DNSSEC validation on its behalf. All Windows DNS clients are nonvalidating security-aware stub resolvers, meaning they do not actually do the DNSSEC validation.

The Windows DNS client is nonvalidating, meaning that the Windows DNS client does not check to see whether the DNS records are secured but instead implicitly trusts the DNS server. The Windows DNS client flags the DNS request based on the NRPT table and expects the DNS server to perform the check for it. The DNS server returns the results regardless and indicates whether the check for DNSSEC was successful. If the check was successful, the Windows DNS client passes the results to the application requesting the DNS lookup.

NOTE

To really ensure the security of the DNS requests, the DNS client must be able to validate the DNS server. The method of doing this for Windows systems is to use IPsec. To really, really secure DNS, IPsec must be deployed as well.

Important Performance Considerations for DNSSEC

Although DNSSEC introduces important security benefits, there are some impacts to deploying it.

Some impacts to consider when deploying DNSSEC are as follows:

- **Increased memory requirements**—A DNSSEC zone may require as much as five times the memory on the Windows Server 2012 server as an unsigned zone.
- **Increased network traffic**—A response to a DNS query against a DNSSEC zone will return additional DNSSEC records as compared to a unsigned zone and will increase the network traffic accordingly.
- **Increased processor utilization**—The additional workload of validating DNSSEC zone data during queries can increase the processor load on the Windows Server 2012 server hosting the DNSSEC zone.
- **Increased number of DNS records**—A DNSSEC zone will have up to four times the number of records as an unsigned zone. For large zones, this can be a significant factor.

It is important to ensure that adequate server-level resources are available when deploying DNSSEC, especially into existing Windows Server 2012 servers. For well-tuned virtual servers that are running at capacity, the additional workload to support DNSSEC on large zones can be a significant increase.

Configuring a DNSSEC Zone

In this scenario, the zone companyabc.com will be encrypted. The zone is unsecured to start and contains several records, shown in Figure 10.18.

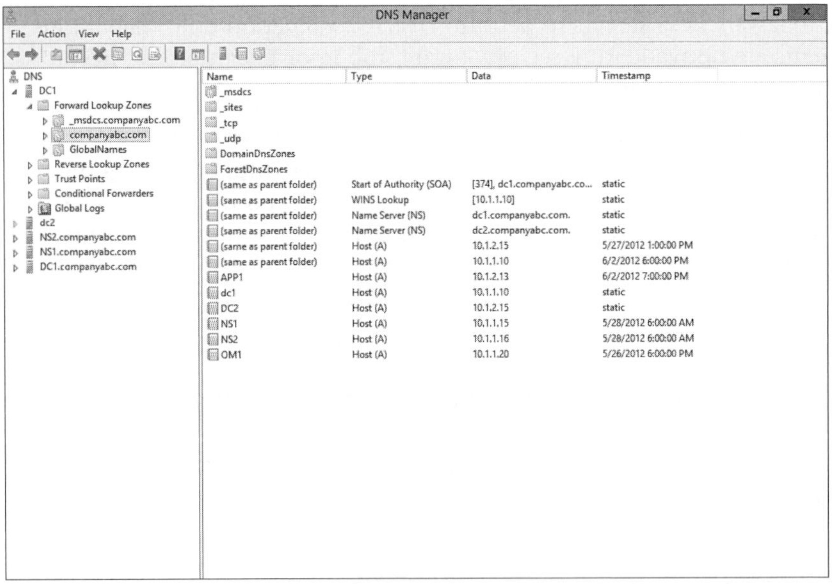

FIGURE 10.18 Unsecured DNS zone.

The DNSSEC configuration and management is done using the DNS Manager utility. To sign a DNS zone, follow these steps:

1. Launch Server Manager from a Windows 2012 server with a full GUI.
2. Select the DNS section. The list of servers in the server pool with the DNS role installed will be shown.
3. Right-click the DNS server to configure and select DNS Manager.
4. Select the DNS server name to configure.
5. Select the Forward Lookup Zones node.
6. Select the zone to sign.
7. Right-click the zone and select DNSSEC and then Sign the Zone.
8. At the Zone Signing Wizard screen, click Next.
9. Select Use recommended setting to sign the zone, then click Next.
10. Review the settings, and then click Next to sign the zone.
11. Click Finish to exit the wizard.

The zone companyabc.com is now encrypted. Figure 10.19 shows the zone records after encryption.

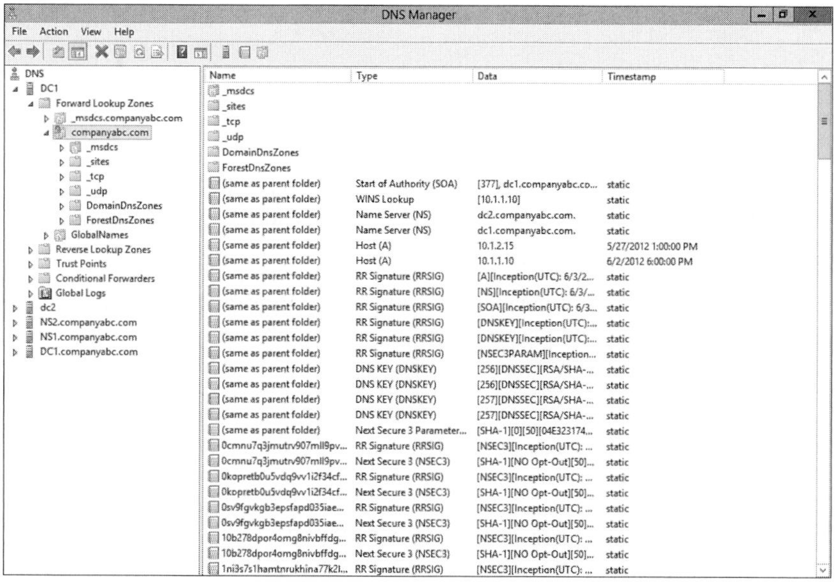

FIGURE 10.19 Encrypted zone records.

There are four records for each previous entry now:

- Standard A Record
- RR Signature (RRSIG) Record for the Standard Record
- Next Secure (NSEC) Record
- RR Signature (RRSIG) Record for the Next Secure Record

To distribute the trust anchor for the DNSSEC zone, follow these steps:

1. Launch Server Manager from a Windows 2012 server with a full GUI.
2. Select the DNS section. The list of servers in the server pool with the DNS role installed will be shown.
3. Right-click the DNS server to configure and select DNS Manager.
4. Select the DNS server name to configure.
5. Select the Forward Lookup Zones node.
6. Select the zone to sign.
7. Right-click the zone and select DNSSEC and then Properties.
8. Select the Trust Anchor tab.
9. Check the Enable the Distribution of Trust Anchors for This Zone box.
10. Click OK to save the changes.
11. Click Yes to confirm the change.
12. Click OK when the setting is complete.

After the setting, there will be a new folder named Trust Points that contains the a pair of records for the zone of type DNS KEY. These contain the public key for the trust anchor for the signed zone.

Without any additional configuration, the DNS clients blissfully ignore the DNSSEC for the zone. To have the clients use the DNSSEC properties of the DNS zone, they must be configured to request secure DNS entries. This is done by configuring a Name Resolution Policy Table (NRPT) policy for clients.

The NRPT policy can be configured through group policy. To create a NRPT group policy for the secure.companyabc.com zone, follow these steps:

1. Launch Server Manager from a Windows 2012 server with a full GUI.
2. Select Tools and then Group Policy Management.
3. Expand Forest: companyabc.com, Domains, and select companyabc.com.

4. Right-click companyabc.com and select Create a GPO in This Domain, and Link It Here.
5. Enter **NRPT Group Policy Object** and click OK.
6. Right-click the NRPT Group Policy Object link and select Edit.
7. Expand Computer Configuration, Policies, Windows Settings, and select Name Resolution Policy.
8. In the To Which Part of the Namespace Does This Rule Apply? Field, select Suffix and enter **companyabc.com**.
9. On the DNSSEC tab, check the Enable DNSSEC in This Rule box.
10. Check the Validation box Require DNS Clients to Check That Name and Address Data Has Been Validated.

NOTE

The wording of this option is precise. The Windows DNS client will check that the DNS server has validated the data, but will *not* do the validation itself.

11. Figure 10.20 shows how the record should look. Click the Create button to create the record in the Name Resolution Policy Table at the bottom of the screen.
12. Close the GPMC editor to save the changes.

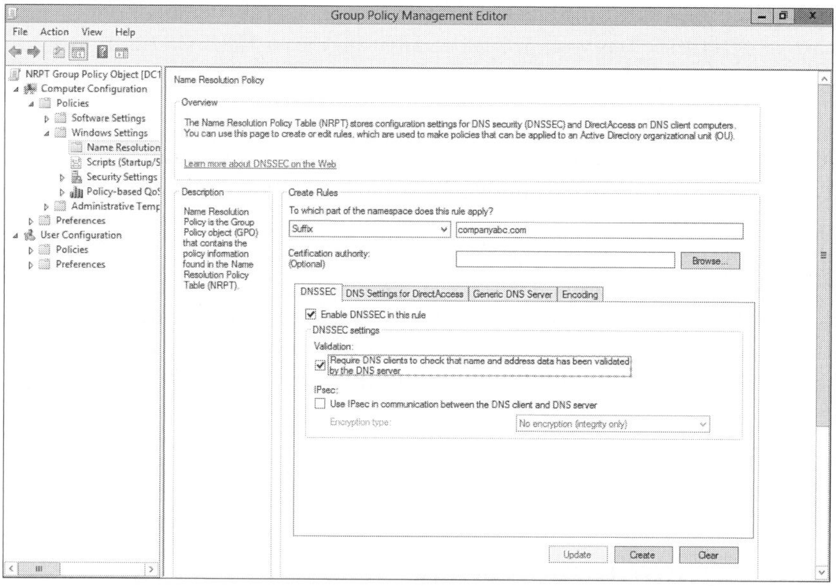

FIGURE 10.20 Name-resolution policy.

Now, all domain DNS clients will request that DNS servers check the validity of the lookups for domain companyabc.com using DNSSEC.

Reviewing the Windows Internet Naming Service

The Windows Internet Naming Service (WINS) has a long history in Microsoft networks. In the beginning, Microsoft networks were primarily broadcast based, using protocols such as NetBEUI to identify local computers. If a user on a Windows client wanted to find a system by name, the Windows client would send out a broadcast message by name, and if the system was on the same network, it would respond so the two systems could establish a connection and begin communication. The problem with this type of name resolution was that it did not scale beyond multiple subnets, and with today's networks, broadcast messages can be blocked by local server and workstation firewalls and antimalware software. With the adoption of TCP/IP as an easily routable protocol, the need to translate NetBIOS or Windows computer names to IP addresses became a reality. This need gave rise to the development of WINS.

WINS provided a central database that can be referenced when a client system is looking up another system by hostname, and that is the key difference between WINS and DNS, hostname versus fully qualified name. As an example of this, a server named SERVER10 in the companyabc.com domain would have a WINS record named SERVER10 and a DNS record in the companyabc.com DNS zone named server10.companyabc.com.

Understanding the Need for Legacy Microsoft NetBIOS Resolution

WINS is effectively a simple database of NetBIOS names and their corresponding IP addresses. Some additional information, such as domain name, server type or service type, and so on, can be determined as well, from the 16th byte in a NetBIOS name stored in WINS.

WINS is considered legacy in the Microsoft world because NetBIOS resolution is being phased out in favor of the domain name system (DNS) form of name resolution. However, it is difficult to divorce WINS from modern networks because of the reliance on WINS by down-level (pre-Windows 2000) clients, legacy applications, and even some Microsoft services, such as the Distributed File System (DFS), that utilize NetBIOS resolution by default. Also, many Independent Software Vendors, or ISVs, develop their software for Microsoft networks, but their test networks sometimes only include a single network with no firewalling between systems. When these software applications are deployed on enterprise networks, they can fall short in name-resolution results, and deploying WINS might be the only viable solution.

As mentioned previously in this chapter, the new DNS GlobalNames feature is designed to remove the need for WINS.

Installing and Configuring WINS

As with many services in Windows Server 2012, the installation and configuration process of a WINS server is streamlined through the Add Features Wizard. This wizard automatically installs all necessary services and databases and configures other settings pertinent to a particular service. Although other methods of installation still exist, this method is the preferred approach in Windows Server 2012.

Installing WINS

Installation of WINS on Windows Server 2012 is straightforward, and no reboot is necessary. To install and configure the WINS feature on a Windows Server 2012 computer, follow these steps:

1. Launch Server Manager from a Windows 2012 server with a full GUI.
2. Select the Dashboard section and click the Add Roles and Features link.
3. Click Next on the Before You Begin page.
4. Leave the default selection Role-Based or Feature-Based Installation and click Next.
5. Select the server from the server pool to add the DNS role to and click Next.
6. Click Next to skip the Roles selection.
7. Select the WINS Server Feature check box, click Add Features button, and then click Next.

NOTE

When the WINS Features box is checked, the Add Roles and Features Wizard does a readiness check to ensure that the target server is ready for the WINS feature.

8. Click Install on the Confirmation page to install the WINS feature.
9. Click Close to exit the Add Roles and Features Wizard.

The DNS role can also be installed locally on a server core installation using PowerShell with the following command:

```
Install-WindowsFeature -Name WINS
```

Configuring Push/Pull Partners

If a WINS server in an environment is the sole WINS server for that network, no additional configuration is required other than ensuring that clients will be pointing to the WINS server in their IP configuration. However, if it has been decided that WINS is required, it is a best-practice recommendation to deploy a secondary WINS server to provide redundancy. Unlike DHCP, however, WINS replication partners will replicate their registered entries between each other. WINS replication is established through the designation of WINS push/pull partners.

A push partner for a particular WINS server is the server that pushes WINS database information to a receiving or pull partner. A pull partner is a WINS server from which changes are "pulled." In a nutshell, if Server1 has Server2 configured as a push partner, Server2 must have Server1 configured as a pull partner, and vice versa.

A WINS push/pull topology should roughly map to an organization's network topology. For example, if an organization is composed of two main offices that serve as network hubs, and several branch offices, each with its own WINS servers, the WINS push/pull topology could look something like Figure 10.21. In many organizations, however, if network connectivity is reliable between locations, it is a best practice to deploy only two WINS servers for the entire organization. This reduces WINS database replication and administration. Remote or branch office WINS servers should only be deployed on networks where network and/or firewall administrators block WINS traffic from remote networks.

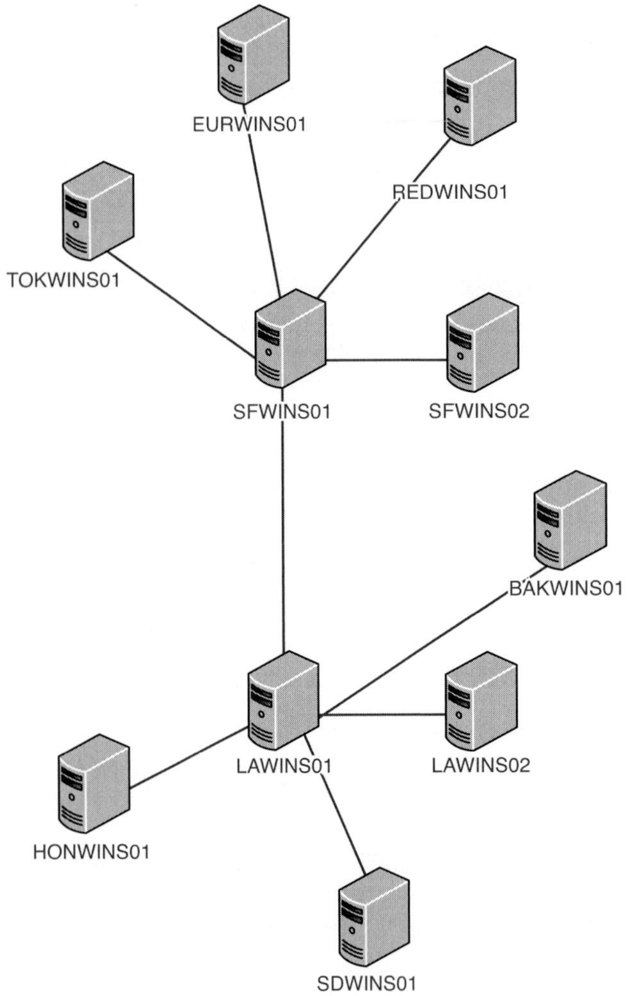

FIGURE 10.21 Sample WINS push/pull topology.

Examining WINS Replication

WINS replicates database changes on a set schedule, which can be modified on a per-connection basis. Just as with any network communications, the replication schedule should be modified to fit the particular needs of an organization. If a WAN link is saturated with traffic, it might be wise to throttle back the WINS replication schedule. However, if a link between push/pull partners is robust, a shorter schedule can be established. To establish WINS replication between two WINS servers, follow these steps:

1. Install WINS on two designated servers as previously outlined. For our example, we will use DC1 and DC2.
2. On one of the servers, log on and open the WINS console (Server Manager, Tools, and select WINS). If prompted, click Continue to confirm the action.
3. Expand the WINS server in the console tree, and then choose Replication Partners. The right pane will display any existing replication partners.
4. If the desired replication partner is not already defined, in the console tree, right-click Replication Partners and select New Replication Partner.
5. Enter the name of the desired WINS server and click OK. This adds the designated WINS server as a push/pull partner, meaning that these servers will replicate and synchronize their database with one another.
6. In the WINS console tree, right-click the WINS node and choose Add Server.
7. Type in the name of the WINS server previously defined as a replication partner.
8. Once the second WINS server is added to the console, repeat the preceding steps to add the first server as a replication partner.

WINS replication partners need to be defined on both systems before replication will function.

WINS replication partners replicate their database information with one another every 30 minutes by default. If you, the WINS administrator, want to change this replication schedule, complete the following steps:

1. Open the WINS console (Server Manager, Tools, and select WINS). If prompted, click Continue to confirm the action.
2. Expand the WINS server in the console tree, and then choose Replication Partners.
3. Right-click Push/Pull Partner (if one does not exist, it will have to be created), and choose Properties.
4. In the replication partner property pages, select the Advanced tab, and change the replication interval time to the desired length, as indicated in Figure 10.22, and click OK to save the settings.
5. Repeat this process on the other replication partner.

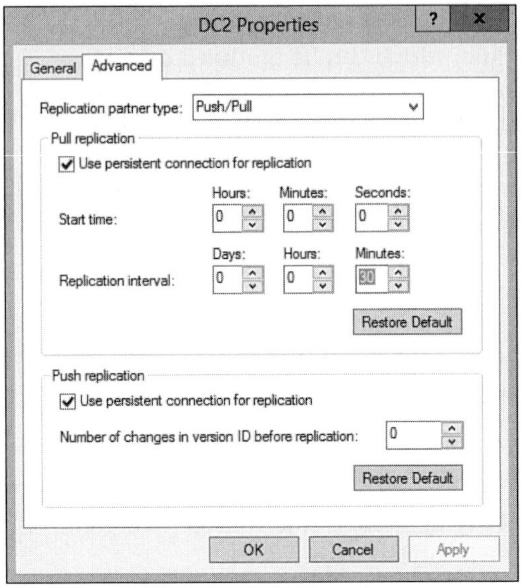

FIGURE 10.22 WINS replication settings.

This can also be used to change other partner replication settings, such as number of retries, start replication at service startup, persistent connections, and other pertinent replication information.

Understanding NetBIOS Client Resolution and the LMHOSTS File

A Windows client does not immediately resort to a WINS server to determine the IP address of a NetBIOS name. This knowledge is essential in the troubleshooting of name resolution on a Windows client. Instead, a client first accesses its local NetBIOS cache for resolution. If an IP address changes, this cache might report the old address, impeding troubleshooting. To flush this cache, run **nbtstat -R** (with an uppercase *R*) at the PowerShell command line.

In addition to the local cache, clients by default always parse an LMHOSTS file, if one exists, before contacting a WINS server. If the LMHOSTS file contains erroneous information, it will impede proper name resolution. Always check to see whether this file is populated (it is usually located in %Systemroot%\System32\Drivers\etc on clients) before beginning to troubleshoot the WINS server.

Planning, Migrating, and Maintaining WINS

As previously mentioned, WINS is necessary in most production environments because the overriding dependencies on NetBIOS that were built in to Windows have not entirely been shaken out. In fresh installations of Windows Server 2012, WINS might not be necessary, but for older, upgraded environments, plans should be made for WINS being around for a few years.

Upgrading a WINS Environment

The WINS service itself is one of the more straightforward services to migrate to a separate set of servers as part of an upgrade to Windows Server 2012. A simple upgrade of the existing WINS server will do the trick for many environments; however, migrating to a separate server or set of servers might be beneficial if changing topology or hardware.

Migration of an existing WINS environment is most easily accomplished through the procedure described in this section. This procedure allows for the migration of an entire WINS database to a new set of servers, but without affecting any clients or changing WINS server settings. Figure 10.23 illustrates a WINS migration using this procedure.

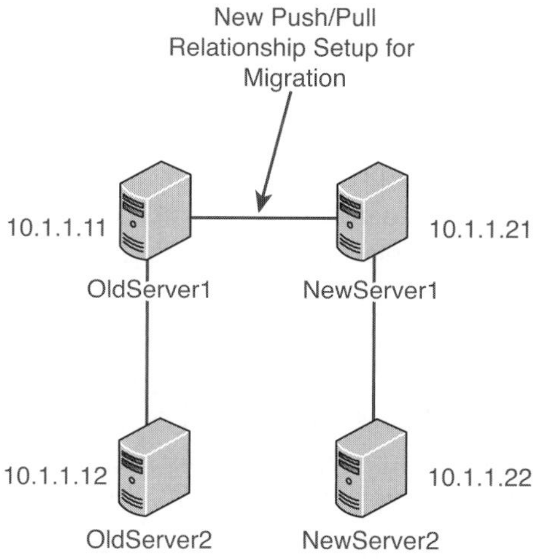

FIGURE 10.23 The first step in the WINS migration procedure.

In Figure 10.23, the existing servers, OldServer1 and OldServer2, handle WINS traffic for the entire network of fictional CompanyABC. They are configured with IP addresses 10.1.1.11 and 10.1.1.12, which are configured in all client IP settings as Primary and Secondary WINS, respectively. OldServer1 and OldServer2 are configured as push/pull partners.

The new servers, NewServer1 and NewServer2, are added to the network with the WINS service installed and configured as push/pull partners for each other. Their initial IP addresses are 10.1.1.21 and 10.1.1.22. OldServer1 and NewServer1 are then connected as push/pull partners for the network. Because the servers are connected this way, all database information from the old WINS database is replicated to the new servers, as illustrated in step 1, shown in Figure 10.23.

After the entire WINS database is replicated to the new servers, the old servers are shut down (on a weekend or evening to minimize impact), and NewServer1 and NewServer2 are immediately reconfigured to take the IP addresses of the old servers, as illustrated in step 2, shown in Figure 10.24.

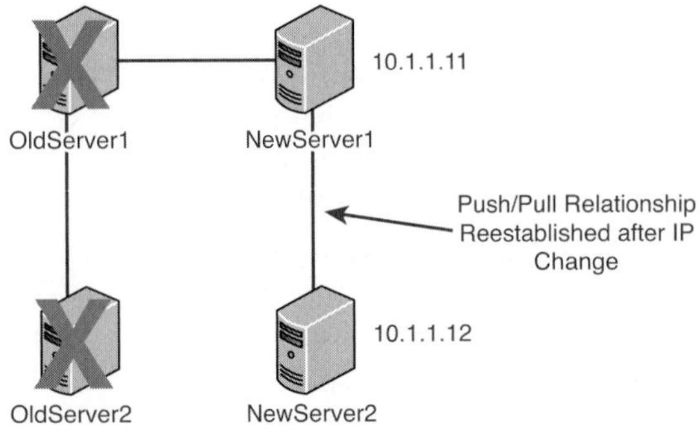

FIGURE 10.24 The second step in the WINS migration procedure.

The push/pull partner relationship between NewServer1 and NewServer2 is then reestablished because the IP addresses of the servers changed. The entire downtime of the WINS environment can be measured in mere minutes, and the old database is migrated intact. In addition, because the new servers assume the old IP addresses, no client settings need to be reconfigured.

There are a few caveats with this approach, however. If the IP addresses cannot be changed, WINS servers must be changed on the client side. If you're using DHCP, you can do this by leaving all old and new servers up in an environment until the WINS change can be automatically updated through DHCP. Effectively, however, WINS migrations can be made very straightforward through this technique, and they can be modified to fit any WINS topology.

Exploring WINS and DNS Integration

DNS can use the WINS database to provide for quasi-DNS resolution of WINS clients. This means that if a name-resolution request is sent to a DNS server to resolve client1.companyabc.com, for example, the DNS server will first look in the companyabc.com zone. If no record exists for client1.companyabc.com, the DNS server will perform a lookup on the WINS database for CLIENT1; if a WINS record exists, the DNS server will take this IP address and send it back to the DNS client as client1.companyabc.com, as illustrated in Figure 10.25.

This functionality must be enabled on the DNS server because it is not configured by default. This feature is configured on a zone-by-zone basis; however, if the forward lookup zone is an AD-integrated zone, each Windows Server 2012 DNS server hosting this zone will copy this WINS setting. To enable WINS resolution on a DNS server, follow these steps:

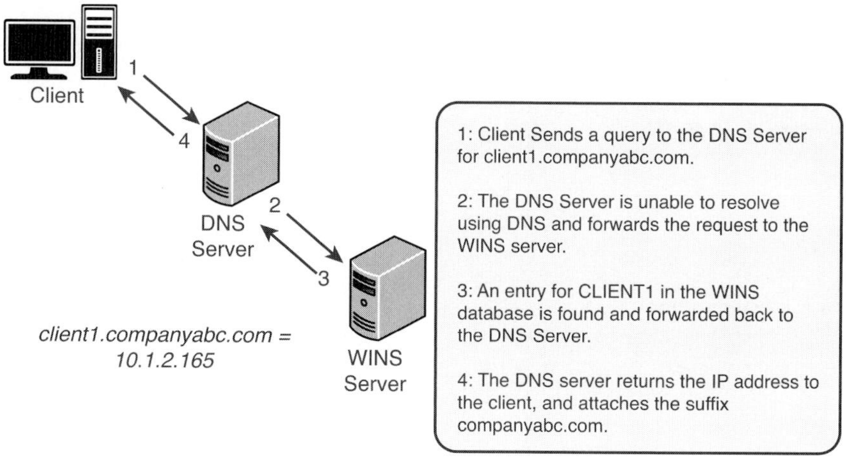

FIGURE 10.25 WINS integration with DNS.

1. Launch Server Manager from a Windows 2012 server with a full GUI.
2. Select the DNS section. The list of servers in the server pool with the DNS role installed will be shown.
3. Right-click the DNS server to configure and select DNS Manager.
4. Select the DNS server name to configure.
5. Select the Forward Lookup Zones node.
6. Right-click the zone in question and click Properties.
7. Choose the WINS tab.
8. Check the Use WINS Forward Lookup check box.
9. Enter the IP address of the WINS servers to be used for resolution of names not found in DNS, and click Add to save the changes, as illustrated in Figure 10.26.
10. If you are replicating this zone between DNS servers that are not running Windows Server 2012 DNS services, make sure to check the Do Not Replicate This Record box. This prevents the records from being replicated to other servers during zone transfers.
11. Click OK to finish and return to the DNS Manager page.

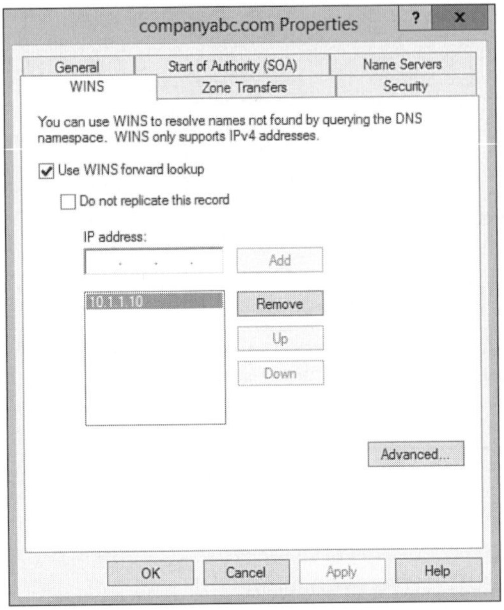

FIGURE 10.26 Configuring WINS resolution in DNS.

Summary

DNS has proven itself over time to be a robust, dependable, and extremely scalable solution to name resolution. Windows Server 2012 takes DNS to the next level and builds on the enhancements introduced with Windows 2000/2003/2008 DNS.

A key improvement in Windows Server 2012 is the enhanced support of the secure DNS (DNSSEC) functionality. Supporting DNSSEC for Dynamic DNS allows for full support of Active Directory and DNSSEC to deployed to large and small organization.

Whether using DNS for a full-fledged AD DS implementation or simply setting up an Internet DNS presence, Windows Server 2012's DNS builds on a successful, road-tested base to provide for a functional, reliable, enterprise name-resolution strategy.

Best Practices

The following are best practices from this chapter:

- Use Windows Server 2012 DNS whenever possible to support AD DS. If you must use a non-Windows DNS to host the AD zone, ensure that it supports SRV records, such as with BIND version 8.1.2 or later.
- Establish a caching-only server in small branch office situations to alleviate large amounts of client query traffic across the network and to eliminate the need to replicate entire DNS zones to remote locations.

- Configure DHCP to dynamically update DNS information for down-level clients if dynamic records are necessary.
- Identify the sources of dynamically updated information to prevent problems with reliability.
- Configure a DNS server to point to itself for DNS queries rather than to another DNS server.
- Make any DNS implementation compliant with the standard DNS character set so that you can support zone transfers to and from non-Unicode-compliant DNS implementations such as UNIX BIND servers. This includes a–z, A–Z, 0–9, and the hyphen (-) character.
- Use the GNZ to reduce the reliance on WINS in the enterprise.
- Turn on Debug Logging on a per-server basis for more advanced DNS event log diagnosis only when required, and turn off this functionality when it's no longer necessary.
- When deploying DNSSEC, ensure that sufficient server resources are allocated to support the increased memory, network and processor requirements that signing the zones will create.
- Implement redundant WINS servers by configuring servers as push/pull partners.
- Limit the number of WINS servers on the network to reduce WINS server replication and administration and to simplify WINS troubleshooting.

CHAPTER 11

DHCP,IPv6 and IPAM

IN THIS CHAPTER

Connecting new servers and workstations to the network requires network connectivity and the ability to find the required resources to properly authenticate the computer and users accounts. This is accomplished with proper network connectivity, network addressing, and name resolution. In the preceding chapter, you learned about the domain name system (DNS) and Windows Internet Naming Service (WINS), which are the primary name-resolution services used by network-connected systems today. This chapter provides an overview and detailed information for system administrators to properly implement automated network addressing solutions using the Dynamic Host Configuration Protocol (DHCP) services provided with Windows Server 2012. This chapter also covers IPv6, DHCP configuration and the new Microsoft feature IP Address Management (IPAM) server and client.

Understanding the Components of an Enterprise Network

Whether an enterprise, midsize, or small business network, all connected systems require proper IP addressing and name resolution to function. When a new system is to be connected to the network, it must be configured with network address settings sufficient enough to authenticate the user logging on and to locate the network resources that the user/computer account require. This is accomplished with a layered approach of network addressing, name resolution, and domain identification and authentication.

The Importance of Network Addressing

This book details the implementation of Windows Server 2012 and assumes that the network will be based on Microsoft networking. Regardless of whether Microsoft, UNIX, Mac, or a different operating system provides the network backbone, network addressing is the key to intercomputer communication. Anything and everything about computer networking is based on locating and accessing resources stored on multiple systems so that users can collaborate and share information. This is possible with network addressing and, to make it simpler, name resolution.

With today's infrastructure consisting of both local company-owned resources intertwining with cloud or Internet-based hosted applications, name resolution is key to successful functionality for computer systems and users on these networks. Name resolution for Internet and intranet connectivity is detailed in the preceding chapter. This chapter focuses more on automated network connectivity provided by DHCP for both IPv4 and IPv6 and also covers the new feature IPAM.

IP address management has always been a task associated with managing an organization's network. Until now, however, this task has mostly been performed by relying on WINS and DNS records and on text files, spreadsheets, custom applications or databases, and third-party products. Microsoft Windows Server 2012 includes the IPAM feature, which provides administrators with a centralized complete view of the IP landscape, to not just to keep track of IP addresses, but also to audit changes and implement changes through the one central console.

Name Resolution

Name resolution refers to the identification of a network-connected system by a friendly name as opposed to a network address. Connecting to a network resource by its actual network address is possible within certain constraints, but with today's security and application features and functionality, connecting to a system by its name is not only ideal, it may be required. For example, in many common hosted implementations, a single network address may resolve to many different names and present different applications, websites, and services based each unique name.

Name resolution is the resolution of a network-connected resource by name and a matched IP address or a different name or alias name. This could be a short name such as WEBSERVER1 or a fully qualified domain name (FQDN) such as www.companyabc.com resolving to an IP address of 10.1.1.10.

Name Resolution and Directory Integration

With Microsoft Active Directory (AD) and many networking services, name resolution provides detailed information about how to connect to a particular service. For example, with Windows Server 2012 DNS servers and clients, a client system looking to find a Global Catalog server is presented not only with a list of names and IP addresses, it is also provided with the closest system to the network the system is connected to, and it also presents the port the client can connect to that service on. So, instead of just a name to IP address, advanced name-resolution services can make distinctions of the client location and provide a detailed response that improves network connectivity.

Network Services Changes in Windows Server 2012

With each new version of the Windows Server operating system, Microsoft improves on the previous release. With Windows Server 2012, Microsoft maintains this tradition and has made a substantial improvement in DHCP services. Windows Server 2012 DHCP services now include a new type of service redundancy named DHCP failover. In the previous DHCP release included with Windows Server 2008 R2, Microsoft introduced a Split-Scope Wizard and a response delay that allowed DHCP administrators to enable redundancy, but some features such as reservations and active leases were still managed separately. Another option was and still is to deploy DHCP services on a failover cluster, but that adds on the complications of managing a failover cluster system and leveraging a shared storage subsystem or an external data replication system.

With Windows Server 2012 DHCP failover, redundancy is achieved through the DHCP services on each system monitoring and updating one another on leases, reservations, scope settings, and service availability. This makes this new enhancement a great addition to the many new features and services already included in the DHCP server role.

Windows Server 2012 IPAM Overview

The IPAM feature included with Windows Server 2012 provides network administrators with a single centralized console from which they can view and manage the IP addresses of the entire enterprise. This feature supports the discovery of servers providing IP-related services and includes tasks to collect and organize data from these servers in single functional console. The IPAM feature collects data from DNS, DHCP, domain controller (DC) and Network Policy Server (NPS) servers that are registered to the particular IPAM server and presents the data in several default views that are searchable and easily manipulated and exportable. IP address audit tracking and even changes to existing service configurations and records are just a few of the tasks that this new feature enables. More information about Windows Server 2012 IPAM is detailed later in this chapter.

Exploring DHCP

Understanding how DHCP works is an important part of a network administrator's list of skills. In today's networks, the DHCP service is used by workstations, some servers, Preboot Execution Environment (PXE) network boot clients, printers, mobile devices such as a smartphone or tablet, IP-based phones and data scanners. Some Windows Server 2012 services, such as the Windows Deployment Server role services interact and depend on DHCP to properly function.

The Need for DHCP

Network administrators cannot expect end users and even IT personnel to be able to manually configure each network device's IP address settings. Furthermore, many end users may not even have the permissions to change network configurations. Because of these and other challenges, DHCP services are required on most networks to enable network connectivity. Also, many devices do not provide an interface simple enough or readily available to configure network settings. DHCP provides a simple way to not only deliver IP addressing from a central administrative point, but it also allows the network administrators to control how these devices actually connect to the network and greatly enhance the management of these network-connected devices through this service.

Outlining DHCP Predecessors: RARP and BOOTP

Before the DHCP service was developed, two predecessors provided the first implementations of automated IP addressing. The first was the Reverse Address Resolution Protocol (RARP), and the second was the Bootstrap Protocol (BOOTP).

To understand RARP, an IT administrator should first understand the Address Resolution Protocol (ARP). Each network adapter, wired or wireless, has a unique address burned into it. This address never changes and it called the Media Access Control (MAC) address. The ARP stores IP address-to-MAC address information. For example, if you know the IP address of a system on the network, the ARP table will provide the corresponding MAC address associated with that IP address. On most systems and network devices, the ARP table is built dynamically based on previous and current connections, but only for systems on the same network segment. RARP tables, however, are the reverse in both the fact that they are not dynamically built and they are MAC-to-IP resolution.

The RARP service allows a newly connected system to broadcast its MAC address on the network and the RARP service will respond with the assigned IP address. This allows the new system to basically connect dynamically to the network. A few catches exist, however. The first catch is that the RARP administrator must first collect that new system's MAC address and create an entry on the RARP table on the service with a corresponding IP address. The next catch is that RARP delivers a system an IP address but no other networking information, such as a subnet mask, router IP address, or DNS server or other networking options. The RARP service was limited to usage on a single flat network, but was useful in its time.

The next predecessor is the BOOTP service. The BOOTP service provided an IP address to clients requesting one, but did not require a predefined table of related MAC and IP addresses. BOOTP was designed to not only get a system connected, but to also provide additional information to systems looking to load or boot an operating system stored on the network. BOOTP is still used today for some network boot implementations but has been superseded by the DHCP service.

Exploring the DHCP Server Service

The DHCP server service is the latest implementation of automated network addressing in use today. The DHCP server service can provide all the same functionality of a BOOTP service, but can also provide additional information to clients who are requesting an IP address. The DHCP server service provides a client an IP address in three steps:

1. DHCP client boots and broadcasts a DHCP IP request to all nodes on the local network.

2. A DHCP server on the local network receives the request and prepares to distribute an IP address to this client in the form of a DHCP IP address lease.

3. After the DHCP server has determined the right prerequisite information from that client request, it issues the client with a DHCP IP address lease, including additional DHCP lease options such as subnet mask, default gateway, and most likely, DNS server IP addresses.

Examining the DHCP Client Service

The DHCP client service is the client-side service that requests an IP address from the network. Depending on the system's network adapter configuration, the DHCP client service may be active or inactive and, if the client is leveraging network boot, can come in the form of a BOOTP or PXE client controlled by the system board. The Windows DHCP client service, however, is managed by the configuration stored within the Microsoft operating system and, furthermore, on each adapter. If the adapter senses a network connection and the IP address configuration is configured for automated IP addressing, the DHCP client service broadcasts the request for an IP address, and when the data is received from the server, the DHCP client service applies the lease information to the appropriate adapter and enables network communications. With the DHCP IP address lease, there is an important piece of information delivered, known as the lease duration. The lease duration informs the client how long the IP address can be used before the client must check back with the DHCP server to renew the lease or get a new lease. The DHCP client caches this information, and when the lease duration is nearly up or when the system is restarted or the network is reinitialized, the DHCP client contacts the DHCP server to ensure the lease can still be used so that it can be renewed or replaced with a new lease.

In addition, on Microsoft systems, the DHCP client service also manages the Dynamic DNS registration of the client if there is a Dynamic DNS server available. This is true unless the DHCP server service is mandating that DHCP leases have their dynamic DNS registration handled by the server itself.

Automatic Private IP Addressing

Automatic Private IP Addressing (APIPA) is a feature of Windows clients and servers that allows systems on the same network to automatically establish network connectivity and communication with one another when no DHCP server is available. This is a great feature for a very small network where a set of machines need to share data and communicate with one another with little or no IT support. The IP addresses automatically assigned to adapters with this configuration are in the 169.254.0.0/16 subnet range. APIPA is enabled on all Windows clients by default. When a Windows client cannot locate a DHCP server and assigns itself with an automatic private IP address, it may not readily detect when a DHCP server comes online and may remain off the network unnecessarily long. APIPA cannot be disabled on Windows 8 and Windows Server 2012 systems except by disabling DHCP altogether.

DHCP Relay Agents

A DHCP relay agent can play a critical role on an enterprise network, allowing DHCP services to be extended across routers and different networks. When a DHCP client broadcasts a DHCP client broadcast, that broadcast is normally only allowed on the local network, which means that if there is no local DHCP server, there is no DHCP server response. Two ways to circumvent this limitation, or really this feature, is to either locate a DHCP server in each network or configure a DHCP relay agent on each remote network. The role of a DHCP relay agent is to pick up the local DHCP client broadcast and to forward that request to a designated DHCP server on a remote network. The remote DHCP server must, of course, be configured with a scope of IP addresses for that network, and when responding provides that lease information to the DHCP relay agent, which delivers that information to the client. This allows for DHCP services to be located centrally and managed by Windows Server 2012 systems, while the DHCP relay agent service can be provided by Windows clients, servers, or network devices such as switches, routers, or firewalls.

DHCP and Dynamic DNS Integration

The Windows Server 2012 DHCP service provides direct integration with the Dynamic DNS (DDNS). All Windows clients and servers are configured by default to register their name and IP address with the designated domain name system (DNS) server as configured manually or by DHCP on their respective network card IP settings. When a DNS server is configured to allow networking clients to automatically register their records within DNS zones, this functionality is referred to as Dynamic DNS registration. With a Windows Server 2012 DHCP server, this functionality can be extended to not only Windows clients leasing an IP address from the DHCP server but to any DHCP client. The DHCP server can, in fact, register the name and IP address on the DNS zone on behalf of the client using its own server computer account or a specified user account that has been granted rights to register DNS records. For more information about Dynamic DNS registration refer to Chapter 10 Domain Name System. For information about configuring Dynamic DNS configuration with DHCP, see the section "DHCP and Dynamic DNS Configuration," later in this chapter.

Installing DHCP Server and Server Tools

The DHCP role can be installed on a Windows Server 2012 system at any time using the Server Manager console. If the DHCP server tools are required on the local DHCP server, they can be selected for installation during the role installation or at a later time. Ideally, IT shops now are making the move toward centralized management, and this in many cases means no management tools on each server. To install the DHCP role and server tools on a single system, follow these steps:

1. Log on to the proposed DHCP server.
2. Click the Server Manager tile on the taskbar.
3. When the Server Manager console opens, on the Welcome to Server Manager page, click Add roles and features in the right pane, as shown in Figure 11.1.

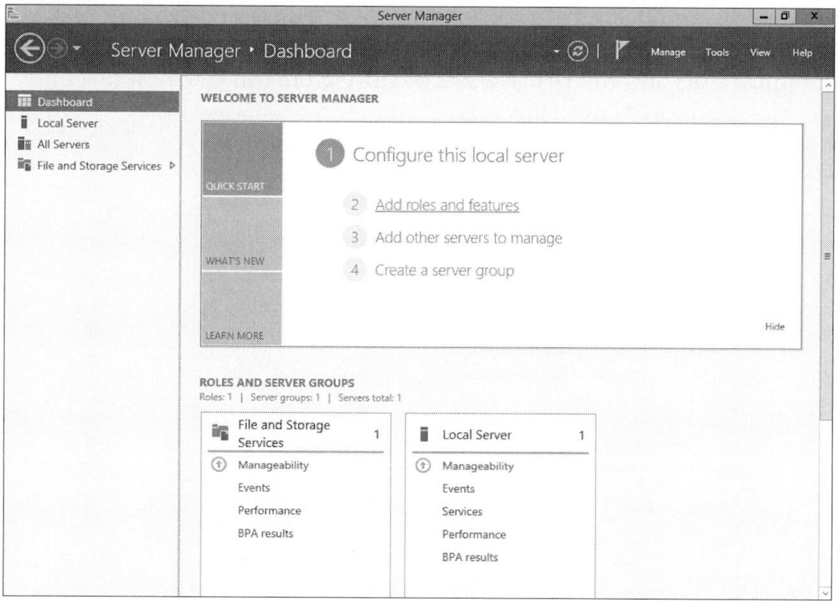

FIGURE 11.1 Starting the Add Roles and Features Wizard from the Server Manager.

4. On the Before You Begin page, in the Add Roles and Features Wizard, click Next to continue.
5. On the Select Installation Type page, select the Role-based or Feature-based Installation radio button, and then click Next to continue.
6. On the Select Destination Server page, select the Select a Server from the Server Pool radio button and select the local server in the window. Click Next to continue.
7. On the Select Server Roles page, check the DHCP Server role, and in the Add Roles and Features Wizard pop-up window, click Add Features to also install the DHCP Server Tools. Click Next to continue.
8. On the Select Features page, scroll down to the Remote Server Administration Tools Features group, expand it, and expand the Role Administration Tools group and verify that the DHCP Server Tools Feature is also selected. Then click Next to continue.
9. On the DHCP Server page, read the information and click Next to continue.
10. On the Confirm Installation Selections page, click Install to begin the installation. If a reboot is required, you are prompted after the installation completes. Reboot as required.
11. From the Installation Progress page, you can monitor the installation progress, but do not close the window.

12. When the installation completes, click the Complete DHCP Configuration link on the Installation Progress page, as shown in Figure 11.2. Running this wizard creates the DHCP Administrators and the DHCP Users security group on the local machine and authorizes this server in Active Directory.

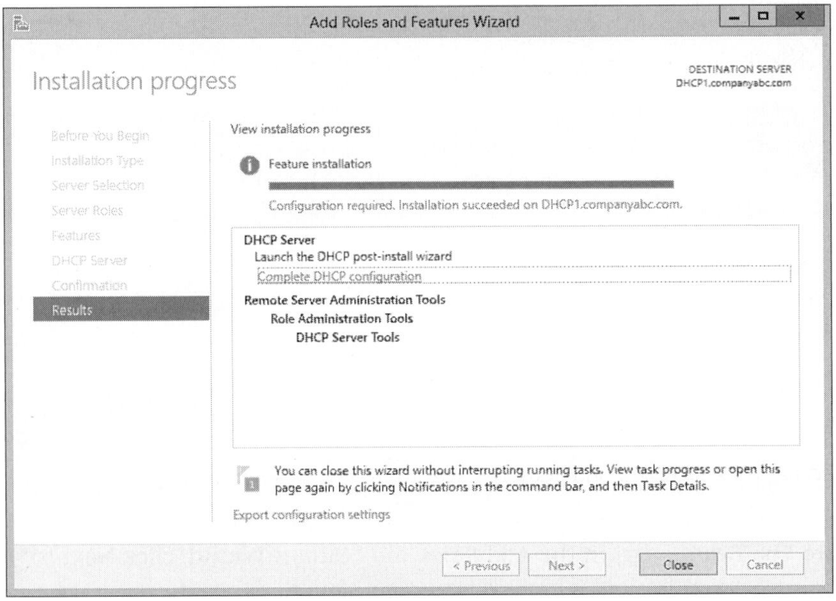

FIGURE 11.2 Launching the DHCP Post-Install Wizard.

13. On the Description page of the DHCP Post-Install Wizard, click Next to continue.

14. On the Authorization page, if the current logon account has the rights to authorize this server in Active Directory, click Commit to complete the task. If another account is required, enter the appropriate credentials and click Commit.

15. On the Summary page, verify the security groups were created and that authorization has completed. Click Close in the Post-Install Wizard window and click Close again in the Add Roles and Features Wizard window.

After the installation completes, you are returned to the Server Manager window. This Post-Install Wizard includes authorizing the DHCP server and creating the local groups DHCP Administrators and DHCP Users for DHCP server delegation.

DHCP authorization is the process of registering a new server in Active Directory to allow it to provide DHCP services on the network. This wizard should be run after all DHCP server installations. However, if DHCP server authorization is not necessary, skip authorization and just let the wizard create the delegation groups.

This completes the DHCP server and server tools installation task.

Creating IPv4 DHCP Scopes

Before a DHCP server can be useful, it must be authorized, and a scope must be created and activated. DHCP authorization can be performed using the DHCP Post-Install Wizard or it can be performed from within the DHCP server console. This section details how to create a basic DHCP IPv4 scope on a newly authorized DHCP server. To create a new DHCP IPv4 scope, follow these steps:

1. On a server with the DHCP Server Tools installed, click the Server Manager tile on the taskbar.
2. When the Server Manager console opens, click Tools, and then select the DHCP option.
3. If no servers are listed when the DHCP console opens, right-click DHCP in the tree pane and select Add Server.
4. In the Add Server windows, if the server is already authorized, select it from the Authorized Server section of the window and click OK, as shown in Figure 11.3. If the server is not yet authorized, type in the server name, and then click OK to continue.

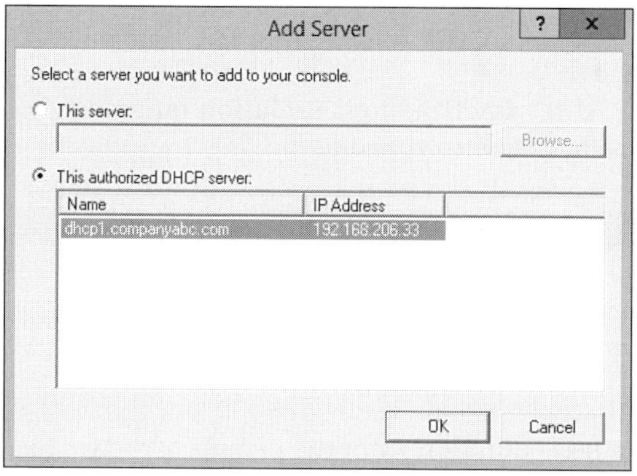

FIGURE 11.3 Selecting an authorized DHCP server.

5. After the server is added to the console, expand the server to reveal the IPv4 and the IPv6 nodes. Verify that both nodes show a green checkmark indicating that the server is properly authorized in Active Directory.
6. Select the IPv4 node, and then right-click and select New Scope.
7. Click Next on the Welcome to the New Scope Wizard.
8. On the Scope Name page, provide a description name and description for the new scope, and then click Next to continue.

9. On the IP Address Range page, enter a starting and ending IP address and a corresponding subnet mask for the new scope, and then click Next to continue, as shown in Figure 11.4.

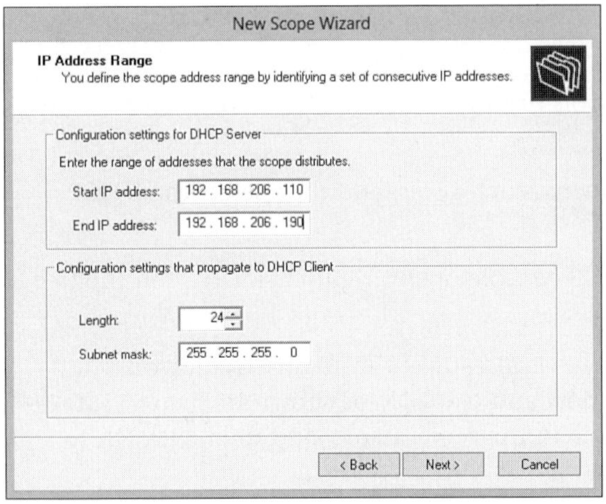

FIGURE 11.4 Defining the new scope IP address range.

10. On the Add Exclusions and Delay page, enter any IP address exclusion ranges or DHCP subnet delay intervals, and then click Next to continue.

NOTE

DHCP administrators wanting to deploy redundant servers or split-scope ranges should leave the fields on the Exclusion and Delay page blank and run the Failover or Split-Scope Wizards to achieve the desired redundancy configuration.

11. On the Lease Duration page, adjust the lease duration from the default of 8 days to the desired IP address lease duration and click Next to continue. Typical durations include 1 day, 8 hours, or 30 days, depending on the organization.

12. On the Configure DHCP Options page, select the Yes I Want to configure Options Now radio button and click Next to continue. The wizard then steps through the configuration for the most common DHCP scope options that administrators desire, such as the Router (Default Gateway) option, the Domain Name Suffix & DNS Servers, and WINS Servers.

13. On each of the options pages, enter the appropriate information and click Next to continue, as shown in Figure 11.5, when configuring the domain name suffix and the DNS servers.

14. On the Activate Scope page, select the Yes, I Want to Activate This Scope Now radio button, and then click Next.

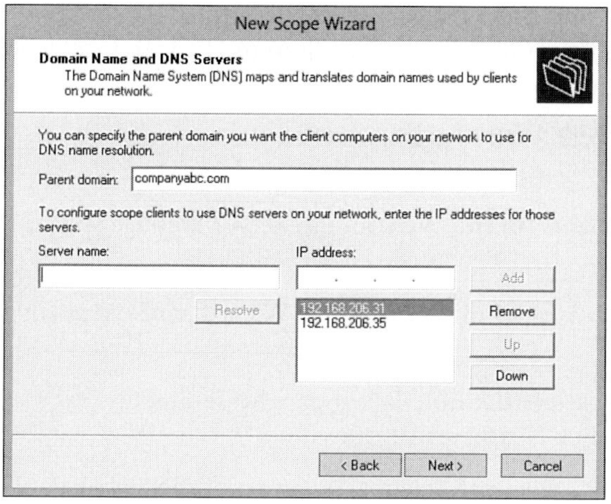

FIGURE 11.5 Configuring the default domain name and DNS server IPv4 DHCP scope options.

15. Click Finish on the Completing the New Scope Wizard page.
16. After the scope has been created, expand the IPv4 node to reveal the new scope and review each of the subnodes to ensure the correct settings were deployed.

This completes the deployment of a new IPv4 DHCP scope.

Exploring DHCP Changes in Windows Server 2012

The Windows Server 2012 DHCP server service has added some new improvements to its features. One of the biggest improvements is the new DHCP failover functionality that allows synchronization of DHCP leases and scope information between servers. Before you can enable that functionality, however, DHCP server roles must be deployed on multiple systems, and at least one of these systems must already have a DHCP scope defined.

On most networks, before this new DHCP feature can be leveraged, existing DHCP servers and their scopes must be migrated/decommissioned. The following section details the migration options available for DHCP migration using the Windows Server 2012 Migration Tools.

Migrating DHCP Servers Using Windows Server Migration Tools

The Windows Server 2012 Window Server Migration Tools are a set of tools designed to aid administrators with the migration of not only DHCP scope information, but also the current leases, reservations, and scope options.

Installing the Windows Server Migration Tools on Windows Server 2012

Before the migration tools can be leveraged, they must be installed on all the source and destination servers. Because the tools are included with Windows Server 2012, they must first be installed on Windows Server 2012, and then a special deployment folder package must be created to support installation on down-level operating systems. To install migration tools on a Windows Server 2012 system, follow these steps:

1. Log on to the proposed Windows Server 2012 system and click the Server Manager tile on the taskbar.
2. When the Server Manager console opens, on the Welcome to Server Manager page, click Add Roles in the center.
3. On the Before You Begin page, in the Add Roles and Features Wizard, click Next to continue.
4. On the Select Installation Type page, select the Role-Based or Feature-Based Installation radio button, and then click Next to continue.
5. On the Select Destination Server page, select the Select a Server from the Server Pool radio button and select the local server in the window. Click Next to continue.
6. On the Select Server Roles page, leave the defaults and click Next to continue.
7. On the Select Features page, scroll down to Windows Server Migration Tools Features group and check the box, and then click Next, as shown in Figure 11.6.

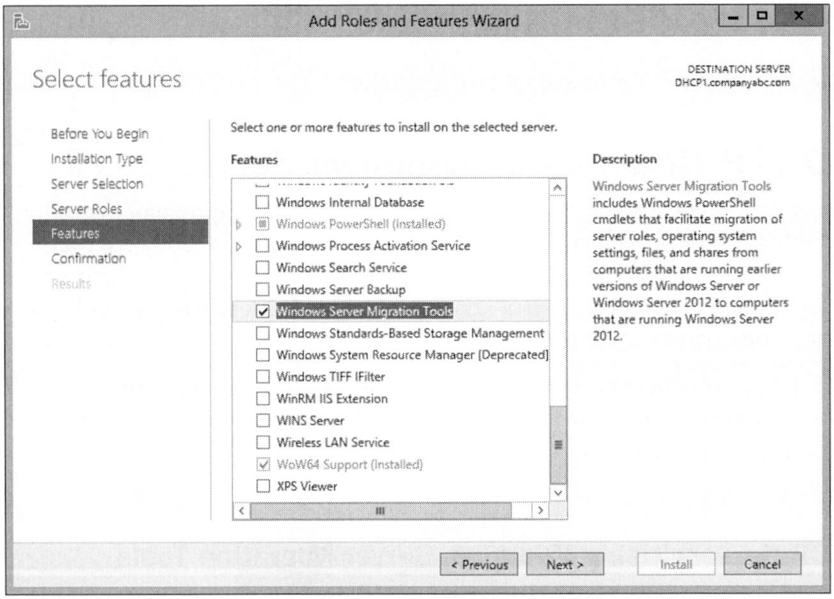

FIGURE 11.6 Installing the Windows Server migration tools.

8. On the Confirm Installation Selections page, click Install to begin the installation. If a reboot is required, you are prompted after the installation completes. Reboot as required.

9. On the Installation Progress page, you can monitor the installation progress. Click Close when the installation completes.

Creating the Deployment Folder Package of the Windows Server Migration Tools for Down-Level Operating System Installation

Before the Windows Server migration tools can be used to migrate DHCP services from older operating systems to Windows Server 2012, the tools must be installed on the down-level operating systems. For the Windows Server 2012 migration tools, this includes Windows Server 2008 R2, Windows Server 2008, and Windows Server 2003. The process is mostly the same for all versions and includes two steps: creating the deployment folder package and then installing that package on the down-level system. To create the deployment folder package for a Windows Server 2008 R2 x64 system, follow these steps:

1. On the Windows Server 2012 system with the Windows Server migration tools installed, open an elevated PowerShell console session.
2. Change directories to C:\Windows\System32\ServerMigrationTools, assuming that the C: drive is the system drive.
3. Type the command **.\SmigDeploy.exe /package /architecture amd64 /OS WS08R2 /path C:\MigTools** and press Enter to create the package.
4. After the package is created, you should have a C:\MigTools\SMT_WS08R2_amd64 folder created. You can repeat the previous command for Windows Server 2008 and Server 2003 for both 32- and 64-bit editions as required. Close the command prompt.

This completes the creation of the down-level deployment folder package.

Installing the Windows Server Migration Tools on Windows Server 2008 R2 64-Bit Edition DHCP Server

Once the deployment folder package has been created, you can copy it over to the destination server and install it. To install the deployment package on a Windows Server 2008 R2 DHCP server, follow these steps:

1. Copy the C:\MigTools\SMT_ws08R2_amd64 folder from the Windows Server 2012 system to the C:\MigTools folder on the destination Windows Server 2008 R2 server. Create the C:\MigTools folder as required or select another desired destination folder.
2. Once the folder is copied over, open an elevated PowerShell console session and change the directory to C:\MigTools\SMT_ws08R2_amd64.
3. Type **SmigDeploy.exe** and press Enter to register and install the tools. If Windows PowerShell is not installed, this process fails, and the PowerShell feature must be installed before this process can continue.
4. When the process completes, both the original PowerShell console session and a new PowerShell window are open. Type **Exit** and press Enter in both windows to close them.

This completes the registration and installation of the Windows Server migration tools on a Windows Server 2008 R2 system. This process is the same for both Windows Server 2008 and 2003, including the prerequisite of Windows PowerShell for installation and operation.

Migrating DHCP Services from 2008 R2 to Windows Server 2012

After all the tools are installed on the source and destination servers, you can perform the export and import process. Aside from the export and import process, after the export is completed on the source server, the source server IP address must be changed, and the original source server IP address must be added to the destination server for the import and DHCP operation to be seamless.

Preparing the Source Windows Server 2008 R2 DHCP Server for Export

After the migration tools are copied to the source Window Server 2008 R2 DHCP server, the migration process can be started.

1. Log on to the source Windows Server 2008 R2 DHCP server and open the DHCP console.
2. Add the local server to the DHCP server console (if not already present), and then select and right-click the server and select Add/Remove Bindings. Note the current IP address of the server because this is used later. Click Cancel in the window to close it.
3. Right-click the server again, select All Tasks, and then select Stop to stop the DHCP service on that system.
4. Select Start, All Programs, Administrative Tools, Windows Server Migration Tools, and then click the Windows Server Migration Tools PowerShell link.
5. When the PowerShell window opens it should default to the C:\MigTools\SMT_ws08R2_amd64 folder. Type **./Servermigration.psc1** and press Enter to open a new PowerShell window. This step may seem redundant, but greatly simplifies the process.
6. In the new PowerShell window type **Export-SmigServerSetting -FeatureID DHCP** and press Enter.
7. When prompted for the path, enter **C:\MigTools\Export** and press Enter
8. When prompted for a password, enter a password with at least six characters and press Enter to continue. The process creates the export folder and returns the results into the PowerShell windows, as shown in Figure 11.7
9. After the export completes, open the services applet on the source server and set the DHCP server service to Disabled, then close the services applet.
10. Copy the C:\MigTools\Export folder to the destination Window Server 2012 system.
11. Once the export has completed and the DHCP server service is disabled, change the IP address of the source server to something other than the IP address that was originally bound to the DHCP service.
12. Shut down or reboot the source server as required.

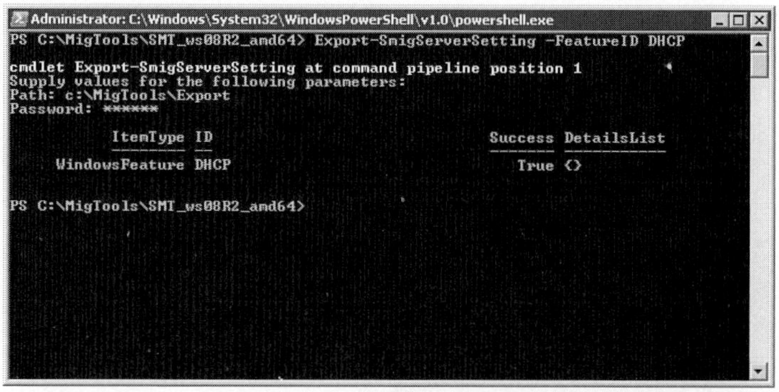

FIGURE 11.7 Exporting the source server DHCP settings.

Preparing the Destination Windows Server 2012 DHCP Server for Import

After the export process has completed and the export data has been copied to the destination server, the original server can have its IP address changed and can be shut down or rebooted. After that process has completed, the import process on the Windows Server 2012 destination server can commence. To perform the import process, follow these steps:

NOTE

Running this import procedure overwrites all DHCP data, so as a best practice do not install the DHCP server service before this import or use the -Force option when running the import.

1. Log on to the destination Windows Server 2012 DHCP server and change the network IP address to the IP address originally bound to the source DHCP server.
2. Reboot the server to ensure that proper DNS registration is now updated and that all services are running under the new IP address.
3. Once the server has rebooted, log back in and open the Server Manager.
4. When the Server Manager console opens, click Tools, and then select the Windows Server Migration Tools option.
5. If necessary change to the C:\Windows\System32\ServerMigrationTools folder. Once at the correct path, type **./Servermigration.psc1** and press Enter to open a new PowerShell window
6. In the new PowerShell window, type the command **Import-SmigServerSetting -FeatureID DHCP -Force -Verbose** and press Enter. For this example, we are using the -Force option because the DHCP server service has already been installed, even though it has not been configured.
7. When prompted for the path, enter **C:\MigTools\Export** and press Enter to continue.

8. When prompted for the password, enter the password previously used during the export process on the source server and press Enter to continue.

   The PowerShell window displays the current status of the import process and when completed displays the results and whether a reboot is required, as shown in Figure 11.8.

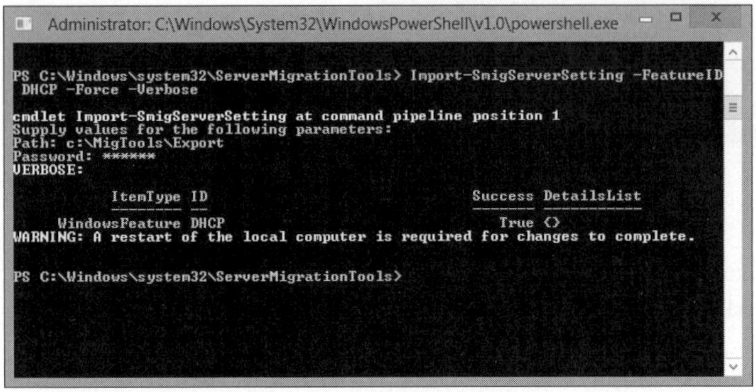

FIGURE 11.8 Importing the DHCP settings to the destination Windows Server 2012 system.

9. If needed, reboot the server and log on and verify that the original source server IP address is still bound to this Windows Server 2012 system.
10. Open the Server Manager, click Tools, and then select the Services option.
11. Verify that the DHCP server service is set to automatic startup and if necessary start the service.
12. After the server has rebooted, log back on and open the Server Manager.
13. When the Server Manager console opens, select Tools, and then select the Windows Server Migration Tools option.
14. Open the DHCP console, and if necessary add the local server to the console. Right-click the DHCP node in tree pane and select Manage Authorized Servers. If the original source server is listed, unauthorize it. If the current destination server is listed with the incorrect IP address, unauthorize it and close that window.
15. Back in the DHCP console, right-click the local server in the tree pane and expand the IPv4 node and verify that the scope has been successfully imported.
16. Right-click the local server in the tree pane and select Authorize as required.
17. Make any necessary modifications to the scope or scope options as required.
18. Right-click the scope beneath the IPv4 node and select Activate as required.
19. Verify that new DHCP clients can obtain a valid IP address lease.

This completes the DHCP migration process from Windows Server 2008 R2 to Windows Server 2012.

Understanding DHCP Client Alternate Network Capability

Earlier in this chapter, the "Automatic Private IP Addressing" section detailed the Windows client automated IP addressing functionality when a DHCP server is not available. As an extension of that protocol, Windows clients and servers can also default to a fallback static IP address that can be used when a DHCP server is offline. This can be beneficial to enable complete network connectivity in the event of a DHCP server outage.

A reasonable application of this functionality can be remote network systems that rely on DHCP relay agents that may be less than reliable. On a Windows Server 2012 system, this functionality can be configured as follows:

1. Log on to a Windows Server 2012 system that is configured with DHCP enabled on the network adapter.
2. On the right side of the taskbar, right-click the Network icon and select Open Network and Sharing Center.
3. When the window opens, in the top-left pane select Change Adapter Settings.
4. In the Network Connections window, right-click the desired network adapter and select Properties.
5. In the Network Adapter window, scroll down and highlight Internet Protocol Version 4 (TCP/IPv4) and press the Properties button.
6. Click the Alternate Configuration tab and select the User Configured Radio button.
7. Enter the desired IP address information and click OK, as shown in Figure 11.9.
8. Click OK twice to save the settings and close the Network Connections window.

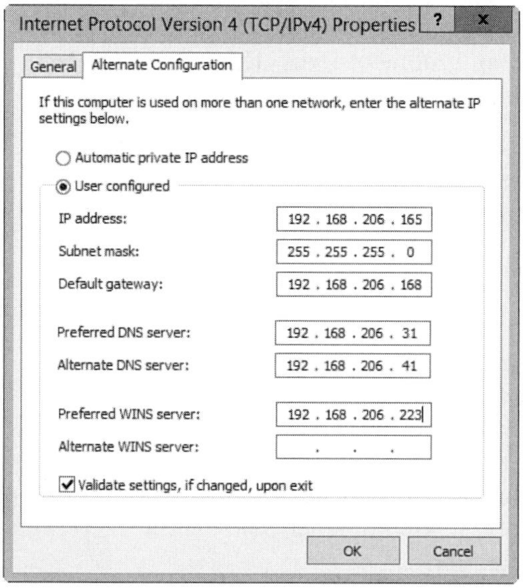

FIGURE 11.9 Configuring a user-configured APIPA address.

This completes the configuration of the DHCP client alternate network configuration.

Enhancing DHCP Reliability

On most networks, DHCP is a critical networking service. When the DHCP service is offline, most clients cannot function and may be unable to work at all. For most organizations building redundancy, reliability, and security into their DHCP service can help alleviate undesired and unexpected DHCP networking outages.

Windows Server 2012 builds on top of previous DHCP server services by leveraging several features that can enhance DHCP reliability as outlined in the proceeding sections.

Link-Layer Filtering

Link-layer filtering or MAC address filtering is a feature of the Windows Server 2012 DHCP service that can be enabled to provide a higher level of security to DHCP leases.

Link-layer filtering basically can restrict which devices are allowed and which devices are denied the ability to obtain a DHCP lease from the DHCP server. For this feature to function, the server must be enabled to support the Allow / Deny Link Layer Filter lists, and the lists must be populated.

In many DHCP deployments, it can be cumbersome for administrators to manually enter each network-connected device's MAC address before it can be granted a DHCP lease, so link-layer filtering may seem like it is out of reach. One way to avoid this issue is to deploy DHCP in a phased approach. First, deploy DHCP services without Link Layer Filtering enabled. Later, after all clients have connected to the network, add leases to the filter lists as leases are obtained. This can even be performed with DHCP reservations. For example, suppose you set up a DHCP scope on Monday morning and later that afternoon most of your clients have obtained a lease. You can simply select and right-click a single or a set of current leases and select Add to Filter and Allow or Deny depending on which filter list you want the system to be on, as shown in Figure 11.10.

After adding all your leases to the appropriate filter list, in the DHCP console right-click the IPv4 node and select Properties. On the Filters tab check the check boxes to enable Allow or Deny Lists, as desired.

DHCP Reservations

A DHCP reservation is a predefined relationship between an IP address and a system's MAC address. This configuration allows a system to remain configured for DHCP, but it will always get the same IP address that is predefined or reserved for it, hence the name reservation. Reservations are quite useful on business networks for mobile devices and printers; the mobile device or printer can always be contacted at the same IP address for access and for remote management and so on. The flip side is that if that printer or mobile device moves to another office or network, it will be DHCP ready and will connect to the network without manual network configuration.

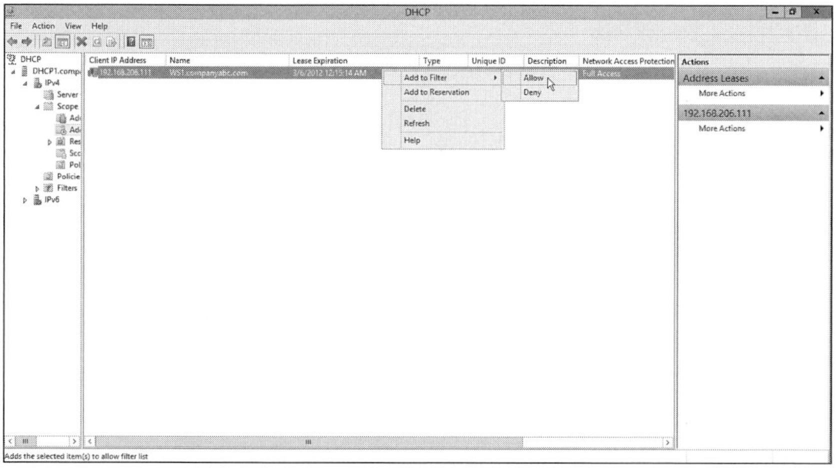

FIGURE 11.10 Adding a DHCP lease to the Allowed link-layer filter list

Using DHCP reservations along with link-layer filtering allows a DHCP administrator to quickly identify new or unidentified machines and quickly block their access. For example, identified machines can be granted leases, and then all of those leases can be converted to reservations and added to Allow filter lists, and finally, an IP address exclusion list can be created for all IP addresses not currently defined in the reservation list, essentially stopping all new leases from occurring. The only issue with this scenario is that when a new valid machine joins the network the DHCP scope changes need adjustments to allow this new system to connect. In addition, when machines have both wireless and wired network cards, each card requires a different reservation.

You can create DHCP reservations using two different processes. The first and most common process is to manually create a reservation; the second much easier process is to convert a DHCP lease into a reservation. To manually create a DHCP reservation, follow these steps:

1. Collect the desired MAC address from the system that will be associated with this reservation. You can do this on a Windows machine in a command prompt by using the **Ipconfig /all** command and recording the physical address entry.
2. Open the DHCP console and expand the IPv4 node.
3. Expand the desired scope, select and right-click the Reservations node, and select New Reservation.
4. Enter a descriptive name, IP address, and MAC address for the system, and click Add to create the reservation, as shown in Figure 11.11.
5. When that reservation is completed, the window clears to allow for another reservation to be created. Click Close to return to the DHCP console.

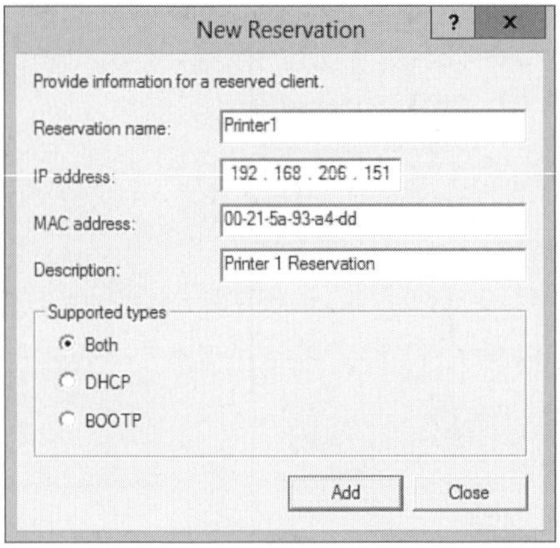

FIGURE 11.11 Manually creating a DHCP reservation.

To create a reservation from an existing lease, simply open the IPv4 scope and select the Address Leases node in the tree pane, locate the lease in the center pane, right-click the desired lease or multiple leases, and select Add to Reservation.

This completes the reservation-creation process.

Configuring Reservation-Specific DHCP Scope Options

Sometimes devices are on the same network but require different DHCP scope options. One example could be a kiosk machine that should not have a default gateway or an IP phone that requires additional scope options that are not desired on all DHCP clients. This can be accomplished with reservation-specific DHCP scope options. To create a reservation-specific scope option, create a reservation in the tree pane, expand the Reservations node, and specifically select the desired reservation and select Configure Options. Proceed to select and configure the desired options and save the changes by clicking OK when completed. These reservation-specific options override both scope and server options when configured.

DHCP Name Protection

DHCP name protection is a feature of the DHCP service that when used with Dynamic DNS registration prevents a DHCP client with a name already in the DNS domain zone from registering or overwriting an existing name that it does not own. This functionality prevents client and server spoofing and name corruption for statically configured systems already registered in DNS. You can enable name protection at either the IPv4 or IPv6 node level or at the scope level. When configured at the scope level, the settings take precedence over the IPv4 or IPv6 node settings. To enable DHCP name protection at the scope level, follow these steps:

1. Open the DHCP console and connect to the desired DHCP server.
2. Expand the IPv4 node, select and right-click the desired scope, and select Properties.

3. Display the DNS tab, and near the bottom in the Name Protection section click the Configure button.
4. In the Name Protection window, check the Enabled Name Protection check box and click OK. Click OK again in the Scope Properties window to save the changes to the scope.

To enable DHCP name protection at the IPv4 node level, follow these steps:

1. Open the DHCP console and connect to the desired DHCP server.
2. In the tree pane, select and right-click IPv4 node and select Properties.
3. Display the DNS tab, and near the bottom in the Name Protection section click the Configure button.
4. In the Name Protection window, check the Enabled Name Protection check box and click OK. Click OK again in the Scope Properties window to save the changes to the scope.

This completes the process of enabling name protection at the IPv4 node and scope level.

DHCP and Dynamic DNS Configuration

When a DHCP server is configured to register DNS records and provide name protection with Dynamic DNS, a few configurations are required to enhance reliability of this server. The first configuration is to set the default DNS registration behavior, and the second is to create a service account and define this account in the DHCP server. To configure DHCP and Dynamic DNS settings, follow these steps:

1. Using Active Directory Users and Computers console, create a user account in the domain named, for example, DHCP-SVC and configure a secure password. No special group membership is required, but set the account to not require a password change at first logon.

NOTE

If you want to avoid DNS registration issues, you can configure this account to have the password never expire. As a best practice, however, you should change the service account password in Active Directory and in the DHCP server settings as frequently as defined in the standard user password policy.

2. Open the DHCP console and connect to the desired DHCP server.
3. Expand the DHCP server, select and right-click the IPv4 node and select Properties.
4. Display the DNS tab. If name protection is enabled, most of the settings will be grayed out. Ensure that the check box to enable DNS dynamic update is checked, as shown in Figure 11.12.

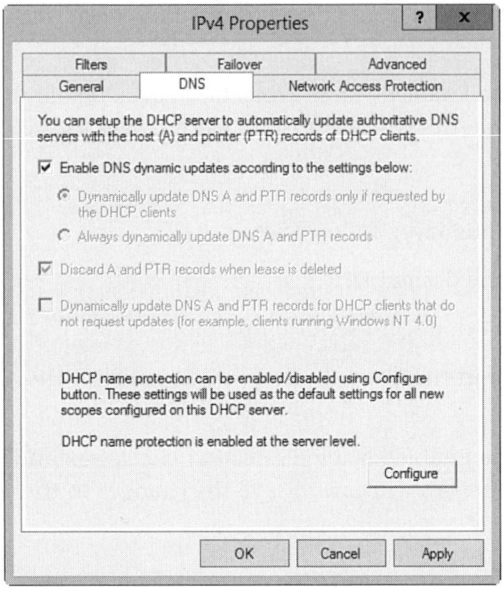

FIGURE 11.12 Enabling DNS dynamic updates for IPv4.

5. Display the Advanced tab and click the Credentials button to open the DNS Dynamic Update Credentials window.
6. Enter the desired service account name, domain, and password. Confirm the password and click OK to validate the credentials, as shown in Figure 11.13.

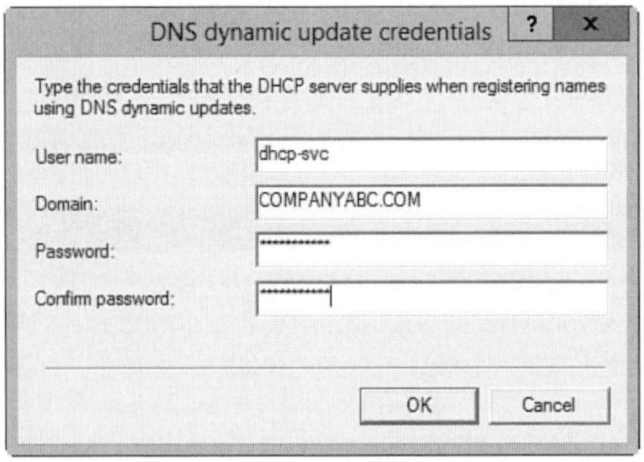

FIGURE 11.13 Defining the DNS dynamic update credentials.

7. Click OK in the IPv4 windows to complete the changes.
8. Restart the DHCP server service.

This completes the DHCP and DNS dynamic update configuration task.

DHCP Network Access Protection Integration

The Windows Server 2012 DHCP server service can interact with the Network Access Protection (NAP) service. NAP consists of administrator-defined policies that include specific criteria to be met before a system is allowed to communicate on the network. In simpler terms, with NAP policies enabled and enforced, an organization can ensure that a connected system has antivirus software and security updates and is a member of the corporate forest of domains, as one example. When tied in with DHCP, you can use NAP to allow a system to get just enough network connectivity to access the NAP policy server to check prerequisites before getting connected to the corporate network. For more information about NAP, see Chapter 15, "Security Policies, Network Policy Server, and Network Access Protection." To enable DHCP NAP integration on a single scope, follow these steps:

1. Open the DHCP console and connect to the desired DHCP server.
2. Expand the DHCP server to reveal the IPv4 node and expand to reveal the DHCP scopes configured on that server.
3. Right-click the desired scope and select Properties.
4. Display the Network Access Protection tab, and under the Network Access Protection Settings section, select the Enable for This Scope radio button.
5. Select to use the default NAP profile or specify a custom profile and click OK to save the settings to the scope.

To enable DHCP NAP integration for all scopes on a DHCP server, follow these steps:

1. Open the DHCP console and connect to the desired DHCP server.
2. Expand the DHCP server right-click and select Properties of the IPv4 node.
3. When the IPv4 Property window opens, display the Network Access Protection tab and click the Enable on All Scopes button.
4. A pop-up window opens stating that all NAP settings on all scopes will be overwritten. Click Yes to confirm.
5. Back in the IPv4 Properties window, select the DHCP server behavior when a Network Policy Server (NPS) server is not available, as shown in Figure 11.14, and then click OK to save the settings.

This completes the DHCP NAP configuration steps.

Access DHCP Activity and Event Logs

Windows Server 2012 includes detailed activity and event logging for the DHCP server service. Historically, reporting or monitoring DHCP usage was quite a challenge, if not impossible. Now DHCP administrators can easily access this data using the built-in logging mechanisms. The DHCP activity log can be read in a text-based editor and is stored in the C:\Windows\System32\DHCP folder. A log is created for each day of the week and named, for example, DHCPSrvLog-Wed.log (for Wednesday). Logs are overwritten each week. The activity log includes startup and shutdown service processing and lease activity. DHCP event logging has also been increased and can be accessed in the Event Viewer. The DHCP event logs include Admin, Operational, and FilterNotifications. These logs are located in the in the Applications and Services/Microsoft/Windows/DHCP-Server node.

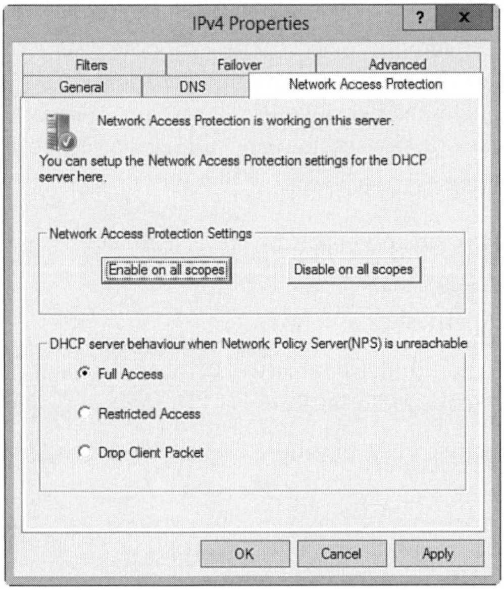

FIGURE 11.14 Configuring NAP settings on the DHCP server.

Implementing Redundant DHCP Services

As stated earlier in this chapter, DHCP is a critical network service and should be treated as such. Building redundancy into DHCP services has been a challenge for years, and with each release of Windows Server, DHCP redundancy options get better. Windows Server 2012 DHCP server service is no different. The biggest improvement for the DHCP server service is the now built-in failover option, but that is not the only option. The following sections detail historic and current DHCP redundancy options that can be leveraged to improved DHCP reliability.

DHCP Split Scopes

Historically, when administrators required DHCP redundancy, DHCP was deployed on a failover cluster or multiple DHCP servers were deployed with split-scope configuration. A split scope is simply the division of the entire pool of DHCP IP addresses across multiple servers. You can split the scope in various ways, as follows:

- **50/50 split-scope configuration**—The 50/50 split-scope configuration, as the name indicates, takes half of the DHCP IP address pool, and a scope is created on each server with nonoverlapping addresses. This can work well if both DHCP servers answer at the same time when a DHCP request comes across the network or if some hardware or software load balancer manages the requests. The challenge arises if all or most of the IP addresses will be leased. When a DHCP server configured with only half of the IP addresses is out of leases, that does not stop it from answering DHCP client requests, and clients can end up without an IP address, even if the second server still has available IP addresses for leasing.

- **The 80/20 split-scope configuration**—The 80/20 split scope configuration is the most ideal configuration for Windows Server 2012 and Windows Server 2008 R2 DHCP servers. With the release of Windows Server 2008 R2 and included with Windows Server 2012, DHCP scope settings now allow for a delayed response interval configuration. With an 80/20 split, the server configured with 20% of the addresses is also configured with a delayed response to DHCP client requests. This results in the 20% server becoming more of a backup DHCP server that will be used only in the event of an issue with the primary DHCP server.
- **The 100/100 split-scope configuration**—The 100/100 split-scope option can be the best configuration, but it requires that 200% of the necessary IP addresses are available to the DHCP IP address pool. For example, if a network will support up to 200 DHCP clients, the DHCP range requires at least 400 IP addresses in the entire DHCP pool. This, of course, is not available in the standard Class C network configuration, so networking changes may be required for this type of configuration to be implemented. With this configuration, no delayed response is required, and clients can get an IP address from either server as required.

Windows Server 2012 Delay Configuration Setting

Windows Server 2012 includes a response delay configuration on the DHCP scope settings. This enables administrators to implement redundant DHCP scope configurations across the network, with different version of DHCP servers. To implement a delayed response to a DHCP server on a particular scope, open the scope properties on the desired DHCP server scope and display the Advanced tab. Near the bottom, under Delay Configuration, enter the delay interval in milliseconds and click OK to save the setting, as shown in Figure 11.15. Administrators must test the amount of delay required to get the desired response time from the redundant or secondary DHCP server.

Windows Server 2012 Split Scope Versus Failover

Windows Server 2012 includes a Split-Scope Wizard and a feature called DHCP failover. The Split-Scope Wizard enables administrators to set up a scope across two DHCP servers, including defining the delay configuration, but leases and reservations are not shared or in sync across servers. Furthermore, DHCP clients get a different IP address from each DHCP server the clients obtain leases from. Windows Server 2012 failover is a single DHCP scope configured across two servers. Lease and reservation information is kept in sync across the servers.

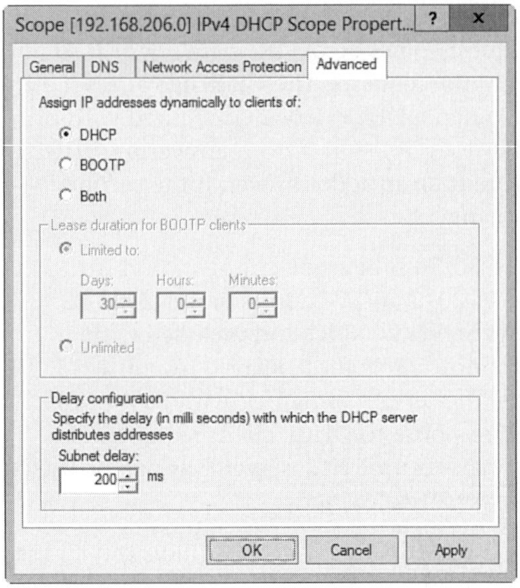

FIGURE 11.15 Implementing a delay configuration on a DHCP scope.

DHCP Split-Scope Configuration Wizard

When a split scope configuration is desired, the DHCP administrator can run the DHCP Split-Scope Wizard to simplify the process. If reservations are already created, the Split-Scope Wizard replicates these reservations, but will not keep these reservations in sync after the split-scope is created. To create a split-scope across two DHCP servers using the wizard, follow these steps.

1. Install the DHCP server service on at least two DHCP servers and authorize them both.
2. Log on to the primary DHCP server and open the console. Expand the IPv4 node and create the desired scope as outlined previously in this chapter.
3. Once the scope is created, right-click the scope in the tree pane and select Advanced and select Split-Scope. The DHCP Split-Scope Wizard opens.
4. On the Welcome page of the DHCP Split-Scope Wizard window, click Next to continue.
5. On the Additional DHCP Server page, click the Add Server button to show the list of authorized DHCP servers. Select the desired server or type the name in and click OK to return to the wizard windows.
6. Once the additional DHCP server is listed, click Next to continue.
7. On the Percentage of Split page, the default is an 80/20 split, with the 20% going to the additional server. If this is the desired configuration, click Next to continue, as shown in Figure 11.16.

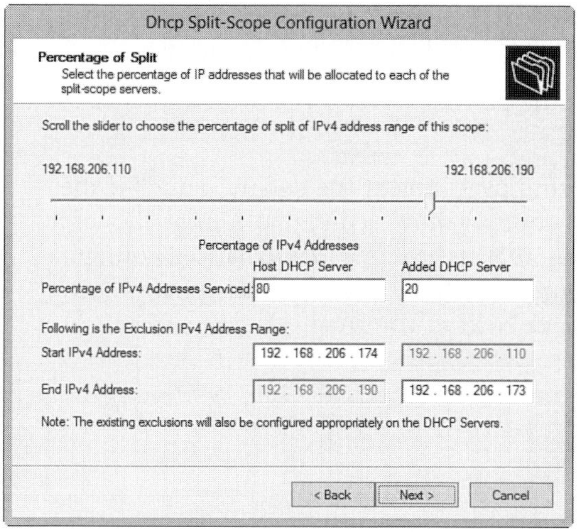

FIGURE 11.16 Configuring the percentage of split IP addresses in the Split-Scope Wizard.

8. On the Delay in DHCP Offer page, enter **0** for the Host DHCP Server and enter the desired delay for the Additional DHCP Server (for example, 200 milliseconds), and then click Next.

9. On the Summary page, review the configuration. If everything looks correct, click Finish to commit the changes and update the scope on both DHCP servers.

10. When the process completes, connect to each of the DHCP servers and verify the scope settings. If the scopes are correct, activate the new scope on the additional DHCP server and on the host DHCP server if not already activated.

This completes the DHCP split-scope configuration task.

Windows Server 2012 DHCP Failover

Windows Server 2012 DHCP includes a failover scope feature. The benefit of this feature is that leases and reservations are synchronized across the DHCP server and a failover cluster is not required. The two different types of failover scopes are a load-balance and hot-standby failover scope. To deploy a failover scope, follow these steps.

1. Install the DHCP server service on at least two DHCP servers and authorize them both.

2. Log on to the primary DHCP server and open the console. Expand the IPv4 node and create the desired scope as outlined previously in this chapter.

3. Once the scope is created, right-click the scope in the tree pane and select Configure Failover. The DHCP Configure Failover Wizard opens.

4. On the Introduction page, leave the check box to apply failover to all scopes or uncheck the box and select the desired scopes and click Next to continue.
5. On the next page, type in the name of the partner server for failover and click Next to continue.
6. On the Create a New Failover Relationship page, accept the default name for the failover relationship and configure the desired failover configurations as shown in Figure 11.17. This example configures a 50/50 split-scope load-balanced configuration. This example also uses message authentication, and we enter a shared secret password that must be documented. Click Next to continue.

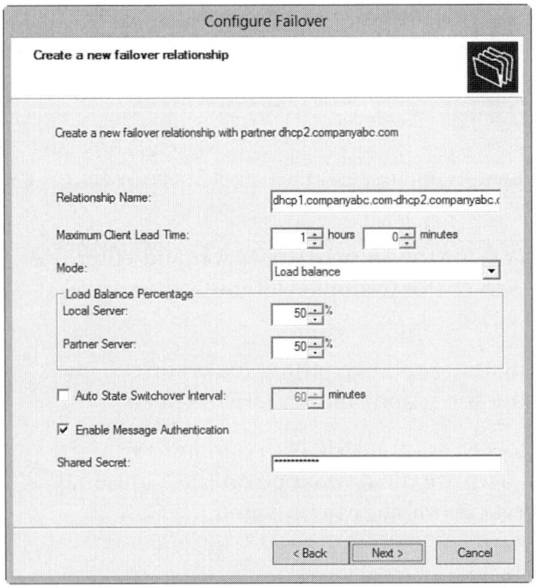

FIGURE 11.17 Defining the failover relationship settings.

7. On the final page, confirm the configurations. If all the settings look correct, click Finish to create the failover scope.
8. A pop-up window opens to detail the status of the configuration. When the configuration completes successfully, click Close to finish the process.

This completes the failover scope configuration task

DHCP Failover Cluster Servers

You can deploy DHCP services on a Windows Server 2012 failover cluster. With this type of DHCP deployment, there is only a single DHCP server database, and configuration is not replicated across servers. Instead, the DHCP data is accessed by one server at a time, and when a software or hardware issue is encountered, the DHCP services are moved to another failover cluster host. Deploying services on failover clusters has its own challenges but can prove to be simpler for a DHCP server deployment if the server and storage hardware meets all the failover cluster requirements. For more information about failover clusters, see Chapter 29, "System-Level Fault Tolerance (Clustering / Network Load Balancing)."

Exploring Advanced DHCP Concepts

DHCP advanced concepts include functionality not used in everyday situations, such as superscopes, multicast scopes, and delegation of DHCP administration. Also, in today's computing environment, managing services through a command line environment is highly desired. The following sections cover these advanced DHCP concepts.

Understanding DHCP Superscopes

A DHCP Superscope is a container that can include several DHCP scopes. A Superscope can be created when a single network includes multiple network ranges. For example, if an organization wanted to support different network clients or organizations with a single router, a superscope with multiple scopes configured with different network address spaces could be created. Policies for each scope range could be configured along with reservations to ensure that the desired clients get the right network scope leases when they request a DHCP lease.

Examining DHCP Multicast Scopes

Organizations that require multicast functionality might want to set up DHCP multicast scopes. Multicast clients are used for media and deployment applications where several systems will be accessing the same content. A few examples are operating system deployments or video or audio presentations that each client will access simultaneously. There are special uses for multicast addressing, and DHCP multicast scopes can simplify the setup and delivery in those scenarios.

Delegating Administration of DHCP

Even though DHCP services are quite critical in most networking environments, organizations usually do not dedicate servers specific for this service. DHCP services are usually bundles on servers that host other services. In situations when DHCP administration needs to be delegated to, say, the networking group or a certain administrator, but access to the host server is not desirable, DHCP delegation is the answer. To delegate DHCP administration, first the administrator needs to have access to the DHCP server tools, and those should be installed on the administrator's IT administrative workstation or on an IT central console server. Once the tools are accessible, the IT administrator's user account, or admin account, can be added to the local DHCP security group named DHCP Administrators.

DHCP Netsh and PowerShell Administration

Like most Microsoft services today, DHCP can be fully managed through a wide array of PowerShell functions and via the Netsh command-line utility. To get a list of the available commands, follow these steps.

1. On a system with the DHCP server tools installed, open a PowerShell console session.
2. Type **get-command *DHCP*** and press Enter to get the list of all the DHCP-related functions or cmdlets.

   For example, type **get-DHCPServerv4Binding -Computername server10.companyabc.com** and press Enter to get the IPv4 address bound to the DHCP server named server10.companyabc.com.
3. To learn how to use any PowerShell function or cmdlet (for example, the get-DHCPServerv4Binding function), in the PowerShell window type **get-help get-DHCPServerv4Binding -Full** and press Enter to list the help information.
4. In the same window or in a command prompt window, to access the DHCP Netsh commands type **Netsh DHCP List** and press Enter to get a list of the commands available.
5. For example, if the DHCP Post-Install Wizard was skipped or closed, the DHCP administrator can add the security groups for delegation to the local server by using the command **Netsh DHCP Add SecurityGroups** and pressing Enter.

This completes the overview of some of the DHCP administrative tasks that you can perform using PowerShell commands or Netsh.

Securing DHCP

DHCP by default is an unsecure service and should be treated as such. For example, in a basic DHCP deployment, if a malicious user gains access to the physical network or a wireless network that the DHCP server provides IP addresses leases for, that user can quickly get on the network and begin to try and hack and communicate with the organizations' systems. Wireless networks get hacked every day, but that is a different topic. Getting access to physical connectivity is less likely, but when it occurs the same risk is presented. This is why every DHCP implementation should include some form of security or frequent auditing. You can secure DHCP services through a number of Windows Server 2012 DHCP server features outlined previously in this chapter, including link-layer filter lists, name protection, NAP, and configuring reservations for known systems and creating exclusion ranges that absorb all remaining available IP addresses. The best method by far is a combination of link-layer filter lists, DHCP reservations, and NAP integration. For detailed information about link-layer filters or DHCP reservations, see those topics detailed previously in this chapter. For more information about NAP, see Chapter 15.

IPv6 Introduction

Internet Protocol version 6 (IPv6) is the updated and revised implementation of the current networking protocol used around the world, IPv4. IPv6 was developed to solve many of the limitations and challenges faced with the IPv4 protocol, initially because of the fast growth of the Internet in the late 1980s and early 1990s and the worry that available addresses would run out. Twenty-plus years ago, the advances in computer networking allowed for huge opportunities for sharing and accessing data between networks, and the Internet Protocol, IPv4, was developed and implemented by the largest Internet service providers (ISPs) that hosted the backbone of the Internet. Organizations, including government institutions, commercial businesses, and schools, started to move their internal networks to this protocol. Although many organizations continued to leverage other networking protocols, if you wanted to share and access data across the Internet, you had to use IPv4. With this big push, operating system development, network-ready applications, and networking devices all included IPv4.

Network administrators had to work hard in some cases to support the quick growth and to troubleshoot issues because IPv4 required manual configuration of addressing on devices and in most cases they also had to deploy and support a method of dynamic addressing provided by, you guessed it, DHCP services. Neither the manual nor automated addressing methods could keep track of all addresses, and administrators had to tightly control and monitor address usage, hence the need for IPAM, covered later in this chapter.

The quick adoption and growth of Internet networking by both private users and businesses began to quickly absorb the usable IP address ranges, and some began to worry that there was a serious risk of running out of IP addresses. When this occurred, private IP ranges were defined, for use on internal networks only, and Network Address Translation (NAT) was developed and leveraged to allow devices on private IP ranges to access the Internet using a shared Internet address. The organizations that used NAT found many uses for this service, mainly managed on routers and firewalls/proxy servers, but in some cases, with certain applications, NAT cannot function at 100%.

Separately, but simultaneously, as organizations moved toward sharing data across the Internet with business partners and between office locations, transmitting data securely over the Internet became a requirement, because supporting private point-to-point lines could not compare on price. Encrypted tunnels, or virtual private networks, were created across the Internet, and this is still in heavy usage today. The use of NAT and VPNs in some earlier implementations proved to be challenging to configure because IPv4 did not have clearly defined or inclusive security standards. Because of this, different hardware and software vendors implemented sometimes similar, but not always compatible versions of IP Security (IPsec). So, for organizations to securely share or securely connect their networks over the Internet, many times they had to use the same vendors for software/hardware or resort to paying for higher-priced private point-to-point connections. As time has passed, IPsec for IPv4 has advanced, and most implementations are compatible, but this IPsec security also comes with more data overhead and utilizes more bandwidth.

Last but certainly not least, with the daily expanding market of Internet services, transferring of data, and the growing number of users on the Internet, network utilization and IP address assignment are always increasing. Streaming music and peer networking were some of the first types of Internet applications to consume large amounts of bandwidth. Now network utilization and bandwidth requirements are being driven higher and higher by streaming video, social networking, Voice over IP (VoIP) phones, email, Internet browsing and shopping, and the ever-growing number of Internet-capable mobile devices (smartphones, tablets, and even gaming consoles). Many organizations, including Internet and telephone service providers, need a way to prioritize their traffic to ensure that the most business-critical or mission-critical applications have all the bandwidth they require and that the less-important applications, such as those for streaming music, can suffer when mission-critical applications require more throughput. To support this, IPv4 quality of service (QoS) features were implemented on many networks. However, because QoS was not a strict requirement for software and hardware developers to support, many applications do not include enough information in their data packets to sufficiently distinguish their data so that QoS could effectively categorize and prioritize the traffic (thus presenting a challenge to IPv4). For example, QoS in many cases uses the port number, like HTTP 80, to identify web browsing traffic. For an application to work through a web proxy server, the application had to run on port 80 (a music or video streaming application, for example). Therefore, categorizing video as web traffic was incorrect, and the video could get the undesired tier of priority, and this could be a good or bad thing depending on the situation. Although deeper examination into an IPv4 packet allows IPv4 QoS to better prioritize traffic, that can also slow down traffic handling, and when IPsec is used and IPv4 packets are encrypted, QoS cannot do its job properly.

Ah, finally, IPv6 is here! IPv6 has been a work in progress since the early1990s when it was first named IP Next Generation. Originally, IPv6 was developed to solve the issue of running out of addresses, but now it has grown to also include many features that IPv4 was lacking or needed improvement/guidelines and standardization. Some of the most prominent improvements IPv6 has over IPv4 are as follows:

- **IP addressing**—IPv6 addresses are 128-bit addresses, IPv4 addresses are 32-bit. Although this might seem only four times larger, the actual number of usable addresses as compared is IPv4 2^{32} addresses versus IPv6 2^{128} addresses.
- **Automated addressing**—IPv4 required manual IP addressing or a DHCP server to provide addressing for newly connected network devices. IPv6 includes both stateful (same as IPv4) and stateless addressing. Stateless addressing can be described as each IPv6 adapter assigns itself a unique address based on discoveries with other neighboring IPv6 stateless devices to enable real automated networking and communication. This self-assigned stateless address is also referred to as the link-local address.
- **Included security**—IPv6 includes detailed specifications for IPsec built in to the protocol. This allows each software and hardware vendor to adopt these standards to make securing communication and traffic between different applications and devices simpler and more reliable. Also, the way IPsec has been implemented in IPv6, encrypted data can still be categorized and prioritized properly with QoS, without compromising the security of the data.

- **Included QoS**—The IPv6 header of each packet of data includes two main fields that allow for QoS to perform better than IPv4. These fields, the Traffic Class and Flow Label fields, can be used by software and hardware developers to properly identify their data so that it can be prioritized and routed correctly. The Traffic Class field is used much like the IPv4 header Type of Service (ToS) field, but the Flow Label field is key to quickly identifying a flow or stream of packets, encrypted or not, to allow the entire dataset to be transmitted without examining each packet individually after the first packet is identified.

This list identifies just a few of the key improvements of IPv6 over IPv4; there are many more. However, if you are still not convinced that you need to learn IPv6, open a PowerShell console session on a Windows Server 2012 Active Directory domain controller and type **Netstat -n** and press Enter. This will show you that without a doubt, IPv6 is in use, whether you want to accept it or not. Just look for the IPv6 link-local address, which will start with fe80:: (the link-local prefix). IPv6 addressing is covered next in this chapter, but the remainder of this IPv6 section provides more detailed information about IPv6 and gives you enough information to set up your first IPv6 network.

IPv6 Addressing

Okay folks, get out your scientific calculators. It is time to do some binary, decimal, and hexadecimal conversions. Fun! With the expanded address space associated with IPv6, the developers of IPv6 decided to leverage the hexadecimal numbering system to simplify and reduce the number of characters to identify the IPv6 address. IPv6 addresses are 128 bits in length and much longer than the 32-bit IPv4 address. But before we can dive deeper, the bit count is actually derived from the binary numbering system, which uses only 0s and 1s to represent any number. Binary numbering is also called base-2, because it uses only two numeric values, 0 and 1. Decimal uses base-10 numbering that ranges from 0 to 9, and hexadecimal uses base-16 numbering that ranges from 0 to f, as shown in Table 11.1.

TABLE 11.1 Number Conversions

Binary	Decimal	Hexadecimal
Base-2	**Base-10**	**Base-16**
0001	1	1
0010	2	2
0011	3	3
0100	4	4
0101	5	5
0110	6	6
0111	7	7
1000	8	8
1001	9	9
1010	10	a

Binary	Decimal	Hexadecimal
Base-2	**Base-10**	**Base-16**
1011	11	b
1100	12	c
1101	13	d
1110	14	e
1111	15	f
11111111	255	ff

From our well-known decimal system to convert to and from binary and hexadecimal, you need to learn how to add in each of the three systems. Figure 11.18 shows the representation of 165 in all three systems and may help explain how addition works in each system.

Decimal								Numeric Expression	Addition	Total
10^7	10^6	10^5	10^4	10^3	10^2	10^1	10^0			
10,000,000	1,000,000	100,000	10,000	1000	100	10	1			
					1	6	5	165 =	(1*100)+(6*10)+(5*1) =	165
Binary								**Numeric Expression**	**Addition**	**Total**
2^7	2^6	2^5	2^4	2^3	2^2	2^1	2^0			
128	64	32	16	8	4	2	1			
1	0	1	0	0	1	0	1	10100101 =	(1*128)+(1*32)+(1*4)+(1*1) =	165
Hexadecimal								**Numeric Expression**	**Addition**	**Total**
16^7	16^6	16^5	16^4	16^3	16^2	16^1	16^0			
268,435,456	16,777,216	1,048,576	65536	4096	256	16	1			
						a	5	a5 =	(10*16)+(5*1) =	165

FIGURE 11.18 Counting in binary, decimal and hexadecimal.

By now, you are probably building a base of information about hexadecimal numbering, and so we will continue with an actual example of an IPv6 IP address.

Network addressing for IPv4 is broken down into four 8-bit groups, totaling 32 bits and divided by periods. Each group can range from 0 to 255 and is represented in three decimal digits, such as the IP address 192.168.101.101. It is common with IPv4 addresses to drop leading 0s. For example, the IP address 192.168.100.010 is normally written as 192.168.100.10. IPv6 addresses, being 128 bits in length, are broken down into eight 16-bit boundaries or groups and are separated by colons. With IPv6 addresses, it is also common to drop leading 0s, but because the addresses are so long, other actions are often taken to shorten the address. The following IPv6 address is written using different forms of character reduction to simplify the notation of the full address, which is listed first:

- 2001:0dba:1234:aaaa:0000:0000:3a5f:0456
- 2001:dba:1234:aaaa:0000:0000:3a5f:456 (leading 0 dropped from last two groups)

- 2001:dba:1234:aaaa:0:0:3a5f:456 (0 groups compressed)
- 2001:dba:1234:aaaa::3a5f:456 (consecutive 0 groups replaced with ::)

Reducing the address as much as possible is highly preferred and now considered the correct way to notate an IPv6 address. You can find more information about notation standards for IPv6 in RFCs 4291, 5952, and 6052. One important point with character reduction, particularly with 0 groups, is that there can only be one set of double colons; if there happens to be more than one consecutive set of 0 groups, the double colon should be used to compress the larger of the two groups to make the biggest character reduction as possible.

NOTE

The IPv6 network prefix of 2001:db8 has been designated as the range to use for IPv6 documentation examples only as detailed in RFC 3849. Do not use this address range on any production IPv6 deployments.

Comprehending IPv6 Addressing

Learning IPv6 notation can be a bit daunting at first, based not only on the use of hexadecimal numbering, but also on the length of a full address. Using notational abbreviations, as described in RFCs 4291, 5952, and 6052, can assist greatly, but hands-on practice implementing IPv6 addressing and gaining familiarity with binary, decimal, and hexadecimal conversion is key to adopting this new protocol. This section covers addition concepts that network administrators need to know, beyond just the IPv6 address itself.

IPv6 Address Prefix

IPv4 address notation is usually written with a 32-bit network address followed by a forward slash (/) and a trailing number used to delineate the network number and the associated subnet mask. This notation tells the network administrator the range of IP addresses available on that particular network segment. For example, the 192.168.1.0/24 network includes a network number of 192.168.1.0 with a 24-bit subnet mask of 255.255.255.0. To understand what that means, remember that everything goes back to binary, and each binary digit represents 1 bit of the address. Binary addition, which you should become familiar with if you are not already, defines that any number added with 1 will equal 1 and any number added with 0 will equal 0. To understand IP addressing, network administrators need to fully understand these binary addition rules. So, moving forward, the term *mask* as it relates to IP networking means performing binary addition of a network address with a predetermined bit length of all 1s. For example, a /24 in an 32-bit IPv4 address includes 24 leading 1s and 8 trailing 0s. Table 11.2 shows how binary addition is used on an existing address of 192.168.1.15, with a subnet mask of 255.255.255.0, to derive the network number.

TABLE 11.2 Binary Addition

Decimal Address	Binary IP Address	
192.168.1.15	11000000.10101000.00000001.00001111	Address
+ 255.255.255.0	11111111.11111111.11111111.00000000	Subnet mask
192.168.1.0	11000000.10101000.00000001.00000000	Network number

Table 11.2 displays the network number that was derived from addition of the IPv4 address and the associated subnet mask. Although IPv6 has changed the terminology some, this example still applies.

In IPv4, the address is divided into the network number and the host number. In IPv6, the network number portion of the address is referred to as the IPv6 prefix. The IPv6 prefix is written in the same form as for an IPv4 network, but with an IPv6 address followed by a forward slash and a trailing number that is simply referred to as the mask length and written as IPv6address/prefix-length. For example, 2001:dba:1234:5678::/64 translates into a network with a mask of 64 bits, and the IP addresses in this network will all start with the prefix of 2001:dba:1234:5678, followed by four other groups that define the host portion of the address. This example made use of an IPv6 notation reduction that truncated the leading 0 in the second group of dba. This and other notation-reduction practices are covered in the section "IPv6 Address Notation Best Practices," later in this chapter.

IPv6 DNS Records

Because IPv6 addresses use a completely different number scheme, a new DNS record format was created to support the lookup of IPv6 hosts. The IPv6 forward, or name to IPv6 address type, is an AAAA address type. This address type is available on Microsoft Windows DNS servers and on most other current DNS server systems. For an organization that will leverage IPv6, network and DNS administrators need to ensure that their DNS server system supports this record type. The same goes for the reverse DNS record, where the IPv6 address lookup needs to resolve to a hostname. With Microsoft DNS, the forward lookup zone can support both the standard IPv4 record type of A and the IPv6 record type of AAAA. The reverse DNS zone must be created and populated manually, but even though there will need to be separate reverse DNS zones for IPv4 and IPv6 networks, the reverse DNS records for both are still the same PTR record type. Microsoft clients and servers will, by default, dynamically register their forward and reverse IPv4 addresses in DNS. With IPv6, only the forward DNS records are registered, and if network administrators require IPv6 reverse DNS records, these must be created manually when needed.

IPv6 Address Notation Best Practices

As stated earlier, IPv6 addresses are long, and RFCs have been written to provide standards and best practices for administrators to follow to simplify notation, when possible. Some of the most common IPv6 character-reduction practices are as follows and are all part of what is referred to as 0 compression:

- **Truncate leading 0s**—Whenever possible, remove one or more leading 0s in an IPv6 address group (for example, by changing the IPv6 address of 2001:0dba:0000:0000:0000:0110:0000:0000 to 2001:dba:0000:0000:0000:110:0000:0000)
- **Compress 0 groups**—When an entire group of an IPv6 address is made up of all 0s (for example, 2001:dba:0000:0000:0000:110:0000:0000), the group can be reduced to a single 0 (2001:dba:0:0:0:110:0:0).
- **Replace consecutive zero groups with double colon**—When consecutive 0 groups are encountered, as shown in the previous example, two or more groups can be replaced with a double colon.
  - Only one set of double colons can be used in an IPv6 address.
  - When there is more than one set of zero groups in an IPv6 address, the double colon should be used to replace the largest set. For this example, that is the last three groups of 0s; the IPv6 address is then written as 2001:dba::110:0:0.
  - When multiple consecutive groups of 0s are replaced with a double colon, administrators can subtract the remaining number of groups from 8 to determine how many groups of 0s were removed. In this case, 8 – 5 = 3, so the double colon has replaced three groups of consecutive 0s.
- **Do not remove trailing or 0s between other numbers**—When a group contains a 0 that is surrounded by other numbers or is the last number in a group, it needs to remain as part of the final address. For example, in the sixth group (originally 0110), removing the trailing 0 would change the number and therefor change the address. This might seem obvious, but with all the available options to reduce the address, it is important to note this rule.

So with all the options previously noted for 0 compression, the original address of 2001:0dba:0000:0000:0000:0110:0000:0000 is now reduced to 2001:dba::110:0:0, and this reduces the original 39 character address to 17 characters (including colons).

One more important point about address notation is that although it is not a standard, a good practice for IPv6 notation is to use all lowercase letters.

IPv6 Addresses and Port Specification

In many documentation cases, it is necessary to also designate the port of a service running on IPv6. IPv4 uses a colon to designate the port (for example, 192.168.1.15:80), but with IPv6 this would cause a lot of confusion. To designate an IPv6 and a port address, you can enclose the address in brackets followed by the colon and port number (for example, [2001:dba::110:0:0]:80); 2001:dba::110:0:0 port 80 is also acceptable.

Unique Local Address

As with IPv4, many organization use the designated IPv4 private IP address ranges of 10.0.0.0/8, 172.16.0.0/16, and 192.168.0.0/24. With IPv6, because there are enough addresses, organizations may not need to use private addressing with NAT at the router or perimeter firewall. Organizations may start to use globally routable IPv6 addresses, or addresses that can be used on the internal network and on the Internet. However, many network administrators may opt to start IPv6 implementations using an internal-use IPv6 address known as the unique local address (ULA). This the IPv6 counterpart to the IPv4 private IP ranges and is detailed in RFC 4193. The ULA prefix is fc00::/7. The addresses within this range are intended to be used on internal site networks, and can even be used to route between internal networks, but are not intended to be routed globally or on the Internet.

The fc00::/7 prefix is divided further into two /8 address prefixes, including fd00:/8, which should be used for actual network deployments and has the eighth bit set to 1, indicating a local network, followed by a randomly generated 40-bit string, known as the global ID and a 16-bit subnet ID allowing network administrators a standard for addressing devices on /64 subnets. The other network is fc00:/8 and has the eighth bit set to 0, but that network has not yet been clearly defined or accepted as a standard. One network range from the fd00::/8 prefix is the fe80::/64 prefix, which is used for link-local addresses. The link-local address is the self-generated address assigned on every IPv6-enabled adapter. This link-local address can be used between IPv6 devices that were not statically configured with an address and did not receive an address from an IPv6 DHCP server (that is, the stateless configuration IPv6 address).

IPv6 Transition Technologies

Today, the Internet (and the world) is mostly running on IPv4 networks. As more and more operating system and devices natively support IPv6, and even require it, making IPv6 work globally will quickly become necessary. Because IPv4 and IPv6 devices cannot natively communicate with one another, protocols have been developed to bridge the gap, and these are known as the IPv6 transition technologies.

Before discussing transition technologies, or how we can make IPv6 devices communicate with IPv4 devices, we need to examine the different types of nodes on the networks, as defined in RFC 2893:

- **IPv4-only node**—This type of nodes uses IPv4 only and most likely does not even have the IPv6 protocol installed. This is Windows XP and Windows Server 2003 and earlier, by default, but IPv6 can be installed and configured on these operating systems.
- **IPv6/IPv4 node**—This is the typical node today, which has both IPv4 and IPv6 protocols installed and uses both protocols. Windows Vista, Windows Server 2008 and later client and server operating systems are IPv6/IPv4 nodes.
- **IPv6-only node**—A node that only has the IPv6 protocol installed and in use. In today's world, finding a node that fits this description is nearly impossible.
- **IPv6 node**—A node that uses IPv6, regardless of whether IPv4 is also used. This is a more generic term
- **IPv4 node**—A node that uses IPv4, regardless of whether IPv6 is also used. This is a more generic term.

Communication between IPv4 and IPv6 devices does not directly occur. Devices need to communicate using the same protocol. You can enable IPv6 devices to communicate over IPv4 networks by using some form of tunneling, but when IPv6/IPv4 nodes are in use on the same network and properly addressed, they use transition technologies built in to the protocol stack architectures. Windows XP and Windows Server 2003 use the dual stack, and later operating systems (Windows Vista and Windows Server 2008 and later) leverage the dual layer. With the dual stack, when data is prepared for the network, it is prepared for both protocols separately, requiring more overhead within the operating system. With the dual layer, the upper-stack layers are shared, thus reducing overhead, and that is the architecture in use with the more recent operating systems. Future releases will most likely do away with the dual layer and move toward an IPv6-only stack. Figure 11.19 compares the dual stack and dual layer architectures.

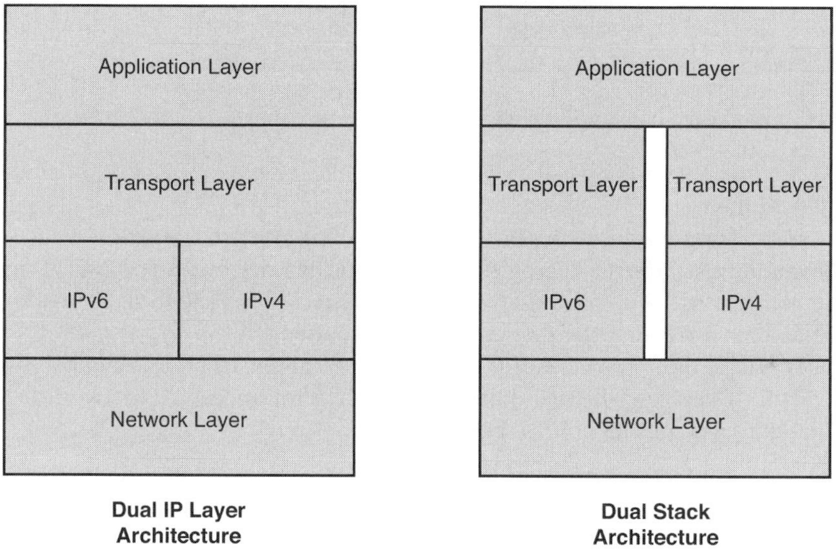

FIGURE 11.19 Dual IP layer and dual stack architectures.

IPv6 Tunneling

When IPv6 nodes are separated between IPv4 networks, they cannot directly communicate. To bridge the gap, the IPv6 nodes can tunnel through the IPv4 network. This tunneling can occur on the host itself or through a designated IPv6 router tunneling router. When IPv6 is tunneled through an IPv4 network, the IPv6 packet is encapsulated within an IPv4 packet. Figure 11.20 shows an example of an encapsulated header.

There are two different IPv6 tunnel configurations. The first is a configured tunnel, in which the endpoints and static routes for IPv6 traffic through an IPv4 network are defined. The second is an automatic tunnel that is created based on the IPv4 address of the device. The automatic tunnel can be leveraged only on devices that are properly configured to use both IPv6 and the IPv4. Configured tunnels, although these can be created on local windows hosts, can also be configured on designated routers to bridge the gap between IPv6-only devices on different networks separated by IPv4 networks.

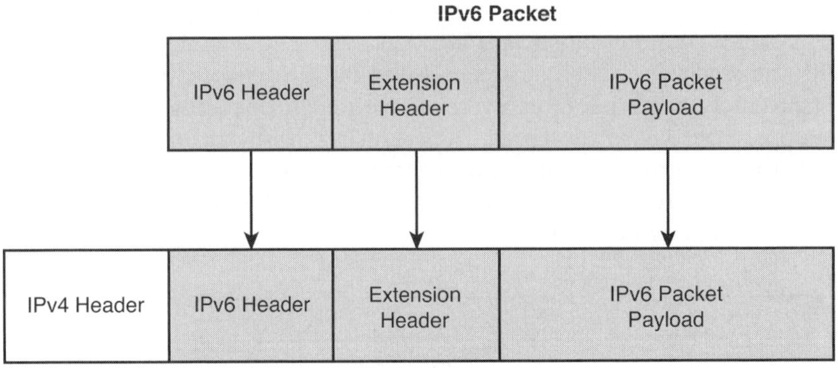

FIGURE 11.20 IPv6 packet encapsulated in IPv4.

The ISATAP Tunneling Protocol

The Intra-Site Automatic Tunnel Addressing Protocol (ISATAP) is an IPv6 transition technology used to allow administrators to deploy IPv6 nodes on IPv4 networks. For ISATAP to be used, an ISATAP router must be deployed and have a DNS record on the local network. ISATAP is not intended for use across the Internet (hence the user of intra-site as part of its name), but ISATAP traffic must traverse an ISATAP router to allow an IPv6-only host to communicate with IPv4 devices. The two main requirements for an ISATAP network to function are an ISATAP router and, of course, ISATAP hosts:

- **ISATAP router**—An ISATAP router advertises subnet prefixes assigned to the ISATAP network, to ISATAP hosts, and the router forwards packets between the IPv4 and IPv6 network.
- **ISATAP hosts**—ISATAP hosts can communicate directly with ISATAP and IPv6 hosts on the local network and with IPv4 hosts through the ISATAP router.

ISATAP addresses are automatically assigned or created on ISATAP hosts, but before that occurs an ISATAP router must be detected by a potential host. A router is detected when a host can resolve the name ISATAP with a DNS lookup within their primary DNS suffix, or through another form of short-name resolution. When an ISATAP router is detected, an address is constructed based on the address prefix provided by the ISATAP router, concatenated with the local IP address of the ISATAP host. The ISATAP address is constructed of the 64-bit IPv6 prefix already defined for the IPv6 network followed by a 32-bit ISATAP designation and then by the 32-bit IPv4 address. For example, with an IPv6 prefix of

2001:0dba:1234:5678::/64 for a host with an IPv4 address in a private network range, the address is as follows:

2001:0dba:1234:5678:0:5efe:w.x.y.z, where the w.x.y.z represents the IPv4 address

The 6to4 Tunneling Protocol

The 6to4 tunneling protocol provides automatic address assignment and tunneling of IPv6 traffic across the IPv4 Internet. This is mainly used when the host or client is connected directly and assigned a public IPv4 Internet address, but can also be used when a host has an IPv4 private address assigned. The 6to4 address format uses an IPv6 global prefix because it is an IPv6 prefix that is okay to route across the Internet. Figure 11.21 shows the 6to4 address format.

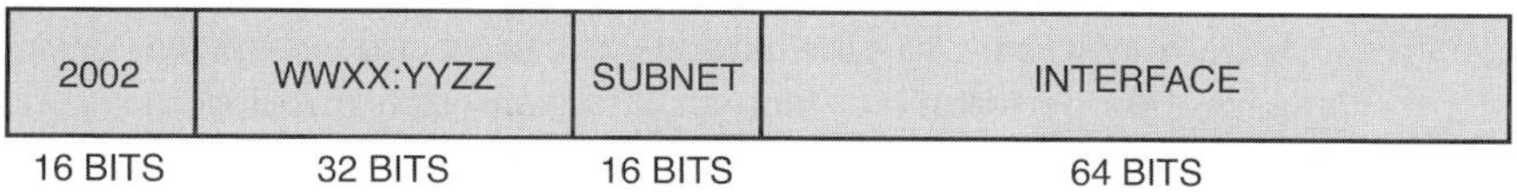

FIGURE 11.21 6to4 IPv6 address format.

A 6to4 global address prefix is in the format of 2002:WWXX:YYZZ::/48, where WWXX:YYZZ is the hexadecimal representation of the public IP address. Each of the two letters represents one of the 32-bit IPv4 octets. As an example of a 6to4 address converted, a public IP address of 72.34.113.11 is converted to 2002:4822:710b::/48.

The 6to4 network can include the following components:

- **6to4 host**—A host that has both IPv4 and IPv6 and is configured with a 6to4 address in the IPv6 global address range of 2002::/16.
- **6to4 router**—An IPv6/IPv4 forwards traffic between 6to4 hosts on the local network to other 6to4 routers and to 6to4 relay routers.
- **6to4 relay**—Forwards 6to4 traffic between the IPv4 Internet and IPv6-only devices directly connected to the Internet.

The Teredo Tunneling Protocol

The Teredo IPv6 transition technology is commonly used when the client system is assigned a private IP address and a 6to4 network is not enabled or preferred. One of the biggest advantages of Teredo over 6to4 is that 6to4 is not so NAT friendly when traversing the Internet and each endpoint needs to have a public IPv4 address. Also, 6to4 traffic has a reasonably high failure rate because the packets are encapsulated and marked with protocol field 41, which is unknown to many firewalls, and unknown protocols are usually blocked by default. Also, using the public Internet, end users cannot control how many NAT traversals (NAT-T) the packets must go through from the sources to the destination, making 6to4 not so resilient to support routing through NATs. This is where Teredo (IPv6 NAT-T) becomes the preferred tunneling protocol. RFC 4380 describes the Teredo tunneling protocol. Teredo makes its way around the NAT challenge by changing the way the IPv6 packet is encapsulated. With the ISATAP and 6to4 tunneling protocols, the IPv6 packet is encapsulated within an IPv4 packet, and the header IP protocol field is set to a value of 41 to identify tunnelled traffic. Teredo tunnels Ipv6 over Ipv4 differently as the IPv6 packet are encapsulated and sent within an IPv4 User Datagram Protocol (UDP) packet that easily gets through NAT traversals. But, the Teredo protocol is considered the protocol of last resort, mainly because of the high overhead associated with the encapsulation mechanism, but also because of security concerns. Teredo basically allows hosts to directly traverse NATs to communicate across the Internet with other Teredo hosts using what is referred to as open-ended tunnels. Because of the way the Teredo protocol encapsulates Ipv6 traffic within Ipv4 UDP packets, it can essentially bypass some of the strict traffic inspection performed by network firewalls and intrusion prevention system (IPS). This leaves the burden of validating the Ipv6 traffic to the Teredo host receiving the data. This might not be the most secure or ideal scenario and in cases where Teredo must be used, network administrators should fully understand Teredo security risks and how to mitigate them.

Until a true IPv6 Internet is configured, there will be security and functionality challenges to make IPv6 work on both the internal network and across the Internet. In some ways, having the transition technologies in place slows down the larger ISPs' adoption of an Ipv6 Internet.

Configuring IPv6 on Windows Server 2012

To begin using IPv6 on your organization's internal network, deploying a DHCP server and manually configuring IP addresses on servers and network devices is a good place to start. A few things to consider when designing your IPv6 network include selecting the IPv6 prefixes for local and remote sites, and determining how clients will be assigned addresses (DHCP or manually) and how or if you will route IPv6 traffic between sites and how IPv6 hostnames will be resolved. A simple IPv6 implementation consists of static or manually configured IPv6 addresses on servers and network devices, an IPv6 DHCP server for client workstations, an IPv6 DNS reverse lookup zone, and IPv6 subnet definitions in Active Directory for each of your IPv6 networks. With these simple steps, you will be well on your way to implementing and using IPv6 on the local network. This simple network design is the basis for the following sections about implementing IPv6 services.

Creating an IPv6 Subnet in Active Directory

For Active Directory clients to properly associate their local services with their respective Active Directory site, all the subnets need to be added to the Active Directory site configuration, and this applies to both IPv4 and IPv6 networks. For this example, we use the documentation IPv6 prefix 2001:dba::/64, but for a real-world implementation a network administrator should design the IPv6 network using a prefix within the ULA range described earlier in this chapter. For our network, the IPv4 network is 192.168.206.0/24, and we will use the IPv6 prefix 2001:dba:ce::/64. To create the IPv6 subnet in the default Active Directory site, follow these steps:

1. Log on to the domain controller.
2. Click the Server Manager tile on the taskbar.
3. Click the AD DS link in the tree pane on the left.
4. In the Servers pane, right-click the domain controller and select Active Directory Sites and Services, as shown in Figure 11.22.

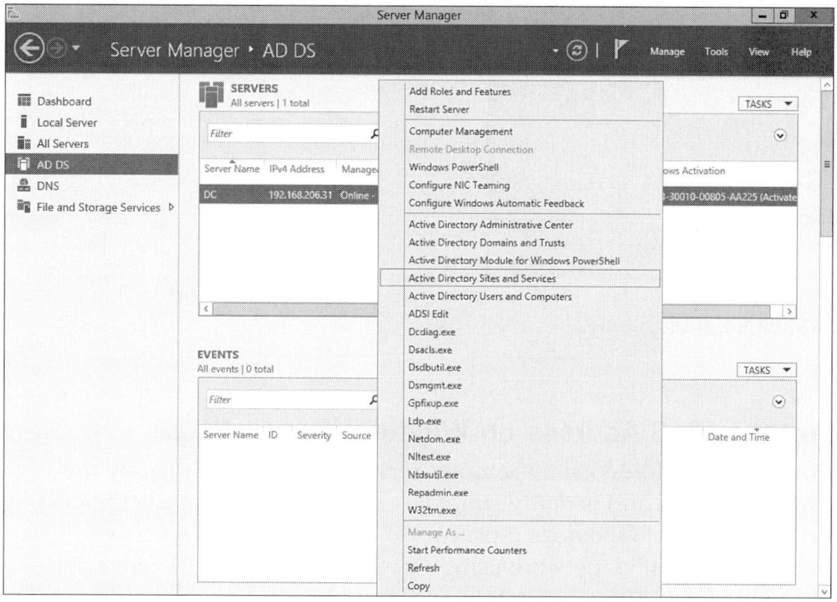

FIGURE 11.22 Opening Active Directory Sites and Services.

5. When the active Directory Sites and Services console open, expand the Sites nodes in the tree pane and select Subnets.
6. Right-click the Subnet node and select New Subnet.
7. When the New Object – Subnet window opens, in the Prefix field type in your IPv6 network prefix and then select the associated site to associate it with, as shown in Figure 11.23. Click OK to create the subnet.
8. Close the Active Directory Sites and Subnet console.

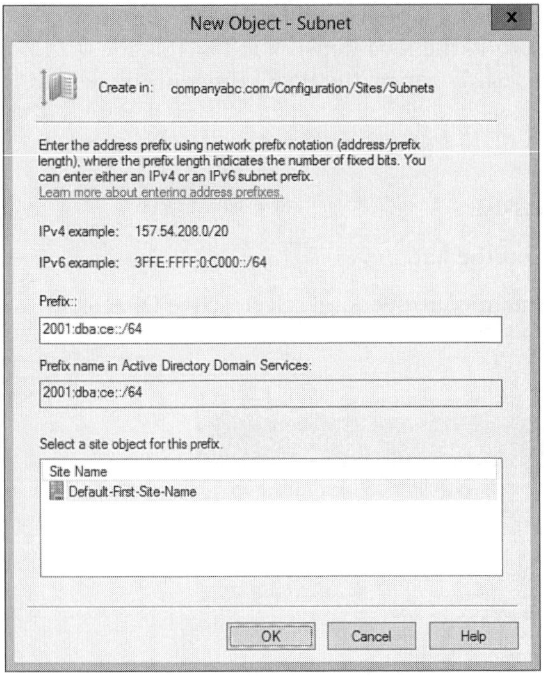

FIGURE 11.23 Creating the IPv6 subnet.

Manually Setting the IPv6 Address on Windows Server 2012

Manually configuring an IPv6 address on a Windows Server 2012 system is nearly the same process as configuring IPv4 and is pretty simple. For this example, we use the documentation IPv6 prefix 2001:dba::/64, but for a real-world implementation a network administrator should design the IPv6 network using a prefix within the ULA range. For our network, the IPv4 range is 192.168.206.0/24, and for the IPv6 to provide some easy-to-remember addressing, we will use 2001:dba:ce::/64. The server in this example has an IPv4 address of 192.168.206.31, and its corresponding IPv6 address will be 2001:dba:ce::1f/64. To configure the address, follow these steps:

1. Log on to the proposed IPv6 server.
2. Click the Server Manager tile on the taskbar.
3. Click the Local Server link in the tree pane on the left.
4. Click the link to the right of the Wired Ethernet Connection in the Properties section, as shown in Figure 11.24.

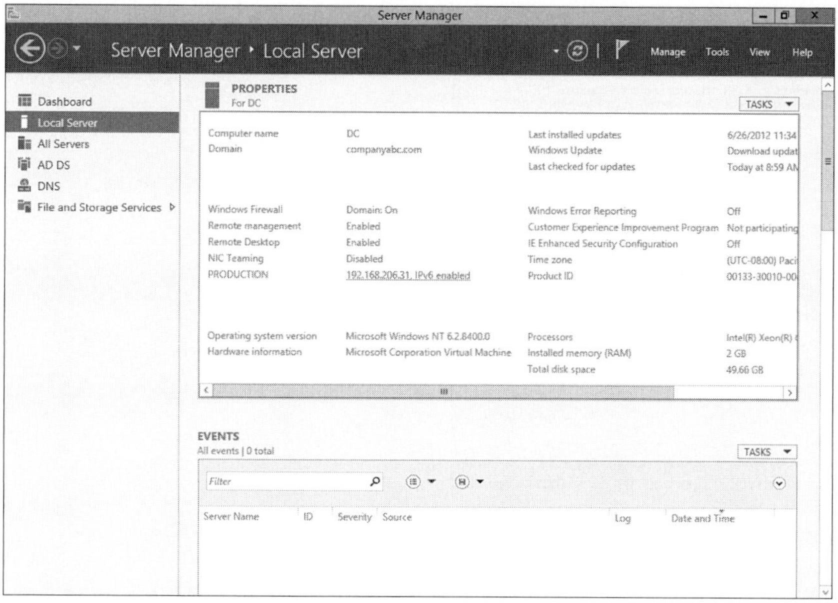

FIGURE 11.24 Selecting the network adapter.

5. When the Network Connections window opens, right-click the Wired Ethernet Connection and select Properties.
6. Scroll down and select Internet Protocol Version 6 (TCP/IPv6) and click the Properties button.
7. In the Internet Protocol Version 6 (TCP/IPv6) Properties window, select the Use the Following IPv6 Address radio button and type in the desired address. When finished, press the Tab key to autopopulate the subnet prefix length of 64.
8. For this example, there is no IPv6 router, so leave that field blank, but enter the IPv6 address of the appropriate DNS server (in this case, the local DNS DC system, as shown in Figure 11.25).
9. Click OK and then click Close to apply the new address and save the configuration to the network connection. Because this is on the DNS server, the DNS service automatically binds to this new IPv6 address, and the network connection dynamically registers the new IPv6 (AAAA) record in the forward DNS lookup zone.
10. Close the Network Connections window.

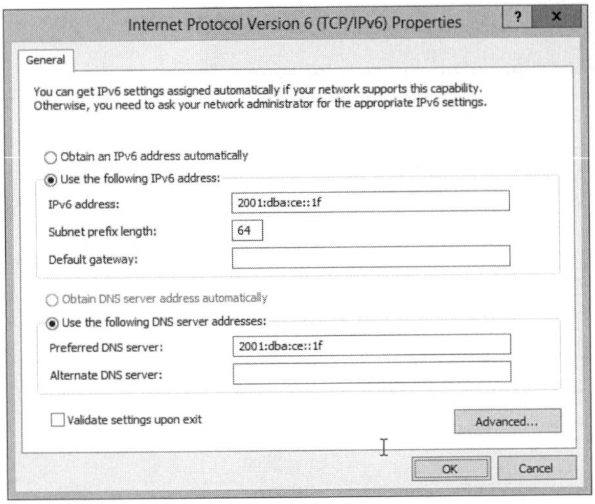

FIGURE 11.25 Manually configuring the IPv6 address of the DNS/DC server.

Creating IPv6 DNS Records and Zones

A Windows Server 2012 DNS server automatically supports IPv6 DNS records. The forward record is the AAAA record, and the reverse is still just a PTR record. When a Windows Server 2012 DNS server is assigned a static IPv6 address, it supports DNS services on this address by default. Also, when the forward DNS zone for the domain is created, AAAA records can be dynamically or statically added to the forward zone without any necessary changes. IPv6 hosts will be able to dynamically register AAAA records immediately. To support IUPv6 reverse DNS lookup, follow the proceeding steps to create the IPv6 reverse DNS zone.

1. Log on to the DNS server.
2. Click the Server Manager tile on the taskbar.
3. Click the DNS link in the tree pane on the left.
4. In the Servers pane, right-click the DNS Server and select DNS Manager from the list.
5. When the DNS Manager console opens, expand the DNS server to reveal the forward and reverse lookup zones.
6. Expand the Forward Lookup Zones node and select the zone for the Active Directory domain to load the records list in the right pane. Scroll up and down to view the existing A and AAAA records, which should already be present for the DNS/DC server.
7. Before we create a new AAAA record, an IPv6 reverse DNS zone should be created. Select and Expand the Reverse Lookup Zones node to reveal the list of existing zones. Right-click the node and select New Zone.
8. Click Next on the Welcome page.

9. On the Zone Type page, accept the defaults of a Primary zone that is stored in Active Directory, and then click Next.
10. On the Active Directory Zone Replication Scope page, accept the defaults and click Next.
11. On the Reverse Lookup Zone Name page, select the IPv6 Reverse Lookup Zone radio button and click Next.
12. On the Reverse Lookup Zone Name page, type **2001:dba:ce::/64** and the zone name will be automatically created based on a four group, 64-bit prefix of 2001:0dba:00ce:0000. Accept the name and click Next.
13. On the Dynamic Updates page, accept the defaults and click Next.
14. On the Completing the New Zone Wizard page, click Finish to complete the process.
15. Now back in the DNS Manager console window, select and expand the new IPv6 reverse zone in the tree pane to load the list of records.
16. Right-click the new IPv6 reverse DNS zone and select New Pointer (PTR) to create a new reverse record for the DNS/DC server.
17. In the New Resource Record window, the 64-bit prefix will be autopopulated. To define the new record, you can either enter the full IPv6 address with no 0 compression or, if the forward AAAA record is created, click the Browse button and search in the forward lookup zone for the corresponding record and select it. This will populate the IPv6 address, as shown in Figure 11.26. Click Next to complete the record creation.

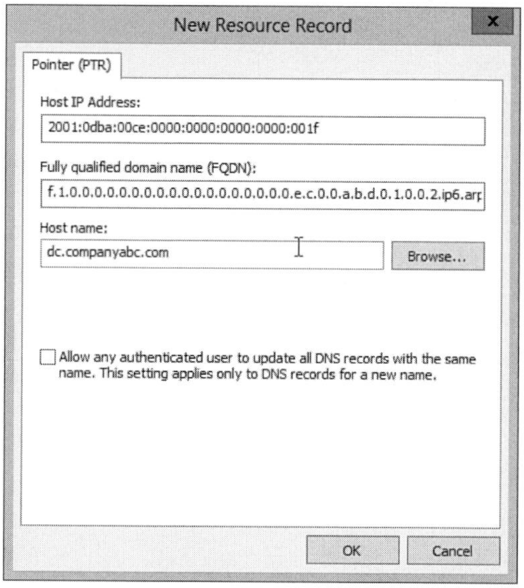

FIGURE 11.26 Creating the IPv6 reverse PTR record for the DNS/DC system.

One important point to remember is that a Windows Server 2012 system, or any IPv6-configured Windows system, will not dynamically register reverse IPv6 records. This is by design and may be changed in the future. But for now, if you require IPv6 reverse DNS resolution, the records will need to be created manually.

Setting Up Windows Server 2012 DHCP IPv6 Scopes

To support stateful IPv6 with DHCP, the network administrator can create IPv6 DHCP scopes on a Windows Server 2012 DHCP server. To create a new IPv6 DHCP scope, follow these steps:

1. Open the DHCP console and connect to the desired DHCP server.
2. When the DHCP Manager console opens, expand the DHCP server to reveal the IPv4 and IPv6 nodes.
3. Select and expand the IPv6 node, right-click the node, and select New Scope.
4. Click Next on the Welcome page.
5. On the Scope Name page, enter a name and description for the scope and click Next.
6. On the Scope Prefix page, enter the scope prefix and leave the default of 0 for the preference. For our example, we use 2001:dba:ce::/64 as the prefix and 0 for the preference. Click Next to continue.
7. On the Add Exclusions page, you need to define the IP addresses that will not be included in this larger DHCP scope range and then click Add. For this example, we retain 255 addresses for statically configured devices and leave the remainder for the DHCP scope. Figure 11.27 shows the exclusion range we define.

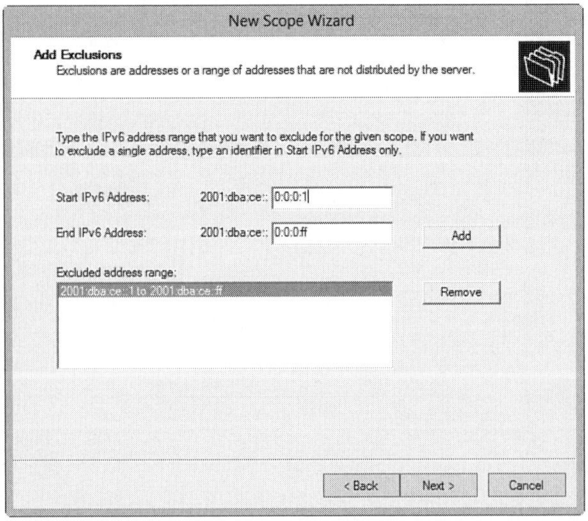

FIGURE 11.27 Defining exclusion ranges in the DHCP scope.

8. On the Scope Lease page, enter the desired time frame for an IPv6 address to be leased and click Next. There are two different entries here: preferred lifetime and valid lifetime. The valid lifetime is when the DHCP server considers an IP address available to be leased again. The preferred lifetime is what is given to the device as the time it should renew the lease by. Leave the defaults, but if you must change them, ensure that the valid lifetime duration is longer than the preferred.
9. On the Completing the New Scope Wizard page, select the desired radio button to activate the scope and click Finish to create the scope.

If necessary, you can create DHCP scope options for the IPv6 scope using the DHCP console after the scope is created. This completes the creation of the DHCP IPv6 scope.

IP Address Management

The IP Address Management (IPAM) feature included with Windows Server 2012 provides network administrators with a single centralized console from which they can view and manage the IP addresses of the entire enterprise. This feature is new to Microsoft Windows servers, but is not new to network administration. Before Windows Server 2012, network administrators had to manage and keep track of IP addresses using a combination of tools such as DHCP Manager and DNS Manager, in addition to third-party products that may have tracked client IP addresses. Commonly, detailed spreadsheets or proprietary databases were created to provide a source that could be referenced when a new device needed addressing or when an audit of an IP address was required. The challenge, however, was that no one place could be reviewed to get the latest and most correct information because keeping the different sources of data in sync and up-to-date was just not reliable enough.

Windows Server 2012 IPAM Server enables network administrators to leverage a built-in product supported by Microsoft that can help reduce or even eliminate the need for manual import or synchronization of IP address data from multiple sources. IPAM can be used to collect and present IP address data from DNS, DHCP, NPS, and domain controllers in a single centralized console. Furthermore, through the Server Manager-integrated IPAM console, network administrators can even manage those services to a degree, and when deeper management is required, the Server Manager console can quickly be used to launch the desired management console for the particular service.

As networks grow, centralized administration is always at the heart of a well-performing and simplified managed infrastructure. The task of managing and tracking IP addresses and networks is no different, and the IPAM feature provides views and functionality for IPAM not included in any other Microsoft role or feature.

IP Address Tracking Today

For IP address auditing or tracking, when a live network IP address needs to be linked or associated with a device, network administrators can use tools such as Nslookup to do a PTR reverse IP-to-name lookup and comb WINS databases or even use **ping -a**. Further testing can even include trying to connect to that system using various techniques like the Computer Management console, Telnet, HTTP, or any other means (such as reviewing firewall logs and so forth). All in all, this task can take some time and might not even produce the correct result; the administrator might have to physically searching that system using network switch ports, the Address Resolution Protocol (ARP) cache, or even tracing network ports to wall jacks and using a wall jack map to find the device. If this seems unrealistic to you, well, it's not, and it happens every day with network and security teams.

Let's consider a different scenario where we need to determine which device was assigned and used a DHCP assigned IP a week ago and that is now leased to a different system. How could we easily perform that task? The only way to do this before was to comb the DHCP activity logs, and if you didn't catch it within a week, you had to look through backups or shadow copies of that file. The DHCP activity logs are located on the local DHCP server in the default location of C:\Windows\System32\DHCP\ and are named DhcpSrvLog-Mon.log and DhcpV6SrvLog-Mon.log (for instance). The daily logs are overwritten each week.

Installing the IPAM Server and Client Features

Deploying IPAM into the network requires several steps. Planning the IPAM infrastructure is not a difficult task, but you must consider which systems will be managed by IPAM, how these systems will be configured to support IPAM, who will be able to view the IPAM information, and who will be able to make changes to IPAM-managed servers. Well, maybe it's not such as simple task from a design standpoint, but in reality, the concept of IPAM will not be new to organizations. So, as always, careful planning makes for the best deployment. The overall planning consists of a few main areas:

- **Discovery and server management**—How servers will be located and added to the IPAM console. Once a server is discovered or added manually, it still needs to be enabled in the IPAM console before it can be monitored and managed by IPAM.
- **Provisioning**—How managed servers will be configured to support IPAM data discovery and remote management. There are several configuration changes that will need to be implemented on a managed server before IPAM can collect data and, as possible, manage the service. This can occur manually or through group policy, and this process is known as provisioning.
- **Task management**—IPAM contains several tasks that are used to discover servers on the network and periodically collect activity, usage, and audit data and perform data maintenance and cleanup. IPAM administrators need to be familiar with task management both manually and through the scheduling to adjust the tasks to fit the organization's data collection and cleanup design.
- **Data sources**—IPAM can collect and organize data from several sources, including text files that can be imported manually by the IPAM administrator and, of course, DNS, DHCP, DC, and NPS servers. IPAM administrators need to understand how

to import data manually and how to add and provision new servers to allow IPAM tasks to collect the data automatically.

- **IP address data presentation**—The IPAM console provides administrators with a few different ways to search and present IP address datasets. Administrators can change the view and add or remove columns and even export to CSV files.
- **Security and permissions**—IPAM contains several security groups, and these groups are granted different levels of permissions, not only within the IPAM console, but also on the managed servers.

The IPAM server must be installed on a member server and should not be attempted on a domain controller. Also, when IPAM is installed on a DHCP server, the server discovery process does not function correctly and is not recommended. IPAM servers should be deployed on dedicated member server systems or at least on systems that do not include any of the ADDS, DHCP, DNS, or NPS roles. To install the IPAM server and client tools, follow these steps:

1. Log on to the IPAM server.
2. Click the Server Manager tile on the taskbar.
3. Click the Dashboard link in the tree pane and select Add Roles and Features to invoke the Add Roles and Features Wizard.
4. On the Before You Begin page, in the Add Roles and Features Wizard, click Next to continue.
5. On the Select Installation Type page, select the Role-Based or Feature-Based Installation radio button and click Next to continue.
6. On the Select Destination Server page, select the Select a Server from the Server Pool radio button and select the local server in the window. Click Next to continue.
7. On the Select Server Roles page, do not check any check boxes. Click Next to continue.
8. On the Select Features page, scroll down to IP Address Management (IPAM) Server Feature and check it. A pop-up window opens showing all the dependencies, including the IPAM client Feature Administration Tool, as shown in Figure 11.28. Click Add Features in the pop-up window, and then click Next on the Select Features page to continue.
9. On the Confirm Installation Selections page, review the list and click Install to begin the installation.
10. When the installation completes, click Close to return to the Server Manager window.

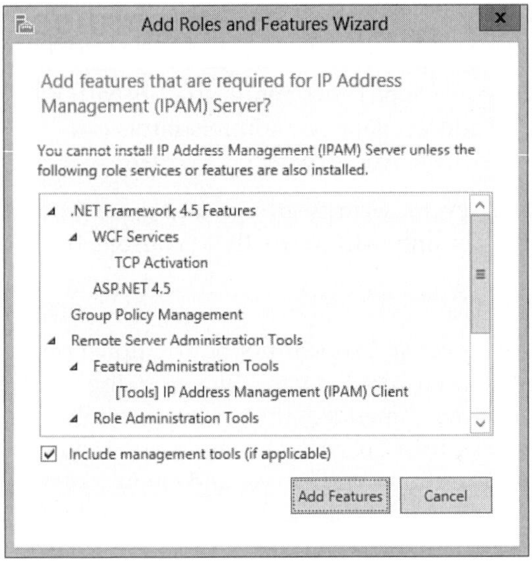

FIGURE 11.28 Install IPAM prerequisites, including client tools.

After the installation of the server feature and client tools, you must complete several steps before you can use IPAM, as follows:

1. Connect to the IPAM server.
2. Configure IPAM server provisioning.
3. Configure servers for IPAM management.
4. Configure and run server discovery.
5. Define discovered servers as IPAM managed.
6. Define IP address blocks.
7. Collect server data.

Connecting to the IPAM Server

When the IPAM client tools are also installed as part of the IPAM server installation, the IPAM server can be managed from Server Manager. To manage the IPAM server on the local system, follow these steps:

1. Log on to the IPAM server.
2. Click the Server Manager tile on the taskbar.
3. Click the IPAM link in the tree pane to display the IPAM console.

   The center console shows a list of six tasks, and the first is Connect to an IPAM Server. This should show that the console is already connected to the local system.

4. For remote administration of an IPAM server, you must perform two steps: install the IPAM client, and add a known IPAM server to the Server Manager server pool. After you complete these tasks, IPAM shows in the tree pane. To connect the IPAM server, select IPAM and then click Connect to IPAM Server.

5. When the Connect to IPAM Server window opens, select the IPAM server in the list and click OK.

NOTE

When the IPAM client is installed on a system that is not the IPAM server, the Group Policy Management Console and the DHCP and DNS tools are also installed; Active Directory tools are not.

Configuring IPAM Server Provisioning

Once the IPAM client is installed and the console is connected to the desired IPAM server, IPAM provisioning should be performed.

Servers that will be monitored and managed by an IPAM server need to be configured so that the IPAM server can connect to its services for data collection and service management. Servers can be configured to support the IPAM server either manually or through group policy. There are several configurations that need to occur on a server that will be managed by an IPAM server, including adding firewall rules, adding security groups to local server and service permissions, and sharing folders for remote IPAM server access. These steps can be manually performed on each server. Servers such as DHCP, DNS, ADDS, and NPS are configured differently, and if many servers require configuration, this can take quite a while.

IPAM server provisioning creates the IPAM database on the IPAM server and defines whether managed servers will be configured manually by the server administrator or through a set of group policies with a specifically defined group policy object (GPO) prefix name. As part of the IPAM provisioning process, local security groups are created, as is a domain security group named IPAMUG, which the local IPAM server is made a member of. This domain\IPAMUG security group is primarily used to grant permission on managed servers, as outlined in the next section.

When configured for manual provisioning, an IPAM server will do nothing when a server is added to the IPAM server as a managed server. When configured for group policy provisioning, the IPAM server, using the logged-in administrator credentials, searches for an existing group policy with the correct name and adds the managed server to the security filtering list. For now, all you need to know is whether your managed servers will be configured manually or through group policy. The IPAM provisioning process gets the IPAM server ready by creating and configuring the IPAM database, local security groups, and IPAM tasks on the local server. The provisioning process does not create any group policies in the domain, regardless of which provisioning method is selected. One thing to keep in mind is that after the provisioning wizard is run, the method of provisioning cannot be changed. To configure provisioning on an IPAM server, follow these steps:

1. Log on to the IPAM server or a server with the IPAM client tools installed and the IPAM server added to the server pool in Server Manager.
2. Click the Server Manager tile on the taskbar.
3. Click the IPAM link in the tree pane to display the IPAM.
4. The IPAM console shows a list of six tasks, and the first is Connect to an IPAM Server. If the console does not indicate that it is connected to an IPAM server, click this first task and follow the steps detailed in the previous section to connect to the desired IPAM server.
5. In the IPAM console, click Provision the IPAM Server, as shown in Figure 11.29.

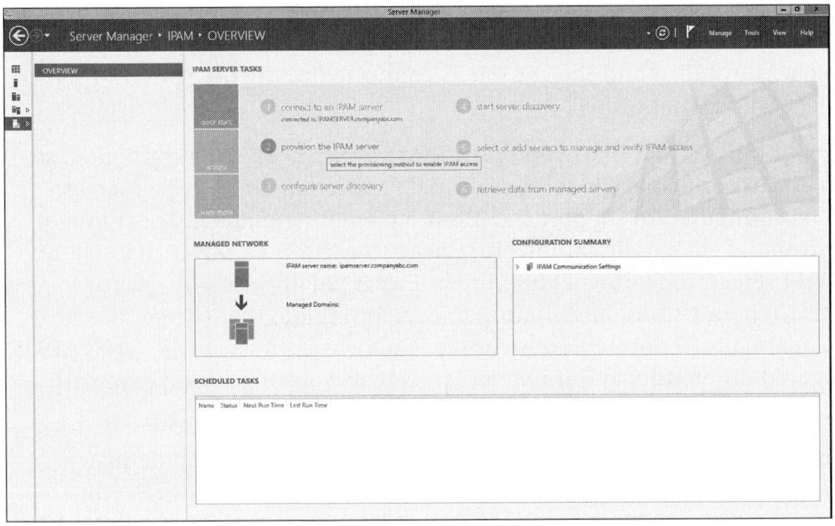

FIGURE 11.29 Provisioning the IPAM server.

6. Click Next on the Before You Begin page.
7. On the Select Provisioning Method page, select Manual if you want to configure each server manually, or select Group Policy Based to allow the IPAM server to add (or remove) managed servers to (or from) the corresponding GPO. For this example, we select the Group Policy Based radio button and then type in **IPAM** in the GPO Name prefix field, as shown in Figure 11.30. Click Next to continue.

NOTE

When the IPAM Group Policy Based Provisioning is selected, the group policies still need to be created using a separate process. Be sure to perform that process before servers are added to the IPAM console.

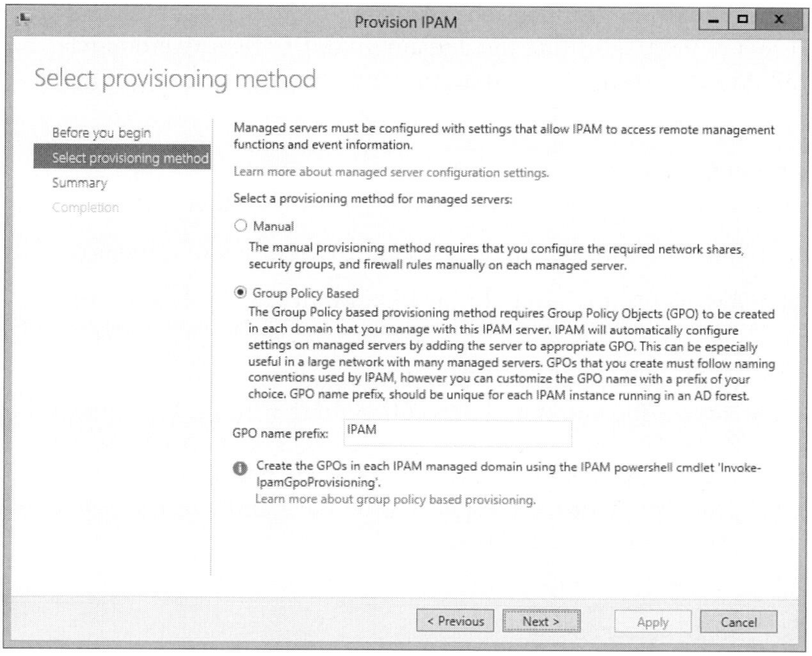

FIGURE 11.30 Selecting Group Policy Based Provisioning for IPAM.

8. On the Summary page, review the details and note that with the IPAM GPO prefix that was entered in the previous section, three GPOs will be referenced by this IPAM server: IPAM_DNS, IPAM_DHCP, and IPAM_DC_NPS. Click Apply to complete the provisioning process on the IPAM server.
9. When provisioning completes, click Close to return to the IPAM console and close the Server Manager window.

This completes the IPAM provisioning process, and no other steps should be performed in the console until the next section is completed.

Configuring Servers for IPAM Management

You can configure IPAM-managed servers manually or through group policies. When done manually, each server type needs specific configurations, and although certain configurations may overlap between a DHCP and DNS server, for example, if you try to put all the configurations on each server you will run into some challenges and might open unnecessary security holes. To perform manual configuration of IPAM-managed servers, follow the steps on the specific server type as detailed in the following sections for DHCP, DNS, DC, and NPS.

When manual configuration is performed, a universal security group can be created in the domain named IPAMUG, and the IPAM server computer account should be made a member of this group. The following manual steps assume this task has been performed earlier. If this group is not desired, substitute the domain\IPAMUG security group reference with the actual IPAM server computer account in the manual server configuration sections that follow.

Manually Configuring DHCP Servers

On all DHCP servers that will be IPAM-managed servers, follow these steps:

1. Add the domain\IPAMUG security group to the local DHCP Users security group.
2. Add the domain\IPAMUG security group to the local Event Log Readers security group.
3. Share the DHCP audit file path as **dhcpaudit** and configure the share and NTFS permissions to contain the domain\IPAMUG security group with read permissions, as shown in Figure 11.31. The default path is C:\Windows\System32\DHCP, but this path can be discovered by opening the DHCP Manager console on the DHCP server, right-clicking the IPv4 node, and displaying the Advanced tab. This is also the default path used for IPv6 DHCP auditing.

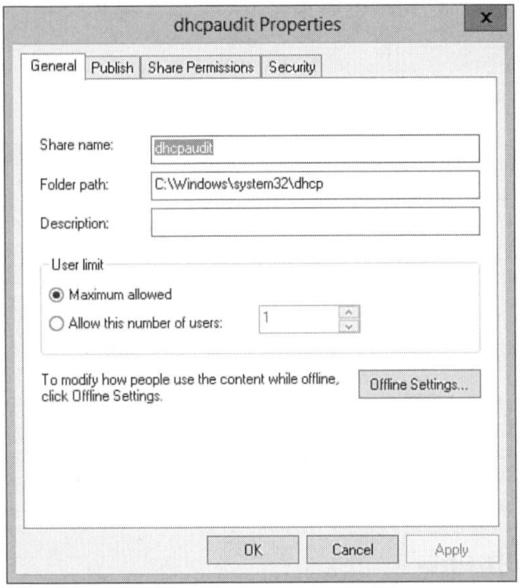

FIGURE 11.31 Sharing the DHCP audit path.

4. Enable the DHCP Server (RPC-In) Inbound Firewall rule.
5. Enable the DHCP Server (RPCSS-In) Inbound Firewall rule.
6. Enable the Remote Service Management (RPC) Inbound Firewall rule.

7. Enable the Remote Service Management (RPC-EPMAP) Inbound Firewall rule.
8. Enable the Remote Event Log Management (RPC) Inbound Firewall rule.
9. Enable the Remote Event Log Management (RPC-EPMAP) Inbound Firewall rule.
10. Enable the File and Printer Sharing (NM-Session-In) Inbound Firewall rule.
11. Enable the File and Printer Sharing (SMB-In) Inbound Firewall rule.

All of these firewall rules are pre-created Windows firewall inbound rules, and no special configuration should be required other than right-clicking the rule and selecting Enable Rule. Some of these rules may already be enabled, and those should be left as is.

Manually Configuring DNS Servers

On all DNS servers that will be IPAM-managed servers, follow these steps:

1. Add the domain\IPAMUG security group to the local Event Log Readers security group for member server DNS servers or the Builtin local security group in the domain on a DNS server running on a domain controller.
2. For a member server DNS server, add the domain\IPAMUG security group to the local Administrators group. For a domain controller DNS server, add the domain\IPAMUG security group with read permissions to the DNS Server Security ACL using the DNS Manager console. Open DNS Manager on the desired DNS server and connect to the server. Right-click the server object and select Properties, and then open the Security tab. Add the domain\IPAMUG group here with read permissions.
3. Enable the Remote Service Management (RPC) Inbound Firewall rule.
4. Enable the Remote Service Management (RPC-EPMAP) Inbound Firewall rule.
5. Enable the Remote Event Log Management (RPC) Inbound Firewall rule.
6. Enable the Remote Event Log Management (RPC-EPMAP) Inbound Firewall rule.

There are also four predefined DNS service group rules that need to be enabled, but these are already enabled when the DNS server role is installed, and no further action is required for IPAM communication.

Manually Configuring Domain Controllers and Network Policy Servers

On all domain controllers and NPS servers that will be IPAM-managed servers, follow these steps:

1. Add the domain\IPAMUG security group to the local Event Log Readers security group for member server NPS servers or the Builtin local security group in the domain for domain controllers.

2. Modify the local security policy on NPS servers and the default domain controller policy for domain controllers with the following setting: Computer Configuration\Policies\Windows Settings\Security Settings\Local Policies\Audit Policy\Audit Account Logon Events (Success/Failure). By default, the Windows Security event log, which will capture these events, is set to overwrite as needed when the log reaches 131MB, so adjust this as required to ensure that IPAM can capture the necessary data before the log rolls over.
3. Enable the Remote Event Log Management (RPC) Inbound Firewall rule.
4. Enable the Remote Event Log Management (RPC-EPMAP) Inbound Firewall rule.

If this seems like maybe just a few too many steps to manage when configuring a server as an IPAM-managed server, you can automate this by creating the appropriate group policies. In our example, we selected Group Policy Based configuration when we ran the IPAM Provisioning Wizard, and the following section details the steps that must be performed after provisioning is run but before servers are added to the IPAM console for management.

Creating Group Policy for IPAM Managed Server Configuration

When an IPAM server is provisioned and Group Policy Based provisioning is selected, the group policies still need to be created in the necessary domains. These group policies include the necessary settings to modify security group membership, enable firewall rules, and other tasks to make IPAM communication work correctly. For this example, the domain name is companyabc.com, and the IPAM GPO prefix is IPAM. To create the GPOs, follow these steps:

1. Log on to the IPAM server using an account with domain administrator rights.
2. Open Windows PowerShell from the taskbar.
3. Type in the command **Invoke-IpamGpoProvisioning -domain companyabc.com -gpoprefixname IPAM** and press Enter. If there are multiple domains in the forest, this task should be performed once per domain.
4. Review the information displayed in the window, press the Y key, and then press Enter to confirm the changes and continue.

When this process completes, three new GPOs will be created in the domain, as shown in Figure 11.32.

Explore each of the three GPOs and notice that they are automatically linked at the domain level but that the Security Filtering section is empty, meaning that in the current state the policy will not be applied by any user or computer. Also during this step, the domain\IPAMUG universal security group is added to the domain in the Users container with the IPAM server as the only member.

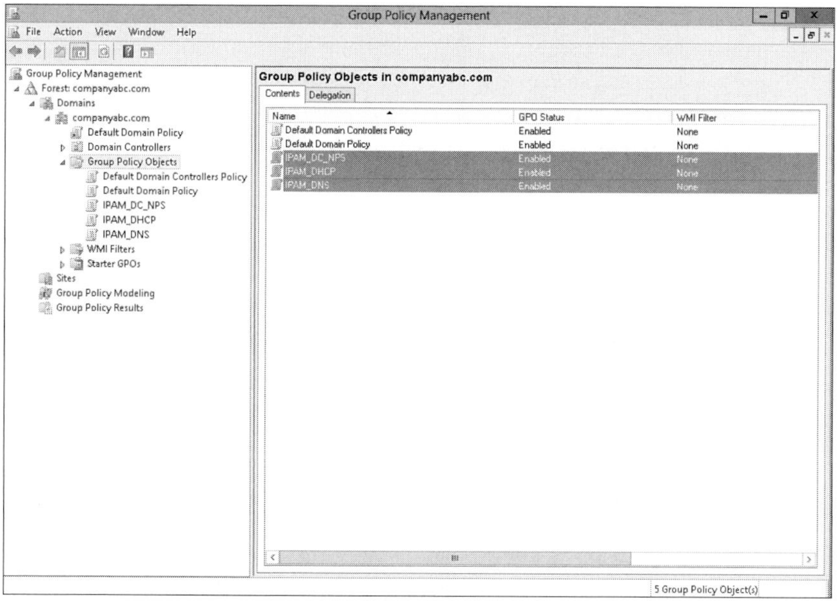

FIGURE 11.32 IPAM GPOs.

Configuring Server Discovery

When an IPAM server is provisioned, several tasks are created within the server's task schedule, including one named the ServerDiscovery task. The ServerDiscovery task searches Active Directory to discover the DHCP, DNS, DC, and NPS servers registered with Active Directory and automatically adds them to the IPAM console. But before discovery can work properly, the domains that the IPAM server will search must be specified. To configure discovery, follow these steps:

1. Log on to the IPAM server or a server with the IPAM client tools installed and the IPAM server added to the server pool in Server Manager.
2. Click the Server Manager tile on the taskbar.
3. Click the IPAM link in the tree pane to display the IPAM console.
4. The IPAM console shows a list of six tasks, and the third one is Configure Server Discovery. Click this task, and when the window opens, select the desired domain from the pull-down list and click Add.
5. Check the type of servers that you want to discover in the domain and click OK, as shown in Figure 11.33.

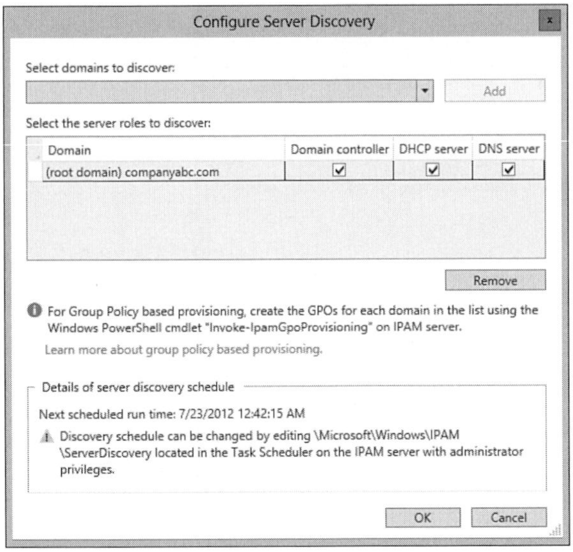

FIGURE 11.33 Defining the domains for IPAM discovery.

6. Once the necessary domains are added to the discovery scope, we can start the discovery process. In the IPAM console, click Start Server Discovery. The discovery task runs for several minutes or longer depending on the number of servers in the domain.

This completes the discovery process.

Defining Discovered Servers as IPAM Managed

After the discovery process has completed, all the discovered servers are listed in the IPAM console. The discovered servers are not yet ready to be managed by the IPAM server; they must first be defined as managed servers. To see the list of discovered servers and configure them as managed servers, follow these steps:

1. Log on to the IPAM server or a server with the IPAM client tools installed and the IPAM server added to the server pool in Server Manager.
2. Click the Server Manager tile on the taskbar.
3. Click the IPAM link in the tree pane to display the IPAM console.
4. The IPAM console shows a list of six tasks, and is the fifth is Select or Add Servers to Manage and Verify IPAM Access. Click this task, and when the window opens, all the discovered servers should be listed.
5. Discovered servers have a manageability status set to Unspecified. Right-click a discovered server and select Edit Server, as shown in Figure 11.34.

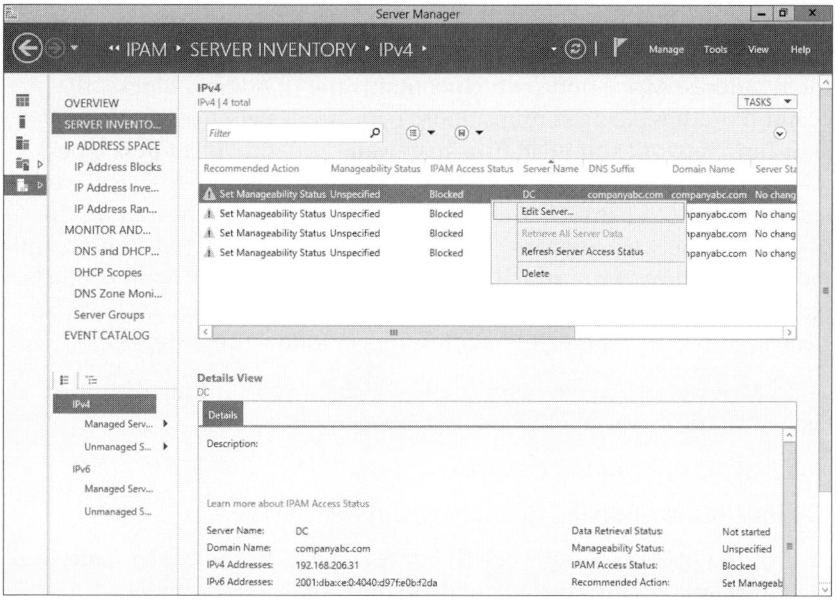

FIGURE 11.34 Configuring a discovered server for IPAM management.

6. When the Add or Edit Server window opens, pull down the Manageability Status menu and select Managed, and then click OK to close the window.

7. Repeat this process on all the discovered servers, and they should then reflect a Managed state, but the Recommended Action column will show as Unblock IPAM Access. This is because the necessary firewall rules and security group membership changes have not yet occurred.

8. Open the Group Policy Management Console from the IPAM server or a domain controller and review the security filtering ACL of the IPAM GPOs. They should now include the discovered servers that were just configured as managed. If this is not the case, the problem might be that the user logged on to the IPAM console does not have the rights to edit these GPOs and that should be updated on the GPOs themselves.

9. After the discovered servers are set to Managed and appear in the GPO security filtering, to speed up IPAM management, you can reboot these servers to force group policy application and to run startup scripts that will need to be processed.

10. After the servers are rebooted and have run for at least 1 hour, return to the IPAM console, right-click each server, and select Refresh Server Access Status. When all servers show up in the Recommended Action column as IPAM Access Unblocked with a green check mark, you are ready to proceed with the collection of server data.

Defining IP Address Blocks

The IPAM console contains several nodes that include different sets of information. The core of all this is the IP Address Space node, which contains the IP Address Blocks, IP Address Inventory, and IP Address Range groups nodes beneath it. Before server data collection is forced or run, network administrators may want to define IP address blocks to ensure address data gets sorted appropriately. An IP address block is the highest-level address space defined in the IPAM console. The IP block should be created based on the actual IPv4 subnets and IPv6 network prefixes. DHCP IP Ranges and discovered and manually entered or imported IP addresses are sorted beneath the appropriate IP address blocks. For our network examples, we have an IPv4 IP address block of 192.168.206.x/24 and an IPv6 prefix of 2001:dba:ce::/64. To create an IP address block, follow these steps:

1. Log on to the IPAM server or a server with the IPAM client tools installed and the IPAM server added to the server pool in Server Manager.
2. Click the Server Manager tile on the taskbar.
3. Click the IPAM link in the tree pane to display the IPAM console.
4. In the tree pane of the IPAM console, click IP Address Space. In the center pane, you can review the terms and definitions of IP address blocks, IP address ranges, and IP addresses as desired.
5. In the IPAM tree pane, click the IP Address Blocks node beneath the IP Address Space node.
6. In the center pane near the top-right corner, click the Tasks link and select Add IP Address Block.
7. When the Add or Edit IPv4 Address Block window opens, type in **192.168.206.0** and click the Prefix pull-down menu to select the appropriate subnet mask of 24. Add a description and click OK, as shown in Figure 11.35.

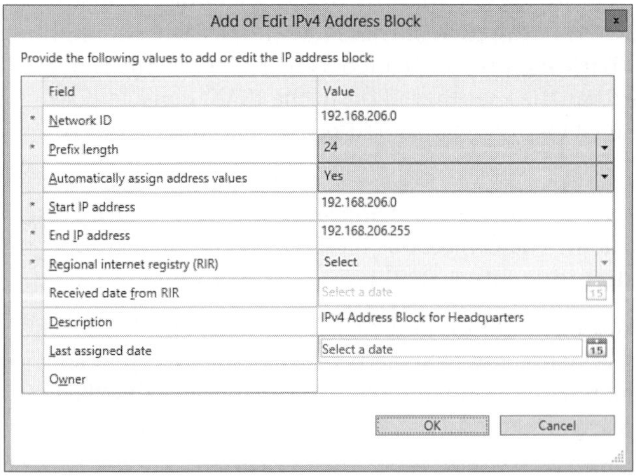

FIGURE 11.35 Defining an IPv4 IP address block.

8. After returning to the IP address block, pull down the current view option and select IP Address Blocks to view the block just created.

9. In the IPAM console tree pane, near the bottom left, select IPv6, and in the center pane near the top-right corner, click the Tasks link and select Add IP Address Block once again.

10. Type in the IPv6 network ID of **2001:dba:ce::** and specify the prefix length of 64. Add a description and click OK, as shown in Figure 11.36.

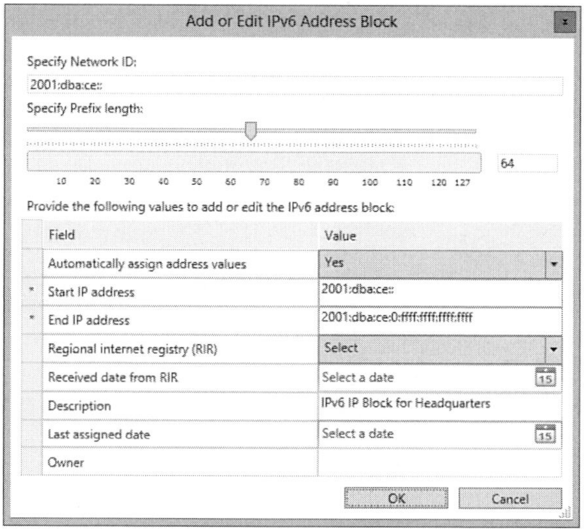

FIGURE 11.36 Defining an IPv6 IP address block.

This completes the creation of the IP address blocks.

Collecting Server Data

Server data collection will occur on a scheduled basis, as will event log collection. This is controlled by the default schedule set on the seven tasks, which can be view using the Task Scheduler console, as shown in Figure 11.37.

When data collection needs to be forced, you can do so as follows:

1. Log on to the IPAM server or a server with the IPAM client tools installed and the IPAM server added to the server pool in Server Manager.

2. Click the Server Manager tile on the taskbar.

3. Click the IPAM link in the tree pane to display the IPAM console.

4. The IPAM console shows a list of six tasks, and is the sixth one is Retrieve Data from Managed Servers. Click this task and all the tasks will be started.

5. When the tasks complete, you can drill down in the tree pane under the IP Address Space node and the Monitor and Manage node to view the status of the servers and the IP address data.

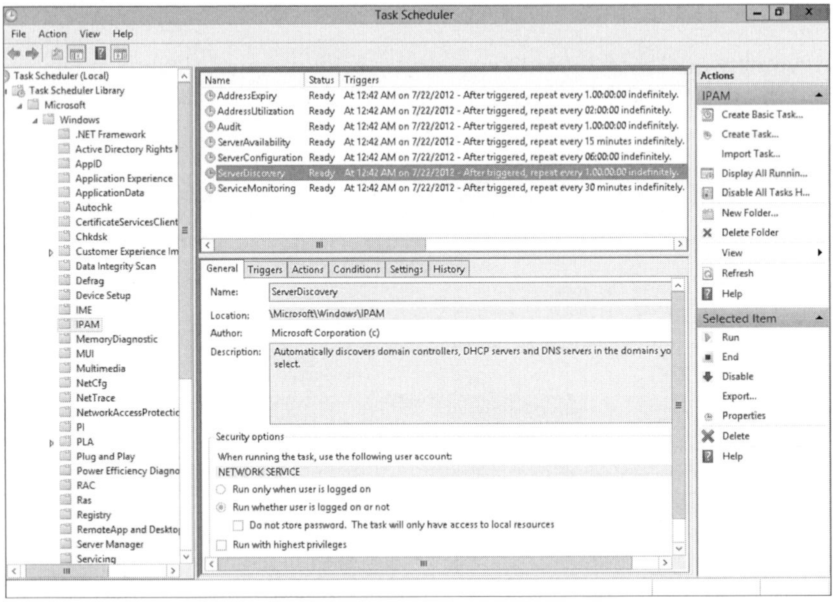

FIGURE 11.37 IPAM scheduled tasks.

Exploring the IPAM Console

The IPAM console has a lot of areas that contain different information. You might find it overwhelming at first, but after browsing through it and using it regularly, administrators should become comfortable retrieving information from this console and launching the management of DHCP and DNS services from it.

Overview Node

The Overview node of the IPAM console is always the place to start. From this node, you can jump right into tasks such as running discovery, collecting servers, or viewing the status of a managed server just by clicking on one of the numbers 1 through 6.

Server Inventory Node

The Server Inventory node is just as the name implies. This node shows the status of each of the discovered or manually added servers known by the IPAM server. In this node, when a server is selected, below it there will be a summary of the server IP information and IPAM configuration status. By right-clicking a single server or multiple servers, administrators can forcibly refresh IPAM server access data or kick off a server data collection cycle. Tasks available from this node enable an administrator to manually add servers that may have not been discovered by IPAM, such as a firewall, router, switch, or just a server that is not managed within Active Directory. Adding a server to the console does not mean that IPAM can manage it, but as a true IPAM solution, adding servers and IP information manually will be required in most enterprise and even smaller network. Remember that the goal is to be able to account for all IP addresses and managed devices.

IP Address Space Node

The Address Space node is where all the IP address information is stored. From here, administrators can view IP information for the enterprise and add or import data. When you select the IP Address Space node, only an informative page opens. Just select a subnode to view data or perform IP-related tasks.

IP Address Block Node

The IP Address Block node stores and details the state of the hierarchy of IP networks. When this node is selected, it displays only the IPv4 or the IPv6 information. This can be changed by selecting IPv4 or IPv6 in the bottom left of the IPAM tree pane. From this node, all IP-related tasks can be performed, such as adding IP address blocks, adding IP ranges, and importing data from external sources.

IP Address Inventory Node

Individual IP addresses can be tracked, and information will display within this node.

IP Address Ranges Node

The IP Address Ranges node displays all defined, imported, and discovered IP ranges. These include DHCP scopes and static IP ranges as defined by administrators, as shown in Figure 11.38.

Monitor and Manage Node

The Monitor and Manage node displays the status of the managed servers and the status of their services.

DNS and DHCP Servers

This node includes all the DNS and DHCP servers that are managed by the IPAM server. When a server is selected in this node, more information will be displayed below. If desired, this is where the actual services on that managed system can be configured, as shown in Figure 11.39.

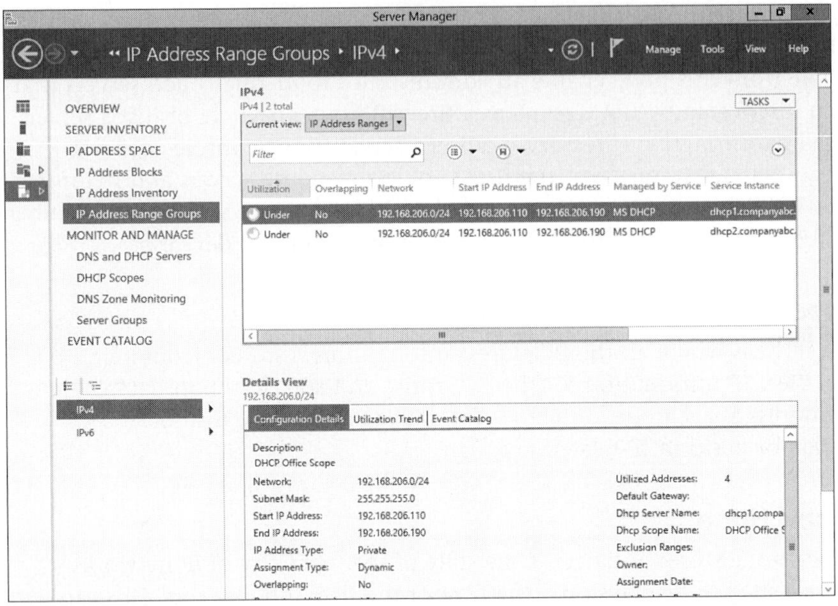

FIGURE 11.38 DHCP scope and static IP ranges.

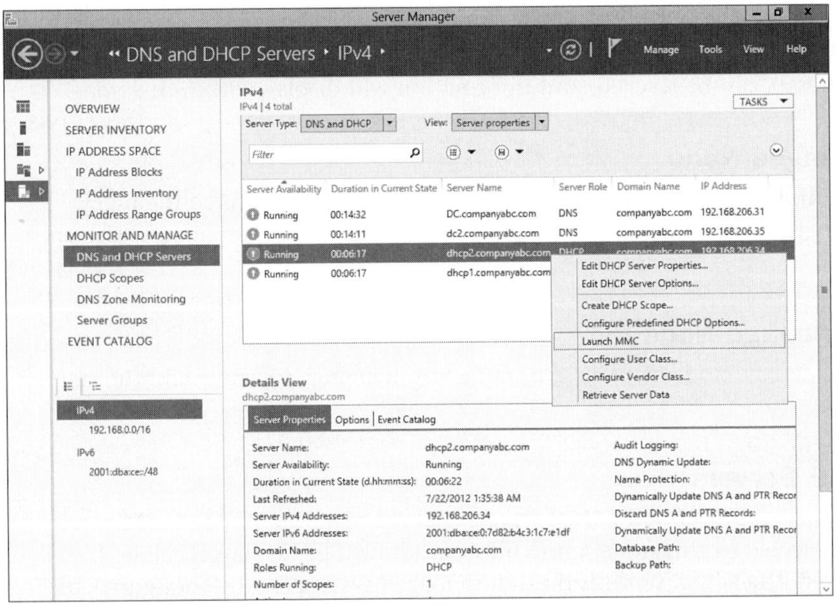

FIGURE 11.39 Launching the DHCP Management console from the IPAM console.

DHCP Scopes Node

In the DHCP Scopes node detailed information about DHCP scopes on managed servers will be presented. Right-clicking on a specific scope will present the administrator with options specific for managing the desired scope.

DNS Zone Monitoring Node

DNS servers' zone files can be monitored from this node, and the status of the DNS zone will be displayed.

Event Catalog Node

The Event Catalog node is where in-depth analysis of managed server and services can be viewed. Event log data is collected and presented in this view for quick and easy access. IP address tracking data and DHCP and IPAM configuration changes can be viewed and searched from within this node.

Summary

This chapter details the DHCP service and IPv6 and the new IPAM server feature. With the growth and adoption of IPv6 expanding every day, administrators who do not learn the technology now are already behind the time. The new features of DHCP (including IPv6 scopes) can help administrators catch up to support IPv6 on their network sooner rather than later. With the addition of IPAM server on the network as well, network administrators have a powerful set of tools and functionality to take their network management to the next level. This gives network administrators the information they need to support and properly manage their network.

Best Practices

The following are best practices from this chapter:

- Perform all tests with DHCP split scope, failover scope, and security configurations in an isolated lab environment before deploying on a production network.
- When migrating DHCP services to a Windows Server 2012 system using the Windows Server migration tools, only install the DHCP service on the destination server but do not configure it (to avoid losing configuration settings or issues with DHCP authorization that might be presented after the import overwrites all the existing configurations).
- To avoid issues with the DHCP service account used for dynamic DNS registration, configure the account with a password that never expires, but change the password as frequently as the standard user password policy of the organization defines on the user account and in the DHCP configuration of each server using that account.

- Deploy DHCP services with some level of redundancy on all deployments, leveraging split scopes, failover scopes, and clusters.
- When designing IPv6 networks for internal usage, always use ULA range to conform to RFC 4193.
- When notating IPv6 addresses, use notation standards to reduce the total number of characters required to properly represent the IPv6 address or network prefix.
- When deploying IPAM server, use group policy provisioning to simplify managed server configuration, and deploy the GPOs before configuring servers as managed.

CHAPTER 12

Internet Information Services

IN THIS CHAPTER

- Understanding Internet Information Services 8
- Planning and Designing IIS 8
- Installing and Upgrading IIS 8
- Installing and Configuring Websites
- Installing and Configuring FTP Services
- Securing IIS 8

Internet Information Services (IIS) has been going through continuous change for years, so it isn't surprising that the most current version of IIS is Microsoft's most scalable, most reliable, and most secure web server. Without a doubt, the fundamental capabilities of IIS 8 are exhilarating. The new web server includes a plethora of new features and functionality that provide numerous benefits to organizations hosting applications and developers creating web applications with the latest .NET Framework. Among other things, organizations can also simplify management, reduce attack surface areas, benefit from improved diagnostic and troubleshooting capabilities, and enjoy greater scalability.

To reap the full benefits of IIS 8, this chapter gives web administrators the knowledge base necessary to understand the improvements and new management user interface in IIS 8. The first sections of the chapter focus on planning an IIS 8 infrastructure and installing or upgrading to IIS 8. The second sections focus on creating both web and File Transfer Protocol (FTP) sites, and discuss how to configure the new settings. The final sections of the chapter discuss how to secure IIS 8.

Understanding Internet Information Services 8

Organizations and web administrators must fully understand IIS 8 before installing, upgrading, or creating sites with the product. Specifically, they should be familiar with the new improvements, the new look and feel of the management tools and user interface, and be comfortable with the new working panes associated with administration. The next few sections examine these areas of interest.

Improvements in IIS 8

Several key enhancements and structural changes have been made to the new IIS 8 web and application platform. These enhancements are designed not only to build upon the latest version of .NET, but also to improve overall scalability, performance, security, and administration. Some of the major IIS 8 improvements that IT professionals, web admins, and developers will take pleasure in having include the following:

- **Dynamic IP restrictions**—IIS 8 supports automatic blacklisting of IP addresses based on the number of requests. This feature is supported for both the website and FTP site functions of IIS. The FTP feature behaves somewhat differently in that IP addresses are blacklisted as a result of failed authentication attempts rather than a number of requests.
- **SSL host header support**—IIS 8 expands the support for host headers to Secure Sockets Layer (SSL)-protected sites using Server Name Indication (SNI). The addition of this feature now allows administrators to protect multiple websites with a single SSL certificate and improves security and scalability of the platform.
- **Central certificate store (CCS)**—A welcome addition for administrators who support large farms with multiple SSL protected websites is the introduction of a central certificate store. The CCS resides on a file share accessible to all farm members and can contain all the certificates required for the operation of the web server. Certificate binding is performed automatically based on the name of the certificate (PFX) file in the CCS. The naming convention of the files supports wildcard and Unified Communication Certificates (UCC). Certificate upgrades become a simple matter of replacing the PFX file in the CCS and restarting each web server.
- **CPU throttling**—A much-desired and requested feature was to have a usable mechanism to control CPU load for each website. With earlier versions of IIS, throttled sites were disabled entirely, which was frequently unacceptable. With IIS 8, sites can be throttled to reduce performance but still provide service. Throttling control is even provided as a full-time configuration or only when the server load requires it.
- **Application Initialization Module**—IIS 8 provides administrator control over the initialization of a web application. Web applications can now be initialized in advance so that the first end user to access the application doesn't experience a delay as the application is initialized. The new module can support a server wide setting or integration with URL Rewrite rules for more granular control. The module's configuration also supports integration with load-balancer health pages to ensure that a node isn't considered available for requests until the application is fully initialized.
- **Scalability**—In addition to the features listed already, the SSL and configuration file-handling components of IIS have been revised to handle much higher scale and support thousands of website and certificates, if not more.
- **WebSocket support**—Now, it is possible to configure web socket support directly within IIS and establish two way, real-time communication between a client and server using HTTP.

Understanding the New IIS Manager Tools

The centerpiece of IIS 8 is the now familiar IIS Manager user interface. The updated user interface, which was introduced with IIS 7 and Windows Server 2008, is the primary tool used to manage IIS and ASP.NET, health and diagnostics, and security.

In addition to the GUI management console, IIS 8 can also be managed using a variety of command-line tools. First and foremost, the PowerShell provider included with IIS is a powerful tool for common management tasks as well as for automation requirements. Although other command-line tools, such as `iisreset`, are still available, many other tools have been deprecated, especially VBS scripts such as `iiscnfg`, `iisback`, and others. The functionality of those tools is available with PowerShell.

Because understanding the console is a must to successfully administer IIS and know where to conduct each task, the next sections examine the layout of the new user interface.

Exploring the IIS Manager Administration Panes

Each area within the IIS Manager console is referenced by a descriptive word, as shown in Figure 12.1. For example, the descriptive words associated with the areas or panes, such as the Connections pane, make it easier to identify the location of the IIS features. The following is a list of the panes included in the IIS Manager console and their respective functions:

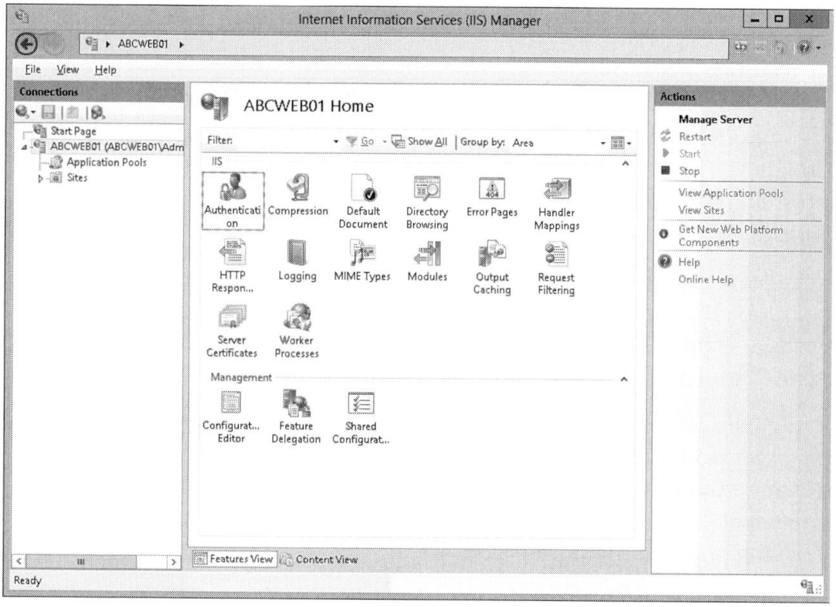

FIGURE 12.1 The IIS Manager user interface.

- **The Connections pane**—The Connections pane is located on the left side of the console and displays the IIS console tree, which is also known as the node tree. Web administrators can conduct the following tasks from within this pane:
  - View the start page
  - Connect to a server, site, or application
  - Manage server settings
  - Configure IIS, application pools, FTP, and websites
  - Change view settings for the Central Details pane
- **Central Details pane**—Also known as the *workspace*, this large pane is located in the center of the IIS 8 management console. This pane can operate in one of two views: feature and content. The feature view displays the configuration options for each IIS feature installed. Each feature is represented by a new icon and replaces the legacy property sheets and tabs that most administrators in the industry were not too fond of in the past. The feature icons can be grouped by category or area; otherwise, grouping can be turned off. The content view displays the actual content files that are part of the selected node in the Connections pane.
- **Actions pane**—The Actions pane is located on the right side of the console and displays common actions, including wizards associated with each task. This pane also usually contains multiple tabs for the different options available based on the node chosen.

IIS Manager Administration Nodes in the Connections Pane

Many web services components need to be configured to optimize IIS for security, functionality, and redundancy. The IIS snap-in is the interface used to administer IIS services. In the left pane of the snap-in, as shown in Figure 12.2, you will see folders or nodes similar to the following:

- **Start Page**—The Start Page is the first item within the Connections pane and is a digital dashboard for IIS. It provides users with a wealth of information by displaying IIS newsfeeds and links to online resources. In addition, the Start Page includes recent connection information and connection tasks.
- **IIS Server**—The main place to administer and manage server properties and features is the server node. After being selected, the IIS feature icons are displayed in the central pane. An administrator must double-click a feature to configure property settings specific to that feature. Examples of feature icons include Feature Delegation, Logging, and Configuration Editor.
- **Application Pools**—Application pools are actually sections of physical memory dedicated to the applications running within a pool. Application pools segment applications from the rest of the memory resources used by other IIS services. This promotes higher reliability and security, but it also requires more memory to be

configured on the web server. The application pool elements can be sorted based on name, status, .NET Framework version, managed pipeline mode, identify, and applications.

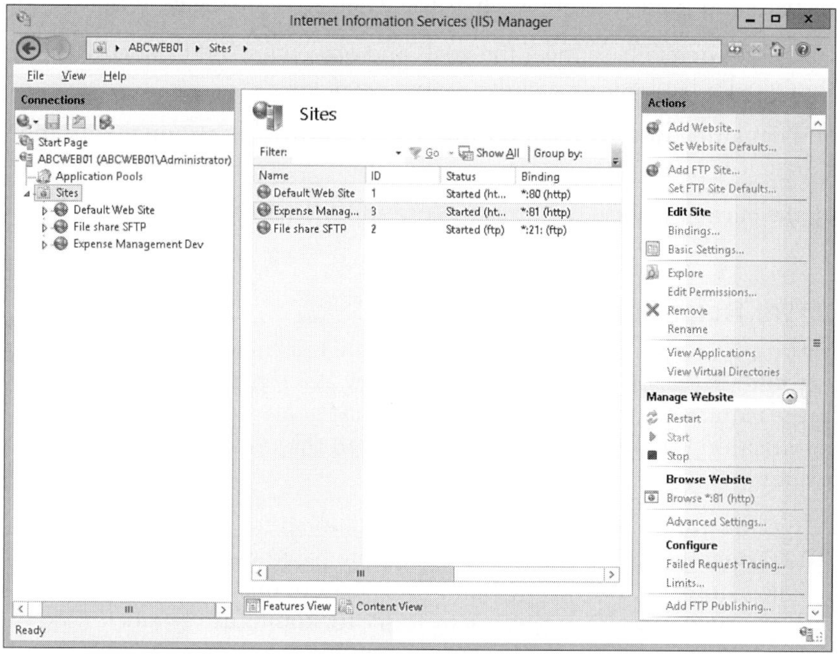

FIGURE 12.2 The IIS 8 Connections pane.

- **Sites**—This folder contains all the websites and FTP sites being hosted on the web server. The Default Web Site is created during the installation of IIS 8.

NOTE

An Internet Information Services (8) Manager can be started from the Metro screen, from the Tools menu in Server Manager, or by typing **start inetmgr** at the command prompt.

Planning and Designing IIS 8

Two of the most important tasks to accomplish before implementing IIS 8 are thorough planning and designing. Planning and designing are the beginning phases to properly implementing IIS, and they can consist of the following:

- Defining goals and objectives of the IIS 8 project
- Identifying and reviewing IIS application types and requirements
- Designing the IIS infrastructure to support the goals and objectives

- Deciding on which IIS 8 features will be utilized during the installation process to meet the goals of the organization
- Defining fault-tolerance requirements
- Designing the back-end infrastructure, such as the database or application tier
- Defining security requirements to meet the goals and objectives and balancing the security methodologies between risks and end-user experience
- Examining and designing disaster recovery plans, and monitoring requirements and maintenance practices
- Documenting the current or new IIS infrastructure and the IIS design decisions

Determining Server Requirements

Hardware and software requirements are usually based on the information gathered and the requirements set forth in the design and planning stages of a project. The necessary hardware and software requirements should always match the goals and objectives of the project. This information is very detailed and describes all the resources necessary for hardware and software.

IIS 8 does not have specific minimum server requirements tailored toward running IIS on Windows Server 2012. The minimum server requirements are based on Windows Server 2012. It is a best practice, however, to stick with multiple dual- or quad-core processors; to use fault-tolerant disks such as RAID 1, RAID 5, or RAID 10; and to use as much RAM as needed, depending on how many sites and users you will be hosting as well as the complexity of the web applications. For more information about recommended Windows Server requirements, review Chapter 1, "Windows Server 2012 Technology Primer," or for server performance tuning, network optimization, and SSL offloading, see Chapter 34, "Capacity Analysis and Performance Optimization."

Determining Fault-Tolerance Requirements

Fault tolerance is a key aspect of any web infrastructure and should be addressed during planning and designing phases, regardless of whether an organization can afford downtime of its websites or requires 99.999% uptime. In view of this, service-level agreements (SLAs) are highly recommended and should be determined from the operational goals during the design and planning phase. After an SLA is in place, it will be easy to apply the appropriate fault tolerance to the web infrastructure because expectations and tolerances are clearly defined and previously agreed upon by everyone involved in the process.

Various technologies can be applied to a Windows Server 2012 web infrastructure to support even the most demanding SLAs. For example, Windows Server 2012 web servers can use Network Load Balancing (NLB) to distribute the load and client requests among multiple web servers and to provide fault tolerance. This is also known as scaling IIS by creating a web server farm. NLB is more suited to provide fault tolerance for scaling web servers than Windows failover clusters because the IIS components are not cluster aware.

NLB on Windows Server 2012 also offers many advanced features and functionality, which makes it more appealing. For instance, NLB offers support for multiple dedicated IP addresses per node. For a complete list of NLB features, benefits, and step-by-step procedures, see Chapter 29, "System-Level Fault Tolerance Clustering/Network Load Balancing.

Installing and Upgrading IIS 8

The installation process and architecture for many recent and upcoming Microsoft product families are completely modularized like Internet Information Services 8 on Windows Server 2012. By providing a modularized approach, web administrators have complete control over the footprint of IIS when customizing the installation. This results in the surface area being reduced, which, in turn, drastically minimizes the chances of a security compromise.

NOTE

As part of the Microsoft Trustworthy security campaign, IIS 8, as was the case with IIS 7 and 7.5, is not installed on Windows Server 2012 by default. You have to add the Web Server (IIS) role via Server Manager if you want IIS installed.

Before installing or upgrading IIS, it is a best practice to fully understand the new modular installation process, including the features associated with the installation.

Understanding the Modular Approach to Installing IIS 8

The buzzword for Internet Information Services 8 modularized installation process is *slim and efficient*. The modular setup is made up of more than 40 separate role services and features allowing for complete customization when deploying IIS 8. This typically results in minimal surface area and more granularity compared with legacy editions of IIS. In addition, patching is also based on a component level, reducing the frequency of patching and overall patching time required to keep the system updated and secure. All of this translates to a customized footprint for each organization running IIS 8.

As illustrated in Figure 12.3, the modules that can be selected during the installation process of the Web Server (IIS) role are organized in the following categories:

- Management Tools
- Web Server
- FTP Server

The following subsections cover these modular role services.

Management Tools Modular/Role Service

The first role service set associated with the Web Server (IIS) role installation is Management Tools. The management tools enable you to manage and administer the IIS 8 infrastructure. The following management tools are available for installation:

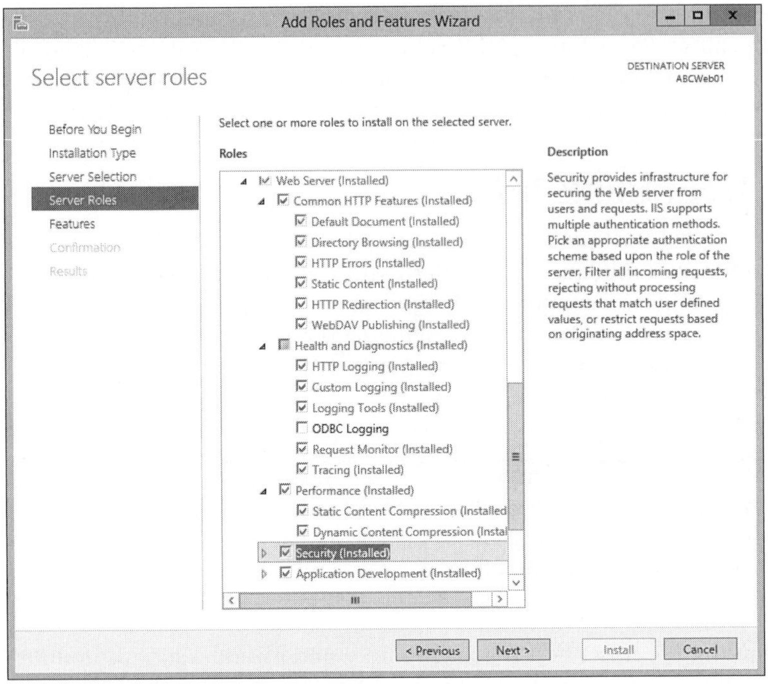

FIGURE 12.3 Reviewing the role services and feature installation options.

- **IIS Management Console**—If selected, the IIS Management Console role service installs the latest User Interface tool for managing, administering, monitoring, and securing IIS 8. The tool has been much improved and provides support for both IIS and ASP.NET.
- **IIS 6 Management Compatibility**—This set of role services provides the tools for backward compatibility when managing an IIS 6.0 infrastructure from a Windows Server 2012 system running IIS 8. In addition, it lets IIS 6.0 management scripts run on IIS 8, provides Windows Management Instrumentation (WMI) compatibility with IIS 6.0, and enables metabase compatibility.
- **IIS Management Scripts and Tools**—It is possible to manage all the IIS settings and configurations based on automated script commands. This feature provides the infrastructure that allows IIS to be managed by scripts. This is great when you need to manage many IIS 8 servers within an infrastructure. Note that much of the functionality provided by these tools is also available with the IIS PowerShell provider.
- **Management Service**—This feature provides the foundation within the IIS 8 infrastructure for remote management.

Web Server Modular/Role Service

The Web Server modular is the main service role within IIS 8. It can be considered the chief functionality for a web server because it provides the foundation for supporting websites and provides developers with a foundation for development. The Web Server role is further broken down into more types of features, which can be independently installed, which promotes further customization of the installation:

- **Common HTTP Features**—A set of role services that allow for static content to be delivered, the creation of customized HTTP errors, directory browsing, and selection of default documents are enabled by default. The HTTP Redirection and WebDAV publishing features are disabled by default.
- **Health and Diagnostics**—Select this feature to install the tools associated with monitoring, managing, and troubleshooting an IIS installation. The independent role services include HTTP Logging, Custom Logging, Logging Tools, Request Monitor, Tracing, and ODBC Logging.
- **Performance**—Performance role services supporting compression for either static or dynamic content are available in this section. Static Content Compression and Dynamic Content Compression bolster website performance by managing bandwidth and compression.
- **Security**—The Security role services includes security features for controlling website authorization based on a variety of authentication mechanisms and certificate-based solutions. In addition, it provides the infrastructure for securing IIS and the websites associated with the installation. The features that can be selected include Basic Authentication, Windows Authentication, Digest Authentication, Client Certificate Mapping Authentication, IIS Client Certificate Mapping Authentications, URL Authorization, Centralized SSL Certificate Support, Request Filtering, and IP and Domain Restrictions.
- **Application Development**—This role service set is not enabled by default during the installation. If selected, the Application Development role service makes available features for creating and hosting web applications. These features include ASP.NET 3.5/4.5, .NET Extensibility 3.5/4.5, Application Initialization, ASP, CGI, ISAPI Extensions, ISAPI Filters, WebSocket Protocol, and Server-Side Includes.

FTP Server Modular/Role Service

The last role service section is known as the FTP Server. It provides a reliable method for making files available for download and also offers a reliable place for users to upload files if needed. The two FTP features that can be installed are as follows:

- **FTP Service**—The FTP Service feature provides the infrastructure for creating and hosting FTP sites within IIS.
- **FTP Extensibility**—This features enables support for custom providers and ASP.NET/ IIS Manager users.

IIS Hostable Web Core Role Service—The last role service enables you (an administrator) to write custom code that will host core IIS functionality in your own application. The use of hostable web core (HWC) requires that IIS 8 be installed but uses a separate configuration file and only supports a single application pool and a single web site. Because HWC is embedded within an application, it does not integrate with IIS monitoring and process recovery features. Application developers are expected to write those features into their applications if needed.

Installing the Web Server (IIS) Role

Now that you understand the installation process, including the modules, the next step is to install the Web Server (IIS) role. You must have Local User Administrator (LUA) security privileges on the Windows Server 2012 system to be able to install IIS. There are two ways to begin the installation: adding the Web Server (IIS) role via Server Manager or installing the services via PowerShell.

To install the Web Server (IIS) server role using Server Manager, follow these steps:

1. Start Server Manager using the taskbar icon.
2. From the Manage menu, select Add Roles and Features.
3. Click Next on the Before you Begin page after reading the notes provided.
4. Click Next to accept the default installation type of Role-Based or Feature-Based Installation.
5. Select the web server from the server pool and click Next.
6. On the Select Server Roles page, install IIS 8 by selecting Web Server (IIS) in the Roles section, as shown in Figure 12.4. A new section will be added to the Installation Wizard to allow selection of specific role services for the installation. Click Next.
7. Click Next to accept the existing features.
8. Review the introduction messages and notes on the Web Server Role (IIS) page, and then click Next.
9. Select the desired Web Server IIS role services to install. The default settings include Static Content, Default Document, Directory Browsing, HTTP Errors, HTTP Logging, Request Monitor, Request Filtering, Static Content Compression, and the IIS Management Console. Click Next.

NOTE

When installing some of the IIS role services, the wizard warns you that additional role services and features are required as dependencies. Click Add Features to install the dependencies.

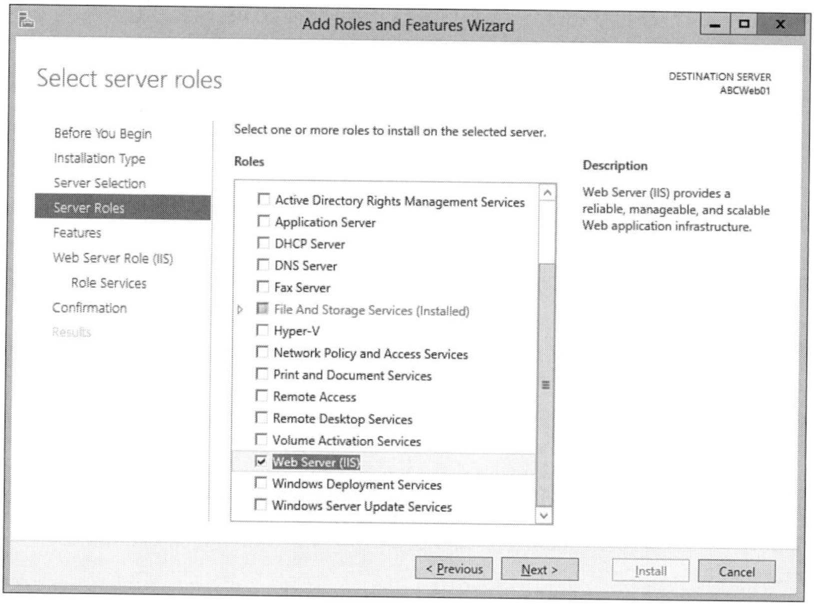

FIGURE 12.4 Selecting the Web Server (IIS) role during the installation process.

10. On the Confirm Installation Selections page, review the roles, services, and features that have been selected for installation, and then click Install to commence the installation process.

11. Ensure the installation succeeded by reviewing the messages on the Installation Results page, and click Close.

NOTE

After the installation is complete, you can add or remove IIS role services and features by clicking either Add Role Services or Remove Role Services within Server Manager based on the Web Server (IIS) role.

Installing the Web Server (IIS) Role via PowerShell

Windows features and roles such as IIS 8 can be installed using the command line with Windows PowerShell. To install a default installation of IIS 8, run the following script from an elevated PowerShell window:

```
add-windowsfeature Web-Server,Web-WebServer,Web-Common-Http,web-Static-Content,
Web-Default-Doc,Web-Dir-Browsing,Web-Http-Errors,Web-Http-Logging,
Web-Log-Libraries,Web-Request-Monitor,Web-Http-Tracing,Web-Security,
Web-Filtering,Web-Stat-Compression, Web-Mgmt-Console
```

Alternatively, the following syntax install alls the IIS 8 features and functionality:

```
add-windowsfeature Web-Server, Web-Mgmt-Tools,Web-Mgmt-Console,Web-Mgmt-Compat,
Web-Metabase,Web-Lgcy-Mgmt-Console,Web-Lgcy-Scripting,Web-WMI,
Web-Scripting-Tools,Web-Mgmt-Service,Web-WebServer,Web-Common-Http,
web-Static-Content,Web-Default-Doc,Web-Dir-Browsing,Web-Http-Errors,
Web-Http-Redirect,Web-DAV-Publishing,Web-Health,Web-Http-Logging,
Web-Custom-Logging,Web-Log-Libraries,Web-ODBC-Logging,Web-Request-Monitor,
Web-Http-Tracing,Web-Performance,Web-Stat-Compression,Web-Dyn-Compression,
Web-Security,Web-Basic-Auth,Web-CertProvider,Web-Windows-Auth,Web-Digest-Auth,
Web-Client-Auth,Web-Cert-Auth,Web-Url-Auth,Web-Filtering,Web-IP-Security,
Web-App-Dev,Web-ASP,Web-Asp-Net,Web-Asp-Net45,Web-CGI,Web-Includes,
Web-WebSockets,Web-Net-Ext,Web-Net-Ext45,Web-ISAPI-Ext,Web-ISAPI-Filter,
Web-AppInit,Web-FTP-Server,Web-FTP-Service,Web-FTP-Ext,Web-WHC
```

NOTE

To get a list of available features and which role services in Server Manager they map to, use the `Get-WindowsFeature` cmdlet.

Upgrading from Other Versions of IIS

In many situations, a fresh installation of IIS 8 and Windows Server 2012 will not occur because organizations might want to preserve the existing IIS settings and content. Therefore, organizations must upgrade their existing IIS infrastructure to IIS 8. With the upgrade of the earlier version of Windows to Windows Server 2012, IIS is also automatically upgraded, allowing web content to be preserved, translated, and, finally, transitioned. However, you should note early in the process that Windows Server 2012 only supports a direct upgrade path from Windows Server 2008 R2, which means only an in-place upgrade from IIS 7.5 is supported. Likewise, if legacy versions of IIS need upgrading, such as IIS 6.0 or 7.0, you must first upgrade the operating system to Windows Server 2008 R2 and then to Windows Server 2012.

The upgrade process for IIS is conducted in three major phases. In the first phase, the new operating system detects and performs an inventory of IIS components and features already installed on the operating system. The second phase of the upgrade process involves upgrading the legacy operating system to Windows Server 2012. After the Windows Server 2012 upgrade is complete, the final phase kicks in and automatically upgrades the legacy IIS components to IIS 8 and installs the appropriate IIS 8 features.

NOTE

For more information about how to upgrade a system to Windows Server 2012, see Chapter 3, "Installing Windows Server 2012 and Server Core."

As is typically the case with most revised products, Windows Server 2012 IIS is inherently superior to its earlier versions. In particular, it lays claim to being more secure. This is witnessed during upgrades of websites to IIS 8. Website services are stopped after the upgrade and must be manually restarted, thus minimizing IIS security vulnerabilities due to previous Windows defaults and configuration. To allow for more clarity, suppose you have a Windows server with IIS installed, but it isn't hardened appropriately; the server will be more secure by default after you upgrade to IIS 8 because it will not be serving websites and FTP sites automatically and be a target for attacks.

Another appealing reason for upgrading from earlier versions of IIS is that IIS 8 includes improved security features such as dynamic IP restrictions and improved SSL support. After upgrading, it is best to review the security requirements of the organization and the application and implement any additional relevant features.

Installing and Configuring Websites

As mentioned earlier, IIS can support thousands of websites on a single web server. The number of websites that you can reasonably support depends on the way the system is configured, including the number of processors, the amount of RAM, bandwidth, and more. Historically, for every website that the system supports for the Internet, there must be a public IP address and registered domain name. With IIS 8, as with recent versions of the platform, if you have only one public IP address and you want to support multiple websites, you can also create virtual directories or leverage host headers to have those sites serving users on the Internet.

Creating a Website with IIS 8

The Default Web Site is located within the Web Sites folder in the IIS Management console. You can use the default website to publish content, but it is possible and typically advisable to create and configure a separate website.

To begin creating a new website, follow these steps:

1. In Internet Information Services (IIS) Manager, right-click the Sites node in the Connections pane, and click Add Website.
2. The Add Website page is opened; enter a website name such as **ExpenseReport**.
3. If desired, click the Select button in the Application Pool section to modify the application pool settings for this new site. The default application pool drop-down option available is DefaultAppPool.
4. In the Content Directory section, enter the physical path to where the Web Sites folder resides. Alternatively, navigate to the folder by clicking the ellipses button.

NOTE

A user can also choose a remote share when providing the location of the content directory's physical path. If a remote share is used, you must ensure IIS has access to that folder by clicking the Connect As button and specifying connectivity to the remote share by choosing a specific user account that has appropriate permissions or you can select the Pass-Through Authentication option.

5. You must now specify whether this new site will use HTTP or HTTPS, provide an IP address to the new site or leave the IP address setting unassigned, and indicate which port this new site will listen on. These settings are configured in the Binding section of the Add Website page.
6. An optional host header setting can be configured before completing the page. A user can enter a host header for the new site, such as expensereport.companyabc.com.
7. Check the option to start the website immediately.
8. Review all the configuration settings inputted, as illustrated in Figure 12.5, and then click OK to finalize the creation of the new website.

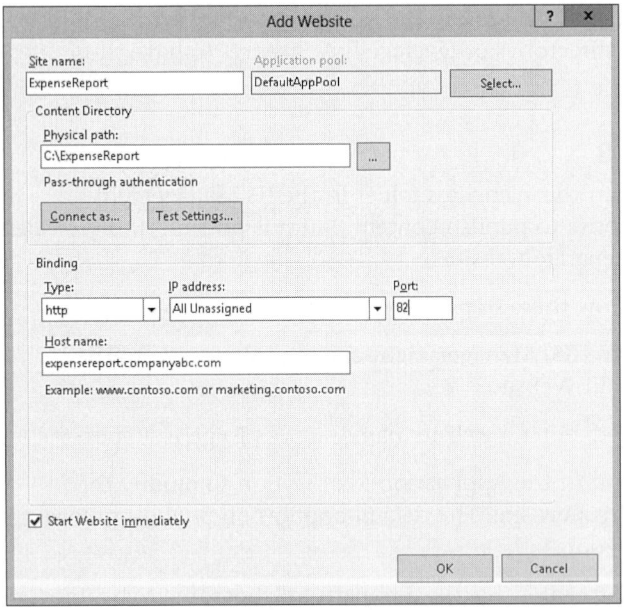

FIGURE 12.5 Creating a new website using the Add Website dialog box.

Creating a Virtual Directory

Virtual directories extend the home directory of your website by providing an alias linking another directory not contained within the home directory. This alias will appear to users as simply a subfolder to the website even though it might be located on an entirely different server.

The virtual directory can contain documents and other information for the website as well as a new website. For example, if CompanyABC's website (www.companyabc.com) wants to host a temporary website for another organization, it could use a virtual directory to contain the website. In this scenario, CompanyXYZ would have its own website located at www.companyabc.com/companyxyz/. You must be a server, site or application administrator to create a virtual directory.

To create a virtual directory using the IIS Manager, follow these steps:

1. Start Server Manager using the taskbar icon. From the Tools menu, run Internet Information Services (IIS) Manager.
2. In the Connections pane, expand the IIS server, and then expand the Sites node within the tree.
3. Select the desired website that will contain the new virtual directory. Right-click the website, and select Add Virtual Directory.
4. Enter the virtual directory's alias, such as **Images**.
5. Enter the physical path to the content folder of the virtual directory, or alternatively, navigate to the folder by clicking the ellipses button.
6. Review the settings, as displayed in Figure 12.6, and click OK to finalize the creation of the virtual directory.

NOTE

If the content folder specified is a remote share, click Connect As and enter credentials for an account that has permissions to access the remote share. Alternatively, select the application user (Pass-Through Authentication) option.

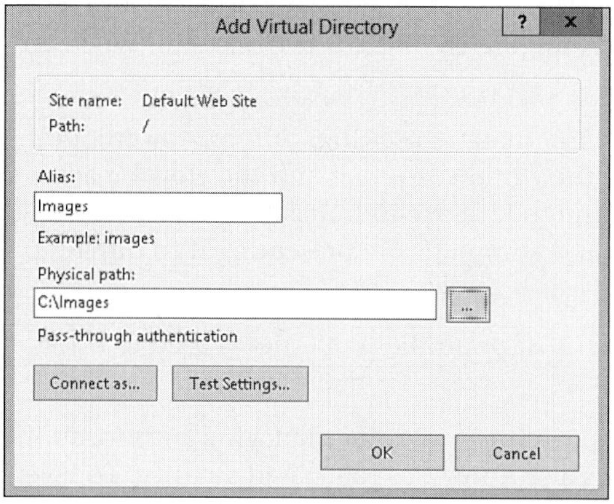

FIGURE 12.6 Add Virtual Directory dialog box.

Configuring IIS 8 Website Properties

In the not-so-recent past, right-clicking a website or the Default Web Site in IIS Manager and then selecting Properties gave you options for modifying the default settings and properties for a website. This is no longer the case because the property pages and tabs have been overhauled starting with IIS 7 and continuing with IIS 7.5 and now IIS 8. In their place are feature icons in the Central Details pane and tasks in the Actions pane. For simplicity, this section describes only the feature icons associated properties pages in IIS 8.

The Features View tab is located in the Central Details pane. Some of the feature icons are connected to this tab for the purpose of configuring properties associated with a website. From here, you can control everything associated with application development, HTTP features, health, diagnostics, performance, and security. The specific features available in the Central Details pane depend on the role services installed and on the object selected in the Connections pane. By default, these options are organized into the following categories:

- ASP.NET features
- IIS features
- Management features

ASP.NET Features

The following feature icons and respective configuration pages are associated with an ASP.NET configuration:

- **.NET Authorization Rules**—Use this page to control access to a website and application by configuring Allow and Deny rules and specifying users, roles, and user groups.
- **.NET Compilation**—Use this page to configure ASP.NET configuration settings. Settings are configured based on the following high-level elements: Batch, Behavior, General, and Assemblies.
- **.NET Error Pages**—This page is used to configure HTTP error responses for when an error occurs on a website or application.
- **.NET Globalization**—This page controls international settings tailored toward local language and cultural environments. As the world converges and the global reach of applications grows, this is a great feature to leverage to translate and format content by reutilizing the existing code and automatically presenting it to different geographic locations.
- **.NET Profile**—This feature page contains a list of profile properties is used to track custom data about an application.
- **.NET Roles**—This page is used to create predefined roles for managing authorization access for groups of users. This concept is also known as role-based security. To leverage this feature, a default provider must be configured. The two options available are AspNetWindowsTokenRoleProvider and AspNetSqlRoleProvider.

- **.NET Trust Levels**—This page is used to specify the trust level for managed objects, such as modules, handlers, and applications in the Web.config file.
- **.NET Users**—This feature page identifies and manages the identities of users for an application. The feature controls the identity management behavior for users defined for an application. When a user is created, the page displays name, email addresses, date created, and last logon.
- **Application Settings**—To manage the variables associated with key/value pairs stored in the website's .config file, this feature page is recommended. The application setting variables and value elements are created by selecting the Add from the Actions pane. These settings can be accessed from anywhere within the application.
- **Connections Strings**—This page is dedicated to creating and managing connections strings for managed web applications. By selecting the Add in the Actions pane, you can create connections strings to SQL Server or other data sources for database access. Typically, the credentials used to access the database are Windows Integrated; however, it is possible to specify a SQL Server account as well.
- **Machine Key**—Because IIS 8 is tightly integrated with .NET web services and security is a primary design factor, this page is available to manage encryption and hashing keys for applications. You can enter encryption and decryption methods, including key generations to secure forms-based authentication, cookie, and page-level view state data.
- **Pages and Controls**—This page manages how the setting of ASP.NET pages and controls are compiled on the web server. New controls can be registered by selecting the task from the Actions pane. Additional elements can be configured, such as the behavior, user interface, view state, compilation, general, and services.
- **Providers**—This feature page is used to manage and administer a list of providers the web server can leverage. Providers are available for .NET Roles, .NET Users, and .NET Profiles. Default providers include AspNetSqlRoleProvider and AspNetWindowsTokenRoleProvider role providers, AspNetSqlMembershipProvider user provider, and AspNetSqlProfileProvider profile provider. In addition, providers can be added by users by selecting Add from the Actions pane.
- **Session State**—This page, as displayed in Figure 12.7, is leveraged when it is necessary to control the behavior of information across browser sessions. It is possible to enable or disable a session state or store a session state in the web browser or in a SQL Server database. Additional elements include defining how cookies are processed when managing session states. Options are Auto Detect, Use Cookies, Use Device Profile, or Use URI.
- **SMTP E-Mail**—The final ASP.NET feature is SMTP E-Mail, which uses the System.Net.Mail API. The feature page, as illustrated in Figure 12.8, includes properties that need to be specified, such as email address, SMTP server name, and port to control message-sending functionality from the web server.

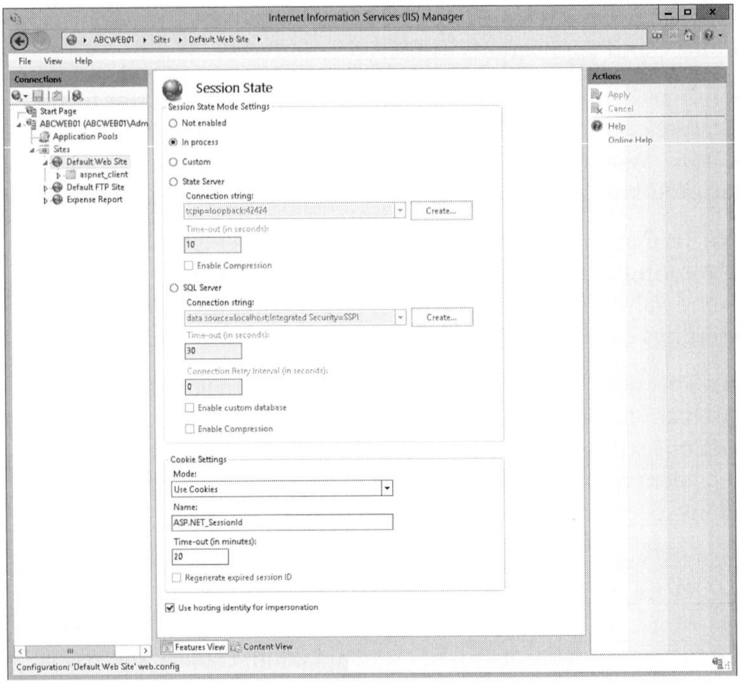

FIGURE 12.7 The Session State feature page.

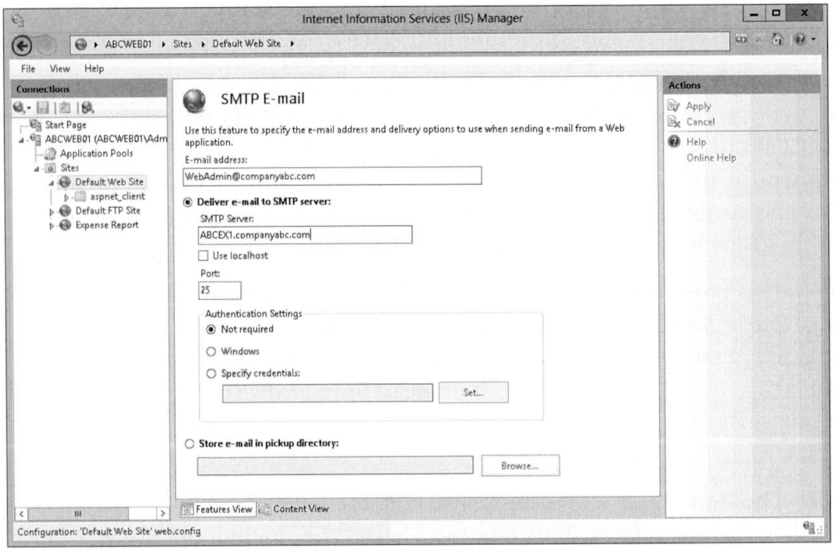

FIGURE 12.8 The SMTP E-Mail feature page.

IIS Features

The following feature icons and respective configuration pages are associated with IIS configurations:

- **ASP**—The first IIS feature page in the list is ASP. This page is meant for managing classic ASP settings, such as the following elements: Behavior, Compilation, Debugging, Services, Caching Properties, Com Plus Properties, and Sessions Properties.
- **Authentication**—The Authentication page is synonymous with the legacy Security tab in IIS 6 and earlier. This page is used to configure security authentication methods. Security can be administered for a web server, website, or a specific page. Authentication methods such as anonymous, ASP.NET impersonation, Basic authentication, digest authentication, forms authentication, and Windows authentication can be configured. Take note as anonymous authentication is enabled by default and might have to be disabled before a different authentication method can be used. In legacy versions, these authentication types were installed and enabled out of the box. However, with the modularized installation approach and security-minded product design, each element now needs to be selected separately during the installation process and then enabled using this page.
- **Authentication Rules**—Use this page to enforce control of web content access by utilizing Allow or Deny rules. Other IIS features such as Users and Roles are associated with this feature as you can specify Allow and Deny rules to already created users and roles.
- **CGI**—IIS 8 supports CGI applications. This page is used to configure CGI properties, which allows these applications to run on an IIS 8 web server. Additional elements on this page control other aspects of CGI applications, including CGI timeout values, whether a CGI application runs in its own console, and, finally, the security context the application will utilize.
- **Compression feature page**—Two options available on this page enhance transmission times between the server and browsers. The compression elements that can be configured consist of compressing static content and compressing dynamic content.

NOTE

For clients to leverage this feature, they must use a web browser that supports compression, such as Microsoft Internet Explorer 7.0 or later. In addition, the use of dynamic compression can increase processor utilization on the server.

- **Default Document**—Similar to the concept in earlier versions of IIS, the Default Document page is used to select the default web page that appears when a user connects to a site. An example is default.htm. Multiple default documents can be provided with an order-based precedence. This feature can be enabled or disabled via the Actions pane.

- **Directory Browsing**—This feature is disabled out of the box. By selecting the Enable task in the Actions pane, this page can be used to configure directory browsing functionality. The elements that can be selected include Time, Size, Extension, Date, and Long Date.
- **Errors feature page**—The Errors feature page is similar to the Custom Errors tab on legacy versions of IIS. An administrator can use this page to create custom error messages for web server clients. It is possible to edit a default error or create a new error page.
- **Failed Request Tracing Rules**—This setting is used to manage a list of tracing rules for failed requests. The Failed Request Tracing Rules Wizard is invoked by clicking Add in the Actions pane. The wizard walks you through the creation of the trace by first requesting information about what will be traced. The options include All Content, ASP.NET, ASP, and Custom. Trace Conditions are defined on the next page. Conditions include Event Severity, Status Codes, or Time Taken in Seconds. The final page is utilized to select the trace providers.

NOTE

When configuring Failed Request Tracing Rules for a site, logging of failed requests must be enabled for the site. If it is not, Failed Request Tracing Rules will not generate a trace.

- **FastCGI Settings**—Use this server-level page to configure FastCGI applications that are used by the IIS servers and hosted websites.
- **Handler Mappings**—Use this page to specify resources that will handle responses for specific request types. Actions include Add Managed Handler, Add Script Map, Add Wildcard Script Map, and Add Module Mapping.
- **HTTP Redirect**—Sometimes there is a need to redirect incoming requests to an alternate uniform resource locator (URL) or website. To achieve this goal, the HTTP Redirect page can be used to redirect requests to a specific destination.
- **HTTP Response Headers**—This feature should be used to configure HTTP headers based on entering name and values to responses from the web server.
- **IP Address and Domain Restrictions**—This page is used to create and manage rules that grant or deny computer networks and IP addresses access to specific web content. The rules available consist of Allow or Deny, and it is possible to enter a single IP address, range of IP addresses, or domain name. Finally, rules can be added to a page, site, or inherited from the parent. New to IIS 8, dynamic restrictions can be edited using the appropriate task from the Action pane. Dynamic restrictions can automatically deny access to an IP address based on the number of concurrent requests or based on a number of requests over a period of time.
- **ISAPI Filters**—ISAPI filters are programs that respond to certain events during HTTP request processing. You can add, enable, and disable filters for a website on this page.

- **Logging**—The Logging feature page configures how IIS log requests will be handled for the web server. For more information about logging, see the section "Using IIS Logging" later in this chapter.
- **MIME Types**—The MIME Types feature page is utilized for managing a list of Multipurpose Internet Mail Extensions (MIME) types for the web server or website. When creating or managing MIME types, the extension and MIME type must be entered.
- **Modules**—This feature should be used when managing or adding managed code modules and configuring native modules to a web server or website. Authentication and compression are examples of native code modules.
- **Output Caching**—The Output Caching features page is leveraged when defining a set of rules associated with caching content. Some of the cache settings include defining file extensions, maximum cache response sizes, and cache size limit in megabytes (MB).
- **Request Filtering**—The page is used to configure filtering rules for a website or application. Components that can be allowed or denied using this feature are File Name Extensions, Rules (strings), Hidden Segments, URL, HTTP Verbs, Headers, and Query Strings.
- **SSL Settings**—This page helps an administrator require SSL for a website or virtual directory and configure support for client certificates. For more information about creating certificates and assigning them to a website, review the section "Using SSL Certificates."
- **Server Certificates**—This feature page, which is available for the server only, provides an interface to install, manage, and configure SSL certificates used by IIS. For more information about creating certificates and assigning them to a website, review the section "Using SSL Certificates."
- **WebDav Authoring Rules**—This feature page is used for managing a list of authoring rules that control access to content.
- **Worker Processes**—This server-level feature page provides information about worker processes running on the IIS server. Detailed information provided for each process includes Application pool name, process ID, state, CPU %, private bytes (KB), and virtual bytes (KB).

Management Features

The following feature icons and respective configuration pages are associated with Management configurations:

- **Central Certificates**—This new server-level page allows an administrator to configure a location for where the central certificate store (CCS) is stored. A password for private keys can also be entered.

- **Configuration Editor**—This new page allows an administrator to access and manage configuration files affiliated with sections such as server, site, or application within IIS Manager.
- **Feature Delegation**—This server-level feature page is used to delegate configuration of various IIS features. Configuring feature delegation unlocks the appropriate section within the IIS configuration files to allow the configuration to be changed at a lower-level configuration file such as those for a site or application.
- **IIS Manager Permissions**—This feature page is used to allow or deny users access to various components in IIS, including websites and applications.
- **IIS Manager Users**—This feature page is used for managing and provisioning IIS Manager users that can be assigned roles as well as access to a website or application.
- **Management Service**—This server-level feature page is used to configure remote management access to the IIS server. The page allows for configuration of credentials, protocol information, logging, and IP address restrictions for remote management connections.
- **Shared Configuration**—This server-level feature page is used for managing configuration files for farms of IIS servers. A shared configuration location can be configured for farms that are deployed using a centralized shared configuration model. IIS configuration files can also be exported using the Action pane tasks on this page.

Installing and Configuring FTP Services

It's hard to find a person today who hasn't used File Transfer Protocol (FTP). FTP can be considered the backbone for transferring files to and from a website. The basic premise of an FTP server is based on placing files in directories and allowing users to access or publish information with an FTP client or an FTP-enabled web browser, such as Microsoft Internet Explorer. Depending on the placement and configuration of the FTP server, amateurs and professionals alike can either upload or download data from the Internet or intranet.

With Windows Server 2008 R2, Microsoft listened to the needs of its IT community and accordingly reengineered the FTP service for IIS after several years of neglecting the component. It is now more robust, dependable, and it supports SSL for data encryption. With Windows Server 2012, the revamped version of FTP Server services is included with the product as an optional component to be installed with IIS 8. It is fully integrated and can be managed with the same IIS 8 administrative interface. FTP Server Services with IIS 8 includes extended support for Internet standards, such as FTP over Secure Sockets Layer (SSL), support for extended character sets by including UTF-8 support, support for IPv6, and newly added with IIS 8, dynamic IP restrictions.

IIS 8 FTP Server Service Features

Microsoft has made many improvements to the FTP Service for IIS 7.5 and IIS 8. First, the FTP Service has been completely rewritten from scratch for IIS 7.5. As a result, it is more secure and meets today's industry standards for publishing content in a secure fashion. The following is a list of features for the FTP Service running on IIS 7.5 on Windows Server 2008 R2:

- Tight integration now exists with IIS 8 websites and IIS Manager.
- It supports today's demanding security needs by supporting FTP over SSL.
- Organizations can now host multiple FTP sites with the same IP address, because the bindings support host headers.
- Both web and FTP content can be hosted from the same site.
- UTF8, IPv6, and integration with other repositories such as SQL Server are supported.
- Improved logging and diagnostics are now available.

In addition to the IIS 7.5 features, IIS 8 FTP introduces one additional powerful improvement:

- Dynamic logon attempt restrictions now provide protection against brute-force attacks by dynamically blacklisting IP addresses based on failed logon attempts.

Microsoft certainly realizes FTP is not going away and is still the preferred method for publishing content and exchanging large pieces of data between organizations. By rewriting the FTP service, utilizing Extensible Markup Language (XML) configuration files, and providing secured FTP, the product meets today's industry FTP requirements out of the box without the need to purchase third-party plug-ins.

Installing the FTP Server

Similar to the earlier version of IIS, the FTP publishing service is not installed by default. To add the FTP role service included with IIS 8 running on Windows Server 2012, complete the following steps in Server Manager after IIS has been installed:

1. From the Manage menu, select Add Roles and Features.
2. Click Next on the Before you Begin page after reading the notes provided.
3. Click Next to accept the default installation type of Role-Based or Feature-Based Installation.
4. Select the web server from the server pool and click Next.
5. On the Select Server Roles page, install FTP 8 by expanding Web Server (IIS) (Installed) in the Roles section and then expanding the FTP Server section and selecting the FTP Service role service below it as well as the FTP Extensibility role service if needed (see Figure 12.9). Click Next.
6. Click Next to accept the existing features.

7. On the Confirm Installation Selections page, review the FTP roles, services, and features selected for installation, and then click Install to initiate the installation process.
8. Ensure the installation succeeded by reviewing the messages on the Installation Results page, and then click Close.

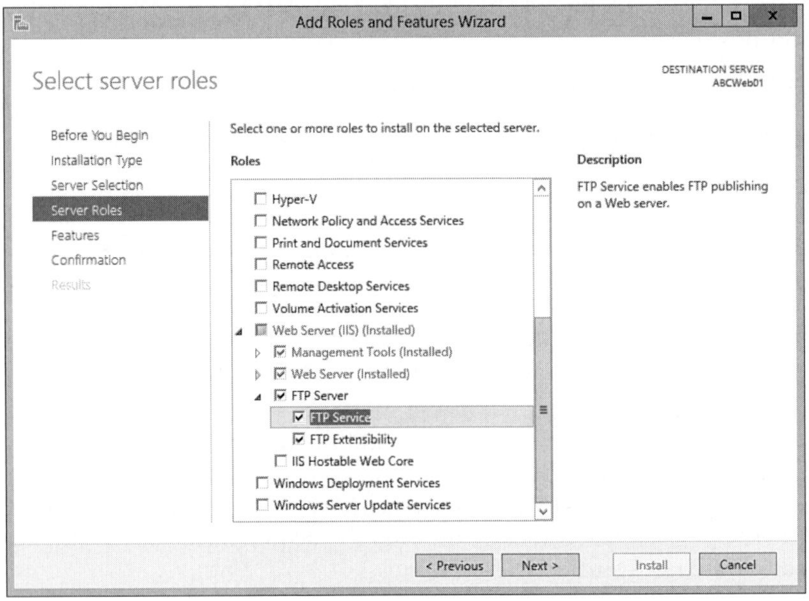

FIGURE 12.9 Selecting the FTP 8 features to install.

Creating a Secure FTP 8 Site Using SSL

With IIS 8, it is not only possible to create a new FTP site or add FTP publishing to an existing website, but it is also possible to have both FTP and HTTP coexist. To create a new FTP site, in addition to the Default Web Site, follow these steps:

1. Start Server Manager using the taskbar icon.
2. From the Tools menu, select Internet Information Services (IIS) Manager.
3. In the Connections pane, expand the IIS server, and then expand the Sites node within the tree.
4. Right-click Sites and select Add FTP Site.
5. Enter the FTP site name and specify the physical path for the FTP site you will use. Click Next.
6. In the Binding section of the Binding and SSL Settings page, enter the IP address and port of the FTP server.

7. From within the Binding and SSL Settings page, specify a certificate and select the Require SSL option in the SSL section.

NOTE

When using SSL, an IIS 8 certificate should be created prior to these procedures. For more information about creating an IIS 8 certificate, review the "Using SSL Certificates" later in this chapter.

12

8. Select the Start FTP Site Automatically option, and click Next, as displayed in Figure 12.10.

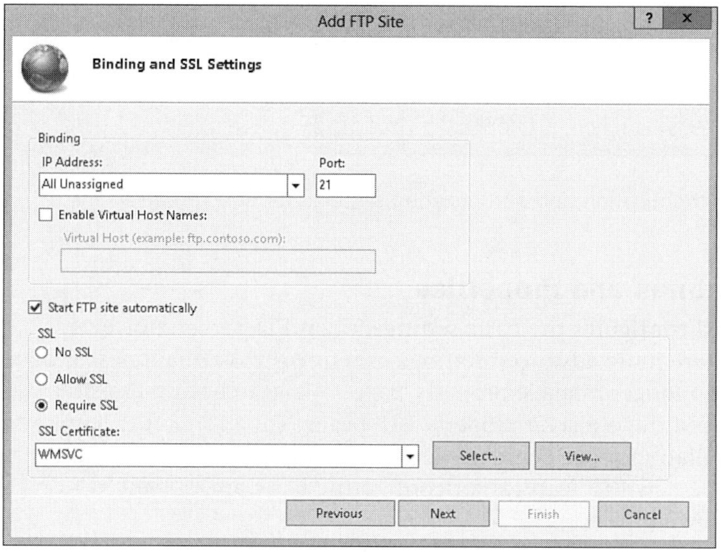

FIGURE 12.10 Setting the binding and SSL settings for FTP.

9. On the Authentication and Authorization Information page, specify how users will authenticate to the site by choosing Anonymous or Basic in the Authentication section.

10. In the Authorization section, specify who has authorization to the site by selecting from the following: All Users, Anonymous Users, Specified Roles or Users Groups, and, finally, Specified Users.

11. The final setting on the Authentication and Authorization Information page is the Permissions section. Specify the permissions for the FTP site. You can choose from Read and/or Write.

12. Review the settings, as illustrated in Figure 12.11, and then click Finish to finalize the FTP site creation.

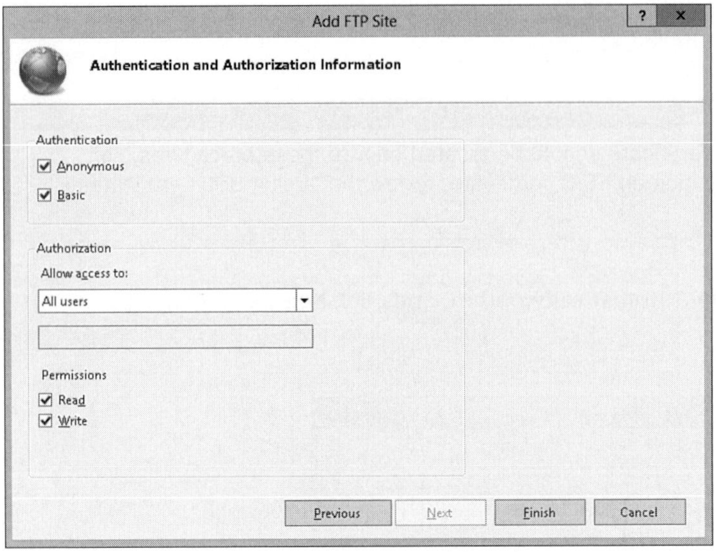

FIGURE 12.11 Specifying authentication and authorization settings for an FTP site.

Configuring FTP 8 Features and Properties

The FTP Site Creation Wizard configures the basic settings for an FTP server; however, there is still a need to configure more advanced settings or refine the original ones. Similar to managing websites, you no longer manage property pages by right-clicking the site. The FTP feature icons have replaced the old style property FTP pages. The FTP feature icons are installed during the installation process and are located in the Central Details pane, as shown in Figure 12.12. The new FTP features for configuring basic and advanced FTP properties consist of the following:

- FTP Authentication
- FTP Authorization Rules
- FTP Current Sessions
- FTP Directory Browsing
- FTP Firewall Support
- FTP IP Address and Domain Restrictions
- FTP Logging
- FTP Logon Attempt Restrictions
- FTP Messages
- FTP Request Filtering
- FTP SSL Settings
- FTP User Isolation

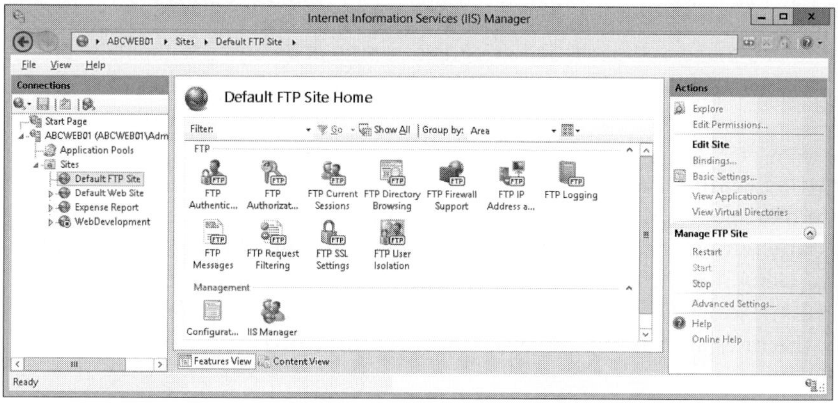

FIGURE 12.12 The FTP features.

FTP Authentication Feature Page

The FTP Authentication feature page is used to configure authentication methods for FTP clients. By default, an FTP site does not have authentication configured, and all mechanisms are disabled out of the box. An administrator must grant the desired authentication to the FTP site. The authentication mechanisms for FTP consist of the following items:

- **Anonymous authentication**—This built-in authentication mechanism should be selected when you want to provide public access to an FTP site without having end users pass credentials.
- **Basic authentication**—Another built-in authentication mechanism for FTP sites. Basic authentication requires the FTP clients to enter a valid Windows user account and password when gaining access to the FTP site. Basic authentication sends password credentials in clear text, which is a security hazard. Therefore, implement SSL when using this mechanism to encrypt passwords in transit.
- **ASP.NET authentication**—The FTP site will provide authorization to FTP clients by having them enter a valid ASP.NET user account and password. This is a custom authentication mechanism that requires a provider and connection string to an ASP.NET user database. This authentication mechanism must be added using the Custom Providers task in the Action pane.
- **IIS Manager authentication**—This is another custom authentication mechanism similar to ASP.NET. An FTP client must provide a legitimate IIS Manager username and password to gain access to FTP content. Similar to basic authentication, the credentials are not encrypted, so it is recommended for this authentication to be used in conjunction with SSL. This authentication mechanism must be added using the Custom Providers task in the Action pane.

NOTE

Don't forget that to use these authentication mechanisms, the appropriate authentication role services must be installed prior to configuration.

FTP Authorization Rules Feature Page

This page is used to manage Allow and Deny authorization rules that control access to FTP sites. The Actions pane options Add Allow Rule and Add Deny Rule should be selected to invoke the Allow or Deny Authorization Rule page. After the page is invoked, rules can be applied to All Users, All Anonymous Users, Specified Roles or User Groups, and Specified Users. In addition, the rules are based on Read or Write permissions.

FTP Current Sessions Feature Page

This page is used to monitor current sessions for an FTP site. The following elements are displayed: User Name, Session Start Time, Current Command, Previous Command, Command Start Time, Bytes Sent, Bytes Received, Session ID, and Client IP Address.

FTP Directory Browsing Feature Page

The FTP Directory Browsing page, illustrated in Figure 12.13, is divided into two sections. The first section is called Directory Listing Style. The format presentation options include MS-DOS and UNIX. The second section, Directory Listing Options, controls how directory information is displayed. The display options include the following:

- **Virtual Directories**—With this option, you can specify whether to include virtual directories.
- **Available Bytes**—This setting controls the display behavior of the available bytes remaining on the disk or in the quota when a disk quota is enabled.

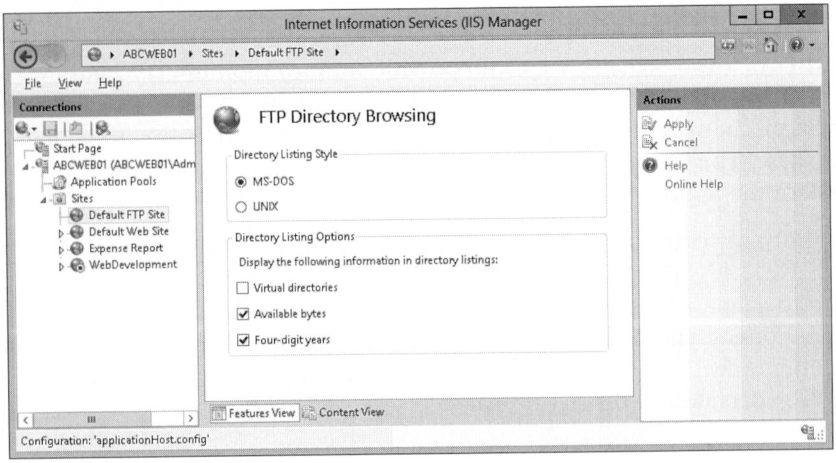

FIGURE 12.13 The FTP Directory Browsing feature page.

- **Four-Digit Years**—When enabled, this setting displays the last modified date for a file based on the four-year date, such as 1974, and not a two-year date format, such as 74.

FTP Firewall Support Feature Page

This feature allows the server to accept passive connections when the FTP client is behind a firewall. An administrator must enter the Data Channel Port Range and External IP Address of the Firewall settings and then click Apply in the Actions pane.

FTP IP Address and Domain Restrictions Feature Page

The FTP IP Address and Domain Restrictions feature page is used to create and manage rules that allow or deny computer networks and IP addresses access to the FTP site. Rules can be configured using a single IP address, a range of IP addresses, or a domain name. Finally, rules can be added to a page, site, or inherited from the parent.

FTP Logging Feature Page

The FTP Logging feature page includes the exact same logging settings as for a website. This page controls the type of log file to use, the location to be stored, and the log file rollover settings.

FTP Logon Attempt Restrictions Feature Page

This server-level only feature page was introduced with IIS 8 for Windows Server 2012 to assist with preventing brute-force attacks on the server. The feature can be configured to block IP addresses based on the number of failed authentication requests within a period of time. Blacklisted IP addresses are prevented from accessing the server until the FTP service is restarted. This feature can be configured to enforce the restriction or just to log IP address that violate the parameters.

FTP Messages Feature Page

The FTP Messages feature page illustrated in Figure 12.14 is a great way to create a series of banners that are presented when a user connects to the FTP server, authenticates successfully to the FTP server, disconnected from the FTP server or is prevented from connecting because the server has reached its connection limit.

The message behavior is controlled by the following elements:

- **Suppress Default Banner**—If enabled, this option suppressed the default welcome banner, including FTP server type and version. This option doesn't impact the display of a custom banner message.
- **Support User Variables in Messages**—By enabling this setting, user variables such as `BytesReceived`, `BytesSent`, `SessionID`, `SiteName`, and `UserName` can be included in the messages.
- **Show Detailed Messages for Local Requests**—This setting controls the behavior for displaying FTP error messages. If enabled, detailed FTP error messages are displayed for connections made locally on the server to facilitate troubleshooting.

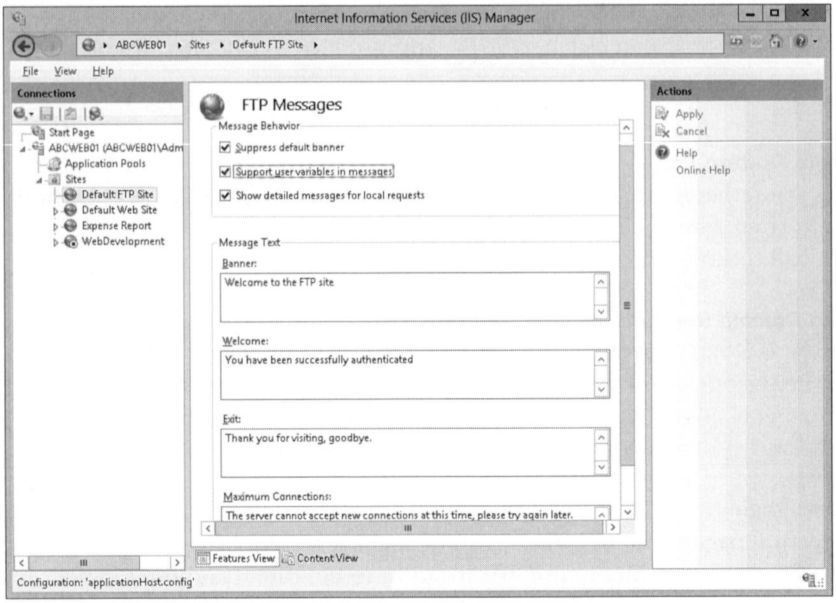

FIGURE 12.14 The FTP Messages feature page.

FTP Request Filtering

The FTP Request Filtering feature page is used to define the list of Allow or Deny rules based on the specific elements:

- **File Name Extensions**—This tab allows for the creation of filename extensions for which the FTP service will either allow or deny access to the site. For example, an administrator can prevent Internet clients from uploading any files with the extension of *.txt or *.com.
- **Hidden Segments**—The Hidden Segments tab should be used if you want to hide specific areas of your FTP site. If hidden, the specific section will not be displayed in the directory listings.
- **Defined URL Sequences**—This setting should be used to define the list of URL sequences for which the FTP service will deny access.
- **Commands**—The final tab Commands defines the list of commands for which the FTP service will either allow or deny access to further tighten security.

FTP SSL Settings Feature Page

This page should be utilized for enabling and configuring SSL settings for an FTP site. The options include a drop-down menu for selecting the SSL certificate you will use and SSL policy. The SSL Policy options include Allow SSL Connections, Require SSL Connections, and Advanced Custom Settings which provides for granular control over the control and data channels separately. You will also have the chance to choose whether to use 128-bit encryption for SSL connections.

FTP User Isolation Feature Page

Similar to legacy versions of FTP, IIS 8 can still isolate FTP users so FTP content is protected. This is an especially useful feature for Internet service providers (ISPs) and application service providers (ASPs) servicing a large number of users. FTP users can have their own separate directory to upload and download files to the web or FTP server. Users who connect see only their directory as the top-level directory and can't browse other FTP directories. Permissions can be set on the FTP home directory to allow create, modify, or delete operations.

It is worth noting that FTP user isolation is based on an FTP site rather than at the server level and is either enabled or disabled. However, sites that need to enable FTP user isolation aren't forced to strictly use this feature. You can enable anonymous access in conjunction with FTP user isolation by creating a virtual directory within the FTP site and allowing read-only access. The only limitation to mixing the FTP user isolation and anonymous access is that information can be downloaded only from the public or read-only virtual directory.

The configuration settings on the FTP User Isolation page, as shown in Figure 12.15, consist of the following options for where to start the user when they connect. The options include the FTP Root Directory or User Name Directory when users are not isolated. In addition, it is possible to isolate users by restricting them to following directories:

- User Name Directory (Disable Global Virtual Directories)
- User Name Physical Directory (Enable Global Virtual Directories)
- FTP Home Directory Configured in Active Directory

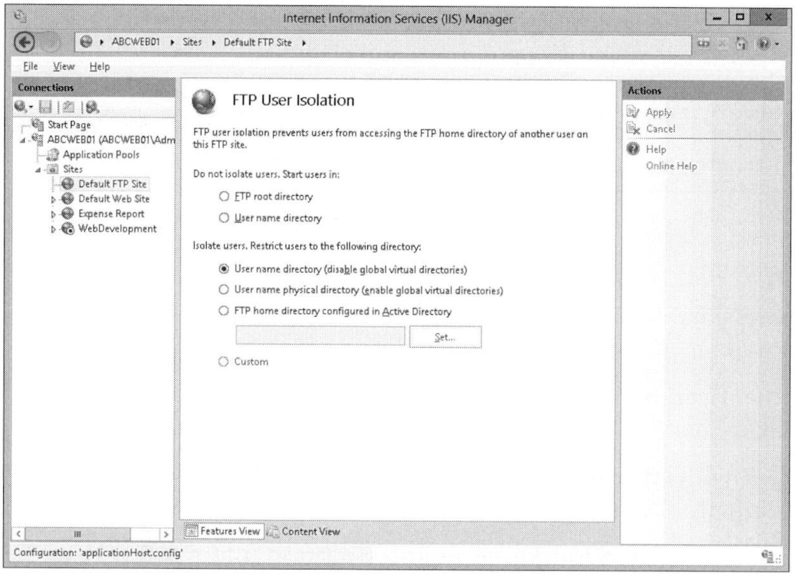

FIGURE 12.15 The FTP User Isolation feature page.

Securing IIS 8

There shouldn't be any question that IIS 8 is significantly more secure than its predecessors. Several key enhancements made over the past several versions such as a reduced attack surface, minimum install by default, and enhanced application isolation deliver a robust and secure web platform. IIS 8 is also configured by default to present only static information. To use applications or other dynamic content, you must manually enable the required features individually.

However, Microsoft products are also very common and therefore present a common target for attacks. For this reason, it's important to secure the web server as much as possible. The more barriers there are, the less inclined a hacker will be to try to gain unauthorized access. Each component on the web server must be secure; the server is only as secure as its weakest point.

Windows Server 2012 Security

Windows Server 2012 security actually begins during the planning and designing phases so that every conceivable security aspect is addressed. This can entail physical, logical (Windows Server 2012, applications, and so on), and communications security.

When you're securing the Windows Server 2012 system with the Web Server (IIS) role, it's important to keep the server updated and apply the latest service pack and security patches. Keeping up-to-date with service packs and patches ensures that Windows Server 2012 is operating with the greatest amount of protection.

Application security on the Windows Server 2012 system with the Web Server (IIS) role should be carefully reviewed, especially if it's a custom-built application. If the application is developed by a vendor, make sure that you have an application that is certified to run on Windows Server 2012 and that all vendor recommendations for configuration and security have been reviewed, vetted and if appropriate, implemented.

NOTE

For more information about securing Windows Server 2012, see Part IV, "Security."

IIS Authentication

Authentication is a process that verifies that users are who they say they are. IIS supports a multitude of authentication methods, including the following:

- **Anonymous authentication**—Users can establish a connection to the website without providing credentials.
- **Active Directory client certificate authentication**—Users can establish a connection by using their Active Directory client certificate for authentication.
- **ASP.NET impersonation**—Users can utilize an impersonation context other than the ASP.NET account.

- **Windows authentication**—This authentication method can be integrated with Active Directory. As users log on, the hash value of the password is sent across the wire instead of the actual password.
- **Digest authentication**—Similar to Integrated Windows authentication, a hash value of the password is transmitted. Digest authentication requires a Windows Server domain controller to validate the hash value.
- **Basic authentication**—Basic authentication sends the username and password over the wire in clear-text format. This authentication method offers little security to protect against unauthorized access by itself and is typically used in conjunction with SSL-based protection of the site or page.
- **Forms authentication**—Users are redirected to a secure page where they enter their credentials. After they have been authenticated, they are redirected back to the page they originally requested.

These authentication methods can be enabled under the Authentication feature page, as illustrated in Figure 12.16. You can view this window by selecting the feature under the IIS section at the server, site, or virtual directory level.

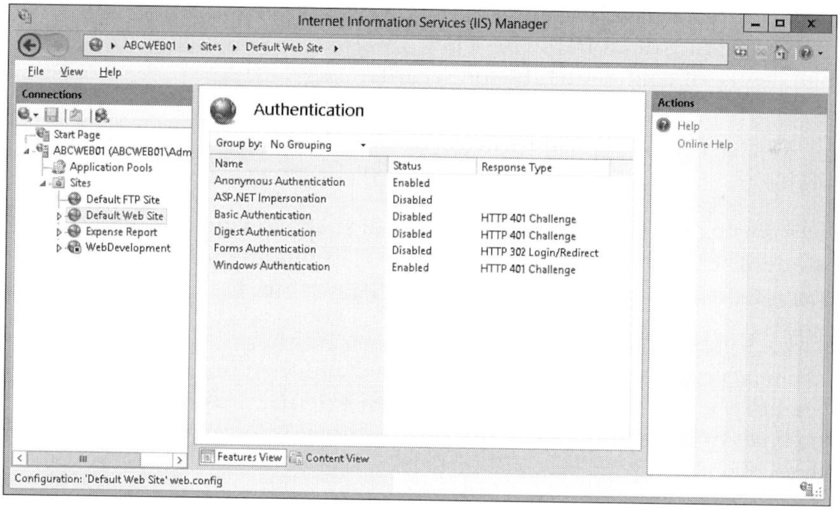

FIGURE 12.16 Authentication feature page.

Auditing Web Services

Windows Server 2012 auditing can be applied to web and FTP sites to document attempts (successful and unsuccessful) to log on, gain unauthorized access to service accounts, modify or delete files, and execute restricted commands. These events can be viewed through Event Viewer. It's also important to monitor IIS logs in conjunction with audited events to determine how, when, and if external users are trying to gain unauthorized access.

Using SSL Certificates

Secure Sockets Layer (SSL) encryption preserves user and content integrity and confidentiality so that communications between a client and the web server, containing sensitive data such as passwords or credit card information, are protected. SSL is based on the public key infrastructure (PKI, X.509) security standards that protect communication by encrypting data before being transmitted.

Earlier versions of IIS supported SSL, and IIS 8 is no different. IIS 8, however, introduces significant improvements to the use of SSL for securing websites, especially when it comes to scalability.

The use of certificates with IIS can serve three primary purposes, although they are typically used to encrypt connections:

- **SSL server authentication**—This allows a client to validate a server's identity. SSL-enabled client software can use a PKI to check whether a server's certificate is valid and has been issued by a trusted certificate authority (CA).
- **Client authentication**—This allows a server to validate a client's identity. IIS can validate that a client's certificate is valid as well as check whether the certificate is from a trusted CA.
- **Encrypting SSL connections**—The most common reason for deploying certificates is for SSL based encrypting of all traffic for a given website or virtual directory. This provides a high degree of confidentiality and security.

From an IIS perspective, SSL can be applied to an entire website, directories, or specific files within the website. SSL configuration can be done through IIS Manager.

The high-level steps for using certificates and SSL consist of the following: The first step is to obtain a certificate. The second step is to create an HTTPS binding for a specific site that needs to be encrypted. The final step is to configure SSL settings for a site, application, or physical directory.

To use SSL on a website, a certificate must first be requested and then installed. The request can be created to obtain a certificate either from an external, trusted CA or from an internal PKI. The types of server requests available in Internet Information Services include the following:

- **Create certificate request**—This option is typically used for creating a certificate request, which will be submitted to a trusted CA. The certificate's distinguished name properties, cryptographic service provider, and bit-length information are entered into a file and then submitted to a public CA for approval.

TIP

When creating the certificate request to a public CA, it is recommended to use 2048 (the default) or higher as the bit length. Keep in mind that higher bit lengths enforce stronger security; however, a greater length can decrease performance.

- **Create domain certificate request**—A domain certificate request is used when providing a request to an internal certificate authority. Typically, the internal certificate authority would be an enterprise certificate authority associated with the company's Active Directory domain. This approach reduces the cost of purchasing third-party certificates and also simplifies the certificate deployment.
- **Create Self-Signed Certificate Request**—The final option available when creating a certificate request is to use a self-signed certificate. This method is usually only used for maintaining certificates for a testing environment because the certificates are not from a trusted CA.

This example illustrates the procedures to create a domain-based certificate request. To complete this task, this example requires an internal CA running within your domain. For more information about creating an internal CA, see Chapter 15, "Security Policies, Network Policy Server, and Network Access Protection."

To create a domain-based certificate request, follow these steps:

1. Launch IIS Manager.
2. In the Connections pane, highlight the IIS server that will request an Internet Server Certificate.
3. In the Feature view, double-click the Server Certificates element.
4. In the Actions pane, select Create Domain Certificate Request.
5. On the Distinguished Name Properties page, specify the required information for the certificate, as displayed in Figure 12.17. The common name is typically the fully qualified domain name (FQDN) of the URL users will use to connect to the website (for example, www.companyabc.com). Click Next to continue.
6. Because this is a domain-based certificate request, the next page presented is the Online Certificate Authority. Specify the online certificate authority that will accept the request by selecting the CA from a list. In addition, a friendly name is also required. Click Finish to finalize the request.

When this process has been completed, either the administrator of the CA must approve the request or it can be automatically approved based on the auto-enrollment feature of the domain-based CA. The CA in this example automatically fulfilled the request; therefore, the certificate resides on the Server Certificates page and can be viewed by selecting it and clicking View Task in the Actions pane. If auto-enrollment is not available, the certificate is installed after an administrator approves the request on the CA.

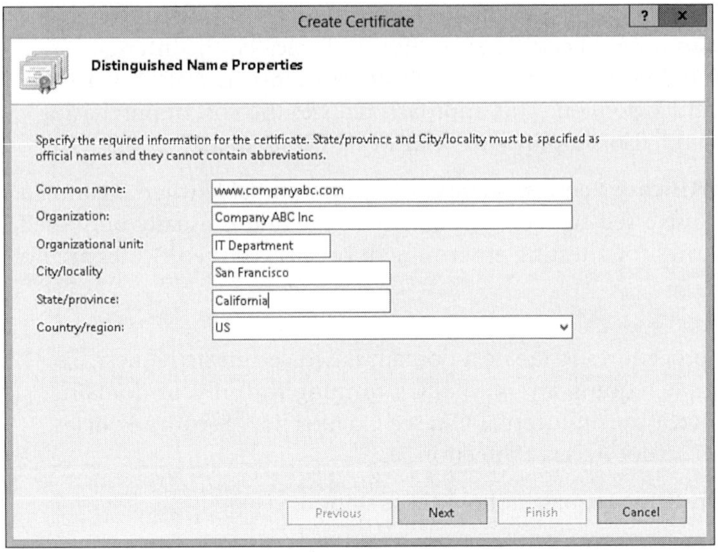

FIGURE 12.17 Creating a domain-based certificate request.

Once the certificate is installed, the next step in the process is to bind the Internet server certificate for the desired website and enable SSL. To do this, follow these steps:

1. Open IIS Manager and select the website for which the certificate will be used.
2. In the Actions Pane, select Bindings to launch the Site Bindings configuration page.
3. In the Site Bindings dialog box, click Add.
4. In the Add Site Binding dialog box, select the HTTPS option from the Type drop-down menu, assign an IP address, and verify the port is 443, as shown in Figure 12.18.

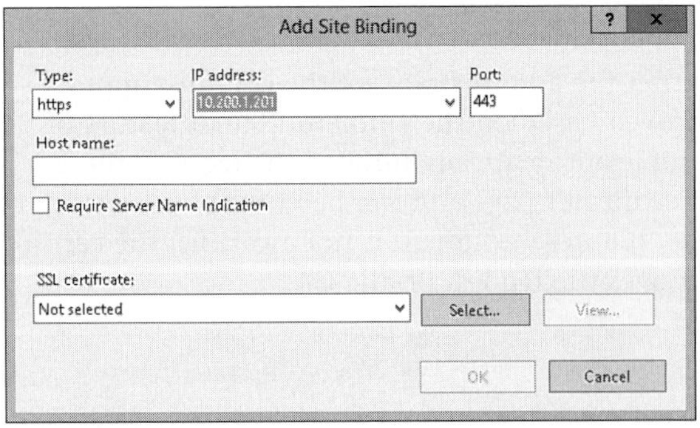

FIGURE 12.18 Adding SSL site binding.

5. Select a certificate, such as the one that was created in the preceding section. You can view the certificate selected by clicking the View button. Click OK to return to the Site Bindings dialog box.
6. Click Close in the Site Bindings dialog box to finalize the binding process.

The final process when configuring a site to utilize SSL is to configure the SSL settings for the site, application, physical directory, or virtual directory. To configure SSL settings on the default website, follow these steps:

1. In IIS Manager, navigate to the Default Web Site.
2. Double-Click the SSL Settings icon in Features view.
3. On the SSL Settings page, enable the Require SSL option. Alternatively, select the Require 128-bit SSL option to force 128-bit encryption.
4. The final setting is to configure whether to accept, ignore, or require client certificates. Choose the appropriate Client Certificates option, and click Apply in the Actions pane to save the changes, as shown in Figure 12.19.

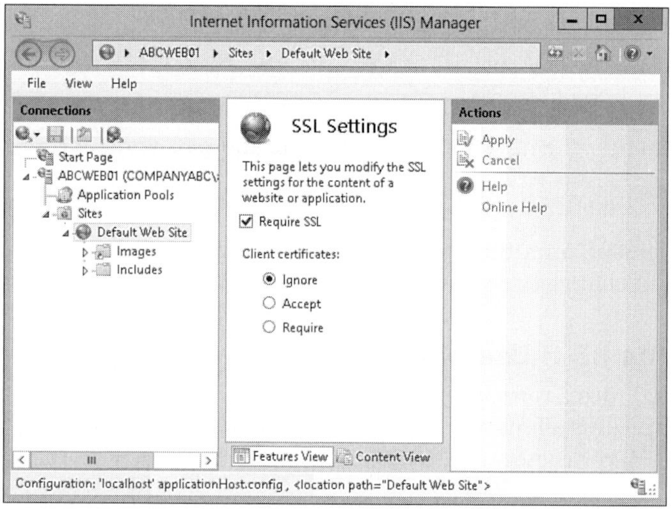

FIGURE 12.19 Configuring properties on the SSL Settings feature page.

Administering IIS 8 Administrator and User Security

Administrative permissions for IIS 8 servers, websites, directory, applications and pages can be granted to Active Directory and to local Windows users. In addition, IIS specific accounts can be added and used for administration purposes. The use of Active Directory accounts is usually recommended as it is easier to manage and scales well when more than one or two IIS servers are used. Account and security management within IIS 8 requires installation of the Management Service role service.

Creating an IIS 8 User Account

In some situations, you might need to provide management capabilities and not want to use an Active Directory or Windows account. Examples of this scenario are often related to vendor support of an application. In this case, an IIS 8 user account is used. This IIS-only, non-Windows user can then be delegated permissions to manage components of the IIS infrastructure.

Follow these steps to enable support for IIS user accounts:

1. In IIS Manager, navigate to the Connections pane and select the IIS server.
2. Open the Management Service feature, which is located in the Central Details pane.
3. In the Identity Credentials section, select Windows Credentials or IIS Manager credentials.
4. Click Apply in the Action pane.

Follow these steps to create an IIS 8 user account:

1. In IIS Manager, navigate to the Connections pane and select the IIS server.
2. Open the IIS Manager Users feature, which is located in the Central Details pane.
3. On the IIS Manager Users feature page, click the Add User task, which is located in the Actions pane.
4. In the Add User dialog box, enter the new user account name and password, and then click OK.

For ongoing user account management, after the user account is created, use the additional tasks on the Actions pane to change the password, disable, or remove the account.

Assigning Permissions to an IIS 8 User Account

The next step in the user-creation process is to assign the appropriate permissions to the newly created user account. This process allows the user to configure delegated features for a specific website or application. Follow these steps to authorize a user account to connect to a site or an application:

1. In IIS Manager, navigate to the Connections pane, expand the IIS server, and then expand the Sites node.
2. Specify the site to which the user account will be granted authorization, and then open the IIS Manager Permissions feature, which is located in the Central Details pane.
3. On the IIS Manager Permissions feature page, click the Allow User task, which is located in the Actions pane.
4. In the Allow User dialog box, first select the IIS Manager option, then enter the account that was created in the previous steps, and then click OK.

NOTE

If the IIS Manager option is not available in the Allow User dialog box, the Management Service is not set to accept connections from IIS users. To do so, use the Management Service page to enable remote connections as outlined previously.

Configuring Feature Delegation

To allow users who have been granted permission to a site, application, directory, or page to make changes to configurations, feature delegation must be used to unlock the relevant portion of the configuration file for the element. Follow these steps to configure feature delegation for a newly created website:

1. In IIS Manager, navigate to the Connections pane and select the IIS server.
2. Select the Feature Delegation feature icon, which is located in the Central Details pane.
3. On the Features Delegation page, select the Custom Site Delegation task from the Actions pane.
4. Select the site to be delegated from the Sites drop-down menu on the Custom Website page.
5. Select the appropriate feature in the list and then set the desired feature delegation from the Actions pane. The delegations include: Read/Write, Read Only, Not Delegated, and Reset to Inherited.

NOTE

In some circumstances, you might need to reset delegation or restore the defaults. When you find this necessary, click the Reset All Delegation or Default Delegation in the Actions pane.

Using IIS Logging

IIS logging should be viewed as a necessity rather than an optional feature of IIS because it helps to ensure IIS security and is also extremely useful for maintenance and troubleshooting. For example, in the event of a system compromise, logs can be used and a forensic review performed on the extensive details contained in them. This information can then be used to review maintenance procedures and identify problems in the system. Equally important, many organizations now require logging because of regulatory compliance or other business policies.

IIS text-based logging, using formats such as the W3C Extended Log File Format, Microsoft IIS Log File Format, and NCSA Common Log File Format, is controlled by Http.sys, which is a kernel-mode process. This is a significant change from legacy versions where logging was a user-mode process. The only other log file format that comes close to legacy versions is Open Database Connectivity (ODBC) logging, because it is implemented using a user mode worker process.

Another bonus about logging is its ability to be implemented at the server, site, web application, file, and directory level. Specific scoping helps minimize the number of logs collected and simplifies log analysis. For organizations that want to configure IIS logging for a specific website, follow these steps:

1. Launch IIS Manager.
2. In the Connections pane, select the desired website for which you want to configure logging.
3. Double-click the Logging feature in the Actions pane.
4. On the Logging page, select the desired logging format to be used.
5. Specify the location of the log file by typing a log path into the Directory text box. Alternatively, click the Browse button and select a directory to store the files.

   In the Log File Rollover section, select the method to create the new log file. The options include specifying an hourly, daily, weekly, or monthly schedule; entering a maximum file size (in bytes); or selecting the option that puts a stop to the creation of new log files.

   The final option requires you to determine whether to use local time for file naming and rollover.
6. After all the log file settings have been entered, select Apply in the Actions pane to commit the changes.

NOTE

It is possible to either enable or disable a log file for a specific site by selecting Enable or Disable in the Actions pane of the Logging feature page. To enable logging for IIS 8, the HTTP Logging Module must be installed.

Summary

IIS 8 is a major improvement over earlier versions in terms of security, reliability, availability, and performance. These facets have been a top priority for Microsoft. Microsoft has incorporated both internal and customer-based feedback to provide a robust platform for providing web, application, and FTP services.

Key points in this chapter covered the planning and design of the new IIS 8 capabilities built in to Windows Server 2012. The features have been greatly enhanced to provide better management, scalability, modification, and reporting of web services operations.

Instead of having IIS installed on every installation of Windows server, an administrator now needs to add the IIS server role to the system and then go through a process of enabling functionality and configuring the web services function to meet the needs of the organization. This approach that starts out with a minimal configuration and requires the server administrator to configure all required functions provides better security for the server systems, but also requires a better understanding of which services to add, and which services to modify to meet the needs of the organization's applications.

And even with IIS requiring deliberate installation and configuration, there are still key security practices that need to be performed to ensure that web services are not attacked and compromised, thus creating a security hole in the organization's network security.

The IIS 8 server role is a robust, flexible, secure web server platform in Windows Server 2012, and one that administrators from early adopter organizations have found to be a welcome improvement for ongoing operations.

Best Practices

The following are best practices from this chapter:

- Use IIS 8 to improve performance and strengthen security.
- Thoroughly design and plan the IIS 8 environment.
- Define the goals and objectives of the IIS 8 project.
- Identify and review IIS application types and requirements.
- Define security requirements to meet the goals and objectives.
- Balance the security methodologies to be used with the associated risks and end-user experience.
- Examine and design disaster recovery plans, and monitor requirements and maintenance practices.
- Document the current IIS infrastructure and the IIS design decisions.
- Build fault tolerance in to the web infrastructure based on how much downtime can be afforded and existing SLAs.
- Use IIS to monitor applications such as pinging worker processes after a specified period of time, monitoring for failed applications, and disabling the application pool after a certain number of failures or a set number of failures within a given time frame.
- Isolate FTP users so that FTP content is protected.
- Carefully review application security on the Windows Server 2012 web server, especially if using a custom-built application.
- Choose an authentication method carefully depending on business and technical requirements.

- Apply auditing to web and FTP sites to document successful and unsuccessful attempts to log on, gain unauthorized access to service accounts, modify or delete files, and execute restricted commands.
- Use SSL to ensure confidentiality.
- Monitor disk space and IIS logs to ensure that a hacker isn't attempting to gain unauthorized access.
- Use logging not only to review IIS security, but also to assist with maintenance and troubleshooting.

CHAPTER 13

Server-Level Security

IN THIS CHAPTER

Starting with Windows Server 2003, Microsoft has made security a top priority for the Windows Server team (in addition to many other teams). As a result, subsequent versions of the operating system have included many changes designed to improve the security of Windows Server. Features such as Core Edition, role-based installation, Windows Server Update Service, AppLocker, and many more have contributed to a more and more secure operating system. Windows Server 2012 continues this trend, with improvements in functionality such as dynamic access control and the trusted boot architecture.

This chapter focuses on the server-side security mechanisms in Windows Server 2012. Advanced features such as the intelligent integrated firewall, dynamic access control, and BitLocker are explained in this chapter. Particular emphasis is placed on the importance of keeping servers up-to-date with security patches through such utilities as Windows Server Update Services, a key feature of Windows security. In addition, file-level security, physical security, and other critical server security considerations are presented.

Defining Windows Server 2012 Security

Security on the server level is one of the most important considerations for a network environment. Servers in an infrastructure not only handle critical network services, such as domain name system (DNS), Dynamic Host Configuration Protocol (DHCP), directory lookups, and authentication, but they also serve as a central location for most, if not all, critical files in an organization's network.

Subsequently, it is important to establish a server security plan and gain a full understanding of the security capabilities of Windows Server 2012.

Outlining Microsoft's Trustworthy Computing Initiative

On the heels of several high-profile viruses and security holes, Bill Gates developed what became known as the Trustworthy Computing initiative. The basics of the initiative boiled down to an increased emphasis on security in all Microsoft technologies. Every line of code in Windows Server was combed for potential vulnerabilities, and the emphasis was shifted from new functionality to security. What the initiative means to users of Microsoft technology is the fact that security has become a major priority for Microsoft, and Windows Server 2012 now takes advantage of almost 10 years of platform development using this concept.

Common Language Runtime

All Microsoft code is verified through a process called common language runtime. It processes application code and automatically checks for security holes that can be caused by mistakes in programming. In addition, it scrutinizes security credentials that are used by specific pieces of code, making sure that they perform only those actions that they are supposed to. Through these techniques, the common language runtime effectively reduces the overall threat posed to Windows Server by limiting the potential for exploitations and vulnerabilities.

Understanding the Layered Approach to Server Security

Security works best when it is applied in layers. It is much more difficult to rob a house, for example, if a thief not only has to break through the front door, but also has to fend off an attack dog and disable a home security system. The same concept applies to server security: Multiple layers of security should be applied so that the difficulty in hacking into a system becomes exponentially greater.

Windows Server 2012 seamlessly handles many of the security layers that are required, using Kerberos authentication, NTFS file security, and built-in security tools to provide for a great deal of security right out of the box. Additional security components require that you understand their functionality and install and configure their components. Windows Server 2012 makes the addition of extra layers of security a possibility and positions organizations for increased security without sacrificing functionality.

Deploying Physical Security

One of the most overlooked but perhaps most critical components of server security is the actual physical security of the server itself. The most secure, unbreakable web server is powerless if a malicious user can simply unplug it. Worse yet, someone logging interactively on to a critical file server could potentially copy critical data or sabotage the machine directly.

Physical security is a must for any organization because it is the most common cause of security breaches. Despite this fact, many organizations have poorly implemented physical security standards for their mission-critical servers. An understanding of what is required to secure the physical and logon access to a server is, consequently, a must.

Restricting Physical Access

Servers should be physically secured behind locked doors, in a controlled-access environment. It is unwise to place mission-critical servers at the feet of administrators or in similar unsecure locations. Rather, a dedicated server room or server closet that is locked at all times is the most ideal environment for the purposes of server security.

Most hardware manufacturers also include mechanisms for locking out some or all the components of a server. Depending on the other layers of security deployed, it might be wise to use these mechanisms to secure a server environment.

Restricting Logon Access

All servers should be configured to allow only administrators to physically log on to the console. By default, such use is restricted on domain controllers, but other servers such as file servers, utility servers, and the like must be configured to specifically forbid these types of logons. To restrict logon access, follow these steps:

1. Open Server Manager, select Tools, and then click the Local Security Policy option.
2. In the node pane, navigate to Security Settings, Local Policies, User Rights Assignment.
3. Double-click Allow Log On Locally.
4. Remove any users or groups that do not need access to the server, as shown in Figure 13.1. Click OK when you have finished.

NOTE

The Allow Log On Locally right can also be configured for an entire domain or organizational unit (OU) using a domain-based group policy, but that mechanism only allows granting users or groups the right rather than removing it. To prevent users or groups from logging on locally with a group policy, use the Deny log On Locally right. For more information about setting up these types of group policies, see Chapter 27, "Group Policy Management for Network Clients."

Using Smart Cards for Logon Access

Increased security is provided for the logon process in secured infrastructures using so-called smart cards for logon access; these smart cards are fully supported in Windows Server 2012. A smart card can exist in multiple forms, commonly as a credit card-sized piece of plastic with an encrypted microchip embedded within or as a USB key. Each user is assigned a unique smart card and an associated PIN. Logging on to a workstation or server is as straightforward as inserting the smart card into a smart card reader and entering in the PIN, which can be a combination of numbers and letters, similar to a password.

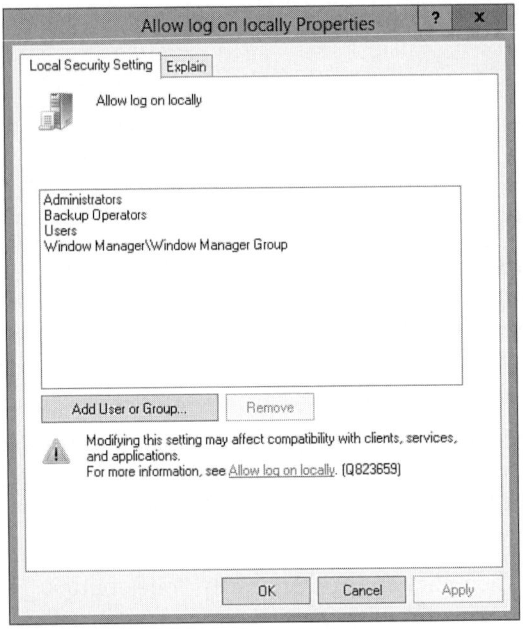

FIGURE 13.1 Restricting logon access.

Security can be tightened further by requiring that when the smart card is removed the user is automatically logged off the console. In this scenario, users insert into the smart card reader a smart card that is physically attached to their person via a chain or string. After entering their PIN, they log on and perform all necessary functions. Upon leaving, they just remove the smart card from the reader, which automatically logs them off the workstation. In this scenario, it is nearly impossible for users to forget to log off because they must physically detach themselves from the computer to leave.

Securing Wireless Networks

Wireless security has always been an issue, but recent trends in the proliferation of wireless networks have made it even more so. Most organizations are shocked to see the kind of damage that can be done to a network by an authorized person being able to connect via a network port. The deployment of wireless networks makes access much easier. An unsavory individual can simply pull up to the parking lot and access an organization's local-area network (LAN) via a laptop computer and a standard wireless card. The standard security employed by many wireless networks, Wi-Fi Protected Access (WPA) is significantly better than past solutions, but is still unsecure, as is any solution using a pre-shared secret or key.

Controlling the network ports and securing network switches are common parts of an organization's security policy. For organizations with deployed wireless networks, similar policies must be created and monitored to ensure the protection of wireless access to internal networks. Deployment of wireless networks protected using network access control with the 802.1x protocol vastly increases the security of the network. Microsoft uses 802.1x to secure its vast wireless network, and Windows Server 2012 fully supports the protocol.

For those organizations without the time or resources to deploy 802.1x, the simple step of placing wireless access points outside the firewall and requiring virtual private network (VPN) access through the firewall can effectively secure the wireless network. Even if trespassers were to break the shared key, they would be connected only to a public network, with no access to internal networks.

Firewall Security

Deployment of an enterprise firewall configuration is a must in any environment that is connected to the Internet. Servers or workstations directly connected to the Internet are prime candidates for hacking. Modern firewall implementations such as Microsoft's Forefront Threat Management Gateway (TMG) 2010 offer advanced configurations, such as web proxying and demilitarized zone (DMZ) configuration, as well. Proper setup and configuration of a firewall in between a Windows Server 2012 network and the Internet is a must.

Using the Integrated Windows Firewall with Advanced Security

Windows Server 2012 includes a vastly improved integrated firewall that is turned on by default in all installations of the product. The firewall, administered from an MMC snap-in shown in Figure 13.2 (Server Manager, Tools menu, Windows Firewall with Advanced Security) gives unprecedented control and security to a server.

Understanding Windows Firewall Integration with Server Manager

The firewall with advanced security is fully integrated with the Server Manager utility and the Add Roles and Features Wizard. For example, if an administrator runs the Add Roles and Features Wizard and chooses to install file services, only then are those ports and protocols that are required for file server access opened on the server.

NOTE

It is instinctual for most administrators to disable software firewalls on servers because they have caused problems with functionality in the past. This is not recommended in Windows Server 2012, however, because the product itself is tightly integrated with its firewall, and the firewall itself provides for a much greater degree of security than earlier versions of Windows Server provided.

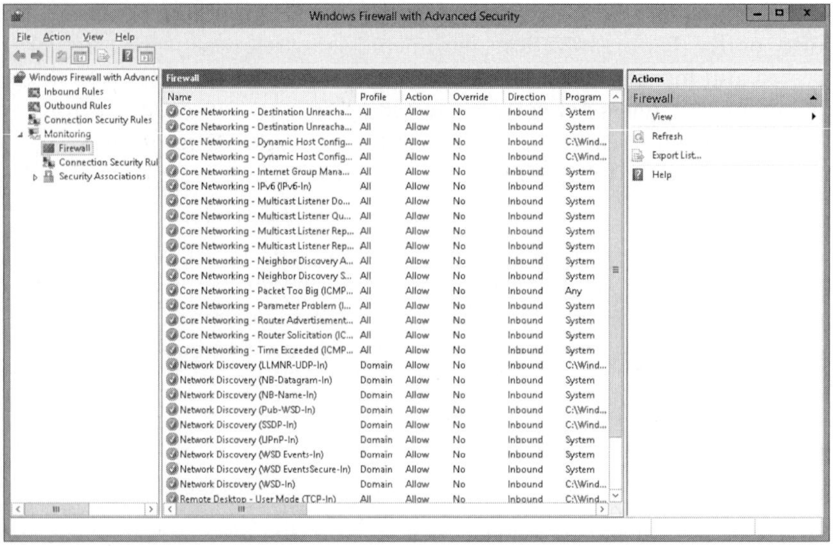

FIGURE 13.2 Monitoring rules with the Windows Firewall with Advanced Security.

Creating Inbound and Outbound Rules on the Windows Firewall

In certain cases, when a third-party application is not integrated with the firewall, or when needing to open specific individual ports, it might become necessary to create firewall rules for individual services to run properly. Both inbound rules, addressing traffic to the server, and outbound rules, addressing how the server can communicate out, can be created. Rules can be created based on the following factors:

- **Program**—A rule can be created that allows a specific program executable access. For example, you can specify that the C:\Program Files\Custom Program\myprogram.exe file has full outbound access when running. The Windows Firewall program will then allow any type of connections made by that program full access. This can be useful in scenarios when a specific application server uses multiple varied ports, but the overall security that the firewall provides is still desired.
- **Port**—Entering a traditional UDP or TCP port into the New Rule Wizard is supported. This covers traditional scenarios such as "We need to open port 8787 on the server."
- **Predefined**—Windows Server also has built-in predefined rules, such as those that allow AD DS, DFS, BITS, HTTP, and many more. The advantage to using a predefined rule is that Microsoft has done all the legwork in advance and so it becomes much easier to allow a specific service. Some predefined rules are not available unless the relevant role or feature are installed.
- **Custom**—The creation of custom rule types not covered in the other categories is also supported.

For example, the following procedure details the creation of an inbound rule to allow a custom application to use TCP port 8787 for inbound communication:

1. Open the Windows Firewall with Advanced Security management console (Server Manager, Tools menu, Windows Firewall with Advanced Security).
2. Click the Inbound Rules node in the node pane.
3. In the Actions pane, click the New Rule link.
4. On the Rule Type page of the New Inbound Rule Wizard, shown in Figure 13.3, select Port to create a rule based on the port, and then click Next to continue.

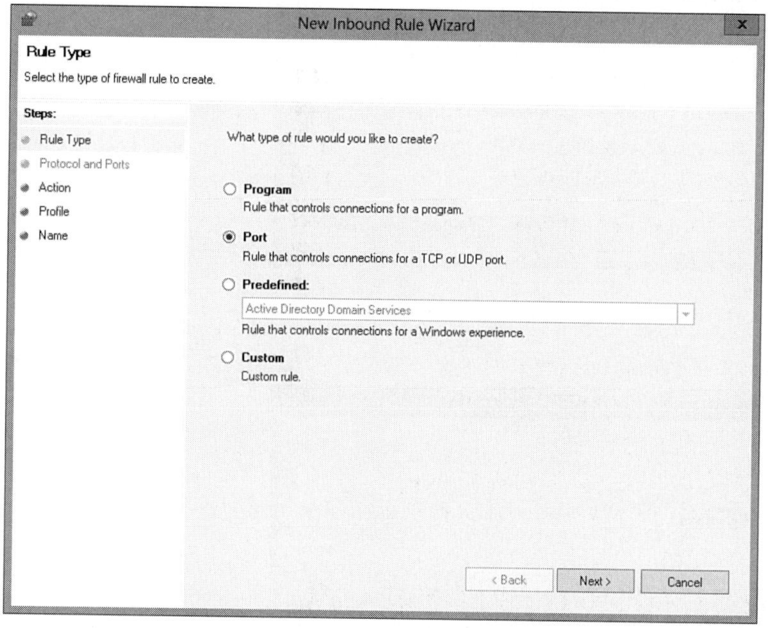

FIGURE 13.3 Creating a rule on the Windows Firewall.

5. On the Protocol and Ports page, shown in Figure 13.4, select TCP, and enter 8787 in the Specific Local Ports field. Click Next to continue.
6. On the Action page, select Allow the Connection, and then click Next.

NOTE

The Action page of the New Inbound Rule Wizard also allows for a rule to be configured that only allows the connection if it is secured using IPsec technologies. For more about IPsec, see Chapter 14, "Securing Data in Transit."

7. On the Profile page, shown in Figure 13.5, check all three check boxes. This enables an administrator to specify that a rule only applies when connected to specific networks. Click Next to continue.
8. Enter a descriptive name for the rule, and then click Finish.

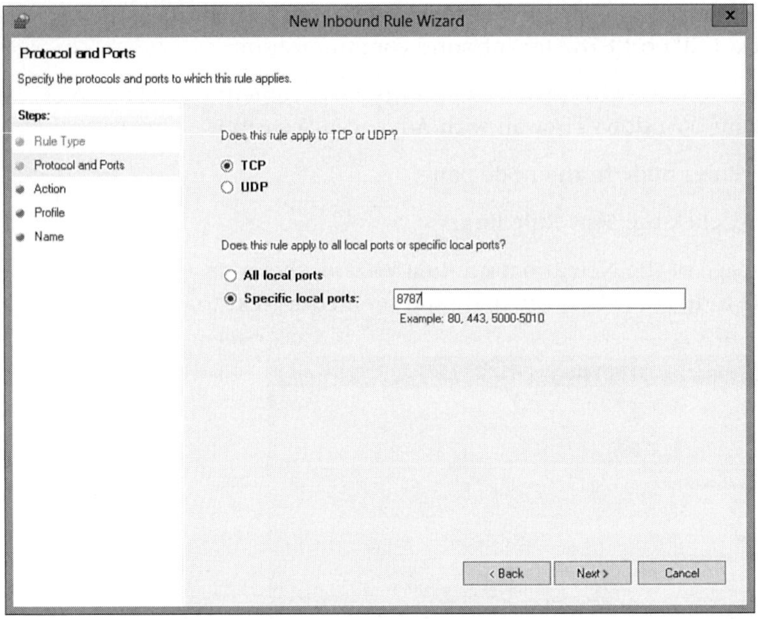

FIGURE 13.4 Entering port information for the firewall rule.

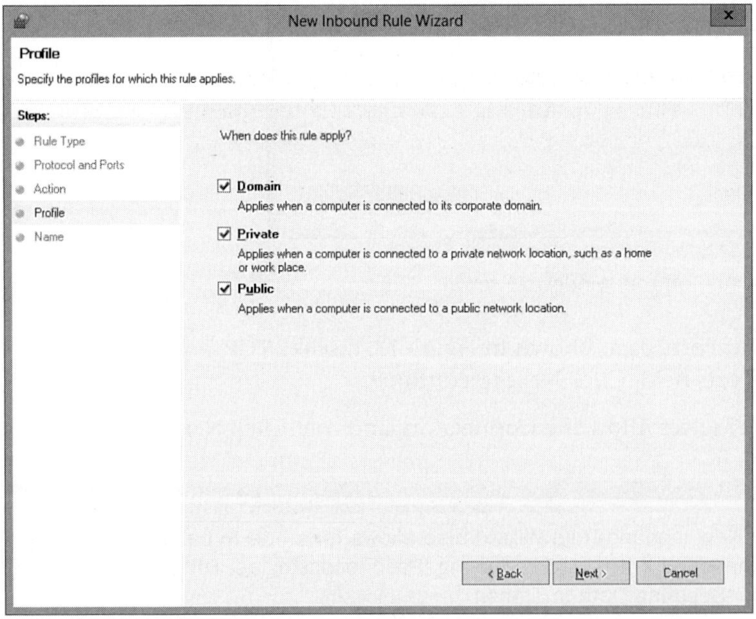

FIGURE 13.5 Specifying the profile of a firewall rule.

Review the rule settings in the Inbound Rules node, shown in Figure 13.6. This allows for a quick-glance view of the rule settings. You can also include a rule in a rule group, which allows for multiple rules to be tied together for easy on/off application.

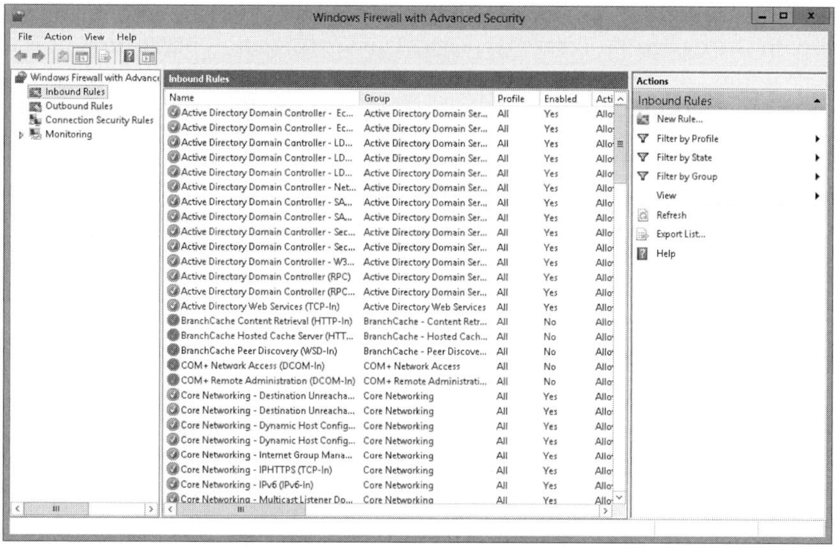

FIGURE 13.6 Viewing the firewall rules.

Using the integrated Windows firewall is no longer just a good idea, it's a vital part of the security of the product. The addition of the ability to define rules based on factors such as scope, profile, IPsec status, and the like further positions the Server OS as one with high levels of integrated security and control.

Hardening Servers

Earlier versions of Windows Server required a great deal of configuration after installation to "harden" the security of the server and ensure that viruses and exploits would not overwhelm or disable the server. The good news with Windows Server 2012 is that, by default, many less commonly used services are turned off. In fact, a fresh installation of Windows Server 2012 only has those services enabled that are vital for the OS to run properly, and everything else must be enabled, typically by adding roles and features using Server Manager. In addition, by default an intelligent firewall is enabled, and only those network services that absolutely needed are allowed through the firewall.

Therefore, in Windows Server 2012, it is important to first define which roles a server will use and then to turn on only those services that are necessary using Server Manager or PowerShell to automate the deployment and configuration of server roles and features.

Defining Server Roles

Depending on the size of an organization, a server might be designated for one or more system roles. Planning the roles deployment is an important and complex exercise that must take into account available hardware, role compatibility, anticipated workloads, a variety of best practice guidelines, and security concerns. One tool that help provide flexibility and scalability in the design process is Hyper-V. The virtualization platform that is now a part of both Windows 8 client and Windows server 2012 provides an opportunity for organizations of every size to provision multiple guests on a small number of physical hosts.

Because any service that is enabled increases the overall risk, it is important to fully define which roles a server will take on so that those services can be properly configured and protected. Although these components can be set up manually, the process of turning on these services is streamlined through the use of Server Manager.

Securing a Server Using Server Manager

With the list of roles that a server will perform in hand, the ideal utility for installing these roles and securing them is the newly renovated Server Manager. By default, if a server is a DNS server but does not provide file and print services, Server Manager not only opens the ports required for DNS, but also blocks any file and print access to the server.

Windows Server 2012 Server Manager, shown in Figure 13.7, allows for individual roles to be installed on a server. After being installed, those roles are enabled, and the proper ports to run those roles are opened on the server.

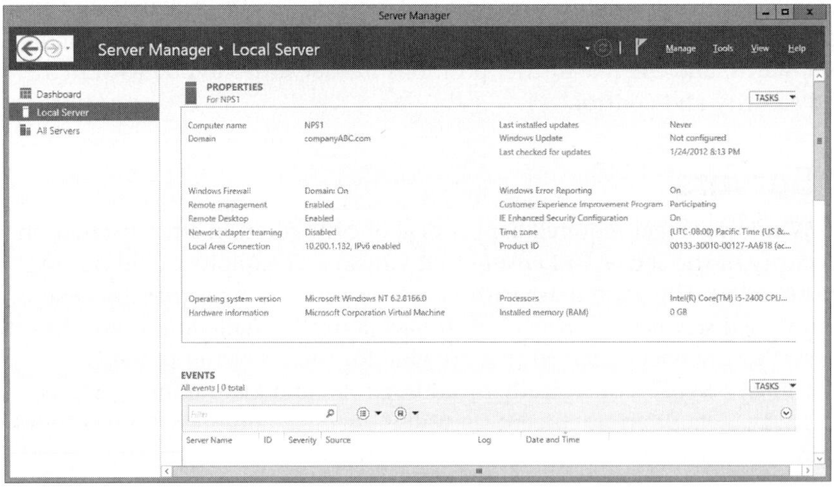

FIGURE 13.7 Server Manager Local Server console.

Reducing Attack Surface

Windows Server 2012 installs with basic functionality and uses the server role management model to ensure that the attack surface of the system is as small as it can be while allowing the system to fulfill its function. Even in that basic functionality, however, there are features that impact attack surface and are not needed for many server environments. Features such as the GUI, Internet Explorer, or .NET applications are features that increase the attack surface of a system and are not always necessary for roles such as a file server or DNS server.

In addition to the familiar full-feature edition, also called the Server Graphical Shell, Windows Server 2012 provides several other minimalistic modes of operation. Each mode sacrifices some functionality to reduce the attack surface of the server. To assist with configuring the various modes of operation, two new features were introduced in Windows Server 2012: the Server Graphical Shell and the Graphical Management Tools and Infrastructure.

Removing the Server Graphical Shell feature transitions the system to the Minimal Server Interface, which doesn't include a desktop or Windows Explorer but still includes PowerShell and a variety of graphical management tools. Some of these can be removed to further reduce the server attack surface.

To reduce the attack surface to a minimum, Windows 2008 introduced the Core Edition of the operating system, available as an option during installation. The Windows Server 2012 version includes some managed code, most importantly PowerShell and a subset of the .NET Framework. A welcome addition to the Windows Server 2012 version of Core Edition is the ability to install the Serve Graphical Shell on the system, converting it to a full interface using the following PowerShell commands:

```
Import-Module Dism
Enable-WindowsOptionalFeature -online -Featurename ServerCore-FullServer,
Server-Gui-Shell,Server-Gui-Mgmt
```

The Core Edition is an excellent fit for several roles, including Hyper-V, Active Directory Domain Services, File Server, Print Server, and more. The Core Edition also represents a highly secure version of the platform that not only reduces the attack surface but also requires less resources and fewer patches and is simple to administer using remote tools and consoles.

AppLocker

A powerful security tool introduced with Windows Server 2008 R2 and expanded in Windows Server 2012, AppLocker is a group policy based component providing an application whitelisting feature set. Application whitelisting restricts software running on the system to a predefined list of allowed software (white list). The configuration and management of the list is based on granular business logic combining filenames, locations, unique hash values, and even digital signatures.

To provide additional support during deployments, AppLocker can be run in audit only mode, recording applications that would be blocked if the policy was enforced. The combination of audit mode, the inherent flexibility of group policies, and the limited set of required applications makes AppLocker a very efficient tool in protecting server against current and future threats.

Deploying AppLocker involves five steps:

1. Group servers by workload.
2. Create a GPO and scope to a server type.
3. Configure AppLocker rules and set to audit mode.
4. Monitor and review AppLocker audit logs.
5. Adjust rules and enable enforcement mode.

Each step is discussed in detail in the following sections.

Grouping Servers by Workload

Servers must be grouped to allow scoping of group policy objects to servers of a specific workload (file, print, SQL, Exchange, and so on). Some workload types, such as Exchange or Remote Desktop Services servers are at times grouped by OU, but using universal security groups is more flexible and easier to implement.

To support dynamic server environments, an automated script can be created to add the server to the correct group automatically based on deployed roles. Such a script could be attached to a virtual management and deployment platform such as System Center Virtual Machine Manager 2012 or an operational monitoring solution such as System Center Operations Manager 2012.

Creating a GPO Scoped to a Server Type

Using the groups created previously, follow this process to create a new GPO that is scoped only to a specific server group:

1. From the Server Manager Tools menu, run Group Policy Management. (If needed, the tools can be installed from the features list.)
2. Expand the nodes within the console until the servers OU is available. Right-click the servers OU and select Create a GPO in This Domain, and Link It Here.
3. Enter a name for the new GPO, such as AppLocker for File Servers, and then click OK.
4. Expand the OU and select the newly created GPO.
5. Open the Scope tab, and in the Security Filtering section, remove Authenticated Users from the delegate list.
6. Click Add and enter the name of the server group being configured (for instance, ABC_FileServers) and click OK.

Figure 13.8 shows the result.

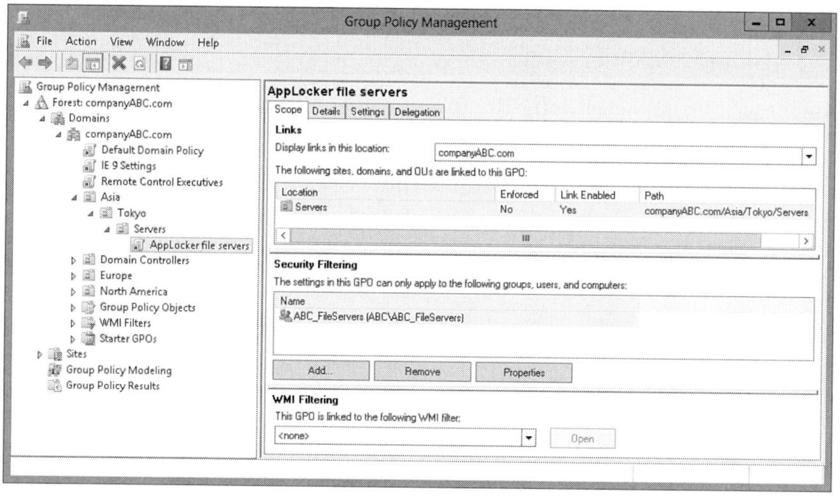

FIGURE 13.8 Scoping the AppLocker GPO.

Configuring AppLocker Rules for Audit Mode

After the GPO has been created using the steps outlined previously, the correct AppLocker policy must be configured as follows:

1. Within the Group Policy Management console, right-click the newly created AppLocker policy and select Edit.
2. Navigate to Computer Configuration\Policies\Windows Settings\Security Settings\Application Control Policies\AppLocker.
3. Under the AppLocker container, four containers correspond to the four different rule types supported by AppLocker. Select the appropriate container, and then right-click it and select one of the following options:
   - **Create New Rule**—The first and most commonly used option allows the manual configuration of a rule.
   - **Automatically Generate Rules**—A wizard-based configuration import based on the existing configuration or files and folders.
   - **Create Default Rules**—A default set of rules to allow access to commonly used files such as those in the Windows or Program Files folder.

These options can be used to create allow or deny rules for specific users or group on selected files or folders based on digital signature (publisher, product, filename, or version), filename, or file hash. The rules can be configured in one of these four categories:

- **Executable rules**—These rules can allow or deny specific executables (*.EXE and *.COM) or folders.
- **Windows Installer rules**—These rules allow or deny the use of a specific windows installer files (*.MSI and *.MSP) or folders.
- **Script rules**—These rules allow or deny the use of a specific windows installer files (*.PS1, *.BAT, *.JS, *.CMD and *.VBS).
- **AppX rules (Packaged app rules)**—These rules allow or deny the use of specific Windows Metro-based AppX packages based on digital signature only.

To configure audit mode, follow these steps:

1. Within the Group Policy Management Editor, right-click the AppLocker container and select Properties.
2. On the Enforcement tab, check the check boxes to enable the requires rule types.
3. For each selected rule type, extend the pull-down list and select the Audit Only option.

And finally, to start the Application Identity service on all scoped servers, follow these steps:

1. Within the Group Policy Management Editor, navigate to Computer Configuration\Policies\Windows Settings\Security Settings\System Services
2. Double-click the Application Identity service and check Define This Policy Setting check box.
3. Set the startup mode to Automatic and click OK.

NOTE

In many environments, there are a large variety of server workloads, and many servers will end up with a unique AppLocker ruleset. As a result, it can be tempting to configure AppLocker rules using the local policy. This approach should be reserved for servers that are not members of a domain because this approach is more difficult to manage, nearly impossible to audit, and scales poorly.

Monitoring and Reviewing AppLocker Audit Logs

With the rules running in audit mode, the server's event logs should be reviewed to confirm that required applications are not within the configuration of the policy before activating enforcement.

AppLocker events appear in a set of dedicated event logs based on the rule types used. You can find all the event logs in Event Viewer under Applications and Services Logs\Microsoft\Windows\AppLocker. Event IDs 8002–8007 in each event log should provide information about file that were allowed (IDs 8002 and 8005) and those that were allowed but would have been blocked (8003 and 8006), as shown in Figure 13.9.

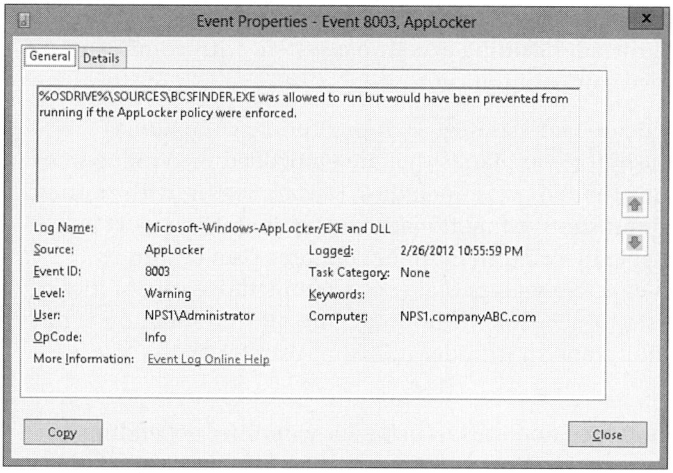

FIGURE 13.9 Auditing AppLocker rulesets.

Adjusting Rules and Enabling Enforcement Mode

The final step in the implementation is to revise the rules as necessary based on the monitor phase and enable enforcement mode.

Based on the audit logs reviewed in the previous phase, rules should be modified to include necessary files, expand allowed digital certificates, or deny access to untrusted sources. A thorough testing cycle should follow each rule change to confirm the desired result.

When the ruleset is finalized, the following process activates enforcement for the current configuration:

1. Within the Group Policy Management Editor, right-click the AppLocker container and select Properties.

2. On the Enforcement tab, for each selected rule type, extend the pull-down list and select the Enforce Rules option.

NOTE

You can use the Advanced tab to activate the DLL rule collection. This feature can have a significant impact on performance and can be very complex to configure correctly. As a result, DLL protection should be used only when necessary and after the effects have been understood and tested.

Using Administration-Only Accounts with Run As

High-privilege administration accounts represent a security challenge. The use of these accounts as primary network accounts for routine tasks and workstation login greatly increases the challenge. The potential damage of an administrator making a mistake while performing routine tasks or of an intruder gaining access to a system with administrative credentials that was left unattended can be significant.

For this reason, it is wise to consider a logon strategy that incorporates the Run as Different User and Run as Administrator commands that are embedded in Windows Server 2012. Essentially, this means that all users, including IT staff, log on with restricted, standard user accounts. When administrative functionality is required, IT support personnel can invoke the tool or executable by using the Run as Different User or Run as Administrator commands, which effectively gives that tool administrative capabilities. If an administrator leaves a workstation console without logging off, the situation is not critical because the console will not grant an intruder full administrator access to the network.

When using a two account logon model, application behavior will differ depending on application security requirements:

Applications that support User Account Control (UAC) prompt the user for credentials when requiring elevation.

UAC-aware applications that do not always require elevation can be executed in elevated mode by right-clicking the application and selecting Run as Administrator.

Applications that do not support UAC or that require elevated network credentials can be executed by holding down the Shift key, right-clicking the application, and selecting Run as Different User.

And, of course, applications that do not require elevation will execute as always.

The following example illustrates how to invoke the Computer Management console using the Run as Different User command from the GUI:

1. Open the Metro interface and start to type the name of the program **Computer Management**.
2. When the search result appears, right-click it, and then click the Advanced button at the bottom of the screen.
3. Select Open File Location, and then click the Computer Management tool icon.
4. Hold down the Shift key, right-click Computer Management in the program list, and then choose Run as Different User.
5. In the Windows Security dialog box, choose the credentials under which you want to run the program, and then click OK.

In addition to the manual method of using Run as Different User, an administrator's desktop can be configured to have each shortcut automatically run as a computer administrator. For example, the Active Directory Users and Computers MMC snap-in can be set to permanently run with elevated privileges as follows:

1. Open the Metro interface and start to type the name of the program **Active Directory Users and Computers**.
2. When the search result appears, right-click it, and then click the Advanced button at the bottom of the screen.
3. Select Open File Location, right-click the Computer Management tool icon, and select Properties.
4. On the Shortcut tab, click the Advanced button.
5. Check the Run as Administrator check box, as shown in Figure 13.10, and click OK twice to save the settings.

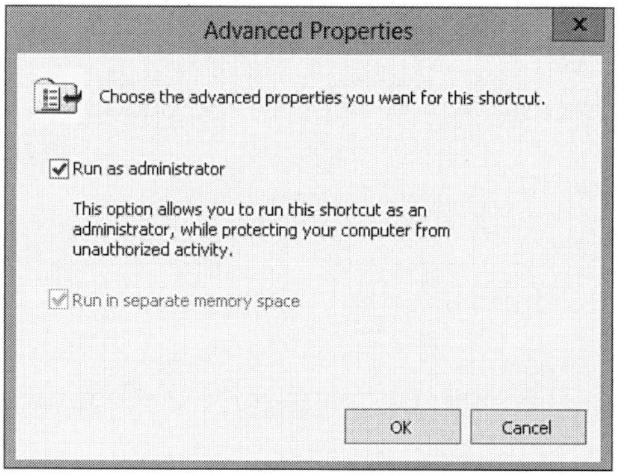

FIGURE 13.10 Running a shortcut with administrator privileges.

NOTE

Ironically, administrative access is sometimes required to be able to change some of the shortcut properties. Consequently, you might need to log on as a user with higher privileges to set up the shortcuts on other users' profiles.

Examining File-Level Security

Files secured on Windows Server 2012 are only as secure as the permissions that are set on them. Subsequently, it is good to know that Windows Server 2012 does not grant the Everyone group full control over share-level and NTFS-level permissions. In addition, critical operating system files and directories are secured to disallow their unauthorized use.

Despite the overall improvements made, a complete understanding of file-level security is recommended to ensure that the file-level security of a server is not neglected, especially for those servers hosting the file server role.

Understanding File System Security

Windows Server 2012 introduced a new file system, ReFS, or Resilient File System. The file system is backward compatible with NTFS. In fact, because the focus of the updated file system is data integrity, scalability, reliability, and ease of management, security mechanisms are largely unchanged from the earlier version of the product.

Each object that is referenced in ReFS, which includes files and folders, is marked by an access control list (ACL) that physically limits who can and cannot access a resource. File and folder permissions utilize this concept to strictly control read, write, and other types of access on files.

File servers should make judicious use of file-level and folder-level permissions, and all directories should have their permissions audited to determine whether there are any unexpected entries or unprotected resources in the permission set. Changing ReFS permissions in Windows Server 2012 is a straightforward process. Just follow these steps:

1. Right-click the folder or file onto which the security will be applied, and choose Properties.
2. Open the Security tab.
3. Click the Advanced button.
4. Click the Disable Inheritance button.
5. Click Remove All Inherited Permissions from This Object when prompted about the application of parent permissions.
6. While you're in the Advanced Security Settings dialog box, use the Add button to give access to the groups/users who need access to the files or folders.
7. Check the Replace All Child Object Permissions with Inheritable Permissions from This Object check box, as shown in Figure 13.11, and then click OK.
8. When prompted about replacing security on child objects, click Yes to replace child object security and continue.
9. Click OK and then click OK again to close the property pages.

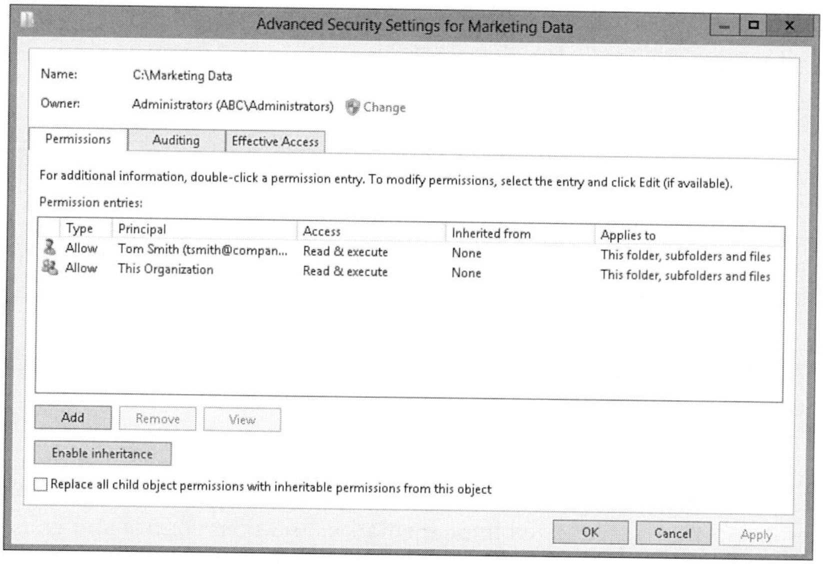

FIGURE 13.11 Setting NTFS permissions.

Dynamic Access Control

A more modern approach to managing file system permissions was introduced in Windows Server 8. Dynamic access control brings a new format to ACLs on files and folders, one that can include expressions. The expressions are based on three components:

- **User/device claims**—These properties of users and devices are stored in the token, making them as fast to verify as group membership. The properties can represent any claims that the user or device make about themselves. For example:

  User.Department = "Human Resources"

  User.Role = "Executive"

  Device.Location = "Los Angeles"

  Device.Type = "Desktop"

- **Resource properties**—Specific properties associated with protected resources (files and folders), typically used to classify the data. For example:

  Resource.Sensitivity = "High"

  Resource.Location = "Los Angeles"

- **Permissions**—The familiar permissions available in standard ACLs, including whether the entry is an allow or a deny.

A resulting access policy might look like this:

```
Apply To: $Resource.Sensitivity="High" | Allow Read/Write | If
{$User.Role = "Executive"} and {$Device.Type = "Desktop"}
```

The use of dynamic access control requires an initial investment in data classification and access validation. For many organizations, this effort has already begun because of regulatory requirements. The result is a structure that reduces administration, improves overall security, and facilitates auditing and oversight. For more information about dynamic access control, see Chapter 28, "File System Management and Fault Tolerance."

Examining Share-Level Security

Most data on Windows file servers is accessed using a share. The share is a network alias assigned to a folder (for example, \\file\marketing). Shares can also be assigned security settings for access control. These share-level permissions are a legacy component left over from legacy file systems that did not support file and folder permissions (for example, FAT, FAT32). As a result, they are an outdated implementation and poor control and granularity. In many situations, share permissions only serve to make troubleshooting more complex, and data is secured with file-level permissions only. However, for more sensitive systems or shares, it may be prudent to use both layers of protection in case of an error in configuration that removes a layer of security.

Auditing File Access

A good practice for file-level security is to set up auditing on a particular server, directory, or file. Auditing on ReFS volumes enables administrators to be notified of who is accessing, or attempting to access, a particular directory. For example, it might be wise to audit access to a critical network share, such as a finance folder, to determine whether anyone is attempting to access restricted information.

NOTE

Audit entries are another example of security settings that can be automatically set via security templates in Windows Server 2012. It is wise to consider the use of security templates to more effectively control audit settings.

The following steps illustrate how to set up simple auditing on a folder in Windows Server 2012:

1. Right-click the folder or file onto which the auditing will be applied, and choose Properties.
2. Open the Security tab.
3. Click the Advanced button.
4. Open the Auditing tab.

5. Using the Add button, enter all users and groups that will be audited. If you're auditing all users, enter the Everyone group.

6. On the Auditing property page, select all types of access that will be audited. If you're auditing for all success and failure attempts, select all the options, as indicated in Figure 13.12.

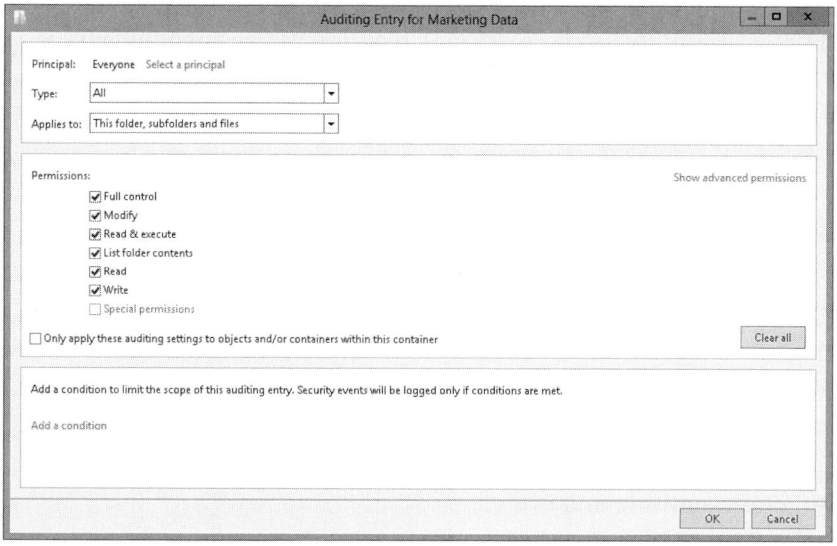

FIGURE 13.12 Configuring file auditing.

7. Click OK to apply the settings.

8. Click OK twice to save the settings.

NOTE

An effective way of catching "snoops" in the act is to create serious-looking shares on the network, such as Financial Statements, Root Info, or similar such shares, and audit access to those folders. This mechanism, known as a honeypot, has been successfully used to identify internal (or external) saboteurs before they could do some serious damage.

Encrypting Files with the Encrypting File System

Windows Server 2012 continues support for the Encrypting File System (EFS), a method of scrambling the contents of files to make them unintelligible to unauthorized users. EFS has proven to be valuable for organizations that desire to keep proprietary data, especially those stored on laptops, out of the wrong hands. A more comprehensive approach to client encryption is with BitLocker Drive Encryption, which encrypts all files on the entire hard drive, with the exception of a few files required for startup.

BitLocker for Servers

BitLocker Drive Encryption was introduced with Windows Vista and continued to mature and improve with the release of Windows 7 and now Windows 2012. In fact, the current release includes several features that make it a great candidate for servers. Providing an additional layer of physical security can be a welcome tool in sensitive environments or ad hoc facilities.

The following features of BitLocker should be of interest to server and security administrators:

- **Support for BitLocker for clustered disks**—Including failover cluster disks and cluster shared volumes.
- **Faster provisioning**—Faster initial encryption with option to encrypt used disk space only, faster deployment by integrating encrypted volumes into the imaging process.
- **Network unlock**—Used in conjunction with TPM, the server is automatically unlocked on the corporate network but requires a PIN when not connected to the corporate network.
- **Improved BitLocker auditing and events.**

For more information about BitLocker, including deployment instructions and best practices, see Chapter 32, "Optimizing Windows 2012 for Branch Office Communications."

Malware and Backup Protection

In an unsecure world, a server is only as secure as the software that runs on it. Windows Server 2012 is the most secure Windows yet, and includes many built-in mechanisms to keep a server secure. All the protection mechanisms are useless, however, if malicious or inadvertent action results in malware being installed on the server. Therefore, implementing measures to protect the server from malware is a necessity.

Well-crafted security policies must also account and plan for eventual security breaches. Implementing effective and secured backup and recovery procedures is a key component in recovering from an incident and protecting data.

Antivirus Precautions

Viruses might be one of the most dangerous threats faced by servers. Many viruses are written to specifically exploit key vulnerabilities that are present in server infrastructure. Others infect files that might be held on a server, spreading the infection to clients who download files. Consequently, it is extremely important to consider the use of an enterprise antivirus solution on all file servers in a network. All the major antivirus manufacturers include robust file-level scanners, and administrators should consider using them.

Microsoft itself has released a line of antivirus products with tight integration with the Windows Server line. This is part of the Forefront line of security products. An advantage to using the Forefront product suite is that it uses five antivirus engines all running at the same time. This way, if one of the engines does not catch a virus or is not updated quickly enough, there is a good chance that one of the other vendors' engines will detect the virus. You can find more information about the Forefront line at http://www.microsoft.com/forefront.

An aggressive plan should be in place to keep antivirus patterns and engines up-to-date. Because virus outbreaks can wreak havoc worldwide in a matter of hours, rather than days, it is wise to have servers check for updates at least daily.

Trusted Boot Architecture with Secure Boot, AM Preloading, and Measured Boot

A new set of features, collectively called the Trusted Boot Architecture, or Platform Integrity Architecture, is being introduced with Windows Server 2012. These features do not require any action on behalf of the administrator but provide a significant improvement in protecting the server against malware, especially low-level threats such as rootkits and bootkits.

The following security features are now part of every Windows Server 2012 (and Windows 8 Client) installation:

- **Secure boot**—The OS firmware will only boot using a signed trusted loader. The loader requires signature verification from later components. This additional check should target boot kits trying to introduce a payload into the boot process.
- **Anti-Malware preboot**—Compatible anti-malware software is loaded first by the OS loader before any third-party drivers and many malware packages. As with other boot components, the anti-malware driver must be signed and trusted.
- **Measured boot**—Throughout the secure boot process, client status and metrics are recorded to the TPM. The anti-malware client can access this record and use it to influence the boot process and to upload the data to an attestation server for analysis.

Deploying Backup Security

Although the need for a backup strategy might seem obvious to most people, it is often surprising to find out how inadequately prepared many organizations are with regard to their backups. All too often, a company will discover that it is very easy to back up a server but often more difficult to restore. In addition to disaster recovery issues, the issue of backup security is often neglected.

File server backups require that an authenticated user account with the proper privileges copy data to a storage mechanism. This requirement ensures that not just anyone can back up an environment and run off with the tape. Keeping this point in mind, the tapes that contain server backups should be protected with the same caution given to the server itself. All too often, a big pile of server backup tapes is left out on unsecured desks, and there is often no mechanism in place to account for how many tapes are in which location. Implementing a strict tape retention and verification procedure is, subsequently, a must.

Using Windows Server Update Services

One of the main drawbacks to Windows security has been the difficulty in keeping servers and workstations up-to-date with the latest security fixes. For example, the security fix for the Index Server component of Internet Information Services (IIS) was available for more than a month before the Code Red and Nimbda viruses erupted onto the scene. If the deployed web servers had downloaded the patch, they would not have been affected. The main reason that the vast majority of the deployed servers were not updated was that keeping servers and workstations up-to-date with the latest security patches was an extremely manual and time-consuming process. For this reason, a streamlined approach to security patch application was required and realized with the formulation of Windows Server Update Services (WSUS).

Understanding the Background of WSUS: Windows Update

In response to the original concerns about the difficulty in keeping computers properly patched, Microsoft made available a centralized website called Windows Update to which clients could connect, download security patches, and install those patches. Invoking the Windows Update web page remotely installed an executable, which ran a test to see which hotfixes had been applied and which were needed, based on the Microsoft components installed on the machine. Those that were not applied were offered up for download, and users could easily install these patches.

Windows Update streamlined the security patch verification and installation process, but the major drawback was that it required a manual effort to go up to the server every few days or weeks and check for updates. A more efficient, automated process was required.

Deploying the Automatic Updates Client

The Automatic Updates client was developed to automate the installation of security fixes and patches and to give users the option to automatically "drizzle" patches across the Internet to the local computer for installation. Drizzling, also known as Background Intelligent Transfer Service (BITS), is a process in which a computer intelligently utilizes unused network bandwidth to download files to the machine. Because only unused bandwidth is used, there is no perceived effect on the network client itself.

All currently supported versions of Microsoft clients include the Automatic Updates client built in to the OS.

Understanding the Development of Windows Server Update Services

The Windows Update website and the associated client provided for the needs of most home users and some small offices. However, large organizations, concerned about the bandwidth effects of hundreds of machines downloading large numbers of updates over the Internet, often disabled this service or discouraged its use. These organizations often had a serious need for Windows Update's capabilities. This fact led to the development of Software Update Services (SUS), which was later improved into the new product, Windows Server Update Services (WSUS).

WSUS started as a free download from Microsoft that effectively gives organizations their own, independent version of the Windows Update server. The latest version of WSUS is integrated into the operating system and deployed using System Manager. Clients connect to a central intranet WSUS server for all their security patches and updates.

WSUS is not considered to be a replacement technology for existing software deployment solutions such as System Center Configuration Manager (SCCM), but rather it is envisioned as a solution for all organizations from small businesses to large enterprises to take control over the fast deployment of security patches as they become available. It also offers a myriad of reports for administrators.

Examining WSUS Prerequisites

Deploying WSUS on a dedicated server is preferable, but it can also be deployed on a Windows Server 2012 server that is running other tasks, as long as that server is running IIS. The following list details the software requirement for WSUS:

- Internet Information Services (IIS)
- Background Intelligent Transfer Service (BITS)
- Windows Internal Database role or SQL Server 2005 (or later) installed locally or on a remote server
- Microsoft .NET Framework 2.0 or later

Installing WSUS on a Windows Server 2012 Server

The installation of WSUS is very easy because it is installed as a server role from Server Manager. The guided setup installs WSUS and any required components.

To complete the initial installation of WSUS, follow these steps:

1. Launch Server Manager.
2. From the Manage menu, select Add Roles and Features to start the wizard.
3. Click Next three times.
4. Select Windows Server Update Services, and click Next.

5. The Add Role Services and Features Required for Windows Server Update Services window prompts for additional components to install, if necessary. Required components are the Web Server (IIS) web server and management tools, the Windows Process Activation Service, and the .NET Framework. Click Add Features to continue.
6. Click Next twice.
7. Read the Introduction to Web Server (IIS) overview, and click Next.
8. Click Next to select the default role services to install for Web Server (IIS).
9. Read the Introduction to Windows Server Update Services overview, and click Next.
10. Leave the default role services to install using Windows Internal Database. To install using an existing SQL server installation, remove the WID Database role server and select the Database role service. Click Next.
11. Enter a local disk location for the WSUS updates themselves and click Next.
12. Read the summary of installation selections, and click Install.
13. When the installation completes, click the Launch Post-Installation Tasks link.

To complete the initial configuration for WSUS, follow these steps:

1. From the Tools menu in Server Manager, launch Windows Server Update Services. This launches the Configuration Wizard.
2. Click Next past the initial page and past the Update Improvement Program page.
3. Select the default upstream configuration, which is to obtain data directly from Microsoft servers. Click Next.
4. Complete the proxy configuration if necessary and click Next.
5. Click the Start Connecting button to have the Configuration Wizard download data required for the configuration process. Click Next when the initial download is complete.
6. Select required languages for the patch. Keep in mind that selecting many languages can greatly increases the time and storage requirements for the update system and processes. It is therefore recommended to install only the required languages.
7. Select the products for which you want updates, as shown in Figure 13.13, and click Next.
8. Select the classifications of updates you want to download, and then click Next.
9. Configure the schedule that you want WSUS to synchronize with the Microsoft Update servers or select Synchronize Manually. Click Next.
10. Ensure that Begin Initial Synchronization is selected, and then click Finish.
11. Review the installation results and click Close.

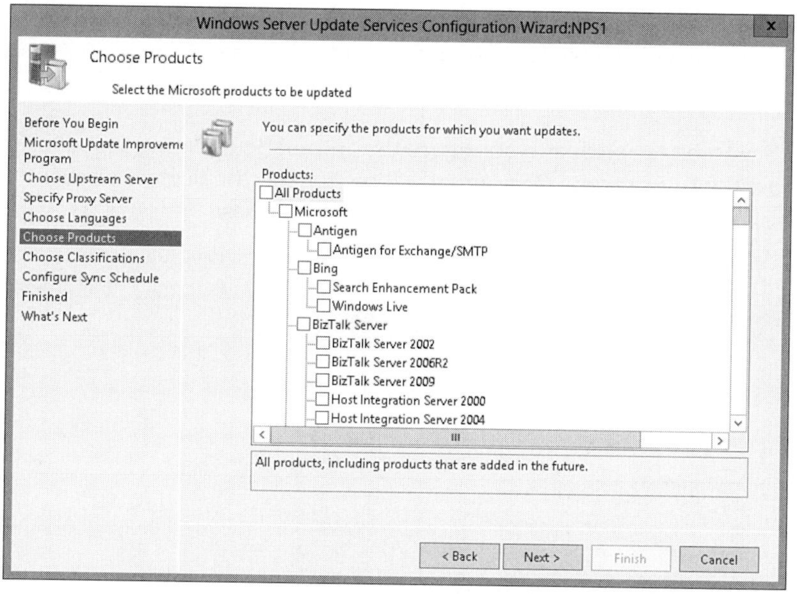

FIGURE 13.13 Choose initial products to be updated by WSUS.

WSUS administration is performed from the Update Services management console. This console is the main location for all configuration settings for WSUS and is the sole administrative console. You can access it from Server Manager, Tools menu, Windows Server Update Services.

Automatically Configuring Clients via Group Policy

The configuration of the Automatic Updates client included with all current versions of Windows can be streamlined by using a group policy in an Active Directory environment. Windows Server 2003 or later domain controllers automatically contain the proper Windows Update Group Policy extension, and a group policy can be defined by following these steps:

1. Open Group Policy Management using the Tools menu in Server Manager.
2. Navigate to the organizational unit that will have the group policy applied, right-click the name of the OU, and choose Create a GPO in This Domain, and Link It Here.
3. Enter a name for the GPO, such as WSUS GPO. You also have the option to start from the settings of an existing GPO. Click OK.
4. Right-click the newly created GPO, and select Edit to invoke the Group Policy Management Editor.

5. Expand the Group Policy Management Editor to Computer Configuration\Policies\Administrative Templates\Windows Components\Windows Update.
6. Double-click the Configure Automatic Updates setting.
7. Set the group policy to be enabled, and configure the automatic updating sequence as desired. The three options given—2, 3, and 4—allow for specific degrees of client intervention. For automatic download without installation, choose option 3, as shown in Figure 13.14.

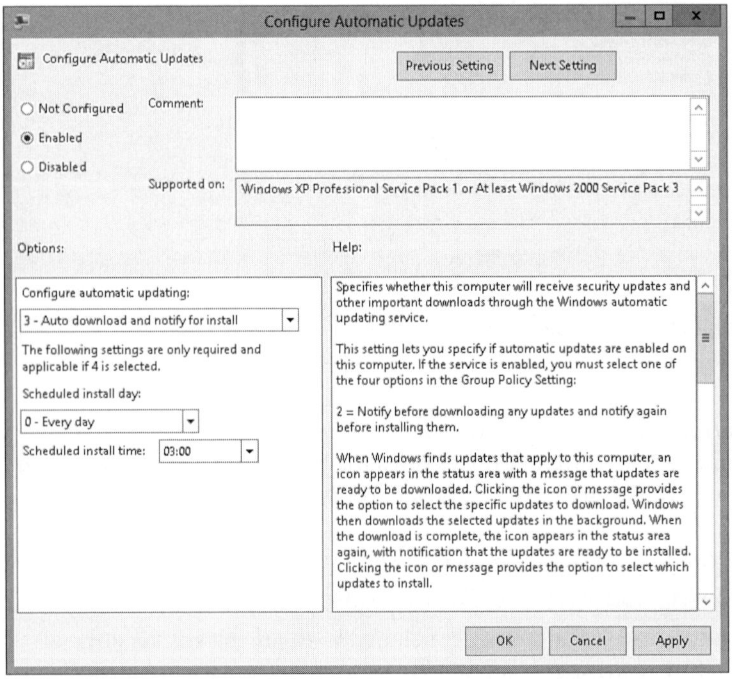

FIGURE 13.14 Configuring Windows Update Group Policy settings.

8. Schedule the interval that updates will be installed, bearing in mind that some updates require reboots.
9. Click Next Setting to configure more options.
10. Click Enabled to specify the web location of the WSUS server. Entering the fully qualified domain name of the server is recommended. Enter both settings (usually the same server), and click OK to save the Group Policy settings. Click Next Setting.

NOTE

Organizations that choose to use a custom web IIS website are required to use port 8530 for client access to WSUS. In this case, enter the web location with the port number, such as http://sfwsus.companyabc.com:8530, for both settings.

11. Enter how often the client checks for updates, and then click Next Setting.
12. Review the remaining option settings and configure as desired. Click OK when you have finished.
13. Repeat the procedure for any additional organizational units. (The same group policy can also be linked in more than one location.)

NOTE

Organizations that do not use Active Directory or group policies have to manually configure each client's settings to include the location of the WSUS server. This can be done through a local policy or manually through Registry settings, as defined in the WSUS Help.

Deploying Security Patches with WSUS

Depending on the settings chosen by the group policy or the Registry, the clients that are managed by WSUS automatically download updates throughout the day and install them at a specified time. Some computers might be configured to allow for local interaction, scheduling proper times for the installation to take place and prompting for "drizzle" downloading.

Clients that are configured to use WSUS are not prompted to configure their Automatic Update settings, and they are grayed out to prevent any changes from occurring. Users without local administrative access cannot make any changes to the installation schedule, although local admin users can postpone forced installs.

NOTE

Generally, it is good practice to allow servers to control the download and installation schedule, but to force clients to do both automatically. Depending on the political climate of an organization, this might or might not be a possibility.

Summary

Out of the box, Windows Server 2012 is by far the most secure Windows yet. Increased security emphasis through the Trustworthy Computing initiative helps to increase overall server security by disabling unnecessary services and locking out file-level permissions by default. In addition to the standard features, advanced options in Windows Server 2012, such as the integrated intelligent firewall, AppLocker, and dynamic access control enable administrators to add multiple layers of security to servers, further protecting them from attacks and vulnerabilities. In addition, the automatic updating capabilities of tools such as Windows Server Update Services give organizations an edge in protecting servers and workstations from constantly changing security threats.

Best Practices

The following are best practices from this chapter:

- Physically secure servers behind locked doors, in a controlled-access environment.
- Apply security in layers.
- Use the Server Roles and Features Wizard for turning on server roles and having them automatically secured.
- Use the integrated Windows Firewall for enhanced security, and only open ports or allow protocols when necessary.
- Use both inbound and outbound firewall rules to limit the exposure a compromised server would have.
- Reduce server attack surface by removing the server graphical shell and using Core Edition.
- Use the Run as Administrator command when administrative access is required instead of logging on as an administrator.
- Deploy AppLocker for as many servers as possible.
- Configure AppLocker using digital signature-based rules.
- Consider a honeypot solution by creating serious-looking shares on the network, such as Financial Statements, Root Info, or similar such shares, and audit access to those folders to identify internal (or external) saboteurs before they can do some serious damage.
- Plan to run the initial synchronization of WSUS over a weekend, beginning the download on Friday evening.
- Test and approve WSUS patches before deploying them to production, either manually or through a process of setting up a pilot WSUS server and a production WSUS server.

CHAPTER 14

Securing Data in Transit

IN THIS CHAPTER

- Introduction to Securing Data in Transit with Windows Server 2012
- Deploying a Public Key Infrastructure with Windows Server 2012
- Understanding Active Directory Certificate Services in Windows Server 2012
- AD DS Rights Management Services
- Using IPsec Encryption with Windows Server 2012

In the past, networks were closed environments, insulated from each other and accessible only on internal segments. Data usage was limited to each network and rarely shared across untrusted networks. Over time, a need developed to share information between these networks, and connections were established to transmit data from network to network. The transmission of this information often crosses untrusted networks such as the Internet and was originally insecure. As a result, if the information was intercepted, it could easily be read or modified by unauthorized persons. The need to secure this information during transit was subsequently made a priority and became a critical component of network and data infrastructures.

Over time, the technology used to keep this information safe evolved along with the technology available to exploit and obtain unauthorized access to data. Despite these threats, intelligent design and configuration of secure data transport solutions using Windows Server 2012 greatly increase the security of a network. In many cases, they are absolutely required, especially for data sent across uncontrolled network segments, such as the Internet.

This chapter focuses on the mechanisms that exist to protect and encrypt information sent between computers on a network. New and improved data transport security features in Windows Server 2012 are highlighted, and sample situations are detailed. IPsec, public key infrastructure (PKI), and virtual private network (VPN) use is outlined and illustrated. In addition, specific server functionality, such as that provided by Windows Server 2012 Active Directory Certificate Services (AD CS) and Active Directory Rights Management Services (AD RMS), is outlined.

Introduction to Securing Data in Transit in Windows Server 2012

Securing data in transit refers to preventing unauthorized access to data as part of the communications between client and server and between servers. In addition to physical security and network-level security, the implementation of security at the data transit layer is yet another level of security important in the design and implementation of a protected network environment.

The Need for Another Layer of Security

The very nature of interconnected networks requires that all information be sent in a format that can easily be intercepted by any client on a physical network segment. The data must be organized in a structured, common way so that the destination server can translate it into the proper information. This simplicity also gives rise to security problems, however, because intercepted data can easily be misused if it falls into the wrong hands.

The need to make information unusable if intercepted is the basis for all transit-level encryption. Considerable effort goes into both sides of this equation: Security specialists develop schemes to encrypt and disguise data, and hackers and other security specialists develop ways to forcefully decrypt and intercept data. The good news is that encryption technology has developed to the point that properly configured environments can secure their data with a great deal of success, as long as the proper tools are used. Windows Server 2012 offers much in the realm of transit security, and deploying some or many of the technologies available is highly recommended to properly secure important data.

Modern businesses and the technology that supports them have also created a diverse group of users and entities which interact with each system and are trusted to varying degrees. The security layer that protects network data presents some challenges in such a nuanced environment. An addition layer of tools that are flexible, dynamic, and can protect data based on content and context is required.

Deploying Security Through Multiple Layers of Defense

Because even the most secure infrastructures are subject to vulnerabilities, deploying multiple layers of security on critical network data is recommended. If a single layer of security is compromised, the intruder must bypass the second or even third level of security to gain access to the vital data. For example, relying on a complex 256-bit "unbreakable" encryption scheme is worthless if an intruder simply uses social engineering to acquire the password or PIN from a validated user. Putting in a second or third layer of security, in addition to the first one, makes it that much more difficult for intruders to break through all layers.

Securing data in transit with Windows Server 2012 uses multiple levels of authentication, encryption, and authorization to provide for an enhanced degree of security on a network. The configuration capabilities supplied with Windows Server 2012 allow for the establishment of several layers of transport-level security focused on protecting the confidentiality and integrity of the data.

NOTE

Security through multiple layers of defense is not a new concept, but is rather adapted from military strategy, which rightly holds that multiple lines of defense are better than one.

Understanding Encryption Basics

Encryption, simply defined, is the process of taking intelligible information and scrambling it so as to make it unintelligible for anyone except the user or computer that is the destination of this information. Without going into too much detail on the exact methods of encrypting data, the important point to understand is that proper encryption allows this data to travel across unsecured networks, such as the Internet, and be translated only by the designated destination. If packets of properly encrypted information are intercepted, they are worthless because the information is garbled. All mechanisms described in this chapter use some form of encryption to secure the contents of the data sent.

Deploying a Public Key Infrastructure with Windows Server 2012

The term public key infrastructure (PKI) is often loosely thrown around, but is not often thoroughly explained. PKI, in a nutshell, is the collection of digital certificates, registration authorities, and certificate authorities that verify the validity of each participant in an encrypted network. Effectively, a PKI itself is simply a concept that defines the mechanisms that ensure that data in transit cannot be read and validates the identity of the user or entity that sent the data. PKI implementations are widespread and are becoming a critical component of modern network and system implementations. Windows Server 2012 fully supports the deployment of multiple PKI configurations, as defined in the following sections.

PKI deployments can range from simple to complex, with some PKI implementations utilizing an array of smart cards (or other two factor authentication tokens) and certificates to verify the identity of all users with a great degree of certainty. Understanding the capabilities of PKI and choosing the proper deployment for an organization are subsequently a must.

Defining Private Key Versus Public Key Encryption

Encryption techniques can primarily be classified as either symmetric or asymmetric. Symmetric encryption requires that each party in an encryption scheme hold a copy of a private key, which is used to encrypt and decrypt information sent between the two parties. The problem with private key encryption is that the private key must somehow be transmitted to the other party without it being intercepted and used to decrypt the information. In addition, each unique two parties would need a unique key to protect the data. The resulting key management is the main obstacle to implementing private key encryption, which is a must-have technology.

Public key, or asymmetric, encryption uses a combination of two keys, which are mathematically related to each other. The first key, the private key, is kept closely guarded and is used to digitally sign or decrypt the information. The second key, the public key, can be used to verify the digital signature or encrypt the information. The integrity of the public key is ensured through certificates, which is explained in depth in the following sections of this chapter. The asymmetric approach to encryption makes key management much easier because the public key does not need to be protected and each user only has a single private key. This improved management comes at a performance cost due to the mathematics involves.

Many implementations of encryption and asymmetric keys (including most PKI implementations) actually use an asymmetric process to select a private key, which is then used for data protection. This combines the benefits of both approaches.

Exploring Digital Certificates

A certificate is essentially a digital document that is issued by a trusted authority (central, internal or local)which can then be used by others to validate a user's identity. Central, trusted authorities such as VeriSign, Thawte or DigiCert are widely used on the Internet to ensure that software from Microsoft, for example, is really from Microsoft, and not a virus in disguise.

Certificates are used for multiple functions, such as the following:

- Secure email
- Web-based authentication
- IP Security (IPsec)
- Code signing
- Certification hierarchies

However, all of these functions amount to either encrypting data, as in the case of securing email or protecting web-based passwords and content, or digitally signing data to ensure integrity and identity, as in the case of code signing or digital email signatures.

Certificates are signed using information from the subject's public key, along with identifying information, such as name, email address, and so on, and a digital signature of the certificate issuer, known as the certificate authority (CA). As long as both users or computers trust the same central authority that issued the certificates, they can trust each other.

Understanding Active Directory Certificate Services in Windows Server 2012

Windows Server 2012 includes a built-in CA technology that is known as Active Directory Certificate Services (AD CS). The first iteration of AD CS emerged with Windows Server 2008, though previous versions of the technology were simply known as Certificate Services. AD CS can be used to issue certificates and subsequently manage them; it is responsible for ensuring their validity and managing their revocation and expiration. AD CS is often used in Windows Server 2012 if there is no particular need to have a third-party verify an organization's certificates. It is common practice to set up an internal certificate authority for uses which are limited to internal users and systems. Third-party certificate authorities such as DigiCert are frequently used when external users and systems are involved and typically require an additional recurring cost.

NOTE

Although the term *Active Directory* has been incorporated into the name of the Windows Certificate Services function, it should be understood that AD CS does not necessarily require integration with an existing Active Directory Domain Services (AD DS) forest environment. Although this is commonly the case, it is important to understand that AD CS has independence over AD DS forest design. For more information about AD DS, see Chapter 4, "Active Directory Domain Services Primer," and Chapter 5, "Designing a Windows Server 2012 Active Directory."

Windows Server 2012 includes several key AD CS features, including the following:

- **Certificate Enrollment Web Service and Certificate Enrollment Policy Web Service**—This feature, introduced with Windows Server 2008 R2, allows certificates to be enrolled directly over HTTP and HTTPS, enabling non-domain or Internet-connected clients to connect and request certificates from a CA server.
- **Automatic renewal for nondomain members**—Extending the support for nondomain members, the Certificate Enrollment Policy Web Service in Windows Server 2012 now supports automatic renewal.
- **Support for Windows Server 2012 Core Edition**—AD CS is now supported on Core Edition servers.
- **Support for cross-forest certificate enrollment**—Introduced to AD CS in Windows Server 2008 R2, the platform allows for CA consolidation across multiple forests.

Reviewing the CA Roles in AD CS

AD CS for Windows Server 2012 can be installed as one of the following CA types:

- **Enterprise root CA**—The enterprise root CA is the most trusted CA in an organization and should be installed before any other CA. All other CAs are subordinate to an enterprise root CA. This CA should be highly physically secured because a compromise of the enterprise CA effectively makes the entire chain compromised.

- **Enterprise subordinate CA**—An enterprise subordinate CA must get a CA certificate from a root CA, but can then issue certificates to all users and computers in the enterprise. These types of CAs are often used to provide a scalable, highly available set of certificate authorities while protecting the root CA.
- **Standalone root CA**—A standalone root CA is the root of a hierarchy that is not related to the enterprise domain information. Multiple standalone CAs can be established for particular purposes. A standalone root CA is often used as the root for other enterprise subordinate CAs to improve security in an environment because a standalone root can be taken offline. In other words, the root is configured as standalone, and subordinate enterprise domain integrated CAs are set up within the domains in a forest to provide for auto-enrollment across the enterprise.
- **Standalone subordinate CA**—A standalone subordinate CA receives its certificate from a standalone root CA and can then be used to distribute certificates to users and computers associated with that standalone CA.

CAUTION

Making decisions about the structure of AD CS architecture is no small task, and should not be taken lightly. Simply throwing AD CS on a server as an enterprise CA and letting it run is not the best approach from a security perspective because compromise of that server can have a disastrous effect. Subsequently, it is wise to carefully consider AD CS design before deployment. For example, one common best practice is to deploy a standalone root CA, then several enterprise subordinate CAs, and then to take the standalone root CA physically offline and secure it in a very safe location, only turning it on again when the subordinate CAs need to have their certificates renewed.

Detailing the Role Services in AD CS

AD CS is composed of several role services that perform different tasks for clients. One or more of these role services can be installed on a server as required. These role services are as follows:

- **Certification Authority**—This role service installs the core CA component, which allows a server to issue, revoke, and manage certificates for clients. This role can be installed on multiple servers within the same root CA chain.
- **Certification Authority Web Enrollment**—This role service handles the web-based distribution of certificates to clients. It requires Internet Information Services (IIS) to be installed on the server.
- **Online Responder**—The role service responds to individual client requests regarding information about the validity of specific certificates. It is used for complex or large

networks, when the network needs to handle large peaks of revocation activity, or when large certificate revocation lists (CRLs) need to be downloaded.

- **Certificate Enrollment Web Service**—This service enables users and computers to enroll for certificates remotely or from nondomain systems via HTTP.
- **Certificate Enrollment Web Policy Service**—This service works with the related Certificate Enrollment Web Service, but simply provides policy information rather than certificates.
- **Network Device Enrollment Service**—This role service streamlines the way that network devices such as routers receive certificates.

Installing AD CS

To install AD CS on Windows Server 2012, determine which server will serve as the root CA, keeping in mind that it is highly recommended that this be a dedicated server and also recommended that it be physically secured and shut off for most of the time to ensure integrity of the certificate chain. It is important to note that an enterprise CA cannot be shut down; however, a standalone root with a subordinate enterprise CA can be shut down. If the strategy of having a standalone root with a subordinate enterprise CA is taken, the root CA must first be created and configured, and then an enterprise subordinate CA must then be created.

In smaller scenarios, an enterprise root CA can be provisioned, though in many cases, those smaller organizations might still want to consider a standalone root and a subordinate enterprise CA. For the single enterprise root CA scenario, however, the following steps can be taken to provision the CA server:

CAUTION

After AD CS is installed onto a server, the name of that server and the domain status of that server cannot change. Also, the server name must not change while it is a CA.

1. Open Server Manager.
2. From the Manage menu, select the Add Roles and Features.
3. Click Next at the Before You Begin page.
4. Accept the default installation type and click Next.
5. Select the AD CS server from the list and click Next.
6. On the Select Server Roles page, check the box for Active Directory Certificate Services, click Add Features to accept the required features and click Next.
7. Click Next to accept the list features.
8. Review the information about AD CS on the Introduction page, and then click Next to continue.

9. On the Select Role Services page, shown in Figure 14.1, choose which role services will be required. A base install will need only the Certificate Authority role. Click Next to continue.

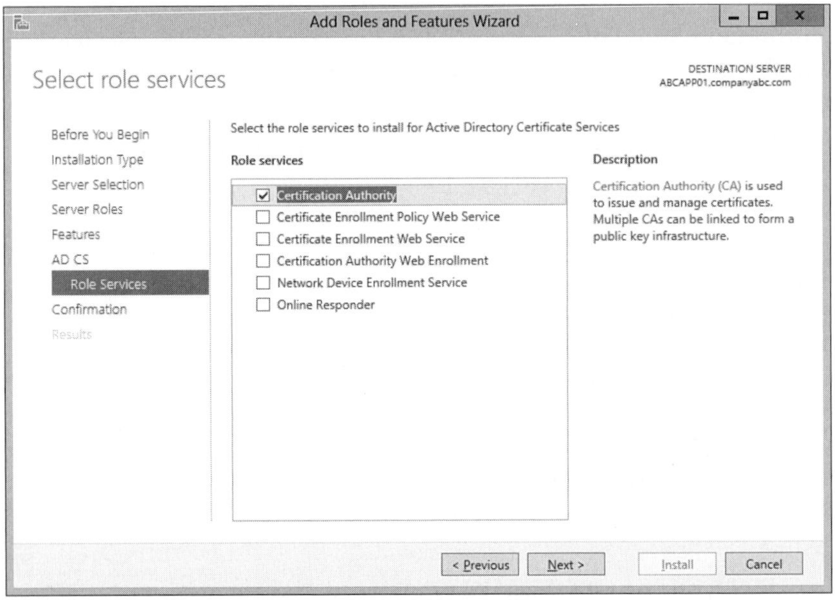

FIGURE 14.1 Installing AD CS.

10. Click Install.

11. When the installation is complete, click the Configure Active Directory Certificate Services on the destination server link.

12. If needed, click Change to change the credentials, and then click Next.

13. Select the Certificate Authority role service to be configured and click Next.

14. Select whether to install an Enterprise (integrated with AD DS) CA or a Stand-alone CA on the subsequent page. In this example, we are installing a domain-based enterprise root CA. Click Next to continue.

15. On the Specify CA Type page, specify the CA type, as shown in Figure 14.2. In this case, we are installing a root CA on the server. Click Next to continue.

16. On the following Private Key page, you can choose whether to create a new private key from scratch or reuse an existing private key from a previous CA implementation. In this example, we create a new key. Click Next to continue.

17. On the Configure Cryptography for CA page, enter the private key encryption settings, as shown in Figure 14.3. Normally, the defaults are fine, but there might

be specific needs to change the CSP, key length, or other settings. Click Next to continue.

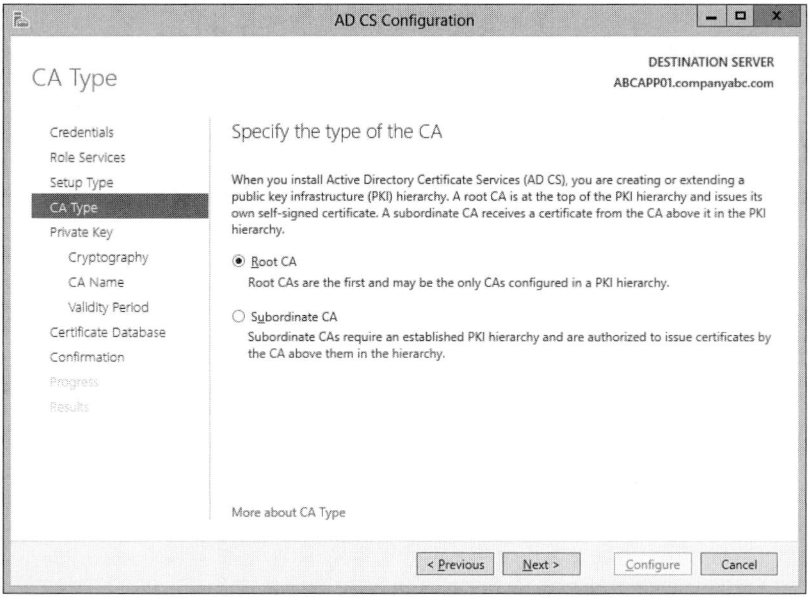

FIGURE 14.2 Specifying a CA type.

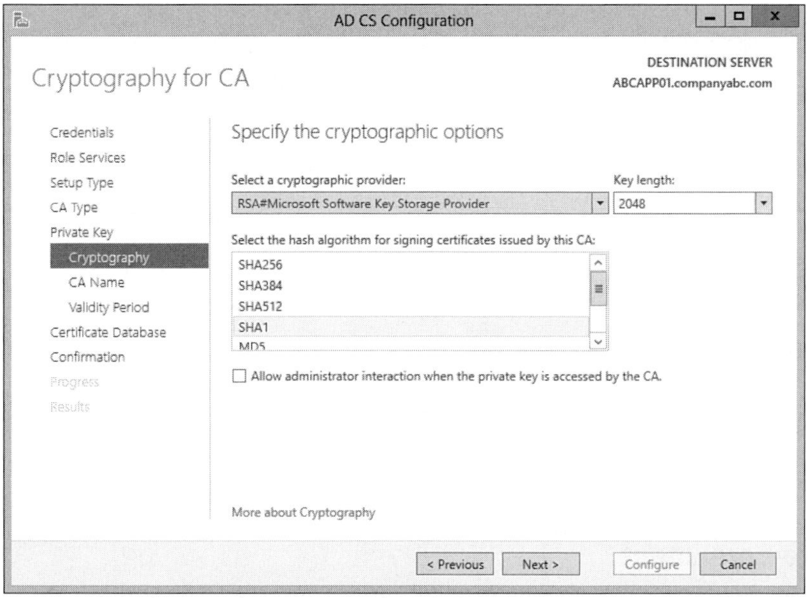

FIGURE 14.3 Choosing cryptography settings.

18. Choose a common name that will be used to identify the CA. Remember that this name will appear on all certificates issued by the CA. In this example, we enter the common name **CompanyABC-CorpCA**. Click Next to continue.

19. Set the validity period for the certificate that will be installed on this CA server. If this is a root CA, the server will have to reissue the certificate chain after the expiration period has expired. In this example, we choose a 5-year validity period, though many production scenarios will have a 20-year CA created for the root. Click Next to continue.

20. Specify a location for the certificate database and log locations, and click Next to continue.

21. Review the configuration selections on the confirmation page, as shown in Figure 14.4, and click Configure.

22. Click Close when the wizard is complete.

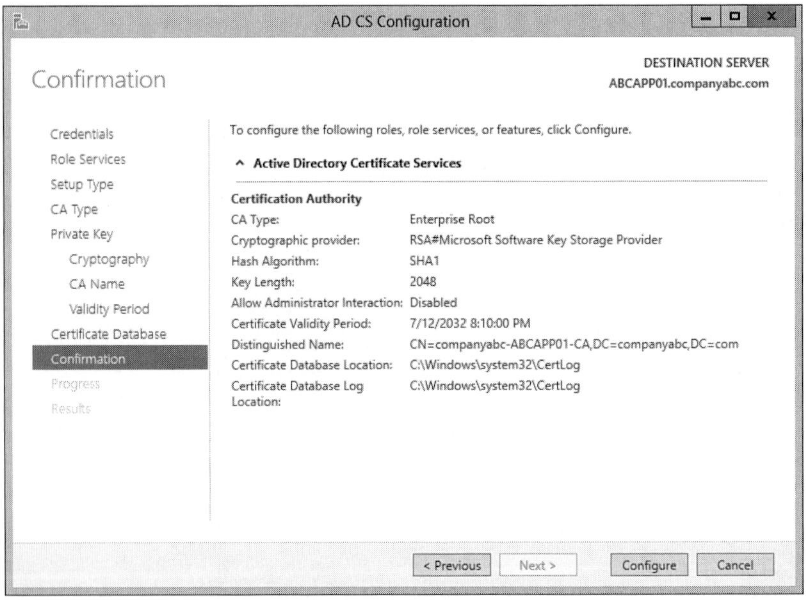

FIGURE 14.4 Reviewing AD CS installation options.

After you install AD CS, you can install additional CAs as subordinate CAs, and administration of the PKI can be performed from the Certification Authority console. (From the Server Manager Tools menu, choose Certification Authority.)

Configuring Auto-Enrollment

With the CA installed, certificates can now be issued. Certificates for application servers such as web servers, Microsoft Exchange servers, Microsoft Lync servers, and so on are often deployed manually by an administrator. Larger deployments of certificates, however, could involve hundreds, thousands, or more certificates and therefore require an automated enrollment process. Windows Server 2012 provides such an automated process, both for domain members and nondomain members.

The following example demonstrates the deployment of a computer certificate to all domain members. The following high-level steps are involved:

1. Assign template permissions.
2. Enable the template on the CA.
3. Configure a group policy object (GPO) for auto-enrollment of domain members.
4. Configure auto-enrollment for nondomain members.

To assign the required template permissions, follow these steps:

1. Click the Start button to open the Metro screen.
2. Enter **mmc** to open the search field and find the mmc executable.
3. Run mmc using the search results.
4. Select File, Add/Remove Snap-In.
5. Add the Certificate Templates snap-in and click OK.
6. Select the Certificate Templates root folder.
7. In the results pane, right-click the Workstation Authentication template and select Duplicate Template. Give the new template a name..
8. Click the Security tab.
9. Select the Domain Computers entry and check the Auto-Enroll check box in the Allow column, as shown in Figure 14.5.
10. Click OK.

To enable the template on the CA, follow this process on the AD CS server:

1. Open Server Manager.
2. From the Tools menu, select Certification Authority.
3. Expand the root authority folder.
4. Right-click the Certificates Templates folder and select New, Certificate Template to Issue.
5. Select the duplicated copy of the Workstation Authentication template and click OK.

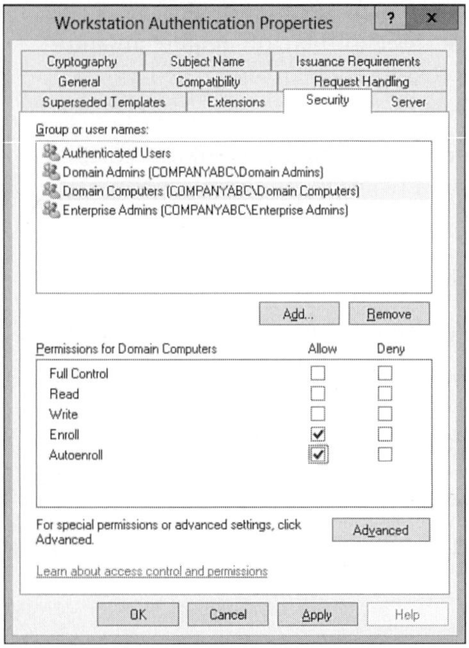

FIGURE 14.5 Configure template permissions for auto-enrollment.

To configure a GPO for auto-enrollment, following this process on a domain controller:

1. Open Server Manager
2. From the Tools menu, select Group Policy Management.
3. Expand the forest name Domains and the domain name folders.
4. Right-click the domain and select Create a GPO in This Domain, and Link It Here.
5. Enter a name for the new GPO, such as Computer certificate auto-enrollment, and then click OK.
6. Right-click the newly created GPO and select Edit.
7. Expand Computer Configuration\Policies\Windows Settings\Security Settings\Public Key Policies.
8. In the results pane, double-click the Certificate Services Client – Auto-Enrollment.
9. Change the Configuration Model setting to Enabled.
10. Check both the Renew Expired Certificates, Update Pending Certificates, and Remove Revoked Certificates and the Update Certificates That Use Certificate Templates check boxes. Click OK.

Use the following process to validate the certificate enrollment:

1. Click the Start button to open the Metro screen.
2. Enter **mmc** to open the search field and find the mmc executable.
3. Run mmc using the search results.
4. Select File, Add/Remove Snap-In.
5. Select the Certificates snap-in and click Add.
6. Select Computer Account Management Scope and click Next.
7. Accept the Local Computer target, click Finish, and then click OK.
8. Expand the Certificates (Local Computer) folder, the Personal folder, and select the Certificates subfolder.
9. Review and validate the certificate listed in the results pane.

Using Smart Cards in a Public Key Infrastructure

A robust solution for a PKI network can be found in the introduction of smart card authentication for users. Smart cards can be microchip enabled plastic cards, USB keys, or other devices.

User logon information, as well as certificates installed from a CA server, can be placed on a smart card. When a user needs to log on to a system, she places the smart card in a smart card reader or simply swipes it across the reader itself. The certificate is read, and the user is prompted only for a PIN, which is uniquely assigned to each user. After the PIN and the certificate are verified, the user is logged on to the domain.

Smart cards are a form of two-factor authentication and have obvious advantages over standard forms of authentication. It is no longer possible to simply steal or guess someone's username and password in this scenario because the username can be entered only via the unique smart card. If stolen or lost, the smart card can be immediately deactivated and the certificate revoked. Even if a functioning smart card were to fall into the wrong hands, the PIN would still need to be used to properly access the system. Smart cards are fast becoming a more accepted way to integrate the security of certificates and PKI into organizations.

Using the Encrypting File System

Just as transport information can be encrypted via certificates and PKI, so too can the Resilient File System (ReFS) on Windows Server 2012 be encrypted to prevent unauthorized access. The Encrypting File System (EFS) option in Windows Server 2012 allows for this type of functionality and improves on previous EFS models by allowing offline folders to maintain encryption sets on the server. EFS is advantageous, particularly for laptop users who tote around sensitive information. If the laptop or hard drive is stolen, the file information is worthless because it is scrambled and can be unscrambled only with the proper key. EFS is proving to be an important part of PKI implementations.

Windows BitLocker goes one step further than EFS, allowing for the entire hard drive, aside from a few boot files, to be encrypted.

Integrating PKI with Non-Microsoft Kerberos Realms

Windows Server 2012's Active Directory component can use the PKI, which utilizes trusts between foreign non-Microsoft Kerberos realms and Active Directory. The PKI serves as the authentication mechanism for security requests across the cross-realm trusts that can be created in Active Directory.

Active Directory Rights Management Services

Active Directory Rights Management Services (AD RMS) is a Digital Rights Management (DRM) technology that allows for restrictions to be placed on how content is managed, transmitted, and viewed. RMS uses like PKI technology to encrypt content such as documents and email messages, and only allows access to view said content if restrictions are placed on the content, such as disabling the ability to print, cut/paste, or forward information.

AD RMS in Windows Server 2012 is the next iteration of the Windows Rights Management Server technology that has been developed over a period of several years. In addition to retaining existing functionality, it adds tighter integration with Active Directory Domain Services (AD DS) and greater scalability.

Understanding the Need for AD RMS

Many organizations are faced with the problem of defining how their intellectual property can be managed after it has been distributed. Several high-profile leaks of sensitive internal emails from major corporations have exposed the need to manage and restrict how email that contains sensitive corporate information is disseminated.

The problem stems from the fact that computer systems have historically been good at restricting information to unauthorized individuals, but as soon as an authorized individual gains access to that data, those organizations have traditionally lost control over what is done with the content. Authorized individuals have copied documents offsite, emailed sensitive information, had their laptops stolen, and have found a myriad of other ways to lose control of an organization's confidential information.

Active Directory RMS was designed to give the control back to an organization. It allows enforcement personnel the ability to restrict how a document is transmitted, printed, copied, or when it expires. Integration with Active Directory Domain Services allows the content to be only decrypted by individuals stipulated in the policies as well.

NOTE

Changes to RMS-protected documents are not reflected unless the document itself is "republished" and the client does not have the use license cached in conjunction with a local copy of the RMS-protected document. If the original use license has not expired, users continue to have access to protected documents that have either not been republished or have been moved from the location of the newly published document.

AD RMS also includes a role service known as Identity Federation Support. Installing this service allows an organization to share rights-protected content with other organizations.

Understanding AD RMS Prerequisites

Before installing AD RMS, the following prerequisites must be satisfied:

- Create a service account for RMS within AD DS. The service account must be different from the account that is used to install RMS.
- The AD RMS server must be a domain member within the domain of the user accounts that will use the service.
- An AD RMS root cluster for certification and licensing must be created.
- A fully-qualified domain name (FQDN) resolvable from the locations where RMS files will be consumed needs to be set up. For example, rms.companyabc.com can be set up for clients to be able to connect to the AD RMS server to validate their RMS rights.
- A server running SQL Server must be available to store the AD RMS databases. It is highly recommended to use an alternate server than the one where AD RMS is installed.

Installing AD RMS

Installation of AD RMS can be performed using the Server Manager utility by adding the AD RMS role to the server. The process of adding the AD RMS role is as follows:

1. Open Server Manager.
2. From the Manage menu, select Add Roles and Features.
3. Click Next at the Welcome page and at the Installation Type page.
4. Select the AD RMS server from the list and click Next.
5. On the Select Server Roles page, check the box for Active Directory Rights Management Services, click Add Features to accept the required features, and then click Next.
6. Click Next to accept the list features.

7. Review the information about AD RMS on the Introduction page, and then click Next to continue.
8. On the Select Role Services page, choose which role services will be required. A base install needs only the Active Directory Rights Management Server role. Click Next to continue.
9. Click Install and monitor the installation progress, as shown in Figure 14.6.
10. When the installation completes, click the Perform Additional Configuration link.

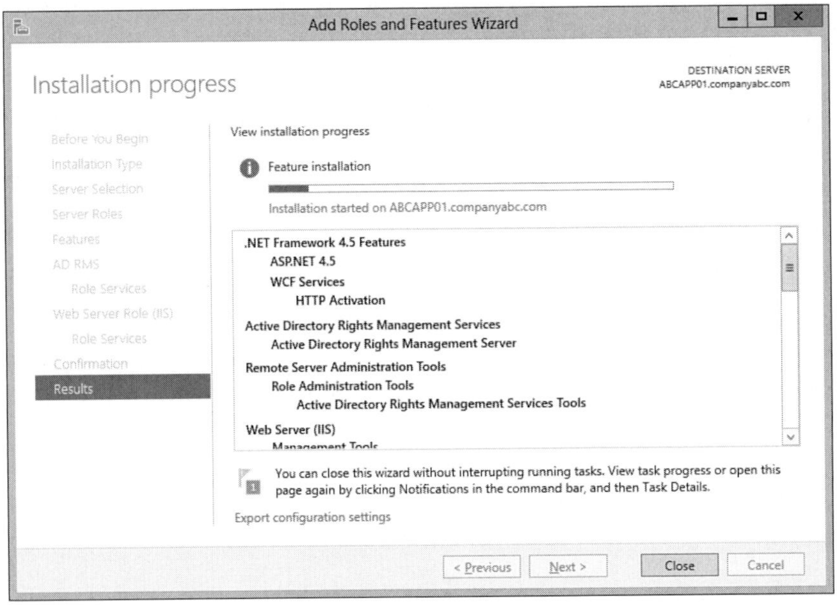

FIGURE 14.6 Installing AD RMS.

Complete the configuration wizard as follows:

1. Review the introductory description and click Next.
2. Accept the default select to create a new cluster and click Next.
3. Select the Use Windows Internal Database on This Server option. Click Next.

NOTE

While the Windows Internal Database is appropriate for nonproduction environments and this example, it does not scale well and does not support high-availability options and is therefore not recommended for production deployments.

4. Enter the service account credentials and click Next.
5. Accept the default cryptographic mode and click Next
6. Accept the default of centralized key storage and click Next..
7. Enter a password for the key and click Next.
8. Accept the default web site and click Next.
9. Select the security connection type and enter the RMS URL and click Next.

NOTE

Production deployments are strongly encouraged to use HTTPS for all RMS access. Environments with internal only content consumers can use internet certificates. If integration with external consumers is required, a third-party certificate should be used.

10. Select the certificate to be used for the cluster and click Next.
11. Enter a descriptive name for the certificate that will establish your RMS identity. It is recommended to use the same host name as the URL. Click Next.
12. Select when to register an AD Service Connection Point (SCP). In projects, the SCP is typically published at a later date after RMS templates have been configured and tested. Once the SCP is published, RMS features and templates immediately become available to Office and Windows users. Click Next.
13. Review the installation parameters and click Install.
14. When the installation completes, click Close to complete the install.

Using IPsec Encryption with Windows Server 2012

IP Security (IPSec), mentioned briefly in previous sections, is essentially a mechanism for establishing end-to-end encryption of all data packets sent between computers. IPsec operates at Layer 3 of the OSI model and subsequently uses encrypted packets for all traffic between members.

IPsec is often considered to be one of the best ways to secure the traffic generated in an environment, and is useful for securing servers and workstations both in high-risk Internet access scenarios and also in private network configurations for an enhanced layer of security.

Understanding the IPsec Principle

The basic principle of IPsec is this: All traffic between clients—whether initiated by applications, the operating system, services, and so on—is entirely encrypted by IPsec, which then puts its own header on each packet and sends the packets to the destination server to be decrypted. Because every piece of data is encrypted, this prevents electronic eavesdropping, or listening in on a network in an attempt to gain unauthorized access to data.

Several functional IPsec deployments are available, and some of the more promising ones are actually built in to the network interface cards (NICs) of each computer, performing encryption and decryption without the operating system knowing what is going on. Aside from these alternatives, Windows Server 2012 includes a robust IPsec implementation by default, which you can configure to use a PKI certificate network.

Detailing Key IPsec Functionality

IPsec in Windows Server 2012 provides for the following key functionality that, when combined, provides for one of the most secure solutions available for client/server encryption:

- **Data privacy**—All information sent from one IPsec machine to another is thoroughly encrypted by such algorithms as 3DES, which effectively prevents the unauthorized viewing of sensitive data.
- **Data integrity**—The integrity of IPsec packets is enforced through ESP headers, which verify that the information contained within an IPSec packet has not been tampered with.
- **Antireplay capability**—IPsec prevents streams of captured packets from being re-sent, known as a *replay* attack, blocking such methods of obtaining unauthorized access to a system by mimicking a valid user's response to server requests.
- **Per-packet authenticity**—IPsec uses certificates or Kerberos authentication to ensure that the sender of an IPsec packet is actually an authorized user.
- **NAT Traversal or Teredo**—Windows Server 2012's implementation of IPsec now allows for IPSec to be routed through current Network Address Translation (NAT) implementations, a concept that is defined more thoroughly in the following sections.
- **Diffie-Hellman 2048-bit key support**—Nearly unbreakable Diffie-Hellman 2048-bit key lengths are supported in Windows Server 2012's IPsec implementation, essentially ensuring that the IPsec key cannot be broken.

Exploring IPsec NAT Traversal

As previously mentioned, IPSec in Windows Server 2012 supports the concept of Network Address Translation Traversal (NAT-T). Understanding how NAT-T works first requires a full understanding of the need for NAT itself.

Network Address Translation was developed simply because not enough IP addresses were available for all the clients on the Internet. Because of this, private IP ranges were established (10.x.x.x, 192.168.x.x, and 172.16-31.x.x) to allow all clients in an organization to have a unique IP address in their own private space. These IP addresses were designed to not route through the public IP address space, and a mechanism was needed to translate them into a valid, unique public IP address.

NAT was developed to fill this role. It normally resides on firewall servers or routers to provide for NAT capabilities between private and public networks. Routing and Remote Access Service (RRAS) for Windows Server 2012 provides NAT capabilities as well.

Because the construction of the IPsec packet does not allow for NAT addresses, IPsec traffic has, in the past, simply been dropped at NAT servers, because there is no way to physically route the information to the proper destination. This posed major barriers to the widespread implementation of IPsec because many of the clients on the Internet today are addressed via NAT.

NAT-T, which was introduced in Windows Server 2008 and is available in Windows Server 2012's IPsec implementation, was jointly developed as an Internet standard by Microsoft and Cisco Systems. NAT-T works by sensing that a NAT connection will need to be traversed and subsequently encapsulating the entire IPsec packet into a User Datagram Protocol (UDP) packet with a normal UDP header. NAT-T handles UDP packets flawlessly, and they are subsequently routed to the proper address on the other side of the NAT.

NAT-T works well but requires that both ends of the IPsec transaction understand the protocol so as to properly pull the IPsec packet out of the UDP encapsulation. With the latest IPsec client and server, NAT-T becomes a reality and is positioned to make IPsec into a much bigger success than it is today.

NOTE

NAT-T was developed to keep current NAT technologies in place without changes. However, some implementations of NAT have attempted to make IPsec work natively across the translation without NAT-T. Disabling this functionality with NAT-T might not be wise, however; it might interfere with IPsec because both NAT-T and the NAT firewall will be attempting to overcome the NAT barrier.

Summary

In today's interconnected networks, securing data in transit is a major, if not one of the most important, security consideration for any organization. Securing the communications between users and computers on a network is vital, and in some cases required by law. Windows Server 2012 builds on the strong security base of Windows Server 2008 and Windows Server 2008 R2 to include support for transport-level security mechanisms, such as IPsec and PKI, using technologies such as AD CS and AD RMS. Proper configuration and use of these tools can effectively lock down an organization's transmission of data and ensure that it is used only by the appropriate persons.

Best Practices

The following are best practices from this chapter:

- To secure a networking environment, deploy some or many of the transit-level security technologies available.
- Because even the most secure infrastructures are subject to vulnerabilities, it is recommended to deploy multiple layers of security on critical network data.
- It is highly recommended to avoid installing the AD RMS database locally on the RMS server. Instead, use a remote full SQL Server instance.
- Take extra care to secure the Active Directory Certificate Services root CA server because a security breach of this server would compromise the entire CA chain.
- Store a standalone root CA server in a physically locked location and shut it down when not in use. This best practice does not apply to enterprise root CAs, which cannot be shut down for long periods of time.
- Implement IPsec to secure the traffic generated in an environment and for securing servers and workstations both in high-risk Internet access scenarios and also in private network configurations.

CHAPTER 15

Network Policy Server, Network Access Protection and Routing and Remote Access

IN THIS CHAPTER

- Understanding Network Access Protection in Windows Server 2012
- Deploying a Windows Server 2012 Network Policy Server
- Enforcing Policy Settings with a Network Policy Server
- Verifying the Client-Side Configuration
- Deploying a Virtual Private Network Using RRAS

Windows Server 2012 contains built-in support for services and an application programming interface (API) known as Network Access Protection (NAP). NAP supports the ability to restrict network clients based on the overall health of their systems. If, for example, the client attempting to connect to the network does not have the compliant security patches or antivirus definitions installed, the technology disallows those clients from connecting to the network.

The Windows Server 2012 NAP enforcement role service is known as a Network Policy Server (NPS). An NPS system controls and manages a series of defined health policies, and enforces those policies on clients that have their own local Windows System Health Agent. This chapter covers this technology in Windows Server 2012. Particular attention is focused on the Network Policy Server role service, and how it can be used to restrict Dynamic Host Configuration Protocol (DHCP), IPsec, 802.1X, and virtual private network (VPN) access to an environment. Further, an example for NAP is demonstrated through a DHCP implementation.

Understanding Network Access Protection in Windows Server 2012

NAP in Windows Server 2012 is composed of a series of components that enable you to restrict client access to networks through various mechanisms, such as controlling who gets an IP address from a DHCP server or who issues an IPsec certificate. NAP itself was developed as an industry-independent technology, and was made with a published set of APIs that allow third-party vendors, such as network device makers and other software companies, to develop their own set of devices that integrate together with Windows Server 2012 devices.

Exploring the Reasons for Deploying NAP

NAP was developed as a technology in response to the threats faced by computers that are not up-to-date with the latest security patches or do not have other security controls in place, such as current versions of antivirus software, or lack a local software firewall. These systems are often the first to be compromised, and are often the target of spyware attacks; they are, therefore, especially vulnerable.

Simply allowing these clients unfettered access to a network is no longer an option. Compromised systems inside an internal network pose an especially strong security risk because they could easily be controlled by malicious entities and could compromise sensitive data. Identifying a method for controlling these clients has become critical, which is why Microsoft developed the NAP concept.

Outlining NAP Components

There are four primary functions of NAP, almost all of which are included within Windows Server 2012 natively:

- **Health policy compliance**—The ability to correct issues and return a system to compliance is central to a NAP platform. Therefore, compliance mechanisms, such as Windows Server Update Services (WSUS) servers, System Center Configuration Manager 2012, and other remediation services fill the health policy compliance space of a NAP platform. Windows Server 2012 can automatically refer clients to a remediation server before granting full network access. For example, a client that is out-of-date with patches can be referred to a WSUS server to have their patches installed.

- **Health state validation**—Through agents on the client systems, the specific state of an individual client can be monitored and logged. The administrator of a NAP platform can tell how many systems on the network are out-of-date with patches, how many don't have their firewalls turned on, and many other health-state statistics. In some cases, health status is simply noted; in others, it is used to block access to clients.

- **Access limitation**—The cornerstone to an effective NAP platform is the ability to restrict access to networks based on the results of the health-state validation. The type of access granted can be very granular. For example, clients can have access to specific systems for patching, but not to other clients. Windows Server 2012 includes custom access limitation capabilities in NAP, allowing administrators to create flexible policies.

- **Ongoing compliance**—NAP will only permit access to the network as long as a client system meets health policy requirements.

Understanding Windows Server 2012 NAP Terminology

The following terms are useful to understand NAP concepts used in Windows Server 2012:

- **Enforcement Client (EC)**—A client that takes part in a NAP infrastructure. Windows 8, Windows 7, Windows Vista, and Windows XP SP3 support NAP and can be an EC in a NAP topology, because they all contain the System Health Agent component.
- **Enforcement Server (ES)**—A server that takes part in a NAP infrastructure and enforces the policies. In Windows Server 2012, this is the Network Policy Server (NPS) role service.
- **System Health Agent (SHA)**—The client agent that sends health information to the NAP ES servers. In Windows 8, Windows 7, Windows Vista, and Windows XP SP3, this is the Windows Security Health Agent (WSHA), which is a service that runs on each client and monitors the local Windows Security Center on the machines.
- **System Health Validator (SHV)**—An SHV is the server-side component of NAP that processes Statements of Health (SoHs) from the SHAs and returns Statement of Health Responses (SoHRs). By default Windows Server 2012 includes the Windows Security Health Validator (WSHV), but additional third-party SHVs can be registered with the NPS service via the SHV API.
- **Remediation Server**—A server that is made accessible to clients that have failed the NAP policy tests. These servers generally provide for services that clients can use to comply with policies, such as WSUS servers, DNS servers, and System Center Configuration Manager servers.

15

NAP and NPS features in Windows Server 2012

NAP and NPS concepts were originally built in to the original Windows Server 2008 operating system. Windows Server 2008 R2 and Windows Server 2012 have added features and improvements to both technologies, including the following:

- **Multiconfiguration Service Health Validators**—The biggest change to NAP that was added in Windows Server 2008 R2 is the ability to create multiple SHVs across a single set of NAP health policy servers. This allows for multiple policies, creating some which might be more or less restrictive and providing for the creation of exceptions.
- **NPS templates**—Templates are now provided for elements such as Remote Authentication Dial-In User Service (RADIUS) clients or shared secrets. These templates can be exported for use on other NPS servers.

- **Accounting improvements in NPS**—RADIUS accounting improvements have been added to NPS along with full support for international character sets providing better logging and tracking capabilities.
- **Support for Windows PowerShell**—You can now use Windows PowerShell for installing Network Policy and Access Services server role. In addition, you can now also deploy and configure some aspects of Network Policy Server by using Windows PowerShell.

Deploying a Windows Server 2012 Network Policy Server

The Windows Server 2012 role service that handles NAP is the Network Policy Server role. Installing this role on a server effectively makes it an SHV and an Enforcement Server. The specific role added to the Server Role Wizard is called the Network Policy and Access Services role, and includes the following components:

- **Host Credential Authorization Protocol (HCAP)**—An industry-standard protocol that is used when integrating Microsoft NAP with the Cisco Network Access Control Server. This allows the Windows NPS role to examine Cisco 802.1X access client health.
- **Health Registration Authority (HRA)**—A server that distributes health certificates to clients that pass health policy checks. The HRA is only used in Microsoft's NAP implementation for IPSec enforcement.
- **Network Policy Server**—The Windows Server 2012 role that acts as a NAP Health Policy Server and a RADIUS server for authentication and authorization.

NOTE

In Windows Server 2008 R2 and Windows Server 2008, Network Policy and Access Services included the Routing and Remote Access Service (RRAS) role service, but in Windows Server 2012 RRAS is now a separate role just named Remote Access.

Exploring NPS Concepts

The Network Policy Server role in Windows Server 2012 allows for the creation of enforcement policies that apply to the following types of network access:

- **Internet Protocol Security (IPsec)**—IPsec encryption allows for all communications, even those that would normally be unencrypted, to be highly secured through public key infrastructure (PKI)-based encryption. IPsec can be configured to be required between servers, and a system configured with the NPS role can regulate which clients are allowed as IPsec clients based on their local health.

- **802.1X authentication—**802.1X is a network-based authentication method that uses PKI-based certificates to authenticate that the user who attaches to the network is who he claims to be. 802.1X authentication is often used on wireless fidelity (Wi-Fi) networks. A system with the NPS role in Windows Server 2012 can add clients to the 802.1X network based on their health status.
- **Virtual private network (VPN) connections—**A VPN connection allows for traffic to be sent in an encrypted tunnel across an untrusted network such as the Internet. VPNs are often used by roaming users to connect to the internal local-area network (LAN) of an organization. The NPS role includes support for restricting client VPN access based on system health.
- **Dynamic Host Configuration Protocol (DHCP) addresses—**One very useful NPS enforcement method is the ability to restrict which clients get DHCP addresses based on their system health. Although this is the easiest NAP policy to set up, this is also the easiest to circumvent as clients could set their own IP addresses.
- **Remote Desktop Services (RDS) Gateway connections–** Systems that connect to virtual sessions hosted on an RDS session host using the RDS Gateway component can be integrated into and managed by the NAP system.

Understanding RADIUS Support on a Network Policy Server

As previously mentioned, installing the Network Policy and Access Services role adds support for the RADIUS protocol, an industry-standard authentication mechanism supported by a wide range of clients.

NOTE

The NPS role in Windows Server 2012 is the replacement for the legacy Internet Authentication Service (IAS) role. The old IAS role provided simple RADIUS authentication support to Active Directory sources.

RADIUS authentication allows for Active Directory users to be authenticated using RADIUS authentication, rather than AD DS authentication. This is commonly used in scenarios where VPN access requires RADIUS authentication or when other devices cannot use AD-based authentication.

Installing a Network Policy Server

Installation of the Network Policy and Access Services role installs the Network Policy Server component. To install, follow these steps:

1. Open Server Manager.
2. Click Manage and select Add Roles and Features.
3. On the Before you Begin page, click Next.

4. Select Role-Based or Feature-Based Installation and click Next to continue. On the Select Destination Server page, select a server from the server pool.
5. From the list of roles to install, select Network Policy and Access Services, and click Next to continue.
6. On the Select Features page click Next, read the information provided on the page, and then click Next to continue.
7. On the Select Role Services page shown in Figure 15.1, select which role services to install on the server. For this example, we will select Network Policy Server. Click Next to continue.

NOTE

Installing a NAP server might prompt you to install additional tools, and you can deploy NPS as a RADIUS and as a NAP policy server.

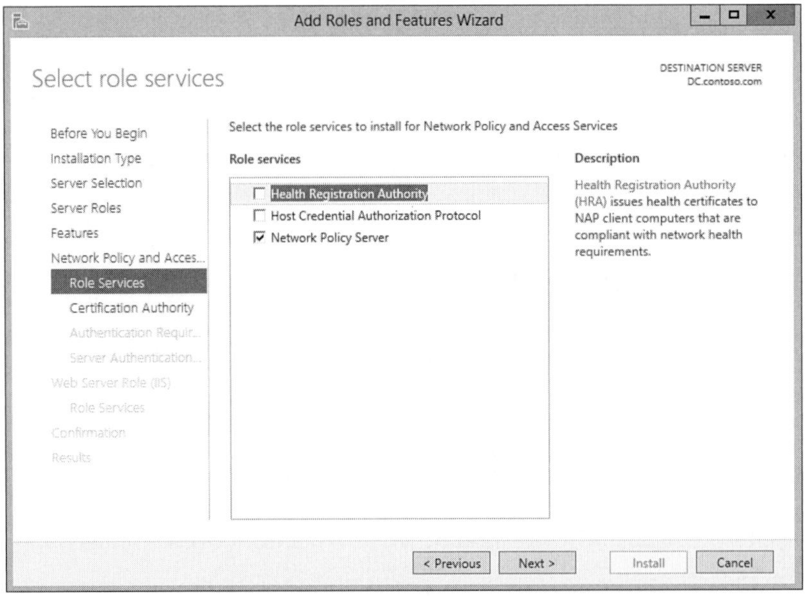

FIGURE 15.1 Installing the Network Policy and Access Services roles.

NOTE

Adding the Health Registration Authority role service requires the IIS Web Server role to be installed on the server as well as a valid certificate (and potentially the Active Directory Certificate Services role). Selecting the role service might prompt you to install these services, as well.

8. On the Confirm Installation page, choose whether to reboot the server automatically and select Install.

9. Click Close when the wizard completes.

Enforcing Policy Settings with a Network Policy Server

The goal of an NPS is to enforce policy settings defined by the administrator (for example, to configure the NPS role to block clients from connecting if they do not have an antivirus application installed). There are multiple variations on this theme, but the same principles apply to each of the variations.

This section describes a scenario where NPS is configured to block DHCP clients from receiving IP addresses if they do not have an antivirus application installed or if their antivirus definitions are out-of-date. The same overall process can be used for 802.1X validation, VPN validation, or IPsec validation.

After installing the NPS, three additional steps are required for a successful NAP implementation using a DHCP validation:

- Create and configure the NAP server's system health validator setting.
- Configure DHCP server for the scope on which NAP would be implemented.
- Configure Group Policy to activate the NAP agent on the client computer.

Creating a System Health Validator

The first step to enabling NPS validation is to create and configure a System Health Validator (SHV). The validator is where the settings are stored and what will be enforced on the client, such as if a firewall is needed, should antispyware software be installed, and so on. To create the SHV for the example we are outlining, follow these steps:

1. Hover the mouse at the lower right and choose Start and select Network Policy Server. From the left pane, select NPS (Local). Then in the right pane, select NAP from the drop-down list and choose the Configure NAP option, as shown in Figure 15.2.

2. In the Select Network Connection Method for Use with Nap screen, choose DHCP in from the drop-down list and assign an appropriate name, as shown in Figure 15.3. Then click Next.

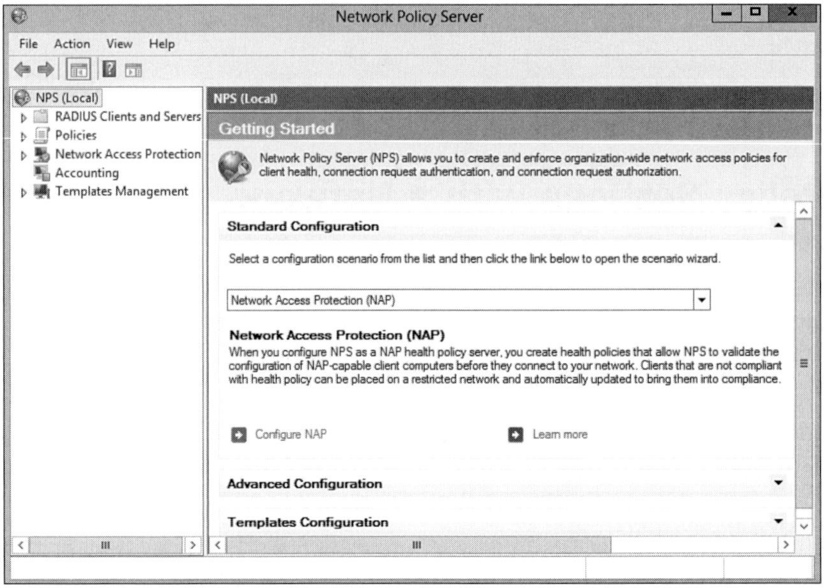

FIGURE 15.2 Configuring the NAP server.

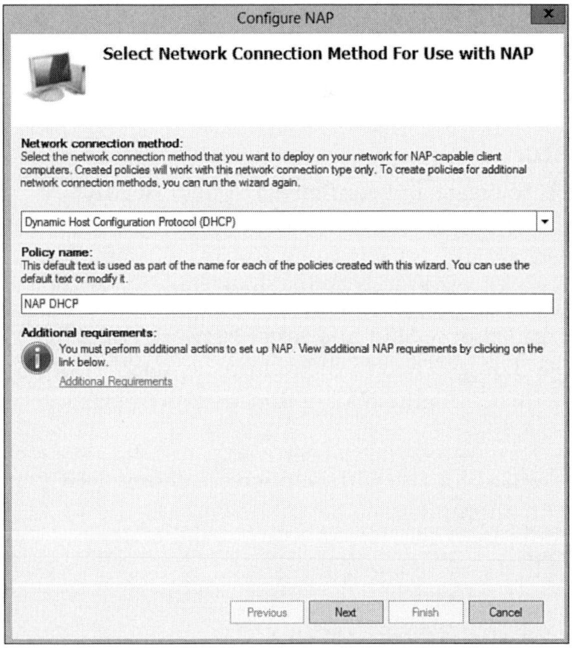

FIGURE 15.3 Choosing the NAP method.

3. Next to the RADIUS list, click Add, and then assign the name and the IP address for the DHCP server that will listen on the client requests, as shown in Figure 15.4, and then click Next.

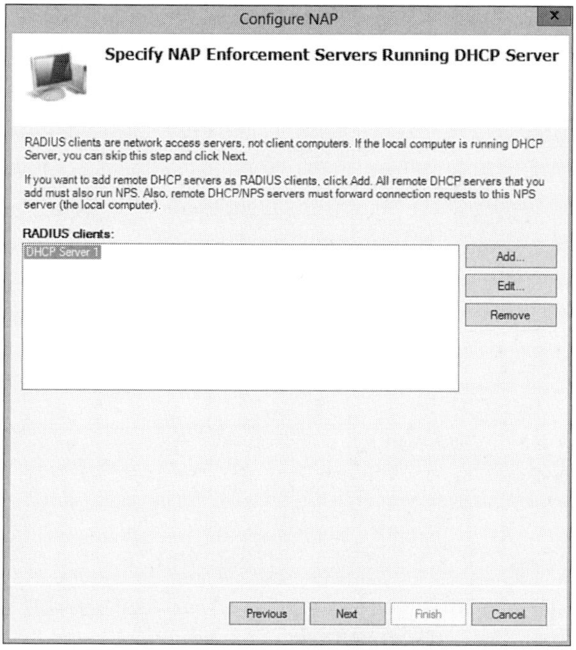

FIGURE 15.4 Choosing the DHCP server.

4. For this example, we want to assign NAP implementation on all the DHCP scopes, so we will leave the DHCP Scope blank. Otherwise, choose the scopes from the DHCP server to be assigned NAP, and then click Next.

5. For this example, leave the Machine Groups as blank and click Next.

6. Click New Group to choose the remediation group servers that will be accessible for the client to fulfill the compliance policies, give a name to the group, and press Add, enter a friendly name for the server and the remediation server (in this case the DHCP server) IP address. For a production environment, you might also want to add the WSUS server to the group.

7. Click Next and then click Next again to accept the NAP default settings. Then click Finish to implement the configuration, as shown in Figure 15.5.

8. Next, in the left pane of the NPS console, browse to Network Access Protection, System Health Validator, Windows Security Health Validator, Settings, right-click, and select Properties for the Default Configuration. Only enable the first option (A Firewall Is Enabled for All Network Connections), as shown in Figure 15.6.

15

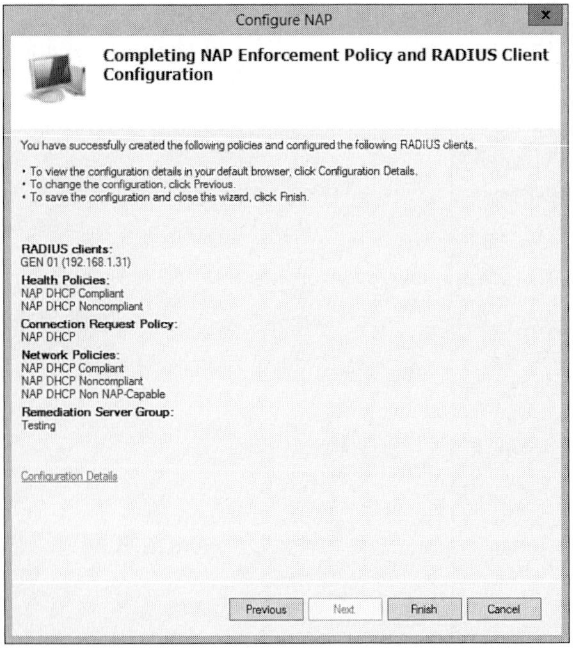

FIGURE 15.5 Reviewing the settings.

FIGURE 15.6 Configuring a Security Health Validator.

Configuring a DHCP Server to Restrict Client Leases Based on the NPS Policy

After NPS has been set up, the DHCP scope needs to be configured to use the NAP server to validate the client's health before granting them unrestricted IP addresses to the corporate network. In the example we've been using so far, this would restrict only those clients without an enabled firewall from getting a valid IP address to the corporate network.

To configure all DHCP scopes for NAP, follow these steps:

1. On a server with the DHCP Server Tools installed, click the Server Manager tile on the taskbar.
2. When the Server Manager console opens, click Tools, and then select the DHCP option.
3. When the DHCP console opens, navigate to Server Name, IPv4.
4. Right-click IPv4 and choose Properties.
5. Select the Network Access Protection tab, select the Restricted Access option, and then click the Enable on All Scopes button, as shown in Figure 15.7. Click Yes when prompted.

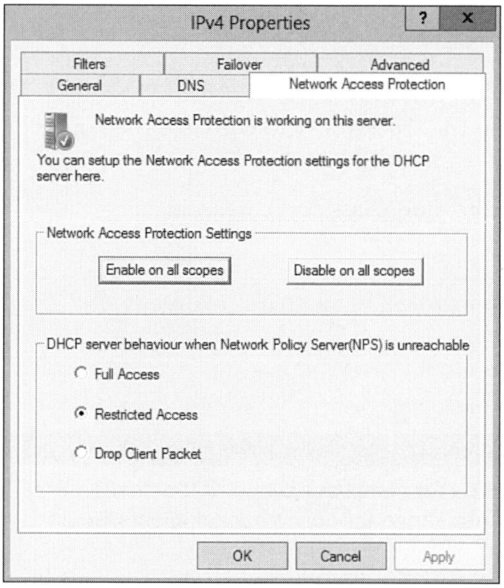

FIGURE 15.7 Enabling NAP on a DHCP server.

TIP

NAP functionality can also be enabled for a specific scope by opening the properties page for the scope and selecting

NOTE

Configuring the default DHCP action when the NPS server is unavailable is an important consideration as part of the overall availability of network access to clients. If this behavior is a concern, a highly available multiserver NPS installation is recommended.

To configure a DHCP scope and options for noncompliant clients, follow these steps:

1. On a server with the DHCP Server Tools installed, click the Server Manager tile on the taskbar.
2. When the Server Manager console opens, click Tools, and then select the DHCP option.
3. When the DHCP console opens, navigate to Server Name, IPv4.
4. Right-click IPv4 and choose New Scope.
5. Follow the wizard prompts and complete the required information for a DHCP scope for noncompliant clients. These settings should provide access to a remediation network.
6. Once the scope has been created, select the Policy node of the scope, right-click, and then choose New Policy.
7. Enter a policy name and description and click Next.
8. Click Add to add a condition for the policy.
9. Select the Criteria User Class and make sure the Operator field contains the Equals operator.
10. Select the value Default Network Access Protection Class and click Add.
11. Click OK and Next.
12. Finish configuring any other required options for the remediation network.
13. Click Next and Finish.

NOTE

You can use the same process to modify the scope for compliant clients if the desired IP range is within the compliant scope. The IP address range for noncompliant clients would then be specified on the appropriate wizard page.

Configuring and Deploying Group Policy on the Systems

After the scopes on the DHCP have been configured for NAP, it is time for the client systems to inherit certain setting through the group policy.

To configure the settings for all domain members, follow these steps:

1. Open the Group Policy Management console from the Tools menu in Server Manager.
2. Expand Forest, Domains, Domain Name.
3. Create a new GPO linked to the domain, and then right-click the new GPO and choose Edit.
4. In the Group Policy Object Editor, expand Computer Configuration, Policies, Windows Settings, Security Settings, Network Access Protection, NAP, Client Configuration, Enforcement Clients.
5. Select the DHCP Quarantine Enforcement Client and enable it as shown in Figure 15.8.

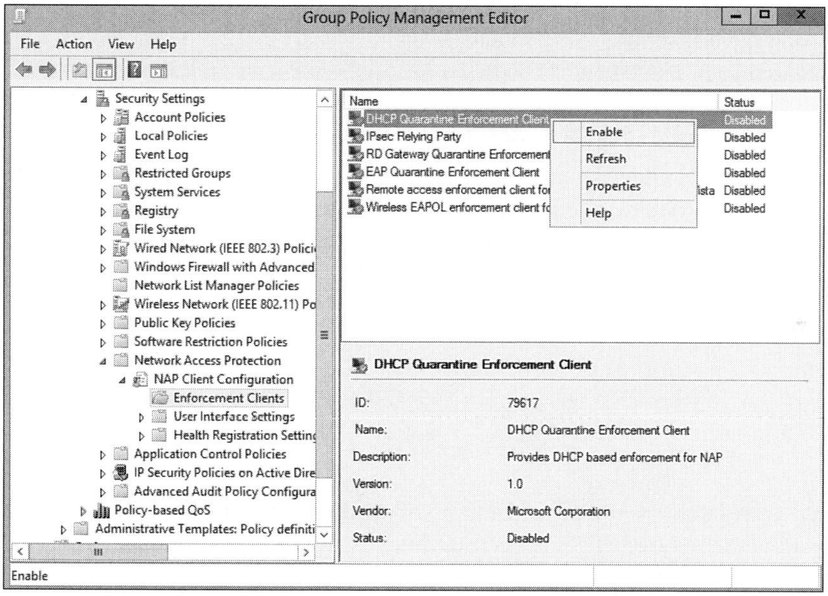

FIGURE 15.8 Enabling the DHCP Quarantine Enforcement Client.

6. Navigate to Policies, Windows Settings, Security Settings, System Services.
7. Right click the Network Access Protection Agent and select Protection. Define the policy as Automatic startup mode, as shown in Figure 15.9.
8. Browse to computer configuration navigate to Policies\Administrative Templates\Windows Components\Security Center.
9. Select Turn on Security Center, right click and select edit then choose Enabled.

FIGURE 15.9 Enabling the Network Access Protection Agent.

Verifying the Client-Side Configuration

Make sure that the Windows 8 client that is connected to the network was assigned an IP from the DHCP scope before making the scope NAP enabled and implementing the Group Policy settings on the domain. In addition, make sure it can access network resources on the network.

To verify that the NAP has been implemented on the client end, follow these steps:

1. From the command prompt, run **ipconfig /all**. (For example, if you are using the DHCP scope range from 192.168.1.20 to 192.168.1.40 with the subnet mask 255.255.255.0 and your client was assigned 192.168.1.20, you will see your subnet mask as 255.255.255.0).

2. Make sure that your client is joined to the domain and verify from the control panel that the firewall is turned on; this has been defined as the only compliance criteria in the System Health Validator.

3. From an elevated command prompt, run **gpupdate /force** to deploy the client-end settings you defined in your NAP Group Policy object (GPO).

4. Now try to turn off the firewall for all three networks (private, domain, public). Notice that it automatically turns back on; this is being enforced by the NAP server.

5. Now go to the NAP server and open Network Policy Server and browse down to the System Health Validator, Windows Security Health Validator, Settings and open the default configuration. Then select An Antivirus Application Is On and click OK.

6. To test the new policy on the client, disable the Windows Defender service, the default Anti-malware protection in Windows 8. To disable the service, hover the mouse at the lower left corner, select Start, type services and select the Services icon to open the services console.

7. Notice that you immediately get warning messages, as shown in Figures 15.10 and 15.11.

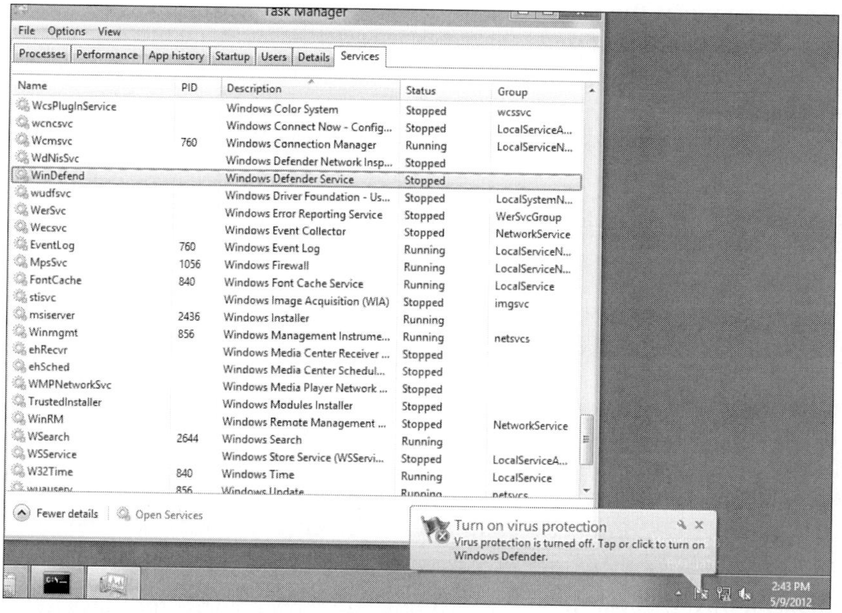

FIGURE 15.10 NAP client-end messages.

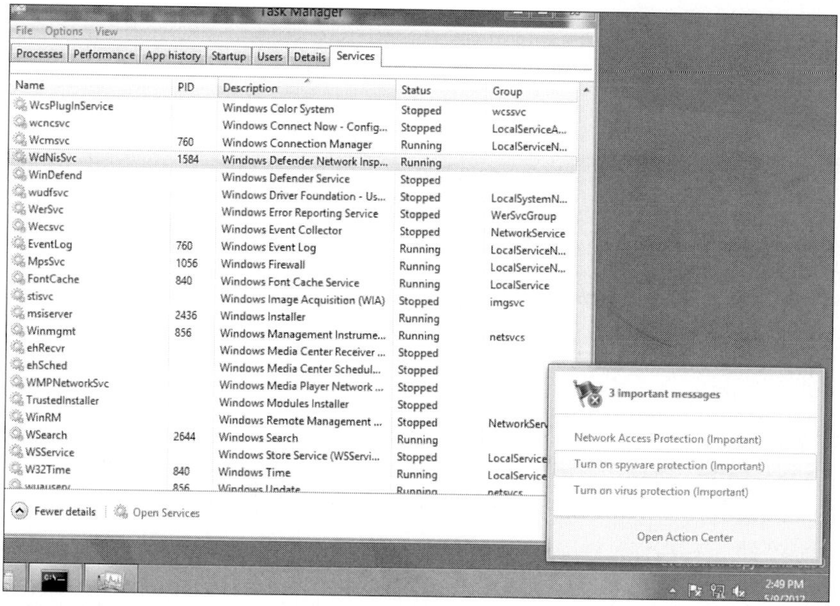

FIGURE 15.11 NAP client-end messages.

8. From the command prompt, execute **ipconfig /all**. Notice how your subnet mask has changed to 255.255.255.255. Also notice that the DNS server settings are there but will only service fully qualified domain name (FQDN) requests for the DHCP server; this is because it was the only server that you had defined in the Remediation server group. If you have another server or a client joined to the domain and on the same subnet, try pinging their FQDN. You will get this response: "Ping request could not find host SERVER-FQDN-NAME. Please check the name and try again." If you ping their IP address, you will receive this response: "PING: transmit failed. General failure."

9. Start the Windows Defender service, to become compliant and gain access to the network.

Deploying a Virtual Private Network Using RRAS

A common method of securing information sent across unsecured networks is to create a virtual private network (VPN), which is effectively a connection between two private nodes or networks that is secured and encrypted to prevent unauthorized snooping of the traffic between the two connections. From the client perspective, a VPN looks and feels just like a normal network connection between different segments on a network—hence the term *virtual private network*.

Data that is sent across a VPN is encapsulated, or wrapped, in a header that indicates its destination. The information in the packet is then encrypted to secure its contents. The encrypted packets are then sent across the network to the destination server, using what is known as a VPN tunnel.

The Windows Server 2012 Remote Access role allows for the creation of VPNs and integrates with the NPS role to provide for validation of client health before creating a VPN session.

NOTE

VPN support in Windows Server 2012 provides for simple VPN tunnels to be created. For more complex scenarios where specific rules need to be created and application-layer filtering of the VPN traffic is needed, look at Microsoft's Forefront Edge line of products, which includes the Forefront Threat Management Gateway and the Forefront Unified Access Gateway products.

Exploring VPN Tunnels

The connection made by VPN clients across an unsecured network is known as a VPN tunnel. It is named as such because of the way it "tunnels" underneath the regular traffic of the unsecured network.

VPN tunnels are logically established on a point-to-point basis, but can be used to connect two private networks into a common network infrastructure. In many cases, for example, a VPN tunnel serves as a virtual wide-area network (WAN) link between two physical locations in an organization, all while sending the private information across the Internet. VPN tunnels are also widely used by remote users who log on to the Internet from multiple locations and establish VPN tunnels to a centralized VPN server in the organization's home office. These reasons make VPN solutions a valuable asset for organizations, and one that can be easily established with the technologies available in Windows Server 2012.

NOTE

VPN tunnels can either be voluntary or compulsory. In short, voluntary VPN tunnels are created when a client, usually out somewhere on the Internet, asks for a VPN tunnel to be established. Compulsory VPN tunnels are automatically created for clients from specific locations on the unsecured network, and are less common in real-life situations than are voluntary tunnels.

Tunneling Protocols

The tunneling protocol is the specific technology that defines how data is encapsulated, transmitted, and unencapsulated across a VPN connection. Varying implementations of tunneling protocols exist and correspond with different layers of the Open System Interconnection (OSI) standards-based reference model. The OSI model is composed of seven layers, and VPN tunneling protocols use either Layer 2 or Layer 3 as their unit of exchange. Layer 2, a more fundamental network layer, uses a frame as the unit of exchange, and Layer 3 protocols use a packet as a unit of exchange.

The most common Layer 2 VPN protocols are the Point-to-Point Tunneling Protocol (PPTP) and the Layer 2 Tunneling Protocol (L2TP), both of which are fully supported protocols in Windows Server 2012.

PPTP and L2TP Protocols

Both PPTP and L2TP are based on the well-defined Point-to-Point Protocol (PPP) and are consequently accepted and widely used in VPN implementations. L2TP is the preferred protocol for use with VPNs in Windows Server 2012 because it incorporates the best of PPTP, with a technology known as Layer 2 Forwarding. L2TP allows for the encapsulation of data over multiple network protocols, including IP, and can be used to tunnel over the Internet. The payload, or data to be transmitted, of each L2TP frame can be compressed, as well as encrypted, to save network bandwidth.

Both PPTP and L2TP build on a suite of useful functionality that was introduced in PPP, such as user authentication, data compression and encryption, and token card support. These features, which have all been ported over to the newer implementations, provide for a rich set of VPN functionality.

L2TP/IPSec Secure Protocol

Windows Server 2012 uses an additional layer of encryption and security by utilizing IP Security (IPsec), a Layer 3 encryption protocol, in concert with L2TP in what is known, not surprisingly, as L2TP/IPsec. IPsec allows for the encryption of the L2TP header and trailer information, which is normally sent in clear text. This also has the added advantage of dual-encrypting the payload, adding an additional level of security into the mix.

L2TP/IPSec has some distinct advantages over standard L2TP, namely the following:

- L2TP/IPSec allows for data authentication on a packet level, allowing for verification that the payload was not modified in transit, as well as the data confidentiality that is provided by L2TP.
- Dual-authentication mechanisms stipulate that both computer-level and user-level authentication must take place with L2TP/IPSec.
- L2TP packets intercepted during the initial user-level authentication cannot be copied for use in offline dictionary attacks to determine the L2TP key because IPSec encrypts this procedure.

An L2TP/IPSec packet contains multiple, encrypted header information and the payload itself is deeply nested within the structure. This allows for a great deal of transport-level security on the packet itself.

Enabling VPN Functionality on a Remote-Access Server

By installing the Remote Access role on the server, the ability to allow VPN connections to/from the server is enabled. The following type of VPN connections can be created:

- **VPN gateway for clients**—The most common scenario, this involves the RRAS server being the gateway into a network for VPN clients. This scenario requires the server to have two network cards installed.
- **Site-to-site VPN**—In this scenario, the RRAS server creates a VPN tunnel between another RRAS server in a remote site, allowing for traffic to pass unimpeded between the networks, but in an encrypted state.
- **Dial-up RAS server**—In this layout, the server is installed with a modem or pool of modems and provides for dial-in capabilities.
- **NAT between networks**—On an RRAS server installed in Routing mode, this deployment option provides for Network Address Translation (NAT) between network segments. For example, on one network, the IP addresses might be public, such as 12.155.166.x, while on the internal network they might be 10.10.10.x. The NAT capability translates the addresses from public to private and vice versa.
- **Routing between networks**—On an RRAS server installed in Routing mode, this deployment option allows for direct routing of the traffic between network segments.
- **Basic firewall**—The RRAS server can act as a simple Layer 3 router, blocking traffic by port. For more secure scenarios, use of an advanced Layer 7 firewall such as Microsoft's Forefront Threat Management Gateway (previously called Internet Security and Acceleration or ISA Server) is recommended.

NOTE

Setting up a VPN connection requires the server to have at least two network cards installed on the system. This is because the VPN connections must be coming from one network and subsequently passed into a second network, such as from the demilitarized zone (DMZ) network into the internal network.

To install the Remote Access role, follow these steps:

1. In Server Manager, click Manage, and then click Add Roles and Features.
2. On the Before you Begin page, click Next.
3. On the Select Installation Type page, click Role/Feature Based Install, and then click Next.
4. On the Select Destination Server page, click Select a Server from the Server Pool, click the names of the servers onto which you want to install the Remote Access role, and then click Next.
5. On the Select Server Roles page, click Remote Access, and then click Next three times. On the Select Role Services page, click Direct Access and VPN (RAS), and then click Next.
6. On the Confirm Installation Selections page, click Install.
7. On the Results page, verify that the installation succeeded.

To set up the Remote Access server for the most common scenario, VPN gateway, follow these steps:

1. Open the Routing and Remote Access management console from the Tools menu in Server Manager.
2. Select the local server name or connect to a remote Remote Access server by right-clicking Routing and Remote Access and selecting Add Server.
3. Click Action, Configure, and Enable Routing and Remote Access.
4. Click Next at the Welcome page.
5. Choose from the list of configuration settings, as shown in Figure 15.12. Different scenarios require different settings. For example, if setting up a site-to-site VPN, you should select the Secure Connection Between Two Private Networks option. In this case, we are setting up a simple VPN, so we select Remote Access (Dial-Up or VPN).
6. On the Remote Access page, check the box next to VPN. If enabling dial-up, such as in scenarios when the VPN box has a modem attached to it, you can check the Dial-Up box, as well. Click Next to continue.

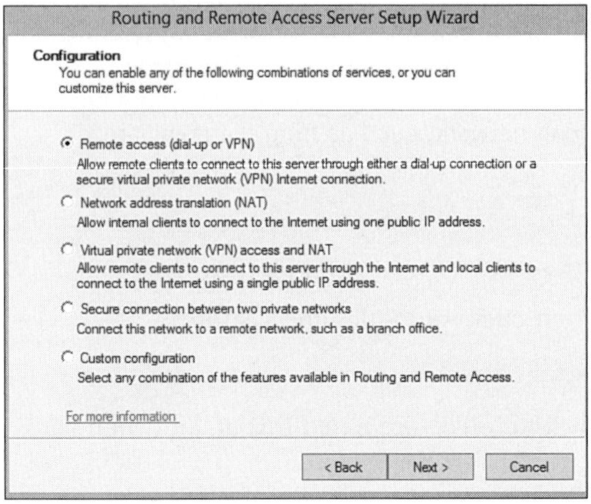

FIGURE 15.12 Enabling VPN functionality.

7. On the VPN Connection page, shown in Figure 15.13, select which network card is connected to the network where VPN clients will be coming from. This might be the Internet, or it might be a secured perimeter network such as a DMZ. Click Next to continue.

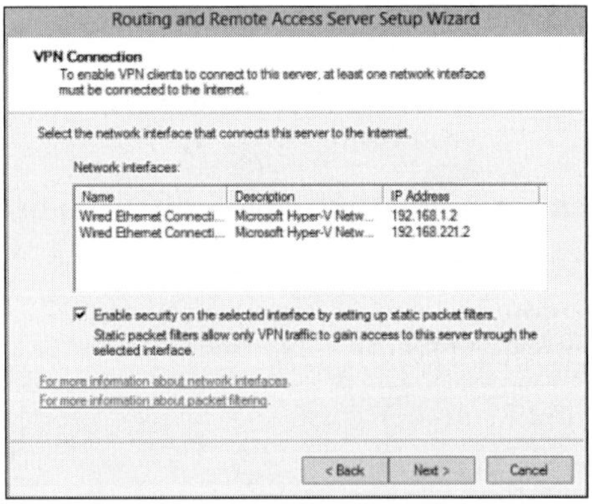

FIGURE 15.13 Specifying the network card for VPN clients.

8. On the IP Address Assignment page, select how VPN clients will get their IP addresses (typically Automatically). In addition, you can specify a manual range. Click Next to continue.

9. On the Managing Multiple Remote Access Servers page, shown in Figure 15.14, select whether to use RRAS to authenticate locally or to use a remote RADIUS server. Click Next to continue.

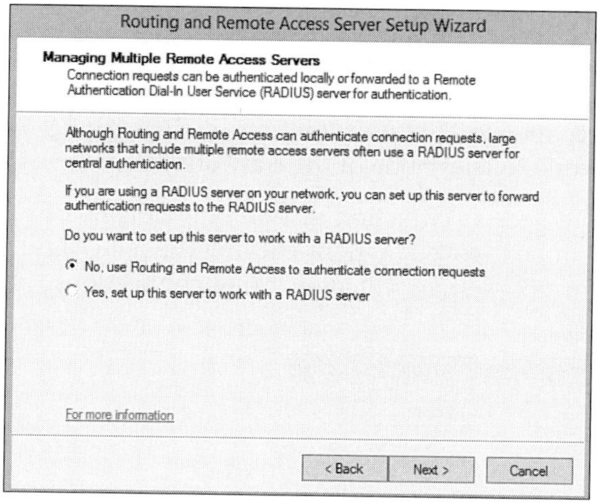

FIGURE 15.14 Specifying RADIUS settings for the VPN server.

10. Review the wizard settings and click Finish when complete.
11. Click OK when prompted about the default connection request policy being created, and click OK again if prompted about the DHCP Relay Agent.
12. Click Finish when the wizard is complete.

The wizard will enable RRAS on the server and allow for administration of the VPN settings and client from the Routing and Remote Access dialog box, shown in Figure 15.15. Review the settings within this tool to familiarize yourself with how the system is configured.

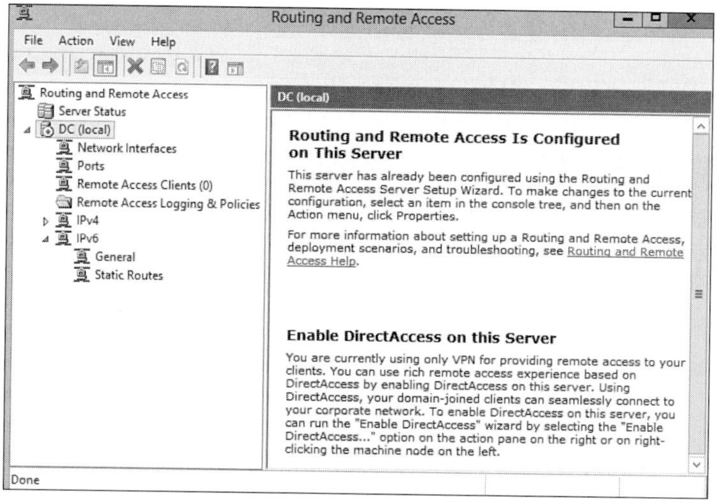

FIGURE 15.15 Administering the server from the RRAS console.

Modifying the Remote Access Network Policy

After installing and configuring Remote Access, the NPS system will deny access by default to the Remote Access server for clients, unless the network policy generated is modified. The network policy, which is labeled Connections to Microsoft Routing and Remote Access Server, can be found under the Network Policies node of the Network Policy Server.

The policy must be set to Grant Access in the Access Permission section of the dialog box, as shown in Figure 15.16. This dialog box can be invoked by right-clicking the policy and choosing Properties. After this is enabled, the NPS system will allow client connections.

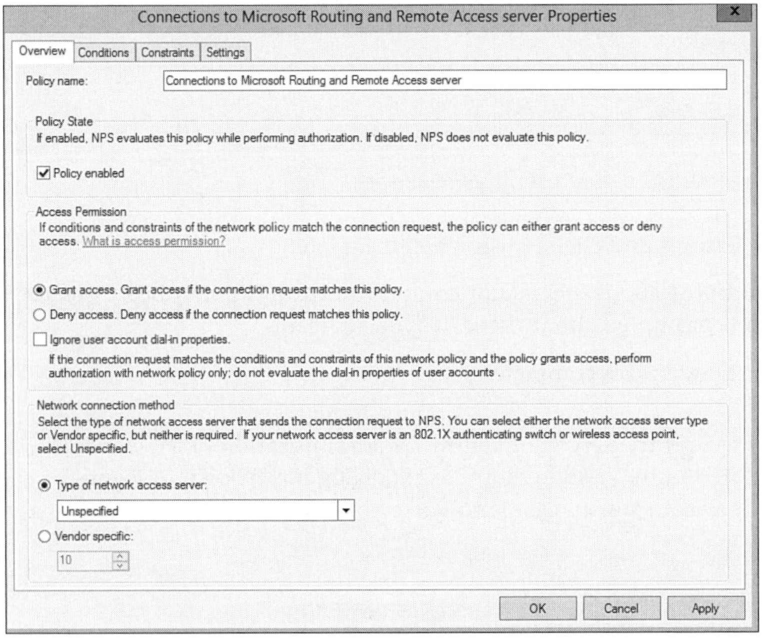

FIGURE 15.16 Modifying the RRAS network policy on the NPS server.

NOTE

VPN clients can be controlled and monitored using the NPS role just like the IPsec, 802.1X, and DHCP clients can. Use the NPS Admin tool and the techniques described earlier in this chapter to enable client health monitoring.

Summary

Network Access Protection in Windows Server 2012 provides for much-needed capabilities to isolate and control clients that don't conform to an organization's policies. By limiting the type of network access these clients can obtain, organizations can greatly reduce their overall security risk. NAP support in Windows Server 2012 is built in to the operating system on both the server and client operating systems running Windows 8, Windows 7, Windows Vista, and Windows XP SP3.

Windows Server 2012 NAP implementation provides for a robust set of tools in the Network Policy Server role service that can be used to restrict clients using NAP. The NPS role contains built-in support for abilities to limit DHCP, IPsec, 802.1X, and VPN clients if they do not pass system health checks. In addition, Windows Server 2012 has improved VPN capabilities, allowing administrators to control and encrypt the connections clients make to the internal network. Using a combination of these technologies can greatly improve the security in an environment.

Best Practices

The following are best practices from this chapter:

- Install the Network Policy Server role service to limit client access according to networks and services.
- Use a dedicated certificate authority server for generation of health certificates for IPsec.
- Ensure that the server certificate used for the Network Policy Server is issued from a certificate authority that is trusted by the clients that will be connecting.
- Install at least two network cards in a server that will handle VPN client connections.
- Although Windows Server 2012 VPN functionality is strong, consider the use of an advanced firewall/VPN solution, such as Forefront Threat Management Gateway or Forefront Unified Access Gateway to further improve VPN security.
- Use L2TP over IPsec encryption for VPN connections when possible. Avoid using the less-secure PPTP VPN connection type.

CHAPTER 16

Migrating from Active Directory 2008 / 2008 R2 to Active Directory 2012

IN THIS CHAPTER

In many ways, a migration from Windows Server 2003/2008 R2 Active Directory to Windows Server 2012 Active Directory Domain Services is more of a service pack upgrade than a major migration. The architectures are fundamentally the same and require mainly upgrades to the schema and domains. The differences between the operating systems (OSs) are more evolutionary than revolutionary, and, subsequently, there are fewer design considerations than in upgrades from the NT 4.0 OS.

That said, several immediate improvements to the OS can be realized through migration to Windows Server 2012, whether by migrating all servers immediately or by using a slow, phased approach. Improvements to Active Directory Domain Services (AD DS), such as the ability to use read-only domain controllers as Global Catalog servers, the GUI Recycle Bin for AD, and greater scalability, provide incentive for Windows Server 2003/2008 R2 Active Directory environments to begin migration. Standalone server improvements such as Hyper-V, Remote Desktop Services, File and Print Server improvements, Automated Server Recovery, and many more also serve to encourage migrations.

This chapter focuses on the planning, strategy, and logistics of migration from Windows Server 2003/2008 R2 Active Directory to Windows Server 2012 AD DS. Several scenarios for migration are considered, including a Big Bang upgrade, a phased upgrade, and a consolidation migration.

Beginning the Migration Process

Any migration procedure should define the reasons for migration, steps involved, fallback precautions, and other important factors that can influence the migration process. After finalizing these items, the migration can begin.

Identifying Migration Objectives

Two underlying philosophies influence technology upgrades, each philosophy working against the other. The first is the expression "If it ain't broke, don't fix it." Obviously, if an organization has a functional, easy-to-use, and well-designed Windows Server 2003/2008 R2 infrastructure, popping in that Windows Server 2012 DVD and upgrading might not be so appealing. The second philosophy is something along the lines of "Those who fail to upgrade their technologies perish." Eventually, all technologies become outdated and unsupported. As modern technology threats attack systems that have unpatched vulnerabilities, being on an unsupported system is inviting disaster.

Choosing a pragmatic middle ground between these two philosophies effectively depends on the factors that drive an organization to upgrade. If the organization has critical business needs that can be satisfied by an upgrade, such an upgrade might be a good idea. If no critical need exists, however, it might be wise to wait until the next iteration of Windows or a future service pack for Windows Server 2012.

A typical scenario involves upgrading Active Directory to the new version to enable any new functionality, with existing domain controllers often being upgraded through attrition. When it is time to replace a domain controller (DC) because of age or warranty or whatever, the opportunity is taken to replace it with the newer OS.

Establishing Migration Project Phases

After the decision is made to upgrade, a detailed plan of the resources, timeline, scope, and objectives of the project should be outlined. Part of any migration plan requires establishing either an ad hoc project plan or a professionally drawn-up project plan. The migration plan assists the project managers of the migration project to accomplish the planned objectives in a timely manner with the correct application of resources.

The following is a condensed description of the standard phases for a migration project:

- **Discovery**—The first portion of a design project should be a discovery, or fact-finding, portion. This section focuses on the analysis of the current environment and documentation of the analysis results. Current network diagrams, server locations, wide-area network (WAN) throughputs, server application dependencies, and all other networking components should be detailed as part of the Discovery phase.

- **Design**—The Design portion of a project is straightforward. All key components of the actual migration plan should be documented, and key data from the Discovery phase should be used to draw up design and migration documents. The project plan itself would normally be drafted during this phase. Because Windows Server 2012 Active Directory is not dramatically different from Windows Server 2003 or 2008 R2, significant reengineering of an existing Active Directory environment is not necessary. However, other issues such as server placement, new feature utilization, and changes in AD DS replication models should be outlined. If migrating from a non-2008 R2 domain, it is worthwhile to consider where read-only domain controllers (RODCs) might fit into the design to improve security in locations where the server might not be well secured physically.
- **Prototype**—The Prototype phase of a project involves the essential lab work to test the design assumptions made during the Design phase. The ideal prototype involves a mock production environment that is migrated from Windows Server 2003/2008 R2 to Windows Server 2012. For Active Directory, this means creating a production DC and then isolating it in the lab and seizing the Flexible Single Master Operations (FSMO) roles with a server in the lab. The Active Directory migration can then be performed without affecting the production environment. Step-by-step procedures for the migration can also be outlined and produced as deliverables for this phase. The goal of this phase is to validate that no errors exist in the production directory that would prevent the upgrade from succeeding. Optimally, the prototype phase would include samples of key systems to ensure that they are compatible with the Windows Server 2012 OS and the Windows Server 2012 Active Directory Schema.
- **Pilot**—The Pilot phase, or Proof-of-Concept phase, involves a production "test" of the migration steps, on a limited scale. For example, a noncritical server could be upgraded to Windows Server 2012 in advance of the migration of all other critical network servers. In a slow, phased migration, the Pilot phase would essentially transition into Implementation, as upgrades are performed slowly, one by one.
- **Implementation**—The Implementation portion of the project is the full-blown migration of network functionality or upgrades to the OS. As previously mentioned, this process can be performed quickly or slowly over time, depending on an organization's needs. It is, subsequently, important to make the timeline decisions in the Design phase and incorporate them into the project plan.
- **Training and support**—Learning the ins and outs of the new functionality that Windows Server 2012 can bring to an environment is essential in realizing the increased productivity and reduced administration that the OS can bring to the environment. Consequently, it is important to include a Training portion into a migration project so that the design objectives can be fully realized.

For more detailed information about the project plan phases of a Windows Server 2012 migration, see Chapter 2, "Best Practices at Planning, Prototyping, Migrating, and Deploying Windows Server 2012."

Comparing the In-Place Upgrade Versus New Hardware Migration Methods

Because of the changes in Windows Server 2012, the in-place upgrade path is limited to servers using Windows Server 2008 R2 only. Although it might be tempting to simply upgrade Windows Server 2008 R2 servers in place, often it is more appealing to simply introduce newer systems into an existing environment and retire the current servers from production. This technique normally has less impact on current environments and can also support fallback more easily.

Determining which migration strategy to use depends on one additional factor: the condition of the current hardware environment. If Windows Server 2003/2008 R2 is taxing the limitations of the hardware in use, it might be preferable to introduce new servers into an environment and simply retire the old Windows Server 2003/2008 R2 servers. This is particularly true if the existing servers are veterans of previous upgrades, maybe transitioning from Windows 2000 Server to Windows Server 2003 to Windows Server 2008. If the hardware in use for Windows Server 2003/2008 R2 is newer and more robust, and could conceivably last for another 2 to 3 years, however, it might be easier to simply perform in-place upgrades of the systems in an environment.

In most cases, organizations take a hybrid approach to migration. Older hardware, 32-bit systems, or Windows Server 2003 DCs are replaced by new hardware running Windows Server 2008 R2. Newer Windows Server 2008 R2 64-bit systems are instead upgraded in place to Windows Server 2012. Consequently, auditing all systems to be migrated and determining which ones will be upgraded and which ones will be retired are important steps in the migration process.

Identifying Migration Strategies: "Big Bang" Versus Phased Coexistence

As with most technology implementations, there are essentially two approaches in regard to deployment: a quick "Big Bang" approach or a slower phased coexistence approach. The Big Bang option involves the entire Windows Server 2003/2008 R2 infrastructure being quickly replaced, often over the course of a weekend, with the new Windows Server 2012 environment; whereas the phased approach involves a slow, server-by-server replacement of Windows Server 2003/2008 R2.

Each approach has its own advantages and disadvantages, and key factors to Windows Server 2012 should be taken into account before a decision is made. Few Windows Server 2012 components require a redesign of current Windows Server 2003/2008 R2 design elements. Because the arguments for the Big Bang approach largely revolve around not maintaining two conflicting systems for long periods of time, the similarities between Windows Server 2003/2008 R2 and Windows Server 2012 make many of these arguments moot. Windows Server 2012 DCs can easily coexist with Windows Server 2003/2008 R2 domain controllers. With this point in mind, it is more likely that most organizations will choose to ease into Windows Server 2012, opting for the phased coexistence approach to the upgrade. Because Windows Server 2012 readily fits into a Windows Server 2003/2008 R2 environment, and vice versa, this option is easily supported.

Exploring Migration Options

As previously mentioned, the Windows Server 2012 and Windows Server 2003/2008 R2 Active Directory DCs coexist together very well. The added advantage to this fact is that there is greater flexibility for different migration options. Unlike migrations from NT 4.0 or non-Microsoft environments such as Novell NDS/eDirectory, the migration path between these two systems is not rigid, and different approaches can be used successfully to achieve the final objectives desired.

In this chapter, three Windows Server 2012 migration scenarios are explored:

- **Big Bang migration**—This scenario upgrades all DCs in a short span of time. This is usually suitable only for single domain and small organizations.
- **Phased migration**—This scenario takes a phased coexistence approach and upgrades the DCs in phases over an extended period of time. During this time, there is coexistence between the existing versions of Active Directory and the new Windows Server 2012 AD DS. This is usually the approach used when there are multiple domains or for large organizations.
- **Multiple domain consolidation migration**—A variation on the phased upgrade, the multiple domain consolidation migrates the existing domains to a new Windows Server 2012 Active Directory domain. This is the typical approach when there are problems with the existing domains, too many domains, or when merging organizations.

The remainder of this chapter walks through each of these scenarios step by step.

Big Bang Migration

The Big Bang approach to migrate from Windows Server 2003/2008 R2 to Windows Server 2012 is the most straightforward approach to migration. An upgrade simply takes any and all settings on the DCs and upgrades them to Windows Server 2012. If a Windows Server 2008 R2 server handles Windows Internet Naming Service (WINS), domain name system (DNS), and Dynamic Host Configuration Protocol (DHCP), the upgrade process will upgrade all WINS, DNS, and DHCP components, as well as the base OS. This makes this type of migration very tempting, and it can be extremely effective, as long as all prerequisites described in the following sections are satisfied.

The prerequisites are as follows:

The OS on the DCs is Windows Server 2008 R2.

The DC hardware meets or exceeds the Windows Server 2012 requirements and all software is compatible with Windows Server 2012, including antivirus software and drivers.

There is enough disk space free to perform the OS and Active Directory upgrade. Specifically, verify that your free space is at least twice the size of your Active Directory database plus the minimum 32GB needed to install the OS.

The current domain functional level is Windows 2003 Native or higher.

Often, upgrading any given server can be a project in itself. The standalone member servers in an environment are often the workhorses of the network, loaded with myriad different applications and critical tools. Performing an upgrade on these servers would be simple if they were used only for file or print duties and if their hardware systems were all up-to-date. Because this is not always the case, it is important to detail the specifics of each server that is marked for migration.

Verifying Hardware Compatibility

It is critical to test the hardware compatibility of any server that will be directly upgraded to Windows Server 2012. The middle of the installation process is not the most ideal time to be notified of problems with compatibility between older system components and the drivers required for Windows Server 2012. Subsequently, the hardware in a server should be verified for Windows Server 2012 on the manufacturer's website or on Microsoft's Hardware Compatibility List (HCL), currently located at http://www.microsoft.com/whdc/hcl/default.mspx.

Microsoft suggests minimum hardware levels on which Windows Server 2012 will run, but it is highly recommended that you install the OS on systems of a much higher caliber because these recommendations do not take into account any application loads, DC duties, and so on. The following is a list of Microsoft's minimum hardware levels for Windows Server 2012:

- 1.4GHz 64-bit processor
- 512MB of RAM
- 32GB free disk space

That said, it cannot be stressed enough that it is almost always recommended that you exceed these levels to provide for a robust computing environment. See Chapter 3, "Installing Windows Server 2012 and Server Core," for additional details on hardware requirements.

NOTE

One of the most important features that mission-critical servers can have is redundancy. Putting the OS on a mirrored array of disks, for example, is a simple yet effective way of increasing redundancy in an environment.

Verifying Application Readiness

Nothing ruins a migration process like discovering a mission-critical application that is installed on the current Windows Server 2003 server will not work in the new environment. Subsequently, it is very important to identify and list all applications on a server that will be required in the new environment. Applications that will not be used or whose functionality is replaced in Windows Server 2012 can be retired and removed from consideration. Likewise, applications that have been verified for Windows Server 2012 can be designated as safe for upgrade. For any other applications that might not be compatible but are necessary, you either need to move them to another Windows Server 2003 server or delay the upgrade of that specific server.

In addition to the applications, the version of the OS that will be upgraded is an important consideration in the process. A Windows Server 2008 R2, Standard Edition DC can be upgraded to Windows Server 2012, Standard Edition or Windows Server 2012, Datacenter Edition. However, a Windows Server 2003 SP2 or R2, Enterprise Edition installation can only be upgraded to Windows Server 2008 R2, Enterprise Edition.

Backing Up and Creating a Recovery Process

It is critical that a migration does not cause more harm than good to an environment. Subsequently, we cannot stress enough that a good backup system is essential for quick recovery in the event of upgrade failure. Often, especially with the in-place upgrade scenario, a full system backup might be the only way to recover; consequently, it is very important to detail fallback steps in the event of problems. The backup should include the boot and system partitions as well as the system state.

Virtual DC Rollback Option

It is always good to have several fallback options in case one of the options is unsuccessful. Another option to consider, in addition to a full backup, is to create a virtual DC. Using a virtual server platform such as Hyper-V or VMware Server, you can create a DC for little or no cost.

A virtual machine is created on the host, which can be an existing installation or even on a desktop with Virtual PC or VMware Workstation. This virtual machine is then joined to the domain and promoted to be a DC.

Before the upgrade, the virtual DC is shut down. Backup copies of the virtual DC files can even be made for safekeeping.

In the event of a major failure in the upgrade process, the virtual DC can be used to rebuild the domain from scratch. If the upgrade is successful, the virtual DC can either be turned back on and demoted, or simply be deleted and cleaned from the domain.

Performing an Upgrade on a Single DC Server

After all various considerations regarding applications and hardware compatibility have been thoroughly validated, a standalone server can be upgraded.

The health of the DCs should be verified before upgrading the DCs. In particular, the Domain Controller Diagnostics (DCDIAG) utility should be run and any errors fixed before the upgrade. The Windows Server 2003 DCDIAG utility is part of the Support Tools, which can be found on the installation media under \support\tools\. The Support Tools are installed via an MSI package named SUPTOOLS.MSI in Windows Server 2003. After installing the tools, you can run the DCDIAG utility. The same utility is included in Windows Server 2008 R2 with no additional installs required. Execute the tool and verify that all tests passed.

The AD DS forest and the domain need to be prepared before the upgrade. This installs the schema updates that are new to Windows Server 2012 Active Directory. The following steps should be run on the FSMO role holders, specifically the schema master for forest-prep and the infrastructure master for domainprep. In a small environment or a single domain, all these roles are typically on the same DC. To prepare the forest and domain, complete the following steps on the DC with the roles:

1. Insert the Windows Server 2012 DVD into the drive. If the Install Windows Autorun page appears, close the window.

NOTE

When preparing the forest, be sure to log on to the schema master as a member of the Schema, Enterprise, and Domain Admins group.

2. Select Start, and launch a command prompt.
3. Enter **D:\Support\Adprep\Adprep.Exe /forestprep** and click OK, where D: is the DVD drive.
4. A warning appears to verify that all DCs are running Windows Server 2003 or higher. Confirm by pressing C and then Enter.
5. Enter **d:\support\adprep\adprep.exe /domainprep /gpprep** and click OK.
6. Enter **d:\support\adprep\adprep.exe /rodcprep** and click OK. This update allows RODCs.

Now that the schema updates have been installed and the domain preparation is done, the domain is ready to be upgraded. The FSMO role holder should be the first Windows 2008 R2 DC to be upgraded. Follow these steps to upgrade:

1. Insert the Windows Server 2012 DVD into the DVD drive of the server to be upgraded.
2. The Install Windows page should appear automatically. If not, choose Start, Run, and then type **D:\Setup**, where D: is the drive letter for the DVD drive.
3. Click Install Now.
4. Click the large Go Online to Get the Latest Updates button. This ensures that the installation has the latest information for the upgrade.
5. Select the OS you want to install and click Next.
6. Select the I Accept the License Terms option on the License page, and click Next to continue.
7. Click the large Upgrade button.
8. Review the compatibility report and verify that all issues have been addressed. Click Next to continue.

The system then copies files and reboots as a Windows Server 2012 server, continuing the upgrade process. After all files are copied, the system is then upgraded to a fully functional install of Windows Server 2012 (see Figure 16.1) and will then reboot again. All this can take some time to complete.

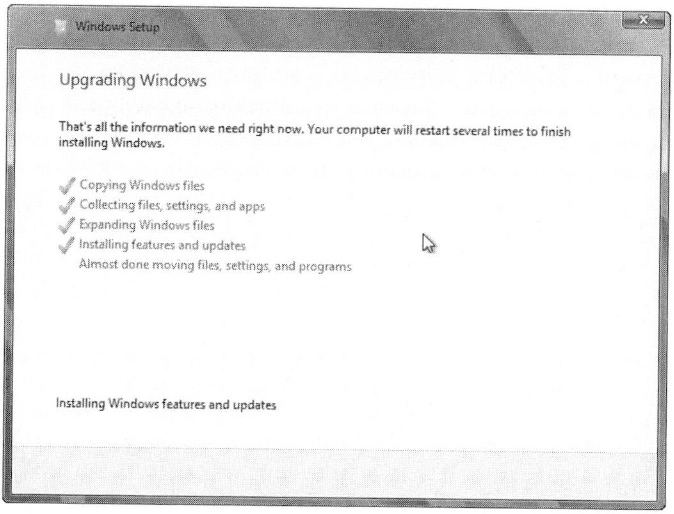

FIGURE 16.1 Big Bang upgrade.

9. After the final reboot, the DC is at the familiar Ctrl+Alt+Del screen. After logon, the DC opens to the Server Manager console, as shown in Figure 16.2. The Windows OS upgrade is complete.

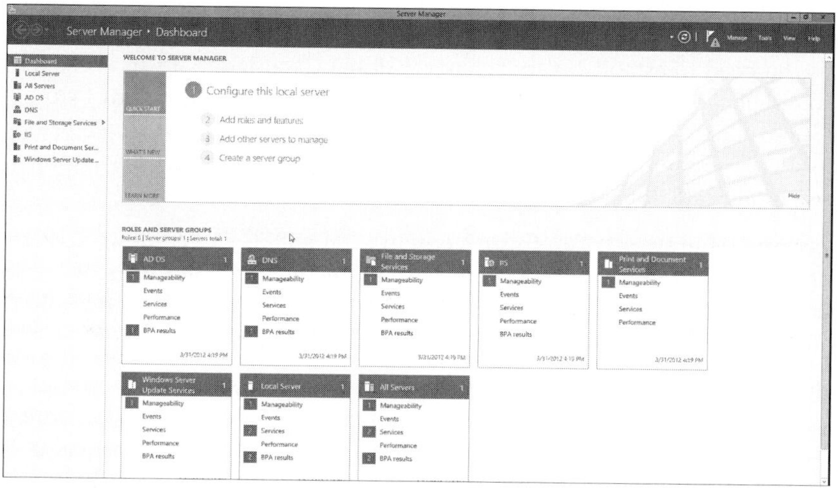

FIGURE 16.2 Server Manager console after upgrade.

The upgrade process shown in steps 1 through 9 is then repeated for each of the remaining 2008 R2 DCs.

Phased Migration

In many cases, the Windows Server 2003/2008 R2 environment that will be migrated includes one or more Active Directory domains and forests. Because Active Directory is one of the most important portions of a Microsoft network, it is subsequently one of the most important areas to focus on in a migration process. In addition, many of the improvements made to Windows Server 2012 are directly related to Active Directory, making it even more appealing to migrate this portion of an environment.

The decision to upgrade Active Directory should focus on these key improvement areas. If one or more of the improvements to AD DS justifies an upgrade, it should be considered. Improvements were introduced in Windows Server 2003 and Windows Server 2008, and yet more improvements were made in Windows Server 2012.

The following list details some of the many changes made to Active Directory in Windows Server 2003 that improved on the original Windows 2000 Server Active Directory:

- **Domain rename capability**—Windows Server 2003 Active Directory supported the renaming of either the NetBIOS name or the Lightweight Directory Access Protocol / domain name system (LDAP/DNS) name of an Active Directory domain. The Active Directory domain rename tool can be used for this purpose, but only in domains that have completely upgraded to Windows Server 2003 or later DCs.
- **Cross-forest transitive trusts**—Windows Server 2003 supports the implementation of transitive trusts that can be established between separate Active Directory forests. Windows 2000 supported only explicit cross-forest trusts, and the trust structure did not allow for permissions to flow between separate domains in a forest. This limitation has been lifted in Windows Server 2003 or later.
- **Universal group caching**—One of the main structural limitations of Active Directory was the need to establish very "chatty" Global Catalog servers in every site established in a replication topology, or run the risk of extremely slow client logon times and directory queries. Windows Server 2003 or later enables remote DCs to cache universal group memberships for users so that each logon request does not require the use of a local Global Catalog server.
- **Intersite topology generator (ISTG) improvements**—The ISTG in Windows Server 2003 was improved to support configurations with extremely large numbers of sites. In addition, the time required to determine site topology has been noticeably improved through the use of a more efficient ISTG algorithm.
- **Multivalued attribute replication improvements**—In Windows 2000 Server, if a universal group changed its membership from 5,000 users to 5,001 users, the entire group membership had to be re-replicated across the entire forest. Windows Server 2003 addressed this problem and allowed incremental membership changes to be replicated.

- **Lingering objects (zombies) detection**—Domain controllers that have been out of service for a longer period of time than the Time to Live (TTL) of a deleted object could theoretically "resurrect" those objects, forcing them to come back to life as zombies, or lingering objects. Windows Server 2003 properly identified these zombies and prevented them from being replicated to other DCs.
- **AD-integrated DNS zones in application partitions**—Replication of DNS zones was improved and made more flexible in Windows Server 2003 by storing AD-integrated zones in the application partition of a forest, thus limiting their need to be replicated to all DCs and reducing network traffic. Conversely, the DNS zones could be configured to replicate them to the entire forest if that was appropriate.

The Windows Server 2008 Active Directory retained all the new features of Windows Server 2003 Active Directory and adds several key new features, as follows:

- **Fine-grained password policies**—Password policies can be customized to different users within the same Active Directory domain.
- **Read-only DCs**—These DCs are designed for branch offices and for extranet scenarios, in that they allow directory information to be accessed but not changed. This adds an element of security to scenarios that require directory services but are not as secure as the corporate data center.
- **Granular auditing**—The Active Directory auditing is much more granular and allows tracking of some objects but not others. This reduces the volume of security logs; however, it provides less information for the auditor or analyst to review during an audit or information acquisition process.
- **Distributed File System Replication (DFSR)**—DFSR is now used for SYSVOL replication, replacing the File Replication Service (FRS) that is used to replicate SYSVOL in Windows 2000 Server and Windows Server 2003. This feature provides more robust and detailed replication of SYSVOL contents and is available when the domain functional level is raised to Windows Server 2008.

Features introduced with the upgrade to Windows Server 2008 R2 include the following:

- **Active Directory Module for Windows PowerShell**—The Active Directory Module for Windows PowerShell is a consolidated group of Windows PowerShell cmdlets you can use to manage Active Directory.
- **Active Directory Administrative Center**—The Active Directory Administrative Center is a task-oriented AD management console that allows for the management of users, groups, computers, sites, and domains from one console.
- **Recycle Bin for AD**—Previously deleted objects can now be restored from the Recycle Bin.
- **Offline domain join**—Join Windows machines to the domain, while offline, via an XML file.

- **Managed service accounts**—This feature greatly improves the daunting task of managing service account passwords by automatically updating all services when the service account password is changed.

Windows Server 2012 adds even more new functionality, including the following:

- **Support for DC snapshots**—The ability to roll back changes on a virtualized DCs without the issues caused by reusing relative identifiers (RIDs).
- **DC cloning**—The ability to deploy a new DC that already contains a mostly replicated copy of Active Directory. This reduces the replication traffic load and brings new DCs online faster.
- **GUI-based AD Recycle Bin**—The AD recycle bin introduced in Server 2008 R2 that was command line only now has a GUI.
- **Improved fine-grained password policies**—The process of creating a fine-grained password policy used to require ADSIEDIT. Windows Server 2012 enables you to configure these using the new Active Directory Administrative Center.
- **Active Directory Administrative Center**—Server 2012 offers a more consolidated and feature rich interface for administering Active Directory.

NOTE

For more information about the improvements to Active Directory and the ways they can be used to determine whether your organization should upgrade, see Chapter 4, "Active Directory Domain Services Primer," Chapter 5, "Designing a Windows Server 2012 Active Directory," Chapter 6, "Designing Organizational Unit and Group Structure," and Chapter 7, "Active Directory Infrastructure."

In the scenario in this section, there are two domains (companyabc.com and asia.companyabc.com), which are members of the same forest (shown in Figure 16.3). The companyabc.com domain has all Windows 2003 Server SP3 DCs, and the asia.companyabc.com domain has all Windows Server 2008 SP2 DCs. The entire forest will be upgraded to Windows Server 2012, but they need to be migrated over time. Therefore, a phased migration will be used.

Migrating DCs

There are two approaches to migrating DCs, similar to the logic used in the "Performing an Upgrade on a Single Domain Controller Server" section. The DCs can either be directly upgraded to Windows Server 2012 or replaced by newly introduced Windows Server 2012 DCs. The decision to upgrade an existing server largely depends on the hardware of the server in question. The rule of thumb is if the hardware will support Windows Server 2012 now and for the next 2 to 3 years, and is running an OS that supports an upgrade to Windows Server 2012, a server can be directly upgraded. If this is not the case, using new hardware for the migration is preferable.

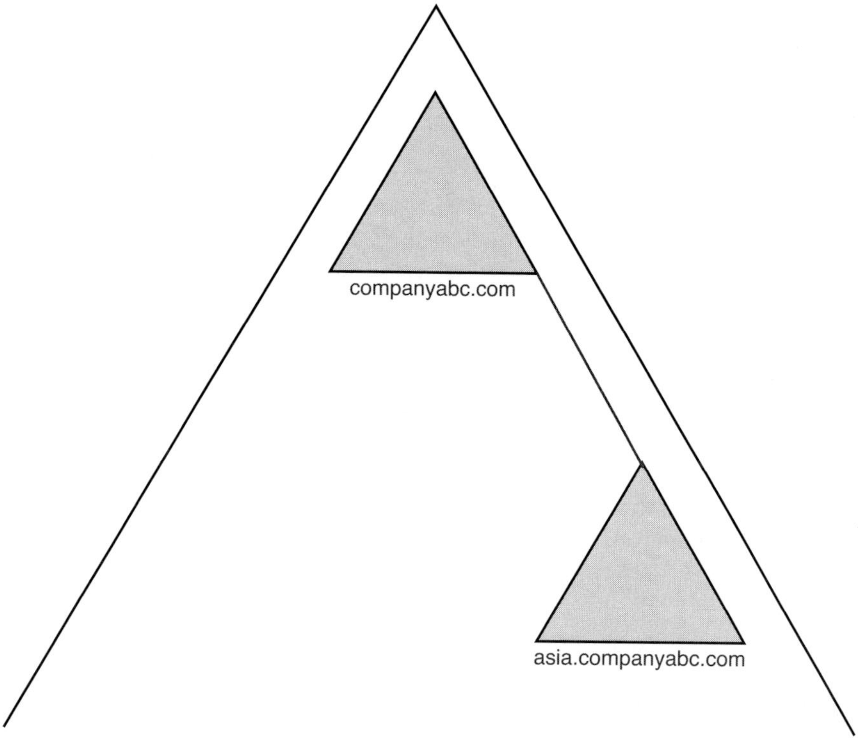

FIGURE 16.3 Company ABC forest.

The prerequisites for upgrading an Active Directory forest and domain discussed earlier still apply. The prerequisites to upgrade to Windows Server 2012 Active Directory are as follows:

- The OS on the DCs is Windows Server 2003 SP3 or higher.
- The current domain functional level is Windows 2003 Native.

These prerequisites are required to upgrade to Windows Server 2012.

NOTE

A combined approach can be and is quite commonly used, as indicated in Figure 16.4, to support a scenario in which some hardware is current but other hardware is out-of-date and will be replaced. Either way, the decisions applied to a proper project plan can help to ensure the success of the migration.

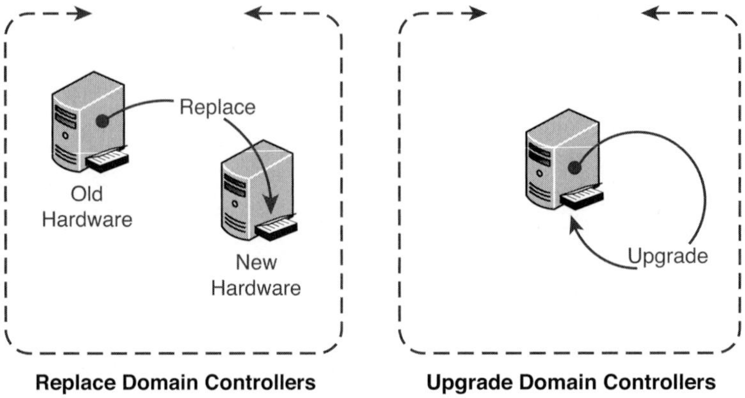

FIGURE 16.4 Combined approach to the upgrade process.

The scenario in this section uses the combined approach to the upgrade, replacing the Windows 2003 SP3 companyabc.com DCs and upgrading the Windows Server 2008 asia. companyabc.com DCs.

The health of the DCs should be verified before upgrading the DCs. In particular, the Domain Controller Diagnostics (DCDIAG) utility should be run and any errors fixed before the upgrade. The Windows Server 2003 DCDIAG utility is part of the Support Tools, which you can find on the installation media under \support\tools\. The Support Tools are installed via an MSI package named SUPTOOLS.MSI in Windows Server 2003. After installing the tools, the DCDIAG utility can be run. The `dcdiag /e` option should be used to check all DCs in the enterprise. Verify that all tests passed.

Preparing the Forest and Domains Using Adprep

The introduction of Windows Server 2012 DCs into a Windows Server 2003/2008 R2 Active Directory requires that the core AD database structure, the schema, be updated to support the increased functionality. In addition, several other security changes need to be made to prepare a forest for inclusion of Windows Server 2012. The Windows Server 2012 DVD includes a command-line utility called adprep that will extend the schema to include the extensions required and modify security as needed. Adprep requires that both forest-prep and domainprep be run before the first Windows Server 2012 DC can be added.

The adprep utility must be run from the Windows Server 2012 DVD or copied from its location in the \support\adprep\ folder. This installs the schema updates that are new to Windows Server 2012 Active Directory. The following steps should be run on the FSMO role holder, specifically the Schema Master role holder:

1. Insert the Windows Server 2012 DVD into the drive. If the Install Windows Autorun page appears, close the window.
2. Select Start, Run.

3. Enter **d:\support\adprep\adprep.exe /forestprep** and click OK, where d: is the DVD drive.

4. A warning appears to verify that all DCs in the forest are running Windows Server 2003 or later. Press C and then press Enter to start the forest preparation.

NOTE

Any previous extensions made to the Active Directory schema, such as those made with Exchange or Lync, are not affected by the adprep procedure. This procedure simply adds additional attributes and does not change those that currently exist.

Now that the schema updates have been installed, the domain is ready to be prepared. The operation must be run once in every domain in a forest. It must be physically invoked on the server that holds the Infrastructure Master role. The steps for executing the domainprep procedure are as follows:

1. On the Infrastructure Master DC, insert the Windows Server 2012 DVD into the drive. If the Install Windows Autorun page appears, close the window.

2. Select Start, Run.

3. Enter **d:\support\adprep\adprep.exe /domainprep /gpprep** and click OK, where d: is the DVD drive. This update updates the permissions on group policy objects (GPOs) in AD DS and Sysvol.

4. Enter **d:\support\adprep\adprep.exe /rodcprep** and click OK. This update allows RODCs by updating the permissions on all the DNS application directory partitions in the forest and allows them to be replicated by all RODCs that are also DNS servers.

Repeat steps 1 through 4 for each domain that will be upgraded.

After the forestprep and domainprep operations are run, the Active Directory forest is ready for the introduction or upgrade of Windows Server 2012 DCs. The schema is extended and includes support for Active Directory Recycle Bin and other enhancements. After these updates have had sufficient time to replicate across all domains, the process of upgrading the DCs to Windows Server 2012 can commence.

Upgrading Existing Domain Controllers

If the decision has been made to upgrade all or some existing hardware to Windows Server 2012, the process for accomplishing this is straightforward. However, as with the standalone server, you need to ensure that the hardware and any additional software components are compatible with Windows Server 2012. The requirements for the server to upgrade are as follows:

- The OS on the DCs must be a 64-bit OS.
- The OS on the DCs is Windows Server 2003 SP3 or Server 2008 (or higher). The DC hardware exceeds the Windows Server 2012 requirements and all software is compatible with Windows Server 2012, including antivirus software and drivers.
- There is enough disk space free to perform the OS and Active Directory upgrade. Specifically, verify that your free space is at least twice the size of your Active Directory database plus the minimum 32GB needed to install the OS.

After establishing this, the actual migration can occur. The procedure for upgrading a DC to Windows Server 2012 is nearly identical to the procedure outlined in the previous section "Performing an Upgrade on a Single Domain Controller Server." Essentially, simply insert the DVD and upgrade, and an hour or so later the machine will be updated and functioning as a Windows Server 2012 DC.

The specific steps are as follows:

1. Insert the Windows Server 2012 DVD into the DVD drive of the server to be upgraded.
2. The Install Windows page should appear automatically. If not, choose Start, Run, and then type **d:\Setup**, where d: is the drive letter for the DVD drive.
3. Click Install Now.
4. Click the large Go Online to Get the Latest Updates button. This ensures that the installation has the latest information for the upgrade.
5. Select the OS you want to install and click Next.
6. Select the I Accept the License Terms option on the License page, and click Next to continue.
7. Click the large Upgrade button.
8. Review the compatibility report and verify that all issues have been addressed. Click Next to continue.

   The system then copies files and reboots as a Windows Server 2012 server, continuing the upgrade process. After all files are copied, the system is then upgraded to a fully functional install of Windows Server 2012 and then reboots again. All this can take some time to complete.
9. After the final reboot, the DC is at the familiar Ctrl+Alt+Del screen. After logon, the DC opens to the Server Manager console. The DC upgrade is complete.

Repeat for all DCs that will be upgraded.

Replacing Existing Domain Controllers

If you need to migrate specific DC functionality to the new Active Directory environment but plan to use new hardware, you need to bring new DCs into the environment before retiring the old servers.

Windows Server 2012 uses a roles-based model. To make a Windows Server 2012 server a DC, the AD DS role is added. This is the most thorough approach, and the following steps show how to accomplish this to establish a new Windows Server 2012 DC in a Windows Server 2003/2008 R2 Active Directory domain:

NOTE

This procedure assumes that the Windows Server 2012 OS has been installed on the server. See Chapter 3 for steps to do this. The server does not need to be a domain member.

1. Log on to the new server as an administrator.
2. Launch Server Manager.
3. Click Add Roles and Features.
4. Select Role-Based or Feature-Based Installation and click Next.
5. Select the appropriate server from the server pool and click Next.
6. From the Select Server Roles page, check the box for Active Directory Domain Services, chick Add Features to accept the additional features, and click Next.
7. Click Next again to skip past the features.
8. Review the reminders related to AD DS installation and click Next.
9. Optionally check the box for Restart the Destination Server Automatically If Required and click Install.
10. Click Close.

NOTE

In Windows Server 2012, you can close the wizard for adding roles and features before the process is done. The notification area of Server Manager will notify you when the process is completed.

11. In Server Manager, click the notifications to see that the role has been installed.

    Figure 16.5 shows the alert that the AD DS role has been installed and indicates that additional configuration is required.

12. Click the Promote This Server to a DC link. This launches the Active Directory Domain Services Configuration Wizard.

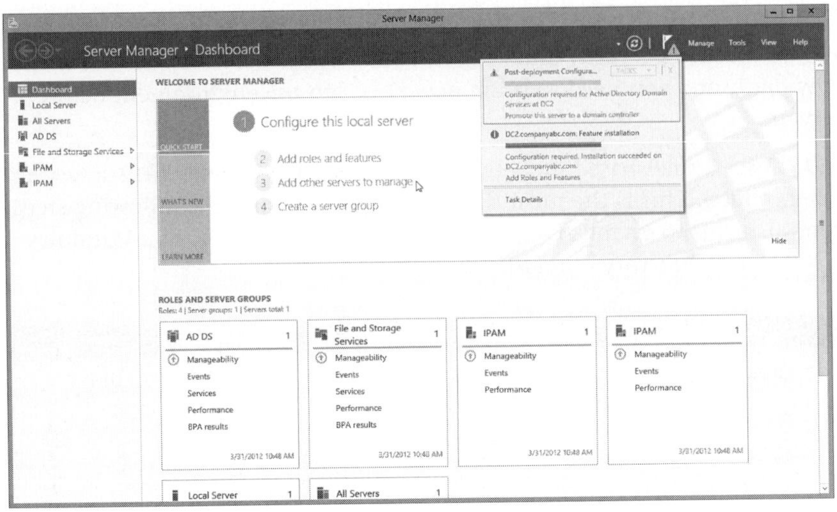

FIGURE 16.5 Reviewing task details.

13. Choose Add a Domain Controller to an Existing Domain, specify the name of the domain, and optionally change credentials if needed and click Next.

14. Optionally check the boxes to add DNS services and to make the DC a Global Catalog (GC) or to make the server an RODC. Select the appropriate site for the DC and enter the Directory Services Recovery Mode (DSRM) password. Click Next.

15. If the DNS box was selected in step 14, there will be an option to update DNS delegations. Click Next.

16. If Install from Media is being utilized to seed the initial AD database from a recent backup, check the box and enter the path to the content. For traditional replication-based creation, you can now select the source DC for replication. You can also add application partitions to be replicated. Click Next.

17. Select the destination paths for the AD database, log files and the SYSVOL folder. Click Next.

18. Review the options and click Next.

19. Read and understand the prerequisites check. If it passed and there are no warnings that need to be addressed, click Install.

The installation process can be observed to verify that it is completed successfully. Repeat this process for each new replacement DC.

NOTE

The ability to choose the source DC for replication via the GUI is a feature available in Windows Server 2012. This feature should be greatly appreciated by any administrator who has ever brought up a second DC in a local site only to watch the DC choose to replicate from a DC on the opposite side of the world that's connected through a single channel of ISDN.

Moving Operation Master Roles

AD DS uses a multimaster replication model, in which any one server can take over directory functionality, and each full DC contains a read/write copy of directory objects (with the exception of RODCs, which hold, as their name suggests, a read-only copy). There are, however, a few key exceptions to this, in which certain forestwide and domainwide functionality must be held by a single DC in the forest and in each domain respectively. These exceptions are known as Operation Master (OM) roles, also known as Flexible Single Master Operations (FSMO) roles. There are five OM roles, as shown in Table16.1.

TABLE 16.1 FSMO Roles and Their Scope

FSMO Roles	Scope
Schema master	Forest
Domain naming master	Forest
Infrastructure master	Domain
RID master	Domain
PDC emulator	Domain

If the server or servers that hold the OM roles are not directly upgraded to Windows Server 2012 but will instead be retired, these OM roles will need to be moved to another server. The best tool for this type of move is the NTDSUTIL command-line utility.

Follow these steps using NTDSUTIL to move the forestwide OM roles (schema master and domain naming master) to a single Windows Server 2012 DC:

1. Open a command prompt on the Windows Server 2012 DC. (Hover the mouse in the upper right, click Search, and type **CMD** in "apps" and press Enter).
2. Type **ntdsutil** and press Enter. The prompt will display "ntdsutil:".
3. Type **roles** and press Enter. The prompt will display "fsmo maintenance:".
4. Type **connections** and press Enter. The prompt will display "server connections:".
5. Type **connect to server Servername**, where <Servername> is the name of the target Windows Server 2012 DC that will hold the OM roles, and press Enter.

6. Type **quit** and press Enter. The prompt will display "fsmo maintenance:".
7. Type **transfer schema master** and press Enter.
8. Click Yes at the prompt asking to confirm the OM change. The display will show the location for each of the five FSMO roles after the operation.
9. Type **transfer naming master** and press Enter.
10. Click Yes at the prompt asking to confirm the OM change.
11. Type **quit** and press Enter, and then type **quit** and press Enter again to exit the NTDSUTIL.
12. Type **exit** to close the command prompt window.

Now the forestwide FSMO roles will be on a single Windows Server 2012 DC.

The domainwide FSMO roles (infrastructure master, RID master, and PDC emulator) need to be moved for each domain to a DC within the domain. The steps to do this are as follows:

1. Open a command prompt on the Windows Server 2012 DC. (Hover the mouse in the upper right, click Search and type **CMD** in "apps" and press Enter.)
2. Type **ntdsutil** and press Enter.
3. Type **roles** and press Enter.
4. Type **connections** and press Enter.
5. Type **connect to server <Servername>**, where <Servername> is the name of the target Windows Server 2012 DC that will hold the OM roles, and press Enter.
6. Type **quit** and press Enter.
7. Type **transfer pdc** and press Enter.
8. Click Yes at the prompt asking to confirm the OM change.
9. Type **transfer rid master** and press Enter.
10. Click Yes at the prompt asking to confirm the OM change.
11. Type **transfer infrastructure master** and press Enter.
12. Click Yes at the prompt asking to confirm the OM change.
13. Type **quit** and press Enter, then type **quit** and press Enter again to exit the NTDSUTIL.
14. Type **exit** to close the command prompt window.

The preceding steps need to be repeated for each domain.

Retiring Existing Windows Server 2003/2008 R2 DCs

After the entire Windows Server 2003/2008 R2 DC infrastructure is replaced by Windows Server 2012 equivalents and the OM roles are migrated, the process of demoting and removing all down-level DCs can begin. The most straightforward and thorough way of removing a DC is by demoting it using the dcpromo utility, per the standard Windows Server 2003/2008 R2 demotion process. After you run the `dcpromo` command, the DC becomes a member server in the domain. After disjoining it from the domain, it can safely be disconnected from the network.

Retiring “Phantom” DCs

As is often the case in Active Directory, DCs might have been removed from the forest without first being demoted. They become phantom DCs and basically haunt the Active Directory, causing strange errors to pop up every so often. This is because of a couple remnants in the Active Directory, specifically the NTDS Settings object and the SYSVOL replication object. These phantom DCs might come about because of server failure or problems in the administrative process, but you should remove those servers and remnant objects from the directory to complete the upgrade to Windows Server 2012. Not doing so will result in errors in the event logs and in the DCDIAG output as well as potentially prevent raising the domain and forest to the latest functional level.

Just deleting the computer object from Active Directory Sites and Services does not work. Instead, you need to use a low-level directory tool, ADSIEdit, to remove these servers properly. The following steps outline how to use ADSIEdit to remove these phantom DCs:

1. Hover the mouse in the upper right, click Search, and type **adsiedit.msc** in “apps” and press Enter.
2. In the ADSIEdit window, select Action, Connect To.
3. From the Select a Well Known Naming Context drop-down menu, select Configuration, and click OK.
4. Select the Configuration node.
5. Navigate to Configuration\CN=Configuration\CN=Sites\CN=<Sitename>\CN=Servers\CN=<Servername>, where <Sitename> and <Servername> correspond to the location of the phantom DC.
6. Right-click the CN=NTDS Settings, and click Delete, as shown in Figure 16.6.
7. At the prompt, click Yes to delete the object.
8. In the ADSIEdit window, select the top-level ADSIEdit node, and then select Action, Connect To.
9. From the Select a Well Known Naming Context drop-down menu, select Default Naming Context, and click OK.
10. Select the Default Naming Context node.

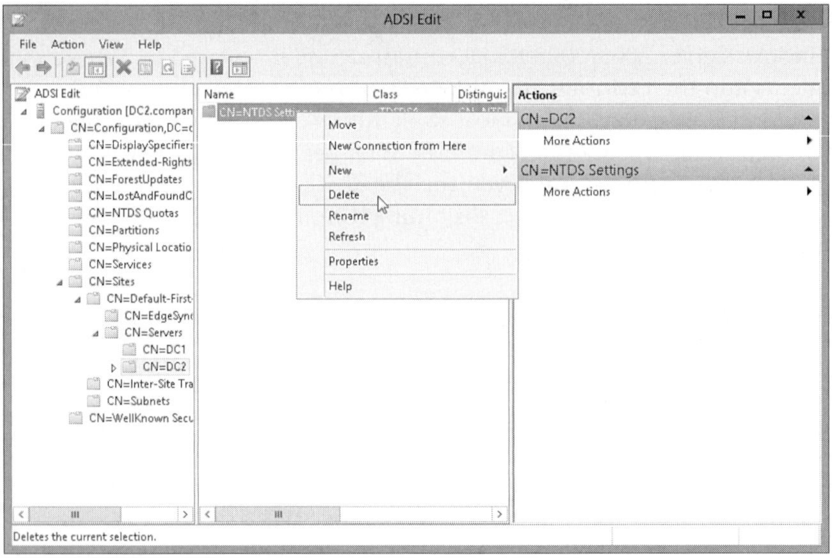

FIGURE 16.6 Deleting phantom DCs.

11. Navigate to Default naming context\<Domain DN>\CN=System\CN=File Replication Service\CN=Domain System Volume(SYSVOL share)\CN=<Servername>, where <Servername> corresponds to the name of the phantom DC and <Domain DN> corresponds to the distinguished name of the domain.
12. Right-click the CN=<Servername>, and select Delete.
13. At the prompt, click Yes to delete the object.
14. Close ADSIEdit.

At this point, after the NTDS Settings are deleted, the server can be normally deleted from the Active Directory Sites and Services snap-in.

NOTE

ADSIEdit was included in the Support Tools in Windows Server 2003, but is now included in the AD DS Tools that are installed automatically with the Active Directory Domain Services role in Windows Server 2012.

Upgrading Domain and Forest Functional Levels

Windows Server 2012 AD DS does not immediately begin functioning at a new level, even when all DCs have been migrated. The domains and forest will be at the original functional levels. You first need to upgrade the functional level of the domain to Windows Server 2012 before you can realize the full advantages of the upgrade. See Chapter 4 for a detailed discussion of the forest and domain functional levels.

NOTE

The act of raising the forest or domain functional levels is irreversible. Be sure that any Windows Server 2003/2008 R2 DCs do not need to be added anywhere in the forest before performing this procedure.

After all DCs are upgraded or replaced with Windows Server 2012 DCs, you can raise the domain level by following these steps:

1. Ensure that all DCs in the forest are upgraded to Windows Server 2012.
2. Launch Active Directory Users and Computers snap-in.
3. Right-click the domain name, and select Raise Domain Functional Level.
4. In the Select an Available Domain Functional Level drop-down menu, select Windows Server 2012, and then select Raise.
5. Click OK at the warning, and then click OK again to complete the task.

Repeat steps 1 through 5 for each domain in the forest. Now the forest functional level can be raised. Depending on the current forest functional level, this change might not add any new features, but it does prevent non-Windows Server 2012 DCs from being added in the future. To raise the forest functional level, follow these steps:

1. Launch Active Directory Domains and Trusts (reachable from the Start menu).
2. Right-click Active Directory Domains and Trusts and select Raise Forest Functional Level, as shown in Figure 16.7.
3. From the Select an Available Forest Functional Level drop-down menu, select Windows Server 2012, and then select Raise.
4. Click OK at the warning, and then click OK again to complete the task.

After each domain functional level is raised, as well as the forest functional level, the Active Directory environment is completely upgraded and fully compliant with all the AD DS improvements made in Windows Server 2012.

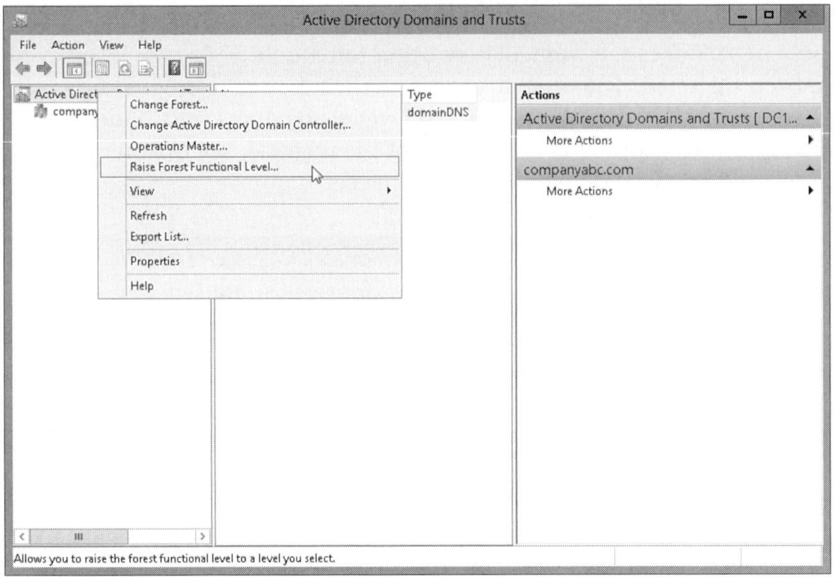

FIGURE 16.7 Raising the forest functional level.

Moving AD-Integrated DNS Zones to Application Partitions

The final step in a Windows Server 2012 Active Directory upgrade is to move any AD-integrated DNS zones into the newly created application partitions that Windows Server 2008 R2 uses to store DNS information. To accomplish this, follow these steps:

1. Launch DNS Manager.
2. Navigate to DNS\<Servername>\Forward Lookup Zones and select the zone to be moved.
3. Right-click the zone to be moved, and click Properties.
4. Click the Change button to the right of the replication description.
5. Select either To All DNS Servers Running on Domain Controllers in This Forest or To All DNS Servers Running on Domain Controllers in This Domain, depending on the level of replication you want, as shown in Figure 16.8. Click OK when you have finished, and then click OK again to save the changes.

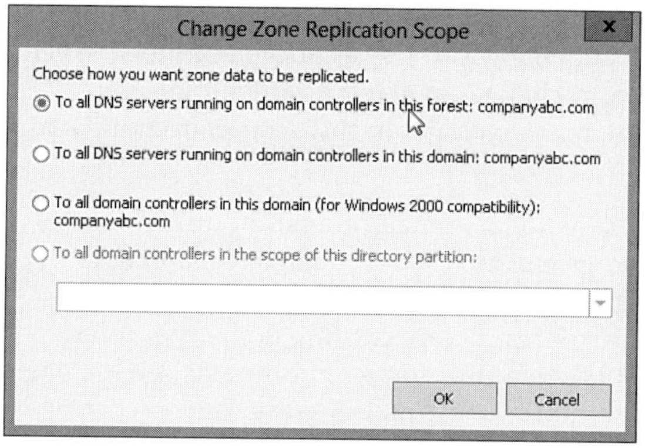

FIGURE 16.8 Moving AD-integrated zones.

Repeat the process for any other AD-integrated zones.

Multiple Domain Consolidation Migration

Sometimes it is better to migrate to a new forest and domain, instead of bringing along the baggage of a legacy Active Directory. This includes needing to consolidate names, concerns with the legacy Active Directory schema, or simply to consolidate Active Directory services. The consolidation migration allows an administrator to, in effect, start fresh with a clean installation of Active Directory. Figure 16.9 shows an example of the migration scenario used in this section, where the companyabc.com and asia.companyabc.com will be consolidated to a new forest with the domain companyxyz.com.

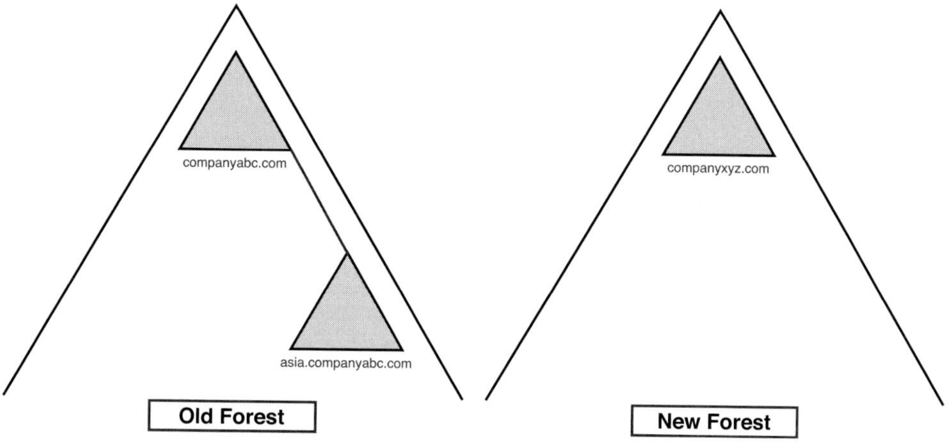

FIGURE 16.9 CompanyXYZ forest.

However, this can be disruptive to the users and applications if not handled carefully. Migrating to a new domain and forest results in changes to the security identifiers, which can impact access. It can also result in password changes, making it difficult for users. However, there are tools and techniques, which are explored in this section, to mitigate the impact to the users and applications.

The Active Directory Migration Tool, a fully functional domain migration utility, allows Active Directory users, computers, and groups to be consolidated, collapsed, or restructured to fit the design needs of an organization. With regard to Active Directory migrations, ADMT v3.2 provides the flexibility to restructure existing domain or forest environments into new Windows Server 2012 Active Directory environments, by keeping security settings, user passwords, and other settings. By maintaining the source security identifier (SID) as a SIDHistory attribute in the target environment, the object is effectively both the old and new object at the same time and can access resources assigned to either, so long as trusts are in place and SIDHistory filtering has been disabled.

Understanding ADMT Functionality

ADMT is an effective way to migrate users, groups, and computers from one domain to another. It is robust enough to migrate security permissions and Exchange mailbox domain settings. ADMT is composed of the following components and functionality:

- **ADMT migration wizards**—ADMT includes a series of wizards, each designed to migrate specific components. You can use different wizards to migrate users, groups, computers, service accounts, and trusts.
- **Low client impact**—ADMT automatically installs a service on source clients negating the need to manually install client software for the migration. In addition, after the migration is complete, these services are automatically uninstalled.
- **SID History and security migrated**—Users can continue to maintain network access to file shares, applications, and other secured network services through migration of the SID History attributes to the new domain. This preserves the extensive security structure of the source domain.

ADMT installs very easily but requires a thorough knowledge of the various wizards to be used properly. In addition, best-practice processes should be used when migrating from one domain to another.

The migration example in the following sections describes the most common use of the Active Directory Migration Tool: an interforest migration of domain users, groups, and computers into another domain. This procedure is by no means exclusive, and many other migration techniques can be used to achieve proper results. Subsequently, matching the capabilities of ADMT with the migration needs of an organization is important.

Using ADMT in a Lab Environment

You can develop the most effective lab by creating new DCs in the source and target domains and then physically segregating them into a lab network, where they cannot contact the production domain environment. The Operations Master (OM) roles for each domain can then be seized for each domain using the NTDSUTIL utility, which effectively creates exact replicas of all user, group, and computer accounts that can be tested with the ADMT.

ADMT v3.2 Installation Procedure

Install the ADMT component on a Windows Server 2012 DC in the target domain to which the accounts will be migrated. To install, follow these steps:

NOTE

As of this writing, ADMT 3.2 does not support installation on Windows Server 2012. To use the tool, install it on a Windows Server 2008 R2 server. After migration, decommission the Windows Server 2008 server.

1. Ensure a SQL Server instance is available or install SQL Server Express.
2. Download ADMT 3.2 from the Microsoft download site.
3. Choose Start, Run. Then browse to the download location, select admtsetup32.exe, and click Open. Click OK.
4. Click Run to launch the setup.
5. On the Welcome page, click Next to continue.
6. Accept the end-user license agreement (EULA), and click Next to continue.
7. On the Customer Improvement Program page, click Next
8. Define the required database server\instance name information, and then click Next to continue.
9. Leave the default No, Do Not Import Data from an Existing Database (Default). Click Next to continue.
10. After installation, click Finish to close the wizard.

ADMT Domain Migration Prerequisites

As previously mentioned, the most important prerequisite for migration with ADMT is lab verification. Testing as many aspects of a migration as possible can help to establish the procedures required and identify potential problems before they occur in the production environment.

That said, several technical prerequisites must be met before the ADMT can function properly. These are as follows:

- **Create one or two-way trusts between source and target domains**—The source and target domains must each be able to communicate with each other and share security credentials. Consequently, it is important to establish trusts between the two domains before running the ADMT.

- **Assign proper permissions on source domain and source domain workstations**—The account that will run the ADMT in the target domain must be added into the Builtin\Administrators group in the source domain. In addition, each workstation must include this user as a member of the local Administrators group for the computer migration services to be able to function properly. Domain group changes can be easily accomplished, but a large workstation group change must be scripted, or manually accomplished, before migration.
- **Create the target OU structure**—The destination for user accounts from the source domain must be designated at several points during the ADMT migration process. Establishing an organizational unit (OU) for the source domain accounts can help to simplify and logically organize the new objects. These objects can be moved to other OUs after the migration and this OU collapsed, if you want.

Exporting Password Key Information

The Password Export Server (PES) service is used to migrate passwords during interforest migrations. This service must be installed on the source domain and uses a password key generated previously.

A 128-bit encrypted password key must be installed from the target domain on a DC in the source domain. This key allows for the migration of password information from one domain to the next.

To create this key, follow these steps from the command prompt of the ADMT server in the target domain:

1. Insert a USB drive to store the key. (The key can be directed to the network, but for security reasons, directing to a USB drive is better.)
2. Open a command prompt.
3. Type **admt key /option:create /sourcedomain:<SourceDomainName> /keyfile:f:\domain.pes /keypassword:***, where <SourceDomainName> is the NetBIOS or DNS name of the source domain, f: is the destination drive for the key, and domain.pes is the password encryption filename. Then press Enter.

   The utility prompts for the password and confirmation of the password. Then the utility creates the password onto the destination drive.
4. Upon successful creation of the key, remove the USB drive and keep it in a safe place.

This needs to be repeated for each domain to be migrated.

Installing PES on the Source Domain

After exporting the password key from the target domain, you need to install the encrypted password key on a DC in the source domain. The procedure uses the key generated previously. The following procedure outlines this installation:

1. Insert the USB drive with the exported key from the target domain into the server's disk drive.
2. The installation source is a separate download from Microsoft with a version for 32-bit servers and one for 64-bit servers. This should be downloaded to the source DC.
3. Start the Password Migration Installer by browsing to find the downloaded file, PwdMig.msi, and running it.
4. On the Welcome page, click Next.
5. Accept the license agreement, and then click Next.
6. Enter the location of the key that was created on the target domain; normally, this is the USB drive that was used to transfer the key. Click Next to continue.
7. Enter and confirm the password that was set on the key file, and then click Next.
8. On the Verification page, click Next to continue.
9. Select an administrator account in the target domain for the service in the form domain\account and the password, and then click OK.
10. Click Finish when the installation is complete.
11. Open the Services console (Start, Administrative Tools, Services). Select the Password Export Server service and change its startup type to Automatic.
12. The system must be restarted, so click Yes when prompted to automatically restart. Upon restarting, the proper settings are in place to make this server a Password Export Server.

The account used for the service will be granted the Logon as a Service right. This needs to be installed on at least one source DC in each domain to be migrated.

Setting Proper Registry Permissions

The installation of the proper components creates special Registry keys, but leaves them disabled by default for security reasons. One of these is the `AllowPasswordExport` value. You need to enable this Registry key on the source domain to allow passwords to be exported from the Password Export Server. The following procedure outlines the use of the Registry Editor to perform this function:

1. On the PES DC in the source domain, open the Registry Editor (Start, Regedit).
2. Navigate to HKEY_LOCAL_MACHINE\SYSTEM\CurrentControlSet\Control\LSA.

3. Double-click the AllowPasswordExport DWORD value.
4. Change the properties from 0 to 1 (Hexadecimal).
5. Click OK and close the Registry Editor.
6. Reboot the machine for the Registry changes to be enacted.

This allows passwords to be exported from the source domain to the target domain.

Configuring Domains for SID Migration

Migration of the source security identifiers (SIDs) into the target domain SID History allows the security assigned in access control lists (ACLs) to work transparently after the migration. This gives the administrator time to reset ACLs on a gradual basis or even after all objects are migrated.

Several settings need to be configured to allow for the SIDs to be transferred. These settings include creating a local group in the source domain for auditing, enabling TCP/IP client support on the source PDC emulator, and, finally, enabling auditing on both the source and target domains.

To create the local group on the source domain for auditing, follow these steps:

1. Log on to a DC on the source domain.
2. Launch Active Directory Users and Computers.
3. Create a domain local group named SourceDomain$$$, where SourceDomain is the NetBIOS name of the source domain. For example, the local group for the companyabc.com domain would be companyabc$$$.

Do not add any members to the group; if you do, the migration process will fail.

To enable TCP/IP client support, follow these steps:

1. Log on to the PDC emulator DC in the source domain.
2. Launch the Registry Editor.
3. Navigate to \HKEY\LocalMachine\System\CurrentControlSet\Control\LSA.
4. Create the value TcpipClientSupport REG_DWORD and assign it a value of 1.
5. Exit the Registry Editor and restart the computer.

To enable auditing in Windows Server 2008 R2 domains, follow these steps:

1. Select Start, Administrative Tools, Group Policy Management.
2. Drill Down to Forest, Domains, Domain, Domain Controllers, Group Policy Objects. Right-click and choose New.

3. Enter a name for the new policy and click Ok. Right-click the new policy in the main pane and choose Edit.
4. Drill down to Computer Configuration, Policies, Windows Settings, Security Settings, Local Policies, and select the Audit Policy node.
5. Double-click the Audit Account Management policy.
6. Check the Define These Policy Settings and select both Success and Failure.
7. Click OK to save the changes.
8. Right-click the domain name object and select Link and Existing GPO. Select the new auditing GPO and click OK.
9. Exit the Group Policy Management Editor.
10. Repeat the preceding steps for all source and target domains.

Administrators of domains that are 2008 or higher can configure more granular auditing policies at Computer Configuration, Policies, Windows Settings, Security Settings, Advanced Audit Policy Configuration, Audit Policies.

Now the source and target domains will be prepared to transfer SIDs into the SID History.

Migrating Groups

In most cases, the first objects to be migrated into a new domain should be groups. If users are migrated first, their group membership will not transfer over unless that setting is explicitly added. However, if the groups exist before the users are migrated, they will automatically find their place in the group structure. To migrate groups using ADMT v3.2, use the Group Account Migration Wizard, as follows:

1. Using your migration service account, open the ADMT MMC snap-in (Start, Administrative Tools, Active Directory Migration Tool).
2. Right-click Active Directory Migration Tool in the left pane, and choose Group Account Migration Wizard.
3. Click Next to continue.
4. Type the source and destination domains, select the source and destination DCs, and click Next to continue.
5. Choose the Select Groups from Domain option, and click Next.
6. On the subsequent page, you can select the group accounts from the source domain. Select all the groups required by using the Add button and selecting the objects. After you select the groups, click Next to continue.
7. Enter the destination OU for the accounts from the source domain by clicking Browse and selecting the OU created in the steps outlined previously. Click Next to continue.

8. On the following page, you have several options to choose from that determine the nature of the migrated groups. Clicking the Help button details the nature of each setting. In the sample migration, choose the settings to update user rights, fix membership of groups, and migrate group SIDs to target domain. Click Next to continue.

9. Enter a user account with proper administrative rights on the source domain on the following page. Then click Next to continue.

10. The subsequent page allows for the exclusion of specific directory-level attributes from migration. If you need to exclude any attributes, they can be set here. In this example, no exclusions are set. Click Next to continue.

11. Naming conflicts often arise during domain migrations. In addition, different naming conventions might apply in the new environment. Objects will not be migrated if conflicts occur. Click Next.

12. The verification page is the last wizard page you see before any changes are made. Once again, make sure that the procedure has been tested before running it because ADMT will henceforth write changes to the target Windows Server 2012 Active Directory environment. Click Finish when you are ready to begin group migration.

13. The group migration process then commences. The window shows the migration progress. Click Close when it completes.

The groups are now migrated to the new domain.

Migrating User Accounts

User accounts are the "bread and butter" of domain objects and are among the most important components. The biggest shortcoming of older versions of ADMT was their inability to migrate passwords of user objects, which effectively limited its use. However, ADMT v3.2 does an excellent job of migrating users, their passwords, and the security associated with them. To migrate users, follow these steps:

1. Using your migration service account open the ADMT MMC snap-in (Start, Administrative Tools, Active Directory Migration Tool).

2. Right-click the Active Directory Migration Tool, and choose User Account Migration Wizard.

3. Click Next on the Welcome page.

4. Select the source and target domains on the subsequent page, and click Next to continue.

5. Choose the Select Users from Domain option, and click Next.

6. The following page allows you to choose user accounts for migration. Just click the Add button and select the user accounts to be migrated. After you select all the user accounts, click Next to continue.

7. The next page allows you to choose a target OU for all created users. Choose the OU by clicking the Browse button. After you select it, click Next to continue.
8. Select Migrate Passwords, and then select the server in the source domain in which the Password Export Server (PES) service was installed, as covered in the "Installing PES on the Source Domain" section. Click Next to continue.
9. On the Account Transition Options page, leave the default transition options, and click Next.
10. Enter the account to use when adding SID History, which has to have administrative rights on the source domain. Then click Next.
11. The subsequent page deals with User Options settings. Click Help for an overview of each option. Select Translate Roaming Profiles. Then click Next to continue.
12. The next page is for setting exclusions. Specify any property of the user object that should not be migrated here. In this example, no exclusions are set. Click Next to continue.
13. Naming conflicts for user accounts are common. Designate a procedure for dealing with duplicate accounts in advance and enter such information about the next wizard page. Select the appropriate options for duplicate accounts and click Next to continue.
14. The following verification page presents a summary of the procedure that will take place. This is the last page before changes are written to the target domain. Verify the settings and click Finish to continue.
15. The Migration Progress status box displays the migration process as it occurs, indicating the number of successful and unsuccessful accounts created. When the process is complete, review the log by clicking View Log and verify the integrity of the procedure. Click Close when you have finished.

NOTE

Depending on if other wizards have already been run, there might be additional steps at this point that happen one time only to set up proper Registry settings, reboot DCs, and create special groups.

Migrating Computer Accounts

Another important set of objects that must be migrated is also one of the trickier ones. Computer objects must not only be migrated in AD, but they must also be updated at the workstations themselves so that users will be able to log on effectively from their consoles. ADMT seamlessly installs agents on all migrated computer accounts and reboots them, forcing them into their new domain structures.

The account running the ADMT must have local administrator rights to the computers being migrated. The agents must also be accessible over the network, so any firewalls should be disabled for the migration or grant exceptions.

Follow these steps to migrate computer accounts:

1. Using your migration service account open the ADMT MMC snap-in (Start, Administrative Tools, Active Directory Migration Tool).
2. Right-click the Active Directory Migration Tool, and choose Computer Migration Wizard.
3. Click Next on the Welcome page.
4. Type the names of the source and destination domains in the drop-down boxes on the next page, and click Next to continue.
5. Choose the Select Computers from Domain option, and click Next.
6. On the following page, select the computer accounts that will be migrated by clicking the Add button and selecting the appropriate accounts. Click Next to continue.
7. Select the OU the computer accounts will be migrated to, and click Next to continue.
8. The next Translate Objects page allows for the option to specify which settings on the local clients will be migrated. Click the Help button for a detailed description of each item. In this example, select all items. Click Next to continue.
9. The subsequent page prompts to choose whether existing security will be replaced, removed, or added to. In this example, replace the security. Click Next to continue.
10. A prompt then informs you that the user rights translation will be performed in Add mode only. Click OK to continue.
11. The next page is important because it allows an administrator to specify how many minutes a computer will wait before restarting itself (the default is 5 minutes). Click Next to continue.
12. Just as in the previous wizards, exclusions can be set for specific attributes in the following wizard page. Select any exclusions needed and click Next to continue.
13. Naming conflicts are addressed on the subsequent page. If any specific naming conventions or conflict resolution settings are required, enter them here. Click Next to continue.
14. The Completion page lists a summary of the changes that will be made. Review the list and click Finish when you are ready. All clients that will be upgraded are subsequently rebooted.
15. When the migration process is complete, you can view the Migration log by clicking the View Log button. After verifying all settings, click Close.

16. The ADMT Agent Dialog window opens. This tool enables the administrator to control the agent operations. Click Start to run pre-check. This identifies any potential issues with the agent migration. The results of the pre-check will be displayed in the Pre-check column. Verify that all computers passed.

17. In the Agent Actions box, select the Run Pre-Check and Agent Operations option button. Then click Start to perform the migration operations.

18. The client agents are subsequently distributed to all clients that have been migrated. Click Close on the ADMT MMC snap-in to end the wizard.

Each agent is installed automatically and counts down until the designated time limit set during the configuration of the Computer Migration Wizard. Then the migrated computers reboot into the new domain with the designated settings migrated.

Migrating Other Domain Functionality

In addition to the Group, User, and Computer Migration Wizards, you can use several other wizards to migrate specific domain-critical components. These wizards operate using the same principles as those described in the preceding sections and are straightforward in their operation. The following is a list of the additional wizards included in ADMT v3.2:

- Security Translation Wizard
- Reporting Wizard
- Service Account Migration Wizard
- Managed Service Account Migration Wizard
- Retry Task Wizard
- Password Migration Wizard

Almost all necessary functionality that needs replacing when migrating from one domain to another can be transferred by using ADMT v3.2. It has proven to be a valuable tool that gives administrators an additional option to consider when migrating and restructuring Active Directory environments.

Migrating Server Roles to Windows Server 2012

Migrating server roles, system settings, and data from your 32-bit and older Windows OSs to Windows Server 2012 has been made easier with the updated version of the Windows Server Migration Tools, the Printer Migration Wizard, and the printbrm.exe command-line utility. The following sections go over the installation, setup, and usage of these tools.

Windows Server Migration Tools

The Windows Server migration tools are a Windows Server 2012 feature, installed via the Add Feature Wizard within Server Manager, that uses PowerShell cmdlets to facilitate the migration of server roles, system settings, and data from older versions of Windows and 32-bit versions of Windows to Windows Server 2012. Before you can use the Windows

Server migration tools to migrate services from one server to another, the tools need to be installed on both the source and destination servers. Because the Windows Server migration tools are included with Windows Server 2012, the tools must be packaged and installed on Windows Server 2003 or Windows Server 2008 systems if the source servers are running either of these OSs.

Windows Server migration tools source server requirements are as follows:

- Windows Server 2003 SP2 or later
- 25MB of free space to store the Windows Server Migration Tools folder
- Microsoft .NET Framework 2.0
- Windows PowerShell 1.0 or later

As with any migration, a backup of the system or data being migrated is recommended before using the Windows Server migration tools. Before decommissioning any migrated server, confirm the new server is functioning properly.

To prepare the target Windows Server 2012 server for migration, follow these steps:

1. On the target server, open Server Manager, and then click Add Roles and Features.
2. Choose Role-based or feature-based installation, and click Next.
3. Select the server from the server pool, and click Next.
4. Click Next to skip past the roles.
5. On the Features page, check Windows Server Migration Tools, and then click Next.
6. Click Install, and then click Close when installation is complete.
7. On the target server, open a PowerShell console session as an administrator.
8. Type **CD $env:windir\system32\servermigrationtools**, and then press Enter.
9. Type **.\smigdeploy /package /architecture x86 /os ws03 /path <folderpath>**.

NOTE

If the source server is 64-bit, change x86 to amd64, and if the source server is Windows Server 2008, change WS03 to WS08. The previous command creates an appropriately named folder in the path specified.

To prepare the source server for migration, follow these steps:

1. Copy <folderpath>\SMT_WS03_x86 from the target server to the source server.
2. Open a command prompt, type **cd <folderpath>\SMT_WS03_x86**, and then press Enter.
3. Type **smigdeploy.exe**, and then press Enter.

You have now installed the Windows Server migration tools and are ready to start migrating.

Migrating DHCP

DHCP server migration to Windows Server 2012 can be accomplished quickly and easily using the Windows Server migration tools. In the following example, we use the Windows Server 2012 migration tools to migrate DHCP server settings from a 32-bit Windows Server 2008 server. The following steps assume you have already followed the procedures for installing the Windows Server migration tools and have configured both source and target servers. The overall process of using the Windows Server migration tools to migrate DHCP services is as follows:

1. Verify the DHCP configuration on the source server is current and working correctly.
2. Click Start, Administrative Tools, expand the Windows Server Migration Tools folder, and then click Windows Server Migration Tools.
3. Type **stop-service dhcpserver**, and press Enter.
4. Type **get-smigserverfeature**, and press Enter.

NOTE

`Get-SmigServerFeature` is the command that scans the source computer for roles or features supported for migration using the Windows Server migration tools.

5. Type **export-smigserversetting -featureid dhcp -ipconfig -user ALL -group -path <folderpath> -verbose**.

NOTE

The `-user` and `-group` switches are optional and only used when migrating the DHCP Administrators group membership. The `-user` switch is used only if there are local user accounts listed as members.

6. Type a password when prompted, and press Enter to start the export.
7. After the export completes, move the export created in <folderpath> to the target server.
8. Unauthorize the source DHCP server.
9. On the target server, open Server Manager, click Tools, and then select the Windows Server Migration Tools option.
10. Type **import-smigserversetting -featureid dhcp -path <folderpath> -verbose**.
11. Type the password used to create the migration file earlier.

NOTE

The Windows Server migration tools install the required roles and features to complete the migration. In this case, the DHCP server role has been installed. However, the DHCP server tools are not installed and need to be installed afterwards as a follow-up task.

12. Confirm Success is marked as True to confirm migration is complete and if a reboot is required reboot the server.
13. Once the server has rebooted log back in, start a PowerShell console session, and then type **start-service dhcpserver**.
14. Next, open Server Manager, click Task Details (the flag), and select the Complete DHCP Configuration option. Running this wizard will create the DHCP Administrators and the DHCP Users security groups on the local machine.
15. On the Description page of the DHCP Post-Install Wizard, click Commit to continue.
16. On the Summary page, verify the security groups were created and that authorization has completed. Click Close in the Post-Install Wizard window.
17. Finally, authorize the new DHCP server to complete the server migration.

Migrating IP Configuration

You can use the Windows Server migration tools to migrate the IP configuration from your source Windows Server 2003, Windows Server 2008, or Windows Server 2008 R2 server to your target Windows Server 2012 system. The IP configuration migration can be included in any other service migration by simply adding the `-ipconfig` switch to the `export-smigserversetting` command.

The overall process of using the Windows Server migration tools to migrate DHCP services is as follows:

1. On the source server, click Start, Administrative Tools, Windows Server Migration Tools, right-click Windows Server Migration Tools, and click Run as Administrator.
2. Type **Export-smigserversetting -ipconfig -path <datapath> -verbose**.
3. Provide a password when prompted.
4. When the export is complete, you can copy the export file to your destination server and then start the import process.

NOTE

Take a snapshot of your current IPConfig by typing **ipconfig /all > C:\ipconfig.txt**. This can be used to verify settings postmigration if needed.

5. On the source server, change the IP address or disconnect it from the network.

6. On the target server, open Server Manager, click Tools, and then select the Windows Server Migration Tools option.

7. Type **import-smigserversetting -ipconfig ALL -sourcephysicaladdress "<sourcephysicaladdress1>","<sourcephysicaladdress2>" -targetphysicaladdress "<targetphysicaladdress1>","<targetphysicaladdress2>" -path <datapath> -verbose**.

8. When prompted, provide the password set during export.

NOTE

You must specify the physical mapping for each adapter indicated by <sourcephysicaladdress1> and <targetphysicaladdress1>. Use the physical address for each adapter where indicated.

9. A restart is required for some of the settings to take effect.

Migrating Print Services

Migrating printer settings from an older environment can be accomplished by first exporting print queues, printer ports, and settings before importing them to Windows Server 2012. The tools at your disposal for this job are the Printer Migration Wizard or the printbrm.exe command-line utility.

NOTE

Migrating printer settings directly from Windows 2000 servers and older using the Printer Migration Wizard or the printbrm.exe command-line tool is not supported. An interim migration to Windows Server 2003 or 2008 is required before migrating to Windows Server 2012.

The Printer Migration Wizard gives you the GUI that walks you through the migration process. This is the easiest method of migrating printers. The steps to migrate print servers are as follows (assuming the Print and Document Services role has already been installed):

1. Open Print Management from the Start menu.

2. If not already there, add the remote print server using Add/Remove Servers.

3. Right-click the remote server and select Export Printers to a File to launch the Printer Migration Wizard.

4. Review the list of items to be exported, and then click Next.

5. Browse to the location on the local server to save the export file, and then click Next.

6. Click Finish when the export is complete.

7. Still in Print Management, right-click the target server, and click Import Printers from a File to launch the Printer Migration Wizard.

8. Browse to the export file location on the local server, click Open, and then click Next.
9. Review the list of items to be imported, and then click Next.
10. Select Import mode, specifying if you want to overwrite or keep existing printers.
11. Select List in the Directory to specify your preferences for listing the imported printers in the Active Directory.
12. Check Convert LPR Ports to Standard Port Monitors if you want to take advantage of the faster Standard Port Monitor.
13. Click Next to start the import.
14. When the import has completed, click Finish.

NOTE

For in-place-upgrades, use the Printer Migration Wizard to export printer settings before the upgrade and then import printer settings back to the same server after the upgrade has completed.

An alternative method of migrating the printer servers is to use the command-line utility printbrm.exe. This utility is not as "pretty" to use as the Printer Migration Wizard, but it enables you to automate the migration process and reduces the number of steps. The steps to migrate using the command line are as follows:

1. On the target server, open a PowerShell console session as an administrator.
2. Type **CD env:windir\system32\spool\tools** and press Enter.
3. Type **printbrm -s \\<SourceServer>\ -b -f <filename>.printerexport** and press Enter.
4. Type **printbrm -s \\<TargetServer>\ -r -f <filename>.printerexport** and press Enter.

Summary

Although Windows Server 2003/2008 R2 and Windows Server 2012 are close cousins in the OS family tree, there are some compelling reasons to upgrade to Windows Server 2012 AD DS. The evolutionary nature of Windows Server 2012 makes performing this procedure more straightforward because the upgrade does not require major changes to Active Directory architecture or the OS design.

In addition, advanced tools such as ADMT v3.2 provide for a broad range of options to bring organizations to Windows Server 2008 R2 functionality and closer to realizing the benefits that can be obtained through a migration.

Best Practices

The following are best practices from this chapter:

- Ensure that one of the post-upgrade tasks performed is an audit of all services so that servers that need IIS have the service reenabled after migration.
- Because prototype phases of a project are essential to test the design assumptions for a migration or implementation, create a production DC and then isolate it in the lab for testing.
- Test the hardware compatibility of any server that will be directly upgraded to Windows Server 2012 against the published HCL from Microsoft.
- Keep in mind that Windows Server 2012 is only available as 64-bit when developing migration plans. Older 32-bit hardware will need to be decommissioned or repurposed.
- Because the decision to raise the forest or domain functional levels is irreversible, ensure that there is no additional need to add Windows Server 2003/2008 R2 DCs anywhere in the forest and that there are no other compatibility issues before performing this procedure.
- If the server or servers that hold the OM roles are not directly upgraded to Windows Server 2012 but will instead be retired, move these OM roles to another server.
- When using ADMT, migrate groups into a new domain first to keep users' group memberships intact.
- Use the new Windows Server migration tools to migrate server roles to Windows Server 2012.

CHAPTER 17
Compatibility Testing

IN THIS CHAPTER

- The Importance of Compatibility Testing
- Preparing for Compatibility Testing
- Researching Products and Applications
- Verifying Compatibility with Vendors
- Microsoft Assessment and Planning Toolkit
- Lab-Testing Existing Applications
- Documenting the Results of the Compatibility Testing
- Determining Whether a Prototype Phase Is Required

At this point in the book, the new features of Windows Server 2012 have been presented and discussed in depth, as have the essential design considerations and migration processes. The goal of this chapter is to examine the process of testing the actual applications that rely on the Windows Server 2012 infrastructure.

This chapter provides insight into the steps necessary to gather information before the testing process begins, how to actually test the applications and document the results, and how to determine whether a more extensive prototype testing process is needed. Going through this process is vital to ensure the success of the project and to avoid a displeased end-user community. The application testing process is intended as a quick way to validate the compatibility and functionality of the proposed end state for the upgrade.

Currently, many companies are seeking to optimize their network environment, whether that is getting the best use out of servers on-premise or migrating server services to the cloud. Migrating to Windows Server 2012 with its higher capacity limits and multitenant capabilities is a chance to optimize servers within the network infrastructure. At the end of the process, fewer servers will handle the same tasks as before, and new functionality and cloud-based services might have been added, making the configurations of the environment that much more complex, and making it even more important to thoroughly test the mission-critical networking applications for compatibility. For example, Windows Server 2012 introduces a tremendous number of new technologies that enhance failover clustering, web applications, virtualization, security, Remote Desktop

Services, improved branch office deployments, and much more, prompting some organizations to replace existing Windows systems with Windows Server 2012. Therefore, it is even more important to test this configuration to ensure that the hardware and software are compatible, the performance meets user expectations, and the everyday features used by the employees to share knowledge and collaborate are in place.

The results of the application compatibility testing process will validate the goals of the project or reveal goals that need to be modified because of application incompatibility or instability. If one key application simply will not work reliably on Windows Server 2012, the legacy Windows system might need to be kept as part of the networking environment, which changes the overall design. As discussed in Part II of this book, "Windows Server 2012 Active Directory," a variety of different combinations of Windows Server system configurations can be combined in the end configuration, so the chances that there will be a way to keep the troublesome applications working in the new environment are good.

NOTE

Many legacy systems running old applications and operating systems cannot be upgraded to Windows Server 2012. This is because the application is not compatible with 64-bit operating systems like what Windows Server 2012 is built under. A direct upgrade from the legacy operating system is not supported, and the hardware is not compatible with Windows Server 2012. When these circumstances exist, it is common for organizations to utilize virtualization technologies such as Hyper-V Server or VMware to emulate and maintain these legacy applications and operating systems.

The Importance of Compatibility Testing

The process presented in this chapter is an essential step to take in validating the design for the end state of the migration or upgrade. The size of the organization and the breadth and scope of the upgrade are important factors to consider in determining the level of testing needed and whether a full prototype should be conducted.

The differences between a prototype phase and an application testing phase can be dramatic or negligible based on the nature of the upgrade. A prototype phase replicates the end state as completely as possible, often using the same hardware in the test lab that will be used in the production rollout.

CAUTION

Application testing can be performed on different hardware with different configurations than the end state, but be aware that the more differences there are between the testing environment and the actual upgraded environment, the greater the risk for unexpected results. Essentially, you can do an application testing phase without a complete prototype phase, but you shouldn't do a prototype phase without a thorough application testing process. This recommendation also applies when planning to use virtual technologies such as Hyper-V.

Most network users do not know or care which server or how many servers perform which task or house which application, but they will be unhappy if an application no longer works after a migration to Windows Server 2012. If the organization already has Active Directory in place and is running Windows Server 2008 / 2008 R2 systems, the risk of application incompatibility is likely to be less than if the organization is migrating from an older operating system, such as Windows 2000 (or earlier) or a competing operating system, such as Novell NetWare.

Preparing for Compatibility Testing

Although the amount of preparation needed will vary based on a number of factors, certain steps should be followed in any organization—the scope of the testing should be identified (what's in and what's out), the goals of the testing process should be clarified, and the process should be mapped out.

A significant advantage of following a phased design methodology, as presented in Chapter 2, "Best Practices at Planning, Prototyping, Migrating, and Deploying Windows Server 2012," is in the planning discussions that take place and in the resulting statements of work, design, and migration documents that are created as deliverables. Often, companies contract with migration experts or Microsoft partners—such as Convergent Computing, also known as CCO—to help companies avoid classic mistakes in the upgrade process. By the end of this planning process, it will be clear why the project is happening, which departments need which features and capabilities, and what budget is available to perform the work. The timeline and key milestones also will be defined.

If a phased discovery and design process hasn't been followed, this information needs to be gathered to ensure that the testing process addresses the goals of the project stakeholders, and that the right applications are in fact tested and verified by the appropriate people.

Determining the Scope for Application Testing

At this point in the process, a list should be put together that clarifies which Windows Server 2012 version is to be used, which version of server software will be used, which add-in features are required, and which third-party applications are needed. As discussed previously, Windows Server 2012 comes in Standard and Datacenter Editions. Windows Server 2012 comes in a 64-bit version only, eliminating the 32-bit version of the server operating system. Smaller organizations might choose to use the Standard Edition of Windows Server 2012 operating system, whereas larger organizations might require the Datacenter Edition on their server systems to support greater densities of virtual guest sessions.

A key issue to discuss at this point is whether it is acceptable to have multiple versions of the Windows Server operating system in the final solution. Some organizations want to control standards on both software and support services and require just a single network operating system such as Windows Server 2012 across the board.

NOTE

Although the Standard Edition of Windows Server 2012 is less expensive than the Datacenter Edition of the license, cost should not be the primary reason for choosing one version over another. The way Microsoft is doing licensing of Windows Server 2012, the versions are no longer limited in basic features like clustering, load balancing, or support for memory per guest session and rather focused on the number of virtual instances that can be run on the operating systems. Organizations that need to run more than a couple virtual guest sessions on a host system will buy the Datacenter Edition of the software just to increase the density of guest sessions per host server.

Third-party applications should be identified as well. The applications most often used include tape-backup software modules or agents, antivirus software, fax software, and voicemail integration products. Additional third-party add-on products might include the following:

- Administration
- Antispam
- Backup and storage
- Customer relationship management (CRM)
- Log monitoring
- Line-of-business applications
- Migration
- Reporting
- Security and encryption

The hardware to be used should be listed, as well, to ensure that it is available when needed. Ideally, the exact hardware to be used in the upgrade will be ordered for the application testing process, but if that is not possible, hardware with specifications similar to that of the servers that will eventually be used should be allocated. Although processor speed and amount of RAM will most likely not make a difference to whether the application functions properly on the server platform, certain hardware devices should be as similar as possible. Tape drives, for example, should have the same features as the ones to be used in the production environment because this is one of the most critical components. If an autoloader will be used in the production environment, one should be made available for the application testing process. If faxing from the Outlook Inbox is required, the same faxing hardware should also be allocated. Another example is implementing clustering with a storage-area network (SAN) back end. If a SAN will be used in production and the test criteria of the lab is to validate clustering functionality, the same production SAN should be used in the test environment. By using the same SAN solution, clustering test criteria and clustering functionality can be validated and guaranteed.

Some applications require clients to be present for the testing process, so at least one workstation class system should be available for this purpose. Connectivity to the Internet might also be necessary for testing the functionality of remote access products and antivirus software.

Table 17.1 shows a sample checklist of requirements for summarizing the scope of the application testing phase.

TABLE 17.1 Checklist for Application Testing

Server #1 Details (Include Version Numbers)
Server specs required:
Processor
RAM
Hard drive configuration
Other
Network operating system and service packs:
Tape backup software version and agents:
Additional third-party apps required:
Virtualization? Yes/No
Additional hardware required:
SAN device
Tape drive
UPS
Switch/hub
Other
Internet access required? Yes/No

This process should not take a great deal of time if previous planning has taken place. If the planning phase was skipped, some brainstorming will be required to ensure that the scope includes all the key ingredients required for the application testing. The goals for the application testing process will also affect the scope, which is covered in the following section.

Defining the Goals for Compatibility Testing

As with the previous step of defining the scope of the testing process, defining the goals might be a very quick process, or could require some discussions with the stakeholders involved in the project.

One useful way of looking at the goals for the project is to treat them as the checklist for successful completion of the testing. What conditions need to be met for the organization to confidently move forward with the next step in the Windows migration? The next step might be a more complete prototype testing phase. For smaller organizations, it might be a pilot rollout, where the new networking environment is offered to a select group of savvy users.

These goals are separate from the business goals the company might have, such as a more reliable network infrastructure or improved security. A more complete prototype phase could seek to address these goals, while the application testing process stays focused on the performance of the specific combinations of the operating system and embedded and connected applications.

A convenient way to differentiate the goals of the project is to split them into key areas, as described in the following sections.

Time Frame for the Testing

This goal can be defined with this statement: "The testing must be completed in X days/ weeks."

If there is very little time available to perform the testing, this limits how much time can be spent on each application and how many end users can put each through its paces. It also necessitates a lesser degree of documentation. Remember to include time for researching the applications' compatibility with the vendors as part of the timeline. A quick project plan might be useful in this process as a way of verifying the assumptions and selling the timeline to the decision makers.

Contingency time should ideally be built in to this goal. Resources assigned to the testing can get sick or might be pulled back into the office for production support, or applications might require additional testing when problems are encountered. Vendors might not provide trial versions of the software as quickly as desired, or new versions of software or even the hardware itself can be delayed. With many companies seeking to consolidate the number of servers in use, it is not uncommon to see labs evolve through the testing process. Different versions of the Windows operating system are used, as are different versions of various application software programs.

ESTIMATING THE DURATION OF THE APPLICATION TESTING PROCESS

A good rule of thumb is to allow 4 hours per application to be tested for basic testing and 8 hours for a more thorough testing process. This allows time for the initial research with the vendors, configuration of the Windows Server 2012 operating system, and testing of the applications. Of course, the total time required will vary based on the types of applications to be tested.

For example, a Windows Server 2012 system with a line-of-business application, such as an enterprise resource planning (ERP) program with a front-end web application, would take an estimated 1 or 2 days to test for basic compatibility and functionality, and potentially a week for more rigorous testing.

Note that if more than one resource is available to perform the testing, these configurations can be tested in parallel, shortening the *duration* of the process, but not the *work effort*.

It is always better to have some extra time during the testing phase. This time can be used for more extensive user testing, training, or documentation.

Budget for the Testing

This goal can be defined with this statement: "The testing must be completed within a budget of $X."

Of course, there might be no budget allocated for testing, but it is better to know this as soon as possible. A lack of budget means that no new hardware can be ordered, evaluation copies of the software (both Microsoft and the third-party applications) need to be used, and no external resources will be brought in. If the budget is available or can be accessed in advance of the production upgrade, a subset of the production hardware should be ordered for this phase. Testing on the exact hardware that will be used in the actual upgrade rather than a cast-off server will yield more valuable results.

More and more virtualization technology is being utilized in test labs for reducing costs associated with hardware procurement. Virtualization is an excellent way to reduce capital expenditures. Keep in mind that hardware-specific prototype testing cannot be achieved when using virtualization as the guest operating system. In addition, performance metrics might get skewed when running more than one guest operating system on a virtual server.

Resources to Be Used

This goal can be defined with this statement: "The testing will be completed by in-house resources or external consultants."

Often, the internal network administration staff is too busy with daily tasks or tackling emergencies that spring up (which might be the reason for the upgrade in the first place), and staff personnel should not be expected to dedicate 100% of their time to the testing process.

If an outside consulting firm with expertise in Windows Server 2012 is going to be used in the testing process, it can be a good leverage point to have already created and decided on an internal budget for the testing process. This cuts down on the time it takes to debate the approaches from competing firms.

Extent of the Testing

The extent of compatibility testing can be defined with this statement: "Each application will be tested for basic, midlevel, or complete compatibility and feature sets."

This goal might be set for different types of applications where some mission-critical applications would need to have extensive testing, whereas less-critical applications might have more basic testing performed. A short time frame with a tightly limited budget will no allow for extensive testing, so basic compatibility will most likely be the goal.

DEFINING THE DIFFERENT LEVELS OF COMPATIBILITY TESTING

Basic compatibility testing, as used in this chapter, essentially means that the mission-critical applications are tested to verify that they load without errors and perform their primary functions properly with Windows Server 2012. Often the goal with basic testing is to simply see whether the application works, without spending a lot of time or money on hardware and resources, and with a minimum amount of documentation and training. Note that this level of testing reduces but does not eliminate the risks involved in the production rollout.

Midlevel testing is defined as a process whereby Windows Server 2012 is configured with *all* the applications that will be present in the eventual implementation, so that the test configuration matches the production configuration as closely as possible to reduce the chance of surprise behavior during the rollout. This level of testing requires more preparation to understand the configuration and more involvement from testing resources, and should include end users. Some training should take place during the process, and documentation is created to record the server configurations and details of the testing process. Although this level of testing greatly reduces the risks of problems during the production migration or upgrade, the migration process of moving data between servers and training the resources on this process hasn't been covered, so some uncertainty still exists.

Complete testing adds additional resource training and possibly end-user training during the process and should include testing of the actual migration process. Complete training requires more documentation to record the processes required to build or image servers and perform the migration steps. Complete testing is what is typically defined as the prototype phase.

Training Requirements During Testing

This goal can be defined with this statement: "Company IT resources will/will not receive training during the application testing process."

Although the IT resources performing the testing will learn a great deal by going through the testing process, the organization might want to provide additional training to these individuals, especially if new functionality and applications are being tested. If external consultants are brought in, it is important that the organization's own resources are still involved in the testing process for training and validation purposes. The application testing phase might be an excellent time to have help desk personnel or departmental managers in the user community learn more about new features that will soon be offered so they can help support the user community and generate excitement for the project.

Documentation Required

This goal can be defined with this statement: "Documentation will/will not be generated to summarize the process and results."

Again, the budget and timeline for the testing will affect the answer to this question. Many organizations require a paper trail for all testing procedures, especially when the Windows infrastructure will have an impact on the viability of the business itself. For other organizations, the networking environment is not as critical, so less or no documentation might be required.

The application testing phase is a great opportunity to document the steps required for application installations or upgrades if time permits, and this level of instruction can greatly facilitate the production rollout of the upgraded networking components.

Extent of User Community Involvement

This goal can be defined with this statement: "End users will be included/will not be included in the testing process."

If there are applications—such as customer relationship management (CRM), document routing, voicemail or paging add-ons, or connectivity to PDAs and mobile devices—a higher level of user testing (at least from the power users and executives) should be considered.

Fate of the Testing Lab

This goal can be defined with this statement: "The application testing lab will/will not remain in place after the testing is complete."

Organizations decide to keep labs in place after their primary purpose has been served for a number of reasons. Whenever a patch or upgrade to Windows Server 2012 or to a third-party application integrates with Windows Server 2012, it is advisable to test it in a nonproduction environment. Even seemingly innocent patches to antivirus products can crash a production server. Other items might require user testing to see whether they should be rolled out to the production servers.

Documenting the Compatibility Testing Plan

The information discussed and gathered through the previous exercises needs to be gathered and distributed to the stakeholders to ensure that the members of the team are working toward the same goals. These components are the scope and the goals of the application testing process and should include the timeline, budget, extent of the testing (basic, midlevel, complete), training requirements, documentation requirements, and fate of the testing lab. This step is even more important if a formal discovery and design phase was not completed.

By taking the time to document these constraints, the testing process will be more structured and less likely to miss a key step or get bogged down on one application. The individuals performing the testing will essentially have a checklist of the exact testing process, and are less likely to spend an inordinate amount of time on one application, or "get creative" and try products that are not within the scope of work. After the testing is complete, the stakeholders will also have made it clear what is expected in terms of documentation so the results of the testing can be presented and reviewed efficiently.

This summary document should be presented to the stakeholders of the project for review and approval. The organization is then ready to proceed with the research and testing process for Windows Server 2012 compatibility.

Researching Products and Applications

The next step in the compatibility testing process is to actually begin research on the products and applications being tested. With the documented goals and expectations of the necessary compatibility testing process, the organization can proceed with information gathering.

Taking Inventory of Network Systems

The first step of the information-gathering process is to take inventory of the network systems that will be part of the Windows Server 2012 environment. These systems include domain controllers, application servers, gateway systems, and utility servers.

NOTE

When you are identifying the systems that are part of the Windows Server 2012 environment, you should create separate lists that note whether a server is a domain controller or member server of the environment, or whether the server is standalone and does not directly interact with the domain. Usually, standalone servers that are not integrated into the domain are significantly less likely to require a parallel upgrade to Windows Server 2012. Because the system is operating as a standalone, it will typically continue to operate in that manner and can be removed from the scope of testing and migration during the initial migration phase. Removing this server can also greatly minimize the scope of the project by limiting the number of servers that need to be included in the testing and migration process.

For systems that are part of the network domain, the devices should be identified by which network operating system they are running. Another item that should be captured is whether the server is physical or virtual. Table 17.2 shows a sample system device inventory sheet.

TABLE 17.2 System Device Inventory Table

Server Name	Member of Domain (Y/N)	Domain Controller (Y/N)	Virtual Server (Y/N)	General Functions	Operating System
SERVER-A	Y	Y	Y	DC, DNS, DHCP	Windows 2003 R2
SERVER-B	Y	N	N	Exchange Server	Windows 2008 R2
SERVER-C	Y	N	Y	File/Print Server	Windows 2008
SERVER-D	N	N	N	WWW Web Server	Windows 2003 SP2

Taking Inventory of Applications on Existing Servers

Now that you have a list of the server systems on your network, the next step is to take inventory of the applications running on the systems. Take care to identify all applications running on a system, including tape software, antivirus software, and network monitoring and management utilities.

The primary applications that need to be upgraded will be obvious, as will the standard services such as data backup and antivirus software. However, in most organizations, additional applications hiding on the network need to be identified. If System Center Configuration Manager 2007/2012 (ConfigMgr) is in use, or another network management tool with inventory capabilities, it should also be able to provide this basic information.

NOTE

Another angle to validating that all applications are tested before a migration is to just ask all departmental managers to provide a list of applications that are essential for them and their employees. This takes the opposite angle of looking not at the servers and the applications, but looking at what the managers or employees in the organization say they use as part of their job responsibilities. From these lists, you can put together a master list.

Understanding the Differences Between Applications and Windows Services

We need to make a distinction as it pertains to the Windows Server 2012 operating environment. Applications are programs that run on top of Windows Server 2012, such as application tools or front-end services, and services are programs that integrate with the operating system, such as SQL, Exchange, antivirus applications, and so on. As discussed previously, in the .NET Framework, applications are designed to sit on top of the Windows platform, so the more embedded the legacy application is in the operating system, the greater the potential for problems.

It is also helpful to separate the Microsoft and non-Microsoft applications and services. The Microsoft applications that are to be upgraded to the new Windows Server 2012 environment are likely to have been thoroughly tested by Microsoft. Possible incompatibilities should have been identified, and a great deal of information will be available on Microsoft TechNet or on the Microsoft product page of its website. For non-Microsoft applications and services, however, weeks could pass after a product's release before information about any compatibility problems with the Microsoft operating system surfaces. This holds true for service packs and product updates, as well, where problems might be made public weeks or months after the release of the update.

Furthermore, many organizations that create custom applications will find that little information is available on Windows Server 2012 compatibility, so they could require more complex lab tests to validate compatibility.

Completing an Inventory Sheet per Application

An organization should create an inventory sheet for each application being validated. Having an inventory sheet per application can result in dozens, if not hundreds, of sheets of paper. However, each application needs to go through extensive verification for compatibility, so the information gathered will be helpful.

A sample product inventory sheet includes the following categories:

- Vendor name
- Product name
- Version number
- Application or service?
- Mission-critical?
- Compatible with Windows Server 2012 (Y/N)?
- Vendor-stated requirements to make compatible
- Decision to migrate (update, upgrade, replace, remain on existing OS, stop using, proceed without vendor support)

Additional items that might be relevant could include which offices or departments use the application, how many users need it, and so on.

Any notes from the vendor, such as whitepapers for migration, tip/trick migration steps, upgrade utilities, and any other documentation should be printed, downloaded, and kept on file. Although a vendor might state that a product is compatible on its website today, you might find that by the time an upgrade occurs, the vendor has changed its statement on compatibility. Any backup information that led to the decision to proceed with the migration might also be useful in the future.

Prioritizing the Applications on the List

After you complete and review the list, you have specific information showing the consensus of which applications are critical and which are not.

There is no need to treat all applications and utilities with equal importance because a simple utility that does not work and is not identified as a critical application can be easily upgraded or replaced later and should not hold up the migration. However, problems with a mission-critical business application should be reviewed in detail because they might affect the whole upgrade process.

Remember that certain utility applications should be considered critical to any network environment. These include tape backup (with the appropriate agents) and virus-protection software. In organizations that perform network and systems management, management tools and agents are also essential.

Verifying Compatibility with Vendors

Armed with the full list of applications that need to be tested for compatibility, the application testing team can now start hitting the phones and delving into the vendors' websites for the compatibility information.

For early adopters of certain application software programs, more research might be necessary because vendors tend to lag behind in publishing statements of compatibility with new products. Past experience has shown that simply using the search feature on the vendor's site can be a frustrating process, so having an actual contact who has a vested interest in providing the latest and greatest information (such as the company's sales representative) can be a great time-saver.

Each vendor tends to use its own terminology when discussing Windows Server 2012 compatibility (especially when it isn't 100% tested); a functional way to define the level of compatibility is with the following four areas:

- Compatible
- Compatible with patches or updates
- Not compatible (requires version upgrade)
- Not compatible and no compatible version available (requires new product)

When possible, it is also a good practice to gather information about the specifics of the testing environment, such as the version and service pack (SP) level of the Windows operating system the application was tested with, along with the hardware devices (if applicable, such as tape drives, specific mobile devices, and so forth) tested.

Tracking Sheets for Application Compatibility Research

For organizational purposes, a tracking sheet should be created for each application to record the information discovered from the vendors. A sample product inventory sheet includes the following categories:

- Vendor name
- Product name and version number
- Vendor contact name and contact information
- Level of criticality: Critical, near-critical, or nice to have
- Compatible with Windows Server 2012: Yes/No/Did not say
- Vendor-stated requirements to upgrade or make application compatible
- Recommended action: None, patch/fix/update, version upgrade, replace with new product, stop using product, continue using product without vendor support
- Operating system compatibility: Windows Server 2012, Windows Server 2008 / 2008 R2, Windows Server 2003, other
- Processor architecture compatibility: 64-bit compatible?
- Notes: Conversation notes, URLs used, copies of printed compatibility statements, or hard copy provided by vendor

It is a matter of judgment as to the extent of the notes from discussions with the vendors and materials printed from websites that are retained and included with the inventory sheet and kept on file. Remember that URLs change frequently, so it makes sense to print the information when it is located.

In cases where product upgrades are required, information can be recorded on the part numbers, cost, and other pertinent information.

Six States of Compatibility

There are essentially six possible states of compatibility that can be defined, based on the input from the vendors, and that need to be verified during the testing process. These levels of compatibility roughly equate to levels of risk of unanticipated behavior and issues during the upgrade process:

1. The application version currently in use is compatible with Windows Server 2012.
2. The application version currently in use is compatible with Windows Server 2012, with a minor update or service patch.
3. The application currently in use is compatible with Windows Server 2012, with a version upgrade of the application.
4. The application currently in use is not compatible with Windows Server 2012 and no upgrade is available, but it will be kept running as is on an older version of Windows Server (or other network operating system) in the upgraded Windows Server 2012 networking environment.
5. The application currently in use is not compatible with Windows Server 2012 and will be phased out and not used after the upgrade is complete.
6. The application currently in use is not compatible with Windows Server 2012 per the vendor, or no information about compatibility was available, but it apparently runs on Windows Server 2012, so the organization needs to determine whether it will run the application on an operating system potentially not supported by the application vendor.

Each of these states is discussed in more detail in the following sections.

Using a Windows Server 2012–Compatible Application

Although most applications require some sort of upgrade, the vendor might simply state that the version currently in use will work properly with Windows Server 2012 and provide supporting documentation or specify a URL with more information about the topic. This is more likely to be the case with applications that do not integrate with the Windows Server components, but instead interface with certain components, and might even be installed on separate servers.

It is up to the organization to determine whether testing is necessary to verify the vendor's compatibility statement. If the application in question is critical to the integrity or security of the Windows Server 2012 operating system or provides the users with features and capabilities that enhance their business activities and transactions, testing is definitely recommended. For upgrades that have short time frames and limited budgets available for testing (basic testing as defined earlier in the chapter), these applications might be demoted to the bottom of the list of priorities and would be tested only after the applications requiring updates or upgrades had been tested.

A clear benefit of the applications that the vendor verifies as being Windows Server 2012 compatible is that the administrative staff will already know how to install and support the product and how it interfaces with Windows Server 2012 and the help desk; end users will not need to be trained or endure the learning curves required by new versions of the products.

NOTE

As mentioned previously, make sure to clarify what network operating system and which specific version of Windows operating system were used in the testing process, including the processor architecture version, because seemingly insignificant changes, such as security patches to the OS, can influence the product's performance in your upgraded environment. Tape backup software is notorious for being very sensitive to minor changes in the version of Windows, and tape backups can appear to be working when they aren't. If devices such as text pagers or mobile devices are involved in the process, the specific operating systems tested and the details of the hardware models should be verified if possible to ensure that the vendor testing included the models in use by the organization.

If a number of applications are being installed on one Windows Server 2012 system, unpredictable conflicts are possible. Therefore, testing is still recommended for mission-critical Windows Server 2012 applications, even for applications the vendor asserts are fully compatible with Windows Server 2012.

Requiring a Minor Update or Service Patch for Compatibility

When upgrading from Windows Server 2008 or Windows Server 2008 R2, many applications simply need a relatively minor service update or patch for compatibility with Windows Server 2012. This is less likely to be the case when migrating from Windows Server 2003 or a completely different operating system, such as Novell NetWare or Linux. This is also evident when running web applications because IIS Web Services has evolved and been completely rewritten.

During the testing process, the service updates and patches are typically quick and easy to install, are available over the Internet, and are often free of charge. It is important to read any notes or readme files that come with the update because specific settings in the Windows Server 2012 configuration might need to be modified for them to work. These updates and patches tend to change and be updated themselves after they are released, so it is worth checking periodically to see whether new revisions have become available.

These types of updates generally do not affect the core features or functionality of the products in most cases, although some new features might be introduced; so they have little training and support ramifications because the help desk and support staff will already be experienced in supporting the products.

Applications That Require a Version Upgrade for Compatibility

In other cases, especially when migrating from Windows 2000 or another network operating system, a complete migration strategy is required, and this tends to be a more complex process than downloading a patch or installing a minor update to the product. The process varies by product, with some allowing an in-place upgrade, where the software is not on the Windows Server 2012 server itself, and others simply installing from scratch.

The amount of time required to install and test these upgrades is greater, the learning curve steeper, and the danger of technical complexities and issues increases. Thus, additional time should be allowed for testing the installation process of the new products, configuring them for optimal Windows connectivity, and fine-tuning for performance factors. Training for the IT resources and help desk staff will be important because of the probability of significant differences between the new and old versions.

Compatibility with all hardware devices should not be taken for granted, whether it is the server itself, tape backup devices, or SAN hardware.

If a new version of the product is required, it can be difficult to avoid paying for the upgrade, so budget can become a factor. Some vendors can be persuaded to provide evaluation copies that expire after 30 to 120 days.

Handling an Incompatible Application That Will Remain "As Is"

As discussed earlier in this chapter, Windows Server 2012 can coexist with earlier versions of the Windows operating system, so a Windows Server 2012 migration does not require that every server be upgraded. In larger organizations, for example, smaller offices might choose to remain on legacy versions for a period of time if there are legitimate business reasons or cost concerns with upgrading expensive applications. If custom scripts or applications have been written that integrate and add functionality to Windows 2000 Server or Windows Server 2003, it might make sense to keep those servers intact on the network, or better yet put in a strategy to upgrade the scripts to support a more currently supported operating system.

Although it might sound like an opportunity to skip any testing because the server configurations aren't changing, connectivity to the new Windows Server 2012 configurations still needs to be tested, to ensure that the functionality between the servers is stable.

Again, in this scenario, the application itself is not upgraded, modified, or changed, so there will not be a requirement for administrative or end-user training.

Incompatible Applications That Will Not Be Used

An organization might decide that because an application is incompatible with Windows Server 2012, no upgrade is available, or the cost is prohibitive, so it will simply retire it. Windows Server 2012 includes a variety of new features, as discussed throughout the book, which might make certain utilities and management tools unnecessary. For example, a disaster recovery module for a tape backup product might no longer be necessary after clustering is implemented.

Take care during the testing process to note the differences that the administrative staff, help desk, and end users will notice in the day-to-day interactions with the networking system. If features are disappearing, a survey to assess the impact can be very helpful. Many users will raise a fuss if a feature suddenly goes away, even if it was rarely used, whereas the complaints could be avoided if they had been informed in advance.

Officially Incompatible Applications That Seem to Work Fine

The final category applies to situations in which no information can be found about compatibility. Some vendors choose to provide no information and take no stance on compatibility with Windows Server 2012. This puts the organization in a precarious situation, as it has to rely on internal testing results to make a decision. Even if the application seems to work properly, the decision might be made to phase out or retire the product if its failure could harm the business process. If the application performs a valuable function, it is probably time to look for or create a replacement, or at least to allocate time for this process at a later time.

If the organization chooses to keep the application, it might be kept in place on an older version of Windows or moved to the new Windows Server 2012 environment. In either case, the administrative staff, help desk, and end users should be warned that the application is not officially supported or officially compatible and might behave erratically.

Creating an Upgrade Decision Matrix

Although each application will have its own inventory sheet, it is helpful to put together a brief summary document outlining the final results of the vendor research process and the ramifications to the network upgrade project. As with all documents that affect the scope and end state of the network infrastructure, this document should be reviewed and approved by the project stakeholders.

This document can be expanded to summarize which applications will be installed on which network server if there are going to be multiple Windows Server 2012 servers in the final configuration. In this way, the document can serve as a checklist to follow during the actual testing process.

Assessing the Effects of the Compatibility Results on the Compatibility Testing Plan

After all the data has been collected on the compatibility, lack of compatibility, or lack of information, the compatibility testing plan should be revisited to see whether changes need to be made. As discussed earlier in the chapter, the components of the compatibility testing plan are the scope of the application testing process and the goals of the process (timeline, budget, extent of the testing, training requirements, documentation requirements, and fate of the testing lab).

Some of the goals might now be more difficult to meet, and require additional budget, time, and resources. If essential network applications need to be replaced with version upgrades or a solution from a different vendor, additional time for testing and training might also be required. Certain key end users might also need to roll up their sleeves and perform hands-on testing to ensure that the new products perform to their expectations.

This might be the point in the application testing process at which a decision is made that a more complete prototype testing phase is needed, and the lab would be expanded to more closely, or exactly, resemble the end state of the migration.

Microsoft Assessment and Planning Toolkit

As mentioned throughout the chapter, it is important to conduct compatibility testing when upgrading or migrating to Windows Server 2012. It is essential to have specific knowledge about each server within the infrastructure and whether the server and associated hardware and software are ready for Windows Server 2012. Microsoft has a free toolkit that will help accelerate your migration to Windows Server 2012.

The Microsoft Assessment and Planning (MAP) toolkit can assist with a migration or upgrade to Windows Server 2012 by conducting inventory, assessments, and reporting on servers throughout the infrastructure. In addition, unlike other tools, it can gather information without installing agents on servers.

You can download the toolkit from http://technet.microsoft.com/en-us/library/bb977556.aspx. Once the toolkit is installed, you can create a server inventory report, which will identify currently installed operating systems. The report will also include detailed analysis of software and hardware readiness and compatibility with Windows Server 2012.

Lab-Testing Existing Applications

With the preparation and research completed and the compatibility testing plan verified as needed, the actual testing can begin. The testing process should be fairly anticlimactic at this point because the process has been discussed at length, and it will be clear what the testing goals are and which applications will be tested. Due diligence in terms of vendor research should be complete, and now it is just a matter of building the test server or servers and documenting the results.

The testing process can yield unforeseen results because the exact combination of hardware and software might affect the performance of a key application; but far better to have this occur in a nonproduction environment in which failures won't affect the organization's ability to deliver its services.

During the testing process, valuable experience with the installation and upgrade process will be gained and will contribute to the success of the production migration. The migration team will be familiar with—or possibly experts at—the installation and application migration processes when it counts, and are more likely to avoid configuration mistakes and resolve technical issues.

Allocating and Configuring Hardware

Ideally, the budget will be available to purchase the same server hardware and related peripherals (such as tape drives, UPSs, mobile devices, and applications) that will be used in the production migration. This is preferable to using a server machine that has been sitting in a closet for an undetermined period of time, which might respond differently than the eventual hardware that will be used. Using old hardware can actually generate more work in the long run and adds more variables to an already complex process.

If the testing process is to exactly mirror the production environment, this would be considered to be a prototype phase, which is generally broader in scope than compatibility testing, and requires additional hardware, software, and time to complete. A prototype phase is recommended for more complex networks in which the upgrade process is riskier and more involved and in which the budget, time, and resources are available.

Don't forget to allocate a representative workstation for each desktop operating system that is supported by the organization and a sample remote access system, such as a typical laptop or mobile device that is used by the sales force or traveling executive.

Allocating and Configuring Windows Server 2012

By this point, the software has been ordered, allocated, downloaded, and set aside for easy access, along with any notes taken or installation procedures downloaded in the research phase. If some time has elapsed since the compatibility research with the vendors, it is worth checking to see whether any new patches have been released. The upgrade decision matrix discussed earlier in the chapter is an excellent checklist to have on hand during this process to ensure that nothing is missed that could cause delays during the testing process.

When configuring the servers with the appropriate operating systems, the company standards for configurations, based on industry best practices, should be adhered to, if they have been documented. Standards can include the level of hard drive redundancy, separation of the application files and data files, naming conventions, roles of the servers, approved and tested security updates, and security configurations.

Next, Windows Server 2012 should be configured to also meet organization standards and then for the essential utilities that will protect the integrity of the data and the operating system, which typically include the backup software, antivirus software, and management utilities and applications. After this base configuration is completed, it can be worth performing a complete backup of the system or taking a snapshot of the server configuration in case the subsequent testing is problematic and a rollback is necessary.

Loading the Remaining Applications

With Windows Server 2012 configured with the core operating system and essential utilities, the value-added applications can be tested. Value-added applications enhance the functionality of Windows and enable the users to perform their jobs more efficiently and drive the business more effectively. It is helpful to provide a project plan calendar or schedule to the end users who will be assisting in the testing process at this point so they know when their services will be needed.

So many different combinations of applications might be installed and tested at this point that the different permutations cannot all be covered in this chapter. As a basic guideline, first test the most essential applications and the applications that were not identified previously as being compatible. By tackling the applications that are more likely to be problematic early on in the process, the testing resources will be fresh, and any flags can be raised to the stakeholders while there is still time left in the testing process for remediation.

Thorough testing by the end users is recommended, as is inclusion of the help desk staff in the process. Notes taken during the testing process will be valuable in creating any configuration guides or migration processes for the production implementation.

NOTE

Beyond basic functionality, data entry, and access to application-specific data, some additional tests that indicate an application has been successfully installed in the test environment include printing to different standard printers, running standard reports, exporting and importing data, and exchanging information with other systems or devices. Testing should be done by end users of the application and administrative IT staff who support, maintain, and manage the application. Notes should be taken on the process and the results because they can prove very useful during the production migration.

Certified for Windows Server 2012

Microsoft offers a program that enables vendors to innovate on the Windows Server 2012 platform and related technologies. This program is called Innovate on Windows Server, and it allows vendors, organizations, and partners to build, test, and certify that their applications and products are compatible with Windows Server 2012. Once certified, a logo is placed on the product stating Certified for Windows Server 2012.

During the analysis phase of whether existing applications will be compatible with Windows Server 2012, it is a best practice to validate that the applications do carry the Certified for Windows Server 2012 logo by contacting the manufacturer. By having the logo, application testing and additional analysis of a specific application is minimized when upgrading to Windows Server 2012.

You can find the ISV Application Readiness and Certification program at http://www.windowsservercatalog.com. The program provides guidelines and validation that an application meets the standards for application compatibility and integration support expected in a tightly integrated Microsoft-based solution.

Testing the Migration and Upgrade Process

This section touches on the next logical step in the testing process. After it has been verified that the final configuration agreed on in the planning process is stable and which applications and utilities will be installed on which server, the actual upgrade process can be tested. The upgrade process is covered in Chapter 16, "Migrating from Active Directory 2008 / 2008 R2 to Active Directory 2012."

Documenting the Results of the Compatibility Testing

A number of documents can be produced during the compatibility testing process. Understanding the expectations of the stakeholders and what the documents will be used for is important. For example, more detailed budgetary information might need to be compiled based on the information, or go/no-go decisions might need to be reached. Thus, a summary of the improvements offered by Windows Server 2012 in the areas of reliability, performance visible to the user community, and features improved and added might need to be presented in a convincing fashion.

At a minimum, a summary of the testing process should be created, and a final recommendation for the applications to be included in the production upgrade or migration should be provided to the stakeholders. This can be as simple as the upgrade decision matrix discussed earlier in the chapter, or it can be more thorough, including detailed notes of the exact testing procedures followed. Notes can be made available summarizing the results of end-user testing, validating the applications, and describing results—both positive and negative.

If the testing hardware is the same as the hardware that will be used in the production upgrade, server configuration documents that list the details of the hardware and software configurations can be created; they will ensure that the servers built in the production environment will have the same fundamental configuration as was tested in the lab.

A more detailed build document can be created that walks the technician through the exact steps required to build the Windows Server 2012 system, in cases where many network servers need to be created in a short period of time.

The level of effort or the amount of time to actually perform the upgrade or the migration of a sample subdirectory can be recorded as part of the documentation, and this information can be very helpful in planning the total amount of time that will be required to perform the upgrade or migration.

Determining Whether a Prototype Phase Is Required

The issue of whether a more complete prototype phase is needed or if a more limited application compatibility testing phase is sufficient has come up several times in this chapter. The essential difference between the two is that the prototype phase duplicates as exactly as possible the actual end state of the upgrade, from server hardware to peripherals and software, so that the entire upgrade process can be tested to reduce the chance of surprises during the production upgrade. The application testing phase can be less extensive, involve a single server or virtual servers, and be designed to verify that the applications required will work reliably on the Windows Server 2012 configuration. Compatibility testing can take as little time as a week—from goal definition, to research, to actual testing. A prototype phase takes considerably longer because of the additional steps required.

The following is a checklist that will help your organization make the decision:

- Is sufficient budget available for a subset of the actual hardware that will be used in the upgrade?
- Is sufficient time available for the configuration of the prototype lab and testing of the software?
- Are the internal resources available for a period of time long enough to finish the prototype testing? Is the budget available to pay for external consulting resources to complete the work?
- Is the Windows networking environment mission-critical to the business's capability to go about its daily activities and generate revenues, and will interruption of Windows services cost the company an unacceptable amount of money?
- Does the actual migration process need to be tested and documented to ensure the success of the upgrade?
- Do resources need to be trained on the upgrade process (building the servers, and configuring the network operating system and related applications)?
- Do the applications that will be tested need to be compatible with 64-bit processor architecture?

If you find that the answer to more than half of these questions is yes, it is likely that a prototype phase will be required.

Summary

Windows Server 2012 compatibility testing should be performed before any upgrade or migration. The process can be completed very quickly for smaller networks (basic testing) or for larger networks with fairly simple networking environments.

The first steps include identifying the scope and goals of the project to ensure that the stakeholders are involved in determining the success factors for the project. Then research needs to be performed, internal to the company, on which in-place applications are network-related. This includes not only Windows Server, but also tape backup software, antivirus software, network management and monitoring tools, add-ons, and inventory sheets created summarizing this information. Decisions as to which applications are critical, near-critical, or just nice to have should also be made. Research should then be performed with the vendors of the products, tracking sheets should be created to record this information, and the application should be categorized in one of six states of compatibility. Next, the testing begins, with the configuration of the lab environment that is isolated from the production network, and the applications are loaded and tested by both administrative and end user or help desk staff. The results are then documented, and the final decisions of whether to proceed are made.

With this process, the production upgrade or migration is smoother, and the likelihood of technical problems that can harm the business' ability to transact or provide its services is greatly reduced. The problems are identified beforehand and resolved, and the resources who will perform the work gain familiarity with all the products and processes involved.

Best Practices

The following are best practices from this chapter:

- Take the time to understand the goals of the project (What will the organization gain by doing the upgrade?) and the scope of the project (What is included and what is excluded from the project?).
- Understand all the applications that connect with Windows Server 2012 and whether they are critical, near-critical, or simply nice to have.
- Accelerate a migration to Windows Server 2012 by using the MAP toolkit.
- Document the research process for each application because this will prove to be very valuable if problems are encountered during the testing process.
- Create a lab environment that is as close to the final end state of the upgrade as possible. This reduces the variables that can cause problems at the least opportune time.
- Test applications for compatibility with both typical end users of the application and application administrators who support, maintain, and manage the application.
- Leverage virtual server technology to minimize the cost associated with procuring hardware for a test lab.
- Ensure that applications have been tested for compatibility with a 64-bit operating system, such as Windows Server 2012.

CHAPTER 18

Windows Server 2012 Administration

IN THIS CHAPTER

- Defining the Administrative Model
- Examining Active Directory Site Administration
- Configuring Sites
- Examining Windows Server 2012 Active Directory Groups
- Creating Groups
- Managing Users with Local Security and Group Policies
- Managing Printers with the Print Management Console

Administrators can administer a Windows Server 2012 infrastructure by learning only a few simple tasks and applying them at different levels and to different objects. This enables the administrator to easily scale the administration of the infrastructure without proportionally increasing the work. However, this requires defining and enforcing an administrative model.

The overall management of an environment is composed of administrative tasks that touch almost every aspect of the network, including user administration, server and workstation administration, and network administration. For example, in a single day, an administrator might check for a successful server backup, reset a user's password, add users to or remove them from existing groups, or manage local-area network (LAN) and wide-area network (WAN) hardware. Although each of these tasks can independently be very simple or difficult in nature, administrators should at least understand their portion of the overall enterprise network and understand how the different components that make up the network communicate and rely on one another.

Active Directory forms the basis for the administrative model in Windows Server 2012. The Active Directory structure is used to control the authorization and access to other technologies such as Microsoft Exchange Server 2010, System Center Operations Manager 2012, and SharePoint 2010. This chapter focuses on the common Windows Server 2012 Active Directory Domain Services (AD DS) user and group administrative tasks and touches on the management of Active Directory sites to optimize user access and replication performance.

Defining the Administrative Model

Before the computer and networking environment can be managed effectively, an organization and its IT group must first define how the systems and components will be assigned and managed. The job of delegating responsibility for the network defines the organization's administrative model. Three different types of administrative models can be used to logically break up the management of the enterprise network between several IT specialists or departments within the organization's IT division. These models are as follows:

- Centralized
- Distributed
- Mixed

When there is no administrative model, the environment is managed chaotically, and the bulk of work is usually made up of reactive troubleshooting (that is, firefighting). This can often require server updates and modifications to occur with short notice and proper planning or testing. Also, when administrative or maintenance tasks are not performed correctly or consistently, securing the environment and auditing administrative events are nearly impossible. Environments that do not follow an administrative model are administered inefficiently and problems are addressed reactively rather than proactively.

To choose or define the correct administrative model, the organization must discover what services are needed in each location and where the administrators with the skills to manage these services are located. Placing administrators in remote offices that require very little IT administration might be a waste of money, but when the small group is composed of VIPs in the company, it might be a good idea to give these elite users the highest level of service available.

The Centralized Administration Model

The centralized administration model is simple in concept: All the IT-related administration is controlled by one group, usually located at one physical location. In the centralized model, all the critical servers are housed in one or a few locations instead of distributed at each location. This arrangement allows for a central backup and always having the correct IT staff member available when a server fails. For example, if an organization uses the Microsoft Exchange Server 2010 messaging server and a server is located at each site, a qualified staff member might not be available at each location if data or the entire server must be recovered from backup. In such a scenario, administration would be handled remotely with inherent challenges related to distance, time zone and more. However, in a centralized administration model, both the Exchange Server 2010 administrator and the servers would be located in a single, central location (often the same location). This allows administration, support and data protection/recovery to be handled as efficiently and effectively as possible.

The Distributed Administration Model

The distributed administration model is the opposite of the centralized model in that tasks are divided among IT and non-IT staff members in various locations. The rights to perform administrative tasks can be granted based on geography, department, or job function. Also, administrative control can be granted for a specific network service such as domain name system (DNS) or Dynamic Host Configuration Protocol (DHCP). This allows separation of server and workstation administration without giving administrators more rights than are required to fulfill their job requirements.

Windows Server 2012 systems allow for granular administrative rights and permissions, giving enterprise administrators more flexibility when assigning tasks to staff members. Historically, distributed administration based only on geographic proximity is commonly found among organizations. After all, if a physical visit to the server, workstation, or network device is needed, having the closest qualified administrator responsible for it might prove more effective. More recently with the proliferation of server virtualization and advanced remote access technologies, remote management of servers is becoming the norm.

The Mixed Administration Model

The mixed administration model is a mix of administrative responsibilities, using both centralized and distributed administration. One example could be that all security policies and standard server configurations are defined from a central site or headquarters, but the implementation and management of servers are defined by physical location, limiting administrators from changing configurations on servers in other locations. Also, the rights to manage a subset of user accounts can be delegated to provide even more flexibility in a distributed administration model on a per-site or per-department basis.

Examining Active Directory Site Administration

Sites can be different things, depending on whom you ask. If you ask an operations manager, she might describe a site as any physical location from which the organization conducts business. Within the scope of Active Directory, a site defines the internal and external replication boundaries and helps users locate the closest servers for authentication and network resource access. It can also serve as a boundary of administrative control, such as delegating authority to a local administrator to his or her AD site. This section discusses Active Directory site administration.

Sites

A site is made up of a site name; subnets within that site; links and bridges to other sites; site-based policies; and, of course, the servers, workstations, and services residing within that site. Some of the components, such as the servers and workstations, are dynamically assigned to a site based on their network configuration and the site's definition. Domain controller services and Distributed File System (DFS) targets are also assigned to sites based on the network configuration of the server on which the resources are hosted.

Each AD site is typically configured to contain resources that have high-bandwidth connectivity between them. The sites can contain one more physical location depending on the network architecture. Sites can be optimized for replication which, during regular daily operations, require very little network bandwidth. After an AD site is defined, servers and client workstations use the information stored in the site configuration to locate the closest domain controllers, Global Catalog servers, and distributed file shares. Configuring a site can be a simple task, but if the site topology is not defined correctly, network access speed might suffer because servers and users might connect to resources across the WAN instead of using local resources.

As mentioned previously, configuring a site should take only a short time because there are very few components to manipulate. In most cases, defining and setting up an Active Directory site configuration might take only a few hours of work. After initial setup, AD sites rarely need to be modified unless significant changes are made to the network topology, including IP addressing changes, domain controllers added or removed from a site, or new sites added or old ones decommissioned.

Examples of site topologies and names might include the name of the city where the company locations are, airport codes for the cities, or the office identifier if the company already has one.

Subnets

Subnets define the network boundaries of a site and limit WAN traffic by allowing clients to find local services before searching across a WAN link. Many administrators do not define subnets for locations that do not have local servers; instead, they relate site subnets only to Active Directory domain controller replication.

If a user workstation subnet is not defined within Active Directory, the workstation picks another domain controller essentially at random. The domain controller could be one from the same physical location or it could be one on another continent across multiple WAN links. The user workstation might authenticate and download policies or run services from a domain controller that is not directly connected to the same LAN. This authentication and download across a WAN could create excessive traffic and unacceptable response times.

In looking at the Active Directory infrastructure, it might seem that branch offices with no domain controller could simply be lumped with their central office site by adding the branch office subnets to the main office site. This would save a lot of configuration time needed to create those branch office sites.

This is somewhat shortsighted, as many other applications are Active Directory aware and leverage the Active Directory site architecture to control the behavior of their application. This includes the Distributed File System (DFS) and System Center Configuration Manager (SCCM) 2012. Thus, it is important to fully define the Active Directory site architecture, including the subnets to mirror the WAN architecture of the organization.

All subnets should be defined in Active Directory Sites and Services to ensure that the proper domain controller and application server assignments are made to workstations.

And all locations should have their own sites and subnets defined, even if there is no domain controller currently in the location. This ensures that resources are allocated correctly by the Active Directory infrastructure not only for domain services, but for other services as well.

Site Links

Site links control Active Directory replication and connect individual sites directly together. A site link is configured for a particular type of protocol (namely, IP or SMTP) with the frequency and schedule of replication configured within the link. Site links are used by the Active Directory Knowledge Consistency Checker (KCC) to build the proper connections to ensure that replication occurs in the most efficient manner.

Once again, some administrators do not fully define the site architecture and don't create sites for locations that do not have a domain controller. The reasoning is that the sites are used by Active Directory for replication, and so domain controller-challenged locations do not need a site defined.

Just like with subnet design, this is also shortsighted, because many other applications are Active Directory aware and leverage the Active Directory site architecture to control the behavior of their application. Site links are also used by Active Directory-aware applications to understand the physical topology to optimize WAN communications. This includes DFS and SCCM 2012.

Therefore, it is important to fully define the Active Directory site architecture, including both subnets and site links to mirror the WAN architecture of the organization.

Examples of site links include a site link for every WAN link, such as from the main office to each of the branch offices. For fully meshed offices, such as those connected via meshed Multiprotocol Label Switching (MPLS), a single site link can be used. This can be done for all offices or just for a subset of offices (for example, North America offices) if needed.

Site Group Policies

Site group policies allow computer and user configurations and permissions to be defined in one location and applied to all the computers/users within the site. Because the scope of a site can span all the domains and domain controllers in a forest, site policies should be used with caution. Therefore, site policies are not commonly used except to define custom network security settings for sites with higher requirements or to delegate administrative rights when administration is performed on a mostly geographic basis.

NOTE

Because sites are usually defined according to high-bandwidth connectivity, some design best practices should be followed when you're defining the requirements for a site. If possible, sites should contain local network services, such as domain controllers, Global Catalog servers, DNS servers, DHCP servers, and, if necessary, Windows Internet Naming Service (WINS) servers. This way, if network connectivity between sites is disrupted, the local site network will remain functional for authentication, Group Policy, name resolution, and resource lookup. Placing file servers at each site might also make sense unless files are housed centrally for security or backup considerations.

That said, there are some specific applications where site group policies can prove to be very useful. For example, it is a best practice to have virtual private network (VPN) users assigned to a site in Active Directory. This is accomplished by creating a VPN site in Active Directory Sites and Services and assigning the VPN subnet to that site. Then, group policies that add additional controls can be assigned to the VPN site using the Site Group Policy object (GPO). That way, when users use their laptop to connect in the office, they receive the standard set of group policies. However, when they use the same laptop to connect to the office via the VPN, they get the additional policies needed for VPN access.

Configuring Sites

The job of configuring and creating sites belongs to the administrators who manage Active Directory, but those who manage the network must be well informed and possibly involved in the design. Whether Active Directory and the network are handled by the same or different groups, they affect each other, and undesired network utilization or failed network connectivity might result. For example, if the Active Directory administrator defines the entire enterprise as a single site, and several Active Directory changes happen each day, replication connections would exist across the enterprise, and replication traffic might be heavy, causing poor network performance for other networking services. On the other side, if the network administrator allows only specific ports to communicate between certain subnets, adding Active Directory might require that additional ports be opened or involve specific network requirements on the servers at each location.

For these examples, the company locations and IP addresses in Table 18.1 will be used. The company has a hub-and-spoke topology, with each branch office connected to the main office. The main office has an IPv4 and an IPv6 subnet.

TABLE 18.1 Common Subnet Mask to Prefix Length

Location	Role	Subnets	WAN Link
Oakland, USA	Main office	192.168.3.0/24 2001:db8:1234:5678::/64	
Boston, USA	Branch office	192.168.10.0/24	T3
Paris, France	Branch office	192.168.11.0/24	T1
Tokyo, Japan	Branch office	192.168.12.0/24	T1

Creating a Site

When creating a site, Active Directory and network administrators must decide how often AD will replicate between sites. They also must share certain information such as the line speed between the sites and the IP addresses of the servers that will be replicating. Knowing the line speed helps determine the correct cost of a site link. For the network administrator, knowing which IP addresses to expect network traffic from on certain ports is helpful when troubleshooting or monitoring the network. To create a site, the AD administrator needs a site name and subnet and also needs to know which other sites will replicate to the new site.

To create a site, follow these steps:

1. Launch Server Manager on a domain controller.

NOTE

The redesigned Windows Server Manager console is used extensively throughout this chapter and is often the central point of administration. See Chapter 20, "Windows Server 2012 Management and Maintenance Practices," for details on the Server Manager console.

2. Expand the Tools menu and run Active Directory Sites and Services.
3. Right-click the Sites container and choose New Site.
4. Type in the name of the site and select any existing site link, as shown in Figure 18.1. Then click OK to create the site.

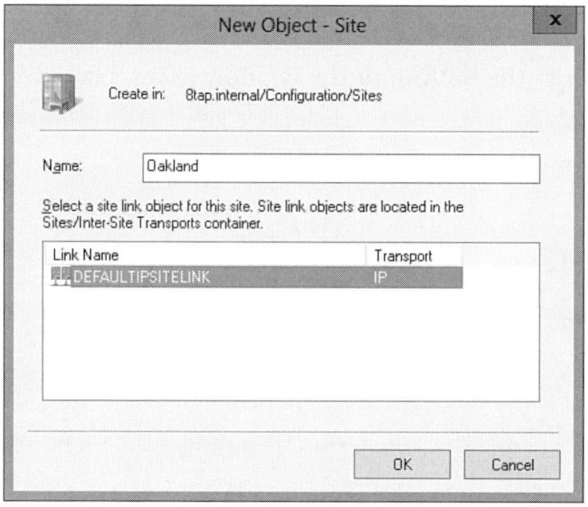

FIGURE 18.1 Creating a new site.

5. A pop-up window might appear, stating what tasks still need to be completed to properly create a site. Read the information, take notes if necessary, and click OK.

Repeat this for each site that needs to be created. For the sample company, Table 18.2 lists the sites that will be created.

TABLE 18.2 Company ABC Sites

Location	Site Name
Oakland, USA	Oakland
Boston, USA	Boston
Paris, France	Paris
Tokyo, Japan	Tokyo

Creating Site Subnets

After you create a site, it should be listed in the console window. To complete the site-creation process, follow these steps:

1. Within the Active Directory Sites and Services console, right-click the Subnets container, and choose New Subnet.
2. Type in the address prefix in the Prefix field (for example, 192.168.3.0/24 for the Oakland site IPv4 subnet).

NOTE

The address prefix is the IP address and the mask entered in network prefix notation. This is the format "IP network address/prefix length." This is very similar to the IP address and subnet mask format. Table 18.3 lists some common subnet masks and their prefix length values.

3. Select the appropriate site from the list at the bottom of the window to associate it with the new subnet.
4. Click OK to create the new subnet.

TABLE 18.3 Common Subnet Mask to Prefix Length

Subnet Mask	Prefix Length
255.0.0.0	8
255.255.0.0	16
255.255.255.0	24

Repeat this for each subnet in the locations. Table 18.4 lists the resulting entries for the sample Company ABC.

TABLE 18.4 Company ABC Sites and Subnets

Location	Site Name	Subnets
Oakland, USA	Oakland	192.168.3.0/24 2001:db8:1234:5678::/64
Boston, USA	Boston	192.168.10.0/24
Paris, France	Paris	192.168.11.0/24
Tokyo, Japan	Tokyo	192.168.12.0/24

Adding Domain Controllers to Sites

If a new domain controller is added to a forest, it will dynamically join a site with a matching subnet if the site topology is already configured and subnets have been previously defined. However, a preexisting domain controller will not change sites automatically, unlike workstations and member servers. A domain controller has to be moved manually if the topology changes. If an existing domain controller is being moved to a new site or the site topology or replication strategy has changed, you can follow these steps to move a domain controller to a different site:

1. Launch Server Manager on a domain controller.
2. Expand the Tools menu and run Active Directory Sites and Services.
3. Expand the Sites folder.
4. Locate the site that contains the desired domain controller to move. You can browse the site servers by expanding the site and selecting the Servers container of the site, as shown in Figure 18.2.

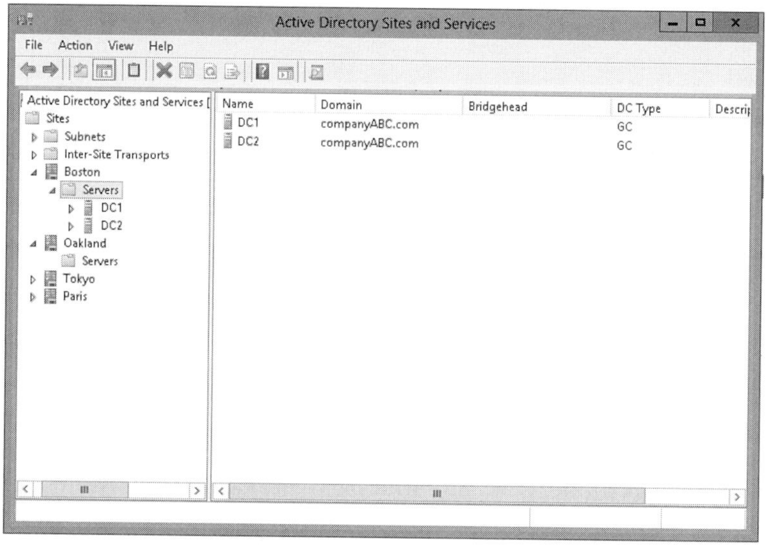

FIGURE 18.2 Browsing for site servers.

18

5. When you locate the desired server, take note of the source site, right-click the server name, and choose Move.
6. When a window opens listing all the sites in the forest, select the destination site, and click OK to initiate the server move.
7. When the move is complete, verify that the domain controller has been placed in the correct Servers container of the desired site.

NOTE

Although you can manually create replication connections if the desired connections are not automatically created by the intersite topology generator (ISTG) within 15 minutes after moving the server, the fact that the automatic creation did not happen usually indicates a problem with site configuration and replication. For more information about the ISTG and replication connections, see Chapter 7, "Active Directory Infrastructure."

Establishing Site Links

Site links establish connectivity between domain controllers to allow Active Directory replication to be managed and scheduled. The Active Directory database, Global Catalog, group policies, and the domain controller SYSVOL directory replicate according to the replication schedule configured in a site link. For more information about site links, see Chapter 7.

To create an IP-based site link, follow these steps:

1. Launch Server Manager on a domain controller.
2. Expand the Tools menu and run Active Directory Sites and Services.
3. Expand the Sites folder.
4. Expand the Inter-Site Transports folder, and select the IP folder.
5. Right-click the IP container and select New Site Link.
6. Enter a name for the site link, select at least two sites that will replicate Active Directory using this site link, and click Add, as shown in Figure 18.3 for Paris and Boston sites.
7. Click OK to create the site link.
8. Back in the Active Directory Sites and Services console, right-click the new site link in the right pane, and choose Properties.
9. At the top of the window, enter a description for the site link. Keep the description simple but informative. For example, enter **Site link between Paris and Boston**.

10. At the bottom of the window, enter a cost for the site link. This determines the preferred link if more than one is available. See the text following these steps for a discussion of site link costs and Table 18.5 for some typical costs. In this example, the connection between Paris and Boston is a T1, and the cost is set to 321.

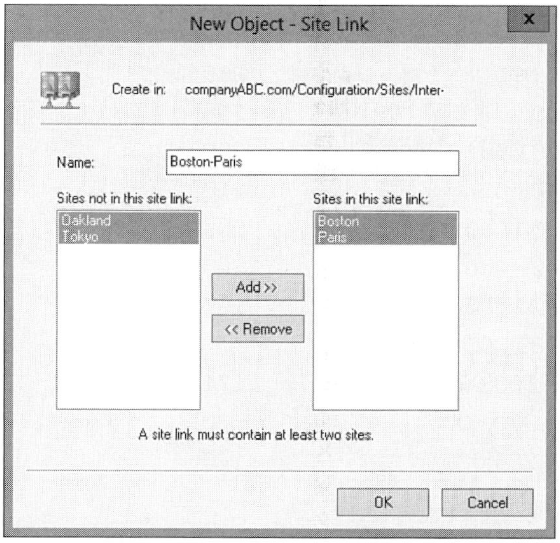

FIGURE 18.3 Adding sites to a site link.

11. Enter the replication frequency. This number indicates how often Active Directory will attempt to replicate during the allowed replication schedule. The default is 180 minutes. The lowest this can be set to between sites is 15 minutes. In most well-connected organizations, the frequency is usually set to 15.

12. Click the Change Schedule button to configure specific intervals when Active Directory should not replicate. This is not typically used in modern well-connected networks. Click OK to leave unchanged.

13. Click OK on the Site Link property page to complete the site link configuration.

After the site link is configured, the Active Directory connections between domain controllers in different sites generate new connections to optimize replication when the KCC runs. The cost of a site link is an arbitrary value that is selected by the administrator to reflect the speed and reliability of the physical connection between the sites. When you lower the cost value on the link, the priority is increased. Site links have a replication interval and a schedule that are independent of the cost. The cost is used by the KCC to prefer one site link path over another.

TABLE 18.5 Typical Link Types, Speeds, and Site Link Costs

Link Type	Link Speed (bps)	Cost
Fractional T1 - 2 Ch	128,000	486
Fractional T1 - 4 Ch	256,000	425
Fractional T1 - 8 Ch	512,000	378
DS1/T1	1,544,000	321
DS2/T2	6,312,000	269
10BaseT	10,000,000	256
DS3/T3	44,736,000	220
OC1	51,840,000	217
100BaseT	100,000,000	205
FDDI	100,000,000	205
OC3/STM1	155,520,000	197
OC12/STM4	622,080,000	177
1000BASE-T	1,000,000,000	171
OC48/STM16	2,488,320,000	160
OC192/STM64	9,953,280,000	146

Cost values determine which connector is preferred for data transfer. When costs are assigned to the links, the KCC computes the replication topology automatically and clients automatically goes to the cheapest link. Link costs can be based on the following formula:

```
Cost = 1024/log(bw/1000)
```

Where

bw = Bandwidth of the link between the two sites in bits per second (bps)

Cost = Site link cost setting

Table 18.5 lists the cost values for some typical bandwidths. The values in the Cost column would be entered into the Cost field of the site link properties.

Of course, in a simple network with only a single WAN connection between locations, the site link cost value can be left at the default value of 100 with little impact. In this configuration, all links are considered equal by the KCC.

In general, a site link topology serves to provide an Active Directory-integrated method for defining preferred routes between physically remote sites connected by WAN links.

The site links created for Company ABC are shown in Table 18.6. The site links represent the hub-and-spoke topology on the Company ABC WAN, with the appropriate costs based on the link speeds.

TABLE 18.6 Company ABC Site Links and Sites

Site Link Name	Cost	Replication Interval	Sites
Oakland-Boston	220	15	Oakland, Boston
Oakland-Paris	321	15	Oakland, Paris
Oakland-Tokyo	321	15	Oakland, Tokyo

NOTE

After the Active Directory site topology has been defined, it is important to remove all the sites from the default site link (DEFAULTIPSITELINK). This prevents replication connections from being generated by the KCC automatically. It is also a best practice to delete or rename the default site and site link—that is, Default-First-Site-Name and DEFAULTIPSITELINK. This ensures that they don't get mistakenly used.

Delegating Control at the Site Level

Control is sometimes delegated at the site level to give network administrators the rights to manage Active Directory replication without giving them the rights to manage any additional Active Directory objects. Site delegation can also do just the opposite, effectively denying network administrators the right to access Active Directory objects on a per-site basis. Specific administrative rights can be granted using the built-in Delegate Control Wizard, whereas others can be set for all the site objects using a site's group policies.

To delegate control at the site level, follow these steps:

1. Launch Server Manager on a domain controller.
2. Expand the Tools menu and run Active Directory Sites and Services.
3. Expand the Sites folder.
4. Right-click the desired site object and select Delegate Control.
5. Click Next on the Delegate Control Wizard Welcome screen.
6. Using the Add button, select the user, users, or groups that will delegate control over the site, and click OK. For example, you can choose an Active Directory group created for the organization's networking team or the default group named Network Configuration Operators.
7. Click Next to continue.
8. On the Tasks to Delegate page, select Create a Custom Task to Delegate, and then click Next.
9. On the Active Directory Object Type page, select This folder, Existing Objects in This Folder, and Creation of New Objects in This Folder, which is the default option to

delegate control. The permissions granted trickle down to each of the containers below the selected container, so you can manage access to all sites by selecting the Sites container itself and using the Delegation Wizard.

10. Click Next to continue.

11. On the Permissions page, check the desired permissions type check boxes and choose each permission the delegated user or group should have.

12. Click Next and then click Finish to complete the Delegate Control Wizard.

Windows Server 2012 Active Directory Groups

An Active Directory group is made up of a collection of objects (groups containing users and computers that are often used to simplify resource access permissions and sending emails). Groups can be used for granting administrative rights, granting access to network resources, or distributing email. There are many flavors of groups, and depending on which mode the domain is running in, certain group functionality might not be available.

Group Types

Windows Server 2012 Active Directory supports two distinct types of groups: distribution and security. Both have their own particular uses and advantages if they are used properly and their characteristics are understood.

Distribution Groups

Distribution groups allow for the grouping of contacts, users, or groups primarily for emailing purposes. These types of groups cannot be used for granting or denying access to domain-based resources. Discretionary access control lists (DACLs), which are used to grant or deny access to resources or define user rights, are made up of access control entries (ACEs). Distribution groups are not security enabled and cannot be used within a DACL. When used with Microsoft Exchange Server 2010, distribution groups, unlike security groups, support the creation and usage of a dynamic distribution group whose membership is defined by a query and reevaluated dynamically as the group is used.

Security Groups

Security groups are security enabled and can be used for assigning user rights and resource permissions or for applying computer and Active Directory-based group policies. Using a security group instead of individual users simplifies administration. Groups can be created for particular resources or tasks, and when changes are made to the list of users who require access, only the group membership must be modified to reflect the changes throughout each resource that uses this group.

To delegate administrative tasks, security groups can be defined for different levels of responsibility. For example, a level 1 server administrator might have the right to reset user passwords and manage workstations, whereas a level 2 administrator might have those permissions plus the right to add or remove objects from a particular organizational unit or domain. The level of granularity possible is immense, so designing and implementing a functional security group structure can be one way to simplify administration and improve security across the enterprise. This is sometimes referred to as role-based access control (RBAC).

Security groups can also be used for emailing purposes, so they can serve a dual purpose.

Group Scopes in Active Directory

To complicate the group design a bit more, after the type of group is determined, the scope of the group must also be chosen. The scope, simply put, defines the boundaries of who can be a member of the group and where the group can be used. While scoping does apply to both group types, because only security groups can be used to delegate control or grant resource access, scoping issues typically impact security groups and therefore they are the focus on the remainder of this section.

Domain Local Groups

Domain local groups can be used to assign permissions to perform domain-based administrative tasks and to access resources hosted on domain members. These groups can contain members from any domain in the forest and can also contain other groups as members. Domain local groups can be assigned permissions only in the domain in which they are hosted.

Global Groups

Global groups are somewhat more functional than domain local groups. These groups can contain members only from the domain in which they are hosted, but they can be assigned permissions to resources or delegated control to perform administrative tasks or manage services across multiple domains when the proper domain trusts are in place.

Universal Groups

Universal groups can contain users, groups, contacts, or computers from any domain in the forest. This simplifies the need to have single-domain groups that have members in multiple forests. Universal group memberships in large, multidomain environments should be used carefully and avoided for groups whose membership changes frequently because group membership is stored in the global catalog and replicated throughout the forest. As a best practice in these environments, create a universal group to span domains but limit its membership to a global group from each domain which can then in turn contain any domain specific members. This practice reduces cross-domain replication.

Creating Groups

When it comes to creating groups, understanding the characteristics and limitations of each different type and scope is only half the battle. Other points to consider for group creation are how the group will be used and who will need to be a member of the group. Groups are commonly used for one or more of the following: delegating administrative rights, distributing email, and securing network resources such as file shares and printer devices. To help clarify group usage, the following examples show how groups can be used in a variety of administrative scenarios.

User Administration in a Single Domain

If a group is needed to simplify the process of granting rights to reset user passwords in a single domain, either a domain local or global security group would suffice. The actual domain user rights can only be granted to domain local groups, but these domain local groups could have global groups as members. For a single-domain model, if the specific user rights need to be granted only at the domain level, a domain local group with users as members would be fine. In more complex situations, if you need to reuse the same group of users for different functions or add domains to the forest, adding the users to global groups that are then added to the domain local group is a good solution.

For most organizations, however, the use of universal groups for most or even all groups is the best solution Thanks to improvements to the speed of networks and the efficiency of directory replication over the past several years, the performance impact of the extensive use of universal groups is often minor. In addition, environments that also use Exchange 2007 or Exchange 2010 must migrate all distribution groups to universal groups, making universal groups a common standard.

User Administration in a Multidomain Forest

When multiple domains need to be supported by the same IT staff, each domain's Domain Admins group should be added to each domain's Administrators group. For example, domain A's Administrators group would have Domain A Domain Admins, Domain B Domain Admins, and Domain C Domain Admins groups as members. You would need to add these domains whenever a resource or administrative task needs to grant or deny groups from each domain access to a resource in the forest.

A common best practice for larger forests is to create a universal security group named Forest Admins with each of the domain's Domain Admin groups as members. Then you would need to configure only a single entry to allow all the administrators access forest-wide for a particular resource or user right. Universal security groups are preferred because they can have members from each domain, but if the group strategy necessitates their use, domain local and domain global groups could still handle most situations.

Domain Functional Level and Groups

There are four different domain functional levels, with each level adding more functionality. The reason for all the different levels is to provide backward compatibility to support domain controllers running on different platforms. This allows a phased migration of the domain controllers. The four domain functional levels are as follows:

- **Windows 2000 Native**—This domain level allows Windows 2000 or later domain controllers in the domain. Universal security groups can be leveraged, along with universal and global security group nesting. This level can be raised to Windows Server 2003 Native level, which also enables you to change some existing groups' scopes and types on-the-fly.

- **Windows Server 2003**—This level allows Windows Server 2003 or later domain controllers. It provides all the features of the Windows 2000 native domain level, plus additional security and functionality features, such as domain rename, logon timestamp updates, and selective authentication.
- **Windows Server 2008**—The Windows Server 2008 functional level allows Windows Server 2008 or later domain controllers. This level supports all the features of the Windows Server 2003 functional level, plus additional features such as AES 128 and AES 256 encryption support for Kerberos, last interactive logon information to provide visibility into true logon activity by the user, fine-grained password policies to allow policies to be set on a per-group and per-user basis, and uses DFSR for Active Directory replication.
- **Windows Server 2008 R2**—The Windows Server 2008 R2 functional level, which allows only Windows Server 2008 R2 and Windows Server 8 domain controllers, adds Authentication Mechanism Assurance. This essentially inserts the type of logon method into the Kerberos token and allows applications to determine authorization or access based on the logon method. For example, an application could only allow logon type 2 (interactive) and not type 3 (network) to ensure that the user was actually at a workstation.
- **Windows Server 2012**—The Windows Server 2012 functional level, which allows only Windows Server 2012 domain controllers provides no additional features.

The most important note is that all the domain functional levels supported by Windows Server 2012 allow universal security groups.

Creating AD Groups

Now that you understand what kinds of groups you can create and what they can be used for, you are ready to create a group. To do so, follow these steps:

1. Launch Server Manager on a machine that has the Remote Server Administration Tools (RSAT) AD DS Tools installed.
2. Expand the Tools menu and run Active Directory Users and Computers.
3. Expand the domain folder (in this example, the companyabc.com folder).
4. Select a container—for example, the Users container or an organizational unit (OU). Right-click it and select New, Group.
5. Enter the group name and select the appropriate group type and scope, as shown in Figure 18.4.
6. Click OK to finish creating the group.

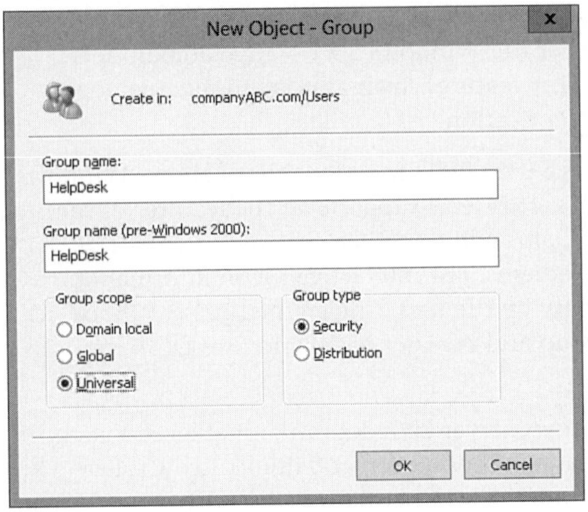

FIGURE 18.4 Creating a group.

Populating Groups

After you create a group, you can add members to it. The domain level that the domain is running in determines whether this group can have other groups as members.

To add members to an existing group, follow these steps:

1. Launch Server Manager on a machine that has the RSAT AD DS Tools installed.
2. Expand the Tools menu and run Active Directory Users and Computers.
3. Expand the domain folder (in this example, the companyabc.com folder).
4. Select the Users container or the OU that was used in the previous section. In the right pane, right-click the group that was created earlier, and select Properties.
5. Enter a description for the group on the General tab, and then click the Members tab.
6. Click Add to add members to the group.
7. In the Select Users, Contacts, Computers, Service Accounts or Groups window, type in the name of each group member separated by a semicolon and click OK to add these users to the group. If you don't know the names, clicking the Advanced button opens a window where you can perform a search to locate the desired members.
8. When all the members are listed on the Members tab of the group's property page, click OK to complete the operation.

Group Management

After a group is created, it needs to be managed by an administrator, users, or a combination of both, depending on the dynamics of the group.

To delegate control of a group to a particular user, follow these steps:

1. Launch Server Manager on a machine that has the RSAT AD DS Tools installed.
2. Expand the Tools menu and run Active Directory Users and Computers.
3. Select Advanced Features from the View menu.
4. Expand the domain folder (in this example, the companyabc.com folder).
5. Select the Users container or the OU that was used in the previous section. In the right pane, right-click the group that was created earlier, and select Properties.
6. Select the Security tab.
7. At the bottom of the page, click the Advanced button.
8. In the Advanced Security Settings for Group dialog box, select the Permissions tab.
9. Click Add and then click Select a Principal.
10. In the Select User, Computer, Service Account or Group window, type in the name of the account for which you want to grant permissions, and click OK.
11. When the Permissions Entry for Group window appears, click the Apply To drop-down list arrow, and then select This Object Only as shown in Figure 18.5.
12. In the Properties section, check the boxes for Read Members and Write Members, and then click OK.
13. Click OK to close the Advanced Security Settings for Group dialog box.
14. Click OK to close the group's property pages.

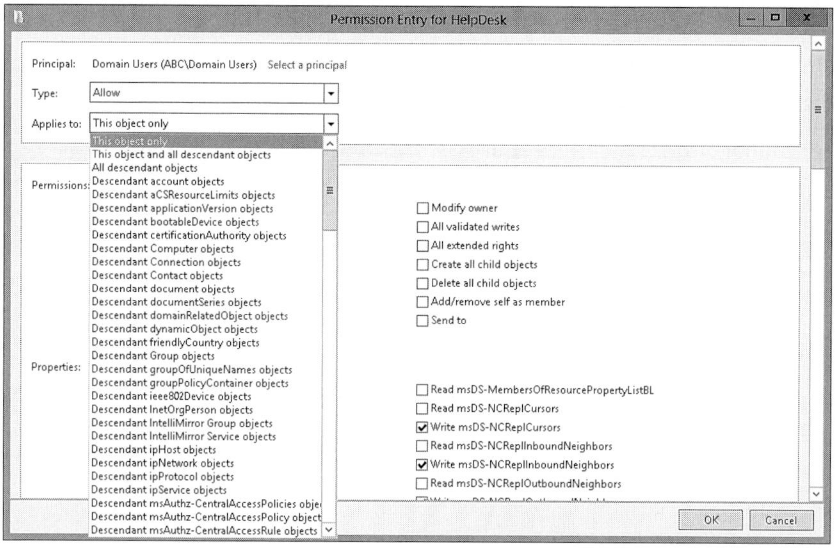

FIGURE 18.5 Granting permissions to modify group membership.

Managing Users with Local Security and Group Policies

Windows Server 2012 systems provide local security policies to manage user and group administrative access on a per-server basis. Within Active Directory, you can use group policies to set configurations and security on a specified collection of computers, users, or groups of users from a single policy. These policies can be used to deliver standard desktop configurations and security settings for server access and application functionality. Also, policies can set user configurations to deliver software on demand, redirect desktop folders, plus affect many more settings. Many settings within each policy explain what the setting controls and whether computer-based settings apply based on the different versions of Windows. Chapter 15, "Security Policies, Network Policy Server, and Network Access Protection," describes security policy in more depth, but the best way to discover and learn about all the Group Policy settings is to open an actual GPO and start browsing each section.

Viewing Policies with the Group Policy Management Console

You can view Active Directory-based group policies with very little effort by using a single console, the Group Policy Management Console (GPMC). This tool is a feature that can installed on any Windows Server 2012 system using Server Manager. The GPMC enables administrators to view group policies, edit group policies, and model the effects of combinations of group policies (that is, model the resulting configuration).

NOTE

Local group policy or security policy changes are made using the Group Policy Object Editor, an MMC snap-in, available on every Windows Server 2012, and the Local Security Policy console, available under the Tools menu in Server Manager.

To open an existing policy, follow these steps:

1. Launch Server Manager on a machine that has the GPMC feature installed.
2. Expand the Tools menu and run Group Policy Management Console.
3. Expand the Forest folder.
4. Expand the Domains folder.
5. Expand the specific domain, such as companyabc.com.
6. Select a GPO, such as the Default Domain Policy. Click OK to close the linked policy warning window.
7. Select the Settings tab to review the settings. Or right-click the GPO and select Edit to change the settings.

After you access the policy, you can view each setting or settings container to determine the default value and, in some cases, learn what the setting controls. Keep in mind that, with the correct level of permissions, any changes you make to this policy are live changes; there is no undo other than reversing the individual setting changes or performing an authoritative restore of Active Directory.

Creating New Group Policies

When changes need to be made or tested using group policies, the administrator should leave the production environment untouched and create test policies in isolated test lab environments. When test labs are not available or cannot replicate the production environment, the administrator can test policies in isolated organizational units within a domain. Also, if domain-based or site-based policies need to be created for testing, security filtering could be modified to apply the policy only to a specific set of test users or groups.

The preceding section described how to locate a group policy. Using the Group Policy Management Console, you can also create, configure, and open site, domain, and organizational unit (OU) group policies for editing.

In some cases, it will be necessary to prevent a GPO from being applied to a user or computer. That is, there might be a GPO that applies to all members of a department, but it is necessary to make a single exception to the rule. Rather than create a specific OU to apply the GPO, security filtering can be used to allow or deny the application of the GPO.

The following steps outline how to create a new domain-based policy and configure its security filtering to apply to a single user:

1. Launch Server Manager on a machine that has the GPMC feature installed.
2. Expand the Tools menu and run Group Policy Management Console.
3. Expand the Forest folder.
4. Expand the Domains folder.
5. Select the specific domain, such as companyabc.com.
6. Right-click the domain and select Create a GPO in This Domain, and Link It Here.
7. Type in a descriptive policy name, leave the source starter GPO set to None, and click OK to create the policy.

NOTE

Source starter GPOs are GPO templates that can be used to prepopulate settings in GPOs. If there are common settings that will go into GPOs, they can be created in starter GPOs and then seeded into new GPOs as they are created.

The starter GPOs are stored in a common folder named StarterGPOs. Any GPOs created in this folder are available for seeding GPOs. There are no starter GPOs in a domain by default.

8. The new policy will be displayed under the domain. Right-click the new policy and select Edit to launch the Group Policy Management Editor snap-in.
9. Right-click the GPO name in the Group Policy Management Editor, and select Properties.
10. Select the Security tab and highlight the Authenticated Users entry.
11. In the Permissions section, scroll down and uncheck the Allow check box for Apply Group Policy. This means that the GPO will not take effect on any user or computer.
12. Select each entry in the Group Policy ACL and verify that no existing groups are allowed to apply Group Policy.
13. Click Add and type in the name of a user or group. To find a list of users and groups within the current domain, click the Advanced button, and in the Search window, click Find Now to return the complete list. Scroll down and select the users or groups you want, and click OK.
14. Click OK to add the entries to the policy.
15. Back in the Security window, select the respective entry and check the Allow check box for Apply Group Policy, as shown in Figure 18.6. This means that the GPO will take effect on the members of this group, which could include both users and computers. Click OK when you're finished.
16. Close the Group Policy Management Editor snap-in.

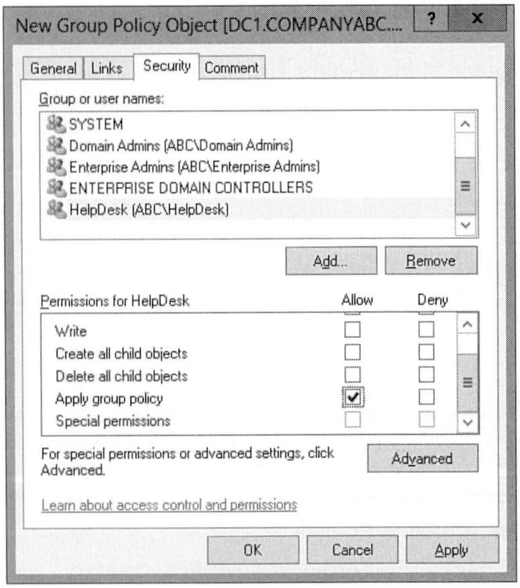

FIGURE 18.6 Modifying a group policy's application scope.

Now the group policies set in the GPO will affect only the users or computers that were specified—in this case, members of the HelpDesk group. This allows for fine-grained application of group policies to targeted groups.

Configuring and Optimizing Group Policy

After a GPO has been created, you should take a few steps to configure how the policy will be applied and to optimize the time to apply the policy. Group policies can be limited to computer-specific or user-specific settings. To determine whether either type of setting can be disabled, the administrator should determine which settings are necessary to provide the desired policy settings. In many cases, a policy uses settings for both types. To disable either user or computer policy settings, select the policy as described in the section "Viewing Policies with the Group Policy Management Console," earlier in this chapter. When the policy is listed, select the Details tab. Adjust the GPO status field to disable computer or user settings as required.

When multiple group policies exist, they are applied in a predefined order. For a particular user or computer, the order can be derived using the Resultant Set of Policies snap-in. The results of standard policies are that if setting X is enabled on a top-level policy and disabled on the last policy to apply to an object, the resulting setting will disable setting X. Many policy settings have three states: Enabled, Disabled, and the default of Not Configured.

You can limit group policies to apply to specific users or computers by modifying the security entries. In addition to disabling portions of each GPO, policy inheritance can be blocked at the domain or OU container level using a setting called Block Policy Inheritance. When blocking or precedence rules need to be ignored for the settings of a particular group policy, you can configure the group policy as Enforced.

Group Policy Objects and Logon Performance

It is important that policies be effectively placed to avoid slow logon performance. For each level in the OU structure where a group policy is linked, the download and application of the policies at that level can cause 15 to 30 seconds of additional logon or startup delay. This is because the GPOs at a particular OU level are evaluated at one time, which takes a few seconds. The process is repeated for each OU level where there are GPOs, and that processing time can really stack up, leading to longer logon delays for the users and complaints to the help desk. Interestingly, the same applies for the computer startup as the policies are applied, but users don't notice that as much.

NOTE

The logon delay is something that can develop over time as the Active Directory infrastructure matures. When initially deployed, the Active Directory will have relatively few GPOs and, consequently, logon delays will be short. As time progresses, more GPOs are added and more OU levels with GPOs are added, with an increase in the logon times that users experience. This creeping logon time can be directly traced to the proliferation of GPOs.

The general guidelines to improve the logon performance of group policies are as follows:

- **Reduce the number of OU levels**—By reducing the number of OU levels, there will be fewer levels to link GPOs to and therefore better performance. The best practice is to have a maximum of three levels, if possible. If more are needed, prohibit the linking of GPOs to some of the levels.
- **Reduce the number of GPOs**—By consolidating settings into fewer GPOs, less processing time is needed to read the GPOs. A single GPO at the same OU level will perform faster than 10 GPOs at the same level.
- **Use security filtering**—If a GPO is security filtered to not apply to a user or computer, the settings do not need to be read or processed. This speeds up logon and startup performance.
- **Disable user or computer settings in GPOs**—Each GPO consists of a user and a computer section. If there are no settings in either of those sections, that section can be disabled and will be ignored. For example, if a GPO only has computer settings and the user settings are disabled, that GPO will be skipped at logon (which only deals with user settings).

These guidelines can dramatically improve logon and startup performance.

The last guideline suggested disabling the user setting or computer settings, because processing a GPO takes a certain amount of time for a computer at startup and for a user at logon. To enable or disable the entire GPO or the user/computer portion of the GPO, follow these steps:

1. Open the Group Policy Management Console.
2. Expand the Forest folder, expand the Domains folder, select the specific domain, and select the Group Policy Objects folder.
3. Right-click the GPO and select GPO Status.
4. Select the appropriate option: Enable, User Configuration Settings Disabled, Computer Configuration Settings Disabled, or All Settings Disabled.

This will take effect immediately. The All Setting Disabled option is useful for troubleshooting when you want to completely disable a GPO without changing the ACLs or the settings.

Block Policy Inheritance

The Block Policy Inheritance option enables an administrator to prevent higher-level policies from applying to users and computers within a certain domain or OU. This capability can be useful to optimize Group Policy applications and protect sensitive user/computer accounts from organizationwide policy settings.

To block policy inheritance, follow these steps:

1. Launch Server Manager on a machine that has the GPMC feature installed.
2. Expand the Tools menu and run Group Policy Management Console.
3. Expand the Forest folder.
4. Expand the Domains folder.
5. Select the specific domain, such as companyabc.com.
6. Locate and right-click the OU for which you want to block inheritance, and select Block Inheritance, as shown in Figure 18.7.

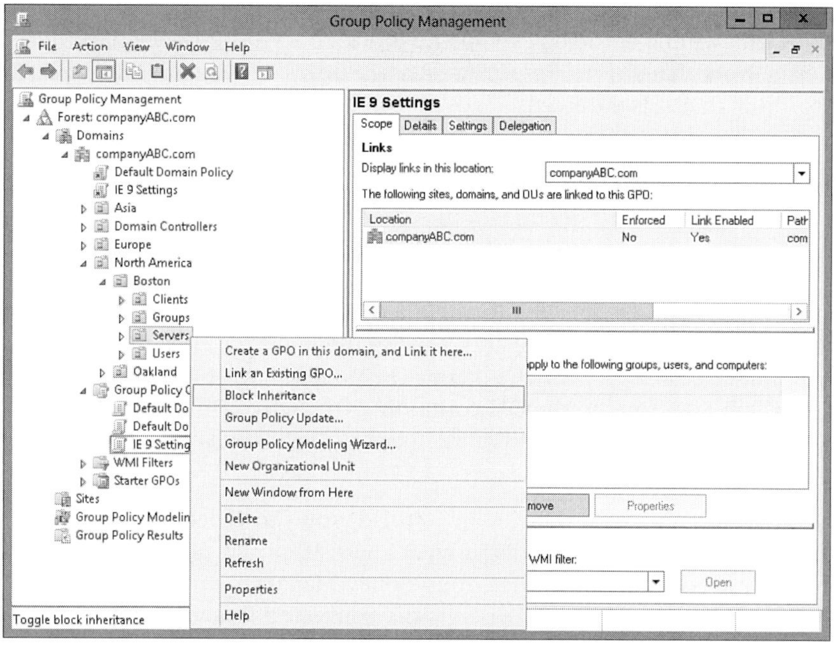

FIGURE 18.7 Blocking policy inheritance for an OU.

In this example, policy inheritance was blocked on the Servers OU. Group policies created above the OU will not affect objects within the OU (unless the group policy is enforced; see the next section). Note the blue exclamation mark icon on the OU to alert the administrator that policy inheritance is blocked.

The Enforce Option

Configuring the Enforce option overrides all other precedence rules for a specific GPO link. Enforcement overrides any inheritance blocking at a lower level OU as well as lower-level policies configured to change any policy settings. This option should be used only if a policy needs to be enforced on AD objects in every container and subcontainer with a link or inheritance to this policy object.

To configure the Enforce option for a policy, follow these steps:

1. Launch Server Manager on a machine that has the GPMC feature installed.
2. Expand the Tools menu and run Group Policy Management Console.
3. Expand the Forest folder.
4. Expand the Domains folder.
5. Expand the specific domain, such as companyabc.com.
6. Right-click the group policy link to enforce, and select Enforce.

Now the group policy link will be enforced even if the Block Policy Inheritance option is set on down-level OUs. Note that the group policy link will now have a small lock icon associated with it to show that it is enforced.

Troubleshooting Group Policy Applications

When policies are used throughout an organization, sometimes the policy settings do not apply to a user or computer as originally intended. To begin basic troubleshooting of Group Policy application issues, you need to understand the policy application hierarchy. First, any local server or workstation policies are applied to the user or computer, followed by site group policies, domain group policies, and, finally, the organizational unit group policies. If nested OUs have group policies, the parent OU policies are processed first, followed by the child OUs, and, finally, the OU containing the Active Directory object (user or computer). You might find it easier to remember LSD-OU—the acronym for local, site, domain, and then OU.

Now that you know the order in which policies are applied, you can proceed to use the Group Policy testing and troubleshooting tools provided with Windows Server 2012, namely the Group Policy Modeling tool in the Group Policy Management Console and the command-line utility GPResult.exe, which is the command-line version of the Resultant Set of Policy (RSoP) snap-in.

The Group Policy Modeling Tool

The Group Policy Modeling snap-in can be used to simulate the policy settings for a user who logs on to a server or workstation after all the respective policies have been applied. This tool is good for identifying which policies are being applied and what the effective setting is based on the defined simulation.

To simulate the policies for a user, use the Group Policy Modeling snap-in as follows:

1. Launch Server Manager on a machine that has the GPMC feature installed.
2. Expand the Tools menu and run Group Policy Management Console.

3. Expand the Forest folder.
4. Select the Group Policy Modeling folder.
5. Select Action, Group Policy Modeling Wizard to launch the wizard.
6. Click Next.
7. Leave the default domain controller selection, which chooses any available domain controller. Click Next.
8. Select the User option button in the User Information box, and click Browse.
9. Enter the name of a user to check, and click OK. Click Next to accept the user and computer selection.

NOTE

In the Group Policy Modeling Wizard, the net effect of the group policies can be modeled for specific users, computers, or entire containers for either object. This enables an administrator to see the effects for individual objects or for objects placed within the containers, making the tool very flexible.

10. Click Next on the Advanced Simulation Options page. The advanced simulation options enable you to model slow network connections, loopback processing mode, or specific sites.
11. Click Next to skip the Alternate AD Paths.
12. The User Security Groups page shows the groups that the user is a member of. You can add additional groups to see the effects of changes. Leave as is and click Next.
13. Click Next to skip the WMI Filters for Users page.
14. Click Next to run the simulation.
15. Click Finish to view the results.
16. Select the Details tab and if needed use Show link next to Group Policy Objects and next to Denied GPOs.

Within the console, you can review each particular setting to see whether a setting was applied or the desired setting was overwritten by a higher-level policy. The report shows why specific GPOs were denied. Figure 18.8 shows that two GPOs were denied to the user object tsmith. The Default Domain Policy GPO was denied because it is empty (of user settings) and the Remote Control Executives GPO was denied because of security filtering. This is the GPO created earlier in the chapter, which was applied only to members of the HelpDesk group. The user tsmith is not a member of this group and, hence, does not have the GPO applied.

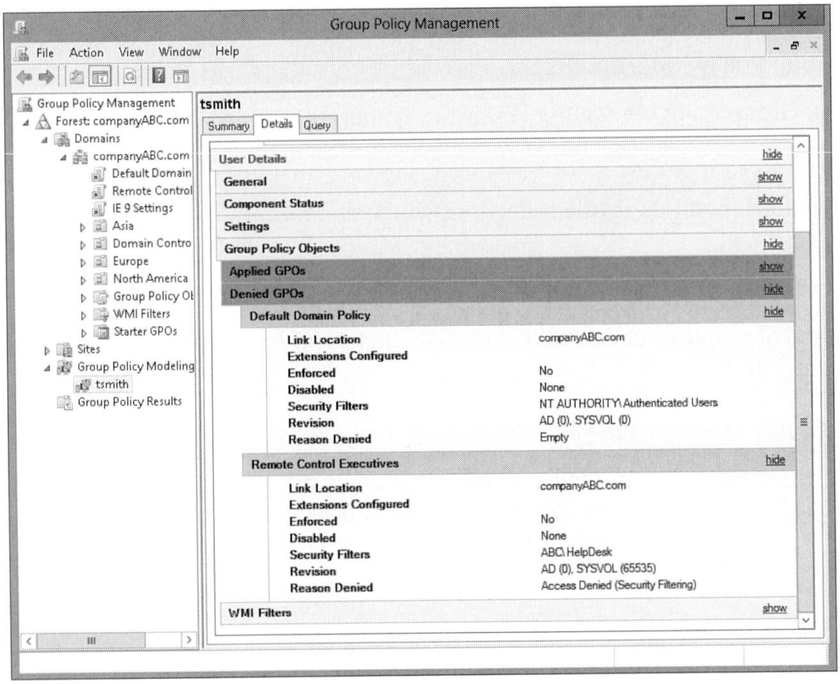

FIGURE 18.8 The Group Policy Modeling report.

Managing Printers with the Print Management Console

The Print Management console in Windows Server 2012 helps organizations better manage and administer printers on an enterprise basis. Before the Print Management console, which was first introduced in the Windows Server 2003 R2 time frame as a standalone installation, a network administrator had to point to each network printer or printer server individually to manage and administer the device. For a large enterprise with hundreds of printers and dozens of printer servers, this was a very tedious task to select print servers each and every time a printer needed to be managed. Furthermore, if the administrator didn't remember which printer was attached to which print server, it could take a while to eventually find the printer and print server that needed management.

The Print Management console, which was later integrated into the Windows operating system, provides a single interface where an administrator can view all printers and print servers in the enterprise. Furthermore, printer resources can be grouped to simplify administration of some of the printers. For example, if an organization has an administrator for a particular building, the Print Management interface could be filtered to only list printers within the building. This would allow the administrator to only see certain printers they are responsible for and to consolidate multiple print server groups of printers into a single interface for management and administration.

The Print Management component only needs to be installed on the system that the administrator is managing from; it does not need to be installed on all print servers or systems in the enterprise. Functionally, Print Management could be installed on just one system. However, it is automatically installed on Windows Server 2012 servers with the Print Service role installed.

Installing the Print Management Console

The Print Management console is installed as one of the Remote Server Administration Tools in the features or as part of the Print Server role of Windows Server 2012. To install the Print Management console on a management server that is not a print server, complete the following steps:

1. Launch Server Manager.
2. Expand the Manage menu and select Add Roles and Features.
3. Accept the default Installation Type.
4. Select the appropriate server on the Server Selection page. Note: If not installing on the local server, the target server must be added to server manager before starting this process.
5. Select no roles and click Next
6. In the feature selection dialog, expand the Remote Server Administration Tools and the Role Administration Tools.
7. Check the Print and Document Services Tools check box.
8. Click Next, Install, and Close to complete the installation process.

Now the Print Management console will be available within Server Manager on the server.

Configuring the Print Management Console

After the Print Management console has been installed on a system, you need to configure the utility to identify the printers and print servers in the enterprise. Printers can be manually added to the Print Management console for administration and management, or the network can be scanned to attempt to automatically identify printers in the enterprise.

To configure print management resources, launch the Print Management console as follows:

1. Select Start.
2. Expand the Manage menu and select the Print Management option.

Upon opening the Print Management console, a screen appears similar to the one shown in Figure 18.9.

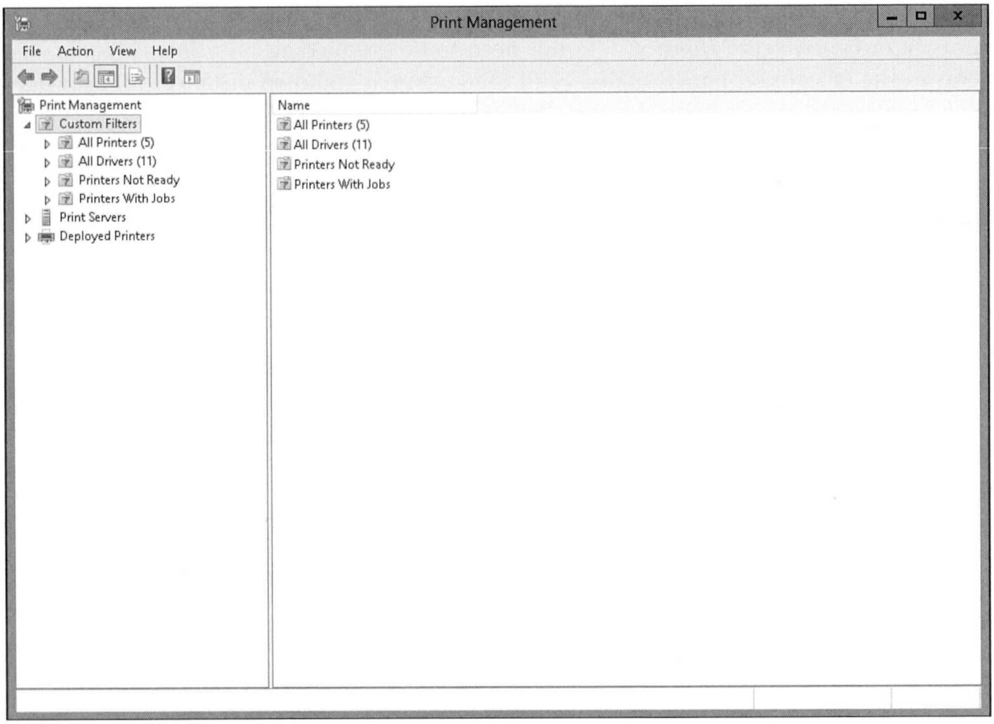

FIGURE 18.9 Print Management console.

Adding New Printers as Network Shared Resources

You can add new printers to a Windows Server 2012 network in two ways. One way is the standard Windows printer installation method of using the Add Printer option. The other option is using the new Print Management console and adding a printer within the utility. Both methods return the same result, so the main reason to use the Print Management console method is to simplify all print management tasks of adding, modifying, and managing printers from a single utility.

Using the Windows Control Panel to Add a Printer

Locally attached printers are typically detected by the operating system and installed automatically. To manually install a local printer or add a network printer, follow these steps:

1. Click the Start button and type the search string **control panel**.
2. Select the Control Panel in the search results.
3. Select the Hardware category within the Control Panel.
4. Select the Advanced Printer Setup link in the Devices and Printers category.
5. After the search completes, select The Printer That I Want Isn't Listed.

6. Select the type of printer being added. For this example, select Add a Printer Using a TCP/IP Address or Hostname, and then click Next
7. Enter the hostname or IP address or the printer and if necessary, also the port and device type, and then click Next.
8. If the automated driver detection fails, select the appropriate driver.
9. When prompted, give the printer a name (such as HP LaserJet P2035 PCL6 in the Marketing Dept), and then click Next.
10. When prompted whether you want to share the printer, select the Share Name option and type in a name that will describe the printer (such as HP2035MKTG), and then click Next.
11. If you want to print a test page, click the Print a Test Page button; otherwise, click Finish to complete the addition of the printer.

Using the Add Printer Option in the Print Management Console

Another way to add a printer to the network is to use the Print Management console. This process is identical to adding the printer using the Windows Add Printer option addressed in the preceding section; however, instead of using two separate interfaces for adding and managing printers, using the Print Management console can centralize the tasks into a single interface.

To start the Network Printer Installation Wizard within the Print Management console, follow these steps:

1. Expand the Print Servers section of the Print Management console.
2. Right-click one of the print servers listed in the Print Servers section of the interface, and choose Add Printer.
3. Follow the wizard prompts to add your printer as outlined in the preceding section.

Adding Print Servers to the Print Management Console

After printers and print servers have been added to the network as noted in the previous sections, an administrator can now begin to add print servers to the Print Management console to centrally view, manage, and maintain the printers on the network.

Adding a print server to the Print Management console allows the administrator to manage the print server and all the printers the print server hosts. To add a print server to the Print Management console, follow these steps:

1. Right-click the Print Servers item in the Print Management console, and choose Add/Remove Servers.
2. Type in the name of the print server you want to add, or click Browse and search the Microsoft Windows network to view the various servers in the environment.
3. Click OK to add the print server.

Using the Print Management Console

With printers added to the network, and print servers added to the Print Management console, an administrator can now begin to centrally view, manage, and administer the printers and print servers. Some of the tasks that an administrator can perform from the Print Management console are tasks that would otherwise require a remote session to each print server, such as change printer ports, add or modify forms, or view the status of printers whether the printers are online or not. Other tasks are new to the Print Management console, such as creating custom printer filters that allow multiple administrators to view and manage selected printers based on their site, rights, and roles.

Performing General Printer Administration Tasks

From within the Print Management console, the administrator can perform general printer administration tasks. These tasks include the following:

- **Updating printer drivers**—By right-clicking the Drivers item in the Print Server section of the Print Management console and choosing Manage Drivers, an administrator can update or change the printer driver of a printer. This is rarely done in a network environment, but sometimes when a new printer add-on, such as an envelope feeder or expansion paper feeder or sorter, is added a new printer driver is needed to support the new add-on.
- **Managing forms**—By right-clicking the Forms item in the Print Server section and choosing Manage Forms, an administrator can create and delete new forms to support different size paper or to specify a custom letterhead paper form.
- **Additional configuration**—Additionally within this interface, an administrator can change the printer port that a printer is attached to on a print server, define log settings, and enable the function to have users notified when a print job has successfully completed printing.

Creating Custom Filters

A unique function of the Print Management console is the Custom Filters function that enables administrators to group printers, typically for the purpose of distributing the administration of printers in the environment. For large organizations that might have multiple buildings, sites, and administration boundaries of devices such as printers, the administrators can perform a filter view to see only the printers that fit within their administrative responsibilities.

First, to view all printers in the environment, an administrator can click the All Printers section of the Custom Filters section of the Print Management console. All the printers for managed print servers will be listed here.

NOTE

If some printers on the network are not listed in the All Printers view, see the section "Adding Print Servers to the Print Management Console."

To create a custom printers view, follow these steps:

1. Right-click the Custom Filters View in the Print Management console, and choose Add New Printer Filter.
2. Type in a descriptive name for this filter view (such as All Printers in the Boston Site).
3. Check the Display the Total Number of Printers Next to the Name of the Printer Filter check box. Click Next.
4. In the Field drop-down list, choose a field that will contain information that can be filtered. In many cases, the print servers can be filtered because a print server frequently services printers in a specific geography. Alternately, organizations that entered in location information for printers such as Building 11 would be able to filter for that designation in a custom printer filter filtered by name. An example might be Field=Location, Condition=Contains, Value=Boston. Click Next to continue.
5. On the Set Notification Options page, an administrator can note an email address where the administrator would be notified on the status of events related to the printers in the filter. You can also run a script. This might include being emailed every time a printer is offline, or every time a printer is out of paper. Enter in the appropriate email information (email address, SMTP mail server to be used, and message desired), or leave this section unchecked, and then click Finish.

By clicking the newly created filter, the filter rule is applied, and the printers noted in the filter will be displayed, as shown in Figure 18.10. In this figure, notice that the environment contains five printers; however, the filter is searching only for printers in Boston, and therefore only three printers are displayed for this administrator to view and manage.

An almost unlimited number of printer filters can be created to show different groupings of printers to be managed or administered. Organizations have created custom printer filters by printer manufacturer such as HP, Xerox, and Sharp or by printer type such as laser, color laser, and plotter to be able to view assets by make, model, or configuration. Printer filters can even be created based on queue length and to run an automatic script to take action in addition to notifying the administrator.

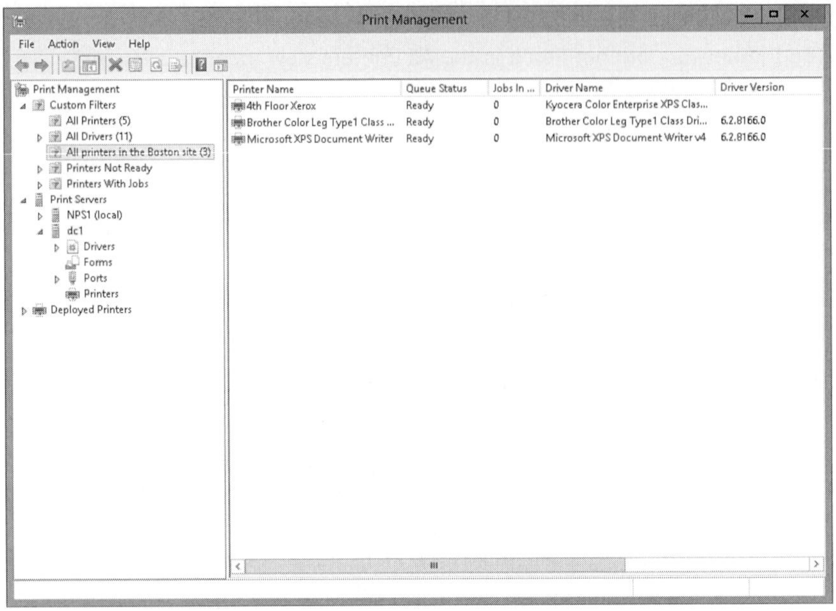

FIGURE 18.10 Custom printer filter.

Summary

Managing Active Directory sites, groups, users, and printers in Windows Server 2012 can be daunting if some of these tasks cannot be automated or simplified. This chapter outlined ways and tools to create these objects and included the information necessary to manage these objects from a standalone and enterprise level.

This chapter addressed options for administration that included centralized, decentralized, and mixed administration, which provides a model that fits pretty much all organizations. Some of the key criteria in administration are addressed when sites and groups are created that identify administration boundaries and define the role of administration within and across the boundaries.

In addition, policies clarify how management and administration will be handled, which ultimately trickle down to profiles and configuration settings to create a managed and administered Windows Server 2012 environment.

Best Practices

The following are best practices from this chapter:

- Clearly understand your roles and responsibilities in the enterprise network, and understand how the different components that make up the network communicate and rely on one another.

- Choose the appropriate administrative model (central, distributed, or mixed) for the organization based on required services and skill sets in each location.
- Always define the Active Directory sites to accurately reflect physical structure even if those locations don't contain domain controllers.
- Always define all subnets in the Active Directory Sites and Services to ensure that all domain computers can be located to their closest Active Directory resources.
- Use site links to accurately reflect the WAN and LAN topology.
- Use site policies to define custom network security settings for sites with unique requirements or to delegate administrative rights when administration is performed on a mostly geographic basis.
- Ensure that sites contain local network services, such as domain controllers, global catalog servers, DNS servers, DHCP servers, and, if necessary, WINS servers.
- For volatile groups, create a universal group to span domains, but have only a global group from each domain as a member.
- Use group policies to manage users and desktops.
- Modify Group Policy security entries to limit Group Policy application to specific users or computers.
- Reduce the OU levels and the number of GPOs by consolidating multiple GPOs into a single GPO where possible to improve logon and startup performance.
- Use Group Policy Modeling to view and troubleshoot the way group policies are applied.
- Use the Print Management console included in to Windows Server 2012 to centrally view, manage, and administer printers in the network environment.

CHAPTER 19

Windows Server 2012 Group Policies and Policy Management

IN THIS CHAPTER

Microsoft has always had a tool or process to create standardized desktop configurations and to roll these configurations out to multiple computers and users. With each new edition of the Microsoft Windows OS (OS), Microsoft has continued to improve these tools and processes, and Windows Server 2012 is no different. Centrally managing computer and user security and configuration settings is achieved by leveraging the Microsoft Windows Group Policy infrastructure.

The Microsoft Windows Group Policy infrastructure included with Microsoft Windows Server 2012 is one of most comprehensive tools created for centralizing and simplifying the implementation of standardized computer configurations and user profile settings across a set of computers or an entire enterprise. Group Policy reduces the need for repetition by enabling the administrator to define configurations and settings just once and then quickly deploy these settings to several computers/users without difficulty.

This chapter provides an overview of the Windows Server 2012 Group Policy infrastructure, particularly with the setup and management of the infrastructure, including design and administrative best practices.

Group Policy Overview

The Microsoft Group Policy infrastructure is a complex system that leverages several features and services included in the Windows server and client OSs and the IP networks that these systems reside on.

At its simplest, a *group policy* is a set of definitions created by administrators to centrally configure and deploy computer and user settings. Group policy contains an extensive set of options right out of the box and can be extended even further through third-party software vendors and through custom development of policy settings by advanced Group Policy administrators. As an example of Group Policy at work, a policy can be created to automatically install a network printer on all machines located in a particular office. Another group policy could define firewall profile definitions that are less restrictive on the corporate network and very secure when a mobile workstation connects to a public wireless network.

Group policy was introduced with Windows 2000 Active Directory. Before Windows 2000, the building blocks of Group Policy were simply known as system policies and had some effective uses, but were still pretty limited. The Windows 2000 version of Group Policy proved to be very useful for security configurations and basic user settings but lacked many features, and when it came to mobile devices, it did not work very well. Microsoft Windows Server 2003 and Windows XP improved on the Windows 2000 Group Policy infrastructure by adding some new network detection features and more computer and user configuration options, including printer deployment. It was not until Windows Vista and Server 2008 were released that a major Group Policy overhaul had taken place.

Starting with Windows Vista and Server 2008, Microsoft now defined two different types of group policies: local and domain-based group policies. The local group policies with Windows Vista and Windows Server 2008 were basically mirrors of the settings available for both computers and users in domain-based group policies. This feature alone extended the application of Group Policy outside of Active Directory environments, making this tool valuable to organizations that use Windows workstations in workgroup configurations or in networks that do not necessarily rely on Microsoft Active Directory as the backbone for network authentication and other services.

Another major change to Group Policy was the introduction of Group Policy Preferences (GPP). GPP includes both computer and user-based preferences, and although these are configured with group policies, by their namesake, they implement the preferred configuration settings, and most can be changed by the user after policy application. GPP included much of the missing functionality that Group Policy administrators had to customize themselves within customized computer startup or user logon scripts to deploy customized desktop profile configurations, Registry settings, and much more. GPP really changed the Group Policy administrative landscape as it moved a lot of advanced customizations away from the cryptic scripts to GUI-based administration that all administrators can review and tune.

As stated earlier in this chapter, many of the new Group Policy features of the Windows Vista and Windows Server 2008 infrastructure have been further improved and extended to provide more out-of-the-box functionality. Group policy is split into four main sections: computer policies, computer preferences, user policies, and user preferences. As a way to understand this quickly, consider the policy sections as enforced and the preference sections as initial configurations that can be changed as desired.

This chapter addresses the administration and management of GPOs for Windows 8 client OS as well as Windows Server 2012, server OS.

Group Policy Processing: How Does It Work?

The first thing an administrator needs to understand about Group Policy is that policies are processed and applied by computers and users. Policy processing occurs during certain events like computer startup and user logon but also at periodic intervals. When policy processing occurs, many factors are taken into account to determine whether a policy will be applied. One determining factor is whether the policy has been previously applied and, if so, whether it has been changed since the last application. This and many other factors are used to check each possible policy before it is applied to the computer/user.

Computer GPO Processing

Computers process group policies during startup, shutdown, and periodic refresh intervals. By default, the refresh interval is every 90 minutes on servers and workstations, with an offset of 0 to 30 minutes. On domain controllers, group policies are refreshed every 5 minutes. The offset ensures that domain-joined computers do not all refresh or process group policies simultaneously and potentially negatively impact the operation of the domain controllers and the computers themselves. When a domain-joined computer starts up, if the computer can successfully locate and communicate with an authenticating domain controller, Group Policy Object (GPO) processing occurs. During GPO processing, the system checks each linked or inherited GPO to verify whether the policy has changed since the last processing cycle, and then runs any startup scripts and checks for any other requirement to reapply the policy. During the shutdown and refresh interval, the GPOs are processed again to check for any updates or changes since the last application cycle.

Computer GPO processing is determined by GPO links, security filtering, and Windows Management Instrumentation (WMI) filters.

User GPO Processing

GPO processing for users is similar to GPO processing for computers. The main difference is that GPO processing for users occurs at user logon, logoff, and periodically. The default refresh interval for user GPO processing is 90 minutes plus a 0- to 30-minute offset. User GPO processing is determined by GPO links and security filtering.

19

Network Location Awareness

Network Location Awareness (NLA) is a service built in to Windows that is used to determine when the computer has connectivity to the Active Directory infrastructure. The Group Policy infrastructure uses NLA to determine whether to attempt to download and apply GPOs. This Group Policy functionality is also used with a connectivity check known as slow-link detection.

In earlier versions, Group Policy processing used slow-link detection to determine whether the network was reliable enough to process and apply policies. Slow-link detection relied on the Internet Control Message Protocol (ICMP) or ping to test for network connectivity and was not very reliable. Because of this specification, group policy processing on mobile and remote client workstations was very unreliable. When a mobile client workstation connected to the corporate network through a virtual private network (VPN) connection or after waking from hibernation or sleep mode, the change in network connectivity usually passed by unnoticed, and GPOs were not applied or refreshed. In these cases, the only way to get these clients to apply their GPOs was to have them manually run a Group Policy update from the command line or have these machines reboot while connected to the corporate network via wired Ethernet connections.

Group policy processing from Windows Vista and later, including Windows 8 and Windows Server 2012, now use the rebuilt NLA service to detect network changes. The new NLA service is much better at detecting changes to network connections, and when a connection is established, NLA checks for domain controller connectivity. If a domain controller can be contacted, the NLA service notifies the computer Group Policy service, which, in turn, triggers Group Policy processing for both computer-based and user-based Group Policy settings. The NLA service is not dependent on ICMP or ping, which on its own makes it more reliable. The NLA service should run on most networks without any special configuration on the network devices or network firewalls, even if ICMP communication is disabled or blocked by the firewall.

Group Policy Client-Side Extensions

Group policies are divided into policies and preferences, but even further within the policy different portions or sections of Group Policy will determine how, when, or if that particular section of a group policy will be processed. Group policy processing on the client side is managed by the Group Policy client-side extensions (CSEs). The CSEs are dynamic link library (DLL) files that are installed on the local client server or workstation OSs. When group policies are processed, it is actually the CSEs that apply the settings on the client. There are both policy and preference CSEs on the client system, and each CSE has its own default processing behavior, as discussed in the next section.

Tuning Group Policy Processing with GPO Settings

Within the Windows OS, there is a default behavior with regard to how Group Policy processing functions. Under these default behaviors, some parts of the group policy run only at computer startup and user logon, whereas some sections are processed during the background refresh interval. In addition, policies that have been processed earlier and have not changed since the last application of the group policy may or may not be processed again. Furthermore, if a computer startup or logon process has occurred off-network, Group Policy processing occurs when the domain network is detected. This is by design, to enhance both Group Policy processing and performance. For example, if all group policies were processed in full at every processing instance, the domain controllers and client system performance or user experience would likely suffer: Users might experience longer logon and logoff intervals, and computers across the organization might experience slower startups/shutdowns and might periodically just slow down. This is why, by default, group policies that have already been applied and have not changed are not processed during the background refresh interval.

Administrators and organizations might want to change the default behavior of Group Policy processing to streamline group policy performance and the user experience, or they might want to tighten security and ensure that all policy settings remain enforced by forcing group policies to reapply every policy processing cycle. To more fully understand the default processing behavior of computer and user Group Policy processing, review the settings within a domain group policy located at Computer Configuration and User Configuration node at Policies\Administrative Templates\System\Group Policy. Within the sections, you can review several Group Policy processing settings. The explanations for each describe their default behavior and provide different options for each setting that is enabled, as shown in Figure 19.1 for the Computer Configuration Drive Maps preference extension policy processing setting.

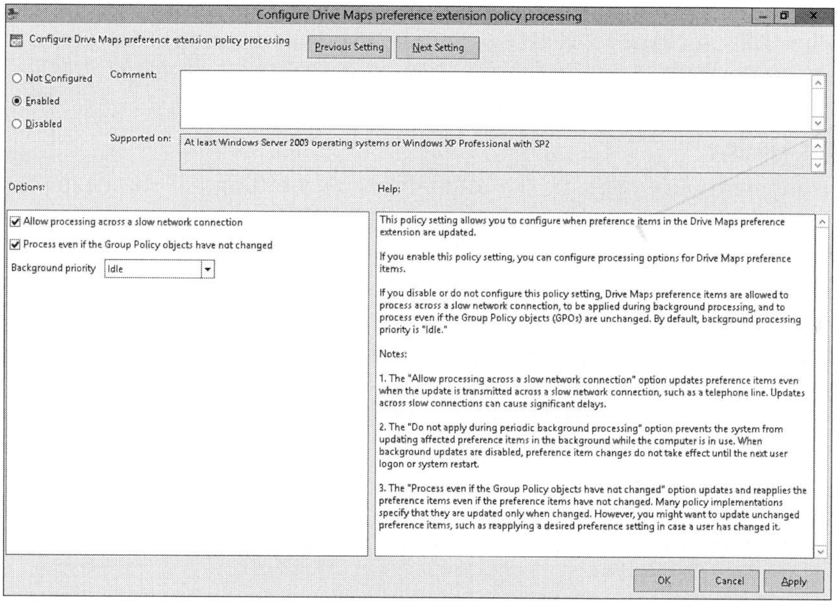

FIGURE 19.1 Group policy drive maps preference policy setting.

Local Group Policies

You can apply two different types of policies to Windows systems and Windows system user accounts: local group policies and Active Directory domain-based group policies. Local group policies exist on all Windows systems, but domain-based group policies are available only in an Active Directory forest. Until the release of Windows Vista and Windows Server 2008, servers and workstations could contain and apply only a single local computer policy. This policy contained settings for both the local computer and the user who logged on to the computer.

In many environments, usually because of legacy or line-of-business application requirements, end users were often granted local Administrators group membership on workstations and essentially excluded from the application of the many configured security settings applied by the local computer group policy. End users with local Administrators group membership could override settings and make configuration changes that could compromise security or, more often, reduce the reliability of the system.

Starting with Windows Vista and Windows Server 2008, administrators could create multiple local computer policies, now known simply as local group policies. One useful feature of local group policies is that specific user group policies can be created for all users, for users who are not administrators, and for users who are members of the local Administrators group on the local computer. This feature increases the security and reliability of computers, both those configured in a workgroup or those configured as standalone. In domain configurations, computer and user-based policy settings are generally configured within domain-based group policies and applied to the Active Directory computers and users. By configuring local group policies, you can ensure that these computers have a base security configuration and user experience that supports the organization's needs, even if the computer is not configured as part of an Active Directory domain.

Local Computer Policy

The default local computer policy contains out-of-the-box policy settings, as shown in Figure 19.2, which are available to configure the computer and user environment. This policy is applied first to both computer and user objects logging on to the workstation in workgroups or domains.

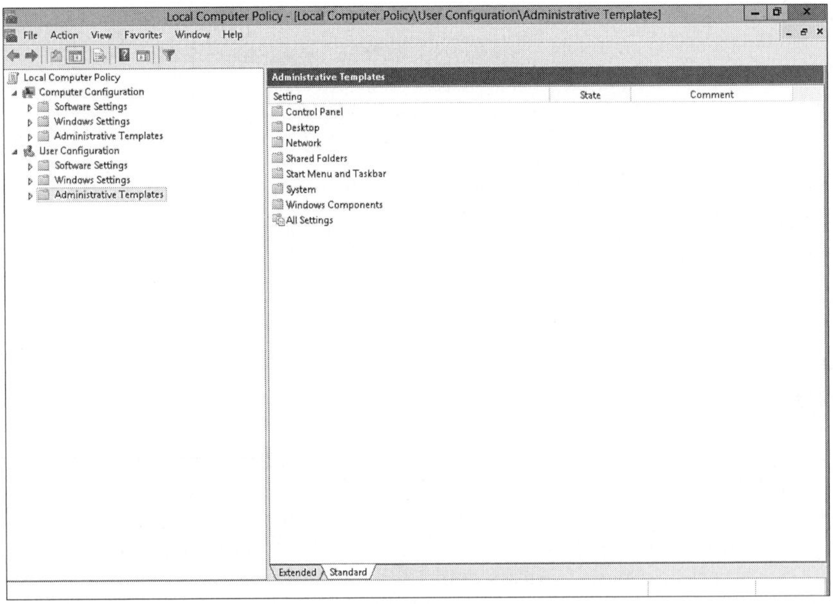

FIGURE 19.2 Local computer policy settings.

Local User Policies for Nonadministrators and Administrators

Starting with Windows Vista and Windows Server 2008, and continuing with Windows 8 and Windows Server 2012, administrators now have the option to create multiple local user group policies on a single machine. In earlier versions, the single local computer policy allowed administrators to apply the single policy settings to all users logging on to a workstation that is part of a workgroup. Now, workgroup computers and domain computers can have additional policies applied to specific local users. Also, policies can be applied to local computer administrators or nonadministrators. This allows the workstation administrator to leave the user section of the default local computer policy blank and create a more-restrictive policy for local users and a less-restrictive policy for members of the local workstation Administrators security group. Local user-based group policies can be created for specific users, for all nonadministrator users and administrators to give a lot of different user configurations based on the user who is logging on to the system.

Domain-Based Group Policies

Domain-based group polices differ significantly from local group policies because you must have an Active Directory environment to create and apply these policies. The settings within the group policies include both policy and preference nodes, which is another major difference (because the local group policies do not include preference settings). After that, however, most of the settings remain the same. Domain-based group policies allow for more flexibility when it comes to actually configuring what criteria is used to apply the policy. With domain-based policies, they can be filtered to apply to specific members of Active Directory security groups, computers, or objects on a particular subnet or stored within an organizational unit (OU), or they can be applied to computers that are running a specific OS version. Also, with preference settings in a domain-based group policy, item-level targeting can be used to determine whether a setting will be applied based on many different types of criteria, as shown in Figure 19.3.

Security Templates

Within each local computer policy and within a GPO Computer Configuration node, there is a section named Security Settings. This section includes settings for computer audit policies, account management settings, and user rights assignments. This section of the policy is unique because it can be imported and exported individually. In earlier versions of Windows, several security templates were provided out of the box to enable administrators to quickly load a set of best-practice security configuration settings. These templates included basic workstation and server templates, along with high security, compatible security, and domain controller security templates.

To manage and apply a standard set of security configurations to workgroup or standalone systems, administrators can leverage the management functions of security templates. Either using the Group Policy Object Editor, the Local Security Policy Editor, or the Security Configuration and Analysis MMC snap-in, administrators can import a base template, configure or adjust settings to meet the desired security settings, and export and save the settings to a custom template file. This custom template file can then be imported or applied to all the desired systems using the tools referenced previously.

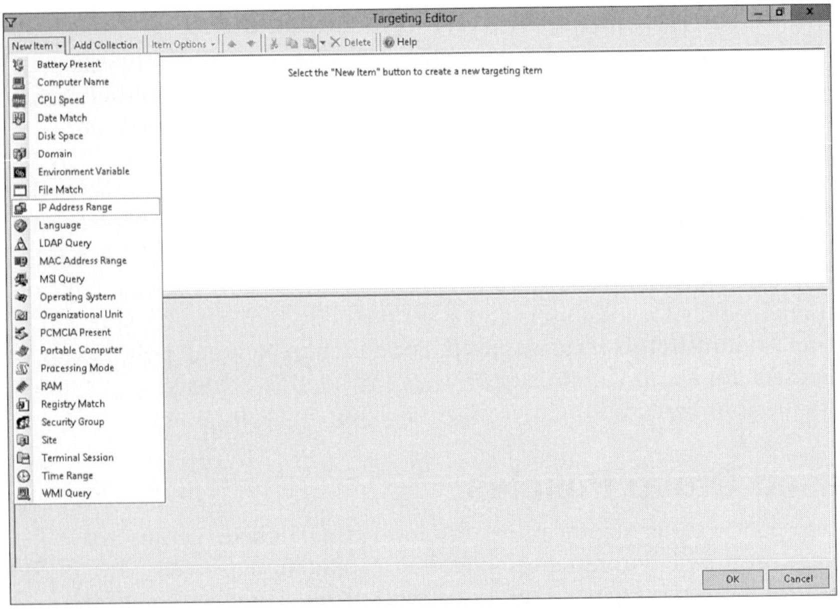

FIGURE 19.3 Domain-based GPP item-level targeting.

Security templates exist for Windows Vista, Windows Server 2008, and later OSs. You can find these base security templates in the %systemroot%\inf folder or on a default install, C:\Windows\Inf. The default security templates all start with the name deflt and end with an .inf extension. For example, on Windows Server 2012, the templates that exist are named defltbase.inf, defltsv.inf, and defltdc.inf. These files can be used to configure a system's security settings to a standard set of security configurations.

CAUTION

Importing security templates on servers, workstations, or domain controllers already deployed can cause several issues, including losing the ability to log on or access the system from the network. Make sure to test any changes to security settings when working with the import and application of security templates.

Understanding Group Policy

This section discusses various concepts and terminology related to Group Policy to provide system administrators with the information required to understand, support, and deploy group policies in an Active Directory forest. As a follow-up to this chapter, Chapter 27, "Group Policy Management for Network Clients," provides useful best-practice examples of how Group Policy can be deployed to simplify the management and configuration of your Active Directory servers, workstations, and users. Although some administrators might be inclined to skip the remainder of this chapter and jump right to Chapter 27, it is highly recommended that you review this chapter to understand how to manage the Group Policy infrastructure before attempting to manage the devices in the Active Directory forest.

Group Policy Objects

Group policy objects (GPOs) are predefined sets of available settings that can be applied to Active Directory computer/user objects. The settings, available within a particular GPO, are created using a combination of administrative template files included or referenced within that GPO. As the particular computer or user management needs change, additional administrative templates can be imported into a particular GPO to extend its functionality.

GPO Storage and Replication

GPOs are stored in both the file system and the Active Directory database. Each domain in an Active Directory forest stores a complete copy of that particular domain's GPOs.

Within Active Directory, the GPO links and version information are stored within the domain naming context partition of the database. Because this partition is replicated only within a single domain, processing GPOs linked across domains, either using sites or just a cross-domain GPO link, can take longer to load and process.

The GPO settings are stored in the file system of all domain controllers within the SYSVOL folder. The SYSVOL folder is shared on all domain controllers. Each domain GPO has a corresponding folder located within the Sysvol\Companyabc.com\Policies subfolder, as shown in Figure 19.4. The GPO folder is named after the globally unique identifier (GUID) assigned to that GPO during creation. The GUID of a GPO is listed when viewing the properties of a domain GPO using the Group Policy Management Console. The GPO folder includes a common set of subfolders and files, including the User folder, Machine folder (and sometimes the ADM, Preferences, Scripts, and other folders) and the gpt.ini file. Each subfolder within a GPO folder hierarchy contains the necessary files and folders associated with the particular policy or preference section.

GPO Replication

Because GPOs are stored within the Active Directory database and on the domain controller file system, all GPO information is replicated by the domain controllers. The file system portion of the domain GPOs is replicated within the Domain System Volume Distributed File System Replication (DFSR) group by the Distributed File System Replication service.

The Domain System Volume replication schedule is controlled by the DFSR schedule, which, by default, follows the same replication cycle as the Active Directory database. Replication occurs every 5 minutes, or immediately between domain controllers in a single Active Directory site, and follows the site link schedule between domain controllers in separate sites. Legacy domains use the File Replication Service instead of DFSR.

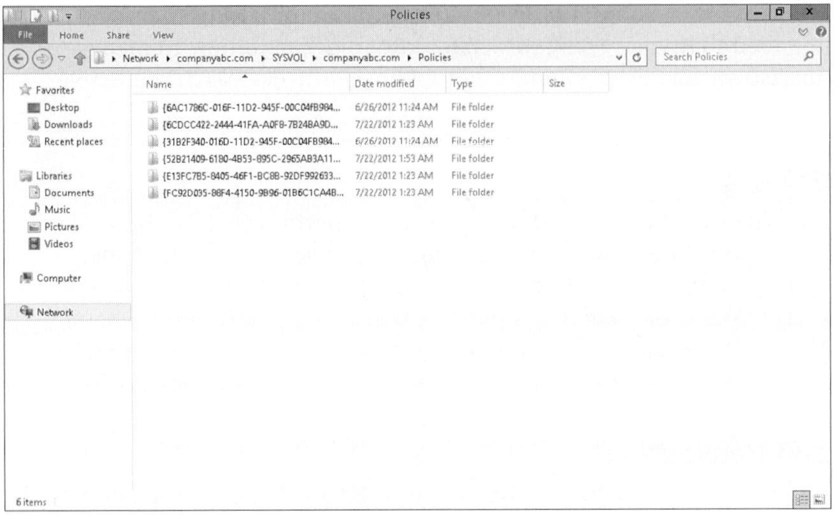

FIGURE 19.4 Examining the SYVOL policies folder.

User Subfolder

The User subfolder contains the files and folders used to store the settings, software, scripts, and any other policy settings specific to user and user object policies configured within a particular GPO.

Machine Subfolder

The Machine subfolder contains the files and folders used to store the settings, software, scripts, and any other policy settings specific to machine or computer object policies configured within a particular GPO.

Preference Subfolder

The Preference subfolder contains the files and folders used to store the settings, tasks, or any other policy settings specific to machine or computer object preference configured within a particular GPO.

ADM Subfolder

The ADM subfolder is created on new GPOs when legacy administrative template files are imported into a GPO. Any GPOs created using Windows 2000 and Windows XP client software, or Windows 2000 Server and Windows Server 2003 system software, contain an ADM subfolder to store all the legacy administrative template files referenced and imported into the GPO. New GPOs created by Window Server 2012 do not contain this subfolder by default.

Registry.pol Files

Within a particular group policy, the settings are segmented into several sections. Many settings within a GPO configure keys and values within the Registry. The configuration status and value of these settings are stored within the registry.pol files in either the User or Machine subfolders. The registry.pol file contains only the configured settings within the GPO to improve processing.

Gpt.ini File

When a GPO is created, a folder for the GPO is created within the connected domain controller's SYSVOL folder. At the root of that GPO folder is a file named gpt.ini. This file contains the revision number of the GPO. The revision number is used when a GPO is processed by a computer or user object. When a GPO is first processed, the revision number is stored on the client system, and when subsequent GPO processing occurs, the reference number in the gpt.ini file is compared with the stored value on the local system cache. If the number has not changed, certain portions of the GPO are not processed by default.

Each time a GPO is changed, the reference or revision number is increased, and even though the gpt.ini file contains a single number, it actually represents a separate revision number for the computer and user section of the GPO.

The default configuration of not processing certain GPO sections if the revision number has not changed can be overridden. In some cases, even though the GPO has not changed, the intended settings could have been changed by the user or a program, and sometimes forcing the entire GPO to always be processed is required. These settings are configurable and are in the "Tuning Group Policy Processing with GPO Settings" section, earlier in this chapter. Chapter 27 also covers these settings.

Group Policy Administrative Templates

Group policy administrative templates are, in most cases, offsets of text or Extensible Markup Language (XML)-based files that include clearly defined settings that can be set to a number of different values.

Administrative templates are provided to give administrators easy access to many configurable settings commonly used to manage server and workstation computers and end users.

When a new GPO is created, a base set of administrative templates are imported or referenced within that policy. Additional administrative templates can be imported to a particular policy to add functionality as required. When new OSs are released on an existing network (for example, Windows 8 and Windows Server 2012), Group Policy administrators will see different values within Group Policy editors when editing a policy on the newer OS. This can cause confusion and issues, and when new OSs are introduced, the new administrative templates should be used by all administrators. A quick way to make this work efficiently is for organizations to leverage the Group Policy central store and to update the administrative templates within that store with each new OS.

Windows 8 and Windows Server 2012 Central Store

As stated earlier in this chapter, each GPO in the Active Directory forest has a corresponding folder stored in the SYSVOL folder on each domain controller in the domain in which the GPO is created. If the domain controllers in the particular domain are running

Windows Server 2003, each of these GPO folders contains a copy of each of the administrative templates loaded in that particular GPO, within the ADM subfolder. This legacy GPO storage scenario created many duplicated administrative template files and required additional storage space and increased replication traffic between domain controllers.

Starting with the new Group Policy infrastructure included with Windows Vista and Windows Server 2008, and continuing with Windows 8 and Windows Server 2012, newly created GPOs only store the files and folders required to store the configured settings, scripts, registry.pol, and other GPO-related files. When the GPO is opened for editing or processed by a Windows Vista, Windows Server 2008, or later OS, the local copy of the administrative templates is referenced but not copied to the new GPO folder in SYSVOL. Instead, the administrative templates are referenced from files stored on the local workstations or the domain central store.

The GPO central store is a file repository that houses each of the next generation administrative templates. The central store contains all the new ADMX and ADML administrative templates, and each workstation references the files on the domain controller they are using to process group policies. With a central store created, when a GPO is opened or processed, the system first checks for the existence of the central store, and then uses only the templates stored in the central store.

The GPO central store can be created within Active Directory infrastructures running any version of Windows Server 2003 or later domain controllers.

Starter GPOs

Windows Server 2008, Windows Server 2008 R2, and the Windows Server 2012 Group Policy Management Console provide a new feature of GPO management called starter GPOs. Starter GPOs are similar to regular GPOs, but they only contain settings available from administrative templates. Just as security templates can be used to import and export the configured settings within the security section of a policy, starter GPOs can be used to prepopulate configured settings in the Administrative Templates sections of the Computer Configuration and User Configuration nodes within a GPO. After the release of Windows Server 2008 and included in Windows Server 2012, Microsoft released a set of predefined starter GPOs for Windows Vista and Windows XP. The predefined settings in these starter GPOs are based on information that can be found in the Windows XP and Windows client security guide published by Microsoft. These particular starter GPOs are read-only policies, but administrators can create their own starter GPOs as needed by the organization.

You learn how to enable starter GPO functionality and how to create and manage starter GPOs in the section, "Creating and Using Starter GPOs," later in this chapter.

Policy Settings

Policy settings are simply the configurable options made available within a particular GPO. These settings are provided from the base administrative templates, security settings, scripts, policy-based quality of service (QoS), and, in some cases, software deployment packages. Many policy settings correspond one to one with a particular Registry key and value. Depending on the particular settings, different values, including free-form text, might be acceptable as a legitimate value.

GPO policy settings are usually configurable to one of three values: Not Configured, Enabled, or Disabled. It is important for administrators to understand not only the differences between these three values, but to also understand what the particular policy setting controls. For example, a policy setting that disables access to Control Panel will block access to Control Panel when enabled but will allow access when disabled.

GPO policy settings apply to either a computer or a user object. Within a particular GPO, an administrator might find the same policy setting within both the Computer Configuration and User Configuration nodes. In cases like this, if the policy setting is configured for both objects, the computer setting overrides the user setting if the policy is linked to the user object and the workstation to which the user is logged on.

Preference Settings

Group policies have two main setting nodes: the Computer node and User Configuration nodes. Each node contains two other nodes: the Policies and Preferences setting nodes. The Group Policy extensions presented in the Preferences node enable administrators to configure many default or initial configuration and environmental settings for users and computers. One really great feature of the GPO Preferences node is item-level targeting, which applies a certain preference (for instance, setting the Start menu on Windows 8 workstations to configure the power button to perform a logoff rather than a computer shutdown) to only defined users or groups within the item-level target definition of that GPO. When a user logs on to a workstation and has that preference applied, this will be the initial setting, but users can change that setting if they want. One important distinction that all GPO administrators must make is that policies set and enforce settings, whereas preferences configure initial settings but do not block the settings from changes. Chapter 27 contains more information about GPO preferences.

GPO Links

GPO links are the key to deploying GPOs to a predetermined set of Active Directory computers/users. GPO links define where the particular policy or policies will be applied in terms of the Active Directory domain and site hierarchy design.

GPOs can be linked to Active Directory sites, domains, and OUs. Also, a single GPO can be linked to multiple sites, domains, and OUs in a single forest. This gives administrators the flexibility to create a single policy and apply it to several different sets of computers and users within an Active Directory forest.

The design of the Active Directory infrastructure, including site design, domain and tree design, and OU hierarchy, is critical to streamlining targeted GPO application. Careful planning and consideration should be taken into account during the Active Directory design phase with regard to how GPOs will be used and how user, group, and computer objects will be organized.

GPO links can also be disabled as required, to assist with troubleshooting GPO application or processing.

Group Policy Link Enforcement

Microsoft provides administrators with many ways to manage their infrastructure, including forcing configurations down from the top. GPO link "enforcement," historically known as No Override, is an option of a GPO link that can be set to ensure that the settings in a particular policy will be applied and maintained even if another GPO has the same setting configured with a different value. GPO link enforcement is shown in Figure 19.5.

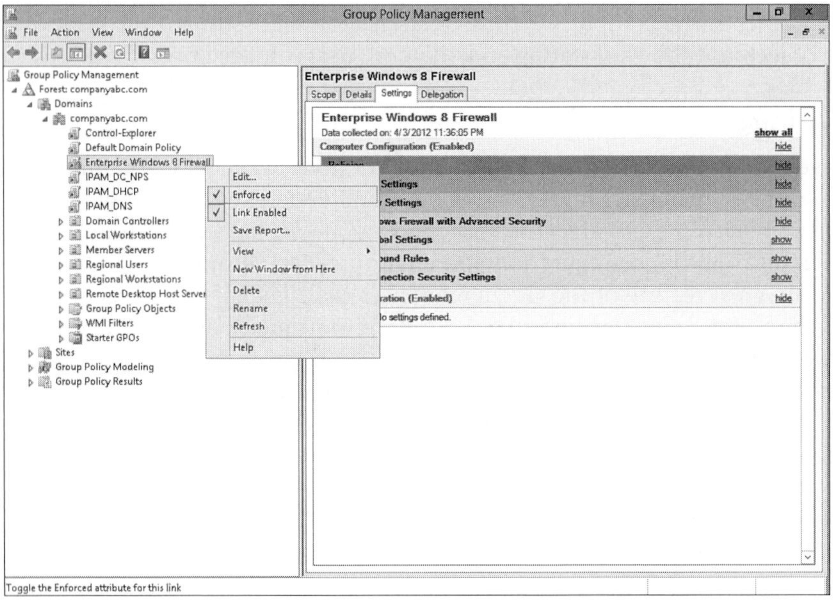

FIGURE 19.5 Group policy link enforcement.

Because this might result in undesired functionality or a different level of security than what is required to run a particular service or application or manage a system, exercise caution when using this function. Before enabling GPO enforcement on any policy, carefully research and test to ensure that this will not break any functionality or violate an organization's IT or regulatory policy.

Group Policy Inheritance

GPOs can be linked at the site, domain, and multiple OU levels. When an Active Directory infrastructure contains GPOs linked at the domain level, for example, every container and OU beneath the domain root container inherits any linked policies. As a default example, the Domain Controllers OU inherits the default domain policy from the domain.

GPO inheritance enables administrators to set a common base policy across an Active Directory infrastructure while allowing other administrators to apply more granular policies at a lower level that apply to subsets of users or computers. As an example of this, a GPO can be created and linked at the domain level that restricts all users from running Windows Update, while an OU representing a branch office in the domain can have a GPO linked that enables the branch office desktop administrators security group to run Windows Update.

GPO links inherited from parent containers are processed before GPO links at the container itself, and the last applied policy setting value is the resulting value, if multiple GPOs have the same configured setting with different values. This Group Policy inheritance is also known as GPO precedence, and is shown in Figure 19.6.

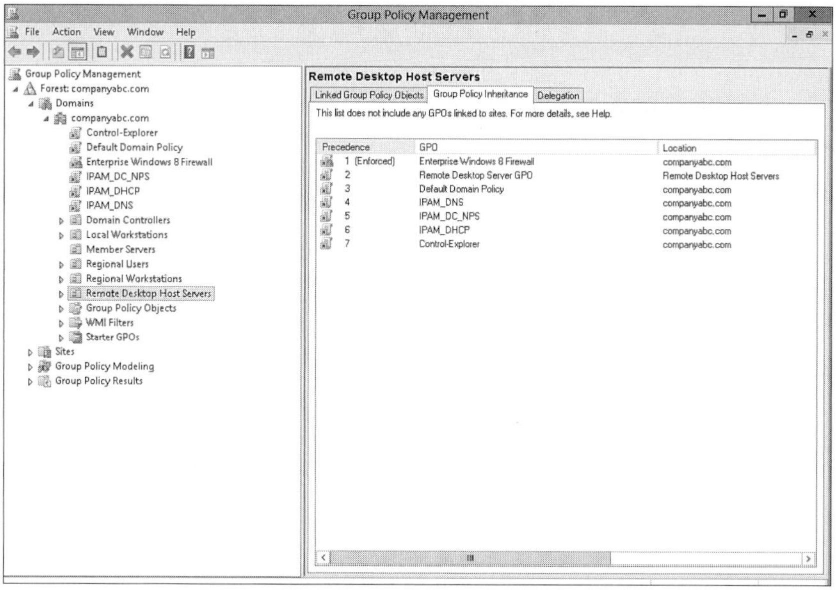

FIGURE 19.6 Group Policy inheritance.

One important point to note: Group Policy processing will start with the highest number in the precedence order and the policy with the precedence of 1 will be processed last to ensure that the settings in that policy are applied and not overwritten. In the example shown in Figure 19.6, the enforced policy from the domain is processed last.

Group Policy Block Inheritance

Just as GPOs can be inherited, Active Directory also provides the option to block inheritance, as shown in Figure 19.7, of all GPOs from parent containers. Figure 19.7 should be compared to Figure 19.6 to show which policies are no longer blocked, but the parent policy that is enforced is still allowed. So, administrators who are granted the rights to manage group policy links on particular organizational units may decide to block inheritance, but if policies are enforced at a parent organizational unit or the domain, they will still be applied.

Block Inheritance is actually an option applied to an Active Directory domain or organizational unit within the Group Policy Management Console and not on an actual policy. The Block Inheritance option can be useful if the container contains users/computer objects that are very security sensitive or business critical. As an example of this option in use, an OU can be created to contain the Remote Desktop Services host systems, which would not function correctly if domain-level GPOs were applied. The OU can be configured to block inheritance to ensure that only the policies linked to the particular OU were applied. If GPOs need to be applied to this container, links would need to be created at that particular container level, or the GPO link from the parent container would need to be enforced, which would override the Block Inheritance setting, as shown in Figure 19.7.

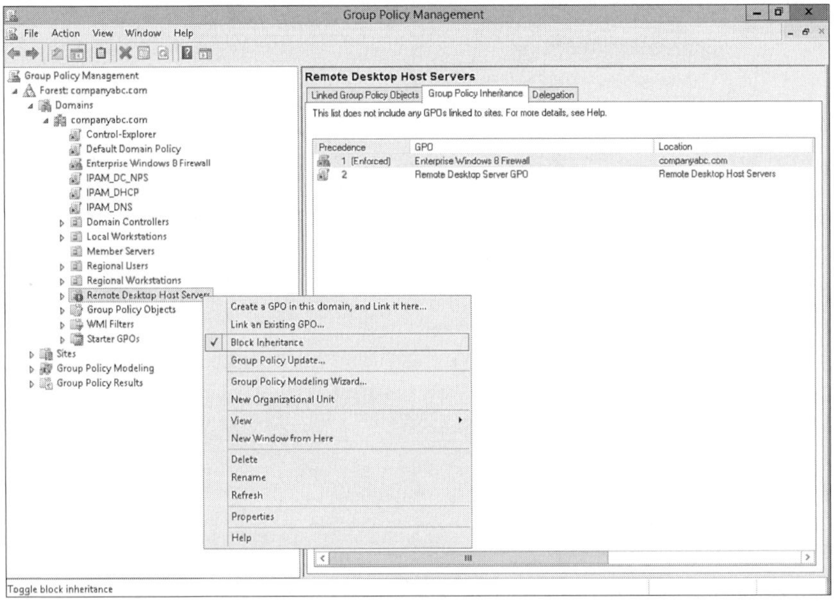

FIGURE 19.7 Group Policy Block Inheritance.

Group Policy Order of Processing

GPOs can be linked at many different levels and in many Active Directory infrastructures; multiple GPOs are linked at the same OU or domain level. This is a common practice because this particular configuration follows a GPO best-practice recommendation, included in a later section in this chapter, of creating separate GPOs for a particular set of functions.

Because GPOs are processed one at a time, the GPO links are processed in a particular order starting with GPOs inherited from parent containers followed by the order of policies that were linked to that container. The resulting impact of this processing order is that when multiple GPOs contain the same configured setting, the last GPO applied provides the resulting setting value. As an example of this, if two GPOs are linked at the domain level, named GPO1 and GPO2, and GPO1 has a configured setting of Remove Task Manager set to disabled and GPO2 has the same setting set to enabled, the end result is enabled for that setting.

To fully understand what the end resulting policy will be in a container that has multiple GPOs linked and inherited, you can run Group Policy Modeling from the Group Policy Management Console. Group Policy Modeling provides a report detailing which policies were applied, in which order the policies were applied, and the resulting policy settings. The steps required to run Group Policy Modeling are detailed in Chapter 27. One easy way to understand this is to know that when looking at a particular Active Directory container in Group Policy Management Console, the group policy link order and the GPP order are processed from the highest number down. This means that the group policy that has a link order of 1 will always be processed last by objects within that container.

GPO Filtering

Applying GPOs can be tricky, and the design of the Active Directory forest, domains, sites, and OU hierarchy plays a major part in this. One of the most important considerations when designing the Active Directory OU hierarchy within a domain is to understand how the domain administrators plan to manage the domain computers and users with group policies. Designing the Active Directory infrastructure is discussed in detail in Chapters 5, "Designing a Windows Server 2012 Active Directory," and Chapter 6, "Designing Organizational Unit and Group Structure."

In many cases, even with the most careful planning of the Active Directory infrastructure, GPOs will be applied to computers/users that do not necessarily need the settings contained within that GPO. To better target which computer and user objects a particular GPO applies to, Microsoft has built in a few different mechanisms to help filter out or include only the necessary objects to ensure that only the desired computers or users actually apply the policy. The mechanisms that control or filter how a policy will be applied are as follows:

- GPO links
- GPO security filtering
- GPO Windows Management Instrumentation (WMI) filtering
- GPO status for the Computer Configuration or User Configuration nodes

GPO Links

Group policy links are required to determine which sites, domains, or organization units the policy will apply to. When a new policy is created, before it can ever be used it must be linked. Before it is linked, though, the security filtering, status, and WMI filters should be configured to further segment policy application to more specific computer and user objects within the linked container hierarchy.

GPO Security Filtering

GPO security filtering is the *group* in Group Policy. Many administrators can get frustrated when having to explain the fact that Group Policy applies to computers and users but not to groups. In fact, the GPO security filtering is where administrators can define which users, computers, or members of security groups will actually apply the group policy.

By default, GPOs apply to the Authenticated Users security group, which includes all users and computers in the domain. The scope of GPO application is then segmented based on the location of the group policy links. It can be segmented even further by removing the Authenticated Users group from the GPO security filtering, as shown in Figure 19.8, and replacing it with specific computer accounts, user accounts, or security groups.

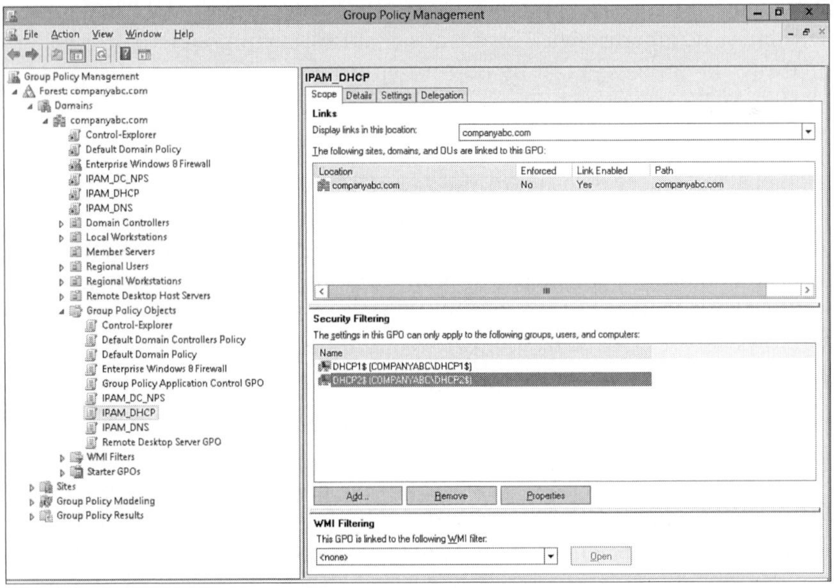

FIGURE 19.8 Group Policy security filtering.

When the security filtering of a GPO is configured to apply to a custom security group, only the members of that group, whether users or computer objects, actually apply that particular policy. Last but not least, it is most important to always keep the group membership current; otherwise, the application of Group Policy might be incomplete or incorrect.

GPO WMI Filtering

GPO WMI filtering is a Group Policy concept introduced in Windows XP and Windows Server 2003. A WMI filter is a query that is processed by computer objects only and can be used to include or exclude particular computer objects from applying a GPO that includes the WMI filter. An example of a WMI filter is a query that includes only computer objects with an OS version of 6.2*, which includes all Windows 8 and Windows Server 2012 systems. Of course, it is important to state that WMI filters will not be processed by legacy Windows 2000 or older systems. The security filtering must also meet the criteria for the GPO to be processed. WMI filters work great when the Active Directory hierarchy is relatively flat, but maintaining computer group membership can be tedious. How to create WMI filters, including a few examples, is included in Chapter 27.

GPO Status

As mentioned previously in this chapter, GPOs are applied to computer and user objects. Within a particular GPO, the settings available are segmented into two distinct nodes: the Computer Configuration node and the User Configuration node.

Configuring or changing the GPO status, shown in Figure 19.9, enables administrators to change the GPO as follows:

- Enabled (Default)
- User Configuration Settings Disabled
- Computer Configuration Settings Disabled
- All Settings Disabled

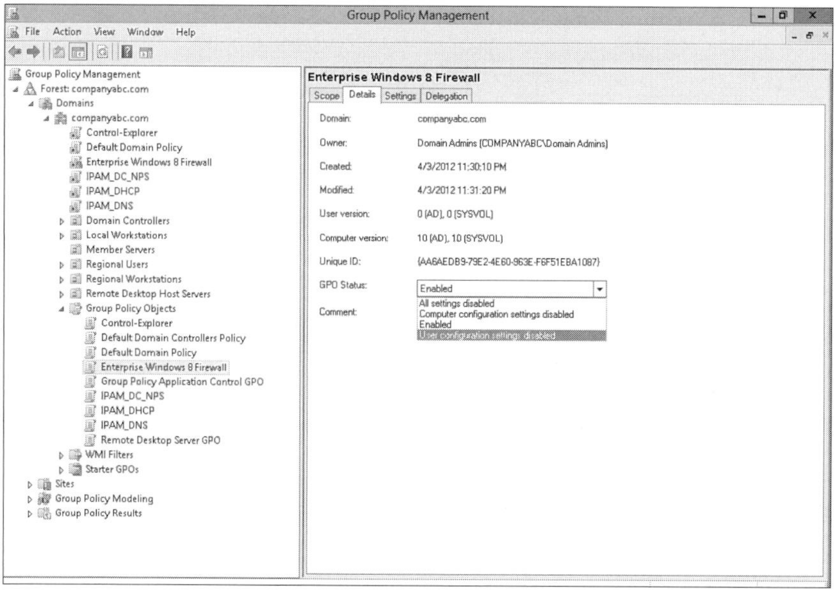

FIGURE 19.9 Group Policy status

This function of a GPO can be a very effective tool in troubleshooting GPOs as well as optimizing GPO processing. For example, if a GPO only contains configured settings in the Computer Configuration node, if any user objects are located in containers linked to that particular GPO, the GPO will still be processed by the user to check for any configured settings. This simple check can add a few seconds to the entire GPO processing time for that user, and if many GPOs are processed, it could increase the logon, logoff, or refresh interval by minutes or more. As a troubleshooting tool, if a user or computer is not receiving the desired end result of a set of applied policies, disabling a node or the entire policy can aid an administrator in identifying the suspect GPO causing the undesired result.

Group Policy Loopback Processing

Group Policy loopback processing, shown in Figure 19.10, allows for the processing of both the Computer Configuration and User Configuration nodes within a policy even if the user object is not in the same container as the computer that the group policy is linked to. As an example, this function would be useful with a Remote Desktop Session Host server deployment where you want to apply computer configuration policies to configure the Remote Desktop server settings but you also want to control the user settings of any user who logs on to the server, regardless of where the actual user account is stored in Active Directory.

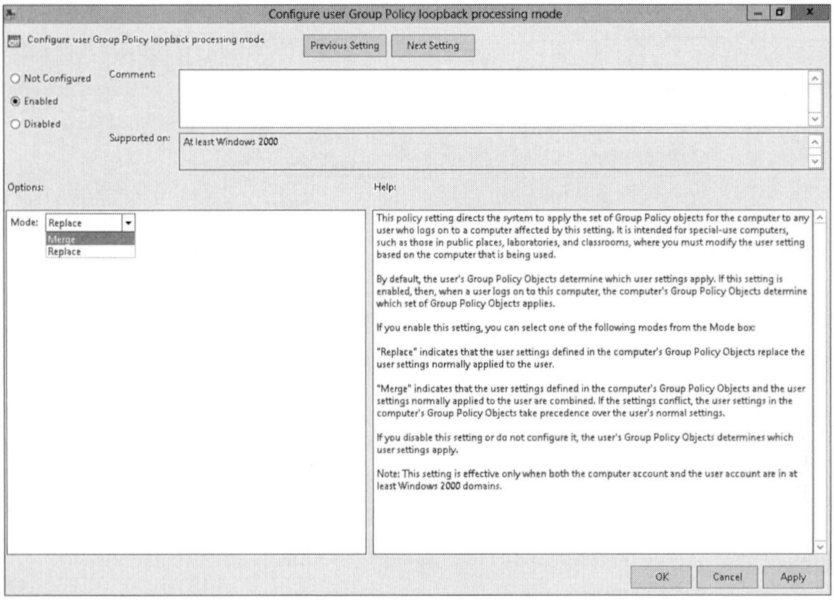

FIGURE 19.10 GROUP Policy loopback processing.

There are two different loopback configurations: replace mode and merge mode. Merge mode applies the user-based policies that would normally apply to the user account as well as the user-based policies on the container that contains the computer account the user is logging on to. Replace mode processes only those user policies applied to the computer the user is logging on to.

Group Policy Slow-Link Detection and Network-Location Awareness

Group Policy uses several mechanisms to determine whether a policy should be processed. One of the mechanisms used by the Group Policy client computer is called slow-link detection. By default, network tests are performed between the client computer and the domain controller to determine the speed of the link between the systems. If the speed is determined to be less than 500Kbps, the Group Policy client does not process any policies. Slow-link detection default settings, along with the ability to disable slow-link detection, is configurable with each policy.

In earlier versions, Group Policy used Internet Control Message Protocol (ICMP) or ping to detect slow links. With Windows Vista, Windows Server 2008, and later OSs, Group Policy now uses the Windows Network Location Awareness service to determine network status. The slow-link detection settings are controlled within the Policies\Administrative Templates\System\Group Policy sections of the GPO. Starting with Windows Server 2012 policy templates, administrators can also configure links detected at 3G connections to be treated as slow links.

Group Policy Policies Node

The Policies node contained in both the computer and user configuration of group policies contain settings that in most cases are enforced and no longer configurable by the client. For settings that can have multiple values, the settings with the Policies node are enforced on the client, but administrators can add or still modify a portion of the setting. For example, if a user right assignment is configured within a domain-based policy, an administrator cannot remove the entries within that user right applied from the policy, but additional entries can be added and allowed. The Policies node contains security settings, including firewall and networking settings, but the bulk of the settings are contained within the Administrative Templates section of the Policies node.

Group Policy Administrative Templates

Administrative templates are the core elements that make up a GPO. Most settings available within an administrative template are used to configure a corresponding Registry value for the computer or a user account, usually defined within the HKEY_Local_Machine or the HKEY_Current_User Registry hive. Other settings are provided to run computer-based and user-based scripts and, in some instances, install or make software packages available to subsets of users or computers.

Administrative templates come in three basic types:

- ADM files for Windows 2000 Client and Server, Windows XP, and Windows Server 2003
- ADMX and ADML files for Windows Vista, Windows Server 2008 and later OSs
- Custom ADM, ADMX, and ADML files used to extend GPO functionality beyond what is already included in the Microsoft provided templates

Administrative Templates for Windows 2000, Windows XP, and Windows Server 2003

Administrative templates for Windows 2000, Windows XP, and Windows Server 2003 have a file extension of .adm. ADM file formats are unlike any other file format and are not the easiest to interpret and create. ADM files include not only the policy settings and their possible values, but they also include the friendly language used to represent the settings to the administrator viewing the policy settings using any of the GPO management tools, detailed later in this chapter.

For each GPO created by an administrator using the Windows XP or Windows Server 2003 GPO tools, a folder for that GPO is created in the connected domain controller's SYSVOL folder. This unique GPO folder contains a common set of ADM files in the language used on the administrative client computer. As a result of this, in an Active Directory infrastructure that has multiple GPOs that use the common administrative templates, each GPO has copies of the same template files within each GPO folder. Each folder is commonly 3MB to 5MB in size and this is commonly referred to as SYSVOL bloat because the GPO folders are stored in the domain controller's SYSVOL folder.

When new policies were created using the Windows XP and Windows Server 2003 GPO tools, a copy of each of the of the ADM template files from the client workstation was pushed up to the SYSVOL folder on the domain controller. When an existing GPO was edited or opened for viewing, the copy of the templates in the GPO folder was compared with the version of the template files on the administrative workstation. If the administrative workstation had a newer version, the workstation template was copied up to the GPO folder and the existing template in the folder was overwritten. This default behavior caused several problems when Microsoft released updated templates with service pack releases of Windows XP and Windows Server 2003.

A common issue related to this feature, as an example, is that if an administrator working on a Windows XP SP2 administrative workstation opened an existing GPO that was created with a Windows XP SP1 workstation, the template files would be updated to the new version, causing a replication of the updated templates across all domain controllers. Another implication of the template file is that the template files included the friendly language of the administrative workstation the GPO was created on and administrators across the globe would be unable to manage the same GPO in their local OS language. This, of course, caused several administration issues and, in some cases, regional Active Directory domains were created to allow regional administrators to manage their client workstations and users with GPOs written and managed in their local language. To support global administration, Active Directory infrastructures have become unnecessarily complicated and moved away from the original reason GPOs were created, to simplify the management, standardize security, and centrally administer and configure companywide resources.

As a means of avoiding the administrative-related and infrastructure-related issues associated with this GPO infrastructure, a common best practice for managing GPOs for XP or later OSs is to only manage GPOs from workstations or servers that meet a single specification for OS version, service pack level, and language. Another means of controlling this is to follow a common practice of configuring all GPOs to not automatically update GPO templates when a GPO is opened for editing. Automatic updates of ADM files are located in the User Configuration\Policies\Administrative Templates\System\Group Policy\ section and is named Turn Off Automatic Updates of ADM Files. As a best practice, many administrators enable this setting to improve GPO reliability and to keep GPO replication traffic at a minimum.

Group Policy Administrative Templates for Windows Vista and Windows Server 2008 and Later

Group Policy for Windows Vista and Windows 2008 has been completely revised and rebuilt from the XP/2003 version, but they still support Windows XP, and Windows Server 2003. Windows 7, Windows Server 2008 R2, and later build on this new revision, adding new settings to support the features of the latest OSs. The original ADM files have been replaced or split into two files:

- ADMX administrative template settings file
- ADML administrative template language file

The original GPO single administrative template ADM file format was replaced to overcome many of the original issues with this file format, including the unique ADM format as well as the inclusive local language of the particular ADM files contained on the administrative workstation.

With the separation of the ADM file into a settings and local language file, the new templates enable the administration of a single GPO using different local languages.

In earlier versions, when an administrator viewed or edited a GPO, the local template files from the administrative workstation were pushed up to the server GPO folder. With the new Windows 8/Windows Server 2012 GPO infrastructure, when the GPO is opened for viewing or editing, the template files located on the local hard drive are loaded to view the GPO. The GPO folder created with the Windows 8 or Windows Server 2012 GPO tools contains only the files and folders that contain the configured settings of the GPO and not the general template files, as with the earlier versions. This improves the GPO processing time as well as reduces the amount of data stored in the SYSVOL folder on each domain controller.

Custom Administrative Templates

Microsoft has provided, in earlier versions as well as the current release, the ability for administrators and independent software vendors (ISVs) to create their own administrative templates. The current administrative templates released with Windows 8 and Windows Server 2012 have all the original ADM settings as well as many of the settings that administrators either had to create custom templates to support or purchase ISV-created templates. But even though the new templates provide many more settings, there will still be custom Registry keys and values, specific application services, and other functions that organizations want to manage with GPOs. These settings will still need to be provided with custom templates or by ISV GPO products. For example, when Microsoft releases a new version of Internet Explorer, they provide a custom administrative template Group Policy administrators can import to block domain computers from downloading, installing, or even presenting the new browser in Windows Updates.

Many ISVs now provide administrative templates for their own applications. Microsoft also provides administrative templates to further manage their own applications and suites such as Microsoft Office include new templates that can be used with each new version of the office suites.

Custom administrative templates can be created in both the ADM and ADMX/ADML file formats. To support the amount of time and effort administrators and ISVs have put into creating custom templates and to support legacy applications, new GPOs will continue to support administrative templates created in the original ADM file format as well as the new ADMX/ADML formats.

Although Microsoft has provided the steps to create custom ADMX and ADML files, the current GPO management tools only allow adding custom ADM templates to specific GPOs. To leverage the settings in a new custom ADM file, the file must be added to each GPO that will use it. ADM files that are added to a GPO are made available beneath the respective Administrative Templates\Classic Administrative Templates (ADM) section of the computer or user configuration Policies node.

NOTE

When Group Policy administrators need to extend Group Policy settings using ADMX/ADML templates, they should consider using a central store and simply add these templates to the store, as explained in Chapter 27.

Group Policy Preferences Node

The Preferences node contained in both the computer and user configuration of group policies contain settings that in most cases are new settings that were previously not included in Group Policy settings and had to be managed with custom scripts and administrative templates. Preference settings are set initially, but in most cases the end user can change those settings after Group Policy processing. Preferences are unique in that within a preference setting there is a function named Item Level Targeting that allows a very granular application of the preference setting based on many different types of criteria. In essence, even though a group policy is applied to a set of users or computers, the preference settings within may only apply to a subset within that group. More information about GPP settings and how to use them is included in Chapter 27.

Policy Management Tools

Microsoft provides several different tools administrators can use to create and manage local and domain-based group policies. The OS version the administrator is using to manage policies determines the functionality the tools provide. As an example, when new group policies are created using the Windows Server 2008 or greater Group Policy Management Console, the GPO folder utilizes the new ADMX/ADML templates, whereas the Windows XP and Windows Server 2003 tool uploads the original ADM template files into the GPO folder.

This section details the tools provided with Windows Vista, Windows Server 2008 and later OSs to manage local and group policies.

Group Policy Management Console

The most functional and useful tool provided to create and manage Active Directory group policies is the Group Policy Management Console (GPMC). The GPMC was introduced after the release of Windows Server 2003; the functionality included with different OSs produces different options and resulting operations when creating and managing Active Directory group policies. This is the main tool for managing the Group Policy infrastructure.

The GPMC is a Microsoft Management Console (MMC) snap-in and can be added to a custom console. The GPMC snap-in provides the most functionality for administrators who want to manage domain group policies. The GPMC provided with Windows Server 2012 can perform the following Group Policy administrative functions:

- Enable starter GPO functionality and create new starter GPOs
- Create new domain group policies
- Create new group policies using starter GPOs as templates
- Create and configure GPO links to sites, domains, and OUs
- View and manage GPOs in domains in the local and trusted Active Directory forests
- Back up and restore a single or all GPOs in a domain
- Back up and restore a single or all starter GPOs in a domain
- Import group policies from external domains and migrate security settings using migration tables to ensure proper import functionality
- Manage GPO link enforcement, enable links, and disable links
- Configure the block inheritance settings for sites, domains, and OUs
- Manage GPO status to control which nodes in a GPO are enabled or disabled
- Create and link WMI filters for GPOs
- Manage GPO security filtering
- Manage GPO delegation and administrative security
- Manage the GPO order of processing on containers with multiple GPO links
- View all configured settings of existing group policies and any additional information, such as the revision number, filtering, delegation, and create exported reports of the configuration
- Check the replication status of the GPO infrastructure
- Generate HTML reports used to summarize Group Policy configurations and settings

- Run the Group Policy Modeling Wizard to determine how group policies will be applied to users or computers in specific containers
- Run the Group Policy Results Wizard to investigate how policies have been applied to specific computer/user objects

Many of the GPMC administrative functions in this list are detailed later in this chapter.

Group Policy Object Editor

The Group Policy Object Editor (GPOE), is the tool used to edit local group computer and user policies. Each server and workstation computer has a default local security policy. This policy is accessed through the shortcut to the specific Local Security Policy MMC snap-in located in the Administrative Tools program folder. Now that Windows Vista, Windows Server 2008, and later OSs support multiple local group policies, the GPOE must be used to manage or create any local group policies other than the default.

The GPOE is used to edit all the configuration settings of a policy. This includes configuring security settings, installing software packages, creating restriction policies, defining the scripts used by computers and users, and many other functions.

Group Policy Management Editor

To manage domain group policies, the Group Policy Management Editor (GPME) is used and provides the same functionality as the GPOE plus additional functionality only available with this tool. One of the biggest differences is that the GPME includes not only the Policy Settings node, but also the Preferences Settings node, which is only available in domains. GPME is installed on Windows Vista and later by downloading and installing the Remote Server Administration Tools (RSAT) tools for the particular service pack and OS. On Windows Server 2008, Windows Server 2008 R2, and Windows Server 2012 OSs, you can install the Group Policy tools from the Add Features applet of Server Manager.

Group Policy Starter GPO Editor

The Group Policy Starter GPO Editor is used to edit starter GPOs created by Group Policy administrators. This console only shows the Administrative Templates nodes under the Computer Configuration and User Configuration sections of a starter GPO. By default, the settings available in the Administrative Templates sections are all that can be set in a starter GPO; however, Microsoft provides read-only starter GPOs for Windows Vista and Windows XP, but the Windows Vista policy best practices still apply to Windows Server 2012 and Windows 8. The Group Policy Starter GPO Editor is included with the Windows Server 2012 Remote Server Administration Tools.

Print Management Console

First introduced with Windows Server 2003 R2, the Print Management console is used to manage Active Directory and local server and workstation printers. The Print Management console, shown in Figure 19.11, can be used to view settings, configure drivers and options, and manage printer and print jobs on a particular system or Active Directory-wide. The Print Management console can also be used to deploy printers to computers or users using the Deployed Printers node. Deploying printers is a function that extends Group Policy functionality to allow printers to be deployed to a predetermined set of users or computer objects to which a GPO is linked.

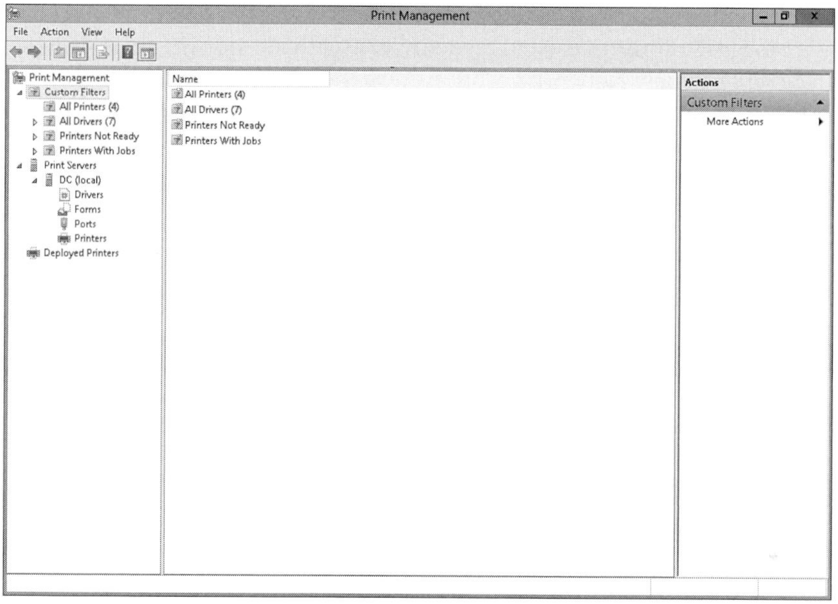

FIGURE 19.11 PRINT Management console.

The GPOE and the GPME on Windows Vista and later include the Deployed Printers node beneath the Windows Settings node in both the Computer Configuration and User Configuration settings nodes. On Windows Server 2008 and later server OSs, the Print Management console must be installed from the Server Manager Features, Add Features link before the Deployed Printers node will be available in the Group Policy Editor consoles. If a policy contains printers defined in the Deployed Printers nodes, and the policy is viewed using the GPMC or GPME on Windows XP, the deployed printers will not be viewed. Furthermore, if the policy is opened on a Windows Server 2003 R2 server, and if the Print Management console is not installed from Windows components, the Deployed Printers node will not be shown. As a best practice, only create GPOs to deploy printers using the GPMC and GPME on Windows Vista, Windows Server 2008, and later OSs. To install the Print Management console on Windows Server 2012, run the Add Features applet from Server Manager and select the Print and Document Services Tools from the Remote Administration Tools submenu.

Gpupdate.exe

The gpupdate.exe tool is a command-line tool that assists administrators in troubleshooting GPO processing and initiating GPO processing on demand. Certain sections of group policies will only be applied at computer startup and user logon, whereas others will be applied during these intervals and during the periodic refresh interval. For the settings that apply during the computer startup and user logon intervals, if network connectivity to the domain controllers is not available during this interval, these settings might not ever be applied. Also, remote or mobile workstations, systems that are put to sleep or hibernated, and users logging on using cached credentials usually do not get these policies applied. This is where the new Network Location Awareness service for Windows Vista, Windows Server 2008, and later OSs come into play; it will notify the system that a domain controller is available and that will trigger a Group Policy refresh cycle.

The gpupdate.exe tool enables you to apply user and computer policies immediately. One common use of this tool is to add the gpupdate.exe to a VPN post-connection script to allow these settings to be applied to remote workstations that belong to the Active Directory infrastructure. This tool provides the following options:

- **gpupdate.exe /Target:{Computer | user}**—This function allows the tool to process only the specified node of the group policy.
- **gpupdate.exe /Force**—This option reapplies all policy settings. This option does not automatically reboot the computer or log off the users.
- **gpupdate.exe /Wait**—This option defines how many seconds to allow GPO processing to complete. The default is 600 seconds, or 10 minutes.
- **gpupdate.exe /Logoff**—This option logs off the user account after GPO processing has completed.
- **gpupdate.exe /Boot**—This option reboots the computer after Group Policy processing completes. This is to apply the GPO settings that are only applied during computer startup.
- **gpupdate.exe /Sync**—This option processes GPO settings that normally only occur during computer startup and user logon. This option requires that the administrator designate whether the system can restart the computer or log off the user.

Group Policy Update from GPMC

New to the GPMC with Windows 8 and Windows Server 2012, administrators can now force a Group Policy update to be processed on all systems within a specific OU from the GPMC. This functionality has been lacking and has a lot of use to administrators who need to create and enforce a policy as soon as possible. This functionality however only applies to computers and not to users. To perform this task, just right-click the desired OU and select Group Policy Update, as shown in Figure 19.12. After the setting is selected, you are required to approve, and the results are shown in a Remote Group Policy Update Results window.

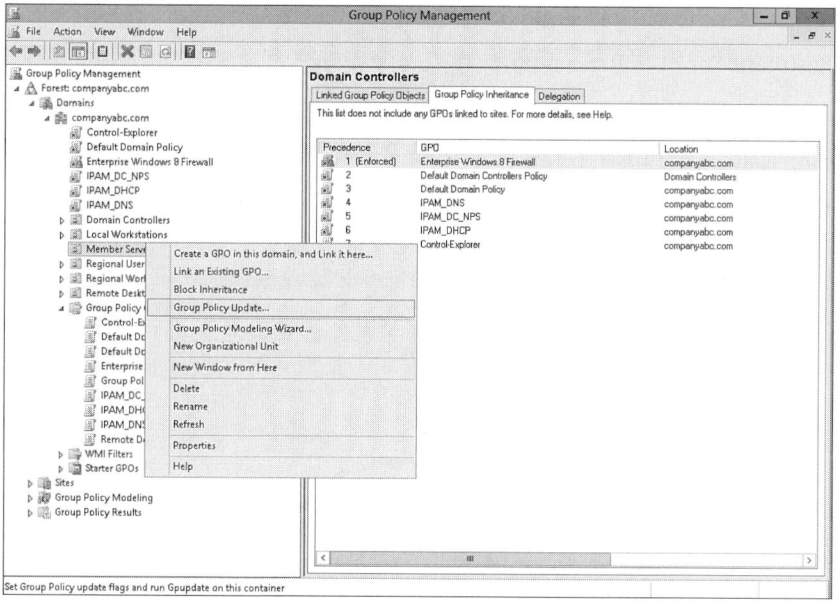

FIGURE 19.12 Group Policy Remote Update from GPMC.

Group Policy Infrastructure Status

One update to the Group Policy Management Console is the domain Group Policy infrastructure status. Now within the GPMC window, Group Policy administrators can check on the replication status of GPOs across all domain controllers in the domain, as shown in Figure 19.13.

PowerShell Management of Group Policies

With the release of Windows 8 and Windows Server 2012, Microsoft has now added functionality to manage group policies with PowerShell. This functionality is automatically enabled when the Group Policy Management feature is installed on a Windows 8 or Windows Server 2012 system. Microsoft includes 28 out-of-the-box PowerShell cmdlets for Group Policy. The cmdlets allow a Group Policy administrator to perform a number of different functions from within PowerShell, including the following:

- Create new GPOs and create new starter GPOs
- Create new GPO links
- Restore or import GPOs
- Remove GPOs and GPO links
- Read/set the properties of an OU to inherit parent GPO links or to block inheritance
- Rename a GPO

- Generate a report of GPO settings and configurations
- Generate a Resultant Set of Policies report
- Generate a Report on Group policy inheritance
- Set GPO administrative permissions and delegation
- Set GPO policy and preference settings that are stored in the Registry

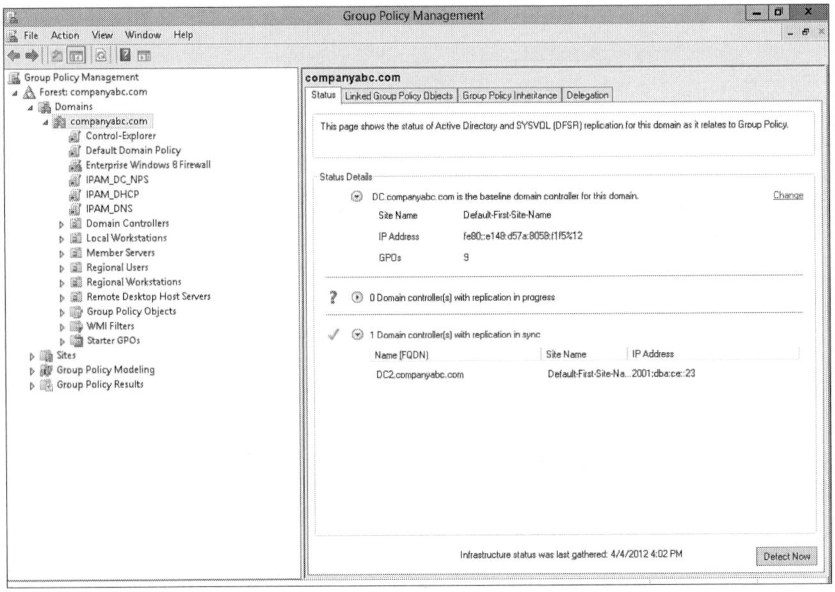

FIGURE 19.13 Group Policy infrastructure status.

To get a list of the Group Policy-related PowerShell cmdlets, follow these steps:

1. Log on to a system that has the Group Policy Management Tools installed. The Group Policy tools can be installed with the remote server administration tools.
2. Move your mouse to the lower-right corner of the Desktop, expose the Charm bar, and click the magnifying glass to open the Search menu.
3. In the Search menu, search Apps and type in **Windows**, and then click the Windows PowerShell ISE tile.
4. When the Windows PowerShell ISE tile opens, pull down the View menu and verify that the Show Command Add-on option is checked.
5. On the right of the console window in the commands pane, pull down the Modules menu and select GroupPolicy to reveal the list of the related cmdlets, as shown in Figure 19.14

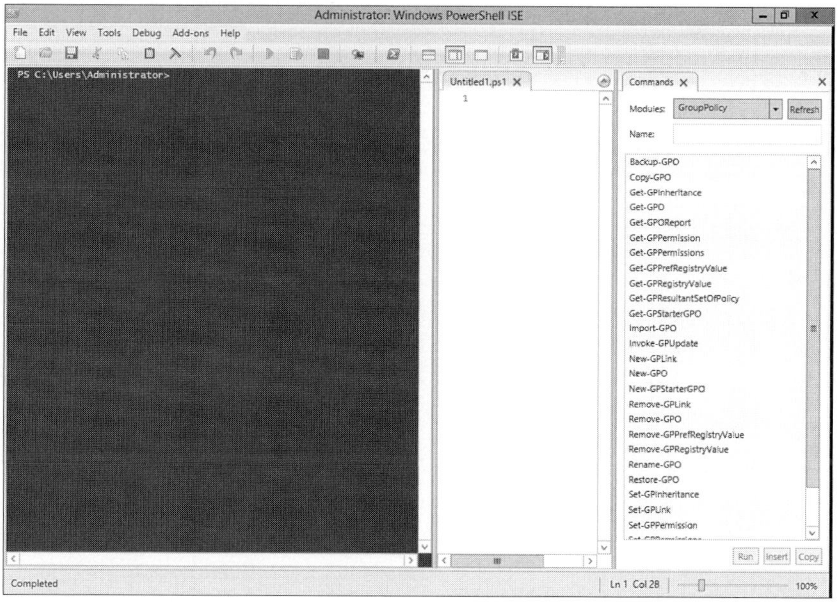

FIGURE 19.14 Group Policy PowerShell cmdlets.

6. As desired, select a particular cmdlets. After a cmdlets is selected, click Show Details to see the parameters or click the question mark icon to show the help information.
7. Close the Windows PowerShell ISE console window.

NOTE

Windows PowerShell Integrated Scripting Environment (ISE) is a powerful tool that enables administrators to search and learn how to leverage PowerShell like never before and should be explored.

Event Viewer

Event Viewer for Windows 8 and Windows Server 2012 includes several new event logs, which now provide additional GPO logging events, similar to those shown in Figure 19.15. GPO logging now includes administrative GPO events, stored in the system log with a source of Group Policy (Microsoft-Windows-GroupPolicy), and GPO operational events, stored in the Applications and Services Logs, which is stored in Microsoft/Windows/GroupPolicy/Operational. By default, minimal logging for Group Policy processing is performed, but if additional logging or troubleshooting is required, you can increase the logging level. Changing Group Policy logging options is covered in the "Troubleshooting Group Policies" section, later in this chapter.

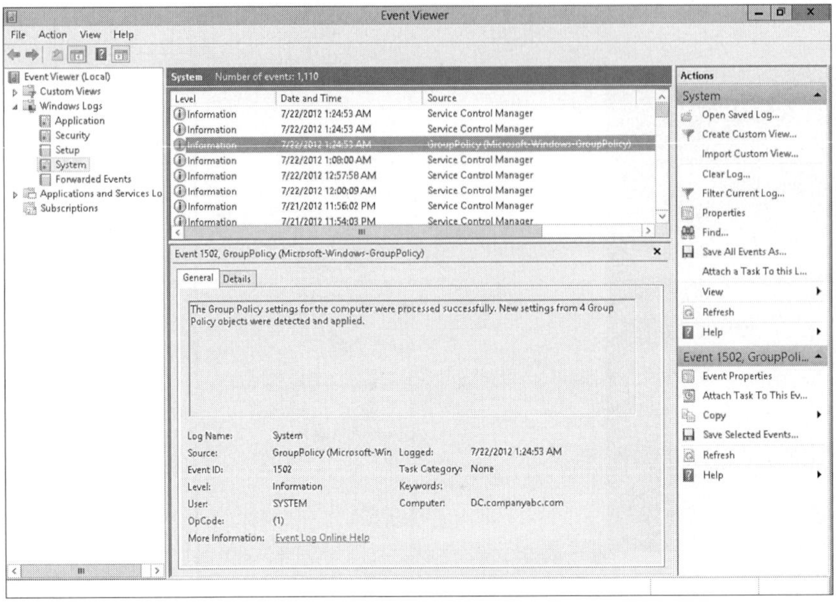

FIGURE 19.15 Group Policy events.

GPO Administrative Events

The administrative events include the state of the GPO processing on a particular computer or user, including high-level information detailing if GPO processing was successful or failed. To view Group Policy administrative events, follow these steps:

1. Log on to a designated administrative server running Windows Server 2012.
2. Open the Event Viewer from the Search Apps menu.
3. When Event Viewer opens, expand Windows Logs.
4. Right-click the System log and select Filter Current Log.
5. In the middle of the filter window, click the Event Sources drop-down arrow.
6. Scroll down and check Group Policy(Microsoft-Windows-GroupPolicy) and click back on the filter window to close the menu.
7. Click OK at the bottom of the window to apply the filter.
8. Review the Group Policy events.
9. If the task is complete, close Event Viewer to clear the filter; otherwise, clear the filter by right-clicking the system log and selecting Clear Filter.
10. Close Event Viewer when you have finished.

GPO Operational Events

The GPO operational events include very granular detail of GPO processing. When GPO processing occurs, the operational events are created almost one for one with each task included within the GPO processing. This new logging functionality simplifies troubleshooting GPO processing tremendously. To view the GPO operational events on a Windows Server 2012 system, follow these steps:

1. Log on to a designated administrative server running Windows Server 2012.
2. Open the Event Viewer.
3. When Event Viewer opens, expand Applications and Services Logs.
4. Expand Microsoft.
5. Expand Windows.
6. Expand Group Policy.
7. Select the Operational log beneath the Group Policy container and view the events in the right pane.
8. Click particular events to see the details.
9. Close Event Viewer when you have finished.

DFS Management

GPO files are stored in the Active Directory domain SYSVOL folder. GPO files in the SYSVOL folder are replicated by the Distributed File System Replication service. The DFS Management console enables administrators to configure the replication options, including scheduling and other DFS management tasks. The SYSVOL share is known as the domain system volume, and the replication of this volume follows the site link replication schedule. You can read more about the DFSR service in Chapter 28, "File System Management and Fault Tolerance." Changing or managing the domain system volume replication schedule between domain controllers in the same Active Directory site is not an option. One thing that has been added to Windows Server 2012 GPMC is the ability to view the Group Policy infrastructure status, which includes the replication status of the GPO back-end files stored on SYSVOL.

Designing a Group Policy Infrastructure

Designing a Group Policy infrastructure requires a detailed understanding of the available configuration settings available in GPOs. Chapter 27 details the available settings administrators can configure with group policies and also covers some best-practice configurations. This section of the chapter covers the high-level steps required to successfully plan and deploy a reliable Group Policy infrastructure.

Active Directory Design and Group Policy

A key to determining how to best design the Group Policy infrastructure is to first understand how the Active Directory infrastructure is configured. The site, domain, and OU design of an Active Directory infrastructure usually follows a few key elements, including physical office locations, network connectivity, and delegation of administration, including branch office management, separation of Active Directory management tasks, desktop and server administration, and, of course, security and reliability.

Site Group Policy Links

Group policies can be linked to Active Directory site objects. There is no default site policy created when Active Directory is first deployed. Common uses of site-linked group policies include settings related to networking, including wireless networking profiles, security configurations, and possibly site printer deployments. Considerations for determining whether a GPO should be linked at a site should include the following:

- Every object in a site, determined by the associated site subnet, will process the policy, regardless of the domain the user or computer account is located in. Is this the desired configuration?
- Does the site contain a domain controller in the domain in which the group policy is created?
- Do any of the associated site subnets include networks across slow links or VPNs? If so, changing the default values or disabling slow link detection on the site policy might be required for proper processing.
- Is there a particular security requirement for the site that required a higher level of enforced security or a required configuration or application?

Before a GPO can be linked to a site, the site must be added into the GPMC. To add an Active Directory site to the GPMC and add a GPO link, follow these steps:

1. Log on to a designated Windows Server 2012 administrative server.
2. Open the Group Policy Management Console.
3. Right-click the Sites container and select Show Sites.
4. In the Show Sites window, click the Select All button or check the box next to the site you want to add to the GPMC. Click OK to add the sites to the console.
5. In the tree pane, expand the Sites container, and right-click the desired site.
6. Select the Link an Existing GPO option.
7. In the Select GPO window, select the source domain from which you want to link the GPO.
8. In the Group Policy Objects section of the window, select the desired GPO or GPOs, and then click OK to create the link.

9. If necessary, configure the link settings for each new site link, and then close the GPMC.

Domain GPO Links

When Active Directory is deployed, two preconfigured default group policies are created. One is linked to the domain named the Default Domain Policy, and the other is linked to the Domain Controllers OU named the Default Domain Controllers Policy.

The Default Domain Policy contains the default security settings for the entire domain, including account and password policies. As a best practice, use this policy only for managing the default account policies for the entire domain. Any additional GPO settings that an organization would desire to apply to all users/computers, including domain controllers, member servers, and client workstations, should be added to new GPOs and linked at the domain level. The number of policies linked at the domain level should be kept to a minimum to ensure quality Group Policy processing performance for the organization. Changes to the default domain controller policy will be applied to all domain controllers and should also be made with caution, or implemented with different GPOs linked at the domain controller organizational unit.

Organizational Unit Links

Linking GPOs to organizational units is the most common use of GPO links. OU GPO links provide the most targeted GPO application and granular administrative control of the OU GPO-related tasks as well as the configuration and management of the objects contained in the OU. The only way to get more granular on an OU GPO link is to apply a security filter or a WMI filter on that particular GPO, but that would affect each GPO link related to that particular policy. One thing to keep in mind is that with the new GPMC functionality, administrators can force an update on computers stored within an OU, and although that doesn't necessarily impact GPO link or placement, it does add some consideration to OU design, which is covered in Chapter 6.

Separation of GPO Functions

Determining which features and settings of a GPO will be utilized is one consideration; another is determining how to deploy those settings. There is one major consideration with GPO management that should be considered: Should a single GPO be created to contain all the necessary settings, or should separate GPOs be created for a particular set of features or functions?

As a best practice, separating GPO functions across multiple GPOs provides more flexibility, but that also adds time to GPO processing and increases the amount of GPO administration that needs to be performed. Separating GPOs for specific functions provides additional troubleshooting options and greater flexibility for how GPOs can be linked and filtered. As an example of how to separate GPO functions, the following list of GPOs can be applied to a Branch Office OU that contains user objects, group objects, and computer objects:

- **Branch Office Help Desk GPO**—This GPO would configure settings to allow help desk administrators to manually run Windows Update, access all Control Panel applets, and run all software with unrestricted access. This would be the last GPO applied and would override any conflicting settings. This GPO status would be set to Computer Configuration Settings Disabled and the security filtering would be configured to use a security group called Branch Office Help Desk, which would include the help desk support staff.
- **Branch Office Server GPO**—This GPO can contain the default security settings and soft-ware packages specific for branch office servers. Also this policy would configure specific audit settings, account management settings, and user rights assignments for servers. The GPO status would be configured for User Configuration Settings Disabled and would have a WMI filter linked that includes computers with an OS name that includes the word server.
- **Branch Office User GPO**—This GPO can contain the default security and configuration settings to configure the end-user desktop environment, including managing Microsoft Internet Explorer settings, redirecting folders to the branch office DFSR shares, enabling offline files, mapping network drives, installing network printers, and configuring settings to hide or restrict access to specific Control Panel applets. The GPO status of this GPO would be configured to Computer Configuration Settings Disabled.
- **Branch Office Workstation GPO**—This GPO can contain the default security settings used to manage the services, install corporate software packages and VPN clients, configure workstation security, and enable remote access. This GPO would be filtered using a WMI filter that includes only computer objects whose OS name value contained Windows 8. The GPO status would be set to User Configuration Settings Disabled. This GPO would be applied first to the workstations after local and inherited GPOs.

Separation of GPO by Targeting Operating System

With each release of a Microsoft client or server OS, Microsoft provides new Group Policy settings and functionality. The release of Windows 8 and Windows Server 2012 is no different; only a few new Group Policy settings will not apply to any other OSs, but most are still compatible Windows 7. These include both policy and preference settings to manage. Some of the preferences include managing power settings on Windows Vista and newer OSs as well as adding scheduled tasks and immediately scheduled tasks that will run at the next Group Policy refresh cycle. These preferences are detailed in Chapter 27.

When OS-specific Group Policy settings will be used, a best practice is to filter out all other OSs the GPO applies to. The best way to do this is with the use of a WMI filter for computers. Security filtering can also be used, but if a security group is used, a computer will only pick up group membership changes during startup, so getting application of a new policy adopted is less successful. A WMI filter will be processed by all Windows XP,

Windows Server 2003, and later OSs. How to create a WMI filter is detailed later in this chapter in the section "Creating and Linking WMI Filters to GPOs."

GPO Administrative Tasks

This section includes detailed steps an administrator can perform to execute GPO-related administrative tasks.

Installing the Group Policy Management Tools

Before Group Policy can be managed, the Group Policy Management Tools must be installed. These tools are installed by default on Windows Server 2012 domain controllers, but for other systems, they must be manually installed. The following sections detail installation steps for Windows Server 2012 and Windows 8 systems.

Installing the Group Policy Management Tools on Windows Server 2012

Before group policies can be managed from a Windows Server 2012 system, the Group Policy Management feature must be installed, as detailed in the following steps:

1. Log on to a designated administrative system running Windows Server 2012.
2. Open Windows PowerShell from the taskbar.
3. Type **Import-Module ServerManager** and press Enter.
4. Type **Add-WindowsFeature GPMC** and press Enter.
5. Review the installation status in the Windows PowerShell window and close the window if the install was successful.

Installing the Group Policy Management Tools on Windows 8 Client

To install Remote Server Administration Tools for Windows Server 2012 on Windows 8 Client, follow these steps:

1. Download the Remote Server Administration Tools for Windows Server 2012 for Windows 8 for x86 or x64 depending on your client OS type.
2. Double-click the downloaded file, and when you are prompted by the Windows Update Standalone Installer dialog box to install the update, click Yes.
3. On the EULA page, read and accept the license terms, and then click I Accept to continue with the installation.
4. When prompted, reboot the system to complete the installation.

After the system reboots, if you are logged on with an account with the necessary permissions, all the Remote Server Administration Tools will be available for remote administration of Windows Server 2012 systems. The tools will be located within an Administrative Tools tile on the Start menu.

Managing Group Policy with Windows PowerShell

From a Windows 8 or a Windows Server 2012 system with the Group Policy Management Tools installed, several new Windows PowerShell cmdlets can be leveraged to manage Group Policy. To access these Group Policy cmdlets, follow these steps:

1. Log on to a designated administrative system running Windows Server 2012.
2. Open Windows PowerShell from the taskbar.
3. In the Windows PowerShell window, type **Import-module grouppolicy** and press Enter to enable Group Policy management.
4. Now in the window, type **Get-command –module grouppolicy** enter to see a list of the 28 different Group Policy cmdlets available.
5. To get help information about a specific Group Policy cmdlet, such as get-gporeport, type **Get-help get-gporeport** and press Enter.
6. And to see syntax usage of a specific cmdlet, such as get-gporeport, type **Get-help get-gporeport –example** and press Enter to see several different examples.

Creating a GPO Central Store

Starting with Windows Vista and Windows Server 2008, administrators can now manually create a folder on the Active Directory domain controller that contains all the necessary ADMX and ADML files. This folder is referred to as the GPO central store and has to be created and managed manually. The GPO central store can be created in a domain that contains at least Windows Server 2003 domain controllers or later.

By default, with Windows Vista, Windows Server 2008, and later OSs, when a GPO is opened for editing the system first checks the domain controller for the existence of a GPO central store. If the central store exists, the GPO loads the templates located in the central store. If the central store does not exist, the local copies of the ADMX and ADML files are loaded to view the GPO.

NOTE

For a central store to work properly, the Active Directory Forest and Domain Schema must be upgraded to at least Windows Server 2008 Schema even though the domain controller requirement is only Windows Server 2003 with the latest service pack.

The creation of the GPO central store provides a simple, yet effective way for administrators to manage administrative templates from the server. To create the GPO central store, follow these steps:

1. Log on to a designated administrative system running Windows 8 or Windows Server 2012.
2. Browse to the C:\Windows\ folder and copy the PolicyDefinitions folder to the Clipboard.

3. In a domain named companyabc.com, open the following folder: \\companyabc.com\sysvol\companyabc.com\policies.

4. Paste the PolicyDefinitions folder from the Clipboard to the folder referenced in the preceding step.

5. Close any open folder windows.

The preceding steps create the central store and populate the store with the ADMX template files and the ADML language files of the administrative workstation or server. If additional language files are required, the language subfolder within the PolicyDefinitions folder of the administrative system can be copied into the domain's central store now located at \\companyabc.com\sysvol\companyabc.com\policies\PolicyDefinitions.

Verifying the Usage of the GPO Central Store

To verify whether the central store is actually being used, follow these steps:

1. Log on to a designated administrative system.

2. Open the Group Policy Management Console.

3. Expand the domain to expose the Group Policy Objects container and expand it.

4. Select any existing GPO that contains at least one configured setting within the Administrative Templates section of either the Computer Configuration or User Configuration node.

5. In the right pane, select the Settings tab to view the settings of the GPO, similar to the settings shown in Figure 19.16.

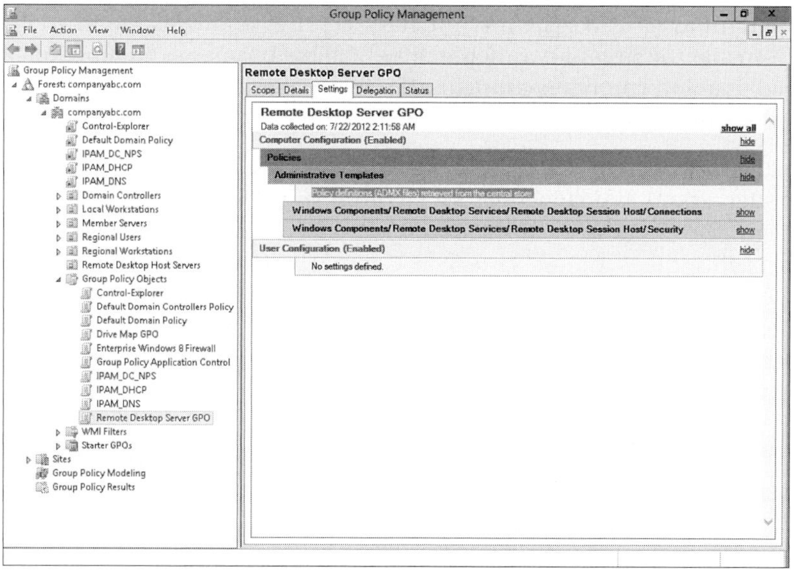

FIGURE 19.16 GPO central store verification.

Under Administrative Templates, it will state whether policy definitions (ADMX) files were retrieved from the local machine or from the central store.

6. Close the Group Policy Management Console.

Creating and Using Starter GPOs

The Windows 8 and Windows Server 2012 GPMC includes a feature and GPO function named Starter GPOs. This function allows administrators to create or load base GPOs with preconfigured administrative template settings and values, which can be used to prepopulate new GPOs. If any starter GPOs exist, an administrator creating a new GPO from a Windows 8 or a Windows Server 2012 GPMC console will have the option of using any existing starter GPO to prepopulate newly created GPOs with a number of setting values. Once the starter GPO functionality is enabled, Group Policy administrators can create new starter GPOs customized for their organization's needs.

Starter GPOs can be viewed within the GPMC and can be edited using the Group Policy Starter GPO Editor, but the files are stored within the domain controller SYSVOL folder. For example, starter GPOs for the companyabc.com domain would be located at the \\companyabc.com\sysvol\companyabc.com\StarterGPOs folder. Microsoft provides some starter GPOs that will be automatically installed when starter GPO functionality is enabled. These currently include templates for two environments as described in the Windows client security guides. These are the Enterprise Client (EC) environment scenario and the Specialized Security Limited Functionality (SSLF) client environment scenario.

The EC environment, as described in the Windows client security guide, is an Active Directory domain infrastructure that runs Windows Server 2003 or Windows Server 2008 or later servers and Windows Vista and later or Windows XP client workstations where functionality is as important as security. The preconfigured settings in the EC starter GPOs have been designed to enable the necessary functionality to allow businesses to function with centrally managed user and computer configuration management as well as security management and audit settings.

The SSLF environment, as described in the Windows client security guide, is designed to provide security configurations and guidelines for environments that require higher security, which outweighs the importance of smoother user experiences and manageability. As an example of this, the Windows Vista SSLF Computer starter GPO would deny logon through Remote Desktop Services functionality, whereas the Windows Vista EC Computer policy leaves this setting undefined. This policy setting allows administrators and members of the Remote Desktop Users groups to connect using Remote Desktop Connection or Terminal Services clients.

CAUTION

Any Group Policy administrator must take the highest precautions to ensure that no group policies deployed on a network are released without thorough testing in an isolated lab environment. This is especially true when considering deploying policies built on the EC or SSLF starter GPO policies.

The starter GPOs included with Windows Server 2012 GPMC are as follows:

- Windows Vista EC Computer
- Windows Vista EC User
- Windows Vista SSLF Computer
- Windows Vista SSLF User
- Windows XP EC Computer
- Windows XP EC User
- Windows XP SSLF Computer
- Windows XP SSLF User

For more information about the EC and SSLF starter GPOs, refer to the Windows client security guides online.

Enabling Starter GPOs

Before starter GPOs can be put to use, the functionality must first be enabled in the domain. Enabling this function is about as simple as pushing a button. To enable the starter GPO feature, follow these steps:

1. Log on to a designated Windows 8 or Windows Server 2012 administrative system.
2. Open the Group Policy Management Console.
3. Expand the domain to expose the Starter GPOs container and select it.
4. In the right pane, click the Create Starter GPOs Folder button.

Once the task is completed, the eight out-of-the-box starter GPOs are available for review in the GPMC. A Group Policy administrator can also create new starter GPOs from scratch and can also create new GPOs by using these default system starter GPOs as templates.

NOTE

The starter GPOs included with Windows 8 and Windows Server 2012 are read-only and cannot be edited directly. Copies of the built-in starter GPOs can be edited.

Creating a Starter GPO

Starter GPOs can be created or added to a domain in a few ways. A starter GPO can be created from scratch using a blank template, it can be created by restoring from a starter GPO backup folder, or it can be imported from a provided starter GPO cabinet file. Before the release of the Windows 7 and Windows Server 2008 R2 Group Policy Management Tools, the Microsoft EC and SSLF starter GPO policies were provided as separate downloads, stored in cabinet backup files. If an organization had not yet adopted Windows Server

2008 R2 domain controllers, this was the only way to import these starter GPO policies. To create a starter GPO from a backup, see the "Backing Up and Restoring Starter GPOs" section. To create a new starter GPO, follow these steps:

1. Log on to a designated Windows Server 2012 administrative system that has the Group Policy Management Tools installed.
2. Open Windows PowerShell.
3. In the Windows PowerShell window, type **import-module GroupPolicy** and press Enter.
4. Type **New-GPStarterGPO -Name "MyStarterGPO"** and press Enter.

   The Windows PowerShell window will show the results of the new starter GPO creation.
5. To check the status of the GPO, type **Get-GPStarterGPO –Name MyStarterGPO**.
6. Close the Windows PowerShell window.

Backing Up and Restoring Starter GPOs

Backing up and restoring starter GPOs is a simple operation that can be performed using the Windows Server 2012 GPMC. Starter GPOs can be backed up individually, or all the starter GPOs can be backed up together.

Starting with Windows Vista and Windows Server 2008, the backup functionality of the GPMC allows for the backup of multiple versions of the same GPOs. In earlier versions, if an organization wanted historical backups of GPOs, or revisions, the GPOs would need to be backed up to separate folder locations. Now, the backups can all be stored in a single folder.

Backing Up All Starter GPOs

Even though there are many Group Policy-related GPO cmdlets, for starter GPOs there are only the New-GPStarterGPO and the Get-GPStarterGPO cmdlets. To perform any other starter GPO-related task, the GPMC must be used. To back up all the starter GPOs in a domain, follow these steps:

1. Log on to a designated Windows Server 2012 administrative system.
2. Open the Group Policy Management Console.
3. Expand the domain to expose the Starter GPOs container and select it.
4. Right-click the starter GPOs container and click the Back Up All button.
5. Specify the folder location to store the backup, enter a description of the backup, and click the Back Up button to back up the starter GPOs.

NOTE

We recommend that the designated backup folder and the description of the backup specify or make it very easy to differentiate between starter GPO backups and domain GPO backups even though they can be stored in the same folder.

6. In the Backup window, review the status of the backup, and click OK when the backup completes.

Backing Up a Single Starter GPO

All starter GPOs can be backed up using the method described in the preceding section, which includes version or revision history, but a single starter GPO can also be backed up individually or it can be saved as a cabinet file. To individually back up a single starter GPO, follow these steps:

1. Log on to a designated Windows Server 2012 administrative system.
2. Open the Group Policy Management Console.
3. Expand the domain to expose the Starter GPOs container and expand it.
4. Select the desired starter GPO, right-click it, and then click the Back Up button.
5. Specify the folder location to store the backup, enter a description of the backup, and click the Back Up button to back up the starter GPO.
6. In the Backup window, review the status of the backup, and click OK when the backup completes.

Saving a Starter GPO as a Cabinet File

Starter GPOs can be exported or saved as individual cabinet (*.cab) files. Starter GPO cabinet files can be used to create new starter GPOs or can be used to move starter GPOs between isolated test and production Active Directory environments. To save an individual starter GPO as a cabinet file, follow these steps:

1. Log on to a designated Windows Server 2012 administrative system.
2. Open the Group Policy Management Console.
3. Expand the domain to expose the Starter GPOs container and select it.
4. In the right pane, select a single starter GPO, and at the bottom of the pane, click the Save as Cabinet button.
5. Browse or type in the location in which to save the cabinet file, specify a name for the cabinet file, and click the Save button to save the starter GPO.

Restoring a Starter GPO from Backup

Restoring a starter GPO can be performed to revert a starter GPO to a previously backed-up state, move a starter GPO from one domain or forest to another, or to recover from a starter GPO deletion.

To restore a deleted starter GPO, follow these steps:

1. Log on to a designated Windows Server 2012 administrative system.
2. Open the Group Policy Management Console.
3. Expand the domain to expose the Starter GPOs container and select it.
4. Right-click the Starter GPO container and select Manage Backups.
5. Browse to or specify the starter GPO backup location to load the starter GPO backup set.
6. In the window, select the desired GPO object.
7. If a filtered view is desired, check the Show Only the Latest Version of Each Starter GPO check box.
8. To view the settings of a particular backed-up GPO, select the desired starter GPO, and click the View Settings button. Close the browser window after the settings are reviewed.
9. After the desired starter GPO is determined, select the starter GPO backup and click the Restore button.
10. Click OK in the Restore confirmation dialog box to restore the starter GPO.
11. Review the GPO restore progress, and click OK when it completes.
12. After all the necessary starter GPOs are restored, close the Manage Backups window.

Disabling Starter GPO Functionality

An organization may determine that starter GPO functionality should be removed. In those situations, it is quite easy to disable starter GPO functionality. If starter GPO functionality needs to be removed from a domain, follow these steps:

1. Log on to a designated Windows Server 2012 administrative system.
2. Open the Group Policy Management Console.
3. Expand the domain to expose the Starter GPOs container and select it.
4. Verify that the starter GPO functionality is enabled by viewing the right pane.
5. If the functionality is enabled, close the GPMC.
6. Click the Windows Explore tile in the task bar and in the location field. Type **\\companyabc.com\sysvol\companyabc.com** and press Enter. This example is for the companyabc.com domain; substitute your Active Directory DNS domain name.

7. When the network path opens, one of the folders shown is the StarterGPOs folder. Right-click and delete that entire folder.
8. Close the Windows explorer window.
9. Open the Group Policy Management Console again.
10. Expand the domain to expose the Starter GPO container and select it.
11. Verify that the Starter GPO functionality is now disabled by viewing the right pane. If starter GPOs are now disabled, there will be a Create Starter GPO Folder button.
12. The task is now complete, so close the GPMC.

Removing Starter GPO functionality will not affect any domain group policies that were previously creating using any starter GPOs.

Creating New Domain Group Policies

To create a new domain GPO, follow these steps:

1. Log on to a designated Windows Server 2012 administrative system that has the Group Policy Management Tools installed.
2. Open Windows PowerShell.
3. In the Windows PowerShell window, type **import-module GroupPolicy** and press Enter.
4. Type **New-GPO –Name MyNewGPO** and press Enter.

Creating and Configuring GPO Links

After a GPO is created and configured, the next step is to link the GPOs to the desired Active Directory containers. To link an existing GPO to an Active Directory container, follow these steps:

1. Log on to a designated Windows Server 2012 administrative system.
2. Open Windows PowerShell, type **Import-Module GroupPolicy**, and press Enter.
3. For this example, we will link the GPO named MyNewGPO to the OU Local Workstations that is located at the root of the companyabc.com domain by typing in **New-GPLink –Name "MyNewGPO" –Target "OU=Local Workstations, DC=companyabc,DC=Com"** and then pressing Enter.
4. The PowerShell window returns the results of that command if successful. Close the Windows PowerShell window.

Advanced GPO Link Configuration

After a GPO link is created, it is enabled by default. Each link has its own configuration options, which include link enforcement and the ability to enable and disable the link. To change the default configuration of a GPO link, follow these steps:

1. Log on to a designated Windows Server 2012 administrative system.
2. Open the Group Policy Management Console.
3. Expand the Domains or Sites node to expose the GPO-linked container.
4. If the GPO link is to be enforced, right-click the desired GPO link, and select Enforced to enforce the link.
5. If the GPO link will be changed from enabled to disabled, right-click the desired GPO link and select Link Enabled to check Link (Enabled) or uncheck Link (Disabled).

Managing GPO Status

GPO status controls whether the entire GPO is enabled, disabled, or if only the Computer Configuration or User Configuration node is enabled. GPO status is applied to the GPO itself, so all links will be affected by any changes to the GPO status. To view or modify the status of a GPO, follow these steps:

1. Log on to a designated Windows Server 2012 administrative system.
2. Open the Group Policy Management Console.
3. Expand the domain to expose the Group Policy Objects container and expand it.
4. Select the desired GPO and select the Details tab in the right pane.
5. On the Details tab, in the GPO Status drop-down menu, note the current status of the GPO.
6. If the GPO status needs to be changed, click the drop-down arrow and select one of the following options:
   - Enabled
   - User Configuration Settings Disabled
   - Computer Configuration Settings Disabled
   - All Settings Disabled
7. After you select the desired GPO status, a confirmation window opens. click OK to complete the status change.

Managing GPO Security Filtering

Managing security filtering is one of the best ways to target a specific group of users and computers for GPO application. Security filtering can be set to a specific user, computer, or security group object or a combination of all three object types. To change the security filtering of a GPO from the default of Authenticated Users, follow these steps:

1. Log on to a designated Windows Server 2012 administrative system.
2. Open the Group Policy Management Console.
3. Expand the domain to expose the Group Policy Objects container and expand it.
4. Select the desired GPO and select the Scope tab in the right pane.
5. In the Security Filtering section of the Scope tab, select the Authenticated Users group, and click the Remove button.
6. Click OK in the confirmation dialog box to remove the security group from the GPO security filtering.
7. In the Security Filtering section of the Scope tab, click the Add button to add an Active Directory object to the security filter for the GPO.
8. Type in the name of the user or security group that will be applied to the GPO security filtering, and click OK.
9. If multiple objects need to be added, repeat this process until all the objects are added to the security filter.
10. If a specific computer object needs to be added, in the Select Users and Group window, click the Object Types button, check the Computers object, and click OK. Type the computer object name or browse for the object, and then click OK.

Creating and Linking WMI Filters to GPOs

When applying security filtering to a GPO is not granular enough to target a specific set of computers, a WMI filter can be linked to the GPO. For this example, we will create a WMI filter that includes a computer with an OS name of Windows 8. To create the example WMI filter, follow these steps:

1. Log on to a designated Windows Server 2012 administrative system.
2. Open the Group Policy Management Console.
3. Expand the domain and select the WMI Filters container.
4. Right-click the WMI Filters container and select New.
5. In the Name section, type in **Windows 8 WMI Filter**.
6. In the Description section, type in **WMI filter to include only Windows 8 workstations**.
7. Click the Add button to create the WMI filter query.
8. In the Query section, type **Select * from Win32_OperatingSystem Where (Name LIKE "%Windows 8%")** to show a GPO WMI filter similar to the one shown in Figure 19.17.

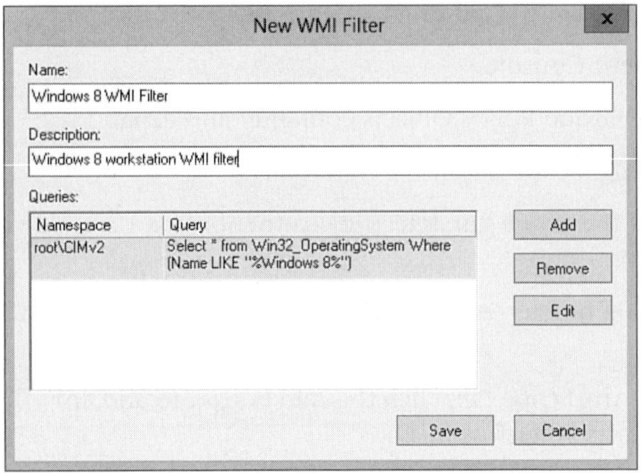

FIGURE 19.17 Creating a Windows 8 WMI GPO filter.

9. Click OK to save the query and return to the WMI Filter window.
10. Click Save to create the WMI filter in the domain.

Managing GPO Link Order of Processing

When an Active Directory container has multiple GPOs linked to it, a specific order of processing will occur. In some instances, the set of linked GPOs can have some conflicting settings, and the order of GPO processing must be modified to produce the desired result. When reviewing both the Linked Group Policy Objects Link order on a container or the Group Policy Inheritance Precedence order, the Group Policies will be applied in a countdown sequence ending with the number 1 policy being applied last. Group Policy Link Order is inherited down from any parent or domain container and can only be adjusted on the actual domain or container the GPO is linked to. To change the GPO link order of processing, follow these steps:

1. Log on to a designated Windows Server 2012 administrative system.
2. Open the Group Policy Management Console.
3. Expand the Forest and Domains or Sites node to expose the container with multiple GPOs linked.
4. Select the desired container.
5. In the right pane, select the Linked Group Policy Objects tab.

NOTE

When the order is presented, the policy with the highest numeric value is applied first and the remainder of the policies are applied sequentially and numerically. The GPO listed as number 1 in the link order is processed last.

6. If the placement or order of a particular GPO needs to be changed, select the GPO and click one of the following buttons on the left:
   - Move Link to Top is a double up arrow.
   - Move Link Up is a single up arrow.
   - Move Link Down is single down arrow.
   - Move Link to Bottom is a double down arrow.
7. When the GPO links are in the correct order, the task is complete.

Viewing GPO Settings and Creating Reports

One of the great features of the GPMC is the ability to view GPO settings from within the window, and to save the settings to share with others as HTML files. To view the settings of a particular GPO, follow these steps:

1. Log on to a designated Windows Server 2012 administrative system.
2. Open the Group Policy Management Console.
3. Expand the forest and domain to expose the Group Policy Objects container and expand it.
4. Select the desired GPO in the tree pane and select the Settings tab in the right pane.
5. Browse the settings by expanding the sections using the Hide and Show hyperlinks.
6. To save the settings to an XML or HTML file, right-click the desired GPO in the left pane, and click Save Report.
7. Specify the location in which to save the GPO report, choose Save the File as an HTML or an XML File, and click Save to save the file.

Backing Up and Restoring Domain GPOs

Backing up GPOs is a task that should be performed regularly. This section contains step-by-step instructions to back up and restore domain group policies.

Backing Up All Domain GPOs

To back up all domain GPOs, follow these steps:

1. Open Windows PowerShell on an administrative system with the Group Policy Management Tools installed.
2. Type **Import-Module GroupPolicy** and press Enter.
3. Type **Backup-GPO –Path C:\GPOBackup -All** and press Enter to back up all GPOs the C:\GPOBackup folder on the local system. The path to the backup folder must exist before running this command or else the task will fail.

Backing Up a Single Domain GPO

1. Open Windows PowerShell on an administrative system with the Group Policy Management Tools installed.
2. Type **Import-Module GroupPolicy** and press Enter.
3. Type **Backup-GPO –Path C:\GPOBackup –Name MyNewGPO** and press Enter to back up the single GPO named MyNewGPO the C:\GPOBackup folder on the local system. The path to the backup folder must exist before running this command or else the task will fail.

Restoring a Domain GPO

Restoring a domain GPO can be performed to revert a GPO to a previously backed-up state or to recover from a domain GPO deletion.

To restore a deleted domain GPO, follow these steps:

1. Log on to a designated Windows Server 2012 administrative workstation.
2. Open the Group Policy Management Console.
3. Expand the forest and domain to expose the Group Policy Objects container and select it.
4. Right-click the Group Policy Objects container, and select Manage Backups.
5. Browse to or specify the domain GPO backup location to load the GPO backup set.
6. Select the desired GPO object.
7. If a filtered view is desired, check the Show Only the Latest Version of Each GPO check box.
8. To view the settings of a particular backed-up GPO, select the desired GPO, and click the View Settings button. Close the browser window after reviewing the settings.
9. After the desired GPO is determined, select the GPO and click the Restore button.
10. Click OK in the Restore confirmation dialog box to restore the GPO.
11. Review the GPO restore progress, and click OK when it is finished.
12. After all the necessary GPOs are restored, close the Manage Backups window and re-create the links as required.

NOTE

Restoring a domain GPO from a backup does not re-create or restore any links previously associated with that GPO. GPO links must be re-created and reconfigured manually, but they can be referenced by viewing the settings within the GPO backup using GPMC.

To change an existing domain GPO to a previously backed-up version, follow these steps:

1. Log on to a designated Windows Server 2012 administrative system.
2. Open the Group Policy Management Console.
3. Expand the domain to expose the Group Policy Objects container and select it.
4. Locate and right-click the desired domain GPO, and select Restore from Backup.
5. In the Restore Group Policy Object Wizard window, click Next on the Welcome page.
6. On the next page, browse to or specify the domain GPO backup location and click Next.
7. To view the settings of a particular backed-up GPO, select the desired GPO, and click the View Settings button. Close the browser window after reviewing the settings.
8. After the desired GPO is determined, select the GPO, and click Next.
9. Review the settings summary on the Completing the Restore GPO Wizard page, and click Finish to start the restore process.
10. Review the GPO restore progress, and click OK when it is finished.

Group Policy Modeling Operations

The GPMC has a function called Group Policy Modeling that enables administrators to run tests to determine the projected outcome of GPO processing. Group Policy Modeling allows administrators to test the outcome of applying new GPOs, changing the status of GPOs, changing the location of a computer or user object, or changing the group membership of a computer or users. Detailed Group Policy Modeling is covered in Chapter 27.

Troubleshooting Group Policies

Group Policy administration also requires the ability to report and troubleshoot Group Policy processing. This topic is covered in Chapter 27, but has been included in this section for convenience.

Managing Group Policy Logging and Tracing

When group policies are not processing as intended, it may become necessary to enable logging to decipher where the issues are occurring. For example, earlier in this chapter the topic of Group Policy client-side extensions elaborated that there are more than a handful of extensions, each responsible for processing a portion of Group Policy. Before logging and tracing defaults are changed, it is important to note that logging for warnings and errors is enabled by default for all extensions. Changing logging and tracing behavior should be done only if the information stored in the event logs on the affected system are not sufficient for determining the cause of the GPO processing issues.

To troubleshoot GPP Drive Maps, for example, you can change the default logging settings for that individual extension. To do so, you must first enable the logging and enable user/computer trace settings within a GPO, and then the GPO must be applied to the affected system by linking the GPO to the appropriate OU.

To enable logging and tracing on the GPP Drive Maps extension, follow these steps:

1. Create a new GPO named GPOLogSettings using the GPMC.
2. Open the GPO for editing and drill down to Computer Configuration\Administrative Templates\System\Group Policy\Logging and tracing and select it.
3. On the Settings page, double-click the Configure Drive Maps Preference Logging and Tracing setting to open it for editing.
4. Read the entire explanation in the Help section, select the Enabled radio button, pull down the Tracing menu, and select On, as shown in Figure 19.18.

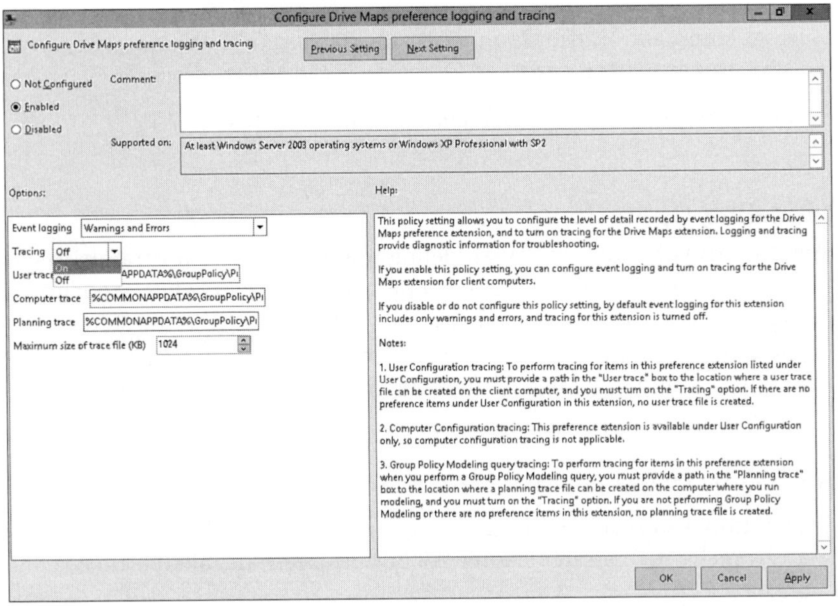

FIGURE 19.18 Enabling GPO Preference Drive Maps Logging and Tracing

5. In the User Trace Form field, note the path to the trace file and click OK to save the settings to the new GPO.
6. Back in the GPMC, link the new GPO to the appropriate OU containing the affected system.
7. Now you can force a Group Policy refresh on the OU within the GPMC by right-clicking the OU and selecting Group Policy Update and then clicking Yes in the confirmation window.

The Remote Group Policy Update results window will show the results of the remote update, and if successful, the new log setting GPO has been applied.

8. Because for this example we used the user-based preference extension Drive Maps, we need to have the user log off and log on to refresh the user-based GPO processing and then we can review the trace file located at %COMMONAPPDATA%\GroupPolicy\Preference\Trace\User.log, which will translate to Windows Vista and later as %systemdrive%\ProgramData or C:\ProgramData.

One important point to note is that if the GPO is not getting applied at all, there will be no tracefile. So, the Group Policy administrator must ensure that the policy is linked correctly and that that the security filtering is applied to the GPO correctly. This is where Group Policy Modeling can be used. Group Policy Modeling is covered in Chapter 27.

Group Policy Results

Now if the Group Policy administrator is sure the GPO is linked and is configured correctly, the actual processing can be checked on the affected system and for the affected user using GPO Resultant Set of Policies (RSoP). Windows 8 and Windows Server 2012, the GPMC includes new reporting capabilities that will assist Group Policy administrators tremendously. To run the Group Policy results tool, follow these steps:

1. Open the GPMC on an administrative system.
2. Expand the forest and select the Group Policy Results container.
3. Right-click the container and select Group Policy Results Wizard. Click Next on the Welcome page.
4. In the Computer Selection page, select the This Computer radio button or the Another Computer radio button and browse or type in the system name, and then click Next.
5. In the User Selection Windows, choose to load the policy processing for the existing user or any other listed that had previously logged on to the system, and then click Next.
6. On the Summary of Selections, review the selections, and then click Next to run the tool.
7. When the wizard completes, click Finish to return to the GPMC window, where the collected data will be presented.
8. In the resulting GPMC windows, the Group Policy administrator can review the results listed on the Summary, Details, and Policy Events tabs to review the GPO processing data, as shown in Figure 19.19.

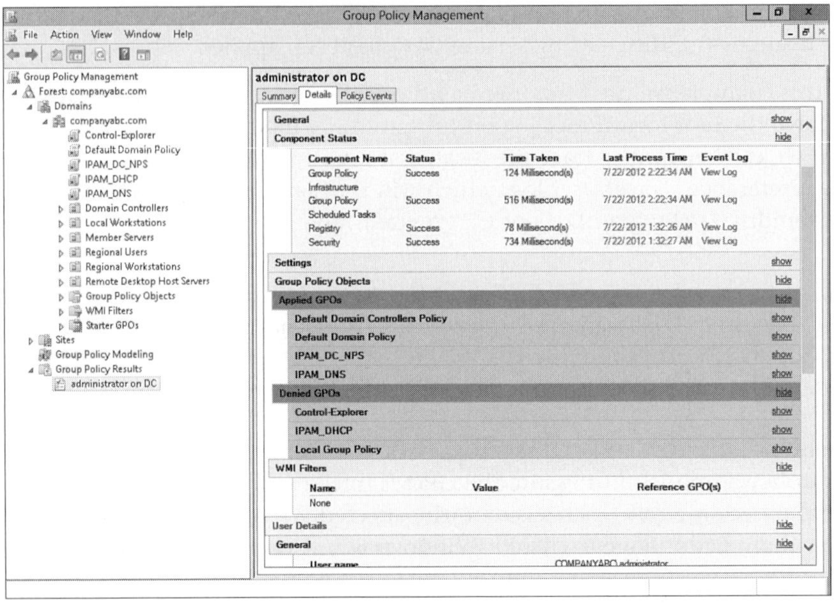

FIGURE 19.19 Review Group Policy results data.

GPO Administrative Delegation

GPO administrative delegation is a process that administrators can follow to delegate permissions to specific users or configure security rights across all GPOs or specific GPOs and GPO-related tasks on specific Active Directory containers, such as sites, domains, and OUs.

GPO delegation or delegation of administration within Active Directory should only be used in organizations that have separate IT groups that manage the infrastructure and servers and other groups that manage the desktop and support the end user. If the IT group of an organization contains administrators who all perform GPO and Active Directory administration, adding a delegation model might not be necessary and can add unnecessary complexity.

All GPO administrative delegation tasks detailed in the following sections are performed using the Group Policy Management Console.

Delegating GPO Creation Rights

The right to create GPOs can be delegated only at the domain's Group Policy Objects container and the Starter GPOs container. After a policy is created, though, the right to completely edit, modify security, and even delete the GPO can be granted on a per-GPO basis. To grant the right to create GPOs in a domain, follow these steps:

1. Log on to a designated administrative system running Windows Server 2012.
2. Open the Group Policy Management Console.

3. Expand the domain to expose the Group Policy Objects container and select it.
4. In the right pane, select the Delegation tab.
5. Click the Add button at the bottom of the pane.
6. Type in the name of the user account or security group, and click OK to apply the changes.

Alternatively, you could add the specific user or security group as a member of the Group Policy Creator Owners security group.

Delegating GPO Management Rights on Existing GPOs

After a group policy is created, it inherits a base set of administrative rights to completely edit the settings and modify the security of the policy. By default, administrative rights are granted to the Domain Admins, Enterprise Admins, and System objects. If the policy was created by a separate group or user that had been granted GPO creation rights, that object would also have these rights. If additional users or security groups need to be granted the right to edit the settings, manage the security, or delete a specific policy, follow these steps:

1. Log on to a designated administrative system running Windows Server 2012.
2. Open the Group Policy Management Console.
3. Expand the domain to expose the Group Policy Objects container and select it.
4. Expand the Group Policy Objects container to expose the domain GPOs.
5. Select the desired GPO and select the Delegation tab in the right pane.
6. At the bottom of the pane, click the Add button.
7. Type in the name of the specific user account or security group, and click OK.
8. In the Add Group or User window, click the Permissions drop-down arrow, and select the appropriate permission of Read, Edit Settings, or Edit Settings, Delete, Modify Security, and click OK to apply the changes.

Delegating GPO Administrative Tasks on Active Directory Containers

The GPMC enables administrators to delegate the rights to manage GPO links and perform testing and troubleshooting tasks at the site, domain, and OU container levels. To delegate GPO administrative rights over an Active Directory container, follow these steps:

1. Log on to a designated administrative workstation running Windows Server 2012.
2. Open the Group Policy Management Console.
3. Expand the Active Directory Forest container.
4. Select either the Domains or Sites node and expand it.

5. If the desired domain or site is not listed, right-click the node and select Show Domains or Show Sites and add the object as required.
6. Expand the Domains or Sites node to expose the container that will have the GPO delegation rights applied to it and select it.
7. In the right pane, select the Delegation tab.
8. On the Delegation tab, near the top of the pane, select the desired permission that will be delegated from the following options:

   Link GPOs

   Perform Group Policy Modeling Analyses

   Read Group Policy Results Data
9. At the bottom of the pane, click the Add button.
10. Type in the name of the specific user account or security group and click OK.
11. In the Add Group or User window, click the Permissions drop-down arrow, and select the appropriate permission of This Container Only or This Container and All Child Containers, and click OK.

NOTE

Even though the right to perform Group Policy Modeling and view results data can be delegated at a container level, if the task is not performed on the domain controller, the user or group will also need to be a member of the domain's Distributed COM Users security group.

Summary

This chapter detailed the Group Policy infrastructure of the Windows 8 and Windows Server 2012 OSs. For an administrator to successfully design and support a Group Policy infrastructure, a thorough understanding of the general GPO functions and how to use the GPO Management Tools is a necessity.

This chapter introduced how policies work, the difference between local group policies and domain policies, and the elements of a group policy. For administrators who are creating multiple policies for their environment, rather than creating individual policies for each user, site, or domain, the concept of creating a starter GPO to use as a template or baseline policy was discussed.

Windows Server 2012 also introduced improvements in the Group Policy Management Console tool that is used for the creation and management of policies throughout the Windows Server 2012 environment, including the Remote Group Policy Update functionality.

After reviewing the tools available for the creation and management of group policies, this chapter provided guidance on the policy management tasks and best practices an administrator should follow when leveraging the capabilities of policies within the Windows Server 2012 environment.

Best Practices

The following are best practices from this chapter:

- Use Windows Powershell ISE to learn how to properly format GPO related PowerShell cmdlets.
- Use commonsense naming conventions for GPOs.
- When you are working with GPOs, disable unused Computer and User Configuration nodes of the policy when possible.
- When you delegate the creation of GPOs to nonadministrators, also consider delegating the capability to manage the links for a specific OU and to allow these administrators to run modeling and to read Group Policy results data.
- Use the Enforced and Block Inheritance settings in GPOs sparingly.
- Only configure the default account policies for the entire domain in the default domain policy. Leave all other settings to separate policies.
- Use fully qualified (UNC) paths (for example, \\server.companyabc.com\share) when referencing shares or paths within a GPO.
- Use starter GPOs to set baseline standards for administrators to create subsequent policies in the environment.
- Try to separate GPO functions across multiple policies to provide more flexibility with regard to targeting GPO application, delegation, and troubleshooting.
- When creating OS-specific Group Policy settings, create separate policies and apply WMI filters for the desired OSs.
- Use Group Policy security and WMI filters to gain more granular control of policies and the application of policies on users and computers.
- Delegate administration of individual existing GPOs to administrative staff instead of allowing the individuals or staff security groups rights to create, edit, or manage policies across the entire domain.
- Leverage the backup and restore capabilities of the Group Policy Management Console as a method to create a copy of the policies so that if a policy is accidentally edited, deleted, or corrupted, the policy can be restored to its original state.

CHAPTER 20

Windows Server 2012 Management and Maintenance Practices

IN THIS CHAPTER

Modern businesses depend on their IT infrastructure in order to keep their processes moving and their products delivering. Most IT infrastructures these days depend fairly heavily on Windows-based servers. These servers need to be managed and maintained to keep the businesses running optimally. Server management and maintenance help maximize investment in infrastructure and productivity. They also keep the IT infrastructure running effectively and efficiently to boost availability and reliability.

Windows Server 2012 brings many new tools and features to help keep the servers managed and maintained and they have been designed to scale to levels never before seen. These tools include the updated Server Manager, better auditing, improved configuration of servers through the roles and features, better remote management, IPAM (IP Address Management), and a slew of other capabilities. Many formerly manual tasks are automated in Windows Server 2012 using the enhanced Task Scheduler. These include tasks such as defragmentation and backup.

Server management entails many different tasks, including administering and supervising servers based on functional roles, proactively monitoring the network environment, keeping track of activity, and implementing solid change-control practices. These management functions for Windows Server 2012 can be performed both locally and remotely.

As systems' workloads, capacities, and usage change in the environment, the systems need to be maintained so that they operate as efficiently as possible. Without such maintenance, systems become more susceptible to causing slower response times and decreased reliability. Efforts to maintain those systems should be made periodically to avoid any inefficiency. This chapter covers best practices on ways an organization can maintain and manage its Windows Server 2012 environment.

Going Green with Windows Server 2012

A big part of server management and maintenance practices is planning for resources, including reducing the environmental impact of servers. Power consumption of servers is a huge environmental concern today and a significant expense for large data centers.

Windows Server 2012 continues the "green" trend with green concerns in mind and specifically with reducing the power consumption, carbon footprint, and therefore, the environmental impact of running a server. This includes server-level improvements and data center-level improvements.

Windows Server 2012 reduces the power consumption of individual servers through several new or improved technologies, as follows:

- **An improved Processor Power Management (PPM) engine**—The new PPM engine adjusts the processor speed and, therefore, power consumption in response to demand. Windows Server 2012 also supports the core-parking feature, which idles processor cores that are not being used, thus reducing their power consumption.
- **Storage power management**—The ATA Slumber feature allows for new power states for a more nuanced power utilization. Windows Server 2012 will recognize solid state drives and power them down when not in use, to reduce their power consumption. And Windows Server 2012 supports boot to storage area networks (SANs), eliminating the need for direct attached drives and thus reducing power consumption.
- **Intelligent Timer Tick Distribution**—This allows processors to skip activation if not needed for work, reducing the power consumption of underutilized systems.
- **Reduced background work**—Windows Server 2012 also has reduced operating system (OS) background work requirements, reducing power draw even further, especially in idle states.

Windows Server 2012 also enables administrators to better manage power consumption across servers through the following:

- **Remote manageability of power policy**—Windows Server 2012 has Group Policy features for controlling power options across a number of servers. Power policy can also be configured remotely with PowerShell and with Windows Management Instrumentation (WMI) scripting via the new root\cimv2\power namespace. These allow for much more sophisticated programmatic control of power consumption.
- **In-band power metering and budgeting**—Power consumption can be displayed as a performance counter in the new Power Meter object. This object allows manufacturers to instrument their platform power consumption live. This can be consumed

by management applications such as Operations Manager 2007 R2 with thresholds and alerts. The Power Meter object also contains a budget counter, enabling you to set power budgets on a server-by-server basis.

- **New additional qualifier designed for Windows Server 2012 Logo program**—This Power Management AQ addition to the program allows manufacturers to distinguish themselves and identify power-saving features in their products, enabling IT managers to purchase power-saving hardware to complement the power-saving Windows Server 2012 OS.
- **Virtualization**—Although virtualization might not initially seem like a power-saving technology, consider the fact that many servers in modern IT infrastructures are not fully using their resources. An application might have justified a high-powered server based on its high I/O requirements or high memory requirements but might not be fully utilizing the CPU power of the server. By creating multiple virtual servers on a physical server and deploying servers based on complementary resource usage, you can more fully utilize modern servers and thus reduce the overall number of physical servers, thus reducing power consumption and eventually resulting in fewer retired servers in landfills.

Many of these features require no specific action on the part of an administrator, but management and maintenance practices can be adjusted to account for these green power features. For example, the power consumption at 100% utilization for Windows Server 2003 SP2 and for Windows Server 2012 servers is roughly the same. However, the power consumption at 30% utilization is approximately 20% higher for Windows Server 2003 SP2 than for Windows Server 2012. At lower workloads, Windows Server 2012 consumes less power. Most servers operate at lower workloads, so the power savings for a Windows Server 2012 server can be significant.

These Windows Server 2012 features help organization move toward greener servers and data centers and protect the environment.

Server Manager Dashboard

One of the new features of Windows Server 2012 is the Dashboard available in Server Manager, which by default will appear at logon. This interface enables an administrator to easily add roles or features, create server groups, and make management changes to groups of servers. This is a departure from the management in Windows Server 2008 R2 in that you no longer have to add roles or features on each server individually. One can create a group and populate it with servers destined to become Internet Information Services (IIS) servers and add the same roles and features to each in a single interface. This greatly improves the ability to manage multiple systems.

As shown in Figure 20.1, the Dashboard gives a quick view of the roles installed, quick access to events specific to that role, a link to see associated services, and links to the management functions of each role.

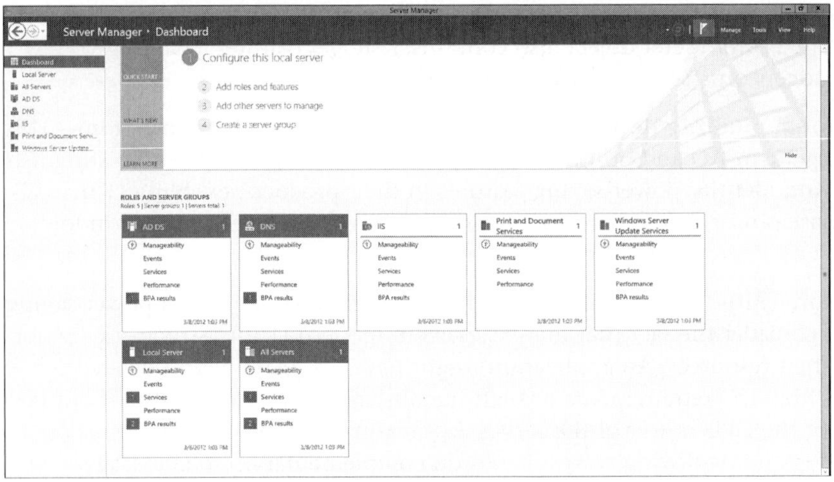

FIGURE 20.1 Server Manager - Dashboard.

For example, clicking Manageability under AD DS brings up the AD DS Manageability Detail view, which shows servers based on status criteria. From here, you can click Go to AD DS and see the full level of detail, including the following:

- **Servers**—This section shows the list of servers associated with the role that was previously chosen (in this example, AD Domain Controllers). The view shows server name, IPv4 address, manageability state, last update, and Windows activation.
- **Events**—This section shows events associated with the role previously selected. Information includes server name, event ID, severity, source, log and date/time.
- **Services**—This section is where the services specific to the role selected are shown. Information includes server name, display name of the service, service name, status, and start type.
- **Best Practices Analyzer**—This section is where BPA scan results are displayed, including server name, severity, title and category. BPA scans can also be launched from the Tasks button here.
- **Performance**—This section shows performance data, including server name, counter status, CPU alert count, memory alert count, first occurrence and last occurrence. Performance alerts can be configured from the Tasks button.
- **Roles and Features**—This section shows the roles and features information, including server name, name, type, and path.

Each of these sections has the ability to filter the view, save queries, or pull up a list of saved queries. This proves exceptionally helpful in large environments where a list of servers could be very large. This is also helpful when viewing events and you are looking for specific events. Each of the views can also sorted based on various clickable fields.

The initial configuration settings in a newly built Windows Server 2012 system are stripped down and basic (as shown in Table 20.1), with little or no security. For example, the latest security updates have not been applied, and the system is not configured to download them automatically. Therefore, the Windows Firewall is enabled by default to protect the server from network access until the initial configuration is completed, and the Remote Desktop feature is turned off.

TABLE 20.1 Default Configuration Settings

Setting	Default Configuration
Time zone	Pacific time (GMT – 8) is the time zone set by default.
Computer name	The computer name is randomly assigned during installation. Administrators can modify the computer name by using commands in the Initial Configuration Tasks Wizard.
Domain membership	The computer is not joined to a domain by default; it is joined to a workgroup named WORKGROUP.
Windows Update	Windows Update is turned off by default.
Network connections	All network connections are set to obtain IP addresses automatically by using Dynamic Host Configuration Protocol (DHCP).
Windows Firewall	Windows Firewall is turned on by default.
Roles installed	No role or features are installed by default.

You can configure each of these settings via the properties of the computer object. Just clicking the Start button (activated by hovering the mouse in the far right side of the screen) and then right-clicking Computer will offer up an Advanced option that exposes Manage, Map Network Drive, Disconnect Network Drive, and Properties. Selecting Properties will provide an interface familiar to Server 2008 R2 administrators where the previously described settings can be modified.

Managing Windows Server 2012 Roles and Features

To help organize and manage the expanded functionality of Windows Server 2012, the platform continues to use the roles and features paradigm. The roles and features enable administrators to add and manage functionality in coherent blocks. This includes tools to summarize, manage, and maintain the installed roles and features with the enhanced ability to configure these roles and features across multiple systems simultaneously.

Roles in Windows Server 2012

Server roles in Windows Server 2012 are used to organize the functionality of the OS. The server roles are an expansion of the server roles of earlier versions of Windows, with significant enhancements. Roles usually include a number of related functions or services that make up the capabilities that the server will offer. A role designates a primary function of the server, although a given server can have multiple roles.

Windows Server 2012 offers the traditional role-based or feature-based installation and introduces a scenario-based installation. Currently the scenario-based installation supports Remote Desktop Services installations only.

Administrators familiar with Server 2008 R2 will notice that the new Add Roles and Features Wizard now offers the option to select multiple servers from a pool or to apply services or roles to a virtual hard disk.

Windows Server 2012 includes the following roles:

- Active Directory Certificate Services
- Active Directory Domain Services
- Active Directory Federation Services
- Active Directory Lightweight Directory Services
- Active Directory Rights Management Services
- Application Server
- DHCP Server
- DNS Server
- Fax Server
- File And Storage Services
- Hyper-V
- Network Policy and Access Services
- Print and Document Services
- Remote Access
- Remote Desktop Services
- Volume Activation Services
- Web Server (IIS)
- Windows Deployment Services
- Windows Server Update Services

Within each role, a number of role services make up the role. The role services allow the administrator to load only the specific services that are needed for a particular server instance. In some cases, such as for the DHCP Server or DNS Server roles, the role and the role service are one and the same. In other cases, the role contains multiple services that can be chosen. For example, the File Services role contains the following role services:

- File Server
- BranchCache for Network Files

- Data Deduplication
- DFS Namespaces
- DFS Replication
- File Server Resource Manager
- File Server VSS Agent Service
- iSCSI Target Server
- Server for NFS

Adding a role and role services installs the binaries (that is, the code) that allow the services to function. Additional installation and configuration usually needs to be done after the roles are installed, such as for the Active Directory Domain Services role.

Only loading the roles required for each server (and therefore only the appropriate binaries) reduces the complexity, the attack surface, and the patch surface of the server. This results in a more-secure, less-complex, and more-efficient server—in short, resulting in fewer headaches for the administrator who has to manage the server!

NOTE

The patch surface of a server is the code in the server that requires patches to be applied. This can increase the need for patches and therefore downtime, as well as administrative overhead. If code is installed on a server, it needs to be patched even if that particular code is not in use on a server. This is analogous to the attack surface of the server.

A good example of this is the Web Server role. If a domain controller has the Web Server role added, any patches that apply to the code base of the Web Server role need to be installed. This is true even if the services are disabled or just not used. Therefore, the patch surface of the domain controller has been increased.

However, if the domain controller only has the roles (and therefore the code) for the roles it needs, the patches for other roles will not need to be applied to the domain controller. Therefore, the patch surface of the domain controller has been reduced.

Features in Windows Server 2012

In addition to the roles and role services, Windows Server 2012 also has the ability to add features. Features are typically supporting components that are independent of the server role but might provide support for a role or role service. For example, a domain controller is configured with the Active Directory Domain Services role. However, in some organizations, the domain controller will also serve as a Windows Internet Naming Service (WINS) server. WINS is a feature in Windows Server 2012.

There are many different features in Windows Server 2012, including the following:

- .NET Framework 3.5.1
- .NET Framework 4.5
- Background Intelligent Transfer Service (BITS)
- BitLocker Drive Encryption
- BitLocker Network Unlock
- BranchCache
- Client for NFS
- Data Center Bridging
- Desktop Experience
- Enhanced Storage
- Failover Clustering
- Group Policy Management
- Ink and Handwriting Services
- Internet Printing Client
- IP Address Management (IPAM) Server
- iSCSI Target Storage Provider (VDS and VSS hardware providers)
- iSNS Server service
- LPR Port Monitor
- Management OData IIS Extension
- Media Foundation
- Message Queuing
- Multipath I/O
- Network Load Balancing
- Peer Name Resolution Protocol
- Quality Windows Audio Video Experience
- RAS Connection Manager Administration Kit
- Remote Assistance
- Remote Differential Compression
- Remote Server Administration Tools
- RPC over HTTP Proxy

- Simple TCP/IP Services
- SMTP Server
- SNMP Services
- Subsystem for UNIX-Based Applications
- Telnet Client
- Telnet Server
- TFTP Client
- User Interfaces and Infrastructure
- Windows Biometric Framework
- Windows Feedback Forwarder
- Windows Identity Foundation 3.5
- Windows Internal Database
- Windows PowerShell
- Windows PowerShell Web Access
- Windows Process Activation Service
- Windows Search Service
- Windows Server Backup
- Windows Server Migration Tools
- Windows Standards-Based Storage Management
- Windows System Resource Manager
- Windows TIFF IFilter
- WinRM IIS Extension
- WINS Server
- Wireless LAN Service
- WoW64 Support
- XPS Viewer

The features are installed with the Server Manager's Add Roles and Features Wizard. To add a feature, follow these steps:

1. Launch Server Manager.
2. From the Server Manager Dashboard, click Add Roles and Features.

3. Choose Role-Based or Feature-Based Installation. Click Next.
4. Select the server from the server pool, and click Next.
5. Click Next to skip past roles and select the features to install. Click Next.
6. Click Install, and then click Close.

The feature will now be installed.

NOTE

Unlike earlier versions of Windows, all the binaries for Windows Server 2012, Windows Vista, Windows 7, and Windows Server 8 are installed in the C:\WINDOWS\WINSXS directory. All the components—that is, roles and features—are stored in the WINSXS directory. This eliminates the need to use the original DVD installation media when adding roles or features.

However, the trade-off is that the WINSXS folder is more than 6GB, because it contains the entirety of the OS. In addition, it will grow over time as updates and service packs are installed. For a physical machine, the additional disk space is not much of an issue. However, for virtual machines, it means that there is an additional 6GB of additional disk space that has to be allocated for each and every Windows server.

Creating a Server Group

To manage Windows Server 2012 systems in groups, it is necessary to create a server group. You can do so from the Server Manager Dashboard as follows:

1. Click Option 4, Create a Server Group.
2. Enter a server group name.
3. Select systems from either the server pool, Active Directory, or DNS, as appropriate. Use the Ctrl or Select key to select more than one server.
4. Click the right-arrow key to add the computers to the Selected list.
5. Click Finish.

This updates the Roles and Server Groups view to include the new group.

Viewing Events

The Windows Server 2012 Event Viewer functionality is located in the new Server Manager. Selecting the Local Server or a Server Group gives administrators access to the event logs from that system. This provides a consolidated view that summarizes application and system event logs.

A more detailed view of event logs can be accessed by selecting a server group, right-clicking a server, and then choosing Computer Management. This will give the Server 2008 R2-style view that places event logs under the System Tools folder. This view gives the more traditional view that includes Application, Security, System, and Setup logs as well as Application and Services logs. The Events Viewer object on this page shows a high-level summary of the administrative events, organized by level:

- Critical
- Error
- Warning
- Information
- Audit Success
- Audit Failure

The view shows the total number of events in the past hour, 24 hours, and 7 days. You can expand each of these nodes to show the counts of particular event IDs within each level. Double-clicking the event ID count shows a detailed list of the events with the matching event ID. This is very useful for drilling on the specific events to see when they are occurring.

The Overview and Summary page also has a Log Summary section, which shows a list of all the various logs on the server. This is important because there are now nearly 220 different logs in Windows Server 2012. In addition to the standard system, security, and application logs, there is a setup log and a forwarded events log. Then there are the numerous application and services logs, including logs for each application and service, and a huge number of diagnostic and debugging logs. For each of the logs, the Log Summary section shows the log name, current size, maximum size, last modification, if it is enabled, and what the retention policy for the log is. This enables administrators to quickly see the status of all the logs, a daunting task otherwise.

Of course, you can view the logs directly by expanding the Windows Logs folder or the Applications and Services Logs folder. The Windows Logs folder contains all the standard application, security, setup, system, and forwarded events logs. The applications and services logs contain all the other ones.

Custom views can be created to filter events and combine logs into a coherent view. There is a default Administrative Events view, which combines the critical, error, and warning events from all the administrative logs. There is also a custom view created for each role that is installed on the server. The administrator can create new ones as needed.

Subscriptions can collect events from remote computers and store them in the forwarded events log. The events to be collected are specified in the subscription. The functionality depends on the Windows Remote Management (WinRM) and the Windows Event

Collector (Wecsvc) services, and they must be running on both the collecting and forwarding servers.

Server Manager Performance Monitor

The Performance Monitor is incorporated into Computer Manager, as well. This diagnostic tool enables the administrator to monitor the performance of the server in real time, generate reports, and also save the performance data to logs for analysis.

The top-level folder of the Performance Monitor displays the System Summary. This gives a comprehensive overview of the memory, network interface, physical disk, and processor utilization during the past 60 seconds (see Figure 20.2). The System Summary is organized in a matrix, with a column for each instance of the network interface, disk, and processor. The information is updated every second. Unfortunately, the pane is still a fixed height, so it is hard to see all the information at once, and excessive scrolling is needed.

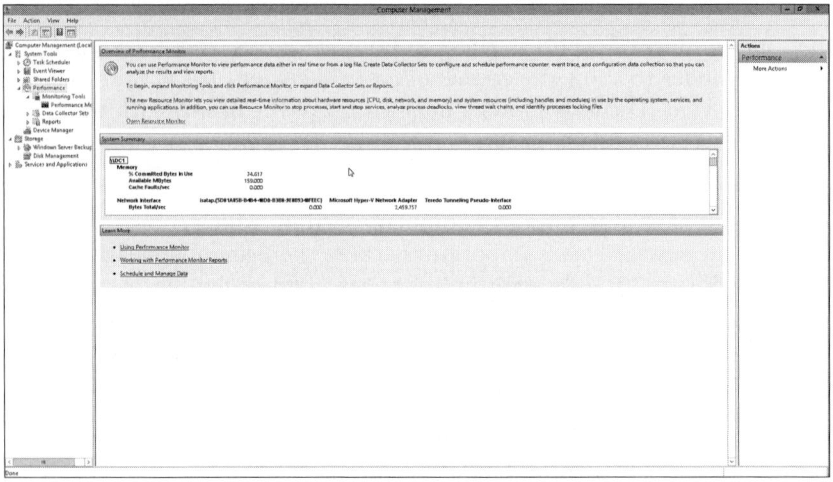

FIGURE 20.2 System Summary in Performance Monitor.

The Monitoring Tools container holds the Performance Monitor tool. This tool enables you to monitor the performance of the server in more detail. The Performance Monitor has not really changed from earlier versions of Windows. It allows you to select performance counters and add them to a graph view for real-time monitoring. The graph can be configured to be a line graph, a bar graph, or even a simple text report of the counters being monitored. The monitor shows the last, average, minimum, maximum, and duration of the windows (1 minute 40 seconds by default).

For longer-term tracking, you can use data collector sets can be used. Data collector sets can log data from the following data sources:

- Performance counters
- Event traces
- Registry key values

This data can be logged over an extended period of time and then reviewed. The data collected will also be analyzed and presented in reports that are very useful. There are two reports defined by default: the System Diagnostics and System Performance. When roles are added, such as the Active Directory Domain Services role, there might be additional data collector sets defined. These datasets gather data that is presented in reports, which is new to Windows Server 2012. There is a new reports folder in the Performance Monitor where the reports are saved.

To generate data for a Performance Monitor report, follow these steps:

1. Launch Server Manager.
2. Expand the Diagnostics node.
3. Expand the Performance node.
4. Expand the Data Collector Sets node.
5. Expand the System node and select the System Performance data collector set. Note that the data collector set includes an NT Kernel trace and performance counters.
6. Right-click the NT Kernel trace object and select Properties. Note the events that will be collected. Click Cancel to exit without saving.
7. Right-click the Performance Counter object and select Properties. Note the performance counters that will be collected. Click Cancel to exit without saving.
8. Right-click the System Performance data collector set and select Start. The data collector set will start collecting data.
9. Right-click the System Performance data collector set and select Latest Report.

The report will show a detailed analysis of the system performance. The Summary and the Diagnostic Results are shown in Figure 20.3. The Diagnostic Results indicate that memory is the busy component on the DC1 server. The report contains a wealth of details on the CPU, network, disk, memory, and overall report statistics.

You can also view the performance data that the report is based on directly. This can be done by right-clicking the specific report and selecting View, Performance Monitor. This shows the graph of all the counters selected during the data collection. You can select which counters to show in the graph.

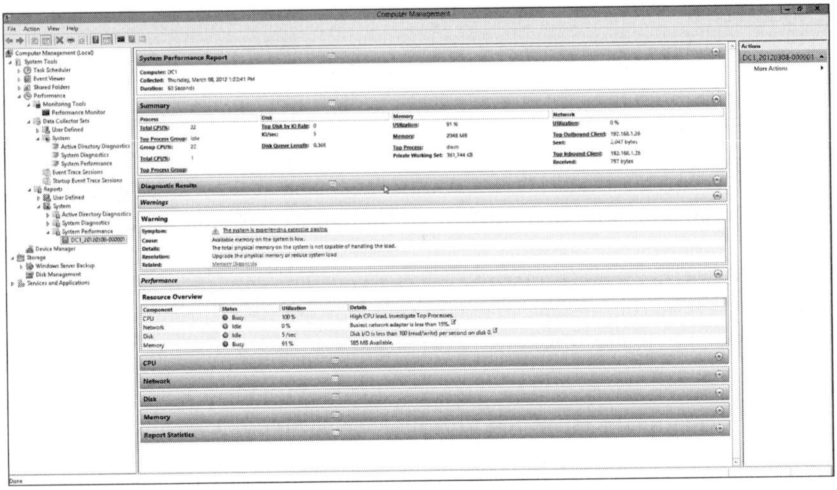

FIGURE 20.3 System Performance Report in Performance Monitor data collector sets.

The System Performance data collector set collects for only 1 minute, which is not long enough for detailed trend analysis. New data collector sets can be defined in the User Defined folder. For example, to create a duplicate of the System Performance data collector set that will run for an hour instead of a minute, follow these steps:

1. Launch Server Manager.
2. Expand the Diagnostics node.
3. Expand the Performance node.
4. Expand the Data Collector Sets node.
5. Select the User Defined node.
6. Right-click the User Defined node and select New, Data Collector Set.
7. Enter **System Performance 1 Hour** for the name and make sure that the Create from a Template is selected. Click Next.
8. Select System Performance and Click Next.
9. Click Next to keep the default root directory.
10. Select the Open Properties for this Data Collector Set option, and click Finish.
11. Click the Stop Condition tab.
12. Change the Overall Duration setting to 1 hour.
13. Click OK to save.

This data collector set can now be run and will collect the same data as the default System Performance, but for 1 hour instead of just 1 minute.

Device Manager

The Device Manager node shows the hardware that is installed on the server. It shows the hardware grouped by type of device, such as disk drives, display adapters, and network adapters. Each instance of the device type is listed in a node underneath the device type.

You can use the Device Manager to update the device drivers of the hardware, to change settings, and to troubleshoot issues with the hardware. Specifically, you can perform the following tasks:

- Scan for new hardware
- Add legacy hardware
- Identify hardware problems
- Adjust configurations
- View device driver versions
- Update the device drivers
- Roll back device driver upgrades
- Enable or disable hardware

For example, sometimes older video drivers or network card drivers will cause problems with the system. It is easy to check the Microsoft online driver repository using Device Manager. To check for an update to the device driver for the network adapter, follow these steps:

1. Expand the Network Adapters node in Device Manager.
2. Select the network adapter to check.
3. Select Action, Update Driver Software from the menu.
4. Click Search Automatically for Updated Driver Software.
5. Click Yes, Always Search Online (Recommended).
6. Install the update if found.
7. Click Close to exit the wizard.

NOTE

Many times, the latest version of the driver will already be installed. In these cases, the message "The best driver for your device is already installed" will be shown.

Task Scheduler

One of the greatly expanded features of Windows Server 2012 is the Task Scheduler. In earlier versions of Windows, this was an anemic service with limited options and auditing features. The Task Scheduler features in Windows Server 2012 have been expanded into a more sophisticated tool. The scheduler can start based on a variety of triggers, can take a number of predefined actions, and can even be mitigated by conditions and the settings.

Appropriately, there are expanded elements to the Task Scheduler, as follows:

- **Triggers**—Tasks run when the trigger criteria are met. This could be a scheduled time, logon, startup, idle, log event, user session connect or disconnect, or workstation lock or unlock. These various triggers give the administrator a wide range of options on when to start a task.
- **Actions**—The actions are the work that the task will perform. This can be executing a program, sending an email via SMTP, or displaying a message on the desktop.
- **Conditions**—Conditions allow the task trigger criteria to be filtered. Conditions include if the computer is idle, on battery power, or connected to a network. This allows administrators to prevent tasks from running if the computer is busy, on battery, or disconnected from the network.
- **Settings**—The settings control how a task can be executed, stopped, or deleted. In the settings of a task, the administrator can control if the task can be launched manually, if it runs after a missed schedule start, if it needs to restart after a failure, if it needs to run multiple tasks in parallel, or to delete it if it is not set to run in the future.

Another big improvement is the Task Scheduler Library, which includes approximately 40 different predefined tasks, including the following:

- **ScheduledDefrag**—This task runs every week and uses the command **defrag.exe –c** to defragment all the volumes on the server. This is a major improvement of earlier versions of Windows, which required this command to be run manually. The task runs at 1 a.m. every Wednesday of every week by default.
- **ServerManager**—This task runs at user logon and runs the ServerManagerLauncher to launch the Server Manager console whenever a user logs on.

Both these tasks demonstrate the capabilities of the Task Scheduler to automate routine tasks or to ensure that certain tasks run at logon.

The Task Scheduler has a new feature that goes hand in hand with the library, namely the ability to create folders to store the tasks. This helps organize the tasks that are created. The scheduler includes a Microsoft folder for the tasks that ship with the OS. Administrators can create other folders to organize and store their tasks.

Selecting the Task Scheduler folder in the Computer Manager configuration shows the Task Scheduler Summary (see Figure 20.4). This window has two sections: Task Status and Active Tasks. The Task Status section shows the status of tasks within a time frame (by default, the last 24 hours). The time frame can be set to the last hour, last 24 hours, last 7 days, or last 30 days. For each task that has run within the time frame, it shows the task name, run result, run start, run end, and triggered by. The section also summarizes the task status; Figure 20.4 also shows that 223 total tasks have run with 3 running and 216 succeeded.

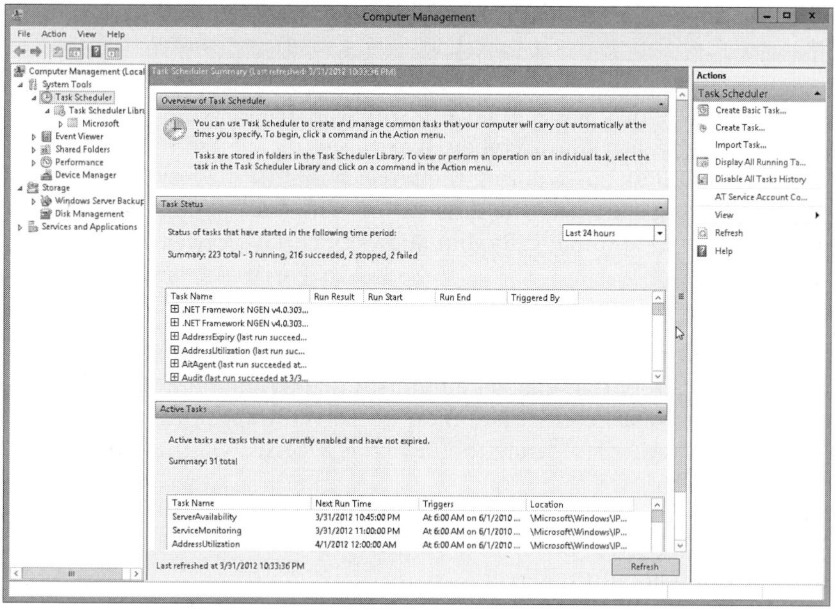

FIGURE 20.4 Task Scheduler Summary window.

The Active Tasks name is somewhat misleading because it shows tasks that are enabled and their triggers. It does not show tasks that are running. For the scheduled tasks, it shows the Next Run Time. This section is very useful for seeing which tasks will run on a given server in response to a trigger, either a schedule or an event. If the task does not appear in this section, it will be run only if executed manually.

Services and Applications

The Services snap-in has been moved to the Services and Applications container in Computer Manager, but is essentially unchanged from the earlier version of Windows. All the services are listed, along with their status, startup type, and logon credentials.

From the Services snap-in, administrators can control services on the server, including the following:

- Start or stop the services
- Change the startup type to set the service to start automatically, be started manually, or even prevent the service from starting at all
- Change the account the service runs under
- Set up recovery actions if the service stops, such as restarting the service or even restarting the server
- View the configuration details of the service, such as what the executable is, what the service name is (which is shown in the Task Manager window), and what dependencies it has

A feature that was added in Windows Server 2008 and still available in Windows Server 2012 is the Automatic (Delayed Start) startup type. This is a setting used to reduce the crunch of services starting simultaneously during the server boot. All the services with the Automatic (Delayed Start) setting start after the services with the Automatic setting. This allows all the services to come up automatically, but allows essential services to start first.

WMI Control

WMI Control has also been moved under the Services and Applications container. Introduced in 2008 R2, this is a tool that enables administrators to maintain the Windows Management Instrumentation (WMI) configuration on the server. Interestingly, the tool is not an integrated snap-in, but rather a separate tool which is accessed via the properties of the WMI Control object.

With the WMI Control tool, an administrator can do the following:

- View general information about the server
- Back up and restore the WMI repository
- Change the default scripting namespace (root\cimv2)
- Manage access to the WMI via the Security tab

Before the introduction of the WMI Control tool, these tasks were difficult to accomplish.

For example, to back up the WMI repository, complete these steps:

1. Open the Server Manager.
2. Click Local Server.
3. In Tasks, select Computer Management.
4. Expand Servers and Applications.
5. Right-click WMI Control and choose Properties.
6. Select the Backup/Restore tab.

7. Select the Back Up Now option.
8. Enter a filename with a full path. The file type will be a WMI Recovery File (.rec).
9. Click Save to save the file.
10. Click OK to exit the tool.

Windows Firewall with Advanced Security

The Windows Firewall with Advanced Security interface is now accessed through Server Manager or through Control Panel. Viewing the Local Server tab via Server Manager shows a high-level status of the Windows Firewall. Clicking its status launches the Windows Firewall MMC.

This feature provides access to the combined Windows Firewall and Connection Security features of Windows Server 2012. These technologies work in tandem to provide protection from network-based attacks to the server. The firewall rules determine what network traffic is allowed or blocked to the server. The connection security rules determine how the allowed traffic is secured.

The Windows Firewall and the Connection Security features are covered in detail in Chapter 13, "Server-Level Security," and Chapter 14, "Transport-Level Security."

The Windows Firewall with Advanced Security folder shows a summary of which profile is active (Domain, Private, or Public), the profile's high-level configuration, and links to the other components of the snap-in.

The other components of the Windows Firewall with Advanced Security snap-in are for configuration and monitoring the features. These components are as follows:

- Inbound rules
- Outbound rules
- Connection security rules
- Monitoring

The inbound and outbound rules control what traffic is allowed in to and out of the server. Several hundred rules govern what traffic is allowed. These are organized into profiles for ease of application. Table 20.2 shows these profiles.

TABLE 20.2 Firewall Profiles

Profile	Description
Domain	Applied when the server is connected to its Active Directory domain
Private	Applied when the server is connected to a private network but not to the Active Directory domain
Public	Applied when the server is connected to a public network

Clearly, the vast majority of services will have the domain profile active because they will likely be on a network with Active Directory. Each of the profiles has a set of rules associated with it. In addition, a number of rules apply to all profiles, which are designated as Any. Some of the rules are disabled by default.

Connection security rules are stored in the likewise named folder. The rules specify how the computers on either side of a permitted connection authenticate and secure the network traffic. This is essentially the IPsec policy from earlier versions of Windows, albeit with a much improved interface. By default, no connection security rules are created in Windows Server 2012. Rules can be created and reviewed in this portion of the snap-in.

The Monitoring folder is somewhat limited in scope. It has a Firewall folder and a Connection Security Rules folder. These two folders simply show what rules are active, but show no traffic details or if the rules have blocked or allowed anything. In effect, they show the net result of the profile that is active.

Server Manager Storage Page

The Storage folder in the Computer Manager has two tools to support storage in Windows Server 2012; Windows Server Backup and Disk Management. These tools are used to manage local backups and locally attached storage respectively.

Windows Server Backup

Assuming the feature is installed, the Windows Server Backup page shows a summary of the backup state of the server. This includes information about the status of backups, how much disk space the backups are using, and what the oldest and newest backups are. This allows an administrator to understand how recoverable the server is at a glance. The backup subsystem in Windows Server 2012 has fundamentally changed from a backup-to-tape job paradigm to a backup-to-disk state paradigm, requiring a different understanding of where backup stands. It is not enough to know that the latest backup job completed, but rather the span of the backups and how much space they take up.

Windows Server 2012 introduces an additional backup option called Online Backup. Online Backup enables administrators to automatically back up a system to online storage. By default, administrators have access via a Windows Live ID to Microsoft's online storage. Clicking the Continue button in this view gives the option to sign up for storage and to download the necessary agent.

For the Windows Server Backup folder to be active, you need to install the Windows Server Backup feature. To do this, follow these steps:

1. Open Server Manager.
2. Click Add roles and features.
3. Click Next and then Next again.
4. On the Select Destination Server page, choose the destination server from the server pool, and then click Next.

5. On the Select Server Roles page, click Next.
6. On the Select Features page, check the Windows Server Backup Features check box.
7. On the Confirm Installation Selections page, click Install to install the new feature.
8. Click Close to close the wizard.

Now the Server Manager Windows Server Backup folder will be active. Selecting the folder shows the Windows Server Backup summary page, shown in Figure 20.5. This figure shows the latest active backup messages, status, scheduled backup, and disk usage. From this page, the administrator can also click links to set the backup schedules, run an immediate backup, start a recovery, and perform other backup-related tasks.

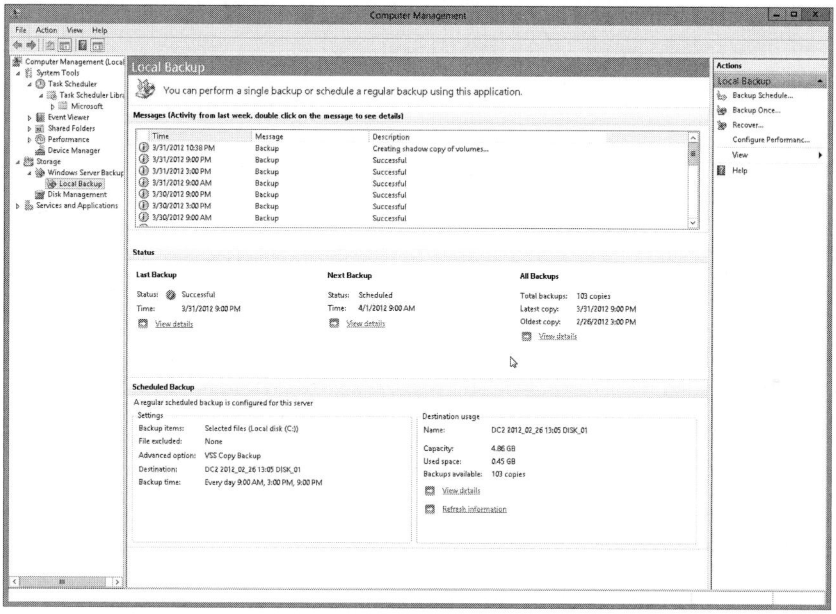

FIGURE 20.5 Windows Server Backup summary page.

The Messages section shows the active messages. You can see in the figure that a backup is running. You can also see that backups completed successfully at 9:00 p.m., 3:00 p.m., 9:00 a.m., 3:00 a.m., and that the current one started at 10:38 p.m.

The Status section shows a summary of the backups, including the last backup, the next scheduled backup, and for all backups. For each of these categories, you can click the View Details link to get additional information. This helps the administrator quickly understand what backups are available for recovery.

The Scheduled Backup section shows a summary of the scheduled backups for the server and the disk usage of the backups. The Settings box shows what is being backed up (backup item), where it is being backed up to (the target disk), and when it is being backed up (the backup time). The backup time can be modified using the Action, Backup Schedule option.

The Destination Usage box shows the capacity, the used space, and the number of backups that are available on the target. You can click the View Details link to see the disk usage and details of the backups. Figure 20.6 shows the disk usage after the backup in the previous figure completed.

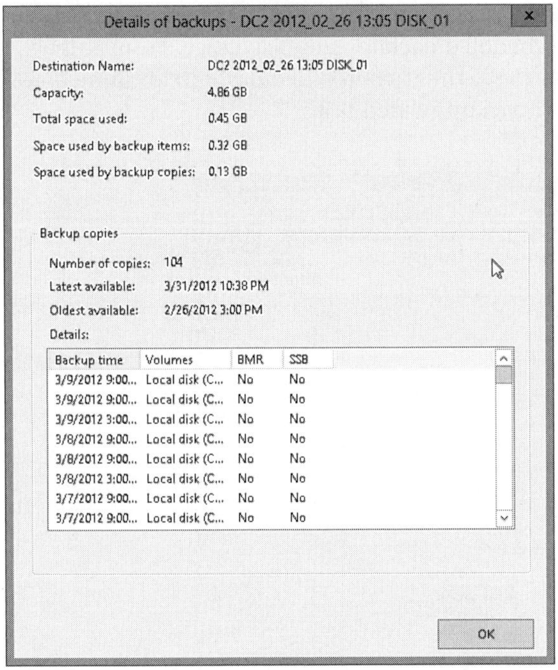

FIGURE 20.6 Windows Server Backup disk usage.

Chapter 30, "Backing Up the Windows Server 2012 Environment," covers the use of Windows Server Backup in more detail.

Disk Management

The Disk Management snap-in is used to conduct storage disk-related tasks. The Disk Management snap-in has not changed substantially from earlier versions, and most administrators will find it to be quite familiar. The snap-in enables administrators to manage disks by doing the following:

- Creating and formatting partitions
- Creating and formatting volumes

- Extending, shrinking, and mirroring volumes
- Assigning drive letters
- Viewing the status of disks, partitions, and volumes

As shown in Figure 20.7, the snap-in shows volumes in the top window with capacity, free space, and status information. This is a logical representation and is independent of the physical media. The bottom window shows the physical disks as recognized by Windows Server 2012 and the position of the partitions and volumes within the disks—that is, the layout of the partitions and volumes. The bottom window also shows the status and the type of disks.

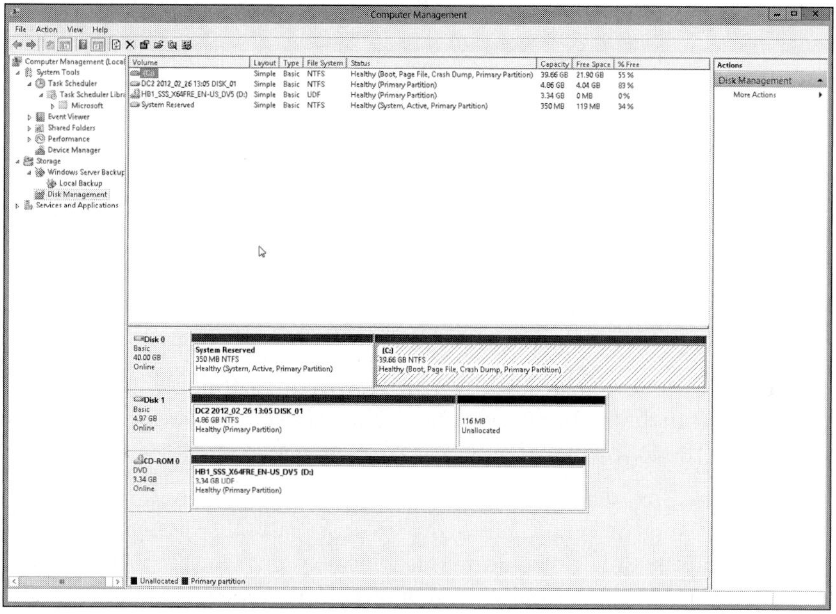

FIGURE 20.7 Disk Management console.

NOTE

The physical disks shown in the Disk Management snap-in are the disk configurations as recognized by Windows Server 2012. The actual hardware configuration of the disks might be very different, as it is abstracted by the hardware controller.

For example, what the OS recognizes as Disk 0 with 32GB might actually be a fault-tolerant RAID-1 configuration of two 32GB physical disks that the hard drive controller presents as one disk to the OS.

Auditing the Environment

Auditing is a way to gather and keep track of activity on the network, devices, and entire systems. By default, Windows Server 2012 enables some auditing, whereas many other auditing functions must be manually turned on. This allows for easy customization of the features the system should have monitored.

Auditing is typically used for identifying security breaches or suspicious activity. However, auditing is also important to gain insight into how the network, network devices, and systems are accessed. Windows Server 2008 greatly expanded auditing as compared with earlier versions of Windows. As it pertains to Windows Server 2012, auditing can be used to monitor successful and unsuccessful events on the system. Windows Server 2012 auditing policies must first be enabled before activity can be monitored.

Audit Policies

Audit policies are the basis for auditing events on a Windows Server 2012 system. Depending on the policies set, auditing might require a substantial amount of server resources in addition to those resources supporting the server's functionality. Otherwise, it could potentially slow server performance. Also, collecting lots of information is only as good as the evaluation of the audit logs. In other words, if a lot of information is captured and a significant amount of effort is required to evaluate those audit logs, the whole purpose of auditing is not as effective. As a result, it is important to take the time to properly plan how the system will be audited. This allows the administrator to determine what needs to be audited, and why, without creating an abundance of overhead.

Audit policies can track successful or unsuccessful event activity in a Windows Server 2012 environment. These policies can audit the success and failure of events. The policies that can be monitored consist of the following:

- **Audit account logon events**—Each time a user attempts to log on, the successful or unsuccessful event can be recorded. Failed logon attempts can include logon failures for unknown user accounts, time restriction violations, expired user accounts, insufficient rights for the user to log on locally, expired account passwords, and locked-out accounts.
- **Audit account management**—When an account is changed, an event can be logged and later examined.
- **Audit directory service access**—Any time a user attempts to access an Active Directory object that has its own system access control list (SACL), the event is logged.
- **Audit logon events**—Logons over the network or by services are logged.
- **Audit object access**—The object access policy logs an event when a user attempts to access a resource (for example, a printer or shared folder).
- **Audit policy change**—Each time an attempt to change a policy (user rights, account audit policies, trust policies) is made, the event is recorded.

- **Audit privilege use**—Privileged use is a security setting and can include a user employing a user right, changing the system time, and more. Successful or unsuccessful attempts can be logged.
- **Audit process tracking**—An event can be logged for each program or process that a user launches while accessing a system. This information can be very detailed and take a significant amount of resources.
- **Audit system events**—The system events policy logs specific system events such as a computer restart or shutdown.

The audit policies can be enabled or disabled through the local system policy, domain controller security policy, or group policy objects (GPOs). Audit policies are located within the Computer Configuration\Policies\Windows Settings\Security Settings\Local Policies\Audit Policy folder of the Group Policy Management Editor, as shown in Figure 20.8.

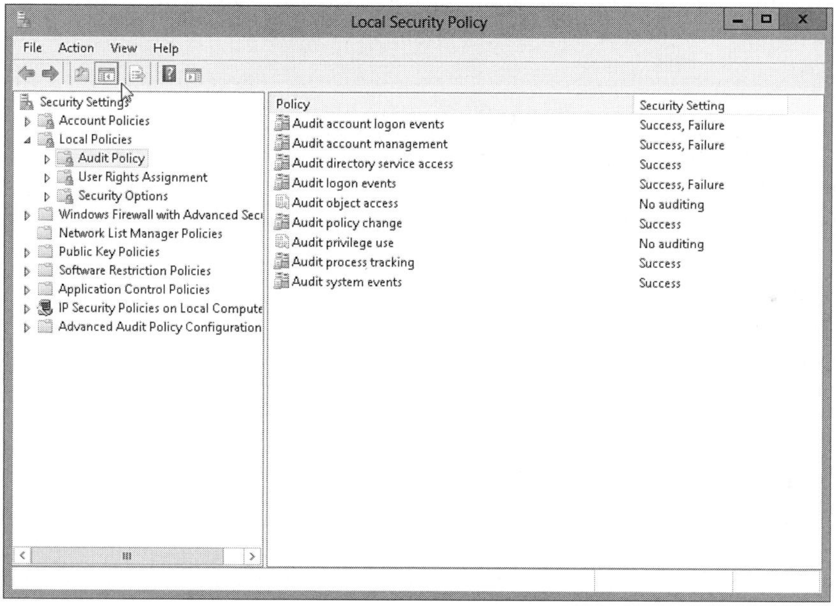

FIGURE 20.8 Audit policies and the recommended settings.

For the audit policies, the commonly used settings are given in Table 20.3. These should be set on custom policies and linked to the same locations as the Default Domain and Default Domain Controller GPOs. By default, all the policies are Not Defined. Table 20.3 also shows the recommended settings.

TABLE 20.3 Matching Audit Policies Recommended Settings

Audit Policy	Recommended Setting
Audit account logon events	Success and Failure
Audit account management	Success and Failure
Audit directory service access	Success
Audit logon events	Success and Failure
Audit object access	Not Defined
Audit policy change	Success
Audit privilege use	Not Defined
Audit process tracking	Success
Audit system events	Success

The recommended settings are designed to address specific threats. These threats are primarily password attacks and misuse of privilege. Table 20.4 matches the threats to the specific audit policies.

TABLE 20.4 Matching Specific Threats to Audit Policy Recommended Settings

Threat Addressed	Audit Policy
Random password attacks	Audit account logon events (failures)
	Audit logon events (failures)
Stolen password attacks	Audit account logon events (successes)
	Audit logon events (successes)
Misuse of privileges	Audit account management
	Audit directory service access
	Audit policy change
	Audit process tracking
	Audit system events

These recommended settings are sufficient for the majority of organizations. However, they can generate a heavy volume of events in a large organization. Or, there might be a subset of security events that an organization needs to track. In those cases, the next section discusses how to fine-tune the audit policy using audit policy subcategories.

Audit Policy Subcategories

Windows Server 2012 allows more granularity in the setting of the audit policies. In earlier versions of the Windows Server platform, the audit policies could only be set on the general categories. This usually resulted in a large number of security events, many of which are not of interest to the administrator. System management software was usually needed to help parse all the security events to find and report on the relevant entries. Windows Server 2012 exposes additional subcategories under each of the general categories, which can each be set to No Auditing, Success, Failure, or Success and Failure. These subcategories allow administrators to fine-tune the audited events.

Unfortunately, the audit categories do not quite match the audit policies. Table 20.5 shows how the categories match the policies.

TABLE 20.5 Matching Audit Policies to Audit Categories

Audit Policy	Audit Category
Audit account logon events	Account Logon
Audit account management	Account Management
Audit directory service access	DS Access
Audit logon events	Logon/Logoff
Audit object access	Object Access
Audit policy change	Policy Change
Audit privilege use	Privilege Use
Audit process tracking	Detailed Tracking
Audit system events	System

There are 57 different subcategories that can be individually set. These give the administrator and security professionals unprecedented control over the events that will generate security log entries. Table 20.6 lists the categories and the subcategories of audit policies.

TABLE 20.6 Audit Subcategories

Audit Category	Audit Subcategory
System	Security State Change
	Security System Extension
	System Integrity
	IPsec Driver
	Other System Events
Logon/Logoff	Logon
	Logoff
	Account Lockout
	IPsec Main Mode
	IPsec Quick Mode
	IPsec Extended Mode
	Special Logon

TABLE 20.6 Continued

Audit Category	Audit Subcategory
	Network Policy Server
	Other Logon/Logoff Events
Object Access	File System
	Registry
	Kernel Object
	SAM
	Certification Services
	Application Generated
	Handle Manipulation
	File Share
	Filtering Platform Packet Drop
	Detailed File ShareFiltering Platform Connection Central Policy StagingRemovable Storage
	Other Object Access Events
Privilege Use	Sensitive Privilege Use
	Non-Sensitive Privilege Use
	Other Privilege Use Events
Detailed Tracking	Process Creation
	Process Termination
	DPAPI Activity
	RPC Events
Policy Change	Audit Policy Change
	Authentication Policy Change
	Authorization Policy Change
	MPSSVC Rule-Level Policy Change
	Filtering Platform Policy Change
	Other Policy Change Events Device Claim Configuration Change* Device Assessment Membership Certificate Requests*
Account Management	User Account Management
	Computer Account Management
	Security Group Management
	Distribution Group Management
	Application Group Management
	Other Account Management Event

TABLE 20.6 Continued

Audit Category	Audit Subcategory
DS Access	Directory Service Access
	Directory Service Changes
	Directory Service Replication
	Detailed Directory Service Replication
Account Logon	Kerberos Service Ticket Operations
	Credential Validation
	Kerberos Authentication Service
	Other Account Logon Events

**These settings are available only on an Active Directory Certificate Services system.*

You can use the `auditpol` command to get and set the audit categories and subcategories. To retrieve a list of all the settings for the audit categories and subcategories, use the following command:

```
auditpol /get /category:*
```

To enable auditing of the Distribution Group Management subcategory of the Account Management category for both success and failure events, use the following command:

```
auditpol /set /subcategory:"Distribution Group Management"
/success:enable /failure:enable
```

This command must be run on each domain controller for the policy to have a uniform effect. To get all the options for the Audit Policy command, use the following command:

```
auditpol /?
```

Auditing Resource Access

Object access can be audited, although it is not one of the recommended settings. Auditing object access can place a significant load on the servers, so it should only be enabled when it is specifically needed. Auditing object access is a two-step process: Step one is enabling audit object access, and step two is selecting the objects to be audited. When enabling audit object access, you need to decide whether both failure and success events will be logged. The two options are as follows:

- Audit object access failure enables you to see if users are attempting to access objects to which they have no rights. This shows unauthorized attempts.
- Audit object access success enables you to see usage patterns. This shows misuse of privilege.

Enable the appropriate policy setting in the GPO. It is a best practice to apply the GPO as close to the monitored system as possible, so avoid enabling the auditing on too wide a set of systems.

NOTE

Monitoring both success and failure resource access can place additional strain on the system. Success events can generate a large volume of events.

After enabling the object access policy, the administrator can make auditing changes through the property pages of a file, folder, or a Registry key. If the object access policy is enabled for both success and failure, the administrator can audit both successes and failures for a file, folder, or Registry key.

After object access auditing is enabled, you can easily monitor access to resources such as folders, files, and printers.

Auditing Files and Folders

The network administrator can tailor the way Windows Server 2012 audits files and folders through the property pages for those files or folders. Keep in mind that the more files and folders that are audited, the more events that can be generated, which can increase administrative overhead and system resource requirements. Therefore, choose wisely which files and folders to audit. To audit a file or folder, follow these steps:

1. In Windows Explorer, right-click the file or folder to audit and select Properties.
2. Select the Security tab and then click the Advanced button.
3. In the Advanced Security Settings window, select the Auditing tab.
4. Click the Add button to display Audit Entry window.
5. Click Select a principal, and then enter the name of the user or group to audit when accessing the file or folder. Click the Check Names button to verify the name.
6. Click OK to return to the Auditing Entries window.
7. In the Auditing Entry window, shown in Figure 20.9, select which events to audit for successes or failures.
8. Click OK three times to exit.

New to Windows Server 2012 is the option to define conditions to help limit the scope of an auditing entry. More specifically, security events would only be logged if the defined condition were met.

Conditions can be created from the Auditing Entry screen by simply clicking Add a Condition. This brings up the interface shown in Figure 20.9. Administrators can set conditions based on the following attributes:

User or Device based on Groups (Member of Each, Member of Any, Not Member of Each, Not Member of Any) with a defined list of groups

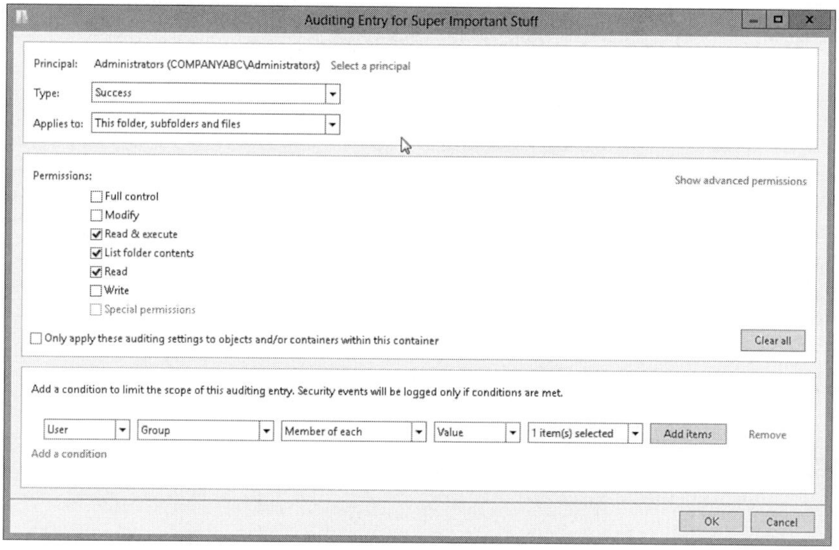

FIGURE 20.9 The Auditing Entry window.

For example, one could set the condition to User, Group, Not Member of Any, and then set the groups to Domain Admins and Enterprise Admins and effectively filter the condition to users who are not a member of either of those groups.

NOTE

This step assumes that the audit object access policy has been enabled.

When the file or folder is accessed, an event is written to Event Viewer's security log. The category for the event is Object Access. An Object Access event is shown in the following security log message:

```
Log Name:       Security
Source:         Microsoft-Windows-Security-Auditing
Date:           4/01/2012 6:22:56 PM
Event ID:       4663
Task Category:  File System
Level:          Information
Keywords:       Audit Success
User:           N/A
```

```
Computer:      DC1.companyabc.com
Description:
An attempt was made to access an object.

Subject:
        Security ID:                COMPANYABC\Administrator
        Account Name:               Administrator
        Account Domain:             COMPANYABC
        Logon ID:                   0x2586e

Object:
        Object Server:   Security
        Object Type:     File
        Object Name:     C:\Confidential\Secret.txt
        Handle ID:       0xec

Process Information:
        Process ID:      0xfd8
        Process Name:    C:\Windows\System32\notepad.exe

Access Request Information:
        Accesses:        WriteData (or AddFile)
                         AppendData (or AddSubdirectory or CreatePipeInstance)

        Access Mask:     0x6
```

The event is well organized into Subject (who attempted the access), Object (what was acted on), Process Information (what program was used), and Access Request Information (what was done). If the event was Audit Success, the attempt was successful. If the event was Audit Failure, the attempt failed. You can see from the event that the administrator wrote to the file Secret.txt at 6:22:56 p.m. and even that the program Notepad was used.

Auditing Printers

Printer auditing operates on the same basic principles as file and folder auditing. In fact, the same step-by-step procedures for configuring file and folder auditing apply to printers. The difference lies in what successes and failures can be audited. These events include the following:

- Print
- Manage this printer
- Manage documents
- Special permissions

These events are stored in Event Viewer's security log, as are all audit events.

To audit a printer, follow these steps:

1. In the Devices and Printers applet, right-click the printer to audit, and select Printer Properties.
2. Select the Security tab and then click the Advanced button.
3. In the Advanced Security Settings window, select the Auditing tab.
4. Click the Add button to display the Auditing Entry window.
5. Click Select a Principal, and then enter the name of the user or group to audit when accessing the file or folder. Click the Check Names button to verify the name.
6. Click OK to return to the Auditing Entries window.
7. In the Auditing Entry window, select which events to audit for successes or failures. The objects to audit will be different than the auditing available for files and folders, as the printer is a different class of object.
8. Click OK four times to exit.

Now access to the printer will generate security log events, depending on the events that were selected to be audited.

Managing Windows Server 2012 Remotely

Windows Server 2012's built-in feature set allows it to be easily managed remotely. This capability reduces administration time, expenses, and energy by allowing administrators to manage systems from remote locations rather than having to be physically at the system.

Server Manager Remote Management

A carryover from earlier versions of Windows Server is the Server Manager Remote Management, which allows the Server Manager console to remotely manage another server. This makes available all the features of Server Manager to the remote computer, allowing administrators to easily manage Windows Server 2012 servers from a central location.

Several functions of Server Manager Remote Management are disabled by default. This is a security feature, much like Remote Desktop, and so Windows Server 2012 defaults to a more secure state out of the box. To enable the Server Manager Remote Management, follow these steps:

1. Launch Control Panel.
2. Click the Check Firewall Status link.
3. Click Advanced Settings.
4. Click Inbound Rules.

5. Enable the remote management rules you plan to use.
6. Close the Windows Firewall control panel.

Now the system is ready to accept connections from remote Server Manager consoles. To connect to a remote computer with the Server Manager console, right-click a member of a defined server group and select Computer Management.

New to Windows Server 2012 is the ability to launch additional remote management events from the Server Manager console. Administrators can also do the following against remotely managed servers:

- Add Roles and Features
- Restart Server
- Computer Management
- Remote Desktop Connection
- Windows PowerShell
- Configure NIC Teaming
- Configure Windows Automatic Feedback
- Manage As

Remote Server Administration Tools

The Remote Server Administration Tools set includes a number of tools to manage Windows Server 2012 remotely. This set of tools replaced the Adminpack.msi set of tools that shipped with Windows Server 2003.

There are different tools for the roles (see Table 20.7) and for the features (see Table 20.8).

TABLE 20.7 Remote Server Administration Tools for Roles

Tool	Description
Active Directory Administrative Center	ADAC is the new primary administrative tool covering object management and dynamic access control.
Active Directory Certificate Services Tools	Active Directory Certificate Services Tools include the Certification Authority, Certificate Templates, Enterprise PKI, and Online Responder Management snap-ins.
Active Directory Domain Services (AD DS) Tools	Active Directory Domain Services Tools include Active Directory Users and Computers, Active Directory Domains and Trusts, Active Directory Sites and Services, and other snap-ins and command-line tools for remotely managing Active Directory Domain Services.

TABLE 20.7 Continued

Tool	Description
Active Directory Lightweight Directory Services (AD LDS) Tools	Active Directory Lightweight Directory Services Tools include Active Directory Sites and Services, ADSI Edit, Schema Manager, and other snap-ins and command-line tools for managing Active Directory Lightweight Directory Services.
Active Directory Rights Management Services (AD RMS) Tools	Active Directory Rights Management Services (AD RMS) Tools includes the Active Directory Rights Management Services (AD RMS) snap-in.
DHCP Server Tools	DHCP Server Tools include the DHCP snap-in.
DNS Server Tools	DNS Server Tools include the DNS Manager snap-in and dnscmd.exe command-line tool.
Fax Server Tools	Fax Server Tools include the Fax Service Manager snap-in.
File Services Tools	File Services Tools include the following: Distributed File System Tools, which include the DFS Management snap-in, and the dfsradmin.exe, dfscmd.exe, dfsdiag.exe, and dfsutil.exe command-line tools. File Server Resource Manager Tools include the File Server Resource Manager snap-in, and the filescrn.exe and storrept.exe command-line tools. Services for Network File System Tools include the Network File System snap-in, and the nfsadmin.exe, showmount.exe, and rpcinfo.exe command-line tools.
Hyper-V Management Tools	Hyper-V Management Tools include the snap-ins and tools for managing the Hyper-V role.
Print and Document Services Tools	Print Services Tools include the Print Management snap-in.
Remote Desktop Services Tools	Remote Desktop Services Tools include the TS RemoteApp Manager, TS Gateway Manager, and TS Licensing Manager snap-ins.
Windows Deployment Services Tools	Windows Deployment Services Tools include the Windows Deployment Services snap-in, wdsutil.exe command-line tool, and Remote Install extension for the Active Directory Users and Computers snap-in.
Windows Server Update Services Tools	Windows Server Update Services Tools includes graphical and PowerShell tools for managing WSUS
Network Policy and Access Services Tools	Network Policy and Access Services Tools includes the Network Policy Server and Health Registration Authority snap-ins.
Remote Access Management Tools	Remote Access Management tools includes graphical and PowerShell tools for managing Remote Access

TABLE 20.7 Continued

Tool	Description
Volume Activation Tools	Volume Activation Tools console can be used to manage volume activation license keys on a Key Management Service (KMS) host or in Active Directory Domain Services. One can use the Volume Activation Tools to install, activate, and manage one or more volume activation license keys, and to configure KMS settings.

TABLE 20.8 Remote Server Administration Tools for Features

Tool	Description
BitLocker Drive Encryption Tools	BitLocker Drive Encryption Tools include the managebde.exe program.
BITS Server Extensions Tools	BITS Server Extensions Tools include the Internet Information Services (IIS) 6.0 Manager and IIS Manager snap-ins.
Failover Clustering Tools	Failover Clustering Tools include the Failover Cluster Manager snap-in and the cluster.exe command-line tool.
IP Address Management (IPAM) Client	Includes the IPAM snap-in.
Network Load Balancing Tools	Network Load Balancing Tools include the Network Load Balancing Manager snap-in and the nlb.exe and wlbs.exe command-line tools.
SMTP Server Tools	SMTP Server Tools include the Internet Information Services (IIS) 6.0 Manager snap-in.
WINS Server Tools	Windows Internet Naming Service (WINS) Server Tools include the WINS snap-in.
SNMP Tool	Simple Network Management Protocol (SNMP) Tools includes tools for managing SNMP.
Windows System Resource Manager	Windows System Resource Manager (WSRM) is an administrative tool that can control how CPU and memory resources are allocated.

The tools are installed as a feature. You can install all the tools or only the specific ones that you need. To install the Remote Server Administration Tools, follow these steps:

1. Launch Server Manager.
2. Click Add Roles and Features, and then click Next.
3. Select the server from the pool, and then click Next.
4. Click Next to skip past the server roles.
5. Expand RSAT and select the RSAT tools desired, and then click Next.

6. Review the options selected and click Install to proceed. Check the Restart Each Destination Server Automatically If Required check box if you want servers to automatically reboot if needed for their new features.

New to Windows Server 2012 is the ability to close the Roles and Features Installation dialog before the completion of the installation. This will not interrupt the process, and it can be checked on later in the Server Manager interface. The flag in the upper right of the tool indicates whether there are task messages waiting for the administrator.

After the tools are installed, you can manage remote computers by selecting the Connect to Another Computer command from the Action menu.

Windows Remote Management

Windows Remote Management (WinRM) enables an administrator to run command lines remotely on a target server. When WinRM is used to execute the command remotely, the command executes on the target server and the output of the command is piped to the local server. This allows administrators to see the output of those commands.

The commands run securely because the WinRM requires authentication and also encrypts the network traffic in both directions.

WinRM is both a service and a command-line interface for remote and local management of servers. The service implements the WS-Management protocol on Windows Server 2012. WS-Management is a standard web services protocol for management of software and hardware remotely.

In Windows Server 2012, the WinRM service establishes a Listener on the HTTP and HTTPS ports. It can coexist with Internet Information Services (IIS) and share the ports, but uses the /wsman URL to avoid conflicts. The IIS role does not have to be installed for this to work.

In most situations, WinRM will work out of the box, but in some situations the WinRM service must be configured to allow remote management of the target server, and the Windows Firewall must be configured to allow Windows Remote Management traffic inbound. The WinRM service can be configured through GPO or via the WinRM command line. To have the WinRM service listen on port 80 for all IP addresses on the server and to configure the Windows Firewall, execute the following commands on the target server:

1. Select Start, Run.
2. Enter the command **winrm quickconfig**.
3. Click OK to run the command.
4. Read the output from WinRM. Answer **y** to the prompt that asks, "Make These Changes [y/n]?"

Fans of PowerShell may recognize that the same task can be accomplished with the `Enable-PSRemoting` cmdlet.

Now the target server is ready to accept commands. For example, suppose an administrator is logged on to a server dc1.companyabc.com and needs to remotely execute a command on branch office server dc3.companyabc.com. These steps assume that WinRM has been configured and the firewall rule has been enabled. To remotely execute the command, follow these steps:

1. Open a command prompt on DC1.
2. Enter the command **winrs –r:http://dc3.companyabc.com ipconfig /all**.

The output of the command will be shown on the local server (DC1)—in this case, the IP configuration of the target server (DC3).

This is particularly useful when executing a command or a set of commands on numerous servers. Instead of having to log on to an RDP session on each server and execute the command, the command can be remotely executed in a batch file against all the target servers.

PowerShell

The powerful new command-line shell is now integrated into Windows Server 2012. PowerShell 3.0 is an administrator-focused shell and scripting language that has a consistent syntax that makes it easy to use. It operates on a cmdlet paradigm, which is, in effect, mini command-line tools. The syntax for the cmdlets is the same as for the PowerShell scripting language, reducing the learning curve of the administrator. In the Windows Server 2012, the PowerShell 3.0 allows for shells to run against remote systems. This enables administrators to execute cmdlets and scripts across the organization from a central console.

PowerShell can run its own scripts and cmdlets, as well as legacy scripts such as VBScript (.vbs), batch files (.bat), and Perl scripts (.perl). The shell can even run Windows-based command-line tools. Many of Microsoft's new applications, such as Microsoft Exchange 2010 and System Center Operations Manager 2007 R2, are integrated with PowerShell and add a host of cmdlets to help automate administration.

Print Management Console

The Print Management console enables administrators to manage printers across the enterprise from a single console. It shows the status of printers on the network. It also allows the control of those printers, such as the following:

- Pausing or resuming printing
- Canceling jobs
- Listing printers in Active Directory

- Deleting printers
- Managing printer drivers

Many of the operational controls support multiselecting printers so that the commands can be run against many printers at once.

The Print Management console is available as a standalone tool as part of the Print and Document Services role installation. It can also be installed on non-print servers as part of the RSAT tools.

The Print Management console supports printers running on a wide variety of OSs, including Windows Server 2012, Windows 7, Windows Server 2008, Windows Vista, Windows Server 2003, Windows XP, and even Windows 2000.

Common Practices for Securing and Managing Windows Server 2012

You can secure and manage a Windows Server 2012 environment with just a few practices. The first is to identify security risks to determine what the organization needs to be concerned about when applying a security policy. The second is that the organization can implement a tool such as Microsoft System Center Operations Manager to monitor the network and simplify management tasks on a day-to-day basis. And the third is to use maintenance practices to help keep the network environment stable and operational.

Identifying Security Risks

A network's security is only as good as the security mechanisms put into place and the review and identification process. Strong security entails employing Windows Server 2012 security measures, such as authentication, auditing, and authorization controls, but it also means that security information is properly and promptly reviewed. Information that can be reviewed includes Event Viewer logs, service-specific logs, application logs, and performance data.

All the security information for Windows Server 2012 can be logged, but without a formal review and identification process the information is useless. Also, security-related information can be complex and unwieldy depending on what information is being recorded. For this reason, manually reviewing the security information might be tedious, but it can prevent system or network compromise.

The formal review and identification process should be performed daily. Any identified activity that is suspicious or could be potentially risky should be reported and dealt with appropriately. For instance, an administrator reviewing a particular security log might run across some data that might alert him of suspicious activity. This incident would then be reported to the security administrator to take the appropriate action. Whatever the course of action might be in the organization, there should be points of escalation and remediation.

Using System Center Operations Manager 2012 to Simplify Management

Many of the recommendations in this chapter focus on reviewing event logs, monitoring the configuration, and monitoring the operations of the Windows Server 2012 system. This can be difficult to do for an administrator on a daily basis and the problem is proportional to the number of servers that an administrator is responsible for. Microsoft has developed a product to make these tasks easier and more manageable, namely System Center Operations Manager 2012.

System Center Operations Manager 2012 is an enterprise-class monitoring and management solution for Windows environments. It is designed to simplify Windows management by consolidating events, performance data, alerts, and more into a centralized repository. Reports on this information can then be tailored depending on the environment and on the level of detail that is needed and extrapolated. This information can assist administrators and decision makers in proactively addressing Windows Server 2012 operation and any problems that exist or might occur.

Many other intrinsic benefits are gained by using System Center Operation Manager 2012, including the following:

- Event log monitoring and consolidation
- Monitoring of various applications, including those provided by third parties
- Enhanced alerting capabilities
- Assistance with capacity-planning efforts
- A customizable knowledge base of Microsoft product knowledge and best practices
- Web-based interfaces for reporting and monitoring

See Chapter 23, "Integrating System Center Operations Manager 2012 with Windows Server 2012," for more details on System Center Operations Manager 2012.

Leveraging Windows Server 2012 Maintenance Practices

Administrators face the often-daunting task of maintaining the Windows Server 2012 environment in the midst of daily administration and firefighting. Little time is spent identifying and then organizing maintenance processes and procedures.

To decrease the number of administrative inefficiencies and the amount of firefighting an administrator must go through, it is important to identify those tasks that are important to the system's overall health and security. After they have been identified, routines should be set to ensure that the Windows Server 2012 environment is stable and reliable. Many of the maintenance processes and procedures described in the following sections are the most opportune areas to maintain.

Keeping Up with Service Packs and Updates

Service packs (SPs) and updates for both the OS and applications are vital parts to maintaining availability, reliability, performance, and security. Microsoft packages these updates into SPs or individually.

An administrator can update a system with the latest SP or update in several ways: Automatic Windows Updates, DVD, manually entered commands, or Microsoft Windows Server Update Services (WSUS).

NOTE

Thoroughly test and evaluate SPs and updates in a lab environment before installing them on production servers and client machines. Also, install the appropriate SPs and updates on each production server and client machine to keep all systems consistent.

Manual Update or DVD Update

Manual updating is typically done when applying service packs, rather than hotfixes. SPs tend to be significantly larger than updates or hotfixes, so many administrators download the service pack once and then apply it manually to their servers, or the SP can be obtained on DVD.

When an SP DVD is inserted into the drive of the server, it usually launches an interface to install the SP.

In the case of downloaded SPs or of DVD-based SPs, the SP can also be applied manually via a command line. This allows greater control over the install (see Table 20.9), such as by preventing a reboot or to not back up files to conserve space.

TABLE 20.9 Update.exe Command-Line Parameters

Parameter	Description
`/Quiet`	Quiet Mode (no user interaction or display)
`/Unattend`	Unattended mode (progress bar only)
`/NoDialog`	Hide the installation result dialog after commpletion
`/NoRestart`	Do not restart when installation is complete
`-/ForceRestart`	Restart after installation
`-/WarnRestart[:<seconds>]`	Warn and restart automatically if required (default timeout 30 seconds)
`/PromptRestart`	Prompt if restart is required

20

Automatic Updates

Windows Server 2012 can be configured to download and install updates automatically using Automatic Windows Updates. With this option enabled, Windows Server 2012 checks for updates, downloads them, and applies them automatically on a schedule. The administrator can just have the updates downloaded, but not installed, to give the administrator more control over when they are installed. Windows Update can also download and install recommended updates, which is new for Windows Server 2012.

When the Windows Server 2012 OS is installed, Windows Update is not configured and, the Server Manager Security Information section shows the Windows Update as Not Configured. This can be an insecure configuration, as security updates will not be applied.

You can configure Windows Updates as follows:

1. Launch Control Panel.
2. Click the System and Security link.
3. Click Windows Update.
4. Click Change Settings.
5. Select Install Updates Automatically (recommended) and click OK.

The Windows Updates status will change to You're Set to Automatically Install Updates.

The configuration of Windows Update can be reviewed by clicking the Windows Updates link again. The Windows Update console appears (see Figure 20.10). The figure shows that updates will be installed automatically at 3 a.m. every day. The console also shows when updates were checked for last. In the console, the administrator can also do the following:

- Manually check for updates
- Change the Windows Updates settings
- View the update history
- See installed updates
- Get updates for more products

The link to get updates for more products allows the administrator to check for updates not just for the Windows Server 2012 platform, but for other products, as well, such as Microsoft Exchange and Microsoft SQL. Clicking the link launches a web page to authorize the server to check for the broader range of updates.

Clicking the Change Settings link allows the Windows Update setting to be changed. The Change Settings window, shown in Figure 20.11, enables the administrator to adjust the time of installs, to install or just download, and to configure whether to install recommended updates.

The Windows Updates functionality is a great tool for keeping servers updated with very little administrative overhead, albeit with some loss of control because it is difficult to centrally manage and it lacks any form on consolidated reporting on results.

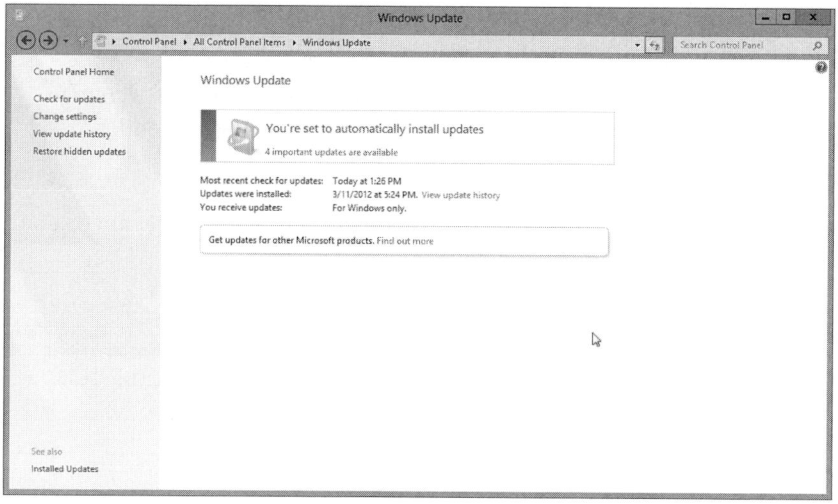

FIGURE 20.10 Windows Update console.

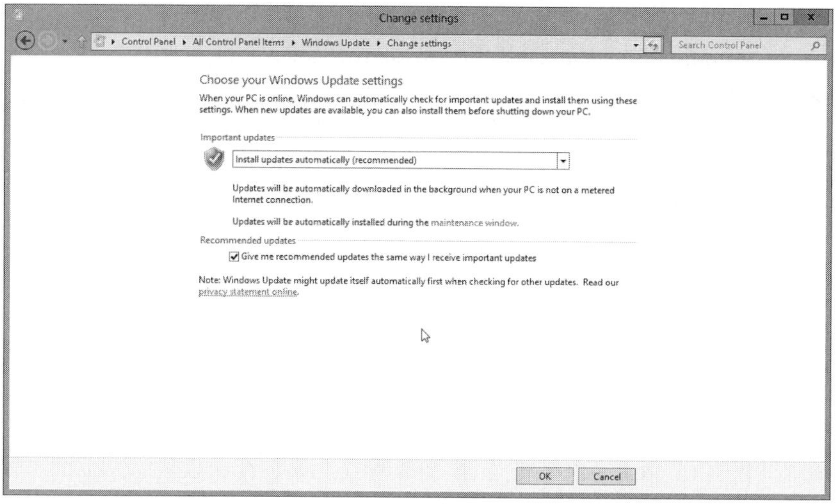

FIGURE 20.11 Windows Update console.

Windows Server Update Services

Realizing the increased administration and management efforts administrators must face when using Windows Update to keep up with SPs and updates for anything other than small environments, Microsoft has created the Windows Server Update Services (WSUS) client and server versions to minimize administration, management, and maintenance of middle- to large-size organizations. WSUS 3.0 SP1 communicates directly and securely with Microsoft to gather the latest SPs and updates.

Microsoft Windows Server Update Services provides a number of features to support organizations, such as the following:

- Support for a broad range of products, such as the Windows OS family, Exchange messaging, SQL Server, Office, System Center family, and Windows Defender.
- Automatic download of updates.
- Administrative control over which updates are approved, removed, or declined. The Remove option permits updates to be rolled back.
- Email notification of updates and deployment status reports.
- Targeting of updates to specific groups of computers for testing and for control of the update process.
- Scalability to multiple WSUS servers controlled from a single console.
- Reporting on all aspects of the WSUS operations and status.
- Integration with Automatic Windows Updates.

The SPs and updates downloaded onto WSUS can then be distributed to either a lab server for testing (recommended) or to a production server for distribution. After these updates are tested, WSUS can automatically update systems inside the network.

The following steps install the Windows Server Update Services role:

1. Open the Server Manager console.
2. Click Add Roles or Features.
3. Click Next.
4. Select Role-Based or Feature-Based Installation and click Next.
5. Select the server to receive the WSUS role and click Next.
6. Select the Windows Software Update Service role and click Add Features to accept the related features, and then click Next.
7. Click Next to skip past the features, and then click Next to accept the IIS installation.
8. Review the role services, and then click Next.
9. Review the WSUS requirements, and then click Next.
10. Review the role services, and then click Next.
11. Select a Content location for WSUS downloads, and then click Next.
12. Review the summary, optionally select Restart the Destination Server Automatically If Required, and click Install.
13. Close the Add Roles and Features Wizard.

Unlike other server roles, the binaries for WSUS are downloaded from Microsoft. This ensures that any time WSUS is installed you will always be installing the most current version.

Maintaining Windows Server 2012

Maintaining Windows Server 2012 systems is not an easy task for administrators. They must find time in their firefighting efforts to focus and plan for maintenance on the server systems. When maintenance tasks are commonplace in an environment, they can alleviate many of the common firefighting tasks.

The processes and procedures for maintaining Windows Server 2012 systems can be separated based on the appropriate time to maintain a particular aspect of Windows Server 2012. Some maintenance procedures require daily attention, whereas others might require only quarterly checkups. The maintenance processes and procedures that an organization follows depend strictly on the organization. However, the categories described in the following sections and their corresponding procedures are best practices for organizations of all sizes and varying IT infrastructures.

Daily Maintenance

Certain maintenance procedures require more attention than others. The procedures that require the most attention are categorized into the daily procedures. Therefore, it is recommended that an administrator take on these procedures each day to ensure system reliability, availability, performance, and security. These procedures are examined in the following three sections.

Checking Overall Server Functionality

Although checking the overall server health and functionality might seem redundant or elementary, this procedure is critical to keeping the system environment and users working productively.

Questions that should be addressed during the checking and verification process including the following:

- Can users access data on file servers?
- Are printers printing properly? Are there long queues for certain printers?
- Is there an exceptionally long wait to log on (that is, longer than normal)?
- Can users access messaging systems?
- Can users access external resources?

Verifying That Backups Are Successful

To provide a secure and fault-tolerant organization, it is imperative that a successful backup be performed each night. In the event of a server failure, the administrator might be required to perform a restore from tape. Without a backup each night, the IT organization is forced to rely on rebuilding the server without the data. Therefore, the administrator should always back up servers so that the IT organization can restore them with minimum downtime in the event of a disaster. Because of the importance of the backups, the first priority of the administrator each day needs to be verifying and maintaining the backup sets.

If disaster ever strikes, the administrators want to be confident that a system or entire site can be recovered as quickly as possible. Successful backup mechanisms are imperative to the recovery operation; recoveries are only as good as the most recent backups.

Monitoring Event Viewer

Event Viewer is used to check the system, security, application, and other logs on a local or remote system. These logs are an invaluable source of information about the system. The Event Viewer Overview and Summary page in Server Manager is shown in Figure 20.12.

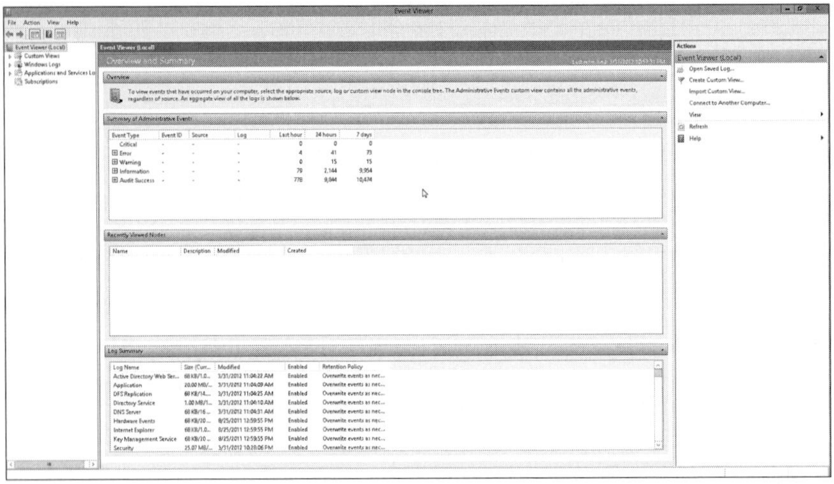

FIGURE 20.12 The Event Viewer snap-in.

> **NOTE**
>
> Checking these logs often helps your understanding of them. There are some events that constantly appear but are not significant. Events will begin to look familiar, so you will notice when something is new or amiss in your event logs.

All Event Viewer events are categorized either as informational, warning, or error. Best practices for monitoring event logs include the following:

- Understanding the events that are being reported
- Setting up a database for archived event logs
- Archiving event logs frequently

To simplify monitoring hundreds or thousands of generated events each day, the administrator should use the filtering mechanism provided in Event Viewer. Although warnings and errors should take priority, the informational events should be reviewed to track what was happening before the problem occurred. After the administrator reviews the informational events, she can filter out the informational events and view only the warnings and errors.

To filter events, follow these steps:

1. Launch Server Manager.
2. Click All Servers
3. Right-click the server whose Event Viewer you want to view and click Computer Management.
4. Expand the Event View folder in Computer Management.
5. Select the log from which you want to filter events.
6. Right-click the log and select Filter Current Log.
7. In the log properties window, select the types of events to filter. In this case, check the Critical, Error, and Warning check boxes.
8. Click OK when you have finished.

Figure 20.13 shows the results of filtering on the system log. You can see in the figure that there are a total of 17,941 events. In the message above the log, the filter is noted and also the resulting number of events. The filter reduced the events by a factor of almost 9,000 to 1. This really helps reduce the volume of data that an administrator needs to review.

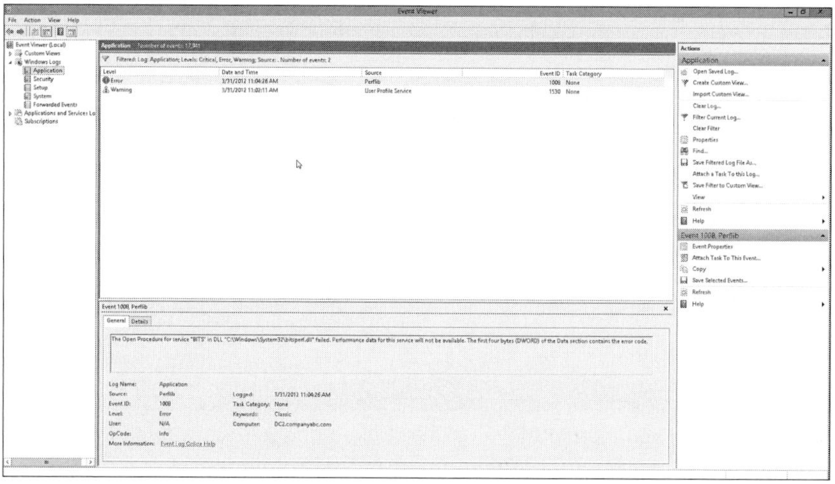

FIGURE 20.13 The Event Viewer filter.

Some warnings and errors are normal because of bandwidth constraints or other environmental issues. The more you monitor the logs, the more familiar you will become with the messages and therefore the more likely you will be able to spot a problem before it affects the user community.

TIP

You might need to increase the size of the log files in Event Viewer to accommodate an increase in logging activity. The default log sizes are larger in Windows Server 2012 than in earlier versions of Windows, which were notorious for running out of space.

Weekly Maintenance

Maintenance procedures that require slightly less attention than daily checking are categorized in a weekly routine and are examined in the following sections.

Checking Disk Space

Disk space is a precious commodity. Although the disk capacity of a Windows Server 2012 system can be almost endless, the amount of free space on all drives should be checked at least weekly if not more frequently. Serious problems can occur if there is not enough disk space.

One of the most common disk space problems occurs on data drives where end users save and modify information. Other volumes such as the system drive and partitions with logging data can also quickly fill up.

As mentioned earlier, lack of free disk space can cause a multitude of problems, including the following:

- Application failures
- System crashes
- Unsuccessful backup jobs
- Service failures
- The inability to audit
- Degradation in performance

To prevent these problems from occurring, administrators should keep the amount of free space to at least 25%.

CAUTION

If you need to free disk space, you should move or delete files and folders with caution. System files are automatically protected by Windows Server 2012, but data is not.

Verifying Hardware

Hardware components supported by Windows Server 2012 are reliable, but this does not mean that they will always run continuously without failure. Hardware availability is measured in terms of mean time between failures (MTBF) and mean time to repair (MTTR). This includes downtime for both planned and unplanned events. These measurements provided by the manufacturer are good guidelines to follow; however, mechanical parts are bound to fail at one time or another. So, hardware should be monitored weekly to ensure efficient operation.

You can monitor hardware in many different ways. For example, server systems might have internal checks and logging functionality to warn against possible failure, Windows Server 2012's System Monitor might bring light to a hardware failure, and a physical hardware check can help to determine whether the system is about to experience a problem with the hardware.

If a failure has occurred or is about to occur, having an inventory of spare hardware can significantly improve the chances and timing of recoverability. Checking system hardware on a weekly basis provides the opportunity to correct the issue before it becomes a problem.

Running Disk Defragmenter

Whenever files are created, deleted, or modified, Windows Server 2012 assigns a group of clusters depending on the size of the file. As file size requirements fluctuate over time, so does the number of groups of clusters assigned to the file. Even though this process is efficient when using NTFS, the files and volumes become fragmented because the file does not reside in a contiguous location on the disk.

As fragmentation levels increase, disk access slows. The system must take additional resources and time to find all the cluster groups to use the file. To minimize the amount of fragmentation and give performance a boost, the administrator should use the Disk Defragmenter to defragment all volumes. As mentioned earlier in this chapter, the Disk Defragmenter is a built-in utility that can analyze and defragment volume fragmentation. Fragmentation negatively affects performance because files aren't efficiently read from disk. There is a command-line version of the tool and a GUI version of the tool.

To use the GUI version of the Disk Defragmenter, follow these steps:

1. Start Disk Defragmenter by running `dfrgui` from a command prompt or from the PowerShell prompt.

   The tool automatically analyzes all the drives and suggests whether to defragment. This only happens if disk defragmentation is not scheduled to run automatically.

2. Select the volumes to defragment.
3. Click Optimize to defragment immediately.
4. The defragmentation runs independently of the Disk Defragmenter GUI, so you can exit the tool while the defragmentation is running by clicking Close.

Unlike earlier versions of the software, the Windows Server 2012 Disk Defragmenter does not show a graphical view of the Disk Defragmenter.

The Disk Defragmenter also enables the administrator to set up a schedule for the backup. This modifies the ScheduledDefrag task in the Task Scheduler (located in Task Scheduler\Task Scheduler Library\Microsoft\Windows\Defrag\). After you select the Run on a Schedule option, you can set the schedule by clicking the Modify Schedule button and select the volumes to be defragmented by clicking the Select Volumes button. New volumes will automatically be defragmented by the task.

Running the Domain Controller Diagnosis Utility

The Domain Controller Diagnosis (DCDIAG) utility is installed with the Active Directory Domain Services roles in Windows Server 2012 and is used to analyze the state of a domain controller (DC) and the domain services. It runs a series of tests, analyzes the state of the DC, and verifies different areas of the system, such as the following:

- Connectivity
- Replication
- Topology integrity
- Security descriptors
- Netlogon rights
- Intersite health
- Roles
- Trust verification

DCDIAG should be run on each DC on a weekly basis or as problems arise. DCDIAG's syntax is as follows:

```
dcdiag.exe /s:<Directory Server>[:<LDAP Port>] [/u:<Domain>\<Username>
/p:*|<Password>|""]
[/hqv] [/n:<Naming Context>] [/f:<Log>] [/x:XMLLog.xml]
[/skip:<Test>] [/test:<Test>]
```

Parameters for this utility are as follows:

- **/h**—Display this help screen.
- **/s**—Use `<Domain Controller>` as the home server. This is ignored for `DCPromo` and `RegisterInDNS` tests, which can only be run locally.
- **/n**—Use `<Naming Context>` as the naming context to test. Domains can be specified in NetBIOS, DNS, or distinguished name (DN) format.
- **/u**—Use domain\username credentials for binding with a password. Must also use the `/p` option.

- **/p**—Use `<Password>` as the password. Must also use the `/u` option.
- **/a**—Test all the servers in this site.
- **/e**—Test all the servers in the entire enterprise. This parameter overrides the `/a` parameter.
- **/q**—Quiet; print only error messages.
- **/v**—Verbose; print extended information.
- **/i**—Ignore; ignore superfluous error messages.
- **/fix**—Fix; make safe repairs.
- **/f**—Redirect all output to a file `<Log>`; `/ferr` redirects error output separately.
- **/c**—Comprehensive; run all tests, including nondefault tests but excluding DCPromo and RegisterInDNS. Can use with `/skip`.
- **/skip:<Test>**—Skip the named test. Do not use in a command with `/test`.
- **/test:<Test>**—Test only the specified test. Required tests will still be run. Do not use with the `/skip` parameter.
- **/x:<XMLLog.xml>**—Redirect XML output to `<XMLLog.xml>`. Currently works with the `/test:dns` option only.
- **/xsl:<xslfile.xsl or xsltfile.xslt>**—Add the processing instructions that reference a specified style sheet. Works with the `/test:dns /x:<XMLLog.xml>` option only.

The command supports a variety of tests, which can be selected. Some tests are run by default and others need to be requested specifically. The command line supports selecting tests explicitly (`/test`) and skipping tests (`/skip`). Table 20.10 shows valid tests that can be run consistently.

TABLE 20.10 DCDIAG Tests

Test Name	Description
Advertising	Checks whether each DC is advertising itself and whether it is advertising itself as having the capabilities of a DC.
CheckSDRefDom	Checks that all application directory partitions have appropriate security descriptor reference domains.
CheckSecurityError	Locates security errors and performs the initial diagnosis of the problem. This test is not run by default and has to be requested with the `/test` option.
Connectivity	Tests whether DCs are DNS registered, pingable, and have LDAP/RPC connectivity. This is a required test and cannot be skipped with the `/skip` option.

TABLE 20.10 Continued

Test Name	Description
CrossRefValidation	This test looks for cross-references that are in some way invalid.
CutoffServers	Checks for servers that will not receive replications because their partners are down. This test is not run by default and has to be requested with the `/test` option.
DCPromo	Tests the existing DNS infrastructure for promotion to the domain controller.
DNS	Checks the health of DNS settings for the whole enterprise. This test is not run by default and has to be requested with the `/test` option.
FrsEvent	Checks to see if there are any operation errors in the file replication server (FRS). Failing replication of the SYSVOL share can cause policy problems.
DFSREvent	Checks to see if there are any operation errors in the DFS.
LocatorCheck	Checks that global role holders are known, can be located, and are responding.
Intersite	Checks for failures that would prevent or temporarily hold up intersite replication.
Kccevent	Checks that the Knowledge Consistency Checker is completing without errors.
KnowsOfRoleHolders	Checks whether the DC thinks it knows the role holders of the five FSMO roles.
MachineAccount	Checks to see whether the machine account has the proper information. Use the `/RecreateMachineAccount` parameter to attempt a repair if the local machine account is missing. Use `/FixMachineAccount` if the machine's account flags are incorrect.
NCSecDesc	Checks that the security descriptors on the naming context heads have appropriate permissions for replication.
NetLogons	Checks that the appropriate logon privileges allow replication to proceed.
ObjectsReplicated	Checks that machine account and DSA objects have replicated. You can use `/objectdn:<dn>` with `/n:<nc>` to specify an additional object to check.
OutboundSecureChannels	Verifies that secure channels exist from all the DCs in the domain to the domains specified by `/testdomain`. The `/nositerestriction` parameter prevents the test from being limited to the DCs in the site. This test is not run by default and has to be requested with the `/test` option.

TABLE 20.10 Continued

Test Name	Description
RegisterInDNS	Tests whether this domain controller can register the Domain Controller Locator DNS records. These records must be present in DNS for other computers to locate this domain controller for the <Active_Directory_Domain_DNS_Name> domain. Reports whether any modifications to the existing DNS infrastructure are required. Requires the /DnsDomain:<Active_Directory_Domain_DNS_Name> argument.
Replications	Checks for timely replication between domain controllers.
RidManager	Checks to see whether RID master is accessible and whether it contains the proper information.
Services	Checks to see whether DC services are running on a system.
Systemlog	Checks that the system is running without errors.
Topology	Checks that the generated topology is fully connected for all DCs. This test is not run by default and has to be requested with the /test option.
VerifyEnterpriseReferences	Verifies that certain system references are intact for the FRS and replication infrastructure across all objects in the enterprise. This test is not run by default and has to be requested with the /test option.
VerifyReferences	Verifies that certain system references are intact for the FRS and replication infrastructure.
VerifyReplicas	Verifies that all application directory partitions are fully instantiated on all replica servers. This test is not run by default and has to be requested with the /test option.

Monthly Maintenance

It is recommended that you perform the tasks examined in the following sections on a monthly basis.

Maintaining File System Integrity

CHKDSK scans for file system integrity and can check for lost clusters, cross-linked files, and more. If Windows Server 2012 senses a problem, it will run CHKDSK automatically at startup.

Administrators can maintain FAT, FAT32, NTFS, and ReFS file system integrity by running CHKDSK once a month. To run CHKDSK, follow these steps:

1. At the command prompt, change to the partition that you want to check.
2. Enter **chkdsk** without any parameters to check only for file system errors. No changes will be made.

3. If any errors are found, run the CHKDSK utility with the `/f` parameter to attempt to correct the errors found.

Testing the UPS

You can use an uninterruptible power supply (UPS) to protect the system or group of systems from power failures (such as spikes and surges) and keep the system running long enough after a power outage so that an administrator can gracefully shut down the system. It is recommended that an administrator follow the UPS guidelines provided by the manufacturer at least once a month. Also, monthly scheduled battery tests should be performed.

Validating Backups

Once a month, an administrator should validate backups by restoring the backups to a server located in a lab environment. This is in addition to verifying that backups were successful from log files or the backup program's management interface. A restore gives the administrator the opportunity to verify the backups and to practice the restore procedures that would be used when recovering the server during a real disaster. In addition, this procedure tests the state of the backup media to ensure that they are in working order and builds administrator confidence for recovering from a true disaster.

Updating Documentation

An integral part of managing and maintaining any IT environment is to document the network infrastructure and procedures. The following are just a few of the documents you should consider having on hand:

- Server build guides
- Disaster recovery guides and procedures
- Checklists
- Configuration settings
- Change configuration logs
- Historical performance data
- Special user rights assignments
- Special application settings

As systems and services are built and procedures are ascertained, document these facts to reduce learning curves, administration, and maintenance.

It is not only important to adequately document the IT environment, but it is also often even more important to keep those documents up-to-date. Otherwise, documents can quickly become outdated as the environment, processes, and procedures change as the business changes.

Quarterly Maintenance

As the name implies, quarterly maintenance is performed four times a year. Areas to maintain and manage on a quarterly basis are typically fairly self-sufficient and self-sustaining. Infrequent maintenance is required to keep the system healthy. This does not mean, however, that the tasks are simple or that they are not as critical as those tasks that require more frequent maintenance.

Checking Storage Limits

Storage capacity on all volumes should be checked to ensure that all volumes have ample free space. Keep approximately 25% free space on all volumes.

Running low or completely out of disk space creates unnecessary risk for any system. Services can fail, applications can stop responding, and systems can even crash if there isn't plenty of disk space.

Changing Administrator Passwords

Administrator passwords should, at a minimum, be changed every quarter (90 days). Changing these passwords strengthens security measures so that systems cannot easily be compromised. In addition to changing passwords, other password requirements such as password age, history, length, and strength should be reviewed.

Summary

Although administrators can easily get caught up in daily administration and firefighting, it is important to structure system management and maintenance of Windows Server 2012 to help prevent unnecessary amounts of effort. Windows Server 2012 provides many tools, such as the server roles and Server Manager, to enable administrators to more effectively manage their servers.

Server Manager is a one-stop shop for the management and monitoring of most of the functions of a Windows Server 2012 server. The OS automatically adds the appropriate snap-ins to manage the features and the roles that are installed on the server as they are installed. This makes it the home base for administrators and simplifies their tasks by placing the tools and techniques in a single location.

Systems management and maintenance is not just about the cool technologies, but also about how those technologies are used. Following a management and maintenance regimen reduces administration, maintenance, and business expenses, while at the same time increasing reliability, stability, and security.

Best Practices

The following are best practices from this chapter:

- Use System Manager as the central point of administration for Windows Server 2012 servers.
- Manage servers based on their roles by placing them into convenient groups.

- Try to maintain the network environment's systems periodically to avoid any inefficiency.
- Audit not only to identify security breaches or suspicious activity, but also to gain insight into how the network, network devices, and systems are accessed.
- Enable audit policies through the local system policy or group policy objects.
- Remotely manage systems using Role and Feature tools, Remote Desktop for Administration, scripting, Windows Remote Management, and command-line utilities.
- Use System Center Operations Manager 2007/2012 to proactively manage Windows Server 2012.
- Identify tasks that are important to the system's overall health and security.
- Install the appropriate service packs and updates on each production server and client machine to keep all systems consistent.
- Thoroughly test and evaluate service packs and updates in a lab environment before installing them on production servers.
- Use Windows Software Update Services to minimize administration, management, and maintenance associated with keeping up with the latest service packs and updates.
- Distribute the service packs and hotfixes downloaded from WSUS to a lab server for testing.
- Categorize and document daily maintenance activities, such as checking server functionality, verifying that backups were successful, and monitoring Event Viewer events.
- Categorize and document weekly maintenance processes and procedures, such as checking disk space, verifying hardware operation, archiving event logs, defragmenting volumes, and diagnosing domain controllers with DCDIAG.
- Categorize and document monthly maintenance processes and procedures, such as maintaining file system integrity, testing UPS functionality, validating backups, and updating documentation.
- Use the data collector sets and reports to analyze server performance and pinpoint problems and resource issues.
- Categorize and document quarterly maintenance processes and procedures, such as checking storage limits and changing administrative passwords.

CHAPTER 21

Automating Tasks Using PowerShell Scripting

IN THIS CHAPTER

- Understanding Shells
- Introduction to PowerShell
- Understanding PowerShell Fundamentals
- Using Windows PowerShell
- PowerShell Integrated Scripting Environment
- Windows Server 2012 Commandlets

Shells are a necessity in using operating systems. They give the ability to execute arbitrary commands as a user and the ability to traverse the file system. Anybody who has used a computer has dealt with a shell by either typing commands at a prompt or clicking an icon to start a word processing application. A shell is something that every user uses in some fashion. It's inescapable in whatever form when working on a computer system.

Until recently, Windows users and administrators primarily have used the Windows Explorer or command prompt (both are shells) to interact with most versions of the Window operating systems. With Microsoft's release of PowerShell, both a new shell and scripting language, the current standard for interacting with and managing Windows is rapidly changing. This change became very evident with the release of Microsoft Exchange Server 2007, which used PowerShell as its management backbone (often providing functions the GUI didn't), the addition of PowerShell as a feature within Windows Server 2008, and now the inclusion of PowerShell as part of the Windows 8 and Windows Server 2012 operating systems.

In this chapter, we take a closer look at what shells are and how they have developed. Next, we review Microsoft's past attempts at providing an automation interface (Windows Script Host [WSH]), and then introduce PowerShell. From there, we step into understanding the PowerShell features and how to use it to manage Windows 2012. Finally, we review some best practices for using PowerShell.

Understanding Shells

A shell is an interface that enables users to interact with the operating system. A shell isn't considered an application because of its inescapable nature, but it's the same as any other process running on a system. The difference between a shell and an application is that a shell's purpose is to enable users to run other applications. In some operating systems (such as UNIX, Linux, and VMS), the shell is a command-line interface (CLI); in other operating systems (such as Windows and Mac OS X), the shell is typically a graphical user interface (GUI).

Both CLI and GUI shells have benefits and drawbacks. For example, most CLI shells allow powerful command chaining (using commands that feed their output into other commands for further processing; this is commonly referred to as the pipeline). GUI shells, however, require commands to be completely self-contained. Furthermore, most GUI shells are easy to navigate, whereas CLI shells require a preexisting knowledge of the system to avoid attempting several commands to discern the location and direction to head in when completing an automation task. Therefore, choosing which shell to use depends on your comfort level and what's best suited to perform the task at hand.

NOTE

Even though GUI shells exist, the term *shell* is used almost exclusively to describe a command-line environment, not a task that is performed with a GUI application, such as Windows Explorer. Likewise, shell scripting refers to collecting commands normally entered on the command line or into an executable file.

A Short History of Shells

The first shell in wide use was the Bourne shell, the standard user interface for the UNIX operating system; UNIX systems still require it for booting. This robust shell provided pipelines and conditional and recursive command execution. It was developed by C programmers for C programmers.

Oddly, however, despite being written by and for C programmers, the Bourne shell didn't have a C-like coding style. This lack of similarity to the C language drove the invention of the C shell, which introduced more C-like programming structures. While the C shell inventors were building a better mousetrap, they decided to add command-line editing and command aliasing (defining command shortcuts), which eased the bane of every UNIX user's existence: typing. The less a UNIX user has to type to get results, the better.

Although most UNIX users liked the C shell, learning a completely new shell was a challenge for some. So, the Korn shell was invented, which added a number of the C shell features to the Bourne shell. Because the Korn shell is a commercially licensed product, the open source software movement needed a shell for Linux and FreeBSD. The collaborative result was the Bourne Again shell, or Bash, invented by the Free Software Foundation.

Throughout the evolution of UNIX and the birth of Linux and FreeBSD, other operating systems were introduced along with their own shells. Digital Equipment Corporation (DEC) introduced Virtual Memory System (VMS) to compete with UNIX on its VAX systems. VMS had a shell called Digital Command Language (DCL) with a verbose syntax, unlike that of its UNIX counterparts. Also, unlike its UNIX counterparts, it wasn't case sensitive, nor did it provide pipelines.

Somewhere along the way, the PC was born. IBM took the PC to the business market, and Apple rebranded roughly the same hardware technology and focused on consumers. Microsoft made DOS run on the IBM PC, acting as both kernel and shell and including some features of other shells. (The pipeline syntax was inspired by UNIX shells.)

Following DOS was Windows, which went from application to operating system quickly. Windows introduced a GUI shell, which has become the basis for Microsoft shells ever since. Unfortunately, GUI shells are notoriously difficult to script, so Windows provided a DOSShell-like environment. It was improved with a new executable, cmd.exe instead of command.com, and a more robust set of command-line editing features. Regrettably, this change also meant that shell scripts in Windows had to be written in the DOSShell syntax for collecting and executing command groupings.

Over time, Microsoft realized its folly and decided systems administrators should have better ways to manage Windows systems. Windows Script Host (WSH) was introduced in Windows 98, providing a native scripting solution with access to the underpinnings of Windows. It was a library that allowed scripting languages to use Windows in a powerful and efficient manner. WSH is not its own language, however, so a WSH-compliant scripting language was required to take advantage of it, such as JScript, VBScript, Perl, Python, Kixstart, or Object REXX. Some of these languages are quite powerful in performing complex processing, so WSH seemed like a blessing to Windows systems administrators.

However, the rejoicing was short-lived because there was no guarantee that the WSH-compliant scripting language you chose would be readily available or a viable option for everyone. The lack of a standard language and environment for writing scripts made it difficult for users and administrators to incorporate automation by using WSH. The only way to be sure the scripting language or WSH version would be compatible on the system being managed was to use a native scripting language, which meant using DOSShell and enduring the problems that accompanied it. In addition, WSH opened a large attack vector for malicious code to run on Windows systems. This vulnerability gave rise to a stream of viruses, worms, and other malicious programs that have wreaked havoc on computer systems, thanks to WSH's focus on automation without user intervention.

The end result was that systems administrators viewed WSH as both a blessing and a curse. Although WSH presented a good object model and access to a number of automation interfaces, it wasn't a shell. It required using Wscript.exe and Cscript.exe, scripts had to be written in a compatible scripting language, and its attack vulnerabilities posed a security challenge. Clearly, a different approach was needed for systems management; over time, Microsoft reached the same conclusion.

Introduction to PowerShell

The introduction of WSH as a standard in the Windows operating system offered a robust alternative to DOSShell scripting. Unfortunately, WSH presented a number of challenges, discussed in the preceding section. Furthermore, WSH didn't offer the CLI shell experience that UNIX and Linux administrators had enjoyed for years, resulting in Windows administrators being made fun of by the other chaps for the lack of a CLI shell and its benefits.

Luckily, Jeffrey Snover (the architect of PowerShell) and others on the PowerShell team realized that Windows needed a strong, secure, and robust CLI shell for systems management. Enter PowerShell. PowerShell was designed as a shell with full access to the underpinnings of Windows via the .NET Framework, Component Object Model (COM) objects, and other methods. It also provided an execution environment that's familiar, easy, and secure. PowerShell is aptly named, as it puts the power into the Windows shell. For users wanting to automate their Windows systems, the introduction of PowerShell was exciting because it combined "the power of WSH with the warm-fuzzy familiarity of a CLI shell."

PowerShell provides a powerful native scripting language, so scripts can be ported to all Windows systems without worrying about whether a particular language interpreter is installed. In the past, an administrator might have gone through the rigmarole of scripting a solution with WSH in Perl, Python, VBScript, JScript, or another language, only to find that the next system that they worked on didn't have that interpreter installed. At home, users can put whatever they want on their systems and maintain them however they see fit, but in a workplace, that option isn't always viable. PowerShell solves that problem by removing the need for nonnative interpreters. It also solves the problem of wading through websites to find command-line equivalents for simple GUI shell operations and coding them into .cmd files. Last, PowerShell addresses the WSH security problem by providing a platform for secure Windows scripting. It focuses on security features such as script signing, lack of executable extensions, and execution policies (which are restricted by default).

For anyone who needs to automate administration tasks on a Windows system or a Microsoft platform, PowerShell provides a much-needed injection of power. As such, for Windows systems administrators or scripters, becoming a PowerShell expert is highly recommended. After all, PowerShell can now be used to efficiently automate management tasks for Windows, Active Directory, Terminal Services, SQL Server, Exchange Server, Internet Information Services (IIS), and even a number of different third-party products.

As such, PowerShell is the approach Microsoft had been seeking as the automation and management interface for their products. Thus, PowerShell is now the endorsed solution for the management of Windows-based systems and server products. Over time, PowerShell could even possibly replace the current management interfaces, such as cmd.exe, WSH, CLI tools, and so on, while becoming even further integrated into the Windows operating system. The trend toward this direction can be seen with the release of Windows Server 2008 R2 and Windows 7, in which PowerShell is part of the operating system.

PowerShell Uses

In Windows, an administrator can complete a number of tasks using PowerShell. The following list is a sampling of these tasks:

- **Manage the file system**—To create, delete, modify, and set permissions for files and folders.
- **Manage services**—To list, stop, start, restart, and even modify services.
- **Manage processes**—To list (monitor), stop, and start processes.
- **Manage the Registry**—To list (monitor), stop, and start processes.
- **Use Windows Management Instrumentation (WMI)**—To manage not only Windows, but also other platforms such as IIS and Terminal Services.
- **Use existing Component Object Model (COM) objects**—To complete a wide range of automation tasks.
- **Manage a number of Windows roles and features**—To add or remove roles and features.
- **Perform administrative tasks**—To perform tasks ranging from resetting passwords to adding DNS entries to modifying virtual machines.

PowerShell Features

PowerShell is a departure from the current management interfaces in Windows. As such, it has been built from the ground up to include a number of features that make CLI and script-based administration easier. Some of PowerShell's more key features are as follows:

- It has thousands of command-line tools (referred to as cmdlets).
- The scripting language is designed to be readable and easy to use.
- PowerShell supports existing scripts, command-line tools, and automation interfaces, such as WMI, ADSI, .NET Framework, ActiveX Data Objects (ADO), and so on.
- It follows a strict naming convention for commands based on a verb-noun format.
- It supports a number of different Windows operating systems ranging from Windows XP SP2 or later and Windows Server 2003 SP1 or later through Windows 8 and Windows Server 2012.
- It provides direct "access to and navigation of" the Windows Registry, certificate store, and file system using a common set of commands.
- PowerShell is object based, which allows data (objects) to be piped between commands.
- It is extensible, which allows third parties (as noted earlier) to build upon and extend PowerShell's already rich interfaces for managing Windows and other Microsoft platforms.

What's New in PowerShell 3.0

PowerShell 3.0 offers several new features and improvement for administrators, including the following:

- **Workflows**—Based on Windows Workflow Foundation, PowerShell workflows allow long running activities to perform larger and more complex management tasks, such as provisioning multiple systems at a time.
- **More robust sessions**—PowerShell 3.0 sessions are able to recover automatically from network failures or other interruptions. One can even disconnect a session, shut down the computer and reconnect from a different computer with the original task uninterrupted.
- **Delegated administration**—PowerShell 3.0 allows administrators to delegate credentials to commands so that they can be run by a person with more limited permissions.
- **Cmdlet discovery**—PowerShell 3.0 makes it easier to find and run cmdlets by discovering and automatically loading modules.
- **Show-Command**—This cmdlet and ISE add-on helps users find the cmdlet they need as well as shows them the parameters they can use.
- **PowerShell web access**—The ability to use Windows PowerShell from a browser.
- **Out-Gridview**—Although it might seem odd to highlight such a specific cmdlet, any administrator that has fought with output to make it "pretty" will absolutely love the ability to output their data to a modifiable grid, making it significantly easier to present and filter on after the fact.
- **Show-Command**—This cmdlet displays a scrollable list of cmdlets that can be filtered by source module
- **Enhanced and Updatable Help**—PowerShell 3.0 has the capability to search online for updated help files and to update the existing help files.

Understanding PowerShell Fundamentals

To begin working with PowerShell, let's start with the fundamentals: accessing PowerShell, working from the CLI, and understanding the basic commands.

Accessing PowerShell

After logging in to your Windows interactive session, there are several methods to access and use PowerShell. The first method is from the Start menu, as shown in the following steps:

1. Hover the mouse in the far right of the desktop until the Search/Start/Settings icons appear.
2. Click Start
3. Click the PowerShell tile.

To use the second method, follow these steps:

1. Hover the mouse in the far right of the desktop until the Search/Start/Settings icons appear.
2. Click Search
3. Type **PowerShell** and press Enter.

For administrators who prefer the classic desktop look to the Metro style tiles, from the desktop just click the PowerShell icon in the Quick Launch bar. Optionally, you can right-click this icon and either choose to launch the command-line PowerShell or the newer Windows PowerShell ISE (Integrated Scripting Environment).

Command-Line Interface

The syntax for using PowerShell from the CLI is similar to the syntax for other CLI shells. The fundamental component of a PowerShell command is, of course, the name of the command to be executed. In addition, the command can be made more specific by using parameters and arguments for parameters. Therefore, a PowerShell command can have the following formats:

- [command name]
- [command name] -[parameter]
- [command name] -[parameter] -[parameter] [argument1]
- [command name] -[parameter] -[parameter] [argument1],[argument2]

When using PowerShell, a parameter is a variable that can be accepted by a command, script, or function. An argument is a value assigned to a parameter. Although these terms are often used interchangeably, remembering these definitions is helpful when discussing their use in PowerShell.

Navigating the CLI

As with all CLI-based shells, an understanding is needed in how to effectively navigate and use the PowerShell CLI. Table 21.1 lists the editing operations associated with various keys when using the PowerShell console.

Luckily, most of the features in Table 21.1 are native to the command prompt, which makes PowerShell adoption easier for administrators already familiar with the Windows command line. The only major difference is that the Tab key autocompletion is enhanced in PowerShell beyond what's available with the command prompt. Tab key autocompletion is one of the most useful features in PowerShell as it allows administrators to find commandlets where they don't remember the exact name. It also saves time by reducing the amount of typing needed to perform a task.

TABLE 21.1 PowerShell Console Editing Features

Keys	Editing Operation
Left and right arrows	Move the cursor left and right through the current command line.
Up and down arrows	Moves up and down through the list of recently typed commands.
PgUp	Displays the first command in the command history.
PgDn	Displays the last command in the command history.
Home	Moves the cursor to the beginning of the command line.
End	Moves the cursor to the end of the command line.
Insert	Switches between insert and overstrike text-entry modes.
Delete	Deletes the character at the current cursor position.
Backspace	Deletes the character immediately preceding the current cursor position.
F3	Displays the previous command.
F4	Deletes up to the specified number of characters from the current cursor.
F5	Moves backward through the command history.
F7	Displays a list of recently typed commands in a pop-up window in the command shell. Use the up and down arrows to select a previously typed command, and then press Enter to execute the selected command.
F8	Moves backward through the command history with commands that match the text that has been entered at the command prompt.
F9	Prompts for a command number and executes the specified command from the command history (command numbers refer to the F7 command list).
Tab	Autocompletes command-line sequences. Use the Shift+Tab sequence to move backward through a list of potential matches.

As with the command prompt, PowerShell performs autocompletion for file and directory names. So, if you enter a partial file or directory name and press Tab, PowerShell returns the first matching file or directory name in the current directory. Pressing Tab again returns a second possible match and enables you to cycle through the list of results. Like the command prompt, PowerShell's Tab key autocompletion can also autocomplete with wildcards. The difference between Tab key autocompletion in the command prompt and PowerShell is that PowerShell can autocomplete commands. For example, you can enter a partial command name and press the Tab key, and PowerShell steps through a list of possible command matches.

PowerShell can also autocomplete parameter names associated with a particular command. Just enter a command and partial parameter name and press the Tab key, and PowerShell cycles through the parameters for the command that has been specified. This method also works for variables associated with a command. In addition, PowerShell performs autocompletion for methods and properties of variables and objects.

Command Types

When a command is executed in PowerShell, the command interpreter looks at the command name to figure out what task to perform. This process includes determining the type of command and how to process that command. There are four types of PowerShell commands: cmdlets, shell function commands, script commands, and native commands.

Cmdlet

The first command type is a cmdlet (pronounced "command-let"), which is similar to the built-in commands in other CLI-based shells. The difference is that cmdlets are implemented by using .NET classes compiled into a dynamic link library (DLL) and loaded into PowerShell at runtime. This difference means there's no fixed class of built-in cmdlets; anyone can use the PowerShell Software Developers Kit (SDK) to write a custom cmdlet, thus extending PowerShell's functionality.

A cmdlet is always named as a verb and noun pair separated by a "-" (hyphen). The verb specifies the action the cmdlet performs, and the noun specifies the object being operated on. An example of a cmdlet being executed is shown here:

```
PS C:\> Get-Process

Handles  NPM(K)    PM(K)      WS(K) VM(M)   CPU(s)     Id ProcessName
-------  ------    -----      ----- -----   ------     -- -----------
    425       5     1608       1736    90     3.09    428 csrss
     79       4     1292        540    86     1.00    468 csrss
    193       4     2540       6528    94     2.16   2316 csrss
     66       3     1128       3736    34     0.06   3192 dwm
    412      11    13636      20832   125     3.52   1408 explorer
...
```

While executing cmdlets in PowerShell, you should take a couple of considerations into account. Overall, PowerShell was created such that it is both forgiving and easy when it comes to syntax. In addition, PowerShell also always attempts to fill in the blanks for a user. Examples of this are illustrated in the following items:

- Cmdlets are always structured in a nonplural verb-noun format.
- Parameters and arguments are positional: **Get-Process winword**.
- Many arguments can use wildcards: **Get-Process w***.
- Partial parameter names are also allowed: **Get-Process –P w***.

NOTE

When executed, a cmdlet only processes a single record at a time.

Windows Server 2012 comes with a large number of new and recycled cmdlets covering all major administrative functions, including the following:

- AD CS Administration Cmdlets
- AD CS Deployment Cmdlets
- AD DS Administration Cmdlets
- AD DS Deployment Cmdlets
- App Installation Cmdlets
- AppLocker Cmdlets
- Best Practices Analyzer Cmdlets
- BranchCache Cmdlets
- Cluster-Aware Updating Cmdlets
- Data Center Bridging (DCB) Quality of Service (QoS) Cmdlets
- Deduplication Cmdlets
- Direct Access Client Cmdlets
- DISM Cmdlets
- DTC Diagnostics Cmdlets
- DTC Management Cmdlets
- Failover Clusters Cmdlets
- Group Policy Cmdlets
- Hyper-V Cmdlets
- International Settings Cmdlets
- iSCSI Cmdlets
- iSCSI Target Cmdlets
- Microsoft Online Backup Cmdlets
- MSMQ Cmdlets
- MultiPath I/O (MPIO) Cmdlets
- Network Connectivity Status Cmdlets
- Network Load Balancing Cmdlets
- Network Quality of Service (QoS) Cmdlets
- Net TCP/IP Cmdlets
- PKI Client Cmdlets
- Print Management Cmdlets
- Remote Access Cmdlets

- Server Manager Cmdlets
- Storage Cmdlets
- VAMT Cmdlets
- Windows Data Access Components (WDAC) Cmdlets
- Web Server (IIS) Administration Cmdlets
- WHEA Cmdlets
- Windows Assessment Services Cmdlets
- Windows PowerShell Web Access Cmdlets
- Windows Server Update Services (WSUS) Cmdlets

Functions

The next type of command is a function. These commands provide a way to assign a name to a list of commands. Functions are similar to subroutines and procedures in other programming languages. The main difference between a script and a function is that a new instance of the shell is started for each shell script, and functions run in the current instance of the same shell.

NOTE

Functions defined at the command line remain in effect only during the current PowerShell session. They are also local in scope and don't apply to new PowerShell sessions.

Although a function defined at the command line is a useful way to create a series of commands dynamically in the PowerShell environment, these functions reside only in memory and are erased when PowerShell is closed and restarted. Therefore, although creating complex functions dynamically is possible, writing these functions as script commands might be more practical. An example of a shell function command is as follows:

```
PS C:\> function showFiles {Get-ChildItem}
PS C:\> showfiles


Directory: C:\


Mode                LastWriteTime     Length Name
----                -------------     ------ ----
d----          3/4/2012  10:36 PM            inetpub
d----         3/17/2012  11:02 PM            PerfLogs
d-r--          3/5/2012  12:19 AM            Program Files
d-r--          3/5/2012  11:01 PM            Users
```

```
d----         4/14/2012  11:42 PM            Windows
-a---         3/26/2012   8:43 PM         24 autoexec.bat
-ar-s         5/13/2012  11:57 PM       8192 BOOTSECT.BAK
```

Advanced Functions

Advanced functions are a feature that was introduced in PowerShell v2.0. The basic premise behind advanced functions is to enable administrators and developers access to the same type of functionality as a compiled cmdlet, but directly through the PowerShell scripting language. An example of an advanced function is shown here:

```
function SuperFunction {
        <#
        .SYNOPSIS
                Superduper Advanced Function.
        .DESCRIPTION
                This is my Superduper Advanced Function.
        .PARAMETER Message
                Message to write.
        #>
        param(
                [Parameter(Position=0, Mandatory=$True, ValueFromPipeline=$True)]
                        [String] $Message
                )

        Write-Host $Message
        }
```

In the previous example, you will see that one of the major identifying aspects of an advanced function is the use of the **CmdletBinding** attribute. Usage of this attribute in an advanced function allows PowerShell to bind the parameters in the same manner that it binds parameters in a compiled cmdlet. For the SuperFunction example, **CmdletBinding** is used to define the **$Message** parameter with position 0, as mandatory, and is able to accept values from the pipeline. For example, the following shows the SuperFunction being executed, which then prompts for a message string. That message string is then written to the console:

```
PS C:\Users\sheldon> SuperFunction

cmdlet SuperFunction at command pipeline position 1
Supply values for the following parameters:
Message: yo!
yo!
```

Finally, advanced functions can also use all the methods and properties of the **PSCmdlet** class, for example:

- Usage of all the input processing methods (Begin, Process, and End)
- Usage of the **ShouldProcess** and **ShouldContinue** methods, which can be used to get user feedback before performing an action
- Usage of the **ThrowTerminatingError** method, which can be used to generate error records
- Usage of a various number of **Write** methods

Scripts

Scripts, the third command type, are PowerShell commands stored in a PS1 file. The main difference from functions is that scripts are stored on disk and can be accessed any time, unlike functions that don't persist across PowerShell sessions.

Scripts can be run in a PowerShell session or at the command prompt. To run a script in a PowerShell session, type the script name without the extension. The script name can be followed by any parameters. The shell then executes the first PS1 file matching the typed name in any of the paths located in the PowerShell **$ENV:PATH** variable.

To run a PowerShell script from a command prompt, first use the CD command to change to the directory where the script is located. Then run the PowerShell executable with the command parameter and specifying which script to be run, as shown here:

```
C:\Scripts>powershell -command .\myscript.ps1
```

If you don't want to change to the script's directory with the **cd** command, you can also run it by using an absolute path, as shown in this example:

```
C:\>powershell -command C:\Scripts\myscript.ps1
```

An important detail about scripts in PowerShell concerns their default security restrictions. By default, scripts are not enabled to run as a method of protection against malicious scripts. You can control this policy with the Set-ExecutionPolicy cmdlet, which is explained later in this chapter.

Native Commands

The last type of command, a native command, consists of external programs that the operating system can run. Because a new process must be created to run native commands, they are less efficient than other types of PowerShell commands. Native commands also have their own parameters for processing commands, which are usually different from PowerShell parameters.

.NET Framework Integration

Most shells operate in a text-based environment, which means you typically have to manipulate the output for automation purposes. For example, if you need to pipe data from one command to the next, the output from the first command usually must be reformatted to meet the second command's requirements. Although this method has worked for years, dealing with text-based data can be difficult and frustrating.

Often, a lot of work is necessary to transform text data into a usable format. Microsoft has set out to change the standard with PowerShell, however. Instead of transporting data as plain text, PowerShell retrieves data in the form of .NET Framework objects, which makes it possible for commands (or cmdlets) to access object properties and methods directly. This change has simplified shell use. Instead of modifying text data, you can just refer to the required data by name. Similarly, instead of writing code to transform data into a usable format, you can simply refer to objects and manipulate them as needed.

Reflection

Reflection is a feature in the .NET Framework that enables developers to examine objects and retrieve their supported methods, properties, fields, and so on. Because PowerShell is built on the .NET Framework, it provides this feature, too, with the Get-Member cmdlet. This cmdlet analyzes an object or collection of objects you pass to it via the pipeline. For example, the following command analyzes the objects returned from the Get-Process cmdlet and displays their associated properties and methods:

```
PS C:\> get-process | get-member
```

Developers often refer to this process as "interrogating" an object. This method of accessing and retrieving information about an object can be very useful in understanding its methods and properties without referring to MSDN documentation or searching the Internet.

Extended Type System

You might think that scripting in PowerShell is typeless because you rarely need to specify the type for a variable. PowerShell is actually type driven, however, because it interfaces with different types of objects from the less-than-perfect .NET to Windows Management Instrumentation (WMI), Component Object Model (COM), ActiveX Data Objects (ADO), Active Directory Service Interfaces (ADSI), Extensible Markup Language (XML), and even custom objects. However, you don't need to be concerned about object types because PowerShell adapts to different object types and displays its interpretation of an object for you.

In a sense, PowerShell tries to provide a common abstraction layer that makes all object interaction consistent, despite the type. This abstraction layer is called the PSObject, a common object used for all object access in PowerShell. It can encapsulate any base object (.NET, custom, and so on), any instance members, and implicit or explicit access to adapted and type-based extended members, depending on the type of base object. Furthermore, it can state its type and add members dynamically. To do this, PowerShell uses the Extended Type System (ETS), which provides an interface that allows PowerShell cmdlet and script developers to manipulate and change objects as needed.

NOTE

When you use the Get-Member cmdlet, the information returned is from PSObject. Sometimes PSObject blocks members, methods, and properties from the original object. If you want to view the blocked information, use the BaseObject property with the PSBase standard name. For example, you could use the **$Procs.PSBase | get-member** command to view blocked information for the $Procs object collection.

Needless to say, this topic is fairly advanced, as PSBase is hidden from view. The only time you should need to use it is when the PSObject doesn't interpret an object correctly or you're digging around for hidden jewels in PowerShell.

Static Classes and Methods

Certain .NET Framework classes cannot be used to create new objects. For example, if you try to create a **System.Math** typed object using the New-Object cmdlet, the following error occurs:

```
PS C:\> new-object system.math
New-Object : Constructor not found. Cannot find an appropriate constructor for
type system.math.
At line:1 char:1
+ new-object system.math
+ ~~~~~~~~~~~~~~~~~~~~~~
    + CategoryInfo          : ObjectNotFound: (:) [New-Object], PSArgumentExce
   ption
    + FullyQualifiedErrorId : CannotFindAppropriateCtor,Microsoft.PowerShell.C
   ommands.NewObjectCommand
PS C:\>
```

The reason this occurs is because static members are shared across all instances of a class and don't require a typed object to be created before being used. Instead, static members are accessed simply by referring to the classname as if it were the name of the object followed by the static operator (::), as follows:

```
PS > [System.DirectoryServices.ActiveDirectory.Forest]::GetCurrentForest()
```

In the previous example, the **DirectoryServices.ActiveDirectory.Forest** class is used to retrieve information about the current forest. To complete this task, the classname is enclosed within the two square brackets ([...]). Then, the **GetCurrentForest** method is invoked by using the static operator (::).

NOTE

To retrieve a list of static members for a class, use the Get-Member cmdlet: **Get-Member -inputObject ([System.String]) -Static**.

Type Accelerators

A type accelerator is simply an alias for specifying a .NET type. Without a type accelerator, defining a variable type requires entering a fully qualified classname, as shown here:

```
PS C:\> $User = [System.DirectoryServices.DirectoryEntry]"LDAP: //CN=Sheldon
Cat,OU=Accounts,OU=Managed Objects,DC=companyabc,DC=com"
PS C:\> $User

distinguishedname:{CN=Sheldon Cat,OU=Accounts,OU=Managed
Objects,DC=companyabc,DC=com}
path             : LDAP: //CN=Sheldon Cat,OU=Accounts,OU=Managed
Objects,DC=companyabc,DC=com

PS C:\>
```

Instead of typing the entire classname, you just use the [ADSI] type accelerator to define the variable type, as in the following example:

```
PS C:\> $User = [ADSI]"LDAP://CN=Sheldon Cat,OU=Accounts, OU=Managed
Objects,DC=companyabc,DC=com"
PS C:\> $User

distinguishedname:{CN=Sheldon Cat,OU=Accounts,OU=Managed
Objects,DC=companyabc,DC=com}
path             : LDAP: //CN=Sheldon Cat,OU=Accounts,OU=Managed
Objects,DC=companyabc,DC=com


PS C:\>
```

Type accelerators have been included in PowerShell mainly to cut down on the amount of typing to define an object type. However, for some reason, type accelerators aren't covered in the PowerShell documentation, even though the [WMI], [ADSI], and other common type accelerators are referenced on many blogs.

Regardless of the lack of documentation, type accelerators are a fairly useful feature of PowerShell. Table 21.2 lists some of the more commonly used type accelerators.

TABLE 21.2 Important Type Accelerators in PowerShell

Name	Type
Int	System.Int32
Long	System.Int64
String	System.String
Char	System.Char
Bool	System.Boolean

Name	Type
Byte	System.Byte
Double	System.Double
Decimal	System.Decimal
Float	System.Float
Single	System.Single
Regex	System.Text.RegularExpressions.Regex
Array	System.Array
Xml	System.Xml.XmlDocument
Scriptblock	System.Management.Automation.ScriptBlock
Switch	System.Management.Automation.SwitchParameter
Hashtable	System.Collections.Hashtable
Type	System.Type
Ref	System.Management.Automation.PSReference
Psobject	System.Management.Automation.PSObject
pscustomobject	System.Management.Automation.PSCustomObject
Psmoduleinfo	System.Management.Automation.PSModuleInfo
Powershell	System.Management.Automation.PowerShell
runspacefactory	System.Management.Automation.Runspaces.RunspaceFactory
Runspace	System.Management.Automation.Runspaces.Runspace
Ipaddress	System.Net.IPAddress
Wmi	System.Management.ManagementObject
Wmisearcher	System.Management.ManagementObjectSearcher
Wmiclass	System.Management.ManagementClass
Adsi	System.DirectoryServices.DirectoryEntry
Adsisearcher	System.DirectoryServices.DirectorySearcher

The Pipeline

In the past, data was transferred from one command to the next by using the pipeline, which makes it possible to string a series of commands together to gather information from a system. However, as mentioned previously, most shells have a major disadvantage: The information gathered from commands is text based. Raw text needs to be parsed (transformed) into a format the next command can understand before being piped.

The point is that although most UNIX and Linux shell commands are powerful, using them can be complicated and frustrating. Because these shells are text based, often commands lack functionality or require using additional commands or tools to perform tasks. To address the differences in text output from shell commands, many utilities and scripting languages have been developed to parse text.

The result of all this parsing is a tree of commands and tools that make working with shells unwieldy and time consuming, which is one reason for the proliferation of management interfaces that rely on GUIs. This trend can be seen among tools Windows administrators use, too; as Microsoft has focused on enhancing the management GUI at the expense of the CLI.

Windows administrators now have access to the same automation capabilities as their UNIX and Linux counterparts. However, PowerShell and its use of objects fill the automation need Windows administrators have had since the days of batch scripting and WSH in a more usable and less parsing-intense manner. To see how the PowerShell pipeline works, take a look at the following PowerShell example:

```
PS C:\> get-process powershell | format-table id -autosize

  Id
  --
3416


PS C:\>
```

NOTE

All pipelines end with the Out-Default cmdlet. This cmdlet selects a set of properties and their values and then displays those values in a list or table.

Modules and Snap-Ins

One of the main design goals behind PowerShell was to make extending the default functionality in PowerShell and sharing those extensions easy enough that anyone could do it. In PowerShell 1.0, part of this design goal was realized through the use of snap-ins. PowerShell snap-ins (PSSnapins) are dynamic-link library (DLL) files that can be used to provide access to additional cmdlets or providers. By default, a number of PSSnapins are loaded into every PowerShell session. These default sets of PSSnapins contain the built-in cmdlets and providers that are used by PowerShell. You can display a list of these cmdlets by entering the command **Get-PSSnapin** at the PowerShell command prompt, as follows:

```
PS C:\> get-pssnapin


Name        : Microsoft.PowerShell.Core
PSVersion   : 3.0
Description : This Windows PowerShell snap-in contains cmdlets used to manage compo-
nents of Windows Powershell.

PS C:\>
```

In theory, PowerShell snap-ins were a great way to share and reuse a set of cmdlets and providers. However, snap-ins by definition must be written and then compiled, which often placed snap-in creation out of reach for many IT professionals. In addition, snap-ins can conflict, which meant that attempting to run a set of snap-ins within the same PowerShell session might not always be feasible.

That is why in PowerShell 2.0, the product team decided to introduce a new feature called modules, which are designed to make extending PowerShell and sharing those extensions significantly easier. In its simplest form, a module is just a collection of items that can be used in a PowerShell session. These items can be cmdlets, providers, functions, aliases, utilities, and so on. The intent with modules, however, was to allow "anyone" (developers and administrators) to take and bundle together a collection of items. These items can then be executed in a self-contained context, which will not affect the state outside of the module, thus increasing portability when being shared across disparate environments.

Remoting

With PowerShell 1.0, one of its major disadvantages was the lack of an interface to execute commands on a remote machine. Granted, you could use Windows Management Instrumentation (WMI) to accomplish this and some cmdlets like Get-Process and Get-Service, which enable you to connect to remote machines. But, the concept of a native-based "remoting" interface was sorely missing when PowerShell was first released. In fact, the lack of remote command execution was a glaring lack of functionality that needed to be addressed. Naturally, the PowerShell product team took this functionality limitation to heart and addressed it by introducing a new feature in PowerShell 2.0, called "remoting."

Remoting, as its name suggests, is a feature that is designed to facilitate command (or script) execution on remote machines. This could mean execution of a command or commands on one remote machine or thousands of remote machines (provided you have the infrastructure to support this). In addition, commands can be issued synchronously or asynchronously, one at time or through a persistent connection called a runspace, and even scheduled or throttled.

To use remoting, you must have the appropriate permissions to connect to a remote machine, execute PowerShell, and execute the desired command(s). In addition, the remote machine must have PowerShell 2.0 and Windows Remote Management (WinRM) installed, and PowerShell must be configured for remoting.

In addition, when using remoting, the remote PowerShell session that is used to execute commands determines execution environment. As such, the commands you attempt to execute are subject to a remote machine's execution policies, profiles, and preferences.

WARNING

Commands that are executed against a remote machine do not have access to information defined within your local profile. As such, commands that use a function or alias defined in your local profile will fail unless they are defined on the remote machine as well.

How Remoting Works

In its most basic form, PowerShell remoting works using the following conversation flow between "a client" (most likely the machine with your PowerShell session) and "a server" (remote host) that you want to execute commands against:

1. A command is executed on the client.
2. That command is transmitted to the server.
3. The server executes the command and then returns the output to the client.
4. The client displays or uses the returned output.

At a deeper level, PowerShell remoting is very dependent on WinRM for facilitating the command and output exchange between a "client" and "server." WinRM, which is a component of Windows Hardware Management, is a web-based service that enables administrators to enumerate information about and manipulate a remote machine. To handle remote sessions, WinRM was built around a SOAP-based standards protocol called WS-Management. This protocol is firewall friendly, and was primarily developed for the exchange of management information between systems that might be based on a variety of operating systems on various hardware platforms.

When PowerShell uses WinRM to ship commands and output between a client and server, that exchange is done using a series of XML messages. The first XML message that is exchanged is a request to the server, which contains the desired command to be executed. This message is submitted to the server using the SOAP protocol. The server, in return, executes the command using a new instance of PowerShell called a runspace. Once execution of the command is complete, the output from the command is returned to the requesting client as the second XML message. This second message, like the first, is also communicated using the SOAP protocol.

This translation into an XML message is performed because you cannot ship "live" .NET objects (how PowerShell relates to programs or system components) across the network. So, to perform the transmission, objects are serialized into a series of XML (CliXML) data elements. When the server or client receives the transmission, it converts the received XML message into a deserialized object type. The resulting object is no longer live. Instead, it is a record of properties based on a point in time and, as such, no longer possesses any methods.

Remoting Requirements

To use remoting, both the local and remote computers must have the following:

- Windows PowerShell 2.0 or later
- Microsoft .NET Framework 2.0 or later
- Windows Remote Management 2.0

NOTE

Windows Remote Management 2.0 is part of Windows 7 and Windows Server 2008 R2. For down-level versions of Windows, an integrated installation package must be installed, which includes PowerShell 2.0.

Configuring Remoting

By default, WinRM is installed on all Windows Server 2008 R2 or later machines as part of the default operating system installation. However, for security purposes, PowerShell remoting and WinRM are, by default, configured to not allow remote connections. You can use several methods to configure remoting, as described in the following sections.

Method One

The first and easiest method to enable PowerShell remoting is to execute the Enable-PSRemoting cmdlet. For example:

```
PS C:\> enable-pssremoting
```

Once executed, the following tasks are performed by the Enable-PSRemoting cmdlet:

- Runs the Set-WSManQuickConfig cmdlet, which performs the following tasks:
    - Starts the WinRM service
    - Sets the startup type on the WinRM service to Automatic
    - Creates a listener to accept requests on any IP address
    - Enables a firewall exception for WS-Management communications
- Enables all registered Windows PowerShell session configurations to receive instructions from a remote computer
- Registers the Microsoft.PowerShell session configuration, if it is not already registered
- Registers the Microsoft.PowerShell32 session configuration on 64-bit computers, if it is not already registered
- Removes the Deny Everyone setting from the security descriptor for all the registered session configurations
- Restarts the WinRM service to make the preceding changes effective

NOTE

To configure PowerShell remoting, the Enable-PSRemoting cmdlet must be executed using the Run As Administrator option.

Method Two

Another method to configure remoting is to use GPO. Follow these steps to use this method:

1. Create a new GPO, or edit an existing one.
2. Expand Computer Configuration, Policies, Administrative Templates, Windows Components, Windows Remote Management, and then select WinRM Service.
3. Open the Allow Automatic Configuration of Listeners Policy, select Enabled, and then define the IPv4 filter and IPv6 filter as *.
4. Click OK.
5. Next, expand Computer Configuration, Policies, Windows Settings, Security Settings, Windows Firewall with Advanced Security, Windows Firewall with Advanced Security, and then Inbound Rules.
6. Right-click Inbound Rules, and then click New Rule.
7. In the New Inbound Rule Wizard, on the Rule Type page, select Predefined.
8. On the Predefined pull-down menu, select Remote Event Log Management. Click Next.
9. On the Predefined Rules page, click Next to accept the new rules.
10. On the Action page, select Allow the Connection, and then click Finish. Allow the Connection is the default selection.
11. Repeat steps 6 through 10 and create inbound rules for the following predefined rule types:
    - Remote Service Management
    - Windows Firewall Remote Management

Background Jobs

Another new feature that was introduced in PowerShell 2.0 is the ability to use background jobs. By definition, a background job is a command that is executed asynchronously without interacting with the current PowerShell session. However, once the background job has finished execution, the results from these jobs can then be retrieved and manipulated based on the task at hand. In other words, by using a background job, you can complete automation tasks that take an extended period of time to run without impacting the usability of your PowerShell session.

By default, background jobs can be executed on the local computer. But, background jobs can also be used in conjunction with remoting to execute jobs on a remote machine.

NOTE

To use background jobs (local or remote), PowerShell must be configured for remoting.

PowerShell ISE

Another new feature that was introduced in PowerShell 2.0 and is improved upon in PowerShell 3.0 is called the Integrated Scripting Environment (ISE). The ISE, as shown in Figure 21.1, is a Windows Presentation Foundation (WPF)–based host application for Windows PowerShell. Using the ISE, an IT professional can both run commands and write, test, and debug scripts.

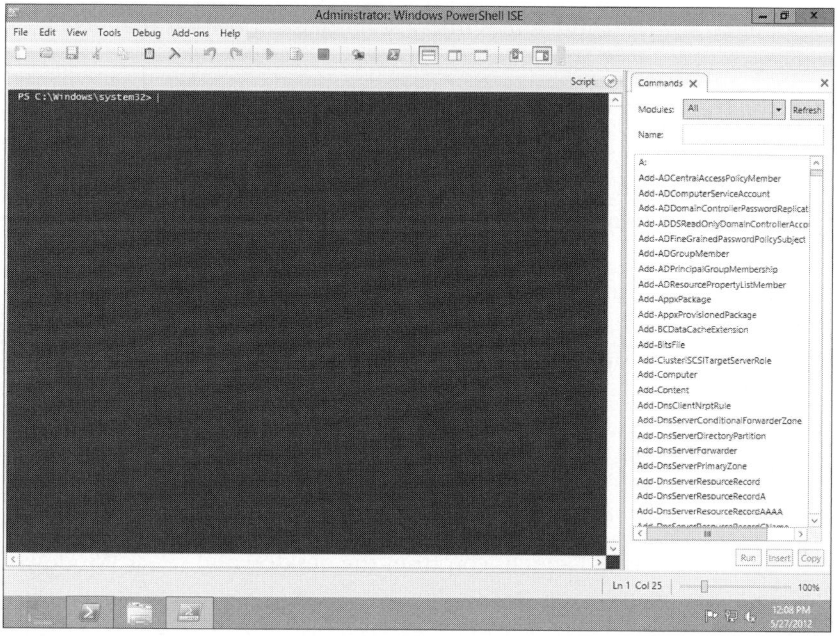

FIGURE 21.1 The PowerShell ISE.

Additional features of the ISE include the following:

- A Command pane for running interactive commands.
- A Script pane for writing, editing, and running scripts. You can run the entire script or selected lines from the script.
- A scrollable Output pane that displays a transcript of commands from the Command and Script panes and their results.
- Multiple independent PowerShell execution environments in the same window, each with its own Command, Script, and Output panes.
- Multiline editing in the Command pane, which lets you paste multiple lines of code, run them, and then recall them as a unit.
- A built-in debugger for debugging commands, functions, and scripts.

- Customizable features that let you adjust the colors, font, and layout.
- A scriptable object model that lets you further customize and extend the PowerShell ISE.
- Line and column numbers, keyboard shortcuts, tab completion, context-sensitive Help, and Unicode support.
- The ability to import a module and all its cmdlets.
- The ability to populate switches and values into a script based on what that given cmdlet supports.
- IntelliSense, which offers clickable menus of matching cmdlets, parameters, values, folders or files as you type.
- Restart Manager and Auto-save, which allow for automatic saving of scripts to protect against unexpected system restarts.

The PowerShell ISE is an optional feature in Windows Server 2012. To use the ISE, it first must be installed using Server Manager. Because the ISE requires the .NET Framework 3.5 with Service Pack 1, the Server Manager will also install this version of the .NET Framework if it is not already installed. Once installed, use any of the following methods to start it:

1. Launch if from the Windows PowerShell ISE tile from the Start menu.
2. Run the powershell_ise.exe executable.
3. Right-click the PowerShell Quick Launch icon from the desktop and select Windows PowerShell ISE.

ISE Requirements

The following requirements must be met to use the ISE:

- Windows 7 and Windows Server 2008 R2 or later versions of Windows
- Microsoft .NET Framework 3.0 or later
- Windows Management Framework 3.0

NOTE

Being a GUI-based application, the PowerShell ISE does not work on Server Core installations of Windows Server.

Variables

A variable is a storage place for data. In most shells, the only data that can be stored in a variable is text data. In advanced shells and programming languages, data stored in variables can be almost anything, from strings to sequences to objects. Similarly, PowerShell variables can be just about anything.

To define a PowerShell variable, you must name it with the $ prefix, which helps delineate variables from aliases, cmdlets, filenames, and other items a shell operator might want to use. A variable name can contain any combination of alphanumeric characters (a–z and 0–9) and the underscore (_) character. Although PowerShell variables have no set naming convention, using a name that reflects the type of data the variable contains is recommended, as shown in this example:

```
PS C:\> $Stopped = get-service | where {$_.status -eq "stopped"}
PS C:\> $Stopped

Status   Name               DisplayName
------   ----               -----------
Stopped  ALG                Application Layer Gateway Service
Stopped  Appinfo            Application Information
Stopped  AppMgmt            Application Management
Stopped  aspnet_state       ASP.NET State Service
Stopped  AudioEndpointBu... Windows Audio Endpoint Builder
Stopped  Audiosrv           Windows Audio
...
```

As you can see from the previous example, the information that is contained within the **$Stopped** variable is a collection of services that are currently stopped.

NOTE

A variable name can consist of any characters, including spaces, provided the name is enclosed in curly braces ({ and } symbols).

Aliases

Like most existing command-line shells, command aliases can be defined in PowerShell. Aliasing is a method that is used to execute existing shell commands (cmdlets) using a different name. In many cases, the main reason aliases are used is to establish abbreviated command names in an effort to reduce typing. For example:

```
PS C:\> gps | ? {$_.Company -match ".*Microsoft*"} | ft Name, ID, Path -Autosize
```

The preceding example shows the default aliases for the Get-Process, Where-Object, and Format-Table cmdlets.

Alias Cmdlets

In PowerShell, several alias cmdlets enable an administrator to define new aliases, export aliases, import aliases, and display existing aliases. By using the following command, an administrator can get a list of all the related alias cmdlets:

```
PS C:\> get-command *-Alias

Capability      Name                          ModuleName
-----------     ----                          ----------
Cmdlet          Export-Alias                  Microsoft...
Cmdlet          Get-Alias                     Microsoft...
Cmdlet          Import-Alias                  Microsoft...
Cmdlet          New-Alias                     Microsoft...
Cmdlet          Set-Alias                     Microsoft...
```

Use the Get-Alias cmdlet to produce a list of aliases available in the current PowerShell session. The Export-Alias and Import-Alias cmdlets are used to export and import alias lists from one PowerShell session to another. Finally, the New-Alias and Set-Alias cmdlets allow an administrator to define new aliases for the current PowerShell session.

Creating Persistent Aliases

The aliases created when using the New-Alias and Set-Alias cmdlets are valid only in the current PowerShell session. Exiting a PowerShell session discards any existing aliases. To have aliases persist across PowerShell sessions, they can be defined in a profile file, as shown in this example:

```
set-alias new new-object
set-alias time get-date
...
```

Although command shortening is appealing, the extensive use of aliases isn't recommended. One reason is that aliases aren't very portable in relation to scripts. For example, if a lot of aliases are used in a script, each alias must be included via a Set-Aliases sequence at the start of the script to make sure those aliases are present, regardless of machine or session profile, when the script runs.

However, a bigger concern than portability is that aliases can often confuse or obscure the true meaning of commands or scripts. The aliases that are defined might make sense to a scripter, but not everyone shares the logic in defining aliases. So if a scripter wants others to understand their scripts, they shouldn't use too many aliases.

NOTE

If aliases will be used in a script, use names that other people can understand. For example, there's no reason, other than to encode a script, to create aliases consisting of only two letters.

Scopes

A scope is a logical boundary in PowerShell that isolates the use of functions and variables. Scopes can be defined as global, local, script, and private. They function in a hierarchy in which scope information is inherited downward. For example, the local scope can read the global scope, but the global scope can't read information from the local scope. Scopes and their use are described in the following sections.

Global

As the name indicates, a global scope applies to an entire PowerShell instance. Global scope data is inherited by all child scopes, so any commands, functions, or scripts that run make use of variables defined in the global scope. However, global scopes are not shared between different instances of PowerShell.

The following example shows the **$Processes** variable being defined as a global variable in the **ListProcesses** function. Because the **$Processes** variable is being defined globally, checking **$Processes.Count** after **ListProcesses** completes returns a count of the number of active processes at the time **ListProcesses** was executed:

```
PS C:\> function ListProcesses {$Global:Processes = get-process}
PS C:\> ListProcesses
PS C:\> $Processes.Count
46
```

NOTE

In PowerShell, an explicit scope indicator can be used to determine the scope a variable resides in. For instance, if a variable is to reside in the global scope, it should be defined as **$Global:variablename**. If an explicit scope indicator isn't used, a variable resides in the current scope for which it's defined.

Local

A local scope is created dynamically each time a function, filter, or script runs. After a local scope has finished running, information in it is discarded. A local scope can read information from the global scope but can't make changes to it.

The following example shows the locally scoped variable **$Processes** being defined in the **ListProcesses** function. After **ListProcesses** finishes running, the **$Processes** variable no longer contains any data because it was defined only in the **ListProcesses** function. Notice how checking **$Processes.Count** after the **ListProcesses** function is finished produces no results:

```
PS C:\> function ListProcesses {$Processes = get-process}
PS C:\> ListProcesses
PS C:\> $Processes.Count
0
PS C:\>
```

Script

In PowerShell 2.0,a script scope is created whenever a script file runs and is discarded when the script finishes running. To see an example of how a script scope works, create the following script and save it as ListProcesses.ps1:

```
$Processes = get-process
write-host "Here is the first process:" -Foregroundcolor Yellow
$Processes[0]
```

After creating the script file, run it from a PowerShell session. The output should look similar to this example:

```
PS C:\> .\ListProcesses.ps1
Here is the first process:

Handles  NPM(K)    PM(K)      WS(K) VM(M)   CPU(s)     Id ProcessName
-------  ------    -----      ----- -----   ------     -- -----------
    105       5     1992       4128    32             916 alg

PS C:\> $Processes[0]
Cannot index into a null array.
At line:1 char:12
+ $Processes[0 <<<< ]
PS C:\>
```

Notice that when the **ListProcesses.ps1** script runs, information about the first process object in the **$Processes** variable is written to the console. However, when you try to access information in the **$Processes** variable from the console, an error is returned because the **$Processes** variable is valid only in the script scope. When the script finishes running, that scope and all its contents are discarded.

What if an administrator wants to use a script in a pipeline or access it as a library file for common functions? Normally, this isn't possible because PowerShell discards a script scope whenever a script finishes running. Luckily, PowerShell supports the dot-sourcing technique, a term that originally came from UNIX. Dot sourcing a script file tells PowerShell to load a script scope into the calling parent's scope.

To dot source a script file, simply prefix the script name with a period (dot) when running the script, as shown here:

```
PS C:\> . .\coolscript.ps1
```

Private

A private scope is similar to a local scope, with one key difference: Definitions in the private scope aren't inherited by any child scopes.

The following example shows the privately scoped variable **$Processes** defined in the **ListProcesses** function. Notice that during execution of the **ListProcesses** function, the **$Processes** variable isn't available to the child scope represented by the script block enclosed by { and } in lines 6–9:

```
PS C:\> function ListProcesses {$Private:Processes = get-process
>>     write-host "Here is the first process:" -Foregroundcolor Yellow
```

```
>>     $Processes[0]
>>     write-host
>>>>     &{
>>         write-host "Here it is again:" -Foregroundcolor Yellow
>>         $Processes[0]
>>     }
>> }
>>PS C:\> ListProcesses
Here is the first process:

Handles  NPM(K)    PM(K)      WS(K) VM(M)   CPU(s)     Id ProcessName
-------  ------    -----      ----- -----   ------     -- -----------
    105       5     1992       4128    32             916 alg

Here it is again:
Cannot index into a null array.
At line:7 char:20
+         $Processes[0 <<<< ]
PS C:\>
```

This example works because it uses the & call operator. With this call operator, you can execute fragments of script code in an isolated local scope. This technique is helpful for isolating a script block and its variables from a parent scope or, as in this example, isolating a privately scoped variable from a script block.

Providers and Drives

Most computer systems are used to store data, often in a structure such as a file system. Because of the amount of data stored in these structures, processing and finding information can be unwieldy. Most shells have interfaces, or providers, for interacting with data stores in a predictable, set manner. PowerShell also has a set of providers for presenting the contents of data stores through a core set of cmdlets. You can then use these cmdlets to browse, navigate, and manipulate data from stores through a common interface. To get a list of the core cmdlets, use the following command:

```
PS C:\> help about_core_commands
...
    ChildItem CMDLETS
    Get-ChildItem

    CONTENT CMDLETS
    Add-Content
    Clear-Content
    Get-Content
    Set-Content
...
```

To view built-in PowerShell providers, use the following command:

```
PS C:\> get-psprovider

Name                 Capabilities                       Drives
----                 ------------                       ------
Alias                ShouldProcess                      {Alias}
Environment          ShouldProcess                      {Env}
FileSystem           Filter, ShouldProcess              {C, D, E}
Function             ShouldProcess                      {Function}
Registry             ShouldProcess, Transactions        {HKLM, HKCU}
Variable             ShouldProcess                      {Variable}
Certificate          ShouldProcess                      {cert}

PS C:\>
```

The preceding list displays not only built-in providers, but also the drives each provider currently supports. A drive is an entity that a provider uses to represent a data store through which data is made available to the PowerShell session. For example, the Registry provider creates a PowerShell drive for the HKEY_LOCAL_MACHINE and HKEY_CURRENT_USER Registry hives.

Administrators familiar with PowerShell 2.0 might notice that WSMan is no longer one of the built-in providers.

To see a list of all current PowerShell drives, use the following command:

```
PS C:\> get-psdrive

Name           Used (GB)     Free (GB) Provider      Root
----           ---------     --------- --------      ----
Alias                                  Alias
C                  68.50        107.00 FileSystem    C:\
cert                                   Certificate   \
D                   8.98          1.83 FileSystem    D:\
E                                      FileSystem    E:\
Env                                    Environment
Function                               Function
HKCU                                   Registry      HKEY_CURRENT_USER
HKLM                                   Registry      HKEY_LOCAL_MACHINE
Variable                               Variable

PS C:\>
```

Security

When WSH was released with Windows 98, it was a godsend for Windows administrators who wanted the same automation capabilities as their UNIX brethren. At the same time, virus writers quickly discovered that WSH also opened up a large attack vector against Windows systems.

Almost anything on a Windows system can be automated and controlled by using WSH, which is an advantage for administrators. However, WSH doesn't provide any security in script execution. If given a script, WSH runs it. Where the script comes from or its purpose doesn't matter. With this behavior, WSH became known more as a security vulnerability than an automation tool.

Execution Policies

Because of past criticisms of WSH's security, when the PowerShell team set out to build a Microsoft shell, the team decided to include an execution policy to mitigate the security threats posed by malicious code. An execution policy defines restrictions on how PowerShell allows scripts to run or what configuration files can be loaded. PowerShell has four primary execution policies, discussed in more detail in the following sections: Restricted, AllSigned, RemoteSigned, and Unrestricted.

NOTE

Execution policies can be circumvented by a user who manually executes commands found in a script file. Therefore, execution policies are not meant to replace a security system that restricts a user's actions and instead should be viewed as a restriction that attempts to prevent malicious code from being executed.

Restricted

By default, PowerShell is configured to run under the Restricted execution policy. This execution policy is the most secure because it allows PowerShell to operate only in an interactive mode. This means no scripts can be run, and only configuration files digitally signed by a trusted publisher are allowed to run or load.

AllSigned

The AllSigned execution policy is a notch under Restricted. When this policy is enabled, only scripts or configuration files that are digitally signed by a publisher you trust can be run or loaded. Here's an example of what you might see if the AllSigned policy has been enabled:

```
PS C:\Scripts> .\happydancinghamsters.ps1
The file C:\Scripts\happydancinghamsters.ps1 cannot be loaded. The file
C:\Scripts\happydancinghamsters.ps1 is not digitally signed. The script will not
execute on the system. Please see "get-help about_signing" for more
details.
At line:1 char:16
+ .\happydancinghamsters.ps1 <<<<
PS C:\Scripts>
```

Signing a script or configuration file requires a code-signing certificate. This certificate can come from a trusted certificate authority (CA), or you can generate one with the

Certificate Creation Tool (Makecert.exe). Usually, however, you want a valid code-signing certificate from a well-known trusted CA, such as VeriSign, Thawte, or your corporation's internal public key infrastructure (PKI). Otherwise, sharing your scripts or configuration files with others might be difficult because your computer isn't a trusted CA by default.

RemoteSigned

The RemoteSigned execution policy is designed to prevent remote PowerShell scripts and configuration files that aren't digitally signed by a trusted publisher from running or loading automatically. Scripts and configuration files that are locally created can be loaded and run without being digitally signed, however.

A remote script or configuration file can be obtained from a communication application, such as Microsoft Outlook, Internet Explorer, Outlook Express, or Windows Messenger. Running or loading a file downloaded from any of these applications results in the following error message:

```
PS C:\Scripts> .\interscript.ps1
The file C:\Scripts\interscript.ps1 cannot be loaded. The file
C:\Scripts\interscript.ps1 is not digitally signed. The script will not execute on
the system. Please see "get-help about_signing" for more details.
At line:1 char:17
+ .\interscript.ps1 <<<<
PS C:\Scripts>
```

Unrestricted

As the name suggests, the Unrestricted execution policy removes almost all restrictions for running scripts or loading configuration files. All local or signed trusted files can run or load, but for remote files, PowerShell prompts you to choose an option for running or loading that file, as shown here:

```
PS C:\Scripts> .\remotescript.ps1

Security Warning
Run only scripts that you trust. While scripts from the Internet can be useful,
 this script can potentially harm your computer. Do you want to run
C:\Scripts\remotescript.ps1?
[D] Do not run  [R] Run once  [S] Suspend  [?] Help (default is "D"):
```

In addition to the primary execution policies, two new execution policies were introduced in PowerShell 2.0, as discussed in the following sections. These two additional policies still exist in PowerShell 3.0.

Bypass

When this execution policy is used, nothing is blocked, and there is no warning or prompts. This execution policy is typically used when PowerShell is being used by another application that has its own security model or a PowerShell script has been embedded into another application.

Undefined

When this execution policy is defined, it means that there is no execution policy set in the current scope. If Undefined is the execution policy for all scopes, the effective execution policy is Restricted.

Setting the Execution Policy

By default, when PowerShell is first installed, the execution policy is set to Restricted. To change the execution policy, you use the Set-ExecutionPolicy cmdlet, shown here:

```
PS C:\> set-executionpolicy AllSigned
```

Or, you can also use a Group Policy setting to set the execution policy for number of computers. In a PowerShell session, if you want to know the current execution policy for a machine, use the Get-ExecutionPolicy cmdlet:

```
PS C:\> get-executionpolicy
AllSigned
PS C:\>
```

Execution policies can not only be defined for the local machine, but can also be defined for the current user or a particular process. These boundaries between where an execution policy resides is called an execution policy scope. To define the execution policy for a scope, you would use the **Scope** parameter for the Set-ExecutionPolicy cmdlet. In addition, if you wanted to know the execution policy for a particular scope, you would use the **Scope** parameter for the Get-ExecutionPolicy cmdlet. The valid arguments for the **Scope** parameter for both cmdlets are Machine Policy, User Policy, Process, CurrentUser, and LocalMachine.

NOTE

The order of precedence for the execution policy scopes is Machine Policy, User Policy, Process, CurrentUser, and LocalMachine.

Using Windows PowerShell

PowerShell is a powerful tool that enables administrators to manage Windows platform applications and to complete automation tasks. This section sheds some light on how PowerShell's many uses can be discovered and how it can be used to manage Windows Server 2012.

Exploring PowerShell

Before using PowerShell, you might want to become more familiar with its cmdlets and features. To assist administrators with exploring PowerShell, the PowerShell team decided to do two things. First, they included a cmdlet that functions very similarly to how the UNIX man pages function. Second, they also included a cmdlet that returns information about commands available in the current session. Together, these cmdlets allow a novice to tap into and understand PowerShell without secondary reference materials; explanations of these cmdlets are discussed in the following sections.

Getting Help

The Get-Help cmdlet is used to retrieve help information about cmdlets, aliases, and from help files. To display a list of all help topics this cmdlet supports, enter **Get-Help *** at the PowerShell command prompt, as shown here:

```
PS C:\> get-help *

Name                          Category  Module          Synopsis
----                          --------  ------          --------
ac                            Alias                     Add-Content
asnp                          Alias                     Add-PSSnapin
clc                           Alias                     Clear-Content
cli                           Alias                     Clear-Item
clp                           Alias                     Clear-ItemProperty
clv                           Alias                     Clear-Variable
cpi                           Alias                     Copy-Item
cpp                           Alias                     Copy-ItemProperty
cvpa                          Alias                     Convert-Path
...
```

If that list seems too large to work with, it can be shortened by filtering on topic name and category. For example, to get a list of all cmdlets starting with the verb Get, try the command shown in the following example:

```
PS C:\> get-help -Name get-* -Category cmdlet

Name                                Category  Module           Synopsis
----                                --------  ------           --------
Get-ADUser                          Cmdlet    ActiveDirectory  Get-ADUser...
Get-ADUserResultantPasswordPolicy Cmdlet    ActiveDirectory  Get-ADUserResult...
Get-AppLockerFileInformation        Cmdlet    AppLocker        Get-AppLockerFil...
Get-AppLockerPolicy                 Cmdlet    AppLocker        Get-AppLockerPol...
Get-BpaModel                        Cmdlet    BestPractices    Get-BpaModel...
Get-BpaResult                       Cmdlet    BestPractices    Get-BpaResult...
Get-BitsTransfer                    Cmdlet    BitsTransfer     Get-BitsTransfer...
Get-CimAssociatedInstance           Cmdlet    CimCmdlets       Get-CimAssociate...
...

PS C:\>
```

After selecting a Help topic, that topic can be retrieved by using the topic name as the parameter to the Get-Help cmdlet. For example, to retrieve help for the Get-Content cmdlet, enter the following command:

```
PS C:\> get-help get-content
```

After executing this command, a shortened view of the help content for the Get-Content cmdlet is displayed. To view the full Help content, include the full switch parameter with the command:

```
PS C:\> get-help get-content -full
```

After executing the command with the full switch parameter, you will find that the full Help content is divided into several sections. Table 21.3 describes each of these sections.

TABLE 21.3 PowerShell Help Sections

Help Section	Description
Name	The name of the cmdlet
Synopsis	A brief description of what the cmdlet does
Syntax	Specific usage details for entering commands with the cmdlet
Description	A detailed description of the cmdlet's behavior, usually including usage examples
Parameters	Valid parameters that can be used with this cmdlet
Inputs	The type of input this cmdlet accepts
Outputs	The type of data that the cmdlet returns
Notes	Additional detailed information about using the cmdlet, including specific scenarios and possible limitations or idiosyncrasies
Examples	Common usage examples for the cmdlet
Related Links	References other cmdlets that perform similar tasks

Get-Command

The Get-Command is used to gather basic information about cmdlets and other commands that are available. For example, when executed, the Get-Command lists all the cmdlets available to the PowerShell session:

```
PS C:\> get-command

Capability      Name                                              ModuleName
----------      ----                                              ----------
Unknown         Add-ProvisionedAppxPackage                        Dism
Unknown         Add-WindowsFeature                                ServerManager
Unknown         Apply-WindowsUnattend                             Dism
Unknown         Begin-WebCommitDelay                              WebAdministration
Unknown         End-WebCommitDelay                                WebAdministration
Unknown         Get-GPPermissions                                 GroupPolicy
Unknown         Get-ProvisionedAppxPackage                        Dism
Unknown         Initialize-Volume                                 Storage
Unknown         Remove-ProvisionedAppxPackage                     Dism
Unknown         Remove-WindowsFeature                             ServerManager
```

```
Unknown         Set-GPPermissions                                GroupPolicy
Script          A:
Script          Add-AppxPackage                                  Appx
CIM             Add-BCDataCacheExtension                         BranchCache
CIM             Add-DnsClientNrptRule                            DnsClient
CIM             Add-DnsServerConditionalForwarderZone            DnsServer...
...
PS C:\>
```

Next, to retrieve basic information about a particular cmdlet, you would then include that cmdlet's name and argument. For example:

```
PS C:\> Get-Command Get-Process

Capability      Name                     ModuleName
----------      ----                     ----------
Cmdlet          Get-Process              Microsoft.PowerShell.Management

PS C:\>
```

The Get-Command cmdlet is more powerful than Get-Help because it lists all available commands (cmdlets, scripts, aliases, functions, and native applications) in a PowerShell session, as shown in this example:

```
PS C:\> get-command note*

Capability      Name                                             ModuleName
----------      ----                                             ----------
Application     notepad.exe

PS C:\>
```

When using Get-Command with elements other than cmdlets, the information returned is a little different from information you see for a cmdlet. For example, with an existing application, the value of the Definition property is the path to the application. However, other information about the application is also available, as shown here:

```
PS C:\> get-command ipconfig | format-list *
HelpUri             :
FileVersionInfo     : File:             C:\Windows\system32\ipconfig.exe
                      InternalName:     ipconfig.exe
                      OriginalFilename: ipconfig.exe.mui
                      FileVersion:      6.2.8250.0 (winmain_win8beta.120217-1520)
                      FileDescription:  IP Configuration Utility
                      Product:          Microsoft® Windows® Operating System
                      ProductVersion:   6.2.8250.0
                      Debug:            False
```

```
                    Patched:          False
                    PreRelease:       False
                    PrivateBuild:     False
                    SpecialBuild:     False
                    Language:         English (United States)

Path                : C:\Windows\system32\ipconfig.exe
Extension           : .exe
Definition          : C:\Windows\system32\ipconfig.exe
Visibility          : Public
OutputType          : {System.String}
Name                : ipconfig.exe
Capability          : Application
CommandType         : Application
ModuleName          :
Module              :
RemotingCapability  : PowerShell
Parameters          :
ParameterSets       :
```

With a function, the Definition property is the body of the function:

```
PS C:\> get-command Prompt

Capability      Name                          ModuleName
----------      ----                          ----------
Script          prompt
PS C:\>
```

With an alias, the Definition property is the aliased command:

```
PS C:\> get-command write

Capability      Name                          ModuleName
----------      ----                          ----------
Cmdlet          write -> Write-Output
PS C:\>
```

With a script file, the Definition property is the path to the script. With a non-PowerShell script (such as a BAT or VBS file), the information returned is the same as other existing applications.

Managing Services

In PowerShell, a number of cmdlets can be used to manage services on a local machine, including the following:

- **Get-Service**—Used to gather service information from Windows
- **New-Service**—Used to create a new service in Windows
- **Restart-Service**—Used to restart services
- **Resume-Service**—Used to resume suspended services
- **Set-Service**—Used to modify service configurations
- **Start-Service**—Used to start services
- **Stop-Service**—Used to stop services
- **Suspend-Service**—Used to suspend services

Getting Service Information

When the Get-Service cmdlet is executed, it returns a collection of objects that contains information about all the services that are present on a Windows system. A representation of that object collection is then outputted into a formatted table, as shown in the following example:

```
PS C:\> get-service

Status   Name               DisplayName
------   ----               -----------
Running  AeLookupSvc        Application Experience
Stopped  ALG                Application Layer Gateway Service
Running  AppHostSvc         Application Host Helper Service
Stopped  Appinfo            Application Information
Stopped  AppMgmt            Application Management
Stopped  aspnet_state       ASP.NET State Service
Stopped  AudioEndpointBu... Windows Audio Endpoint Builder
Stopped  AudioSrv           Windows Audio
...
```

To filter the information returned based on the service status, the object collection can be piped to the Where-Object cmdlet, as shown in the following example:

```
PS C:\> get-service | where-object {$_.Status -eq "Stopped"}

Status   Name               DisplayName
------   ----               -----------
Stopped  ALG                Application Layer Gateway Service
Stopped  Appinfo            Application Information
Stopped  AppMgmt            Application Management
Stopped  aspnet_state       ASP.NET State Service
Stopped  AudioEndpointBu... Windows Audio Endpoint Builder
Stopped  AudioSrv           Windows Audio
...
```

As shown in the preceding example, the Where-Object cmdlet is used in conjunction with a code block {...}, which is executed as the filter. In this case, the code block contained an expression that filtered the object collection based on services that were "stopped." The same type of logic can also be applied to return information about a particular service. For example:

```
PS C:\> get-service | where-object {$_.Name -eq "DNS"} | fl


Name                : DNS
DisplayName         : DNS Server
Status              : Running
DependentServices   : {}
ServicesDependedOn  : {Afd, Tcpip, RpcSs, NTDS}
CanPauseAndContinue : True
CanShutdown         : True
CanStop             : True
ServiceType         : Win32OwnProcess


PS C:\>
```

In the preceding example, the object collection from the Get-Service cmdlet is piped to the Where-Object cmdlet. The filter statement defined script block then instructs the Where-Object cmdlet to return an object for the DNS service. The object that is returned by this cmdlet is then piped to the Format-List cmdlet, which writes a formatted list (containing information about the object) back to the console session.

NOTE

A shorter method for performing the preceding action is to use the name switch, as shown in the following command: **get-service –name DNS**.

Managing Service Statuses

To stop a service in PowerShell, the Stop-Service cmdlet is used, as shown in this example:

```
PS C:\> stop-service -name dns
```

Notice that when the cmdlet has finished executing, no status information about the service's status is returned. To gather that information, the pass-through switch parameter can be used to pass the object created by a cmdlet through to the pipeline. For example:

```
PS C:\> start-service -name dns -pass | ft

Status   Name               DisplayName
------   ----               -----------
Running  DNS                DNS Server
```

In the preceding example, the pass-through switch parameter is used in conjunction with the Start-Service cmdlet. When the cmdlet has finished executing, thus starting the DNS service, the object is piped to the Format-Table cmdlet, which then displays status information about the DNS service.

Modifying Services

The Set-Service cmdlet is used to change a service's properties (such as its description, display name, and start mode). To use this cmdlet, either pass it a service object or specify the name of the service to be modified, plus the property to be modified. For example, to modify the startup type of the DNS service, use the following command:

```
PS C:\> set-service -name DNS -start "manual"
```

A startup type can be defined as Automatic, Manual, or Disabled. To change a service's description, a command might look as follows:

```
PS C:\> set-service -name DNS -description "My Important DNS Service"
```

NOTE

The service management cmdlets in PowerShell are not end-alls for managing Windows services. There are a number of areas in which these cmdlets are lacking—for example, not being able to define a service's logon account or report on its startup type. Luckily, if a more in-depth interface is needed, an administrator can always fall back onto WMI.

Gathering Event Log Information

In PowerShell, the Get-EventLog cmdlet can be used to gather information from a Windows event log and list the event logs that are present on a system. To gather event log information, the name of the event log must be specified, as shown in the following example:

```
PS C:\> get-eventlog -logname application

Index Time          Type Source                EventID Message
----- ----          ---- ------                ------- -------
 1778 Oct 05 19:44  Info MSExchangeFBPublish      8280 When initializing ses...
 1777 Oct 05 19:38  Info MSExchangeIS             9826 Starting from 10/5/20...
 1776 Oct 05 19:38  Info MSExchange ADAccess      2080 Process MSEXCHANGEADT...
 1775 Oct 05 19:16  Info MSExchange ADAccess      2080 Process MAD.EXE (PID=...
...
```

To create a list of all the event logs on the local system, use the **list** switch parameter, as shown in the following command:

```
PS C:\> get-eventlog -list

  Max(K) Retain OverflowAction        Entries Name
  ------ ------ --------------        ------- ----
  20,480      0 OverwriteAsNeeded       1,778 Application
  15,168      0 OverwriteAsNeeded          44 DFS Replication
     512      0 OverwriteAsNeeded       1,826 Directory Service
  16,384      0 OverwriteAsNeeded          38 DNS Server
  20,480      0 OverwriteAsNeeded           0 Hardware Events
     512      7 OverwriteOlder              0 Internet Explorer
  20,480      0 OverwriteAsNeeded           0 Key Management Service
     512      7 OverwriteOlder            155 PowerShell
 131,072      0 OverwriteAsNeeded       9,596 Security
  20,480      0 OverwriteAsNeeded       3,986 System
  15,360      0 OverwriteAsNeeded         278 Windows PowerShell

PS C:\>
```

To gather in-depth information about a particular set of events or event, the information returned from the Get-EventLog cmdlet can be further filtered. For example:

```
PS C:\> $Errors = get-eventLog -logname application | where {$_.eventid -eq 8196}
PS C:\> $Errors[0]  | fl -Property *

EventID            : 8196
MachineName        : dc1.companyabc.com
Data               : {}
Index              : 1772
Category           : (0)
CategoryNumber     : 0
EntryType          : Information
Message            : License Activation Scheduler (SLUINotify.dll) was not able
                      to automatically activate. Error code:
                     0x8007232B
Source             : Software Protection Platform Service
ReplacementStrings : {0x8007232B}
InstanceId         : 1073750020
TimeGenerated      : 4/5/2012 6:56:36 PM
TimeWritten        : 4/5/2012 6:56:36 PM
UserName           :
Site               :
Container          :

PS C:\>
```

In the preceding example, the Get-EventLog cmdlet is used in conjunction with the Where-Object cmdlet to create a collection of objects that all have an EventID equal to 8196. This collection is then defined as the variable **$Errors**. In the next command, the first object in the **$Errors** variable is passed to the Format-List cmdlet, which then writes a list of all the object's properties to the console.

Managing the Files and Directories

As mentioned earlier in this chapter, specifically in the section "Providers," a set of core cmdlets can be used to access and manipulate PowerShell data stores. Because the Windows file system is just another PowerShell data store, it is accessed through the FileSystem provider. Each mounted drive or defined location is represented by a PSDrive and can be managed by using the core cmdlets. Details about how these core cmdlets are used are discussed in the following sections.

Listing Directories of Files

In PowerShell, you can use several cmdlets to explore the file system. The first cmdlet, Get-Location, is used to display the current working location:

```
PS C:\> get-location


Path
----
C:\


PS C:\>
```

To get information about a specified directory or file, you can use the Get-Item cmdlet:

```
PS C:\temp> get-item autorun.inf


    Directory: C:\temp


Mode                LastWriteTime     Length Name
----                -------------     ------ ----
-a---          8/7/2011  11:06 PM         63 autorun.inf


PS C:\temp>
```

To get information about directories or files under a specified directory, you can use the Get-ChildItem cmdlet:

```
PS C:\> get-childitem c:\inetpub\wwwroot


    Directory: C:\inetpub\wwwroot
```

```
Mode                LastWriteTime     Length Name
----                -------------     ------ ----
d----          10/4/2011  11:09 PM            aspnet_client
-a---          10/4/2011   2:10 PM        689 iisstart.htm
-a---          10/4/2011   2:10 PM     184946 welcome.png

PS C:\>
```

Creating Directories or Files

Creating a directory or file in PowerShell is a simple process and just involves the use of the New-Item cmdlet:

```
PS C:\> new-item -path c:\ -name work -type dir

    Directory: C:\

Mode                LastWriteTime     Length Name
----                -------------     ------ ----
d----          10/7/2011  11:44 AM            work

PS C:\>
```

In the preceding example, it should be noted that the **itemtype** parameter is a parameter that must be defined. If this parameter is not defined, PowerShell prompts you for the type of item to be created. An example of this is shown here:

```
PS C:\work> new-item -path c:\work -name script.log
Type: file

    Directory: C:\work

Mode                LastWriteTime     Length Name
----                -------------     ------ ----
-a---          10/7/2011   8:58 PM          0 script.log

PS C:\work>
```

In the previous example, PowerShell prompts you to define the value for the **itemtype** parameter. However, because you wanted to create a file, the value is defined as "file."

NOTE

With files, in addition to using the New-Item cmdlet, you can use several other cmdlets to create files. Examples of these are Add-Content, Set-Content, Out-Csv, and Out-File. However, the main purpose of these cmdlets is for adding or appending content within a file.

Deleting Directories and Files

To delete directories and files in PowerShell, the Remote-Item cmdlet is used. Usage of this cmdlet is shown in the next example:

```
PS C:\work> remove-item script.log
```

Notice how PowerShell doesn't prompt you for any type of confirmation. Considering that the deletion of an item is a very permanent action, you might want to use one of the PowerShell common parameters to confirm the action before executing the command. For example:

```
PS C:\work> remove-item test.txt -confirm


Confirm
Are you sure you want to perform this action?
Performing operation "Remove File" on Target "C:\work\test.txt".
[Y] Yes  [A] Yes to All  [N] No  [L] No to All  [S] Suspend  [?] Help
(default is "Y"):
```

In the preceding example, the **confirm** common parameter is used to verify the deletion of the test.txt file. Usage of this parameter can help prevent you from making mistakes when executing commands that might or might not be intended actions.

NOTE

In addition to the Remove-Item cmdlet, you can use the Clear-Content cmdlet to wipe content from a file instead of deleting it.

Renaming Directories and Files

To rename directories and files in PowerShell, use the Rename-Item cmdlet:

```
PS C:\> rename-item c:\work scripts
```

When using the Rename-Item cmdlet, the argument for the first parameter named path is defined as the path to the directory or file being renamed. The secondary parameter, newName, is then defined as the new name for the directory or file.

Moving or Copying Directories and Files

To move and copy directories or files in PowerShell, you can use either the Move-Item or Copy-Item cmdlets. An example of using the Move-Item cmdlet is as follows:

```
PS C:\> move-item -path c:\scripts -dest c:\work
PS C:\> get-childitem c:\work


    Directory: C:\work
```

```
Mode                LastWriteTime     Length Name
----                -------------     ------ ----
d----         10/7/2011   9:20 PM            scripts

PS C:\>
```

The syntax for using the Copy-Item cmdlet is very similar, as shown in the next example:

```
PS C:\work> copy-item 4444.log .\logs
PS C:\work> gci .\logs
    Directory: C:\work\logs

Mode                LastWriteTime     Length Name
----                -------------     ------ ----
-a---         10/7/2011  10:41 PM          6 4444.log

PS C:\work>
```

Reading Information from Files

To read information from a file, you can use the Get-Content cmdlet. An example of using this cmdlet is as follows:

```
PS C:\work\logs> get-content 4444.log
PowerShell was here!
```

When the Get-Content cmdlet is executed, it reads content from the specified file line-by-line and returns an object for each line that is read. For example:

```
PS C:\work\logs> $logs = get-content 4444.log
PS C:\work\logs> $logs[0]
PowerShell was here!
PS C:\work\logs>
```

Managing the Registry

PowerShell has a built-in provider, Registry, for accessing and manipulating the Registry on a local machine. The Registry hives available in this provider are HKEY_LOCAL_MACHINE (HKLM) and HKEY_CURRENT_USER (HKCU). These hives are represented in a PowerShell session as two additional PSDrive objects named HKLM: and HKCU:.

NOTE

The WshShell object has access to not only the HKLM: and HKCU: hives, but also HKEY_CLASSES_ROOT (HKCR), HKEY_USERS, and HKEY_CURRENT_CONFIG. To access these additional Registry hives in PowerShell, you use the Set-Location cmdlet to change the location to the root of the Registry provider.

Because the Windows Registry is treated as a hierarchy data store, like the Windows file system, it can also be managed by the PowerShell core cmdlets. For example, to read a Registry value, you use the Get-ItemProperty cmdlet:

```
PS C:\> $Path = "HKLM:\Software\Microsoft\Windows NT\CurrentVersion"
PS C:\> $Key = get-itemproperty $Path
PS C:\> $Key.ProductName
Windows Server 8 Beta Datacenter
PS C:\>
```

To create or modify a Registry value, you use the Set-ItemProperty cmdlet:

```
PS C:\> $Path = "HKCU:\Software"
PS C:\> set-itemproperty -path $Path -name "PSinfo" -type "String" -value  "Power-
Shell_Was_Here"
PS C:\>
PS C:\> $Key = get-itemproperty $Path
PS C:\> $Key.PSinfo
PowerShell_Was_Here
PS C:\>
```

Remember that the Windows Registry has different types of Registry values. You use the Set-ItemProperty cmdlet to define the **Type** parameter when creating or modifying Registry values. As a best practice, you should always define Registry values when using the Set-ItemProperty cmdlet. Otherwise, the cmdlet defines the Registry value with the default type, which is String. Other possible types are as follows:

- ExpandString
- Binary
- DWord
- MultiString
- Qword

NOTE

Depending on the Registry value you're creating or modifying, the data value you set the named value to needs to be in the correct format. So, if the Registry value is type REG_BINARY, you use a binary value, such as $Bin = 101, 118, 105.

To delete a Registry value, you use the Remove-ItemProperty cmdlet, as shown here:

```
PS C:\> $Path = "HKCU:\Software"
PS C:\> remove-itemproperty -path $Path -name "PSinfo"
PS C:\>
```

Managing Processes

In PowerShell, you can use two cmdlets to manage processes. The first cmdlet, Get-Process, is used to get information about the current processes that are running on the local Windows system:

```
PS C:\> get-process

Handles  NPM(K)    PM(K)      WS(K) VM(M)   CPU(s)     Id ProcessName
-------  ------    -----      ----- -----   ------     -- -----------
    782      12     2500       4456   113     4.02    448 csrss
    237      10     3064       6228   113    76.70    488 csrss
    292      26    20180      14632   356    12.94   1496 dfsrs
    160      13     3020       5536    55     0.34   2696 dfssvc
    203      24     6368       5888    64     1.75   3220 dns
...
```

To filter the object collection that is returned by the Get-Process cmdlet to a particular process, you can specify the process name or ID, as shown in the following example:

```
PS C:\> get-process dns

Handles  NPM(K)    PM(K)      WS(K) VM(M)   CPU(s)     Id ProcessName
-------  ------    -----      ----- -----   ------     -- -----------
    203      24     6368       5888    64     1.77   3220 dns

PS C:\> get-process -id 3220

Handles  NPM(K)    PM(K)      WS(K) VM(M)   CPU(s)     Id ProcessName
-------  ------    -----      ----- -----   ------     -- -----------
    203      24     6368       5888    64     1.77   3220 dns

PS C:\>
```

In addition to the preceding examples, you could also combine the Get-Process cmdlet with the Where-Object cmdlet. For example:

```
PS C:\> get-process | ? {$_.workingset -gt 100000000} | sort ws -descending

Handles  NPM(K)    PM(K)      WS(K) VM(M)   CPU(s)     Id ProcessName
-------  ------    -----      ----- -----   ------     -- -----------
    471      29   108608     104972   658    95.88   4208 mmc
    629      39   130716     104208   705   108.58   4332 mmc

PS C:\>
```

By using these cmdlets together, a more robust view of the current running processes based on a specified filter statement can be created. In the previous example, the resulting object collection includes processes that only have a working set greater than 100,000,000 bytes. In addition, the Sort-Object cmdlet is used to sort the formatted table's WS(K) column in descending order.

The second cmdlet that is used to manage processes is the Stop-Process cmdlet. Usage of this cmdlet is as follows:

```
PS C:\work\logs> stop-process -name notepad
```

The process that is being stopped can either be defined by its name, ID, or as an object that is passed to the Stop-Process cmdlet via the pipeline.

Using WMI and CIM

Using WMI in PowerShell has similar conceptual logic as in WSH. The main difference is that the PowerShell methods are based on WMI .NET instead of the WMI Scripting API. You have three methods for using WMI in PowerShell: WMI .NET (which is the .NET System.Management and System.Management.Instrumentation namespaces), the Get-WmiObject cmdlet, or the PowerShell WMI type accelerators: [WMI], [WMIClass], and [WMISearcher].

The first method, using the System.Management and System.Management. Instrumentation namespaces, isn't discussed in this chapter because it's not as practical as the other methods. It should be only a fallback method in case PowerShell isn't correctly encapsulating an object within a **PSObject** object when using the other two methods.

The second method, the Get-WmiObject cmdlet, retrieves WMI objects and gathers information about WMI classes. This cmdlet is fairly simple. For example, getting an instance of the local **Win32_ComputerSystem** class just requires the name of the class, as shown here:

```
PS C:\> get-wmiobject "Win32_ComputerSystem"

Domain              : companyabc.com
Manufacturer        : Microsoft Corporation
Model               : Virtual Machine
Name                : DC1
PrimaryOwnerName    : Mark Weinhardt
TotalPhysicalMemory : 1167642624

PS C:\>
```

The next example, which is more robust, connects to the remote machine named Jupiter and gets an instance of the **Win32_Service** class in which the instance's name equals Virtual Server. The result is an object containing information about the Virtual Server service on Jupiter:

```
PS C:\> get-wmiobject -class "Win32_Service" -computerName "Jupiter" -filter
"Name='W32Time'"

ExitCode  : 0
Name      : W32Time
ProcessId : 1016
StartMode : Auto
State     : Running
Status    : OK

PS C:\>
```

The following command returns the same information as the previous one but makes use of a WQL query:

```
PS C:\> get-wmiobject -computerName "Jupiter" -query "Select *From Win32_Service
Where Name='W32Time'"

ExitCode  : 0
Name      : W32Time
ProcessId : 1016
StartMode : Auto
State     : Running
Status    : OK

PS C:\>
```

Finally, here's an example of using Get-WmiObject to gather information about a WMI class:

```
PS C:\> get-wmiobject -namespace "root/cimv2" -list | where {$_.Name  -eq
"Win32_Product"} | format-list *

Name              : Win32_Product
__GENUS           : 1
__CLASS           : Win32_Product
__SUPERCLASS      : CIM_Product
__DYNASTY         : CIM_Product
__RELPATH         : Win32_Product
__PROPERTY_COUNT  : 12
__DERIVATION      : {CIM_Product}
__SERVER          : PLANX
__NAMESPACE       : ROOT\cimv2
__PATH            : \\PLANX\ROOT\cimv2:Win32_Product
...

PS C:\>
```

Although using Get-WmiObject is simple, using it almost always requires typing a long command string. This drawback brings you to the third method for using WMI in PowerShell: the WMI type accelerators.

[WMI] Type Accelerator

This type accelerator for the **ManagementObject** class takes a WMI object path as a string and gets a WMI object bound to an instance of the specified WMI class, as shown in this example:

```
PS C:\> $CompInfo = [WMI]"root\cimv2:Win32_ComputerSystem.Name='DC2'"
PS C:\> $CompInfo

Domain              : companyabc.com
Manufacturer        : Microsoft Corporation
Model               : Virtual Machine
Name                : DC2
PrimaryOwnerName    : William James Worden
TotalPhysicalMemory : 2145566720

PS C:\>
```

NOTE

To bind to an instance of a WMI object directly, you must include the key property in the WMI object path. For the preceding example, the key property is **Name**.

[WMIClass] Type Accelerator

This type accelerator for the **ManagementClass** class takes a WMI object path as a string and gets a WMI object bound to the specified WMI class, as shown in the following example:

```
PS C:\> $CompClass = [WMICLASS]"\\.\root\cimv2:Win32_ComputerSystem"
PS C:\> $CompClass

   NameSpace: ROOT\cimv2

Name                                Methods              Properties
----                                -------              ----------
Win32_ComputerSystem                {SetPowerState, R... {AdminPasswordSt...
PS C:\> $CompClass | format-list *

Name             : Win32_ComputerSystem
__GENUS          : 1
__CLASS          : Win32_ComputerSystem
__SUPERCLASS     : CIM_UnitaryComputerSystem
__DYNASTY        : CIM_ManagedSystemElement
```

```
__RELPATH          : Win32_ComputerSystem
__PROPERTY_COUNT : 54
__DERIVATION       : {CIM_UnitaryComputerSystem, CIM_ComputerSystem, CIM_System,
                      CIM_LogicalElement...}
__SERVER           : DC2
__NAMESPACE        : ROOT\cimv2
__PATH             : \\DC2\ROOT\cimv2:Win32_ComputerSystem
...

PS C:\>
```

[WMISearcher] Type Accelerator

This type accelerator for the **ManagementObjectSearcher** class takes a WQL string and creates a WMI searcher object. After the searcher object is created, you use the **Get()** method to get a WMI object bound to an instance of the specified WMI class, as shown here:

```
PS C:\> $CompInfo = [WMISearcher]"Select * From Win32_ComputerSystem"
PS C:\> $CompInfo.Get()


Domain              : companyabc.com
Manufacturer        : Microsoft Corporation
Model               : Virtual Machine
Name                : DC2
PrimaryOwnerName    : William James Worden
TotalPhysicalMemory : 2145566720



PS C:\>
```

AuthenticationLevel and ImpersonationLevel

When using the Get-WmiObject cmdlet in PowerShell 1.0 in conjunction with the **IIsWebService** class to manage the W3SVC service on a remote machine, the following error would be encountered:

```
PS > get-wmiobject -class IIsWebService -namespace "root\microsoftiisv2" -Computer
sc1-app01
Get-WmiObject : Access denied
At line:1 char:14
+ Get-WMIObject <<<<  -class IIsWebService -namespace "root\microsoftiisv2"
-computer sc1-app01
```

This is normal behavior for any of the IIS WMI classes because they require the **AuthenticationLevel** property defined as PacketPrivacy. The **AuthenticationLevel** property is an integer, which defines the COM authentication level that is assigned to an object and in the end determines how DCOM will protect information sent from WMI. In this case, the IIS WMI classes require that data is encrypted, which is not the default behavior of WMI.

Although defining the **AuthenticationLevel** property in WSH was a simple line of code, in PowerShell 1.0's version of the Get-WmiObject cmdlet, there was no method to define this property. In addition, there wasn't a way to change either the **ImpersonationLevel** property or enable all privileges, both of which are often requirements when working with WMI. To correct this problem, the product team has updated the Get-WmiObject cmdlet in PowerShell 2.0 to include new parameters to define the **AuthenticationLevel** and **ImpersonationLevel** properties, as well as enable all privileges. In addition, these parameters also work with the new WMI cmdlets (Invoke-WMIMethod, Remove-WMIObject, and Set-WMIInstance), which were also introduced in PowerShell 2.0. For example:

```
PS > get-wmiobject -class IIsWebService -namespace "root\microsoftiisv2" -Computer
sc1-app01 -Authentication 6
```

In the preceding example, the **Authentication** parameter is used to define the **AuthenticationLevel** property. In this case, the value is defined as 6 (PacketPrivacy).

Set-WMIInstance Cmdlet

The Set-WMIInstance cmdlet was developed to reduce the number of steps needed to change a read-write WMI property (or property that allows direct modification). For example, in PowerShell 1.0, the following set of commands might be used to change the **LoggingLevel** for the WMI service:

```
PS C:\> $WMISetting = Get-WMIObject Win32_WMISetting
PS C:\> $WMISetting.LoggingLevel = 2
PS C:\> $WMISetting.Put()
```

By using the Set-WMIInstance cmdlet, you can complete the same task using a single command:

```
PS > set-wmiinstance -class "Win32_WMISetting" -argument @{LoggingLevel=2}
```

In the preceding example, the **class** parameter is defined as a **Win32_WMISetting**, and the **argument** parameter is defined as a **HashTable** and contains the property and the value the property will be set to. In addition, because this parameter requires an argument that is a HashTable, then to define multiple property and value pairs, you would separate the pairs with a semicolon, as shown here:

```
-argument @{LoggingLevel=1;MaxLogFileSize=1000}
```

However, the true power of this cmdlet is to use the **computername** parameter to change read-write WMI properties on multiple machines simultaneously. For example:

```
PS > set-wmiinstance -class "Win32_WMISetting" -argument @{LoggingLevel=1}
-computername sc1-app01,sc1-app02
```

The arguments for the **computername** parameter can be either a NetBIOS name, fully qualified domain name (FQDN), or IP address. In addition, each argument must be separated by a comma.

Invoke-WMIMethod Cmdlet

With WMI, there are two different types of methods: instance or static. With static methods, you must invoke the method from the class itself, whereas instance methods are invoked on specific instances of a class. In PowerShell 1.0, working with instance methods were fairly straightforward and only involved creating an object of a particular instance of a WMI class. However, to work with a static method required a fairly complex and unintuitive WQL statement, as shown in the following example:

```
PS > $ProcFac = get-wmiobject -query "SELECT * FROM Meta_Class WHERE __Class
= 'Win32_Process'" -namespace "root\cimv2"
PS > $ProcFac.Create("notepad.exe")
```

Granted, you could also use the [WMIClass] type accelerator, as shown here:

```
PS > $ProcFac = [wmiclass]"Win32_Process"
PS > $ProcFac.Create("notepad.exe")
```

But, if you wanted to use the Get-WMIObject cmdlet or were having problems with the [WMIClass] type accelerator, employing the use of the noted WQL statement wasn't very command-line friendly. To fill this noted gap, the PowerShell product team has introduced the Invoke-WMIMethod cmdlet in PowerShell 2.0.

As its name suggests, the purpose of the Invoke-WMIMethod cmdlet is to make it easier to directly invoke WMI methods. To use this cmdlet to invoke a static method, you use the following command:

```
PS > invoke-wmimethod -path "Win32_Process" -name "create" -argumentList
"notepad.exe"
```

In the preceding command example, the **path** parameter requires the name of the WMI class from which the method is to be invoked. In this case, the method being invoked is the **Create** method as defined for the **name** parameter. If you were invoking an instance method, the argument for the **path** parameter would need to be the complete path to an existing WMI instance. For example:

```
PS > invoke-wmimethod -path "Win32_Process.Handle='42144'" -name terminate
```

Finally, the **argumentList** parameter is used to define any arguments that a method requires when it is invoked. In cases where the method requires multiple values or you want to pass multiple values, you must assign those values into an array. Then, the array must be defined as the argument for the **argumentList** parameter.

NOTE

Values for methods are not in the same order as used with the WMI's scripting API. Instead, values are ordered such as they appear in Wbemtest.exe.

Remove-WMIObject Cmdlet

The last new cmdlet to be introduced in PowerShell 2.0 is the Remove-WMIObject cmdlet. This cmdlet is used to remove instances of WMI objects. For example, to terminate a process using WMI in PowerShell 1.0, you might use the following set of commands:

```
PS > $Proc = get-wmiobject -class "Win32_Process" -filter "Name='wordpad.exe'"
PS > $Proc.Terminate()
```

However, depending on the type of WMI object that you are trying to remove, there can be any number of methods that would need to be used. For instance, to delete a folder using WMI in PowerShell 1.0, you would use the following command:

```
PS > $Folder = get-wmiobject -query "Select * From Win32_Directory Where Name
='C:\\Scripts'"
PS > $Folder.Delete()
```

Conversely, using the Remove-WMIObject cmdlet, you can remove instances of any type of WMI object. For example, to remove an instance of the **Win32_Process** class, you use the following commands:

```
PS > $Proc = get-wmiobject -class "Win32_Process" -filter "Name='wordpad.exe'"
PS > $Proc | remove-wmiobject
```

The following commands are used to remove a directory:

```
PS > $Folder = get-wmiobject -query "Select * From Win32_Directory Where Name
='C:\\Scripts'"
PS > $Folder | remove-wmiobject
```

CIM, or Common Information Model, is the DMTF standard for describing the structure and behavior of managed resources such as network, storage, or software components. CIM is replacing WMI cmdlets in Windows Server 2012 as they lift the "Windows to Windows" limitations and expand Windows Server 2012's ability to manage non-Windows devices. Historically, WMI was Microsoft's original implementation of CIM. Moving toward CIM as a replacement, Windows Server 2012 has added 12 new cmdlets involving CIM, including the following:

- Get-CimAssociatedInstance
- Get-CimClass
- Get-CimInstance
- Get-CimSession

- Invoke-CimMethod
- New-CimInstance
- New-CimSession
- New-CimSessionOption
- Register-CimIndicationEvent
- Remove-CimInstance
- Remove-CimSession
- Set-CimInstance

These cmdlets allow administrators to use PowerShell 3.0 to perform tasks such as these:

- Enumerating instances of a class
- Enumerating associated instances
- Getting instances by running a query on a server
- Getting a specific instance of a class
- Creating a new instance of a class
- Modifying an instance of a class
- Deleting an instance of a class
- Invoking extrinsic methods on a class or instance
- Enumerating classes in a namespace
- Getting a class schema
- Subscribing to indications
- Unsubscribing from indications

CIM indications are a representation of an event in the managed system. CIM clients can subscribe to indications by providing the indication type and the filtering expression, which selects events that are delivered to the client.

Using Snap-Ins

Snap-ins are used to show a list of all the registered PSSnapins outside of the default snap-ins that come with PowerShell. Entering the command **Get-PSSnapin -Registered** on a newly installed PowerShell system will return nothing, as shown in the following example:

```
PS C:\> get-pssnapin -registered
```

In most cases, a setup program will accompany a PowerShell snap-in and ensure that it becomes correctly registered for use. However, if this is not the case, the .NET utility InstallUtil.exe is used to complete the registration process. In the following example, InstallUtil.exe is being used to install a third-party library file called freshtastic-automation.dll:

```
PS C:\> & "$env:windir\Microsoft.NET\Framework\v4.0.30319\InstallUtil.exe"
freshtastic-automation.dll
```

After the DLL library file has been registered with PowerShell, the next step is to register the DLL's snap-in with PowerShell so that the cmdlets contained in the DLL are made available to PowerShell. In the case of the freshtastic-automation library, the snap-in is registered by using the command **Add-PSSnapin freshtastic**, as follows:

```
PS C:\> add-pssnapin freshtastic
```

Now that the freshtastic snap-in has been registered, you can enter the command **Get-Help freshtastic** to review the usage information for the freshtastic cmdlets:

```
PS C:\> get-help freshtastic
```

Now that the registration of the freshtastic library DLL is complete and the associated snap-in has been added to the console, you can enter the command **Get-PSSnapin –registered** again and see that the freshtastic snap-in has been added to the console:

```
PS C:\> get-pssnapin -registered


Name        : freshtastic
PSVersion   : 3.0
Description : Used to automate freshness.



PS C:\>
```

Now that you have registered the third-party library file and added its snap-in to the console, you might find that the library does not meet your needs, and you want to remove it. The removal process is basically a reversal of the installation steps listed previously. First, you remove the snap-in from the console using the command **Remove-PSSnapin freshtastic**, as follows:

```
PS C:\> Remove-PSSnapin freshtastic
```

After the third-party snap-in has been unregistered, you will once again use **InstallUtil.exe** with a **/U** switch to unregister the DLL, as follows:

```
PS C:\> & "$env:windir\Microsoft.NET\Framework\v4.0.30319\InstallUtil.exe" /U
freshtastic-automation.dll
```

Once the uninstall has completed, you can verify that the library file was successfully unregistered by entering the command **Get-PSSnapin -registered** and verifying that no third-party libraries are listed.

Using Modules

In Windows Server 2012, a set of base modules are loaded when the operating system is installed. In addition, modules can be added or removed using the Add Features Wizard in Server Manager.

Default Module Locations

There are two default locations for modules. The first location is for the machine, as follows:

```
$pshome\Modules (C:\Windows\system32\WindowsPowerShell\v1.0\Modules)
```

The second location is for the current user:

```
$home\Documents\WindowsPowerShell\Modules (UserProfile%\Documents\WindowsPowerShell\
Modules)
```

Installing New Modules

As mentioned previously, new modules can be added using the Add Features Wizard in Server Manager. In addition, other modules should come with an installation program that will install the module for you. However, if need be, you can also manually install a new module. To do this, use the following steps:

1. Create a new folder for the module that is being installed. For example:

   PS C:\> New-Item -type directory -path $home\Documents\WindowsPowerShell\Modules\Spammer1000

2. Copy the contents of the module into the newly created folder.

Using Installed Modules

After a module has been installed on a machine, it can then be imported into a PowerShell session for usage. To find out what modules are available for use, use the Get-Module cmdlet:

```
PS C:\> Get-Module -listAvailable
```

Or, to list modules that have already been imported into the current PowerShell session, just use the Get-Module cmdlet without the **listAvailable** switch parameter:

```
PS C:\> Get-Module
```

Next, to import a module into a PowerShell session, use the Import-Module cmdlet. For example, if the ActiveDirectory module has been installed, the following command would be used:

```
PS C:\> Import-Module ActiveDirectory
```

NOTE

A complete path to the module folder must be provided for modules that are not located in one of the default modules locations or any additional module locations that have been defined for the current PowerShell session. This is required when using the Import-Module cmdlet to define the module location used by the cmdlet.

In addition, if you want to import all modules that are available on a machine into a PowerShell session, one of two methods can be used. The first method is to execute the following command, which lists all modules and then pipes that to the Import-Module cmdlet:

```
PS C:\> Get-Module -listAvailable | Import-Module
```

NOTE

By default, modules are not loaded into any PowerShell session. To load modules by default, the Import-Module cmdlet should be used in conjunction with a PowerShell profile configuration script.

Removing a Module

The act of removing a module causes all the commands added by a module to be deleted from the current PowerShell session. When a module is removed, the operation only reverses the Import-Module cmdlet's actions and does not uninstall the module from a machine. To remove a module, use the Remove-Module cmdlet, as shown here:

```
PS C:\> Remove-Module ActiveDirectory
```

Using Remoting

When using remoting, three different modes can be used to execute commands, as follows:

- **1 to 1**—Referred to as Interactive mode. This mode enables you to remotely manage a machine similar to using an SSH session.
- **Many to 1**—Referred to as the Fan-In mode. This mode allows multiple administrators to manage a single host using an interactive session.
- **1 to Many**—Referred to as the Fan-Out mode. This mode allows a command to execute across a large number of machines.

More information about each mode is provided in the following sections.

Interactive Remoting

With interactive remoting, the PowerShell session you are executing commands within looks and feels very much like an Secure Shell (SSH) session, as shown in the following example:

```
PS C:\> enter-pssession abc-util01
[abc-util01]: PS C:\Users\administrator.COMPANYABC\Documents>
```

The key to achieving this mode of remoting is a PowerShell feature called a runspace. Runspaces by definition are instances of the **System.Management.Automation** class, which defines the PowerShell session and its host program (Windows PowerShell host, cmd.exe, and so on). In other words, a runspace is an execution environment in which PowerShell runs.

Not widely discussed in PowerShell 1.0, runspaces in PowerShell 2.0 and 3.0 are the method by which commands are executed on local and remote machines. When a runspace is created, it resides in the global scope and it is an environment upon itself, which includes its own properties, execution polices, and profiles. This environment persists for the lifetime of the runspace, regardless of the volatility of the host machine's environment.

Being tied to the host program that created it, a runspace ceases to exist when the host program is closed. When this happens, all aspects of the runspace are gone, and you can no longer retrieve or use the runspace. However, when created on a remote machine, a runspace will remain until it is stopped.

To create a runspace on a machine, you can use two cmdlets. The first cmdlet, Enter-PSSession, is used to create an interactive PowerShell session. This is the cmdlet that was shown in the previous example. When this cmdlet is used against a remote machine, a new runspace (PowerShell process) is created and a connection is established from the local machine to the runspace on the remote computer. If executed against the local machine, a new runspace (PowerShell process) is created and connection is established back to the local machine. To close the interactive session, you would use the Exit-PSSession cmdlet or the exit alias.

Fan-In Remoting

Fan-in remoting is named in reference to the ability for multiple administrators to open their own runspaces at the same time. In other words, many administrators can "fan in" from many machines into a single machine. When connected, each administrator is then limited to the scope of their own runspace. This partitioning of access can be achieved thanks to PowerShell security model that was introduced in 2.0, which allows for the creation of restricted shells and cmdlets.

However, the steps needed to fully utilize the new security model require a degree of software development using the .NET Framework. The ability of being able to provide secure partitioned remote management access on a single host to a number of different administrators is a very powerful feature. Usage could range from a web hosting company wanting to partition remote management access to each customer for each of their websites to internal IT departments wanting to consolidate their management consoles on a single server.

Fan-Out Remoting

Fan-out remoting is named in reference to the ability to issue commands to a number of remote machines at once. When using this method of remoting, commands are issued on your machine. These commands then "fan out" and are executed on each of the remote machines that have been specified. The results from each remote machine are then returned to your machine in the form of an object, which you can then review or further work with; in other words, the basic definition for how remoting was defined earlier in this chapter.

Ironically enough, PowerShell has always supported the concept of fan-out remoting. In PowerShell 1.0, fan-out remoting was achieved using WMI. For example, you could always import a list of machine names and then use WMI to remotely manage those machines:

```
PS C:\> import-csv machineList.csv | foreach {Get-WmiObject Win32_
NetworkAdapterConfiguration -computer $_.MachineName}
```

Although the ability to perform fan-out remoting in PowerShell 1.0 using WMI was a powerful feature, this form of remoting suffered in usability because it was synchronous in nature. In other words, once a command had been issued, it was executed on each remote machine one at a time. While this happened, further command execution had to wait until the command issued had finished being executed on all the specified remote machines.

Attempting to synchronously manage a large number of remote machines can prove to be a challenging task. To address this challenge in PowerShell 2.0, the product team tweaked the remoting experience such that fan-out remoting could be done asynchronously. With these changes, you could still perform remote WMI management, as shown in the previous example. However, you can also asynchronously execute remote commands using the following methods:

- Executing the command as a background job
- Using the Invoke-Command cmdlet
- Using the Invoke-Command cmdlet with a reusable runspace

The first method, a background job, as its name might suggest, allows commands to be executed in the background. Although not truly asynchronous, a command that is executed as a background job enables you to continue executing additional commands while the job is being completed. For example, to run the previously shown WMI example as a background job, you can simply add the **AsJob** parameter for the Get-WmiObject cmdlet:

```
PS C:\> import-csv machineList.csv | foreach {Get-WmiObject Win32_
NetworkAdapterConfiguration -computer $_.MachineName -asjob}
```

With the **AsJob** parameter (introduced in PowerShell 2.0) being used, each time the Get-WmiObject cmdet is called in the **foreach** loop, a new background job is created to complete execution of the cmdlet. Although more details about background jobs are provided later in this chapter, this example shows how background jobs can be used to achieve asynchronous remote command execution when using WMI.

The second method to asynchronously execute remote commands is by using the new cmdlet called Invoke-Command. This cmdlet was introduced in PowerShell 2.0, and it enabled you to execute commands both locally and remotely on machines—unlike WMI, which uses Remote Procedure Call (RPC) connections to remotely manage machines. The Invoke-Command cmdlet utilizes WinRM to push the commands out to each of the specified "targets" in an asynchronous manner.

To use the cmdlet, two primary parameters need to be defined. The first parameter, **ScriptBlock**, is used to specify a scriptblock, which contains the command to be executed. The second parameter, **ComputerName** (NetBIOS name or IP address), is used to specify the machine or machines to execute the command that is defined in the scriptblock. For example:

```
PS C:\> invoke-command -scriptblock {get-process} -computer dc1,dc2
```

In addition, the Invoke-Command cmdlet supports a set of parameters that make it an even more powerful vehicle to conduct remote automation tasks with. These parameters are described in Table 21.4.

TABLE 21.4 Important Invoke-Command Cmdlet Parameters

Parameter	Details
AsJob	Used to execute the command as a background job
Credential	Used to specify alternate credentials that are used to execute the specified commands
ThrottleLimit	Used to specify the maximum number of connections that can be established by the Invoke-Command cmdlet
Session	Used to execute the command in the specified PSSessions

As discussed previously, the **AsJob** parameter is used to execute the specified command as a background job. However, unlike the Get-WmiObject cmdlet, when the **AsJob** parameter is used with the Invoke-Command cmdlet, a background job is created on the client machine, which then spawns a number of child background jobs on each of the specified remote machines. Once execution of a child background job is finished, the results are returned to the parent background job on the client machine.

If a large number of remote machines are defined using the **ComputerName** parameter, the client machine might become overwhelmed. To help prevent the client machine or your network from drowning in an asynchronous connection storm, the Invoke-Command cmdlet will, by default, limit the number of concurrent remote connections for an issued command to 32. If you want to tweak the number of concurrent connections allowed, you use the **ThrottleLimit** parameter.

NOTE

The **ThrottleLimit** parameter can also be used with the New-PSSession cmdlet.

An important concept to understand when using the Invoke-Command cmdlet is how it actually executes commands on a remote machine. By default, this cmdlet will set up temporary runspace for each of the targeted remote machines. When execution of the specified command has finished, both the runspace and the connection resulting from that runspace are closed. This means, irrespective of how the **ThrottleLimit** parameter is used, if you are executing a number of different commands using the Invoke-Command cmdlet at the same time, the actual number of concurrent connections to a remote machine is the total number of times you invoked the Invoke-Command cmdlet.

If you want to reuse the same existing connection and runspace, you need to use the Invoke-Command cmdlet's **Session** parameter. However, to make use of the parameter requires an already existing runspace on the targeted remote machines. To create a persistent runspace on a remote machine, you use the New-PSSession cmdlet, as shown in the following example:

```
PS C:\> new-pssession -computer "dc1","dc2"
```

After executing this command, two persistent runspaces on each of the specified targets will have been created. These runspaces can then be used to complete multiple commands and even share data between those commands. To use these runspaces, you need to retrieve the resulting runspace objects using the Get-PSSession cmdlet and then pass it into the Invoke-Command cmdlet. For example:

```
PS C:\> $Sessions = new-pssession -computer "dc1","dc2"
PS C:\> invoke-command -scriptblock {get-service "W32Time"} -session $Sessions | ft
PSComputerName, Name, Status

PSComputerName          Name                    Status
------------            ----                    ------
Dc1                     W32Time                 Running
Dc2                     W32Time                 Running
```

First, the **$Sessions** variable is used to store the two resulting runspace objects that are created using the New-PSSession cmdlet. Next, the **$Sessions** variable is then defined as the argument for the **Session** parameter of the Invoke-Command cmdlet. By doing this, the command that is defined as the argument for the **ScriptBlock** parameter is executed within each of the runspaces represented by the **$Sessions** variable. Finally, the results from the command executed within each of the runspaces is returned and piped into the Format-Table cmdlet to format the output. In this case, the output shows the current status of the W32Time service on each of the specified remote machines.

After you have finished executing commands, it's important to understand that the runspaces that were created will remain open until you close the current PowerShell console. To free up the resources being consumed by a runspace, you need to delete it using the Remove-PSSession cmdlet. For example, to remove the runspaces contained in the **$Sessions** variable, you would pass that variable into the Remove-PSSession cmdlet:

```
PS C:\> $Sessions | remove-pssession
```

New-CimSession

With the move toward CIM for managing Windows and non-Windows systems, the **New-CimSession** cmdlet uses WSMAN to access remote computers if they are running PowerShell 3.0 with version 3.0 of the WSMAN stack. Optionally **New-CimSession**, like all CIM cmdlets, can be forced to use DCOM.

For example:

```
PS C:\> New-CimSession -ComputerName dc2

Id           : 2
Name         : CimSession2
InstanceId   : 0b387ab0-1520-42c8-a4e4-c2812876adbc
ComputerName : dc2
Protocol     : WSMAN

As opposed to:
PS C:\> $option = New-CimSessionOption -Protocol DCOM
PS C:\> $out = New-CimSession -ComputerName DC2 -SessionOption $option
PS C:\> $out

Id           : 3
Name         : CimSession3
InstanceId   : 074340ad-eae5-4c85-905b-5dc6e71325a3
ComputerName : DC2
Protocol     : DCOM
```

Both examples make CimSession connections to a remote host, but one uses WSMAN whereas the other is forced to use DCOM.

The established session can then be used to query the remote system for information:

```
PS C:\> get-CimInstance -CimSession $out -ClassName Win32_ComputerSystem

Name          PrimaryOwner Domain        TotalPhysica  Model        Manufacturer
                   Name                                   Memory
----               ------------ ------          ------------ -----         -----------
DC2           Windows User companyab...1073270784  Virtual ... Microsof...
```

While similar to WMI, CIM expands Windows Server 2012's reach into non-Windows devices.

Using the New-Object Cmdlet

The New-Object cmdlet is used to create both .NET and COM objects. To create an instance of a .NET object, you just provide the fully qualified name of the .NET class you want to use, as shown here:

```
PS C:\> $Ping = new-object Net.NetworkInformation.Ping
```

By using the New-Object cmdlet, you now have an instance of the **Ping** class that enables you to detect whether a remote computer can be reached via Internet Control Message Protocol (ICMP). Therefore, you have an object-based version of the Ping.exe command-line tool.

To an instance of a COM object, the **comObject** parameter is used. To use this parameter, define its argument as the COM object's programmatic identifier (ProgID), as shown here:

```
PS C:\> $IE = new-object -comObject InternetExplorer.Application
PS C:\> $IE.Visible=$True
PS C:\> $IE.Navigate("www.cnn.com")
```

Summary

In this chapter, you have been introduced to PowerShell, its features, concepts, and how it can be used to manage Windows. Of all the topics and items covered in this chapter, the most important concept that should be remembered is that PowerShell should not be feared—rather, it should be used. The PowerShell team has produced a CLI shell that is easy and fun to use. With practice, using PowerShell should become second nature.

After all, the writing is on the wall. With the inclusion of PowerShell in the Windows Server 2012 operating system and with the integration into its next generation of products, Microsoft's direction is toward embracing PowerShell. This trend toward all things PowerShell is even clearer when looking at all the community-based projects and third-party products being developed and released that use or enhance PowerShell. After all, PowerShell is the answer that Microsoft has been seeking as the management interface for Windows and its platform products. Thanks to a good feature set, which includes being built around the .NET Framework, being object based, being developed with security in mind, and so on, PowerShell is a powerful tool that should be part of any administrator's arsenal.

Best Practices

The following are best practices from this chapter:

- If a function needs to persist across PowerShell sessions, define that function within your profile.ps1 file.
- To access block information about a base, use the **BaseObject** property with the PSBase standard name.
- When naming a variable, don't use special characters or spaces.
- When using aliases and variables in a script, use names that other people can understand.
- If possible, try not to use aliases in a script.
- In a production environment, don't configure the PowerShell execution policy as unrestricted and always digitally sign your scripts.
- If built-in PowerShell cmdlets don't meet your needs, always remember that you can fall back onto existing automation interfaces (ADSI, WMI, COM, and so forth).
- Useful ISE add-ons are being created all the time. Just click Add-Ons, and then Open Add-On Tools Website to see what's available.

CHAPTER 22

Documenting a Windows Server 2012 Environment

IN THIS CHAPTER

- Benefits of Documentation
- Types of Documents
- Planning to Document the Windows Server 2012 Environment
- Knowledge Sharing and Knowledge Management
- Windows Server 2012 Project Documents
- Administration and Maintenance Documents
- Network Infrastructure
- Disaster Recovery Documentation
- Change Management Procedures
- Performance Documentation
- Baselining Records for Documentation Comparisons
- Routine Reporting
- Security Documentation

As technology advances, we, as implementers, work to learn it, understand it, and figure out how to use it to make our environments more reliable, more secure, and help end users be more productive. We upgrade from one version of an application to the next, and although some of the technology becomes obsolete, the need for accurate documentation remains the same.

Documentation serves several purposes throughout the life cycle of the Windows Server 2012 operating system and is especially important for the planning and execution of a Windows Server 2012 implementation project. In the initial stages of a project, it serves to provide a historical record of the options and decisions made during the design process. During the testing and implementation phases, documents such as step-by-step procedures and checklists guide project team members and help ensure that all steps are completed. When the implementation portion of the project is complete, support documentation plays a key role in maintaining the health of the new environment. Support documents include administration and maintenance procedures, checklists, detailed configuration settings, and monitoring procedures.

This chapter is dedicated to providing the breadth and scope of documentation for a Windows Server 2012 environment. Equally important, it provides considerations and best practices for keeping your messaging environment well documented, maintained, and manageable.

Benefits of Documentation

Documentation that is developed with specific goals and goes through a review or approval process is typically well organized, complete, and contributes to the overall professionalism of the organization and its knowledge base. The following sections examine some of the other benefits of professional documentation in the Windows Server 2012 environment.

Organizational Benefits

Many of the benefits of documenting your Windows Server 2012 environment are obvious and tangible. Documentation is an integral part of the installation or design of a Windows Server 2012 environment as well as the maintenance, support, and recovery of new or existing environments.

Other benefits can be harder to identify. For example, the process of putting the information down on paper encourages a higher level of analysis and review of the topic at hand. The process also encourages teamwork and collaboration within an organization and interdepartmental exchange of ideas.

In today's world of doing more with less, the intangible benefits of good documentation can become a challenge to justify to upper management. Key benefits of documentation include the following:

- **Collaboration**—Producing the documentation to support a good Windows Server 2012 implementation requires input from departments across the organization. This teamwork encourages deeper analysis and more careful review of the project goals. With better base information, the project team can make more informed decisions and avoid having to go back to the drawing board to address missed objectives.
- **Historical records**—Implementation projects are composed of several different stages during which goals are identified and key decisions are made to support them. It is important to ensure these decisions and their supporting arguments are recorded for future reference. As the project moves forward, it is not uncommon for details to get changed because of incomplete information being passed from the design stage on to the implementation stage.
- **Training**—Life is ever-changing. That might sound a bit philosophical for a book on technology, but when it comes to people, we know that some of them move on to other challenges. And that is when good documentation becomes an invaluable tool to provide information to their replacement. This is equally true for the executive sponsor, the project manager, or the engineer building the Windows server.

Financial Benefits

Proper Windows Server 2012 documentation can be time-consuming and adds to the cost of a project. In addition, ongoing costs can come up for maintenance and disaster recovery documents. In lean economic times for a company or organization, it is often difficult to justify the expense of project documentation. However, when looking at documents for maintenance or disaster recovery scenarios, it is easy to see that creating this documentation makes financial sense. For example, in an organization where downtime can cost thousands of dollars per minute, the return on investment (ROI) in disaster recovery and maintenance documentation is easy to calculate. In a company that is growing rapidly and adding staff and new servers on a regular basis, tested documentation on server builds and administration training can also have immediate and visible benefits.

Financial benefits are not limited to maintenance and disaster recovery documentation. Well-developed and professional design and planning documentation helps the organization avoid costly mistakes in the implementation or migration process, such as buying too many server licenses or purchasing too many servers.

Types of Documents

Each document should be created with a specific goal in mind and knowledge of the target audience. The following list specifies the main document categories that are used to implement a Windows Server 2012 project and maintain the environment:

- Historical/planning (who made which decision and how we will manage the project)
- Support and maintenance (to assist with maintaining the hardware and software on the network)
- Policy (service-level agreements)
- Training (for end users or administrators)

It is important that any documentation produced be reviewed by other stakeholders in the organization to ensure that it meets their needs as well, and to simply get input from other sources. For technical procedures, the document must be tested and validated. Ideally, the procedures are written by one resource and validated by one of the target users, be it an end user or one of the administrators. With a review process of this sort, the document will be more useful and more accurate. For example, a server build document that has gone through this process is more likely to be complete and useful in the event the server in question needs to be rebuilt in an emergency.

Documentation that is not historical and that is intended to be used for supporting the network environment or to educate on company policies should be reviewed periodically to ensure that it is still accurate and reflects current corporate policies and processes.

The discipline of creating effective documentation that satisfies the requirements of the appropriate support personnel as well as management is also an asset to the company and can have dramatic effects. The material in this chapter gives a sense of the range of different documents that can have value to an organization and should help in the process of deciding which ones are critical in the organization.

Planning to Document the Windows Server 2012 Environment

When planning documentation (whether for general purposes, specific aspects such as disaster recovery, or a particular project), you should consider several factors:

- The business requirements of the organization
- The technical requirements of the organization
- The audience that will be using the documents
- How and when the documents will be produced and maintained

The extent of the documentation depends on the business and technical requirements of the organization. Some organizations require that each step be documented, and other organizations require that only the configuration be recorded. Careful consideration should be given to any regulatory requirements or existing internal organization policies.

After the specific documentation requirements have been determined, it is important to consider who the audience for each document will be. Who will use each document, in what setting, and for what purpose? It would be impractical to develop a 300-page user guide when all the user wants to do is log on to the messaging system. In that case, all that would be required is a quick reference guide. Properly analyzing the purpose and goals of each document aids in the development of clear and useful documentation.

Planning the schedule for document production often requires a separate project timeline or plan. The plan should include checkpoints, sponsorship or management review, and a clear schedule. Tools such as Microsoft Project facilitate the creation of a documentation project plan. The project plan can also provide an initial estimate of the number of hours required and the associated costs. For instance, based on previous documentation projects, there is an estimate that one to two pages per hour will be produced.

Knowledge Sharing and Knowledge Management

Knowledge sharing is about making the enterprise documentation available to the people who are going to use it. The right documentation enables an organization to organize and manage its data and intellectual property. Company policies and procedures are typically located across multiple locations that include individual files for various departments. Consolidating this information into logical groupings makes it easier to locate for day-to-day usage as well as updating the documents in a timely manner.

TIP

Place documentation in at least two different locations where it is easily accessible for authorized users, such as on the intranet, in a public folder, or in hard-copy format. Also consider using a document management system such as SharePoint 2010.

A complete design document consolidates and summarizes key discussions and decisions, budgetary concerns, and timing issues. This consolidation provides a single source of information for questions that might emerge at a later date. In addition, a document that describes the specific configuration details of the Windows server might prove very valuable to a manager in another company office when making a purchasing decision.

Knowledge management is about keeping the information contained in the documents updated and relevant to the most current environment as well as archiving the historical documentation. All the documents should be readily available at all times. This is especially critical regarding disaster recovery documents. Centralizing the documentation and communicating the location helps reduce the use of out-of-date documentation and reduce confusion during disaster recovery. It is also recommended that documentation be available in a number of formats, such as hard copy, the appropriate place on the network, and even via an intranet.

TIP

Add review and updating of configuration and procedural documents into the recurring maintenance tasks list. This will help keep the task at the forefront of the administrator's responsibilities and ensure the documents are up-to-date when the time comes to use them.

Windows Server 2012 Project Documents

A Windows Server 2012 implementation is a complex endeavor that should be approached in phases. First and foremost, a decision should be made on how the project will be tracked. This can be done using a simple Microsoft Excel spreadsheet, but a tool like Microsoft Project makes mapping out the tasks much easier. Also, the first round of mapping out a project is mostly likely to have at most 15 to 20 lines of tasks. Using a tool like Microsoft Project makes it easier to fill in more line items as you progress in the design and planning stages.

With the tracking method in place, you can move on to address the documents that are typically created for a Windows Server 2012 implementation:

- Project plan
- Design and planning document
- Communication plan
- Migration plan
- Training plan
- Test plan
- Pilot test plan
- Support and project completion document

This chapter discusses each of these documents individually and outlines their key elements.

Project Plan

A project plan is essential for more complex migrations and can be useful for managing smaller projects, even single-server migrations. Tasks should be laid out in the order in which they will occur and be roughly half-day durations or more because a project plan that tries to track a project hour by hour can be overwhelmingly hard to keep up-to-date.

Tools such as Microsoft Project facilitate the creation of project plans and enable the assignment of one or more resources per task and the assignment of durations and links to key predecessors. The project plan can also provide an initial estimate of the number of hours required from each resource and the associated costs if outside resources are to be used. "What-if" scenarios are easy to create by simply adding resources to more complex tasks or cutting out optional steps to see the effect on the budget.

NOTE

It's a great idea to revisit the original project plan after everything is completed (the baseline) to see how accurate it was. Many organizations fail to take this step and miss the opportunity to learn from the planning process to better prepare for the next time.

Design and Planning Document

The first step in the implementation of the Windows Server 2012 environment is the development and approval of a design. Documenting this design contributes to the success of the project. The design document records the decisions made during the design process and provides a reference for testing, implementation, and support. The key components to a design document include the following:

- The goals and objectives of the project
- The background or what led up to the design
- The approach that will be used to implement the solution
- The details of the end state of the project

Goals and objectives can be surprisingly hard to pin down. They need to be detailed and concrete enough to define the results that you want while staying at a high level. For instance, "reduce downtime" is too vague to be considered a functional goal, whereas "implement server clustering with Windows Server 2012 Enterprise Server to reduce downtime to less than 5 minutes in the case of a single-server failure" is much more specific.

Including the background of meetings and brainstorming sessions that led up to the decisions for the end state of the project provides the groundwork for the detailed designs provided later in the document. For example, a decision might have been made "because the CEO wants it that way," which affects the postmigration environment. Other decisions might have come about after many hours of debates over the particulars and required technical research to come up with the "right" answer. Recording this level of information can be extremely useful in the future if performance issues are encountered or additional changes to the network are being considered.

The description of the end state to be implemented can be very high level or can drill down to more specific configurations of each server, depending on the document's audience. However, it is recommended that the design document not include step-by-step procedures or other details of how the process will be accomplished. This level of detail is better handled, in most cases, in dedicated configuration or training documents as discussed later in this chapter.

The Windows Server 2012 design and planning document is the outcome of the design sessions held with the subject matter expert (SME) and the technical staff within the organization. A standard Windows Server 2012 design and planning document will contain the following information:

- Executive Summary
    - Project Overview
- Project Organization
    - Resources
    - Costs
- Risk Assessment
- Goals and Objectives
- Active Directory Architecture
    - Design
    - Domain Design
    - Placeholder Root
    - Namespace
    - Organizational Unit Design
    - Group Design
    - Site Design
    - Group Policy Design
- Mixed Mode Versus Native Mode
- AD Services Design
    - Domain Controller (DC) Placement
    - Global Catalog (GC) Placement

- DNS, DDNS, and Integration
- Platform Selection and Alternatives
- Autosite Coverage
- Flexible Single Master Operations (FSMO) Role Placement
- DC Sizing
- Physical or Virtual Server Setup
- Client Performance
- Service-Level Agreements

- Replication Topology
  - Site Link Topology
  - Site Link Bridges
  - Costs
  - Cost Formula = 1024/log (bw)
  - Schedule
  - Latency/Convergence Time
  - Traffic
- Transport: IP/RPC Versus SMTP
  - Knowledge Consistency Checker (KCC) and Complexity Equation
  - Connection Creation—Automatic Versus Scripted Versus Manual
- Active Directory Database Sizing
  - Domain Database
  - Global Catalog
  - Attributes
  - Exchange 2010 / SharePoint 2010 Extensions
- Security Model
  - Groups
  - Administrators
  - Domain Administrators
  - Schema Administrators
  - Enterprise Administrators
  - DNS Administrators

- Administrative Model
  - Delegation
  - Group Policy
  - Default Domain
  - Default Domain Controller
  - Security Templates
- Directory Integration
  - Existing Windows Environments
  - LDAP
  - AD
- Application Integration
- Desktop Clients
  - Existing Windows Clients
  - UNIX
  - Apple Mac
  - Tablets
  - Apple iOS / Android
  - Group Policy and Lockdown
  - Group Policy Application
  - Templates

Communication Plan

The detail of the communication plan depends on the size of the organization and management requirements. From the project management perspective, the more communication the better! This is especially important when a project touches all aspects of the server environment.

Mapping out the how, when, and who to communicate with allows the project team to prepare well-thought-out reports and plan productive meetings and presentations. This also provides the recipients of the reports the chance to review the plan and set their expectations. Once again, there are no surprises for the project team or the project sponsors.

A good communication plan should include the following topics:

- Audience
- Content

- Delivery method
- Timing and frequency

Table 22.1 gives an example of a communication plan. To make the plan more detailed, columns can be added to list who is responsible for the communication and specific dates for when the communication is delivered.

TABLE 22.1 Communication Plan

Audience	Content (Message)	Delivery Method	Timing Stage/Frequency
Executive sponsor	Project status	Written report	Weekly in email
Project team	Project status	Verbal updates	Weekly in meeting
IT department	Project overview	Presentation	Quarterly meeting

Migration Plan

After the design and planning document has been mapped out, the project team can begin planning the logistics of implementing Windows Server 2012. This document will be a guide that contains the technical steps needed to implement Windows Server 2012 from the ground up. This document goes into great detail on the specific steps for migration. Depending on how the migration team is set up, it might also include logistical instructions, such as the following:

- Communication templates
- Location maps
- Team roles and responsibilities during the implementation

In a large organization, a session or sessions are held to develop the migration plan. An agenda for the development of the plan will look something like this:

- Goals and Objectives
- Project Management
    - Phase I: Design/Planning
    - Phase II: Prototype
    - Phase III: Pilot
    - Phase IV: Implement
    - Phase V: Support
    - Timeline
    - Resource Requirements

- Risk Management
- Iterative Refinement of Plan

- Migration Planning—Active Directory
  - In-Place Versus Restructuring
  - Account Domains
  - Resource Domains
  - Active Directory Migration Tool (ADMT)
  - DNS Integration
- Deployment Tools
  - Scripting
  - Built-In
  - Third-Party
- Building
  - Normalize Environment
  - Data Center First
  - Deployment Strategies
  - Staged Versus Scripted Versus Manual
- Documentation
  - Design
  - Plan
  - Build Guides
  - Migration Guides
  - Administration Guides
  - Maintenance Guides
  - As Builts
  - Disaster Recovery Guides
  - User Guides
- Training
  - Users
  - Administrators
  - Migration Team
  - Technical Experts

- Communications
    - Migration Team
    - Executives and Management
    - Administrators
    - Users
    - Methods
    - Frequency
    - Detail Level
- Administration and Maintenance
    - Administration
    - Maintenance
    - Disaster Recovery
    - Guides
    - Periodic Schedules
    - Daily/Weekly/Monthly
    - Planned Downtime
    - Checklists
- Testing

Note that many of the agenda topics are stated in a way that facilitates discussion. This is a great way to organize discussion points and at the same time keep them on track.

NOTE

The results of testing the design in a prototype or pilot might alter the actual migration steps and procedures. In this case, the migration plan document should be modified to take these changes into account.

Server Migration Procedures

High-level migration procedures should be decided on during a design and planning process and confirmed during a prototype/testing phase. The initial migration document also should focus on the tools that will be used to migrate data, users, and applications, as well as the division of labor for these processes.

A draft of the document can be put together, and when the process is tested again, it can be verified for accuracy. When complete, this information can save you a great deal of time if a number of servers need to be migrated.

TIP

Server migration procedures should be written in such a way so that even less-experienced staff members can use the procedures for the actual migrations.

The procedures covered can include the following:

- Server hardware configuration details
- Windows Server 2012 version for each server
- Service pack (SP) and hotfixes to install on each server
- Services (such as DNS and DHCP) to enable or disable and appropriate settings
- Applications (such as antivirus and SQL Server) to install and appropriate settings
- Security settings
- Steps required to migrate services and data to the new servers
- Steps required to test the new configuration to ensure full functionality
- Steps required to remove old servers from production

Desktop Migration Procedures

As with the documented server migration process, the desktop migration process should be discussed in the design and planning phase and documented in the migration document. In some migrations, the changes might be minimal, whereas other migrations might require dramatic upgrades. For instance, a desktop machine might qualify for an in-place upgrade to Windows 7 or Windows 8 client, whereas another might require hardware or system replacement.

What specifically is documented will vary among organizations; however, the recommended areas to consider documenting are as follows:

- Hardware inventory
- Installation methods, such as Remote Installation Services, third-party imaging software, and network-based installations
- Base installation applications
- Security configuration
- Templates being used
- Language options
- Accessibility considerations

User Migration Procedures

Users and their related information (username, password, and contact information) in other systems or directories need to be migrated to take advantage of Windows Server 2012. The procedures to migrate the users should be examined during the design and planning phases of the project.

User information can exist in many different places such as an Active Directory (AD) domain, an application, and more. The user information might be inconsistent depending on where it exists and how it is stored. Procedures should be documented for migrating the user information from each different location. For example, if some users will be migrated from another operating system or from multiple forests, separate procedures should be documented for each process.

Another scenario to document is the migration of user profiles and desktops. Although some of this information might be redundant with desktop migration scenarios, it is nonetheless important to capture the procedures for making sure that, when clients log on after the migration, all their settings still exist and they will not have any problems with the applications they use. This is a very important consideration for mobile users. For instance, will mobile users need to come back into the office to have settings changed or migrated? Will these changes be performed the next time they log on?

Checklists

The migration process can often be a long process, based on the amount of data that must be migrated. It is helpful to develop both high-level and detailed checklists to guide the migration process. High-level checklists determine the status of the migration at any given point in the process. Detailed checklists ensure that all steps are performed in a consistent manner. This is extremely important if the process is being repeated for multiple sites.

Training Plan

When creating a training plan for a Windows Server 2012 implementation, the first thing that needs to be identified is the target audience. That will determine what type of training needs to be developed. Some of the user groups that need to be targeted for training are as follows:

- **End users**—If the implementation is going to change the desktop client, the end user must receive some level of training.
- **Systems administrators**—The personnel involved in the administration of the messaging systems must be trained.
- **Help desk**—In organizations where the support is divided among different teams, each one must be trained on the tasks he or she will be carrying out.
- **Implementation team**—If the implementation is spread across multiple locations, some project teams choose to create implementation teams. These teams will need to be trained on the implementation process.

After the different groups have been identified, the training plan for each one can be created. The advantage of creating a training plan in-house is the ability to tailor the training to the organization's unique Windows environment. The trainees will not have to go over configurations or settings that do not apply to their network.

As a special note, if the systems administrators and implementation team members can be identified ahead of time, it is wise to have them participate in the prototype stage.

The implementation team can assist by validating procedures and, through the repetitive process, can become more familiar with the procedures. After the prototype environment is set up, administrators and help desk personnel can come in to do the same for the administrative procedures.

This provides the necessary validation process and also allows the systems groups to become more comfortable with the new tools and technology.

Test Plan

Thorough testing is critical in the success of any implementation project. A test plan details the resources required for testing (hardware, software, and lab personnel), the tests or procedures to perform, and the purpose of the test or procedure.

It is important to include representatives of every aspect of the network in the development of the test plan. This ensures that all aspects of the Windows Server 2012 environment or project and its impact will be included in the test plan.

Prototype Test Plan

Going in to the prototype stage, experienced engineers and project managers are aware that the initial plan will probably have to be modified because of reasons such as application incompatibility, administrative requirements, or undocumented aspects of the current environment.

So, if it was important to start out this stage with a well-documented plan, the most important documentation goal for the prototype is to track these changes to ensure that the project still meets all goals and objectives of the implementation.

The document tool the project team will use to do this is the test plan. A well-developed test plan contains a master test plan and provides the ability to document the test results for reference at a later date. This is necessary because the implementation procedures will likely have changes from the first round of testing to the next and the project team will need to refer to the outcome to compare results.

A test plan outline contains the following:

- Summary of what is being tested and the overall technical goals of the implementation
- Scope of what will be tested

- Resources needed
  - Hardware
  - Software
  - Personnel
- Documentation
  - What will be recorded
  - Test plan outline
- Operating system
  - Hardware compatibility
  - Install first domain controller
  - Test replication
  - Install additional domain controllers
  - Client access
  - Role-based configuration
  - Domain name system (DNS)
  - Dynamic Host Configuration Protocol (DHCP)
  - Internet Information Services (IIS)
  - Domain controller
  - Exchange
  - Group policy
  - New settings
  - Group Policy Management Console
  - Resultant set of policies
  - Antivirus
  - Password policy
  - Security templates
  - File migration
  - Print migration
  - Distributed file system
  - Volume Shadow Copy

- Remote Assistance
- Uninterruptible power supply (UPS) battery backup software
- Applications testing
- Backup and restore
- Monitoring software (Systems Center Operations Manager 2012)
- Administrative rights

Each individual test should be documented in a test form listing the expected outcome and the actual outcome. This becomes part of the original test plan and is used to validate the implementation procedure or document a change.

Table 22.2 shows a sample test form.

TABLE 22.2 Sample Test Form

Test Name
Hardware requirements:
Software requirements:
Other requirements:
Expected outcome:
Actual outcome:
Tester:
Date:

At the end of the stage, it should be clearly documented what, if anything, has changed. The documentation deliverables of this stage are as follows:

- Pilot implementation plan
- Implementation plan
- Rollback plan

Pilot Test Plan

Documenting a pilot implementation has special requirements because it is the first time the implementation will touch the production environment. If the environment is a complex one where multiple applications are affected by the implementation, all details should be documented along with the outcome of the pilot.

This is done by having a document similar in content to the test plan form and tracking any issues that come up.

In extreme cases, the project team will have to put into effect the rollback plan. Before starting the pilot implementation, the team should have an escalation process along with contact names and numbers of the personnel with the authority to make the go/no-go decision in a given situation.

Support and Project Completion Document

A Windows Server 2012 implementation should include a plan for handing off administration to the personnel who will be supporting the environment after the implementation is complete. This is especially true if the SMEs are brought in to implement the Windows Server 2012 infrastructure and will not be remaining onsite to support it.

The handoff plan should be included in the original project plan and have a timeline for delivery of the administrative documentation as well as training sessions if needed.

Administration and Maintenance Documents

Administration and maintenance documentation can be critical in maintaining a reliable network environment. These documents help the administrator of a particular server or set of servers organize and keep track of the different steps that need to be taken to ensure the health of the systems under his or her care. They also facilitate the training of new resources and reduce the variables and risks involved in these transitions.

Windows Server 2012 systems can serve several different functions on the network, such as file servers, print servers, web servers, messaging servers, terminal servers, and remote-access servers. The necessary maintenance procedures might be slightly different for each one based on its function and importance in the network.

One key component to administration or maintenance documentation is a timeline detailing when certain procedures should be followed. As Chapter 20, "Windows Server 2012 Management and Maintenance Practices," discusses, certain daily, weekly, monthly, and quarterly procedures should be followed. These procedures, such as weekly event log archiving, should be documented to ensure that there are clearly defined procedures and frequency in which they should be performed.

Step-by-Step Procedure Documents

Administration and maintenance documentation contains a significant amount of procedural documentation. These documents can be very helpful for complex processes, or for processes that are not performed on a regular basis. Procedures range from technical processes that outline each step to administrative processes that help clarify roles and responsibilities.

Flowcharts from Microsoft Visio or a similar product are often sufficient for the administrative processes, such as when testing a new patch to a key software application, approving the addition of a new server to the network, or scheduling network downtime.

Policies

Although policy documents might not be exciting reading, they can be an administrator's best friend in touchy situations. A well-thought-out, complete, and approved policy document makes it clear who is responsible for what in specific situations. It is also important to be realistic about which policies need to be documented and what is excessive—for example, document policies concerning when and how the servers can be updated with patches, newer hardware, or software.

Documented Checklists

Administration and maintenance documentation can be extensive, and checklists can be quick reminders for those processes and procedures. Develop comprehensive checklists that will help administrators perform their scheduled and unscheduled tasks. A timeline checklist highlighting the daily, weekly, monthly, and quarterly tasks helps keep the Windows Server 2012 environment healthy. In addition, these checklists function as excellent auditing tools.

Active Directory Infrastructure

Active Directory is one of the core services for a Windows Server 2012 environment. As such, documenting the AD infrastructure is a critical component to the environment. There are many aspects to documents as they relate to AD, including the following:

- Forest and domain structure, such as DNS names, NetBIOS names, mode of operation, and trust relationships
- Names and placement of domain controllers (DCs) and Global Catalog (GC) servers
- Flexible Single Master Operations (FSMO) locations on DCs or GCs
- Sites, site links, link costs, and site-link bridges
- Organizational unit (OU) topology
- Special schema entries (such as those made by applications)
- Security groups and distribution lists
- AD-integrated DNS information
- AD security
- Group policy object (GPO) configurations and structure

This information can be extremely useful in day-to-day operations as well as when you're troubleshooting AD issues, such as replication latency or logon problems.

Server Build Procedures

The server build procedure is a detailed set of instructions for building the Windows Server 2012 system. This document can be used for troubleshooting and adding new servers, and is a critical resource in the event of a disaster.

The following is an example of a table of contents from a server build procedure document:

Windows Server 2012 Build Procedures

- System Configuration Parameters
- Configure the Server Hardware
  - Install Vendor Drivers
  - Configure RAID
- Install and Configure Windows Server 2012
  - Using Images
  - Scripted Installations
- Applying Windows Server 2012 Security
  - Using a Security Template
  - Using GPOs
  - Configuring Antivirus
  - Installing Service Packs and Critical Updates
- Backup Client Configuration

Configuration (As-Built) Documentation

The configuration document, often referred to as an as-built, details a snapshot configuration of the Windows Server 2012 system as it is built. This document contains essential information required to rebuild a server.

The following is a Windows Server 2012 as-built document template:

Introduction

The purpose of this Windows Server 2012 as-built document is to assist an experienced network administrator or engineer in restoring the server in the event of a hardware failure. This document contains screenshots and configuration settings for the server at the time it was built. If settings are not implicitly defined in this document, they are assumed to be set to defaults. It is not intended to be a comprehensive disaster recovery with step-by-step procedures for rebuilding the server. For this document to remain useful as a recovery aid, it must be updated as configuration settings change.

- System Configuration
  - Hardware Summary
  - Disk Configuration
  - Logical Disk Configuration

- System Summary
- Device Manager
- RAID Configuration
- Windows Server 2012 TCP/IP Configuration
- Network Adapter Local Area Connections

- Security Configuration
    - Services
    - Lockdown Procedures (Checklist)
    - Antivirus Configuration
- Share List
    - Applications and Configurations

Topology Diagrams

Network configuration diagrams and related documentation generally include local-area network (LAN) connectivity, wide-area network (WAN) infrastructure connectivity, IP subnet information, critical servers, network devices, and more. Having accurate diagrams of the new environment can be invaluable when troubleshooting connectivity issues. For topology diagrams that can be used for troubleshooting connectivity issues, consider documenting the following:

- Internet service provider contact names, including technical support contact information
- Connection type (such as T1, T3, 10Mbps fiber, 20Mbps fiber, and so on)
- Link speed
- Committed information rate (CIR)
- Endpoint configurations, including routers used
- Message flow and routing

Administration Manual

The administration manual is the main tool for the administrative group. All the Windows tasks are documented with details specific to the organization. A well-prepared administration manual can also be used for training new administrators.

Using Documentation for Troubleshooting Purposes

Troubleshooting documentation is helpful both in terms of the processes that the company recommends for resolving technical issues and for documenting the results of actual troubleshooting challenges. Often, companies have database and trouble-ticket processes in place to record the time a request was made for assistance, the process followed, and the results. This information should then be available to the appropriate support staff so they know the appropriate resolution if the problem comes up again.

Organizations might also choose to document troubleshooting methodologies to use as training aids and also to ensure that specific steps are taken as a standard practice for quality of service to the user community.

Procedural Documents

Although security policies and guidelines comprise the majority of security documentation, procedures are equally as important. Procedures include not only the initial configuration steps, but also maintenance procedures and more important procedures that are to be followed in the event of a security breach.

Additional areas regarding security that can be documented include the following:

- Auditing policies, including review
- Service packs (SPs) and hotfixes
- Certificates and certificates of authority
- Antivirus configurations
- BitLocker
- Password policies (such as length, strength, age)
- GPO security-related policies
- Registry security
- Lockdown procedures

Network Infrastructure

Network configuration documentation is essential when you are designing technologies that might be integrated into the network, when managing network-related services such as DNS, when administering various locations, and when troubleshooting. Network environments usually don't change as much as a server infrastructure. Nonetheless, it's important to keep this information current and accurate through periodic reviews and analysis.

Documenting the WAN Infrastructure

Network configuration documentation also includes WAN infrastructure connectivity. Consider documenting the following:

- Internet service provider contact names, including technical support contact information

- Connection type (such as T1, T3, 10Mbps fiber, 20Mbps fiber, and so on)
- Link speed
- Committed information rate (CIR)
- Endpoint configurations, including routers used

Enterprise networks can have many different types of WAN links, each varying in speed and CIR. This documentation is useful not only for understanding the environment, but also for troubleshooting connectivity, replication issues, and more.

Network Device Documentation

Network devices such as firewalls, routers, and switches use a proprietary operating system. Also, depending on the device, the configuration should be documented. Some devices permit configuration dumps to a text file that can be used in the overall documentation, whereas others support web-based retrieval methods. In worst-case scenarios, administrators must manually document the configurations.

Network device configurations, with possibly the exception of a firewall, rarely change. If a change does occur, it should be documented in a change log and updated in the network infrastructure documentation. This allows administrators to keep accurate records of the environment and also provides a quick, documented way to rebuild the proper configurations in case of a failure.

NOTE

Step-by-step procedures for rebuilding each network device are recommended. This information can minimize downtime and administration.

Disaster Recovery Documentation

Creating and maintaining a disaster recovery plan for the Windows Server 2012 infrastructure requires the commitment of IT managers as well as the systems administrators in charge of the messaging systems. This is because creating a disaster recovery plan is a complex process and, after it is developed, the only way of maintaining it is by practicing the procedures on a regular schedule. This will, of course, involve the administrative personnel and should be worked into their scheduled tasks.

The initial steps of creating the DR plan involve determining what the desired recovery times are. Then, the team moves on to discuss possible disaster scenarios and maps out a plan for each one. The following table of contents outlines the different topics that are addressed when creating the DR plan:

- Executive Summary or Introduction
- Disaster Recovery Scenarios

- Disaster Recovery Best Practices
  - Planning and Designing for Disaster
- Business Continuity and Response
  - Business Hours Response to Emergencies
  - Recovery Team Members
  - Recovery Team Responsibilities
  - Damage Assessment
  - Off-hours Response to an Emergency
  - Recovery Team Responsibilities
  - Recovery Strategy
  - Coordinate Equipment Needs
- Disaster Recovery Decision Tree
- Software Recovery
- Hardware Recovery
- Server Disaster Recovery
- Preparation
  - Documentation
  - Software Management
  - Knowledge Management
- Server Backup
  - Client Software Configuration
- Restoring the Server
  - Build the Server Hardware
  - Post-Restore
- Active Directory Disaster Recovery
  - Disaster Recovery Service-Level Agreements
  - Windows Server 2012 Disaster Recovery Plan
  - Hyper-V Replication
  - RAID Storage Failure

- SAN Storage Failure
- Complete System Failure
- NIC, RAID Controller Failures
- Train Personnel and Practice Disaster Recovery

Every organization should go through the process of contemplating various disaster scenarios. For instance, organizations on the West Coast might be more concerned with earthquakes than those on the East Coast. Each disaster can pose a different threat. Therefore, it is important to determine every possible scenario and begin planning ways to minimize those disasters.

Equally important is analyzing how downtime resulting from a disaster might affect the company (reputation, time, productivity, expenses, loss in profit or revenue) and determine how much should be invested in remedies to avoid or minimize the effects.

A number of different components make up disaster recovery documentation. Without this documentation, full recovery is difficult at best.

Disaster Recovery Planning

The first step of the disaster recovery process is to develop a formal disaster recovery plan. This plan, although time-consuming to develop, serves as a guide for the entire organization in the event of an emergency. Disaster scenarios, such as power outages, hard drive failures, and even earthquakes, should be addressed. Although it is impossible to develop a scenario for every potential disaster, it is still helpful to develop a plan to recover for different levels of disaster. It is recommended that organizations encourage open discussions of possible scenarios and the steps required to recover from each one. Include representatives from each department because each department will have its own priorities in the event of a disaster. The disaster recovery plan should encompass the organization as a whole and focus on determining what it will take to resume normal business function after a disaster.

Backup and Recovery Development

Another important component of a disaster recovery development process is the evaluation of the organization's current backup policies and procedures. Without sound backup policies and procedures, a disaster recovery plan is useless. It is not possible to recover a system if the backup is not valid.

Backup procedures encompass not only backing up data to tape or other media, but also a variety of other tasks, including advanced system recovery, offsite storage, and retention. These tasks should be carefully documented to accurately represent what backup methodologies are implemented and how they are carried out. Step-by-step procedures, guidelines, policies, and more can be documented.

Periodically, the backup documents should be reviewed and tested, especially after any configuration changes. Otherwise, backup documents can become stale and can only add more work and add to the problems during recovery attempts.

Recovery documentation complements backup documentation. This documentation should include where the backup data resides and how to recover from various types of failures (such as hard drive failure, system failure, and natural disaster). As with backup documentation, recovery documentation can take the form of step-by-step guides, policies, frequently asked questions (FAQs), and checklists. Moreover, recovery documents should be reviewed for validity and revised if necessary.

Monitoring and Performance Documentation

Monitoring is not typically considered a part of disaster recovery documentation. However, alerting mechanisms can detect and bring attention to issues that might arise. Alerting mechanisms can provide a proactive means to determining whether a disaster might strike. Documenting alerting mechanisms and the actions to take when an alert is received can reduce downtime and administration.

Windows System Failover Documentation

Organizations using failover technologies or techniques such as clustering or network load balancing (NLB) can benefit from having documentation regarding failover. When a system fails over, knowing the procedures to get the system back up and running quickly can help you avoid unnecessary risk. These documented procedures must be thoroughly tested and reviewed in a lab setting so that they accurately reflect the process to recover each system.

Change Management Procedures

Changes to the environment occur all the time in an organization, yet often those changes are either rarely documented or no set procedures are in place for making those changes. IT personnel not responsible for the change might be oblivious to those changes, and other administration or maintenance might be adversely affected.

Documented change management seeks to bring knowledge consistency throughout IT, control when and how changes are made, and minimize disruption from incorrect or unplanned changes. As a result, documenting change procedures should entail the processes to request and approve changes, the high-level testing procedures, the actual change procedures, and any rollback procedures in case problems arise.

Performance Documentation

Documenting performance-related information is a continuous process because of the ever-changing metrics of business. This type of documentation begins by aligning with the goals, existing policies, and service-level agreements (SLAs) for the organization. When these areas are clearly defined and detailed, baseline performance values can be established using System Monitor, System Center Operations Manager (SCOM), or third-party tools (such as Nagios or IBM Tivoli). Performance baselines capture performance-related metrics, such as how much memory is being used, the average processor utilization, and more; they also illustrate how the Windows Server 2012 environment is performing under various workloads.

After the baseline performance values are documented and understood, the performance-related information that the monitoring solution is still capturing should be analyzed periodically. More specifically, pattern and trend analysis needs to be examined on a weekly basis if not on a daily basis. This analysis can uncover current and potential bottlenecks and proactively ensure that the system operates as efficiently and effectively as possible.

Baselining Records for Documentation Comparisons

Baselining is a process of recording the state of a Windows Server 2012 system so that any changes in its performance can be identified at a later date. Complete baselining also pertains to the overall network performance, including WAN links, but in those cases it might require special software and tools (such as sniffers) to record the information.

A Windows Server 2012 system baseline document records the state of the server after it is implemented in a production environment and can include statistics such as memory use, paging, disk subsystem throughput, and more. This information then allows the administrator or appropriate IT resource to determine at a later date how the system is performing in comparison to its initial operation.

Routine Reporting

Although System Monitor can log performance data and provide reporting when used with other products such as Microsoft Excel, administrators should use products such as SCOM for monitoring and reporting functionality. For example, SCOM can manage and monitor multiple systems and provide graphical reports with customizable levels of detail.

Management-Level Reporting

Management-level reporting on performance data should be concise and direct but still at a high level. Stakeholders do not require an ample amount of performance data, but it is important to show trends, patterns, and any potential problem areas. This extremely useful information provides a certain level of insight to management so that decisions can be made as to what is required to keep the systems operating in top-notch condition. For instance, administrators identify and report to management that, if current trends on Windows Server 2012 server processor utilization continue at the current rate of a 5% increase per month, this will require additional processors in 10 months or less. Management can then take this report, follow the issue more closely over the next few months, and then determine whether to allocate funds to purchase additional processors. If the decision is made to buy more processors, management has more time to negotiate quantity, processing power, and cost instead of having to potentially pay higher costs for the processors on short notice.

Technical Reporting

Technical performance information reporting is much more detailed than management-level reporting. Details are given on many different components and facets of the system. For example, many specific counter values can be given to determine disk subsystem utilization. In addition, trend and pattern analysis should also be included to show historical information and determine how to plan for future requirements.

Security Documentation

Administrators can easily feel that documenting security settings and other configurations is important but that this documentation might lessen security mechanisms in the Windows Server 2012 environment. Nevertheless, documenting security mechanisms and corresponding configurations is vital to administration, maintenance, and any potential security compromise.

As with many of the documents about the network environment, they can do a lot of good for someone either externally or internally trying to gain unauthorized access. So, security documentation and many other forms of documentation, including network diagrams, configurations, and more, should be well guarded to minimize any security risk.

Areas related to security that should be documented include the following:

- Auditing policies including review
- SPs and hotfixes
- Certificates and certificates of authority
- Firewall and proxy configurations
- Antivirus configurations
- Access control policies, including NTFS-related permissions
- BitLocker
- Password policies (such as length, strength, and age)
- GPO security-related policies
- Registry security
- Security breach identification procedures
- Lockdown procedures

Change Control

Although the documentation of policies and procedures to protect the system from external security risks is of utmost importance, internal procedures and documents should also be established. Developing, documenting, and enforcing a change-control process helps protect the system from well-intentioned internal changes.

In environments with multiple administrators, it is common to have the interests of one administrator affect those of another. For instance, an administrator might make a configuration change to limit volume size for a specific department. If this change is not documented, a second administrator might spend a significant amount of time trying to troubleshoot a user complaint from that department. Establishing a change-control process that documents these types of changes eliminates confusion and wasted resources. The change-control process should include an extensive testing process to reduce the risk of production problems.

Reviewing Reports

A network environment might have many security mechanisms in place, but if the information such as logs and events obtained from them is not reviewed, security is more relaxed. Monitoring and management solutions (such as SCOM) can help consolidate this information into a report that can be generated on a periodic basis. This report can be invaluable to continuously evaluating the network's security.

The reports should be reviewed daily and should include many details for the administrators to analyze. You can customize SCOM, for example, to report on only the most pertinent events for keeping the environment secure.

Management-Level Reporting for Security Assessments

Management should be informed of any unauthorized access or attempts to compromise security. The technical details that an administrator appreciates are usually too detailed for management. Therefore, management-level reporting on security issues should contain only vital statistics and any risks that might be present. Business policy and budget-related decisions can then be made to strengthen the environment's security.

Summary

Most, if not all, aspects of a Windows Server 2012 network environment can be documented. However, the type of documentation that can benefit the environment depends on each organization. Overall, documenting the environment is an important aspect of the network and can assist all aspects of administration, maintenance, support, troubleshooting, testing, and design.

Best Practices

The following are best practices from this chapter:

- Create documents that target a specific audience and meet a particular goal.
- Have documentation reviewed and approved by other stakeholders in the organization to ensure that it meets their needs as well, and to simply get input from another source. For technical procedures, the document also must be tested and walked through.

- Consolidate and centralize documentation for the organization.
- Document the company's policies and procedures for securing and maintaining the Windows environment.
- Create well-thought-out and professional planning and design documentation to avoid costly mistakes in the implementation or migration process, such as buying too many server licenses or purchasing too many servers.
- Baseline and document the state of a Windows Server 2012 server so that any changes in its performance can be identified at a later date.
- Use tools such as Microsoft Project to facilitate the creation of project plans, enable the assignment of one or more resources per task, and enable the assignment of durations and links to key predecessors.
- Create disaster recovery documentation that includes step-by-step procedures for rebuilding each server and network device to minimize downtime and administration.
- Document daily, weekly, monthly, and quarterly maintenance tasks to ensure the health of the systems.
- Use documentation to facilitate training.
- Document business and technical policies for the organization.
- Establish a plan for reviewing and updating documents and make it a part of routine maintenance.

CHAPTER 23

Integrating System Center Operations Manager 2012 with Windows Server 2012

IN THIS CHAPTER

System Center Operations Manager (OpsMgr) 2012 provides the best-of-breed approach to end-to-end monitoring and managing for Windows Server 2012. This includes servers, applications, and devices. Through the use of monitoring and alerting components, OpsMgr helps to identify specific environmental conditions before they evolve into problems.

OpsMgr provides a timely view of important Windows Server 2012 server and application conditions and intelligently links problems to knowledge provided within the monitoring rules. Critical events and known issues are identified and matched to technical reference articles in the Microsoft Knowledge Base for troubleshooting and quick problem resolution.

The monitoring is accomplished using standard operating system components such as Windows Management Instrumentation (WMI), Windows event logs, and Windows performance counters, along with Windows Server 2012 specific application programming interface (API) calls and scripts. OpsMgr-specific components are also designed to perform synthetic transaction and track the health and availability of network services. In addition, OpsMgr provides a reporting feature that allows administrators to track problems and trends occurring on the network. Reports can be generated automatically, providing network administrators, managers, and decision makers with a current and long-term historical view of environmental trends. These reports can be delivered via email or stored on file shares for archive to power web pages.

The following sections focus on defining OpsMgr as a monitoring system for Windows Server 2012. This chapter provides specific analysis of the way OpsMgr operates and presents OpsMgr design best practices, specific to deployment for Windows Server 2012 monitoring.

Windows Server 2012 Monitoring

The Operations Manager 2012 monitoring is organized into management packs (MPs) for ease of installation and versioning. The Operations Manager 2012 includes some of the best MPs for monitoring and maintaining Windows Server 2012. These include the following:

- Windows Server Operating System MPs
- Active Directory Server MPs
- Windows Cluster Management MPs
- Microsoft Windows DNS Server MPs
- Microsoft Windows DHCP Server MPs
- Microsoft Windows Group Policy MPs
- Microsoft Windows Hyper-V MPs
- Windows Server Internet Information Services MPs
- Windows Server Network Load Balancing MPs
- Windows Server Print Server MPs
- Windows Terminal Services MPs

Each of the preceding categories includes several different MPs to support monitoring, discovery, and libraries. These MPs were developed by the product groups and include deep knowledge about the product.

The features of the MPs for the following major systems are as follows:

- **Windows Operating System Management Pack**—Monitors and alerts all the major elements that Windows Server 2012 runs on, including processor, memory, network, disk, and event logs. It gathers performance metrics and alerts on thresholds, as well as critical events.
- **Active Directory Management Pack**—Monitors and alerts on Windows Server 2012 Active Directory key metrics, such as replication latency, domain controller response times, and critical events. The MP generates synthetic transactions to test the response time of the PDC, LDAP, and other domain services.

- **DNS Management Pack**—Monitors and alerts on Windows Server 2012 DNS servers for resolution failures and latency as well as critical events.
- **IIS Management Pack**—Monitors and alerts on Windows Server 2012 IIS services, application pools, performance, and critical events.

On all these elements, administrators can generate Availability reports to ensure that the servers and systems are meeting the service-level agreements (SLAs) set by the organization.

The MP includes a comprehensive set of reports that are specific to Windows Server 2012. These include reports on performance, availability, events, and even configuration for the various Windows Server 2012 roles. These reports can be generated ad hoc, scheduled for email delivery on a regular basis, or even generated into web pages for portal viewing. Figure 23.1 shows a Performance by System utilization report for a server. The report shows that processor utilization is low and that memory utilization is steady, but that the Average Disk sec/Transfer is high.

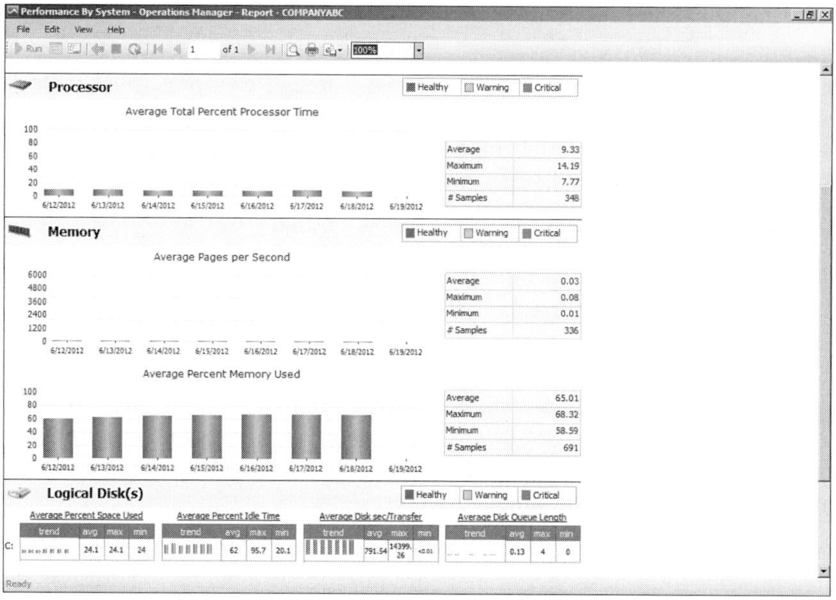

FIGURE 23.1 Performance by System report.

This kind of summary performance report showing trends, analysis, and color-coded problem areas is invaluable to reporting on the Windows Server 2012 infrastructure and really ties together the low-level technical monitoring into a high-level view that support personnel can use.

Understanding How OpsMgr Works

OpsMgr is a sophisticated monitoring system that effectively allows for large-scale management of mission-critical servers. Organizations with a medium to large investment in Microsoft technologies will find that OpsMgr allows for an unprecedented ability to keep on top of the tens of thousands of event log messages that occur on a daily basis. In its simplest form, OpsMgr performs two functions: processing monitored data and issuing alerts and automatic responses based on that data.

The monitoring is accomplished using standard operating system components such as Windows Management Instrumentation (WMI) and WS-Management, Windows and UNIX event logs, and Windows and UNIX performance counters, along with API calls and scripts. OpsMgr-specific components are also designed to perform synthetic transactions and track the health and availability of network services. In addition, OpsMgr provides a reporting feature that allows administrators to track problems and trends occurring on the network. Reports can be generated automatically, providing network administrators, managers, and decision makers with a current and long-term historical view of environmental trends. These reports can be delivered via email or stored on file shares for archiving or to power web pages.

The model-based architecture of OpsMgr presents a fundamental shift in the way a network is monitored. The entire environment can be monitored as groups of hierarchical services with interdependent components. Microsoft, in addition to third-party vendors and a large development community, can leverage the functionality of OpsMgr components through customizable monitoring rules.

OpsMgr provides for several major pieces of functionality, as follows:

- **Management packs**—Application-specific monitoring rules are provided within individual files called management packs. For example, Microsoft provides MPs for Windows Server systems, Exchange Server, SQL Server, SharePoint, domain name system (DNS), and Dynamic Host Configuration Protocol (DHCP), along with many other Microsoft technologies. MPs are loaded with the intelligence and information necessary to properly troubleshoot and identify problems. The rules are dynamically applied to agents based on a custom discovery process provided within the MP. Only applicable rules are applied to each managed server.
- **Monitors**—MPs contain monitors, which allow for advanced state-based monitoring and aggregated health rollup of services. There are monitors for events, performance, logs, services, and even processes. Monitors also provide self-tuning performance threshold monitoring based on a two- or three-state configuration.
- **Rules**—MP rules can monitor for specific event log data, collect performance data, or even run scripts on a timed basis. This is one of the key methods of responding to conditions within the environment. MP rules can monitor for specific performance counters. This data is used for alerting based on thresholds or archived for trending and capacity planning. A performance graph shown in Figure 23.2 shows DNS

Response Time data for the DC1 and DC2 DNS servers. Response time is normally below 0.25 seconds, but DC1 occasionally spikes to above than 1.5 seconds. This would bear investigation, because something seems to be slowing response times.

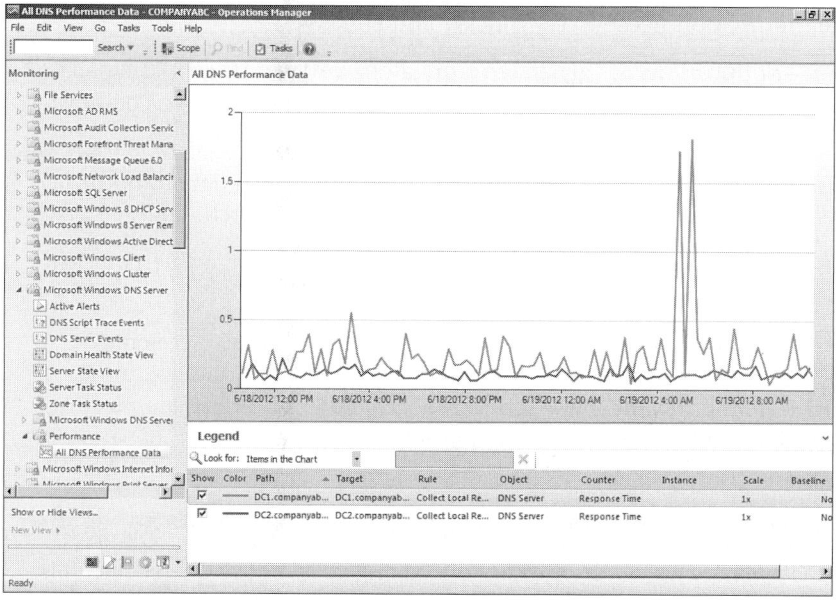

FIGURE 23.2 Operations Manager 2012 performance charts.

- **Alerting and notification**—OpsMgr provides advanced alerting functionality such as alert notifications via email, paging, Short Message Service (SMS), and instant messaging (IM). Alerts are highly customizable, with the ability to define alert rules for all monitored components.
- **End-to-end service monitoring**—OpsMgr provides service-oriented monitoring based on System Definition Model (SDM) technologies. This includes advanced object discovery and hierarchical monitoring of systems, as well as synthetic transactions that confirm the health of the system from a client perspective. This includes URLs, ports, Active Directory, Lightweight Directory Access Protocol (LDAP), database access, and Exchange services.

Operations Manager 2012 can present the collected information in a variety of ways. The OpsMgr monitoring environment can be accessed through three sets of consoles: an Operations console, a Web console, and a command shell. The Operations console provides full monitoring of agent systems and administration of the OpsMgr environment, whereas the Web console provides access only to the monitoring functionality. The command shell provides command-line access to administer the OpsMgr environment.

Major OpsMgr components are as follows:

- **Consoles**—The main method for presenting information is the Operations console and the Web console. The Operations console is the full console and presents alert, event, and performance data in a highly scalable fashion. This allows an operator to drill into the information needed very quickly and effectively.
- **Notifications**—Notifications are generated from alerts and can be sent as email, SMS, or IM messages. There is also a generic command notification, which allows any command line or script to execute.
- **Reports**—Monitoring rules can be configured to send monitored data to both the operations database for alerting and the reporting database for archiving.
- **Dashboards**—Sophisticated dashboards can be configured to display alerts, performance, and state, both in the consoles and in SharePoint.
- **Service-level dashboards**—The Service Level Dashboards Solution Accelerator leverages the Service Level Tracking feature of OpsMgr 2012 and the ubiquitous SharePoint to present a flexible view of how objects and applications are meeting defined service-level objectives (SLOs), such as 99.9% uptime or other metrics.

NOTE

Service-level dashboards are a Solution Accelerator and require Microsoft SharePoint. This is an add-on developed by Microsoft to leverage the functionality of Operations Manager, but is not really a part of the product.

Interestingly, the Service Level Tracking (SLT) feature of Operations Manager was developed expressly to enable service-level dashboards, although SLTs can be used completely independently using the Operations Manager reporting feature.

Processing Operational Data

OpsMgr manages Windows Server 2012 infrastructures through monitoring rules used for object discovery, Windows event log monitoring, performance data gathering, and application-specific synthetic transactions.

Monitoring rules define how OpsMgr collects, handles, and responds to the information gathered. OpsMgr monitoring rules handle incoming event data and allow OpsMgr to react automatically, either to respond to a predetermined problem scenario, such as a failed hard drive, with predefined corrective and diagnostics actions (for example, trigger an alert, execute a command or script), or to provide the operator with additional details based on what was happening at the time the condition occurred.

Another key feature of OpsMgr is the capability to monitor and track service-level performance. OpsMgr can be configured to monitor key performance thresholds through rules that are set to collect predefined performance data, such as memory and CPU usage over time. Rules can be configured to trigger alerts and actions when specified performance thresholds have been met or exceeded, allowing network administrators to act on potential performance issues. Performance data can be viewed from the OpsMgr Operations console.

In addition, performance monitors can establish baselines for the environment and then alert the administrator when the counter subsequently falls outside the defined baseline envelope.

Generating Alerts and Responses

OpsMgr monitoring rules can generate alerts based on critical events, synthetic transactions, or performance thresholds and variances found through self-tuning performance trending. An alert can be generated by a single event or by a combination of events or performance thresholds. Alerts can also be configured to trigger responses such as email, pages, Simple Network Management Protocol (SNMP) traps, and scripts to notify you of potential problems. In brief, OpsMgr is completely customizable in this respect and can be modified to fit most alert requirements. A sample alert is shown in Figure 23.3. The selected alert shows that the database server could not allocate space for an object. Note that the description is clear and specific. Notice also that the figure shows the alert knowledge and suggested resolutions as well, in this case to free disk space.

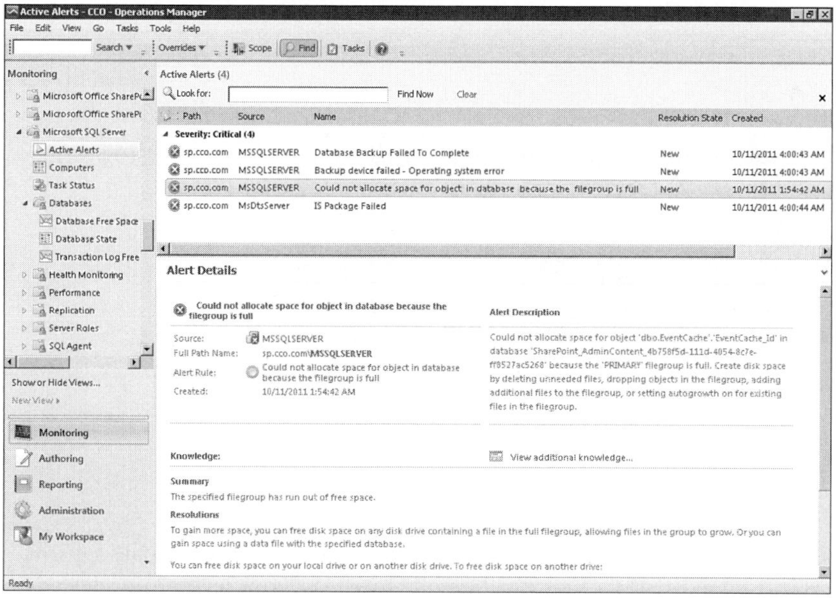

FIGURE 23.3 Operations Manager 2012 alert.

Reporting from OpsMgr

OpsMgr MPs commonly include a variety of preconfigured reports to show information about the operating system or the specific application they were designed to work with. These reports are run in SQL Reporting Services. The reports provide an effective view of systems and services on the network over a custom period, such as weekly, monthly, or quarterly. They can also help you monitor your networks based on performance data, which can include critical pattern analysis, trend analysis, capacity planning, and security auditing. Reports also provide availability statistics for distributed applications, servers, and specific components within a server.

Availability reports are particularly useful for executives, managers, and application owners. These reports can show the availability of any object within OpsMgr, including a server (shown in Figure 23.4), a database, or even a service such as Windows Server 2012 Active Directory that includes a multitude of servers and components. The Availability report shown in Figure 23.4 indicates that the DC1 server has been 100% available for the week.

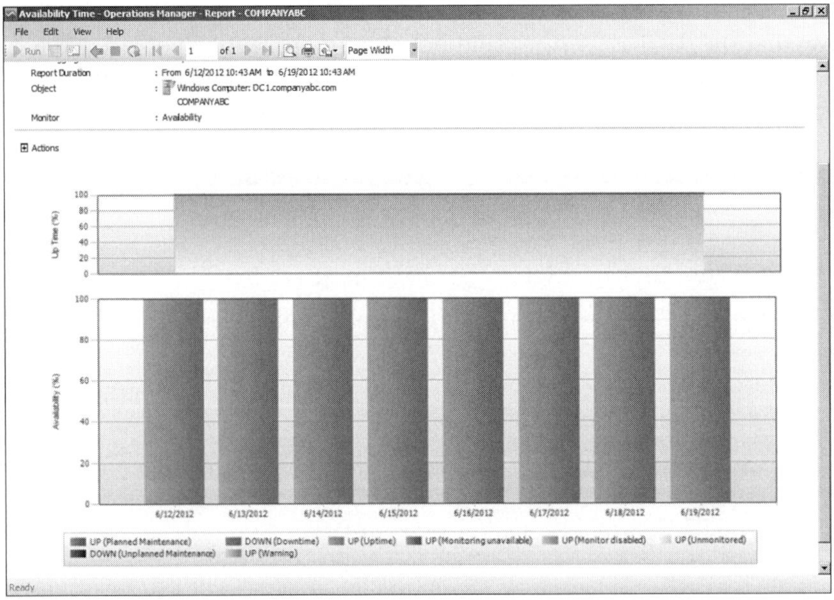

FIGURE 23.4 Availability report.

The reports can be run on demand or at scheduled times and delivered via email. OpsMgr can also generate HTML-based reports that can be published to a web server and viewed from any web browser. Vendors can also create additional reports as part of their MPs.

OpsMgr Architecture Components

OpsMgr is primarily composed of five basic components: the operations database, reporting database, management server, management agents, and Operations console. These components make up a basic deployment scenario. Several optional components are also described in the following bulleted list; these components provide functionality for advanced deployment scenarios.

The following list describes the different OpsMgr components:

- Agents
- Management server
- OperationsManager database
- Reporting data warehouse
- Reporting server
- Operations console
- Web console
- Command shell
- Gateway

OpsMgr was specifically designed to be scalable and can subsequently be configured to meet the needs of any size company. This flexibility stems from the fact that all OpsMgr components can either reside on one server or can be distributed across multiple servers.

Each of these various components provides specific OpsMgr functionality. OpsMgr design scenarios often involve the separation of parts of these components onto multiple servers. For example, the database components can be delegated to a dedicated server, and the management server can reside on a second server.

The Operations Manager 2012 architecture is shown in Figure 23.5, with all the major components and their data paths.

The components are organized by two major architectural structures: the management group and resource pools. All the components are contained within a management group, which can contain only a single operations database and a single reporting database. The management group can contain multiple management servers and other components. For fault tolerance, management servers can be organized into resource pools. Management servers inherently provide fault tolerance for Windows servers, although they are also organized into a default resource pool.

In the next sections, each of the components is discussed in detail.

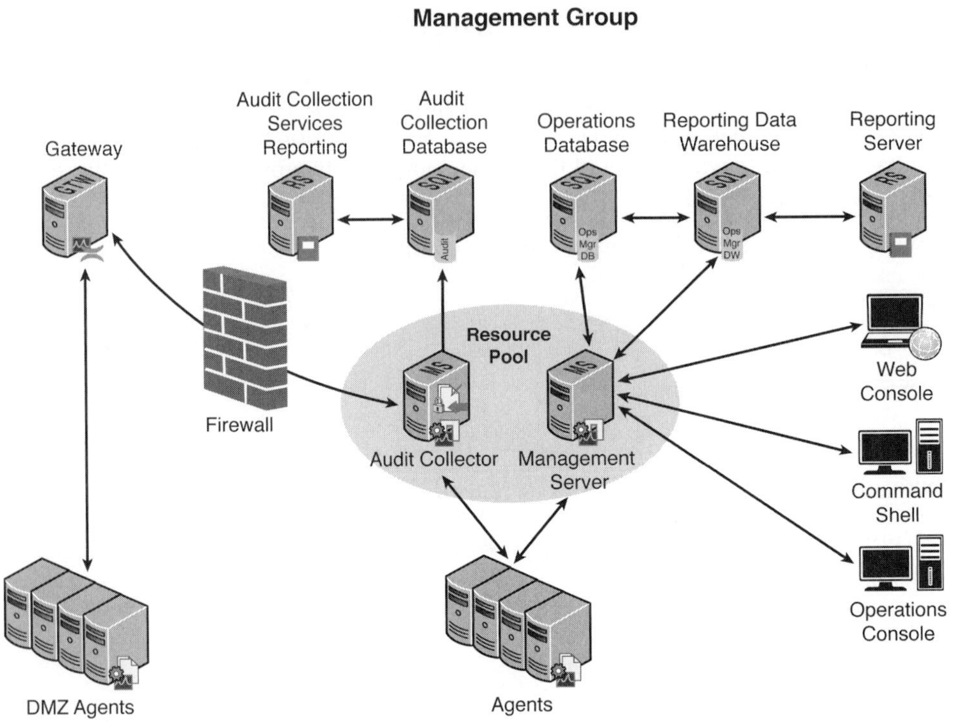

FIGURE 23.5 Operations Manager 2012 architecture.

The Agent Component

Agents are installed on each managed system to provide efficient monitoring of local components. Almost all communication is initiated from the agent with the exception of the actual agent installation and specific tasks run from the Operations console. Agentless monitoring is also available with a reduction of functionality and environmental scalability.

The agent supports all editions and versions of Windows Server 2012, including both core and full installations.

Agents can report to more than one management group at the same time by using multihoming, allowing for different administration and bifurcation of operations. For example, an agent might report to one management group for operations monitoring and to another management group for security monitoring.

Windows computers can also be monitored as agentless, in which case the management server will perform the monitoring. No agent is deployed, but rather the management server makes Remote Procedure Call (RPC) connections to the managed computer to poll the event and performance data. This places a tremendous load on the management server and the network, so agentless monitoring is not recommended.

NOTE

When virtual components are discovered, such as the virtual cluster machines, they are shown as separate monitored objects and are listed in the Administrative space in the Agentless node. The agents are deployed to the physical nodes, but not to the virtual node. These virtual systems are monitored by their physical nodes and not by the management server, thus there is no undue load placed on the management servers. These agentless virtual objects should not be confused with agentless managed computers.

Factors that impact the agent include the following:

- Number of MPs deployed
- Type of MPs deployed

The maximum supported number of agents in a management group is 10,000 agents; however, due to the impact of the consoles, that is with a maximum of 25 open consoles. If 50 consoles will be open (the maximum per management group), only 6,000 agents are supported. The maximum number of agentless managed computers per management group is 60.

The software requirements for the agent component are as follows:

- %SYSTEMDRIVE% must be formatted with the NTFS file system
- .NET Framework 3.5 SP1
- Windows Installer version: at least Windows Installer 3.1
- Microsoft Core XML Services (MSXML) 6.0

The Management Server Component

Optionally, additional management servers can be added for redundancy and scalability. Agents communicate with the management server to deliver operational data and pull down new monitoring rules.

The management server in 2012 is similar to the Microsoft Operations Manager 2007 management server. It manages communication with managed agents and forwards events and performance data to the operations database. The management server also supports agentless monitoring of managed systems, and it provides support for audit collection. Management servers now write directly to the operations database and data warehouse, which eliminates the need to transfer data from one database to another. This arrangement enables near-real-time data for reporting.

Each management server runs the software development kit (SDK) and Configuration service and is responsible for handling console communication, calculating the health of the environment, and determining what rules should be applied to each agent.

Compared with Microsoft Operations Manager 2007, management server fault tolerance, performance, and scalability is generally improved. In OpsMgr 2007, all operational data passed through the Root Management Server (RMS), and it was also responsible for rollups and notifications. Thus, the RMS was a single point of failure unless clustered. Operations Manager 2012 eliminates the single point of failure by grouping management servers into resource pools in which all management servers share in the duties. The most important resource on a management server is the CPU; however, management servers do not typically require high-end hardware.

Factors that impact the management server include the following:

- Number of agents
- Configuration changes to agents
- Number of consoles

The maximum number of open consoles supported by a management group is 50, due to the load that the console places on the RMS SDK service and the database. Operations Manager can support a maximum of 3,000 Windows agents. The maximum number of agentless managed computers per management server is 10.

NOTE

The value of 10 for the maximum number of agentless monitored computers per management server is not a typo. Agentless managed computers place a huge load on the management server, which must gather and process all the workload of the rules, monitors, and other elements. This takes place over RPC, which has a heavy performance penalty on the network and the processor of the management server.

Because of the heavy load and abysmal scalability, agentless managed computers are not recommended.

OpsMgr does not have a hard-coded limit of management servers per management group. However, it is recommended to keep the environment to 10 or fewer management servers per management group.

The minimum supported hardware configuration for the management server component is as follows:

- 2.8GHz or faster x64 processor
- 2GB of RAM or more
- 20GB of available hard disk space (a minimum of 1GB on the OS drive)

The software requirements for the management server component are as follows:

- Windows Server 2008 R2 SP1

NOTE

At time of publication, OpsMgr 2012 does not support installation of server components on Windows Server 2012. Support for installation of OpsMgr 2012 components on Windows Server 2012 will be supported in the System Center SP1.

- .NET Framework 3.5 SP1
- .NET Framework 4.0
- Microsoft Core XML Services (MSXML) 6.0
- Windows PowerShell version 2.0.

The OperationsManager Database Component

The operations database (OperationsManager) stores the monitoring rules and the active data collected from monitored systems. This database has a seven-day default retention period.

The OperationsManager database is a Microsoft SQL Server 2008 database that contains all the data needed by Operations Manager for day-to-day monitoring. Because you can only have a single OperationsManager database, it is very important to ensure that it is sized appropriately. The most critical resource used by the OperationsManager database is the I/O subsystem, but the CPU and RAM are also important.

OpsMgr operates through a principle of centralized, rather than distributed, collection of data. All event logs, performance counters, and alerts are sent to a single, centralized database, and there can subsequently be only a single operations database per management group. Considering the use of a backup and high-availability strategy for the OpsMgr database is, therefore, highly recommended, to protect it from outage.

Factors that impact the OperationsManager database include the following:

- Volume of data collection
- Configuration changes to agents
- Number of consoles open simultaneously

There is only one OperationsManager database per management group. The maximum number of open consoles supported by a management group is 50, due to the load that the consoles place on the OperationsManager database and the RMS SDK service.

It is recommended to keep this database with a 50GB limit to improve efficiency and reduce alert latency.

The minimum supported hardware configuration for the OperationsManager database component is as follows:

- 2.8GHz or faster x64 processor
- 4GB of RAM or more
- 50GB of available hard disk space

The software requirements for the OperationsManager database component consist of the following:

- Windows Server 2008 SP2 64 bit or Windows Server 2008 R2 SP1

NOTE

At time of publication, OpsMgr 2012 does not support installation of server components on Windows Server 2012. Support for installation of OpsMgr 2012 components on Windows Server 2012 will be supported in the System Center SP1.

- SQL Server 2008 SP1 or higher
- SQL Server 2008 R2 or higher
- .NET Framework 3.5 SP1
- .NET Framework 4.0
- SQL Collation—SQL_Latin1_General_CP1_CI_AS
- %SYSTEMDRIVE% formatted with the NTFS file system
- SQL Server Full Text Search

The Reporting Data Warehouse Component

The reporting database (OperationsManagerDW) stores archived data for reporting purposes. This database has a 400-day default retention period.

Operations Manager 2012 uses Microsoft SQL Server Reporting Services 2008 (SRS 2008) for its reporting engine. SRS provides many enhancements to previous reporting solutions, including easier authoring and publishing. Operations Manager 2012 includes an easy-to-use graphical report designer as part of the Operations Manager 2012 console. Several new controls are also included to allow sophisticated reports and dashboards to be created. Most common reports are shipped as part of the MPs, so very little customization is needed to start working with best-practice reports.

Because Operations Manager 2012 inserts data into the Reporting data warehouse in near real time, it is important to have sufficient capacity on this computer that supports writing all data being collected to the Reporting data warehouse. As with the OperationsManager database, the most critical resource on the Reporting data warehouse is the I/O subsystem. On most systems, loads on the Reporting data warehouse are similar to those on the OperationsManager database, but they can vary. In addition, the workload put on the Reporting data warehouse by reporting is different from the load put on the OperationsManager database by Operations console usage.

NOTE

This requirement is relatively new to OpsMgr 2007 and later because in earlier versions the data transfers from the OperationsManager database to the data warehouse database were batched. However, this caused reports to be out of date because of the lag in the transfer and also spikes in load when the transfers took place. Microsoft shifted to a real-time transfer, which improves reporting and increases performance, but it puts the data warehouse in the critical data path.

Factors that impact the Reporting data warehouse include the following:

- Volume of data collection
- Number of consoles generating reports
- Number of Service Level Dashboards open simultaneously

There is only one Reporting data warehouse per management group.

The minimum supported hardware configuration for the Reporting data warehouse component is as follows:

- 2.8GHz or faster x64 processor
- 4GB of RAM or more
- 100GB of available hard disk space

The software requirements for the Reporting data warehouse component consist of the following:

- Windows Server 2008 SP2 64 bit or Windows Server 2008 R2 SP1

NOTE

At time of publication, OpsMgr 2012 does not support installation of server components on Windows Server 2012. Support for installation of OpsMgr 2012 components on Windows Server 2012 will be supported in the System Center SP1.

- SQL Server 2008 SP1 or higher
- SQL Server 2008 R2 or higher
- .NET Framework 3.5 SP1
- .NET Framework 4.0

- SQL Collation—SQL_Latin1_General_CP1_CI_AS
- %SYSTEMDRIVE% formatted with the NTFS file system
- SQL Server Full Text Search

The Reporting Server Component

The Reporting Server component is installed on a Reporting Services instance and provides the extensions needed for the Operations Manager reports. The reports are generated from the Reporting data warehouse and can be generated ad hoc, exported, or scheduled for email delivery.

The reports are accessed via the Operations console and security is integrated with the Operations Manager roles.

Factors that impact the reporting server include the following:

- The size of the Reporting data warehouse database
- The number and complexity of reports being generated

The minimum supported hardware configuration for the Reporting Server component is as follows:

- 2.8GHz or faster x64 processor
- 2GB of RAM or more
- 20GB of available hard disk space

The software requirements for the Reporting Server component are as follows:

- Windows Server 2008 R2 SP1

NOTE

At time of publication, OpsMgr 2012 does not support installation of server components on Windows Server 2012. Support for installation of OpsMgr 2012 components on Windows Server 2012 will be supported in the System Center SP1.

- SQL Server Reporting Services 2008 SP1 or higher
- SQL Server Reporting Services 2008 R2 or higher
- .NET Framework 3.5 SP1
- .NET Framework 4.0
- At least 1024MB free hard disk space on %SYSTEMDRIVE% drive
- SQL Collation: SQL_Latin1_General_CP1_CI_AS

The Operations Console Component

The Operations console is used to monitor systems, run tasks, configure environmental settings, set author rules, subscribe to alerts, and generate and subscribe to reports. The console automatically scopes to the objects that an operator is authorized to manage in his or her user role. This allows the OpsMgr administrator to grant application owners full operator privileges to the Operations console, but to a restricted set of objects. These restrictions are based on Active Directory security principles (users and security groups) and are respected by all consoles, APIs, and even the command shell.

Console performance can be a major issue to contend with in an OpsMgr infrastructure. The Operations console places a substantial load on the operations database, more so than any other factor. This manifests itself in slow console performance, including delays in presenting information, updating views, or switching between views. Because this is the end-user-facing component, this can generate frustration for operators and administrators.

Factors that impact the Operations console include the following:

- Disk latency on the OperationsManager database
- Number of consoles open simultaneously

There can be a maximum of 50 simultaneous open consoles on any management group, which includes the Operations console, the Web console, and the command shell.

The minimum supported hardware configuration for the Operations console component is as follows:

- 2.8GHz or faster processor
- 2GB of RAM or more
- 20GB of available hard disk space

The software requirements for the Operations console component are as follows:

- Windows Vista, Windows 7, Windows Server 2008 64 bit, or Windows Server 2008 R2 SP1

NOTE

At time of publication, OpsMgr 2012 does not support installation of server components on Windows Server 2012. Support for installation of OpsMgr 2012 components on Windows Server 2012 will be supported in the System Center SP1.

- .NET Framework 3.5 SP1
- .NET Framework 3.5 SP1 hotfix KB976898
- .NET Framework 4.0
- Microsoft Windows PowerShell 2.0

- Microsoft Report Viewer 2008 SP1 Redistributable Package
- File system: %SYSTEMDRIVE% must be formatted with the NTFS file system
- Windows Installer version: at least Windows Installer 3.1

The Web Console Component

The Web console is an optional component used to monitor systems, run tasks, and manage Maintenance mode from a web browser. The Web console is very similar to the Monitoring space in the Operations console, but the Web console has some limitations such as only a 24-hour view of performance data.

The Web console is an excellent choice for application administrators who need console access to the Operations Manager infrastructure, but don't want to go through the trouble of installing the full console.

Factors that impact the Web console include the following:

- Disk latency on OperationsManager database
- Number of consoles open simultaneously

There can be a maximum of 50 simultaneous open consoles on any management group, which includes the Operations console, the Web console, and the command shell.

The minimum supported hardware configuration for the Web console component is as follows:

- 2.8GHz or faster x64 processor
- 2GB of RAM or more
- 20GB of available hard disk space

The software requirements for the Web console component are as follows:

- Windows Server 2008 R2 SP1

NOTE

At time of publication, OpsMgr 2012 does not support installation of server components on Windows Server 2012. Support for installation of OpsMgr 2012 components on Windows Server 2012 will be supported in the System Center SP1.

- .NET Framework 3.5 SP1
- .NET Framework 4.0
- Internet Information Services (IIS)
- ASP.NET

The Command Shell Component

This optional component is built on PowerShell and provides full command-line management of the OpsMgr environment. A wide array of PowerShell cmdlets are available that allow for viewing configuration and operations data, as well as setting operational parameters.

Factors that impact the command shell include the following:

- Disk latency on the OperationsManager database
- Number of consoles open simultaneously

There can be a maximum of 50 simultaneous open consoles on any management group, which includes the Operations console, the Web console, and the command shell.

The minimum supported hardware configuration for the command shell component is as follows:

- 2.8GHz or faster processor
- 2GB of RAM or more
- 20GB of available hard disk space

The software requirements for the command shell component are as follows:

- Windows Vista, Windows 7, Windows Server 2008, or Windows Server 2008 R2 SP1

NOTE

At time of publication, OpsMgr 2012 does not support installation of server components on Windows Server 2012. Support for installation of OpsMgr 2012 components on Windows Server 2012 will be supported in the System Center SP1.

- .NET Framework 3.5 SP1
- .NET Framework 4.0
- Microsoft Windows PowerShell 2.0

The Gateway Component

This optional component provides mutual authentication through certificates for non-trusted systems in remote domains or workgroups.

The gateway server is designed to improve management of devices in demilitarized zones (DMZs) or behind firewalls. The gateway server aggregates communication from agents and forwards them to a management server inside the firewall. The gateway server does not have direct access to the database, data warehouse, or root management server. The most important resource on a gateway server is the CPU; however, gateway servers do not typically require high-end hardware.

Factors that impact the gateway server include the following:

- Volume of data collection

Operations Manager can support a maximum of 1,500 Windows agents or 100 UNIX/ Linux agents per gateway server. OpsMgr does not have a hard-coded limit of gateway servers per management group.

The minimum supported hardware configuration for the gateway server component is as follows:

- 2.8GHz or faster processor
- 2GB of RAM or more
- 20GB of available hard disk space

The software requirements for the gateway server component are as follows:

- Windows Server 2008 R2 SP1

NOTE

At time of publication, OpsMgr 2012 does not support installation of server components on Windows Server 2012. Support for installation of OpsMgr 2012 components on Windows Server 2012 will be supported in the System Center SP1.

- .NET Framework 3.5 SP1
- .NET Framework 4.0 (for UNIX/Linux management)
- Microsoft Windows PowerShell 2.0
- Microsoft Core XML Services (MSXML) 6.0

Securing OpsMgr

Security has evolved into a primary concern that can no longer be taken for granted. The inherent security in any IT system is only as good as the services that have access to it; therefore, it is wise to perform a security audit of all systems that access information from servers. This concept holds true for management systems as well because they collect sensitive information from every server in an enterprise. This includes potentially sensitive event logs that could be used to compromise a system. Consequently, securing the OpsMgr infrastructure should not be taken lightly.

Role-Based Security Model

The Operations Manager infrastructure supports a role-based security model, which allows roles to be defined as profiles and assigned to Active Directory security principles.

NOTE

The built-in Operations Manager Administrator profile can only have group security principles assigned to it. Other built-in and custom profiles can have both group and user security principles assigned.

Seven different roles provide a range of authorization options:

- **Administrator**—The Administrator profile includes full privileges to Operations Manager. No scoping of the Administrator profile is supported.

NOTE

The local administrators group is placed in the Administrator profile at installation by default. This means that all members of the local administrators group are by default also Operations Manager administrators. Because the domain administrators group is normally a member of the local administrators group, all members of the domain admins group are also by default Operations Manager administrators.

This can be changed by changing the groups in the Administrator profile.

- **Operator**—The Operator profile includes a set of privileges designed for users who need access to alerts, views, and tasks. A role based on the Operator profile grants members the ability to interact with alerts, execute tasks, and access views according to their configured scope.
- **Advanced Operator**—The Advanced Operator profile includes a set of privileges designed for users who need access to limited tweaking of monitoring configuration in addition to the Operator privileges. A role based on the Advanced Operator profile grants members the ability to override the configuration of rules and monitors for specific targets or groups of targets within the configured scope.
- **Read-Only Operator**—The Read-Only Operator profile includes a set of privileges designed for users who need read-only access to alerts and views. A role based on the Read-Only Operator profile grants members the ability to view alerts and access views according to their configured scope.
- **Report Operator**—The Report Operator profile includes a set of privileges designed for users who need access to reports. A role based on the Report Operator profile grants members the ability to view reports according to their configured scope.
- **Author**—The Author profile includes a set of privileges designed for authoring of monitoring configuration. A role based on the Author profile grants members the ability to create, edit, and delete monitoring configuration (tasks, rules, monitors,

and views) within the configured scope. For convenience, Authors can also be configured to have Advanced Operator privileges scoped by group.

- **Report Security Administrator**—The Operations Manager Report Security Administrator profile is designed to enable the integration of SQL Server Reporting Services security with Operations Manager user roles. This gives Operations Manager administrators the ability to control access to reports. This role cannot be scoped.

For each of the roles, a profile is created at installation that grants the role access across all objects. Additional profiles can be created for the Operator, Advanced Operator, Read-Only Operator, and the Author roles that narrow the scope of objects, allowing flexible access control to different users or groups of users.

NOTE

The access granted by profiles is cumulative. If a user is a member of two profiles, they will have the access granted by the combined profiles. There is no "deny" concept in the access controls within profiles.

The access is granted based on the user's account either directly or via group membership. The access controls are respected across all methods of access, including the Operations console, Web console, command shell, and even API access.

A key part of any Operations Manager design is developing the administrative model that will grant users the appropriate console access they need.

Securing OpsMgr Agents

Each server that contains an OpsMgr agent and forwards events to management servers has specific security requirements. Server-level security should be established and should include provisions for OpsMgr data collection. All traffic between OpsMgr components, such as the agents, management servers, and database, is encrypted automatically for security, so the traffic is inherently secured.

NOTE

In environments with high-security requirements, the organization could investigate the use of encryption technologies such as IPsec to scramble the event IDs that are sent between agents and OpsMgr servers, to protect against eavesdropping of OpsMgr packets.

OpsMgr uses mutual authentication between agents and management servers. This means that the agent and management server must trust a common certificate authority, a simple requirement when the agents reside in the same forest as the management server. If the agent is located in a different forest or workgroup, client certificates can be used to establish mutual authentication. If an entire nontrusted domain must be monitored, the gateway server can be installed in the nontrusted domain, agents can establish mutual authentication to the gateway server, and certificates on the gateway and management server are used to establish mutual authentication. In this scenario, you can avoid needing to place a certificate on each non-trusted domain member.

Understanding Firewall Requirements

OpsMgr servers that are deployed across a firewall have special considerations that must be taken into account. Port 5723, the default port for OpsMgr communications, must specifically be opened on a firewall to allow OpsMgr to communicate across it.

Table 23.1 describes communication ports for this and other OpsMgr components.

TABLE 23.1 OpsMgr Communication Ports

From	To	Port
Agent	Management server	5723
Agent	Gateway server	5723
Agent (ACS forwarder)	Management server ACS collector	51909
Management server	Network device	161, 162
Gateway server	Management server	5723
Gateway server	Management server	5723
Management or gateway server	UNIX or Linux computer	1270
Management or gateway server	UNIX or Linux computer	22
Management server	OperationsManager database	1433
Management server	Management server	5723, 5724
Management server	Reporting data warehouse	1433
Management server ACS collector	ACS database	1433
Operations console	Management server	5724
Operations console (reports)	SQL Server Reporting Services	80
Reporting server	Management server	5723, 5724
Reporting server	Reporting data warehouse	1433
Web console browser	Web console server	51908
Web console server	Management server	5724

The firewall port for the agents is the port that needs to be opened most often, which is only port 5723 from the agent to the management servers for monitoring. Other ports, such as 51909 for ACS, are more rarely needed. Figure 23.6 shows the major communications paths and ports between OpsMgr components.

NOTE

Note the directionality of the management server to UNIX/Linux arrow. This is because the management server collects information from the UNIX/Linux agents, rather than having the UNIX/Linux agents upload the information. This explains the lower scalability numbers for UNIX/Linux agents.

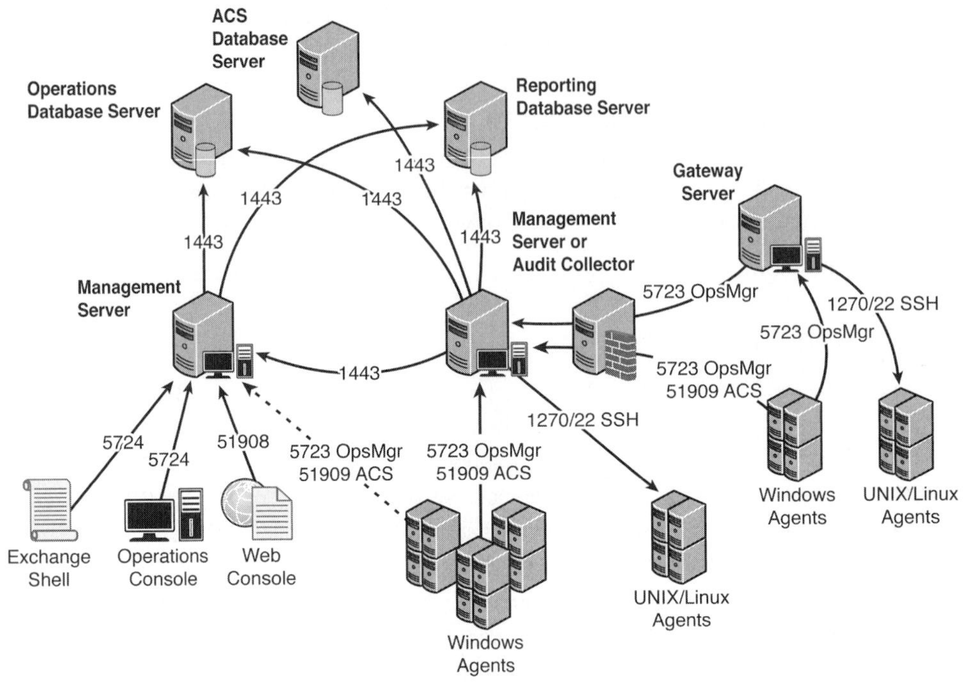

FIGURE 23.6 Communications ports.

Action and RunAs Account Security

In addition to the aforementioned security measures, security of an OpsMgr environment can be strengthened by the addition of multiple service accounts and RunAs accounts to handle the different OpsMgr components and MPs. For example, the Management Server Action account and the SDK/Configuration service account should be configured to use separate credentials, to provide for an extra layer of protection in the event that one account is compromised:

- **Management Server Action account**—The account responsible for collecting data and running responses from management servers.
- **SDK and Configuration service account**—The account that writes data to the operations database; this service is also used for all console communication.
- **Local Administrator account**—The account used during the agent push installation process. To install the agent, local administrative rights are required.
- **Agent Action account**—The credentials the agent will run as. This account can run under a built-in system account, such as Local System, or a limited domain user account for high-security environments.
- **Data Warehouse Write Action account**—The account used by the management server to write data to the Reporting data warehouse.

- **Data Warehouse Reader account**—The account used to read data from the data warehouse when reports are executed.

- **RunAs accounts**—The specific accounts used by MPs to facilitate monitoring. Out of the box, Operations Manager provides a number of RunAs accounts and RunAs profiles, and you can create additional ones as necessary to delegate specific rights as defined in the MP documentation. These accounts are then assigned as RunAs accounts used by the MP to achieve a high degree of security and flexibility when monitoring the environment. New to OpsMgr 2012 is the ability to selectively distribute the RunAs account to just the agents that need them.

Various MPs have their own RunAs accounts, such as the Active Directory MPs and the Exchange MP. These allow accounts with specific elevated privileges to be assigned to execute MP scripts.

Securing DMZ Servers with Certificates

Servers in an organization's DMZ are usually not domain members and, therefore, cannot do automatic mutual authentication with the OpsMgr server. However, these servers are the most exposed in the organization and, thus, a critical asset to be monitored. Thankfully, there is a well-defined process for using certificates to handle the mutual authentication. Certificates on both the management servers and the agents are used to mutually authenticate their communications.

The certificates used for mutual authentication must

- Have the Name field match the computer name in the Computer Properties
- Be configured with server (1.3.6.1.5.5.7.3.1) and client (1.3.6.1.5.5.7.3.2) OIDs
- Be marked as Exportable
- Have their issuing CA trusted by the computer

The agent checks for these conditions at startup and will not use the certificate if these conditions are not satisfied.

Fault Tolerance and Disaster Recovery

The ability to recover from failures is critical to the proper function of any system, including Operations Manager. Although the two concepts are closely related, fault tolerance and disaster recovery are fundamentally different.

Fault tolerance is the ability to continue operating even in the event of a failure. This ensures that failures don't result in loss of service. Fault-tolerance mechanisms, such as clustering or load-balanced components, have activation times typically measured in seconds or minutes. These mechanisms typically also have high costs associated with them, such as duplicated hardware.

In contrast, disaster recovery is the ability to restore operations after a loss of service. This ensures that failures don't result in the loss of data. Disaster recovery mechanisms, such as backups or log shipping, have activation times typically measured in hours or days. Disaster recovery mechanisms generally have lower costs associated with them, though failover sites in backup data centers can be expensive.

As IT organizations mature, the monitoring systems such as Operations Manager become more critical and, thus, require investment in fault tolerance.

NOTE

Depending on the organization, Operations Manager is sometimes considered to be a non-business-critical system and therefore is not implemented with fault tolerance. The rationale for this is that if Operations Manager is down, business-critical systems would still be operational albeit without monitoring or alerting.

In addition to the scalability built in to OpsMgr, redundancy is built in to the components of the environment. Proper knowledge of how to deploy OpsMgr redundancy and place OpsMgr components correctly is important to the understanding of OpsMgr redundancy. The main components of OpsMgr can be made redundant through the following methods:

- **Management servers**—Management servers are automatically redundant and agents will fail over and fail back automatically between them. Simply install additional management servers into the resource pool for redundancy.
- **SQL databases**—The SQL database servers hosting the various databases can be made redundant using SQL clustering, which is based on Windows clustering. This supports failover and failback.

Figure 23.7 shows a fully fault-tolerant architecture.

Management Group Redundancy

Having multiple management servers deployed across a management group allows an environment to achieve a certain level of redundancy. If a single management server experiences downtime, another management server within the management group will take over the responsibilities for the monitored servers in the environment. For this reason, it might be wise to include multiple management servers in an environment to achieve a certain level of redundancy if high uptime is a priority.

Resource Pools

Resource pools provide fault tolerance for the OpsMgr 2012 management group. However, they are used differently by different managed devices, such as Windows computers, UNIX computers, and network devices.

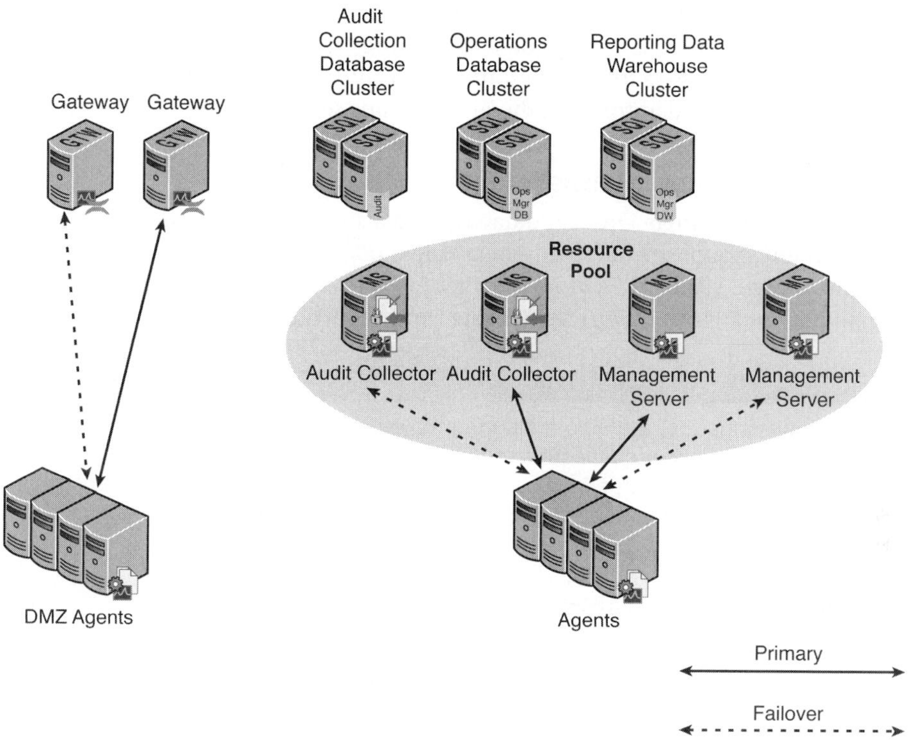

FIGURE 23.7 Operations Manager 2012 fault tolerance.

Windows computers work exactly as they did within OpsMgr 2007 and are assigned a primary management server. The difference with resource pools is that they will failover to management servers within the default resource pool, which is the All Management Servers Resource Pool. All management servers are members of this default resource pool and cannot be removed.

UNIX and Linux computers and network devices function differently. They can be manually assigned to resource pools and will fail over between management servers within their resource pool. The OpsMgr administrator can create resource pools and assign management servers to those pools, allowing different devices to fail over between different management servers.

Resource pools can also be used to control which management servers will send out notifications. The Notifications Resource Pool is created at installation and by default automatically includes all management servers. However, this resource pool can be converted to a manual resource pool, allowing the membership to be selected and thus controlling which management servers will send out notifications. Any management server within this group can send out notifications, allowing for fault tolerance.

Resource pools replace the RMS functionality, or limitations, present in OpsMgr 2007. The Root Management Server (RMS) component was a single point of failure and required complicated clustering to mitigate its loss. Resource pools in OpsMgr 2012 replace this functionality with an easily and automatically fault-tolerant service.

Clustering and Operations Manager

Because there can be only a single OpsMgr database and a single Reporting data warehouse per management group, the databases are a single point of failure and should be protected from downtime. Utilizing Windows Server 2008 R2 clustering for SQL databases helps to mitigate the risk involved with the OpsMgr and reporting databases.

NOTE

Geo-clusters (multisite clusters) are also supported; however, the maximum round-trip latency for the network heartbeat connection must be less than 500ms. This is a technology requirement for Microsoft Cluster Services (MSCS), but a violation of the requirement in an Operations Manager environment might result in inadvertent failover of components.

The following components can be clustered:

- Operations database
- Reporting data warehouse
- Audit collection database

Operations Manager only supports Microsoft Cluster Services quorum node clusters. The clusters should be single active-passive clusters dedicated to the respective components. This is the recommended cluster architecture.

Table 23.2 shows a sample cluster architecture with the components on separate dedicated clusters per recommended best practice.

TABLE 23.2 Sample Recommended Cluster Configuration

Component	Cluster	Node 1	Node 2
Operations database	CLUSTER01	Active	Passive
Reporting data warehouse	CLUSTER02	Active	Passive
Audit collection database	CLUSTER03	Active	Passive

The database components (operations database, Reporting data warehouse, and the audit collection database) can coexist on the same active node of an active-passive cluster. This could be all three or a combination of any two of the three database components. The cluster should be scaled up accordingly to avoid potential resource issues with having the multiple roles on a single node.

Other configurations are possible, but not recommended. For example, active-active SQL cluster configurations where there is a separate database component on each active node, such as the operations database on node 1 and the data warehouse on node 2. This is not recommended due to potential catastrophic performance issues when one of the nodes fails over. The concern is that if node 1 is running at 60% of resource utilization supporting the operations database and node 2 is running at 60% of resource utilization supporting the data warehouse, then when a node fails the single remaining node would suddenly be expected to be running at 120% of resource utilization supporting both components. This typically results in the failure of the second node in the cluster due to resource constraints.

NOTE

Management server clustering is not supported in OpsMgr 2012. This is a change from OpsMgr 2007, where clustering the RMS was the recommended approach to fault tolerance. Resource pools eliminated this need for clustering and are no longer supported.

Disaster Recovery

Disaster recovery in Operations Manager is critical to be able to recover in the event of the loss of any or all of the components. This includes the loss of a database, RMS, or a management server.

The critical items to back up in an Operations Manager infrastructure, that is, the items needed to recover the environment, include the following:

- **Operations database (OperationsManager)**—The OperationsManager database contains almost all of the Operations Manager environment configuration settings, agent information, MPs with customizations, operations data, and other data required for Operations Manager to operate properly.
- **Reporting data warehouse database (OperationsManagerDW)**—The OperationsManagerDW database contains all of the performance and other operational data from your Operations Manager environment. SQL Reporting Services then uses this data to generate reports, such as trend analysis and performance tracking.
- **Audit collection database (OperationsManagerAC)**—The Audit Collection Services (ACS) database, OperationsManagerAC, is the central repository for events and security logs that are collected by ACS forwarders on monitored computers.
- **Master database**—The master database is a system database, which records all of the system-level information for a Microsoft SQL Server system, including the location of the database files. It also records all logon accounts and system configuration settings. The proper functionality of the master database is key to the operation of all of the databases in a SQL Server instance.

- **MSDB database**—The MSDB database, Msdbdata, is a SQL system database, which is used by the SQL Server agent to schedule jobs and alerts and for recording operators. The proper functionality of the MSDB database is key to the operation of all the databases in a SQL Server instance.
- **Internet Information Services**—The Internet Information Services (IIS) contains the custom settings for the Web console and the reporting database. Backing up the IIS 6.0 metabase in Windows Server 2003 or the IIS 7.x configuration in Windows Server 2008/R2 is necessary to restore the full functionality. Loss of this would require reconfiguring the Web console and the reporting database.
- **Override MPs**—These MPs contain the overrides that have been configured as part of tuning MPs. Loss of these MPs will reset the installed MPs to their default state and require all the overrides to be reentered.
- **Custom MPs**—These MPs contain all the custom development. Loss of these would require development to be redone.

Each of the components will have a different backup method and a different impact if the data is not recoverable. The most critical piece of OpsMgr, the SQL databases, should be regularly backed up using standard backup software that can effectively perform online backups of SQL databases. If integrating these specialized backup utilities into an OpsMgr deployment is not possible, it becomes necessary to leverage built-in backup functionality found in SQL Server. Table 23.3 lists the backup methods for each component.

TABLE 23.3 OpsMgr Component Backup Methods and Impacts

Component	Backup Method
Operations database (OperationsManager)	SQL backup
Reporting data warehouse database (OperationsManagerDW)	SQL backup
Audit collection database (OperationsManagerAC)	SQL backup
Master database	SQL backup
MSDB database	SQL backup
IIS 6.0 metabase or IIS 7.0 configuration	IIS backup
Override MPs	Operations console
Custom MPs	Operations console

The schedule of the backups is important. This is especially true because the databases can become quite large and the backup process time-consuming, as well as expensive in terms of tapes and storage. The backup schedule suggested in Table 23.4 is based on a trade-off between the effort to back up and the impact of a loss.

TABLE 23.4 OpsMgr Component Backup Schedules

Component	Full Backup	Incremental Backup
Operations database (OperationsManager)	Weekly	Daily
Reporting data warehouse database (OperationsManagerDW)	Monthly	Weekly
Audit collection database (OperationsManagerAC)	Monthly	Weekly
Master database	Weekly	
MSDB database	Weekly	
IIS 6.0 metabase or IIS 7.0 configuration	Weekly	
Override MPs	Weekly and after changes	
Custom MPs	Weekly and after changes	

Given the volume of data in the Reporting data warehouse and the audit collection database, some organizations might choose to not perform backups of these components. The value of the long-term historical operational and security data might not be worth the storage requirements. Even if that is decided, the OperationsManager database should always be backed up to avoid loss of the valuable configuration, deployment, and tuning information.

TIP

The long-term operational, performance, and security information in the Reporting data warehouse and the audit collection database can be captured in reports as an alternative or supplement to database backups.

Reports that summarize key metrics and information can be scheduled automatically in SQL Reporting Services and stored in a file share, allowing for long-term access to summarized data.

Understanding OpsMgr Components

OpsMgr's simple installation and relative ease of use often belie the potential complexity of its underlying components. This complexity can be managed with the right amount of knowledge of some of the advanced concepts of OpsMgr design and implementation.

Each OpsMgr component has specific design requirements, and a good knowledge of these factors is required before beginning the design of OpsMgr. Hardware and software requirements must be taken into account, as well as factors involving specific OpsMgr components, such as the management server, gateway servers, service accounts, mutual authentication, and backup requirements.

Exploring Hardware Requirements

Having the proper hardware for OpsMgr to operate on is a critical component of OpsMgr functionality, reliability, and overall performance. Nothing is worse than overloading a brand-new server only a few short months after its implementation. The industry standard generally holds that any production servers deployed should remain relevant for three to four years following deployment. Stretching beyond this time frame might be possible, but the ugly truth is that hardware investments are typically short term and need to be replaced often to ensure relevance. Buying a less-expensive server might save money in the short term but could potentially increase costs associated with downtime, troubleshooting, and administration. That said, the following are the Microsoft-recommended minimums for any server running an OpsMgr 2012 server component:

- 2.8GHz processor or faster x64 architecture
- 20GB of free disk space
- 2GB of RAM

These recommendations apply only to the smallest OpsMgr deployments and should be seen as minimum levels for OpsMgr hardware. More realistic deployments would have the following minimums:

- Two to four 2.8GHz cores
- Windows 2008 R2 SP1 operating system
- 64-bit SQL Server
- 100GB free disk space on RAID 1+0 for performance
- 4GB to 8GB of RAM

Operations Manager 2012 is one of Microsoft's most resource-intensive applications, so generous processor, disk, and memory are important for optimal performance. Future expansion and relevance of hardware should be taken into account when sizing servers for OpsMgr deployment, to ensure that the system has room to grow as agents are added and the databases grow.

Determining Software Requirements

OpsMgr components can be installed only on Windows Server 2008 R2 SP1, which is only available in x64 versions. The database for OpsMgr must run on a Microsoft SQL Server 2008 server. The database can be installed on the same server as OpsMgr or on a separate server, a concept that is discussed in more detail in following sections.

NOTE

At time of publication, OpsMgr 2012 does not support installation of server components on Windows Server 2012. Support for installation of OpsMgr 2012 components on Windows Server 2012 will be supported in the System Center SP1.

OpsMgr itself must be installed on a member server in a Windows Active Directory domain. It is commonly recommended to keep the installation of OpsMgr on a separate server or set of dedicated member servers that do not run any other applications that could interfere in the monitoring and alerting process.

A few other requirements critical to the success of OpsMgr implementations are as follows:

- Microsoft .NET Framework 3.5 SP1 and 4.0 must be installed on the management server and the reporting server.
- Windows PowerShell 2.0.
- Microsoft Core XML Services (MSXML) 6.0.
- Client certificates must be installed in environments to facilitate mutual authentication between non-domain members and management servers.
- SQL Reporting Services must be installed for an organization to be able to view and produce custom reports using OpsMgr's reporting feature.

Network Bandwidth Requirements

Each of the communications paths between OpsMgr components requires a certain minimum bandwidth to communicate properly.

Table 23.5 lists the communication bandwidth requirements between OpsMgr components.

TABLE 23.5 OpsMgr Minimum Communications Bandwidth

From	To	Minimum Bandwidth
Agent	Management server or gateway	64Kbps
Management server	Agentless	1024Kbps
Management server	OperationsManager database	256Kbps
Management server	Management server	64Kbps
Gateway server	Management server	64Kbps
Management server	Reporting data warehouse	768Kbps
Management server	Reporting server	256Kbps
Reporting server	Reporting data warehouse	1024Kbps
Operations console	Management server	768Kbps
Operations console	Reporting server	768Kbps
Web console browser	Web console server	128Kbps
ACS collector	ACS database	768Kbps

The values given are minimum requirements, but actual requirements will be based on load factors as well. For example, although the minimum bandwidth for a gateway server to a management server is given as 64Kbps, the actual bandwidth requirements will depend on the number of agents that the gateway is supporting and the workloads on the agents.

NOTE

The agentless bandwidth requirement clearly shows one of the issues with deploying agentless monitoring and why it does not scale. At 1024Kbps, the network requirement alone for agentless monitoring is 16 times that of an agent-based monitoring.

Figure 23.8 shows the communications bandwidth requirements graphically.

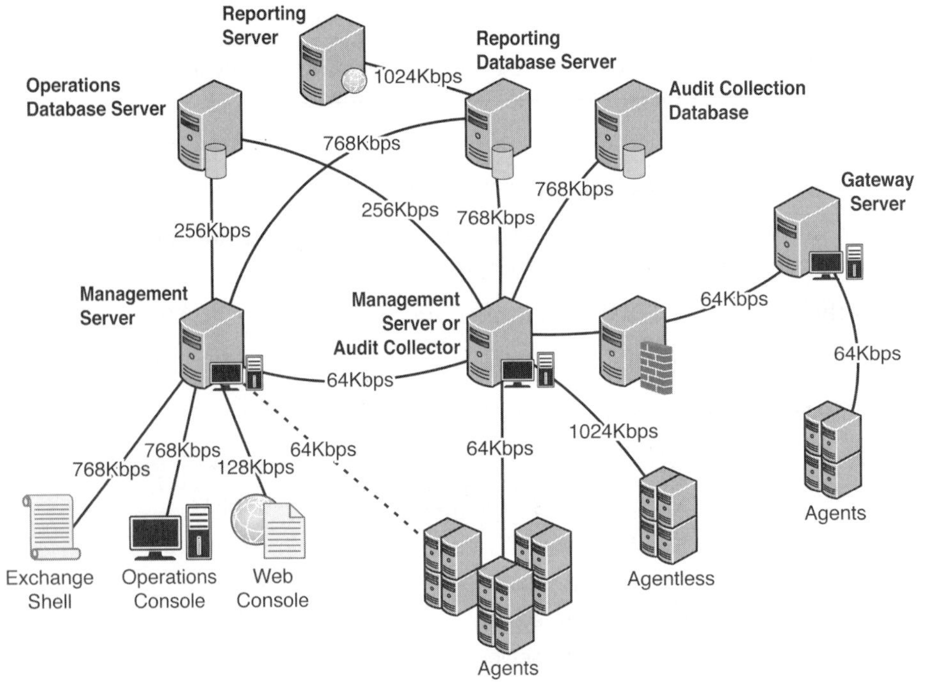

FIGURE 23.8 Communications bandwidth requirements.

Sizing the OpsMgr Databases

Depending on several factors, such as the type of data collected, the length of time that collected data will be kept, or the amount of database grooming that is scheduled, the size of the OpsMgr database will grow or shrink accordingly. It is important to monitor the size of the database to ensure that it does not increase well beyond the bounds of acceptable size. OpsMgr can be configured to monitor itself, supplying advance notice of database problems and capacity thresholds. This type of strategy is highly recommended because OpsMgr could easily collect event information faster than it could get rid of it.

The size of the operations database can be estimated through the following formula:

> Number of agents x 5MB x Retention days + 1024 Overhead
> = Estimated database size

For example, an OpsMgr environment monitoring 1,000 servers with the default seven-day retention period will have an estimated 36GB operations database:

> (1000 agents * 5MB / day per agent * 7 day) + 1024MB = 36024MB

The size of the reporting database can be estimated through the following formula:

> Number of agents x 3MB x Retention days + 1024 Overhead
> = Estimated database size

The same environment monitoring 1,000 servers with the default 400-day retention period will have an estimated 1.2TB reporting database:

> (1000 agents * 3 MB / day per agent * 400 days) + 1024MB = 1201024MB

The size of the audit collection database can be estimated through the following formula:

> Number of agents x 120MB x Retention days + 1024 Overhead
> = Estimated database size

This assumes that 4% of the servers are domain controllers (that is, 40 domain controllers for the 1,000 servers). At that ratio, the domain controllers are contributing 45% of the database size due to their high volume of events.

The environment monitoring 1,000 servers with the default 14-day retention period will have an estimated 1.6TB audit collection database at steady state:

> (1000 agents * 120MB / Agent per day * 14 days) + 1024MB = 1681024MB

Table 23.6 summarizes the estimated daily database growth for each database for each agent.

TABLE 23.6 Database Growth Estimates

Database	Daily Growth Estimate (MB)
OperationsManager database	5MB/day per agent
Data warehouse	3MB/day per agent
Audit collection database	120MB/day per agent

NOTE

It is important to understand that these estimates are rough guidelines only and can vary widely depending on the types of servers monitored, the monitoring configuration, the degree of customization, and other factors.

For example, more or fewer domain controllers will have a huge impact on the audit collection database and a large proportion of Exchange servers will have a similar impact on the OperationsManager database size.

Monitoring Non-Domain Member Considerations

DMZ, workgroup, and nontrusted domain agents require special configuration; in particular, they require certificates to establish mutual authentication. Operations Manager 2012 requires mutual authentication, that is, the server authenticates to the client and the client authenticates to the server, to ensure that the monitoring communications are not hacked. Without mutual authentication, it is possible for a hacker to execute a man-in-the-middle attack and impersonate either the client or the server. Thus, mutual authentication is a security measure designed to protect clients, servers, and sensitive Active Directory domain information, which is exposed to potential hacking attempts by the all-powerful management infrastructure. However, OpsMgr relies on Active Directory Kerberos for mutual authentication, which is not available to non-domain members.

NOTE

Workgroup servers, public web servers, and Microsoft Exchange Edge Transport role servers are commonly placed in the DMZ and are for security reasons not domain members, so almost every Windows Server 2008 R2 environment will need to deploy certificate-based authentication.

In the absence of Active Directory, trusts, and Kerberos, OpsMgr 2012 can use X.509 certificates to establish the mutual authentication. These can be issued by any public key infrastructure (PKI), such as Microsoft Windows Server 2012 Enterprise CA.

Putting It All Together in a Design

To illustrate the concepts discussed in this chapter, three designs are presented. These design scenarios cover a range of organizations from small to medium to large. The profile of the three enterprises is as follows:

- **Small enterprise**—A total of 30 servers in 3 locations, a main office with a shared T1 to the branch offices, and 25% bandwidth availability.
- **Medium enterprise**—A total of 500 servers in 10 locations, a main office with a shared 11Mbps fractional T3 to the branch offices, and 25% bandwidth availability.

- **Large enterprise**—A total of 2,000 servers in 50 locations, a main office with a shared 45Mbps T3 to the branch offices, and 25% bandwidth availability.

Based on these sizes, designs were developed.

In these designs, direct-attached storage (DAS) was used as a design constraint, rather than a storage-area network (SAN). This provides a more realistic minimum hardware specification. Performance could be further improved by using SAN in place of DAS.

Small Enterprise Design

The first design point is for a small enterprise consisting of the following:

- 30 servers
- Three locations, including a main office and two branch offices
- A shared T1 from the main office to the branch offices
- Approximately 25% bandwidth availability

For illustration and sizing, the numbers and types of servers at each location is listed in Table 23.7. Because the types of servers determine which MPs are loaded and determine database sizing, it is important to have some sense of the monitored servers.

TABLE 23.7 Small Enterprise Server Counts

Server Type	Central Office	Each Branch Office	Total
Windows servers	4	2	8
Exchange servers	5	0	5
SQL servers	5	0	5
IIS servers	4	2	8
Active Directory servers	2	1	4

Given the relatively small number of managed computers, a single-server design makes the most sense. The recommended design for the small enterprise is given in Table 23.8.

TABLE 23.8 Small Enterprise OpsMgr Design Recommendation

Server	Components	Processors	Memory	Disk
OM01	Operations database, Reporting data warehouse, reporting server, and management server	4 cores	8GB RAM	4-disk RAID-10 data 2-disk RAID-1 logs

For the server software, the recommendations are as follows:

- Windows Server 2008 R2 SP1, Standard edition 64-bit

NOTE

At time of publication, OpsMgr 2012 does not support installation of server components on Windows Server 2012. Support for installation of OpsMgr 2012 components on Windows Server 2012 will be supported in the System Center SP1.

- SQL Server 2008 R2 Enterprise 64-bit

Given that the components are all on the same server, the single-server option can really use the SQL Enterprise performance improvements. Also, using the Enterprise version of SQL allows the database server to add processors in the future if resource utilization dictates it.

Figure 23.9 shows the architecture for the small organization.

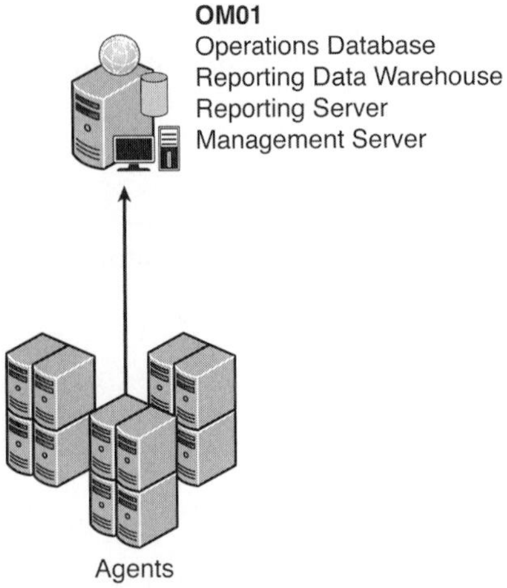

FIGURE 23.9 Operations Manager 2012 small enterprise architecture.

The databases will grow to their steady state sizes proportional to the number of agents being monitored, all other things being equal. Table 23.10 lists the estimated database sizes for the small enterprise databases. These sizes are important for determining the drive sizes and sizing backup solutions.

TABLE 23.10 Small Enterprise Estimated Database Sizes

Database	Agents	MB/Agent/Day	Retention	Database Size (GB)
OperationsManager	30	5	7	1.05
OperationsManagerDW	30	3	400	36

These sizes would be changed by adjustments to the retention periods, managed computer configuration, and MPs.

When determining the sizing of the disk subsystems, it is important to factor in the following:

- Database sizes
- Local backup overhead
- Log overhead
- Operating system overhead
- Application overhead

Typically, there should be a cushion of at least three to four times the database size to account for the overhead factors. The RAID types and number of disks would be changed to accommodate the storage needs.

Medium Enterprise Design

The second design point is for a medium enterprise consisting of the following:

- 500 servers
- 11 locations, including a main office and 10 branch offices
- A shared 11Mbps fractional T3 from the main office to the branch offices
- Approximately 25% bandwidth availability

For illustration and sizing, the numbers and types of servers at each location are listed in Table 23.11. Because the types of servers determine which MPs are loaded and determine database sizing, it is important to have some sense of the monitored servers.

TABLE 23.11 Medium Enterprise Server Counts

Server Type	Central Office	Each Branch Office	Total
Windows servers	150	3	35
Exchange servers	10	1	8
SQL servers	50	1	10
IIS servers	185	3	35
Active Directory servers	5	2	12

Given the number of managed computers, a dual-server design makes the most sense. This would be a database server and a management server. The recommended design for the medium enterprise is given in Table 23.12.

TABLE 23.12 Medium Enterprise OpsMgr Design Recommendation

Server	Components	Processors	Memory	Disk
OM01	Management Server	2 cores	4GB RAM	2-disk RAID 1
OM02	Operations database, Reporting data warehouse, and reporting server	4 cores	4GB RAM	6-disk RAID-10 data 2-disk RAID-1 logs

These are minimum specifications for performance and storage requirements. They can be revised upward based on additional requirements, such as backup storage.

For the server software, the recommendations are as follows:

- Windows Server 2008 R2 SP1, Standard edition 64-bit

NOTE

At time of publication, OpsMgr 2012 does not support installation of server components on Windows Server 2012. Support for installation of OpsMgr 2012 components on Windows Server 2012 will be supported in the System Center SP1.

- SQL Server 2008 R2 Enterprise 64-bit

Given that the database components are all on the same server, the database server can really use the SQL Enterprise performance improvements. Also, using the Enterprise version of SQL allows the database server to add processors in the future if resource utilization dictates it. Using 64-bit versions similarly allows memory to be added and utilized without having to rebuild servers.

Figure 23.10 shows the architecture for the medium-sized organization.

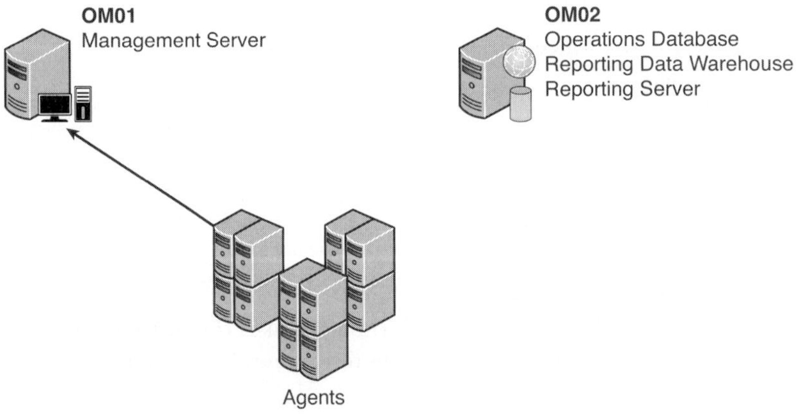

FIGURE 23.10 Operations Manager 2012 medium enterprise architecture.

The databases will grow to their steady state sizes proportional to the number of agents being monitored, all other things being equal. Table 23.14 lists the estimated database sizes for the medium enterprise databases. These sizes are important for determining the drive sizes and sizing backup solutions.

TABLE 23.14 Medium Enterprise Estimated Database Sizes

Database	Agents	MB/Agent/Day	Retention	Database Size (GB)
OperationsManager	500	5	7	17.5
OperationsManagerDW	500	3	400	600

These sizes would be changed by adjustments to the retention periods, managed computer configuration, and MPs.

When determining the sizing of the disk subsystems, it is important to factor in the following:

- Database sizes
- Local backup overhead
- Log overhead
- Operating system overhead
- Application overhead

Typically, there should be a cushion of at least three to four times the database size to account for the overhead factors. The RAID types and number of disks would be changed to accommodate the storage needs.

Large Enterprise Design

The last design point is for a large enterprise consisting of the following:

- 2,000 servers
- 51 locations, including a main office and 50 branch offices
- A shared 45Mbps T3 from the main office to the branch offices
- Approximately 25% bandwidth availability

For illustration and sizing, the numbers and types of servers at each location is listed in Table 23.15. Because the types of servers determine which MPs are loaded and determine database sizing, it is important to have some sense of the monitored servers. This information can also be used with the System Center Capacity Planner tool.

TABLE 23.15 Large Enterprise Server Counts

Server Type	Central Office	Branch Office (Each)	Branch Offices (Total)
Windows servers	575	2	100
Exchange servers	15	2	100
SQL servers	300	2	100
IIS servers	600	2	100
Active Directory servers	10	2	100
Totals	1,500		500

Given the relatively large number of managed computers, a server per component design makes the most sense. This places each component on its own dedicated server, ensuring that there is no contention for resources between components. The recommended design for the large enterprise is given in Table 23.16.

TABLE 23.16 Large Enterprise OpsMgr Design Recommendation

Server	Component(s)	Processors	Memory	Disk
OM01	Management server	4 cores	12GB RAM	4-disk RAID 10
OM02	Operations database	4 cores	8GB RAM	8-disk RAID-10 data 2-disk RAID-1 logs
OM03	Reporting data warehouse	4 cores	8GB RAM	16-disk RAID-10 data 2-disk RAID-1 logs
OM04	Reporting Server	2 cores	4GB RAM	2-disk RAID 1
OM05	Management server	2 cores	4GB RAM	2-disk RAID 10

These are minimum specifications for performance and storage requirements. The 8-disk RAID-10 subsystem for the OperationsManager database is driven mainly by performance considerations, whereas the OperationsManagerDW 16-disk RAID 10 is driven mainly by storage requirements. They can be revised upward based on additional requirements, such as backup storage.

NOTE

This configuration could really benefit from SAN storage to improve performance and scalability. At the very least, the database servers will require external drive enclosures to support the large number of disks.

For the server software, the recommendations are as follows:

- Windows Server 2008 R2 SP1, Standard edition 64-bit

NOTE

At time of publication, OpsMgr 2012 does not support installation of server components on Windows Server 2012. Support for installation of OpsMgr 2012 components on Windows Server 2012 will be supported in the System Center SP1.

▶ SQL Server 2008 R2 Enterprise 64-bit

Given the scale of the infrastructure, the 64-bit platforms are needed to take advantage of the larger memory and to increase the performance of the SQL database servers.

Figure 23.11 shows the architecture for the large-sized organization.

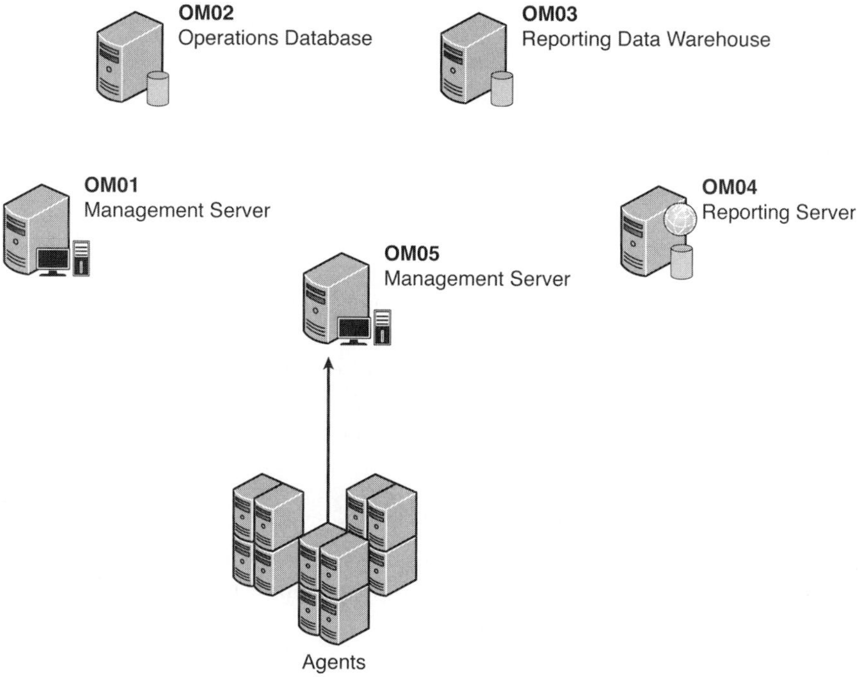

FIGURE 23.11 Operations Manager 2012 large enterprise architecture.

The databases will grow to their steady state sizes proportional to the number of agents being monitored, all other things being equal. Table 23.18 lists the estimated database sizes for the large enterprise databases. These sizes are important for determining the drive sizes and sizing backup solutions.

TABLE 23.18 Large Enterprise Estimated Database Sizes

Database	Agents	MB/Agent/Day	Retention	Database Size (GB)
OperationsManager	2,000	5	7	70
OperationsManagerDW	2,000	3	400	2400

These sizes would be changed by adjustments to the retention periods, managed computer configuration, and MPs.

NOTE

For these larger databases, larger drives can be used to reduce the number of spindles in the RAID-10 arrays. This reduces the performance, but should not be a problem for the Reporting data warehouse and the audit collection databases.

When determining the sizing of the disk subsystems, it is important to factor in the following:

- Database sizes
- Local backup overhead
- Log overhead
- Operating system overhead
- Application overhead

Typically, there should be a cushion of at least three to four times the database size to account for the overhead factors. This is more difficult with large enterprise organizations and their correspondingly large datasets. The RAID types and number of disks would be changed to accommodate the storage needs, especially if online backup to tape or replication to an offsite recovery site might be used instead of local backup.

Installing Operations Manager 2012

Operations Manager 2012 is a multitier and multicomponent application that can be deployed in a variety of architectures. This allows OpsMgr to support scaling from a small organization to a very large enterprise.

Three different installations are performed in this section:

- A small organization install on a single server
- A small organization upgrade from a single server
- A medium-sized organization install on two servers

Single-Server OpsMgr 2012 Install

This section steps through the install of OpsMgr and Reporting Server on a single-server configuration. There will be a single server named OM1 with all the components. Figure 23.12 shows the architecture for the small organization build.

The specification for a single-server configuration of OM1 to support the small organization is as follows:

- 4 cores
- 8GB of RAM
- 4-disk RAID 10 for data and 2-disk RAID 1 for logs

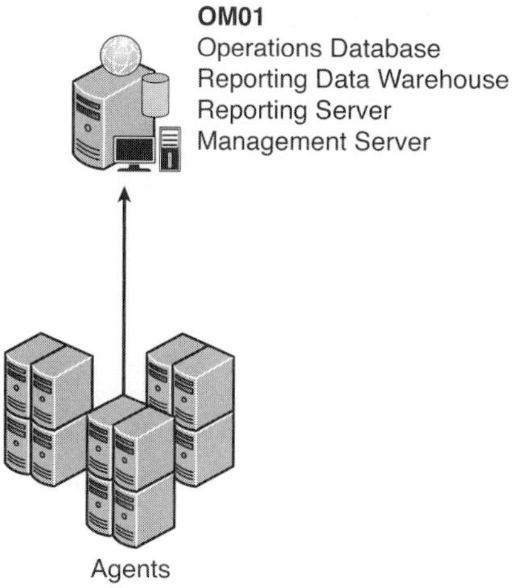

FIGURE 23.12 Operations Manager 2012 small enterprise architecture.

These hardware requirements ensure that the system can perform to specification.

NOTE

If the configuration were to be virtualized on a Windows Server 2008 R2 Hyper-V host, a single-server configuration is not recommended. Instead, a two-server configuration is recommended and SQL Server 2008 R2 should be installed on the second server to balance the load. See the section "Multiserver OpsMgr 2012 Install" later in this chapter.

The steps in this section assume that the single server has been prepared with the following:

- Windows Server 2008 R2 SP1 operating system installed
- Microsoft Core XML Services (MSXML) version 6.0
- Microsoft Report Viewer 2010 Redistributable Package
- Windows Remote Management enabled for the management server
- Web Server (IIS) role with the appropriate role services installed
- .NET Framework 3.5 SP1
- .NET Framework 4.0
- SQL Server 2008 SP1, SQL Server 2008 R2, or SQL Server 2008 R2 SP1 with Reporting Services installed
- SQL Collation: SQL_Latin1_General_CP1_CI_AS
- SQL Server Full Text Search required

- An OpsMgr service account with local administrator rights to the server and system administrator rights to SQL Server 2008

NOTE

It is recommended to install the IIS role before installing .NET Framework 4.0; otherwise, the ASP.NET 4.0 will need to be registered with IIS manually. To register ASP.NET 4.0 manually, execute the following command: c:\windows\Microsoft.NET\Framework64\v4.0.30319\aspnet_regiis.exe –r

To support the OpsMgr 2012 Web Console role, the following Web Server role services are needed:

- Static Content
- Default Document
- Directory Browsing
- HTTP Errors
- HTTP Logging
- Request Monitor
- Request Filtering
- Static Content Compression
- ASP.NET
- Windows Authentication
- IIS 6 Metabase Compatibility

The first eight are selected by default when adding the Web Server role to Windows Server 2008; the other role services must be added manually.

This prepares the system for the install of OpsMgr 2012. Once the server meets all the prerequisites and is ready for installation, complete the following steps to run the install:

1. Log on with the OpsMgr service account.
2. Launch Setup.exe from the OpsMgr installation media.
3. Click Install Hyperlink.
4. Select the features to install; in this example, check all the boxes. These are Management Server, Management Console, Web Console, and Reporting Server.
5. Click Next.

6. Select the installation location and click Next.
7. The prerequisites will be checked. Remediate any issues or click Next to continue if passed.

NOTE

On the Prerequisites screen, the Review Full System Requirements link can be clicked to launch a browser window to see the full list of requirements for each component.

8. Type the management group name in the Management Group text box and click Next.
9. Accept the license agreement and click Next.
10. Enter the server name and the instance of SQL Server on which to install the Operations Manager 2012 operations database, and then click the Tab key to populate the database fields.
11. Leave the default database name OperationsManager and size of 1000MB. Change the data and log file locations if appropriate, and then click Next.
12. Enter the server name and the instance of SQL Server on which to install the Operations Manager 2012 data warehouse database, and then click the Tab key to populate the database fields.
13. Leave the default database name OperationsManagerDW and size of 1000MB. Change the data and log file locations if appropriate, and then click Next.
14. Choose the SQL Reporting Services instance and click Next.
15. Choose the Default Web Site to use for the Web console and click Next.
16. Leave the default selection Use Mixed Authentication and click Next.
17. Enter the account information for the Management Server Action Account, Data Reader Account, and Data Writer Account, and then click Next.

NOTE

If there is an action account warning pop-up, click OK to clear the warning.

18. At the Health Improve Operations Manager 2012 screen, check the appropriate options and click Next to continue.
19. At the Microsoft Update screen, select the recommended On option button.
20. At the Installation Summary screen, review the selections and click Install to continue.
21. Once setup is complete, click Close to exit the Installation Wizard.

Operations Manager 2012 is now installed in a single-server configuration. Although the small organization design was created for 30 servers, this configuration can manage up to 250 servers.

Multiserver OpsMgr 2012 Install

This section steps through the install of OpsMgr and reporting server on a two-server configuration to support a medium-sized organization. The infrastructure is designed to support up to 500 agent systems. There will be two servers, with the management server named OM1 and the database server named OM2. Figure 23.13 shows the architecture for the medium-sized organization build.

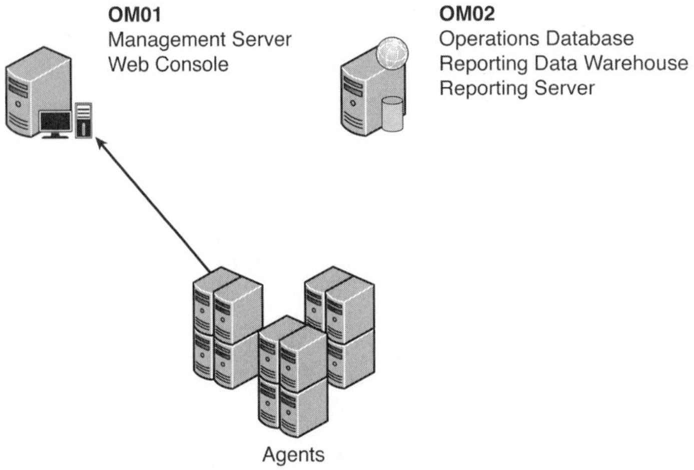

FIGURE 23.13 Operations Manager 2012 medium enterprise architecture.

The hardware specification for the management server OM1 configuration is as follows:

- 2 cores
- 4GB of RAM
- 2-disk RAID 1

The steps in this section assume that the management server OM1 has been prepared with the following:

- Windows Server 2008 R2 SP1 operating system installed

NOTE

At time of publication, OpsMgr 2012 does not support installation of server components on Windows Server 2012. Support for installation of OpsMgr 2012 components on Windows Server 2012 will be supported in the System Center SP1.

- Microsoft Core XML Services (MSXML) version 6.0
- Web Server (IIS) role with the appropriate role services installed
- Microsoft Report Viewer 2010 Redistributable Package
- .NET Framework 3.5 SP1
- .NET Framework 4.0
- An OpsMgr service account with local administrator rights to the server and system administrator rights to SQL Server 2008

NOTE

It is recommended to install the IIS role before installing .NET Framework 4.0; otherwise, the ASP.NET 4.0 will need to be registered with IIS manually. To register ASP.NET 4.0 manually, execute the following command: c:\windows\Microsoft.NET\Framework64\v4.0.30319\aspnet_regiis.exe –r

To support the OpsMgr 2012 Web Console role, the following Web Server role services are needed on the management server OM1:

- Static Content
- Default Document
- Directory Browsing
- HTTP Errors
- HTTP Logging
- Request Monitor
- Request Filtering
- Static Content Compression
- ASP.NET
- Windows Authentication
- IIS 6 Metabase Compatibility

The first eight are selected by default when adding the Web Server role to Windows Server 2008; the other role services must be added manually.

NOTE

The Web Console role requires that the ISAPI and CGI restrictions be allowed for ASP.NET 4.0. This can be done by selecting the web server in the Internet Information Service (IIS) Manager tool and opening the ISAPI and CGI restrictions feature. Click the two ASP.NET v4.0.30319 options and select Allow for each one (as shown in Figure 23.14).

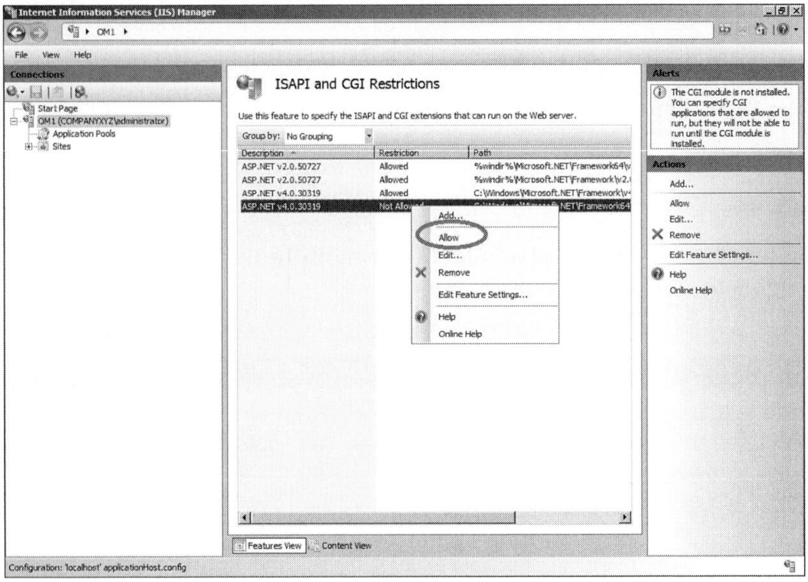

FIGURE 23.14 Allow ISAPI and CGI for ASP .NET 4.0.

The hardware specifications for the database server OM2 configuration are as follows:

- 4 cores
- 4GB of RAM
- 6-disk RAID 10 for data and 2-disk RAID 1 for logs

These hardware requirements ensure that the system can perform to specification.

The steps in this section assume that the database server has been prepared with the following:

- Windows Server 2008 R2 SP1 operating system installed

NOTE

At time of publication, OpsMgr 2012 does not support installation of server components on Windows Server 2012. Support for installation of OpsMgr 2012 components on Windows Server 2012 will be supported in the System Center SP1.

- SQL Server 2008 with Reporting Services installed
- SQL_Latin1_General_CP1_CI_AS Collation selected
- SQL Server Full Text Search installed
- .NET Framework 3.5. SP1

- .NET Framework 4.0
- An OpsMgr service account with local administrator rights to the server and system administrator rights to SQL Server 2008

This prepares the system for the install of OpsMgr 2012.

Because the install is on separate servers, this requires that the installations take place in a specific order. The order of installation is in two parts:

1. Management server, Management console, and Web console components. This will also install the operational database and data warehouse database components.
2. Reporting server component. This will install the report engine that pulls data from the data warehouse database. This step must be run on the server that will hold the Reporting Server role.

The first part is to install the management server, Management console, and Web console components. Once the servers meet all the prerequisites and are ready for installation, the steps to run the install are as follows:

1. Log on to the management server (OM1 in this example) with the OpsMgr service account.
2. Launch Setup.exe from the OpsMgr installation media.
3. Click Install at the System Center 2012 Operations Manager splash screen, as shown in Figure 23.15.

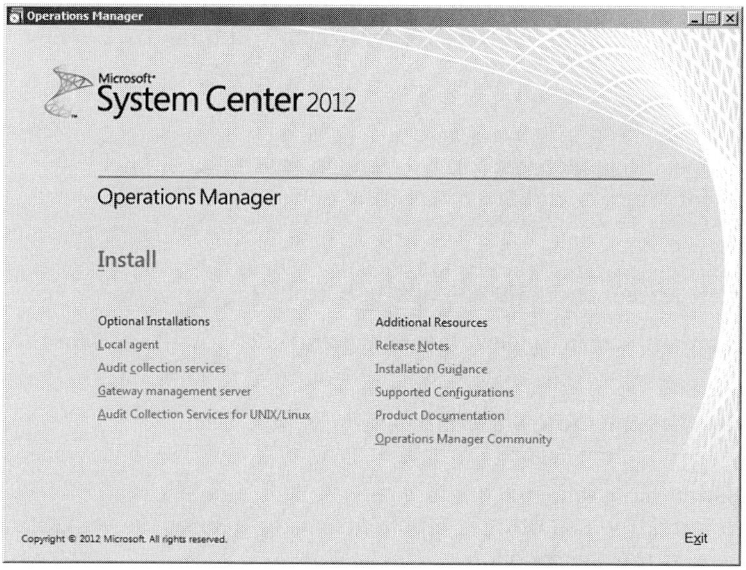

FIGURE 23.15 Operations Manager 2012 installation screen.

4. At the Select Features to Install screen, check off the options: Management Server, Management Console, and Web Console.
5. Click Next.
6. At the Select Installation Location screen, enter the installation location and click Next.
7. Verify the prerequisites have been met and remediate if necessary, and then click Next.
8. Enter a management group name, in this case **COMPANYXYZ**, and then click Next.
9. Accept the license agreement and click Next.
10. Enter the operational database server name and instance, in this case **OM2**. The wizard will automatically initiate a check of the target database server.
11. Leave the database name at the default OperationsManager. Change the data file and log file locations if necessary, and then click Next.
12. Enter the data warehouse database server name and instance, in this case **OM2**. The wizard will automatically initiate a check of the target database server.
13. Leave the database name at the default OperationsManagerDW. Change the data file and log file locations if necessary, and then click Next.
14. Leave the Default Web Site option selected and click Next.
15. Leave the Use Mixed Authentication option selected for the Web console authentication mode and click Next.
16. At the Configure Operations Manager Accounts screen, enter credentials for the Management Server Action Account, the Data Reader Account, and the Data Writer Account.
17. Click Next.
18. At the Help Improve Operations Manager 2012 screen, choose the Customer Experience Improvement Program and Error Reporting options.
19. Click Next.
20. At the Microsoft Update screen, check the On option button and click Next.
21. At the Installation Summary screen, review the choices and click Install to begin the installation.
22. Once setup completes, click the Close button to exit the Setup Wizard.

The first part of the installation has completed and the console will launch automatically. The second part is to install the Reporting components on the database server OM2. Complete the following steps to run the install:

1. Log on to the database server (OM2 in this example) with the OpsMgr service account.
2. Launch Setup.exe from the OpsMgr installation media.
3. Click Install at the System Center 2012 Operations Manager splash screen.
4. At the Select Features to Install screen, only check the Reporting Server option.
5. Click Next.
6. At the Select Installation Location screen, enter the installation location and click Next.
7. Verify the prerequisites have been met and remediate if necessary, and then click Next.
8. Enter a management server name, in this case **OM1**, and then click Next.
9. Choose the SQL Server instance for Reporting Services and click Next.
10. Enter the credentials for the Data Reader Account and click Next.
11. At the Help Improve Operations Manager 2012 screen, choose the Operational Data Reporting option and click Next.
12. At the Microsoft Update screen, check the On option button and click Next.
13. At the Installation Summary screen, review the choices and click Install to begin the installation.
14. Once setup completes, click the Close button to exit the Setup Wizard.

Operations Manager 2012 is now installed in a multiserver configuration. This configuration can manage up to 500 servers.

NOTE

The Operations console will need to be closed and reopened to see the newly installed reports in the console.

Importing Management Packs

After the initial installation, OpsMgr only includes a few core MPs. The MPs contain all the discoveries, monitors, rules, knowledge, reports, and views that OpsMgr needs to be able to effectively monitor servers and applications. One of the first tasks after installing OpsMgr 2012 is to import MPs into the system.

A large number of MPs are in the Internet catalog on the Microsoft website. These include updated MPs, MPs for new products, and third-party MPs. It is important to load only those MPs that are going to be used, as each additional MP increases the database size, adds discoveries that impact the performance of agents, and, in general, clutters up the interface.

The key MPs for a Windows environment are as follows:

- Windows Server Operating System MPs
- Active Directory Server MPs
- Windows Cluster Management MPs
- Microsoft Windows DNS Server MPs
- Microsoft Windows DHCP Server MPs
- Microsoft Windows Group Policy MPs
- Microsoft Windows Hyper-V MPs
- Windows Server IIS MPs
- Windows Server Network Load Balancing MPs
- Windows Server Print Server MPs
- Windows Terminal Services MPs
- SQL Server MPs (to monitor the OpsMgr database roles)

There might be other MPs that are appropriate for the environment, depending on the applications that are installed. For example, if the organization has deployed Exchange Server 2010 and HP Proliant server hardware, it would be good for the organization to deploy the Exchange MPs and the HP Proliant MPs.

For each of these MPs, it is important to load the relevant versions only. For example, if the environment includes Windows Server 2008 only, only load the Windows Server Core OS 2008 Management Pack. If the environment includes both Windows Server 2003 and Windows Server 2008, load both the Windows Server Core OS 2003 and the Windows Server Core OS 2008 Management Packs. In addition, a number of language packs don't need to be loaded unless those particular languages are supported by the organization at the server level.

Some collections of MPs require that all versions be loaded, but the Management Pack Import Wizard checks and warns if that's the case.

In versions of OpsMgr earlier than 2007 R2, the MPs had to be downloaded from the Microsoft website one by one, the MSI installed one by one, and the MPs imported one by one. Dependencies would not be checked unless additional steps were taken to consolidate the MP files prior to importing. This was a very labor-intensive process. Also, there was no easy way to check for updates to previously installed MPs.

In OpsMgr 2012, a new Management Pack Import Wizard was introduced. This wizard connects directly to the Microsoft MP catalog and downloads, checks, and imports MPs.

It even does version checks to ensure that the MPs are the latest versions. This is a huge improvement over the old method of importing MPs.

To import the key MPs, follow these steps:

1. Launch the Operations console.
2. Select the Administration section.
3. Select the Management Packs folder.
4. Right-click the Management Packs folder and select Import Management Packs.
5. Click Add and select Add from Catalog.
6. Click the Search button to search the entire catalog.

NOTE

The View pull-down menu in the Management Pack Import Wizard includes four options: All Management Packs in the Catalog, Updates Available for Installed Management Packs, All Management Packs Released in the Last 3 Months, and All Management Packs Released in the Last 6 Months. The Updates option checks against the previously installed MPs and allows the download of updated versions of those.

7. Select the key MPs from the previous bulleted list and click Add for each of them. Each of the major MPs might include a number of sub-MPs for discovery, monitoring, and other breakdowns of functionality.
8. When done adding MPs, click OK.
9. The wizard now validates the added MPs, checking for versions, dependencies, and security risks. It allows problem MPs to be removed and dependencies to be added to the list.
10. Click Install to begin the download and import process. Progress is shown for each of the MPs being imported.
11. After all the MPs are imported, click Close to exit the wizard.

After the import completes, the MPs take effect immediately. Agents begin discovering based on the schedule specified in the MPs and monitors and rules begin deploying.

Deploying OpsMgr Agents

OpsMgr agents are deployed to all managed servers through the OpsMgr Discovery Wizard, or by using software distribution mechanisms such as Active Directory Group Policy objects (GPOs) or System Center Configuration Manager 2012. Installation through the Operations console uses the fully qualified domain name (FQDN) of the computer. When searching for systems through the Operations console, you can use wildcards to locate a broad range of computers for agent installation. Certain situations, such as monitoring across firewalls, can require the manual installation of these components.

Generally, there are three ways to deploy agents: The first is using software distribution such as Microsoft System Center Configuration Manager or Active Directory GPOs, the second is manual installation using the product media, and the third and most common way is using the SCOM Discovery Wizard to search for and install agents on domain members by executing the following steps:

1. Launch the Operations console and select the Administration section.
2. At the bottom of the navigation pane, click Discovery Wizard.
3. Select Windows Computers and click Next.
4. Select Automatic Computer Discovery and click Next. This scans the entire Active Directory domain for computers.
5. Leave the Use Selected Management Server Action Account selected and click Discover. This starts the discovery process.
6. After the discovery process runs (this might take a few minutes), the list of discovered computers is displayed. Select the devices that should have agents deployed to them, as shown in Figure 23.16.

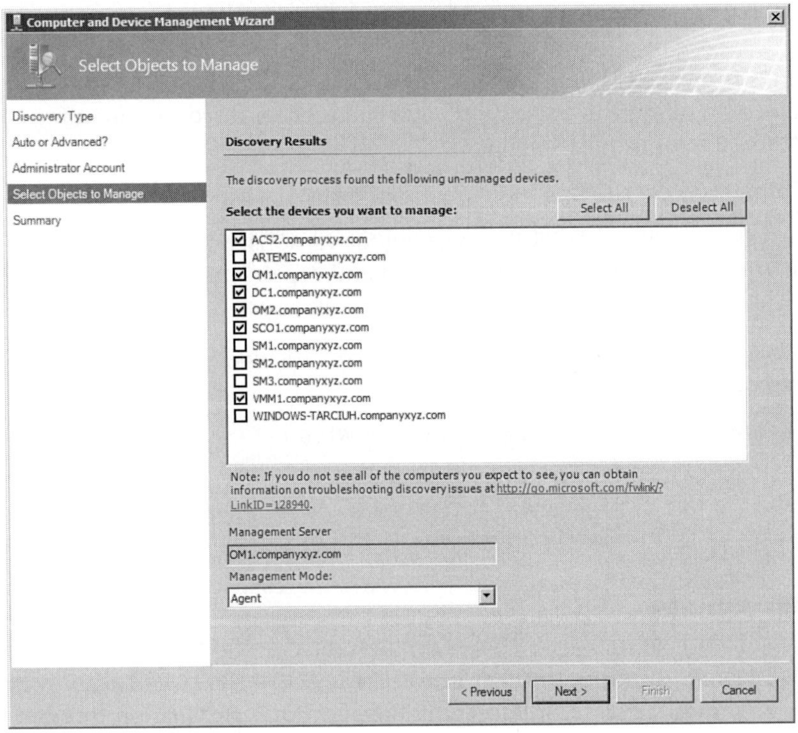

FIGURE 23.16 Discovered computers.

NOTE

The list only includes systems that do not already have agents installed. If a computer has an agent installed, the wizard excludes it from the list of devices.

7. Click Next.
8. Leave the Agent Installation Directory and the Agent Action Account at the defaults, and then click Finish.
9. The Agent Management Task Status window opens, listing all the computers selected and the progress of each installation. As shown in Figure 23.17, the agent installation task started for the selected computers. The ACS2, CM2, and VMM1 agents have been installed successfully and the others are in progress.
10. Click Close when the installation completes.

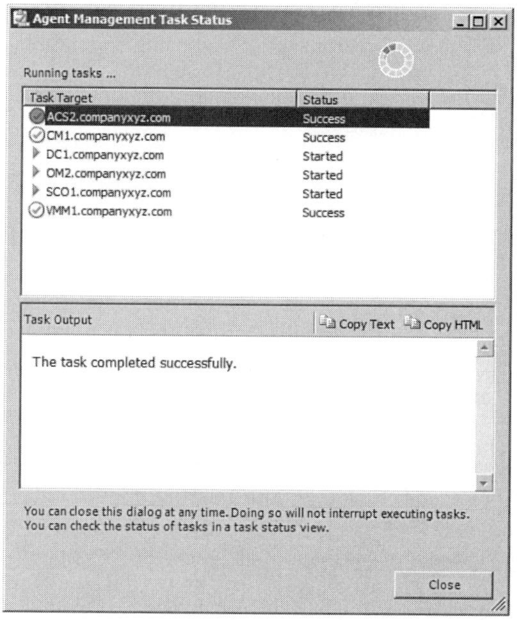

FIGURE 23.17 Agent installation progress.

Even if the window is closed before the installs complete, the results of the installs can be viewed in Task Status view in the Monitoring section of the Operations console.

The agent deployment is very efficient and a large number of computers can be selected for deployment without any issues. The agents start automatically and begin to be monitored as they are discovered.

After installation, it might be necessary to wait a few minutes before the information from the agents is sent to the management server.

During the next few minutes after installation, the agent contacts the management server and establishes a mutually authenticated, encrypted communication channel with the assigned management server. If the agent was pushed through a software delivery system such as System Center Configuration Manager 2012, the agent determines the management server through command-line options or Active Directory-integrated discovery.

Figure 23.18 shows the state of the agents after deployment. The computers show the agent or management server state as Healthy. However, the Windows operating system state shows as Not Monitored. This is because there have been no additional MPs imported on this newly installed Operations Manager infrastructure. MPs must be imported and configured for OpsMgr to monitor additional objects like the Windows operating systems.

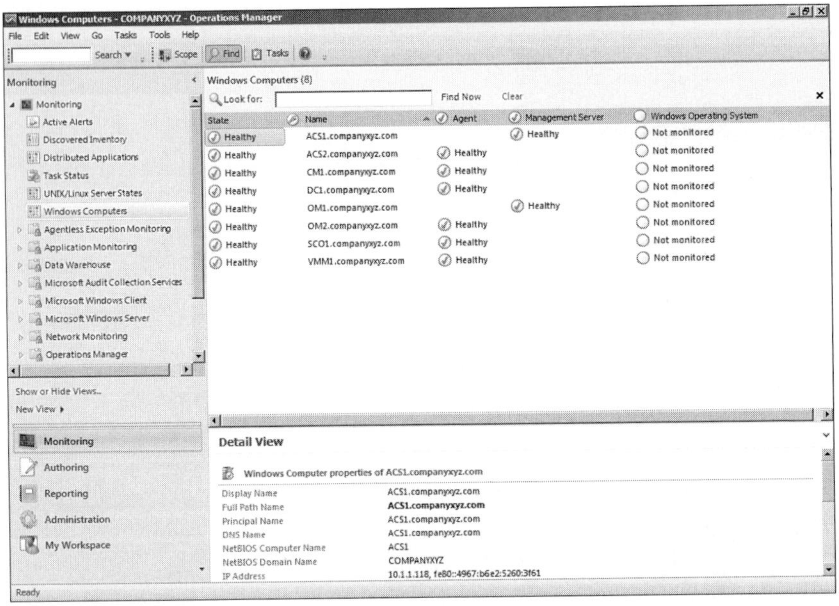

FIGURE 23.18 Agent state in a new infrastructure.

Once MPs are imported, the agent downloads rules to discover the various applications and components it's hosting, allowing the correct application-specific MPs to be applied.

This discovery process runs periodically to ensure the correct rules are always applied to the server.

Configuring OpsMgr

After installing the Operations Manager 2012 infrastructure, several configuration steps should be taken to have the system monitor properly, generate Active Directory synthetic transactions, and send out email notifications of alerts.

Global Management Group Settings

After the installation of the Operations Manager infrastructure, several settings need to be configured for the management group. These settings are called global management group settings. They include a number of settings that control the security, data retention in the operations database, agent heartbeat interval, web addresses for alerts and consoles, and manual agent security. Figure 23.19 shows the Global Management Group Settings page.

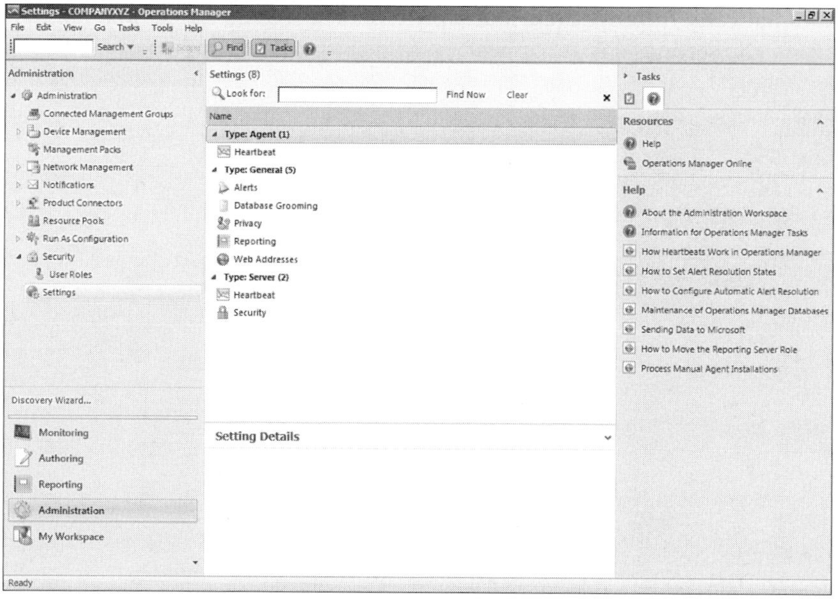

FIGURE 23.19 Global management group settings.

The two key global management group settings that need to be configured are as follows:

- Manual Agent Install Security
- Database Grooming

The manual agent install security controls how Operations Manager handles manual agent installations. If an agent is installed manually—that is, not pushed out from the console—the management servers will by default reject the agent. This is done to ensure that rogue computers are not connecting to the management infrastructure. In reality, this is a relatively low-probability threat. For most organizations, it is more convenient to have the manual agents be automatically accepted.

To configure the management group to accept manual agents, complete the following steps:

1. Launch the Operations console.
2. Select the Administration space.
3. Select the Settings folder.
4. Under the Type: Server section, right-click Security and select Properties.
5. Select the Review New Manual Agent Installations in Pending Management View option.
6. Check the Automatically Approve New Manually Installed Agents check box. Figure 23.20 shows how the settings should appear.

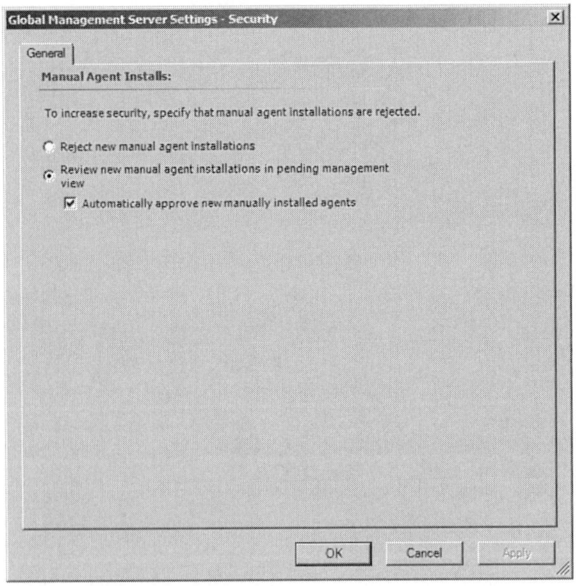

FIGURE 23.20 Manual agent install security.

7. Click OK to save the settings.

Now manual agents will be accepted automatically.

The database grooming controls how long data is retained in the operations database, which, in turn, dictates how much data is visible in the Operations console. Once the data retention period is reached, the data is groomed (that is, deleted) from the operations database. The default grooming settings are set for seven days, which means that after seven days the data is no longer available in the Operations console. However, the data is available in summarized form in the Reporting data warehouse for the retention period of that database, which is approximately a year. This data can then be viewed with the reports.

The biggest impact of the operations database grooming settings is that by default only a week of data is available. When troubleshooting problems using the console, it is important to have more than a week's worth of data. This allows for comparing data week to week to ascertain trends and catch longer-term problems.

However, the longer the grooming settings, the larger the size of the Operations Manager database. Therefore, it is important to balance the data retention against the size of the database.

The best-practice recommendation is to set the database grooming settings to 14 days to have 2 weeks' worth of data for troubleshooting without creating too large a database. These settings will essentially double the size of the Operations Manager database, which is manageable in most cases.

The settings to change are for the following records:

- Resolved Alerts
- Events Data
- Performance Data
- Task History
- Monitoring Job Data
- State Change Events Data
- Maintenance Mode History
- Availability History

WARNING

Do not adjust the Performance Signature grooming interval from the default of two days. This value is used to compute baselines. Changing it negatively affects performance baselines.

To adjust the Database Grooming settings, complete the following steps:

1. Launch the Operations console.
2. Select the Administration space.
3. Select the Settings folder.
4. Under the Type: General section, right-click Database Grooming and select Properties.

5. Select the record to change and click Edit.
6. Change the value to 14 and click OK.
7. Repeat for each of the remaining records. Do not change the Performance Signature record. Figure 23.21 shows how the configuration should look.

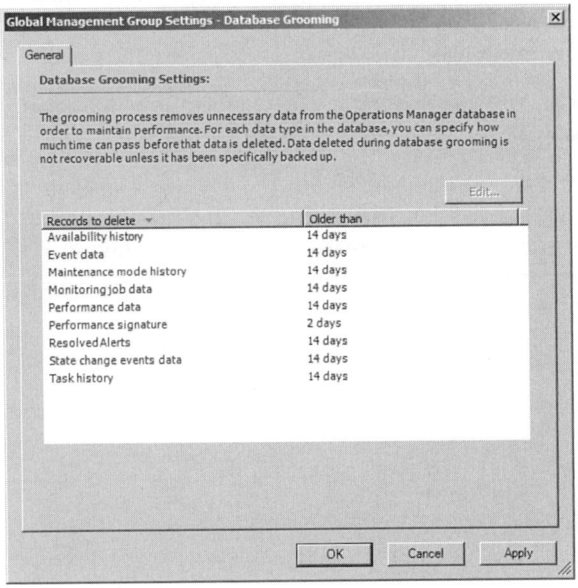

FIGURE 23.21 Database Grooming settings.

8. Click OK to save the configuration changes.

Now the data will be retained in the operations database for 14 days.

Agent Proxy Configuration

Operations Manager 2012 has a variety of security measures built in to the product to prevent security breaches. One measure in particular is the prevention of impersonation of one agent by another. That is, an agent SERVER1 cannot insert operations data into the database about a domain controller DC1. This could constitute a security violation, where SERVER1 could maliciously generate fraudulent emergencies by making it appear that DC1 was having operational issues.

Although this is normally a good feature, this can be a problem if, in fact, SERVER1 is monitoring DC1 from a client perspective. The Operations Manager infrastructure would reject any information presented about DC1 by SERVER1. When this occurs, the system generates an alert to indicate that an attempt to proxy operations data has occurred.

Figure 23.22 shows an example of the alert, where DC1.companyxyz.com is attempting to submit data for another computer. In the normal course of events, this alert is not an indication of an attack but rather a configuration problem.

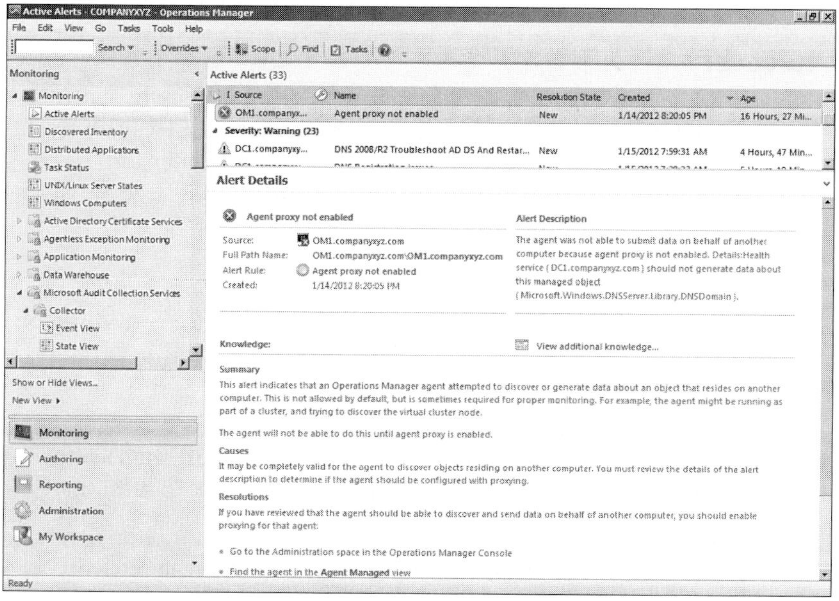

FIGURE 23.22 Agent Proxy alert.

To get around this problem, Agent Proxy can be selectively enabled for agents that need to be able to present operational data about other agents. To enable Agent Proxy for a computer, complete the following steps:

1. Open the Operations Manager 2012 console.
2. Select the Administration section.
3. Expand the Device Management folder and select the Agent Managed node.
4. Right-click the agent in the right pane, in this case SERVER1, and select Properties.
5. Click the Security tab.
6. Check the Allow This Agent to Act as a Proxy and Discover Managed Objects on Other Computers check box.
7. Click OK to save.

Repeat this for all agents that need to act as proxy agents.

NOTE

Because the alerts generated by this condition are rule based and not monitor based, the alert needs to be manually resolved by right-clicking on it and selecting Close Alert.

Agent Restart Recovery

Agents will heartbeat every 60 seconds by default, contacting their management server to check for new rules and upload data. On the management server, there is a Health Service Watcher corresponding to each managed agent. If the Health Service Watcher for an agent detects three missed heartbeats in a row (that is, 3 minutes without a heartbeat), the Health Service Watcher executes a pair of diagnostics:

- First, the Health Service Watcher attempts to ping the agent.
- Second, the Health Service Watcher checks to see if the Health Service is running on the agent.

An alert is then generated for each of the diagnostics if they failed. If the agent is reachable via ping but the Health Service is stopped, there is a recovery to restart the Health Service. This allows the agent to recover automatically from stopped agent conditions.

The Restart Health Service Recovery is disabled by default. To enable the functionality, an override can be created for the Health Service Watcher objects. To enable the recovery, follow these steps:

1. Open the Operations Manager 2012 console.
2. Select the Authoring space.
3. Expand the Management Pack Objects node.
4. Select the Monitors node.
5. Select View, Scope.
6. Click Clear All to clear the scope.
7. Type **health service watcher** in the Look For field and click the View All Targets option button.
8. Select the Health Service Watcher target. Don't pick the ones with additional information in parentheses.
9. Click OK.
10. Type **Heartbeat Failure** in the Look For field and click Find Now.
11. Right-click the Health Service Heartbeat Failure aggregate rollup node and select Overrides, Override Recovery, Restart Health Service, and For All Objects of Class: Health Service Watcher.
12. Check the Override box next to Enabled and set the value to True.

13. In the Select Destination Management Pack pull-down menu, select the appropriate override MP. If none exists, create a new MP named Operations Manager MP Overrides by clicking New and then following the prompts to create a new MP.

NOTE

Never use the Default Management Pack for overrides. Always create an override MP that corresponds to each imported MP.

14. Click OK to save the override.

Now if the Health Service is stopped on an agent, the management server automatically attempts to restart it.

Notifications and Subscriptions

When alerts are generated in the console, a wealth of information is available about the nature of the problem and how to troubleshoot and resolve it. However, most administrators will not be watching the console at all times. Operations Manager has a sophisticated notification mechanism that allows alerts to be forwarded to email, SMS, IM, or even a command-line interface. The most common method of alert notification is email.

However, Operations Manager generates a lot of alerts. If each one of these alerts were forwarded, this would overwhelm the average administrator's Inbox and prove totally useless. Operations Manager has two alert parameters to help categorize the alerts. Each alert has two parameters that help guide the notification process: severity and priority.

Alert Severity is the first and main parameter. There are three severity levels:

- **Critical (2)**—These alerts indicate that there is a problem that needs to be fixed immediately and is directly actionable (that is, something can be done).
- **Warning (1)**—These alerts indicate that there is a problem, but that it might not be immediately impacting the environment or might not be directly actionable.
- **Information (0)**—These alerts indicate that there is something that is good to know, but might not be a problem nor is actionable.

By the nature of things, a lot more warning alerts are generated than critical alerts. In general, notifications should only be sent out for critical alerts. That is, an email should never be sent for a warning or informational alert.

Alert Priority is the second parameter that qualifies the alert status. The priority allows MP authors to make some alerts more important than others. There are three levels of priority, as well:

- High (2)
- Medium (1)
- Low (0)

In general, a high-priority, critical severity alert is very important. This includes events like an agent down or a security breach. A medium-priority, critical severity alert is important. Both are generally actionable.

The best practice is to create two Simple Mail Transfer Protocol (SMTP) channels to deliver the alert notification emails, which are as follows:

- **SMTP (High Priority)**—High-priority email to an SMTP gateway
- **SMTP (Normal Priority)**—Regular email to an SMTP gateway

Then, create two notification subscriptions that use the severity and the priority to select the emails to be sent:

- Notification for All Critical Severity High-Priority Alerts
- Notification for All Critical Severity Medium-Priority Alerts

This provides a configuration that delivers the very important alerts (high-priority, critical severity alerts) via high-priority email and important alerts (medium-priority, critical severity alerts) via regular email. All other alerts will be available in the console and no emails will be sent to notify of them.

The next sections set up the notification infrastructure described previously.

The first step is to set up a channel, that is, how the emails will be sent. To set up a channel, complete the following steps:

1. Launch the Operations Manager 2012 console.
2. Select the Administration space.
3. Expand the Notifications folder and select the Channels node.
4. Right-click the Channels node and select New Channel, E-Mail (SMTP).
5. Enter **SMTP Channel (High Priority)** for the channel name and click Next.
6. Click Add, enter the FQDN of the SMTP server, and click OK.
7. Enter a return SMTP address, such as **opsmgr@companyxyz.com**, and click Next.
8. Change the Importance to High and click Finish. Click Close to close the wizard.
9. Right-click the Channels node and select New Channel, E-Mail (SMTP).
10. Enter **SMTP Channel (Normal Priority)** for the channel name and click Next.
11. Click Add, enter the FQDN of the SMTP server, and click OK.
12. Enter a return SMTP address and click Next.
13. Leave the Importance at Normal and click Finish. Click Close to close the wizard.

The second step is to set up the subscriber, that is, to whom the emails will be sent. The steps are as follows:

1. Launch the Operations Manager 2012 console.
2. Select the Administration space.
3. Expand the Notifications folder and select the Subscribers node.
4. Right-click the Subscribers node and select New Subscriber.
5. Click the ellipsis (...) button and select a user or distribution group. Click OK.
6. Click Next.
7. Click Next to always send notifications.
8. Click Add.
9. Type **Email** for the address name and click Next.
10. Select the Channel Type as E-Mail (SMTP), enter the delivery email address, and then click Next.
11. Click Finish.
12. Click Finish again to save the subscriber. Click Close to exit the wizard.

NOTE

It is a best practice to use distribution lists rather than user email addresses for subscribers.

The last step is to set up the subscriptions, that is, what to notify on. To set up the subscriptions, complete the following steps:

1. Launch the Operations Manager 2012 console.
2. Select the Administration space.
3. Expand the Notifications folder and select the Subscriptions node.
4. Right-click the Subscriptions node and select New Subscription.
5. Enter **Notification for All Critical Severity High Priority Alerts** for the subscription name and click Next.
6. Check the Of a Specific Severity and the Of a Specific Priority check boxes.
7. In the Criteria Description pane, click the Specific Severity link, check the Critical check box, and then click OK.
8. In the Criteria Description pane, click the Specific Priority link, check the High check box, and then click OK.

9. Click Next.
10. Click Add, click Search, select the subscriber, click Add, and then click OK.
11. Click Next.
12. Click Add, click Search, select the SMTP Channel (High Priority) channel, click Add, and then click OK.
13. Click Next, click Finish, and then click Close.
14. Right-click the Subscriptions node and select New Subscription.
15. Enter **Notification for All Critical Severity Medium Priority Alerts** for the subscription name and click Next.
16. Check the Of a Specific Severity and the Of a Specific Priority check boxes.
17. In the Criteria Description pane, click the Specific Severity link, check the Critical check box, and then click OK.
18. In the Criteria Description pane, click the Specific Priority link, check the Medium check box, and then click OK.
19. Click Next.
20. Click Add, click Search, select the subscriber, click Add, and then click OK.
21. Click Next.
22. Click Add, click Search, select the SMTP Channel (Normal Priority) channel, click Add, and then click OK.
23. Click Next, click Finish, and then click Close.

Now, the subscribers will get email notifications for alerts based on the severity and priority. These severities and priorities are based on the judgments of the authors of the MPs, which might or might not be optimal for any given organization. Later in the chapter, the priority and severity of alerts are used to tune the MPs to reduce alert noise.

Administering OpsMgr

After Operations Manager 2012 has been installed and configured, ongoing work needs to be done to ensure that the product performs as expected. The two primary activities are to, first, tune the MPs to ensure that alerts are valid for the environment and that alert noise is reduced and, second, produce reports of the information that Operations Manager 2012 is collecting.

Dip Stick Health Check Tasks

Whenever a motorist is going for a drive, the conscientious driver goes through a set of basic automotive health checks, including the following:

- Check the oil level with the dip stick.
- Check the tire pressure.
- Check the gasoline level.

These are sometimes referred to as the "dip stick health checks" because the oil level is checked with a dip stick.

Like any other complicated technology, Operations Manager 2012 can have problems in a variety of ways, ranging from running out of disk space, to failing to send email notifications, to having agents stopped, and so forth. To make sure that Operations Manager is functioning properly, a set of dip stick health checks can be performed to make sure everything is running smoothly.

These are the health check tasks that the OpsMgr administrator should do every day to verify the health and proper operation of the OpsMgr infrastructure:

1. Verify that you have received notifications by email. Confirm that you are getting notifications within the normal range. Too many is a bad sign and too few (or none) is also a bad sign.
2. Review OpsMgr daily reports sent via email or in the console. If using the console, the reports are stored in the Favorites folder in the Reporting space.
3. In the Operations Manager console, review the Active Alerts view. This shows you new alerts.
4. In the Operations Manager console, review the All Alerts view. This shows you both new and closed alerts.
5. In the Operations Manager console, review the Agent Health State view in the \Operations Manager\Agent Details node. Investigate any Critical, Warning, or Not Monitored states.
6. In the Operations Manager console, review the Active Alerts view in the \Operations Manager\Agent Details node. Investigate any Critical or Warning alerts.
7. In the Operations Manager console, review the Management Server Health State view in the \Operations Manager\Management Server node. Investigate any Critical, Warning, or Not Monitored states.
8. In the Operations Manager console, review the Active Alerts view in the \Operations Manager\Management Server node. Investigate any Critical or Warning alerts.

After reviewing the results of these health check tasks, an administrator can be pretty confident that the Operations Manager 2012 infrastructure is functioning properly.

Health check task number 2 recommends reviewing the daily reports. The recommended Operations Manager health reports to review on a daily basis are as follows:

- **Alert Logging Latency report**—This report tells you the length of time between an event being raised to an alert being generated. This should be under 30 seconds.
- **Send Queue % Used Top 10 report**—This report tells you if agents are having trouble uploading their data to the management servers. These queues should be less than 1%.
- **Top 10 Most Common Alerts report**—This report analyzes the most common alerts that were generated and are good for identifying alert-tuning opportunities.
- **Daily Alert report**—This report gives you a complete list of all the alerts that were generated. This is very detailed, but is good for chasing down problems uncovered in other checks.

These health check tasks should give a good sense of the operational health of the SCOM infrastructure.

Management Pack Updates

Management pack updates are released periodically by Microsoft. The Operations console allows you to update installed MPs from the online catalog.

NOTE

Installing updates by definition changes the rules, alerts, and monitors that are deployed. This can have significant consequences on the alerts that are generated. Any updates should first be tested in a lab setting to ensure that there are no problems.

The online catalog should be checked for updates to the installed MPs on a monthly basis. To do this, complete the following steps:

1. Launch the Operations console.
2. Go to the Administration space.
3. Select the Management Packs node.
4. Right-click the Management Packs node and select Import Management Packs.
5. Click Add and select Add from Catalog.
6. In the View pull-down, select Updates Available for Installed Management Packs.
7. Click the Search button.
8. Review the results in the Management Packs in the Catalog pane.
9. Select the MPs to update and click Add to add them to the Selected Management Packs pane.

10. Click OK.
11. Review the select MPs, the version numbers, and any warnings or informational messages.
12. Click Install to download and import the MPs.
13. After download and import, click Close to close the Import Management Packs Wizard.

The MP updates take effect immediately.

Notification and Alert Tuning

After deploying Operations Manager 2012, there are frequently complaints about the number of alert notifications that get generated. This can cause organizations to decommission the product, ignore the emails, or generally complain about what a bad product it is. In reality, the Operations Manager alert notifications just need to be tuned.

The following process helps tune the MP quickly and effectively to reduce alert and email noise. This is done by adjusting parameters on the rules (Enable/Disable, Severity, and Priority) using overrides.

Alert Severity is the first parameter to be tuned. There are three levels:

- Critical (2)
- Warning (1)
- Information (0)

Alert Priority is the second parameter to be tuned. There are three levels of priority as well:

- High (2)
- Medium (1)
- Low (0)

There are two SMTP channels to deliver the emails:

- **SMTP Channel (High Priority)**—High-priority email to an SMTP gateway
- **SMTP Channel (Normal Priority)**—Regular-priority email to an SMTP gateway

NOTE

These channels were created earlier in the chapter.

There are two notification subscriptions that use the severity and priority to select the emails to be sent:

- Notification for All Critical Severity High-Priority Alerts
- Notification for All Critical Severity Medium-Priority Alerts

These channels and subscriptions automatically send email notifications for critical severity high- and medium-priority alerts.

NOTE

These notification subscriptions were created earlier in the chapter.

However, sometime the alerts that are generated are not appropriate for the environment. This is because the source alert is not appropriate or actionable, so the resulting email is not useful and can be considered noise.

When you get an email from an alert that you don't want, you need to tune the MP monitor or rule. The basic decision tree is as follows:

1. **Alert is noise?** If no, this means that the alert is appropriate and actionable. In this case, the underlying cause of the alert needs to be addressed.
2. **Alert not needed?** If yes, create an override to disable the rule for either the instance of the object, the class of objects, or a group of the objects. This prevents the alert from being generated, so no console alerts and definitely no emails are generated.
3. **Alert severity too high?** If yes, create an override to change the alert severity to warning. This keeps the alert in the console as a warning, but does not generate an email.
4. **Alert priority too high?** If yes, create an override to change the alert priority to low. This keeps the alert as a critical alert, but prevents an email from being generated.

Figure 23.23 shows the decision tree in a flowchart form.

If these are not enough to narrow down the email notification behavior, a custom approach is needed. For example, if you want to get an email when mail flow alerts are generated but only after a couple are generated, do the following:

1. Change the alert priority to low using an override. This prevents the alert from generating a notification from the default subscriptions.
2. Create a notification subscription for the alert, but set an aging to longer than the test interval or whatever you want to wait before sending the email.

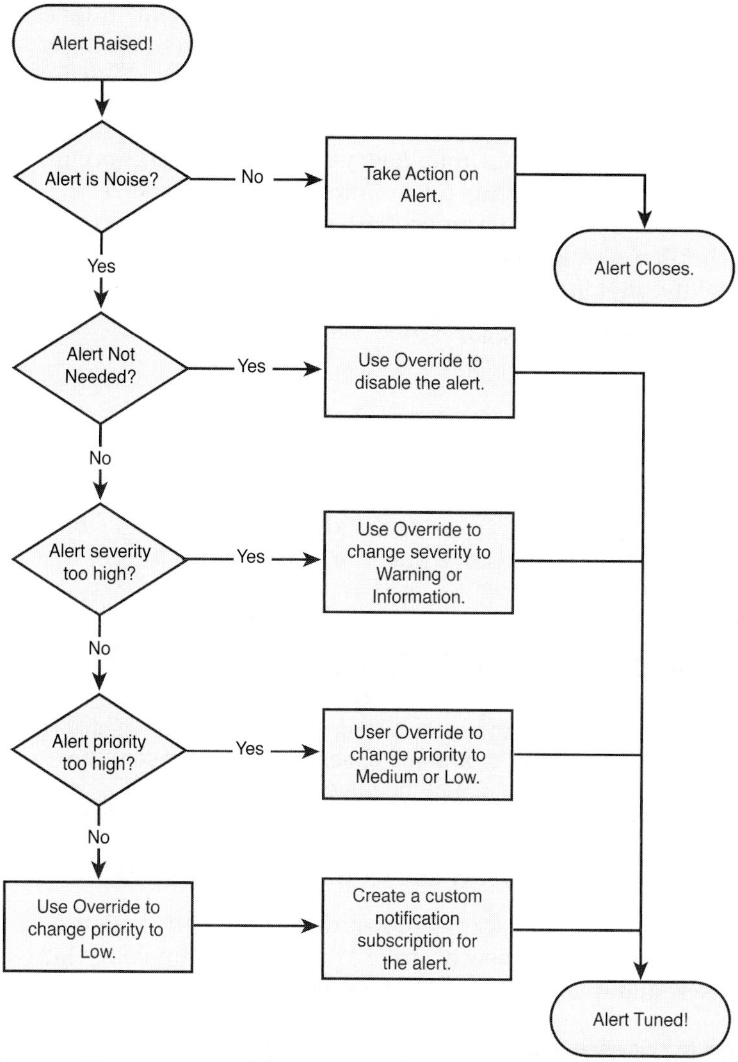

FIGURE 23.23 Alert tuning flowchart.

NOTE

When creating the custom notification subscription, make sure to have the With Specific Resolution State criteria checked and only New resolution states selected. If this is not done, the notification triggers after the aging. This is because even if the alert closes before the aging period is up, the Closed resolution state still triggers the notification.

This process takes care of the majority of cases and reduces spamming by the OpsMgr console.

These options can be taken for all objects of the target class, for just the specific instance that generated the alert, or for a group. The group would have to be created in advance and would have to contain objects of the type targeted by the monitor or rule generating the alert.

For example, let's say there is an Application of Group Policy critical alert that is occurring frequently in the environment. It is occurring on a number of Windows Server 2008 R2 servers and is generating a lot of email notifications. This alert is valid, but does not require immediate action. The alert needs to be tuned to change the severity from critical to warning. The steps to tune the alert are as follows:

1. Open the Operations Manager 2012 console.
2. Select the Monitoring space.
3. Select the Active Alerts view.
4. Locate and select the Application of Group Policy alert that is to be tuned.
5. Right-click the alert and select Overrides, Override the Monitor, and For All Objects of Class: Group Policy 2008 Runtime. This overrides the alert for all objects of that class.

NOTE

The alert is to be tuned for all objects, rather than any specific instances. If the alert is to be tuned for the specific instance that raised the alert, the For the Object option should be chosen. If it is a group of the objects, the For a Group option should be chosen. The group would have to be pre-created and be a group of the target objects.

6. Check the Override box next to Alert Severity and set the value to Warning.
7. In the Select Destination Management Pack pull-down menu, select the appropriate override MP. If none exists, create a new override MP named Group Policy MP Overrides by clicking New and then following the prompts to create a new MP.

NOTE

Never use the Default Management Pack for overrides. Always create an override MP that corresponds to each imported MP.

8. Click OK to save the override.

Now the next time the monitor triggers an alert, it will be of warning severity and will not generate a notification email. However, the alert can still be reviewed in the console.

This approach to tuning will address 90% of the noisy alerts that you get. To target the noisiest alerts, see the Most Common Alerts report in the next section. This helps identify the alerts that are responsible for the most noise. You'll frequently find that 50% of your alerts are coming from less than five rules or monitors. Tuning those gives you the most bang for your buck.

Exploring the Windows 2012 Management Pack

The Windows 2012 Management Pack discovers Windows Server 2012 servers and roles to monitor availability, health, and performance. It is part of the Windows Management Pack, which also manages Windows Server 2000, 2003 and 2008. The MP automatically detects, alerts, and responds to a wide range of critical events and performance metrics to ensure the long-term health and stability of the server operating systems.

NOTE

This MP is also leveraged by other MPs, such as AD, Exchange, and SQL.

How to Configure the Windows Management Pack

With OpsMgr 2012, the MP can be downloaded and imported directly from the Web Catalog. The location in the catalog is Microsoft Corporation\Windows Server\Core OS\. There are eight MPs and also additional language versions.

After downloading and installing this MP, usually the default location of the MP files is located in C:\%Program Files%\System Center Management Packs\Windows Server Base OS System Center Operations Manager 2012 MP\.

NOTE

When installing the MP via executing the downloaded MP source file (usually an MSI), content of the MSI is expanded into the default installation directory. Executing the MSI does not import the MP into Operations Manager.

The MPs that make up the Windows Core OS monitoring are as follows:

- Microsoft.Windows.Server.2000.mp
- Microsoft.Windows.Server.2003.mp
- Microsoft.Windows.Server.2008.Discovery.mp
- Microsoft.Windows.Server.6.2.Discovery.mp
- Microsoft.Windows.Server.2008.Monitoring.mp
- Microsoft.Windows.Server.2008.R2.Monitoring.BPA.mp
- Microsoft.Windows.Server.6.2.Monitoring.mp
- Microsoft.Windows.Server.ClusterSharedVolumeMonitoring.mp
- Microsoft.Windows.Server.Library.mp
- Microsoft.Windows.Server.Reports.mp

The Microsoft.Windows.Server.Library.mp and Microsoft.Windows.Server.Reports.mp are common across all the Windows Server operating systems. The other operating system-specific MPs can be imported as needed.

In the event a manual import is required, the following order of import should be followed:

- First, the Microsoft.Windows.Server.Library.mp
- Second, the Microsoft.Windows.Server.6.2.Discovery.mp

The naming convention for the Windows Server 2012 MP uses the 6.2 version number rather than 2012 version number.

Afterward, any operating system-specific MPs (such as the Microsoft.Windows.Server.2000.mp, Microsoft.Windows.Server.2003.mp, crosoft.Windows.Server.2008.Monitoring.mp or Microsoft.Windows.Server.6.2.Monitoring.mp) can be imported.

NOTE

The naming conventions within the Windows Serve 2012 MP vary considerably. The designation vNext, 8, and 2012 are all used interchangeably within the inner details of the MP. These reference the version name of the product (Windows Server .Next, Windows 8 and finally Windows 2012) evolution over time. This will likely be rectified in a future update to the MP.

The installed agent should be configured to use the Local System account. Using this account grants the agent the ability to process discovery, monitors, rules, tasks, and other Operations Manager-related tasks.

Microsoft has also updated the associated MPs such as whose roles are hosted on Windows Server 2012, such as DNS, File Services, Active Directory, and Internet Information Services.

Tuning the Windows Management Pack

During Windows MP deployment, a couple of items must be tuned to mitigate alerting storms and for baseline monitoring. The tuning points are as follows:

- Logical Disk Free Space Monitor
- Total Processor % Interrupt Time Rule

The Logical Disk Free Space monitor for both Windows Server 2003 Logical Disk and the Windows Server 2008 Logical Disk should be tuned. The way the Logical Disk Free Space is configured, there are two sets of values for error and warning: % Threshold and MByte Threshold. Rather than a logical OR operator, the MP uses a logical AND operator. Both the % Threshhold and the MByte Threshold must be true for the alert to trigger. By configuring one of the value sets to always be true, the monitor is effectively set to trigger on the other value set. Configure overrides for the following items:

- Error Mbytes Threshold for Non-System Drives to Value 10240
- Warning Mbytes Threshold for Non-System Drives to Value 10240
- Warning Mbytes Threshold for System Drives to Value 10240

Setting those to 10GB allows the % Threshold values to trigger alerts properly.

The Rule node contains several rules covering memory and interrupts that should be tuned. By default, many of the performance rules are disabled. This reduces the size of the database, but at the expense of details performance metrics. To take full advantage of OpsMgr 2012, it is a best practice to enable many of these collection rules using overrides for the respective objects.

Each version of the operating system will have its own object, such as Windows Server 2008 Core Operating System or Windows Server 2003 Core Operating System. Each object will have its own set of rules, which need to have the overrides configured to enable the rules. In the following examples, the objects and rules for the Windows Server 2012 operating system will be used. If Windows Server 2003 or Windows Server 2008 Management Packs are in use, then the corresponding overrides will need to be configured.

For the Windows Server vNext Operating System object, five main rules need to be enabled. These rules can be found in the Authoring section of the console in the Management Pack Objects\Rules folder. The rules will be under the Type: Windows Server vNext Operating System class. The rules to override are as follows:

- Page File Percentage Use 8
- Total Processor % Interrupt Time 8
- Memory Page Writes per Second 8
- Memory Page Reads per Second 8
- Memory % Committed Bytes in Use 8

Ten disk-related rules should be enabled to properly monitor disk activity. These are rules that target the Windows Server vNext Logical Disk object. These rules can be found in the Authoring section of the console in the Management Pack Objects\Rules folder. The rules will be under the Type: Windows Server vNext Logical Disk class. The specific rules to override are as follows:

- Collection Rule for Average Logical Disk Seconds per Write 8
- Collection Rule for Disk Writes per Second 8
- Collection Rule for Disk Reads per Second 8
- Logical Disk Read Bytes per Second 8
- Collection Rule for Average Disk Seconds per Read 8
- Average Logical Disk Read Queue Length 8

- Collection Rule for Average Disk Queue Length 8
- Average Logical Disk Write Queue Length 8
- Collection Rule for Disk Bytes per Second 8
- Logical Disk Write Bytes per Second 8

To properly monitor network activity, a number of rules need to be enabled for the Windows Server 2008 Network Adapter object. These rules can be found in the Authoring section of the console in the Management Pack Objects\Rules folder. The rules will be under the Type: Windows Server vNext Network Adapter class. The specific rules to override are as follows:

- Network Adapter Bytes Sent per Second 8
- Percent Bandwidth Used Write
- Percent Bandwidth Used Read
- Network Adapter Bytes Received per Second 8

Enabling the previous rules for the class of objects will allow detailed performance metrics to be collected for the processor, disk, memory, and network for the Windows Server operating system. This will also enable the Windows MP views, discussed in the next section, and reports to show useful information.

Windows Management Pack Views

Upon importing this MP, a Microsoft Windows Server sealed MP folder will appear in the Monitoring view tree.

Included by default are four top-level views in the Microsoft Windows Server:

- Active Alerts
- Operating System Performance (shown in Figure 23.24)
- Task Status
- Windows Server State

In addition, a Health Monitoring subfolder contains the following four Dashboard views, one for each component:

- Cluster Shared Volumes Health
- Disk Health
- Network Adapter Health
- Operating System Health

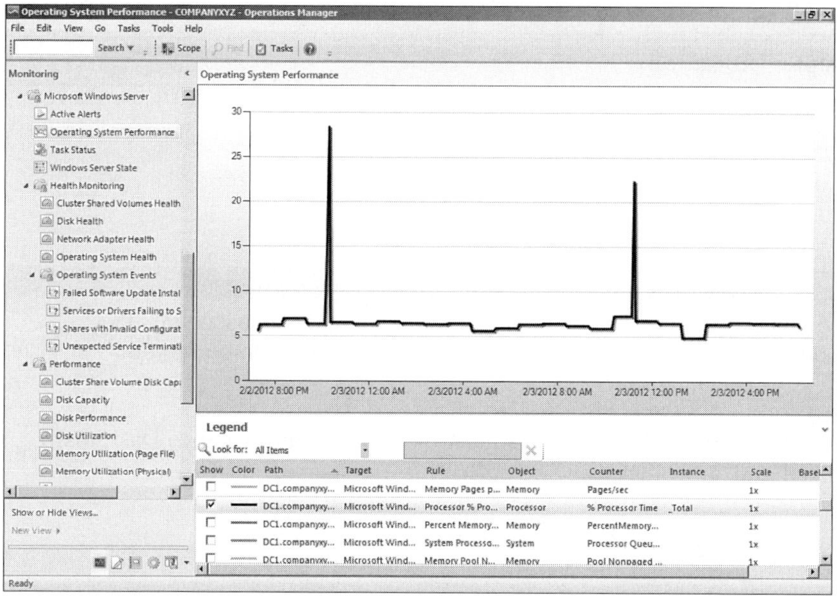

FIGURE 23.24 Operating System Performance view.

Each of these component Dashboard views has two panes, the top pane showing the state of each discovered instance and the bottom pane showing any related alerts.

The Operating System Events subfolder under Health Monitoring contains Event views for Failed Software Updates Installations, Services or Drivers Failing to Start, Shares with Invalid Configuration, and Unexpected Service Terminations. These Event views are useful for detecting failure events.

NOTE

The Operating System Health Dashboard view located in this subfolder is the best location to view operating system health and mitigate open alerts.

For monitoring and graphing performance, the Performance subfolder contains the following eight performance Dashboard views:

- Cluster Share Volume Disk Capacity
- Disk Capacity
- Disk Performance
- Disk Utilization
- Memory Utilization (Page File)

- Memory Utilization (Physical)
- Network Adapter Utilization
- Processor Performance

The views nested under the Performance and Health Monitoring combine like performance captures allowing like data to be viewed from one location.

NOTE

The Performance subfolder of this sealed MP is heavily used for troubleshooting. From this location, in-depth performance metrics for the past seven days can be viewed.

In the sample image in Figure 23.25, each quadrant of the Disk Performance Dashboard view must be selected and subvalues must be defined in the legend.

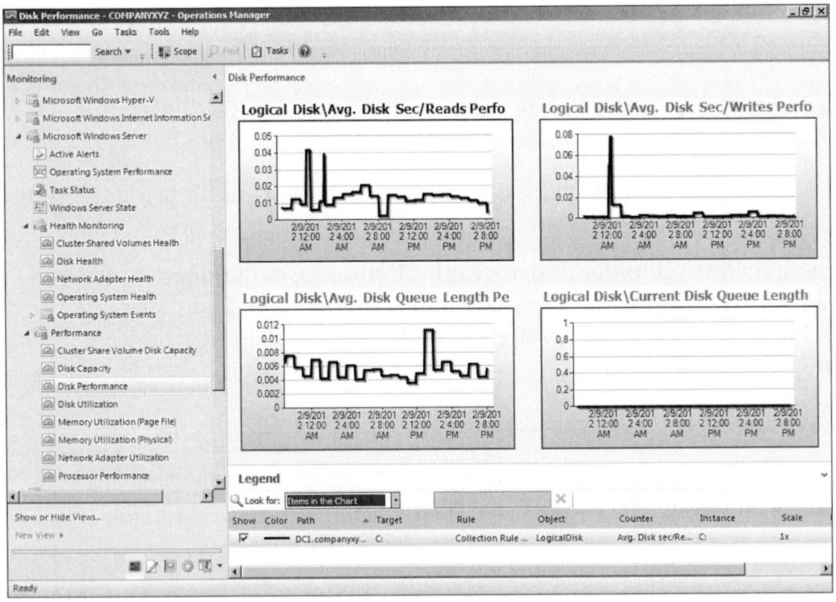

FIGURE 23.25 Disk Performance Dashboard view.

Windows Management Pack Tasks

More than 10 Windows Computer tasks are included in the MP and can be accessed in the Actions pane on the right when selecting a Windows Computer object. In addition, a subset of the Health Service tasks is available (Ping Computer, Remote Desktop, and so on), as shown in Figure 23.26.

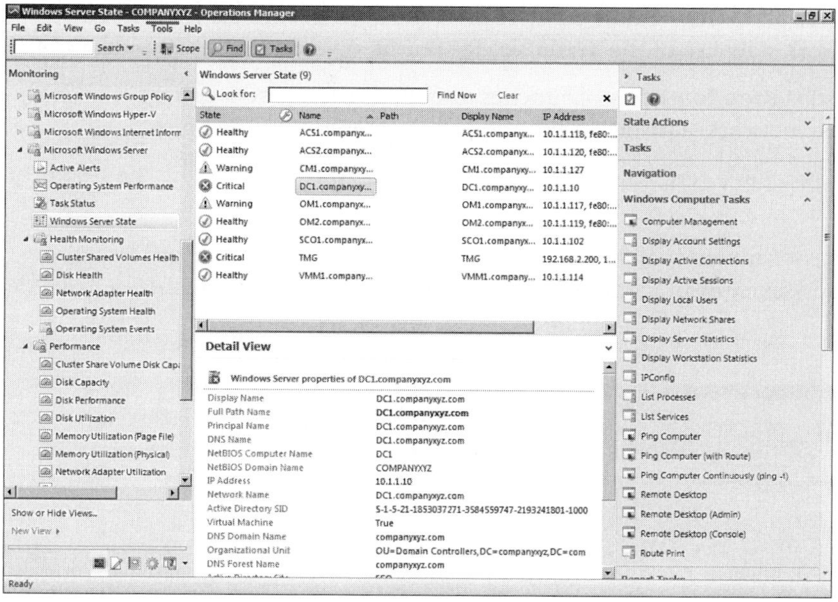

FIGURE 23.26 Windows Computer tasks.

NOTE

The Health Service tasks have a small blue monitor icon on them, whereas the Windows Computer tasks have a small grey server icon on them. The Health Service tasks are executed on the console machine, whereas the Windows Computer tasks are executed on the target Windows Computer by the agent.

The Windows Computer tasks are as follows:

- **Display Account Settings**—Launches a script at the agent; returns a snapshot displaying the current password requirements, settings, and applied server roles for the object.
- **Display Active Connections**—Launches a script at the agent; returns a snapshot displaying a list of active connections (netstat).
- **Display Active Sessions**—Launches a script at the agent; returns a snapshot displaying the open sessions on the object.
- **Display Local Users**—Launches a script at the agent; returns a snapshot enumerating the local users.
- **Display Network Shares**—Launches a script at the agent; returns a snapshot displaying the shares on the object.

- **Display Server Statistics**—Launches a script at the agent; returns a snapshot displaying the network statistics of the Server service on the object.
- **Display Workstation Statistics**—Launches a script at the agent; returns a snapshot displaying the network statistics of the Workstation service on the object.
- **Ipconfig**—Launches a script at the agent; returns a snapshot displaying the results of **ipconfig /all**.
- **List Processes**—Launches a script at the agent; returns a snapshot displaying all running processes, session name, PID, and memory consumption, as shown in Figure 23.27.

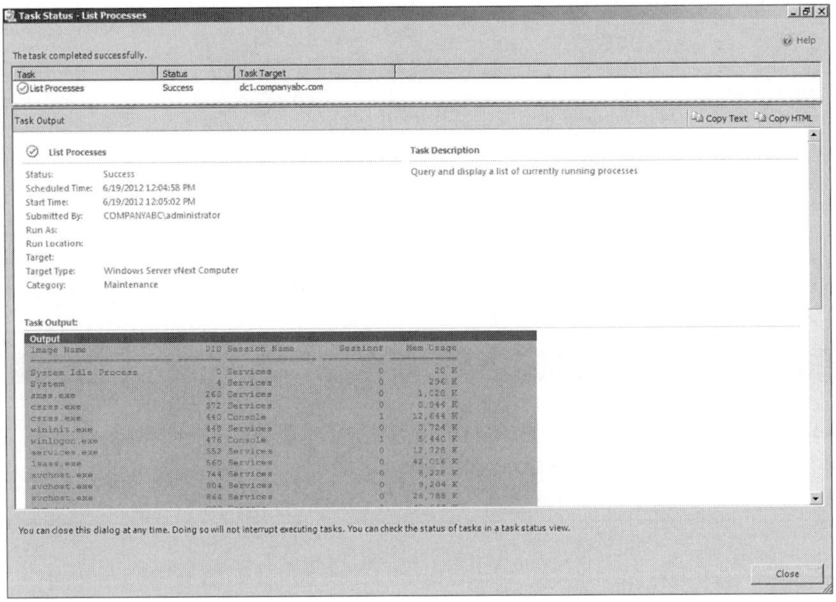

FIGURE 23.27 Windows MP List Processes task results.

- **List Services**—Launches a script at the agent; returns a snapshot displaying all active services.
- **RoutePrint**—Launches a script at the agent; returns a snapshot displaying the results of RoutePrint.

NOTE

The State views always contain tasks in the Actions pane, when an object with tasks is selected.

These tasks are among the most useful tasks when troubleshooting. In particular, the List Processes, the Display Active Connections, and the Display Active Sessions are very helpful for gathering information.

Windows Management Pack Reports

By default, the Windows MP contains 17 reports for Windows Server 2012, as follows:

- Disk Performance Analysis (shown in Figure 23.28)

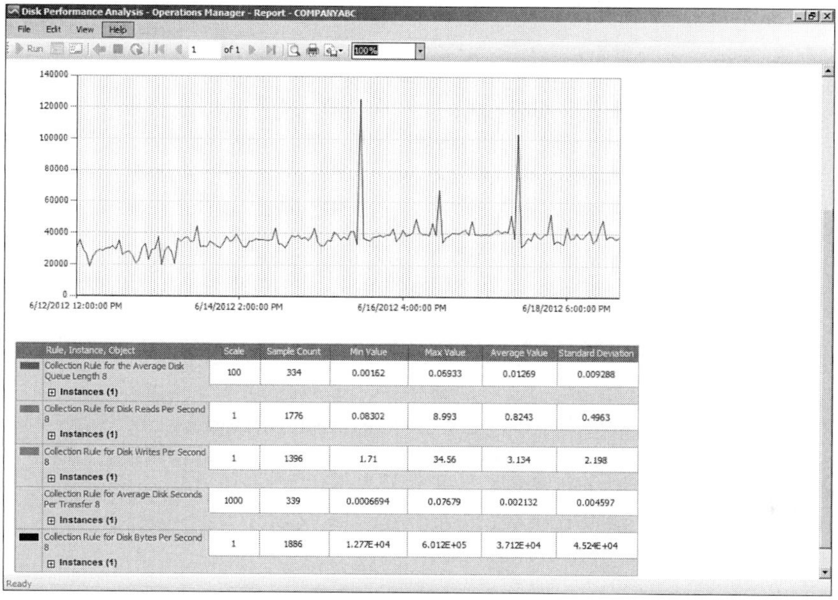

FIGURE 23.28 Disk Performance Analysis report.

- Memory Performance History (Available MB)
- Memory Performance History (Page Reads per Sec)
- Memory Performance History (Page Writes per Sec)
- Memory Performance History (Pages per Sec)
- Operating System Configuration
- Operating System Performance
- Operating System Storage Configuration
- Paging File Performance History (Percentage Usage)
- Performance History

- Performance History (Context Switches per Sec)
- Performance History (Percent Interrupt Time)
- Performance History (Percent Processor Time)
- Performance History (Processor Queue Length)
- Physical Disk Performance History (Avg Disk Queue Length)
- Pool Performance History (Nonpaged Bytes)
- Pool Performance History (Paged Bytes)

In addition to the operating system-specific reports, there are two generic reports for all Windows Server operating systems. These two reports provide a summary of operating system performance by system and a ranking of utilization across systems. The two reports are as follows:

- Performance by System
- Performance by Utilization

You can generate these reports by browsing to the Windows Server Operating System Reports.

The Performance by System report gives a summary of utilization, including processor, memory, logical disk, and network, for each system included in the report. Each server is given its own section in the report. The report can be generated for an individual Windows Computer or for a group of Windows Computer class objects. This report is good for analyzing the performance of individual systems.

The Performance by Utilization report gives a ranking of Windows Computer class objects across processor, memory, logical disk, and network metrics. This report allows you to target a large number of Windows Computer objects, for example the All Windows Computers group, and specify the top number that you want to select for each of the metrics. The top three might be different for each metric, as the top ranking systems are selected from the entire group. This report is very useful for determining which systems are experiencing the most utilization.

Figure 23.29 shows a sample Performance by Utilization report for the All Windows Computers group with the top three most utilized selected.

If you are getting the "too many arguments specified" error when generating the Performance By Utilization report, this is caused by the Windows 2003 MP. It also contains the stored procedure definition for Microsoft_SystemCenter_Report_Performace_By_Utilization, but the definition in the Windows 2003 MP is missing the @DataAggregation INT, variable. Depending on the MP import process, it is possible that the stored procedure from the Mi-crosoft.Windows.Server.Reports.mp will not be deployed, which does contain this variable. To resolve this issue, we need to modify the existing stored procedure.

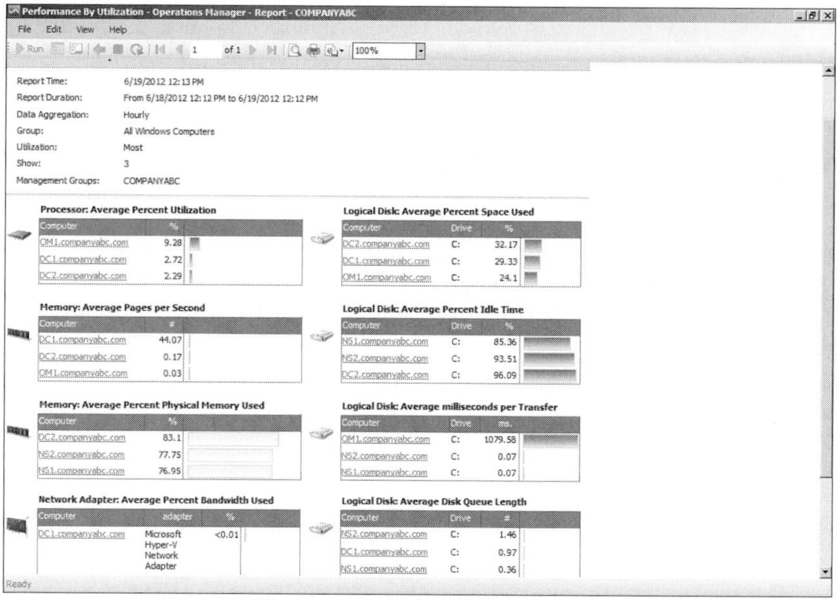

FIGURE 23.29 Performance by Utilization report.

NOTE

Ensure you back up your Data Warehouse database *first*, and if you are not comfortable editing stored procedures, open a case with Microsoft on this issue.

To modify the stored procedure, follow these steps:

1. Launch SQL Studio Manager.
2. Expand Databases.
3. Expand OperationsManagerDW database.
4. Expand Programmability.
5. Expand Stored Procedures.
6. Right-click dbo.Microsoft_SystemCenter_Report_Performance_By_Utilization stored procedure and select Modify.
7. Add the **@DataAggregation INT**, line just below the "Alter procedure" line.
8. Click Execute to save the stored procedure.

The report will now run without any error.

Summary

System Center Operations Manager 2012 is key to managing Windows Server 2012 environments, providing detailed performance monitoring, alerting, and reporting. The Windows Server 2012 MP provides out-of-the-box deep monitoring that that allows administrators to easily understand how their Windows Server 2012 system are performing and quickly pinpoint any problems.

Understanding the components of Operations Manager, their interactions, and their constraints is critical to designing and deploying an effective infrastructure. This type of functionality is instrumental in reducing downtime and getting the most out of an OpsMgr investment.

Best Practices

The following are best practices from this chapter:

- Always create a design and plan when deploying Operations Manager, even if it is a simple one.
- Take future expansion and relevance of hardware into account when sizing servers for OpsMgr deployment.
- Keep the installation of OpsMgr on a separate server or set of separate dedicated member servers that do not run any other separate applications.
- Start with a single management group and add on additional management groups only if they are absolutely necessary.
- Use Windows 2008 R2 SP1 and SQL 2008 R2 together to gain maximum performance from both.
- Use SQL Enterprise when combining components on the same server.
- Use SQL Enterprise when scaling up Operations Manager.
- Allocate adequate space for the databases depending on the length of time needed to store events and the number of managed systems.
- Leverage the reporting database to store and report on data over a long period.
- Always create disaster recovery processes to restore in the event of a failure.
- Deploy fault tolerance (that is, clusters) only when needed.
- Size the disk subsystems to provide sufficient I/Ops to support the anticipated data flows.
- Use a dedicated service account for OpsMgr.
- Allocate adequate space for the databases depending on the length of time needed to store events and the number of managed systems.

- Monitor the size of the OpsMgr database to ensure that it does not increase beyond the bounds of acceptable size.
- Be sure to keep the MPs updated, as Microsoft routinely releases updates to the core MPs.
- When tuning, err on the side of fewer alerts. If nothing will be done about an alert, make sure it doesn't send a notification email.
- Configure OpsMgr to monitor itself.

CHAPTER 24

Server-to-Client Remote and Mobile Access

IN THIS CHAPTER

As the Internet grows year after year, so does the need to work productively away from the office. Companies are always looking for alternative cost-effective methods of connecting their remote and mobile users without sacrificing performance or security. Windows Server 2012 offers Remote Access Service (RAS) in the form of traditional virtual private network (VPN) or dial-up services, as well as an improved DirectAccess as a modern alternative method of remote connectivity.

As the Internet has evolved and become ubiquitous, the vast majority of users have high-speed Internet connections at home, while on the road at hotels, and even while sipping a latte in a coffee shop. The Internet to which they are connecting is full of hackers, worms, and viruses from which the connections need to be protected. These users use remote access in the form of tunnels (shown in Figure 24.1) that connect from their workstation in the coffee shop through the dangerous Internet to the corporate resources. This chapter discusses the traditional VPN components of server-to-client remote and mobile access. This chapter also discusses the new DirectAccess, which makes this process even simpler for the remote worker, allowing application-level access without requiring a traditional VPN.

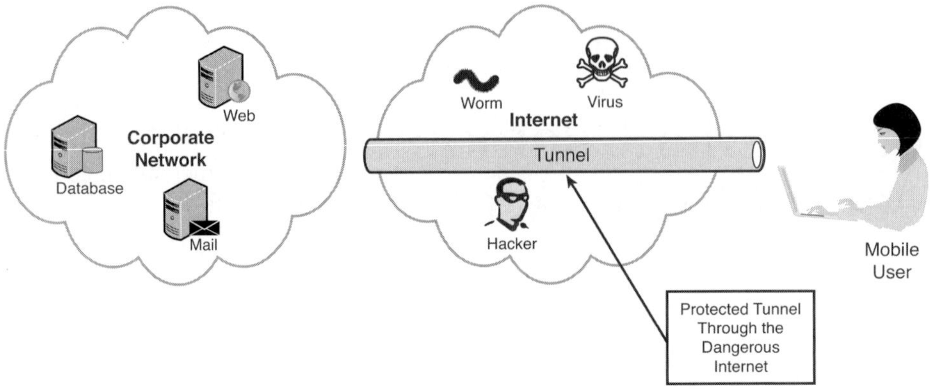

FIGURE 24.1 Connecting securely over the Internet.

A huge problem is ensuring that the resources that are connecting to the internal network are healthy and will not infect internal resources. When the remote and mobile clients are connected to the internal network, they have direct network connectivity to internal resources, such as the database server, file servers, and directory server. This can present a huge risk if not managed and mitigated properly. Windows Server 2003 offered some features, but they were difficult to use.

Windows Server 2008 provided a vastly improved access control mechanism for validating and controlling access to sensitive network resources via the Network Policy Server (NPS). Network Policy Server introduced key features to detect unhealthy systems, control what internal resources they can access, and even remediate the problems on the remote clients.

Windows Server 2008 R2 extended NPS functionality with templates for NPS configuration, SQL logging for RADIUS, and support for non-English languages. DirectAccess, a new feature introduced in Windows Server 2008 R2, seamlessly connects users to the corporate network anywhere they have Internet access. DirectAccess loads as the system boots, extending access into the "office." Remote systems are treated just as if they are on the local network and can be managed in a similar manner with the added quarantine and remediation functionality of the NPS system. However, in Windows Server 2008 R2, DirectAccess had stringent requirements and constraints that made it difficult to implement for many organization.

With Windows Server 2012, the Remote Access Services role provides a single role that encompasses the client-to-server remote-access features. This allows for holistic administration and management of the remote-access services. Windows Server 2012 also introduces a number of improvements, mainly in DirectAccess, that eliminate many of the deployment blockers (such as support for a DirectAccess server behind a Network Address Translation [NAT] device) and will facilitate organizations adopting the DirectAccess technology.

This chapter focuses on client-to-server connectivity in Windows Server 2012, rather than on server-to-server security or site-to-site connectivity. See Chapter 14, "Transport-Level

Security," for a detailed discussion on the server-to-server and site-to-site connectivity features of Windows Server 2012.

What's New for Remote Access in Windows Server 2012

The new features for the Remote Access role in Windows Server 2012 include ease of deployment features, technical improvements, and management features.

Windows Server 2012 makes it easier to deploy the Remote Access role and configure the DirectAccess feature in particular. Improvements include the following:

- **DirectAccess and RAS coexistence**—In Windows Server 2012, both RAS and DirectAccess can now run on the same server. Previously, these roles were antithetical, and installing DirectAccess would block VPN traffic at the IPsec level.
- **Simplified DirectAccess deployment**—The Windows Server 2012 DirectAccess has few requirements and even an understanding of IPv6 is not required and is handled by the wizard behind the scenes. The simpler deployment wizard that makes it easier for administrators to deploy DirectAccess quickly. This is especially true for small and medium-sized organizations that might not have dedicated resources for these tasks.
- **Optional PKI deployment for DirectAccess**—A public key infrastructure (PKI) is no longer a requirement for deploying DirectAccess, though it is still recommended. The wizard can use a server authentication certificate from a public certificate authority (CA) or even use self-signed certificates in small deployments.
- **Windows PowerShell**—Windows Server 2012 provides full support for the Remote Access role through PowerShell, including setup, configuration, monitoring, and troubleshooting.

There are a number of technical improvements to the Remote Access role in Windows Server 2012, although these improvements mainly impact the DirectAccess service. These technical improvements include the following:

- **Integrated NAT64 and DNS64 for accessing IPv4-only resources**—While DirectAccess is an IPv6 technology, supporting only clients that support IPv6, in most organizations these clients need to access resources that only support IPv4. Windows Server 2012 DirectAccess now includes protocol translation with NAT64 and name resolution with DNS64, allowing DirectAccess clients to access IPv4 resources seamlessly. In previous versions, this would have required deployment of Microsoft Forefront Unified Access Gateway.
- **NAT support**—DirectAccess now supports configurations where the server is not directly connected to the Internet. This is the typical configuration for small and medium-sized organizations, where the DirectAccess server is behind a firewall that is using NAT to provide access to the Internet. In this configuration, DirectAccess will use IP over HTTPS to tunnel through the firewall.

24

- **High-availability support**—The Windows Server 2012 DirectAccess now includes high availability by supporting both Network Load Balancing (NLB) and third-party hardware load balancers.
- **Multidomain support**—The Windows Server 2012 allows a single DirectAccess server to support multiple domains, simplifying the infrastructure for multi-domain organizations.
- **NAP integration**—The DirectAccess Wizard now sets up the required Group Policy objects and policies needed for Network Access Protection (NAP), reducing the manual steps needed and simplifying the installation for administrators.
- **Support for RSA SecureID**—Windows Server 2012 now supports third-party One-Time Password (OTP) two factor authentication, such as RSA Secure ID.
- **Integrated force tunneling support**—Normally, DirectAccess creates a split tunnel so that corporate communications travel over the DirectAccess tunnel. However, Internet traffic normally goes over the local Internet connection. This can be a security risk, so all traffic can be administratively forced over the DirectAccess tunnel, ensuring that all traffic is secured by the corporate infrastructure at the cost of bandwidth.
- **Manage-out only support**—Windows Server 2012 allows administrators to configure DirectAccess to provide corporate support of workstations only. This ensures that the corporate IT can always remotely manage the workstations in the field, without needing to provide users access.
- **Server Core support**—The Windows Server 2012 Remote Access role supports both RAS and DirectAccess on the default Server Core installation option as well as the full installation option. This allows the remote-access services to be deployed in the most secure and performing manner possible. When installed on server core, the Remote Access role can be managed via PowerShell or via remote server management.

The new Remote Access role also make it easier for administrators to understand what activity is taking place over the remote access connections and troubleshoot issues. New for Windows Server 2012 are the following:

- **Health monitoring**—The Windows Server 2012 Remote Access role now has user and server health monitoring, which is a greatly expanded set of metrics including summary connections, user connections, and even resources being accessed by users. This is displayed in a dashboard for quick access.
- **Diagnostics**—The Windows Server 2012 Remote Access role now includes diagnostic tools that are integrated into the monitoring dashboard. This includes detailed event logging, trace logs, packet capture, and log correlation to activities and actions.

These new features and improvements make it easier to deploy, support, and use the Windows Server 2012 remote access services.

VPN in Windows Server 2012

A virtual private network (VPN) is the extension of a private network that encompasses links across shared or public networks like the Internet. A VPN allows data to be sent between two computers across the Internet in a manner that emulates a point-to-point private link. With a VPN, illustrated in Figure 24.2, a private link is created between the client and the VPN server by encrypting the data for confidentiality; data packets that are intercepted while traveling through the Internet are unreadable without the proper encryption keys.

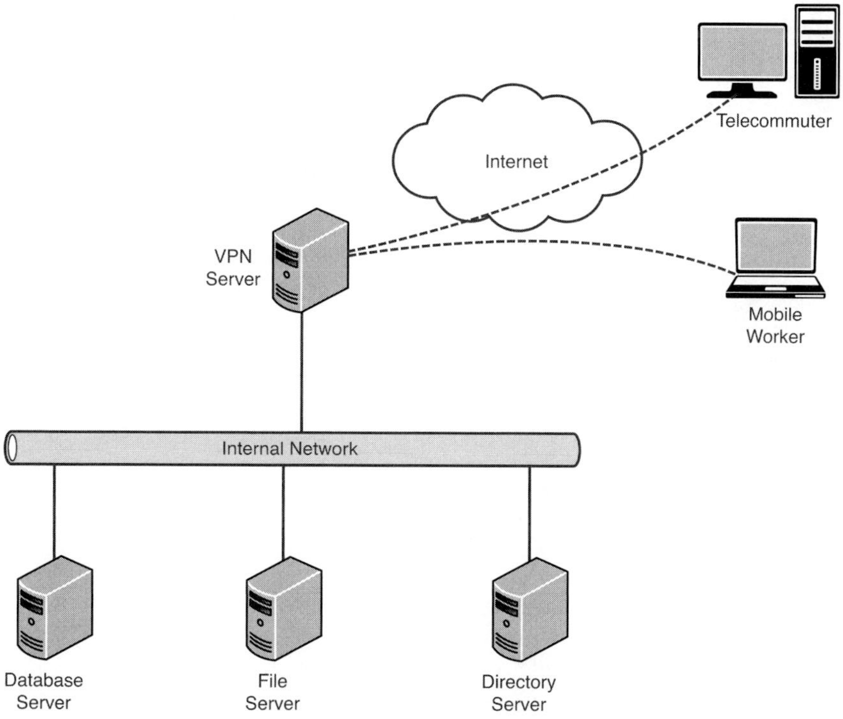

FIGURE 24.2 Virtual private networking across the Internet.

VPN technology provides corporations with a scalable and low-cost solution for remote access to corporate resources, such as database, file, and directory servers. VPN connections allow remote users to securely connect to their corporate networks across the Internet. Remote users would access resources as if they were physically connected to the corporate local-area network (LAN).

NOTE

Later in the chapter, a Windows Server 2012 Remote Access service called DirectAccess is discussed. Microsoft has positioned DirectAccess as being different from a traditional VPN. This positioning is based mainly on the automated nature of DirectAccess, rather than on technical or architectural differences. DirectAccess is technically a VPN, but we'll focus on key differences from traditional VPNs later in this chapter.

Components Needed to Create a Traditional VPN Connection

A point-to-point link, or tunnel, is created by encapsulating or wrapping the data with a header that provides routing information that allows the data to travel through the Internet. A virtual private network connection requires a VPN client and a VPN server or infrastructure. A secured connection is created between the client and server through encryption that establishes the tunnel, as shown in Figure 24.3.

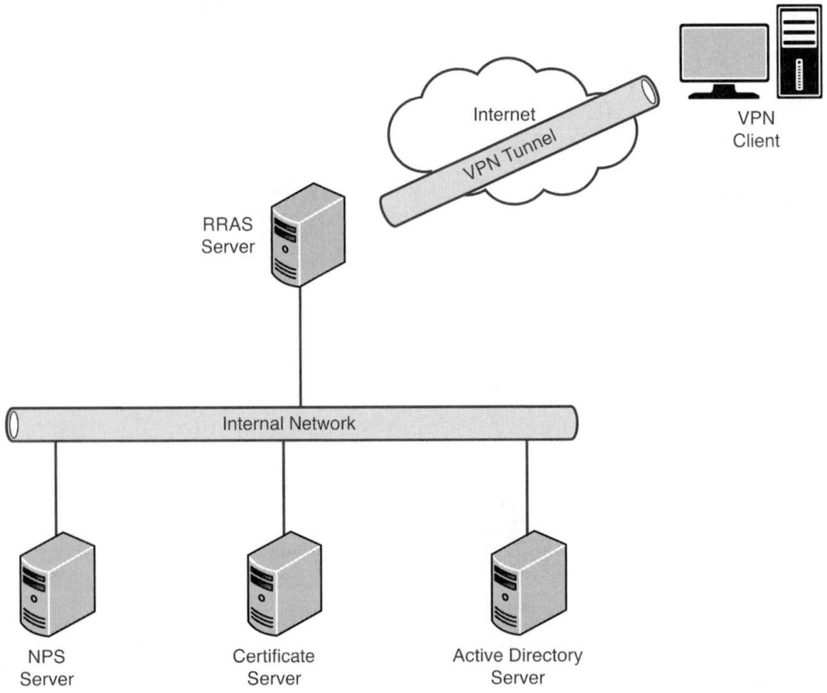

FIGURE 24.3 Establishing a VPN tunnel between a client and server.

The tunnel is the portion of the connection in which data is encapsulated. The VPN connection is the portion of the connection where the data is encrypted. The data encapsulation, along with the encryption, provides a secure VPN connection.

NOTE

A tunnel that is created without the encryption is not a VPN connection because the private data is sent across the Internet unencrypted and can be easily read. This violates the *P* for *private* in a virtual private network (VPN).

The figure also depicts the roles in a typical Windows Server 2012 VPN infrastructure. The roles in Windows Server 2012 consist of the following:

- VPN client
- RAS server
- NPS server
- Certificate server
- Active Directory server

These roles work together to provide the VPN functionality.

A shared or public internetwork is required to establish a VPN connection. For Windows Server 2012, the transit internetwork is always an IP-based network that includes the Internet as well as a corporation's private IP-based intranet.

The topics and examples in this chapter utilize Certificate Services, Network Policy Server, and Network Access Protection to secure VPN access. The details of the CA, the NPS, and NAP in Windows Server 2012 are covered in Chapter 15, "Security Policies, Network Policy Server, and Network Access Protection."

The VPN Client

A VPN client is a computer that initiates a VPN connection to a VPN server. Microsoft clients, including Windows NT 4.0, Windows 9x, Windows 2000, Windows XP, Windows Vista, Windows 7, and Windows 8 can create a remote-access VPN connection to a Windows Server 2012 system.

VPN clients can also be any non-Microsoft PPTP client or L2TP client using IPsec.

The RAS Server

An RAS server is a Windows Server 2012 server with the Remote Access role services installed. This is the server that accepts VPN connections from VPN clients. The RAS server name or IP address must be resolvable as well as accessible through corporate firewalls, which could be by either having a network interface connected to the demilitarized zone (DMZ) or by providing the appropriate access rule on the firewall.

The NPS System

The Network Policy Server (NPS) provides the authentication, authorization, auditing, and accounting for the VPN clients. The NPS system is a Windows Server 2012 server with the Network Policy Server role service installed.

The NPS is used to enforce network access policies for client health, client authentication, and client authorization. NPS works with Network Access Protection (NAP), which is a technology to manage, enforce, and remediate client health. The NPS service provides the policies for NAP to validate against. NPS also has multiple templates for larger-scale deployments or configuring multiple NPS servers identically.

In NAP, system health agents (SHAs) are used to inspect and assess the health of clients according to policies. System health validators (SHVs) are the policies that the agents validate against.

The Network Access Protection agent is the SHA in Windows 7, Windows 8, and in Windows Server 2012. These provide the following features in their SHVs:

- Firewall software installed and enabled
- Antivirus software installed and running
- Current antivirus updates installed
- Antispyware installed and running
- Current antispyware updates installed
- Microsoft Update Service enabled

These are configured in the client health policies or SHVs on the NPS. When a client attempts a connection, the client SHA will send a statement of health (SoH) to the NPS system. The SoH is compared with the health policy, resulting in a pass or a fail. Based on that result, the NPS does one of four actions. In the case of a pass (that is, the client is healthy), it just allows the client to connect. In the case where the SoH fails the policy comparison (that is, the client is unhealthy), the NPS can prevent the client from connecting, connect the client to a restricted network, or even allow the client to connect even though it is unhealthy, as shown in Table 24.1.

TABLE 24.1 NPS Actions

SoH Versus Policy	NPS Action
Passes	Client is allowed to connect.
Fails	Client is not allowed to connect, client is connected to a restricted network, or client is allowed to connect even if it is deemed unhealthy.

When a client fails and is not allowed to connect, that is straightforward. When the client fails and is connected to a restricted network, this allows the client to connect to secured remediation servers to download software, patches, or updates to be remediated. The SHA can even conduct remediation automatically and then allow the client to connect. Interestingly, in some cases, the client might fail and yet the policy still allows it to connect. This might be for reporting purposes.

In addition, third-party SHVs and SHAs can be written that access the NAP application programming interface (API).

Remediation server groups can be configured to restrict noncompliant VPN clients to just those servers where software and updates are stored. After the appropriate software and updates are applied that bring the client into compliance, the NPS will allow the clients full access to the network.

This server handles VPN client authentication requests for the RAS server and validates those requests against its policies. This allows for a centralized policy and access control, while allowing the RAS server role to be scaled out as needed.

See Chapter 15 for more details on the NPS system and NAP technologies.

Certificate Server

The certificate server is a certificate authority (CA) that issues certificates for the servers and clients to use in the authentication and encryption of tunnels. In Windows Server 2012, this is a Windows Server 2012 server with the Active Directory Certificate Services role installed with the Certification Authority and the Certification Authority Web Enrollment role services installed. These roles also require some other supporting roles to be installed, such as the Web Server (IIS) role and the File Services role.

Using Windows Server 2012 allows the administrator to issue and control certificates for the VPN infrastructure. This could also be handled by a third-party CA such as VeriSign, thereby not requiring a server, albeit at a steep annual cost.

Although not a requirement for all configurations of the VPN infrastructure, certificates are considered a best practice to enhance the security of the VPN infrastructure.

Active Directory Server

The Active Directory server provides the authentication database for the VPN client users. In Windows Server 2012, this is a server with the Active Directory Domain Services role installed.

RAS System Authentication Options

Authentication in any networking environment is critical for validating whether the individual wanting access should be allowed access to network resources. Authentication is an important component in the Windows Server 2012 security initiative. Windows Server 2012 can authenticate a remote access user connection through a variety of PPP authentication protocols, including the following:

- Password Authentication Protocol (PAP)
- Challenge-Handshake Authentication Protocol (CHAP)
- Microsoft Challenge Handshake Authentication Protocol (MS-CHAP)
- MS-CHAP version 2 (MS-CHAP v2)

- Extensible Authentication Protocol (EAP)
- Protected Extensible Authentication Protocol (PEAP)

Authentication Protocols for PPTP Connections

For PPTP connections, only four authentication protocols (MS-CHAP, MS-CHAP v2, EAP, and PEAP) provide a mechanism to generate the same encryption key on both the VPN client and VPN server. Microsoft Point-to-Point Encryption (MPPE) uses this encryption key to encrypt all PPTP data sent on the VPN connection. MS-CHAP and MS-CHAP v2 are password-based authentication protocols.

Without a CA server or smart cards, MS-CHAP v2 is highly recommended because it provides a stronger authentication protocol than MS-CHAP. MS-CHAP v2 also provides mutual authentication, which allows the VPN client to be authenticated by the VPN server and the VPN server to be authenticated by the VPN client.

If a password-based authentication protocol must be used, it is good practice to enforce the use of strong passwords (passwords longer than eight characters) that contain a random mixture of uppercase and lowercase letters, numbers, and punctuation. Group policies can be used in Active Directory to enforce strong user passwords.

EAP and PEAP Authentication Protocols

Extensible Authentication Protocol (EAP) and Protected Extensible Authentication Protocol (PEAP) are designed to be used along with a certificate infrastructure that uses user certificates or smart cards.

With EAP, the VPN client sends its user certificate for authentication, and the VPN server sends a computer certificate for authentication. This is the strongest authentication method because it does not rely on passwords. Third-party CAs can be used as long as the certificate in the computer store of the NPS contains the server authentication certificate purpose (also known as a certificate usage or certificate issuance policy). A certificate purpose is identified using an object identifier (OID). If the OID for server authentication is 1.3.6.1.5.5.7.3.1, the user certificate installed on the Windows remote access client must contain the client authentication certificate purpose (OID 1.3.6.1.5.5.7.3.2).

PEAP does not specify an authentication method, but rather secures EAP by creating an encrypted channel between the client and the server. As such, it provides additional security on top of EAP. PEAP can even be used with MS-CHAP v2 to provide additional security to the password authentication protocol.

Authentication Protocols for L2TP/IPsec Connections

For L2TP/IPsec connections, any authentication protocol can be used because the authentication occurs after the VPN client and VPN server have established a secure connection known as an IPsec security association (SA). The use of a strong authentication protocol such as MS-CHAP v2, EAP, or PEAP is recommended to provide strong user authentication.

Choosing the Best Authentication Protocol

Organizations typically spend very little time choosing the most appropriate authentication protocol to use with their VPN connections. In many cases, the lack of knowledge about the differences between the various authentication protocols is the reason a selection is not made. In other cases, the desire for simplicity is the reason heightened security is not chosen as part of the organization's authentication protocol decisions. Whatever the case, we make the following suggestions to assist you in selecting the best authentication protocol for VPN connections:

- Using the EAP or PEAP authentication protocol for PPTP, L2TP, and SSTP connections is highly recommended if the following conditions exist in an organization. If a smart card will be used, or if a certificate infrastructure that issues user certificates exists, EAP is the best and most secure option. Note that EAP is supported only by VPN clients running Windows XP, Windows 2000 client, Windows Vista, Windows 7, Windows 2000 Server, Windows Server 2003, Windows Server 2008, Windows 8, and Windows Server 2012.
- Use PEAP with EAP-MS-CHAP v2 as a method of easing the deployment burden. In this configuration, certificates are required only for the VPN server infrastructure and not for the clients. However, the key generation is done using Transport-Level Security (TLS) with mutual authentication for greatly enhanced security.
- Use MS-CHAP v2 and enforce strong passwords using Group Policy if you must use a password-based authentication protocol. Although not as strong of a security protocol as PEAP or EAP, MS-CHAP v2 is supported by computers running Windows 8, Windows Server 2012, Windows Server 2008, Windows Server 2003, Windows 2000 Server, Windows Vista, Windows 7, Windows XP, Windows 2000 client, Windows NT 4.0 with Service Pack 4 and higher, Windows Me, Windows 98, and Windows 95 with the Windows Dial-Up Networking 1.3 or higher Performance and Security Update.

24

VPN Protocols

PPTP, L2TP, and SSTP are the communication standards used to manage tunnels and encapsulate private data. It is important to note that data traveling through a tunnel must also be encrypted to be a VPN connection. Windows Server 2012 includes PPTP, L2TP, and SSTP tunneling protocols.

To establish a tunnel, both the tunnel client and tunnel server must be using the same tunneling protocol. Tunneling technology can be based on either a Layer 2 or Layer 3 tunneling protocol that corresponds to the Open System Interconnection (OSI) reference model. Layer 2 protocols correspond to the Data-link layer and use frames as their unit of exchange. PPTP and L2TP are Layer 2 tunneling protocols that encapsulate the payload in a PPP frame before it is sent across the Internet. Layer 3 protocols correspond to the Network layer and use packets. IPsec tunnel mode is a Layer 3 tunneling protocol that encapsulates IP packets in an additional IP header before sending them across the Internet.

Windows 8, Windows 7, Windows Vista, Windows XP, and Windows 2000 workstation VPN client and server computers support both L2TP/IPsec and PPTP by default. Both PPTP and L2TP/IPsec use PPP to provide an initial envelope for the data and then append additional headers for transport through the Internet. PPTP and L2TP also provide a logical transport mechanism to send PPP payloads and provide tunneling or encapsulation so that PPP payloads based on any protocol can be sent across the Internet. PPTP and L2TP rely on the PPP connection process to perform user authentication and protocol configuration.

There are a few differences between the three protocols. First, when using PPTP, the data encryption begins after the PPP connection process is completed, which means PPP authentication is used. With L2TP/IPsec, data encryption begins before the PPP connection process by negotiating an IPsec security association. In SSTP, the session is encrypted by SSL before authentication begins.

Second, PPTP connections use MPPE, a stream cipher that is based on the Rivest-Shamir-Adleman (RSA) RC-4 encryption algorithm and uses 40-, 56-, or 128-bit encryption keys. Stream ciphers encrypt data as a bit stream. L2TP/IPsec connections use the Data Encryption Standard (DES), which is a block cipher that uses either a 56-bit key for DES or three 56-bit keys for 3DES. Block ciphers encrypt data in discrete blocks (64-bit blocks, in the case of DES). SSTP uses SSL with RC4 or AES. DirectAccess uses 3DES or AES.

Finally, PPTP connections require only user-level authentication through a PPP-based authentication protocol. L2TP/IPsec connections require the same user-level authentication as well as computer-level authentication using computer certificates or pre-shared keys. In contrast, SSTP and DirectAccess may only require computer-level certificates and user account name and password credentials for the VPN servers.

Table 24.2 compares some of the characteristics of the three tunneling protocols.

TABLE 24.2 Comparing VPN Protocols

Characteristics	PPTP	L2TP/IPsec	SSTP
Encapsulation	Generic routing encapsulation (GRE)	L2TP over UDP	SSTP over TCP
Encryption	Microsoft Point-to-Point Encryption (MPPE) with RC4	IPsec ESP with Triple Data Encryption Standard (3DES) or Advanced Encryption Standard (AES)	SSL with RC4 or AES
Tunnel maintenance protocol	PPTP	L2TP	SSTP
When user authentication occurs	Before encryption begins	After the IPsec session is established	After the SSL session is established

Characteristics	PPTP	L2TP/IPsec	SSTP
Certificates needed	None	Computer certificates on both the VPN client and VPN server	Computer certificate on the VPN server and root CA certificate on the VPN client
Client	Windows 9x and later	Windows 2000 and later	Windows Server 2012, Windows 8, Windows Server 2008, Windows XP SP3, and Windows Vista SP1

Tunneling Within a Windows Server 2012 Networking Environment

For Layer 2 tunneling technologies, such as PPTP, L2TP, and SSTP, a tunnel is similar to a session; both of the tunnel endpoints must agree to the tunnel and must negotiate configuration variables, such as address assignment or encryption or compression parameters. In most cases, data transferred across the tunnel is sent using a datagram-based protocol. A tunnel maintenance protocol is used as the mechanism to manage the tunnel.

Layer 3 tunneling technologies generally assume that all the configuration settings are preconfigured, often by manual processes. For these protocols, there might be no tunnel maintenance phase. For Layer 2 protocols (PPTP, L2TP, and SSTP), however, a tunnel must be created, maintained, and then terminated.

After the tunnel is established, tunneled data can be sent. The tunnel client or server uses a tunnel data transfer protocol to prepare the data for transfer. For example, as illustrated in Figure 24.4, when the tunnel client sends a payload to the tunnel server, the tunnel client first appends a tunnel data transfer protocol header to the payload. The client then sends the resulting encapsulated payload across the internetwork, which routes it to the tunnel server. The tunnel server accepts the packets, removes the tunnel data transfer protocol header, and forwards the payload to the target network. Information sent between the tunnel server and tunnel client behaves similarly.

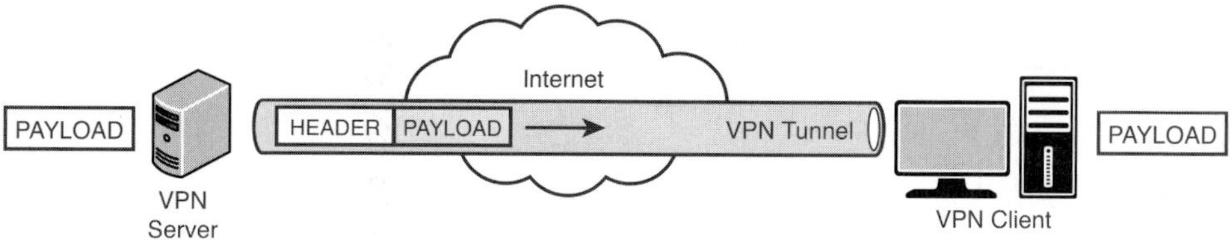

FIGURE 24.4 Tunneling payload through a VPN connection.

Point-to-Point Tunneling Protocol

The Point-to-Point Tunneling Protocol (PPTP) is a Layer 2 protocol that encapsulates PPP frames in IP datagrams for transmission over the Internet. PPTP can be used for remote access and router-to-router VPN connections. It uses a TCP connection for tunnel maintenance and a modified version of GRE to encapsulate PPP frames for tunneled data. The payloads of the encapsulated PPP frames can be encrypted/compressed. Figure 24.5 shows the structure of a PPTP packet containing user data.

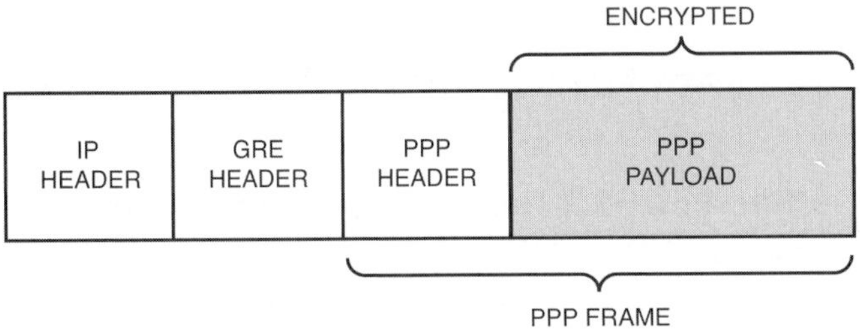

FIGURE 24.5 Structure of the PPTP packet.

Layer 2 Tunneling Protocol

Layer 2 Tunneling Protocol (L2TP) is a combination of the Point-to-Point Tunneling Protocol (PPTP) and Layer 2 Forwarding (L2F), a technology proposed by Cisco Systems, Inc. L2TP encapsulates PPP frames that are sent over IP, X.25, Frame Relay, and ATM networks. The payloads of encapsulated PPP frames can be encrypted/compressed. When sent over the Internet, L2TP frames are encapsulated as User Datagram Protocol (UDP) messages, as shown in Figure 24.6.

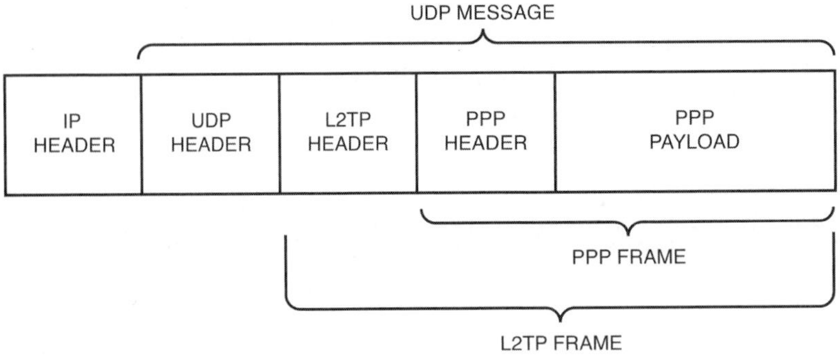

FIGURE 24.6 Structure of the L2TP packet.

L2TP frames include L2TP connection maintenance messages and tunneled data. L2TP connection maintenance messages include only the L2TP header. L2TP tunneled data includes a PPP header and PPP payload. The PPP payload can be encrypted or compressed (or both) using standard PPP encryption and compression methods.

In Windows Server 2012, L2TP connections do not negotiate the use of PPP encryption through Microsoft Point-to-Point Encryption (MPPE). Instead, encryption is provided through the use of the IP Security (IPsec) Encapsulating Security Payload (ESP) header and trailer.

IP Security

IPsec was designed as an end-to-end mechanism for ensuring data security in IP-based communications. Illustrated in Figure 24.7, the IPsec architecture includes an authentication header to verify data integrity and an encapsulation security payload for both data integrity and data encryption. IPsec provides two important functions that ensure confidentiality: data encryption and data integrity. IPsec uses an Authentication Header (AH) to provide source authentication and integrity without encryption and the Encapsulating Security Payload (ESP) to provide authentication and integrity along with encryption. With IPsec, only the sender and recipient know the security key. If the authentication data is valid, the recipient knows that the communication came from the sender and that it was not changed in transit.

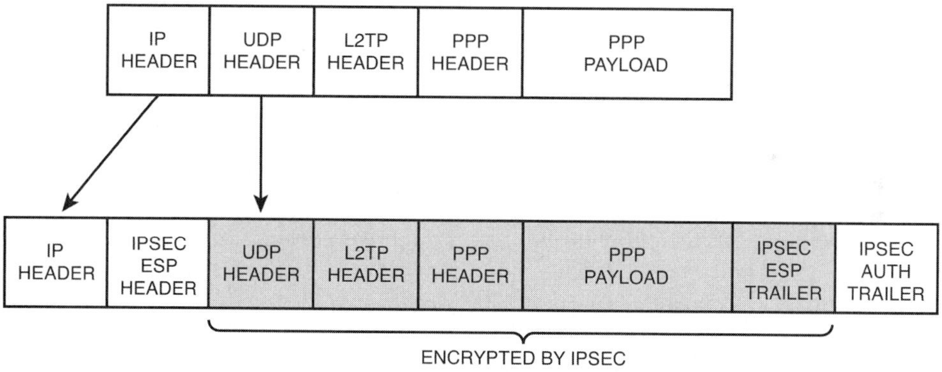

FIGURE 24.7 Structure and architecture of the IPsec packet.

NOTE

IPsec also plays a key role in another remote-access technology, Windows Server 2012 DirectAccess.

Secure Sockets Tunneling Protocol

Introduced in Windows Server 2008, Secure Sockets Tunneling Protocol (SSTP) was specifically developed to get around the difficulties of setting up VPN tunnels through corporate firewalls, which block many of the ports and protocols used by PPTP and L2TP. The SSTP tunnel uses the HTTP over SSL (HTTPS) protocol, which is widely supported for secure web traffic. SSTP uses port 443 for the connection.

The tunneling protocol functions by encapsulating the original IP packet with a PPP header and then an SSTP header. The SSTP header, the PPP header, and the original IP packet are all encrypted by the SSL session. Finally, an IP header is added to the packet and it is routed to the destination. The structure of the packet is shown in Figure 24.8.

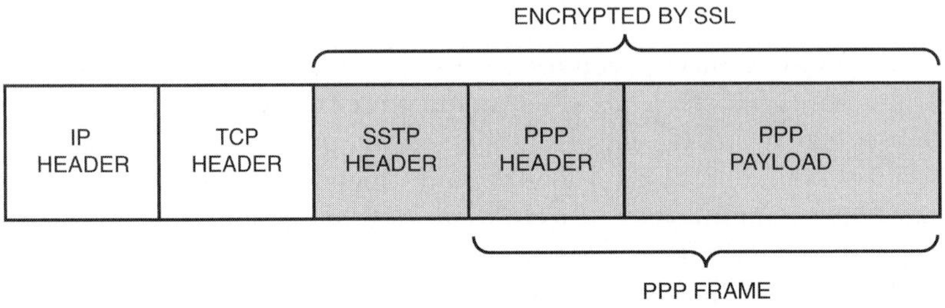

FIGURE 24.8 Structure and architecture of the SSTP packet.

NOTE

Interestingly, even though SSTP is based on the HTTPS web protocol, the VPN server does not have to be configured with Internet Information Services (IIS). The RAS VPN server listens for SSTP connections on the uniform resource identifier (URI) /sra_{BA195980-CD49-458b-9E23-C84EE0ADCD75}/. This does not conflict with or require IIS, so IIS can be installed if needed for other purposes.

Unfortunately, SSTP does not support tunneling through web proxies that require authentication. Another limitation of SSTP is that it does not support site-to-site connections in Windows Server 2012, which both PPTP and L2TP do.

DirectAccess in Windows Server 2012

DirectAccess is a remote-access protocol introduced in Windows Server 2008 and improved in Windows Server 2012 that provides network node connectivity to remote systems without any user login requirements. DirectAccess addresses several challenges with traditional VPN, including the following:

- The need for the user to manually connect to the VPN.
- The delay the user experiences when connecting to the VPN while health checks are completed during the connection process.
- The need for the user to reconnect manually if an established VPN connection is lost.

- The slow performance when all traffic (intranet and Internet) is routed through the VPN connection.

These challenges can cause users to limit the use of traditional VPN solutions. DirectAccess has been designed from the ground up to address those challenges. DirectAccess hides all the connection processes from the users and intelligently routes intranet versus Internet traffic, thereby alleviating the challenges of traditional VPNs. It connects as soon as the computer starts up and conducts the health checks, rather than when the user is logging in. The connection process is transparent to the user and the user never needs to explicitly connect to DirectAccess. Finally, DirectAccess has built-in options to control how DNS requests are handled, effectively bifurcating the Internet and intranet traffic to avoid burdening the remote access connection and improving performance.

DirectAccess creates an encrypted point-to-point tunnel from a remote user—in this case, specifically a remote user on Windows 7 or Windows 8—to the internal "enterprise" network. The difference is that the connection is transparent to the user. Once configured, the computer will automatically connect to the office from any available Internet connection. The user experience is almost identical to being in the office. In addition, through the use of the Windows Server 2012 NPS server, remote-connected clients can be securely managed similarly to internal client systems.

NOTE

Although positioned as an alternative to a VPN, the DirectAccess technology has all the elements of a VPN. It establishes a secure private tunnel through public networks using IPsec and certificates, with an end result functionally not much different from L2TP. The differences are mainly administrative rather than technical.

DirectAccess uses IPv6, IPsec, and if needed certificates to establish secure connections from the DirectAccess clients to intranet resources via the DirectAccess server. To traverse public IPv4 networks, DirectAccess uses IPv6 transition technologies such as ISATAP, Teredo, and 6to4.

DirectAccess in Windows Server 2008 R2 had some specific requirements, as follows:

- The server running DirectAccess needed to have two network cards: one attached to the intranet and one attached to the Internet.
- The Internet network card had to have two consecutive public IPv4 addresses.
- The intranet resources and applications must support IPv6 unless there was a NAT64 device present.
- The DirectAccess clients needed to be running Windows 7; older clients are not supported.
- A domain controller and domain name system (DNS) server that the systems are connected to needed to be running Windows Server 2008 SP2 or later.

- A PKI needs to be available to issue certificates with a published Internet available certificate revocation list (CRL).

These requirements are somewhat stringent and prevented many organizations from deploying Windows Server 2008 R2 DirectAccess.

In Windows Server 2012 DirectAccess, many of these requirements have been relaxed to make it simpler for organizations to deploy DirectAccess. Some of the specific changes are as follows:

- The server running Windows Server 2012 can now have a single network card and can be located behind a firewall.
- The Internet network card must have a single public IPv4 address only if Teredo support is needed.
- The DirectAccess server can act as a gateway between IPv4 and IPv6, allowing DirectAccess clients to access IPv4 only resources.
- The DirectAccess clients can either be Windows 7 or Windows 8; older legacy clients still are not supported.
- A domain controller and DNS server that the systems are connected to need to be running Windows Server 2008 SP2, Windows Server 2008 R2, or Windows Server 2012.
- Client authentication requests can be via Kerberos through the Kerberos proxy service versus requiring server and client certificates.
- The DirectAccess server can also issue self-signed certificates if needed, rather than requiring a PKI solution be in place.

These changes make it easier for small and medium-sized organizations to deploy Windows Server 2012 DirectAccess, as well as provide flexibility to larger organizations. The Configuration Wizard is even intelligent and will examine the configuration of the DirectAccess server and then choose the best DirectAccess deployment options automatically.

DirectAccess and IPv6

DirectAccess is designed on top of IPv6 and requires that all endpoint devices support IPv6. It is one of the first services to require this modern protocol.

DirectAccess is most likely to be deployed in an IPv4 world, given the prevalence of IPv4 on the Internet today. This creates an IPv4 gap (shown in Figure 24.9) across which IPv6 devices like DirectAccess clients need to communicate.

Most organizations will need to use IPv6 transition technologies to bridge the IPv4 gap from their IPv6 enlightened devices to communicate. This, in effect, routes the IPv6 communications through the IPv4 protocol stack, as shown in Figure 24.10. The packets

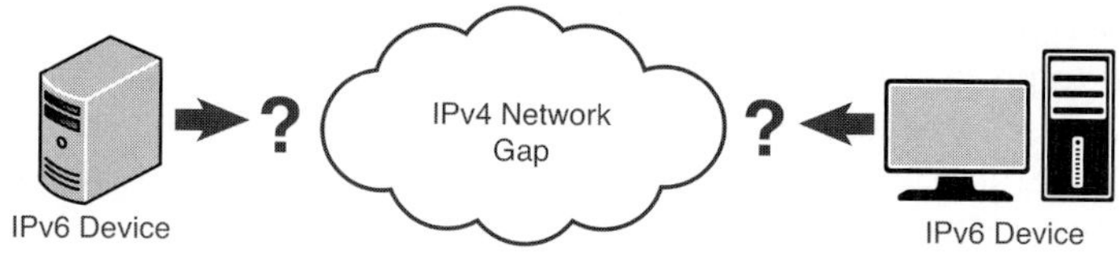

FIGURE 24.9 The IPv4 gap between IPv6 devices.

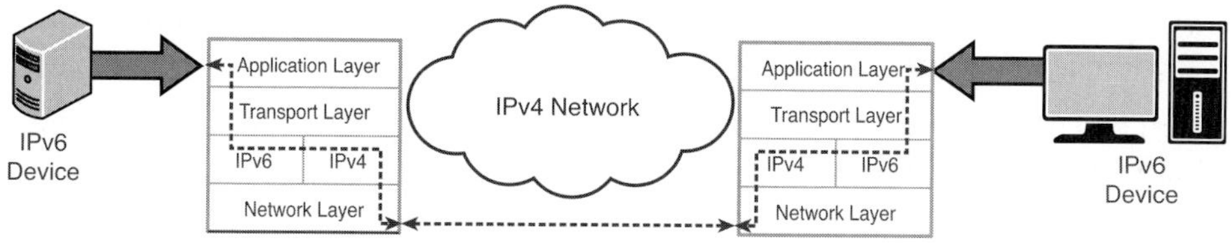

FIGURE 24.10 Bridging the IPv4 gap with transition technologies.

traveling down the IPv6 protocol stack take a sharp turn and move across the protocol stack to the IPv4 protocol stack, allowing them to transit the IPv4 network. On the other side, the same packets come in via the IPv4 protocol stack, but are routed to the IPv6 stack.

Communications between IPv6 devices like DirectAccess clients over IPv4 networks is accomplished with IPv6 over IPv4 tunneling. In tunneling, the IPv6 packets are encapsulated in an IPv4 packet by the source device and routed through the IPv4 network. When the encapsulated packet arrives at the boundary between the IPv4 and IPv6 networks, the IPv4 encapsulation is stripped off and the IPv6 packet continues on its way. The most common tunneling protocols are ISATAP, 6to4, and Teredo.

For organizations, the IPv6 tunneling protocols are used for the following purposes:

- **ISATAP**—This protocol is used to automatically assign IPv6 addresses within the organization's IPv4 intranet.
- **6to4**—This protocol is used to automatically assign IPv6 addresses and route across the public IPv4 Internet.
- **Teredo**—This protocol is used to automatically assign IPv6 addresses and route across the public IPv4 Internet to devices behind NAT firewalls. This is the protocol that requires 2 consecutive public IPv4 addresses.

For organizations that have not deployed IPv6 natively, Microsoft Windows Server 2012, Windows 7, and Windows 8 support ISATAP, 6to4, and Teredo transition protocols. However, even while DirectAccess clients are using IPv6 transitional technologies like Teredo or 6to4, it is ultimately communicating from IPv6 clients to IPv6 hosts.

Internally, DirectAccess can use Network Address Translation-Protocol Translation (NAT-PT) devices, which can be used to provide access to IPv4 resources. Resources that don't support IPv6 natively can be accessed through the use of a NAT-PT device. Microsoft Windows Server 2012 has NAT64 and DNS64 functionality built in, so DirectAccess clients can seamlessly access both IPv6 and IPv4 resources.

For organizations that have not deployed IPv6, the deployment of DirectAccess is an excellent project to test the IPv6 waters with. The infrastructure can be deployed in parallel with existing remote-access solutions and without impacting the existing IPv4 addressing scheme, providing IT personnel with a chance to learn IPv6 and its integration with IPv4 in a low-impact production setting.

See Chapter 11, "DHCP / IPv6 / IPAM," for a detailed discussion of the IPv6 protocol and the transition technologies needed to bridge the IPv4 gap.

A Tale of Two Tunnels

The DirectAccess client establishes two tunnels, which are key to the versatility of this method of remote access. These tunnels are IPsec ESP tunnels that are authenticated and encrypted to ensure the confidentiality. These tunnels are as follows:

- **Computer tunnel**—The computer tunnel is established first when the DirectAccess client starts up. This tunnel is authenticated with the computer certificate only and provides access to the intranet DNS and domain controllers. This tunnel is also used to download the computer group policy and request user authentication.
- **User tunnel**—This tunnel is authenticated with the computer certificate and the user credentials and provides access to the intranet resources. This tunnel is used to download user group policy as well.

Both these tunnels are established transparently to the user. The user does not have to present credentials above and beyond the normal Windows logon to establish remote access. The two tunnels are shown in Figure 24.11.

These tunnels allow for the transparent establishment of remote access, essentially allowing the computer to connect to the intranet even when no user is logged on. This allows the DirectAccess client to receive Group Policy remotely and be managed by the management servers in the intranet. When a user logs on, they are authenticating to the intranet and, thus, ensuring that users are subject to the latest requirements, password changes, and policies. In contrast, other VPN solutions typically have users authenticating using cached credentials against the local machine and then establishing the remote-access connection.

End-to-Edge DirectAccess Model

The end-to-edge model of DirectAccess has the DirectAccess client establish an IPsec tunnel to the DirectAccess server. The DirectAccess server then forwards unprotected traffic to the intranet resources. This is the most common form of DirectAccess and closely follows a standard remote access methodology.

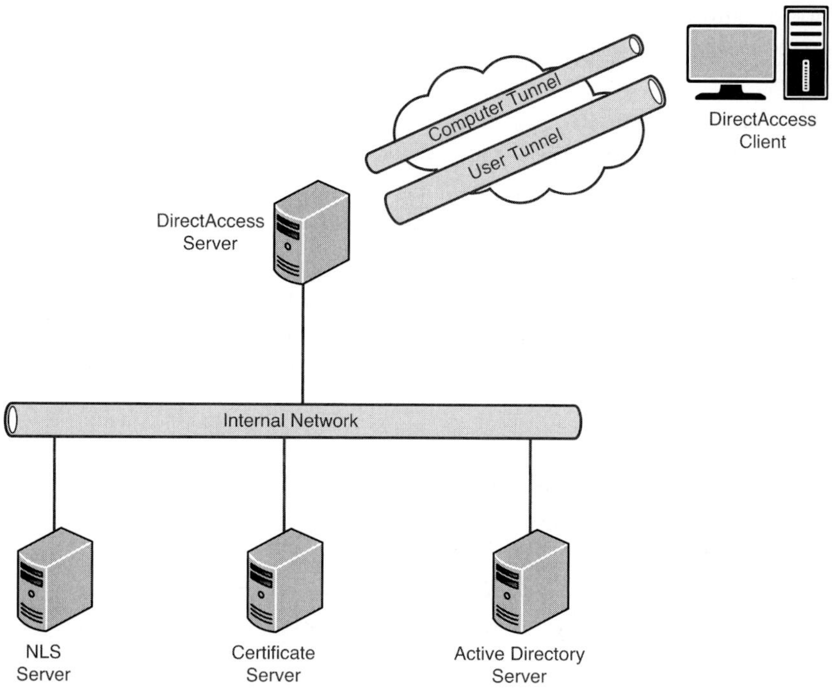

FIGURE 24.11 The two DirectAccess tunnels.

Figure 24.12 shows the end-to-edge connection model. Note that there is a single protected (solid line) connection through the tunnel to the DirectAccess server, which then is forwarded to each of the application servers in three separate unprotected (dashed line) connections.

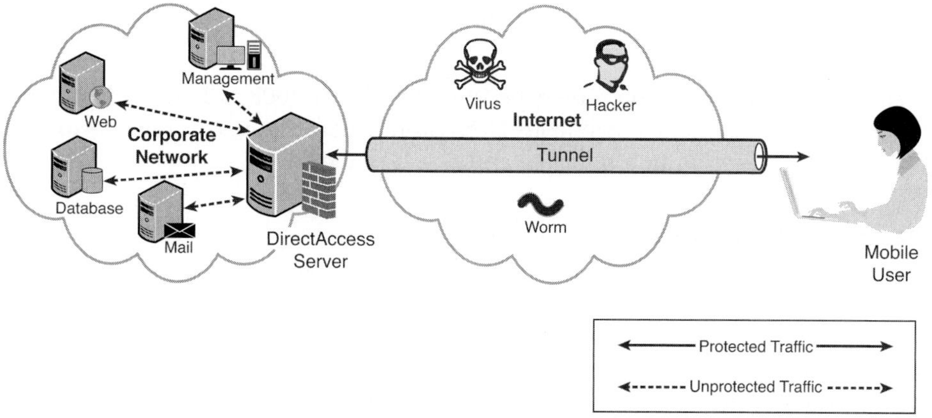

FIGURE 24.12 End-to-edge DirectAccess.

The end-to-edge model requires no IPsec support within the intranet, although the intranet resources still need to support IPv6.

End-to-End DirectAccess Model

The end-to-end model of DirectAccess has the DirectAccess client establish an IPsec tunnel with each application server that they connect to. This ensures that traffic is protected end to end (hence the name) by the IPsec encryption, including while traversing the intranet.

Figure 24.13 shows the end-to-end connection model. Note that there is a protected (solid line) connection through the tunnel and the DirectAccess server to each of the application servers. This indicates that there are separate IPsec connections to each server, which are protected by encryption not only through the Internet but also through the intranet.

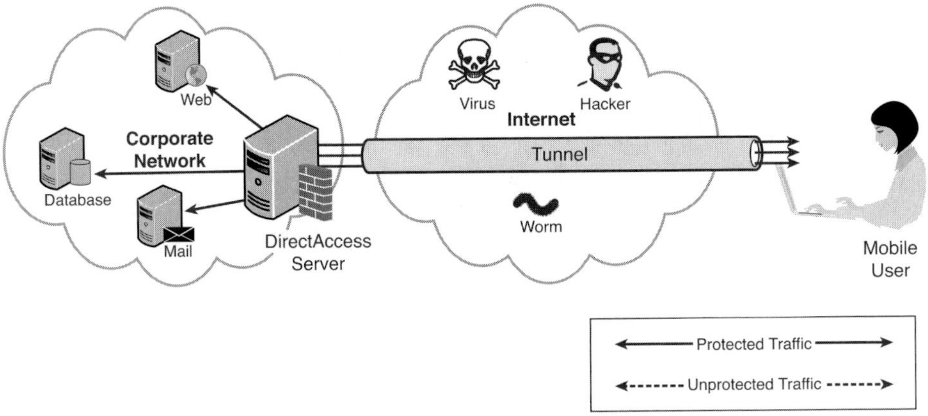

FIGURE 24.13 End-to-end DirectAccess.

The end-to-end model requires that each application server run on Windows Server 2008 or Windows Server 2012, as well as use IPv6 and IPsec. There is also some additional overhead for the IPsec connections.

The requirement that all application servers be Windows Server 2008 or later is a difficult hurdle to overcome in today's heterogeneous IT environments. This makes the end-to-end model of DirectAccess less common than the end-to-edge model.

Managed-Out Support Model

The managed-out support model is used to manage devices in the field without providing user access. This deployment model only allows the DirectAccess computer access to the designated management servers. The management servers can also access the DirectAccess computers. This is illustrated in Figure 24.14. Note that the connection is only to the management server and that it is bidirectional.

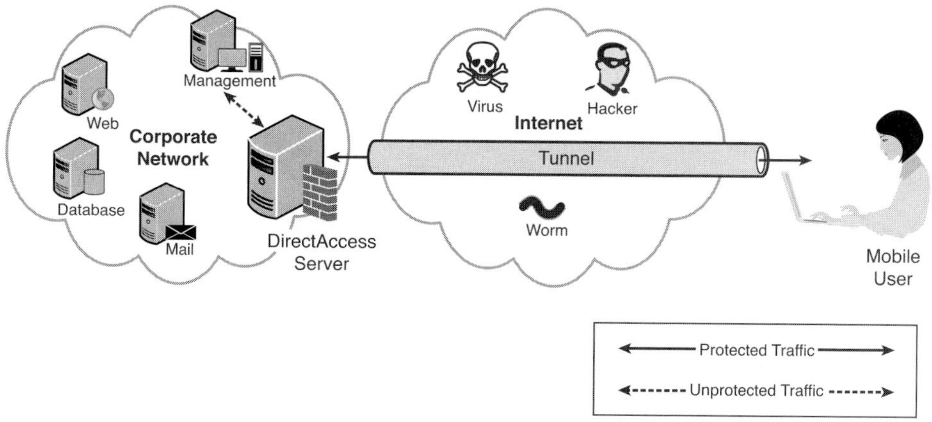

FIGURE 24.14 Managed-out DirectAccess.

This option is useful for providing remote management of computers for patching, inventory, and software distribution and facilitates the use of Microsoft System Center 2012 products such as Configuration Manager, Operations Manager, and Forefront Endpoint Protection.

Internet Versus Intranet Traffic with DirectAccess

One of the benefits of DirectAccess is the ability to separate the intranet traffic (destined for internal servers) from the Internet traffic (destined for external servers). This conserves the corporate bandwidth for access to corporate resources. By specifying the domains and subdomains for which the DirectAccess server provides access, traffic for those domains is directed through the DirectAccess connection. Other traffic is routed through the default routes and bypasses the DirectAccess connection. This is the highest performance configuration and is the default mode of operation.

However, in some cases, administrators might want to have all traffic route through the DirectAccess connection. Examples of this include organizations that want to control or monitor their client communications or prevent access to certain Internet sites. In these cases, the DirectAccess client can be configured to route all traffic through the DirectAccess connection with the force tunneling option in the DirectAccess client setup.

DirectAccess Components

DirectAccess leverages IPv6 technology to provide a seamless secure connection to the enterprise network. DirectAccess runs at boot and connects as soon as Internet connectivity is established. There's no need for a user to configure a VPN client or logon. From an administrative perspective, this technology allows system administrators to manage and monitor remote systems through tools like Microsoft System Center Configuration Manager (SCCM) and Group Policy. DirectAccess finally puts remote workers on equal ground with traditional office employees.

The following list depicts the components found in a DirectAccess deployment:

- **DirectAccess server**—This is the server that connects to the internal network and the Internet. It has to be running Windows Server 2012.
- **DirectAccess client**—This is a computer running Windows 7 or Windows 8, and it must be a domain member.
- **Corporate IPv6 network**—The IPv6 network to which DirectAccess clients will be connecting remotely.
- **Certificate server**—This server issues the certificates that support the tunnel creation, authentication, and security. This certificate server must have a published CRL that is available internally and externally.
- **Network Location Server (NLS)**—This is an HTTPS site that serves as the indicator to the DirectAccess client if it is connected to the Internet or the intranet.
- **Active Directory and DNS server**—This server must be running Windows Server 2008 SP2 or greater. The AD and DNS role can be separate servers, although most organizations will have these services on the same server.

Figure 24.15 shows the components and their connections.

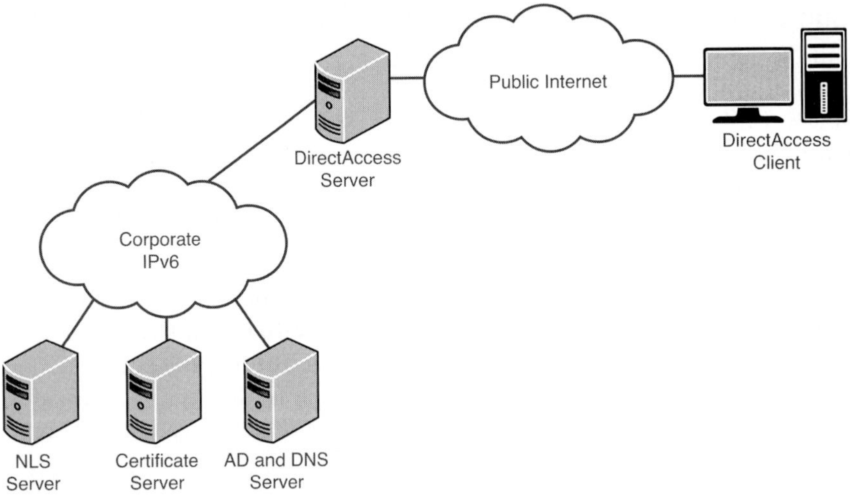

FIGURE 24.15 DirectAccess components.

Smart cards, One-Time-Password (OTP) devices such as RSA SecureID, or NAP protection can also be implemented for additional security if desired.

DirectAccess uses IPv6, but can transparently provide access to IPv4 resources on the internal enterprise network through NAT64 and DNS64. It leverages conversion technology like Teredo, 6to4, and also the new IP-HTTPS for remote clients using IPv4 to connect to the IPv6 enterprise network. These new technologies are described in the following list:

- Teredo is the most common method for DirectAccess. It allows IPv6 traffic to pass through NAT devices that transition out to an IPv4 public network. A good example is many "hot spot" connections at coffee shops and many home networks.
- 6to4 directly translates IPv6 addresses into IPv4 addresses. If remote clients are directly connected to the Internet and have only IPv4 public IP addresses, 6to4 is the preferred method for connectivity.
- IP-HTTPS is a new protocol in Windows 7 and Windows Server 2012. It tunnels IPv6 traffic over an IPv4 HTTPS tunnel between a DirectAccess client and a DirectAccess server. Although this might seem like the simplest option, it comes at a large performance cost due to network overhead and should be used only as a last resort.

The DirectAccess protocol is very robust and will transparently attempt multiple methods of access to establish a connection.

Network Location Service

The Network Location Service (NLS) is a critical component for the DirectAccess architecture. This is a website that clients attempt to connect to determine if they are currently connected to the Internet or to the intranet. It is the URL of a highly available website in the corporate intranet.

There are two behaviors that would be experienced for the DirectAccess client system. They are as follows:

- If the DirectAccess client can reach the NLS URL, it assumes that it is connected to the corporate network and no further action is necessary.
- If the DirectAccess client cannot reach the NLS URL, it assumes that it is not connected to the corporate network and then begins the DirectAccess connection process.

The NLS service is normally a highly available website, such as servers in a Network Load Balanced (NLB) cluster or a Windows cluster.

NOTE

As you can see, if the NLS website is down, this can result in the disastrous situation of all the DirectAccess clients suddenly thinking they are on the Internet, even though they are really in the intranet. They would all then begin the DirectAccess connection process. That's why the NLS website must be highly available.

In Windows Server 2012, the DirectAccess server can act as the NLS. This is typically done for the managed-out model.

DirectAccess Connection Process

The DirectAccess client is very robust and will try a variety of methods to connect to the corporate network. The connection process is started when the DirectAccess client detects that it is connected to a network—that is, a network transition such as the connection to a LAN, wireless access point, or other connection becomes active.

The DirectAccess client goes through the following connection process when it detects that it is connected to a network:

1. The DirectAccess client attempts to connect to the NLS website. If it can reach the site, it determines that it is connected to the intranet and stops the DirectAccess process. If it cannot reach the NLS website, it determines that it is connected to the Internet and continues with the DirectAccess process.
2. The DirectAccess client establishes an IPsec tunnel to the DirectAccess server using IPv6. If there is an intervening IPv4 network, the client uses the Teredo or 6to4 protocols to tunnel IPv6 over IPv4.
3. If the DirectAccess client is unable to connect using the Teredo or 6to4 protocols, the client will attempt to connect using the IP-HTTPS protocol.
4. The DirectAccess client establishes an IPsec tunnel to the DirectAccess server using IPv6. The DirectAccess client and the DirectAccess server mutually authenticate using certificates in the process of setting up the IPsec computer tunnel.
5. The DirectAccess client contacts the domain controller and obtains the computer group policy.

NOTE

The user does not have to be logged on to the computer for this process to complete to this point in the process.

6. The DirectAccess user logs on or the logged-on credentials are used in conjunction with the certificates to establish the IPsec user tunnel. The user group policy is applied to the DirectAccess client.
7. The DirectAccess server begins forwarding traffic from the DirectAccess client to authorized intranet resources.

This entire process is transparent to the user and requires no user interaction. In the event of an interruption in network connectivity, the DirectAccess client will reestablish the connection through this process when it detects network connectivity again.

Choosing Between Traditional VPN Technologies and DirectAccess

One of the choices to make when you're deploying Windows Server 2012-based remote access is the choice between a traditional VPN technology and the new DirectAccess.

Within the VPNs technologies are a number of choices, primarily whether to use L2TP/IPsec or PPTP.

Advantages of L2TP/IPsec

Although PPTP users significantly outnumber L2TP/IPsec users, because of a higher level of security in L2TP/IPsec as well as several other benefits of L2TP/IPsec, organizations that are seeking to improve secured remote connectivity are beginning to implement L2TP/IPsec VPN as their remote and mobile access standard. The following are the advantages of using L2TP/IPsec over PPTP:

- IPsec provides per-packet data authentication (proof that the data was sent by the authorized user), data integrity (proof that the data was not modified in transit), replay protection (prevention from resending a stream of captured packets), and data confidentiality (prevention from interpreting captured packets without the encryption key). PPTP provides only per-packet data confidentiality.
- L2TP/IPsec connections provide stronger authentication by requiring both computer-level authentication through certificates and user-level authentication through a PPP authentication protocol.
- PPP packets exchanged during user-level authentication are never sent unencrypted because the PPP connection process for L2TP/IPsec occurs after the IPsec security associations are established. If intercepted, the PPP authentication exchange for some types of PPP authentication protocols can be used to perform offline dictionary attacks and determine user passwords. If the PPP authentication exchange is encrypted, offline dictionary attacks are possible only after the encrypted packets have been successfully decrypted.

Advantages of PPTP

Although L2TP/IPsec is more secure than a PPTP VPN session, there are significant reasons organizations choose PPTP over L2TP/IPsec. The following are advantages of PPTP over L2TP/IPsec:

- PPTP does not require a certificate infrastructure. L2TP/IPsec, SSTP, and DirectAccess require a certificate infrastructure for issuing computer certificates to the VPN server computer (or other authenticating server) and all VPN client computers.
- PPTP can be used by all Windows desktop platforms (Windows Server 2008, Windows Server 2012, Windows Server 2003, Windows 2000 Server, Windows 8, Windows 7, Windows Vista, Windows XP, Windows 2000 client, Windows NT 4.0, Windows Millennium Edition [Me], Windows 98, and Windows 95 with the Windows Dial-Up Networking 1.3 Performance and Security Update). Windows Server 2012, Windows Server 2008, Windows Server 2003, Windows 2000 Server, Windows 7, Windows Vista, Windows XP, and Windows 2000 Workstation VPN clients are the only clients that support L2TP/IPsec and the use of certificates. Windows 7 is the only client that supports DirectAccess.

IPsec functions at a layer below the TCP/IP stack. This layer is controlled by a security policy on each computer and a negotiated security association between the sender and receiver. The policy consists of a set of filters and associated security behaviors. If a packet's IP address, protocol, and port number match a filter, the packet is subject to the associated security behavior.

Advantages of SSTP

The SSTP protocol in Windows Server 2012 enables administrators to establish tunnels across the majority of corporate networks, bypassing many of the technical hurdles that stop PPTP and L2TP.

The advantages of SSTP are as follows:

- SSTP helps lower administrative costs by reducing the technical steps needed to tunnel between organizations. Because HTTPS is allowed through most firewalls and proxy servers, there is no additional infrastructure changes needed to support SSTP.
- SSTP is certificate-based security implemented via SSL. However, certificates only need to be issued to the servers rather than the clients. This provides the security benefits of L2TP, but with almost the ease of configuration of PPTP.

The benefits are offset by the requirement that the client CA requirements and the operating system requirement. The client requirement is that it trusts the CA issuing the certificates and that it can access the certificate revocation list.

Support for SSTP in clients is available in Windows Server 2008, Windows Server 2012, Windows 7, Windows XP SP3 or later, and Windows Vista SP1 or later.

Advantages of DirectAccess

DirectAccess is a new and improved technology introduced with Windows Server 2008 R2 and enhanced with Windows Server 2012 and is a completely new idea for remote access. Essentially, DirectAccess is a transparent always-on remote access. It allows users to always appear to be on the corporate network and appear as if they are in the office. In addition, it allows administrators to manage systems as local systems through tools like Group Policy and Microsoft System Center Configuration Manager (SCCM). From a user perspective, this is the easiest remote access solution. Once configured, they don't need to perform any action; it just works. From an administrator point of view, however, this solution is the most complex due to the IPv6 and certificate requirements.

The advantages of DirectAccess are as follows:

- DirectAccess provides seamless connectivity wherever a remote system has an Internet connection. No user interaction is required.
- System administrators can manage remotely connected systems as if they were internal systems.

- DirectAccess allows folder redirection so that all critical data is maintained inside the corporate network and backed up using enterprise tools.
- DirectAccess uses a new technology, Name Resolution Policy Table (NRPT), to determine the appropriate DNS server for connection requests. Combined with split tunneling, this makes for a truly transparent solution.

DirectAccess in Windows Server 2012 overcomes many of the limitation in the previous editions, relaxing many of the constraints and simplifying the deployment.

Ports Affecting the VPN Connectivity

Frequently, RAS servers operating as VPN servers have two network cards, one of which is plugged into the external network or DMZ. This is simpler, because there are usually few restrictions on communicating with that external-facing interface. The RAS server is firewalled and the external-facing interface is hardened as a matter of best practice to mitigate the potential risks. In fact, this is a requirement for DirectAccess servers.

However, even with mitigation steps, this external-facing interface can present an unacceptable level of risk to some organizations. In those cases, the VPN infrastructure must remain entirely within the internal network. In that configuration, the firewall must be configured to allow the appropriate traffic to the RAS server.

Table 24.3 and Table 24.4 list the relevant firewall rules needed for the PPTP and L2TP protocols. The IP address for each of the rules is the RAS server address, which is the destination if the direction is inbound and the source if the direction is outbound.

NOTE

Interestingly, because the DirectAccess server must be a dual-homed server with a network interface on the public network, no ports are needed on the firewall for DirectAccess. In effect, it bypasses the firewall completely.

The SSTP protocol is simple and only requires that TCP port 443 be permitted inbound to the RAS server.

TABLE 24.3 Firewall Rules for the RAS Server for PPTP

Direction	Protocol	Port or ID	Why?
Inbound	TCP	1723	Allows PPTP tunnel maintenance traffic from the PPTP client to the PPTP server
Inbound	IP	47	Allows tunneled PPTP data from the PPTP client to the PPTP server
Outbound	TCP	1723	Allows PPTP tunnel maintenance traffic from the PPTP server to the PPTP client
Outbound	IP	47	Allows tunneled PPTP data from the PPTP server to the PPTP client

TABLE 24.4 Firewall Rules for the RAS Server for L2TP

Direction	Protocol	Port or ID	Why?
Inbound	UDP	500	Allows IKE traffic to the VPN server
Inbound	UDP	4500	Allows IPsec NAT-T traffic to the VPN server
Inbound	IP	50	Allows IPsec ESP traffic to the VPN server
Outbound	UDP	500	Allows IKE traffic from the VPN server
Outbound	UDP	4500	Allows IPsec NAT-T traffic from the VPN server
Outbound	IP	50	Allows IPsec ESP traffic from the VPN server

Setting Up the Unified Remote Access Role

Windows Server 2012 now has a unified Remote Access role, which supports both DirectAccess and VPN services on the same server. This allows small and medium-size organizations to deploy a single server that will support all their remote-access services.

To add and configure the Remote Access role to the remote-access server, follow these steps:

1. Launch Server Manager on the VPN server, and select Manage, then Add Roles and Features.
2. Click Next on the Before You Begin screen.
3. At the Installation Type screen, leave the default Role-Based or Feature-Based Installation and click Next.
4. Select the server, in this case RAS1, and click Next.
5. Select the Remote Access role check box.
6. If the Add Features That Are Required for Remote Access box appears, click the Add Features button.
7. Click Next at the Server Roles screen.
8. Click Next at the Features screen.
9. At the Remote Access screen, click Next.
10. Leave the default DirectAccess and VPN (RAS) role service selected and click Next.
11. At the Web Server Role (IIS) screen click Next, and then click Next again on the following Role Services screen.
12. Click Install at the Confirmation screen to install the role.
13. Click Close to exit the Add Roles and Features Wizard.

The Remote Access role has been installed, but still needs to be configured for the appropriate services. This will be done in the DirectAccess scenario and the VPN scenario.

DirectAccess Scenario

Although the prerequisites and associated technologies for DirectAccess can be difficult to implement, DirectAccess configuration is fairly straightforward through a simple wizard. The example walks through the DirectAccess Wizard in Windows Server 2012.

The goal of this scenario is to show that DirectAccess in Windows Server 2012 is very simple and straightforward to setup and can easily coexist with the traditional VPN services. This would be the typical configuration for a small to medium-sized organization. The scenario demonstrates the following:

- **Remote Access Wizard**—This is an easy-to-run wizard that analyzes the system and automatically chooses the best settings for the configuration.
- **DirectAccess**—This will allow workstations to seamlessly access intranet resources as they move from the internal network to a public network.
- **VPN coexistence**—This will allow a single server to support both DirectAccess services and traditional VPN services on a single Windows Server 2012 server. The VPN features will be configured in the "VPN Scenario" section later in this chapter.
- **Use of self-signed certificates**—Rather than require a complex PKI infrastructure for issuing and maintaining certificates, the scenario will use self-signed certificates.
- **Tunneling using IP-HTTPS**—The scenario will demonstrate the IT-HTTPS tunneling protocol, which is the most portable tunneling protocol. This will allow DirectAccess to function across many different networks, including NAT firewalls.

Figure 24.16 shows the DirectAccess scenario components and their connections. This is a straightforward example, with a domain controller (DC1), the DirectAccess server (RAS1), and the Windows 8 workstation (WS1).

There are two servers and a client in the scenario shown in Figure 24.16. These are the systems that will be configured and tested against during the scenario. The systems are as follows:

- **DC1**—Domain controller and DNS server running Windows Server 2012. The Active Directory domain is companyabc.com. The DC1 IP address is 10.1.1.10.
- **RAS1**—DirectAccess server domain member running Windows Server 2012, with two network interface cards, and a public IP address (75.25.156.217) assigned. The internal IP address is 10.1.1.210. This server should also have the Web Server role installed to support IP-HTTPS.

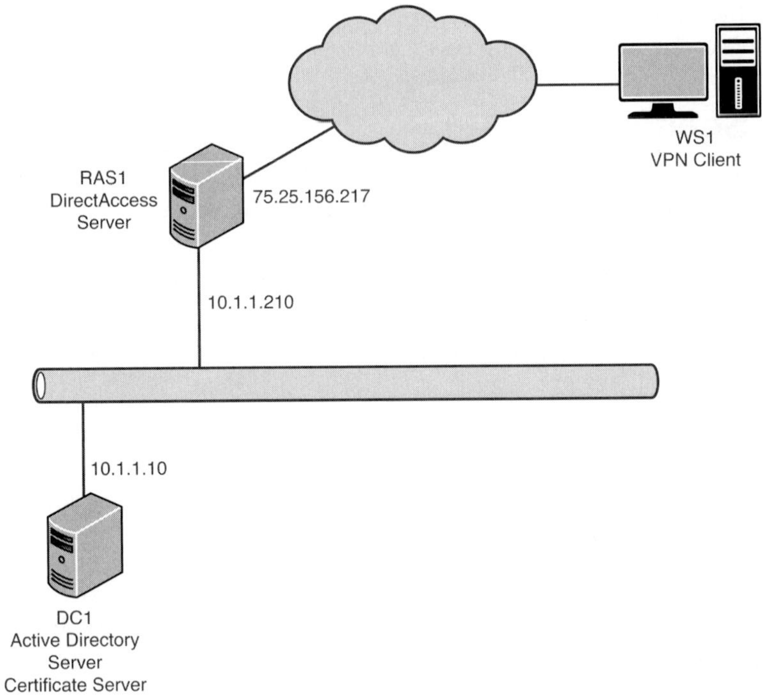

FIGURE 24.16 DirectAccess components.

NOTE

In Windows 2008 R2, DA required two consecutive public IP addresses, which was frequently an issue. The reason for two consecutive public IPv4 addresses on the DirectAccess server's public Internet interface is so that Teredo-based DirectAccess clients can detect the type of NAT that they are located behind. In this example using Windows Server 2012, we'll not be using Teredo tunneling, and so can use a traditional single IP address.

- **WS1**—DirectAccess client domain member running Windows 8. This system will travel between the intranet and Internet networks.

The scenario assumes that split-brain DNS is being used—that is, that there is an internal companyabc.com zone and an external companyabc.com zone. There should be a DNS A record for ras.companyabc.com (75.25.156.217) in the external companyabc.com zone.

It is important to note that the scenario does not require that you have deployed IPv6 throughout the internal network to begin using DirectAccess. The scenario leverages the Windows Server 2012 and Windows 8 technologies that will automatically enable and configure IPv6 using transitional technologies like ISATAP, 6to4, and Teredo.

This scenario assumes that Windows Server 2012 Active Directory and DNS are already deployed. The DirectAccess server must have two physical network interfaces. The first is connected directly to the Internet, no NAT, and must have two consecutive public IP addresses. The second interface is connected to the internal network. This scenario also assumes you have an internal enterprise PKI deployment with CRLs published on the Internet.

There are 2 networks in the scenario. The DirectAccess client is WS1 and will be roaming between these networks, but must be able to access the application server no matter which network they are in. The two networks are as follows:

- **Intranet network**—This is the corporate network and is using an IPv4 address in the 10.1.x.x range.
- **Internet network**—This is a public network and the IP address range is not known in advance, as it could easily be an Internet cafe.

The client WS1 will be tested while connected to the internal network, the public network, and, finally, to the home network. In all cases, the client WS1 will seamlessly transition between the networks with no interruption in access to internal resources.

Configuring the Infrastructure

Create a security group for DirectAccess client computers. This allows the DirectAccess clients to be specified. The group will be named Remote Access Computers. To create the group, follow these steps:

1. On the domain controller, launch Server Manager.
2. Select Tools and then Active Directory Users and Computers, expand the companyabc.com domain, and select the Users container.
3. Right-click on Users, select New, and then click Group.
4. In the Group Name field, type **Remote Access Computers** and click OK.

This group will be used later to assign Group Policy to the DirectAccess clients.

Configuring the DirectAccess Feature

Next, run the DirectAccess Setup Wizard to configure DA1 and the Group Policy settings for DirectAccess clients.

To run the DirectAccess Setup Wizard, complete the following steps:

1. On the DirectAccess server RAS1, launch Server Manager.

NOTE

The Remote Access role was installed on RAS1 in the previous section.

2. Select Tools and then Remote Access Management to launch the console.
3. Click the Run the Getting Started Wizard link.
4. Select the Deploy Both DirectAccess and VPN option to launch the configuration analysis. The VPN configuration will be done in the VPN scenario section later in the chapter.

NOTE

The wizard scans the configuration and automatically detects the best configuration based on the number of interfaces, the assigned IP address (public or private), and other factors.

5. Leave the Automatically Detected Edge option selected, enter the FQDN address of the public interface of the DirectAccess server (in this example, ras.companyabc.com), and then click Next.
6. The wizard automatically selects the most common settings based on the analysis and the basic information given. Click the Click Here to Edit the Wizard Settings link to adjust the settings.
7. Click the Step1 Remote Clients Change Edit link.
8. Select the Domain Computers group and click Remove.
9. Click Add and locate the security group that was set up previously, the Remote Access Computers group.
10. Uncheck the Enable DirectAccess for Mobile Computers Only option. Rather than use the WMI filter, we'll be adding the computers to the security group.
11. Click Next and then Finish to save the Remote Client edits.
12. Click OK to save the edits.
13. Click Finish to apply the DirectAccess configuration. The DirectAccess server will be configured, and the Group Policy objects will be created.
14. Click Close to exit the wizard.

The console will be at the Remote Access Setup screen for the server, with a diagram of the Remote Access server configuration.

There will be two new Group Policy objects: one named DirectAccess Client Settings, and one named DirectAccess Server Settings. The DirectAccess Client Settings GPO has security filtering that applies it only to the DirectAccess clients in the DirectAccessClients security group (in this example, Remote Access Computers). The DirectAccess Server Settings GPO has security filtering that applies it only to the DirectAccess server by computer name

(RAS1$). The DirectAccess server (RAS1) and the DirectAccess clients (WS1) will need to be rebooted or have **gpupdate.exe /force** run to have their group policies applied.

NOTE

The Windows 2012 DirectAccess setup is very easy. Previously in Windows Server 2008 R2, setting up DirectAccess would have taken over 100 steps in 4 different consoles with a lot of data entry. In Windows Server 2012, it takes just 14 easy steps in a single console.

Testing DirectAccess

To test the DirectAccess functionality, the WS3 computer will be added to the Remote Access computer group. This applies the DirectAccess client group policy, DirectAccess Client Settings, to the members of the group.

To add WS1 to the DirectAccess client computers security group, complete the following steps:

1. On the DC1 domain controller, launch Server Manager.
2. Select Tools, Active Directory Users and Computers, the domain companyabc.com, and select the container Users.
3. Right-click the group Remote Access Computers and select Properties.
4. Select the Members tab, and then click the Add button.
5. In the Select Users, Contacts, Computers, or Groups dialog box, click Object Types, check Computers, and click OK.
6. Under Enter the Object Names to Select (Examples), type **WS1**, and click OK.
7. Click OK to save.
8. Restart the WS1 computer to have the changes take effect.

NOTE

The WS1 computer needs to reboot to add the computer group SID to its token.

The DirectAccess group policies will now be in effect on the WS1 computer.

You might need to run **gpupdate.exe/force** on the DirectAccess server DA1 to get the group policies to take effect on it.

As shown in the arrows in Figure 24.17, we will test (A) the connection to the internal network (intranet) and (B) the connection to the public network (Internet).

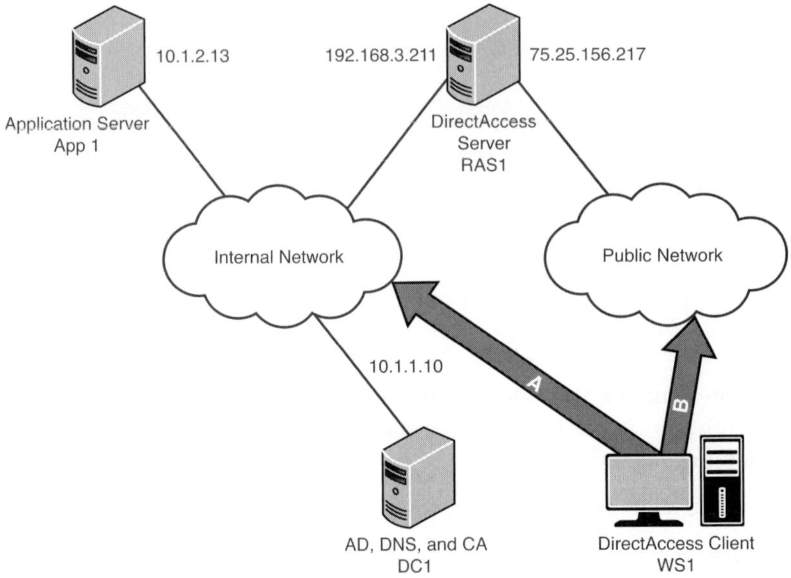

FIGURE 24.17 Testing client connection to networks.

For Test A, the connection to the internal network, follow these steps:

1. Connect the DirectAccess client WS1ipconfig to the internal network.
2. Select Start, type **cmd** and press Enter.
3. At the command prompt, type **ipconfig** and press Enter. Figure 24.18 shows that WS3 has been assigned an IPv4 address (10.1.2.19) on the internal network.

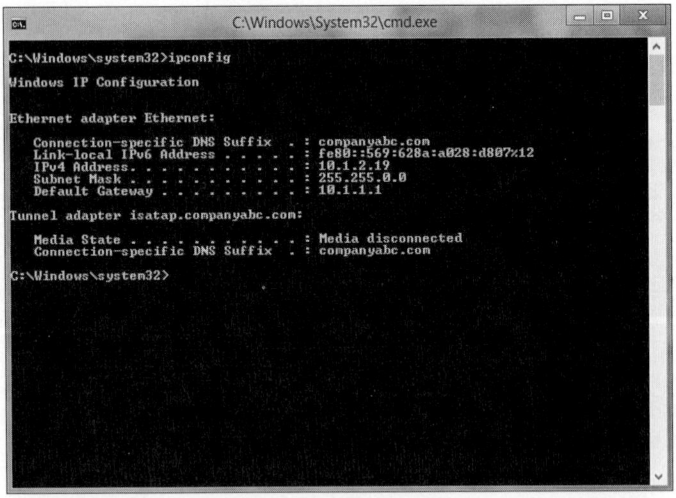

FIGURE 24.18 Test A: internal network.

4. Launch Explorer and access a share (\\APP1\DATA\) on the application server to demonstrate access.
5. Go to the Windows 8 charms bar by moving the cursor to the lower-right corner of the screen.
6. Select the Settings charm, which is the sprocket-shaped icon.
7. Select the Networks icon, which has the name of the current network.
8. In the Networks, there will be an inactive network named Workplace Connection, as shown in Figure 24.19. This is the DirectAccess connection, which is inactive because WS1 is connected to the intranet.

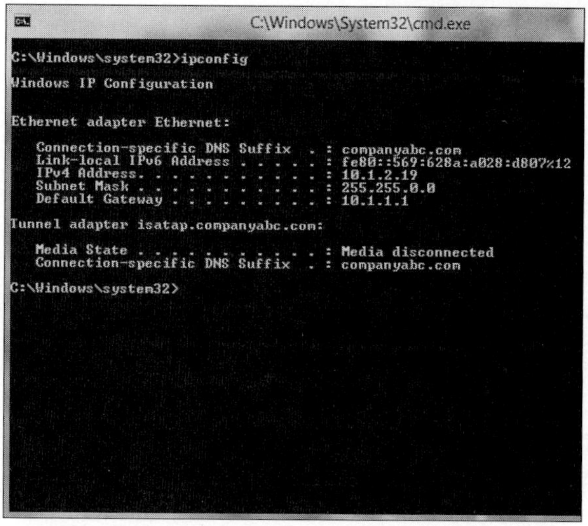

FIGURE 24.19 Inactive DirectAccess connection.

This demonstrates that WS1 is connected to the internal network and is able to access resources.

For Test B, which tests the connection to the public network, follow these steps:

1. Connect the DirectAccess client WS1 to the public network.
2. Select Start, type **cmd** and press Enter.
3. At the command prompt, type **ipconfig** and press Enter. Figure 24.20 shows that WS3 has been assigned an IPv4 address (192.168.2.126) and that an IP-HTTPS tunnel has been established automatically.
4. Launch Explorer and access a share (\\APP1\DATA\) on the application server to demonstrate access.

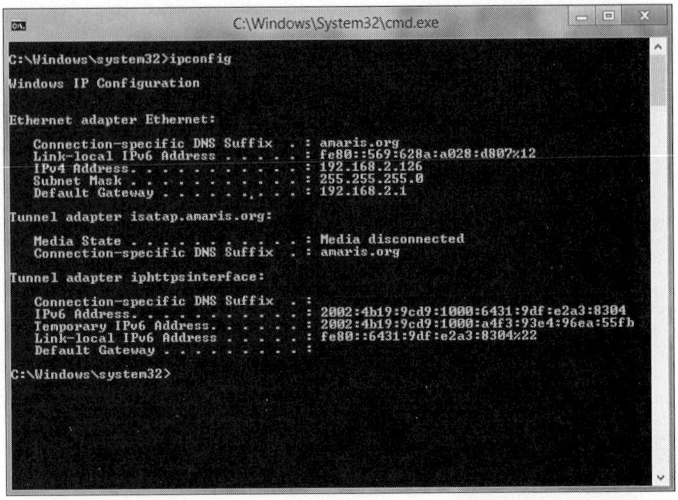

FIGURE 24.20 Test B: IP-HTTPS tunnel established.

5. Go to the Windows 8 charms bar by moving the cursor to the lower-right corner of the screen.
6. Select the Settings charm, which is the sprocket-shaped icon.
7. Select the Networks icon, which has the name of the current network.
8. In the Networks, there will now be an active network named Workplace Connection, as shown in Figure 24.21. This is the DirectAccess connection, which is now active since WS1 is connected to the Internet.

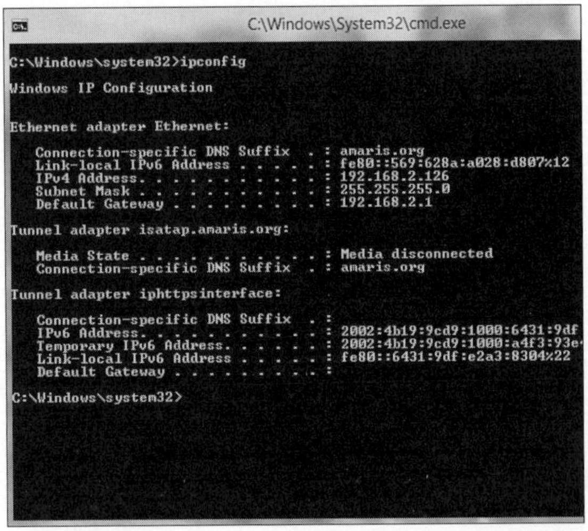

FIGURE 24.21 Test B: workplace connection connected.

This demonstrates that WS1 is connected to the public network and is able to access resources and that the IPv6 transitional technologies are working publicly, specifically IP-HTTPS.

In the course of the testing, no additional configuration was needed, no logon credentials needed to be supplied, and resources were transparently available. This is the seamless nature of DirectAccess, which completely hides the connection complexity from the end user.

VPN Scenario

The best way to illustrate the concepts in this chapter is to walk through a sample VPN scenario. The scenario demonstrates the following:

- The setup and testing of a VPN infrastructure
- Coexisting with the DirectAccess feature (set up in the previous section)
- Health checks and remediation of a client on and during connection

Figure 24.22 shows the VPN scenario architecture.

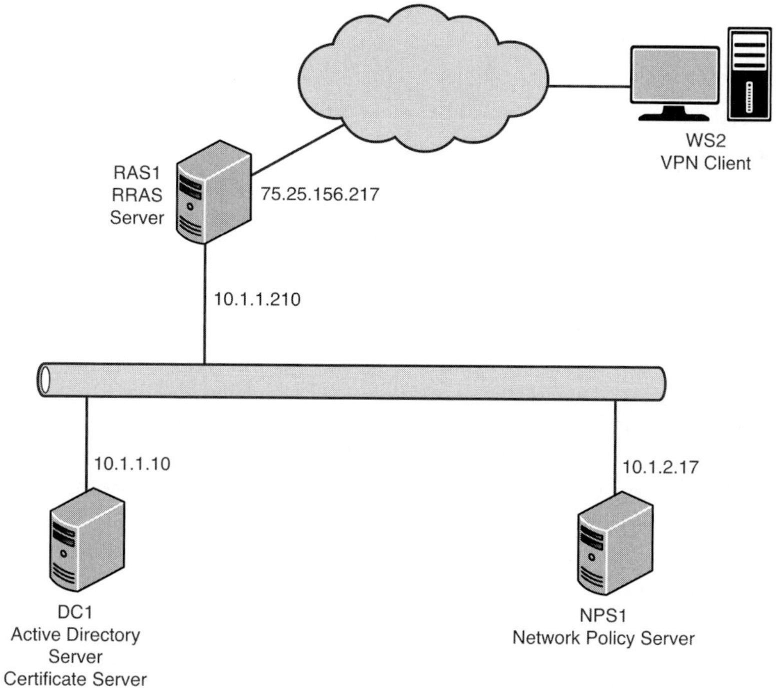

FIGURE 24.22 VPN scenario diagram.

The scenario will use the systems with the basic configuration shown in Table 24.5. These examples assume that an Active Directory domain companyabc.com has been created and that DC1 is the domain controller.

TABLE 24.5 VPN Scenario Servers

Server	Roles	Operating System	IP Address
DC1	Directory server Certificate server	Windows Server 2012	10.1.1.10
NPS1	Network Policy Server	Windows Server 2012	10.1.2.17
RAS1	RAS server	Windows Server 2012	10.1.1.210 (internal) 75.25.156.217 (external)
WS2	VPN client	Windows 7	

The steps to configure the VPN architecture are as follows:

- Configure the NPS.
- Set up the RAS.
- Set up the VPN client.
- Test the VPN connection.
- Control unhealthy VPN clients.

In Windows Server 2012 Active Directory, the users would need to be enabled on the Dial-In tab of the account properties. As you can see in Figure 24.23, the default option is Control Access Through NPS Network Policy.

We'll now step through the setup, configuration, and testing of a Windows Server 2012 traditional VPN infrastructure.

The following sections assume the Remote Access role has been installed and the Configuration Wizard run, configuring the RAS1 server to support both DirectAccess and VPN. The DirectAccess configuration has been completed and tested, so the following steps configure the VPN portion of the Remote Access role.

Certificate Auto-Enrollment

Configure the root CA so that computer certificates are issued automatically through a group policy using a GPO named Cert Auto Enrollment Group Policy Object. This assumes that a Windows Server 2012 Enterprise CA has been set up and configured. See Chapter 15 for details.

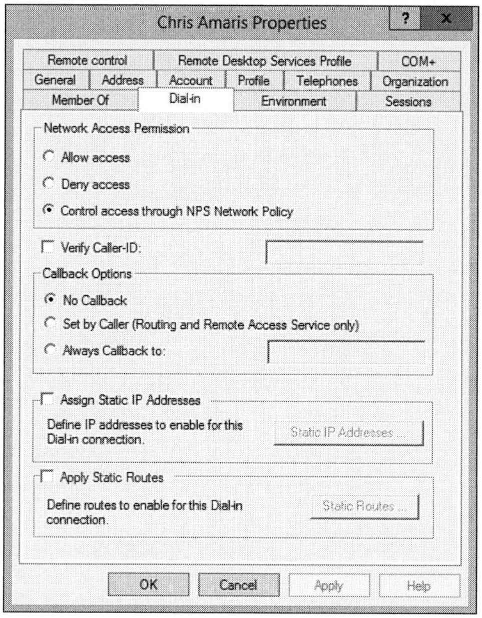

FIGURE 24.23 Dial-In tab in Windows Server 2012 Active Directory.

To configure the computer certificate auto-enrollment using the enterprise CA, follow these steps:

1. On the domain controller DC1, launch Server Manager.
2. Select Tools, Group Policy Management, and expand Forest: companyabc.com, Domains, and select companyabc.com.
3. In the console tree, right-click the domain companyabc.com and select Create a GPO in the Domain and Link It Here.
4. Enter the name **Cert Auto Enrollment Group Policy Object** and click OK.
5. Right-click the Cert Auto Enrollment Group Policy Object and select Edit.
6. In the console tree of the Group Policy Management Editor, open Computer Configuration, Policies, Windows Settings, Security Settings, and select Public Key Policies.
7. In the details pane, right-click Automatic Certificate Request Settings, point to New, and then click Automatic Certificate Request.
8. In the Automatic Certificate Request Wizard, click Next.
9. On the Certificate Template page, click Computer (shown in Figure 24.24), click Next, and then click Finish.

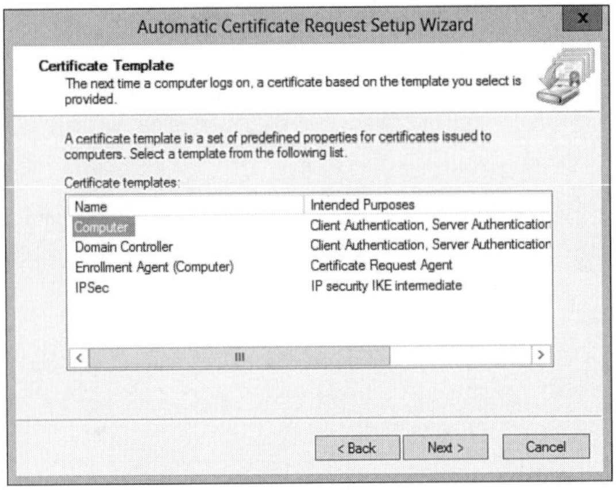

FIGURE 24.24 Certificate auto-enrollment.

10. Close the Group Policy Management Editor and Group Policy Management Console.

Now each computer that is a member of the domain will be enrolled automatically with a computer certificate.

NOTE

The certificate will be issued when the computer next reboots or can be trigger by running the command **gpupdate /force**.

Configuring the Network Policy Server

The next step is to configure the NPS with the appropriate policies to validate and enforce security. This assumes that a Windows Server 2012 NPS has been set up and configured. See Chapter 15 for details.

The process consists of the following elements:

- Health validators
- Health policy
- Network policy
- Connection request policies
- RADIUS client

Because of the interdependencies, they should be configured in the order presented. To set up the health validators in the NPS, follow these steps:

1. On the NPS system, select Start, Administrative Tools, Network Policy Server to launch the console.
2. Expand the Network Access Protection folder, and expand the System Health Validators folder.
3. Expand the Windows Security Health Validation folder and click Settings.
4. Right-click the default configuration and select Properties.
5. Uncheck all options except for the Firewall option. The configuration should look like the example shown in Figure 24.25.
6. Click OK.

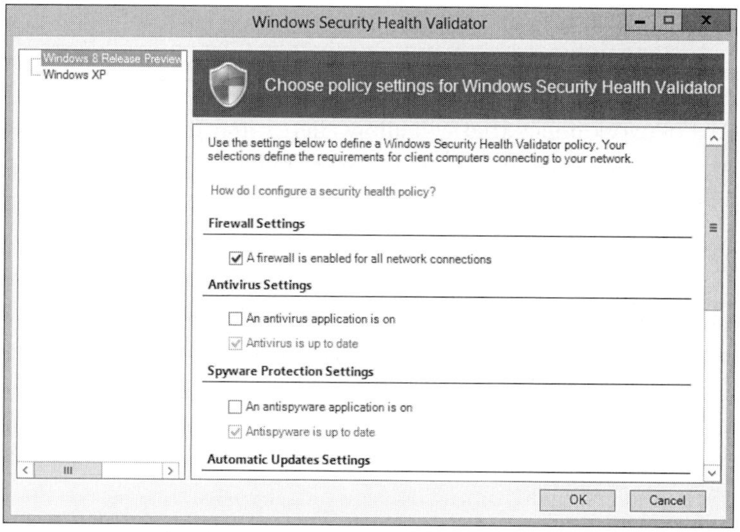

FIGURE 24.25 Validator configuration.

The validator properties are now configured and a health policy needs to be created to use the validator. To configure the health policy, complete the following steps:

1. In the Network Policy Server console, expand the Policies folder and select the Health Policies folder.
2. Select Action, New to create a new health policy.
3. Enter **Pass** for the policy name.
4. Under Client SHV Checks, ensure that the Client Passes All SHV Checks is selected.
5. Select the Windows Security Health Validator in the SHVs Used in This Health Policy window.

6. Click OK to save the health policy.
7. Select Action, New to create a new health policy.
8. Enter **Fail** for the policy name.
9. Under Client SHV Checks, ensure that the Client Fails One or More SHV Checks option is selected.
10. Select Windows Security Health Validator in the SHVs Used in This Health Policy window.
11. Click OK to save the health policy.

Now the conditions (that is, that the firewall is enabled) for the health of a connecting system are established. Now the network policies for systems that pass or fail the health validation need to be created. These policies are separate, so there will be one policy for passing and one policy for failing.

The first part is to configure a network policy that will allow clients that pass the health validation to connect to the network. To configure the network policy for passing health validation, execute the following steps:

1. In the Network Policy Server console, expand the Policies folder, and select the Network Policies folder.
2. Disable the two default policies in the middle pane by selecting each one and then selecting Action, Disable. They should both show as grayed out when this is done.
3. Select Action, New to create a new network policy.
4. Enter **Pass Allow Access** for the policy name.
5. Select Remote Access Server (VPN Dial-Up) for the type of network access server.
6. Click Next.
7. Click the Add button to specify conditions.
8. Select Health Policies and click the Add button.
9. Select the previously created Pass health policy from the drop-down list, and click OK.
10. Click Next.
11. Leave the default Access Granted option, and click Next.
12. Leave the default authentication methods, and click Next.
13. Leave the default constraints, and click Next.
14. In the Configure Settings options, select NAP Enforcement.

15. Leave the default Allow Full Network Access, which will allow the clients that pass the health validation to connect, and click Next.
16. Click Finish to complete the network policy.

The next task is to configure a network policy for those clients that fail the health validation. To configure the network policy for failing health validation, execute the following steps:

1. With the Network Policies folder highlighted, select Action, New to create a new network policy.
2. Enter **Fail Limit Access** for the policy name.
3. Select Remote Access Server (VPN Dial-Up) for the type of network access server.
4. Click Next.
5. Click the Add button to specify conditions.
6. Select Health Policies and click the Add button.
7. Select the previously created Fail Health Policy from the drop-down list, and click OK.
8. Click Next.
9. Leave the default Access Granted option, and click Next. It might be counterintuitive to grant access, but we will be configuring the policy to remediate the condition rather than deny access outright.
10. Leave the default authentication methods, and click Next.
11. Leave the default constraints, and click Next.
12. In the Configure Settings options, select NAP Enforcement.
13. Select Allow Limited Access, which will limit the clients that fail the health validation.
14. Ensure that the default Auto-Remediation option is set to Enable Auto-Remediation of Client Computers.
15. Click the IP Filters option in the Settings window.
16. Click the Input Filters button in the IPv4 window.
17. Click New to add a filter for the domain controller DC1, which is 10.1.1.10 in this example.
18. Check the Destination Network check box, and enter the IP address for the domain controller (**10.1.1.10**) and a subnet mask of **255.255.255.255**.

NOTE

The subnet mask of 255.255.255.255 restricts the access to a single IP address. If a range of IP addresses were needed—for example, a class C subnet (192.168.99.x) that the quarantined client could access—then an address such as 192.168.99.0 and a subnet mask of 255.255.255.0 could be used to permit the clients to access the entire IP address range.

19. Click OK to close the window.
20. Select Permit Only the Packets Listed Below, and click OK.
21. Click the Outbound Filters button in the IPv4 window.
22. Click New to add a filter for the domain controller DC1.
23. Check the Source Network check box, and enter the IP address for the domain controller (**172.16.1.100**) and a subnet mask of **255.255.255.255**.
24. Click OK to close the window.
25. Select Permit Only the Packets Listed Below, and click OK.
26. Click Next.
27. Click Finish to complete the network policy.

Now that the health and network policies have been configured, the next step is to configure the connection request policy. To configure the connection policy, follow these steps:

1. In the Network Policy Server console, expand the Policies folder, and select the Connection Request Policies folder.
2. Highlight the Use Windows Authentication for All Users policy, and select Action, Disable.
3. Select Action, New to create a new connection request policy.
4. Enter **RAS connections** for the policy name.
5. Select Remote Access Server (VPN Dial-Up) for the type of network access server, and click Next.
6. In the Specify Conditions window, click the Add button to create a new condition.
7. Select Client IPv4 Address and click the Add button.
8. Enter the IP address of the RADIUS client, which is the VPN server RAS1 in this example (**10.1.1.210**), and click OK.
9. Click Next.
10. Leave the default Authenticate Requests on This Server, and click Next.

11. In the Specify Authentication Methods window, check the Override Network Policy Authentication Settings check box.
12. Click the Add button in the EAP Types window.
13. Select Microsoft: Protected EAP (PEAP), and click OK.
14. Click the Add button again in the EAP Types window.
15. Select Microsoft: Secured Password (EAP-MS-CHAP v2), and click OK.
16. Select Microsoft: Protected EAP (PEAP) in the EAP Types window, and click Edit.
17. Verify that the certificate requested earlier in the section is selected based on the FQDN in the friendly name.
18. Click OK to close the window. Click Next.
19. Click Next at the Configure Settings window.
20. Verify settings to ensure that they look similar to Figure 24.26.
21. Click Finish to create the connection request policy.

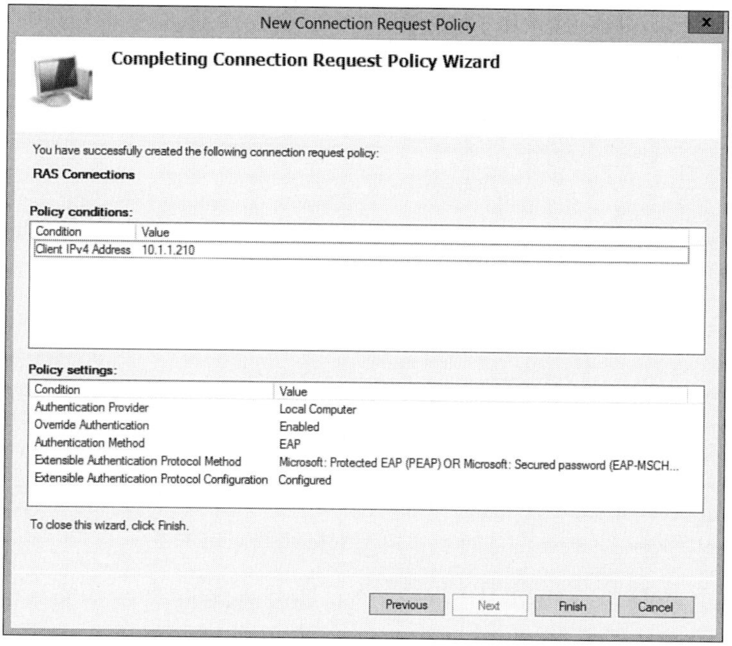

FIGURE 24.26 PEAP properties.

The next step is to configure the RAS server as a RADIUS client on the NPS system. This requires using a shared secret password, which in this example is Secret Password. To configure the RADIUS client, complete the following steps:

1. In the Network Policy Server MMC on NPS1, expand the RADIUS Clients and Servers folder.
2. Select the RADIUS Clients folder and select Action, New RADIUS Client.
3. Enter the friendly name for the client (in this example, **RAS1**).
4. Enter the FQDN or IP address for the client (in this example, **10.1.1.210**).
5. In the Shared Secret text box, enter the secret password **Secret Password**.
6. In the Confirm Shared Secret text box, enter the secret password again, as shown in Figure 24.27.

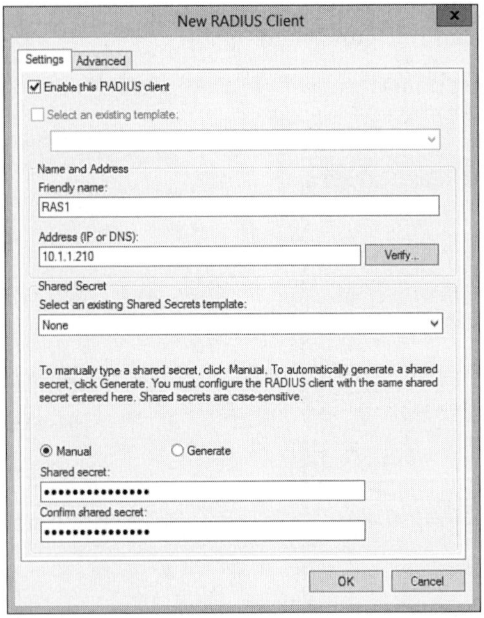

FIGURE 24.27 RADIUS client configuration.

7. Select the Advanced tab and check the RADIUS Client Is NAP-Capable check box.
8. Click OK to create the RADIUS client.

The Network Policy Server configuration is now complete on NPS1. The next step is to create the RAS server.

Setting Up the RAS Server

The RAS server is the entity that will actually connect to the Internet or DMZ, providing the direct communications with the VPN clients, although the NPS system will be authenticating and authorizing those connections.

The following steps assume that Windows Server 2012 is already installed, that the RAS1 server is configured with an internal network interface card (NIC; 10.1.1.210) and an external NIC (75.25.156.217), and that the server is a member of the companyabc.com Active Directory domain. In addition, the Remote Access role has been installed and the Configuration Wizard run, configuring the RAS1 server to support both DirectAccess and VPN.

The DirectAccess configuration has been completed and tested, so the following steps configure the VPN portion of the Remote Access role.

To configure the VPN, follow these steps:

1. On the Remote Access server (RAS1), launch Server Manager and select Tools, Remote Access Management.
2. Select the CONFIGURATION section, which will show a diagram of the configuration.
3. In the Step 2 - Remote Access Server portion of the diagram, click the Edit link.
4. Select the VPN Configuration section.
5. Select the Authentication tab.
6. Check the Use RADIUS Authentication option.
7. In the RADIUS servers box, right-click the first line and click New.
8. Enter the name of the Network Policy Server configured earlier (**NPS1.companyabc.com**) in the Server Name field.
9. Click the Change button to change the Shared Secret.
10. In the New Secret and Confirm Secret text boxes, enter the secret password **Secret Password**. This was set earlier in the RADIUS client setup.
11. Click OK to save the shared secret.
12. Click OK to save the new RADIUS server configuration.
13. Click Finish to save the VPN settings.
14. In the bottom of the diagram, click Finish to update the Remote Access server with the changed settings.
15. After reviewing the changes, click Apply to apply the changes.
16. Click Close to exit the wizard.

The RAS server is now configured and ready to accept VPN client connections.

Setting Up the VPN Client

The next step is to set up the VPN client. For this example, the client will be a Windows 7 system named WS2 that is a member of the companyabc.com domain. The four major tasks in this process are as follows:

- Enable Security Center
- Enable the system health agent (SHA)
- Configure certificate trusts
- Configure the VPN client

These tasks prepare the client to connect and also validate, enforce, and remediate health policies.

If the client is a domain member, the Security Center will be disabled. This can be enabled in the local security policy by executing the following steps:

1. On the VPN Client computer, select Start, Run.
2. Enter **gpedit.msc** and click OK.
3. Expand Local Computer, Computer Configuration, Administrative Templates, Windows Components, and select Security Center.
4. Double-click on Turn on Security Center (Domain PCs Only).
5. Select Enabled and click OK.
6. Close the Group Policy Edit tool.

The Remote Access Quarantine Enforcement Client is normally disabled, so it will need to be enabled on the client. This is done with the NAP Client Configuration MMC (napclcfg.msc), as follows:

1. On the client, select Start, Run.
2. Enter **napclcfg.msc** and click OK.
3. Select the Enforcement Clients folder.
4. Select the EAP Quarantine Enforcement Client.
5. Select Action, Enable to enable the client.
6. Exit the NAP Client Configuration MMC.

The Network Access Protection Agent service is normally set to Manual, so it will need to be started and set to start automatically by executing the following steps:

1. On the client, select Start, Run and then enter **Services.msc**.
2. Highlight the Network Access Protection Agent service, and select Action, Properties.

3. Change the Startup Type to Automatic, and click Start.
4. Click OK to exit the service properties.

The next task is to set up and configure the VPN connection on the VPN client:

1. On the client, select Start, Control Panel.
2. Click Network and Internet.
3. Click Network and Sharing Center.
4. Click Set Up a New Connection or Network.
5. Select Connect to a Workplace, and click Next.
6. Click Use My Internet Connection (VPN).
7. Enter the Internet address (in this case, **75.25.156.217**).
8. Enter a destination name, such as **Company ABC VPN Connection**.
9. Check the Don't Connect Now check box, as we will need to configure additional settings.
10. Click Next.
11. Enter the username, the password, and the domain, and check the Remember This Password check box.
12. Click Create to create the connection.
13. Click Close.
14. Click Change Adapter Settings.
15. Right-click on the Company ABC VPN Connection, and select Properties.
16. Select the Security tab.
17. In the Authentication section, select the Use Extensible Authentication Protocol (EAP) option button.
18. Select Protected EAP (PEAP) (Encryption Enabled) from the drop-down list, and click the Properties button.
19. Uncheck the Connect to These Servers check box.
20. Check the box next to the previously imported CA certificate in the Trusted Root Certification window (in this example, companyabc-DC1-CA).
21. Verify that Secured Password (EAP-MS-CHAP v2) is selected in the Select Authentication Method drop-down list.
22. Uncheck the Enable Fast Reconnect check box.

23. Check the Enforce Network Access Protection check box. The result should look like Figure 24.28.

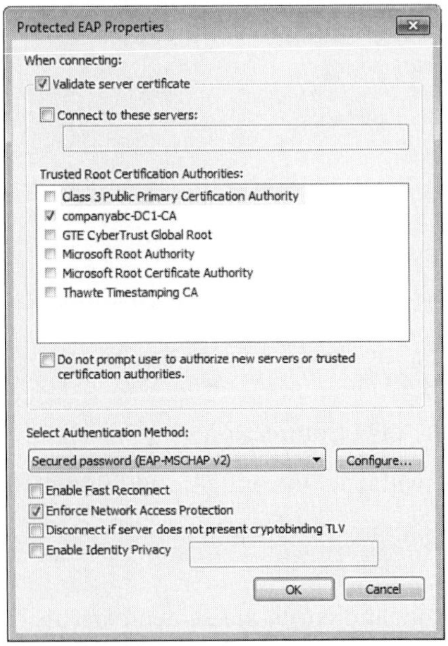

FIGURE 24.28 VPN connection security options.

24. Click OK to close the Protected EAP Properties dialog box.

25. Click OK to close the connection properties.

The connection is now ready for use. The next step is to test the connection.

Testing the VPN Connection

The next step in the working with a VPN connection is to test the configuration to make sure the system can properly VPN into the network. To test the VPN connection, do the following:

1. On the client, right-click on the Company ABC VPN Connection, and select Connect.
2. Click the Connect button.
3. Click OK to accept the credentials. The connection will be established.

The connection can be tested by pinging the domain controller dc1.companyabc.com. Because the system passed the health validation checks, the connection is granted full access to all intranet resources. To test the connection, complete the following steps:

1. With the Company ABC VPN Connection connected, select Start, All Programs, Accessories, and click on Command Prompt.
2. Enter **ping dc1.companyabc.com** and press Enter.
3. You should get a reply from the IP address of DC1.
4. Select Start, Connect To and choose to open the Connections window.
5. Select the Company ABS VPN Connection, and click Disconnect.
6. Click Close.

The NPS system presents a wealth of information on the connection that was sorely lacking in previous versions of Windows. With Windows Server 2012, troubleshooting traditional VPN connection issues is a straightforward endeavor.

Controlling Unhealthy VPN Clients

The previous example had everything going smoothly with no health issues. However, if the client had failed the health validation checks, the failing items will be remediated. The health validation check that was configured was to check for Windows Firewall being enabled. To test the health remediation capabilities, we'll turn off the Windows Firewall and then connect again:

1. On the VPN client, select Start, Control Panel.
2. Click on System and Security.
3. Click on Windows Firewall.
4. Click on Turn Windows Firewall On OR Off.
5. Select the Off (Not Recommended) option button, and click OK.

The client is now in an unhealthy state, as defined by the health policy. Let's see what happens when the client connects to the VPN by executing the following steps:

1. On the client, select Start, Connect To, and then choose to open the Connections window.
2. Right-click on the Company ABC VPN Connection, and select Connect.
3. Click the Connect button.
4. Click OK to accept the credentials.
5. The client firewall will be enabled by the NAP client and then connected to the VPN.

The NAP client continues enforcing the health policy even after the initial connection. You can test this by leaving the connection active and then turning off the Windows Firewall:

1. On the VPN client, select Start, Control Panel.
2. Click on Security.
3. Click on Windows Firewall.
4. Click on Change Settings.
5. Select the Off (Not Recommended) option button, and click OK.

The Windows Firewall will be off briefly and then be turned back on. Just like magic, the EAP agent will fix the problem to ensure that the client stays compliant with the health policy even after the initial connection.

If the client should fall out of compliance with the health policy in such a way as to be irremediable, the connection will drop to a reduced connectivity state as defined by the health policies. For example, if an intrepid user disables the Windows Firewall, the EAP agent will detect that condition and take the appropriate action. The following example illustrates this:

1. On the client, connect to the Company ABC VPN Connection.
2. Select Start, Run.
3. Enter **services.msc** and click OK.
4. Select the Windows Firewall service in the list of services.
5. Select Action, Properties.
6. Change the startup type to Disabled, and click OK.
7. Select Action, Stop to stop the Windows Firewall.

The connection icon will change to show a yellow warning triangle with an exclamation point to indicate limited connectivity. As shown in Figure 24.29, the Action Center shows that the computer does not meet the security standards and network access is limited.

Thus, even if the remediation steps fail, the internal network is protected from noncompliant systems. Even better, when the client returns to compliance, the EAP agent detects that and reestablishes full connectivity. To illustrate that, complete the following steps:

1. Select the Windows Firewall service in the list of services.
2. Select Action, Properties.
3. Change the startup type to Automatic, and click OK.
4. Close the Services MMC.

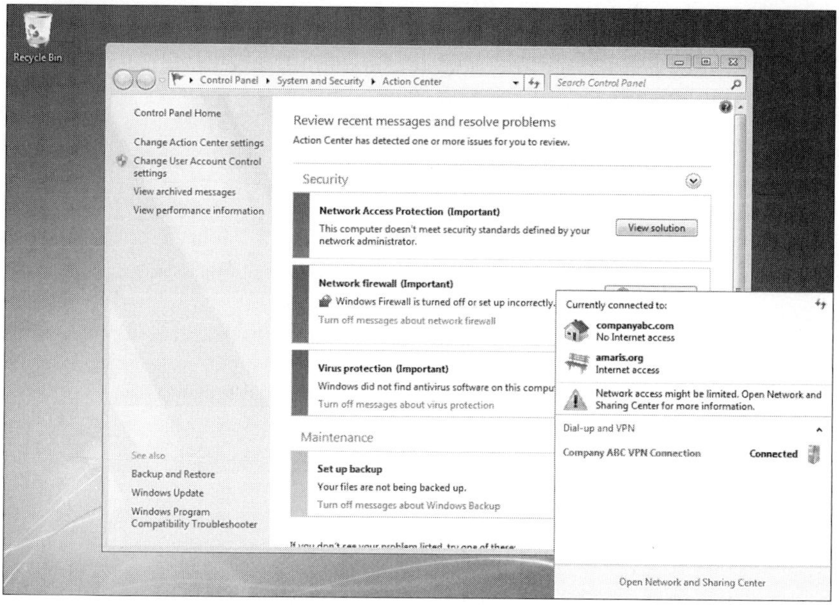

FIGURE 24.29 Failed compliance.

5. In the Network and Sharing Center, click the View Status link in the warning message. A message will appear, indicating that remediation had previously failed, as shown in Figure 24.30.

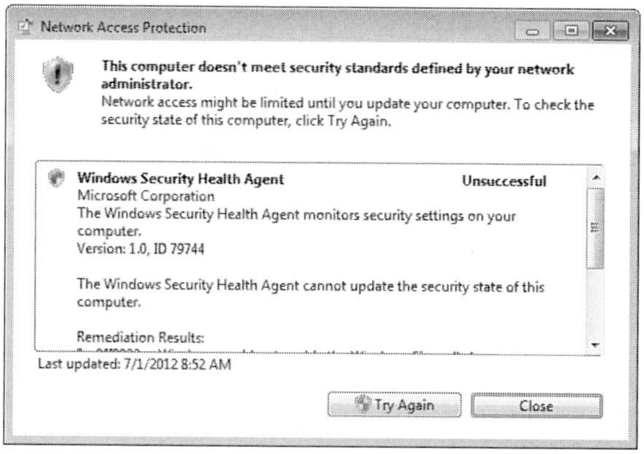

FIGURE 24.30 Network Access Protection remediation message.

6. Click on the Try Again button to attempt the remediation.
7. The NAP agent will restart the service and update the compliance of the client, showing a message similar to the one shown in Figure 24.31.
8. Click Close to close the NAP agent window.

FIGURE 24.31 Successful compliance message.

The NPS and NAP combination is a very powerful tool for ensuring the health of the systems that are connecting to the VPN infrastructure.

Monitoring the Remote Access Server

The Remote Access Management Console includes excellent tools to monitor the activity of the remote clients, including both DirectAccess and traditional VPN remote clients. The console has been completely redesigned to provide administrators with better insight on the overall health of the remote access services, how clients are connecting, and what those clients are doing.

The console has 5 sections: 4 for management (Dashboard, Operations Status, Remote Client Status, and Reporting) and 1 for configuration (aptly named Configuration).

Dashboard

The Dashboard view in the Remote Access Management Console shows a summary of the remote access server. The view shows the:

- **Operations Status**—The operational state of the Remote Access role, the state of the services it is supporting (DirectAccess and VPN), and the state of their subcomponents.
- **Configuration Status**—This is the last time the configuration was updated.

- **Remote Client Status**—These are very useful summary statistics like total active clients, total cumulative connections, maximum number of clients, and total transferred data. The statistics are reset whenever the server is restarted.

An example Remote Access Dashboard is shown in Figure 24.32.

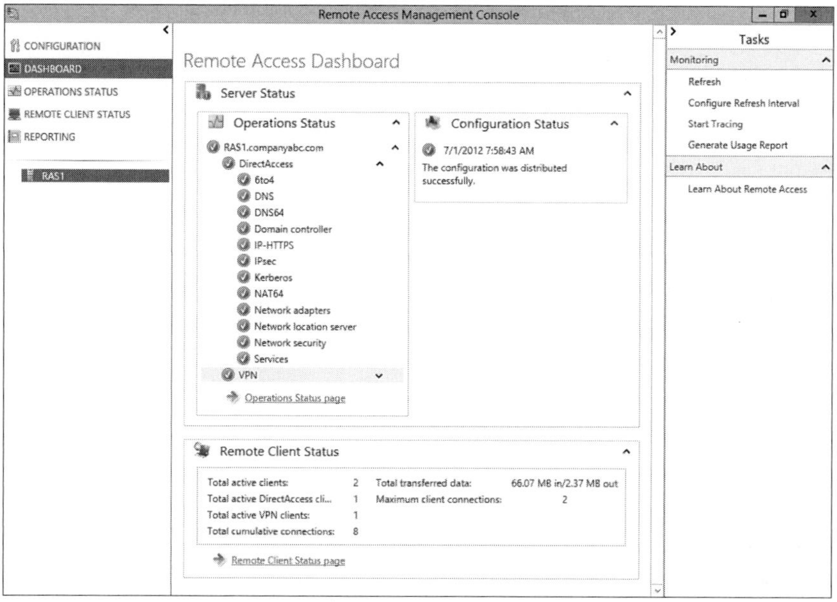

FIGURE 24.32 Remote Access Dashboard View.

There is also a task to generate a usage report. This functionality requires some configuration and will be discussed in the Reporting section.

From the dashboard, tracing can be started to capture packets for analysis. The tracing logs are stored in C:\Windows\DirectAccess\RemoteAccessLog.etl. The Enterprise Tracing for Windows (ETW) is a framework for implementing tracing providers, which output files with the extension ETL. These are not natively readable and need to be converted with a utility such as the Log Parser 2.2 (http://www.microsoft.com/en-us/download/details.aspx?id=24659) from Microsoft.

Operations Status

The Operations Status view in the Remote Access Management Console shows a more state and detailed status for each remote access server, services on the server, and the components for each service.

Each component can be selected to give a detailed status and analysis. For example, Figure 24.33 shows the Network Adapter in a critical state with the details indicating possible causes and resolutions. In this case, simply a disconnected adapter is the cause.

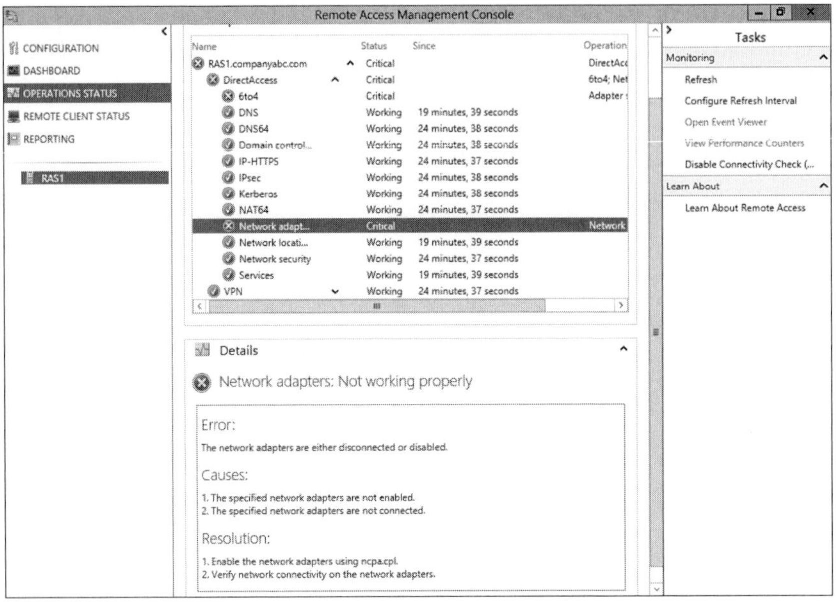

FIGURE 24.33 Remote Access Dashboard View with Critical State Details.

Remote Client Status

The Remote Client Status view shows a detailed view of the connected clients. This includes the user name, machine name (for DirectAccess), ISP address, the connection protocol (for VPN) or tunneling protocol (for DirectAccess), and the duration of the connection.

For the selected client, there are two details panes in the bottom of the view. The Access Details pane shows the most recent packets with the protocol, port and destination IP address. The Connection Details pane shows the details for the client connections including the connection type (VPN or DirectAccess), total bytes in and out, the connection start time, and the authentication method.

An example Remote Client Status view is shown in Figure 24.34.

These details are very useful for seeing real-time what the traffic and connections are going through the Remote Access server. There is even a task to Disconnect VPN Clients, which as the name implies, only works for disconnecting VPN client connections. DirectAccess connections cannot be disconnected in this way,

Reporting

The final view is the Reporting view or Remote Access Reporting. However, this view requires some configuration before being used. Specifically, Inbox Accounting must be configured to be able to view reports.

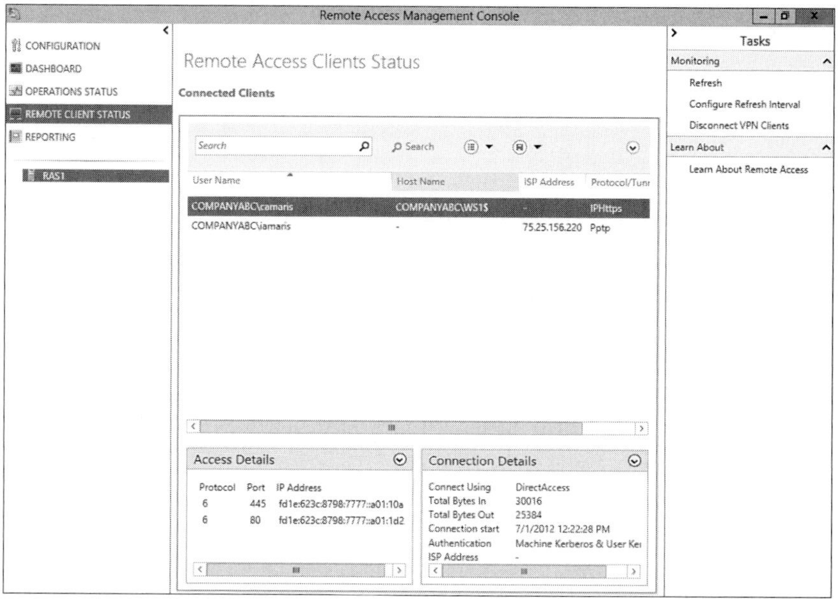

FIGURE 24.34 Remote Client Status View.

To configure Inbox Accounting, follow these steps:

1. On the Remote Access server (RAS1), launch Server Manager and select Tools, Remote Access Management.
2. Select the REPORTING section, which will show a warning "Inbox accounting must be configured before reporting can be used."
3. Click the Configure Accounting link.
4. Check the Use Inbox Accounting box.
5. Click the Apply button. The DirectAccess Server Settings GPO will be modified and applied to the Remote Access server.
6. Click Close to exist the wizard.

The server will now begin to gather data.

The reporting feature will allow administrators to review statistics for specific periods of time, rather than just relying on statistics as of the last restart of the server. The reports are also searchable, allowing administrators to do some forensic analysis of clients and activities.

An example Remote Access Reporting view is shown in Figure 24.35. The highlighted entry shows that the user accessed the website of the target system over port 80 on 7/1/2012 after being connected for 7 minutes and 45 seconds.

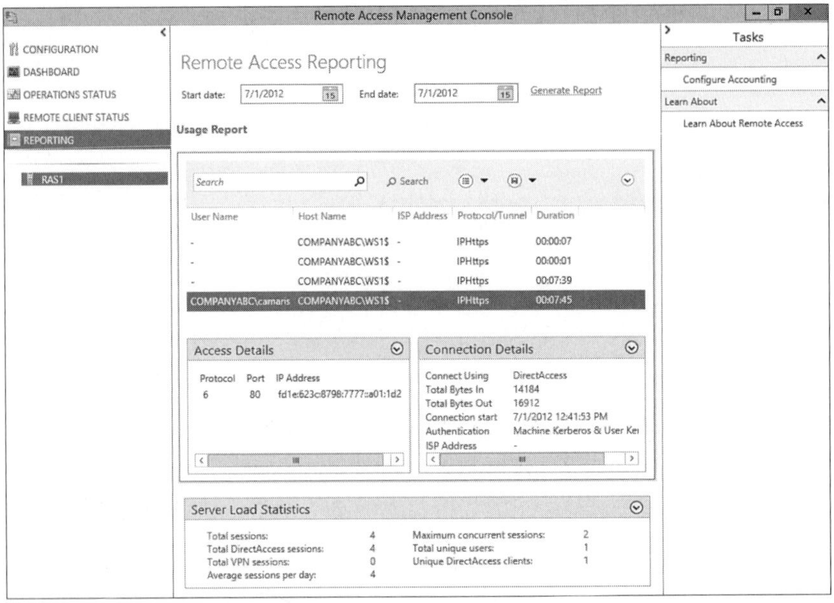

FIGURE 24.35 Remote Access Reporting View.

Summary

Remote and mobile connectivity has increased over the years because the extended office now includes hotels, airports, client sites, other campus buildings, and even wireless coffee shop users. With the expansion of the network from which users need to connect to a Windows Server 2012 environment, the improvement of security, reliability, compatibility, and performance becomes extremely important for an organization. The Windows Server 2012 Remote Access technologies meet the needs of these increasingly mobile and remote users.

Windows Server 2012 DirectAccess is a compelling solution for enterprises with extensive infrastructure already in place, allowing seamless and transparent access to corporate resources while users are in the field. Windows Server 2012 still contains all the legacy VPN technologies from the previous version of Windows.

These new technologies allow the Windows Server 2012 Remote Access role to extend further with increased security and reliability, while making the end user experience painless.

Best Practices

The following are best practices from this chapter:

- Use DirectAccess to provide remote users a simpler no-touch method of securely connecting back to the office.
- Use the Network Policy Server to validate and remediate the health of clients.
- Use certificates for authentication where possible.
- For increased security, choose DirectAccess, SSTP, or L2TP with IPsec as the VPN protocol.
- Use PEAP as the preferred authentication protocol.
- Use the more secure MS-CHAP v2 if password authentication must be used.
- Use the Remote Access Management Console to troubleshoot and monitor remote access clients.

CHAPTER 25

Remote Desktop Services

IN THIS CHAPTER

Remote Desktop Services (RDS, previously named Terminal Services) is a component of Microsoft Windows (server and client operating systems) that enables users to remotely run applications or manage a server from any machine that has the Remote Desktop Connection (RDC) client and network access. In a Remote Desktop Services session, whether a client requires a complete Remote Desktop environment or just needs to run a single application, the Remote Desktop Session Host uses its hardware resources to perform all the application processing. In a basic Remote Desktop Services session, the client sends out only keyboard and mouse signals and receives screen images, which requires only a small amount of bandwidth on the network. For a more robust session that might need access to local resources, Remote Desktop Services can provide audio, local printer, COM port, local disk, and plug-and-play device redirection (for media players and digital cameras) to provide ease of data transfer between the client and server through a single network port. RDS also provides local time zone redirection, which allows users to view time stamps of email and files relative to their location. Lastly, RDS can also support high-resolution desktop computers (up to 4096 x 2048) and spanning multiple monitors horizontally to form a single, large desktop, and using the Client Experience feature, users can be given an RDS desktop experience that feels and looks like Windows 8.

RDS was first introduced in Windows NT 4.0 Terminal Server Edition. Through subsequent versions of Windows, both RDS and its subject protocol Remote Desktop Protocol (RDP) have been significantly improved. With the latest release of RDS in Windows Server 2012, the focus of this update includes key enhancements, such as the following:

- True concept of a "session collection" from deployment through ongoing administration and management focused on simplifying the RDS "farm" of servers
- Significant improvements in user profile management and RemoteApp program management
- Automation and simplification of image management and user personalization in Microsoft's Virtual Desktop Infrastructure (VDI) offerings
- Further improvements in rich user experience for graphics and full-motion video leveraging RemoteFX technologies first introduced in Windows 2008 R2 SP1

This chapter reviews features and discusses how to plan, implement, and support a Windows Server 2012 RDS deployment. The chapter addresses not only the new features added in Windows Server 2012, but also how these new technologies can be leveraged to improve remote-access services by users and by network administrators.

Why Implement Remote Desktop Services?

RDS is a versatile product that can be implemented to meet many different business needs. In some cases, it is implemented to enable administrators to remotely administer a server, group of servers, or applications. RDS can also be used to allow users access to applications and network resources through a terminal session. Or, RDS can be implemented by a cloud service provider to create managed application services, eliminating the need for its customers to buy server hardware, software, and support.

Regardless of the reason why RDS is implemented, there are several benefits to implementing it:

- **Centralized deployment of applications**—By deploying applications using RDS, those applications reside only on RDS and can be centrally managed. In addition, deploying applications in this manner allows them to be rapidly deployed and updated.
- **Remote access to applications**—RDS allows users to access applications within a local network and remotely. Connections can even be made to applications in bandwidth-constrained connections, such as dial-up or shared wide-area network (WAN) links, and over Hypertext Transfer Protocol Secure (HTTPS).
- **Windows Anywhere**—RDS allows users to access feature-rich Windows applications from many different devices. These devices can include underpowered hardware, non-Windows desktops, thin clients (terminals), and even mobile devices.
- **Virtual desktops**—Using RDS in conjunction with Remote Desktop Virtualization, users can be allocated their own personal virtual desktop or given access to a virtual desktop instance within a virtual desktop pool.

NOTE

Windows XP, Windows Vista, Windows 7, Windows 8, Apple Macs, and other systems that support the Remote Desktop Client (RDC) can be enabled and used for remote system access.

Remote Desktop for Administration

As a remote administration tool, RDS gives an administrator the option of performing server administration from a server console or from any other server or workstation using the RDC client (previously known as the Terminal Services Client). Remote Desktop is installed by default, but is not automatically enabled. Using Remote Desktop can simplify server administration for an IT department by allowing personnel to do their jobs from almost any console on the network. This can improve IT response times to complete trouble tickets concerning access to network resources or user account management. Server maintenance tasks such as reviewing logs or gathering server performance data can be accomplished through the client. Applications and updates can be installed through a Remote Desktop session.

Remote Desktop for Users

There are many benefits of making Remote Desktop available to users. For example, company hardware costs can be reduced, application availability and licensing management can be simplified, and network performance can increase.

Because a Remote Desktop session is really a remote session running on the Remote Desktop Server Session Host system, all Remote Desktop users run applications on a Windows server, utilizing the processing power of the server while reducing the load on the local workstation. This can extend the life of an underpowered machine whose deficient resources might impede workflow through high processor, memory, or disk utilization.

From a desktop support perspective, a Remote Desktop Session Host can be put in place and used as a secondary means of providing users access to their applications if problems are encountered with the applications on their local workstations. Although this approach might seem to be overkill, providing a secondary means of application access can be vital to user productivity and company revenue when support personnel might not be readily available to fix end-user application issues.

Providing centralized applications for users though RDS can also simplify application management by reducing the number of machines on which application upgrades, security updates, and fixes need to be installed. Because all the applications run on the Remote Desktop Session Host, only the server itself needs to be updated, and the entire user base benefits from the change immediately. This way, the updates can be performed for all Remote Desktop Session Host users at one time.

Remote Desktop for Remote User Support

Remote Desktop can be used to provide application support for end users within a Remote Desktop session. When users are running in a Remote Desktop session, an administrator can configure remote control or shadowing functionality to view or completely interact with a user's session. This feature can be used to train users, provide application support, or create configuration changes, such as installing a printer or connecting to a network file share. This capability can greatly reduce the number of administrators needed during the regular workday because multiple users can be assisted from one location.

NOTE

To comply with many organizations' security and privacy policies, RDS provides an option for the remote control function to be completely disabled. Alternatively, rather than completely disabling the function for all users, RDS can be configured enable users to choose whether to allow an administrator to interact with their Remote Desktop session.

Remote Desktop for Cloud Service Providers

Installing the RDS Role Service allows applications and services to be made available to users in any location. Companies that provide services to businesses through proprietary applications can standardize and provide their applications exclusively through RDS and gain all the benefits outlined in the preceding sections. An added bonus for these companies is that RDS reduces the need to send application media out to each client, and end-user support can be provided in a way never before possible.

Cloud service providers that make several applications available to clients can use RDS to service hundreds or thousands of users from different organizations while charging a fee for application usage or terminal session time usage.

How Remote Desktop Works

Remote Desktop allows users to connect to a remote machine and access applications or an entire desktop. To establish their client/server session, users utilize the RDC client. The RDC client, in turn, uses a multichannel protocol called the Remote Desktop Protocol (RDP), which is an extension of the ITU T.120 family of protocols. By default, RDP-based connections are made over TCP 3389, or if Remote Desktop Gateway is used, the connections are made over TCP 443 (HTTPS).

When a user uses RDP, client mouse and keyboard events are redirected from the client to the remote machine. On the remote machine, RDP uses its own onscreen keyboard and mouse driver to receive these keyboard and mouse events from RDC clients. Then to render a user's actions, RDP uses its own video driver. Using this video driver, RDP constructs the display output into network packets, which are then redirected back to the RDC client. On the client, the rendering data is received and translated into corresponding Microsoft Win32 graphics device interface (GDI) application programming interface (API) calls.

Because RDP is multiple-channel capable, separate virtual channels are used for carrying device communication, presentation data, and encrypted client mouse and keyboard data between the RDC client and a remote machine. RDP's virtual channel base is extensible and supports up to 64,000 separate channels for data transmissions or multipoint transmissions.

NOTE

Using a multipoint transmission data from an application can be sent to multiple clients in real time without sending the same data to each session individually (for example, virtual whiteboards).

Modes of Operation

Remote Desktop can be run in two different modes of operation. The first mode is called the Remote Desktop for Administration, and the other is called Remote Desktop Services.

Remote Desktop for Administration

Remote Desktop for Administration is included and installed with the Windows Server 2012 operating system and only needs to be enabled. This eases automated and unattended server deployment by allowing an administrator to deploy servers that can be managed remotely after the operating system has completed installation. This mode can also be used to manage a headless server or a virtual guest session on a host virtual server, which reduces the amount of space needed in any server rack. More space can be dedicated to servers instead of switch boxes, monitors, keyboards, and mouse devices.

The Remote Desktop for Administration limits the number of terminal sessions to only two parallel connections (three, if the administrator uses session 0, the local console), and only local administrators can connect to these sessions by default. No additional licenses are needed to run a server in this Remote Desktop mode, which allows an administrator to perform almost all the server management duties remotely.

Even though Remote Desktop for Administration is installed by default, it has to be enabled. Some organizations might see using this feature as an unneeded security risk and choose to keep it disabled or limit access to remote sessions. However, Remote Desktop for Administration can also easily be enabled by using a group policy, a PowerShell-based command/script, or good old manual means. Lastly, this mode of Remote Desktop is available in every Windows Server 2012, Windows Server 2008, and Windows Server 2003 version and, as mentioned before, Windows XP Professional, Windows Vista, Windows 7, and Windows 8 systems.

Remote Desktop Services

RDS allows any authorized user to connect to the server and run a single application or a complete desktop session from their client workstation. Running RDS requires the purchase of a RDS client access license (CAL) for each simultaneous connection. To manage these CALs, a Remote Desktop licensing server is needed to allocate and track the licenses for RDS. The Remote Desktop Licensing role service can be installed on any Windows Server 2012 Standard or Datacenter edition member server.

It should also be noted that before installing applications that will be used in RDS, it is recommended that administrators follow a strict validation process to ensure that each application runs as it should in multiple user sessions. Some applications might not be properly suited to run on a Remote Desktop server; in such cases, extensive RDS application compatibility testing should take place before deployment. The results of such testing can both determine whether an application is compatible and if any custom installation steps or scripts need to be created for these applications to run correctly.

Client-Side RDS

Windows XP, Windows Vista, Windows 7, and Windows 8 all have a scaled-down version of Remote Desktop. This version of Remote Desktop allows a user to connect to a workstation and remotely take over the workstation to run applications that he or she would normally run from their desk locally. As an administration tool, this client-side Remote Desktop can be used to install software on an end user's workstation from a remote machine. Also, it can be used to log on to a user's desktop environment to remotely configure a user's profile settings.

Remote Assistance

Remote Assistance is a feature that has been present in Windows since Windows Server 2003 and Windows XP Professional. This feature allows a user to request assistance from a trusted friend or administrator to help deal with desktop issues and configurations. This feature gives the end user the power to control what level of participation the remote assistant can have. The remote assistant can be granted the ability to chat with the end user, view the desktop, or remotely control the desktop. During remote assistance sessions, both the end user and remote assistant can hand off control of the keyboard and mouse. Remote assistance uses the underlying RDP used by Remote Desktop.

Remote Desktop Connection

The RDC client is the name of the client that is installed on systems that allows users at the system to connect to RDS systems. This full-featured client allows end users to control Remote Desktop session settings such as local disk, audio, and port redirection, plus additional settings such as running only a single program or logging on automatically and so on. RDC information can be saved and reused to connect to RDS with previously defined session specifications.

Understanding the Name Change

As mentioned earlier in this chapter, many Windows old-timers will remember the name of Remote Desktop Services as Terminal Services (TS) and may be more familiar with the TS designation than with the RDS designation. Windows Terminal Services was renamed to RDS in Windows Server 2008 R2. Table 25.1 lists the Terminal Services role, role services, and related components and the corresponding Windows Server 2012 name.

TABLE 25.1 Parameters and Values for Creating an Unattended Answer File

Previous Name	Windows Server 2012 Name
Terminal Services	Remote Desktop Services
Terminal Server	Remote Desktop Session Host (RD Session Host)
Terminal Services Licensing (TS Licensing)	Remote Desktop Licensing (RD Licensing)
Terminal Services Gateway (TS Gateway)	Remote Desktop Gateway (RD Gateway)
Terminal Services Session Broker (TS Session Broker)	Remote Desktop Connection Broker (RD Connection Broker)
Terminal Services Web Access (TS Web Access)	Remote Desktop Web Access (RD Web Access)

RDS Roles

Although some of the features in RDS have already been touched on, this section covers features that are important, new, or improved in Windows Server 2012-based RDS.

RD Session Host

The Remote Desktop Session Host (RD Session Host) is used to host Windows-based applications or a full Windows desktop for users who connect to an RD Session Host using either RDC or RemoteApp.

The new features that have been introduced in Windows Server 2012 for the RD Session Host role service are discussed in the following sections.

Fair Share Experience

In previous versions of TS and RDS, the Windows scheduler had a fair scheduling policy that distributed processor time evenly across all threads of the same priority level. Although this scheduling methodology was a good mechanism to prevent any one user from completely monopolizing the CPU, it was not able to evenly distribute the processor time based on dynamic loads. To better handle dynamic loads, the Fair Share CPU Scheduling feature in RDS has been improved to better use the Windows Server 2012 kernel-level scheduling mechanism to dynamically distribute processor time across sessions based on the number of active sessions and load on those sessions. In addition to CPU Fairshare, Microsoft also includes Network Fairshare and Disk Fairshare in Windows Server 2012.

Network Fairshare dynamically distributes network bandwidth across guest sessions based on the number of active guest sessions. Disk Fairshare equally distributes disk I/O among sessions to prevent sessions from overutilizing disk usage.

Centralized Deployment and Configuration

With Windows Server 2012, deployment and configuration management are all handled through the Server Manager console. Instead of simply configuring individual servers,

Server Manager assists with the configuration of all RDS roles at the same time, better known as a session collection (formerly called an RDS farm). Centralized deployment and configuration ensures that the association between server roles such as the relationship between the RD Web, RD Connection Broker, and the RD Session Hosts is all tied together. In addition, when multiple RD Session Hosts or Broker servers, or the like are configured, the links between similar servers for load balancing, redundancy, and common configuration are associated, as well. For an administrator, RDS configuration used to take several hours to complete can now be done from the Server Manager of a single system in minutes.

Centralized Administration and Management

Once an RDS session collection has been created, the administration and management of the RDS servers is also greatly simplified. Common configuration settings of Broker servers, or Web servers, or the like are managed by the same centralized Server Manager console screen. This greatly assists the administrator in ensuring common configurations are maintained across common server systems.

User Profile Disks

In addition to centralized deployment, configuration, administration, and management from an RDS administrator's perspective, RDS in Windows Server 2012 also provides the ability to collectively centralize user profile settings and personalization configurations. In the past, user-specific settings were configured specifically to the user's local profile on the Terminal Server or RDS (2008) server. Each server typically had its own profile settings. With Windows 2012 RDS and the user of user profile disks, a user configuration settings follow the user no matter which RDS host server the user is connected to.

RD Virtualization Host

The Remote Desktop Virtualization Host (RD Virtualization Host) role service works in conjunction with Hyper-V to host virtual machines for Windows client users sessions. Users can connect to a virtual machine using either RemoteApp and Desktop Connection or Remote Desktop Web Access (RD Web Access). These virtual machines can either be deployed as a personal virtual desktop (each user is assigned a unique virtual machine) or part of a shared virtual desktop pool (a virtual machine is dynamically assigned).

Personal virtual desktops are assigned to individual users by using the Remote Desktop Connection Manager. Users can only be assigned one virtual desktop; additionally, a virtual desktop can only be assigned to one user. By keeping the relationship one to one, all customizations that are made to a personal virtual desktop by a user are preserved and available for future use.

In contrast, the goal with a virtual desktop pool is to have the same user experience across all virtual desktops regardless of the virtual desktop that a user is connected to. To achieve this type of experience, all virtual machines in a virtual desktop pool must be configured identically (in addition to not already being assigned as a personal virtual desktop). In addition, virtual desktop pools can be configured to roll back changes to a previous state when a user logs off of the virtual machine.

To redirect users to the correct virtual machine, the RD Virtualization Host uses the Remote Desktop Connection Broker (RD Connection Broker). When a user is assigned to a personal virtual desktop, the RD Connection Broker redirects a user's session request to the appropriate virtual machine. For cases when the virtual machine is not powered on, the RD Virtualization Host will power on the virtual machine before completing the session request. When a user attempts to open up a connection to a shared virtual desktop pool, the RD Connection Broker does either of the following:

- If the user already has a disconnected session to a virtual machine, the RD Connection Broker simply redirects the connection request to that virtual desktop.
- If the user doesn't already have a disconnected session, the RD Connection Broker dynamically assigns a virtual machine from the pool.

NOTE

Using the RD Virtualization Host role service requires that Hyper-V also be installed.

RD Gateway

The Remote Desktop Gateway (RD Gateway) role service allows users to access network resources (like RD Session Host servers, RD Session Host servers running RemoteApp programs, RD Virtualization Host-based virtual machines, or computers with Remote Desktop enabled) that are located behind firewalls in a private network from any Internet-based client (or internally based clients if TCP 3389 is an internally restricted port). To do this, the RD Gateway employs something that is called an SSL relay (also known as an SSL VPN). In short, an SSL relay allows clients to connect to internal resources over a secure, encrypted HTTPS connection. In this case, the traffic that is being passed through the SSL relay is just RDP (TCP 3389).

RD Gateway was first introduced in Windows Server 2008 as the TS Gateway. Microsoft included this feature in Windows Server 2008 because security measures were typically put into place to block traffic such as RDP (TCP 3389). In other words, IT security departments typically blocked RDP or were reluctant to open ports on their firewalls for it. Microsoft took a card from networking companies and built an SSL VPN solution in to their RDS offerings. The result of this effort is the RD Gateway, which allows users to gain access to the services that are provided by RDS, regardless of their location.

As hinted previously, the RD Gateway uses an HTTP Secure Sockets Layer/Transport Layer Security (SSL/TLS) tunnel to transmit RDP traffic. Because the RD Gateway server is using HTTPS, a server authentication certificate needs to be installed. Furthermore, the certificate that is installed needs to be issued by a certificate authority (CA) that is trusted on clients accessing the RD Gateway. In other words, the certificate of the CA that signed the RD Gateway server certificate must be located in the client's Trusted Root Certification Authority store. A trusted certificate can either be obtained from a publicly trusted CA or an internal CA to your organization that is already trusted by clients.

The following are some additional requirements that should be taken into account when using the RD Gateway:

- The Remote Procedure Call (RPC) over HTTP Proxy service must be installed. (This is installed when you install the RD Gateway role service.)
- Internet Information Services must be installed and running for the RPC over HTTP Proxy service to function.
- The Network Policy Server (NPS) service must be installed or an existing NPS server must be present that can be used by the RD Gateway.
- RD Gateway servers and RDS clients can be configured to use Network Access Protection (NAP).
- Active Directory Domain Services is required if the RD Gateway authorization policy is defined such that clients must be a member of a domain-based group.

NOTE

The RD Gateway feature is only supported on clients running Windows XP with Service Pack 2 or higher, or Windows Server 2003 with Service Pack 1 or higher that have the RDC client installed.

RD Web Access

The Remote Desktop Web Access role service is designed to allow users (internally and remotely) to access RemoteApp programs, session-based remote desktops, or virtual desktops from within a website. Using RD Web Access, a user accessing a website (hosting the RD Web Access web part) would be presented with a single consolidated list of published RemoteApps. This list consists of the application icons for each RemoteApp that has been published either from a single RD Session Host server or RD Session Host server farms. By clicking one of these icons, a session would then be launched on the remote RD Session Host or RD Virtualization Host that is hosting the published resource. RD Web Access is especially useful to administrators who want to deploy RDS-based programs from a central location, from a customized web page, or from a Windows SharePoint Services site.

To use RD Web Access, clients must meet the following requirements:

- Internet Explorer 6.0 or later
- RDC that supports RDP 6.1 or later

The version of the RDC client on Windows 7 and Windows Server 2008 R2 support RDP 7.0, and the version of RDC client on Windows 8 and Windows Server 2012 support RDP 8.0. The RDC client that is being used determines which RD Web Access features will be available to users.

RD Connection Broker

In Windows Server 2003, the feature named Session Directory was introduced to maintain user connection states across load-balanced terminal servers. This feature kept a list of sessions indexed by username. Then, when a user became disconnected from that session and attempted to reconnect, the Session Directory redirected the user back to the same terminal server that held their disconnected session.

In Windows Server 2008, the Session Directory was renamed to the Terminal Services Session Broker (TS Session Broker). The renamed TS Session Broker also contains a new feature called TS Session Broker load balancing. Microsoft introduced the load-balancing feature to allow administrators to distribute session loads between terminal servers without having to use Windows Network Load Balancing (NLB). A typical deployment for the TS Session Broker load-balancing feature is for terminal server farms that consist of 2 to 10 servers.

For Windows Server 2012, the Broker is called the RD Connection Broker. Like before, the RD Connection Broker role service still performs load balancing and ensures that users get connected to the correct Remote Desktop session. However, the RD Connection Broker also supports load balancing and session state management for session-based desktops, virtual desktops, and RemoteApp programs accessed by using RemoteApp and RDC.

NOTE

When the RD Connection Broker role service is installed, the RD Web Access role service is also installed.

To track user sessions in a load-balanced RD Session Host server farm, an RD Connection Broker server stores information in its local database for each and every session. This session information includes where the session resides, its state, the session ID, and the username associated with the session. Using this information, the RD Connection Broker redirects users with an already existing session to the correct RD Session Host server or virtual desktop.

With RD Connection Broker load balancing, users with existing sessions are still redirected to those sessions if they attempt to reconnect to them. However, for new session connections, the RD Connection Broker attempts to distribute the session load between more-powerful and less-powerful servers in the farm based on an assigned server weight value and which server has the least load.

To configure RD Connection Broker load balancing, an administrator must create an A or AAAA record for each RD Session Host in a farm. The hostname for the record is then set to the farm's name and the IP address to the RD Session Host server that is being added. The RD Connection Broker then uses round-robin DNS to distribute a user's initial connection to an RD Session Host server farm. After the user has connected and authenticated to the initial RD Session Host server, that server then queries the RD Connection Broker for where to redirect the user to. The final RD Session Host server that is returned from the RD Connection Broker is based on the following two decisions:

- Does the user have an existing session? If so, redirect that user to the RD Session Host server where that session exists.
- If the user doesn't have an existing session, which RD Session Host server has the least load? Redirect that user to the RD Session Host server with the least load.

RD Licensing

In addition to purchasing a Windows Server 2012 server license, administrators must also have the correct number of Windows Server client access licenses (CALs). When utilizing RDS functionality, an additional set of RDS client access licenses (RDS CALs) is needed for each user or device. For certain types of deployments, RDS External Connector or Service Providers License Agreement (SPLA) licenses can be purchased as well.

RDS License Types

The following Remote Desktop licensing types are available for use:

- **RDS Device CAL**—This CAL type permits one device (used by any user) to utilize RDS functionality on any server.
- **RDS User CAL**—This CAL type permits one user (using any device) to utilize RDS functionality on any server.
- **RDS External Connector**—Using this type of license allows for multiple external users to access a single Remote Desktop server; when multiple servers are being used, additional RDS External Connectors and Windows Server External Connectors must be purchased.
- **Service Providers License Agreement (SPLA)**—Using this type of license provides a service provider with a more flexible and robust licensing solution when hosting RDS to a number of different organizations and end users.

NOTE

Any combination of RDS device CALs and RDS user CALs can be simultaneously used.

RDS Client Access Licensing Mode

When using RDS CALs (Per-User or Per-Device modes), a separate RDS CAL is required for each user or device that is accessing RDS. CALs may be reassigned from one user or device to another. This assignment can be either permanent or temporary, depending on the need at the time.

Virtual Desktop Infrastructure Licensing

To correctly license a Virtual Desktop Infrastructure (VDI) environment also requires the purchase of licenses for both the Windows operating system being used for the virtual machines and the infrastructure/management components needed for an end-to-end VDI deployment.

To license Windows as a guest operating system for any VDI environment, regardless of the choice of infrastructure or hypervisor vendor, a Virtual Enterprise Centralized Desktop (VECD) licensing agreement must be purchased. This agreement is available both for client devices that are covered by Software Assurance (VECD for SA) or just VECD for devices such as thin clients.

To license the rest of a VDI environment requires using one of two paths. The VDI infrastructure components can be licensed using RDS CALs, whereas the VDI management components are separately licensed. Or, the environment can be licensed using either Microsoft Virtual Desktop Infrastructure Standard Suite or the Microsoft Virtual Desktop Infrastructure Premium Suite. Both suites are volume license offerings that combine the products for an optimum VDI experience in a value package.

RD Licensing Features

The new features that have been introduced in recent updates to the RD Licensing role service are discussed in the following sections.

Automatic License Server Discovery No Longer Supported for Remote Desktop Servers

In earlier versions of Windows Server, the licensing server was automatically discovered on the network. In Windows Server 2012, automatic discovery is no longer supported. Instead, administrators must now specify the name of a licensing server to use for each RD Session Host server.

Changes to the Licensing Tab in Remote Desktop Server Configuration

When configuring an RD Session Host server, an administrator can use the Licensing tab in the Remote Desktop Server Configuration tool to specify the licensing server. When using this tab, a licensing server can be chosen from a list of servers that have been registered as a service connection point in Active Directory or can be manually defined by entering its name. If more than one license is added, an RD Session Host server attempts to contact licensing servers in the order in which they appear in the Specified License Servers box.

The Manage RDS CALs Wizard

A new wizard has been introduced in the RD Licensing Manager, which allows the following tasks to be performed:

- Migrate RDS CALs from one licensing server to another
- Rebuild the RD Licensing database

It is important to understand that the Manage RDS CALs Wizard can only be used against licensing servers running Windows Server 2012. Therefore, if a licensing server is not running Windows Server 2012, the original CALs on that server should be manually removed as part of the migration process to a Windows Server 2012 licensing server.

CAUTION

When rebuilding the RD Licensing database, all RDS CALs are deleted and, therefore, will need to be reinstalled.

Service Connection Point Registration

While installing the RD Licensing role service, the licensing server will attempt to register itself as a Service Connection Point (SCP) in Active Directory. Once registered, the licensing server then shows up as a known licensing server in the Remote Desktop Server Configuration tool's Licensing tab. If Active Directory is not available during the role service installation, or the SCP registration fails, an administrator must manually register the licensing server by using Review Configuration in the RD Licensing Manager.

RemoteApp and Desktop Connection

Windows Server 2008-based Terminal Services introduced a feature called RemoteApp, or Seamless Windows. This feature allows applications that are accessed through RDS to appear as if they are running locally on an end user's machine. By using this feature, a user would run their remote application side by side other applications allowing them to minimize, maximize, and resize the application window as if it were a location application. In addition, if a user were to launch more than one RemoteApp, each RemoteApp would reuse the existing RDS session.

In Windows Server 2012 RDS, the RemoteApp feature has been expanded to include the ability to group and personalize RemoteApp programs, session-based desktops, and virtual desktops while making them available to users on the Windows 8 or Windows Server 2012 Start menu. As a result, the expanded RemoteApp feature has been renamed to RemoteApp and Desktop Connection.

To deploy RemoteApp and Desktop Connection, an administrator must first deploy and configure both the RD Connection Broker and the RD Web Access role services. Then, once RemoteApp programs have been defined on a source, administrators can use the Remote Desktop Connection Manager tool to configure virtual desktops or define which RemoteApp sources will be used for RemoteApp and Desktop Connection.

Once configured by and deployed by administrators, users on Windows 7 or Windows Server 2012 machines can use RemoteApp programs, session-based desktops, and virtual desktops that were defined as part of the RemoteApp and Desktop Connection. The items from the connection can be found by users on the Start menu. As changes are made to RemoteApp and Desktop Connection, such as adding or removing RemoteApp programs, these changes are then automatically reflected on the Start menu. In addition, users can use the RemoteApp and Desktop Connection notification area icon in the taskbar to follow these steps:

- See the connection status for RemoteApp and Desktop Connection
- Manage the connection status (disconnect) for RemoteApp and Desktop Connection if needed

Configuration Options and Fine-Tuning Terminology

To understand why some applications can run on RDS and why other applications cannot (and how some system configurations work one way in RDS, and others require special settings), you want to understand a number of fine details about RDS. This section covers some of the key configuration options and the terminology related to the fine-tuning options available for RDS.

Granular Session Configuration Control

With the addition of many great features in RDS also comes the ability for an administrator to granularly control the configuration of Remote Desktop sessions. All the features available to the end user's Remote Desktop session can be managed, limited, and overridden by the administrator. Configuring administrative settings through Group Policy or Remote Desktop Management tools can override/control most user-configurable settings. This can greatly benefit an RD Session Host server by freeing up valuable server resources for features that might not be required in an enterprise deployment, such as audio redirection or high-color resolution. With this granular administrative capability, the administrator can also improve RD Session Host server or virtual desktop security by requiring high encryption for sessions, force certain types of strong authentication, or even lock the session down to prevent users from making operating system changes.

Session 0 Isolation

In Windows Server 2003, Windows XP, and earlier versions of Windows, a console session was called Session 0. In addition to being an interactive logon session, Session 0 was also the session where all services were running. Unfortunately, having services run within the same session that hosted interactive logons presented a possible attack vector. Services run with elevated rights. Because of this, Session 0 services were a target for a malicious agent attempting to elevate their rights.

Microsoft addressed this threat in Windows Vista and Windows Server 2008 and later versions of Windows by making Session 0 a noninteractive session. Now, when a user logs on to an interactive session, he or she is given Session 1, the next parallel user is given Session 2, and so on. As a result of this change, a number of consequences apply to how Remote Desktop for Administration works in Windows Server 2012:

- **No /console switch**—The **/console** switch does not work when connecting to Windows Server 2012 Remote Desktop session.
- **Only two Remote Desktop sessions can connect at the same time**—There is a maximum of two parallel Remote Desktop sessions allowed in Windows Server 2012.
- **Session 0 user interface (UI) interaction**—What if a service presents a user with a UI to interact with? Because Session 0 is no longer interactive, Windows Server 2012 allow the user to interact with the Session 0 UI in a special desktop.
- **Disconnected session dialog box**—With Windows Server 2012, when there are too many parallel sessions, the client displays a selection dialog box that allows an administrator to disconnect an existing session.

- **Users are restricted to one session by default**—By default in Windows Server 2012 RDS, all users are restricted to one interactive session. This setting can be changed through the management console or Group Policy.

Local Resource Redirection

RDS enables an RDC client to redirect many of the local resources so that they can be easily used within a Remote Desktop session. Serial and printer ports can be made available in Remote Desktop sessions to allow a user to send RD Session Host server print jobs to locally configured printers, as well as access serial devices such as modems from within the Remote Desktop session. Audio can also be redirected from a session to local sound cards to enable sound from the Remote Desktop session to be heard from local speakers. Also, the Windows Clipboard can be redirected to allow cutting and pasting between the Remote Desktop session and the local workstation console.

Each of these resource redirections works only if the operating system and the RDC client on the end user's workstation support these configurations. Some of these local resource redirections require user modification or reconfiguration for proper use.

The various redirection support features built in to RDS are described in the following sections.

Disk Drive Redirection

Local disk drives can be redirected to Remote Desktop sessions and appear in Windows Explorer as networked drives using the naming convention local drive letter on computer name—for example, C on workstation5. To access from a graphical window, simply browse the drive as you would a local or networked drive. Accessing this drive from the command prompt requires a little bit of education. Within a command prompt, the redirected local drives are referenced as \\tsclient\Drive letter. Directory listings can be created using this universal naming convention (UNC), but for file transfer or quick browsing, a client should map a network drive letter to this local drive resource. To do so, follow these steps:

1. Open a command prompt.
2. Type **net use * \\tsclient\c**, where the local **c** drive is the disk you want to access within the command prompt window. The local drive is automatically mapped to the next available drive letter, starting from drive letter Z: and working backward through the alphabet.
3. At the command prompt, type **Z:** and press Enter to connect directly to the mapped local drive and begin using this drive.
4. After you finish working with this resource, disconnect the drive by typing **net use Z: /delete**, where the Z: drive is the local mapped drive.
5. Close the command prompt window.

CAUTION

The preceding steps refer to a machine called tsclient. You should not replace this name with the actual machine account name. The Remote Desktop session recognizes the machine's local disk resources only from within a command window as tsclient, so do not consider this a substitute for the actual machine name.

Printer Redirection

Locally defined print devices can also be redirected. This includes printers directly attached to the client workstation as well as network printers. When a client opens a Remote Desktop session that is configured to redirect Windows printers as well as LPT ports, the RD Session Host server attempts to install each printer for use in the Remote Desktop session. Integrated into Windows Server 2012 RDS are the following functionality:

- RDS uses a universal printer driver. Because it is universal, this driver supports legacy and new printer drivers without the need for administrators to install these drivers on the RD Session Host server.
- RDS enables users to view their local printer driver's printing preferences. They can do so because the driver acts as a proxy and redirects all calls for the GUI to the actual driver on the client side. The result is the RDC client actually just launches the GUI for the client-side printer on top of the remote session.

In the past few years, Microsoft has made improvements to RDS to improve a user's experience with printer redirection, including the following:

- **Scope limitations for redirected printers**—The visibility of redirected printers is limited to the session where they are installed. The spooler service does not need to enumerate as many redirected printers. This reduction both improves the time when a user tries to enumerate their printers during a session and during initial logon.
- **Per-session default printers**—In Windows Server 2008 or later, a user's default printer is on a per-session basis. This is a change from Windows Server 2003, where the default printer for a user was the same for all sessions.
- **Redirected printer names are shorter**—In Windows Server 2003, redirected printer names were %PRINTER_NAME% (from %CLIENT_MACHINE_NAME%) in session %Session_ID%. In Windows Server 2008 or later, these names have been shortened to %PRINTER_NAME% (%SESSION_ID%).

Local Time Zone Redirection

RDS also supports local time zone redirection. This feature allows RDC clients connecting from a separate time zone to have the session time reflect the user's local time, enabling users to more easily comprehend the times, especially when reviewing emails.

Plug-and-Play Device Redirection

Using plug-and-play device redirection, a user can redirect Windows portable devices that support the Media Transfer Protocol (MTP) and digital cameras that support the Picture Transfer Protocol (PTP). Plug-and-play device redirection works so that when a terminal session is launched, a user's plug-and-play devices are automatically installed on the RD Session Host server, virtual machine, or remote computer if just Remote Desktop for Administration is being used. After being connected, any plug-and-play notifications then appear above the taskbar in the Remote Desktop session.

Users can also configure plug-and-play device redirection so that devices connected after a session has already been established are then redirected. To do this, a user would select the Devices That I Plug in Later check box in the RDC client before connecting to a remote machine. Then after a device has been redirected, it will become available for use within the current session. For example, if a digital camera is redirected, that device would be directly accessible from an application such as the Scanner and Camera Wizard on the remote machine.

NOTE

Plug-and-play device redirection is not supported over cascaded Remote Desktop sessions. A cascading session is when a user connects to one remote machine and then from within that session connects to a second remote machine.

Redirection Features

The following are redirection features support in Windows Server 2012 RDS:

- **Multimedia redirection**—This feature redirects multimedia files and streams such that audio and video content is received in its original form from the server to a client. By doing this, multimedia content is then rendered using a client's local media playback capabilities.
- **Audio input and recording**—This feature enables audio recording support for remote clients using Voice over IP (VoIP) or speech-recognition applications.
- **Language bar redirection**—Users can now control the language setting (for example, right to left) for RemoteApp programs using the local language bar.

Single Sign-On

This feature allows a user with a domain account to log on once (via a password or smart card) and access RD Session Host servers and virtual desktops without being prompted for credentials again.

The following are some important considerations when using Single Sign-On:

- Single Sign-On is supported from Windows XP with Service Pack 3 or more current clients to a Windows Server 2012 RD Session Host server.

- The remote machine that a client is connecting to must be authenticated via Kerberos or a server authentication certificate such as SSL. Or, an administrator must enable the Allow Default Credentials with NTLM-Only Server Authentication policy.
- When saved credentials for a remote machine are already present, those credentials take precedence over the current credentials.

Remote Desktop Connection Display

In the Remote Desktop Connection 6.0 client and more recent, support was added for several new features that are geared toward improving the end-user experience: custom display resolutions, horizontal monitor spanning across multiple monitors, Desktop Experience, Font Smoothing, and Display Data Prioritization.

Custom Display Resolutions

In the previous Terminal Services Client, only 4:3 display resolution ratios and a maximum resolution of 1600 x 1200 were supported. In the new client, additional display resolution ratios, such as 16:9 or 16:10, and maximum resolution of 4096 x 2048 are now supported.

There are two ways to set a custom display resolution. The first method is to edit an RDP file with a text editor. In the file, add or change the following settings:

- **desktopheight:i:***value*
- **desktopwidth:i:***value*

The variable *value* should be defined as the desired resolution. The second method is to define the custom resolution from the command prompt:

- **mstsc.exe /w:***width* **/h:***height*

Monitor Spanning

With the monitor spanning feature, a Remote Desktop session can now be spanned across multiple monitors. To use this feature, the monitors used must meet the following requirements:

- The monitors must use the same resolution.
- The monitors must be aligned horizontally.
- The total resolution across all monitors cannot exceed 4096 x 2048.

Monitor spanning can be enabled using two methods. The first method is to edit an RDP file with a text editor. In the file, add or change the following setting: **Span:i:***value*.

- *Value* = 0, monitor spanning is disabled.
- *Value* = 1, monitor spanning is enabled.

25

The second method is to enable spanning from the command prompt:

- **mstsc.exe /span**

Desktop Experience

The Desktop Experience feature is used to make a desktop session on an RD Session Host server look and feel like a Windows desktop setup. When enabled, this feature does the following things:

- Installs a Windows client-like desktop, which then enables features such as Windows Media Player, desktop themes, photo management, and so on
- Allows another feature called Desktop Composition to function; Desktop Composition is used for Windows Aero over an RDC

NOTE

Desktop Composition is not supported on a multiple-monitor-based Remote Desktop session.

Font Smoothing

An RD Session Host server can provide ClearType functionality to clients via a feature called Font Smoothing. ClearType is a feature that is used to display fonts such that they are clearer and smoother on displays such as an LCD monitor.

By default, ClearType is enabled in Windows Server 2008 and more current. To enable Font Smoothing, follow these steps on a RDC client:

1. Open the RDC client.
2. In the Remote Desktop Connection dialog box, click Options.
3. Now select the Experience tab, and select the Font Smoothing check box.

Display Data Prioritization

In past versions of Terminal Services, a user's remote session would often become frozen when printing or transferring files. In Windows Server 2008, a feature called Display Data Prioritization was introduced, this feature has continued to be implemented in Windows Server 2012. By design, this feature gives display, keyboard, and mouse data a higher priority over other virtual channel traffic. The result of this design is that virtual channel traffic, such as disk or file transfers, does not adversely affect a user's ability to interact with a remote session.

By default, the bandwidth ratio with the Display Data Prioritization feature is 70:30. This means that 70% of the bandwidth is reserved for display and input data and 30% is reserved for all other traffic. An administrator can adjust the bandwidth ratios by changing the following Registry values on a Terminal Server or RD Session Host server under the HKEY_LOCAL_MACHINE\SYSTEM\CurrentControlSet\Services\TermDD subkey:

- **FlowControlDisable**—Enables and disables flow control
- **FlowControlDisplayBandwidth**—Determines relative bandwidth priority for display (and input data)
- **FlowControlChannelBandwidth**—Determines relative bandwidth priority for other virtual channels
- **FlowControlChargePostCompression**—Determines bandwidth allocation based on precompression or postcompression bytes

New RDC Display Features

The following are new RDC display features that are introduced in Windows Server 2012 RDS:

- **True multiple-monitor support**—Now up to 16 monitors of almost any size, resolution, or layout are supported with RemoteApp and Remote Desktop.

Planning for RDS

To successfully deploy a RDS environment requires thorough planning and testing prior to production rollout. Criteria such as application resource usage, security requirements, physical location, network access, licensing, fault tolerance, and information indicating how users will be utilizing their sessions all contribute to the way RDS implementation should be designed.

Planning for Remote Desktop for Administration

Unless RDS is viewed as a security risk, it is recommended to enable Remote Desktop for Administration on all internal servers to allow for remote administration. For servers that are on the Internet and for demilitarized zone (DMZ) networks, RDS can be used, but access should be limited to predefined separate IP addresses using firewall access lists to eliminate unauthorized attempts to log on to a server. In addition, those servers should be closely monitored for unauthorized attempts to access the system.

Planning for RD Session Host Requirements

Deploying RD Session Host servers can require a lot of planning. Because the goal is to make applications and entire desktops available to end users, server hardware specification and application compatibility are key components to test before a production rollout.

User Requirements

It is important to determine user requirements based on typical usage patterns, the number of users accessing the system, and the number of applications that are required to run. For instance, the more applications that a user will run in a session, the more processing power and memory will be required to optimize session performance. On average, a Remote Desktop user who runs one application might take 256MB of RAM and use little more than 3% of a server's total processing time per session. A power user who runs three or more applications simultaneously might require 2GB of RAM or much more, depending on the applications and features being used. Use the Performance Monitor MMC snap-in to test and validate usage statistics. The key is to not overload the server to the point where performance is too slow to be cost effective. In addition, the bandwidth required by each user session will also affect how well the system performs under various workloads.

Antivirus on RDS

Just as standard servers require operating system (OS)-level antivirus software, so do RDS servers. When choosing an antivirus product, be sure to choose one that is certified to run on Windows Server 2012 RDS. In addition, for RD Session Host servers, install the antivirus software after adding the role service so that scanning will work for all Remote Desktop sessions. Be sure to also follow installation guidelines for installing applications as outlined in the "Installing Applications" section later in this chapter.

Application Compatibility

In RDS, *application compatibility* is a term used to describe a number of issues that might be encountered when trying to deploy an application on an RD Session Host server. For example:

- Some applications are written such that only a single user can use the application at a time. With such applications, conflicts with system resources—such as files, Registry entries, pipes, IP addresses, and ports, which are used concurrently by multiple instances of applications—might prevent an application from being concurrently executed on an RD Session Host server.
- In some cases, an application's preferences might persist or manifest from one user to the next. When this scenario occurs, there is concern with user data privacy because settings (data) are transiting from one user to the next.
- In addition, an application might be written such that execution of the application requires administrative privileges. However, in most RDS deployments, regular users are not granted administrative access on an RD Session Host server.
- Applications might also be written such that network bandwidth or hardware constraints cause application performance to suffer in a multiuser usage scenario. For example, a large amount of video or animation content might overwhelm the RD Session Host's network connection, video card, and so on, thus reducing response time. Or, the application was simply written such that it requires a large amount of CPU or memory, thus monopolizing resources.

- In some cases, an application might require devices that are not redirected by default, for example, devices such as CD drives, hard disk drives, and other special devices that are not available as native devices.
- Or, an application is written for a particular version of Windows (32-bit version of Windows, a version of Windows that supports 16-bit runtime, and so on) and, thus, its API usage and behavior might differ on Windows Server 2012.

A good way to confirm the successful operation of an application (besides asking or checking with the application vendor) is to test the application to see whether it works or not on an RD Session Host system. Additional information can be found off the Internet with a simple search query to determine whether other users have successfully gotten an application to work under Windows 2012 RD Session Host, or what problems exist.

Planning for RD Session Host Sizing and Optimization

An RD Session Host server can be sized to deliver high-performance Remote Desktop sessions by estimating the amount of resources each user will require and the number of users who will utilize RDS. Performing frequent performance testing on the RD Session Host server helps generate accurate information about Remote Desktop session usage. You should perform performance testing during both peak and nonpeak times to ensure proper data collection. Increase memory and processors or introduce additional RD Session Host servers as necessary. Understanding the users' resource needs and the number of users will help you decide how to specify the server hardware requirements and determine how many RD Session Host servers you need to support the load.

Scaling RD Session Host Servers

Scaling RD Session Host servers can be achieved by increasing server resources, such as the number of processors and the amount of memory, as well as by increasing the number of servers that are servicing requests. When determining how to scale, also consider manageability, cost, and how end users might be affected if a server goes offline. For instance, using a greater number of servers might decrease manageability (such as updating applications, keeping up with operating system updates, and other maintenance), but if a server goes down, fewer users will be affected. The solution will vary depending upon your organization's needs and circumstances.

Another consideration is the amount of flexibility your organization requires. Using more instead of bigger servers gives more flexibility because of the redundancy as well as the capability to take servers offline for maintenance. In this scenario, it is important to use servers with enough power to sustain slightly greater workloads during those times when other servers in the farm go offline.

Optimizing RD Session Host Performance

Optimizing performance on an RD Session Host is a challenging task because of the complexities in any environment. Hardware resources, applications, usage, the number of users to support, and much more can affect how well a Remote Desktop session responds to user interaction. There are rarely cases where there is one "silver bullet" that can improve overall performance; it takes a combined approach. For instance, from a user perspective, video, color depth, audio redirection, printer redirection, and encryption level all affect how well a system performs.

The following are best practices for ensuring that an RD Session Host server runs as efficiently and effectively as possible:

- Limit users to a single session.
- Log off disconnected or idle sessions after a specified period of time.
- If using vendor printer drivers, only use drivers that have been certified for Windows Server 2012.
- Use applications that are certified to run on Windows Server 2012 RD Session Host servers.
- Use System Center Operations Manager 2012 or other operations management software to monitor an RD Session Host server farm.
- For medium and enterprise deployments, use a separate server or group of servers with a fast disk subsystem to store redirected folders.
- Block Internet websites that use a lot of animation.
- Prevent the usage of applications that use a lot animation.
- Prevent users from installing applications such as games or desktop enhancements/themes.
- Utilize folder redirection to roam user data between RD Session Host servers.

Monitoring RD Session Host Servers

The Performance Monitor tools that comes in Windows Server 2012 can be used to monitor a Remote Desktop Session Host server and to gather session statistics. The two specific performance monitoring objects for an RD Session Host server are Terminal Services and Terminal Services Session.

NOTE

These performance monitoring objects, as shown in Figure 25.1, have not been renamed in Windows Server 2012 and as such reflect the old Terminal Services naming convention.

The first object, Terminal Services, has only three counters: active sessions, inactive sessions, and total sessions. Gathering this session data and teaming it with information such as Server Memory\Available Bytes and Processor\% Idle can give an administrator a clear understanding of RD Session Host usage and load. This information can be used to determine whether additional resources or servers need to be added to accommodate load or enhance performance. For example, one adjustment that can be made after taking readings from these counters is the implementation of disconnected session time limits to free server hardware resources for active sessions. The second performance object, Terminal Services Session, has a number of different performance counters available in relation to Remote Desktop sessions. When using this performance object, an administrator can then gather statistical information, such as how much memory and processor time the average Remote Desktop session uses. Lastly, be sure to also monitor network interfaces for available bandwidth to ensure that the RD Session Host server is not creating a bottleneck between clients and other back-end servers.

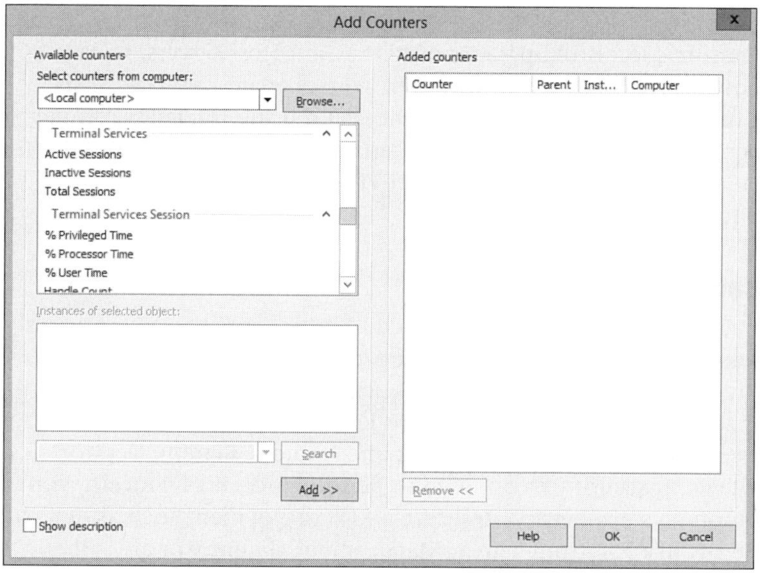

FIGURE 25.1 Performance Monitor for an RDS environment.

Planning for RD Session Host Upgrades

Upgrading an RD Session Host server can be tricky and should be handled with caution. Before any operating system or application updates or patches are applied on a production RD Session Host server, they should be thoroughly tested in an isolated lab server. This process includes knowing how to properly test the application before and after the update to be sure the update does not cause any problems and, in some cases, adds the functionality that you intended to add.

When an RD Session Host server's operating system is to be upgraded to the next version, many issues can arise during the upgrade process. Applications might not run properly in the next version because key system files might be completely different. Even printer drivers can be changed drastically, causing severe performance loss or even loss of functionality. Lastly, you need to consider that the existing RD Session Host server could have been modified or changed in ways that can cause the upgrade to fail, requiring a full restore from backup.

NOTE

Complete disaster recovery and rollback plans should be available during upgrades. This way, if problems arise, the administrator does not have to create the plan on the spot, ensuring that no important steps are overlooked.

In addition, with the user of virtualization technologies (where an RD Session Host is running as a guest session within a Hyper-V host server), a "snapshot" is a simple way of protecting the configuration of an RD Host server before updates are applied, therefore if the updates failed, the snapshot can be applied and the system rolled back to the pre-update state.

As a best practice and to ensure successful upgrades of RD Session Host servers, replace existing servers with cleanly built RD Session Host servers with the latest updates. This includes re-creating each of the file shares and print devices and using the latest compatible drivers to support each of your clients. If necessary, an existing server can also be rebuilt from scratch and redeployed to the production environment if the hardware can still meet performance requirements.

Planning the Physical Placement of RDS

Place your RDS servers where they can be readily accessed by the clients that will primarily be using them. Also, to keep network performance optimized, try to place RD Session Host and RD Virtualization Host servers on the same network segment as other servers that clients might use in their session, such as domain controllers, database servers, and mail servers. This way, you can reduce traffic on the network and improve Remote Desktop session performance. However, if security, as opposed to performance, is of concern, you should also take any appropriate steps needed to secure a RDS deployment such as deploying Application-layer firewalls like Forefront Threat Management Gateway or any other needed network controls.

Planning for Networking Requirements

To keep Remote Desktop sessions running efficiently, adequate available network bandwidth is a must. In addition, it's important to remember that a Remote Desktop session not only requires network access to the RD Session Host, but might need access to other servers depending on the application being used. For optimum performance for multi-tiered applications, install two or more network cards on an RD Session Host server and either configure the server to use one exclusively for Remote Desktop session connectivity and the others for back-end server communication or consider leveraging teaming technology to aggregate the bandwidth provided by all the network cards.

Planning for RD Session Host Tolerance

A fault-tolerant RD Session Host farm can be created using load balancing or clustering of RD Session Host systems. Alternatively, using other hardware vendor load-balancing technologies or using the RD Connection Broker to distribute load across RD Host servers is an option. If the RD Connection Broker is being used, an administrator needs to create the correct DNS records for the RD Session Host farm and all of its servers. In addition, an administrator will need to add each RD Session Host server to the RD Connection Broker's Session Broker Computers Local Group. If a third-party load-balancing technology is being used, a preference should be for a technology that can either manage Remote Desktop sessions or use information from the RD Connection Broker. Lastly, if NLB is being used, load balancing of the Windows Server 2012 servers should be configured per the best practices outlined in Chapter 29, "System-Level Fault Tolerance (Clustering / Network Load Balancing)."

Deploying RDS

After the RDS deployment has been planned, an RDS environment can be built in a limited production environment with a handful of users testing applications and validating that the configuration if working as they expect. Because RDS is nonintrusive to the network, meaning that it can be easily installed and easily uninstalled, it is common for organizations to just build RDS right into a production environment and build applications and do live testing. After an RDS environment has been verified to work with a handful of test users, the deployment can be expanded to more and more users. By following this process, administrators can reduce many of the inherent risks associated with deploying RDS while also verifying the infrastructure is ready to support end users.

The following subsections contain detailed instructions on how to install and configure Windows Server 2012-based RDS for a typical enterprise deployment that only includes several RDS servers.

Enabling Remote Desktop for Administration

Remote Desktop for Administration is installed on all Windows Server 2012 servers by default and only needs to be enabled. To enable this feature, follow these steps:

1. Log on to the desired server with local administrator privileges.
2. Launch the Server Manager console if it is not already running, and click Local Server.
3. On the main Properties page, click to the right of the Remote Desktop naming, select the Allow Connections Only from Computers Running Remote Desktop with Network Level Authentication (recommended) option button, as shown in Figure 25.2.
4. Click OK in the Systems Properties dialog box to complete this process.

NOTE

Allow Connections Only from Computers Running Remote Desktop with Network Level Authentication (recommended), only allows a client that is using a version of the RDC client that supports Network Level Authentication (NLA) to connect to RDS. When disabled, a client using any version of the RDC client can connect to RDS.

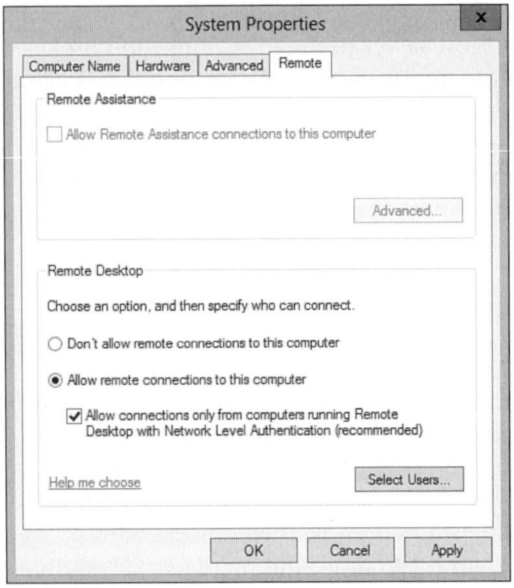

FIGURE 25.2 Allowing users to connect to the system remotely.

Alternatively, Remote Desktop for Administration can also be enabled via GPO using the following policy options:

- Computer Configuration\Policies\Administrative Templates\Windows Components\Remote Desktop Services\Remote Desktop Session Host\Connections\Allow allows users to connect remotely using RDS.
- Computer Configuration\Policies\Administrative Templates\Windows Components\Remote Desktop Services\Remote Desktop Session Host\Security\Require requires user authentication for remote connections by using Network Level Authentication.

Or, administrators can also use PowerShell and the following commands to enable Remote Desktop for Administration:

- (Get-WmiObject -Class "Win32_TerminalServiceSetting" -Namespace root\cimv2\terminalservices).SetAllowTsConnections(1)
- (Get-WmiObject -class "Win32_TSGeneralSetting" -Namespace root\cimv2\terminal-services -Filter "TerminalName='RDP-tcp'").SetUserAuthenticationRequired(1)

NOTE

Although the Server Manager method described previously will also configure the required host firewall rules for Remote Desktop, the other two methods leave it to the administrator to configure the necessary firewall rules.

Deploying the Remote Desktop Service Role Service

When deploying the Remote Desktop Service role service, two things must be done to start the RDS implementation process:

1. The Remote Desktop Service role service must be installed on all servers that'll participate in the RDS farm.
2. The RDS scenario-based installation configuration needs to be run to identify which servers in the farm will host which RDS roles (that is, RD Gateway, RD Web, RD Session Host, and so on).

Installing and Configuring the Remote Desktop Service Role Service

The Remote Desktop Service role can be installed on one server at a time, or if you have several servers to configure for your RDS collection, you can install the RDS role on several servers at the same time. This is new to Windows Server 2012 RDS installation and is a quicker and easier way to set up and configure a collection of RDS servers.

To install and configure the Remote Desktop Service role service on one or more servers, follow these steps:

1. Log on to the desired server with local administrator privileges.
2. Launch Server Manager, if it isn't already running.
3. Right-click the All Servers on the left pane of Server Manager and choose Add Servers
4. Search for the servers you plan to add for management. In my scenario all of my RDS servers start with RD, so I just typed in RD and clicked Find Now, and it listed the servers as shown in Figure 25.3.
5. Highlight the servers and click the right arrow to add the servers to the Selected list, and then click OK.
6. Now that you see all the servers you want to manage for your RDS farm, highlight the first server you want to add the RDS role service to, and then click Manage on the upper right of the Server Manager console.
7. Choose Add Roles and Features.
8. On the Before You Begin page, click Next.
9. On the Select Installation Type page, choose Remote Desktop Services scenario-based installation, and then click Next.

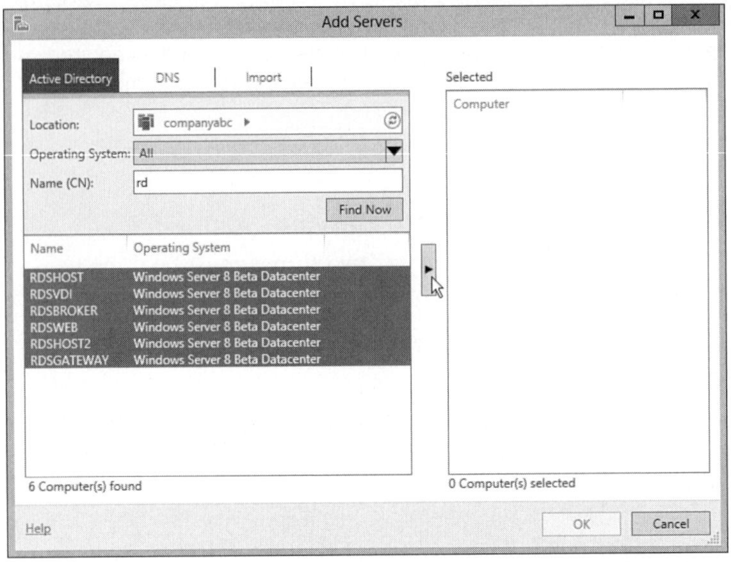

FIGURE 25.3 Selecting servers to manage in Server Manager.

10. On the Select Deployment Type page, you can choose either a Standard Deployment or a Quick Start deployment. The Quick Start deployment is intended for a single server configuration where one server holds all the RDS roles and the configuration is simple. If you have more than a single-server configuration, choose Standard deployment so that you can pick and choose which servers hold which roles. Click Next.

11. On the Select Deployment Scenario page, you can choose Virtual Desktop Infrastructure (VDI) or a Session Virtualization configuration. The VDI scenario is covered later in this chapter in the "Virtual Desktop Infrastructure" section. Assuming you want to build a traditional RDS Session Virtualization configuration, select Session Virtualization and click Next.

12. Click Next through the Review Role Services page.

13. On the Specify RD Connection Broker server page, click to highlight the server you plan to make your RD Connection Broker server, click the right arrow to move the server into the right window pane as a selected object, and then click Next.

14. On the Specify RD Web Access Server page, click to highlight the server you plan to make your RD Web Access server, click the right arrow to move the server into the right window pane as a selected object, and then click Next.

15. On the Specify RD Session Host Servers page, click to highlight the server you plan to make your RD Session host servers, click the right arrow to move the servers into the right window pane as a selected object that will show something similar to Figure 25.4, and then click Next.

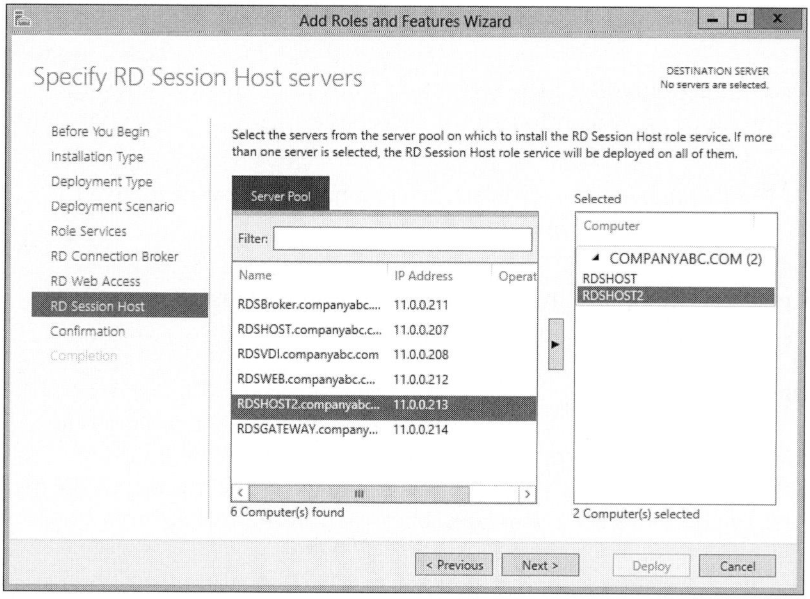

FIGURE 25.4 Selecting the RD Session Host servers.

16. On the Confirm selections page, make sure the Restart the Destination Server Automatically If Required option is selected, and then click Deploy.

The server roles will begin to install, installing both the server roles on all the RDS servers, but also configuring the roles as you identified with servers setup as RD Connection Brokers, RD Web Access, and RD Session Host systems. When the servers are configured, rebooted, and ready to go, you can click Close to close the configuration window.

Completing the RDS Collection Configuration

With the RDS role services installed, the basis of the collection configuration started, the final step in configuration is to add RD Gateway servers, RD Licensing servers, and if desired, RD Virtualization Host servers.

In the Server Manager console, click Remote Desktop Services. Then click the Overview page, where you will see the current framework of the collections. Some of the items will have icons set (like on the RD Web Access, RD Connection Broker, and RD Session Host), but some of the items will have a green plus sign (+) noting that those server roles can be added to the collection.

Adding an RD Gateway Server to the Collection

An RD Gateway Server can be added to the collection, including adding a needed SSL certificate on the system to be a valid remote desktop gateway system. To add and configure the RD Gateway, follow these steps:

1. From Server Manager/Remote Desktop Services/Overview, click the RD Gateway green + icon.
2. In the Select Server screen, highlight the server you want to be the RD Gateway server and click the right arrow icon to add the server as an RD Gateway Server, and then click Next
3. For the name of the self-signed SSL certificate, select a name you want to give the system (such as rds.companyabc.com) and click Next.

The installation will proceed and finally show Succeeded. Before clicking Close to close the View Progress page, configure the RDS Certificates as noted in the next section.

Configuring RDS Certificates

After you add an RD Gateway Server, the View Progress page will note "The role service installed needs certificate to be configured." Click the Configure Certificate link. An option to Configure the Deployment will show up; this is where certificates will be created for all the role services. To configure the certificates, click each of the role services and follow these steps:

1. Click Create New Certificate Options.
2. In the Create New Certificate page, enter the name of the certificate (for the RD Gateway server, possibly something like RDGateway.yourdomain.com), enter in a password, and click the Allow the Certificate to Be Added to the Trusted Root Certification Authorities option, and then click Apply.
3. Repeat these steps for all RDS role services that need certificates created.

Alternatively, a certificate that is trusted by a trusted root can be used and added into the RDS certificates store for the collection. To configure the certificates by choosing an existing certificate, click each of the role services and follow these steps:

1. Click the Select existing certificate option.
2. On the Select Existing Certificate page, select the Choose a Different Certificate and click Browse.
3. Select a saved certificate (typically in a PFX format), enter in the password, click the Allow the Certificate to Be Added to the Trusted Root Certification Authorities option, click OK, and then click Apply.

NOTE

The certificate for the RD Gateway and RD Web Access should be certificates for the respective RD Gateway and RD Web Access servers. The Redirector certificate is frequently the same certificate used for remote access, such as the certificate used for the RD Gateway server. If no RD Gateway is used and users access directly to the RD Session Host, use a certificate for the RD Session Host. And lastly, the Publishing certificate is a valid certificate for signing RemoteApp RDP files, which frequently an RD Web Access certificate is selected for this certificate.

4. Repeat these steps for all RDS role services that need certificates that have been previously created. Click Close when complete.

Configuring the RD Licensing Server

The RD Licensing server needs to be identified and configured. To configure the RD Licensing server, follow these steps:

1. From Server Manager/Remote Desktop Services/Overview, click the RD Licensing Server green + icon.
2. In the Select server screen, highlight the server you want to be the RD Licensing server and click the right arrow icon to add the server as an RD Licensing Server, and then click Next.
3. When prompted to confirm selections, click Add.
4. After the Remote Desktop Licensing role service has been installed, click Close.

Making Applications Available for User Access

Once the base RDS roles are installed and the base RDS systems are configured properly, the collection is ready for the next two steps:

1. Applications that are to be hosted by the RDS farm need to be installed on an RD Session Host server.
2. Users or groups are granted the required privileges to connect to the RD Session Host server and configure RD Licensing, covered in the "Deploying RD Licensing" section later in this chapter.

Installing Applications

Applications should be installed on an RD Session Host server only after the RD Session Host role service has been installed. Applications that are installed prior to installing the RD Session Host role service might not function properly for all users. In addition, applications must only be installed on an RD Session Host server when it is in a special installation mode. To put an RD Session Host server into this installation mode, use either of the following methods:

- Use the Install Application on Remote Desktop Session Host option under Programs in Control Panel.
- Use the following command before installing an application: **change user /Install**.

If the **change user /Install** command is used and then the server needs to be changed back to Execute mode, use the following command: **change user /Execute**. The server should be in Execute mode before users access the newly installed application. To see the current mode, use the following command: **change user /Query**.

NOTE

When installing applications that use an MSI package from Microsoft, an RD Session Host server typically does not need to be switched to Install mode. Instead, just install the application using the MSI package or the related installation executable.

Creating a Session Collection of RD Session Host Servers and Granting Access Rights

When you have more than one RD Session Host server, you can group the RD Session Host systems into a collection so that the servers work together and load balance one another. Even if you only have 1 RD Session Host server, you'll still want to create a session collection for the 1 RD Session Host server so that you can provide access rights to the servers. To create a session collection of RD Session Host servers, follow these steps:

1. Log on to the desired server with local administrator privileges.
2. Launch Server Manager, if it isn't already running.
3. Click Remote Desktop Services in the left column of Server Manager.
4. Right-click the RD Session Host icon, and on the Overview page, choose Create Session Collection.
5. On the Before You Begin option, click Next.
6. For the name of the collection, enter in what you want, and then click Next.
7. To specify RD Session Host servers, select the servers, click the right arrow to add, and then click Next.
8. For Specify User Groups, either keep the default Domain Users, or remove it and add in the group that should have access to the RDS collection, and then click Next.
9. For Specify User Profile Disks, for the location of user profile disks, choose a common share to which all RD Session Host servers have access, and then click Next.
10. Review and confirm selections, and click Create.

Additional RD Session Host Server Configuration Tasks

In addition to just installing the RD Session Host role service, administrators might want to complete several additional configuration tasks on an RD Session Host server. These tasks are described in the following sections.

Denying New User Logons

Called Terminal Services Server Drain mode in Windows Server 2008, an RD Session Host server can be configured to prevent new user sessions from being created. Reasons why an administrator might want to prevent new user sessions from being created include planned server outages for maintenance or to install new applications. Called User Logon mode in Windows Server 2012, the following modes can be used:

- **Allow All Connections**—This is the default setting that is selected and allows users to connect remotely to the RD Session Host server.
- **Allow Reconnections, but Prevent New Logons**—When selected, users are prevented from creating new sessions on an RD Session Host server. However, users that already have a Remote Desktop session running can still use and even reconnect to their session. Once the RD Session Host server is rebooted, no users will be able to connect to that server.
- **Allow Reconnections but Prevent New Logons Until the Server Is Restarted**—When selected, users who already have a remote session can connect to the RD Session Host server. However, new users without a session will not be able to create new sessions. Then once the RD Session Host server is restarted, the User Logon mode is reset to Allow All Connections.

The User Logon mode can be configured using the command line:

- **change logon /drain**—No additional users will be able to log on to this system.
- **change logon /drainuntilrestart**—After the server is restarted, user logons will automatically be reenabled.
- **change logon /enable**—User logons are enabled.

Setting Up Printer Support

By default, when printer redirection is enabled, an RD Session Host server first attempts to use the Remote Desktop Easy Print driver. If the client cannot use this driver, the server then attempts to match the printer driver on the client. To support the usage of other printer drivers, administrators mush either preinstall the matching printer driver on an RD Session Host server or create a custom printer mapping file.

To change the default printer driver behavior, an administrator can use GPOs to modify the Use Remote Desktop Services Easy Print Printer Driver First policy setting. This setting is located under the following node: Computer Configuration\Policies\Administrative Templates\Windows Components\Remote Desktop Services\Remote Desktop Session Host\Printer Redirection. When enabled or set to Do Not Configure, this policy setting forces the RD Session Host server to use the Remote Desktop Easy Print driver first. If that fails, the server then looks for a matching printer driver. Conversely, when disabled, the policy setting forces the RD Session Host server to look for a matching printer driver first. If that fails, the server attempts to use the Remote Desktop Easy Print driver.

Other printer redirection policy settings available under the noted node include the following:

- Do Not Allow Client Printer Redirection
- Do Not Set Default Client Printer to Be Default Printer in a Session
- Redirect Only the Default Client Printer

Modifying the Session Collection Sessions

There are several configuration options that can be revised or changed from the defaults created in the Installation Wizard. Some of the options that can be changed include user groups, connections, security, load balancing, client settings, and user profile disks.

To access the session collection configuration settings, follow these steps:

1. Log on to the desired server with local administrator privileges.
2. Launch Server Manager, if it isn't already running.
3. Click Remote Desktop Services in the left column of Server Manager
4. Expand the Collections and click the desired Session Collection.
5. In the Properties window in the upper middle of the page, click Tasks; so doing will bring up a window similar to the one shown in Figure 25.5.

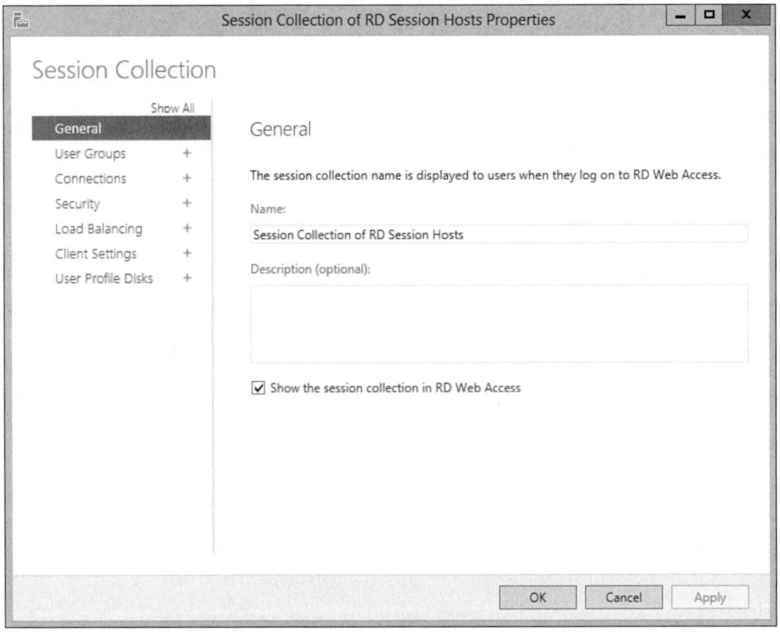

FIGURE 25.5 Session collection option configurations.

You can change the following configurations:

- **General**—Changing of the session collection name, including the option to show the session collection name on the RD Web Access page.
- **User Groups**—Selecting which groups of users can access RD Session Host servers.
- **Session**—Specifying timeouts for End a Disconnected Session, Active Session Limit, and Idle Session Limit. In addition, configuring what happens when a connection is

broken (user session is disconnected and available for reconnection, or the session is immediately ended). In addition, there's an option to delete temporary folders to clean up traces of users on host servers.

- **Security**—The security layer can be configured whether the session security is negotiated, SSL is used, or basic RDP security is enabled.
- **Load Balancing**—RD Session Host limits on the number of guest sessions on a host and the relative weight of the host server relative to other servers can be defined.
- **Client Settings**—Default client settings can be changed, such as whether audio and video playback can be allowed, whether audio recording can be allowed, whether smart cards are required, the use of plug and play devices, whether drives are enabled, and whether information can be cut/pasted from the Clipboard. In addition, printer redirection settings and default printer configurations can be set.
- **User Profile Disks**—Whether user profile disks are enabled, including the common disk share folder as well as the ability to store user settings and data in the user profile disk location.

All of these settings can be modified, and clicking Apply or OK will set the configuration settings.

Adding Programs to the RemoteApp Programs

RemoteApp programs, available from RD Web Access servers, are programs that are made available from a web page or as executable launch files to access specific applications. To create a RemoteApp program, follow these steps:

1. Log on to the desired server with local administrator privileges.
2. Launch Server Manager, if it isn't already running.
3. Click Remote Desktop Services in the left column of Server Manager.
4. Expand the collections and click the desired session collection.
5. In the RemoteApp Programs window in the middle of the page, click Tasks and choose Publish RemoteApp Programs.
6. On the Select RemoteApp Programs page, choose the program you want to publish. The list of programs will be from applications installed on the RD Session Host servers. If the program does not show on the screen, you can click Add Another Program to manually select the program on the RD Session Host system you want to make available. Click Next.
7. Click Publish to make the program available on the RemoteApp page.
8. Click Close

Modifying RemoteApp Program Settings

Each RemoteApp program can have key settings modified, including whether the application is shown on the RD Web Access page, user access, and file type associations. To access property configurations for RemoteApp applications, follow these steps:

1. Log on to the desired server with local administrator privileges.
2. Launch Server Manager, if it isn't already running.
3. Click Remote Desktop Services in the left column of Server Manager.
4. Expand the collections and click the desired session collection.
5. In the RemoteApp Programs window in the middle of the page, right-click any of the applications you have set up to be published in RemoteApp and choose Edit Properties.

You can change the following configurations:

- **General**—Changing the name of the RemoteApp program, whether the RemoteApp program is visible on the RD Web Access page, and any subfolder you might want to put the program in to. The setting options are similar to those shown in Figure 25.6.

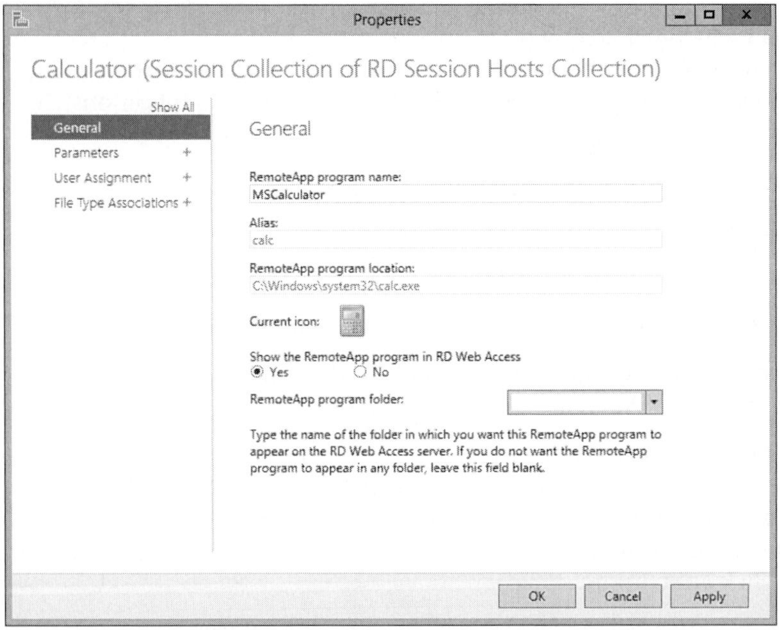

FIGURE 25.6 Property configurations for RemoteApp modifications.

- **Parameters**—The ability to allow or deny command-line parameters then an application is launched.

- **User Assignment**—By default, all users and groups that have access to the collection have access to the RemoteApp programs. However, if you want to lock down access to a program, you can specific that the application is only available to a specified user/group.
- **File Type Association**—Allows the changing of file type associations so that when specific an application is launched, that RemoteApp application will execute. The file type association can be assigned from the Group Policy object User Configuration/Administrative Templates/Windows Components/Remote Desktop Settings/RemoteApp and Desktop Connections as a Default Connection URL.

All of these settings can be modified, and clicking Apply or OK sets the configuration settings.

Accessing RemoteApp and Desktop Connection

When using Windows client or Windows Server systems, users can access RemoteApp and Desktop Connection using a RemoteApp and Desktop Connection URL, which is provided by administrators. For example, such a URL might be formatted as https://rdsweb.companyabc.com/RDWeb. Using this URL, a user can then create a new connection to RemoteApp and Desktop Connection using the Control Panel, RemoteApp, and Desktop Connection.

NOTE

To determine what the default RD Web App URL is, go to Server Manager/Remote Desktop Services/Overview, click Tasks in the Deployment Overview pane, choose Edit Deployment Properties, and then click RD Web Access.

Deploying Virtual Desktops

Virtual Desktops, or effectively Windows 7 or Windows 8 guest sessions running on an RD Virtualization Host server can provide organizations a way of supporting a standard "desktop configuration' for users so that applications, configurations, and settings are all within virtual desktop systems on RDS host servers instead of distributed to systems throughout the organization. It is this centralization of guest sessions that helps an organization provide standards in an environment where "bring your own device" (BYOD) is common. The steps in this section describe how to deploy virtual desktops.

Installing the RD Virtualization Host Role Service and Configuration Settings

If you already have an RDS collection and you want to add the RD Virtualization Host to the collection, you can simply add the RD Virtualization Host to the server that'll become your VDI host server and then join the server to the collection. To do so, follow these steps:

1. Log on to the desired server with local administrator privileges.
2. Launch Server Manager, if it isn't already running.
3. Right-click the All Servers in the left pane of Server Manager and choose Add Servers.
4. Search for the servers you plan to add for management. In my scenario, all of my RDS servers start with RD, so I just typed in RD and clicked Find Now, and it listed.
5. Highlight the servers and click the right arrow to add the servers to the Selected list, and then click OK.
6. Now that you see all the servers you want to manage for your RDS Virtualization Host farm, highlight the first server you want to add the RDS role service to, and then click Manage on the upper right of the Server Manager console.
7. Choose Add Roles and Features.
8. On the Before you begin page, click Next.
9. On the Select Installation Type page, choose Remote Desktop Services Scenario-Based Installation, and then click Next.
10. On the Select Deployment Type page, you can choose either a Standard deployment or a Quick Start deployment. The Quick Start deployment is intended for a single-server configuration where one server holds all the RDS roles and the configuration is simple. If you have more than a single-server configuration, choose Standard deployment so that you can pick and choose which servers hold which roles. Click Next.
11. On the Select Deployment Scenario page, you can choose Virtual Desktop Infrastructure (VDI) or a Session Virtualization configuration. In this scenario, we will be building the VDI environment, so select Virtual Desktop Infrastructure Scenario, and then click Next.
12. Click Next through the Review Role Services page.
13. On the Specify RD Connection Broker Server page, click to highlight the server you plan to make your RD Connection Broker server, click the right arrow to move the server into the right window pane as a selected object, and then click Next.
14. On the Specify RD Web Access Server page, click to highlight the server you plan to make your RD Web Access server, click the right arrow to move the server into the right window pane as a selected object, and then click Next.
15. On the Specify RD Virtualization Host Server page, click to highlight the servers you plan to make your RD Virtualization host servers, click the right arrow to move the servers into the right window pane as a selected object, and then click Next.
16. On the Confirm Selections page, make sure the Restart the Destination Server Automatically If Required option is selected, and then click Deploy.

The server roles will begin to install, installing both the server roles on all the RDS servers, but also configuring the roles as you identified with servers set up as RD Connection Brokers, RD Web Access, and RD Virtualization Host systems. Once the servers are configured, rebooted, and ready to go, you can click Close to close the configuration window.

NOTE

If Hyper-V is not installed, it will be installed automatically by the Installation Wizard.

Completing the RDS Collection Configuration

With the RDS role services installed, and the basis of the collection configuration started, the final step in configuration is to add RD Gateway servers, RD Licensing servers, and if desired, RD Session Host servers.

In the Server Manager console, click Remote Desktop Services. Then click the Overview page where you will see the current framework of the collections. Some of the items will have icons set (like on the RD Web Access, RD Connection Broker, and RD Virtualization Host), but some of the items will have a green plus sign (+) noting that those server roles can be added to the collection.

Adding an RD Gateway Server to the Collection

An RD Gateway Server can be added to the collection, including adding a needed SSL certificate on the system to be a valid remote desktop gateway system. To add and configure the RD Gateway, follow these steps:

1. From Server Manager/Remote Desktop Services/Overview, click the RD Gateway green + icon.
2. In the Select Server screen, highlight the server you want to be the RD Gateway server and click the right arrow icon to add the server as an RD Gateway Server, and then click Next.
3. For the name of the self-signed SSL certificate, select a name you want to give the system (such as rds.companyabc.com), and then click Next.

The installation will proceed and finally show Succeeded. Before clicking Close to close the View Progress page, configure the RDS certificates as noted in the next section.

Configuring RDS Certificates

After adding an RD Gateway server, the View Progress page will note "The role service installed needs certificate to be configured." Click the Configure Certificate link. An option to configure the deployment will show up; this is where certificates will be created for all the role services. To configure the certificates, click each of the role services and follow these steps:

1. Click Create New Certificate Options.
2. On the Create New Certificate page, enter in the name of the certificate (for the RD Gateway server, possibly something like RDGateway.yourdomain.com), enter in a password, and click the Allow the Certificate to Be Added to the Trusted Root Certification Authorities option, and then click Apply.
3. Repeat these steps for all RDS role services that need certificates created.

Alternatively, a certificate that is trusted by a trusted root can be used and added into the RDS certificates store for the collection. To configure the certificates by choosing an existing certificate, click each of the role services and follow these steps:

1. Click the Select Existing Certificate option.
2. On the Select Existing Certificate page, select the Choose a Different Certificate and click Browse.
3. Select a saved certificate (typically in a PFX format), enter in the password, click the Allow the Certificate to Be Added to the Trusted Root Certification Authorities option, click OK, and then click Apply.

NOTE

The certificate for the RD Gateway and RD Web Access should be certificates for the respective RD Gateway and RD Web Access servers. The Redirector certificate is frequently the same certificate used for remote access, such as the certificate used for the RD Gateway server. If no RD Gateway is used and users access directly to the RD Virtualization Host, use a certificate for the RD Virtualization Host. And lastly, the Publishing certificate is a valid certificate for signing RemoteApp RDP files, which frequently an RD Web Access certificate is selected for this certificate.

4. Repeat these steps for all RDS role services that need certificates that have been previously created. Click Close when complete.

Creating a Virtual Desktop Template

When you are building out a VDI environment, the RD Virtualization Host server needs to have a working template on the system that'll be the basis of the creation of other virtual guest sessions.

1. Log on to the server that'll be your RD Virtualization host.
2. Launch Server Manager, if it isn't already running.
3. Launch Hyper-V Manager by clicking on Tools in the upper right of Server Manager.

4. Create a guest session in Hyper-V; from the actions pane, choose New, Virtual Machine. The New Virtual Machine Wizard will launch.
5. Click Next to continue past the initial Before You Begin screen.
6. Give your virtual machine a name that will be descriptive of the virtual guest session you are creating, such as Win8Guest or Win7Template.
7. If you had set the default virtual machine folder location where guest images are stored, the new image for this virtual machine will be placed in a subfolder of that default folder. However, if you need to select a different location where the image files should be stored, click Store the Virtual Machine in a Different Location, and select Browse to choose an existing disk directory or to create a new directory where the image file for this guest session should be stored. Click Next to continue.
8. Enter in the amount of RAM you want to be allocated to this guest image (in megabytes), and then click Next.

NOTE

When assigning memory, you can choose the option Use Dynamic Memory for This Virtual Machine, which is a good option to choose when optimizing the memory in a server. Instead of randomly picking (typically more) memory than is needed for a guest session that might not be fully utilized, choosing dynamic memory allows you to configure a range of memory. If the additional memory is not needed, the guest session "gives back" the unused memory for other guest sessions to use.

9. Choose the network segment to which you want this guest image to be initially connected: External, Internal, or Private Network. Click Next.

NOTE

You can also choose Not Connected during this virtual machine creation process and change the network segment option at a later date.

10. The next option enables you to create a new virtual hard disk or use an existing virtual hard disk for the guest image file. Creating a new virtual hard disk creates a VHDX disk image in the directory you choose. By default, a dynamic virtual disk image size setting is set to 127GB. The actual file itself will only be the size of the data in the image (potentially 4GB or 8GB to start, depending on the operating system) and will dynamically grow up to the size indicated in this setting. Click Next to continue.
11. The next option allows for the installation of an operating system on the disk image you created in the previous step. You can choose to install an operating system at a later time, install an operating system from a bootable CD/DVD or ISO image

file, install an operating system from a boot floppy disk image, or install an operating system from a network-based installation server (such as Windows Deployment Services). Typically, operating system source discs are on either a physical disc or ISO image file, and choosing a CD or DVD or an associated ISO image file will allow for the operating system to be installed on the guest image. Select your option, and then click Next to continue.

12. Review the summary of the options you have selected and either click Finish if the settings you've chosen are fine or click Previous to go back and make changes. Click Finish to create the new virtual machine.

Once the guest session has been created, you'll likely want to install your common applications onto the guest session so that when you duplicate the template for additional VDI guests, they will already have their applications on the guest session. So at this point, install things such as Microsoft Office, Adobe Acrobat, your line-of-business applications, and the like to make a working user template.

After the template is created and you have added your core applications, you need to run sysprep on the template and "generalize" the template, effectively clearing the template of any personalized configuration settings, yet leaving the base applications installed on the template. To sysprep a template, follow these steps:

1. Launch and log in to the virtual guest session template that you have prepared in the previous section with the application software you want on the template.

NOTE

Make sure to install the Integration Tools to the guest session; this is required to create a guest session template. To install the Integration tools, while the guest session is running, on the Hyper-V options, choose Actions, Insert Integration Services Setup Disk.

2. Drop to a command prompt on the system. In Windows Vista or Windows 7, Start, All Programs, Accessories, command prompt. In Windows 8, press the Windows key to bring up the Metro window, type on the keyboard **command prompt**, and when the auto-search finds the command prompt program, run it and you'll end up at the C> prompt.
3. From the command prompt, type **cd \windows\system32\sysprep**.
4. In the sysprep folder, type **sysprep** to launch the sysprep program.
5. Choose Enter System Out-of-Box Experience (OOBE), click Generalize to select the option, and choose Shutdown, as shown in Figure 25.7.

Once the template shuts down, you can proceed with creating a virtual desktop collection to replicate the template for additional VDI user guest sessions.

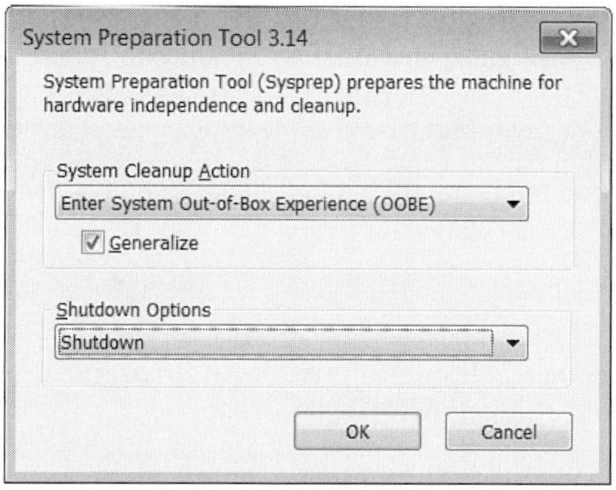

FIGURE 25.7 Running sysprep to generalize a system configuration.

Creating a Virtual Desktop Collection

Personal virtual desktops are specific virtual machines hosted on an RD Virtualization Host server that have been assigned to a user account in Active Directory. The following steps describe how to assign an existing virtual machine to a user. These steps should be carried out on the server that has the RD Connection Broker role service installed:

1. Log on to the desired server with local administrator privileges.
2. Launch Server Manager, if it isn't already running.
3. Click Remote Desktop Services, Collections.
4. In the Collections pane at the top right of the page, click Tasks, Create Virtual Desktop Collection.
5. On the Before You Begin page, click Next.
6. On the Name the Collection page, enter in a name for the collection, like **RD Virt Collection**, and then click Next.
7. For Specify the Collection Type, you can create a pooled virtual desktop collection or a personal virtual desktop collection. Choose which one you want, and then click Next.

NOTE

A personal virtual desktop collection is one where each VDI user gets his or her own/private virtual guest session. The guest sessions are dedicated to specific users. The pooled virtual desktop collection is a series of virtual guest sessions that are pooled or shared among users. So from a pool of say six guest sessions, the sessions are made available to whichever user logs in to the guest session.

Pooled virtual desktop sessions are lower cost to create and manage in that users will theoretically be sharing guest sessions, whereas the personal virtual desktops are dedicated 1:1 to users.

8. For Virtual Desktop Template, choose the template you created in the previous section that you want to replicate for additional guest sessions, and then click Next.

NOTE

If you get an "Could not retrieve the virtual desktop template details for..." error, you need to make sure the template you are working from has 1024MB of memory or more before running this step.

9. On the Specify the Virtual Desktop Settings page, choose to provide an unattended settings file, or use a sysprep answer file, and then click Next.
10. If choosing an unattended setting option, you will be prompted for information that'll allow you to join the virtual desktop system to Active Directory by providing the information for the domain, OU, a local administrator name and password, and the time zone. Click Next to continue.
11. On the Specify Users and Collection Size page, specify what group of users you want to make available to the collection and the number of base configurations you want to automatically build, and then click Next.
12. On the Specify virtual desktop allocation page, confirm the number of new virtual desktops you want to create, and then click Next.
13. For the storage of the virtual desktops, you can choose to locally store the guest sessions (which is typically the default) or choose to place the guest sessions on an external storage system, and then click Next.
14. When prompted to specify user profile disks, choose a network share where user profile information is stored. This is configuration information, Registry information, roaming data that will be stored outside of the VDI guest sessions so that in pooled image scenarios, or where multiple RD Virtualization hosts exist, the user's profile information is available for common user configuration settings. Click Next.
15. Review the settings, and click Create to build out the virtual desktop systems. This takes a while because the VHDX images need to be prebuilt and configured.
16. When finished and after viewing the results, click Close.

Accessing the VDI Guest Sessions

Once the VDI guest sessions have been created, users can log on to the RD Virtualization host infrastructure and access their guest sessions. If personal virtual guests were selected and created, a user will be assigned a guest session, and the user will always use the same guest session. If a virtual desktop pool was selected and created, users retain their profile configuration information, but the base operating system used by the user is shared among other pool users.

To log on and access a VDI guest session, do one of the following:

- **Accessing from RD Gateway**—A VDI guest session can be accessed directly from an RDS client. Launch the Remote Desktop Client (RDC) from any computer that has network connectivity to the RD Gateway server, enter in the server name or IP address of the RD Gateway server, and when prompted, type in a valid logon name and password of a user account that is part of the group you gave access to the VDI guest session earlier.
- **Accessing from RD Web Access**—A VDI guest session can also be accessed from an RD Web Access session connected to the VDI collection. Launch a browser and type in the URL of the RD Web Access server. Log on to the Web Access server; there will be an icon for the RD Virtualization server collection. Click the collection that'll start the logon process to the RD virtual guest session.

NOTE

To determine what the default RD Web App URL is, go to Server Manager, Remote Desktop Services, Overview and click Tasks in the Deployment Overview pane, choose Edit Deployment Properties, and then click RD Web Access.

Enabling RemoteFX

Starting with Windows Server 2008 R2 and then further enhanced in Windows Server 2012 is RemoteFX, a technology that greatly improves graphical performance for Remote Desktop sessions. Normally when graphics are rendered on a Remote Desktop session (such as the playback of a full-motion video, or display of heavily graphics-based applications), not only does the motherboard CPU have to support the processing of the Remote Desktop sessions, but it also has to handle the rendering of graphics. Therefore in the past, heavy graphics-based applications greatly slowed down the performance of Remote Desktop servers to the point where graphics applications were discouraged from execution on Remote Desktop systems.

However, with RemoteFX technology, video rendering is offloaded from the Remote Desktop CPU to a graphics processor (or GPU) on a separate video adapter on the RDS server. The GPUs used for RemoteFX have traditionally been used for gaming (online games, computer-based live action games). By offloading graphical processes to the GPU, organizations can now provide graphics support for business applications to users, which in this day and age, rich content such as video streaming, video and graphics-based web content, and the like is important to serve the business needs of an organization.

Integrating and Supporting RemoteFX for VDI Guests

RemoteFX requires a standard Windows 2012 Remote Desktop Server that also has a Second-Level Address Translator (SLAT)-supported motherboard processor and a RemoteFX-supported GPU video adapter.

To support RemoteFX, it is as simple as having a server with the SLAT-supported processor and the RemoteFX-supported GPU video adapter installed, and then install Windows Server 2012 on the system as an RD Virtualization Host (for VDI-enabled RemoteFX) or set up a system as an RD Session Host server (for RD Session Host-enabled RemoteFX). When Remote Desktop Services is operational, it recognizes that a GPU is available, and RemoteFX is supported.

Specifically, in the configuration of a RemoteFX VDI guest session, follow these steps:

1. On an RD Virtualization Host server that is operational, after the basic VDI Guest session is configured, go to Actions, Settings for the guest session.
2. Click Add Hardware, and the hardware option RemoteFX 3D Video Adapter is available. Select the RemoteFX option and click Add.
3. Click OK and launch the guest session as normal to run the virtual guest session.
4. Once the guest session has been created, boot the guest session and insert the Integration Services (drivers) for the guest session (Action, Insert Integration Services Setup Disk). This installs the drivers for the guest session and the drivers for RemoteFX.

NOTE

You may choose to configure the guest session with software applications, tools, and so on *before* adding the RemoteFX 3D Video Adapter hardware configuration to the guest session settings, or alternatively, before you insert the integration services to load the RemoteFX drivers. Once you install the RemoteFX drivers, it requires a system reboot, and once the system reboots, the *only* way you can access the RemoteFX-enabled guest session is to log on as a VDI guest session. You cannot log on from the Hyper-V or RD Virtualization Host console. The graphical resolution of RemoteFX prevents running the guest sessions from the console, and therefore you must log on to the guest sessions through the RDC.

Integrating and Supporting RemoteFX for RD Session Host Guests

The installation and configuration for RemoteFX improved client performance for RD Session Host guests as well as made it much easier to configure an RD Session Host. Because the RD Session Host users share the processors, disk, and guest session operating system with one another, RemoteFX is configured once for a server. You do not have to create RemoteFX hardware configuration or drivers for each individual guest session like you do with VDI. VDI is personalized, each user having his or her own guest session, and thus the individualized configuration.

With RemoteFX for RD Session Host guests, simply install Windows Server 2012 on a server that has the GPU video adapter in the system. For the Windows host server, load up the video drivers for the GPU video adapter so that the entire host system boots and acknowledges the video adapter in the system. Windows RD Session Host is configured, it automatically acknowledges the video adapter and prepares the entire RD Session Host server to for RemoteFX operations.

Securing and Supporting RDS

Remote Desktop Services should be secured using standard security guidelines and policies defined by an organization. In addition to an organization's security standards and guidelines, it is advisable that administrators use recommended best practices compiled by Microsoft, as well as the National Institute of Standards and Technologies (NIST) and the National Security Agency (NSA). Both NIST and NSA provide security lockdown configuration standards and guidelines that can be downloaded from their websites (http://www.nist.gov and http://www.nsa.gov, respectively).

Securely Building Remote Session Services

When building security into RDS, keep in mind that you are giving users certain levels of access to a shared resource. Essentially, users are logging on to a system and using the applications and services installed on that server or virtual machine. With this in mind, it is important to strike a balance between a user's productive capability and what the user can do (intentionally or accidentally) to a system. Otherwise, a single session can significantly affect other user sessions, as well as the entire RD Session Host server or an individual shared virtual machine. In addition, administrators should also consider that depending on their deployment strategy, users might be accessing RDS from external systems. Therefore, a comprehensive approach around end-to-end security (from the client to RD Session Host/virtual machine) needs to be implemented.

Segmenting Resources

RD Session Host server resources should be segmented in such a way that users can only modify specific settings. This sounds simple, but requires careful planning. For instance, partitioning the server's disk subsystem can keep the operating system, logs, applications, and profiles separated. Each of these partitions should also be formatted with NTFS so that the proper permissions can be applied. This also makes it easier for administrators to manage and lock down specific resources.

The profile partition should be given particular attention because of the nature of the content it stores. One of the new improvements in Windows Server 2012 RDS is its support for profile disks. The profile disk allows the administrator to target profiles to be stored on a drive share of another server. Not only does this centralize and simply profiles to a centralized model, but it also provides a second level of redundancy and protection for profiles because they are a separate process and task for RDS.

Another option built in to Windows Server 2012 is the ability to remove temporary folders off the Remote Desktop servers. To configure the removal of temporary folder settings, follow these steps:

1. From a Server Manager console, click Remote Desktop Services.
2. Click to expand collections, and choose the collection created.

3. On the Properties pane in the upper middle of the screen, click Tasks and choose Edit Properties.
4. On the Connections option settings, ensure that the check mark is on for Delete Temporary Folders on Exit as well as on Use Temporary Folders per Session, as shown in Figure 25.8.

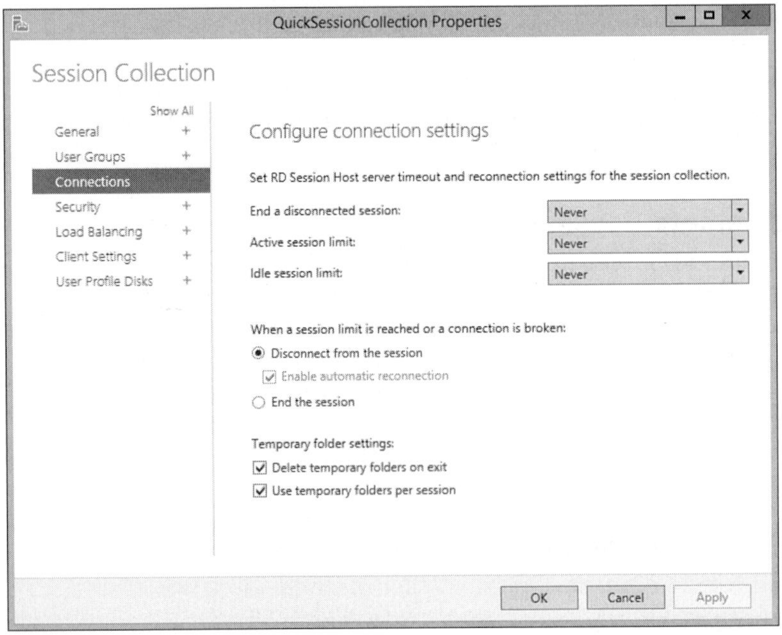

FIGURE 25.8 Configuring connections to delete temporary folders.

Securing RDS with GPOs

As mentioned earlier in the "Group Policy for RD Session Host Servers" section, GPOs can and should be used to secure the RDS environment. For instance, if an application or department working with sensitive information uses RDS, the Remote Control setting can be disabled to ensure that only authorized users can view these sessions. Group Policy can also be used to set disconnect timeout values and allow reconnections from only the original client. For more complex security requirements, Group Policy can also be used to secure and customize a user's session. For example:

- GPO can be used to create a secure desktop that gives users limited Windows functionality based on their needs.
- Or, if supported, a GPO can be used to customize and restrict individual application features.

Network Level Authentication

A couple years ago when RDP 6.0 was introduced, a feature called Network Level Authentication was included in RDS. This feature enhanced RDP security by providing an interface for user authentication earlier in the connection process of a session (before a Remote Desktop connection and the logon screen appears). The following are the benefits of configuring RDS to require Network Level Authentication:

- Fewer resources are used validating users before presenting them with a full session.
- Remote computer authentication can be used to preauthenticate servers, as well.
- It can reduce the risk of a denial-of-service attack.

Changing the RDP Port

As mentioned earlier, RDS securely communicates over TCP port 3389 using RDP. Organizations requiring even greater security can change the default port by modifying the following Registry key:

HKEY_LOCAL_MACHINE\System\CurrentControlSet\Control\Terminal Server\WinStations\RDP-Tcp\PortNumber

Or, if RemoteApp programs are being used, the RDP settings can be modified to specify a different port for RDP traffic.

NOTE

Only clients using RDP version 5.1 or later can connect to the nonstandard port. Also, after the port is changed, the RD Session Host server or RD Virtualization Host server must be restarted.

Remotely Managing a Remote Desktop Session

Remote Desktop users might require support for tasks such as mapping to a file share, installing a third-party printer driver, or just troubleshooting issues within the terminal session. While using the remote control features of RDS, an administrator can interact with users in active sessions with view-only access or complete remote control functionality. The amount of access given to an administrator during a remote control session can be set by the user, but it can be configured at the server level by the administrator.

An administrator can remotely control a user's session only from within a separate Remote Desktop session. The remote control command can be initiated using Remote Desktop Services Manager or the command-line tool Shadow.exe.

Managing RDS with PowerShell

When the Remote Desktop Services role is installed, a PowerShell provider is also installed that enables administrators to manage Remote Desktop settings using PowerShell. Once installed, and a PowerShell console is opened, administrators can access the resulting RDS: drive to manage a number of different settings that are organized into the following directories:

- **RDSConfiguration**—Contains settings that apply to the RD Session Host role service
- **Gateway**—Contains settings that apply to the RD Gateway role service
- **LicenseServer**—Contains settings that apply to the RD Licensing role service
- **ConnectionBroker**—Contains settings that apply to the RD Connection Broker role service
- **RemoteApps**—Contains a list of published applications and their settings
- **RDFarms**—Contains settings that apply to RD Session Host server farms

Group Policy for RD Session Host Servers

Group Policy contains several RDS user and computer settings to configure Remote Desktop sessions. An administrator can modify existing group policies or create new group policies to manage RDS machine and user settings. These Group Policy objects (GPOs) can then be applied to RD Session Host servers, virtual machines, or users located in an Active Directory site, domain, or organizational unit (OU) or based on a GPO filter.

Group Policy is the preferred method of standardizing RDS configurations throughout Active Directory because user and machine configurations can be centrally administered. Because so many RDS settings are available in Group Policy, the following list outlines where RDS settings can be found:

- **Computer Configuration\Windows Settings\Security Settings\Local Policies\User Rights Assignment**—User rights assignment can allow logon through RDS as well as deny logon through RDS, depending on the configuration setting.
- **Computer Configuration\Administrative Templates\Windows Components\Remote Desktop Services**—Almost all RDS settings can be configured here. Settings here override user or client configurations and also override settings made in the User Configuration section of Group Policy.
- **User Configuration\Administrative Templates\Windows Components\Remote Desktop Services**—User session settings can be configured in this section. Settings here override user or client configurations.

A simple and effective way to manage the GPOs for your RD Session Host servers is to create an OU for your RD Session Host servers and apply GPOs to the OU. Enabling the Computer Configuration\Administrative Templates\System\Group Policy\User Group Policy Loopback Processing mode is very important if you want the user-context GPO settings to take effect. The loopback processing can be set to either merge or replace. Merging allows existing domain-based GPOs to merge with the ones for RDS, whereas the replace option overrides all other settings and the RDS-specific settings are only applied.

Applying Service Packs and Updates

Applying service packs and updates on an RD Session Host server or virtual machine should follow the same strategy as outlined in the previous section, "Installing Applications." Test all service packs and updates in an isolated lab environment prior to production release and always create a backup of the system first to allow for rollback, if necessary.

Performing Disaster Recovery

The steps for backing up and restoring an RD Session Host server or virtual machine should follow the same procedures as backing up and restoring a standalone server. Administrators must be sure to back up any local user data, including profiles, and back up the current server System State. The data and System State backup, accompanied with a server build document, are all that an administrator needs to recover the RD Session Host server or virtual machine. For detailed steps concerning the creation of server build documents and Windows Server 2012 backup and recovery techniques, see Chapter 22, "Documenting a Windows Server 2012 Environment," Chapter 30, "Backing Up the Windows Server 2012 Environment," and Chapter 31, "Recovering from a Disaster."

Summary

Windows Server 2012 RDS is a flexible tool that can be used to provide administrative, server-based computing, and virtual desktop functionality. Depending on the needs of your organization, RDS can be deployed to meet needs that range from centralized administration to remote access for business-critical applications. With features like RD Web Access, RD RemoteApp, RD Gateway, RD Virtualization Host, and so on, the ease and simplicity of using RDS has never been more compelling.

RDS enables users and system administrators alike to perform job functions productively from the office or remotely with simplicity.

Best Practices

The following are best practices from this chapter:

- Drain Remote Desktop connections when performing scheduled maintenance on an RD Session Host server.
- When an RD Session Host server or virtual machine is due for an operating system upgrade, if possible replace the server with a clean build and test all applications, instead of performing in-place upgrades to avoid server or application failures.
- Place your RD Session Host and RD Virtualization Host servers where they can be readily accessed by the clients that will primarily be using them.
- Whenever possible, choose applications that have been tested and certified by the vendor to run on Windows Server 2012 RDS.

- For optimum performance for multitiered applications, install two or more network cards on an RD Session Host server and configure the server to use one exclusively for RDC client connectivity and the others for back-end server communication.
- Use Group Policy to limit client functionality as needed to enhance server security, and if increased network security is a requirement, consider requiring clients to run sessions in 128-bit high encryption mode.
- When possible, try to never install the Remote Desktop Services role and then host applications on a domain controller.
- It is recommended that applications always be grouped together based on usage. If an application behaves badly or isn't certified to run Remote Desktop Services, it should be separated to dedicated servers in a farm.
- Try to treat RD session host servers as nodes that are dispensable. So, try to always build your RD session host servers using the same hardware and install the same applications on them.

CHAPTER 26

Windows Server 2012 Administration Tools for Desktops

IN THIS CHAPTER

- Managing Desktops and Servers
- Operating System Deployment Options
- Windows Server 2012 Windows Deployment Services
- Installing Windows Deployment Services
- Customizing Boot Images
- Creating Discover Images
- Pre-creating Active Directory Computer Accounts for WDS (Prestaged Systems)
- Creating Custom Installations Using Capture Images
- Automating Image Deployment Using Unattend Files
- General Desktop Administration Tasks

Windows Server 2012 contains several services and features that can be leveraged to simplify the management of an organization's computer and network infrastructure. Managing an organization's computer and network infrastructure requires the ability to support users from any location, perform remote configuration and administration of servers and workstations, and deploy or replace servers and workstations in an efficient manner.

When an organization's computer and network infrastructure utilizes Windows Server 2012 servers and Active Directory Domain Services (AD DS), many of the local and remote administrative tasks are simplified with PowerShell, Server Manager, Group Policy, Remote Desktop, and many other tools administrators have in their arsenal. For example, domain group policies can be created and applied to different sets of users and computers to automatically deploy printers, map drives, change security policy, and install software, just to name a few. To support and simplify server and workstation operating system deployment in an Active Directory infrastructure, organizations can deploy and leverage a Windows Server 2012 role named Windows Deployment Services (WDS). WDS enables administrators to deploy Windows Vista, Windows Server 2008, and later server and workstation operating systems through a single console (although some minor work will need to be performed on the system that will be imaged). Other legacy operating systems such as Windows XP and Windows Server 2003 can also be deployed using WDS, but as these operating systems get closer to end of life, finding hardware and drivers that support these operating systems will become more difficult.

This chapter focuses on using WDS to automate the deployment of operating systems to both physical and virtual servers and workstations. Also included in this chapter are some general overviews of the roles and features included with Windows Server 2012 that can assist with the management, configuration, and support of existing servers and workstations.

Managing Desktops and Servers

When planning how the information technology department will manage desktops and servers for a particular organization, many different support scenarios should be considered. Deploying operating systems is only one of the many tasks that fall under the managing desktops and servers umbrella. Additional tasks include deploying and updating software to existing systems, generating reports that detail the status of the overall computer and network infrastructure, supporting end users, and managing backup and recovery processes. There are, of course, many more tasks, but this chapter is limited to these types of IT-related tasks and primarily focuses on the automation of operating system deployment using Windows Server 2012 WDS.

Operating System Deployment to Bare-Metal Systems

When choosing to deploy an operating system to a bare-metal system, all you need is the operating system media, the correct product key, and the supporting driver disks for your hardware. In today's computer and network infrastructure, many workstations come with operating systems preinstalled, and servers usually contain vendor-specific installation disks that not only deploy the operating system, but also install vendor-specific drivers, services, and applications specific to the particular server hardware. Deploying operating systems to bare-metal systems, or systems with no existing operating system, is still a common scenario when organizations want to ensure that a very clean, unmodified operating system is deployed without any unnecessary applications or services. Also, this method might be required to meet specific security and licensing requirements or to be able to easily leverage WDS to quickly roll out new servers and desktops.

Managing Windows and Security Updates

Managing the deployment of security and application updates to Microsoft Windows workstation and server operating systems can be very challenging. This challenge applies not only to systems already deployed on the network, but it also applies to systems recently deployed from a WDS server and virtual servers and offline virtual disks.

Many organizations utilize domain group policies to configure the Windows Update settings on the organization's servers and workstations to ensure that all systems adhere to a policy that automatically keeps the systems updated and secure. The Windows Server 2012 Windows Server Updates Services role can be used in conjunction with the Windows Updates settings in domain policies to allow an organization to centrally manage and report on which updates will be deployed and which client and server systems are in and out of security update compliance.

Regarding WDS images, the longer they remain on the WDS server, the longer they are outdated. These images need to be deployed, updated and recaptured to the WDS server to ensure faster and more secure deployments of systems using WDS. For example, if a 6-month-old WDS image is deployed to a workstation, it may take more than an hour after deployment to download and install the latest Windows security and application updates before the system can be delivered to the end user.

Another common issue faced today with regard to maintaining security updates is dealing with offline virtual machines or virtual disk files. Many organizations leverage virtual machines for production and test usage and many test systems remain offline or powered off most of the time. To keep these offline systems updated with the latest security updates, Microsoft has created a product named the Microsoft Virtual Machine Servicing Tool. This tool integrates with System Center Virtual Machine Manager to enable virtual machine administrators to create and run tasks that install the updates on the normally offline virtual systems.

Supporting End Users and Remote Administration

Supporting end users and performing remote workstation administration of the computer and network infrastructure is a requirement for most organizations. Each organization should determine what the particular end-user support requirements will be and how support will be provided. If remote support of end users is the preferred approach, the organization needs to decide on whether Microsoft-specific tools will be used or if third-party applications or cloud-based services will be necessary to meet the support requirements.

Operating System Deployment Options

When new servers or workstations need to be deployed, one of the big decisions to make is whether these systems will be built and deployed manually or if the system deployment process will be automated. Automating system deployment is not a task that can be completed in a few hours or days, at least not the first time. On the contrary, building a functional operating system deployment infrastructure takes careful planning, sometimes expensive licenses, and many hours and days or weeks worth of testing and tuning the images and the automation. There are many different ways Windows server and business desktop operating system deployments can be performed. Some of these deployment options include manual installation, 100% unattended installations, manufacturer-assisted or customized unattended installations, and through the deployment of prebuilt and possibly customized operating system images.

Manual Installation Using Installation Media

Manual installation is rather straightforward. Insert the installation media and run through the step-by-step installation, documenting all of your settings as you move forward. This method is sometimes required when administrators do not have an image suitable for the particular hardware platform or when only a small number of systems are regularly deployed and taking the time to create unattended or image type installations is unnecessary and provides no real value to the organization.

Unattended Installation

Unattended installations can be helpful when deploying a large number of desktops and servers that have the same hardware model and specifications. An unattend file is simply a file created that answers all the questions asked during a manual installation. Unattended configuration files were historically referred to as answer files. Options in some unattended answer files can include accepting the end-user licensing agreement, entering a volume license product key, choosing to format the drive, specifying a particular partition or volume size for the operating system, and much more. This is now referred to as an unattended installation file.

Windows Deployment Server performs some of the tasks of the unattended installation, primarily the post image deployment task of joining the Active Directory domain. When a default WDS installation is not acceptable, unattend files can be created to support the installation steps like partitioning the hard drives a certain way and post image steps like domain joins, creating local administrator accounts and many more options. Creating and testing unattend files is a tedious step and requires the use of the Windows System Image Manager from the Windows Assessment and Deployment Kit or manually editing the XML files.

Manufacturer-Assisted Installation

Some manufacturers provide automated installation media that, upon boot, prompts the administrator to answer a few questions and the remainder of the installation is automated. This is a very common scenario encountered in the retail sector for home user and business desktops that are shipped with preinstalled operating systems. These types of installations usually include original equipment manufacturer (OEM) licensed software. One important point to note is that when an organization wants to move toward the automated deployment of servers or desktops using an imaging or deployment system, an OEM operating system license and media cannot be used with deployment systems as it usually violates the licensing agreement.

Server systems can also be sold with OEM preinstalled operating systems. Others, however, come with no operating system and require either retail or volume license media for installation. Many manufacturers will also have installation CD's that will have the administrator go through an installation interview of sorts, then will build the unattend files and install the Windows server operating system based on the interview questions. Depending on the scenario and the software, this is a very viable scenario because it can usually include necessary hardware-related drivers and support software for monitoring the hardware.

Cloning or Imaging Systems

Cloning or imaging systems can be helpful when deploying a series of identical desktops and servers. You build up a desktop or a server, prepare the system for cloning/imaging, and copy/capture the system image using third-party tools or Microsoft deployment tools such as WDS. Microsoft only supports the cloning and imaging of servers and desktops when the application Sysprep.exe is used to generate new machine security identifiers (SIDs). WDS can be used to deploy both default installation images and customized or captured installation images to Windows servers and desktops.

Microsoft and Independent Software Vendors have supported the imaging and rapid deployment of Windows systems for years. Today Microsoft has three different imaging deployment tools: Windows Deployment Services, System Center Configuration Manager, and the Microsoft Deployment Toolkit (MDT) 2012; and in earlier versions of Microsoft Windows Server, Microsoft has also released deployment tools with the server operating system and as separate feature packs.

Remote Installation Services

Remote Installation Services (RIS) was released with Windows 2000 Server and was Microsoft's first successful "over the network" operating system deployment services. Windows 2000 Server RIS did not support server operating systems and had many limitations, but it was a very functional and valuable tool.

Automated Deployment Services

Automated Deployment Services was an add-on feature pack to Windows Server 2003 Enterprise edition, and was designed to assist with the rapid deployment of Windows 2000/2003 server operating systems only. For organizations that utilized Windows Server 2003 and required desktop deployment options, Windows Server 2003 RIS was still required.

Windows Server 2003 SP2 Windows Deployment Services

With the release of Windows Server 2003 Service Pack 2, administrators could upgrade their Windows Server 2003 RIS systems to Windows Server 2003 WDS. If RIS had previously been deployed with existing images, the upgrade took the existing RIS (RIPREP and RISETUP) images and placed them in the Legacy Image folder within the WDS MMC snap-in, and upon your initial launch of the WDS console, the administrators were prompted to choose whether the WDS system would run in Legacy or Mixed mode. After a few more simple configurations, existing RIS images would work successfully in the environment.

Windows Server 2008 and 2008 R2 WDS

Windows Deployment Services (WDS) running on Windows Server 2008 or Windows Server 2008 R2 systems provides many of the same features and functions of RIS, Automated Deployment Services, and Windows Server 2003 SP2 WDS combined. Windows Server 2008 R2 WDS also provides additional functionality not included in any of its predecessors. Two of the distinct features of Windows Server 2008 and Windows

Server 2008 R2 Windows Deployment Services are that both server and desktop operating systems can be deployed and images can be deployed using multicast communication. New specifically on Windows Server 2008 R2 WDS systems is the ability to support directly adding drivers or driver provisioning to Windows 7 and Windows Server 2008 R2 boot images using the WDS console and the support for network booting on x64-based computers with Extensible Firmware Interface (EFI) support.

System Center Configuration Manager 2007 and 2012

For medium-sized and enterprise-sized organizations, additional deployment options can be leveraged when the organization has deployed System Center Configuration Manager 2007 or 2012. Utilizing the Operating System Deployment feature, organizations can leverage a zero-touch or lite-touch deployment of operating systems. As evident by the name zero-touch, if configured properly, the workstation or server never needs a visit. For example, an existing Windows XP or later workstation operating system can be tested for Windows 8 compatibility. If the tests pass, the user state can be exported and saved and a customized Windows 8 image can be pushed down to the system, followed by post-image processing to install applications. And then, the compatible portions of the exported user state can be restored. The end result delivers Windows 8 to the end-user desktop with the user's profile already configured. More information about this and many of the other valuable features included with System Center Configuration Manager 2007 and 2012 can be found on the System Center 2012 website.

Windows Server 2012 Windows Deployment Services

Windows Server 2012 WDS is a server role that is designed to assist organizations that utilize Active Directory Domain Services with the deployment of Windows systems. The WDS system typically is set up to provide the storage and image retrieval services necessary for image deployment, the client components such as the PXE boot images, and the management components used to configure WDS settings, including adding images to the WDS server and creating multicast transmissions.

As previously stated, Windows Server 2012 WDS includes the best features of all its predecessors released with Windows 2000 Server, Windows Server 2003, Windows Server 2008, and Windows Server 2008 R2. Some of the features include the following:

- Support for Windows Vista SP1, Windows 7, Windows 8, Windows Server 2008, 2008 R2, and Windows Server 2012 operating systems images.
- Support for Windows Server 2003 and Windows XP Professional images.
- The ability to deploy images using multicast communication.
- The ability to use boot and installation images included with Windows Vista, Windows Server 2008 and later workstation and server operating systems using the .wim extension. These WIM files can be copied directly from the respective installation media right into the WDS server to provide base images for these operating systems within minutes, without any customization.

- Support for both 32- and 64-bit operating system deployment.
- WDS deployment as a standalone server without Active Directory.

Because of the nature of the Preboot Execution Environment (PXE), Dynamic Host Configuration Protocol (DHCP) and domain name system (DNS) services are required. Of course, for WDS to function properly, the desktop or server hardware must also be compatible and must support PXE boot and have at a minimum of 512MB of RAM and a 1.4GHz or faster processor to install Windows Server 2012, or 1GB of RAM and a 1 GHz or faster processor for Windows 8. Although the WDS server can be configured to use IPv6, all client and WDS server communication will use IPv4.

WDS Image Types

Windows Server 2012 WDS includes several different image types. WDS administrators need to understand each of these image types to understand the documentation and how WDS works and also to be able to communicate the inner workings of WDS to management and other administrators or clients as required. WDS image types include boot images, installation images, discover images, and capture images.

Boot Images

A boot image contains the Windows Deployment Services client and the Windows Preinstallation Environment (Windows PE), which is basically a mini operating system used to connect the system to the WDS server and provide the means to select and install a WDS installation image. The boot image included in the Windows Server 2012 installation media as an example, is appropriately named boot.wim and can be used to boot systems that will install Windows Vista SP1 Windows 2008 or greater server and workstation x64 operation system. The Windows Server 2012 boot image can also be used to install images using multicast transmissions. If x86 images will be deployed, it is a best practice to boot those systems using the compatible x86 Windows 8 or Windows Vista SP1 boot image because Windows Server 2012 does not have a x86 compatible version. Maintaining both x86 and x64 boot images on the WDS server will help simplify issues with driver provisioning and manual driver injection as necessary. Also, even if a Windows XP or Windows Server 2003 custom install image will be deployed, the x86 or x64 boot image from the Microsoft Deployment Toolkit will be required as well as the appropriate storage, system bus, and networking drivers for that boot image. To be very specific, if a hardware platform that will be used for a Windows XP or Windows Server 2003 system does not contain storage, network, and system bus hardware that has a compatible driver that matches the MDT boot image, that hardware might not be a feasible candidate for WDS deployment.

Installation Images

The installation images are the actual Windows installation media, packaged into a single WIM file. Depending on the actual media used to provide the WIM files, many different installation images might be included. For example, organizations that receive volume license media from Microsoft might have received a Microsoft Windows Server 2012 DVD that contains the full installation and the Server Core images for Standard and Datacenter editions and older server installation images may include also the Web and Enterprise editions. On a WDS server, normally only a single boot image is required per platform, x86 or x64, but it can contain many different installation images.

Discover Images

A discover image is created from a boot image and is used to boot a system and load the Windows Preinstallation Environment (Windows PE) and locate and connect to a WDS server. A discover image is commonly used when the network does not support PXE boot or the system does not support it. Discover images can be exported to ISO files and then burned or stored on removable media, such as CDs, DVDs, or USB memory sticks, for portability. In some cases, when hardware is not booting and connecting properly to a WDS server using a boot image, a discover image can be tested as an alternative for both deploying installation images and capturing a system to an image.

Capture Images

A capture image is also created from a boot image, but instead of running setup like an installation image, the capture image runs the WDS capture utility. The WDS capture utility is used to connect to a system that has been prepared for imaging or cloning, using the appropriate system preparation tools, to the WDS system to create a new installation image that can be deployed later to WDS clients. Before a capture image is used, a system with an operating system is customized by adding applications, custom configurations, and other system changes that are required by the particular organization. When the system is ready for imaging, it is prepared using sysprep, a Microsoft deployment tool used to clear the machine's SID and operating system configurations that are specific to the system that will be imaged. Many times however, additional steps must be taken before running sysprep to ensure a successful capture, such as clearing out application specific certain Registry keys, deleting user profiles and possibly removing software applications themselves. To be certain about third-party or even Microsoft applications or suites, review the manufacturer documentation with specific emphasis on system imaging, cloning, or sysprep.

Installing Windows Deployment Services

You can install WDS on Windows Server 2012 using the Server Manager console, or through Windows PowerShell. Windows Deployment Services can be installed on the Standard or Datacenter edition of Windows Server 2012, but it is not included on any Server Core editions. If the WDS role is installed on a Server Core installation, this will also install the GUI on that system, essentially changing it from a Server Core installation to a GUI installation. Before installing the WDS role, ensure that all volumes on the WDS server are formatted as NTFS volumes. Also, it is not recommended to install the WDS images into the same volume as the operating system (to allow for customized security and to remove any risk of filling up the system drive when adding images to the WDS server). To add the WDS role using Windows PowerShell, follow these steps:

1. Log on to the Windows Server 2012 system that will have the WDS role installed with an account with local administrator and domain administrator rights.
2. Open Windows PowerShell from the taskbar.
3. Type the command **Add-WindowsFeature WDS** and press Enter. This will install the WDS role, including both the Transport and Deployment service as well as the WDS tools.
4. The installation progress will be shown in the PowerShell Windows. After the installation completes, close the PowerShell Window.

Configuring the WDS Server

After the WDS role is installed, the initial boot and installation image can be added. Locate the Windows Server 2012 installation media because the boot image from this media can and will be used to deploy Windows Vista SP1, Windows 7, and Windows 8 64-bit edition images. If x86 images will be deployed, you can use the Windows 8 x86 boot image, which can be used to deploy both x86 and x64 install images. For the remainder of this chapter, the tasks will be associated with a WDS server that is part of an Active Directory domain with DHCP services running on a separate Windows Server 2012 server. To install the initial boot image on the WDS server, follow these steps:

1. Log on to the Windows Server 2012 system that has the WDS role installed with an account with local administrator and domain administrator rights.
2. Open Server Manager from the taskbar.
3. When Server Manager opens, click the WDS icon in the tree pane.
4. In the Servers pane, right-click the WDS server and select Windows Deployment Services Management Console. The WDS console can also be opened from the Start menu using the WDS console tile.
5. When the WDS Management console opens, expand the Servers node in the tree pane, and the local WDS server will be listed with a warning symbol on it indicating that the WDS server needs to be configured. Right-click the server and select Configure Server, as shown in Figure 26.1.
6. Review the requirements that are detailed on the Before You Begin page, and click Next to continue.
7. On the Install Options page, select to install Integrated with Active Directory or Standalone Server, and then click Next to continue. For this example (and the remainder of this chapter), we will select Integrated with Active Directory.

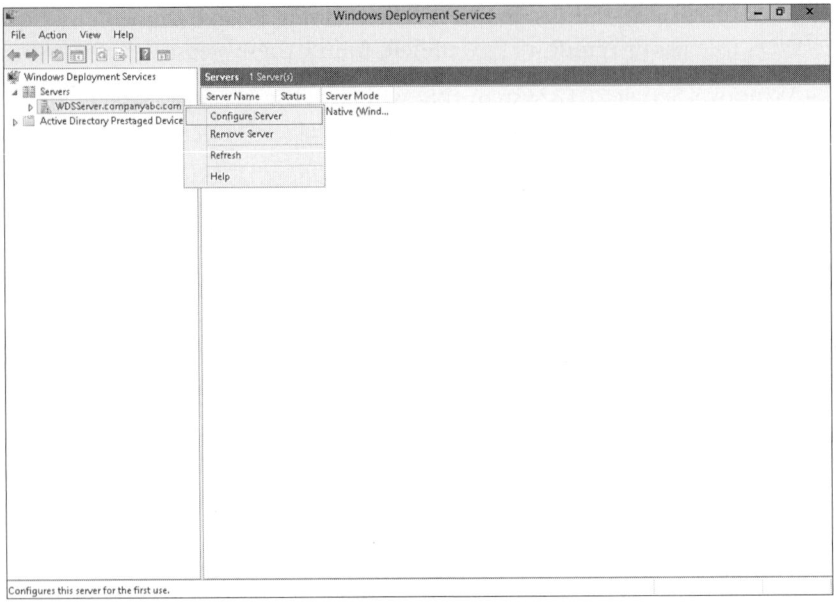

FIGURE 26.1 Configuring the WDS server.

8. On the Remote Installation Folder Location page, specify the default installation path for the WDS images. For our example, we will use a separate drive and specify the path of E:\RemoteInstall and then click Next.

NOTE

If the WDS server only has a single disk and is selected for the installation folder, a pop-up notification opens stating that it is recommended that you create the remote installation disk on a different volume and, if possible, a different disk.

9. On the PXE Server Initial Settings page, review the options for PXE boot settings:

- **Do Not Respond to Any Client Computer**—This option essentially disables the WDS server from responding to any PXE boot attempts.
- **Respond Only to Known Client Computers**—This option requires that each system that will have an image deployed or captured will need to have an existing Active Directory computer account with a predefined globally unique identifier (GUID). This is the desired configuration after the WDS infrastructure is tested and working properly and after the WDS administrator understands how to locate the GUID of a system and pre-create a computer account in Active Directory.

- **Respond to All Client Computers (Known and Unknown)**—This option allows any machine that is PXE boot capable to connect to the WDS server and load a boot image. Of course, to install an image, the user needs to specify domain credentials.

When Respond to All Client Computers (Known and Unknown) is selected, the WDS administrator can also select an additional check box that would require WDS administrators to approve connected WDS clients in the console before an image can be deployed to that system. This added security removes the requirement for the collection of system GUIDs before a system can connect to WDS but also adds the necessary security to allow the WDS administrator to control the deployment of WDS images.

10. For the initial WDS installation, select the Respond to All Client Computers (Known and Unknown) option button, and click Next, as shown in Figure 26.2.

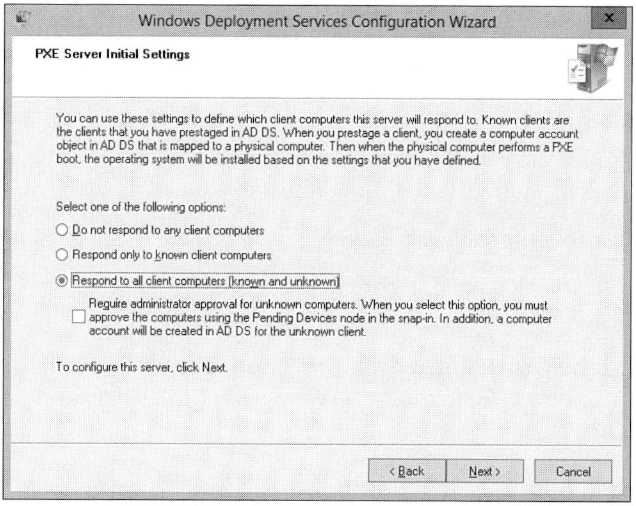

FIGURE 26.2 Configuring WDS to respond to all PXE clients.

11. The Operation Complete page appears, and an Add Images to the Server Now check box is displayed. Uncheck the check box and click Finish to close the wizard.

After the wizard closes, the Windows Deployment Services console is displayed. Review each of the nodes that are now displayed beneath the WDS server, such as the Install Images, Boot Images, Pending Devices, Multicast Transmissions, and the Drivers node. As we move forward in our WDS server configuration, each of these nodes will be reviewed, but at this time, additional configuration of the WDS server might be required. To review the WDS server settings, follow these steps:

1. Open the WDS Management console on the WDS server.
2. When the WDS Management console opens, if the local server is not listed under the Servers node, it must be added by right-clicking Servers in the tree pane and selecting Add Server. Specify the local server and click OK to add it to the console.
3. When the WDS server is listed in the tree pane, right-click the server and select Properties.
4. Review each of the property pages to become familiar with the WDS server configuration options and update as necessary or click Cancel to close the property pages.

DHCP Configuration

You must have a working DHCP server with an active scope on the network and, of course, DNS and Active Directory Domain Services are also required. The DHCP services are used to supply the PXE client computer with an IPv4 address during the installation of the image. When the WDS server is installed, it automatically registers in Active Directory with a DHCP server to allow for PXE clients to locate the WDS server without having to reconfigure any DHCP options. Of course, the WDS server also registers with the DNS server so that it can be located during the network boot process. If this registration process by the WDS server is successful, it should have a DNS record, and it will need to be authorized in DHCP. To authorize the WDS server in DHCP, follow these steps:

1. Open the WDS Management console on the WDS server.
2. When the WDS server is listed in the tree pane, right-click the server and select Properties.
3. Select the Advanced tab, and in the DHCP Authorization section select the radial button labeled Authorize this Windows Deployment Services Server in DHCP, and then click OK, as shown in Figure 26.3.

In situations when the WDS server is also the DHCP server, additional changes to the WDS server will need to be adjusted. To adjust the WDS server DHCP settings when the two roles are hosted on the same system, follow these steps:

1. Open the WDS Management console on the WDS server.
2. When the WDS server is listed in the tree pane, right-click the server and select Properties.
3. Select the DHCP tab and in the DHCP page select both check boxes to configure the DHCP server to not listen on port 67 and to configure option 60 to indicate that the DHCP server is also a PXE server, as shown in Figure 26.4.

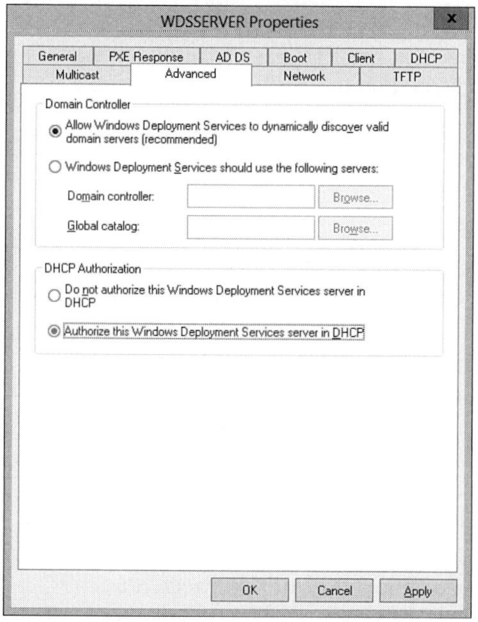

FIGURE 26.3 Configuring DHCP authorization in the WDS console.

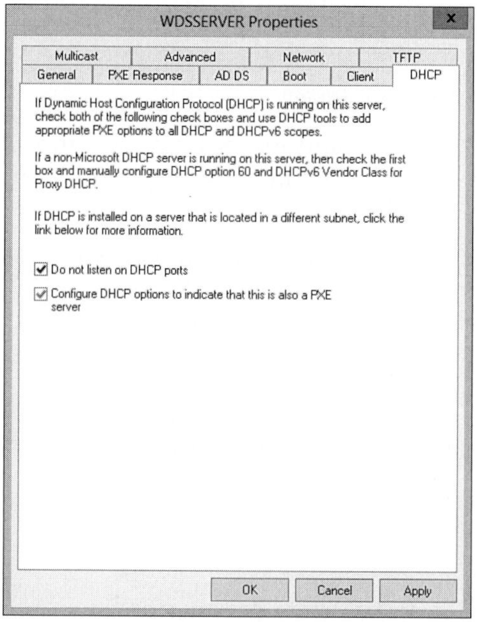

FIGURE 26.4 Configuring DHCP server settings on the WDS server.

NOTE

If there is a DHCP server running on the network but it is not a Microsoft DHCP server, option 60 will need to be manually added and configured on the DHCP server to enable PXE clients to locate the WDS server.

Adding a Boot Image to the WDS Server

After the WDS server is configured as desired, it is time to add the initial boot image to the server. When a system is booted using PXE boot and connects to a WDS server, a boot image is used to prepare the client system to install a Windows image. The boot image contains the WDS client and Windows PE. With the Windows 8 default boot image, boot.wim, the Windows PE contains an extensive list of network drivers, and most systems can be booted to WDS and successfully install an image. Using the Windows 8 or Windows Server 2012 boot.wim images allows for the largest inclusion of network and storage drivers for image deployment. Boot images are also used to create capture images and discover images. One important point to note is that the boot.wim from Windows 8 x86 architecture will list both x86 and x64 install images if the WDS client architecture can support both. x64 boot images will only list x64 install images once connected to the WDS server even if the hardware supports both x86 and x64. To add a boot image to the WDS server, follow these steps:

1. Open the WDS Management console on the WDS server.
2. In the tree pane, expand the Servers node, and then select and expand the WDS server.
3. Right-click the Boot Images node and select Add Boot Image.
4. When the Add Image Wizard opens, the first page prompts for the location of the boot image file. If the Windows 8 installation media is not in the WDS server's local CD/DVD drive, locate it on the network.
5. Click the Browse button to locate the Windows installation media on the server or on the network. Using the DVD media, open the Sources folder on the root of the Windows 8 installation media and select the boot.wim file, and click Open to add it.
6. Back in the Add Image Wizard window, if the boot image path and file are listed, click Next to continue.
7. On the Image Metadata page, either accept the default boot image name and description or type in a new one, and click Next to continue.
8. Next review the Summary page and click Next to continue. This starts the process of adding the boot image to the WDS server.
9. After the process completes, click Finish on the Task Progress page to close the wizard.

10. Back in the Windows Deployment Services console, select the Boot Images node in the tree pane, and in the Tasks pane verify that the new boot image has been added.
11. Close the Windows Deployment Services console and log off of the server.

Adding Install Images to the WDS Server

After the initial boot image is added to the WDS server, installation images can be added. Windows Vista, Windows Server 2008, and later workstation and server Windows operating system installation media contain the compatible Windows Imaging (WIM) format file. These WIM files can be directly added to the WDS server as install images. To install the initial install image, follow these steps:

1. Open the WDS Management console on the WDS server.
2. In the tree pane, expand the Servers node, and then select and expand the WDS server.
3. Right-click the Install Images node and select Add Install Image.
4. On the Image Group page, either select an existing image group to store the file in, or create a new image group by typing in a valid name. For this example, we will create a new image group named Windows 8. When you are finished, click Next.
5. On the Image File page, browse to the location of the install.wim Install Image file. For our example, in the Windows 8 DVD installation media, browse to the Sources folder and select the install.wim file, and click Open.
6. Back on the Image File page, verify the path, and click Next to continue.
7. On the Available Images page, depending on the particular install.wim file a single image or several images may be listed. Select only the images that the company or organization is licensed for or only the images that will be uploaded into the WDS server and click Next to continue.
8. On the Summary page, review the list of install images that will be loaded into the WDS server, and click Next to begin the process.
9. After the images are uploaded into the WDS server, click Finish on the Task Progress page to return to the WDS console.

If necessary or desired, the WDS administrator can now also add additional boot and install images for both x86 and x64 architectures.

Deploying the First Install Image

After a WDS server has at least one boot image and one install image, the imaging process should be tested before any additional configurations are performed. Before testing the imaging process, we need to check the properties of the WDS server and the DHCP server scope options. To verify these settings, perform the following tasks:

- Using the WDS console, open the properties of the WDS server and click the Advanced tab to verify or to select the appropriate option buttons to ensure that both the Authorize This Windows Deployment Services Server in DHCP and the Allow Windows Deployment Services to Dynamically Discover Valid Domain Servers (Recommended) check boxes are checked. Click OK to update the server settings if any changes were made; otherwise, click Cancel to close the WDS server property pages.
- Using the WDS console, open the properties of the WDS server again and click the PXE Response tab and verify that the Respond to All Client Computers (Known and Unknown) option button is selected and verify that the check box that would require administrator approval is not checked. Click OK to update the server settings if any changes were made; otherwise, click Cancel to close the WDS server property pages.
- Using the DHCP console on the appropriate DHCP server, open the properties of the appropriate IPv4 DHCP scope, assuming a Microsoft Windows Server 2012 DHCP server is deployed, and verify that the DNS domain name and DNS server DHCP options contain the proper values for your company's environment. DHCP option 60 is not required if the DHCP server is on the same subnet as the WDS server and both of the servers are running Windows Server 2008, 2008 R2 or Windows Server 2012.

After these precheck steps are completed, the imaging process can begin. To deploy an image to a system using PXE boot, follow these steps:

1. Select the desired system that will be imaged using WDS and connect the system's primary network adapter to a live switch port that is on the same network as the DHCP and WDS server.
2. Boot the system and enter the system BIOS. Verify that PXE network boot is enabled for the primary adapter and verify that PXE network boot is listed in the boot menu before the system optical drive, hard disk or disk arrays.
3. Save the BIOS settings and exit the BIOS to start a system boot sequence. When the PXE network boot starts, keep a close eye on it to verify that the PXE client is obtaining a DHCP IPv4 lease. When prompted with the Press F12 for Network Boot message, press the F12 key to start the WDS imaging process. If PXE boot is getting an IPv4 address from the DHCP server but the system never prompts to press F12 for network boot, there is most likely some issue with the DHCP server configuration and defined options. This needs to be resolved before moving forward or an alternative is to create and use a discover image to start the imaging process. Creating and using discover images are detailed in the next section, "Creating Discover Images."
4. If the system is able to connect to the WDS server after the prompt and after the F12 key is pressed, the boot image is downloaded from the WDS server to the client and the imaging process starts. If multiple boot images have been added to the WDS server, pressing F12 will use the network boot to connect to the WDS server to get

the list of boot images, then the boot image selected will be loaded, including the appropriate network drivers to allow the WDS client to connect to the WDS server to locate and begin installation of the install image selected.

5. After the system completes loading the boot image system files, the Windows Preinstallation Environment is loaded and the WDS client install application is started. The page name that appears is named Windows Deployment Services. Select the desired locale and keyboard or input method, and click Next to continue.

6. An authentication window opens. Enter the domain and username of the account used to install WDS and the password, and click OK. For a domain with a NetBIOS name of COMPANYABC, the username should be entered as **COMPANYABC\username** along with the correct password for that user account. If the authentication window never opens or does not connect to the WDS server after the correct username and password combination are entered, this most likely means that the boot image does not contain suitable network drivers for the client hardware and network drivers will need to be added to the boot image and this process should be started over.

7. On the Select the Operating System You Wish to Install page, each of the install images that are compatible with the boot image architecture, x86 or x64, will be listed as available selections. Select the desired operating system install image, and click Next to continue.

8. The next page lists the available or detected disks that can be used for the image installation. If no disks are listed, this is a red flag for WDS imaging and requires adding disk controller driver files to a boot image for WDS imaging to work on this particular hardware platform. Select the disk to install the operating system on, click Next to allow the imaging process to create the volume, format it, and install Windows 8 on the WDS client system.

NOTE

When selecting hardware for server and desktops that will be deployed using WDS images, ensure that the hardware is certified to work with the operating system that you are deploying to that hardware and verify that all the drivers are certified and signed by the Windows Hardware Quality lab to simplify operating system deployment to these systems.

9. After the disk selection is made and the Next button is clicked, the disk volume is created and formatted and the operating system installation begins by expanding and copying the necessary files and installing the default operating system selections. When this phase of the installation completes, Windows Setup begins.

10. Depending on the install image and the network configuration, after the install image is deployed the first screen may prompt for the product key, accepting the end-user licensing agreement, Windows Update settings, date and time, and network zone settings. Also a new local user account or online Microsoft account will need to

be created or associated with the image. These pages will appear in a different order depending on the install image and on a default Windows 8 install image the setting page has an option to accept the express settings to complete the installation. Follow the necessary steps to complete the installation of this image to the WDS client.

By default, the WDS server when configured with Active Directory integration will join the newly imaged machines to the domain and will automatically name the systems. When this is not the desired behavior, the WDS server properties can be modified to not join the domain or a custom unattended file can be created. This completes the installation process of a default WDS image.

Creating Multicast Images

A feature of WDS is that images can be deployed to servers and workstations using multicast transmissions. For multicast imaging to work properly, the network devices that connect the WDS multicast clients to the WDS server providing the multicast transmission must support and allow multicast traffic. Creating a multicast transmission is a very straightforward process and can be created within a few minutes, if the WDS server already contains tested boot and install images. To create a multicast transmission, follow these steps:

1. Open the WDS Management console on the WDS server.
2. In the tree pane, expand the Servers node, and then select and expand the WDS server.
3. Right-click Multicast Transmissions node and select Create Multicast Transmission.
4. On the Transmission Name page, enter a name for the multicast transmission, and click Next. For example, enter **MultiCast-Windows8**. Click Next to continue.
5. On the Image Selection page, select one of the WDS install images that will be transmitted to clients through this multicast transmission, and click Next. If the desired image is not listed, pull down the image group pull-down menu and select the correct image group that contains the desired install image.
6. On the Multicast Type page, select Auto-Cast, which will start the transmission automatically when a client connects to the WDS server and selects the install image that is defined within this multicast transmission, and click Next. Alternatively, select Scheduled-Cast to define a number of clients or a start time that will kick off the multicast transmission, as shown in Figure 26.5. Click Next after the multicast type is selected.
7. On the Operation Complete page, click Finish to return to the WDS console.
8. In the tree pane, select and expand the Multicast Transmissions node to reveal the new multicast transmission.
9. Select the new multicast transmission, and in the Tasks pane, after clients connect to the transmission, each client will be listed and their progress can be tracked.

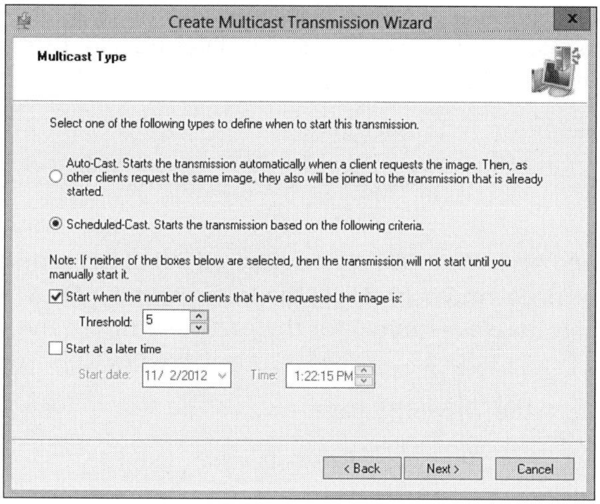

FIGURE 26.5 Configuring a multicast image transmission type.

10. When the multicast transmission is no longer required, right-click the multicast transmission, and select Delete. Confirm the deletion by clicking Yes, and then close the WDS console and log off of the server.

When WDS clients need to connect to the multicast transmission, they only need to select the install image used to create the multicast transmission and they will connect appropriately. This also means that this install image cannot be used by unicast clients until the multicast transmission is removed.

Customizing Boot Images

Depending on the hardware and images being deployed it may become necessary to customize boot images. The boot image loads the initial network and storages drivers required to connect to the WDS server to find and download the install images. This sections details customizations for boot images and describes some troubleshooting steps for boot and image deployment issues that WDS administrators may encounter.

Adding Drivers to Boot and Discover Images

Windows Server 2012 WDS supports adding drivers to Windows Server 2012 and Window 8 boot images from within the WDS console. This also includes any Windows Server 2012 or Windows 8 discover and capture images that are loaded as boot images on a WDS system. For all other boot, discover images, and capture images, drivers will need to be injected manually to the WIM file using the tools in the Windows Assessment and Deployment Kit (ADK). To add drivers into a Windows Server 2012 WDS infrastructure into a Windows Server 2012 or Windows 8 boot image, complete the steps detailed in the following sections.

Adding Drivers to the WDS Server Console

When drivers need to be added to Windows 8 or Windows Server 2012 boot images, they can be installed using the WDS console as follows:

1. Open the WDS Management console on the WDS server.
2. In the tree pane, expand the Servers node, and then select and expand the WDS server.
3. Download the appropriate drivers and save the drivers to a folder on WDS server or a network location. Expand the drivers download to reveal the folder that contains the necessary INF, SYS, and other files that are required for the particular driver and note the exact location.
4. Right-click the Drivers node and select Add Driver Package.
5. On the Driver Package Location page, select the Select Driver from an INF File option button.
6. In the Location field, click the Browse button and browse to the folder that contains the drivers INF, SYS, and other files. Once back on the Driver Package Location page, click Next to continue.
7. On the Available Driver Packages page, check or uncheck the desired drivers that will be added to the WDS server and click Next to continue. Many drivers are packaged together and the driver file may include many different drivers. As a best practice, limit the drivers added to the WDS server and the boot images to only the necessary drivers and no more to avoid unnecessary driver conflicts or file size bloat.
8. Review the selections on the Summary page and click Next to continue.
9. On the Task Progress page, once the drivers are added, click Next to continue.
10. On the Drivers Group page, if a driver group exists, the driver can be added to the group; otherwise, a new driver group can be created or the driver can be added to the root without creating a group. Select the desired option button, enter or select the driver group, and click Next to continue.
11. On the Task Completed page, click Finish to complete the driver addition.

Adding a Driver Package to a Boot Image Using the WDS Console

After a driver package has been added to the WDS Server, it can be added into an existing boot or install image using the WDS console. To perform this task, follow these steps:

1. Open the WDS Management console on the WDS server.
2. In the tree pane, expand the Servers node, and then select and expand the WDS server.
3. Select the Boot images node, and in the Boot Images pane right-click the desired boot image and select Add Driver Packages to Image.
4. On the Before You Begin page, click Next to continue.

5. On the Select Driver Packages page, click the Search for Packaged button on the right center of the window.
6. Select the desired driver package in the Search results section of the window by checking the check box, and then click Next, as shown in Figure 26.6.

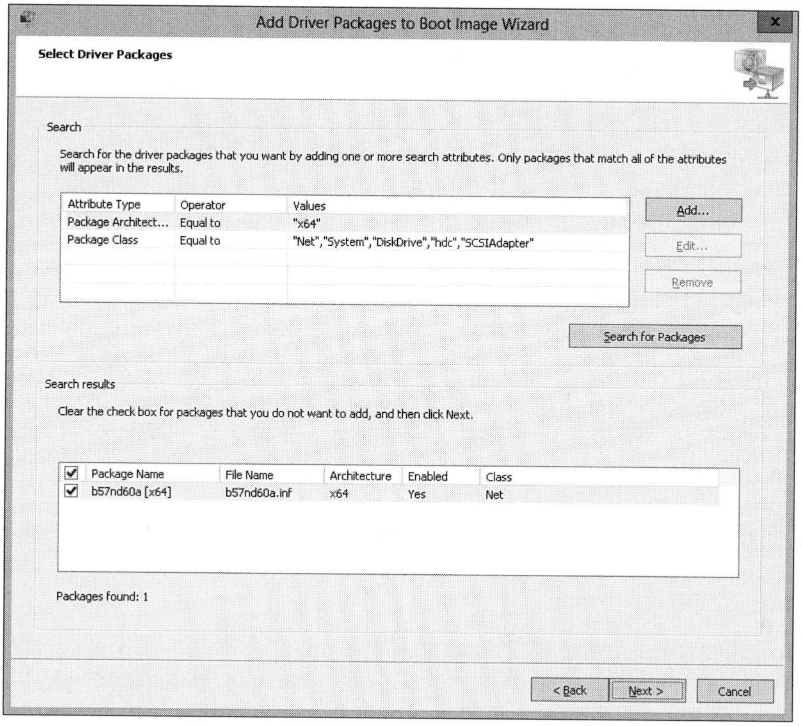

FIGURE 26.6 Selecting a driver package to add to a boot image.

7. In the Selected Driver Packages window, click Next to add the package to the boot image.
8. Review the results in the Operation Complete Page and click Finish.

This task should only be performed if there are systems that cannot boot properly into the WDS deployment image, and when this task is executed, it should be performed on a separate test boot image to retain the integrity of the original working boot images.

WDS Boot and Install Image Troubleshooting

Getting a WDS system and images to work the first time will either work without issue or it can take a little bit of work. This section provides a short list of issues and troubleshooting steps that might help make the implementation of WDS more successful.

Issue 1: WDS clients never prompt to boot from network by pressing F12.

When this occurs, the issue might be related to the boot order on the client. Go into the BIOS on the client and first verify that the network interface card has network boot functionality enabled. Next, set the boot order to make the network interface card first in the boot list or boot priority and try again.

If the PXE boot option starts, the administrator should see the IP address that is leased from the DHCP server. If no IP address is leased, check to see that the WDS server is listed as an authorized DHCP server using the Microsoft Windows Server 2012 DHCP console. If it is not listed, add it by changing the DHCP server advanced property page settings. If DHCP is on the same server as WDS, check the WDS server DHCP property page settings to ensure that both check boxes are checked. Also verify normal DHCP server operation by checking that a client on the same network can acquire a DHCP IP address.

Issue 2: WDS clients can press F12 and get the list of boot images. After the boot image is loaded and the locale and keyboard layout are chosen, they are never prompted for credentials or cannot proceed any further even after entering the correct credentials.

When this occurs, the most likely issue is that the boot image selected does not contain a suitable network card driver for that workstation or server network interface card. To determine whether this is the case, after the boot image is loaded at the Windows Deployment Services page, press Shift and F10 to drop to a command prompt. Type in **Ipconfig** and press Enter. If an IP address is listed, run **Ipconfig /all** to check the DNS server settings as the DHCP server might not be giving the correct scope options. If no IP address is listed, the network interface card drivers for this hardware will need to be added to the boot image using the WDS console.

Another issue that can cause this is if the NTFS and share permissions of the deployment share on the WDS server are not configured correctly. The share and NTFS permissions should allow all desired user groups to read and execute. These groups might be limited based on the delegation of administration desired to control who can deploy WDS images.

Issue 3: After entering credentials, the list of install images only shows x64 images.

This issue is by design if the boot image selected is an x64-based boot image. Selecting an x86 boot image, for example from Windows 8, allows the WDS client to show both x86- and x64-based images.

Issue 4: The WDS client can boot into the boot image and select the install image, but no disks are listed as options to install the WDS image on to.

This issue is most likely caused by a missing storage controller driver in the boot image. The resolution to this issue is to add storage controller drivers to the boot image the same way network card drivers are added using the WDS console.

Issue 5: After selecting the install image and the destination disk, the installation starts but after the install completes, many devices are listed as unknown in Device Manager.

This issue indicates that the drivers for these unknown devices are not included in the install image and they should be added to the desired install image the same way drivers are added to the boot image.

Creating Discover Images

In cases when PXE boot is not supported on the system or on the network, it might be necessary to use bootable media to start a WDS imaging process. This can be accomplished with a WDS discover image. A discover image is created from an existing WDS boot image that contains Windows PE and the WDS client, but can be stored on removable media making it easier to deploy images to older systems or on heterogeneous networks that have PXE issues. To create a discover image, follow these steps:

1. Open the WDS Management console on the WDS server.
2. When the Windows Deployment Services console opens, in the tree pane expand the Servers node, expand the WDS server, and select the Boot Images node.
3. In the Tasks pane, locate and right-click the desired boot image, and select Create Discover Image.
4. On the Discover Image Metadata and Location page, enter a name and description for the new discover boot image. In the Location and File Name section, browse to a folder on the local system where the new discover boot image can be created, type in a name for the discover image, and click Open to return to the Discover Image Metadata and Location page.
5. Enter the fully qualified domain name of the WDS server that the discover image will connect to after booting into the Windows PE and loading the WDS client. Figure 26.7 shows the discover metadata that will be used for this example; the path to the file is important as it will be required later. Click Next to create the discover image.
6. When the discover image is created, click Finish to close the window and return to the WDS console.

At this point, a new discover image has been created, but a few additional steps are required before it can be used to boot a system and connect to a WDS server.

The discover image can now be added to the WDS server as a boot image, by following the steps in the previous section on adding boot images to the WDS server. You might ask why a WDS administrator would want to do this—there have been documented issues where a WDS client PC cannot connect to the WDS server using a standard boot image but can connect using a discover image. Perhaps it has to do with the fact that the WDS server is already selected, but this is an out-of-the-ordinary case that is only listed here because it might add value to a WDS administrator troubleshooting an implementation.

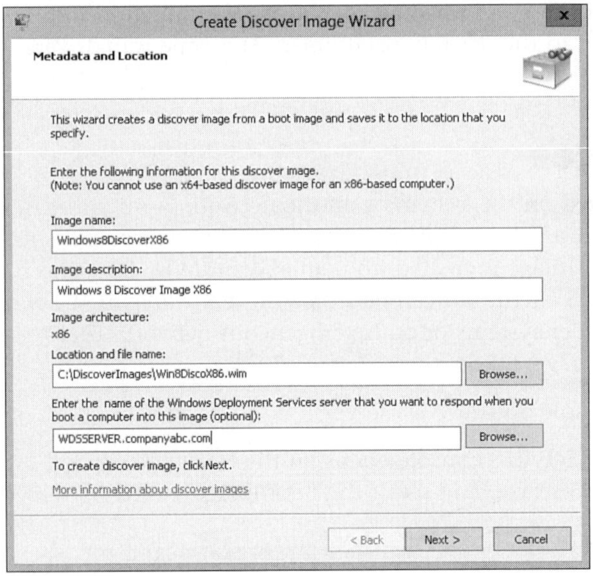

FIGURE 26.7 Sample discover boot image metadata.

An alternate and more common use of discover images is to create bootable media that can be used on client or server hardware that does not support PXE boot. To create a bootable CD or DVD that will use the new discover boot image, the tools included in the Windows Assessment and Deployment Kit (ADK) are required. The ADK for Windows 8 and Windows Server 2012 is new and includes many updated features and settings.

Pre-Creating Active Directory Computer Accounts for WDS (Prestaged Systems)

When imaging a system using the default boot and install images, WDS automatically generates the name of the computer and uses the credentials specified during the image deployment to add the imaged system to the Active Directory domain of which the WDS server is a member. WDS uses the configuration settings in the WDS Properties, AD DS tab, as shown in Figure 26.8, to define the Client Naming Policy format for computers and to define which domain and container the new computer accounts will be created in.

The configuration options in the WDS Property page, AD DS tab, work well for new computer account placement, but are not very flexible for naming computer accounts. When many computers will be deployed and will require specific computer names in Active Directory, the computer accounts can be pre-created. For the pre-created computer accounts to be linked to the actual systems, the associated system's network card MAC address or GUID is required. On most systems, the MAC address and the GUID will be displayed during the PXE boot sequence, as shown in Figure 26.9. Either of these can be used to predefine the computer account in the WDS console. Creating prestaged systems is quite helpful for tracking systems. For example, in one deployment, an organization always created prestaged systems based on the serial number of the system, and on others the systems were named to reflect the user the system is assigned to.

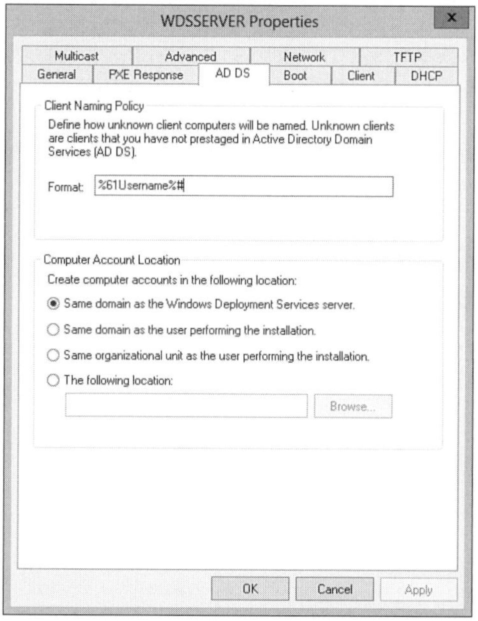

FIGURE 26.8 WDS Properties page for new computer account, AD DS tab.

26

Creating prestaged systems is not only useful for custom naming, it also can be used to choose which boot and install image will be deployed to a system, but for that an unattend file will need to be created. For this example of creating a prestaged device, we will simply customize the name of the system and associated it with the known MAC address as captured previously and shown in Figure 26.9. After the MAC address has been identified and recorded, the account can be prestaged in the WDS console. To create a prestaged device in the WDS console, follow these steps:

FIGURE 26.9 Gathering a system's network adapter MAC or GUID from the Network boot screen.

1. Open the WDS Management console on the WDS server.
2. When the Windows Deployment Services console opens, select the Active Directory Prestaged Devices node.

3. In the Active Directory Prestaged Devices pane, all the machines that have been imaged on the WDS server will be listed. In the tree pane, right-click the Active Directory Prestaged Devices node and select Add Device.

4. When the Add Prestaged Device Wizard opens on the Identity page, enter the desired name of the computer in the Name field. In the Device ID field, enter either the MAC address or the GUID of the system. In the Device Group field, you can optionally enter a desired group name used only for identification within the console, such as Workstations. In the OU field, you can enter a specific OU to place the system in Active directory using Lightweight Directory Access Protocol (LDAP) format, as shown in Figure 26.10. Click Next to continue.

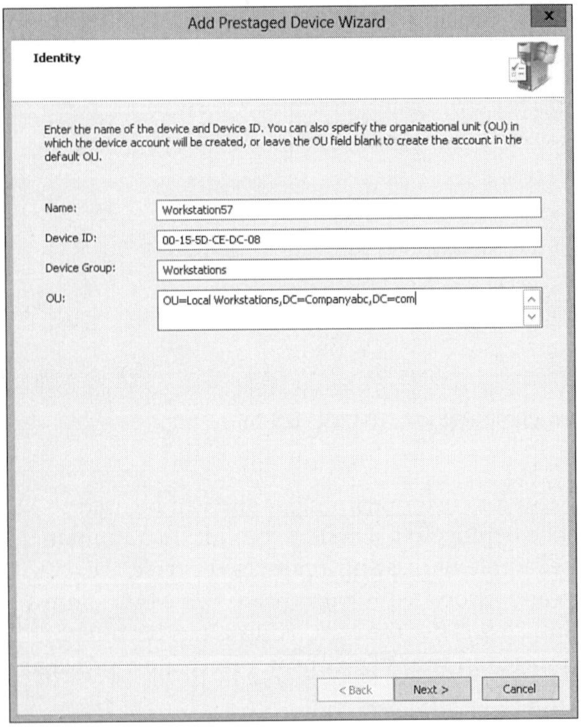

FIGURE 26.10 Configuring the prestaged device identity.

5. On the Boot page, you can adjust the PXE Boot Policy to predetermine whether or not pressing the F12 key will be required to start the network boot. You can also select the boot image you want to use with this device if your WDS implementation has more than one boot image. With the defaults, F12 will need to be pressed on the prestaged system, ensuring that imaging will be performed only when desired.

6. On the Client Unattend page, click the Create New button to create a customized unattend file.

7. When the Create Client Unattend Window opens, specify the following information as shown in Figure 26.11, and click Save to return to the Client Unattend page in the Add Prestaged Device Wizard:

   - Setup language.
   - Credentials to connect to the WDS server.
   - Specify the install image by selecting the radial button and clicking the Select button to browse the install image group and desired image.
   - Installation info related to disk and partition selection. If this is a new disk, no partitions exist, and this process will fail. If the device already has had a default installation of Windows 7 or Windows 8, both a partition 1 for the system files and a partition 2 for the operating system will exist. Selecting partition 2 as shown in the figure will work.

When deploying images to newly unformatted disks, custom unattend files will need to be created manually or using the Windows Assessment and Deployment Kit's Windows System Image Manager (SIM) tool. After a custom unattend is created using that tool, it can be referenced directly with the boot or install image or within the prestaged device as outlined in this set of steps.

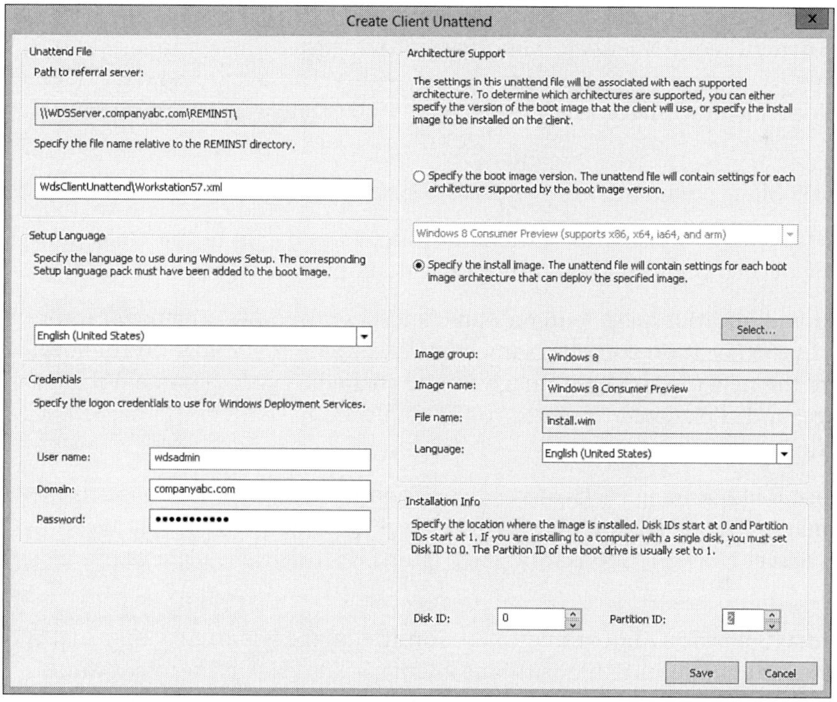

FIGURE 26.11 Configuring the prestaged device client unattend file.

8. Click Next on the Client Unattend page after the unattend file has been created.
9. On the Join Rights page, leave the checkbox checked to join the computer to the domain and click the Configure User button to add the credentials specified in the unattend file to give this user the right to join the computer to the domain. Click Next to continue.
10. Click Finish to complete the wizard, and then click OK the results pop-up window.

After this prestaged device is created, the system with the matching MAC address can be booted up and will process the WDS configuration as determined by the prestaged device properties including the unattend file.

CAUTION

The unattend files, when credentials are specified, will contain the credentials password in clear text within the XML file, so securing the shares on WDS server as well as only using accounts with join rights is most important to maintain a high level of security.

Creating Custom Installations Using Capture Images

When the default install images included with Windows Server 2012 or Windows 8 do not meet the deployment requirements for an organization, custom install images can be created by preparing the system using Sysprep.exe and with WDS, a capture boot image can be used to upload the new image to the WDS server. To create a new capture image, follow these steps:

1. Open the WDS Management console on the WDS server.
2. When the WDS console opens, select the Boot Images node, and in the Tasks pane, right-click the desired boot image and select Create Capture Image.
3. On Metadata and Location page, enter a name and description for the new capture boot image. In the Location and File Name section, browse to a folder on the local system where the new capture boot image can be created, type in a name for the capture image, and click Open to return to the Capture Image Metadata page. Click Next to continue.
4. When the capture boot image is created, we will add the new capture image to the WDS boot images. On the Task Progress page, check the Add Image to the Windows Deployment Server Now check box, and click Finish to close the Create Capture Image Wizard.
5. In the Add Image Wizard window that opens, on the Image File page, verify that the file path represents the capture file path and filename and click Next to continue.
6. On the Image Metadata page, be certain to change the name so that it reflects a capture image, as shown in Figure 26.12. Click Next to continue.

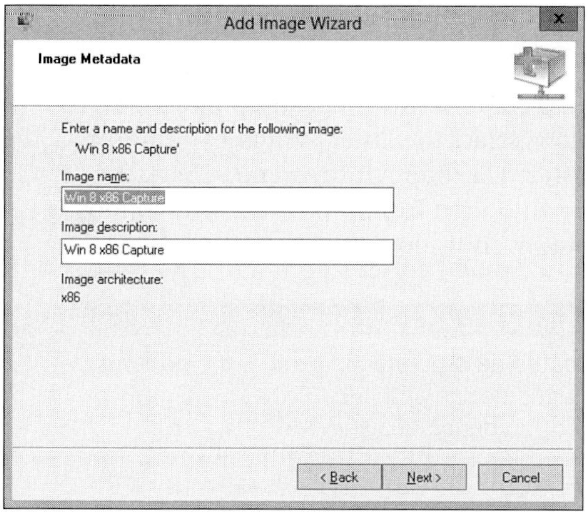

FIGURE 26.12 Naming the new capture boot image.

7. Review the settings on the Summary page, and click Next to import the capture boot image to the WDS server.

8. After this process completes, click Finish, and close the WDS console and log off of the server.

Typically, when organizations decide to use a product to image servers or desktops, the main driving force is to reduce the effort required to deploy the systems. If only base operating systems were deployed using WDS, the time savings would not be much, but when several hours of post operating system software installations and custom configurations are part of this process, creating and deploying customized images can be very valuable. To create an image of a preconfigured Windows Server 2012 or a Windows 8 system, follow these steps:

1. Deploy the image to a system using a default boot and install image from the WDS server.

2. Customize the newly deployed system by installing any necessary applications or drivers and customizing the system based on the organization's requirements. Also make sure to install the latest operating system and application service packs and security updates.

3. Many applications that register with a central server (for example, antivirus applications and backup agents) will not image well and will require special steps before imaging. For any third-party applications, either make these post-image installs or follow the manufacture recommendations of pre-imaging and post-imaging steps that may include wiping out certain Registry settings or running clean up processes, then continue with the next steps.

4. Delete any user profiles on the system except for the logged on user profile that will run sysprep and the system profiles.

5. Run the Sysprep.exe utility from The C:\Windows\System32\Sysprep folder. In the System Preparation Tool 3.14 window, select the Enter System Out-of-Box Experience (OOBE) option from the System Cleanup Action menu. Check the Generalize check box, select the Shutdown option from the Shutdown Options menu, and click OK. After this completes, it shuts down the system.

NOTE

If the system being used for imaging was created as a prestaged device, the boot image must be changed or cleared out in the prestaged device settings for that system so that the capture image can be selected during boot up during imaging.

6. On the WDS server, create a capture boot image and add the capture boot image to the WDS boot images that matches the systems platform version. This step is only necessary if no compatible capture image already exists and is loaded in the WDS server.

7. Boot the system that has been prepared for imaging using PXE boot, press F12 when required, and when the available boot images are presented, select the previously created capture boot image.

8. When the Windows Deployment Services Image Capture Wizard is displayed, click Next on the Welcome page to continue.

9. On the Directory to Capture page, select the volume that will be captured from the drop-down menu, type in a name and description for the new install image, and click Next to continue.

10. Next, on the New Image Location page, enter the name and location for the image by clicking the Browse button. For this example, we will enter **D:\Win8CustomX86.wim**, as shown in Figure 26.13.

11. Also on the New Image Location page, check the check box to upload the image to the WDS server. Enter the fully qualified name of the WDS server and click the Connect button. When prompted, enter WDS administrative credentials, and then select the desired image group, as shown in Figure 26.13, and click Finish to start the upload. Once the process completes, shut down the system used for imaging.

12. Log on to the WDS server, and from the WDS console, verify that the new install image that was just created is listed in the designated install image group.

13. Boot a different system using PXE into a WDS boot image, and select the new install image to test the deployment of this image. Customize the image or prepare the system again and recapture.

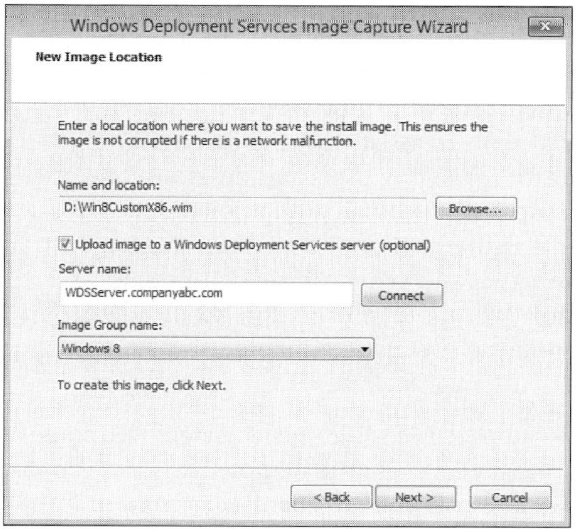

FIGURE 26.13 Configuring the name and location of the custom install image.

Additional customization to captured install images might be required using the Windows System Image Manager (SIM) tool included in the Windows Assessment and Deployment Kit (ADK).

Automating Image Deployment Using Unattend Files

Using the default install images, or install images created from the WDS capture process, there are still several options available that allow administrators to interact and manipulate how the install image will be deployed. If the imaging process needs to be customized to remove options from the end-user experience, such as entering the product key, wiping out any existing partitions on a hard drive, and creating a custom partition size for the operating system, these can be accomplished by creating a customized unattended answer file using the Windows Assessment and Deployment Kit (ADK)

To create an answer file, you need to copy the install image that will be customized. This can be accomplished by exporting an install image from the WDS console if the install image is custom, or by simply copying the install.wim file from the Windows 8 or Windows Server 2012 installation media. After the install image is copied to the server, if the ADK is not installed, it needs to be downloaded from Microsoft and installed on the server.

The ADK programs group contains documentation that can be used to provide all the necessary information about how to create and customize an unattend answer file. This is by no means a quick-and-easy process; it requires several iterations of the file and several tests until the desired result is achieved. For detailed information about how to create and configure unattended answer files using the ADK, install the ADK and reference the documentation related to the Windows System Image Manager tool.

General Desktop Administration Tasks

Aside from deploying operating systems to servers and desktops, managing or remotely updating the systems and the end users after deployment can be an even more challenging task. Windows Server 2012 provides several tools to assist with the management of the computer and network infrastructure, but for managing users and desktops, one of the most functional tools is domain-based group policies. With group policies, Windows Update settings can be configured, network configurations can be managed from a central console, end-user data can be migrated to the server and synchronized with the local desktop folder for mobile users, and much more. For more information about how group policies can be used to manage Windows systems and users, see Chapter 27, "Group Policy Management for Network Clients."

In addition, when end users need one-on-one support, Windows systems deployed in an Active Directory Domain Services domain can easily leverage the Remote Assistance application. This application enables administrators and end users to share their desktop in either a view-only or fully interactive sessions. Remote Assistance works outside of domain deployments, but within a domain, the IT staff can offer Remote Assistance to the user. To start the process, the user only needs to accept the offer by clicking the link. Going even one step further, when organizations leverage Remote Desktop Services Host systems, administrators can also interact with end users within their session using a remote control function that allows both the end user and administrator to view and share control of the shared desktop.

Summary

Windows Server 2012 provides administrators and organizations with many features, applications, and services that can be used to help deploy and manage Windows servers and desktops. Tools such as Windows Deployment Services and domain group policies allow organizations to define configurations and security settings as standards once, and then automate the process to reduce the risk of user error or inconsistent configurations across the infrastructure. Of course, as with any powerful technology or service, before any new applications or services are introduced in an existing computer and network infrastructure, the applications and services should be carefully tested and reviewed in an isolated lab environment to ensure that they are really necessary and will increase productivity or enhance the infrastructure's functionality or security.

Best Practices

The following are best practices from this chapter:

- Deploy Windows Deployment Services on the computer and network infrastructure only if the organization frequently deploys many servers or desktops or wants to ensure consistent and quickly recoverable systems.
- Place the WDS image repository on a separate volume dedicated for images, and not on the system volume.

- When customized desktop images will be captured to the WDS server as new install images, ensure that the sysprep utility is run before booting into a capture image; otherwise, the image will be a duplicate of the workstation, and there will be name and computer SID conflicts.
- When utilizing unattend files, make sure to secure access to these files as some will contain credential passwords in clear text. Furthermore, always use less-privileged accounts for WDS imaging to avoid security breaches.
- Update images when hardware platforms change enough that heavy customization to the install and boot images are required to support the deployment of WDS images to the systems or when major operating system upgrades have been released.
- When selecting new server and desktop hardware, ensure that the systems and all related hardware components are certified to work with Windows 8, Windows Server 2012, or whichever operating system is being deployed. Also ensure that all the necessary drivers are digitally signed by the Windows Hardware Quality labs.
- After images are deployed, the systems should be placed on isolated networks until post-imaging deployment tasks can be completed, including installing any security updates and software packages to provide adequate security to the production network and the newly deployed system.

CHAPTER 27

Group Policy Management for Network Clients

IN THIS CHAPTER

The management and configuration of Windows Server 2012, Windows 8, and some legacy Windows systems can be simplified and standardized with the use of group policies. Group policies are designed to centralize the administration of Windows systems and the users who log on to these systems. Group policy management is divided into two policy nodes: Computer Configuration and User Configuration. The settings contained in the Computer Configuration node can be used to configure Registry and file system permissions, define user password policies, restrict the use of removal media, change network configuration and firewall settings, manage system services, define and control power profiles and much more. The User Configuration node contains settings that can manage desktop environment settings, including automatically enforcing a standard screensaver and lockout duration, installing printers, running logon scripts, adding shortcuts to desktops, redirecting user folders to a network share and configuring folder synchronization, securing down the desktop environment, and much more.

Windows systems can be managed individually with local group policies, and when the systems are members of Active Directory domains, they can also be managed using domain group policies. Local group policies and domain group policies are similar in function but domain group policies provide additional functionality as many of the settings included within the group policy templates apply only to Active Directory domain members. One of the reasons many organizations deploy Active Directory domains is to leverage the capabilities of domain

Group Policy Objects. Chapter 19, "Windows Server 2012 Group Policies and Policy Management," details Group Policy infrastructure concepts and how to create, link, back up, and manage Group Policy objects.

This chapter provides an overview and examples of how local and domain Group Policy objects can be used to manage and configure Windows systems and users.

The Need for Group Policies

Many businesses today are challenged and short-staffed when it comes to managing the configuration and security of their information technology (IT) systems. For IT staff, managing the infrastructure involves standardizing and configuring application and security settings, keeping network resources readily available, and having the ability to effectively support end users. Providing a reliable computer and network infrastructure is also a key task for these administrators and part of that requirement includes deploying reliable servers and end-user workstations.

Providing reliable servers and workstations often includes tuning the system settings, installing the latest security updates and bug fixes, and managing the end-user desktop. For small environments, performing these tasks manually can be effective and the right approach, but, in most cases, this can result in inconsistent configurations and an inefficient use of the technical staff member's time.

Using group policies to control the configuration of computer and user settings and centrally managing these settings can help stabilize the overall computer network and greatly reduce the total number of hours required to manage the infrastructure. For example, if a network printer is replaced, the new printer can be deployed using Group Policy; the next time a user logs on, the printer can be automatically installed and the original can be automatically removed. Without Group Policy, each user desktop would need a visit to manually install and replace the printers.

Only 10 years ago, the bulk of computer and user configuration and management tasks were performed on a per-user and per-computer basis. Organizations that required higher efficiency had to hire specialized staff to develop and support standard desktop building and cloning procedures and had to create their own applications and scripts to perform many of the management functions that are now included with Windows Server 2012 and Windows 8 group policies. With more specialized technical staff members, the ratio of technical staff to end users commonly ranged from 5 to 8 technical resources for every 200 employees. Even at this ratio however, when corporate wide changes were necessary, outside consultants and contractors were commonly brought onboard to provide expertise and extra manpower to develop custom applications or processes and to implement the necessary changes.

In many of today's organizations, with the advancements in systems and end-user management, it is not uncommon to find organizations now able to support an average of 100 to 250 users with 1 to 2 technical resources. This is only possible when desktop and end user management policy and procedural standards are developed and group policies are leveraged to support these standards.

Windows Group Policies

Windows Server 2012 and Windows 8 provide several different types of policies that can be used to manage computer systems and user accounts. Depending on the security groups a user account is a member of, and whether or not the computer system is a member of an Active Directory domain or a Windows workgroup, the number of policy settings applicable will vary.

Local Computer Policy

Every Windows system will contain a default local computer policy. The local computer policy is a Local Group Policy Object (LGPO). The local computer policy contains separate Computer and User Configuration nodes. The local computer policy only applies configured settings to the individual local computer system and the users who log on. The local computer policy on a new system is blank, except for the default settings defined within the Computer Configuration\Windows Settings\Security Settings policy node. The Security Settings policy node is also the local security policy.

Local Security Policy

The local security policy of a system contains the only configured policy settings on newly deployed Windows systems. Settings such as user rights assignments, password policies, Windows Firewall with advanced security settings, and system security settings are managed and configurable within the local security policy. Furthermore, the local security policy can be exported from one system as a single text file and imported to other systems to simplify security configuration in workgroup environments and to customize security for new system deployments.

Local Administrators and Non-Administrators User Policies

Windows Server 2012 and Windows 8 support multiple local group policies for user accounts. If any settings are configured in the User Configuration node of the local computer policy, the settings are applied to all users who log on to the system, including the local Administrators group. In earlier versions of Windows, if the local computer policy restricted an administrator from performing a specific function, the policy would need to be changed and reapplied before the administrator could perform the function. Starting with Windows Vista and Windows Server 2008 including continued support in Windows 8 and Windows Server 2012, additional user-only policies can be created to provide override settings to either further restrict or reduce security to allow the particular user to perform their tasks. As an example, if the local computer policy setting was enabled to restrict read and write access to removal disks no users would be able to access externally connected disks or thumb drives. This is a great setting to maintain both system and data security. If an Administrators local group policy was created, this same setting could be set to disabled and any administrator would be able to connect and read and write to external drives.

For local administrators, the Administrators local group policy can be configured as stated previously. In addition, separate local user policies can be created for the non-Administrators users. If the system has local user accounts, specific local user policies can be created for each user. This allows for very granular assignment of rights and functionality for systems that use local accounts but require specific configurations and security settings on a per-user basis.

By default, users logging on to Windows Server 2008 or Windows Vista and later operating systems will apply the local computer policy, followed by either the Administrators or Non-Administrators policy and any specific local user policy. To clarify how multiple policies will be processed, using the previous example, the local computer policy could be configured to restrict read and write access to all removable media for all users and the Administrators local user policy that allows read and write access to removable storage. Because the Administrators local user policy is applied after the local computer policy, only administrators will be able to write to removable storage media.

Domain Group Policies

Domain group policies are very similar to local group policies, but many additional settings are included and these policies are managed and applied within an Active Directory environment. For clarification, documentation might refer to local policies as Local Group Policy Objects and group policies as domain-based policies. For the remainder of this chapter, they will be referred to as local policies and domain policies.

Local policies are very close to domain policies, but there are several key differences. Domain policies are managed using the Group Policy Management Editor, which allows administrators to view all available settings or to filter out only configured settings when managing a policy. Many settings that only apply to a domain environment are still available in a local policy but when configured will not function if the computer is not a member of an Active Directory domain. One of the biggest differences between domain and local group policies is the separation of settings into the Policies and Preferences nodes, which is detailed later in this chapter in the "Policies and Preferences" section.

Security Configuration Wizard

Windows Server 2012 contains a tool called the Security Configuration Wizard (SCW). The SCW contains different templates that can be applied to systems that meet specific criteria.

For example, on a system running only the Windows Server 2012 File Services role, when examined and secured by the SCW, a File Server role template will be applied that will configure the firewall, disable unnecessary services, and tune the system to provide access to the necessary functions of the File Services role but not much else. The SCW should be used only when properly tested because the security changes can impact functionality if incorrect settings are applied to a system. Also, it is highly recommended to configure the server 100% ready for production then run the security configuration wizard to perform the final lock down. Alternatively, the SCW can be used to create the necessary security template which can then be exported, and later imported into a domain policy and applied to the necessary servers that match the appropriate configuration. Finally, if the SCW is used as a standard, it must be run again if the roles and services of a system are changed, to ensure continued and proper functionality. Additional information about how to use the Security Configuration Wizard is detailed in Chapter 13, "Server-Level Security."

Policy Processing Overview

When a Windows system contains multiple local policies or is a member of an Active Directory domain, more than one policy will be processed when the computer boots or when a user logs on. Each policy that applies to the particular computer or user is processed sequentially and it is important to understand the policy processing order. In cases where multiple policies have the same settings configured, but with different values, the resulting setting value will match the last policy processed.

Policy Processing for Computers

Policy settings are applied to computers during computer startup, shutdown, and background refresh intervals. Policy processing for computer objects is performed in the following order:

1. Local computer policy
2. Domain policies linked to the Active Directory site
3. Domain policies linked to the Active Directory domain
4. Domain policies linked to the organizational unit hierarchy in which the computer account is located

Policy Processing for Users

Policy settings are applied to users during user logon, logoff, and background refresh intervals. Policy processing for domain and local users is performed in the following order:

1. Local computer policy
2. Local Non-Administrators policy or local Administrators policy if these policies exist
3. Local user-specific policy; only applies if the user is a local user account and a policy exists for the user
4. Domain policies linked to the Active Directory site
5. Domain policies linked to the Active Directory domain
6. Domain policies linked to the organizational unit hierarchy in which the user account is located

Group Policy Order of Processing

When multiple policies are linked to a single Active Directory site, domain, or organizational unit, each policy will be applied sequentially. The order of policy application or processing is based on the policy link order. The policy link with the number 1 associated to the policy name is the last policy applied at the container and, therefore, takes precedence for policy link order of processing.

Loopback Processing

When a user is processing domain policies, the policies that apply to that user are based on the location of the user object in the Active Directory hierarchy. The same goes for domain policy application for computers. There are situations, however, when administrators or organizations want to ensure that all users get the same policy when logging on to a particular computer or server. For example, on a computer that is used for training or on a Remote Desktop Session Host, when the user desktop environment must be the same for each user, this can be controlled by enabling loopback processing.

There are two different loopback configurations: replace and merge mode. Merge mode will apply the user-based policies that would normally apply to the user account as well as the user-based policies on the container that contains the computer account the user is logging on to. Replace mode will only process user policies applied to the computer the user is logging on to.

Group Policy Feature Set

The Group Policy Feature Set is the collection of all the available settings within a group policy. The available policy settings are created from the basic policy template, which includes the general hierarchy, the local security policy, and the default administrative templates stored in the local file system. The administrative templates that present their settings within a policy are referenced from the files stored in the c:\windows\policydefinitions folder or in the Active Directory domain central store.

The policy settings available within a particular policy or all policies can be extended by importing additional administrative templates. This can be accomplished by simply adding the correct ADMX and ADML files to the PolicyDefinitions folder on the local system or in the central store or by importing a legacy administrative template file with the ADM extension into a particular policy.

By default, the Windows Server 2012 group policies administrative templates contain approximately 1,860 settings in the Computer Configuration node and another 1,560 in the User Configuration node. There are many more settings in the Windows Settings nodes and the Preferences node that extend this number dramatically. This, of course, makes detailing each of the settings a very inconvenient and lengthy process. Instead of covering every setting, this section and many of the proceeding sections in this chapter highlight the types of settings available that might be the most common and useful settings for managing Windows environments.

Many of the policy settings contained in both the Computer and User Configuration policy nodes apply only to specific Windows Server 2012 role services such as the Encrypting File System (EFS), Remote Desktop Services (RDS), Network Access Protection (NAP), or the Distributed File System (DFS) role services. For these particular services, as with any group policy settings, it is very important that the administrator understands the potential impact of configuring these settings. Before any production group policies are created, modified, or linked, the policy should be tested in an isolated environment and a rollback plan should be created and also tested. For more information about how to plan for Group Policy deployment, see Chapter 19.

Computer Configuration Policy Node

The Computer Configuration node of a group policy contains settings designed to configure and manage a Windows system. Many of the settings found in this node also exist in the User Configuration node, and when both settings are configured, different outcomes will result. In some cases, computer policy settings will always be used even if the user configuration policy setting is configured as well. In other cases, the last policy setting applied will be used. For example, in a local group policy, within each node under Administrative Templates\System\Scripts, there is a setting named Run Logon Scripts Synchronously, and if this setting is configured in the Computer Configuration section, it will be enforced regardless of how the setting is configured in the User Configuration policy node.

At the root of the Computer Configuration node, there are three policy nodes: the Software Settings node, the Windows Settings node, and the Administrative Templates node. In domain group policies, these three nodes are located beneath the Computer Configuration\Policies node.

Computer Configuration Software Settings Node

The Software Settings node is used to add software application packages to the computers that process the particular policy. Prepackaged or custom Windows Installer MSI software packages can be added to this Software Settings node and used to automatically install software on the computer during the next reboot cycle. This is known as an assigned software package.

Computer Configuration Windows Settings Node

The Windows Settings node provides administrators with the ability to manage the overall security and configuration of the Windows system. The settings contained beneath the Windows Settings node can be used to define how local and domain users can interact and manage the system and how the system will communicate across the network. The five nodes contained within the Windows Settings node are as follows:

- **Name Resolution Policy**—This node allows group policy administrators to create rules to build the content of the Name Resolution Policy Table to support DNSSEC implementations and to configure Windows Server 2012 Direct Access DNS Settings centrally.
- **Scripts (Startup/Shutdown)**—The Scripts node allows administrators to add startup or shutdown scripts to computer objects.
- **Deployed Printers**—This node allows administrators to automatically install and remove printers on the Windows systems. Using the Group Policy Object Editor on

Windows Server 2008 or Windows Server 2012 systems, this node might not appear unless the Print Management console is also installed.

- **Security Settings**—This node is a replica of the local security policy although it does not sync or pull information from the local security policy. The settings in this node can be used to define password policies, audit policies, software restrictions, services configuration, Registry and file permissions, and much more.
- **Policy-Based QoS**—The Policy-Based Qos node can be configured to manage, restrict, and prioritize outbound network traffic between a source Windows system and a destination host based on an application, source, or destination IP address or source and destination protocols and ports.

Security Settings

The Security Settings node allows a security administrator to configure security levels assigned to a domain or local Group Policy object. This can be performed manually or by importing an existing security template.

The Security Settings node of the Group Policy object can be used to configure several security-related settings, including file system NTFS permissions and many more settings contained in the nodes beneath Security Settings, as follows:

- **Account Policies**—These computer security settings control password policy, lockout policy, and Kerberos policy in Windows Server 2000 through Windows Server 2012 Active Directory domains.
- **Local Policies**—These security settings control audit policy, user rights assignment, and security options, including setting the default User Account Control settings for systems the policy applies to.
- **Event Log**—This setting controls security settings and the size of the event logs for the application, security, and system event logs.
- **Restricted Groups**—These settings allow the administrator to manage local or domain group membership from within this policy node. Restricted group settings can be used to add members to an existing group without removing any existing members or it can enforce and overwrite membership based on the policy configuration.
- **System Services**—These settings can be used to control the startup mode of a service and to define the permissions to manage the service configuration or state. Configuring these settings does not start or stop any services, but the state will be changed upon Group Policy application.
- **Registry**—This setting is used to configure the security permissions of defined Registry keys and, if desired, all subkeys and values. This setting is useful in supporting legacy applications that require specific Registry key access that is not normally allowed for standard user accounts.

- **File System**—This setting is used to configure NTFS permissions on specified folders on NTFS formatted drives. Also, enabling auditing and configuring folder ownership and propagating these settings to subfolders and files is an option.
- **Wired Network (IEEE 802.3) Policies**—This policy node can be used to configure additional security on wired network adapters to allow for or require smart card or computer-based certificate authentication and encryption.
- **Windows Firewall with Advanced Security**—This policy node enables administrators to configure the Windows Firewall on Windows Vista, and Windows 2008 and later operating systems. The configured settings can configure specific inbound or outbound rules and can define how the firewall is configured based on the firewall profile. The configuration can overwrite the local firewall rules or the group policy and local rules can be merged.
- **Network List Manager Policies**—Windows Firewall on Windows Vista, and Windows Server 2008 and later operating systems use firewall profiles based on the network. This setting node can be used to define the permissions end users have regarding the identification and classification of a new network as public or private to allow for the proper firewall profile to be applied.
- **Wireless Network (IEEE 802.11) Policies**—These policies help in the configuration settings for a wide range of devices that access the network over wireless technologies, including predefining the preferred wireless network, including the service set identifier (SSID) and the security type for the network. This node includes Windows Vista and Windows XP compatible policies.
- **Public Key Policies**—These settings are used to specify that computers automatically submit a certificate request to an enterprise certification authority and install the issued certificate. Public Key Policies are also created and are used in the distribution of the certificate trust list. Public Key Policies can establish common trusted root certification authorities. EFS settings use this policy node, as well.
- **Software Restriction Policies**—These policies enable an administrator to control the applications that are allowed to run on the Windows system based on the file properties and not the filename. In addition, software restrictions can be created based on certificates or the particular network zone from which the application is being accessed or executed. For example, a rule can be created to block application installations from the Internet zone as defined by Microsoft Internet Explorer.
- **Network Access Protection**—This setting can be used to deploy the configuration of the NAP client.
- **Application Control Policies**—This node enables group policy administrators to create rules that define which security groups or specific users can run executables, scripts or Windows Installer files and can also be used to granularly define which file paths, filenames, and digitally signed publishers of files will be allowed or denied on the computers these policy settings apply to.

- **IP Security Policies on Active Directory**—IP Security (IPsec) policies can be applied to the GPO of an Active Directory object to define when and where IPsec communication is allowed or required.
- **Advanced Audit Policy Configuration**—This node can be used to define more detailed and granular audit settings for use on Windows Server 2012 and Windows 8 systems.

Computer Configuration Administrative Templates Node

The Computer Configuration Administrative Templates node contains all the Registry-based policy settings that apply to the Windows system. These settings are primarily used to control, configure, and secure how the Windows system is set up and how it can be used. This is not the same as the security settings configuration where specific users or groups are granted rights because the configuration settings available within the administrative templates apply to the system and all users who access the system. Many settings, however, are not applied to users who are members of the local administrators group of a system.

User Configuration Policy Node

The User Configuration node contains settings used to configure and manage the user desktop environment on a Windows system. Unlike the computer configuration settings that define system settings and restrict what users can do on a particular system, the user configuration settings can customize the desktop experience for a user, including setting Start menu options, hiding or disabling Control Panel applets, redirecting folders to network shares, restricting write access to removable media, and much more. At the root of the User Configuration node are three policy nodes named the Software Settings node, the Windows Settings node, and the Administrative Templates node, but the settings contained within these nodes are different from the settings included in the Computer Configuration node, and in a domain group policy, these nodes are located beneath the User Configuration\Policies\ node.

User Configuration Software Settings Node

The Software Settings node in the User Configuration section of a policy allows administrators to publish or assign software applications to individual users to which the policy applies. When a packaged software application is assigned to a user, it can be configured to be installed automatically at user logon or it can just be available in the Control Panel Programs applet for installation by the user the same as when it is published. When a packaged application is published to a user, it can be installed by that user by accessing the application in the following section of the Control Panel:

- **Windows Server 2012**—Control Panel, Get Programs
- **Windows Vista**—Control Panel, Programs, Get Programs and Features
- **Windows 7**– Control Panel, Programs, Get Programs

- **Windows 8**—Control Panel, Programs, Get Programs
- **Windows XP**—Control Panel, Add or Remove Programs, Add New Programs

User Configuration Windows Settings Node

The Windows Settings node in the User Configuration section of a policy allows administrators to configure logon scripts for users, configure folder redirection of user profile folders, define software restriction policies, automatically install and, if necessary, remove printers.

User Configuration Administrative Templates Node

User Configuration Administrative Templates are the most commonly configured policy settings in domain group policy deployments. Settings contained within the User Configuration Administrative Templates node can be used to assist administrators with the automated configuration of a user's desktop environment. Of course, now with domain Group Policy preferences, many of these newly available settings will also be highly used once group policy administrators begin to explore and find the best ways to use preference settings.

Planning Workgroup and Standalone Local Group Policy Configuration

Many organizations deploy Windows servers and workstations in workgroup configurations and for these organizations, local group policies can play a vital role in simplifying Windows system administration. Some of the benefits of leveraging local group policies in workgroup deployments include the following:

- **Standardizing workgroup and image deployments**—Define the base local computer, Administrators, and Non-Administrators local policies on a machine that will be used as a template for a desktop or server image to reduce security exposure, improve standardization, and reduce user error when many systems are deployed.
- **Standardizing User Configuration settings**—The User Configuration section of the local computer policy can be configured to install specific printers for users, customize the Start menu and display settings, predefine settings for Windows programs such as Remote Desktop Connection, and much more. For the most part, however, the settings are standardized to give every user the same experience.
- **Preconfiguring policies for shared or public Windows systems**—Systems that are made available for public use or are utilized by several different users require more restrictive configurations to increase the security and reliability of the system. In these types of deployments, Windows administrators can configure tight security settings in the local computer policy, very restrictive settings in the Non-Administrators policy, and less-restrictive settings in the Administrators policy to allow for updates and management. Also, audit settings can be enabled to track logon/logoff, file and folder access, and much more.

- **Preconfiguring security updates and remote administration settings**—Windows systems that are deployed in workgroups can be difficult to remotely support and administer if the proper configurations are not created prior to deployment. Using the local computer policy, firewall rules can be created to allow for remote management, Remote Desktop can be enabled and enforced, and Windows Update settings can also be configured to enable automated security update installation and remote management options.

Creating Local Administrators and Non-Administrators Policies

When a Windows system is first deployed, only the local computer group policy is created. Local group policies for Administrators, Non-Administrators, and individual local users need to be manually created if they are to be utilized. The process of creating the Administrators or Non-Administrators policy must be performed from the local machine using the Group Policy Object Editor. In the following example, create a local group policy for the Administrators group. To create a local user group policy for administrators, follow these steps:

1. Log on to the Windows Server 2012 system with an account with administrator privileges.
2. Open the charms bar by moving your cursor to the lower-right corner, and then select the search icon (magnifying glass). In the Search field, type **MMC**, and when the MMC tile appears, click it to open the Microsoft Management Console. If the MMC does not appear, ensure that Apps is selected for searching and try again.
3. When the Microsoft Management Console opens, click File on the menu bar, and select Add/Remove Snap-in.
4. In the Add or Remove Snap-ins window, in the Available Snap-Ins pane on the left, scroll down and select the Group Policy Object Editor, and click the Add button.
5. The Select Group Policy Object window opens and defaults to the local computer policy. Click the Browse button to choose a different policy.
6. In the Browse for a Group Policy Object window, select the Users tab.
7. On the Users tab, each local user account will be listed as well as Administrators and Non-Administrators. Select Administrators and click OK, as shown in Figure 27.1.
8. Back in the Select Group Policy Object window, the Group Policy Object name should reflect Local Computer\Administrators. If the name matches, click Finish to return to the Add or Remove Snap-Ins window.
9. In the Add or Remove Snap-Ins window, click OK to complete adding snap-ins to this console window.
10. In the MMC window, the Local Computer\Administrators policy will be available for editing. Because this policy only applies to users in the Administrators group, only the User Configuration node is present.

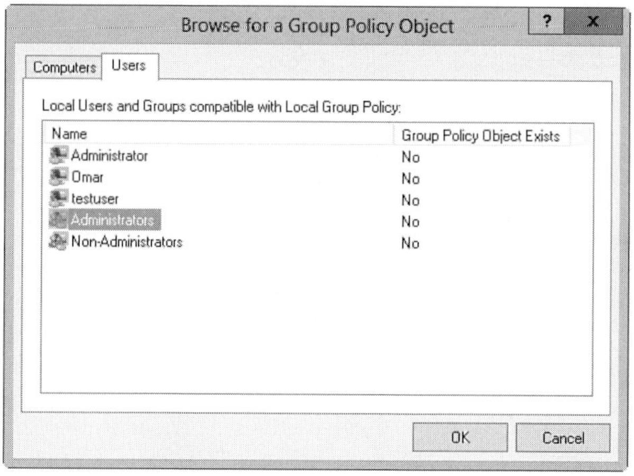

FIGURE 27.1 Selecting the local group policy for administrators.

11. Configure at least one setting in this policy to create it and close the MMC window when the configuration of the local user group policy for administrators is complete.
12. When prompted to save the console, click No and proceed to sign off (log off) of the server.
13. Log back on to the server with an account with local Administrator rights.
14. Open the charms bar, select the search icon and in the Search pane, type **cmd**, and press Enter.
15. Type **gpresult /h LGPO-Administrators.html** and press Enter. The **gpresult** command with the **/h** option generates an HTML file that will be used to determine whether the local user group policy for administrators has been applied. This option is only available on Windows Vista, Windows Server 2008, and later workstation and server operating systems, but the tool can be run against remote systems with the proper permissions and firewall settings configured.
16. After **gpresult** completes, in the command prompt type the name of the file created, in this example **LGPO-Administrators.html**, and press Enter.
17. This launches Internet Explorer. Notice that the browser might require permission to allow the ActiveX content to load. Click the Show Blocked Content button if presented.
18. Scroll down to the User Configuration Summary section and click the Group Policy Objects link.
19. Click Applied GPOs and Denied GPOs to reveal which policies were applied to the user, as shown in Figure 27.2.
20. Review the HTML report and when finished, close Internet Explorer and log off.

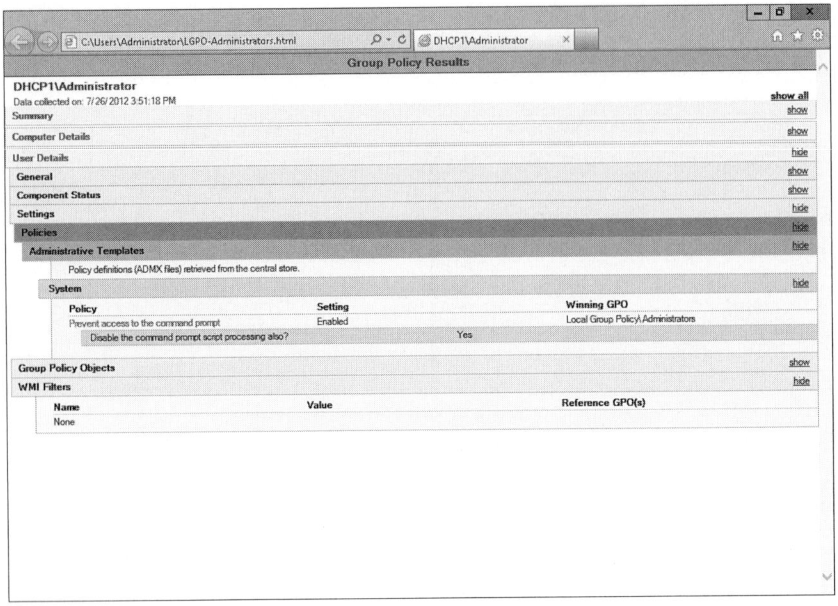

FIGURE 27.2 Verifying GPO application using the gpresult HTML report.

The same procedure can be used to create local group policies for non-administrators or individual local user accounts.

Planning Domain Group Policy Objects

Group Policy objects (GPOs) can be used to perform many functions across a diverse or standard computer and network infrastructure built on Microsoft Windows and Active Directory Domain Services (AD DS). Considering how to best utilize group policies to manage any one particular environment and deciding on which GPO settings to leverage can be a lengthy process. To simplify this process and to keep from rethinking GPO usage each time, a base set of GPOs should be created and stored as starter GPOs.

A starter GPO is a feature of the Group Policy infrastructure that first became available with the release of the Windows Server 2008 Group Policy Management Console. A starter GPO can contain a set of Group Policy administrative template settings that have been preconfigured or defined to meet an organization's security or configuration requirements. When a new GPO is created, a starter GPO can be leveraged to prepopulate the defined settings into the new GPO. The benefit is that each time a new GPO is needed, it does not have to be created from scratch and the administrator does not need to search for each of the settings that are necessary to meet the specific object of the new GPO. Windows Server 2012 provides several starter GPOs for Windows XP and Windows Vista systems that have been created to provide pre-configured security settings to meet the best practice recommendations outlined in the Windows Vista and Windows XP security guides. For more information about starter GPOs, see Chapter 19. The remainder of this section outlines common scenarios for GPO usage to assist administrators with the planning, deployment, and configuration of GPOs across an organization's Active Directory infrastructure.

Policies and Preferences

GPOs are segmented into policy settings and preference settings for both Computer and User objects, as shown in Figure 27.3. Preferences provide many of the features that the group policy infrastructure was lacking in earlier versions, and preferences also provide many functions that were commonly handled with complex logon and startup scripts, with Registry file import tasks, and by administrators configuring the default user profile on workstations and servers. Many preference settings, such as the Registry and Drive Maps settings, would have previously been applied with scripts that required the workstation to be logged on to or started up on the internal network. With preference settings in domain group policies, these settings can now be applied during the Group Policy refresh interval, which can greatly increase the successful application of these types of settings.

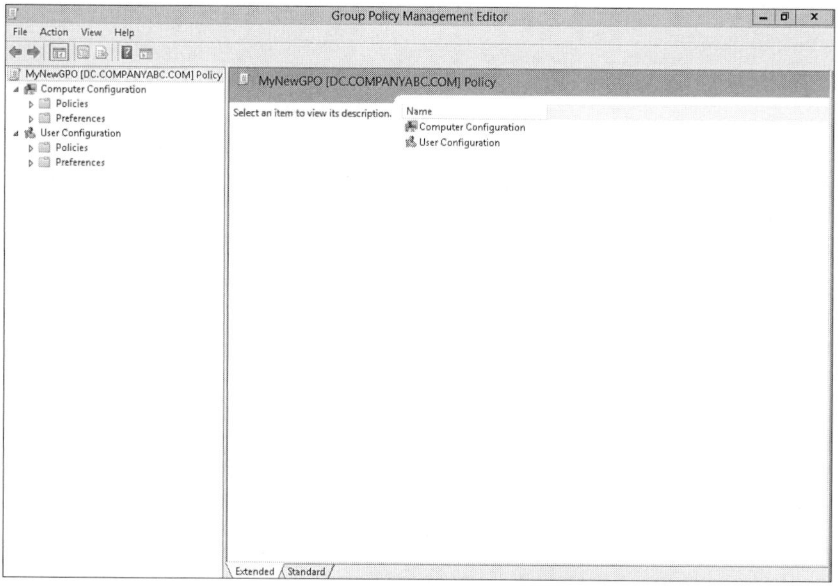

FIGURE 27.3 Group Policy User Configuration preferences.

Policy settings and preference settings have different characteristics. Policy settings are enforced and all users are commonly restricted from changing any configured policy setting. If a policy setting contains a graphic interface, when configured, the setting is normally grayed out to the end user, as shown in Figure 27.4 for the policy-configured Remote Desktop settings. Policy settings such as software installations and computer or user scripts are only processed during computer startup or shutdown and user logon and logoff cycles.

27

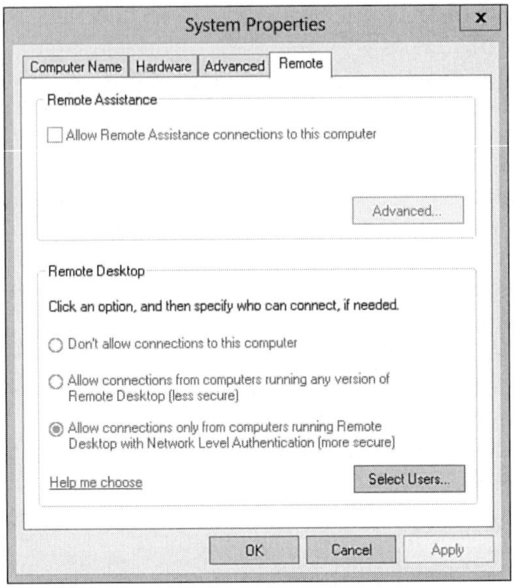

FIGURE 27.4 Enforced Remote Desktop policy setting.

Preference settings are applied to computers and users the same as policy settings: during startup, shutdown, and refresh cycles for computers and logon, logoff, and refresh cycles for users. Preferences settings, however, are configured but not enforced. As an example of this, using a user printer preference, a printer can be installed in a user profile and set to be the default printer, but the end user will still retain the ability to define a different default printer if necessary. Preference settings are applied during refresh intervals, but certain settings, such as creating Registry keys and values, might require a computer reboot or user logoff/logon cycle to actually apply the new setting. One important point to note is that the domain group policy preferences are supported on Windows 7, 8, Windows Server 2008, 2008 R2, and Windows Server 2012, but all other operating systems, including Windows Vista, will need an update or the latest service pack to support preference settings.

Preference settings are all different, but they each share common administrative functionality. Each preference setting will either be presented in a graphic interface similar to, if not exactly, what the end user can see and access within the user profile. This is one distinction between preference and policy settings, as most policy settings are enabled, disabled, or not configured whereas a preference setting can contain several configuration features. Furthermore, each preference setting can have multiple items defined within it, each with a separate configuration value. For example, a drive map preference can have a setting item of a mapped drive P and a mapped drive U defined within the single domain group policy preference setting.

In addition to the specific setting options that are unique to each preference, such as the drive letter designation for a map drive or a folder path to a network share preference, each setting also contains a set of common options and many also include a preference action.

Preference Actions

Many preference settings contain an option called the preference action. Preference actions determine how a preference setting will be applied to a user or computer. The most common preference actions are Create, Replace, Update, and Delete:

- **Create**—The Create action creates or configures the preference setting if the setting does not already exist. If the setting already exists, no action is taken.
- **Replace**—The Replace action deletes and recreates the setting on the computer or within the user profile.
- **Update**—The Update action creates the setting if it does not exist, but if the setting already exists, part or all of the setting configurations are updated to match the preference setting. Update is the default action and is less intrusive than the Replace action. It can be used to ensure that the setting is configured as desired, but processing speed will be optimized because if the setting already matches it will be skipped.
- **Delete**—The Delete action simply deletes the preference setting from the computer or user profile. For example, a Delete action can remove a mapped drive, delete a Registry key, or delete a printer from a computer or a user profile.

Preference Common Options

Each preference setting contains a common tab that contains several options that can be enabled for the particular setting. A list of the common options is shown in Figure 27.5. Common options include the ability to process the setting only once, which is great for setting default configurations for new user profiles or a new preference settings on existing domain group policies.

Item-Level Targeting

One of the most functional preference common options is the item-level targeting option. Item-level targeting enables administrators to define the scope of application for a particular preference setting item such as a drive map. So with item-level targeting an administrator can create a single domain group policy and have a single drive map preference defined that will apply different preference setting items to subsets of computers or users based on the specifications of the item-level target. For example, a drive map preference that defined the G drive for a group-based network drive, can be configured to map \\FileServer1\GroupShare\Sales to members of the domain security group named sales, based on the item-level targeting option configuration settings for security groups. The same preference can also define the G drive to \\FileServer1\GroupShare\HR for members of the domain Human Resources group based on a different configuration for item-level targeting.

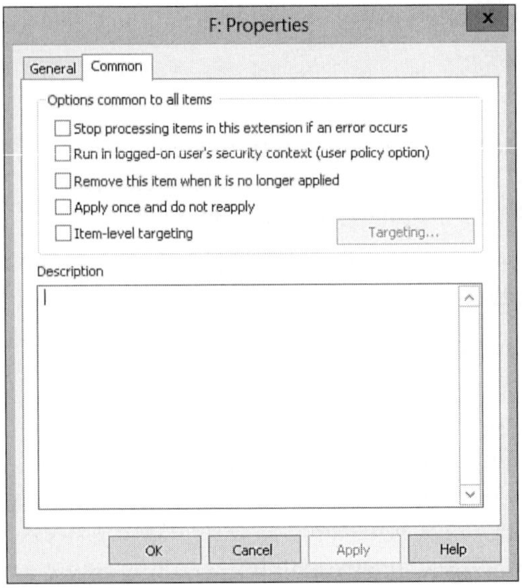

FIGURE 27.5 Group Policy preference common options.

Domain GPOs

When an Active Directory domain is deployed, a default domain policy and a default domain controller policy are created. The default domain policy defines the password and account policies for all domain user accounts and local user accounts for domain member servers and workstations. A few additional settings are also defined within the default domain policy regarding the EFS, Kerberos authentication, and a few other network-related security settings.

As a best practice, the only changes that should be made to the default domain policy should be modifying the password and account policy settings and nothing else. Additional settings that are required at the domain level should be defined in separate policies linked to the domain. The settings configured on domain-linked GPOs will be applied to all computer and user accounts in the domain, including all domain controllers. Settings configured at the domain level should be deployed as default settings and not as organizational standards. For example, as a domain default, the organization might want to configure all computers to enable Windows Update and get updates from the Windows Software Update Services (WSUS) at headquarters and to configure a few default firewall exceptions to allow for remote administration from the IT department. Common default settings applied at the domain level, but not in the default domain policy, can include the following:

- Default screensaver settings
- Default Windows Update settings
- Default firewall profile and rule configurations

- Default EFS settings and recovery agent
- Trusted root certification authorities
- Certificate enrollment configurations

All Windows systems that are members of an Active Directory domain will inherit the user password and account policies from the domain and apply this policy to local accounts on these systems. In some cases, it might be necessary to leverage local user accounts on systems with a less-restrictive password policy to support a particular service or application. This task can be accomplished by adding a GPO at the organizational unit that defines a less restrictive password and account lockout policy. This particular password and account lockout policy will only apply to local user accounts on the computers contained within the linked organizational unit. The only thing that will break this configuration is if the default domain policy is enforced. For more information about domain policy enforcement, see Chapter 19.

In situations when special or specific domain user accounts cannot adhere to the domain password policy, if the domain is operating in Windows Server 2008 or greater domain functional level, a fine-grained password policy can be created and applied to the necessary user accounts. Fine-grained password policies are detailed later in this chapter in the section "Fine-Grained Password Policies."

Domain Controller GPOs

When an Active Directory domain is deployed, a default domain controller policy is created. This is different from the default domain policy in many ways, but the most prevalent distinction is that this policy is applied to the Domain Controllers organizational unit and not the entire domain. The default domain controller policy only applies to objects in this organizational unit, which should contain all of domain controllers of the specific domain, and no other objects.

The Domain Controllers organizational unit inherits all policies linked to the domain, and each domain controller also inherits any site-linked GPOs if any exist. These policies will be applied by the domain controllers and might not be desirable. As a best practice, to avoid impacting domain controller security and reliability, try to limit the configuration settings defined within domain-linked policies or specifically deny the application of these group policies to the Enterprise Domain Controllers security group within each domain of the forest.

NOTE

Moving a domain controller out of the Domain Controllers organizational unit is not recommended as adverse effects could result, including compromising the security of the entire domain and breaking authentication and replication functionality.

The default domain controller policy defines user rights assignment settings for domain controller management as well as defining settings to control the security of network communication. Most organizations do not require any changes made to the default domain controller policy or any additional policies linked to the Domain Controllers organizational unit. Common settings applied at the domain controller organizational unit level can include the following:

- User rights assignment updates for domain controllers (commonly used for backup agent accounts)
- Event Viewer settings
- Audit settings for domain controllers
- Domain controller-specific Windows Update settings
- Remote administration settings for domain controllers

Active Directory Site GPOs

By default, no group policies are created for Active Directory sites. Policies linked to Active Directory sites will be applied to all computers that connect to the domain from the particular subnets associated with the site and, of course, the users who log on to these site associated computers. If computers are moved to new sites, these computers will pick up and process any policies linked to the new site and none from the original site. For example, if an Active Directory site is created for the virtual private network (VPN) network, when a computer is connected to the corporate network using the VPN, any policies linked to the VPN site will be applied to the computer.

Site policies can be a very effective way to simplify administration of mobile users, but if used incorrectly, site policies can cause a lot of issues. For example, using site policies to deploy printers can simplify end-user management for visiting employees. However, installing software for all computers in a site or enforcing networking settings might impact mobile computers if these settings are not overwritten or restored when the user and the system return back to the main office or disconnect from the corporate network. Site GPOs are not commonly used, but when they are, some of the common settings can include the following:

- Wireless and Wired Network Policies
- Deployed Printers (User Configuration)
- Internet Explorer Proxy Configuration

Small Business

Many small businesses run Windows Server systems and Active Directory domains. Unless these businesses run an edition of Small Business Server, most small business Active Directory infrastructures do not effectively leverage local or domain group policies using the default configuration. Many of these Active Directory deployments are flat and all computers and users remain in the default containers and only apply the default domain policy. For small businesses with limited IT resources and budget, aside from updating the password and account lockout settings in the default domain policy, there are a few GPO settings that can enhance management and reliability. Please keep in mind that the following small business group policies are not recommended for Small Business Server (SBS) because SBS includes a number of preconfigured policies that provide some of the features included in the following policies and much more.

Group Policy management for small businesses should be kept simple. The following list of recommendations should be considered for small business Group Policy configurations:

1. Review and, if necessary, adjust the password and account lockout policy in the default domain policy to match the requirements of the organization.

2. Create a new policy named Company Computer Policy and disable the User Configuration section of this policy. Within this policy, configure Windows Update settings, deploy network printers, enable remote administration and configure firewall exceptions or rules to allow for proper communication between the servers and workstations on the network. If necessary, also configure Internet Explorer Security Zone settings. Link this policy to the domain.

3. Create a new policy named Company User Policy and disable the Computer Configuration section of this policy. Within this policy, configure user mapped drives, default screensaver settings, and, if necessary, lock down the desktop, Start menu, and Control Panel. In some cases, folder redirection configuration would also be recommended, but this is an advanced configuration and might not be feasible for small businesses. Link this policy to the domain.

4. Create a new policy named Company Domain Controller Policy and configure the Windows Update settings to download and notify the administrator when updates are ready. Many organizations configure Windows Update on workstations to auto-install and auto-reboot, but on a domain controller (or any server for that matter), this might be risky. For a small business, allowing for auto-install and auto-reboot might present more of a risk than having a tech regularly perform a manual update task.

Delegated Administration

Delegating administration to perform Active Directory functions is becoming a very common task in medium-size and large-size organizations. Delegation tasks, such as allowing the telecom group to update telephone numbers for all Active Directory user accounts or allowing help desk staff to unlock user accounts and reset user passwords, are simple to implement using the Active Directory Users and Computers snap-in. To configure delegation of Active Directory objects such as user accounts, security and distribution groups, and computer objects, this task is not best handled with domain policies. Instead, these delegation tasks are handled by configuring security permissions at the domain level, organizational unit level, or on the particular object itself. One way to simplify or clarify this concept is to remember that if the task will be performed using the Active Directory Administrative Center console, this is delegated by configuring security permissions on a container or object. If the task would normally be performed by logging on to a computer and configuring settings or configuring the profile of a user or group of users, most functions related to this type of task can be performed using domain policies.

GPOs are, in fact, Active Directory objects and delegating Group Policy administration rights is also performed by configuring security access on Active Directory containers, such as domains and organizational units. Group Policy management includes several tasks, which can be delegated in the following configurations:

- **New domain group policy creation**—This is performed by adding the user account or security group to the domain Group Policy Creator Owners security group or delegating this right using the Group Policy Management Console (GPMC) at the Group Policy Objects container. Although delegating this right allows the user to create new policies and GPO creation delegation allows the added user or group to create new GPOs, this user or group is not granted the right to edit settings or modify security on existing GPOs.

- **Edit settings on an existing GPO**—After a GPO is created, the right to edit that particular GPO can be delegated using the GPMC.

- **Edit settings, modify security, and delete a GPO**—These tasks are delegated using the GPMC on a single GPO at a time. The Modify security right allows the designated user to change the security filtering, basically defining which users and computer objects will apply the policy if these objects are in containers linked to that particular GPO.

- **Link existing GPOs**—The ability to link GPOs to Active Directory containers is performed by editing the security settings on the particular Active Directory site, domain, or OU. This is known as the Manage Group Policy Links security right.

- **Create and edit WMI filters**—The right to create new WMI filters or have full control over all WMI filters in a domain can be delegated at the WMI Filters container using the GPMC. Also, the right to edit or grant full control over an existing WMI filter can be delegated to a user or group. Delegating the right to edit or to grant full control does not enable linking WMI filters to GPOs as that requires edit rights permissions on a particular GPO.

- **Perform GPO modeling using GPMC**—GPO modeling delegation is performed by editing the security settings on the particular Active Directory site, domain, or OU. This task allows a designated user the ability to perform dry runs or simulated tests to determine the results of linking a policy to a particular container or moving a user or computer object to a different container in Active Directory. This is also known as the Generate Resultant Set of Policy (Planning) security right. If the user running GPMC is not running GPMC on the domain controller, the user needs to be added to the domain's Distributed COM Users security group to run Group Policy Modeling from another system.

- **Perform GPO results using GPMC**—This task can be performed on local machines if the user is a local administrator and the GPMC is installed. It can also be run by using the GPresult.exe from the command line or by loading the rsop.msc Microsoft Management Console snap-in. By default, local administrators can run this tool against all users on a machine. To delegate this right in Active Directory, edit the security settings on the particular Active Directory domain or OU that contains the computer and user accounts. This task allows the user to remotely connect to the computer to query the Group Policy logs to generate a historical report of previously logged Group Policy processing events. This is also known as the Generate Resultant Set of Policy (Logging) security right. To run this task against a remote computer, aside from having this right in Active Directory, the user also needs to be a member of the computer's local Distributed COM Users security group or the local administrators group, or the domain Distributed COM or Administrators group if running modeling or results against a domain controller. Additional configuration might also include possible firewall policy changes on the required computers to enable the remote administration firewall exception.

Managing Computers with Domain Policies

Managing the configuration and settings of domain servers and workstations can be standardized using domain group policies. Domain group policies offer the advantage of taking user error and mistakes out of the loop by pushing out the configuration and security of computers from a single or a set of group policies. Of course, with this much control it is essential that group policies are tested to verify that the correct configuration and desired results are achieved with the policies before they are released to production systems. In the early days of Active Directory domain-based group policies, a few organizations, which will go unnamed in this book, found themselves locked out of their own computers and Active Directory domain controllers because of over restrictive Group Policy security settings and application of these settings to all computers and users, including the domain administrators. When this situation occurs, a domain controller can be rebooted into Directory Services Restore Mode (DSRM), and an authoritative restore of Active Directory might be required.

Before domain group policies can be created and managed, the Group Policy Management Console needs to be installed. Also, if printers will be installed using the Deploy Printer function of Group Policy, the Print Services Tools should also be installed. To install the GPMC and Print Services Tools, follow these steps:

1. Log on to a designated administrative system running Windows Server 2012.
2. Open the Windows PowerShell from the taskbar
3. Type **Add-WindowsFeature GPMC, RSAT-Print-Services** and press enter.
4. After the process completes, close the Windows PowerShell window.

Creating a New Domain Group Policy Object

To create a new domain GPO, follow these steps:

1. Log on to a designated Windows 8 or Windows Server 2012 administrative system.
2. Open the Group Policy Management Console tile from the Start menu.

3. Expand the forest node, expand the domain node, and expand the domain to expose the Group Policy Objects container and select it.
4. Right-click the Group Policy Objects container, and select New.
5. Type in a name for the new GPO (for example, **MyFirstGPO**). If the starter GPO functionality in the domain is enabled and if a suitable starter GPO exists, click the Source Starter GPO drop-down list arrow, and select either (None) or the desired starter GPO and the click OK to create the GPO.
6. In the tree pane of the Group Policy Management Console windows expand the Group Policy Objects container to reveal the newly created GPO.
7. After the GPO is created, it can be edited by right-clicking the GPO and selecting Edit.
8. Close Group Policy Management Console and log off of the server.

Creating and Configuring GPO Links

After a GPO is created and configured, the next step is to link the GPOs to the desired Active Directory containers. To link an existing GPO to an Active Directory container, follow these steps:

1. Log on to a designated Windows 8 or Windows Server 2012 administrative system and open the Group Policy Management Console.
2. Expand the forest node, expand the domain node, and expand the domain to expose the Group Policy Objects container and all the other domain containers and organizational units.
3. Right-click the desired site, domain, or organizational unit, and select Link an Existing GPO.
4. In the Select GPO window, select the desired domain and GPO, and click OK to link it.

Managing User Account Control Settings

Windows Vista, Windows Server 2008 and later workstation and server operating systems contain a security feature named User Account Control (UAC). UAC was created primarily to provide greater control over changes to the operating system configuration or file system. UAC interacts with both non-administrators and administrators in their desktop environment and runs almost all applications in Standard User mode. When an administrator, regular user, or application attempts to perform an action that can result in a system configuration change or require access to sensitive areas of the operating system or file system, UAC stops the change and prompts for authorization or credentials to validate the change. The response will require the user to approve the change by either clicking the Allow button and administrative credentials may or may not be required.

UAC settings are pretty flexible in allowing applications to run as desired but can require some tuning on the part of the desktop administrator. Many independent software vendors have been able to produce applications that can interact with UAC but in some cases where functionality or usability of a PC is impacted by UAC, some administrators or organizations may decide to disable UAC completely or just certain UAC settings to optimize the user experience. For situations when UAC is causing undesired issues with applications, if adjusting file security, user rights assignments, or running applications in legacy mode do not work, it may be necessary to adjust or disable User Account Control functions. The likely candidates are applications that formerly required the end user to be a member of the local Power Users or Administrators group.

UAC settings should not adversely affect the functionality and operation of standard users. On the contrary, UAC actually allows standard users to be prompted for credentials to allow elevation of rights to install software or components that would have failed with previous operating systems with an Access Denied message. If, for some reason, the end user requires local administrator rights to run a legacy application and all other options have failed, changing UAC security settings in a local computer policy or domain GPO is required. When UAC security setting changes are required, follow these steps:

1. Log on to a designated Windows 8 or Windows Server 2012 administrative system and open the Group Policy Management Console.
2. Expand the forest node, expand the domain node, and expand the domain to expose the Group Policy Objects container and select it.
3. Either create a new GPO or edit an existing GPO.
4. After the GPO is opened for editing in the Group Policy Management Editor, expand the Computer Configuration node, expand the Policies node, select the Windows Settings node, and expand it.
5. Expand the Security Settings node, expand Local Policies, and select Security Options.
6. In the Settings pane, scroll to the bottom of the pane to locate the UAC settings. The following list displays the default UAC settings in the Local Computer Policy for Windows Server 2012 as an example:
   - Admin Approval mode for the Built-in Administrator account—Disabled
   - Allow UIAccess applications to prompt for elevation without using the secure desktop—Disabled
   - Behavior of the elevation prompt for administrators in Admin Approval mode—Prompt for consent for non-Windows binaries
   - Behavior of the elevation prompt for standard users—Prompt for credentials
   - Detect application installations and prompt for elevation—Enabled
   - Only elevate executables that are signed and validated—Disabled

- Only elevate UIAccess applications that are installed in secure locations—Enabled
- Run all administrators in Admin Approval mode—Enabled
- Switch to the secure desktop when prompting for elevation—Enabled
- Virtualize file and Registry write failures to per-user locations—Enabled

7. To disable all UAC functionality, using domain policies, create and link a new GPO for UAC and edit the setting named Run All Administrators in Admin Approval mode, and configure the setting value to Disabled. If this setting is configured as Disabled, all other UAC settings are ignored. Also, this setting change will be applied during startup, shutdown, and background refresh, but a reboot is required to complete the setting change.
8. To disable UAC prompts when logged on with an account with local administrator rights and leave all other settings functional, using domain policies, create and link a new GPO for UAC and edit the setting named Behavior of the Elevation Prompt for Administrators in Admin Approval Mode, and configure the setting value to Elevate Without Prompting, as shown in Figure 27.6. Click OK to save the setting and close the Group Policy Management Editor window.

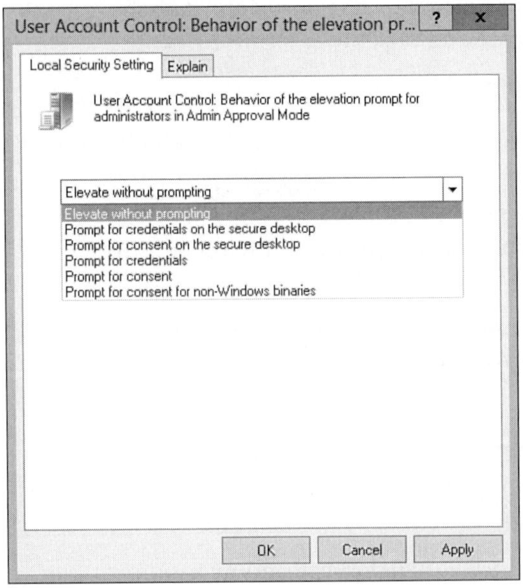

FIGURE 27.6 Configuring User Account Control to allow administrators to elevate privileges without prompting.

9. After the GPO is configured as desired, save the GPO and link it to an organizational unit that has a test Windows Vista, Windows Server 2008, or later workstation or

server operating system to verify that the desired functionality has been achieved. Remember that a reboot is required before the results of this setting change will take affect.

10. After the testing is completed, configure security filtering and possibly also WMI filtering to limit the application scope of this policy and link it to the desired organizational units.

Creating Application Control Policies (AppLocker)

Application control policies implement software restriction on computers and user profiles to prevent users from running undesired programs that might impact system configuration and reliability. Application control policies are supported on Windows 7 Enterprise and Ultimate editions, Windows 8 Pro, and on all editions of Windows Server 2008 R2 and Windows Server 2012. Application control policies or AppLocker, when enabled, will not allow users to run any executables except those defined as allowed. This can of course cause serious functionality issues if deployed improperly so Microsoft has developed an audit-only mode that can be used to test a policy with AppLocker settings to start gathering a list of applications end users need to run in order to perform their job.

Before AppLocker policies can function and be applied to the desired Windows 8 and Windows Server 2012 systems, the Application Identity service needs to be running. This service can be set to automatic startup on the desired systems by configuring and applying domain policy. To configure this service to automatic startup on the desired systems, create a new domain policy and in the Computer Configuration node beneath Windows Settings and System Services, locate the Application Identity service, define the policy setting and set the startup mode to Automatic. Apply this policy to the desired systems but understand that the service, even when set to automatic, will not start until the next reboot or until the service is started by a local user, through a remote management console or script, or through the use of a scheduled or immediate task, which is discussed later in this chapter.

AppLocker policies are based on rules. These rules include the following:

- **Publisher rules**—Rules based on the digital signature of the application the rule is defined for.
- **File hash rules**—Rules based on the specifics of the actual application file itself.
- **Path rules**—Rules based on the location of the applications the rule is define for.

File hash rules are the most specific, but publisher rules and path rules can include all applications signed by the same software vendor and certificate or the if all applications fall under a specific pat they also can be grouped together.

To configure AppLocker settings, follow these steps:

1. Log on to a designated Windows 8 or Windows Server 2012 administrative system and open the Group Policy Management Console.

2. Expand the forest node, expand the domain node, and expand the domain to expose the Group Policy Objects container and select it.
3. Either create a new GPO or edit an existing GPO.
4. After the GPO is opened for editing in the Group Policy Management Editor, expand the Computer Configuration node, expand the Policies node, expand the Windows Settings node, and select the Security Settings node.
5. Expand the Security Settings node, and select Application Control Policies.
6. Expand the Application Control Policies node and select AppLocker.
7. In the Settings pane, click the Configure Rule Enforcement link in the center of the page.
8. In the AppLocker Properties window, check the four check boxes for Executable, Windows Installer, Script, and Packaged App rules and select the Audit Only option from the pull-down menus, as shown in Figure 27.7. Then, click OK to define the rule enforcement properties.

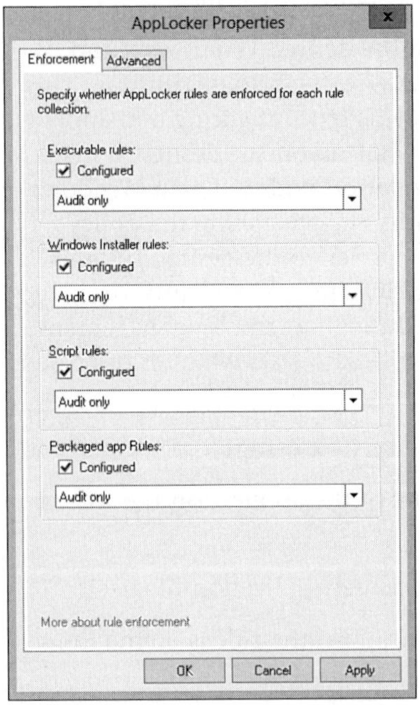

FIGURE 27.7 Configuring the AppLocker enforcement rules to audit only.

9. Now before any auditing can be logged, new rules will need to be created. For this example, right-click the Executable Rules node beneath AppLocker and select Automatically Generate Rules.

10. On the Folders and Permissions page, leave the default group of Everyone and the default path of C:\Program Files and rule name of Program files as it and then click Next to continue.

11. On the Rules Preferences page, leave the defaults of creating publisher rules for files that are digitally signed and grouping similar rules together as shown in Figure 27.8, but choose whether your organization desires to use file hash or path rules for unsigned applications. The default will create file hash rules, which are more secure. Click Next to continue.

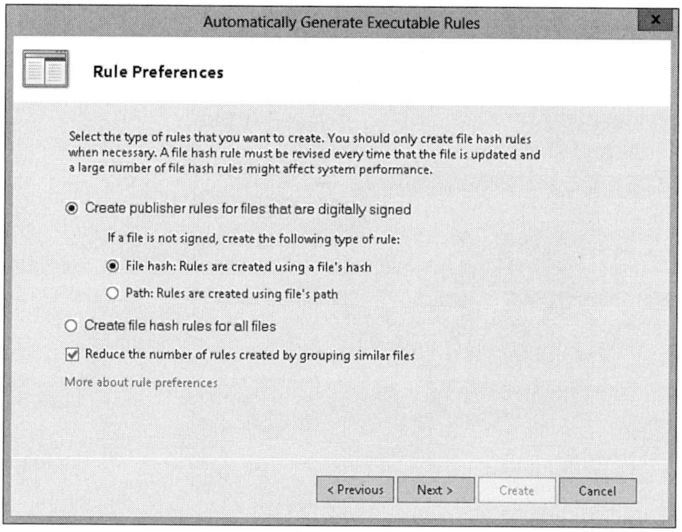

FIGURE 27.8 Creating publisher rules for digitally signed executables.

NOTE

If the APP Locker GPO will be applied to Windows 7 or Windows Server 2008 Publishing rules are not compatible and file hash rules should always be used.

12. In the Rules Review page, review the proposed rules and click Create to actually create the rules within the group policy. A pop-up window will open asking to also create the default rules, click Yes to complete the task.

13. Once this is completed, save the domain policy and link it to an organizational unit that contains Windows 8 Pro or Ultimate or Windows Server 2012 systems.

14. Log on to the desired test system, verify that the new AppLocker policy has been applied and that the Application Identity service is set to Automatic and is running on the desired machine. Reboot the machine.

15. Log back on to the test machine and run Internet Explorer or any other executable that is located beneath the C:\Program Files folder.

16. Now open the Event Viewer console using an elevated account so the audit events can be reviewed.

17. In the Event Viewer window, expand Applications and Services Logs, expand Microsoft, and expand AppLocker.

18. Select the EXE and DLL log and in the Settings pane and review the AppLocker events, as shown in Figure 27.9. Warning events are logged for executables that would have been blocked by the rule. If no events are logged, the Application Identity service may not be running or a reboot might not have been performed after the initial AppLocker policy was applied.

19. Close the event log on the test machine to complete this exercise.

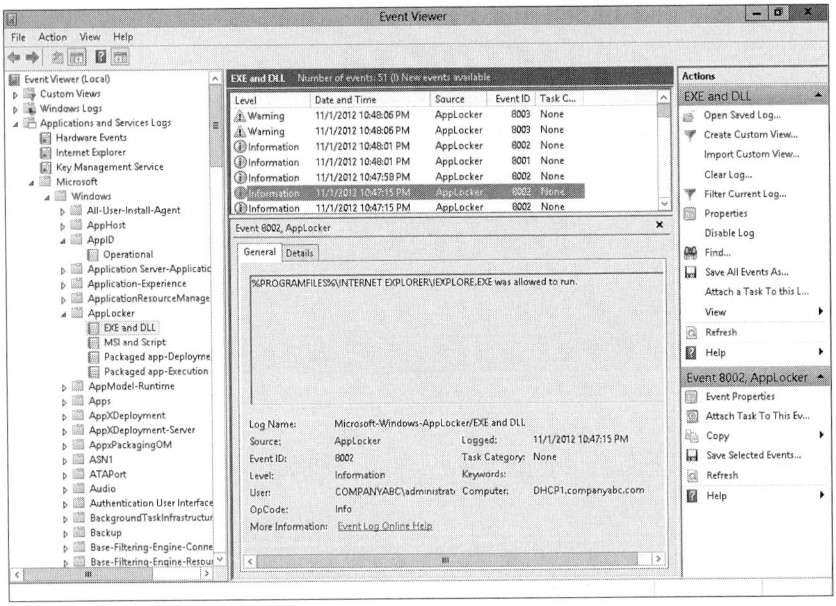

FIGURE 27.9 Viewing AppLocker EXE and DLL event log audit events.

AppLocker rules applied to a computer can be defined or configured to apply on a per-user or per-security group basis. Specific AppLocker policies can be configured to block all executables, Windows Installer files, and scripts after each of those rules are enforced. Applocker is broken into four different policy rule groups including Executable rules, Windows Installer rules, Script rules and Packaged App rules. Each of these policy rule groups support administrator created rules or rules can be generated automatically. As an example, the C:\program files folder can be scanned for Executable files and rules will be generated based on the contents of that folder. Also, administrators can choose to add in a default rule set when creating Applocker policy rules. The default executable rules, for example, will define that everyone can run executables in the program files and Windows folders, including all subfolders, but only administrators can run executables without path restrictions. To create or populate the default rules for executables, in the tree pane under AppLocker, expand AppLocker and right-click the Executable Rules node and click Create Default Rules. This will generate the three rules described previously.

Configuring Preference Item-Level Targeting

There are many instances in Group Policy deployments when an administrator desires to apply a particular preference setting to only a subset of computers or users. When this is the case, preference item-level targeting can be used. For example, a Group Policy administrator can create a single domain policy named UserDriveMapGPO and leave the policy filtering set to authenticated users, and it can be linked to the domain. In this case, if a drive map preference is defined, all users in the domain will map the same drive. Now within this single policy several drive maps can be created, but each drive map can be applied to only specified users or security groups using item-level targeting with the drive map preference options. The following steps detail segmenting the application of a drive map setting to a security group named sales, using item-level targeting:

1. Log on to a designated Windows Server 2012 administrative server and open the GPMC.
2. Expand the tree view to reveal the desired domain and expand the domain to reveal the Group Policy Objects container.
3. Create a new GPO named UserDriveMapGPO and open it for editing.
4. In the Group Policy Management Editor window, select and expand the User Configuration node in the tree pane, and expand the Preferences node and Windows Settings node.
5. Select the Drive Maps preference setting in the tree pane and in the Drive Maps pane right-click and select create New Mapped Drive.
6. When the New Drive Properties window opens, leave the Action setting as Update and type in the appropriate UNC path to the network share folder (in this example, **\\FILESERVER1\GroupShare\Sales**). Check the box to reconnect and label as Sales.
7. Select the drive letter G, as shown in Figure 27.10.
8. Select the Common tab and check the Item-Level Targeting check box and click the Targeting button to open the Targeting Editor.
9. In the Targeting Editor window, click the arrow in the New Item pull-down menu to reveal each of the different options that can be used for item-level targeting and select Security Group.
10. When the security group item is added to the window, in the lower pane next to the group form field click the ellipsis (...) button to locate and add a security group from the domain; for this example, it is the companyabc\sales secuity group, as shown in Figure 27.11.

27

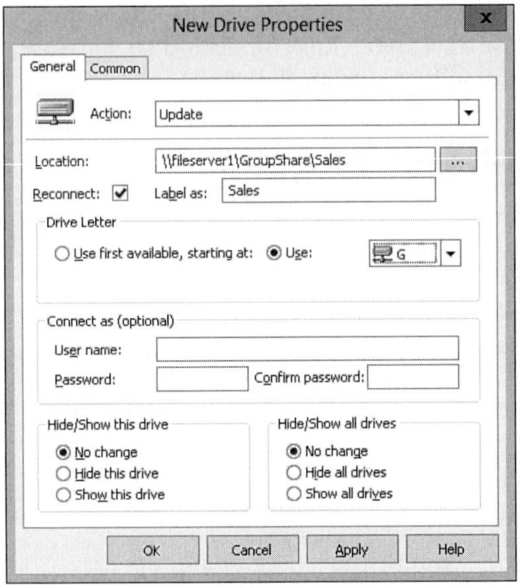

FIGURE 27.10 Configuring the drive map settings.

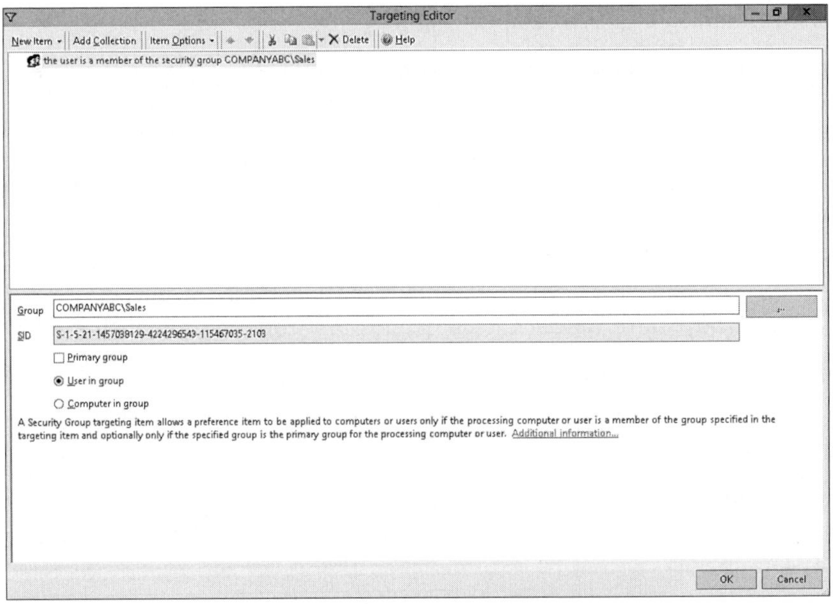

FIGURE 27.11 Configuring a security group item-level target

11. Click OK to close the item-level targeting windows, and click OK in the New Drive Properties window.

12. Back in the Group Policy Management Editor window, additional drive maps can be created, even with the same drive letter, as long as they all have a different item-level target configuration, such as the security group targeting as created in this example.

13. Close the Group Policy Management Editor window and test the application of the policy on a test system with a test user account that is in the security group.

Configuring Remote Desktop and Remote Administration Support

A common Group Policy request from IT administrators who need to support Windows XP, Windows Server 2003, and later workstation and server operating systems is to enable and allow for remote administration. Group Policy can manage this task with minimal configuration. To enable Remote Desktop on Windows XP, Windows 2003, Windows Vista, or Windows Server 2008 systems, enable the Allow Users to Connect Remotely Using Remote Desktop Services setting. This setting is located in Computer Configuration\Policies\Administrative Templates\Windows Components\Remote Desktop Services\Remote Desktop Session Host\Connections node, as shown in Figure 27.12. When this GPO is saved and linked to a GPO with computers in it, all the computers will have Remote Desktop enabled. By default, only members of the Administrators group will be able to connect using Remote Desktop. If this needs to be changed, additional users can be added to the local Remote Desktop Users group.

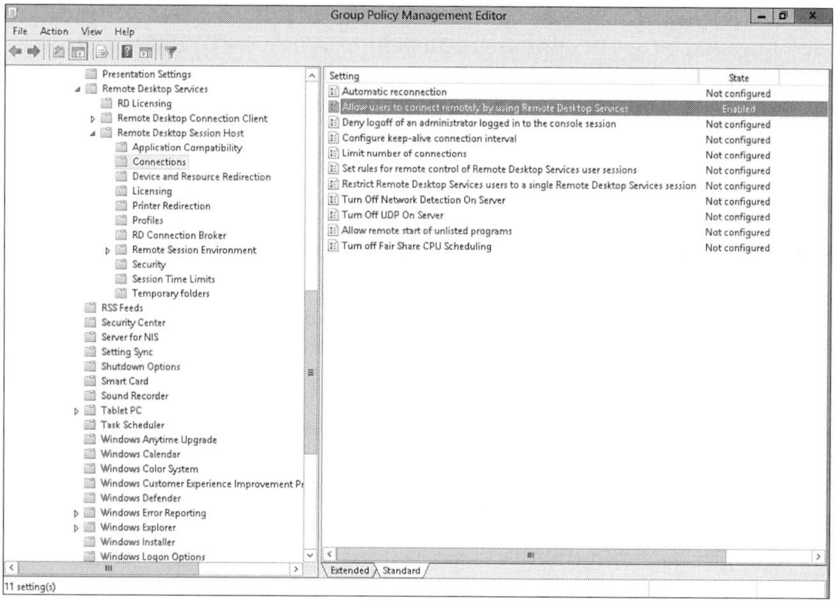

FIGURE 27.12 Enabling Remote Desktop using a GPO.

After Remote Desktop is enabled on a system with the previous setting, administrators will also need to configure the authentication security level as well as the firewall exceptions. To configure the authentication level (for example, to allow older clients to connect to the server or workstation using any version of remote desktop), configure the setting named Require User Authentication for Remote Connections by Using Network Level Authentication to Disabled. With this setting set to Disabled, any version of Remote Desktop can connect to the system. This may be ideal for support scenarios that contain older clients such as thin clients or third-party Remote Desktop implementations, but in general this setting should be set to Enabled to require higher authentication security. This setting is located in the Computer Configuration\Policies\Administrative Templates\Windows Components\Remote Desktop Services\Remote Desktop Session Host\Security node.

The Remote Desktop firewall exceptions still need to be configured; otherwise, Remote Desktop is not possible. Remote Desktop is a built-in exception in the Windows XP, Windows Server 2003, and later client and server basic and advanced firewall rule sets. In addition, remote administration is a built-in exception. To configure these exceptions, see the following section, "Configuring Basic Firewall Settings with Group Policy."

Configuring Basic Firewall Settings with Group Policy

In many organizations, part of the responsibility of supporting end users requires the ability to remotely manage the desktop. Many organizations leverage the built-in Windows tools for remote management, whereas many others utilize third-party products. Remote management tasks of workstations can include installing custom software for a particular user, computer or set of computers, installing Windows Updates, assisting with the installation of local printers, adding local user accounts, changing local group membership, or troubleshooting reported issues with or without the end user's interaction and approval.

The Microsoft Windows Firewall includes multiple firewall profiles that contain separate firewall rules and firewall exceptions. In many situations, remote administration included, the Windows Firewall rules can block the undesired as well as the desired traffic from passing through. In the case of remote desktop and remote administration, Windows XP, Windows Server 2003, and later client and server operating system firewalls contain precreated rules to quickly enable this functionality.

When managing firewall rules through group policies, administrators need to consider several configuration options, including which firewall profiles require the rule changes, does the rule need to be filtering by the source IP address, and should certain systems be targeted with these changes. For example, with Remote Desktop and Remote Administration, organizations may want to allow this functionality through the firewall only on the domain profile and only from certain IP ranges or subnets where the company servers and administrator workstations reside. This will reduce the security exposure of the system when connected to public network and even tightly control who can remotely connect to these systems when on the company network.

Windows XP and Windows Server 2003 include a standard and domain firewall profile. The domain profile is activated when the desktop is on a network that is defined in Active Directory Sites and Subnets and can communicate with a domain controller. The standard profile is activated when the desktop is on a remote or public network; in many cases, however, if the machine is connected to a VPN that does not support proper communication, it might also remain in the standard firewall profile. Windows Vista, Windows Server 2008, and later workstation and server operating systems contain three firewall profiles: the domain profile, the private profile, and the public profile. The domain profile remains the same, but the previous standard profile has now been segmented into the private and public profiles. Any network that is different from the domain network is initially categorized as an untrusted network, and the public firewall profile is activated. End users, with the appropriate rights, can recategorize a public network as a private network, which can then activate the private firewall profile and the appropriate firewall rule set, which is likely to be less restrictive. Private networks can be used in workgroup settings and for users to define their home networks as well. Windows Firewall design and configuration planning is a very important task for Windows administrators to execute and should not be taken lightly. Also, disabling firewalls in any profile is not recommended and is a poor approach to enabling systems and applications to function on an organization's network.

To allow Windows administrators to continue to manage and administer Windows server and desktop systems remotely, certain firewall exceptions should be defined. Aside from enabling Remote Desktop, as outlined in the previous section, remote administrators might need to copy files to and from systems and utilize Microsoft Management Console snap-ins such as Windows Backup, Event Viewer, Computer Management, and many others from remote administrative workstations. To enable the Remote Desktop and Remote Administration exceptions in the Windows Firewall using domain group policies, follow these steps:

1. Log on to a designated Windows Server 2012 administrative server and open the GPMC.

2. In the GPMC, expand the forest and domains node to reveal the desired domain and the Group Policy Objects container within.

3. Select the Group Policy Objects container and either create a new GPO or edit an existing GPO.

4. After the GPO is opened for editing in the Group Policy Management Editor, expand the Computer Configuration node, expand the Policies node, and select the Administrative Templates.

5. Expand the Administrative Templates node, expand the Network node, expand the Network Connections node, and select the Windows Firewall node. Configurations made in this section will apply to Windows XP, Windows Server 2003 and greater client and server operating systems but this section is really created for Windows XP and Windows Server 2003. For more granular firewall configuration for Windows Vista, Window Server 2008 and greater operating systems, the Windows Firewall with Advanced Security settings can be used.

6. In the tree pane, expand the Windows Firewall node to reveal the Domain Profile node, and select it.
7. In the Settings pane, locate the setting named Windows Firewall: Allow Inbound Remote Administration Exception, and double-click it to open the setting for editing.
8. In the Setting window, click the Enabled option button, and type in the network from which inbound remote administration will be allowed. For this example, consider an organization that utilizes the 10.0.0.0 network with a subnet mask of 255.0.0.0. This would be defined as 10.0.0.0/8 in the properties of this exception, as shown in Figure 27.13. When finished, click OK to update the setting.

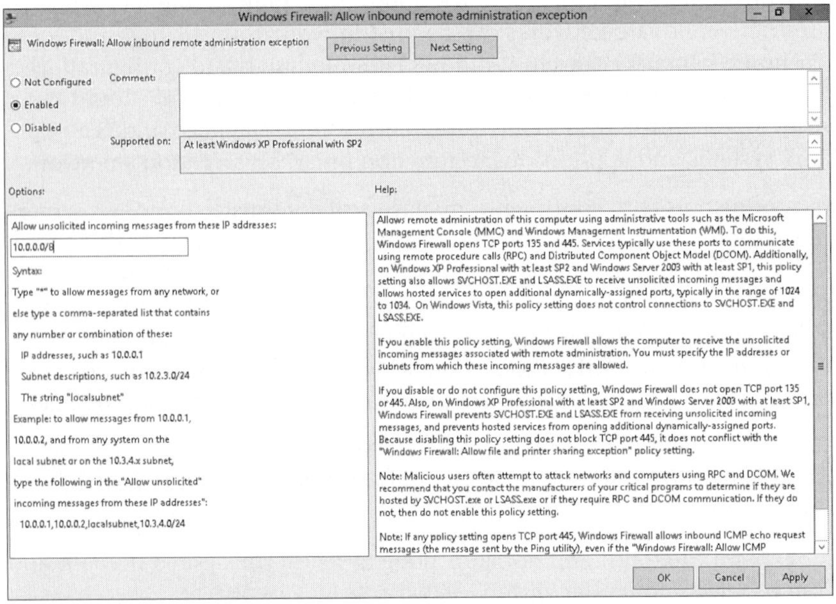

FIGURE 27.13 Configuring the Remote Administration basic firewall rule.

9. After the previous setting has been configured, back in the Settings pane, select the Windows Firewall: Allow Inbound Remote Desktop Exceptions, and double-click it to open the setting for editing.
10. In the setting window, click the Enabled option button, and type in the network from which inbound Remote Desktop connections will be allowed. When finished, click OK to update the setting.
11. If necessary, repeat the process of configuring the inbound remote administration and Remote Desktop exception in the standard profile to ensure that remote management from the defined network will function regardless of which firewall profile is currently activated on the client.

NOTE

If the network defined within a Windows firewall exception is a common network, such as 192.168.0.0/24, the configuration of these exceptions in the standard profile are considered risky and should not be performed. Instead, work with the networking group and VPN configurations to ensure that when users connect remotely to the network from remote sites and through VPN connections, the system will always recognize and apply the domain profile.

12. Back in the GPMC, link the new remote administration firewall exception GPO to an OU with a computer that can be used to test the policy.

13. After the testing is completed, configure security filtering and possibly also WMI filtering to limit the application scope of this policy and link it to the desired organizational units.

Configuring Advanced Firewall Settings

Windows Vista, Windows Server 2008, and later client and server operating systems have a new and improved firewall that enables administrators to manage granular inbound and outbound firewall rules within the three the default firewall profiles. Even though the Windows Firewall is enabled and active by default on Windows Server 2012, when the Add Roles Wizard is run and a role, role service, or feature is added to the Windows Server 2012 system, the necessary firewall exceptions are also configured as part of the process. This is a major advantage compared with what was included in Windows Server 2003. However, be aware that when adding additional applications or services (that are not included with the product) to a Windows Server 2012 system, unless the installation of that product also has a built-in feature to enable and configure the necessary exceptions in the firewall, the exceptions will need to be defined and configured manually. When custom firewall rules, exceptions, and changes to the default behavior and configuration of the firewall profiles are required, the settings need to be defined using the Windows Firewall with Advanced Security console. If these settings need to be defined using a domain policy, access to these policy settings are included in the Computer Configuration\Policies\Windows Security\Security Settings\Windows Firewall with Advanced Security settings node. One advantage of using Windows Firewall with Advanced Security is that when a system is configured manually and all the necessary exceptions and rules are defined within the firewall, these rules can be exported from the firewall and imported into a domain policy and applied from the central location to all the desired servers. You can find more information about creating Windows Firewall rules in Chapter 13, "Server-Level Security."

27

Configuring Windows Update Settings

Many organizations utilize the Internet services provided by Microsoft known as Windows Update and Microsoft Update. The main difference between the two is that Microsoft Update also includes updates for other products such as Microsoft Office, Microsoft Exchange Server, Microsoft SQL Server, and many more. Starting with Windows XP and

Windows Server 2003, all Windows systems are now capable of downloading and automatically installing Windows Update out of the box. To upgrade the Windows Update client to support updates for other Microsoft applications through Microsoft Update, these machines might need to be upgraded manually, upgraded using a GPO software installation, or upgraded using Microsoft Windows Server Update Services (WSUS). A WSUS server can be configured to auto-update the client software automatically, which is the preferred approach. Depending on whether the organization utilizes an internal WSUS server running on Windows Server 2012 or wants to utilize the Windows/Microsoft Internet-based services to configure these settings using group policies, the settings are located in the following sections:

- Computer Configuration\Policies\Administrative Templates\Windows Components\Windows Update
- User Configuration\Policies\Administrative Templates\Windows Components\Windows Update

For more information and recommendations on best practices for configuring Windows Updates, see the section, "Using Windows Server Update Services," in Chapter 13.

Configuring Power Options Using Domain Policies

Using group policies to manage the power profiles on Windows systems is a feature that was introduced with Windows Vista and Windows Server 2008 Group Policy preference templates and continues. Computer preferences for power include three types:

- **Power Options (Windows XP)**—This preference item can be used to define the action of pressing the power button or closing the lid of a notebook on an XP system.
- **Power Schemes (Windows XP)**—This preference item can be used to set the power-usage scenario that controls when an XP system will go to sleep.
- **Power Plan (At Least Windows 7)**—This preference item will apply to Windows Vista, 7, and 8 clients as well as Windows Vista, 7, 8 clients as well as Windows Server 2008 and will contain all the settings necessary to configure the power button actions, closing the lid on notebooks, and power management of the hardware components of the system, as well as the sleep and hibernation settings.

Starting with Windows Server 2008 and Windows Vista, power plans can be defined and applied using domain policies using computer preference settings. To configure a centrally managed power plan for Windows Vista, Windows Server 2008, and later client and server operating systems follow these steps:

1. Log on to a designated Windows Server 2012 administrative server and open the GPMC.
2. In the GPMC, expand the forest and domains node to reveal the desired domain and the Group Policy Objects container within.

3. Select the Group Policy Objects container and create a new GPO named PowerProfileGPO and open it for editing.
4. After the PowerProfileGPO is opened for editing in the Group Policy Management Editor, expand the Computer Configuration node, expand the Preferences node
5. Expand the Control Panel Settings, right-click the Power Options node, and select New - Power Plan (At Least Windows 7).
6. On the Advanced Settings page, leave the default Action on Update and change the power plan from Balanced to High Performance. Also, check the Set as the Active Power Plan check box, and then click OK to complete the settings, as shown in Figure 27.14. If you want to, change any of the default settings to other values.

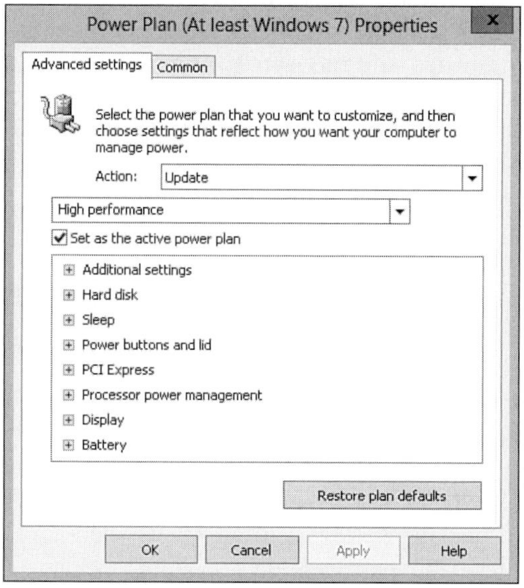

FIGURE 27.14 Configuring the power plan settings.

7. Close the Group Policy Management Editor and link the policy in the Group Policy Management Console to a test organizational unit.
8. Once the new policy passes validation testing, link it to a production organizational unit as desired.

This will make the High Performance power plan the default for the computer and for all users who log on, although power plans are in fact unique to the user logon and some implementations of such a policy will require the user-based power plan preference settings.

Managing Scheduled Tasks and Immediate Tasks with Domain Policies

There are many times when Group Policy administrators would have liked to run an application or a command on a remote machine without having to reboot or log on to that particular system. For example, there may be a critical security or application update that needs to be rolled out and executed immediately. Historically, this would require a new group policy with a script or software package assigned, and the machine would need to be rebooted to run the script or install the application. With Windows Server 2012, this can be accomplished with the Scheduled Task and Immediate Task preference settings for both Windows XP and Windows 7 and later operating systems. As an example of this that ties to the previous section on AppLocker, the policy administrators can create a policy that immediately starts the Application Identity Service to automatic startup mode, since this is required to support Applocker policy rules. This can be accomplished by creating a group policy that defines the Scheduled Tasks\Immediate task computer preference and runs the **Net Start AppIDSvc** command. To perform the previously cited example, create a new domain policy, open the policy for editing, and navigate to the Computer Configuration\Preferences\Control Panel\Scheduled Tasks node. Right-click the node and select New- Immediate Task (At Least Windows 7). Configure and save the task settings as shown in Figures 27.15 and 27.16. Save the policy and test it out to verify it works as desired, and then deploy it in production or save it as a quick policy that can be updated and used for a different purpose later.

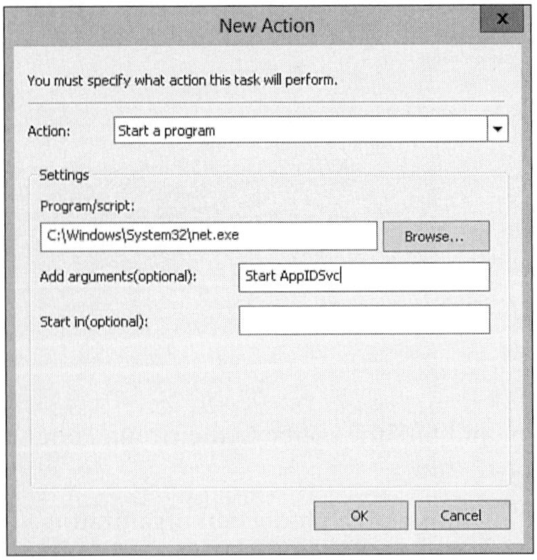

FIGURE 27.15 Configuring the Start a Program action.

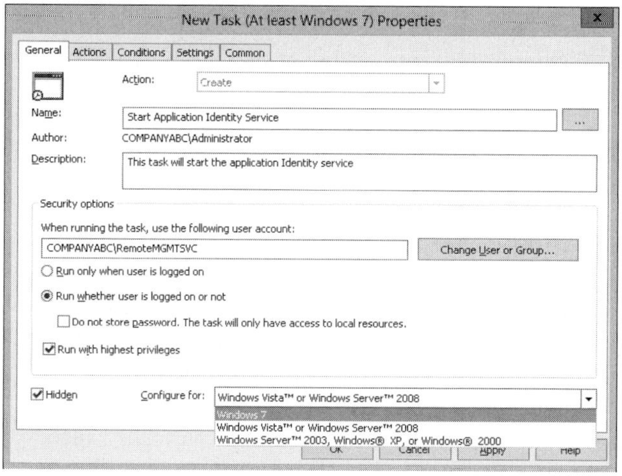

FIGURE 27.16 Defining a new Immediate Task preference setting for Windows 8 systems.

Managing Users with Policies

Group Policy enables administrators to define how the end-user experience and desktop will be configured. Also, with user-based group policies, end users can be granted or denied access to certain Windows applications and features and even can be limited from reading or writing to removable media. Common user Group Policy configurations include the following:

- Start menu configuration
- Restricting Control Panel and display settings
- Internet Explorer settings
- Software restrictions
- Microsoft Management Console restrictions
- Screensaver settings
- Mapping network drives
- Installing printers

- Creating desktop shortcuts
- Application-specific configurations, including customizing Microsoft Office if the administrative templates are loaded and used in the policy
- Network configuration settings
- Power plans
- Folder redirection and offline file settings

Managing the user environment and desktop with group policies, for the most part, can be used to configure the GUI for the user and to impose security restrictions to increase the reliability of the computer systems in use. In some cases, application shortcuts can be added to the desktop and applets can be hidden from view in the Control Panel or Start menu, but in more restrictive cases, they can be hidden and restricted from execution. Many organizations would like the end-user desktop to be very simple and present the end users with only the necessary applications relevant to their job. Although this is an extreme case, it can be performed by configuring the settings located in the User Configuration\Policies\Administrative Templates\Start Menu and Taskbar settings node. A more functional start menu GPO extension can also be used to manage the configuration of the start menu for XP, Vista, Windows 7, and Windows 8 clients by configuring settings located in the User Configuration\Preferences\Control Panel Settings\Start Menu settings node.

Desktop security is a big concern for companies, now more than ever. One easy configuration organizations can use to better secure end-user desktops is to implement a password-locking screensaver. Automatic desktop locking with screensavers can be a very handy configuration, but sales and remote users should be granted extended computer idle time to prevent a password protected screensaver from executing in the middle of a sales presentation or a web based meeting. Screensaver settings can be configured in the User Configuration\Policies\Administrative Templates\Control Panel\Personalization settings node. To enable a password-protected screensaver with a blank screen screensaver that works on every version of Windows, the following four settings must be configured:

- **Enable Screen Saver**—Enabled
- **Password Protect the Screen Saver**—Enabled
- **Force Specific Screen Saver**—Enabled scrnsave.scr
- **Screen Saver Time Out**—Enabled 900, to go to screensaver after 15 minutes of inactivity

Another of the biggest pain points for companies is being able to back up end-user data, which, by default, is stored on the local profile folder on the local drive of the computer. When users log on to multiple computers or Remote Desktop Services systems, administrators can configure users with roaming profiles and/or specific Remote Desktop Services profiles, which follow them between systems and are stored on server shares. This configuration is set on the actual user object and is not necessarily a Group Policy setting.

Remote Desktop Services profiles are great for Remote Desktop Services systems, but implementing roaming profiles for an entire company on every computer is not the best solution because each time the user logs on to a system, the entire profile is copied to the local computer and when the user logs off, the profile is copied back to the server. The larger the profile gets, the longer it takes to copy the profile between the server shares and the computer system. On Remote Desktop Services systems, it is very easy for administrators to remotely log off and complete the copy of the profile back to the server share. However, for end-user workstations, when roaming profiles get large, many users may not wait for the profile copy to complete and manually shut down the system, or they unplug it from the network or put it to sleep and take it with them. This, of course, can cause profile corruption and, even worse, data loss. To improve Remote Desktop Services profile and standard roaming profile performance, administrators can use Group Policy to redirect user folders to server shares using folder redirection.

Configuring Folder Redirection

Folder redirection can be used to redirect certain special folders in the end user's profile to server shares. Special folders such as the Documents, which is the default folder for users to store and access their data, can be redirected to server shares. The following are some basic rule-of-thumb guidelines when using this Group Policy extension:

- **Allow the system to create the folders**—If the folders are created by the administrator, they will not have the correct permissions. But properly configuring the share and NTFS permissions on the server share is essential in providing a functional folder redirection experience.
- **Enable client-side caching or offline file synchronization**—This is important for users with portable computers but is not the desired configuration for folder redirection on Remote Desktop Services systems. Furthermore, when storing data on end-user workstations, it may violate regulatory or security requirements to allow for cached local copies.
- **Use fully qualified (UNC) paths or DFS paths for server share locations**—For example, use \\Server1.companyabc.com\UserProfiles or \\companyabc.com\UserProfiles\ if DFS shares are deployed.

Before folder redirection can be expected to work, share and NTFS permissions must be configured appropriately. For folder redirection to work properly, configure the NTFS as follows:

- Configure the share folder to not inherit permissions and remove all existing permissions.
- Add the file server's local member server's Administrators group with Full Control of This Folder, Subfolders, and Files.
- Add the Domain Admins domain security group with Full Control of This Folder, Subfolders, and Files.

- Add the System account with Full Control of This Folder, Subfolders, and Files.
- Add the Creator Owner with Full Control of Subfolders and Files only.
- Add the Authenticated Users group with both List Folder/Read Data and Create Folders/Append Data - This Folder Only rights. To set these two permissions, you will need to configure the permissions using the advanced permission dialog box. The Authenticated Users group can be replaced with the desired group, but, as a best practice, do not choose the Everyone group.

The share permissions of the folder can be configured to grant administrators Full Control or owner and Authenticated Users Read/Write permissions.

To redirect the Documents folder to a network share for Windows Vista, Windows Server 2008, and later client and server operating systems, follow these steps:

1. Log on to a designated Windows Server 2012 administrative server and open the GPMC.
2. In the GPMC, expand the forest and domains node to reveal the desired domain and the Group Policy Objects container within.
3. Select the Group Policy Objects container and create a new GPO named UserFolderRedirectGPO and open it for editing.
4. After the UserFolderRedirectGPO is opened for editing in the Group Policy Management Editor, navigate to User Configuration\Policies\Windows Settings and select the Folder Redirection node to display the user profile folders that are available for redirection, as shown in Figure 27.17. Keep in mind that the folders in this section and detailed in Figure 27.17 represent the folders available in Windows Vista, Windows Server 2008, and later client and server operating systems user profiles. If Windows 2000, Windows XP, or Windows Server 2003 profiles require folder redirection, configuring the Documents folder for redirection should work but will require additional testing against each edition and service pack level of the legacy operating system that this policy applies to.
5. In the Settings pane, right-click the Document folder and select Properties.
6. On the Target tab, click the Setting drop-down list arrow, and select Basic - Redirect Everyone's Folder to the Same Location, which reveals additional options. There is another option to configure folder redirection to different locations based on group membership, but for this example, select the basic redirection option.
7. In the Target Folder Location section, there are several options to choose from and each should be reviewed for functionality; for this example, select Create a Folder for Each User Under the Root Path. This is very important if multiple folders will be redirected; more details are explained in the following steps.
8. In Root Path field, type in the server and share name (for example, **\\CompanyABC.com\UserShare**), as shown in Figure 27.18. Notice how the end-user name and Document folder will be created beneath the root share folder. This

requires that the end users have at least Change rights on the share permissions, and they must also have the Create Folder NTFS permission on the root folder that is shared.

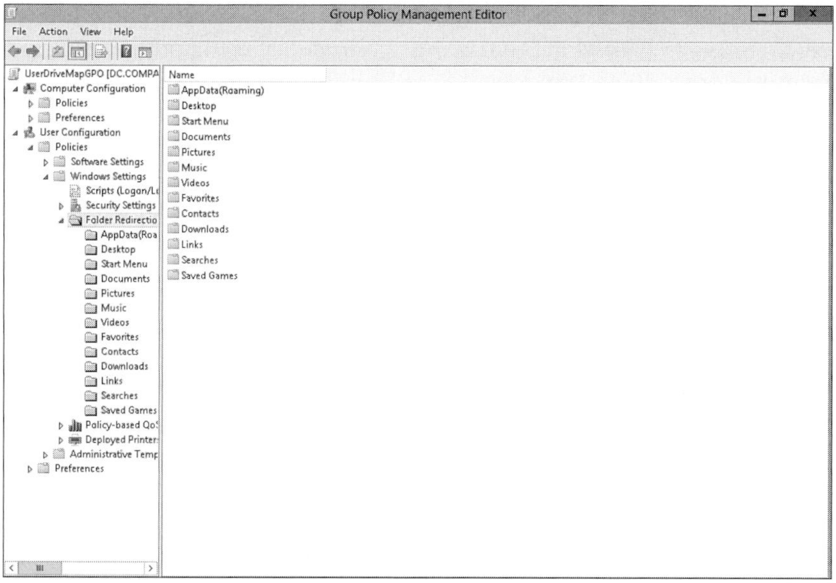

FIGURE 27.17 Windows Server 2012 and Windows 8 folder redirection.

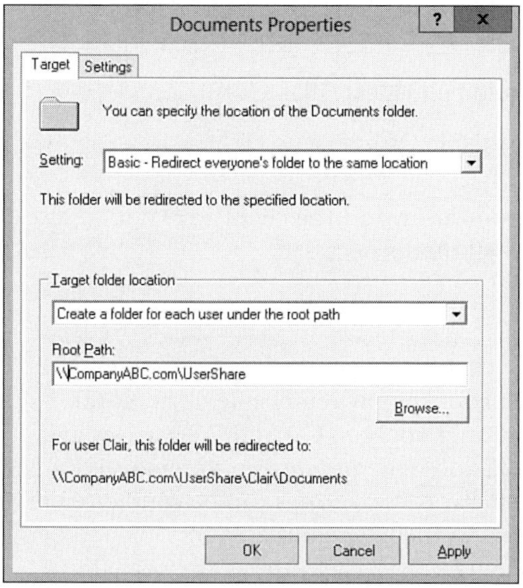

FIGURE 27.18 Folder redirection with basic redirection to a target root folder.

9. Select the Settings tab and uncheck the Grant the User Exclusive Rights to Documents check box. If necessary, check the check box to also apply redirection to Windows 2000, XP, and Windows Server 2003 operating systems.
10. Click OK to complete the folder redirection configuration. A warning pop-up opens that states that this policy will not display the Folder Redirection node if an administrator or user attempts to configure or view this group policy using policy management tools from Windows 2000, Windows XP, or Windows Server 2003. Click Yes to accept this warning and configure the folder redirection.
11. Back in the Group Policy Management Editor window, close the GPO.
12. In the GPMC, link the new UserFolderRedirectGPO policy to an OU with a user account that can be used to test this policy.
13. Log on to a Windows Vista, Windows Server 2008 or greater client or server operating systems with the test user account. After the profile completes loading, click the Start button, and locate and right-click the Documents folder. Select the Location tab and verify the path. For example, for a user named Jamil, the path should be \\companyabc.com\UserShare\Jamil\Documents.

If the folder is not redirected properly, the Windows Vista or greater operating system might need to have a domain policy applied that forces Synchronous Foreground Refresh of group policies. Also a very common configuration error is incorrect NTFS and share permissions on the share's root folder. In most cases, however, a few logons by the particular user will get the settings applied properly.

Each of the folder redirection folders will automatically be configured to be synchronized with the server and be available offline. When additional server folders need to be configured to be available offline, follow these steps:

1. Locate the shared network folder that should be made available offline.
2. Right-click the folder and select Always Available Offline.

As long as the server share allows offline synchronization and the client workstation also supports this, as they both do by default, that is all that is necessary.

Removable Storage Access

Windows Vista, Windows Server 2008, and later client and server operating system group policies provide several settings that can be used control how removable devices and removable storage can be used. Some of these settings apply to CD and DVD drives and media, but many are designed to control the read and write permission to removable disks such as external USB drives and memory sticks. These settings can be configured in a computer group policy but can also be configured in the User Configuration node to deny write access to removable media, as shown in Figure 27.19. The settings are located in User Configuration\Policies\Administrative Templates\System\Removable Storage Access.

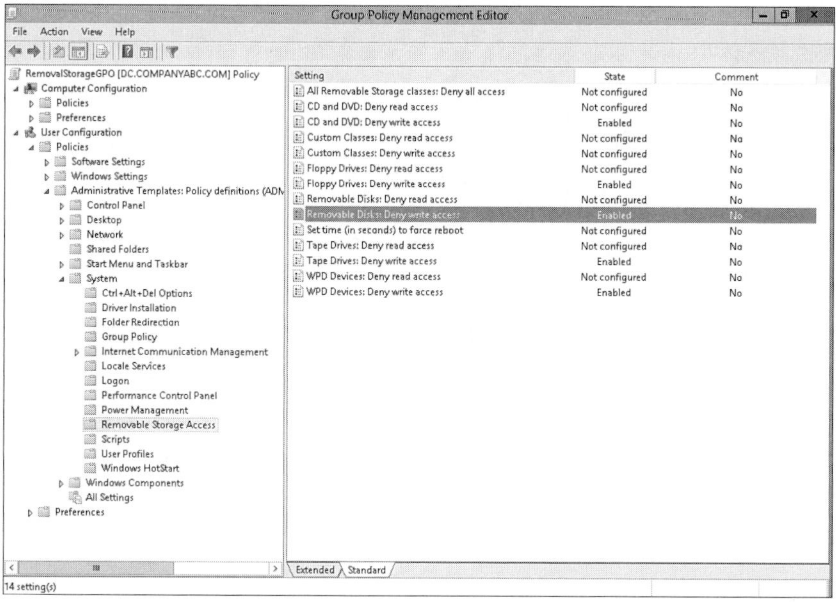

FIGURE 27.19 Denying write access to removable storage devices.

Managing Microsoft Management Console Access

Microsoft has standardized the deployment of management and configuration tools to use Microsoft Management Console (MMC) snap-ins. By default, all users can open a blank MMC and add snap-ins to the console. Which snap-ins are loaded on a particular machine determines or limits which snap-ins can be added. Having access to each snap-in can unnecessarily expose configuration information to undesired individuals. Also, depending on the function of the snap-in, functions might be available to standard users that can impact the performance of production systems. For example, a user can add the Active Directory Users and Computer snap-in to an MMC console and can then create queries that run against the domain controller, causing unnecessary load on the system. To restrict access to the MMC or specific MMC snap-ins using domain group policies, follow these steps:

1. Log on to a designated Windows Server 2012 administrative server and open the GPMC.
2. In the GPMC, expand the forest and domains node to reveal the desired domain and the Group Policy Objects container within.
3. Select the Group Policy Objects container and create a new GPO named MMCManagementGPO and open it for editing.
4. After the GPO is opened for editing in the Group Policy Management Editor, navigate to UserConfiguration\Policies\Administrative Templates\Windows

Components, select the node and scroll down and select Microsoft Management Console in the tree pane.

5. Expand the Microsoft Management Console node, and then select the Restricted/Permitted snap-ins node and select it.
6. With the Restricted/Permitted snap-ins node selected in the tree pane, a list of well-known snap-ins is displayed in the Settings pane. Select and open the Active Directory Users and Computers snap-in. Configure the setting to Disabled to block the use of this snap-in for the users to whom this policy will apply, and then click OK.
7. After the snap-in is disabled, close the policy and link it to the desired OU that contains the users who need to be restricted from using the disabled snap-in.

If this policy is to also be applied to administrators, the default security filtering of the GPO may need to be changed. For example, if an organization wants to restrict all administration to certain workstations or servers, this GPO could be applied to the domain and even domain admins, and loopback processing could be enabled for designated administrative workstations and servers, and a policy that enables MMC consoles could be linked to it, also with security filtering applying to administrators. Using a configuration like this can be great for security management and auditing.

Managing Active Directory with Policies

Many Group Policy settings detailed in the previous sections of this chapter for computer and user management apply only to domain environments. Group Policy can and is also used to manage security and configuration settings within Active Directory. Many settings apply to server role configurations to standardize security and configurations, but one main configuration of the Active Directory domain group policies is to set the password policy for all the users in the domain. To configure the setting values for the domain password policy, the default domain policy needs to be edited. The password policy settings are contained in the Computer Configuration\Policies\Windows Settings\Security Settings\Account Policies\Password Policy settings node. Figure 27.20 displays the default password policy settings for Windows 2012 domains.

When administrators review or need to update the domain password policy, an account lockout policy should be defined. The account lockout policy determines how many failed password attempts will be tolerated before a user account is locked, and whether the account will be automatically unlocked. The following list contains the three account lockout settings:

- **Account Lockout Duration**—This setting defines how many minutes an account will remain locked out before it is automatically unlocked by the system.
- **Account Lockout Threshold**—This setting defines the number of failed logon attempts that will be allowed before the user account is locked out.

- **Reset Account Lockout Counter After**—This setting defines the number of minutes before the bad logon count is returned to zero.

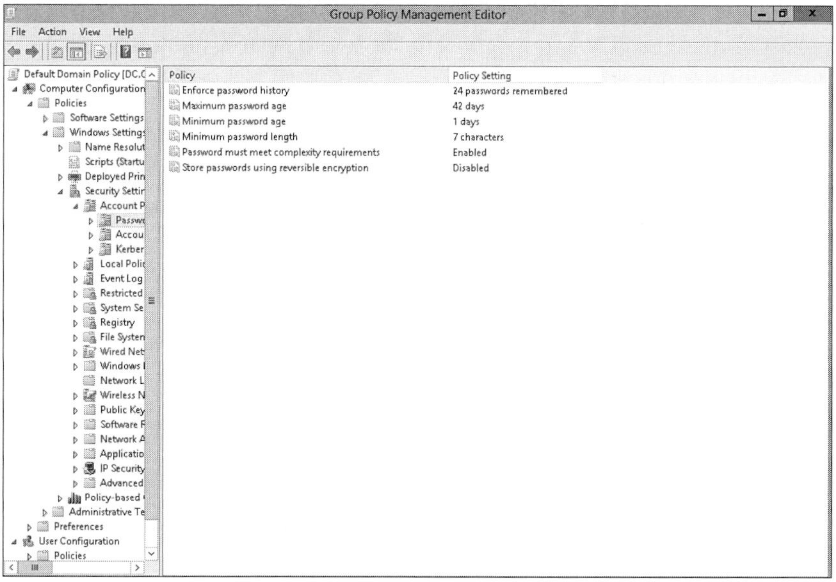

FIGURE 27.20 Default domain password policy settings.

Fine-Grained Password Policies

New for Windows Server 2008 and also included with Windows Server 2012 domains is a feature called fine-grained password policies. This feature is only available in domains operating in Windows 2008 or greater domain functional level. A fine-grained password policy is a password policy that can be defined and applied to a single domain user or a set of domains users that require looser or tighter password policies that the organization's current domain password policy. This can be a very valuable feature for organizations that require interoperability with legacy systems or applications that require service accounts that cannot adhere to the standard domain password policy. Fine-grained password policies are stored in the domain Password Settings Container and are defined as Password Settings Objects. To create a new password settings object, follow these steps:

1. Log on to the designated Windows Server 2012 system with the ADDS tools installed.
2. Open Server manager from the taskbar and from the Server Manager tools menu select Active Directory Administrative Center (ADAC).
3. When the ADAC window opens, in the tree pane double-click on the desired domain, for this example, the companyabc.com domain.
4. In the center pane scroll down and double-click on the System container.

5. In the center pane scroll down and select the Password Settings Container.

6. Once the Password Settings Container is select, in the Task pane on the right, select New and then select Password Settings to create a new Password Settings Object.

7. In the Create Password Settings Window give the Password Settings object a name and enter a value for the precedence.

8. Configure the desired Password Settings Object settings to the desired values.

9. Under the Directly Applies to section, click the Add button and specify the users and/or security groups that this Password Settings Object will apply to as shown in Figure 27.21.

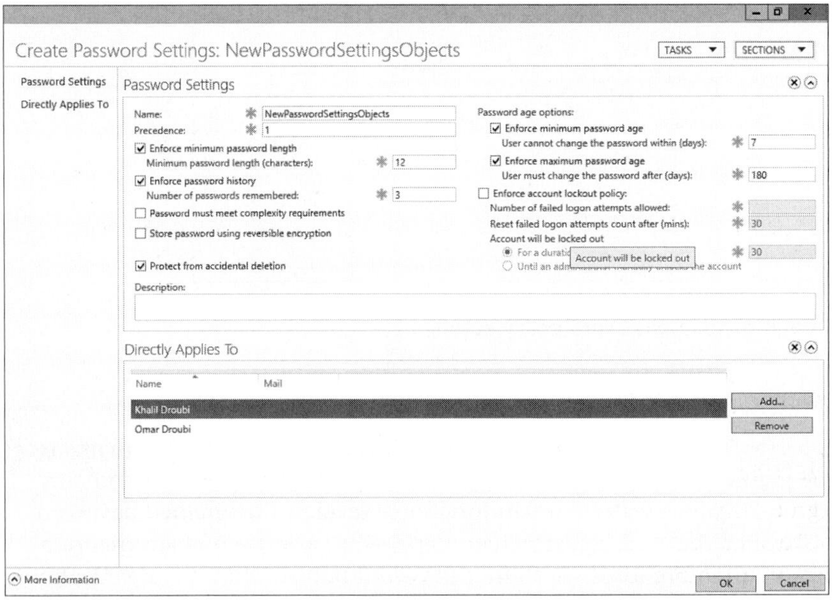

FIGURE 27.21 Review the PSO settings.

10. Click Ok to save the new Password Settings Object.

    If a user account needs to be checked to see if a fine grain Password Setings object is applied to it, simply right-click on a user account from within Active Directory Administrative Center and select View Resultant Password Settings as shown in Figure 27.22.

11. Log on to a workstation or server with a user account added to the policy, change the password to verify that the Fine-Grained PSO has been applied properly.

Even though fine-grained password policies should only be used if necessary and sparingly, after administrators know about it, many accounts will suddenly need to be added to a PSO that is less restrictive than the domain password policy. To audit the users to whom PSOs apply, the PSOs in the Password Settings Container should be reviewed regularly.

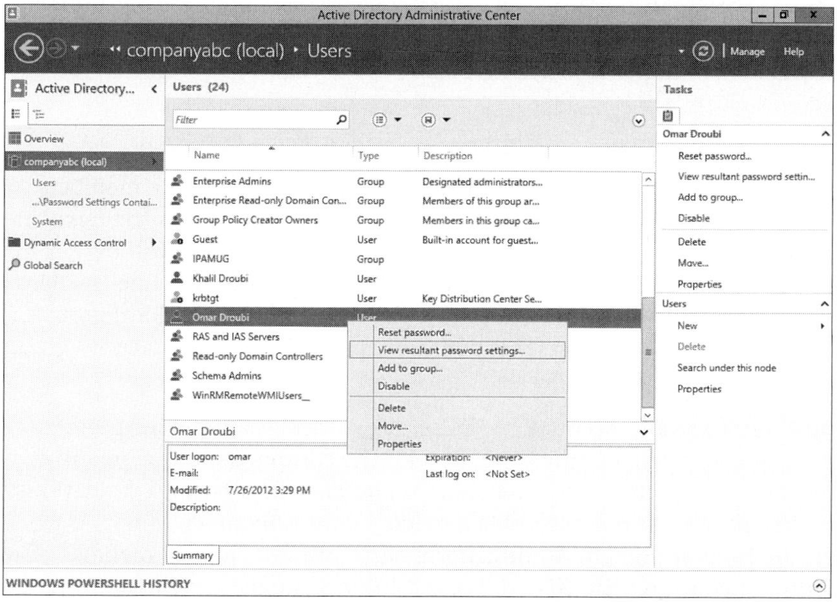

FIGURE 27.22 Checking a user account for password settings configuration

Configuring Restricted Groups to manage Computer Local Groups

A great feature of group policies that commonly goes unused is restricted groups. Restricted groups Group Policy settings enable an administrator to manage the membership of local groups on domain member servers and workstations.

NOTE

Unless the impact is completely understood and desired, never link a group policy with restricted group settings to a domain or a site object because the settings will be inherited by all computers in the domain or site, including domain controllers and Active Directory security groups. Managing Active Directory security groups using Group Policy restricted groups is not supported by Microsoft.

Restricted groups can be used to populate and control the members of a designated local group, or they can be used to add members to a specific group. Using restricted groups requires a deep understanding of how the settings work. Testing should always be performed before linking a restricted group GPO to an domain organizational unit in a production environment. There are a few scenarios that Group Policy administrators and organizations commonly utilize restricted groups domain policies for, including the following:

- Define and restrict the membership of a local security group by adding users or other groups using the members setting of restricted groups.
- Add Universal and Global Domain groups to local computer or local domain groups using the member of setting of restricted groups.

Controlling Group Membership Using Restricted Groups

Restricted groups can be used to control the membership of a group using the member setting, which is detailed next. When this setting is defined for a group, only the members added to this list will be a member of the group, and any existing members will be removed when the policy is applied or refreshed. The only exception to this rule is when the local Administrator user account is a member of a server Administrators local group or the Administrators domain security group. This does not apply to any other security group that the Administrator account is a member of.

The restricted groups Administrator account exception was added as a fix with specific service pack revisions in a legacy operating systems, so if the computers in the organization are not up-to-date on supported operating systems and current service pack revisions, the Administrator account may be removed by a restricted groups member policy. As a best practice, when the local or domain Administrator account needs to be a member of a restricted group, do not count on the GPO to leave it in; instead, define it within the member policy setting. As an example of how to control membership of a local group on a member server or workstation using restricted groups, follow these steps:

1. Log on to a designated Windows Server 2012 administrative server and open the GPMC.
2. In the GPMC expand the forest and domains node to reveal the desired domain and the Group Policy Objects container within.
3. Select the Group Policy Objects container and create a new GPO named NetCfgOpsRestrictedGroupGPO and open it for editing.
4. Open the NetCfgOpsRestrictedGroupGPO policy for editing and in the Group Policy Management Editor, navigate to the Computer Configuration\Policies\Windows Settings\Security Settings node, and select Restricted Groups beneath it.
5. In the tree pane, right-click the Restricted Groups node and select Add Group.
6. When the Add Group window opens, do not browse; just type in **Network Configuration Operators** and click OK.
7. When the Network Configuration Operators window opens, click the Add button in the Members of This Group section.
8. When the Add Member window opens, type in the name of a user or group and click OK for local user accounts, or click the Browse button to locate and select users

or groups from the domain, click OK, and click OK again. Domain accounts should be entered as domain\username and multiple entries should be separated by semicolons or they can be added one by one.

9. After all the entries are added, click OK to finalize the settings, as shown in Figure 27.23.

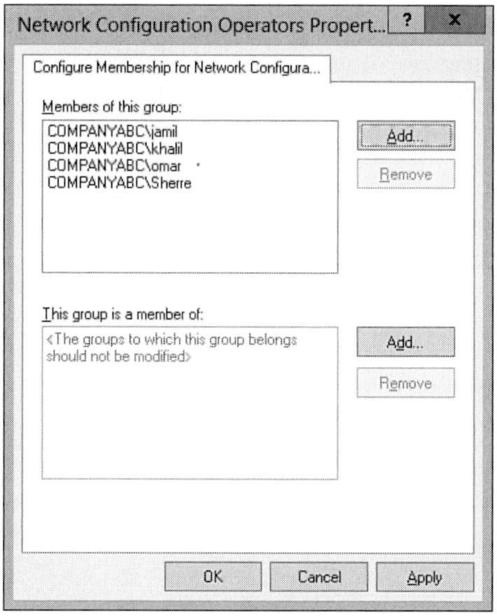

FIGURE 27.23 Configuring members using restricted groups.

10. Back in the Group Policy Management Editor window, close the GPO.

11. In the GPMC, link the new NetCfgOpsRestrictedGroupGPOpolicy to an OU with a computer account that can be used to test this policy. Network Configuration Operators groups exist in Windows XP, Windows Server 2003 and later client and server operating systems.

12. Log on to a system to which the policy applies with an account with administrator group membership and verify the membership of the group. If the policy has not yet been applied, run the **gpdate.exe /force** command in a command prompt window.

13. Add additional users to the group and reapply the GPO by running the **gpupdate.exe /force** command in a command prompt window. Verify that the new users have been removed by the domain group policy.

14. Log off of the workstation and log back on to the Windows Server 2012 system. Link the GPO to the appropriate organizational unit to complete this task.

Using this function of restricted groups is not recommended for the Administrators local group on domain workstations unless the organization is certain that no users have been added to allow for legacy application or other additional rights. For this example, the Network Configuration Operators group membership has been defined by the policy. This group has the rights to completely manage and configure network settings of the computer.

Augmenting Group Membership Using Restricted Groups

When strictly controlling the membership of a group is not the desired change, the restricted group's Member Of function can be used. This is a less-invasive method of updating or modifying group membership using domain policies. For example, if an organization wants to add the COMPANYABC\IT domain security group to the local Administrators group of all computers in the Local Workstations organizational unit, the following process can be followed:

1. Create an OU named Local Workstations and place all the necessary computer accounts into the OU.
2. Create a new domain group policy called LocalWorkstationsRestrictedGroupGPO and open it for editing.
3. In a GPMC windows, open the Computer Configuration\Policies\Windows Settings\Security Settings\Restricted Groups node. Right-click the node and select Add Group.
4. Type in or browse to locate the desired domain group; for this example, we will use the COMPANYABC\IT group. Click OK when the group is designated.
5. In the properties of the COMPANYABC\IT restricted group, click the Add button in the This Group Is a Member Of section. In the Add window, do not browse; simply type in **Administrators** and click OK. The properties of the group should appear, as shown in Figure 27.24.
6. Click OK again to close the COMPANYABC\IT Restricted Group Properties window.
7. Back in the Group Policy Management Editor window, close the GPO.
8. In the Group Policy Management Console, link the new LocalWorkstationsRestrictedGroupGPO policy to an OU with a computer account that can be used to test this policy.
9. Log on to a system that the policy applies to using an account with Administrators group membership, and verify the membership of the local Administrators group includes the designated domain group as configured in the GPO.
10. Log off of the workstation and log back on to the Windows Server 2012 system. Link the GPO to the appropriate organizational unit.

FIGURE 27.24 Adding members to the local Administrators group using the restricted group Member Of function.

Synchronous Foreground Refresh

Group Policy processing occurs at computer startup, shutdown, and periodically at during the background refresh interval for computers. Processing for users occurs at user logon and logoff and periodically during the background refresh interval. Certain functions of Group Policy, including software installation, user folder redirection, computer startup and shutdown scripts, and user logon and logoff scripts require the network to be available during processing. Windows XP and greater client operating systems do not wait for the network during computer startup and user logon by default and by design. This feature provides faster computer reboots and faster user logon processes but can also cause some Group Policy processing issues. When software installations, folder redirection, computer startup, and/or user logon scripts are defined within domain group policies, it might be required to also enable the Always Wait for the network at Computer Startup and Logon setting within group policies. The setting is stored in the Computer Configuration node and can be configured as follows:

1. Log on to a designated Windows Server 2012 administrative server and open the GPMC.
2. In the GPMC, expand the forest and domains node to reveal the desired domain and the Group Policy Objects container within.
3. Select the Group Policy Objects container and create a new GPO named WaitForNetworkGPO and open it for editing.

4. When the Group Policy Management Editor opens, navigate to Computer Configuration\Policies\Administrative Templates\System node.
5. Expand the System node and select Logon in the tree pane.
6. In the Settings pane, double-click the Always Wait for the Network at Computer Startup and Logon setting.
7. On the Setting tab, select the Enabled option button, and click OK.
8. Close the Group Policy Management Editor, and return to the GPMC.
9. In the GPMC, if necessary, adjust the links to the updated GPO and close the GPMC when finished.

There is also a corresponding setting in the User Configuration section of GPOs, but if this setting is configured in the Computer Configuration section, it will run for all users who log on to the system.

GPO Modeling and GPO Results in the GPMC

When an organization decides to perform administrative and management tasks using group policies, it is essential that the system administrators understand how to check to see whether Group Policy processing is working correctly. In the case when Active Directory hierarchies are being reconstructed or if new policies are being deployed, performing a simulated application of group policies to review the results can help avoid unexpected issues. To perform Group Policy simulations, an administrator can use Group Policy modeling, available in the GPMC. Group Policy modeling is the equivalent of Resultant Set of Policies (Planning), which is the name of the administrative right that must be delegated in Active Directory to run this tool. To perform Group Policy modeling, complete the following steps:

1. Log on to a designated Windows Server 2012 administrative server and open the GPMC.
2. In the tree pane, select the Group Policy Modeling node, right-click the node, and select Group Policy Modeling Wizard.
3. On the Welcome page, click Next to continue.
4. On the Domain Controller Selection page, specify a domain controller or accept the default of using any domain controller, and click Next.
5. On the User and Computer Selection page, the Group Policy Modeling Wizard can be used to run a simulation based on a specific user and computer in their current locations, or containers can be specified for either the user or computer to simulate GPO processing of a specific user, logging on to a Computer in a specific container. For this example, we will use root OUs named Corporate Users for users and for computers we will use the Local Workstations OU, as shown in Figure 27.25. Click Next to continue.

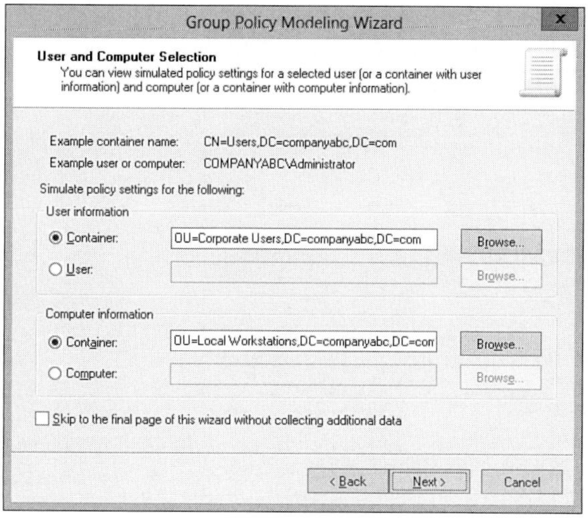

FIGURE 27.25 Selecting the Desired user and computer OUs for GPO modeling.

6. On the Advanced Simulations page, loopback processing, slow network connections, and site-specific testing can be specified. Accept the defaults and click Next to continue.

7. On the User Security Groups page, specific security groups can be specified to run policy modeling against. Accept the defaults and click Next to continue.

8. On the Computer Security Groups page, specific security groups can be specified to run policy modeling against. Accept the defaults and click Next to continue.

9. On the WMI Filters for Users page, select the All Linked Filters option button, and click Next to continue.

10. On the WMI Filters for Computers page, select the All Linked Filters option button, and click Next to continue.

11. On the Summary of Selections page, review the choices and if everything looks correct, click Next to run the GPO modeling tool.

12. When the process completes, click Finish to return to the GPMC and review the modeling results.

13. In the Settings pane, the summary of the computer and user policy processing will be available for view. Review the information about this page, and then click the Details tab to review the final GPO settings that would be applied, as shown in Figure 27.26.

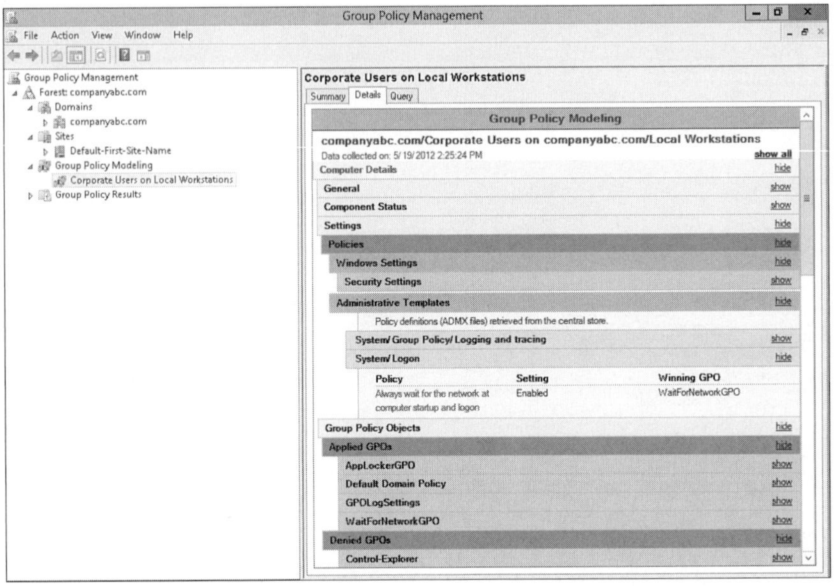

FIGURE 27.26 Reviewing the GPO modeling resultant settings.

In situations when Group Policy is not delivering the desired results, GPO results can be run to read and display the Group Policy processing history. GPO results are run against a specific computer, but can also be used to collect user policy processing. For the following example, we will use an existing system named WS1 and an existing user named Jamil. To run GPO results to review the GPO processing history, follow these steps:

1. Log on to a designated Windows Server 2012 administrative server and open the GPMC

2. In the tree pane, select the Group Policy Results node, right-click the node, and select Group Policy Results Wizard.

3. On the Welcome page, click Next to continue.

4. On the Computer Selection page, choose to run the policy against Another Computer and locate a Windows 8 system that a user has already logged on to such as WS1 for our example. Also be sure to uncheck the Do Not Display Policy Settings for the Selected Computer in the Results check box, and click Next. For this example, we only want to display user processing results.

5. On the User Selection page, select the Display Policy Settings For option button, and then select the Select a Specific User option button. Select a user from the list, and click Next to continue. Only users who have previously logged on to the selected computer will be listed and they will only be listed if the user running the tool is a domain admin or has been granted the right to run Resultant Set of Policies (Logging) for the particular users.

6. On the Summary of Selections page, review the choices and click Next to start the GPO Results collection process.
7. When the process completes, click Finish to return to the GPMC.
8. When the process completes, the results will be displayed in the Settings pane on the Summary, Settings, and Policy Events tabs. Review the results and close the GPMC when finished.

Managing Group Policy from Administrative or Remote Workstations

It is common for Windows system administrators to manage group policies from their own administrative workstations. To manage a Windows Server 2012 environment properly, domain Group Policy administration should only be performed using a Windows Server 2012 system with the Group Policy Management tools and the Print Services tools installed or a Windows 8 system with the Group Policy and Print Services tools installed. The main reason for this is that only the Windows Server 2012 and Windows 8 GPMC exposes the Starter GPOs node and functions and the Print Services tools provide more functional management of network shared printers and GPO deployed printers. Of course, Windows Server 2008 GPMC can also be used, but the Vista GPMC does not provide the Starter GPO node if needed.

Group Policy management, aside from creating and managing policies, enables administrators to simulate policy processing for users and computers in specific containers in Active Directory using the Group Policy Modeling node in the GPMC. Furthermore, the previous application of Group Policy for users and computers can be collected and reviewed in the Group Policy Management Console using the Group Policy Results node in the GPMC. For an administrator, even a member of the Domain Admins group, to perform remote Group Policy modeling using the GPMC from a machine other than a domain controller, the following requirements must be met:

- The administrator must be a member of the domain Distributed COM Users security group.
- The administrator must be delegated the Generate Resultant Set of Policy. This right must be applied to the domain, OU, container, or site that contains all the computers and users the administrator will run simulated GPO processing against.
- The administrator must have the right to read all the necessary group policies, and this should be allowed by default.

To perform remote Group Policy results tasks using the GPMC from a machine other than a domain controller, the following requirements must be met:

- The administrator must be a member of the computer's local Distributed COM Users security group for Windows XP, Windows Server 2003, and later client and server operating systems.

- The administrator must be a member of the computer's local Administrators security group for the remote system and the remote system must be live on the network.
- The Windows Firewall must be configured to allow the inbound Remote Administration exception, and the remote workstation must be on a network that is defined within this exception.
- The administrator must be delegated the Generate Resultant Set of Policy (Logging) right in Active Directory. This right must be applied to the domain, OU, container, or site that contains all the computers and users the administrator will run simulated GPO processing against.
- The administrator must have the right to read all the necessary group policies, and this should be allowed by default.

Summary

Windows Server 2012 Group Policy provides administrators with many options to standardize configuration and management of users and computer settings. Management policies can be fine-tuned based on the function, location, and the security requirements of the organization. This chapter offers many suggestions and examples of how Group Policy can be leveraged in any organization. Although group policies are very functional and can be a very attractive option for user and computer management, the planning and testing of group policies is essential in delivering the desired configuration and security settings to users and computers in an Active Directory or Windows workgroup environment.

Best Practices

The following are best practices from this chapter:

- The only changes that should be made to the default domain policy should be modifying the password and account policy settings and nothing else.
- When the local or domain Administrator user account is a member of a group that will be managed with domain group policy restricted groups, do not count on the GPO to leave it in; instead, define it within the member policy setting of a restricted group.
- When naming group policies, try to use naming conventions that easily identify the function of the policies for the organization.
- When using folder redirection for user profile folders, allow the system to create the folders and ensure that the share and root folder permissions are set up appropriately to allow this.
- Configure policies with application control policies to be processed by machines only running Windows 7 Enterprise and Ultimate, Windows 8 Professional client operating systems, and Window Server 2008 R2 or later server operating systems.

- When defining network paths to scripts, software or shared folders, always use fully qualified domain names in the path, such as \\server.companyabc.com\share or DFS links such as \\companyabc.com\share.
- Limit the computer configuration setting GPOs linked to the domain to avoid making undesired changes to domain controllers, or specifically deny the application of those policies to the Enterprise Domain Controllers security group.
- Have systems administrators use standard user accounts to do their day-to-day tasks and use User Account Control to allow for prompting of elevation when administrator privileges are required.

CHAPTER 28

File System Management and Fault Tolerance

IN THIS CHAPTER

- Windows Server 2012 File System Overview
- File System Access Services and Technologies
- Managing Windows Server 2012 Disks
- Adding the File and Storage Services Role
- Managing Data Access Using Windows Server 2012 Shares
- File Server Resource Manager
- The Distributed File System
- Planning a DFS Deployment
- Installing and Configuring DFS
- Using the Volume Shadow Copy Service
- Configure Data Deduplication
- Configuring Storage Spaces
- Dynamic Access Control

Computer networks were developed for the sharing of data and collaboration. Some of the first ways to share data, of course, is by simply accessing files and folders stored on networked systems or central file servers, such as Windows Server 2012 or other types of file servers.

As data storage and computer service needs have evolved in the past 25 or so years, many different methods have become available to present, access, secure, and manage data. For example, data can be accessed through a web browser through SharePoint document libraries, through network shares, through external media such as USB drives, floppy disks, CDs, and DVDs, tape devices and by accessing data stored on any of the other types of media for the many different operating systems, network storage devices and file systems available.

This chapter covers the file system features and services included with Windows Server 2012. The goal of this chapter is to introduce administrators to Windows Server 2012 file services and give them the tools they require to deploy reliable enterprise file services for their organizations using Windows Server 2012.

Windows Server 2012 File System Overview

Windows Server 2012 provides many services that can be leveraged to deploy a highly reliable, manageable, and fault-tolerant file system infrastructure. This section of the chapter provides an overview of these services.

Windows Disk Properties

Before file services can be leveraged in Windows Server 2012, disks must be added and configured in the Windows server operating system. When a new disk is added to a Windows Server 2012 system, it must be configured by choosing what type of partition style, type of disk, type of volume, and volume format type will be used. To introduce some of the file system services available in Windows Server 2012, you must understand each of these disk properties.

Windows Server 2012 allows administrators to format Windows disk volumes by choosing either the file allocation table (FAT) format, FAT32 format or NT File System (NTFS) format. FAT format is legacy and provides no security while the NTFS format has been available since Windows NT 3.51 and enables administrators to secure files and folders as well as the ability to leverage many of the services provided with Windows Server 2012.

Master Boot Record Partition Style

Master Boot Record (MBR) disks utilize the traditional disk configuration. The configuration of the disk, including partition configuration and disk layout, is stored on the first sector of the disk in the MBR. Traditionally, if the MBR became corrupted or moved to a different part of the disk, the data became inaccessible. MBR disks have a limitation of three primary partitions and a single extended partition that can contain several logical drives. Choosing to create an MBR disk should provide administrators with a more compatible disk that can easily be mounted or managed between different operating system platforms and third-party disk management tools.

GUID Partition Table Partition Style

GUID Partition Table (GPT) disks were first introduced in Windows with Windows Server 2003 Service Pack 1. GPT disks are recommended for disks that exceed 2TB in size. GPT disks can support an unlimited number of primary partitions and this can be very useful when administrators are leveraging large external disk arrays and need to segment data for security, hosting, or distributed management and access. GPT disks are only recognized by Windows Server 2003 SP1 and later Windows operating systems. Attempting to manage a GPT disk using a previous operating system or third-party MBR disk management tool will be blocked and virtually inaccessible.

Basic Disk

A Windows disk is defined as a basic or a dynamic disk regardless of whether the disk is an MBR or a GPT disk. A basic disk supports only simple volumes or volumes that exist on a single disk and partition within Windows. Basic disks contain no fault tolerance managed by the Windows operating system, but can be fault tolerant if the disk presented to Windows is managed by an external disk controller and is configured in a fault-tolerant array of disks.

Basic disks are easier to move across different operating systems and usually are more compatible with Windows and third-party disk and file system services and management tools. Basic disks also support booting to different operating systems stored in separate partitions. Furthermore, and most importantly, if the disk presented to Windows is from a storage-area network (SAN) that include multiple paths to the disk, using a basic disk will provide the most reliable operation as a different path to the disk may not be recognized if the disk is defined within windows as a dynamic disk.

Dynamic Disk

Dynamic disks extend Windows disk functionality when managing multiple disks using Windows Server 2012 is required. Windows administrators can configure dynamic disks to host volumes that span multiple partitions and disks within a single system. This allows administrators to build fault-tolerant and better performing volumes when RAID controllers are not available or when a number of smaller disks need to be grouped together to form a larger disk.

In some server deployments, dynamic disks are required as the disk controllers do not support the necessary performance, fault-tolerance, or volume size requirements to meet the recommended system specifications. In these cases, dynamic disks can be used to create larger volumes, fault-tolerant volumes, or volumes that can read and write data across multiple physical disks to achieve higher performance and higher reliability. Dynamic disks are managed by the operating system using the Virtual Disk Service (VDS).

Simple Volume Type

A simple volume is a single partition created on a single basic or dynamic disk. On a basic disk, simple volumes can be extended to include free, unallocated space that exists in a sequential section of the disk. To extend a simple volume to a noncontiguous, unallocated space on the same disk or a different disk, the disk will need to be upgraded to a dynamic disk.

Spanned Volume Type

A spanned volume is treated as a single drive, but the volume spans two or more disks or different noncontiguous areas of the same disk. Spanned volumes provide no disk fault tolerance, but can be used to meet disk storage needs that exceed the capacity of a single disk or volume. Spanned volumes are slowest when it comes to reading and writing data and are recommended only when the space of more than a single disk is necessary or an existing simple volume needs to be extended to add disk space and there is no available, unallocated space located next to the volume. For instance, if an application, file share, or service is dependent on the drive letter, does not support the moving of data or system files to another drive, and the current drive is nearly full, a simple volume can be upgraded to a spanned volume and extended with unallocated space on the same or another disk to add additional disk space. A simple volume that has been extended with unallocated space on the same disk is still considered a simple volume. If the simple volume is extended to a different disk, it is automatically converted to a spanned volume. The allocated space on each of the disks can be different sizes and there is no space lost when creating a spanned volume. One thing to keep in mind though is that a spanned volume can never be reverted to a simple volume.

Striped Volume Type

A striped volume or RAID-0 compatible volume requires two or more Windows dynamic disks and provides the fastest of all disk configurations. Striped volumes read and write data from each of the disks simultaneously, which improves disk access time. Striped volumes utilize all the space allocated for data storage but provide no disk fault tolerance. If one of the disks should fail, the entire data set would become inaccessible. Stripe sets require the exact amount of disk space on each of the allocated disks. For example, to create a 15GB stripe set array with three disks, 5GB of unallocated space would be required on each disk.

Mirrored Volume Type

Mirrored or RAID-1 compatible volumes require two separate disks to create. Furthermore, the size of the volume must be equal and available in one contiguous, unallocated section of each of the disks. Mirrored volumes duplicate data across each disk and can withstand the failure of a single disk. Because the mirrored volume is an exact replica of the first disk, the total space capacity is the capacity of one disk.

RAID-10 Volume Type

RAID-10 volumes are now considered the most desirable RAID configurations. A RAID-10 volume consists of two RAID-1 volumes that are striped together to extend the total usable volume. A typical configuration includes 4 disk and the total usable space is the equivalent of two disks. The set provides high performance for read and write operations and also provides high redundancy as the volume can suffer the failure of one of the RAID-1 disk from each set.

RAID-5 Volume Type

Software-based RAID-5 volumes require three or more Windows dynamic disks and can provide faster read disk access than a single disk because all disks in the set can be read at the same time. Write performance is slower than a striped set with the same number of disks because of the parity stripe that must be generated and written. The space allocated to the RAID-5 volume on each disk in the volume must be equal and contiguous unallocated space. For example, to create a RAID-5 volume that requires 100GB on each disk, a disk with two separate areas of 50GB of unallocated space cannot be used to participate in the volume.

RAID-5 sets can withstand the failure of a single disk in the volume. During a disk failure, the remaining disks in the volume will continue to provide access to data but at a slower or degraded rate. This capability is achieved by reserving a small portion of each disk's allocated space to store data parity information that can be used to rebuild a failed disk and to continue to provide data access. This is called a parity stripe. RAID-5 parity information requires the total space of a single disk in the array. For example, if five 10GB dynamic disks are used to create a single RAID-5 volume, 40GB would be available for data storage. The reserved 10GB would be spread evenly across all five disks. The formula for usable capacity of a RAID-5 array is $(N - 1) * S$, where N is the total number of drives in the array and S is the capacity of the smallest drive in the array.

Partition or Volume

When referring to Windows disks, administrators might consider partitions and volumes interchangeable. In fact, even though the graphical user interface makes no clear distinction and might refer to everything as a volume, volumes only exist on dynamic disks and partitions only exist on basic disks. This is especially important when managing disks using the diskpart.exe command-line utility, which defines a clear delineation between partitions and volumes.

Mount Point

When a new volume is created in Windows, it can be assigned a drive letter or mounted into an existing empty folder on an existing volume. When a volume is mounted into a folder, this is known as a mount point or junction point. Mount points can be very useful in situations where administrators want to simplify disk access for end users, but must also make use of a number of small disks versus a single large disk. For example, on a database server with three disks, an administrator might assign disk1 the D drive, disk2 would be mounted in d:\data, and disk3 would be mounted in d:\logfiles. Any administrator would only need to connect to the D drive to access the databases or log files. One thing that administrators must test before using mount points is to see that all clients, applications, and backup agents support the use of mount or junction points and can successfully access and back up data stored within them. With many backup applications, enabling a backup job to back up data stored on a mounted volume is not the default and can cause major problems if the right backup configuration is not selected before a failure occurs.

FAT, FAT32, and exFAT Formatted Volumes Features

FAT-formatted volumes are legacy-type volumes used by older operating systems and floppy disk drives. FAT volumes are limited to 2GB in size. FAT32 is an enhanced version of FAT that can accommodate partitions up to 2TB and is more resilient to disk corruption. Data stored on FAT or FAT32 partitions are not secure and does not provide many features. exFAT format is the same as FAT32 but it can accommodate file sizes larger than 4GB, which is a FAT32 limitation. Also, exFAT format was designed with flash drives in mind.

NTFS Formatted Volume Features

NTFS enables many features that can be leveraged to provide a highly reliable, scalable, secure, and manageable file system. Base features of NTFS formatted partitions include support for large volumes, configuring permissions or restricting access to sets of data, compressing or encrypting data, configuring per-user storage quotas on entire partitions or specific folders, and file classification tagging, which will be discussed later in this chapter.

Several Windows services require NTFS volumes; as a best practice, we recommend that all partitions created on Windows Server 2012 systems are formatted using NT File System (NTFS).

reFS Formatted Volume Features

New with Windows Server 2012 is reFS, or the Resilient File System. The resilient file system may in fact be the next-generation file system to replace NTFS and has been developed to work in conjunction with storage spaces. The reFS will retain many of the same features as NTFS, but will also add in the ability to locate and repair data corruption on volume or storage pools, while keeping the unaffected data storage available to clients. The reFS file system was developed in conjunction with the Storage Spaces service and is the back-end infrastructure that provides the fault tolerance and reliability included with the new service.

File System Quotas

File system quotas allow administrators to configure storage thresholds on particular sets of data stored on server NTFS volumes. This can be handy in preventing users from inadvertently filling up a server drive or taking up more space than is designated for them. Also, quotas can be used in hosting scenarios where a single storage system is shared between departments or organizations and storage space is allocated based on subscription or company standards.

The Windows Server 2012 File System Quota service provides more functionality than included in versions older than Windows Server 2008. Introduced in Windows 2000 Server as an included service, quotas could be enabled and managed at the volume level only. This did not provide granular control; furthermore, because it was at the volume level, to deploy a functional quota-managed file system, administrators were required to create several volumes with different quota settings. Windows Server 2003 also included the volume-managed quota system and some limitations or issues with this system included the fact that data size was not calculated in real time. This resulted in users exceeding their quota threshold after a large copy was completed.

Windows Server 2008 through Windows Server 2012 includes the volume-level quota management feature but also can be configured to enable/enforce quotas at the folder level on any particular NTFS volume using the File Server Resource Manager service. Included with this service is the ability to screen out certain file types as well as real-time calculation of file copies to stop operations that would exceed quotas thresholds. Reporting and notifications regarding quotas can also be configured to inform end users and administrators during scheduled intervals or when a quota threshold is nearing or, when the threshold is actually reached.

Data Compression

NTFS volumes allow administrators to enable data compression on an entire volume and enable all users to compress data at the folder and file level. Data compression reduces the required storage space for data. Data compression, however, does have some limitations, as follows:

- Additional load is placed on the system during read, write, and compression and decompression operations.
- Compressed data cannot be encrypted.

Data Encryption

NTFS volumes support the ability for users and administrators to encrypt the entire volume, a folder, or a single file. This provides a higher level of security for the data. If the disk, workstation, or server the encrypted data is stored on is lost or stolen, the encrypted data cannot be accessed. Enabling, supporting, and using data encryption on Windows volumes and Active Directory domains needs to be considered carefully. If proper planning and testing is not performed, access to encrypted data may be lost forever.

File Screening

File screening enables administrators to define the types of files that can be saved within a Windows volume and folder. File screening is a feature of the File Server Resource Manager service and file screening can be managed with templates. When a file screen is created for a folder or volume, all file write or save operations are intercepted, screened and only files that comply with the screen settings are allowed to be saved to that particular volume or folder. File screening can also be passive and just report on the existing activity data on a volume. File screening is covered later in this chapter in the "File Server Resource Manager (FSRM)" section.

File Classification Infrastructure

Windows Server 2012 includes a feature called the File Classification Infrastructure (FCI) first introduced with Windows Server 2008 R2. FCI can be managed by using the File Server Resource Manager console and allows file server administrators to identify and classify files by applying specific FCI property values onto these files based on their folder location or based on the content stored within the file itself. When a file is classified by FCI, if the file is a Microsoft Office file as an example, the FCI information will be stored within the file itself and will follow the file where ever it is copied or moved to. If the file is a different type of file, the FCI information will stored within the NTFS volume itself, but the FCI information will follow the file to any location it is copied or moved to, provided that the destination is an NTFS volume hosted on a Windows Server 2012 system. More information about FCI will be detailed later in this chapter.

Virtual Hard Disks

Virtual hard disks (VHDs) are used by virtual machines to emulate Windows disks. VHDs can be created on an existing Windows Server 2012 system using the Hyper-V Management console, or they can be created directly using the Disk Management console. VHD are primarily created on the Windows host system as a file with a .vhd extension on an existing windows volume. VHD files can easily be moved across servers and between virtual machines, and also can be expanded quite easily, granted that the VHD is not in use and there is ample free space on the host volume. VHD files can be attached directly to a Windows Server 2012 host using the Disk Management console, unlike in previous releases which required scripts to mount the file. This added functionality is a needed improvement to the integrated VSS Hyper-V backup functionality, included with Windows Server Backup and available to third-party backup software vendors. Creating and attaching a VHD file to a Windows Server 2012 host is detailed later in this chapter, but for more information about VHD files and their management, see Chapter 37, "Deploying and Using Windows Virtualization."

Windows Server 2012 VHDX Virtual Hard Disks

With the release of Windows Server 2012 is a new virtual disk format VHDX. The older VHD file has a 2TB limit, but the new VHDX file has a 64TB limit and is better protected again data corruption due to the way changes are logged within the file itself.

Fixed Size Disk

VHD disks can be created to be fixed size or dynamically expanding. A fixed-sized VHD that is 10GB in size will equate to a 10GB file on the Windows host server volume. With the new VHDX format, the actual fixed disk size may even be a bit smaller, but not by much. Fixed-size virtual disks should be used as a preference to deliver better performance for the virtual guest and host/parent system when used in production deployments of servers. The key benefit of a fixed disk related to performance is that the actual file itself will not become fragmented over time if the disk shares space on the same host/parent volume.

Dynamically Expanding

Dynamically expanding virtual disks are configured with a maximum value, but only take up the necessary space on the host/parent system. For example, if a 25GB dynamically expanding virtual disk is created on a host and added to a Hyper-V virtual guest system, the guest system will see a 25GB disk available. The host system file size for that disk will only be as large and the used space within the guest OS disk. These disks are best used for test machines and machines that do not require the highest performance.

Differencing Disk

With Hyper-V guest systems, disks can be created with a parent/child relationship. The parent disk is created with the base operating configuration and then it can have a single or multiple differencing or child disks attached it to. The differencing disk is used to isolate changes to the guest system, and the changes are kept in this disk while the parent disk remains unchanged. Differencing disks are also used/created when creating snapshots for Hyper-V guest systems.

Volume Shadow Copy Service

Windows Server 2003 introduced a file system service called the Volume Shadow Copy Service (VSS). The VSS allows administrators and third-party independent software vendors to take snapshots of the file system to allow for faster backups and, in some cases, point-in-time recovery without the need to access backup media. VSS copies of a volume can also be mounted and accessed just like another Windows volume if that should become necessary.

Shadow Copies of Shared Folders

Volume shadow copies of shared folders can be enabled on Windows volumes to allow administrators and end users to recover data deleted from a network share without having to restore from backup. The shadow copy runs on a scheduled basis and takes a snapshot copy of the data currently stored in the volume. In earlier versions of Windows prior to Windows Server 2003, if a user mistakenly deleted data in a network shared folder, it was immediately deleted from the server and the data had to be restored from backup. A Windows server running Windows Server 2003 or a later Windows server operating system with an NTFS volume that has shadow copies enabled, allows a user with the correct permissions to restore deleted or overwritten data from a previously stored shadow copy backup. It is important to note that shadow copies are stored on local volumes and if the volume hosting the shadow copy becomes inaccessible or corrupted, so does the shadow copy. Shadow copies are not a replacement for backups and should not be considered a disaster recovery tool.

Volume Shadow Copy Service Backup

VSS in Windows Server 2012 also provides the ability for Windows Backup and third-party software vendors to utilize this technology to improve backup performance and integrity. A VSS-compatible backup program can call on the VSS to create a shadow copy of a particular volume, database or application, and then the backup can be created using that shadow copy. A benefit of utilizing VSS-aware backups is that the reliability and performance of the backup is increased as the backup window will be shorter and the load on the system disk will be reduced during the backup. More information about volume shadow copy backups is detailed in Chapter 30, "Backing Up the Windows Server 2012 Environment."

BranchCache for Network Files

BranchCache is a feature of Windows Server and Windows workstations that enable the intelligent synchronization and data access of centrally stored data to be accessible in remote branch offices. When a file is accessed in a branch office, the workstation will search the local network for a current copy of that file before traversing the network to download from the central site. The BranchCache for Network File service is the server side portion of the BranchCache infrastructure. More information about installing BranchCache is highlighted later in this chapter. You can also find additional information in Chapter 32, "Optimizing Windows Server 2012 for Branch Office Communications."

Data Deduplication Service

The Data Deduplication service is not data duplication. In fact, it is just the opposite, because the Deduplication service removes duplicate data. In short, the Data Deduplication service optimizes file storage by breaking down files into smaller chunks, identifying duplicate chunks and retaining only a single copy of that chunk. This results in less required storage space for the same amount of data previously required on older operating systems.

Continuously Available File Shares

Continuously Available File Shares is a new Windows Server 2012 Failover Cluster feature. In earlier Windows Server failover cluster file servers, when file services were transferred between cluster nodes, client connections would be disrupted or completely disconnected. With Windows Server 2012, when clustered file servers are configured with continuous availability, client connections will not be disrupted or disconnected during group transfers between cluster nodes. This functionality is named SMB2 transparent failover. You can find more information about Continuously Available File Shares in Chapter 29, "System-level Fault Tolerance (Clustering / Network Load Balancing)."

ISCSI Target Server Service

The ISCSI Target Server Service in Windows Server 2012 provides the ability for a Windows server to host ISCSI storage and make this storage available to ISCSI initiators (clients) to mount this storage as local drives. ISCSI storage is accessed across the Ethernet and when connected, ISCSI storage can be assigned a drive letter and used just like local storage. Many applications on a server can leverage ISCSI storage, but be sure to check the system requires of any particular application before deploying it on ISCSI storage. Also, Windows backup and other backup software will treat ISCSI storage differently so before ISCSI is used be sure to verify full functionality.

Distributed File System

In an effort to create highly available file services that reduce end-user impact and simplify file server management, Windows Server 2012 includes the Distributed File System (DFS) service. DFS provides access to file data from a single namespace that can be used to represent a single server or a number of servers that store unique or replicated sets of the data. For example, when using DFS in an Active Directory domain, a DFS namespace named \\companyabc.com\UserShares could redirect users to \\FILESERVER1\UserShares or to a replicated copy of the data stored at \\FILESERVER2\UserShares.

Users and administrators both can benefit from DFS because they only need to remember a single server or domain name to locate all the necessary file shares. DFS will be detailed later in this chapter.

Distributed File System Replication

With the release of Windows 2003 R2 and continuing through Windows Server 2012, DFS is constantly improving. In previous versions, DFS Replication was performed by the File Replication Service (FRS). Starting with Windows Server 2003 R2, DFS Replication is now performed by the Distributed File System Replication service, or DFSR. DFSR uses the Remote Differential Compression (RDC) protocol to replicate data. The RDC protocol improves upon FRS with better replication stability, more granular administrative control, and additional replication and access options. DFSR and RDC are discussed in detail in the section "The Distributed File System" later in this chapter.

Storage Spaces and Storage Pools

Storage Spaces is a new Windows Server 2012 service that enables the pooling of storage on a server to deliver essentially virtual disks to the server operating system. Unlike VHD or VHDX virtual disk, which is a file on single volume, and unlike a striped or fault-tolerant volume that requires several dynamic disks, Storage Spaces leverages storage pools and allows administrators to create and present a single virtual disk that can reside on a single or several windows disks. Storage pools can be easily extended to include new disks and can be created in fault tolerance or resilient configurations. Another great feature is that a storage pool can be configured as a thin provisioned pool that will grow as necessary. While storage spaces are new to Windows Server 2012, the concepts and features are not new, and storage and server administrators will be able to quickly come up to speed and learn this new service quite easily. There is no installation necessary to leverage storage spaces and create a storage pool because it is a service installed by default, and administrators only require a minimum of one unused disk to create their first storage pool.

NOTE

With the introduction of storage pools, there may be some confusion with the terms *virtual disk* and *virtual hard disk*. Administrators should use caution and always define virtual hard disks as VHD or VHDX files, and virtual disks should be defined as part of a particular storage pool for clarity.

File System Access Services and Technologies

Windows Server 2012 provides administrators with many different options to present file data to end users. These, of course, include the traditional file sharing methods, but also include presenting file data using web services. By default, Windows Server 2012 systems running the File Services role support Windows 2000 clients and later. To support legacy Windows clients, UNIX clients, or legacy Macintosh clients, may require additional services and security modifications to the data. Several of the options available for presenting file data to end users are included in the proceeding sections.

Windows Folder Sharing

This is the traditional and most commonly used method to access server data using the server message block (SMB) protocol over TCP/IP. Windows systems, many UNIX systems, and current Mac systems can access Microsoft servers using this protocol. The path to access the data uses the Universal Naming Convention (UNC) path of \\server\sharename.

DFS Namespaces and Replication

This method utilizes Windows folder sharing under a unified namespace. The main difference between standard Windows Server folder sharing and DFS shares is that the actual server name is masked by a unified name, commonly the Active Directory domain name, but in some cases a single server name and share can be used to access data stored on several servers. Also with DFS, the underlying data can be replicated between servers. One limitation of DFS is that the client accessing the DFS namespace must be a DFS-aware client so that it can utilize the benefits of DFS and, in some cases, just to locate and access the data.

WWW Directory Publishing

Using this method, administrators can make folders and files available through a web browser for read/write operations. This can be a useful tool to make files available to remote users with only Internet access. Some common types of files typically published in websites can include employee handbooks, time sheets, vacation requests, company quarterly reports, and newsletters. In addition, web based file access can be performed using Windows SharePoint Services, Microsoft Office SharePoint Server, and Microsoft Exchange 2007 and 2010..

File Transfer Protocol Service

The File Transfer Protocol (FTP) service is one of the oldest services available to transfer files between systems. FTP is still commonly used to make large files available and to present remote users and customers alike with a simple way to send data to the organization. FTP is very efficient, and that is why it still has a place in today's computer and network infrastructure. Standard FTP, however, is not secure by default and should be used only with secure and monitored connections. FTP is compatible with most web browsers, making it very easy to include and utilize links to FTP data within websites to improve file transfer performance. Some common types of files typically made available using FTP sites include company virtual private network (VPN) clients, software packages, product manuals, and to present a repository for customers and vendors to transfer reports, large databases, and other types of data.

Server and Client for NFS

Server and Client for NFS are included in Windows Server 2012 to allow for storage interoperability with the Network File System commonly used with the UNIX and LINUX compatible operating systems. Server for NFS presents the windows storage to NFS clients for use, and Client for NFS acts as a gateway for the Windows server to access NFS data stored on UNIX type servers.

Managing Windows Server 2012 Disks

Disks in Windows Server 2012 can be managed using a few different tools included with the operating system. Most disk-related tasks can be performed using the Disk management console, the Server Manager, PowerShell, or the diskpart.exe command-line utility. Windows Server 2012 introduces several new disk management PowerShell cmdlets which was not an option in previous versions.

The Disk Management MMC Snap-In

The Disk Management console, or snap-in, can be used to initialize and configure new disks; import previously configured disks; convert basic disks to dynamic disks; create, extend, and shrink disk volumes; format disk volumes; enable shadow copies; and many more disk-related tasks. Disk Management can also be used to create and attach or mount VHD and VHDX files to the host operating system for quick volume access and data management. This snap-in is included as part of the Computer Management console, but it can also be added to a separate Microsoft Management Console window. The Disk Management console can be used to manage disks on remote machines as well as local disks.

Diskpart.exe Command-Line Utility

Diskpart.exe is a command-line utility that administrators can use to manage Windows disks. Most disk tasks that can be performed using the Disk Management console can also be performed using this command-line utility except for initializing new disks. When issues are encountered with a Windows Server 2012 that won't boot, diskpart.exe may be the only option available when booting into the recovery environment, so administrators should be well versed and comfortable with this tool.

PowerShell Disk Management Cmdlets

Windows Server 2012 and Windows 8 introduce several new cmdlets developed to manage windows disks. In addition to the usual disk functions such as initializing, formatting, and assigning drive letters to windows disks, you can create new storage pools and virtual disks and create virtual ISCSI disks from within the PowerShell.

Server Manager File and Storage Services

In Windows Server 2012, the preferred method for managing server roles and features has moved primarily to the PowerShell, but for GUI management Server Manager is the console to leverage. For file and storage management, Server Manager has integrated the management of storage pools, windows disks, virtual disks, ISCSI, and shares into one central location.

Adding New Disks and Volumes to Windows

When a disk is added to a Windows Server 2012 system, the disk must first be brought online and initialized before it can be configured for use within the operating system. Windows Server 2012 can detect most new disk additions most disks without a reboot, but this, of course, depends on the disk and controller type. For example, if a new disk is added to a system with a RAID-compatible disk controller, it will not be detected or available to Windows until the new disk is configured using the RAID controller configuration utility. When a new disk is ready to be added into the Windows Server 2012 operating system, follow these steps:

1. Log on to the Windows Server 2012 system with an account with administrator privileges.
2. Open Windows PowerShell, type in **Get-Disk**, and press Enter to show the list of detected disks. New disks will be listed with an offline operational status and a partition style of raw, as shown in Figure 28.1.
3. Now for this example, in Figure 28.1 disks 2, 3, 4, and 5 need to be initialized. In the PowerShell window, type **Initialize-Disk 2,3,4,5 –PartitionStyle GPT** and press Enter.

After the disks are initialized, they will be configured as basic disks by default and can be configured with volumes and formatted for use.

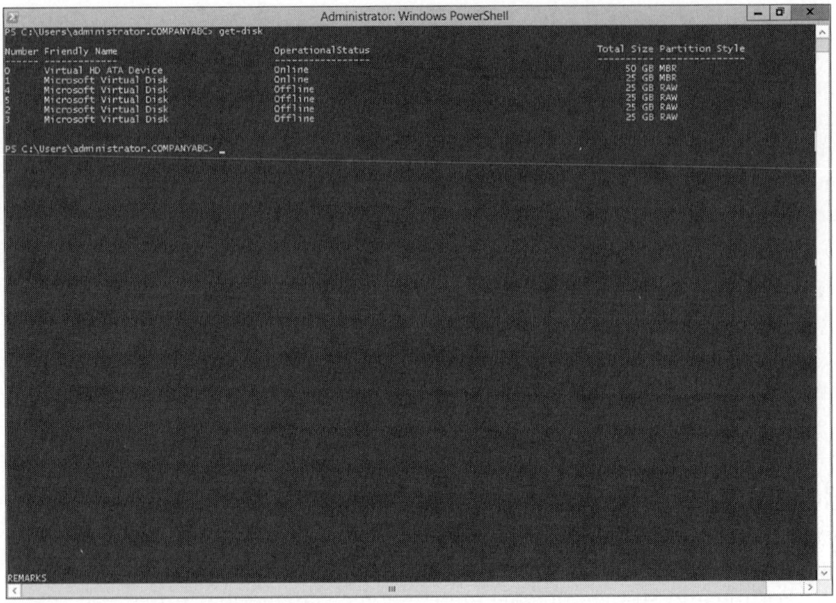

FIGURE 28.1 Displaying detected disks with **get-disk**.

If the disks will be configured with traditional advanced volume types such as striped, mirrored, or RAID-5, they must be converted to dynamic disks (which can be done automatically during volume creation if you are using the Disk Management console). If you are using diskpart.exe, however, they will need to be converted manually. To create a traditional Windows disk volume such as a simple, spanned, striped, mirrored, or RAID-5 volume, follow these steps:

1. In the Windows PowerShell Window, type in **Diskpart.exe** and press Enter.
2. Once you know the disk you will use (for this example, we will use disks 2, 3, 4, and 5, and we will create a RAID-5 volume), type **List Disk** and press Enter. Note that all of our disks are not dynamic, as indicated with no * in the Dyn column, as shown in Figure 28.2.
3. Based on the disk configuration detailed in Figure 28.2, disk 2, 3, 4, 5 need to be converted to dynamic disks. In the PowerShell window, type **select disk 2** and press Enter. Now type **convert dynamic** and press Enter. Repeat these steps for disks 3, 4, and 5.
4. Now that all the disks are initialized, online, and dynamic, we can create the RAID-5 volume. Type **Select disk 2** and press Enter. Now type **create volume RAID disk 2,3,4,5** and press Enter.
5. Now that the RAID-5 volume is created, we will format it, but the volume will need to be identified. In the command prompt window, type **List volume** and press Enter.

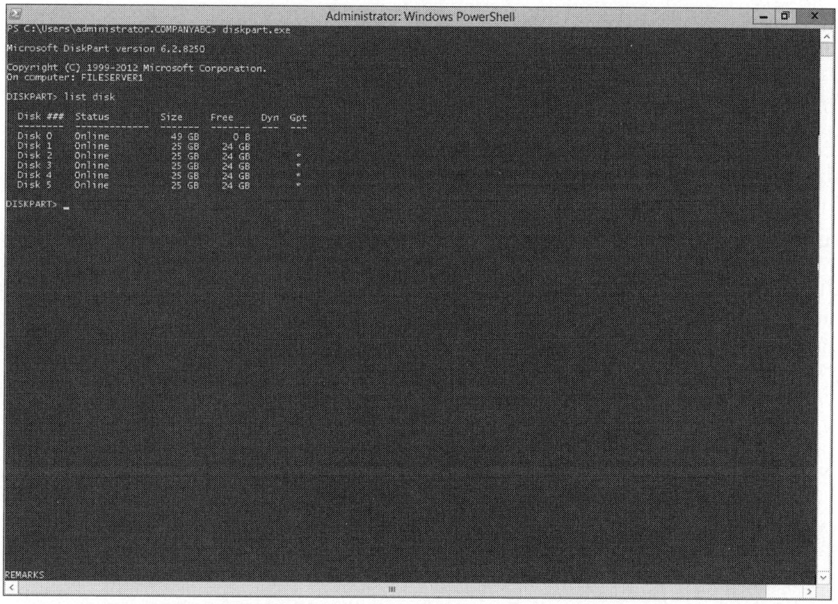

FIGURE 28.2 Listing disk status using diskpart.exe.

6. The new volume should be listed as a RAID-5 volume. In Figure 28.3, the new volume is listed as volume 3.

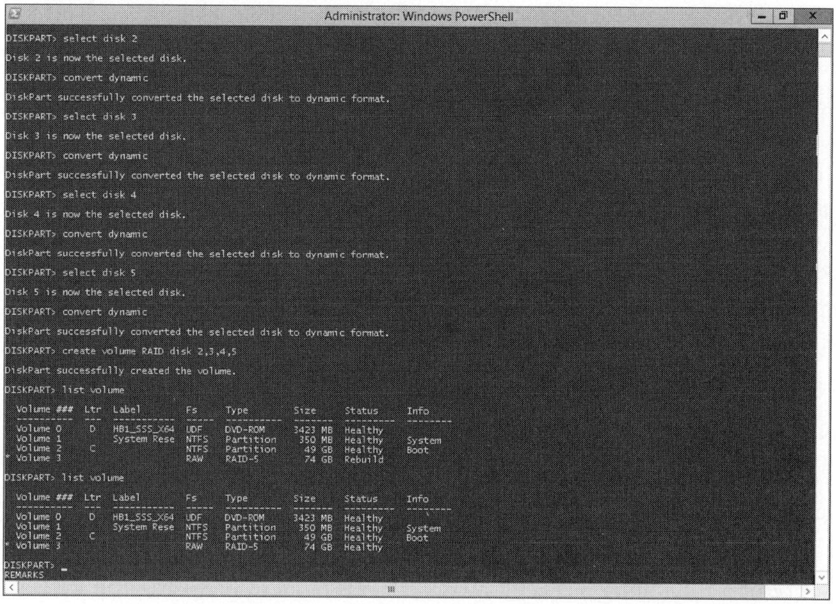

FIGURE 28.3 Identifying the new RAID-5 volume using diskpart.exe.

7. In the command prompt window, type **Select volume 3** and press Enter.
8. In the command prompt window, type **Format FS=NTFS label=New_RAID5_Volume** and press Enter to format the volume. This will perform a full format of the volume.
9. When the format completes, the window details if the format completed successfully. If the format completed successfully Once the volume is formatted, type **Assign Letter=F** and press Enter to assign the new volume the letter F.
10. When the drive letter is assigned, in the command prompt window type **exit** and press Enter to close diskpart.exe and return to the PowerShell window.
11. In the PowerShell window type **get-volume** and press Enter to see the complete list of volumes. Type **exit** to close the PowerShell window.

The new RAID-5 volume should now be accessible from the operating system

TIP

To get a list of disk and volume management PowerShell cmdlets, open PowerShell and type **get-command *disk*** or **get-command *volume*** and press Enter. To get a list of commands when in diskpart, type **?** and press Enter.

Working with Virtual Hard Disk Files

Virtual hard disks have been around since virtual machines appeared on the scene in the late 1990s. Windows Server 2012 can create and directly attach Microsoft virtual hard disks or VHD/VHDX files. VHD files are used in Windows Server 2008, Windows Server 2008 R2, and Windows Server 2012 Hyper-V guest systems as well as Microsoft Virtual Server 2005 and Microsoft Virtual PC, although not all VHD versions are 100% interchangeable. Starting with Windows Server 2012, Hyper-V guest systems also can use the new VHDX file format to leverage larger file sizes. VHD and VHDX files can be created and mounted into a Windows Server 2012 operating system using the disk manager console and also the Windows PowerShell. To create and attach a new virtual hard disk file using the Disk Manager console follow these steps:

1. Log on to the Windows Server 2012 system, open the charms bar, and select the magnifying glass icon to open the search window.
2. In the Search field, type in **Computer Management** press Enter.
3. When the Computer Management window opens, select the Disk Management node under Storage.
4. Right-click the Disk Management node and select Create VHD. For this example, we will create a mount a file named F:\Test1.VHDX that is a 50GB file using the VHDX format and defined as a dynamically expanding disk.

5. When the Create and Attach Virtual Hard Disk window opens, type in the full path and name in the Location field, type in the desired size and size increment, choose the desired virtual hard disk format and type, and then click OK, as shown in Figure 28.4.

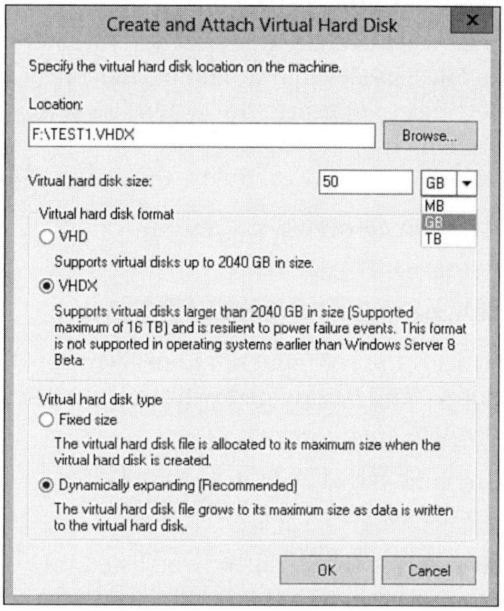

FIGURE 28.4 Creating a new virtual hard disk.

6. Once the process completes, scroll down in the disk management Tasks pane to locate the new virtual hard disk, which should be listed as the last disk and should be listed as Unknown and Not Initialized. Right-click the disk in the left section of the task pane and select Initialize Disk.

7. In the Initialize Disk window, choose to create an GPT partition style for the disk, ensure that the correct disk is checked in the window, and then click OK to initialize the disk.

8. Once initialized, the disk will be listed as Basic and Online. Right-click the volume in the Tasks pane and select New Simple Volume.

9. Follow the steps to format the disk as NTFS and assign a drive letter.

10. Once the process has completed, the virtual hard disk will be available in My Computer and Windows Explorer just as any other local drive.

11. Once the usage of the disk is complete, from within Disk Manager right-click the attached virtual hard disk and select Detach VHD.

12. In the Detach Virtual Hard Disk window, the disk that was selected will be listed. Click OK to detach the disk.

Once the virtual hard disk is detached, it can be copied to any other Windows Server 2012 system and mounted or attached to the host operating system or a Hyper-V guest virtual machine.

Adding the File and Storage Services Role

Windows Server 2012 systems, out of the box, can be used to share folder data right after installation. To get the most out of the system, the File Services role should be added. Adding the File Services role not only configures settings to optimize the system for file sharing, but also allows the administrator to choose which additional file server role services will be installed. To install the File Services role and services, follow these steps:

1. Log on to the Windows Server 2012 system with an account with administrator privileges and open Server Manager.
2. In Server Manager, click Number 2 in the Dashboard to add roles and features.
3. On the Before You Begin page, if the system meets the recommendations to have a strong administrator password, static IP address, and be updated with the latest Windows security updates, click Next to continue.
4. On the Select Installation Type page, select the Role-Based or Feature-Based Installation radial button and click Next to continue.
5. On the Select Destination Server page, the local server should already be listed in the server pool section. Click the local server to select it, and then click Next to continue.
6. On the Select Server Roles page, expand the File and Storage Services node and expand the File Services node beneath it. Note how the Storage Services node is already checked. Underneath the File Services node, check the file services that you want to install, as shown in Figure 28.5.
7. When selecting certain file services, a pop-up window will open giving the option to also install the role administration tools. Click the Add Features button to accept the prompts and install the tools. Click Next to continue.
8. On the Select Features page, you have the option to also install the Client for NFS, if this file server will also access NFS data on UNIX type systems. Click Next to continue
9. On the Confirm Installation Selections page, review the selections, and if desired, check the check box to Restart the Destination Server Automatically. Then, click the Install button to start the File Server role service installation.
10. Once the services are installed, click the Close button to return to Server Manager. Close Server Manager.

After the installation, many of the role services will require additional configuration before they can be of use. This post-installation configuration is covered in later in this chapter.

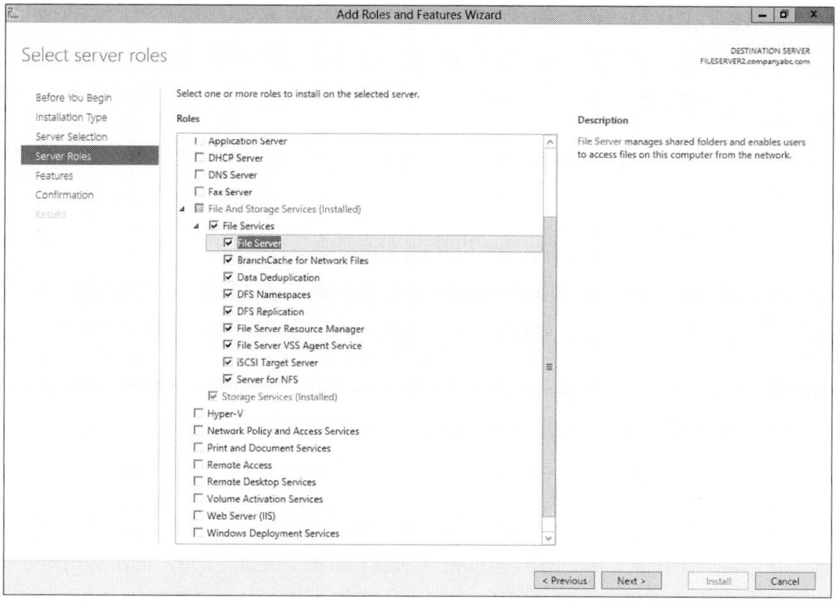

FIGURE 28.5 Selecting the desired File Server role services for installation.

Managing Data Access Using Windows Server 2012 Shares

Providing access to data stored on a Windows Server 2012 server can be very simple to configure using Windows shares. Existing folders and entire volumes can be shared with a few clicks, but understanding who can access that data is critical to security and, in some cases, licensing. Shares are accessed using the UNC or Universal Naming Convention of \\server\sharename or when configured within domain-based DFS names spaces the shares can be accessed at \\companyabc.com\sharename for the example companyabc.com domain. Administrators can configure a few different settings when creating or updating shares. Share options or features include the following:

- Determining whether the share will be visible or hidden, based on the share name ending with a $ symbol
- Setting the description of the share
- Configuring the type of share; if Server for NFS is installed, there will be two options
- Configuring the number of simultaneous connections allowed through the share
- Configuring the cache or offline sync settings of the share
- Enabling or disabling BranchCache
- Configuring access-based enumeration to control folder and file visibility based on NTFS permissions

- Configuring share permissions to manage whether users can read, change, or have full control over a share
- Configuring NTFS permissions on the folder or volume hosting the file share

Share Permissions

The first line of security for shares is in the share permissions. Share permissions are limited as shares can be enabled on CD/DVD drives, FAT volumes, NTFS volumes, and reFS volumes. The configurable share permissions are limited to Full Control, Change, and Read. Full Control permissions allow users to manage all data and to reset permissions. Change allows users to manage all data, and Read just allows users to read the data. Because share permissions are not very granular, as a best practice shares should be created only on NTFS and reFS volumes to allow for increased data security.

When shares are created on NTFS or reFS volumes, both the Share and NTFS folder and file permissions are applied to the user. Windows Server 2012 will combine the permissions, and the most restrictive permissions will apply. For example, if a folder located at C:\UserShare is shared and testuser1 is granted Read permission at the share and Change or Modify NTFS permissions on the folder, testuser1 will only have Read permission when accessing the data across the network through the share. If testuser1 logs on to the system console and accesses the C:\UserShare folder directly, testuser1 will have Change or Modify permissions.

Access-Based Enumeration

A share feature included with Windows Server 2008 and later server operating systems is Access-based enumeration. Access-based enumeration, when enabled on a share, hides the folders or files within the share from view for users who do not have access to the data. Access-based enumeration, however, does not hide the share itself. This feature can simplify data access for end users as they will only see what they can access, but, on the flip side, users who are collaborating and trying to instruct their co-workers on where to locate the data might be confused when the folders cannot be located.

Share Caching and Offline Files

To provide flexibility for mobile users and to provide centralized storage for end-user data, Windows Server 2012 shares can be configured to allow or disable client-side caching of shared server data. Client-side caching (CSC) is a feature that enables data shared on a server to be synchronized between the server and end-user workstations. This enables end users to access data when the server is unavailable or when the workstation is not connected to the company network. This feature also can be used to ensure that any data stored in a synchronized end-user workstation folder is copied to the server for centralized storage and backup and recoverability.

For CSC to function properly, both the workstation and the server must be configured to support it. CSC from the workstation and server side is more commonly referred to as offline files. Depending on the workstation operating system version, different synchronization options are available. A common usage of offline files is to couple offline files with a Group Policy setting called Folder Redirection.

Folder Redirection can be used to redirect the end user's My Documents or Documents folder to a server share. When an end user's My Documents or Documents folder is redirected to a server share with caching enabled, enforced or not, the folder is automatically configured to synchronize with the server. This functionality ensures that any file an end user saves to their default documents folder will be copied up to the server during synchronization. Folder Redirection is covered in Chapter 27, "Group Policy Management for Network Clients." The default offline file synchronization settings for Windows 8 and Windows Server 2012 will synchronize with the server at logon, logoff, and when a file is opened or saved. In addition, synchronization can be configured to run when a computer has been idle or when a user locks or unlocks a workstation.

Caching can be configured on a per-share basis using the shared folder's share property page. By default, all shares allow end users to cache data as they desire. Certain folders (for example, the My Documents or Documents folders) when redirected to a Windows Server 2003 or later server operating system, will automatically enable and configure the folder to be synchronized. To enable or disable share caching functionality, follow these steps on the server:

1. Log on to the Windows Server 2012 system with the share that will be modified and open Server Manager.
2. In the tree pane, click File and Storage Services link, and when that opens, click Shares on the left.
3. In the Shares pane, select and right-click the desired share.
4. When the share properties window opens, click the Settings link, and in the Settings pane check or uncheck the Allow Caching of Share check box, as shown in Figure 28.6.
5. Note that in this window Access-based enumeration and encryption of data access can also be enabled. Click the OK button to complete any setting changes.

To enable caching from the workstation, simply right-click the desired share or folder beneath a share and select the Always Available Offline link. This will perform the initial sync and set up the sync relationship.

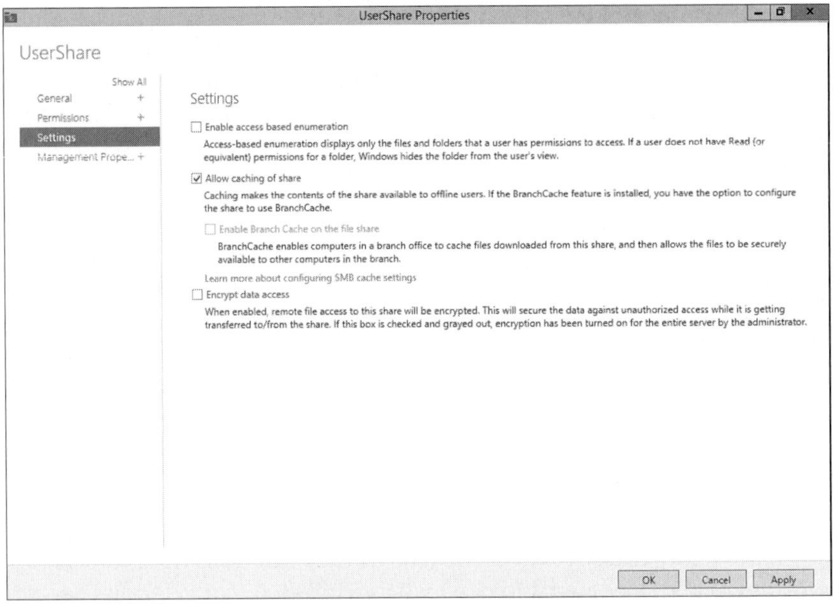

FIGURE 28.6 Managing cache settings on a share.

BranchCache

BranchCache is a feature for Windows Server 2008 R2, Windows 7, and later client and server operating systems. BranchCache enables a branch office workstation to locate and locally store copies of files and folders hosted on remote Windows Server 2012 BranchCache file servers. When BranchCache is installed on a Windows Server 2012 file server, and BranchCache is enabled on a particular file share, when a remote branch office user on a Windows 7 or Windows 8 workstation requests the file from the file server, it broadcasts the request on the local network. If no copy exists, it pulls a copy to the local machine. The updates to that file are sent across the network as changes are made. When the next Windows 8 workstation attempts to access this same file from across the network, the broadcast for that file is sent on the local network, and in this particular example, the file is referenced from the original workstation that copied the file over during the initial request, thus improving access performance to the file and reducing network traffic. You can find more detailed information about BranchCache in Chapter 32.

To enable BranchCache on a Windows Server 2012 system, install the BranchCache for Network Files service as outlined earlier in this chapter. Once the service is installed, open the share properties from the Server Manager File and Storage Services link and in the share settings property page check the Allow Caching of Share check box and also check the Enable Branch Cache on the File Share check box, and click OK to save the settings.

Before BranchCache functionality is enabled, network administrators will need to understand the service in greater details, especially based on the fact that it is currently only supported on Windows 7, Windows Server 2008 R2, and later client and server operating systems. Any lower-level client cannot make use of this feature. In cases where Windows Vista or older clients still exist on remote or branch office networks, administrators should continue to deploy remote file servers with replicated DFS file shares when access to large or numerous files are required.

File Server Resource Manager

Windows Server 2012 includes a file system management and reporting configuration tool named the File Server Resource Manager (FSRM). This service and tool was first introduced in Windows Server 2003 R2 and enables administators to configure quota management at the volume and folder level, create and apply file screening policies, generate alert notifications and reports on a schedule and in real time, and to classify files and folders based on administratively defined criteria.

With the volume-level quota management, previously included with Windows Server versions, administrators were very limited on how quotas could be applied and several issues were encountered. With the quota management functionality included with the FSRM service in Windows Server 2012, administrators can create quotas at a volume or folder level and create exceptions or tighter restrictions in specific subfolders. With this level of functionality, a standard quota size can be established, and different quota policies can be applied on a per-group or per-user basis if different quota settings are required.

With the file screening functionality of FSRM, organizations can restrict all users from storing certain types of files on server storage (for example, music and video files or executable files are common files that are screened for end users). Of course, this can be overridden using file screen exceptions as required.

Windows Server 2012 FSRM includes the File Classification Infrastructure (FCI) that can be used to run scheduled tasks that identify and tag or classify files based on their storage location or the content of the file itself. Of course, FCI can only search through the content of certain file types, which cannot include encrypted files. The FCI is also leveraged when Dynamic Access Control (DAC) is deployed on a network. On overview of DAC is included later in this chapter.

Uses of File Server Resource Manager

FRSM allows administrators to set quotas on volumes and folders as well as implementing file screening functionality or file classification by location or content. Even though in today's market disk storage is much more affordable than in previous years, the amount of time required to back up and restore the data still needs to be managed. Furthermore, many more organizations need to ensure that their file systems meet certain security and regulatory compliance policies and FSRM can assist with these tasks. Some of the most common uses of FSRM are as follows:

- **Setting limits on storage**—An administrator can set the limit on how much disk space a user or group of users can store within a system volume or folder. This is the traditional quota limit item that can limit users to store (for example, 10GB of files on the network).

- **Providing storage limit flexibility of group data**—When a user or group of users need to have different storage limits, instead of allowing these users unlimited access, FSRM can be configured to allow the extension of storage usage beyond the default within specific, designated folders. This can be achieved by applying a strict quota policy on a parent folder and either disabling the quota on a subfolder or applying a less-restrictive quota policy on the necessary folder or folders.
- **Enforcing storage policies**—FSRM does more than just define storage policies. It also help administrators enforce the policies by creating reports and generating notifications of policy violations and predefined storage threshold limits, on a real-time or scheduled basis, that can be sent via email, stored in event logs, or stored in designated report folders.
- **File screen policies**—Administrators can block the storing of a particular type of file or sets of files. In previous years, many organizations were surprised to discover that a significant source of increased data storage requirements had to do with end users downloading and storing music, videos and personal picture files on file servers. File screen exceptions can be created and applied to subfolders as necessary.
- **File classification**—Administrators can define file classification properties and rules that can be manually run or run on a schedule to check files and tag files based on administratively defined rules. This can be useful in identifying data based on usage characteristics or identifying data based on content to ensure higher security and management of sensitive data.

Leveraging the FSRM Features

Before FSRM features can be configured, the FSRM services and management tools must be installed. The File Server Resource Manager services and tools can be installed separately or can be installed during the installation of the File Services role as outlined previously in this chapter.

FSRM Global Options

After the FSRM services and management tools are installed, the global options should be configured. FSRM global options include settings such as the SMTP server to use for email notifications, notification limits, the default location of reports, and enabling file screen auditing. The global options can be configured can be configured as follows:

1. Log on to the Windows Server 2012 system with the share that will be modified and open Server Manager.
2. In the tree pane, click the File and Storage Services link, and when that opens, click Servers on the left.
3. In the Servers pane, right-click the desired server and select File Server Resource Manager to open the FSRM console.

4. When the console opens, in the tree pane right-click File Server Resource Manager (servername) and select Configure Options.
5. In the File Server Resource Manager Options window, review and configure the desired settings in each of the option pages, and then click OK save the changes.

Configuring Quotas with File Server Resource Manager

To create and configure FSRM quotas, follow these steps:

1. Log on to the Windows Server 2012 system with the share that will be modified and open Server Manager.
2. In the tree pane, click the File and Storage Services link, and when that opens, click Servers on the left.
3. In the Servers pane, right-click the desired server and select File Server Resource Manager to open the FSRM console.
4. Double-click the Quota Management node under the FSRM console.
5. Select the Quotas node in the tree pane.
6. In the actions pane, click the Create Quota link to begin the process.
7. When the Create Quota window opens, specify the path for the quota, such as E:\GroupShare.
8. Select the Auto Apply Template and Create Quotas on Existing and New Subfolders option button.
9. In the Quota properties section of the widow, select the Derive Properties from This Quota Template option button, and from the drop-down menu, select the 200 MB Limit Reports to User, and then click Create, as shown in Figure 28.7.
10. After the quota is created, click the Refresh link in the actions pane.
11. In the Tasks pane, the new quota will be listed, along with the quotas applied to all existing subfolders and the current status of each quota.

Adjusting Quotas

When a quota is created on a folder, all subfolders of that parent folder will inherit the quota. In some cases, it might be necessary to exclude a particular subfolder from the parent folder quota or to modify the quota of that particular subfolder. When this is necessary, an administrator simply needs to right-click the quota of the particular folder and select Edit Quota Properties. In the Quota Properties window, the quota can be disabled by checking the Disable Quota check box or the quota space limit can be adjusted.

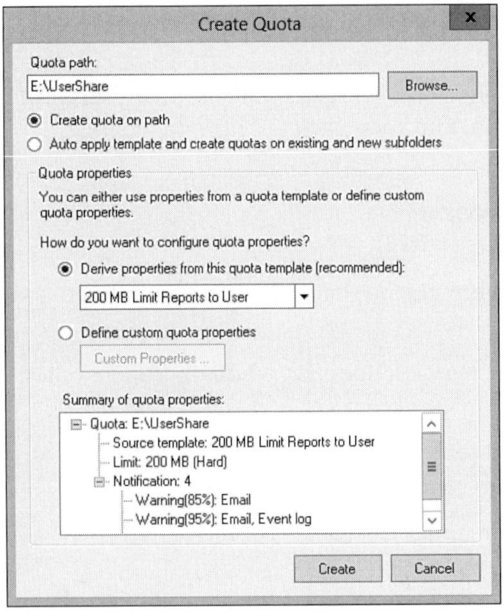

FIGURE 28.7 Creating a new FSRM quote.

Creating a Quota Template

When working with quotas, rather than defining the storage limits on each and every folder being issued a quota, an administrator can create a quota template and apply the template to the folder, simplifying the quota policy creation process. Within the quota template, the administrator can define the following:

- **Amount of disk space of the quota**—The administrator can define in kilobytes (KB), megabytes (MB), gigabytes (GB), or terabytes (TB) the amount of space to be set as the quota for the template.
- **Hard limit or soft limit**—A hard limit does not allow a user to extend beyond the hard limit for storage, whereas a soft limit gives the user a warning they have exceeded the policy limit; however, it allows the user to continue to save files beyond the limit.
- **Notification thresholds**—When the storage limit nears or reaches the quota limit, a series of events can occur, such as the automatic generation of an email warning, event log entry, or a script can be executed.

To create a new quota template, click the Quota Templates node beneath the FSRM console and follow these steps:

1. Open the FSRM console and click Create Quota Template in the actions pane to open the Create Quota Template window.

2. Type in a name of the template (for example, **500mb Hard Limit for Sales**), and enter a description (**Template for Sale Staff Users**).
3. Specify the storage limit for the quota; for this example, enter **500** and choose MB from the list.
4. Pick whether you want a hard limit or soft limit for the quota; for this example, select Hard Quota: Do Not Allow Users to Exceed Limit.
5. Create notification thresholds by clicking the Add button and defining limits. A common threshold is an 85% limit that notifies users via email that they have achieved 85% of their limit and to consider deleting files so that they do not exceed their limit.
6. The quota limit will look similar to Figure 28.8. Click OK when you are satisfied with your settings.

The administrator can now create quotas and apply this template or other templates to the quota settings.

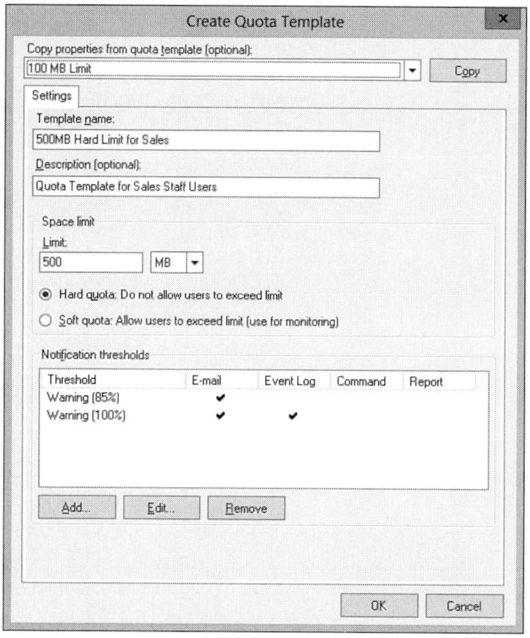

FIGURE 28.8 Creating a new FSRM quota template.

Creating File Screens

File Server Resource Manager also enable you to create file screens. A file screen applied to a folder inspects the file to be written and either allows or disallows a user from saving the file based on the screen. A file screen blocks files from being written within a folder and all subfolders. For example, an organization can allow the storage of all undefined documents and deny the storage of *.mp3 audio files and *.mpg video files by applying a file screen that contains these two file types to a particular folder or set of folders.

To create a file screen, follow these steps:

1. Open the File Server Resource Manager and expand it.
2. Double-click File Screening Management.
3. Select the File Screens node. In the actions pane, click Create File Screen.
4. In the Create File Screen window, specify the path for the file screen, such as E:\UserShare.
5. In the File screen properties section of the windows, select the Derive properties from This File Screen Template option button, or choose Define Custom File Screen Properties, depending on whether you want to apply a template or create a custom screen. For this example, choose the Derive Properties from This File Screen Template option button, and select Block Audio and Video Files from the drop-down menu, as shown in Figure 28.9. Click Create to create the new file screen.

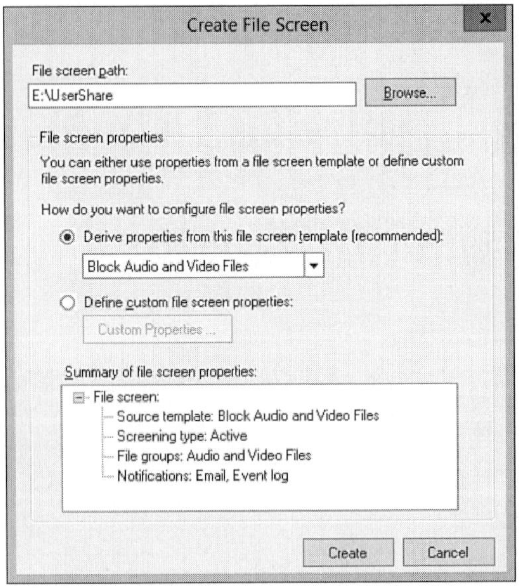

FIGURE 28.9 Creating a new file screen.

Generating Storage Reports with FSRM

The File Server Resource Manager enables you to create or automatically generate general storage reports as well as quota and file screen activity reports. The various reports that can be generated include the following:

- Duplicate Files
- File Screening Audit
- Files by File Group
- Files by Owner
- Files by Property
- Folders by Property
- Large Files
- Least Recently Accessed Files
- Most Recently Accessed Files
- Quota Usage

Generating Reports in Real Time

Reports can be generated on a real-time basis to view the file storage information on demand. To generate a report, right-click the Storage Reports Management node of the FSRM console, and choose Generate Reports Now. Then do the following:

1. On the Settings tab, choose which report or reports will be generated by checking the desired check boxes for the particular report type.
2. On the Settings tab, also select the report formats to generate by checking the appropriate check boxes in the Report formats section of the tab.
3. Click the Scope tab and click Add button to define the scope of the volumes or folders that the report will be based on (for example, E:\UserShare), and then click OK to return to the Storage Report Task Properties window.
4. Click OK when the report options are configured.
5. A new window opens prompting you to decide to wait for the report to generate and automatically display the report or to generate the report in the background and store it in the default report location. Select the Wait for Reports to be Generated and Then Display Them option, and then click OK.
6. Once completed, the folder containing the reports will be opened for review.

28

Scheduling Reports to Be Generated on a Regular Basis

Reports can also be generated on a regular basis (such as weekly or monthly), typically for the purpose of reporting file storage information to management. To schedule a report, right-click the Storage Reports Management node of the FSRM console, and choose Schedule a New Report Task. Define the report name, formats, scope of the report, the schedule, and whether the report will be delivered via email or just stored in the default folder.

File Classification Management

File classification allows an organization to define properties and rules that will add specific file properties to better define the characteristics of the classified files. File classification properties are supported on Windows Server 2012 NTFS volumes. When files are classified, they are tagged, and this information is stored within the actual file for Microsoft Office 2007/2010 files and SharePoint files. For all other files, however, the FCI data is stored on an NTFS volume where the files are stored. When classified or tagged files are moved to other Windows Server 2012 NTFS volumes, these properties follow the files.

File classification allows administrators to create file properties and automatically classify files with these properties based on the file location and, in some cases, also based on the content stored within the file. The steps to file classification include, first enabling and defining file properties that can be used for classification and secondly creating classification rules that will actually classify files according to the criteria defined within the rule. Once files are classified, file management tasks can be created to perform tasks upon classified files, such as moving files to designated folders or performing custom tasks such as running automated scripts to perform any number of tasks related to the particular file classifications.

The best way to understand file classification is to start defining file classification properties, file classification rules, and file management tasks on data that has been copied from a server share to an isolated lab server running Windows Server 2012.

CAUTION

Once a file is classified and has properties defined, these properties cannot be removed, they can only be overwritten or merged with other properties.

To begin using the file classification features of Windows Server 2012, install the File Server Resource Manager service and tool as previous described in this chapter, and then complete the steps outlined in the proceeding sections.

Classification Properties

Classification properties are used to categorize files to be used later for file management tasks or reporting. A classification property, as included with Windows Server 2012, includes the following classification property types:

- Yes/No
- Date-time
- Number
- Multiple Choice List
- Ordered List
- Single Choice
- String
- Multi-string

Two properties are created by default: Folder Usage and Folder Owner Email. The Folder Usage property has been created to enable administrators to quickly classify folders to simplify running reports based on the three types of predefined folder usage: Application Data, Group Data, and User Data. This can be modified to include additional types such as software or something else. The Folder Owner Email property has been created to enable administrators to tag folders with email addresses to create reports and send notifications to designated email addresses without having to define this for each folder.

To get a good understanding of how classification can be used, this section and the following sections provide an example of how to classification can be used to classify files based on content that includes the word *password*. To do this, we will create a file property type of Yes/No and create a classification rule to search the E:\GroupShare folder for any files containing the word and classify these files as necessary. To perform this task, we must first create the classification property. Follow these steps to create the classification property:

1. Open the FSRM console and double-click Classification Management and select the Classification Properties node.
2. In the actions pane, click the Create Local Property link to start the creation of the classification property.
3. In the Create Local Classification Property window, type **Password Property** in the Property Name section, enter a description, and choose the property type of Yes/No, as shown in Figure 28.10.

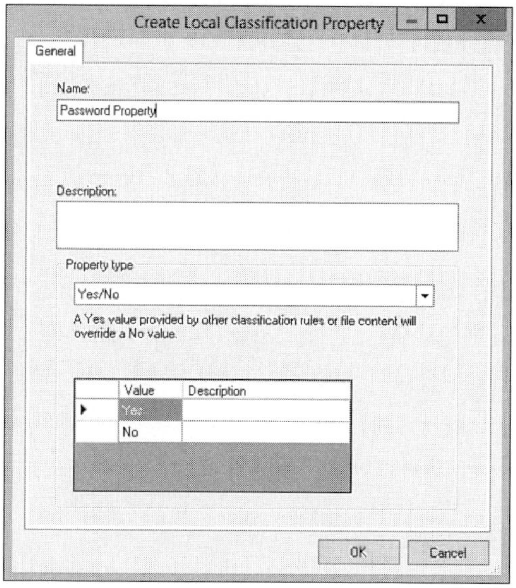

FIGURE 28.10 Creating a new classification property.

Once the new classification property is created, we can create a classification rule that will use this property to classify files that the rule determines to meet the criteria.

Classification Rules

Once the file administrator has created the necessary file classification properties, they can proceed in creating classification rules that will actually process and classify the files that meet the rule criteria, by applying the necessary classification property values to the file collections. To create a new classification rule, follow these steps:

1. Log on to the same Windows Server 2012 system that the Password Property classification property was previously defined on, and open the FSRM console.
2. Double-click Classification Management and select the Classification Rules node.
3. In the actions pane, click the Create Classification Rule.
4. In the Create Classification Rule window, type in the name of the rule as **Classify files with passwords** and be sure to check the Enabled check box. Do not close the window or click OK yet.
5. Select the Scope tab and click the Add button to add the folder or volume that this classification rule will be applied to. For our example, we will apply this rule to E:\GroupShare folder. When the location is specified, all subfolders will also be included. Do not close the window or click OK yet.
6. Select the Classification tab and select Content Classifier from the Classification Mechanism drop-down menu.
7. In the Property Name section, select the Password Property and set the property value to be assigned as Yes, as shown in Figure 28.11.

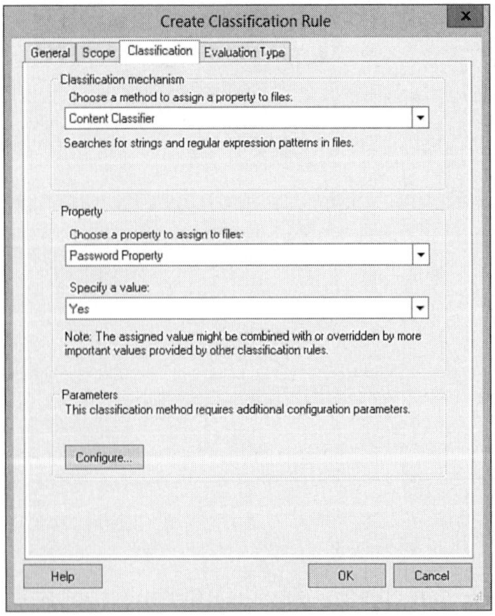

FIGURE 28.11 Defining the classification criteria on a file classification rule,

8. Click the Configure button in the Parameters section of the Classification tab.
9. In the Classification Parameters window, the administrator can define three different types of criteria used to search for specific file content:
   - **RegularExpression**—The RegularExpression is the same as is used with .NET programming and can be used to find complex or multiple types of data formats, for more complex searches.
   - **String (case-sensitive)**—The StringCaseSensitive is the same as the string, in that the entire string must be an exact match, but the case must also match. For example, the StringCaseSensitive string of Password will not match the string password.
   - **String**—The String type is used to find a very specific string, such as password that will not be dependent on the case of the string, although the string must be an exact match. For example, the string password will not match passwords, because that is a different string.
10. For our example, we will specifically look for the string of password and will not care about the case. Pull down the Expression Type menu and select String. In the Value field, type in **password**, as shown in Figure 28.12. Click OK after doing so.
11. Back in the Create Classification Rule window, click OK to complete the rule creation.

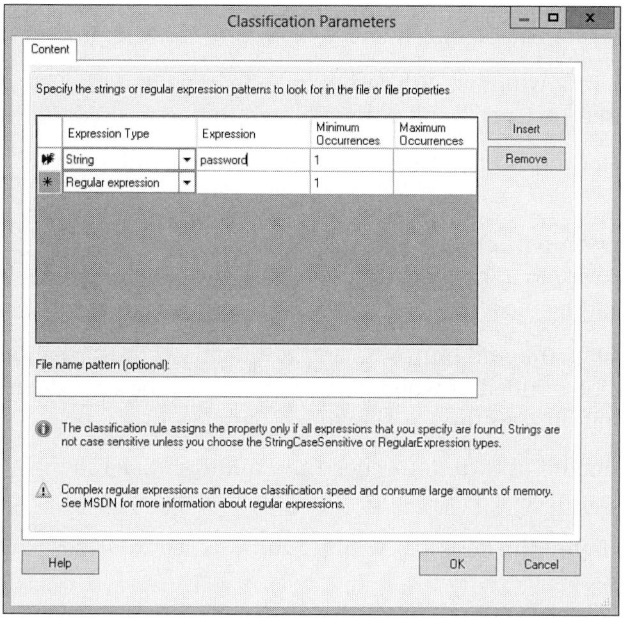

FIGURE 28.12 Defining the additional content parameter for content classification by string.

28

Once the rule is created, it can be scheduled or run manually. To run all the rules manually, in the Tasks pane, right-click the Classification Rules node and select Run Classification with All Rules Now. Follow the steps to select the type of report that will be generated and whether the administrator will wait for the classification to complete and display the window or to have the process run in the background. If a schedule or a manual run is performed, any files that meet the properties of any enabled classification rules will be classified, unless these files have been previously classified.

File Management Tasks

File management tasks can be run on a Windows Server 2012 system to expire classified files that meet a certain criteria (by moving these files to a designated folder location), perform RMS encryption, or a custom task can be performed. To perform any related RMS-related tasks, the RMS infrastructure will need to be deployed and configured on this system, and this is beyond the scope of this book.

File management tasks can be handy to automatically move files that have not been accessed in an extended period of time, or in the case of sensitive data, it can be moved to a secured folder or protected by RMS. To create a new file management task to move expired files that have not been accessed in over a year, for example, follow these steps on a Windows Server 2012 system with the FSRM services and tool installed:

1. Log on to the FSRM Windows Server 2012 system and open the FSRM console.
2. Double-click the File Management Tasks node beneath the File Server Resource Manager node.
3. In the actions pane, click the Create File Management Task link to start the process.
4. In the Create File Management Task window, on the General tab, type in a task name of **Move Data not accessed in 1 year**, and enter a description as desired.
5. On the Scope tab, click Add to locate and add the folder, folders, or volumes to this task.
6. Click the Action tab, and for action type choose File Expiration, and in the Expiration directory, type or browse to a volume and folder location to where the files that meet this criteria should be moved.
7. Click the Notification tab and click the Add button to add notifications to users and administrators so that they can be notified of when particular files will be considered expired and moved to the expiration directory, as shown in Figure 28.13.
8. Back in the Create File Management Task window, click the Condition tab and check the Day Since File Was Last Accessed check box and enter a value of **365**.
9. Click the Schedule tab and configure the desired schedule, and then click OK to complete the creation of the task.

When the task is completed, it will run on the designated schedule and will begin notifying administrators and users when files will be moved. One important point to consider is that once a file is expired and moved, there will be no indication of where or when that file was moved when users go to the original location of the expired file.

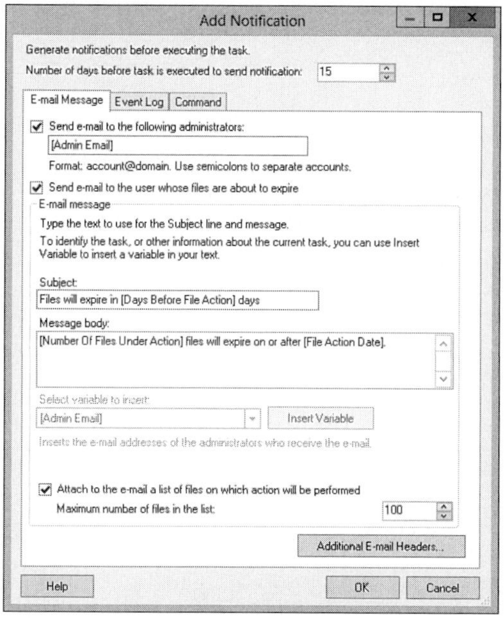

FIGURE 28.13 Defining the notification settings for a file management task.

The Distributed File System

To improve the reliability and availability of file shares in an enterprise network, Microsoft has developed the Distributed File System (DFS). DFS improves file share availability by providing a single, unified namespace to access shared folders hosted across one or more servers. A user needs to only remember a single server or domain name and share name to connect to a DFS shared folder.

DFS has many benefits and features that can simplify data access and management from both the administrator and end-user perspective. DFS provides four main functions:

- **Unified namespace**—DFS data is located under a single server name or a single domain name.
- **Data redundancy**—DFS can provide access to a single share that is hosted on multiple servers. This allows clients to get referred to or fail over to a different server if the primary server cannot be contacted.
- **Automated data replication**—DFS can be configured to utilize the Distributed File System Replication (DFSR) service, and can be configured to automatically synchronize folders between DFS servers to provide data redundancy or centralized storage of branch office data.

- **Distributed Data Consolidation**—DFS can be used to provide a single namespace that can contain several distinct or unique datasets, that can be hosted on separate servers. This allows administrators to provide access to existing file shares hosted many different file servers, from the single name space, without adding replication or redundant data sets.

DFS Namespaces

DFS can be used in a few different ways, but it will always require the creation of a DFS namespace. A DFS namespace can be the name of a single server and share folder or the DNS and NetBIOS name of an Active Directory domain and share folder. The DFS namespace has also historically been referred to as the namespace root. The namespace allows connections to automatically be redirected to different servers without user knowledge. Using Figure 28.14 as an example, when a client connects to the domain-based DFS namespace \\Companyabc.com\Users, the client will be redirected to \\FILESERVER1\Users, and the client will be unaware of this redirection.

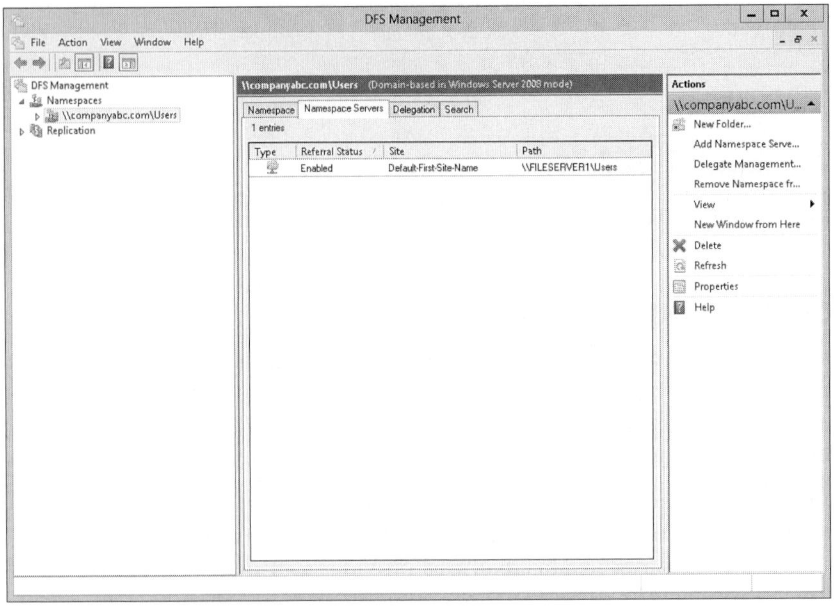

FIGURE 28.14 Domain DFS namespace.

For DFS to function properly with regard to client redirection and just basic connectivity, a compatible DFS client is required. In a network that supports different versions of Windows, Mac, and UNIX clients, DFS should be tested on all clients before it is released to production. DFS-compatible clients are currently available for the following Microsoft Windows operating systems:

- Windows 2000 Professional and Server
- Windows XP Professional
- Windows Server 2003 and later server operating systems
- Windows Vista Business, Ultimate and Enterprise
- Windows 7 Professional, Ultimate and Enterprise
- Windows 8 Pro
- Windows NT Server and Workstation 4.0 with Service Pack 6a and the Active Directory Client Extension found on the Windows 2000 Server CD
- Windows 98 with the Active Directory Client Extension found on the Windows 2000 Server CD

Because DFS clients do not connect to the actual server by name, administrators can move shared folders to new servers and user logon scripts and mapped drive designations never need to be changed. In fact, DFS data presented in a single namespace can be hosted on multiple servers to provide redundancy and distribution of large amounts of data.

Standalone DFS Namespace

A standalone DFS namespace uses the name of the server hosting the DFS namespace. Standalone DFS namespaces should be used when file system access needs to be simplified and the amount of data exceeds the capacity of a single server. Also, standalone DFS namespaces are good if an old file server needs to be replaced but the paths should remain fully functional. Also, if no Active Directory domain exists, a standalone DFS namespace is still supported. When a standalone DFS namespace is created on a Windows Server 2012 server that is a member of an Active Directory domain, DFSR can be configured.

Domain-Based DFS Namespace

A domain-based DFS namespace utilizes the name of the Active Directory domain the DFS namespace server is a member of. A domain-based DFS namespace is created upon deployment of an Active Directory domain at the location of \\domain\SYSVOL to replicate the domain group policies and logon script folders. Domain-based DFS namespaces support replication using either the File Replication Service or the new DFSR service.

Domain-Based DFS Namespace Windows 2008 Mode

When a new domain-based DFS namespace is created on a Windows Server 2012 system, an option to enable Windows Server 2008 mode is presented. This option is available on Windows Server 2008 and later server operating systems when the namespace is hosted on a server where the domain is running in Windows Server 2008 domain functional level or higher. Also, the forest must be running in at least Window Server 2003 forest functional level. This means that the domain must have only Windows Server 2008 or later domain controllers and the entire forest must have only Windows 2003 or later domain controllers.

Windows Server 2008 mode enables the namespace to contain more than 5000 DFS folders, and it also enables access-based enumeration within the DFS namespace. It is important to note that the same functionality enabled for a Windows 2008 mode domain-based namespace exists on standalone DFS namespaces when the namespace server is hosted on a Windows Server 2012 server, so this functionality can be leveraged immediately, even in organizations that are far from meeting the requirements for Windows 2008 mode domain-based namespaces.

DFS Replication

When an Active Directory domain exists, standalone and domain-based DFS namespaces support the replication of DFS data stored on multiple servers. This can be a valuable tool used to distribute company applications to each site or to provide centralized storage of remote office data for redundancy, centralized backup, and to support users who travel and work in different offices.

With the release of Windows Server 2003 R2 and further improved in Window 2008 R2, a new service to extend the functionality and optimize DFS Replication has been created. This new service is called the Distributed File System Replication (DFSR) service, which utilizes the new Remote Differential Compression (RDC) protocol. DFSR replaces the legacy File Replication Service (FRS) that was previously used to replicate DFS data. As long as all the DFS servers defined in a DFSR group are running Windows Server 2003 R2 or later, the DFSR service will be used to replicate the data. If any of the systems are running an earlier version of the operating system, DFS data will be replicated using the FRS. There is one exception to this rule: The domain system volume (SYSVOL) will be replicated between domain controllers using the FRS, even if all the domain controllers are running Windows Server 2012, until the domain functional level is raised to the Windows Server 2012 level and the SYSVOL is migrated from FRS to DFSR.

DFSR and DFS namespaces are independent of one another, but they can be used together, as they are commonly deployed in this fashion. Replication of folders can be set up between servers that do not host any DFS namespaces or namespace folders but the DFSR service must be installed on all systems participating in the replication. Windows Server 2012 increases DFSR security and performance as all DFSR is compressed and encrypted. And just so you know, the data stream cannot be set to run without encryption.

DFS Terminology

A number of technical terms are used when referring to deploying, configuring, and referencing DFS. The DFS namespace and DFSR have already been described, but the remaining terms should also be understood before reading the remainder of this chapter or deploying a new DFS infrastructure:

- **DFS namespace**—A unified namespace that presents a centralized view of shared folder data in an organization.
- **DFS namespace server**—A Windows server that hosts a DFS namespace.

- **DFS namespace root**—The top level of the DFS tree that defines the namespace for DFS and the functionality available. The namespace root is also the name of the DFS namespace. A domain-based root adds fault-tolerant capabilities to DFS by allowing several servers to host the same DFS namespace root.
- **DFS folder**—A folder that will be presented under the root when a DFS client connects. When a root is created, folders can be created within the file system, but DFS folders allow the system to redirect clients to different systems other than the namespace server hosting the root.
- **Folder target**—A share hosted on a Windows server. The DFS folder name and the share name do not need to be the same, but for troubleshooting purposes, it is highly recommended. Multiple folder targets can be assigned to a single DFS folder to provide fault tolerance. If a single folder target is unavailable, clients will be connected to another available target. When DFS folders are created with multiple folder targets, replication can also be configured using DFSR groups to keep the data across the targets in sync. Folder targets can be a share name or a folder beneath a share. For example, \\server1\userdata or \\server1\userdata\Finance are both valid folder targets.
- **DFS tree**—The hierarchy of the namespace. For example, the DFS tree begins with the DFS root namespace and contains all the defined folders below the root.
- **Referrals**—A configuration setting of a DFS namespace/folder that defines how DFS clients will connect to the namespace server, a folder in the namespace, or a particular folder target server. Referral properties include limiting client connections to servers in the local Active Directory site and how often to check the availability of a DFS server. Disabling a target's referral keeps it from being used by clients. Target referral can be disabled when maintenance will be performed on a server.

DFS Replication Terminology

DFS uses either the FRS or the DFSR service to automatically replicate data contained in DFS folder targets. To understand the replication concepts, you must understand some key DFSR terminology. Here are some important terms:

- **Replication**—The process of copying data from a source server folder to a destination server folder.
- **Replication connection**—The directory object that defines and manages the replication between a sending and receiving replication member server. The replication connection defines the replication schedule, which service will replicate the data, the sending and receiving members, and any bandwidth restrictions for the connection. Each replication connection has only a single sending and receiving replication member.
- **Replication member**—A server that shares a common replication connection. The receiving replication server receives data from a sending member server specified in

the replication connection. The sending replication partner sends data to the receiving member specified in the replication connections.

- **Read-only replication folders**—Windows Server 2012 supports read-only replication sets. This can be useful for auditing or centralized backup or managing datasets. Only the replication members that are not defined as the primary source can host read-only replication folders made read-only. Read-only domain controllers host the SYSVOL as a read-only replication folder. When read-only replication folders exist, it is a best practice to ensure that replication is only one way to the read-only replication folder.
- **Replication group**—All the servers, folders, and connections that define a replication set of data.
- **Multimaster replication**—This defines two-way replication between multiple servers in a replication group. With multimaster replication, data changed on any server in the group will be replicated to every other server in the group.

Planning a DFS Deployment

Planning for a DFS implementation requires an administrator to understand the different types of DFS namespaces and the features and limitations of each type, including which operating system versions and domain functional levels are required to enable certain functionality. Also, the administrator must understand which tasks can be automated using DFS and which must be configured manually. For instance, DFS can create the file share for namespace roots, folders, or folder targets, including setting share permissions, but the NTFS permissions would be set to match the share permissions and advanced share features cannot be configured during this process. As a best practice, DFS administrators should create and define shares, share permissions, and NTFS permissions on the shared folder before defining these shares as DFS folder targets.

When an organization wants automated file replication, domain-based DFS and standalone DFS namespaces deployed in an Active Directory domain can use Windows Server 20012 DFSR using the RDC to replicate shared folders if all the participating DFS servers are running Windows Server 2012.

Choosing a DFS Namespace Type

As mentioned previously, DFS namespaces can be based on the server name (standalone) or the domain name hosting the namespace (domain based). Both provide a single namespace, but only domain-based namespaces can provide redundancy at the namespace root level.

Standalone DFS Namespace

A standalone DFS namespace provides the characteristic DFS single namespace. The namespace is defined by the name of the server that hosts the root target and the share. Standalone roots can support only a single root target, but an administrator can configure multiple folder targets. Data stored within multiple folder targets must be kept in sync manually unless the standalone namespace server and all the folder target servers are members of a single Active Directory domain and will use DFSR.

Domain-Based DFS Namespace

For an administrator to create a domain DFS root, the initial namespace root server must be a member of an Active Directory domain. A domain-based DFS namespace provides a single namespace that is based on the DNS and NetBIOS domain name plus a root name, when the namespace is created. Domain-based DFS namespaces can use DFSR to replicate data between multiple folder targets.

Windows Server 2008 Mode for DFS Domain-Based DFS Namespace

Windows 2008 mode for domain-based namespaces enables the namespace to contain more than 5,000 folders, and access-based enumeration can also be enabled. To enable this functionality, the forest must be set to Windows 2003 or later forest functional level, and the domain that contains the namespace servers must be in Windows Server 2008 domain functional level. Once a namespace it created. it cannot be changed to Windows Server 2008 mode, so this option must be configured during creation.

Planning for DFS Replication

When an organization wants to replicate data stored on Windows Server 2012 systems published in DFS namespaces, administrators must create the namespaces on servers that are members of an Active Directory domain. Replication can be configured between multiple targets on a DFS folder or on Windows Server 2008 or later server operating systems that do not participate in a DFS namespace. When multiple targets are defined for a folder, DFS can use the FRS or the DFSR service to create replication connection objects and automatically synchronize data between each target.

Initial Master

When replication is first configured using the DFS console and the New Replication Group Wizard, the administrator can choose which target server will be the initial master. The data contained on the initial master is replicated to the remaining targets. For targets on servers other than the initial master, existing data is moved to a hidden directory, and the current folder is filled with the data contained only in the initial master folder. After initial replication is complete, the administrator can restore data moved to the hidden folder back to the working directory, where it can trigger replication outbound to all the other replicas in the replica set, if replication is two way and neither target is set to read-only. As a best practice, when adding additional targets to a replica set, try to start with empty folders.

The Staging Folder

The staging folder is the location where a DFSR member stores the data that will be replicated to other replication members with a replication group. In a fully synchronized replication group, the staging folder on all servers will be empty. Because replication data will travel through this folder, the drive hosting the staging folder must have sufficient free space to accommodate the maximum size of the staging folder, and should be able to handle the additional disk load. The default location for the staging folder will be located in the target share folder in a hidden directory named E:\Users\DfsrPrivate\Staging, if the target is located in E:\Users, for example. The staging folder of any DFSR group is set to 4GB by default. Be sure to understand the data that will be replicated and adjust the staging folder size as necessary to avoid filling up the staging folder.

Determining the Replication Topology

Windows Server 2012 DFS provides a number of built-in replication topologies to choose from when an administrator is configuring replication between DFS folder targets or replication group members; they're described next. As a general guideline, it might be prudent to configure DFSR connections and a schedule to follow current Active Directory site replication topology connections or the existing network topology when the organization wants true multimaster replication.

Hub and Spoke

A hub-and-spoke topology is somewhat self-descriptive. A single target is designated as the replication hub server, and every other target (spoke target) replicates exclusively with it. The hub target has two replication connections with each spoke target: sending and receiving. A hub-and-spoke topology requires three or more servers and when the hub target is unavailable, replication updates stop between all replication members. Windows Server 2012 includes the ability to specify more than one hub when creating a hub-and-spoke replication topology.

Full Mesh

Using a full-mesh topology, each target has a connection to every other target in the replication group. This enables replication to continue among available replication members when any member becomes unavailable. Because each member has a connection to every other member, replication can continue with as few as two replication members. Using this topology with read/write replication sets can lead to data conflicts if data is being changed in multiple sites, so this topology should be used with caution.

No Topology

During the creation of a replication group, one of the topology options is the No Topology option. Selecting this option allows an administrator to create a custom replication topology after the replication group is created. A custom topology allows an administrator to define specific replication connections for each target. This option can be useful if an organization wants to define one way replication for centralized backup or to optimize read only replicated folders. Also, this can be most useful when creating a topology for a network that is connected using different speed WAN links or each connection needs to have a specific schedule and bandwidth setting.

Replication Schedule and Bandwidth Throttling

Windows Server 2003 R2 and later server operating systems support scheduling replication as well as restricting the amount of bandwidth a replication connection can utilize. For large datasets that will initially replicate across the WAN, the initial replication connections can be configured to run limited bandwidth during business hours and full bandwidth after hours until replication has completed and restrictions can be removed if desired.

Installing and Configuring DFS

To install DFS, an administrator of a file server on the network needs to install the File System role and select the necessary DFS-related role services. Also, when the DFS role services are selected, the necessary DFS tools will be installed as part of the installation.

Creating the DFS Namespace and Root

When creating a DFS namespace, the administrator requires local administrator group access on each of the servers hosting the namespace, and if a domain namespace is selected, domain administrator rights are also required to either create or delegate permissions to create as the domain-namespace information is stored in Active Directory.

A DFS namespace requires a file share. When the DFS root is created, the name can be matched to an existing file share name or a custom name can be selected. The wizard searches the specified server for an existing file share matching the DFS root name; if it does not locate one, the wizard can create the share as part of the process.

As a best practice, the file share should be created and have share and NTFS permissions configured prior to the DFS namespace creation. One thing to keep in mind, though, is that the share name must match the DFS namespace name. Preconfiguring the NTFS permission will help simplify troubleshooting and administration of the namespace.

To create a DFS namespace, follow these steps:

1. Log on to the Windows Server 2012 system with an account with local server Administrator privileges. If a domain-based DFS namespace will be created, ensure that the account is also a member of the Domain Admins group.
2. Pre-create the share and set share and NTFS permissions on the servers and shares that will host the DFS namespace root.
3. Open Server Manager, and in the tree pane click the File and Storage Services link, and when that opens, click Servers on the left.
4. In the Servers pane, right-click the desired server and select DFS Management.
5. In the DFS Management console, expand DFS Management and select the Namespaces node. In the actions pane, click the New Namespace link.
6. When the New Namespace Wizard opens, type in the name of the server that will host the namespace, and then click Next.
7. On the Namespace Name and Settings page, type in the name of the share previously created, and then click Next. For our example, we will use the root share named CorpShares on a folder named C:\CorpShares.

8. A pop-up window opens asking whether the existing share should be used, as shown in Figure 28.15. Click Yes to use the previously configured share and configured security.

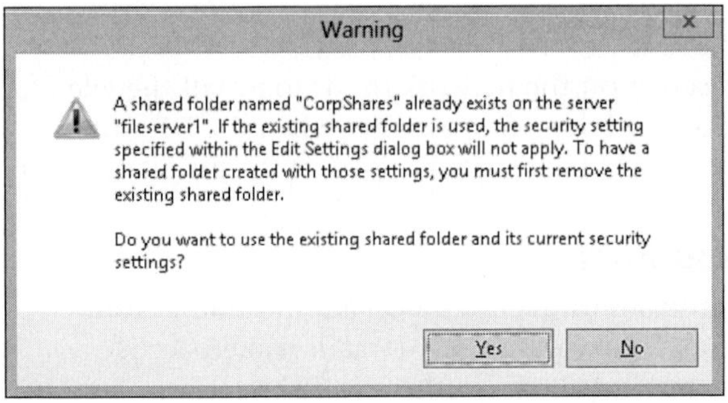

FIGURE 28.15 Using an existing share for the DFS namespace.

9. On the Namespace Type page, to create a domain-based namespace, select the appropriate option button and check the Enable Windows Server 2008 Mode check box to enable scalability and allow for access-based enumeration within the namespace. Click Next to continue.
10. On the Review Settings and Create Namespace page, review the namespace settings, and if everything looks correct, click Create to start the namespace creation.
11. On the Confirmation page, if the result status is reported as a Success, click Close to complete the process. If the creation failed, select the Errors tab to review the issues, repair the problems, and attempt the namespace creation again.

Adding an Additional Namespace Server to a Domain-Based Namespace

After a domain namespace has been successfully created, it is a best practice to add an additional server to host the namespace. To add an additional server to an existing domain-based namespace, follow these steps:

1. On the same server used to create the original namespace, open the DFS Management console as previously outlined.
2. Pre-create the share and configure the desired share and NTFS permissions on the additional server and that will also host the DFS namespace root.
3. Back in the DFS Management console, expand DFS Management, and then expand the Namespaces node. If the existing \\companyabc.com\CorpShares namespace is listed, select it. If the desired namespace is not listed, right-click the Namespaces node, select Add Namespaces to Display, and follow the steps to locate and add the namespace.

4. Select the desired existing domain namespace, and in the actions pane, click the Add Namespace Server link to begin the process.
5. Type in the name of the server, and click OK to continue.
6. If the share already exists, click Yes on the pop-up window to use the existing share and existing configured security. If the share does not exist, it will be created under c:\DFSRoots\ by default.
7. In the Tasks pane, select the Namespace Servers tab to verify that the additional namespace server was successfully added, as shown in Figure 28.16. Also note that in the top of the pane it shows that the namespace is a domain-based in Windows Server 2008 mode.

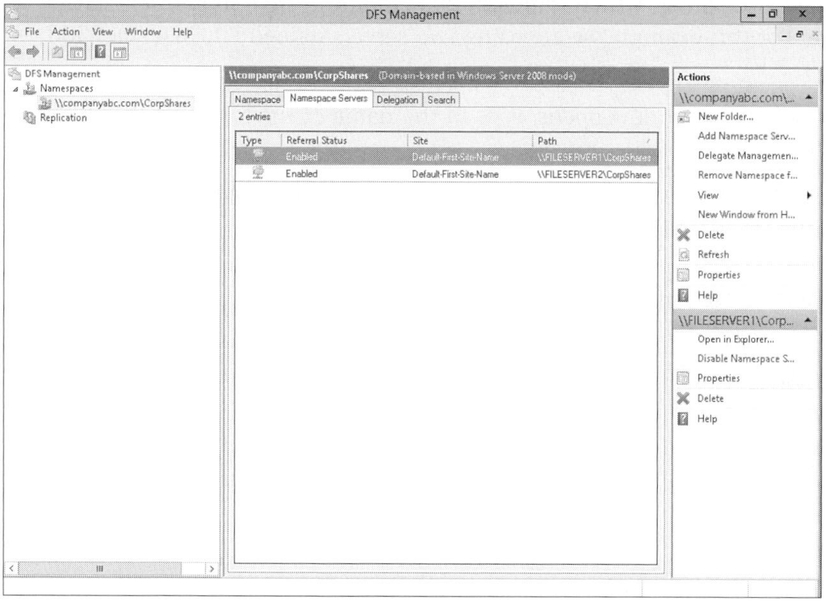

FIGURE 28.16 Verify the successful addition of a namespace server.

Creating a DFS Folder and Replication Group

Creating a DFS folder is similar to creating the DFS namespace. A folder can be created to target existing shares, folders beneath existing shares, or a new share can be created on the desired server or servers. As recommended previously, pre-create the file share on an NTFS folder and properly configure the share and NTFS permissions for each folder target that will be added to the DFS folder.

When a new folder is created with multiple folder targets, a replication group can be created at the same time. To create a folder within an existing namespace, follow these steps:

1. On the same server used to create the original namespace, open the DFS Management console as previously outlined.
2. Pre-create and set NTFS permissions on the servers and shares that will host the DFS namespace folder targets.
3. In the DFS Management console, expand DFS Management, and then expand the Namespaces node to expose the existing namespaces and select the desired namespace. If the desired namespace does not appear, in the actions pane click the Add Namespaces to Display link and follow the steps to search for and add an existing namespace to the console view.
4. Select the desired existing namespace, and in the actions pane, click the New Folder link. For our example, we will use the CorpShares name space and we will create a folder named UserShares, which is already shared and hosted on two servers at E:\UserShare. For this example we are using two servers named FILESERVER1 and FILESERVER2.
5. When the New Folder window opens, type in the name of the folder and click the Add button to locate the folder targets.
6. After all the folder target servers have been added to the New Folder window, click OK to continue, as shown in Figure 28.17.

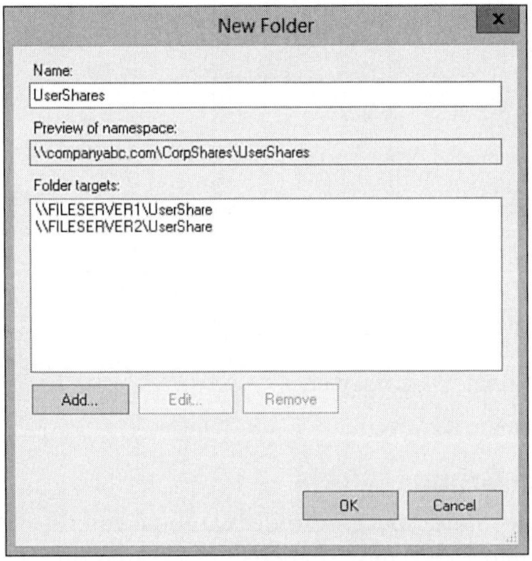

FIGURE 28.17 Defining a new folder and folder targets.

7. When a new folder is created and multiple targets are specified, a Replication pop-up window opens asking whether a replication group should be created. Click Yes to create a new replication group for the folder targets.

8. When the Replication Folder Wizard opens, on the Replication Group and Replicate Folder Name Window page, review the name of the proposed replication group and the replicated folder name, and click Next to continue. The prepopulated names will match the namespace folder path and folder names, as shown in Figure 28.18.

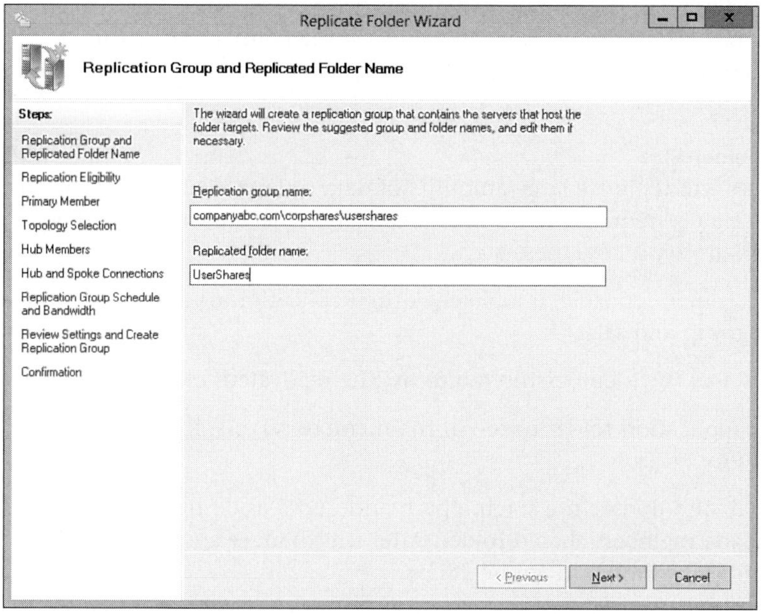

FIGURE 28.18 New replication group name.

9. The Replication Eligibility page will display whether or not each of the folder targets are capable of DFSR. If all targets are eligible, click Next to continue.

10. On the Primary Member page, click the Primary Member drop-down list arrow and select the folder target server that will be used to populate the remaining member folder targets. The data that exists in the folder of the primary target member will be replicated to each of the other targets. After selecting the desired primary server, click Next to continue.

11. On the Topology Selection page, select the desired replication topology. For this example, select the Full mess radial button and click Next to continue.

12. On the Replication Group Schedule and Bandwidth page, select the desired bandwidth limitation or set the hours replication to allowed, and click Next to continue.

13. On the Review Settings and Create Replication Group page, review the selections, and if everything looks correct, click Create.

14. On the Confirmation page, if the replication group creation tasks were all completed successfully, click Close. Otherwise, select the Errors tab and review and repair the errors, and rerun the Replication Group Creation Wizard. A Replication Delay

28

pop-up window will open stating that replication will begin after replication is picked up by all members. Click OK to close this window and return to the DFS Management console.

15. Back in the DFS Management console, double-click the Replication node to reveal the new replication group and select it.

16. In the Tasks pane, select the Connections tab to review the connections created from the previous steps.

Configuring the Staging Folder Size

When a DFSR group server will replicate large amounts of data or large files, increasing the size of the staging folder may be required to optimize replication. To adjust the staging folder size in a replication group, follow these steps:

1. Open the DFS Management console, double-click the Replication node to reveal the desired replication group and select it.

2. In the Tasks pane, select the Membership tab to list the replicated folders.

3. Expand the desired replication folder to reveal the member servers. Right-click one member and select Properties.

4. Select the Staging tab and update the staging path and quota as desired. The default path will be within the members shared folder. After the changes are updated, click OK to save the settings, as shown in Figure 28.19.

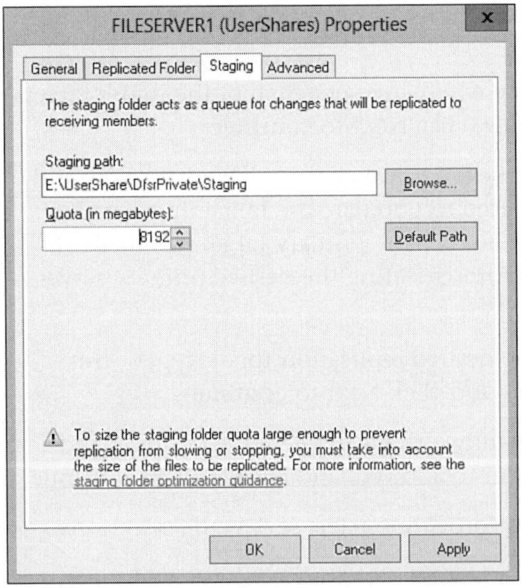

FIGURE 28.19 Adjusting the staging folder quota.

5. Back in the DFS Management console, right-click each of the other member servers in the replicated folder group and adjust the staging folder quota to match the first server.

Enabling Access-Based Enumeration on a Domain-Based Namespace in Windows Server 2008 Mode

When a domain-based namespace is created and Windows 2008 mode is enabled, access-based enumeration can be enabled, but it is not by default. To enable access-based enumeration on a domain-based namespace in Windows Server 2008 mode, locate the namespace in DFS Management. Right-click the namespace and select Properties. Select the Advanced tab and check the check box at the bottom of the Enable Access-Based Enumeration for this Namespace window, and then click OK to complete the change. One thing to keep in mind is that this will apply to the entire namespace and any and all folders and folder targets defined in the namespace.

Disabling Replication for Extended Downtime

When a server containing a replicated folder target will be offline for an extended period of time, for upgrades or due to unexpected network downtime, removing that server's targets from all replication groups is recommended. Doing this relieves the available replica servers from having to build and store change orders and staging files for this offline server. Because the staging folder has a quota limit, an offline server might cause the active server's staging folders to reach their limit, essentially shutting down all replication.

When the server is once again available, the administrator can add this server back to the list of targets and configure replication. The data will be moved to the preexisting folder where it can be compared with file IDs sent over on the change orders from the initial master. If the file ID is the same, it will be pulled from the preexisting folder instead of across the WAN to reduce network traffic.

Using the Volume Shadow Copy Service

The Windows Server 2012 Volume Shadow Copy Service (VSS) is a feature available for NT File System (NTFS) and Resilient File System (reFS) volumes. VSS is used to perform a point-in-time backup of an entire volume to the local disk. This backup can be used to quickly restore data that was deleted from the volume locally or through a network-mapped drive or network file share. VSS is also used by Windows Server Backup and by compatible third-party backup applications to back up local and shared NTFS volumes.

Using VSS and Windows Server Backup

When the Windows Server Backup program runs a backup of a local NTFS volume, VSS is used by default to create a snapshot or shadow copy of the volume's current data. This data is saved to the same or another local volume or disk. The Backup program then uses the shadow copy to back up data, leaving the disk free to support users and the operating system. When the backup is complete, the shadow copy is automatically deleted from the local disk. For more information about VSS and Windows Server Backup, see to Chapters 30 and 31, "Backing Up the Windows Server 2012 Environment," and "Recovering from a Disaster," respectively. One important point is that for VSS backups to work properly, shadow copies should be enabled on every volume and enough free space should exist to store the shadow copies. Even if the schedule is set to once a year, enabling shadow copies on the volume enables shadow copies with the Volume Shadow Copy provider and reduces VSS errors on backups.

Configuring Shadow Copies

Enabling shadow copies for a volume can be very simple. Administrators have more options when it comes to recovering lost or deleted data and, in many cases, can entirely avoid restoring data to disk from a backup tape device or tape library. In addition, select users can be given the necessary rights to restore files that they've accidentally deleted.

From a performance standpoint, it is best to configure shadow copies on the same volume as recommended by Microsoft and required to be compliant for certain VSS backup support scenarios. The VSS is already installed and is automatically available using NTFS-formatted volumes.

To enable and configure shadow copies, follow these steps:

1. Log on to the Windows Server 2012 system with an account with administrator privileges.
2. Open Windows Explorer from the taskbar.
3. Navigate to the Computer node to list all local volumes/drives. Right-click any NTFS drive and select properties
4. Select the Shadow Copies tab, and in the Select a Volume section, click the desired volume, and click the Settings button.
5. The Settings page allows you to choose an alternate volume to store the shadow copies. Select the default of storing the shadow copies on the same volume and set the storage space limit for the volume. The default is usually set to 10% of the volume size, accepting the defaults is recommended.
6. After the location and maximum size are configured, click the Schedule button and define the schedule. The defaults create a shadow copy at 7:00 a.m. and 12:00 p.m., but for this example, set up an additional shadow copy to run at 5:00 p.m., as shown in Figure 28.20.
7. Click OK to close the Schedule window and click OK again to close the Volume Shadow Copy Settings window. The shadow copy for the originally selected volume is now enabled.
8. If necessary, select the next volume and enable shadow copies; otherwise, click the Create Now button to create the initial shadow copy.

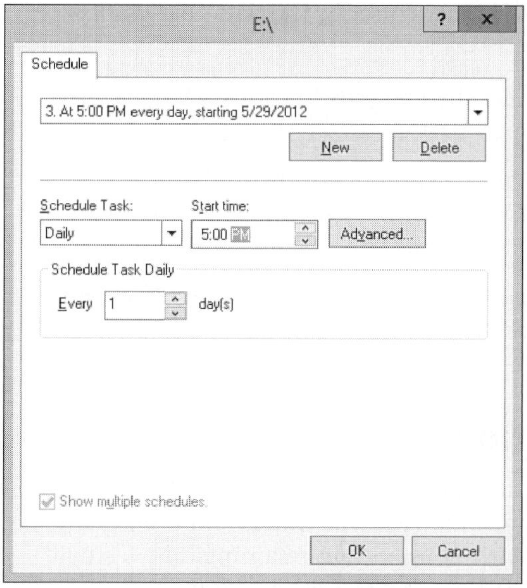

FIGURE 28.20 Creating an additional schedule for volume shadow copies.

9. If necessary, select the next volume and immediately create a shadow copy by clicking the Create Now button.
10. After the shadow copies are created, click OK to close the disk volume window and close the Windows Explorer window.

For more detailed information concerning the VSS and how to recover data using previously created volume shadow copies, see Chapters 30 and 31.

Recovering Data Using Shadow Copies

The server administrator or a standard user who has been granted permissions can recover data using previously created shadow copies. The files stored in the shadow copy cannot be accessed directly, but they can be accessed by connecting the volume that has had a shadow copy created.

To recover data from a file share, follow these steps:

1. Log on to a Windows Server 2012 system or Windows XP SP1 or later workstation with either administrator rights or with a user account that has permissions to restore the files from the shadow copy.
2. Click Start and select Run or type in the server and share name in the Search pane (for example, *servername*\sharename, where *servername* represents the NetBIOS or fully qualified domain name of the server hosting the file share). The share must exist on a volume in which a shadow copy has already been created.

3. When the folder opens, right-click the folder that contains the data that will be restored and select Properties
4. When the window opens, if necessary, select the Previous Versions tab, and select the desired folder version and click the Open button.
5. An Explorer window then opens, displaying the contents of the folder when the shadow copy was made. If you want to restore only a single file, locate the file, right-click it, and select Copy.
6. Open the server share location the restored file will be placed in, right-click, and choose Paste. Overwrite the file as required and close all the windows as desired.

Configuring Data Deduplication

The Data Deduplication service removes duplicate data stored on file server storage. It can perform this task by breaking down file and folder storage into chunks and then identifying duplicate chunks and replacing duplicates with pointers and retaining only a single copy of that chunk. To get a detailed overview of how this process actually works, review the online Microsoft Technical information about data deduplication.

Before attempting to leverage data deduplication, administrators should run the evaluation tool to determine whether there will be a benefit to enabled deduplication on the data volume. Deduplication is not available for the system volume. To check the impact of data deduplication, the administrator can run the Data Deduplication Savings Evaluation Tool as follows:

1. Open and command prompt on a Windows Server 2012 system with the Data Deduplication service installed.
2. Browse to C:\Windows\System32, and for this example we will examine the E:\GroupShare\IT folder. Type the command **DDPEval.exe e:\GroupShare\IT** and press Enter. This will start the DDP eval tool's examination of that particular folder and subfolders.
3. When the process completes, the calculated results display in the window, as shown in Figure 28.21.

NOTE

Even though the DDPEval.exe tool can examine individual folders, data deduplication can only be enabled at a volume level.

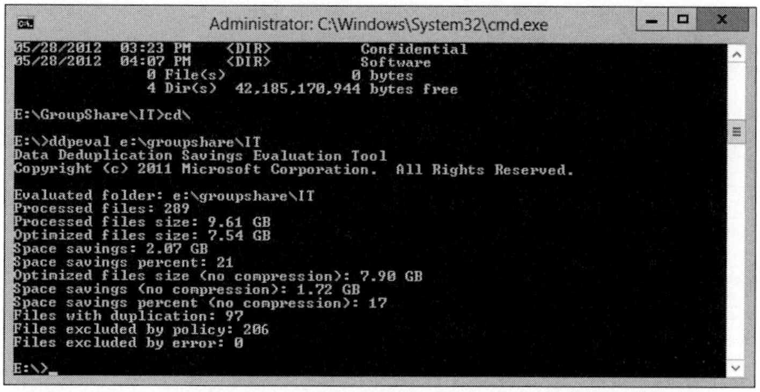

FIGURE 28.21 Displaying the results of the DDPEVAL.exe tool.

To enable data deduplication on a desired data volume, follow these steps:

1. Log on to the Windows Server 2012 system with the Data Deduplication service installed and open Server Manager.
2. In the tree pane, click the File and Storage Services link, and when that opens, click Volumes on the left.
3. In the Volumes pane, right-click the desired volume and select Configure Data Deduplication.
4. Check the Enable Data Deduplication check box.
5. Adjust the Duplicate Files Older Than (In Days) Setting as desired. This setting ensures that new files that may be changing regularly are not modified until they have been stored on the system for a reasonable duration. The default is 30 days.
6. Add in any necessary file extension exclusions and add any excluded folders, as shown in Figure 28.22
7. Click the Set Deduplication schedule button. Enable Background Optimization is the default and provides the least amount of server performance impact. Select the Enable Throughput Optimization to set a hard schedule, such as after-hours or weekends, to keep tighter controls on when deduplication processing will occur. Click OK to close the Deduplication Schedule window, and click OK again to close the Deduplication Settings window.
8. After deduplication processing occurs, right-click the volume and select Properties to reveal the deduplication settings.

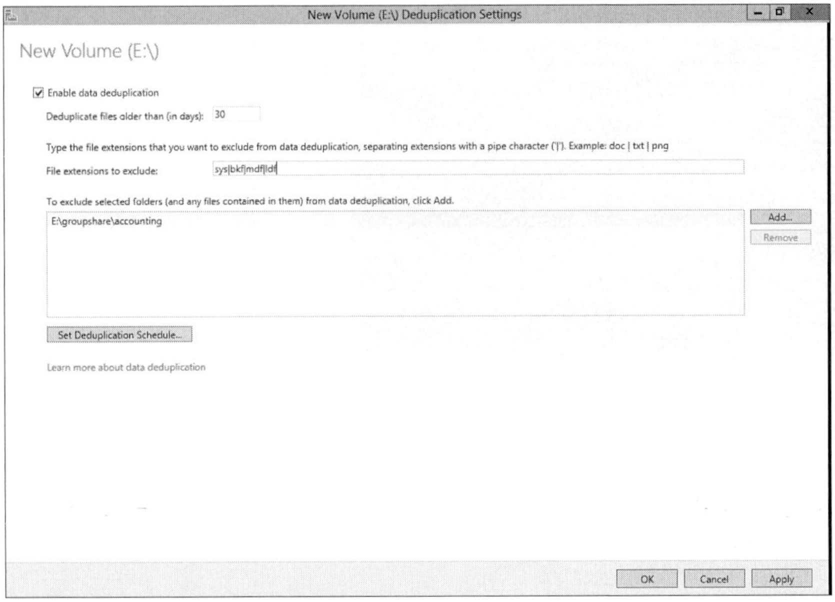

FIGURE 28.22 Configuring data deduplication.

Configuring Storage Spaces

Storage Spaces is a new feature for Windows Server 2012 and Windows 8 that enables the pooling of disks on a server or workstation to deliver virtual disks to the operating system. Storage spaces are made up of storage pools, which include the physical disks, and virtual disks, which are hosted and defined within a storage pool.

Storage pools are very flexible; they can be changed to add or replace physical disks as necessary. This is a unique feature because the storage pool can be changed, but the virtual disk can remain the same, and when additional disks are added to the storage pool, the virtual disks can be expanded quite easily.

A storage pool can be created with a single disk, but when a storage pool contains multiple disks, fault-tolerant or resilient virtual disks can be created. Storage spaces need no special installation on Windows Server 2012, and to create a storage pool and virtual disks, administrators only need to add new disks to the system and perform a few simple tasks. To create a storage pool and a virtual disk, follow these steps:

1. Connect additional disks to the Windows Server 2012 system. Do not configure the disks.

2. Log on to the Windows Server 2012 system with the new unconfigured disks and open Server Manager.

3. In the tree pane, click the File and Storage Services link, and when that opens, click Storage Pools on the left.
4. In the Storage Pools pane, note the existing Primordial storage pool, which includes all server disks. Right-click a blank spot underneath the Primordial storage pool and select New Storage Pool.
5. When the New Storage Pool Wizard window opens, review the information on the Before You Begin page, and then click Next to continue.
6. On the Specify a Storage Pool Name and Subsystem page, enter the desired name for the pool, and then click Next to continue.
7. On the Select Physical Disks for Storage page, check the check box next to the disks that will be added to the pool. Also, in the Allocation column, pull down the menu and choose if each disk will be allocated as a data store, manually or as a hot spare, as shown in Figure 28.23

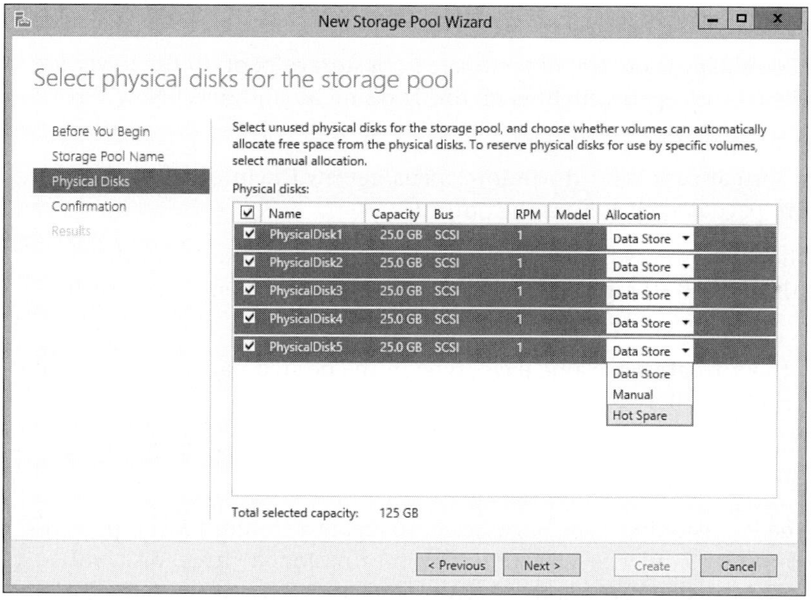

FIGURE 28.23 Defining disks within the new storage pool.

8. On the Confirm Selections page, review the settings and click Create to create the new storage pool.
9. After the storage pool has been created, click Close in the View Results page to return to Server Manager.

Creating Virtual Disks

Once a storage pool is created, virtual disks can be added to it. Virtual disks can be configured with a striped, mirror, or parity storage layout. Striped virtual disks can be created on storage pools that contain only a single physical disk because it includes no fault tolerance or resilience. Mirror and parity storage layout disks require that the storage pool contains multiple physical disks. Mirror virtual disks will be configured to replicate data to two or more physical disks. Parity disks will store parity information about the data stored on all disks within the storage pool. The parity information is stored across all disks in the set and is used to maintain data integrity when data is written to, or moved within, the disk set. Parity information is also used to recover data and rebuild data in the event of a physical disk failure. To create a virtual disk, follow these steps on a system with a storage pool created:

1. Log on to the Windows Server 2012 system with the new storage pool and open Server Manager.
2. In the tree pane, click the File and Storage Services link, and when that opens, click Storage Pools on the left.
3. In the Storage Pools pane, note the new storage pool storage pool. In the lower-left corner is the Virtual Disks pane. Right-click the Tasks menu and select New Virtual Disk.
4. When the New Virtual Disk Wizard window opens, review the information on the Before You Begin page and click Next to continue.
5. On the Select the Server and Storage Pool page, click the desired server in the top pane, and the desired storage pool in the lower pane, and then click Next to continue.
6. On the Specify the Virtual Disk Name page, type in the desired name and optionally a description, and then click Next to continue.
7. On the Select the Storage Layout page, select the Simple, Mirror, or Parity storage layout, and then click Next to continue.
8. On the Select the Provisioning Type page, select to create a thin or fixed type and click Next to continue. Similar to VHD files, a thin-provisioned virtual disk will only take up the needed space, whereas a fixed type will claim all the space defined for the maximum virtual disk size.
9. On the Specify the Size of the Virtual Disk page, enter the size in GB for the disk and click Next to continue.
10. On the Confirm the Selections page, review and the settings, and then click Create to create the disk, as shown in Figure 28.24.
11. On the View Results page, review the creation results, and click Close to complete the virtual disk creation process.

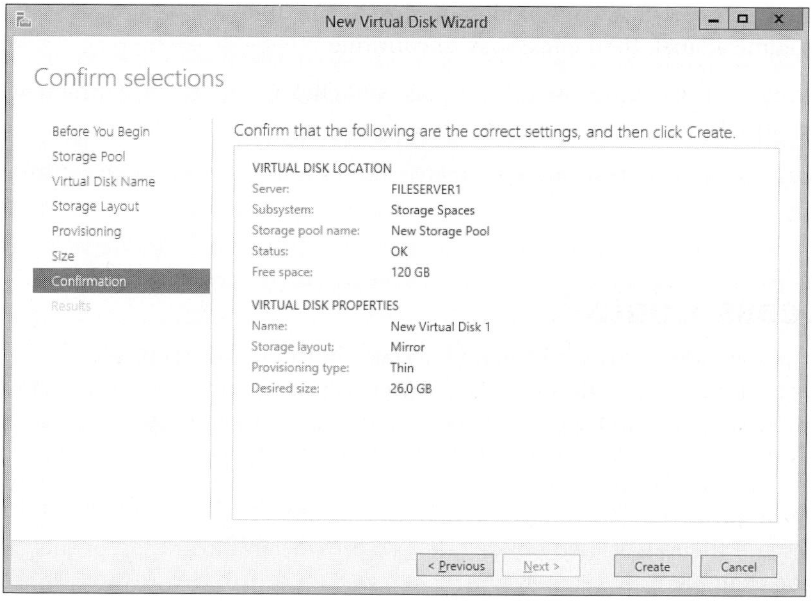

FIGURE 28.24 Creating the virtual disk.

Creating Volumes on Virtual Disks

After a virtual disk is created, a volume must also be created on it before the operating system can make it usable for users and applications. To create a volume on a new virtual disk, follow these steps:

1. Log on to the Windows Server 2012 system with the new virtual disk and open Server Manager.
2. In the tree pane, click the File and Storage Services link, and when that opens, click Storage Pools on the left.
3. In the Storage Pools pane, select the new storage pool. In the lower-left corner is the Virtual Disks pane. Right-click the desired virtual disk and select Create Volume.
4. Review the information on the Before You Begin page, and then click Next to continue.
5. On the Select Server and Disk page, select the desired server and disk, and then click Next to continue.
6. On the Specify the Size of the Volume page, accept the default to create the maximum volume size in the virtual disk, and then click Next to continue.
7. On the Assign a Drive Letter or Folder page, configure the desired settings and click Next.

8. In the Select file system settings page, choose to format the drive as NTFS or reFS and give the volume a label, then click Next to continue.
9. Review the settings in the Confirm selections page and click Create to create the new volume on the virtual disk.
10. On the View Results page, if the volume is created successfully, click Close to return to Server Manager.

Dynamic Access Control

A new feature for Windows Server 2012 is Dynamic Access Control (DAC). DAC is an entirely new way to control access to file share data. Whereas share permissions and NTFS permissions manage share, folder, and file access by referencing the user account and security group membership, DAC extends that functionality by adding in an additional layer of security. This layer includes, as one example, comparing additional user attribute values with folder classification property values, and then granting or denying access based on central access policies and their associated policy rules. To provide an illustration of this, consider the following example.

Jamil and Colby are both in the Human Resources department of a global organization. Jamil is located in the Brazil office, and Colby is located in the United States office. To meet some Human Resources compliance requirements, Human Resources departmental data from the United States should not be accessible to department members in other countries. Traditionally this would be accomplished by creating several security groups, managing the membership of these groups, and appropriately securing the folder data with NTFS permissions based on these groups. An example of the security groups could be as follows:

- **Human Resources Global**—This group would contain all the country-specific security groups and no users.
- **Human Resources United States**—This group would contain the specific U.S. Human Resource departmental employees.
- **Human Resources Brazil**—This group would contain the specific Brazil Human Resource departmental employees.

When data storage for the Human Resources department is created, it will need to be designated and secured as available for the global department or specifically for each country's department. This can be challenging and will periodically involve IT support to configure the permissions appropriately, but the Human Resource users, or content owners, may be able to identify and group this data more easily.

Now enters DAC and folder classification properties. For the previously cited scenario, the following chapter sections detail the configuration of a sample Active Directory DAC infrastructure to restrict access to a shared folder to users with the Human Resources department in the United States. Instead of security groups, the actual user attributes will be used to evaluate and grant/deny access to the data. This DAC sample scenario requires that the domain controllers, file servers, and clients are all running Windows Server 2012 and Windows 8. The following processes include steps that build the DAC infrastructure from the bottom up, specifically for this scenario, but these same steps can be updated to meet many different scenarios.

1. **Creating DAC claim types**—A claim is simply a stated condition supported with a matching attribute value. An example is that the user Colby is in the Human Resources department in the United States. This claim is supported by the configured attributes in Colby's user account matching the values stated in the claim for the Department and Country attribute.

2. **Configuring DAC resource properties**—The resource properties that we configure and enable will be made available to define folder classification properties. These resource property values will be used to compare against the user claims to control access to the data in the folder.

3. **Adding configured resource properties to a Resource Property list**—File servers will only download Resource Property lists and not individual resource properties. The list will allow for the grouping and segmentation of only the desired resource properties required for the classification design.

4. **Creating a central access rule**—The central access rule will define the criteria for allowing or denying access to DAC secured data.

5. **Creating a central access policy**—A central access policy can contain one or many central access rules and will be applied or assigned to file servers as a single unit using group policies.

6. **Creating and assigning a central access policy GPO to file servers**—This step involves creating a new Group Policy object, configuring that object, and then applying the policy to designated Windows Server 2012 file servers.

7. **Enabling Kerberos armoring for domain controllers**—This step involves updating the domain controller Kerberos configuration to include DAC information when generating Kerberos tickets for users and computers.

8. **Creating and updating a file share to Leverage Dynamic Access Control**—This step involves updating the security configuration of a file server's shared folder to support the classification data and criteria desired by the organization.

9. **Configuring user accounts and testing data access**—This step involves configuring the user account and testing access to the DAC secured folder.

Creating DAC Claim Types

At the heart of the DAC infrastructure is the claims that will be made available to present options for folder classification and processing access requests. To create a new DAC claim type, follow these steps:

1. Log on to a Windows Server 2012 domain controller with an account in the Domain Admins and Enterprise Admins security groups.
2. Open Server Manager, click Tools, and open the Active Directory Administrative Center console.
3. When the console opens, in the tree pane on the left, click Dynamic Access Control, and in the center pane, double-click Claim Types.
4. In the Tasks pane, click New Claim Type.
5. When the Create Claim Type window opens, scroll down in the Source Attribute list and locate the source attribute with the display name of C, which is the Country field. Select this source attribute, and in the Display Name field in the top-right corner type in **Country**, and then click OK in the bottom-right corner, as shown in Figure 28.25.

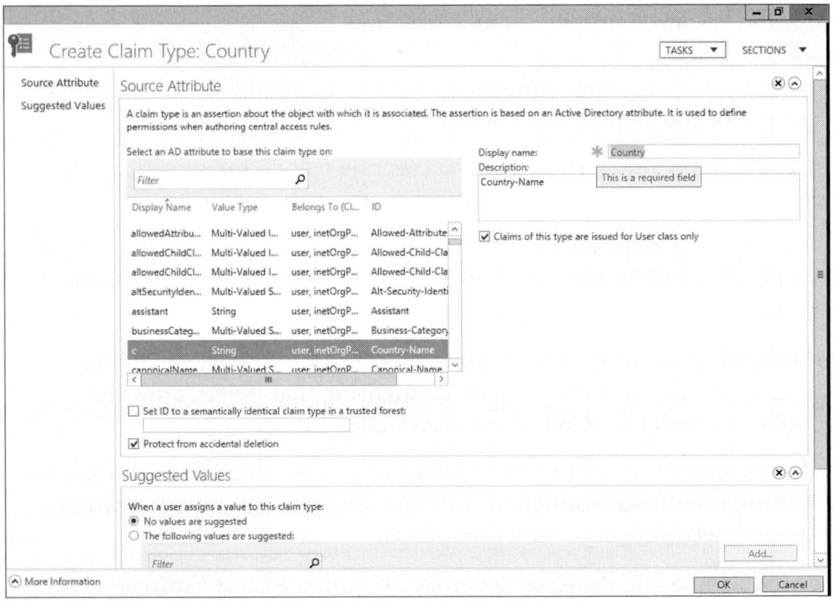

FIGURE 28.25 Creating the Country claim type.

6. Back in the Claim Type window, click New Claim Type to create another. When the Create Claim Type window opens, scroll down in the Source Attribute list and locate the source attribute with the display name of Department, and select this attribute. In the Display Name field, in the top-right corner, change the name to **Department**, and then click OK in the bottom-right corner to create the claim type.

Configuring DAC Resource Properties

Once the two claim types are created, we can define the resource properties that will be compared to the user claims to allow or deny DAC secured data access. To configure the resource properties, follow these steps:

1. Log on to a Windows Server 2012 domain controller with an account in the Domain Admins and Enterprise Admins security groups.
2. Open Server Manager, click Tools, and open the Active Directory Administrative Center console.
3. When the console opens, in the tree pane on the left, click Dynamic Access Control, and in the center pane, double-click Resource Properties.
4. Unlike the claim types, Windows Server 2012 Active Directory already includes several predefined resource properties. Existing resource properties can be used or modified, and new properties can also be created. In the Resource Properties pane, scroll down and select the property with the ID of Department_MS, and then in the Tasks pane in the top right of the window, click the Enable link, as shown in Figure 28.26.

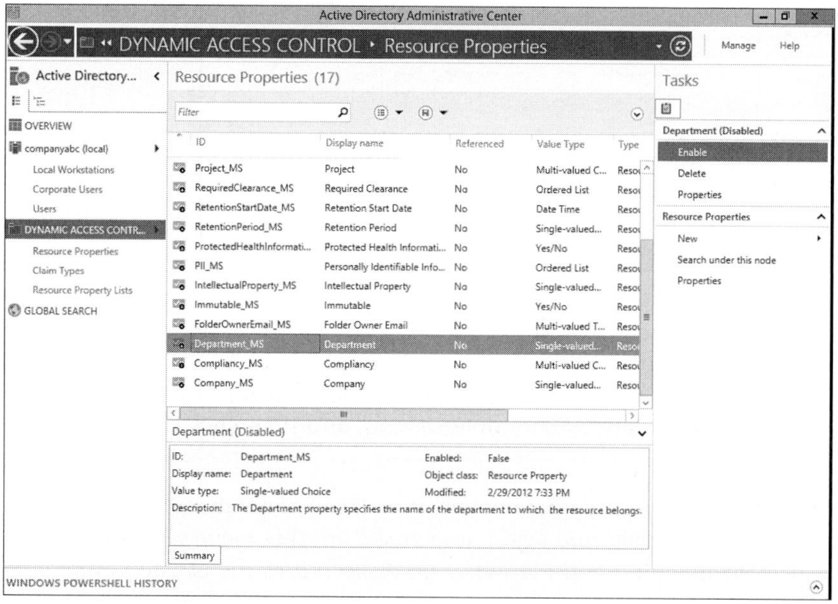

FIGURE 28.26 Enabling the existing Department_MS resource property.

5. The Department_MS resource type has been pre-created by Microsoft, hence the trailing _MS, and this resource has existing values. Click the Properties link in the Tasks pane to review the existing list of Departmental values. If the organization leverages different departments, they can be added into the Suggested Values section of the resource property, or existing values can be edited. Click Cancel to close the Department_MS resource property.

6. Back in the Resource Property window, in the Tasks pane, click New Resource Property, as shown in Figure 28.27.

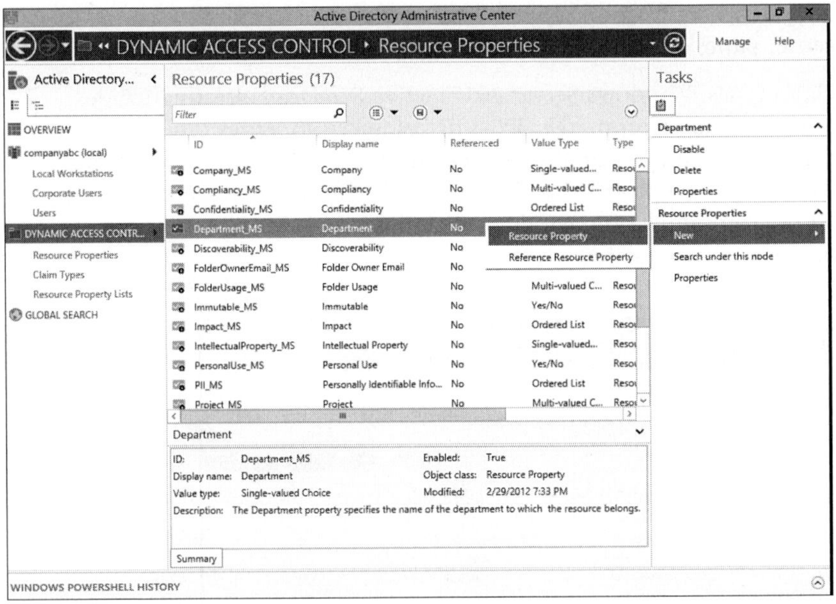

FIGURE 28.27 Creating a new resource property.

7. When the Create Resource Property window opens, type **Country** in the Display Name field and in the lower Suggested Values section, and then click the Add button.

8. When the Add Suggested Value window opens, type **US** in the Value and Display Name fields and click OK. Click Add again, and create another value with **BR** in the Value and Display Name fields, and then click OK to return to the Create Resource Property window.

9. Back in the Create Resource Property window, click OK to create the resource property, as shown in Figure 28.28.

10. Back in the Resource Properties window, select the new Country resource property and verify that it is enabled, which it should be by default after creation.

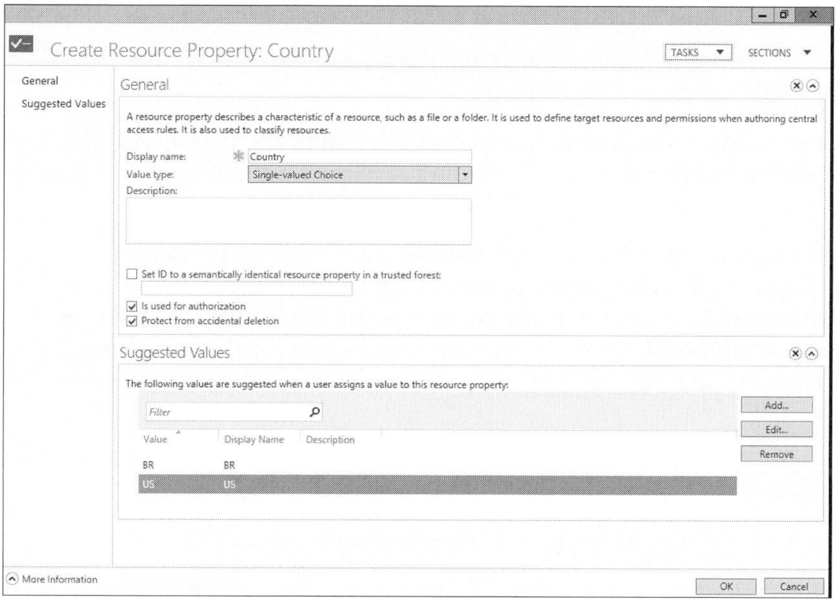

FIGURE 28.28 Creating the Country resource property.

Adding Configured Resource Properties to a Resource Property List

After the necessary resource properties are enabled, edited, or created, as outlined in the previous section, the properties can be added to a Resource Property list. To add the desired resource properties to a list, follow these steps:

1. Open the Active Directory Administrative Center console, and in tree pane on the left, click Dynamic Access Control, and in the center pane, double-click Resource Property List.
2. In the Resource Property List pane, one list already exists by default. This is the Global Resource Property List, and it contains all the resource properties defined in Active Directory, including the new Country resource property.
3. At this stage, a new Resource Property list can be created and the Department and Country resource properties can be added to the list. For this example, we will leverage the Global Resource Property List and not create a new one.

Creating a Central Access Rule

A central access Rule will define the criteria the user claims must meet to access the DAC secured data on the file server. To create a new central access rule, follow these steps:

1. Open the Active Directory Administrative Center console, and in the tree pane on the left, click Dynamic Access Control, and in the center pane, double-click Central Access Rules.

28

2. In the Tasks pane, click New Central Access Rule.
3. In the Create Central Access Rule window, type in a name, such as **HR-US-CentralAccessRule**, but do not click OK yet.
4. In the Target Resources section, click the Edit button and in the pop-up window click the Add a Condition link near the bottom left. Create a condition where the Country resource property is equal to US, but do not click OK yet.
5. Click the Add a Condition link again and add another condition where the Department resource property is equal to Human Resources, as shown in Figure 28.29. Once completed, confirm that the conditions are joined with an AND condition expression, meaning that both conditions must be met for the rule to true. Click OK to close the pop-up condition window and return to the Central Access Rule window.

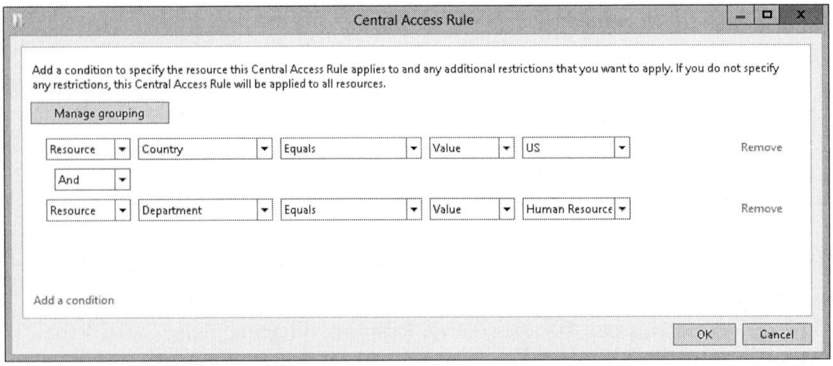

FIGURE 28.29 Defining the central access rule target resource conditions.

6. Back in the Central Access Rule window, in the Permissions section, there are two radial buttons. The top button, Use the Following Permissions as Proposed Permissions, will enable the rule as an auditing-only rule. Select the second radial button labeled Use the Following Permission as Current Permissions. and then click OK to save the new rule, as shown in Figure 28.30.

Creating a Central Access Policy

Once the rule is created, it can be added to a central access policy as follows:

1. Open the Active Directory Administrative Center console, and in the tree pane on the left, click Dynamic Access Control, and in the center pane, double-click Central Access Policies.
2. In the Tasks pane, click New Central Access Policy.
3. In the Create Central Access Policy window, type in a name for the policy, such as **DAC Central Access Policy**, but do not click OK yet.

4. In the Member Central Access Rules section, click Add on the right. In the Add Central Access Rules pop-up window, double-click the previously created rule to add it, and then click OK to return to the Central Access Policy window. Click OK again to close the policy window.

At this stage, the DAC infrastructure configuration has been completed, and we can proceed to configuring the file servers and the domain controller to support DAC.

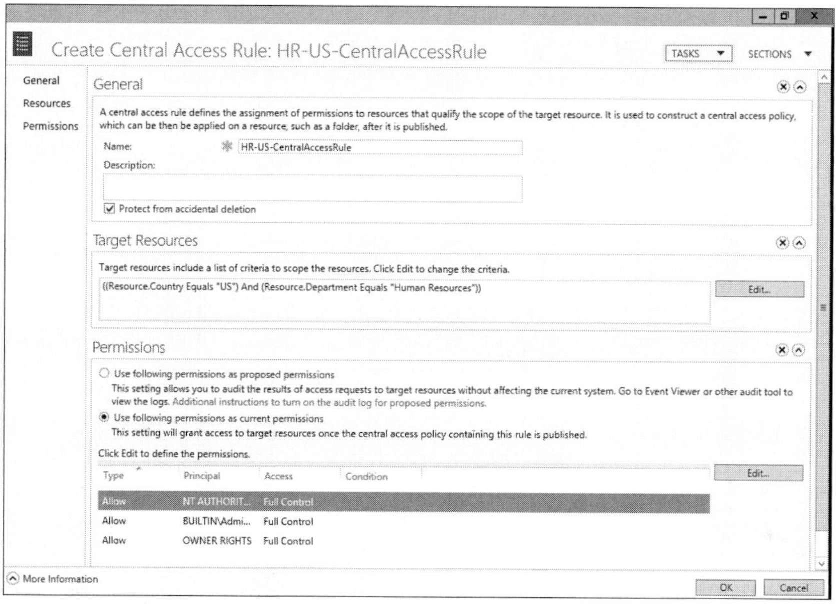

FIGURE 28.30 Creating the central access rule.

Creating and Assigning a Central Access Policy GPO to File Servers

To allow file servers to leverage the DAC infrastructure, a few tasks need to be performed. One requirement is that the desired file servers are running Windows Server 2012 and the File Server Resource Manager file role service has already been installed. The service installation is covered earlier in this chapter. Another requirement is that the file server is configured to use a central access policy. This can be performed by creating and assigning a group policy to delivers the required settings, as outlined in the following steps:

1. Log on to a Windows Server 2012 domain controller with an account in the Domain Admins group.

2. Open Server Manager, click Tools, and open the Group Policy Management Console.

3. In the GPMC, expand the Forest and Domains node to reveal the desired domain and the Group Policy objects container within.

4. Select the Group Policy Objects container and create a new GPO named DACFileServerGPO.

5. Once the new GPO is created, select it, and in the Security Filtering section, remove the Authenticated Users security group and add in the desired file server computer objects, as shown in Figure 28.31 (for our example, file server FILESERVER1 and FILESERVER2).

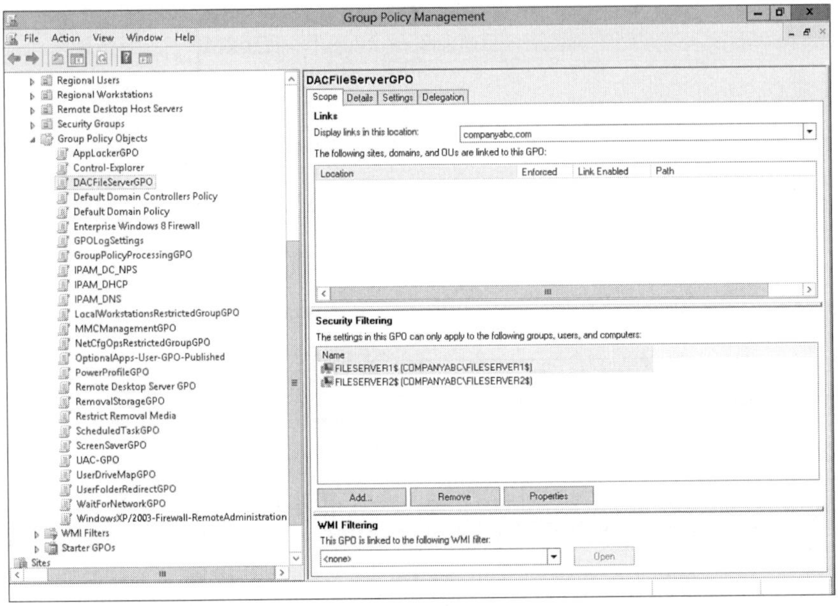

FIGURE 28.31 Configuring the security filtering on the DAC GPO.

6. Once the Security Filtering is configured property, right-click the GPO and open it for editing.

7. In the Group Policy Management Editor window, navigate to Computer Configuration\Policies\Windows Settings\Security Settings\File System, and then click the Central Access Policy node.

8. Right-click the Central Access Policy node and select Manage Central Access Policies. When the Central Access Policies window opens, the previously created policy should be listed. Double-click the policy to move it from the Available Policies to the Application Policies section of the window, as shown in Figure 28.32, and then click OK.

9. The central access policy previously created should now be listed in the right-hand pane of the GPO. Close the Group Policy Management Editor window.

10. Once the policy has been defined, link the new policy to the OU that contains the desired file servers, or link the policy to the domain since the security filtering is configured to only include the desired file servers.

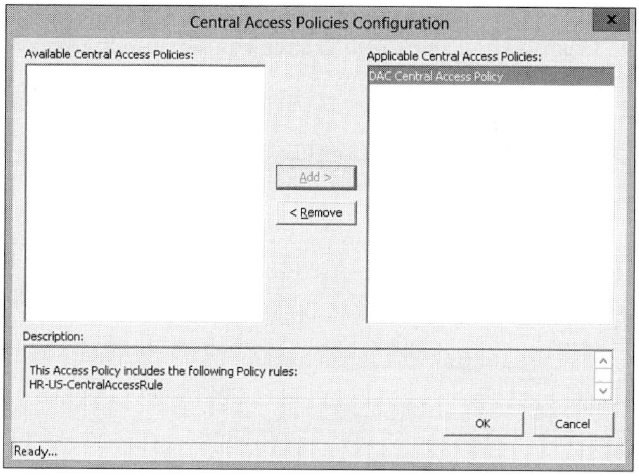

FIGURE 28.32 Adding the central access policy to the GPO.

After this policy has been created and linked, the desired file server should be forced to update group policy, or the administrators should give ample time for background policy processing to run so this new policy can be applied.

Enabling Kerberos Armoring for Domain Controllers

The next step is to configure the domain controllers to include DAC information in the Kerberos authentication tickets that are granted to users for data access and authorization. The basis for DAC is Kerberos authentication and authorization, and DAC will not function if organizations' Active Directory infrastructures rely on third-party Kerberos realm trusts or NTLM as the primary authentication and authorization systems. To enable DAC functionality for Kerberos, known as Kerberos armoring, on the organization's domain controllers, all domain controllers will require this change.

This change will be applied to all domain controllers by creating a new GPO and linking it to the domain controllers Organizational Unit. To enable Kerberos armoring on all the domain controllers, follow these steps:

1. Log on to a Windows Server 2012 domain controller with an account in the Domain Admins group.
2. Open Server Manager, click Tools, and open the Group Policy Management Console.
3. In the GPMC, expand the Forest and Domains node to reveal the desired domain and the Group Policy Objects container within.
4. Select the Group Policy Objects container, create a new GPO named KerberosArmoringGPO and open it for editing.
5. In the Group Policy Management Editor window, navigate to the Computer Configuration\Policies\Administrative Templates\System\KDC node and open the Support Dynamic Access Control and Kerberos Armoring setting.

6. Select the Enabled radial button, and in the Options leave the default option of Supported, as shown in Figure 28.33, and then click OK to save the setting changes. Then close the Group Policy Management Editor window.

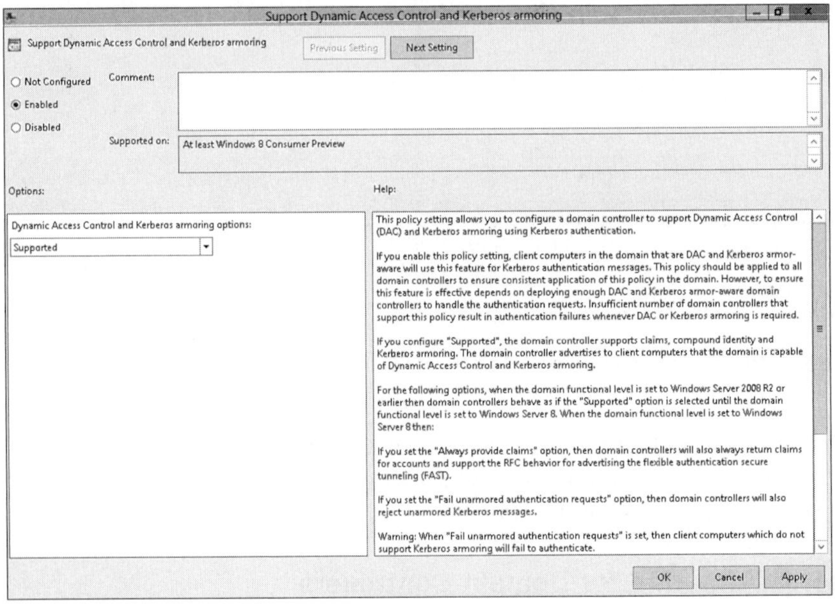

FIGURE 28.33 Enabling DAC and Kerberos armoring in the default domain controller policy.

7. After the policy setting has been updated and the policy has been closed, back in the GPMC window and link the new GPO to the Domain Controllers OU.

8. Navigate to the Domain Controllers OU, right-click the OU, and select Group Policy Update. Then, click Yes in the confirmation window to kick off Group Policy processing on all the domain controllers. Close the results window and close the GPMC.

Creating and Updating a File Share to Leverage Dynamic Access Control

Now the only remaining configuration steps include configuring the data on the file servers themselves. To configure a shared folder on a file server to leverage DAC, follow these steps:

1. Log on to a Windows Server 2012 file server that has the FSRM file role service installed and the previously created Central Access Policy GPO applied to it. Make sure the logon account is a domain user and is a member of the local administrators group on the file server.

2. Open the desired NTFS volume, and as an example, on the F drive create a root folder named DeptShare and share it with default share and NTFS permission to give administrators Full Control and Users Read/Write Access.
3. Create a subfolder name HR-US-DATA beneath the F:\DeptShare folder. Right-click the new folder and select the Classification tab.
4. On the Classification tab, if group policy processing has already occurred, the resource properties previously assigned to the central access rule should be listed. Select the Country property in the top of the window, and in the Value section below, select US. Select the Department property, and in the Value section, select Human Resources, and then click Apply, as shown in Figure 28.34.

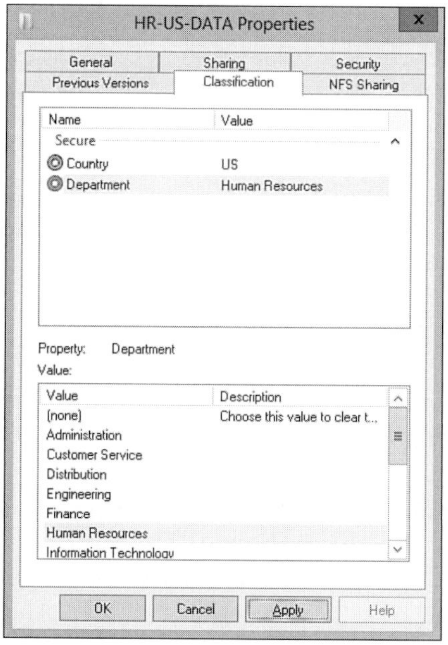

FIGURE 28.34 Configuring the folder classification property values.

The previous four steps assigned the property values to the folder. Now we will configure the security settings of the folder to force uses to match their claims to the folder's classification properties, as follows:

1. On the same folder that was previously configured, open the properties of the folder and select the Security tab and click the Advanced button.
2. Select the Central Policy tab and click the Change link. Pull down the Central Policy menu and select the DAC Central Policy that was previously created, and the rule will be listed below, as shown in Figure 28.35.

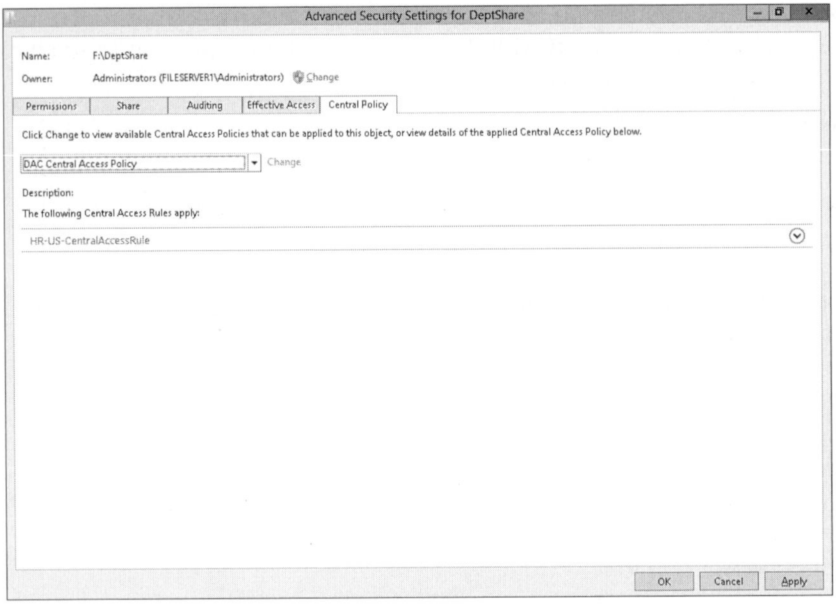

FIGURE 28.35 Assigning the central access policy to the folder.

This completes the file server configuration steps. Repeat these steps on any other folders and on additional file servers as required.

Configuring User Accounts and Testing Data Access

After the file servers are configured, the user accounts will need to be configured. For our example, we had a user name Colby in the Human Resources department in the United States, and a user named Jamil in the Human Resource department in Brazil. To configure the user account attributes to enable the user claims to match the folder resource properties and the rules, follow these steps:

1. Log on to a Windows Server 2012 domain controller with an account in the Domain Admins and Enterprise Admins security groups.
2. Open Server Manager, click Tools, and open the Active Directory Administrative Center console.
3. In the tree pane, click Global Search, and in the Search pane, type in the username and press Enter (for this example, we will search for Colby).
4. When the user is located, double-click the user to open the user account property pages.
5. Add in the desired value for the department attribute and pull down and select the desired country and click OK, as shown in Figure 28.36. Repeat this process for other users.

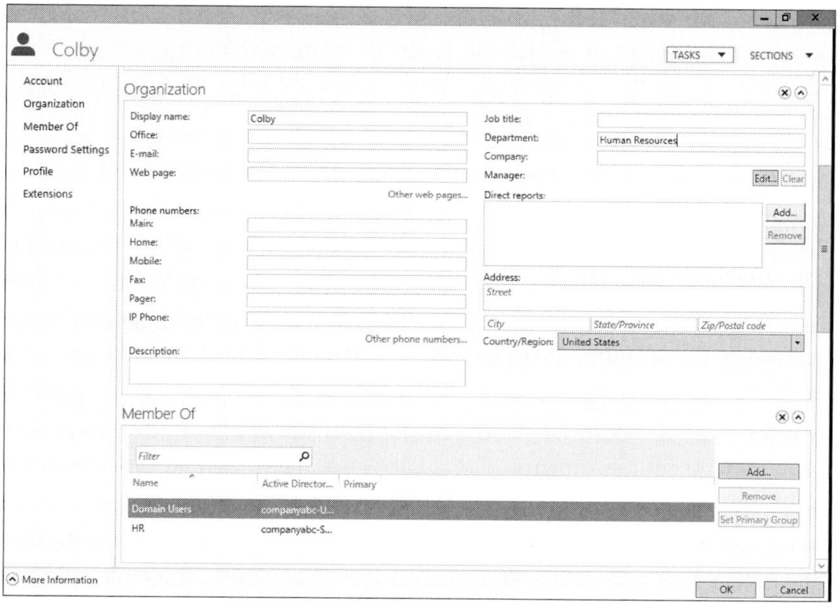

FIGURE 28.36 Configuring the user account properties.

6. Log on to a Windows Server 2012 or a Windows 8 system with the user account and try to access the DAC secured data to verify that users with the correct matching attributes can access the data, and that those not matching are denied.

One important point to note with the previously outlined scenario and solution is that the department value is a string that needs to match exactly, and using attributes like this can become problematic if the data is entered manually. Also, certain user contact attributes can be edited by the end user. So, when configured central access rules are going to compare resource properties against user claims based on attributes, ensure that the user attributes selected are not editable by the end users themselves.

Summary

Windows Server 2012 file services give administrators several options when it comes to building fault-tolerant servers, configuring data storage, and securing access to data. Through services such as the Volume Shadow Copy Service, deleted or overwritten files can be restored automatically or by an administrator without restoring from backup. Using services such as the Distributed File System and Distributed File System Replication, administrators have more flexibility when it comes to deploying, securing, and providing high-availability file services. Through the new Storage Spaces feature, administrators have a lot of flexibility with building and expanding fault-tolerant virtual disks. Through the Data Deduplication service, administrators can maximize storage usage by removing duplicate data. And finally, with this first release of Dynamic Access Control, administrators and organizations can easily add in additional layers of security to control access to sensitive data. Using just one or a combination of these file system services, organizations can truly make their file systems optimized, fault tolerant, easy to recover, very scalable, and tightly secured.

Best Practices

The following are best practices from this chapter:

- Use the Volume Shadow Copy Service to provide file recoverability and data fault tolerance to minimize the number of times you have to restore from backup.
- Try to provide disk fault tolerance for your operating system and data drives, preferably using hardware-based RAID sets, through the use of Windows fault-tolerant volumes or by deploying resilient mirrored or parity virtual disks on storage pools that include multiple physical disks.
- Use NTFS or reFS on all volumes to enable additional file system functionality and security. Only use NTFS on system drives and on drives that will leverage file classification and Dynamic Access Control.
- Always define share permissions for every share regardless of the volume format type.
- Replace the Everyone group with the Domain Users group when shares are created on domain servers and anonymous or guest access is not required, and set the share permissions accordingly.
- Use domain-based DFS roots whenever possible.
- Use DFS to provide a unified namespace to file data.
- Use Window Server 2008 mode on domain-based namespaces to enable access-based enumeration and more scalability.
- Start with an empty DFS root folder to keep from having to replicate any data at the root level, and do not create any replication groups based on the namespace root folder.
- When deploying domain-based DFS namespace, add additional namespace servers for redundancy.
- Replicate DFS data only during off-peak hours to reduce network congestion or restrict replication with bandwidth constraints if WAN links are heavily used during business hours.
- Back up at least one DFS folder target, and configure the backup to not update the archive bit to avoid possible unnecessary replication.
- Test antivirus programs thoroughly to ensure that no adverse effects are caused by the scanning of files on a replicated DFS folder target.

- Verify that the drive containing the staging folder for a replication connection contains ample space to accept the amount of replicated data inbound and outbound to this server and adjust the staging folder quote for each replication group as required.
- When creating virtual disks within storage pools, create resilient disks by selecting either a mirror or parity disk layout.
- If user claims based on attributes will be used to compare against resource properties assigned to folder classifications, ensure that the user attributes selected are not editable by the end users themselves.

CHAPTER 29

System-Level Fault Tolerance (Clustering / Network Load Balancing)

IN THIS CHAPTER

- Building Fault-Tolerant Windows Server 2012 Systems
- Windows Server 2012 Clustering Technologies
- Determining the Correct Clustering Technology
- Overview of Failover Clusters
- Deploying Failover Clusters
- Backing Up and Restoring Failover Clusters
- Deploying Network Load Balancing Clusters
- Managing NLB Clusters
- Network Teaming

Most businesses today rely heavily on their computer and network infrastructure. Internet access and email rate among the more important, but Voice over IP (VoIP), file, print, and of course, core authentication and networking services can be just as critical to many businesses. If service is interrupted to one or more of these systems, the impact to the business can be huge. When computer and network operation is critical to business operations, deploying a fault-tolerant computer and network infrastructure might be required.

Windows Server 2012 provides several methods of improving system-level fault tolerance by leveraging some of the roles, role services, and features included in the different editions of the operating system. For example, as detailed in Chapter 28, "File System Management and Fault Tolerance," the Distributed File System (DFS) can be used to create and deploy redundant and automatically synchronized file data through DFS shares and DFS Replication (DFSR). Another example of providing redundant services is to design an infrastructure that includes multiple Dynamic Host Configuration Protocol (DHCP) servers configured with DHCP failover scopes.

Windows Server 2012 provides many functions and services that can extend and enhance the reliability and resilience of computer and networking services. Many services, however, are only available when deployed on specific hardware platforms and when deployed on the Enterprise or Datacenter Editions of Windows Server 2012.

This chapter covers system-level fault tolerance using Windows Server 2012 Network Load Balancing (NLB) and failover clusters. These built-in clustering technologies provide load-balancing and failover capabilities that can be used to increase fault tolerance for many different types of applications and network services. Choosing the right Windows Server 2012 clustering technology depends on the roles that will be hosted by the cluster.

This chapter focuses on the setup and deployment of the Windows Server 2012 clustering technologies, NLB, and failover clusters, including predeployment checklists to ensure that the server hardware is more reliable.

Building Fault-Tolerant Windows Server 2012 Systems

Building fault-tolerant Windows Server 2012 systems by utilizing the built-in clustering technologies consists of carefully planning and configuring of server hardware and software, planning and configuring the network devices that connect the server to the network, and providing reliable power for the systems. Purchasing high-quality server, network, and storage hardware is a good start to building a reliable system, but the proper configuration of this hardware is equally, if not more important. Also, providing this equipment with reliable power and redundant backup power from can increase reliability of the servers as well as the networking infrastructure. Last, but not least, properly tuning the server operating systems to streamline performance for the desired roles, role services, features, and applications helps enhance server availability and stability.

Powering the Computer and Network Infrastructure

Powering Windows Server 2012 servers and network hardware with battery/generator-backed power sources not only provides these devices with conditioned line power by removing voltage spikes and providing steady line voltage levels, but it also provides alternative power when unexpected blackouts or brownouts occur. Many organizations cannot afford to implement redundant power sources or generators to power the offices, datacenters, and server rooms. For these organizations, the best approach to providing reliable power to the computer and network infrastructure is to deploy uninterruptible power supplies (UPSs) with battery-backed power. When the line power fails, the UPS can provide ample time for end users to save their data to the server and to gracefully shut down the server or network device without risk of damaging hardware or corrupting data.

UPS manufacturers commonly provide software that can send network notifications, run scripts, or even gracefully shut down servers automatically when power thresholds are reached. Of course, if end-user data is important, each end-user workstation and the network infrastructure should also be protected with battery-backup UPSs.

One final word on power is that most computer and network hardware manufacturers offer device configurations that incorporate redundant power supplies designed to keep the system powered up in the event of a single power supply failure.

Designing Fault-Tolerant IP Networks

Network design can also incorporate fault tolerance by creating redundant network routes and by utilizing technologies that can group devices together for the purposes of load balancing and device failover. Load balancing is the process of spreading requests across multiple devices to keep individual device load at an acceptable level. Failover is the process of moving services offered on one device to another upon device failure, to maintain availability. Common scenarios for creating fault-tolerant IP networks can include the following:

- **Acquiring multiple Internet connections**—This includes using different Internet service providers and, hopefully, each of the connections is not connected to the same external telco box on the street as this becomes the single point of failure if hit by a car, truck, or cut off from communications.
- **Deploying multiple and redundant firewalls, virtual private networks (VPNs), and network routers that will failover to one another**—These devices, when deployed in redundant load balanced configurations, can be leveraged in an active/passive or in active/active configuration that disperses or distributes the load and requests across each device and when a single device fails, the remaining device handles the entire load.
- **Deploying critical servers with multiple network adapters connected to separate network switches**—This allows a server to be connected and available on different switches in case a single network card in the server fails or if the port or the entire network switch.
- **Deploying hardware-based NLB devices**—Many network switches, routers, and certain devices created just for this purpose can provide the functionality also included in Windows Server 2012 NLB. This, of course, might be the best choice for load balancing at the network level when organizations deploy and support systems other than Windows Server 2012 and when they also need to load-balance network devices, such as firewalls and VPN devices.

Designing Fault-Tolerant Server Disks

Windows Server 2012 systems that will be used for NLB or failover clusters are usually deployed with local disk storage. When local disks are used to provide the operating system and application or service core files, the local disks should be deployed using redundant, fault-tolerant configurations. There are three ways to add fault tolerance to the local disks in a Windows Server 2012 system. The first is creating redundant arrays of inexpensive disks (RAID) using hardware-based disk controller configuration utilities (hardware-level RAID), the second is creating the RAID disks using dynamic disks using the Disk Management console from within the operating system (known as software-level RAID), and the third is by using resilient virtual disks in storage pools. The resilient virtual disks however cannot be used or configure for disks that contain operating system files.

Using two or more disks, different RAID types can be configured to provide fault tolerance that can withstand disk failures and still provide uninterrupted disk access. Implementing hardware-level RAID, which is configured, stored, and managed by the system's disk controllers is preferred over the software-level RAID configurable within Windows Server 2012. Windows Server 2012 dynamic disk mirrored and RAID-5 volumes are managed by the system and add some load to the system. In addition, another good reason to provide hardware-level RAID is that the configuration of the disks does not depend on the operating system, which gives administrators greater flexibility when it comes to recovering server systems and performing upgrades. For more information about disk configuration options, see Chapter 28 of this book. For detailed information about how to best configure RAID arrays using local disk controllers, refer to the manufacturer's documentation.

As a best practice, Windows Server 2012 can be deployed with the operating system disks stored on hardware based RAID-1 (mirrored) disks and presented to the operating system as disk zero, where the system "C" volume is created. A second disk and volume in the system can be used to store application data and files and, when possible, this data should be placed on different redundant disks as a best practice.

Increasing Windows Server 2012 Role Availability

A Windows Server 2012 role's reliability is greatly dependent on the underlying software code, the hardware the system is running on, and how it interacts with the host operating system. Windows Server 2012 is a very stable platform partly because third-party applications and services must use only the system files provided by Microsoft when interacting with the operating system and the system hardware. Furthermore, when third-party roles require additional drivers, these drivers must be certified for Windows Server 2012 and the drivers must be digitally signed by the Windows Quality Hardware labs to ensure the highest reliability. Administrators can disable the strict device driver signing requirements, but on failover clusters, this would place the system in an unsupported configuration and is not advisable. Remember that the only reason to deploy failover clusters or NLB clusters is to provide high availability or very scalable services; deploying systems using unsigned or untested drivers can reduce the overall reliability of each system and the entire cluster.

Windows Server 2012 Clustering Technologies

Windows Server 2012 provides two clustering technologies, which are included in all editions. Clustering is the grouping of independent server nodes that are accessed and viewed on the network as a single system. When a service/application is run from a cluster, the end user can connect to a single cluster node to perform his work, or each request can be handled by multiple nodes in the cluster. In cases where data is read-only, the client might request data from one server in the cluster and the next request might be made to a different server and the client may never know the difference. Also, if a single node on a multiple node cluster fails, the remaining nodes continue to service client requests, and depending on the clustered service or application, the client may never experience a disruption in service.

The first clustering technology provided with Windows Server 2012 is failover clusters. Failover clusters provide system fault tolerance through a process called failover. When a system or node in the cluster fails or is unable to respond to client requests, the clustered role service that were running on that particular node are possibly taken offline and moved to another available node where functionality and access are fully restored. The reason the services are possibly taken offline is that some services can make use of the latest Windows Server 2012 failover cluster features that share memory and client sessions across nodes, to allow for seamless service moves between cluster nodes. In most deployments, however, clients may experience slight interruptions in service or may need to reconnect to the service after a failover process has occurred. Many failover cluster designs require access to shared storage and are best suited, but not necessarily limited to, the deployment of the following roles:

- **File servers**—File services on failover clusters provide much of the same functionality a standalone Windows Server 2012 system can provide, but when deployed as a clustered file server, a single data storage repository can be presented and accessed by clients through the currently assigned and available cluster node without replicating the file data.
- **Print servers**—Print services deployed on failover clusters have one main advantage over standalone print servers: If the print server fails, each of the shared printers is made available to clients using the same print server name. Although deploying and replacing printers to computers and users is easily managed using Group Policy deployed printers, when standalone print servers fail, the impact can be huge.
- **Database servers**—When large organizations deploy critical business systems that require a back-end database server, deploying the database servers on failover clusters is the preferred method. In many cases installing and configuring an enterprise database server can take hours and the size of the databases can be huge, so deploying database servers on standalone systems and rebuilding these systems in the event of a single server system failure might take several hours or days to rebuild. This is another reason building databases on failover clusters is beneficial.
- **Back-end enterprise messaging systems**—For many of the same reasons as cited previously for deploying database servers, enterprise messaging services have become critical to many organizations and are best deployed in failover clusters. Microsoft Exchange 2010 leverages failover cluster services, but does not however get configured and managed within the failover cluster tools. For more information about deploying redundant Exchange messaging services, refer to Microsoft Exchange documentation.
- **Hyper-V virtual machines**– As many organizations continue to move toward server consolidation and conversion of physical servers to virtual servers, providing a means to also maintain high availability and reliability has become even more important when a single physical Hyper-V host has several critical virtual machines running on it. Windows Server 2012 Hyper-V and failover cluster include several

new features that make Hyper-V even more resilient to single system issues. For more information about Hyper-V high-availability designs, see Chapter 36, "Deploying and Using Windows Virtualization."

The second Windows Server 2012 clustering technology is Network Load Balancing (NLB), which is best suited to provide fault tolerance for front-end web applications and websites, Remote Desktop Services Session Host server systems, VPN servers, and proxy servers. NLB provides fault tolerance by having each server in the cluster individually run the network-based service or application, removing any single points of failure. Depending on the particular needs of the service or application deployed on an NLB cluster, there are different configuration or affinity options to determine how clients will be connected to the back-end NLB cluster nodes. For example, on a read-only website, client requests can be directed to any of the NLB cluster nodes; during a single visit to a website, a client might be connected to different NLB cluster nodes. As another example, when a client attempts to utilize an SSL secured website, the client session should be initiated and serviced by a single node in the cluster, as this session will contain specific session data.

NOTE

Microsoft does not support running failover clusters and NLB on the same Windows Server 2012 system.

Windows Server 2012 Cluster Terminology

Before failover or NLB clusters can be designed and implemented, the administrator deploying the solution should be familiar with the general terms used to define the clustering technologies. The following list contains the many terms associated with Windows Server 2012 clustering technologies:

- **Cluster**—A cluster is a group of independent servers (nodes) that are accessed and presented to the network as a single system.
- **Node**—A node is an individual server that is a member of a cluster.
- **Cluster resource**—A cluster resource is a service, application, IP address, disk, or network name defined and managed by the cluster. Within a cluster, cluster resources are grouped and managed together using cluster resource groups, now known as role groups.
- **Role group**—Cluster resources are contained within a cluster in a logical set called a role group or historically referred to as a cluster or services and applications group. Role groups are the units of failover within the cluster. When a cluster resource fails and cannot be restarted automatically, the role group this resource is a part of will be taken offline, moved to another node in the cluster, and the group will be brought back online.
- **Client access point**—A client access point is a term used in Windows Server 2012 failover cluster that represents the combination of a network name and associated IP

address resource. By default, when a new role group is defined, a client access point is created with a name and an IPv4 address. IPv6 is supported in failover clusters, but an IPv6 resource either needs to be added to an existing group or a generic role group needs to be created with the necessary resources and resource dependencies.

- **Virtual cluster server**—A virtual cluster is a service or application group that contains a client access point, a disk resource, and at least one additional role resource. Virtual cluster server resources are accessed either by the domain name system (DNS) name or a NetBIOS name that references an IPv4 or IPv6 address. A virtual cluster server can in some cases also be directly accessed using the IPv4 or IPv6 address. The name and IP address remain the same regardless of which cluster node the virtual server is running on.
- **Active node**—An active node is a node in the cluster that is currently running at least one role group. A role group can only be active on one node at a time and all other nodes that can host the group are considered passive for that particular group.
- **Passive node**—A passive node is a node in the cluster that is currently not running any role groups.
- **Active/passive cluster**—An active/passive cluster is a cluster that has at least one node running a role group and additional nodes the group can be hosted on, but are currently in a waiting state. This is a typical configuration when only a single role group is deployed on a failover cluster.
- **Active/active cluster**—An active/active cluster is a cluster in which each node is actively hosting or running at least one role group. This is a typical configuration when multiple groups are deployed on a single failover cluster to maximize server or system usage. The downside is that when an active system fails, the remaining system or systems need to host all the groups and provide the role service on the cluster to all necessary clients.
- **Cluster heartbeat**—The cluster heartbeat is a term used to represent the communication that is kept between individual cluster nodes to determine node status. Heartbeat communication can occur on a designated network but is also performed on the same network as client communication. Due to this internode communication, network monitoring software and network administrators should be forewarned of the amount of network chatter between the cluster nodes. The amount of traffic that is generated by heartbeat communication is not large based on the size of the data but the frequency of the communication may initially trigger monitoring notifications.
- **Cluster quorum**—The cluster quorum maintains the definitive cluster configuration data and the current state of each node, each role group, and each resource and network in the cluster. Furthermore, when each node reads the quorum data, depending on the information retrieved, the node determines whether it should remain available, shut down the cluster, or activate any particular role groups on the local node. To extend this even further, failover clusters can be configured to use one of four different cluster quorum models. The quorum type used within a cluster

also defines the type cluster. For example, a cluster that utilizes the Node and Disk Majority Quorum can be called a Node and Disk Majority cluster.

- **Cluster witness disk or file share**—The cluster witness or the witness file share are used to store the cluster configuration information and to help determine the state of the cluster when some, if not all, of the cluster nodes cannot be contacted.
- **Generic cluster resources**—Generic cluster resources were created to define and add new or undefined services, applications, or scripts that are not already included as available cluster resources. Adding a custom resource provides the ability for that resource to be failed over between cluster nodes when another resource in the same role group fails. Also, when the group the custom resource is a member of moves to a different node, the custom resource will follow. One disadvantage or lack of functionality with custom resources is that the Failover Cluster feature cannot actively monitor the resource and, thereby, cannot provide the same level of resilience and recoverability as with predefined cluster resources. Generic cluster resources include the generic application, generic script, and generic service resource.
- **Shared storage**—Shared storage is a term used to represent the disks and volumes presented to the Windows Server 2012 cluster nodes as logical unit numbers (LUNs).
- **Cluster Shared Volumes (CSV)**– A disk or LUN defined within the cluster that can be accessed by multiple nodes in the cluster simultaneously. This is unlike any other cluster volume, which normally can only be accessed by one node at a time. CSVs are one of the main building blocks for clusters that cannot tolerate any downtime. CSVs have their uses, but be sure that the actual role, service, or application that will be clustered is supported on CSV volumes, and be sure the backup software can support it.
- **LUN**—LUN stands for logical unit number. A LUN is used to identify a disk or a disk volume that is presented to a host server or multiple hosts by a shared storage device or storage-area network (SAN). Of course, there are shared storage controllers, firmware, drivers, and physical connections between the server and the shared storage, but the concept is that a LUN or set of LUNs is presented to the server for use as a local disk.
- **Failover**—Failover is the process of a role group moving from the current active node to another available node in the cluster. Failover occurs when a server becomes unavailable or when a resource in the cluster group fails and cannot recover within the failure threshold. Failover can also be performed manually for maintenance of a cluster node.
- **Failback**—Failback is the process of a cluster group automatically moving back to a preferred node after the preferred node resumes cluster membership. Failback is a nondefault configuration that can be enabled within the properties of a role group. The cluster group must have a preferred node defined and a failback threshold configured for failback to function. A preferred node is the node you would like your cluster group to be running or hosted on during regular cluster operation when all cluster nodes are available. When a group is failing back, the cluster is performing

the same failover operation but is triggered by the preferred node rejoining or resuming cluster operation instead of by a resource failure on the currently active node.

- **Live Migration**—Live Migration is a feature of failover clusters running Windows Server 2008 R2 or Windows Server 2012. Live Migration enables Hyper-V virtual machines on the failover cluster to be moved between cluster nodes without disrupting communication or access to the virtual machine. Live Migration utilizes a cluster shared volume that is accessed by all nodes in the group simultaneously and it transfers the memory between the nodes during active client communication to maintain availability.
- **Quick Migration**—With Hyper-V virtual machines on failover clusters, a quick migration provides the option of failover cluster administrators to move the virtual machine to another node without shutting the virtual machine off. This utilizes the virtual machines shutdown settings options, and if set to Save, the default setting, performing a quick migration will save the current memory state, move the virtual machine to the desired node, and resume operation shortly. End users should only encounter a short disruption in service but should reconnect usually without issue depending on the service or application hosted within that virtual machine, Quick Migration does not require CSVs to function.
- **Storage Migration**—Hyper-V failover cluster virtual machines can now have their underlying storage moved to different disk using a wizard. This enables a lot of flexibility when adding, removing or taking storage offline as the virtual machine never needs to be exported/imported or recreated.
- **Continuously Available file shares**—Continuously Available (CA) file shares is a new file sharing feature that is built to run on top of Window Server failover clusters. In previous Windows Server failover cluster file servers, when file services were transferred between cluster nodes, client connections would be disrupted or completely disconnected. With Windows Server 2012 File Services, file servers clusters include a new type named Scale-Out file servers that enable failover to occur without client connections being disrupted or disconnected during the transfer between cluster nodes. This functionality requires the file server cluster to be deployed on cluster shared volumes.
- **Geographically dispersed clusters**—These are clusters that span physical locations and sometimes networks to provide failover functionality in remote buildings/datacenters, usually across a wide-area network (WAN) link. These clusters can now span different networks and can provide failover functionality but network response and throughput must be good. Data replication is not handled by the failover cluster.
- **Multisite cluster**—Geographically dispersed clusters can and are commonly referred to as multisite clusters as cluster nodes are deployed in different Active Directory sites. Multisite clusters can provide access to resources across a WAN and can support automatic failover of role groups defined within the cluster.
- **Stretch clusters**– Stretch clusters is a common term thrown around that, in some cases, refers to geographically dispersed clusters in which different subnets are

used but each of the subnets are part of the same Active Directory site (hence the term *stretch*, as is stretch the AD site across the WAN). Otherwise this term is used to describe a geographically dispersed cluster, as in the cluster stretches between geographic locations.

Determining the Correct Clustering Technology

For either of the Windows Server 2012 fault-tolerant clustering technologies to be most effective, administrators must carefully choose which technology and configuration best fits their application or service requirements. NLB is best suited to provide connectivity to TCP/IP-based services such as Remote Desktop Services, web-based roles, VPN services, streaming media, and proxy services. NLB is easily scalable, and the number of clients that can be supported is based on the number of clients a single NLB cluster node can support multiplied by the number of nodes in the cluster. Windows Server 2012 failover clusters provide system failover functionality for mission-critical applications, such as enterprise messaging, databases, file servers, print services, DHCP services, Hyper-V virtualization services, and many other built-in Windows Server 2012 roles, role services, and features.

Although Microsoft does not support using both NLB and failover clusters on the same server, multitiered applications can take advantage of both technologies by using NLB to load-balance front-end application servers and using failover clusters to provide failover capabilities to back-end databases that contain data too large to replicate during the day or if the back end cannot withstand more than a few minutes of downtime if a node or service encounters a failure.

Failover Clusters

Windows Server 2012 failover clusters are a clustering technology that provides system-level fault tolerance by using a process called failover. Failover clusters are best used to provide access to resources such as file shares, print queues, email or database services, and back-end applications. Applications and network services defined and managed by the failover cluster, along with cluster hardware including shared disk storage and network cards, are called cluster resources. When roles are cluster aware or certified to work with Windows Server 2012 failover clusters, they are monitored and managed by the cluster service to ensure proper operation.

When a problem is encountered with a cluster resource, the failover cluster service attempts to fix the problem by restarting the resource and any dependent resources. If that doesn't work, the role group the resource is a member of is failed over to another available node in the cluster, where it can then be restarted. Several conditions can cause a role group to failover to a different cluster node. Failover can occur when an active node in the cluster loses power or network connectivity or suffers a hardware or software failure. In most cases, the failover process is either noticed by the clients as a short disruption of service or is not noticed at all. Of course, if failback is configured on a particular role group and the group is simply not stable, it will be continually moved back and forth between nodes until the failback threshold is reached. When this happens, the group will be shut down and remain offline by the cluster service.

To avoid unwanted failover, power management should be disabled on each of the cluster nodes in the motherboard BIOS, on the network interface cards (NICs), and in the Power applet in the operating system's Control Panel. Power settings that allow a display to shut off are okay, but the administrator must make sure that the disks are configured to never go into Standby mode as well as each of the network cards.

Cluster nodes can monitor the status of resources running on their local system, and they can also keep track of other nodes in the cluster through private network communication messages called heartbeats. Heartbeat communication is used to determine the status of a node and send updates of cluster configuration changes and the state of each node to the cluster quorum.

The cluster quorum contains the cluster configuration data necessary to restore a cluster to a working state. Each node in the cluster needs to have access to the quorum resource, regardless of which quorum model is chosen or the node will not be able to participate in the cluster. This prevents something called split-brain syndrome, where two nodes in the same cluster both believe they are the active node and try to control the shared resource at the same time or worse, each node can present their own set of data, when separate datasets are available, which will cause changes in both datasets and a whirlwind of proceeding issues. Windows Server 2012 provides four different quorum models, which are detailed in the section "Failover Cluster Quorum Models" later in this chapter.

Network Load Balancing

The second clustering technology provided with Windows Server 2012 is Network Load Balancing (NLB). NLB clusters provide high network performance, availability, and redundancy by balancing client requests across several servers with replicated configurations. When client load increases, NLB clusters can easily be scaled out by adding more nodes to the cluster to maintain or provide better response time to client requests. One important point to note now is that NLB does not itself replicate server configuration or application datasets.

Two great features of NLB are that no proprietary hardware is needed and an NLB cluster can be configured and up and running literally in minutes. One important point to remember is that within NLB clusters, each server's configuration must be updated independently. The NLB administrator is responsible for making sure that application or service configuration, version and operating system security, and updates and data are kept consistent across each NLB cluster node. For details on installing NLB, see the "Deploying Network Load Balancing Clusters" section later in this chapter.

Network Teaming

Network teaming is a function of networking that ties multiple network adapters together to provide load balancing and redundancy across multiple adapters on the single server or host. Failover clustering and NLB enable redundancy across multiple servers. Network teaming is configured on a per-host basis and can be used in conjunction with failover clustering or NLB to add network redundancy to the each cluster node before the cluster is even created.

Network teaming has been supported by Microsoft in previous Windows Server versions, on failover and NLB clusters, but with Windows Server 2012, this service is now built in. Creating a network team is detailed later in this chapter.

Overview of Failover Clusters

After an organization decides to cluster an application or service using failover clusters, it must then decide which cluster configuration model best suits the needs of the particular deployment. Failover clusters can be deployed using four different configuration models that will accommodate most deployment scenarios and requirements. The four configuration models in this case are defined by the quorum model selected: the Node Majority Quorum, Node and Disk Majority Quorum, Node and File Share Majority Quorum, and the No Majority: Disk Only Quorum.

Failover Cluster Quorum Models

As previously stated, Windows Server 2012 failover clusters support four different cluster quorum models. Each of these four models is best suited for specific configurations, but if all the nodes and shared storage are configured, specified, and available during the installation of the failover cluster, the best-suited quorum model is automatically selected.

Node Majority Quorum

The Node Majority Quorum model has been designed for failover cluster deployments that contain an odd number of cluster nodes. When determining the quorum state of the cluster, only the number of available nodes is counted. A cluster using the Node Majority Quorum is called a Node Majority cluster. A Node Majority cluster remains up and running if the number of available nodes exceeds the number of failed nodes. For example, in a five-node cluster, three nodes must be available for the cluster to remain online. If three nodes fail in a five-node Node Majority cluster, the entire cluster is shut down. Node Majority clusters have been designed and are well suited for geographically or network dispersed cluster nodes, but for this configuration to be supported by Microsoft, it takes serious effort, quality hardware, a third-party mechanism to replicate any back-end data, and a very reliable network. Once again, this model works well for clusters with an odd number of nodes.

Node and Disk Majority Quorum

The Node and Disk Majority Quorum model determines whether a cluster can continue to function by counting the number of available nodes and the availability of the cluster witness disk. Using this model, the cluster quorum is stored on a cluster disk that is accessible and made available to all nodes in the cluster through a shared storage device using Serial Attached SCSI (SAS), Fibre Channel, or iSCSI connections. This model is the closest to the traditional single-quorum device cluster configuration model and is composed of two or more server nodes that are all connected to a shared storage device. In this model, only one copy of the quorum data is maintained on the witness disk. This model is well suited for failover clusters using shared storage, all connected on the same network with an even number of nodes. For example, on a 2-, 4-, 6-, 8-, or 16-node cluster using this model, the cluster continues to function as long as half of the total nodes are available and can contact the witness disk. In the case of a witness disk failure, a majority of the nodes need to remain up and running for the cluster to continue to function. To calculate this, take half of the total nodes and add one, and this gives you the lowest number of available nodes that are required to keep a cluster running when the witness disk fails or goes offline. For example, on a six-node cluster using this model, if the witness disk fails, the cluster remains up and running as long as four nodes are available; but on a two-node cluster, if the witness disk fails, both nodes need to remain up and running for the cluster to function.

Node and File Share Majority Quorum

The Node and File Share Majority Quorum model is very similar to the Node and Disk Majority Quorum model, but instead of a witness disk, the quorum is stored on file share. The advantage of this model is that it can be deployed similarly to the Node Majority Quorum model, but as long as the witness file share is available, this model can tolerate the failure of half of the total nodes. This model is well suited for clusters with an even number of nodes that do not utilize shared storage or clusters that span sites. This is the preferred and recommended quorum configuration for geographically dispersed failover clusters.

No Majority: Disk Only Quorum

The No Majority: Disk Only Quorum model is best suited for testing the process and behavior of deploying built-in or custom services/applications on a Windows Server 2012 failover cluster. In this model, the cluster can sustain the failover of all nodes except one, as long as the disk containing the quorum remains available. The limitation of this model is that the disk containing the quorum becomes a single point of failure and that is why this model is not well suited for production deployments of failover clusters.

As a best practice, before deploying a failover cluster, determine whether shared storage will be used, verify that each node can communicate with each LUN presented by the shared storage device, and when the cluster is created, add all nodes to the list. This ensures that the correct recommended cluster quorum model is selected for the new failover cluster. When the recommended model utilizes shared storage and a witness disk, the smallest available LUN will be selected. This can be changed, if necessary, after the cluster is created.

Choosing Applications for Failover Clusters

Many applications can run on failover clusters, but it is important to choose and test those applications thoroughly. Although many can run on failover clusters, the application might not be optimized for clustering or may not be supported by the software vendor or Microsoft when deployed on Windows Server 2012 failover clusters. Work with the vendor to determine requirements, functionality, and limitations (if any). Other major criteria that should be met to ensure that an application can benefit and adapt to running on a cluster are the following:

- Because clustering is IP based, the cluster application or applications must use an IP-based protocol.
- Applications that require access to local databases must have the option of configuring where the data can be stored so a drive other than the system drive can be specified for data storage separate from the storage of the application source files.
- Some applications need to have access to data regardless of which cluster node they are running on. With these types of applications, it is recommended that the data is stored on a shared disk resource that will fail over with the role group. If an application will run and store data only on the local system or boot drive, the Node Majority Quorum or the Node and File Share Majority Quorum model should be used, along with a separate file replication mechanism for the application data.
- Client sessions must be able to reestablish connectivity if the application encounters a network disruption or fails over to an alternate cluster node. During most failover processes, there is no client connectivity until an application or service is brought back online. If the client software does not try to reconnect and simply times out when a network connection is disrupted, this application or service might not be well suited for failover or NLB clusters.

Cluster-aware applications that meet all the preceding criteria are usually the best applications to deploy in a Windows Server 2012 failover cluster. Many services built in to Windows Server 2012 can be clustered and will failover efficiently and properly. If a particular application is not cluster-aware, be sure to investigate all the implications of the application deployment on Windows Server 2012 failover clusters before deploying or spending any time prototyping the solution.

NOTE

If you're purchasing a third-party software package to use for Windows Server 2012 failover clustering, be sure that both Microsoft and the software manufacturer certify that it will work on Windows Server 2012 failover clusters; otherwise, support will be limited or nonexistent when troubleshooting is necessary.

Shared Storage for Failover Clusters

Shared disk storage is a requirement for Windows Server 2012 failover clusters using the Node and Disk Majority Quorum and the Disk Only Quorum models. Shared storage devices can be a part of any cluster configuration, and when they are used, the disks, disk volumes, or LUNs presented to the Windows systems must be presented as basic Windows disks.

All storage drivers must be digitally signed and certified for use with Windows Server 2012. Many storage devices certified for Windows Server 2003 or even Windows Server 2008 or 2008 R2 may not work with Windows Server 2012 and either simply cannot be used for failover cluster shared storage, or might require a firmware and driver upgrade to be supported.

When LUNS are presented to failover cluster nodes, each LUN must be presented to each node in the cluster. Also, when the shared storage is accessed by the cluster and other systems, the LUNs must be masked or presented only to the cluster nodes and the shared storage device controllers to ensure that no other systems can access or disrupt the cluster communication. There are strict requirements for shared storage support, especially with failover clusters. Using SANs or other types of shared storage must meet the following list of requirements and recommendations:

- All Fibre, SAS, and iSCSI host bus adapters (HBAs) and Ethernet cards used with iSCSI software initiators must obtain the Designed for Microsoft Windows logo for Windows Server 2012 and have suitable signed device drivers.
- SAS, Fibre, and iSCSI HBAs must use StorPort device drivers to provide targeted LUN resets and other functions inherent to the StorPort driver specification. SCSIport was at one point supported for two-node clusters, but if a StorPort driver is available, it should be used to ensure support from the hardware vendors and Microsoft.
- All shared storage HBAs and back-end storage devices, including iSCSI targets, Fibre, and SAS storage arrays, must support SCSI-3 standards and must also support persistent bindings or reservations of LUNs.
- All shared-storage HBAs must be deployed with matching firmware and driver versions. Failover clusters using shared storage require a very stable infrastructure and applying the latest storage controller driver to an outdated HBA firmware can cause very undesirable situations and might disrupt access to data.
- All nodes in the cluster should contain the same HBAs and use the same version of drivers and firmware. Each cluster node should be an exact duplicate of each other node when it comes to hardware selection, configuration, and driver and firmware revisions. This allows for a more reliable configuration and simplifies management and standardization.
- When iSCSI software initiators are used to connect to iSCSI software- or hardware-based targets, the network adapter used for iSCSI communication should be connected to a dedicated switch, should not be used for any cluster communication, and cannot be a teamed network adapter as teamed adapters are not supported with iSCSI.

Serial Attached SCSI Storage Arrays

Serial Attached SCSI, or SAS, storage arrays provide organizations with an affordable, entry-level, hardware-based direct attached storage arrays suitable for Windows Server 2012 clusters. SAS storage arrays commonly are limited to four hosts, but some models support extenders to add additional hosts as required. One of the major issues with direct attached storage is that replication of the data within the storage is usually not achievable without involving one of the host systems or software provided by the hardware vendor.

Fibre Channel Storage Arrays

Using Fibre Channel (FC) HBAs, Windows Server 2012 can access both shared and nonshared disks residing on a SAN connected to a common FC switch. This allows both the shared-storage and operating system volumes to be located on the SAN, if desired, to provide diskless servers. In many cases, however, diskless storage might not be desired if the operating system performs many paging actions because the cache on the storage controllers can be used up very fast and can cause delays in disk read and write operations for dedicated cluster storage. If this is desired, however, the SAN must support this option and be configured to present the operating system dedicated LUNs to only a single host exclusively. The LUNs defined for shared cluster storage must be zoned and presented to every node in the cluster, and no other systems. The LUN zoning or masking in many cases is configured on the Fibre Channel switch that connects the cluster nodes and the shared-storage device. This is a distinct difference between direct attached storage and FC or iSCSI shared storage. Both FC and iSCSI require a common fiber or Ethernet switch and network to establish and maintain connections between the hosts and the storage.

A properly configured FC zone for a cluster will include the World Wide Port Number (WWPN) of each cluster host's FC HBAs and the WWPN of the HBA controllers from the shared-storage device. If either the server or the storage device utilizes multiple HBAs to connect to a single or multiple FC switches to provide failover or load-balancing functionality, this is known as multipath I/O (MPIO), and a qualified driver for MPIO management and communication must be used. Also, the function of either MPIO failover or MPIO load balancing must be verified as approved for Windows Server 2012. Consult the shared-storage vendor, including the Fibre Channel switch vendor for documentation and supported configurations, and check the cluster hardware compatibility list (HCL) on the Microsoft website to find approved configurations.

iSCSI Storage and iSCSI Targets

When organizations want to utilize iSCSI storage for Windows Server 2012 failover clusters, security and network isolation is highly recommended. iSCSI utilizes an initiator or the host that requires access to the LUNs or iSCSI targets. Targets are located or hosted on iSCSI target portals. Using the target portal interface, the target must be configured to be accessed by multiple initiators in a cluster configuration. Both the iSCSI initiators and target portals come in software- and hardware-based models, but both models utilize IP networks for communication between the initiators and the targets. The targets need to be presented to Windows as basic disks. When standard network cards will be used for iSCSI communication on Windows Server 2012 systems, the built-in Windows Server 2012 iSCSI initiator can be used, provided that the iSCSI target can support the authentication and security options included.

Regardless of the choice of the Microsoft iSCSI initiator, software- or hardware-based initiators, or targets, iSCSI communication should be deployed on isolated network segments and preferably dedicated network switches and network interface cards Furthermore, the LUNs presented to the failover cluster should be masked from any systems that are not nodes participating in the cluster by using authentication and IPsec communication, as possible. Within the Windows Server 2012 operating system, the iSCSI HBA or designated network card should not be used for any failover cluster communication.

NOTE

When deploying a failover cluster, pay close attention to the results of the Validate a Cluster Wizard to ensure that the system has passed all storage tests to ensure a supported configuration is deployed.

Multipath I/O

Windows Server 2012 supports multipath I/O to external storage devices such as SANs and iSCSI targets when multiple HBAs are used in the local system or by the shared storage. Multipath I/O can be used to provide failover access to disk storage in case of a controller or HBA failure, but some drivers also support load balancing across HBAs in both standalone and failover cluster deployments. Windows Server 2012 provides a built-in multipath I/O driver for iSCSI that can be leveraged when the manufacturer conforms to the necessary specifications to allow for the use of this built-in driver. The iSCSI initiator built in to Windows Server 2012 is very user friendly and makes adding iSCSI targets simple and easy by making new targets reconnect by default and MPIO support is also installed by default.

Volume Shadow Copy for Shared Storage Volume

The Volume Shadow Copy Service (VSS) is supported on shared-storage volumes. VSS can take a point-in-time snapshot of an entire volume, enabling administrators and users to recover data from a previous version. Furthermore, failover clusters and the entire Windows Server Backup architecture utilize VSS to store backup data. Many of today's roles that are certified to work on Windows Server 2012 failover clusters are VSS compliant; consider carefully when choosing an alternative backup system, unless the system is provided by the shared-storage manufacturer and certified to work in conjunction with VSS, Windows Server 2012, and the service or application running on the failover cluster.

Clustered Storage Pools

Windows Server 2012 failover clusters support storage spaces and storage pools. This is a new concept for Windows servers and is outlined in Chapter 28. Storage spaces allow disks to be grouped together in storage pools, and then resilient virtual disks can be created within those pools. These storage pools and virtual disks are supported in failover clusters and allow cluster administrators to take smaller disks presented from shared-storage arrays and layer on additional functionality to increase reliability and capacity, all supported and managed within the failover cluster.

Failover Cluster Node Operating System Selection

Windows Server 2012 supports only the 64-bit operating systems. If any services or applications require deployment on 32-bit operating systems, and if this application is deployed on a Windows Server 2012 failover cluster, performance of that application may suffer and should be tested thoroughly before deployment on production failover clusters. Also, verify that these 32-bit applications are indeed supported on Windows Server 2012 failover clusters and not just on Windows Server 2008 or Windows Server 2003 32-bit failover clusters.

Deploying Failover Clusters

The Windows Server 2012 Failover Cluster feature is not installed on a system by default and must be installed before failover clusters can be deployed. Alternatively, for administrative workstations, the Remote Server Administration Tools features can be installed, which includes the Failover Cluster Manager snap-in, but the feature needs to be installed on all nodes that will participate in the failover cluster. Even before installing the Failover Cluster features, several steps should be taken on each node of the cluster to help deploy a reliable failover cluster. Before deploying a failover cluster, follow these steps on each node that will be a member of the failover cluster:

- Configure fault-tolerant volumes or LUNs using local disks or SAN-attached storage for the operating system volume.
- Configure at least two network cards, one for client and cluster communication and one for dedicated cluster communication.
- For iSCSI shared storage, configure an additional, dedicated network adapter or hardware-based iSCSI HBA.
- For Hyper-V clusters, configure an additional, dedicated network adapter on each node for virtual guest communication.
- Rename each network card properties for easy identification within the Failover Cluster Manager console after the failover cluster is created. For example, rename Local Area Connection to PRODUCTION and Local Area Connection 2 to iSCSI NIC and Local Area Connection 3 to HEARTBEAT, as required and possible. Also, if network teaming will be used with third-party software or using Microsoft Windows Server 2012 network teaming, configure the team first, excluding teaming from iSCSI connections, and rename each physical network adapter in the team to TEAMMEMBER1 and 2. The virtual team adapter should then get the name of PRODUCTION or HEARTBEAT.
- Configure all necessary IPv4 and IPv6 addresses as static configurations.
- Verify that any and all HBAs and other storage controllers are running the latest firmware and matched driver version suitable for Windows Server 2012 failover clusters.
- If shared storage will be used, plan to utilize at least two separate LUNs, one to serve as the witness disk and one to serve as the cluster disk for a high-availability role group.
- If applications or services, not included with Windows Server 2012, will be deployed in the failover cluster, as a best practice add an additional fault-tolerant array or LUN to the system to store the application installation and service files.
- Ensure that proper LUN masking and zoning has been configured at the FC or Ethernet switch level for FC or iSCSI shared-storage communication, suitable for failover clustering. Each node in the failover cluster, along with the HBAs of the

shared-storage device, should have exclusive access to the LUNs presented to the failover cluster.

- If multiple HBAs will be used in each failover node or in the shared-storage device, ensure that a suitable multipath I/O driver has been installed. The Windows Server 2012 multipath I/O feature can be used to provide this function if approved by the HBA, switch, and storage device vendors and Microsoft.
- Shut down all nodes except one and on that node, configure the shared storage LUNs as Windows basic disks, format as a single partition/volume for the entire span of the disk, and define an appropriate drive letter and volume label. Shut down the node used to set up the disks and bring each other node up one at a time and verify that each LUN is available, and, if necessary, configure the appropriate drive letter if it does not match what was configured on the first node.
- When cluster storage pools will be utilized, leave these disks unconfigured until after the failover cluster is created.
- As required, test multipath I/O for load balancing and failover using the appropriate diagnostic or monitoring tool to ensure proper operation on each node one at a time.
- Designate a domain user account to be used for Failover Cluster Manager, and add this account to the local administrators group on each cluster node. In the domain, grant this account the Create Computer Accounts right at the domain level to ensure that when the administrative and high-availability role groups are created, the account can create the necessary domain computer accounts.
- Create a spreadsheet with the network names, IP addresses, and cluster disks that will be used for the administrative cluster and the high-availability role group or groups that will be deployed in the failover cluster. Each role group requires a separate network name and IPv4 address, but if IPv6 is used, the address can be added separately in addition to the IPv4 address or a custom or generic role group needs to be created.

After the tasks in the preceding list are completed, the Failover Cluster feature can be installed. Failover clusters are deployed using a series of steps, including the following tasks:

1. Preconfigure the nodes, as listed previously, and create a domain user account to be used as the cluster service account.
2. Install any necessary Windows Server 2012 roles, role services, or features that will be deployed on the failover cluster. If any wizards are included with the role installation, like creating a DFS namespace or a DHCP scope, skip those wizards. Repeat this installation on all nodes that will be in the cluster.
3. Install the Failover Clustering feature on each node.

4. Run the Validate a Configuration Wizard and review the results to ensure that all tests pass successfully. If any tests fail, the configuration will not be supported by Microsoft and can be prone to several different types of issues and instability.
5. Run the Create a Cluster Wizard to actually deploy the administrative cluster.
6. Customize the failover cluster properties, including configuring storage as required.
7. Install any Microsoft or third-party applications that will be added as application-specific cluster resources so that the application can be deployed using the High Availability Wizard.
8. Run the High Availability Wizard to create a high-availability role group within the failover cluster, such as a file server, print server, DHCP server, virtual machine, or another of the included or separate services or applications that will run on a Windows Server 2012 failover cluster.
9. Test the failover cluster configuration and back it up.

Installing the Failover Clustering Feature and Tools

Before a failover cluster can be deployed, the necessary feature must be installed. To install the Failover Clustering feature, follow these steps:

1. Log on to the Windows Server 2012 system and open Windows PowerShell.
2. Type in **Install-WindowsFeature Failover-Clustering** and press Enter. This installs the Failover Clustering feature, but not any tools to manage failover clustering.
3. To install the graphic failover clustering management tools, in the Windows PowerShell window type in **Install-WindowsFeature RSAT-Clustering-MGMT** and press Enter.
4. To install the Windows PowerShell failover clustering module, in the Windows PowerShell window type in **Install-WindowsFeature RSAT-Clustering-PowerShell** and press Enter.
5. Repeat these steps on each server that will be configured as a failover cluster node.

This completes the installation of the Failover Clustering feature and tools.

Configuring Disks for Cluster Usage

For the storage that will be used in the cluster, the storage can be added before cluster creation or after. Before disks can be used within the cluster however, they will need to be initialized and brought online on one of the cluster nodes. Of course, this only applies to new unformatted disks, but regardless, if the operating system seems them as offline on all cluster nodes, the storage will not be available for use within the cluster.

When the cluster is created, as detailed in the preceding section, we will deploy a two-node cluster that leverages a shared storage disk as the quorum resource. For this process, we will not only initialize and bring online the desired disk for the quorum, but we will also create an NTFS volume and give it the drive letter of Q. To initialize and bring online new disks, follow these steps:

1. Log on to one of the Windows Server 2012 cluster nodes and open Server Manager.
2. Click the Tools menu and select Computer Management.
3. In the Computer Management window, expand Storage and select Disk Management in the tree pane.
4. Right-click the desired disk that is listed as Unknown and Offline and select Online.
5. Right-click the disk again and select Initialize. When the Initialize Disk window opens, select the GPT(GUID Partition Table) option button and click OK to initialize the disk.
6. Repeat this process for each new disk, but this process only needs to be performed on one of the cluster nodes.
7. After all the disks are brought online and initialized, if a disk quorum will be used, as will be in the following example, select the desired disk, right-click the disk, and select New Simple Volume. Follow the steps to create an NTFS volume and set the drive letter to Q for quorum.

The additional disks can be formatted as NTFS volumes and assigned drive letters after the cluster is created to avoid the cluster selecting the wrong disk for quorum. Normally the cluster creation process will select the smallest volume available as the quorum, but only formatting and assigning a drive letter to the desired quorum disk avoids any unnecessary work.

Running the Validate a Configuration Wizard

Failover Cluster Manager is the graphic management console used to administer the Failover Clustering feature. After the feature is installed on the prospective cluster nodes, the next step is to run the Validate a Configuration Wizard from the Tasks pane of the Failover Cluster Manager console. All nodes should be up and running when the wizard is run. To run the Validate a Configuration Wizard, follow these steps:

1. Log on to one of the Windows Server 2012 cluster nodes and open Server Manager.
2. Click the Tools menu and select Failover Cluster Manager.
3. When the Failover Cluster Manager console opens, click the Validate Configuration link in the actions pane.
4. When the Validate a Configuration Wizard opens, click Next on the Before You Begin page.
5. On the Select Servers or a Cluster page, enter the name of a cluster node, and click the Add button. Repeat this process until all nodes are added to the list, as shown in Figure 29.1, and click Next to continue.

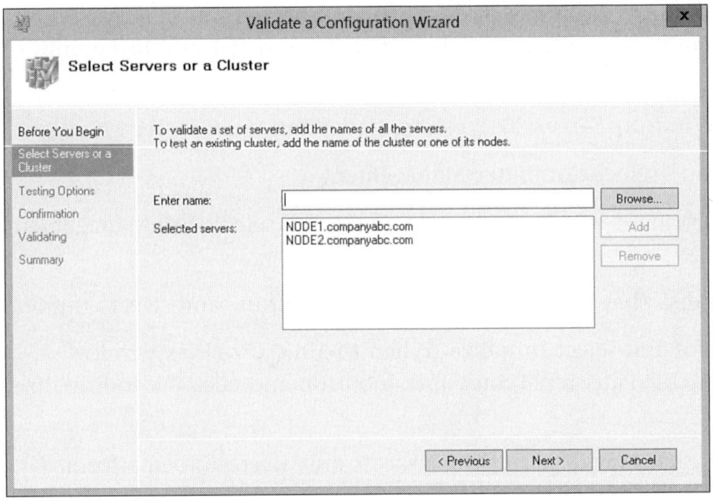

FIGURE 29.1 Adding the servers to be validated by the Validate a Configuration Wizard.

6. On the Testing Options page, read the details that explain the requirements for all tests to pass to be supported by Microsoft. Select the Run All Tests (Recommended) option button, and click Next to continue.
7. On the Confirmation page, review the list of servers that will be tested and the list of tests that will be performed, and click Next to begin testing the servers.
8. When the tests complete, the Summary page displays the results and if the tests pass it will be indicated by stating that the test has completed successfully. Click the View Report button to see the detailed report in a web browser, as shown in Figure 29.2.
9. Close the browser window after viewing the report, and back in the Validate a Configuration Wizard window, uncheck the Create the Cluster Now Using the Validated Nodes check box, and then click Finish to close the wizard.

Even if the Validate a Configuration Wizard does not pass every test, depending on the test, creating a cluster might still be possible. After the Validation a Configuration Wizard is completed successfully, the cluster can be created. One common mistake is that the disks that will be used for the cluster are not defined on any of the cluster nodes, and these should be defined and active on at least one node, and listed as offline on the remaining nodes. Alternatively, the cluster can be deployed with only a single node, the cluster can be created, and additional nodes can be deployed later.

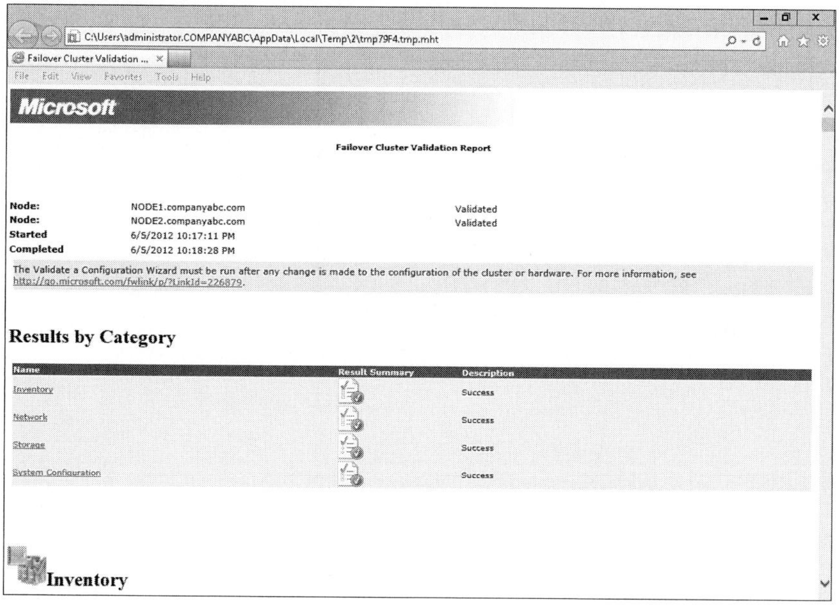

FIGURE 29.2 A successful Cluster Validation Report.

Creating a Failover Cluster

When the failover cluster is first created, all nodes in the cluster should be up and running. To create the failover cluster, follow these steps:

1. Log on to one of the Windows Server 2012 cluster nodes and open Server Manager.
2. From the Tools menu, select Failover Cluster Manager. When the Failover Cluster Manager console opens, click the Create Cluster link in the actions pane.
3. When the Create Cluster Wizard opens, click Next on the Before You Begin page.
4. On the Select Servers page, enter the name of each cluster node, and click the Add button. When all the nodes are listed, click Next to continue.
5. On the Access Point for Administering the Cluster page, type in the name of the cluster, complete the IPv4 address, and click Next, as shown in Figure 29.3.
6. On the Confirmation page, review the settings, and note that the Add all eligible storage to the Cluster check box is checked by default. Click Next to create the cluster.

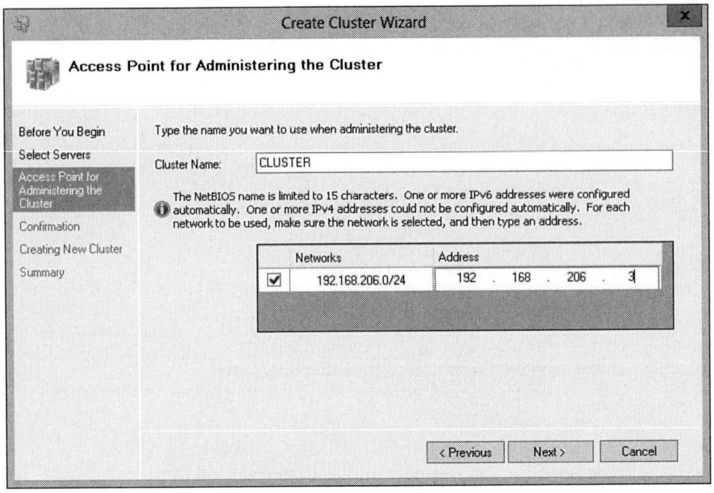

FIGURE 29.3 Defining the network name and IPv4 address for the failover cluster.

7. On the Summary page, review the results of the cluster creation process, and click Finish to return to the Failover Cluster Manager console. If there are any errors, you can click the View Report button to reveal the detailed cluster creation report.

8. Back in the Failover Cluster Manager console, select the cluster name in the tree pane, if not already selected by default, and in the Tasks pane, review the configuration of the cluster.

9. In the tree pane, select and expand the cluster to reveal the Nodes group to list all the cluster nodes.

10. Select Storage and review the cluster storage in the Tasks pane listed under Storage, as shown in Figure 29.4. Also click Storage Pools to list any storage pools, which will be created later in this chapter.

11. Expand Networks in the tree pane to review the list of networks. Select each network and review the names of the adapters in each network.

12. When reviewing is completed, the initial cluster deployment is complete. Close the Failover Cluster Manager console and log off of the cluster node.

After the cluster is created, additional tasks should be performed before any role groups are created using the High Availability Wizard. These tasks can include, but might not require, customizing the cluster networks, adding storage to the cluster, adding nodes to the cluster, and changing the cluster quorum model.

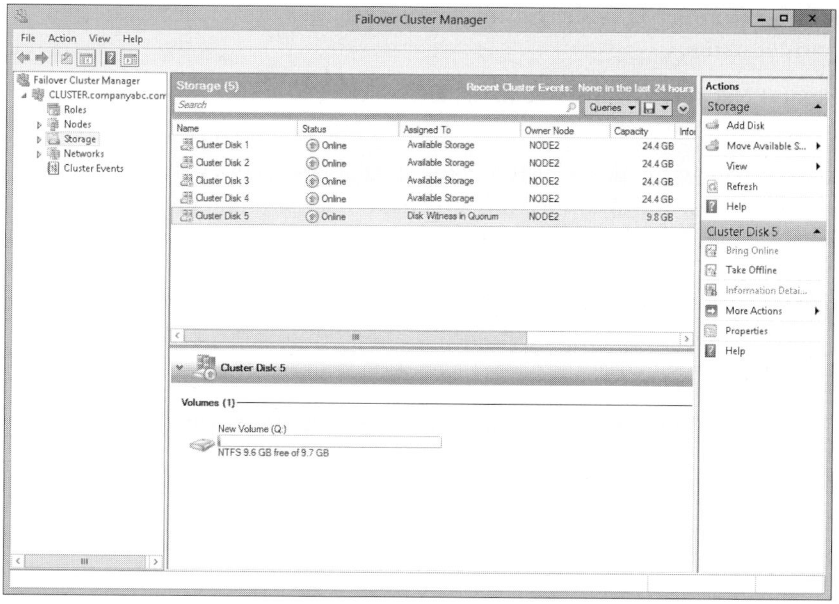

FIGURE 29.4 Displaying the dedicated cluster storage.

Configuring Cluster Networks

After the cluster is created, several steps should be taken to improve cluster management. One of these tasks includes customizing the cluster networks. Each node in the cluster should have the same number of network adapters and each adapter should have already been renamed to describe a network or to easily identify which network a particular network adapter belongs to. After the nodes are added to the failover cluster for each network card in a cluster node, there will be a corresponding cluster network. Each cluster network will be named by default as Cluster Network 1, Cluster Network 2, and so forth for each network. Each network can be renamed and can also be configured for use by the cluster and clients, for internal cluster use only, or the network can be excluded from any cluster use. Networks and network adapters used for iSCSI communication must be excluded from cluster usage. Now excluding iSCSI networks from cluster usage may seem strange, especially if iSCSI disks are used for the cluster, but this is intended to ensure that only iSCSI communication is passed to that network and no unnecessary cluster communication is competing for NIC resources when disk access may be critical. To customize the cluster networks, follow these steps:

1. Log on to one of the Windows Server 2012 cluster nodes and open Server Manager.
2. Click the Tools menu and select Failover Cluster Manager.
3. When the Failover Cluster Manager console opens, if necessary type in the name of the local cluster node to connect to the cluster.

4. When the Failover Cluster Manager console connects to the cluster, select and expand the cluster name.

5. Select and expand Networks in the tree pane, and select Cluster Network 1 as an example.

6. In the Tasks pane, review the name of the network adapters in the network, as shown in Figure 29.5, for the iSCSI network adapters that are members of Cluster Network 1.

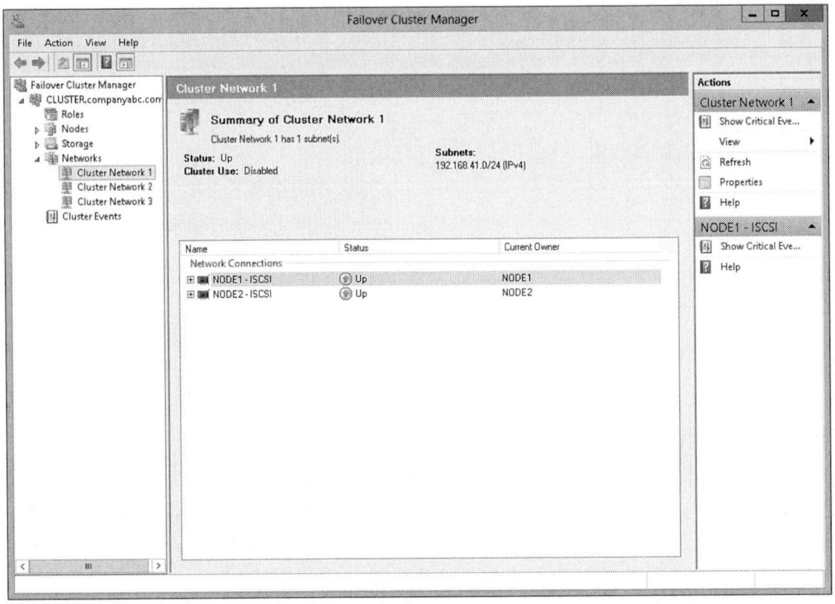

FIGURE 29.5 Displaying the network adapters in a cluster network.

7. Right-click Cluster Network 1, and select Properties. Rename the cluster to match the network adapter name and select the Do not allow cluster communication on this Network option button, and then click OK to save the changes.

8. Back in the Failover Cluster Manager console, rename the remaining cluster networks and verify that each network is configured for the proper cluster only or cluster and client communication. HEARTBEAT network interface cards should be configured to not allow clients to connect through this network, and the PRODUCTION network should be configured to allow cluster network communication and to allow clients to connect through the network.

9. When all the networking changes are complete, click the Networks node in the tree pane and the networks should be listed similarly to Figure 29.6. Notice the value of each network in the Cluster Use column of Figure 29.6. Close the Failover Cluster Manager console and log off of the server.

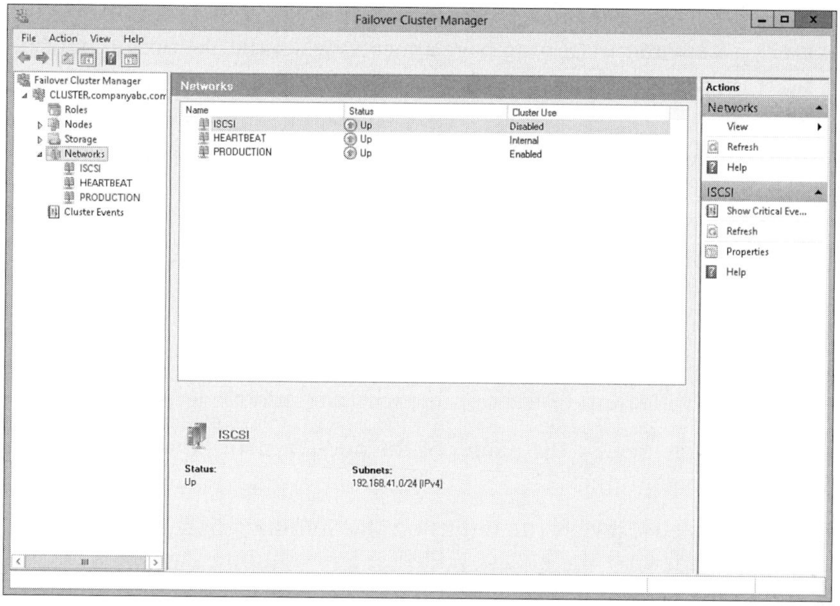

FIGURE 29.6 Cluster networks defined for Internal, Disabled, and Enabled.

Adding Nodes to the Cluster

If additional nodes need to be added to the cluster after the initial cluster creation process, first join that server to the domain, add the failover cluster feature, configure the network interface cards and storage configuration per cluster specifications, and then follow these steps:

1. Log on to one of the Windows Server 2012 cluster nodes and open Server Manager.
2. Click the Tools menu and select Failover Cluster Manager.
3. When the Failover Cluster Manager console opens, if necessary type in the name of the local cluster node to connect to the cluster.
4. When the Failover Cluster Manager console connects to the cluster, select and expand the cluster name.
5. Select and expand Nodes in the tree pane.
6. Right-click Nodes and select Add Node.
7. When the Add Node Wizard opens, click Next on the Before You Begin page.
8. On the Select Servers page, type in the name of the cluster node, and click the Add button. After the node is added to the list, click Next to continue.

9. If this node was not previously included with the original run of the Cluster Validation Wizard, a Validation Warning page appears. Select the Yes option button to check this node for cluster validation before adding it to the cluster and click Next to continue.

10. If you selected Yes, the Validate a Configuration Wizard will open. Follow the steps through the wizard and choose to test all nodes for all tests. Once completed, if validation results are successful, continue with the remaining steps in the Add Node process. If the cluster contains Cluster Shared Volumes, stop any role groups that utilize these volumes before running the Validate a Configuration Wizard and test all the Cluster Shared Volumes. Restart the Add Node Wizard if necessary to ensure that the role groups are stopped.

11. After the nodes pass all validation tests, continue with the Add Node Wizard.

12. On the Confirmation page, review the names of the node or nodes that will be added, and click Next to continue.

13. When the process completes, review the results on the Summary page, and click Finish to close the wizard. After the node is added, if a new quorum model is recommended, the summary page will display a warning. If necessary after closing the wizard, change the quorum configuration of the cluster.

14. Close the Failover Cluster Manager console and log off of the server.

Adding Storage to the Cluster

When shared storage is used with failover clusters, all the LUNs or targets presented to the cluster hosts might not have been added to the cluster during the initial configuration. When this is the case, and additional storage needs to be added to the cluster, follow these steps:

1. Log on to one of the Windows Server 2012 cluster nodes and open Server Manager.

2. Click the Tools menu and select Failover Cluster Manager.

3. When the Failover Cluster Manager console opens, if necessary type in the name of the local cluster node to connect to the cluster.

4. When the Failover Cluster Manager console connects to the cluster, select and expand the cluster name.

5. In the tree pane, expand the cluster and select Storage, right-click Storage, and select Add Disk.

6. If suitable storage is ready to be added to the cluster, it will be listed in the Add Disks to a Cluster window. If a disk is listed, check the box next to the desired disk or disks, and click OK to add the disks to the cluster. The disks will need to be configured as basic disks online and initialized in Disk Manager and have an NTFS volume and a drive letter assigned on it.

7. After the process completes, the disks will be listed as Available Storage in the Assigned To column. At this stage, it is ready to be assigned to a role group.
8. Close the Failover Cluster Manager console.

NOTE

For disks that will be used in cluster storage pools, do not create volumes and assign drive letters outside of the Failover Cluster Manager tool.

Cluster Quorum Configuration

If all cluster nodes and shared storage were available during the creation of the cluster, the best-suited quorum model would have been automatically selected during the cluster-creation process. In some cases, the selected quorum model may need to be changed if the cluster configuration changes by adding or removing nodes or by deploying geographically dispersed clusters. When the existing cluster quorum needs to be validated or changed, follow these steps:

1. Log on to one of the Windows Server 2012 cluster nodes, open Failover Cluster Manager, and connect to the cluster.
2. In the tree pane, select the cluster name; in the Tasks pane, the current quorum model is listed.
3. Review the current quorum model, and if it is correct, close the Failover Cluster Manager console. If the current quorum model is not the desired model, right-click the cluster name in the tree pane, click More Actions, and select Configure Cluster Quorum Settings.
4. If the Before You Begin page opens, click Next, and then on the Select Quorum Configuration page, select the option button of the desired quorum model or select the option button of the recommended model, and click Next to continue, as shown in Figure 29.7.
5. If a quorum model contains a witness disk or file share, select the designated disk or specify the path to the file share, and then click Next.
6. On the Confirmation page, review the settings, and click Next to update the cluster quorum model for the failover cluster.
7. Review the results on the Summary page, and click Finish to return to the Failover Cluster Manager console.
8. Close the Failover Cluster Manager console and log off of the server.

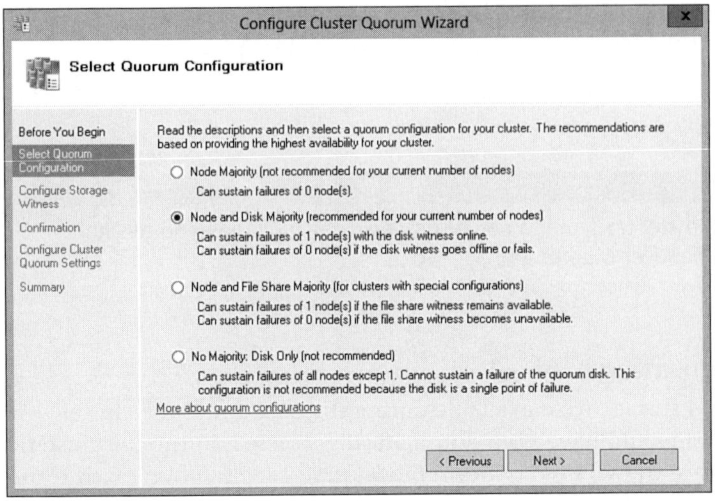

FIGURE 29.7 Configuring the cluster quorum model for a failover cluster.

Enabling Cluster Shared Volumes

Cluster Shared Volumes (CSV) can be enabled for use with Hyper-V virtual machines deployed on failover clusters and for the new Scale-Out file server failover cluster. CSV is currently only supported for these two deployment scenarios, and unlike other cluster shared storage, these designated volumes can be read and written to by all nodes in the cluster simultaneously. One important point to note is that for a virtual machine or a Scale-Out file server to use a CSV, it must be configured prior to deployment of the new role group. To learn how to create CSVs and deploy virtual machines using CSV storage, see Chapter 36. To create a CSV, follow these steps:

1. Log on to one of the Windows Server 2012 cluster nodes, open Failover Cluster Manager, and connect to the cluster.
2. Click Storage, and in the Storage pane select each of the desired disks by holding down the Shift key, then right-click and select Add to Cluster Shared Volumes, as shown in Figure 29.8.
3. When the process completes, each of the selected disks will show as Assigned to Cluster Shared Volume.

Deploying Roles on Failover Clusters

After the desired cluster configuration is achieved, the cluster is ready for the creation of role groups. Windows Server 2012 provides several out-of-the-box cluster resources that can be used to deploy Windows roles using failover clusters, as shown in Figure 29.9.

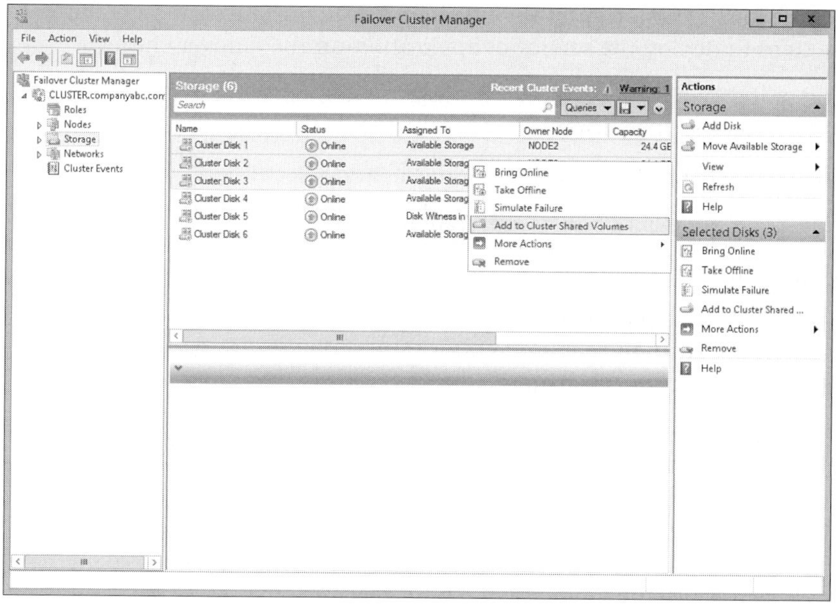

FIGURE 29.8 Assigning available disk to a CSV.

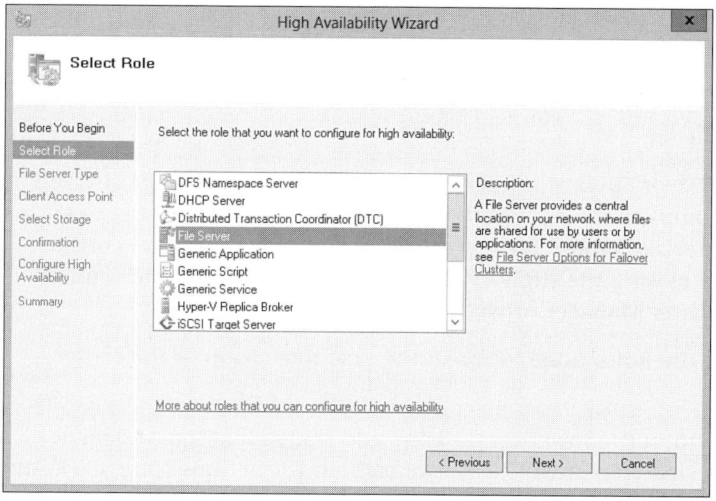

FIGURE 29.9 Windows Server 2012 built-in cluster roles resources.

Before a particular built-in service or application can be deployed in the cluster, the role, role service, or feature associated with it needs to be installed on each node prior to running the High Availability Wizard. For example, before the File Server role can be deployed on a failover cluster for high availability, the File Services role will need to be installed on each node in the cluster. After the prerequisites are installed on each cluster node, follow these steps to deploy the service or application on the failover cluster:

1. Log on to one of the Windows Server 2012 cluster nodes, open Failover Cluster Manager, and connect to the cluster.
2. In the tree pane, select the cluster name, expand it, and select Roles.
3. Right-click the Roles node, and select Configure Role.
4. When the High Availability Wizard opens, click Next on the Before You Begin page.
5. Select the desired role and click Next to continue. If the necessary roles, role services, or features are not installed on each node prior to selecting the desired entry, an error is displayed, and the process cannot continue. For this example, we have selected File Server as the role that will be deployed on the failover cluster.
6. For the File Server role, the next page will be the File Server Type page. Windows Server 2012 includes the traditional File Server for general use type and the new File Server for Scale-Out application data type. The Scale-Out type is designed for use with the hyper-v role and with applications like SQL Server where the file share will be used for connections that will remain open for extended periods of time. Scale-out will require a cluster shared volume on the cluster. Select the file server type and click Next to continue.
7. In the Client Access Point page, type in the name for the new file server and click Next. This is the name that will be used by clients to connect to the clustered file server.
8. Review the settings on the Confirmation page, and click Next to deploy the new file server in the failover cluster.
9. Depending on the service or application deployed, there can be specific post-creation wizards that open to complete the configuration. Complete the steps in the wizards as required or close the wizard and return to the Failover Cluster Manager console. Otherwise, click Finish, closing the High Availability Wizard window, and return back to the Failover Cluster Manager console.
10. In the tree pane, select the Roles node to reveal the new role group in the center Roles pane.
11. Select the new role group in the lower-center pane and notice that a new default share has already been created named ClusterStorage$. In the actions pane, click Add Shared Folder to create a new share
12. In the New Share Wizard window, select the share profile as shown in Figure 29.10. For this example, since a Scale-Out file share was created, NFS type shares are not supported. Instead, select an SMB Share – Server Application and click Next.

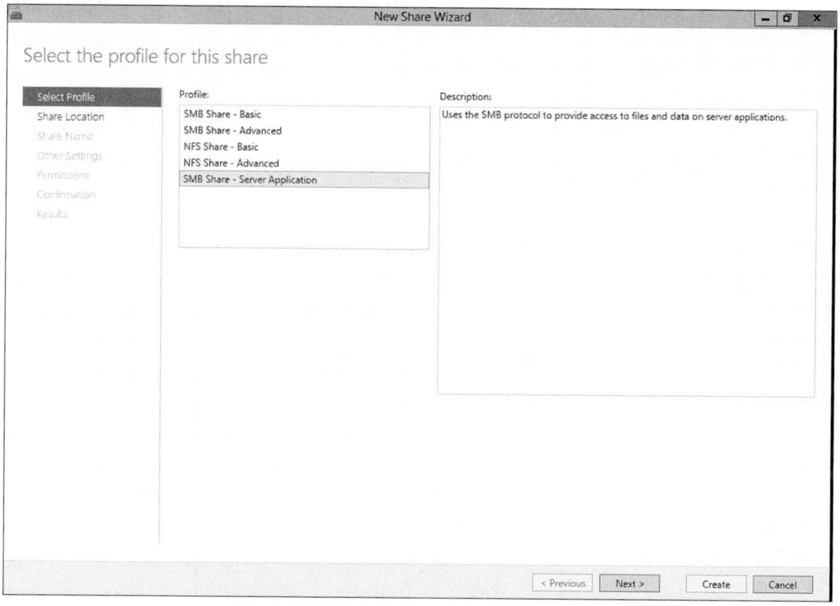

FIGURE 29.10 Selecting the new share profile.

13. On the Select a Server and Path for the Share page, if multiple CSV volumes are listed, select the desired volume and click Next.

14. On the Specify Share Name page, type in the desired share name, enter a share description, and click Next.

15. In the Configure Share Settings page, select the desired check boxes to enable access-based enumeration, continuous availability, share caching, BranchCache and encryption, as shown in Figure 29.11. Continuous availability is checked by default because this is what enables the application support by allowing the service to fail over between cluster nodes without service disruption.

16. On the Specify Permissions to Control Access page, click the Customize permissions button to modify NTFS share or central access policy rules and permissions. For more information about central access policies and Dynamic Access Control, see Chapter 28.

17. On the Confirm Selections page, review the settings and click Create to create the share.

18. On the View Results page, if the creation was successful click Close to return to the Failover Cluster Manager window.

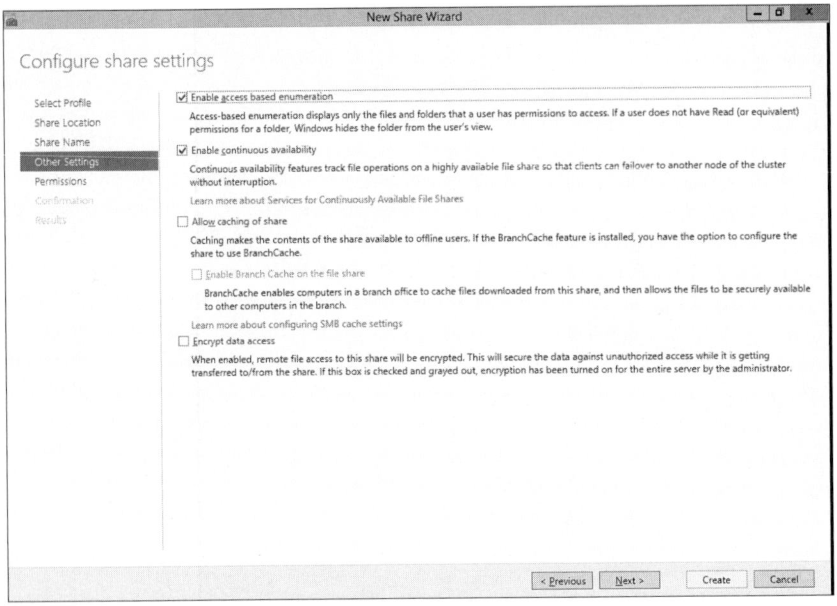

FIGURE 29.11 Selecting the desired share settings.

Configuring Failover and Failback

Clusters that contain two or more nodes automatically have failover configured for each role group as long as each node has the necessary services or applications installed to support running the group locally. Failback is never configured by default and needs to be manually configured for each role group if desired. Failback allows a designated preferred server or "preferred owner" to always run a particular cluster group on the preferred node, when it is available. When the preferred owner fails and the affected groups failover to alternate nodes, once the preferred node is back online and functioning as desired, the failback configuration options are used to determine whether the group will automatically fail back immediately or after a specified time period. Also, with regard to failover and failback configuration, the Failover and Failback properties define how many failures in a specified number of hours will be tolerated before the group is taken offline and remains offline. To review and if necessary change the failover and failback configuration options on a particular role group, follow these steps:

1. Log on to one of the Windows Server 2012 cluster nodes with an account with administrator privileges, open Failover Cluster Manager and connect to the desired cluster.
2. When Failover Cluster Manager opens, select the Roles node, and in the Roles center pane, right-click the desired role group and select Properties.
3. In the role group properties on the General tab, in the Preferred Owner section, check the box next to the desired node if failback will be configured. Do not close the group property window.

4. Select the Failover tab and review the number of allowed failures in a specified number of hours. The default is one group failure allowed in 6 hours.
5. In the lower section of the tab, if desired, enable failback and configure whether failback will be allowed and whether it will occur immediately when the preferred node is online or if the failback can only occur during after-hours, such as between the hours of 10:00 p.m. and 6:00 a.m. or 22 and 6, as shown in Figure 29.12.

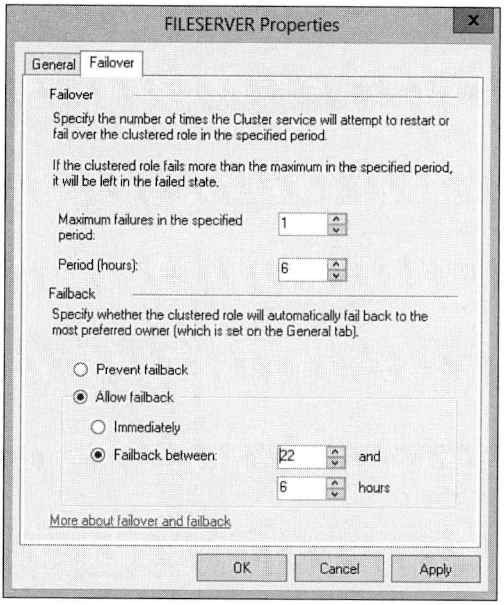

FIGURE 29.12 Configuring a role group's failover threshold and failback configuration.

NOTE

To reduce the chance of having a group failing back to a node during regular business hours after a failure, configure the failback schedule to allow failback only during nonpeak times or after hours using settings similar to those made in Figure 29.12 based on the organization's work hours and backup schedule.

Testing Failover Clusters

After all the desired cluster nodes to the failover cluster are added and failover and failback configuration options are set for each role group, each group should be verified for proper operation on each cluster node. For these tests to be complete, failover and, when applicable, failback of role groups need to be tested. They can be tested by simulating a cluster resource failure or by manually moving the role groups between nodes. To move a role group to another node, follow these steps:

1. Open Failover Cluster Manager and navigate to the desired role group. Right-click the group and click Move, Select Node, as shown in Figure 29.13.

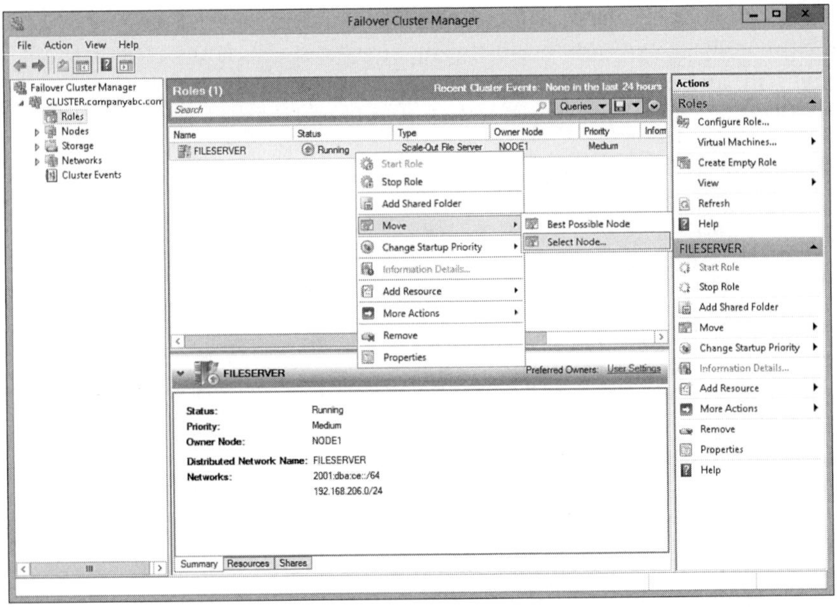

FIGURE 29.13 Moving a role group to another available node.

2. In the Move Clustered Role window, the available nodes will be listed. Select the desired node and click OK to move the group. Depending on the type of role group, a confirmation dialog box may open to confirm moving the group to the alternate node.

Failover Cluster Maintenance

Roles are deployed on failover clusters based on the fact that they are critical to business operations. The reliability of each cluster node is very important, and making any changes to the software or hardware configuration of each node can compromise this reliability. Before any changes are implemented on a production failover cluster, a few pre-maintenance tasks should be performed. To prepare a cluster node for maintenance, do the following:

1. Whether you're planning a software or hardware upgrade, research to see whether the changes will be supported on Windows Server 2012 failover clusters.

2. Log on to one of the Windows Server 2012 cluster nodes with an account with administrator privileges over all nodes in the cluster and open Failover Cluster Manager and connect to the desired cluster.

3. In the tree pane, select the cluster name, and in the tree pane, note the current host server. If the current host server is the node that will be taken offline for maintenance, the cluster will be automatically moved to an alternate node if the maintenance node is rebooted.
4. In the tree pane, select and expand Roles to reveal each of the groups.
5. For cluster groups that do not support Live migration, Select each of the respective groups and in the Tasks pane, note which node is the owner node of the group. Manually move each group to the node that will remain online if any of the groups are currently running on the node that will be taken offline for maintenance.
6. After all the groups that do not support live migration are moved to a node that will remain online, in the tree pane expand Nodes to reveal all the nodes in the failover cluster.
7. Locate the node that will be taken offline for maintenance, right-click the node, and select Pause Drain Roles. The drain roles option is new for Windows Server 2012 and will ensure that all client connections completed before pausing the node. This features requires live migration support on the group and works well with Scale-Out file server groups because all nodes will service clients even when the node is not the group owner. Pause Drain ensures that no clients are being serviced by the node before maintenance is performed.
8. Once the node is paused, resources cannot fail over and come online, and the system can have the software/hardware configuration or updates applied and, if necessary, rebooted.
9. After the maintenance tasks are completed, the node can be configured to be active in the failover cluster by right-clicking the node in the Failover Cluster Manager console and selecting Resume Do Not Fail Roles Back. This option will have the node rejoin the cluster, but will not move any groups, even if the resuming node is a preferred node of a group.
10. When the node resumes operation, if necessary, move the groups to this node and perform the maintenance tasks on the remaining nodes in the cluster.
11. When the maintenance tasks have been completed on all the cluster nodes, close the Failover Cluster Manager console and log off of the server.

Cluster-Aware Updating

A new feature of failover clustering for Windows Server 2012 is Cluster-Aware Updating. This feature is directly tied to Windows Updates and allows failover cluster administrators to select between two different models for the purposes of managing Windows-related and Microsoft-related updates on a failover cluster. One method is simply to allow administrators to run this wizard when updates need to be installed. The feature will manage the installation of the updates on all nodes in the cluster and move groups automatically.

Another method is to install the Cluster-Aware Updating role and then configure a run profile. To manually run Cluster-Aware Updating, follow these steps:

1. Log on to a Windows Server 2012 or Windows 8 system with an account that has local administrator rights and also has administrative rights on all nodes in the desired cluster.

2. On this system, install the failover cluster management tools, and then open Failover Cluster Manager and connect to the desired cluster.

3. Once connected to the desired cluster, right-click the cluster in the tree pane and select More Actions Cluster-Aware Updating, as shown in Figure 29.14.

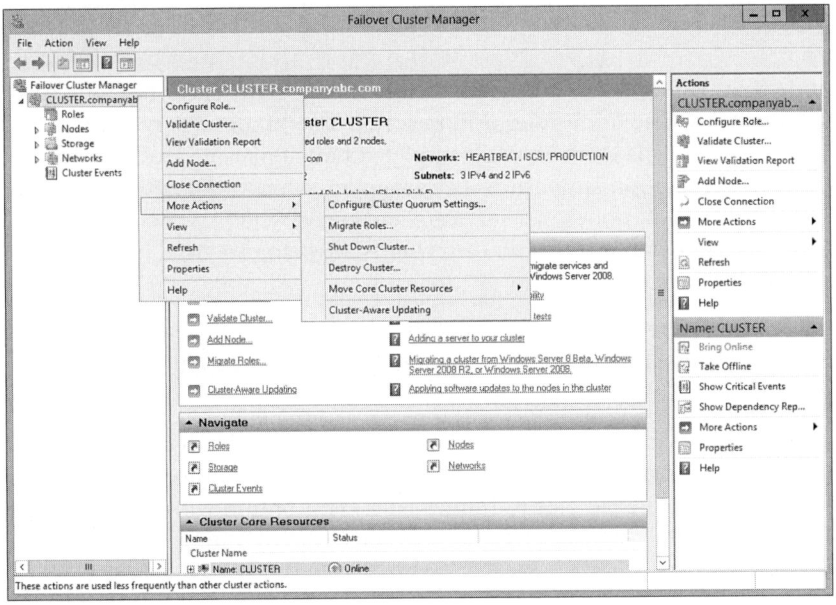

FIGURE 29.14 Launching the Cluster-Aware Updating Wizard.

4. In the Cluster-Aware Updating window, click the Preview updates for this cluster link on the right.

5. When the Preview Updates window opens, click the Generate Update Preview List button near the bottom to have Windows Update search for updates to install.

6. After the list is generated, click each update to review detailed information about the update. Note that this will show all the updates that will apply to each of the nodes in the cluster. After reviewing updates, click the Close button to return to the Cluster-Aware Updating window.

7. Now click the Apply updates to this cluster link on the right.

8. On the Getting Started page of the Cluster-Aware Updating Wizard, click Next to continue.
9. On the Advanced Options page, configure the desired options for the update process, and then click Next to continue.
10. On the Additional Update Options page, select whether recommended updates will be delivered the same way as important updates and click Next to continue.
11. On the Confirmation page, review the settings and click Update to start the process.
12. Once the configuration is delivered, click Close on the Completion page to close the wizard.
13. Back in the Cluster-Aware Updating window, the progress of the updates will be displayed. If reboots are required, the process will fail over role groups and restart each node before the other nodes are updated.
14. After the updates are installed successfully on all nodes, the administrator can click Generate Report on Past Updating Runs to view update history.
15. In the Generating Update Run Report windows, click the Generate Report button to list the report run history. Click Close when done reviewing.
16. Click the Cluster-Aware Updating windows and close Failover Cluster Manager.

Another way to update is to configure the cluster self-updating options of the Cluster-Aware Updating feature. This option enables administrators to set up scheduling to run the update processes on the cluster. To configure this option, open the Cluster-Aware Updating Wizard and click the Configure Cluster Self-Updating Options link and follow the wizard to set up a schedule and the updating options.

Because of the critical nature of failover clusters, this is not the preferred or best-practice selection for updates. In high-security deployments, however, this might in fact be the best selection. Your organization will need to determine which approach is best suited for your failover clusters. One other point to note is that Cluster-Aware Updating will install all important updates, and the administrator cannot choose updates to exclude. When administrators want to maintain greater control of which updates are installed on failover cluster nodes, they can implement Windows Server Update Services (WSUS) and configure the nodes to get their list of approved updates from the WSUS server. Then the administrators can leverage Cluster-Aware Updating, but only the WSUS approved updates will be applied to the cluster nodes.

Removing Nodes from a Failover Cluster

Cluster nodes can be removed from a cluster for a number of reasons, and this process can be accomplished quite easily.

NOTE

If you're removing nodes from a cluster that utilizes the Node Majority Quorum model, be sure that a majority of the nodes remain available; otherwise, the cluster might be shut down. If this is not possible, the quorum model might need to be changed before a node is removed from the failover cluster.

To remove a node from a failover cluster, follow these steps:

1. Log on to one of the Windows Server 2012 cluster nodes with an account with administrator privileges, open Failover Cluster Manager, and connect to the desired cluster.
2. When Failover Cluster Manager opens, expand the cluster name and select Nodes.
3. Expand Nodes to reveal all the cluster nodes.
4. Right-click the node that will be removed from the cluster, select More Actions, and click Evict.
5. A confirmation window opens. Click the Yes button to evict the desired node from the cluster. After the process starts, if the cluster or any role groups are running on this node, they will be moved to a remaining node before this node is removed from the cluster.
6. After the node is removed, close the Failover Cluster Manager console and log off of the server.

Cluster Migration and Upgrades

If an organization currently supports Windows Server 2003 clusters, the nodes in the cluster cannot be upgraded to Windows Server 2012 failover cluster nodes. This is mainly because the requirements of Windows Server 2003 server clusters and Windows Server 2012 failover clusters are very different. Even hardware requirements between Windows Server 2008 or 2008 R2 and Windows Server 2012 are different in terms of what actual configurations have been tested and are certified for failover clusters on each operating system version. Windows Server 2012 does provide a tool that can be used to collect data and migrate built-in Windows services between Windows Server 2008 or 2008 R2 or Windows Server 2012 failover clusters to a new destination Windows Server 2012 failover cluster. For more information about migrating services between Windows Server 2003 and Windows Server 2008 failover clusters to Windows Server 2012, review the Help topic "Migrating a Service or Application from One Failover Cluster to Another" in the Help file. Note that most default services and application groups that were able to run on a Windows Server 2008 or 2008 R2 failover clusters will also work on a Windows Server 2012 failover cluster, only the hardware that is supported may differ.

Backing Up and Restoring Failover Clusters

Windows Server 2012 contains a backup program appropriately named Windows Server Backup. Windows Server Backup can be used to back up each cluster node and any cluster disks that are currently online on the local node. Also, the system state of the cluster node can be backed up individually or as part of a complete system backup.

To successfully back up and restore the entire cluster or a single cluster node, the cluster administrator must first understand how to troubleshoot, back up, and restore a standalone Windows Server 2012 system using Windows Server Backup. Some basic and some advanced Windows Backup and Restore topics and procedures are detailed in this book in Chapters 30 and 31, "Backing Up the Windows Server 2012 Environment" and "Recovering from a Disaster," respectively. The process of backing up cluster nodes is the same as for a standalone server, but restoring a cluster might require additional steps or configurations that do not apply to a standalone server. To be prepared to recover different types of cluster failures, you must take the following steps on each cluster node:

- Back up each cluster node's local disks.
- Back up each cluster node's system state.
- Back up the cluster quorum from any node running in the cluster.
- For failover clusters using shared storage, back up shared cluster disks from the node on which the disks are currently hosted.

Failover Cluster Node: Backup Best Practices

As a backup best practice for cluster nodes, administrators should strive to back up everything as frequently as possible. Because cluster availability is so important, here are some recommendations for cluster node backup:

- Back up each cluster node's system state daily and immediately before and after a cluster configuration change is made.
- Back up cluster local drives and system state daily if the schedule permits or weekly if daily backups cannot be performed.
- Back up cluster shared volumes daily if the schedule permits or weekly if daily backups cannot be performed.
- Using Windows Server Backup, perform a full system backup before any major changes occur and monthly if possible. Although if a full system backup is scheduled using Windows Server Backup, this task is already being performed.

For detailed information about how to perform any of the backup tasks previously listed, see Chapter 30.

Restoring an Entire Cluster to a Previous State

Changes to a cluster should be made with caution and, if at all possible, should be tested in a nonproduction isolated lab environment first. When cluster changes have been implemented and deliver undesirable effects, the way to roll back the cluster configuration to a previous state is to restore the cluster configuration to all nodes. This process is simpler than it sounds and is performed from only one node. There are only two caveats to this process:

- All the cluster nodes that were members of the cluster previously need to be currently available and operational in the cluster. For example, if Cluster.companyabc.com was made up of Node1 and Node2, both of these nodes need to be active in the cluster before the previous cluster configuration can be rolled back.
- To restore a previous cluster configuration to all cluster nodes, the entire cluster needs to be taken offline long enough to restore the backup, reboot the node from which the backup was run, and manually start the Cluster service on all remaining nodes.

To restore an entire cluster to a previous state, follow these steps:

1. Log on to one of the Windows Server 2012 cluster nodes with an account with administrator privileges over all nodes in the cluster. (The node should have a full system backup available for recovery.)
2. Open Server Manager and from the Tools menu select Failover Cluster Manager.
3. Right-click the cluster and select More Actions and then select Shutdown Cluster as shown in Figure 29.15.

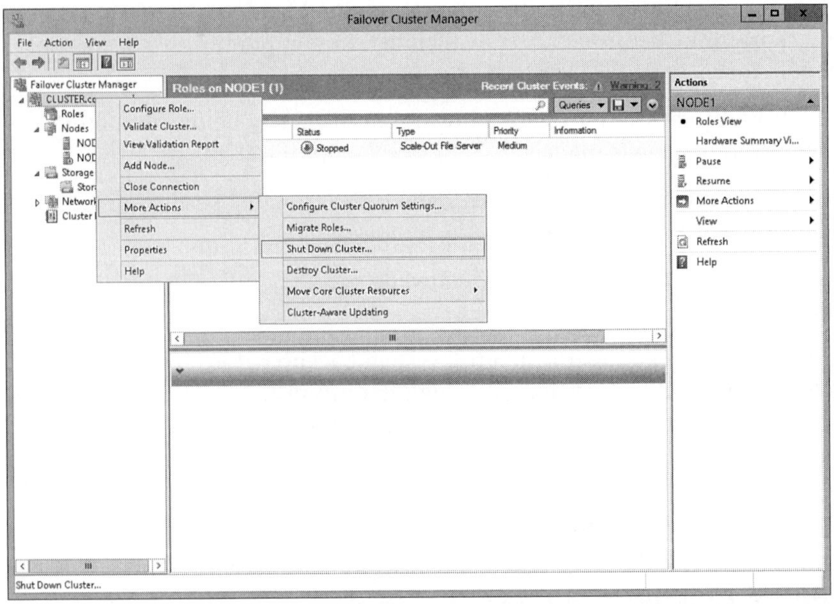

FIGURE 29.15 Shutting down the cluster to perform recovery.

4. Open Server Manager and from the Tools menu select Windows Server Backup.
5. From the Actions menu, click Recover.

6. When the Recover window opens, select the This Node(servername) option button on the Getting Started page and click Next.
7. On the Select Backup Date page, select the correct date, and if multiple backups were performed on that date, pull down the Time menu and select the desired time. Click Next to continue.
8. On the Select Recovery Type page, select the Applications option button and click Next.
9. On the Select Application page, select Cluster from the Applications field and click Next.
10. On the Specify Recovery Options page, the only option is to Recover to Another Location. Click the Browse button, select the C: drive, and create a new folder named ClusterRestore, and then select it and click OK. Back on the Specify Recovery Options page, the path should show as C:\ClusterRestore. Click Next to continue. The recovery process will create the folder, and the cluster database file is all that will be recovered (and the size is quite small).
11. On the Summary page, verify that only the cluster database will be restored, as shown in Figure 29.16, and click Recover to start the process.

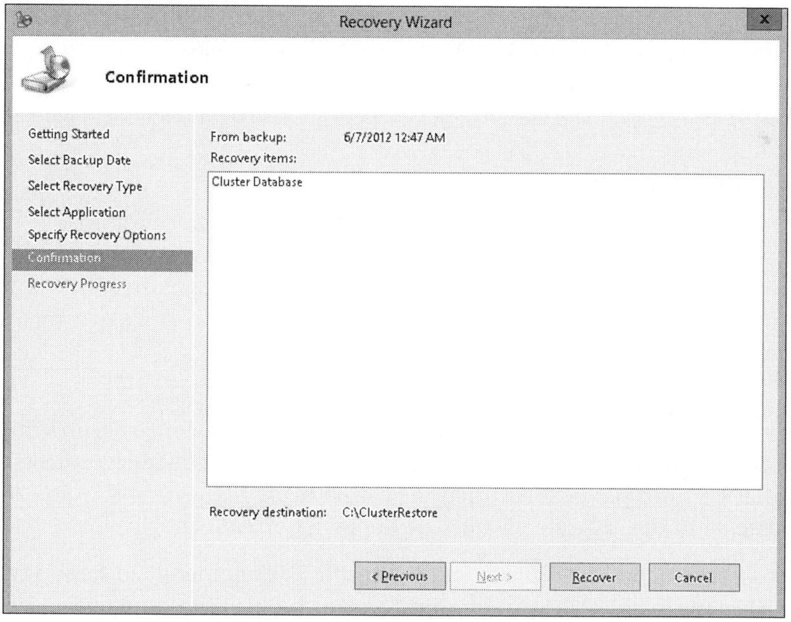

FIGURE 29.16 Recovering the cluster database using Windows Server Backup.

12. After the recovery process completes, click Close.

13. Open the C:\ClusterRestore folder using Windows Explorer and copy the CLUSDB file from the C:\ClusterRestore\Cluster Database\C_\Windows\cluster folder to the C:\Windows\Cluster folder and choose to overwrite the existing file. Copy this same file to all nodes in the cluster into the C:\Windows\Cluster folder and overwrite the existing file.
14. On the node that the CLUSDB file was just originally restored, open Failover Cluster Manager, right-click the cluster, and select Start Cluster.
15. After the cluster starts, verify that the restore has completed successfully. Start any role groups, and then close the console and log off of the server when you are finished and run a backup.

Deploying Network Load Balancing Clusters

The other clustering technology included in Windows Server 2012 is Network Load Balancing (NLB). NLB clusters can easily be deployed on Windows Server 2012 systems. Before an NLB cluster can be deployed, the Network Load Balancing feature needs to be installed on all servers that will be members or nodes in the NLB cluster. To properly configure an NLB cluster, the administrator needs to research the type of network traffic the application or service utilizes. For example, a standard website uses TCP port 80 and standard Remote Desktop Services (RDS) utilizes port 3389. NLB is intended to intelligently load balance client connections based on the incoming traffic across multiple servers. If network redundancy on a single server is required, network teaming can be configured on a single server.

NLB Applications and Services

NLB is well equipped to distribute user connections and create fault tolerance for a number of different applications and network services across multiple servers. Because NLB does not replicate data across cluster nodes, and neither does failover clusters for that matter, using applications that require access to local data that is dynamic or frequently changes is not recommended for NLB clusters.

Applications well suited for NLB clusters are web-based applications and services, proxy services, virtual private network (VPN), SMTP gateways, and Remote Services Session Host systems. Typically in multitier applications, the top and middle tiers that clients connect to and those systems that perform processing functions would be deployed on NLB clusters, and the lower or back-end database tiers would be deployed on failover clusters.

NLB clusters are based on client connections made to a specific DNS name, IP address, and TCP/UDP port using either IPv4 or IPv6. It's important to read the vendor's application documentation regarding how the client communicates with the application and how this communication can be configured on load-balancing devices or services such as Microsoft Windows Server 2012 NLB clusters. For instance, certain applications use cookies or other stateful session information that can be used to identify a client throughout the entire session, and it is important that the client maintains a connection to the same cluster node during the entire session. Other applications, such as a website that serves up static pages, can spread out and respond to client requests from multiple nodes in the NLB cluster. For a web-based application, such as an e-commerce application, an encrypted Secure Sockets Layer (SSL) session, or an application that is authenticated by the actual web server, the NLB cluster would need to direct all communication between the client and a specific cluster node. Considering these types of scenarios in advance helps determine how the NLB cluster will be defined.

Installing the Network Load Balancing Feature

Before an NLB cluster can be created, the feature needs to be installed on all servers that will participate in the cluster. To install the Network Load Balancing feature, follow these steps:

1. Log on to each Windows Server 2012 system with an account that has local administrator rights.
2. Open Windows PowerShell from the taskbar.
3. In the Windows PowerShell window, type in **Add-WindowsFeature NLB** and press Enter. This command installs the Network Load Balancing feature.
4. In the Windows PowerShell window, type in **Add-WindowsFeature RSAT-NLB** and press Enter. This command installs the NLB tools. Perform this step only on the desired nodes and on any additional administrative systems that will be used to manage the NLB cluster.
5. Repeat this process on all nodes that will be in the NLB cluster.

Creating Port Rules

When an NLB cluster is created, one default port rule is created for the cluster. The NLB cluster default port rule and any additional rules define what type of network traffic the cluster will load balance and how the connections will be managed. The default rule can be modified and augmented with other rules, but within this rule the filtering option is what defines how the traffic will be balanced across each node.

In an NLB cluster, because each node can answer for the clustered IP address, all inbound traffic is received and processed by each node. When a node receives the request, it either handles the request or drops the packet if another node has already established a session or responded to the initial request. When an administrator discards or modifies the default NLB cluster port rule and creates additional rules that only allows specific ports and block all other traffic destined for the cluster IP address, each cluster node can quickly eliminate and drop packets that do not meet the allow port rule and in effect improve network performance of the cluster. The security benefit of this configuration also removes any risk of attacks on any other port using the cluster IP address.

Port Rules Filtering Mode and Affinity

Within an NLB cluster port rule, the NLB administrator must configure the appropriate filtering mode. This allows the administrator to specify whether only one node or multiple nodes in the cluster can respond to requests from a single client throughout a session. There are three filtering modes: Single Host, Disable This Port Range, and Multiple Host.

Single Host Filtering Mode

The Single Host filtering mode ensures that all traffic sent to the cluster IP address that matches a port rule with this filtering mode enabled is handled exclusively in the cluster by one particular cluster node.

Disable This Port Range Filtering Mode

The Disable This Port Range filtering mode tells the cluster which ports are not active on the cluster IP address. Any traffic requests received on the cluster IP address that match a port rule with this filtering mode result in the network packets getting automatically discarded or dropped. Administrators should configure specific port rules and use this filter mode for ports and port ranges that do not need to be load balanced across the cluster nodes.

Multiple Host Filtering Mode

The Multiple Host filtering mode is probably the most commonly used filtering mode and is also the default. This mode allows traffic to be handled by all the nodes in the cluster. When traffic is balanced across multiple nodes, the application requirements define how the Affinity mode should be set. There are three types of multiple host affinities:

- **None**—This affinity type can send unique clients' requests to all the servers in the cluster during the span session. This can speed up server response times, but is well suited only for serving static data to clients. This affinity type works well for general web browsing, read-only file data, and FTP servers.
- **Network**—This affinity type routes traffic from a particular Class C address space to a single NLB cluster node. This mode is not used too often, but can accommodate client sessions that use stateful applications and when different client requests are serviced by down-level proxy servers. This is a useful affinity type for companies that direct traffic from several remote offices through proxies before connecting to the services/applications managed by the port rules in the NLB cluster.
- **Single**—This affinity type is the most widely used. After the initial request is received by the cluster nodes from a particular client, that node will handle every request from that client until the session is completed. This affinity type can accommodate sessions that require stateful data such as an encrypted SSL web application or a Terminal Server session. This is the default filtering mode on a port rule and is well suited to handle almost any NLB clustered service or application.

Using Cluster Operation Mode

There are three different cluster operation modes: Unicast, Multicast, and IGMP Multicast. Most traditional network traffic is unicast traffic where clients and servers maintain a one-to-one network connection. Multicast networking allows a server to send out information to one multicast address that is then processed by a number of clients. To receive multicast data, a client joins a multicast group associated with the multicast address, and one data feed or transmission is presented to the group by the server, thereby streamlining and improving network performance of the application. Multicast traffic is usually one direction and when the multicast client joins the group, it begins to receive the transmission. Common applications that use multicast are streaming music and video websites, Internet radio, and Internet training or online noninteractive courses. IGMP multicast can be used in place of multicast and enhances overall network performance when multicast is required. Selecting this management protocol allows for the multicast clients to register with the IGMP multicast server, and afterward the multicast traffic will only be sent to the switch ports or trunks that connect to the multicast clients, reducing traffic on the remaining ports of the network switches. One more important point to mention about multicast traffic is that the network switches and routers that the traffic will pass through must support multicast traffic and allow it. Many enterprise-class switches and routers have multicast support disabled by default.

Configuring Network Cards for NLB

Configuring the network cards on the NLB cluster nodes is the first step in building the cluster. Although these steps can be performed during cluster creation using the NLB Manager, the same result can be achieved by editing the TCP/IP properties of each of the cluster node's network cards. Best practice for NLB cluster nodes running in Unicast mode is to have two network cards to allow host communication to occur on one network interface card (NIC) while cluster communication is isolated on the cluster NIC. Multiple NICs can also add greater flexibility when it comes to controlling traffic and managing network security.

Creating an NLB Cluster

Before an NLB cluster can be created, a few bits of information are required. The NLB cluster is actually load balancing traffic based on a defined clustered IP address, the DNS name, and the TCP/IP ports that will be allowed. Each NLB cluster node can also be configured with multiple network cards. Each card can be associated with a different NLB cluster, and a single card can support multiple clusters, but each cluster must have a different DNS name and IP addresses. For this example, a new NLB cluster will be created for the name NLB.companyabc.com using the IP address of 192.168.206.25. To create an NLB cluster, follow these steps:

1. Log on to a Windows Server 2012 system with an account that has local administrator rights and that has the NLB feature already installed.
2. Open Server Manager and from the Tools menu select Network Load Balancing Manager.

3. When Network Load Balancing Manager opens, click the Cluster menu, and select New to create a new cluster.
4. When the New Cluster window opens, type in the name of the first server that will be added to the new NLB cluster, and click Connect. If the server is a remote system and cannot be contacted, check the firewall configuration to ensure that remote administration is allowed.
5. When the server is contacted, each of the network adapters will be listed. Select the adapter that will be used for the NLB cluster, as shown in Figure 29.17, and then click Next.

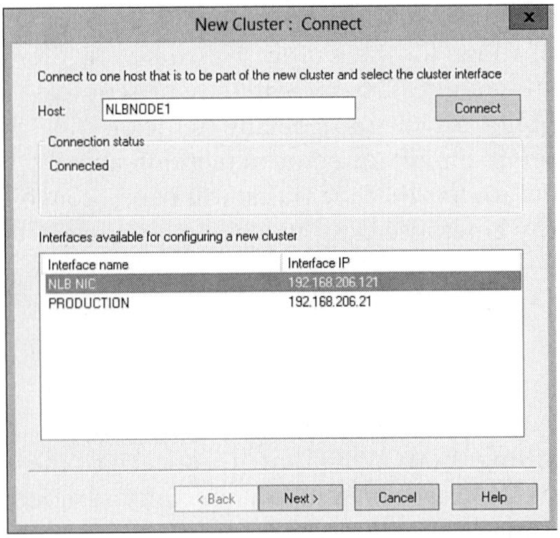

FIGURE 29.17 Selecting the network adapter that will be used for the NLB cluster.

6. On the Host Parameters page, accept the defaults of giving this first server the Host ID of 1 and select the dedicated IP address that will be used when communication is received for the NLB cluster IP address, which will be specified next. Click Next to continue.
7. On the Cluster IP Addresses page, click the Add button to specify an IPv4 address and subnet mask or an IPv6 address to use for the NLB cluster, and click OK. For our example, we will use the IPv4 configuration of 192.168.206.125/255.255.255.0.
8. Back on the Cluster IP Addresses page, add additional cluster IP addresses as required, and click Next to continue.
9. On the Cluster Parameters page, enter the fully qualified DNS name that is associated with the IP address specified on the previous page, and select whether it will be used for unicast traffic, multicast traffic, or IGMP multicast. This choice depends on the network communication of the service or application that will be used in this NLB cluster. For this example, we are creating an NLB cluster for standard web

traffic, so we will use NLB.companyabc.com as the Internet name and select Unicast as the cluster operation mode, as shown in Figure 29.18.

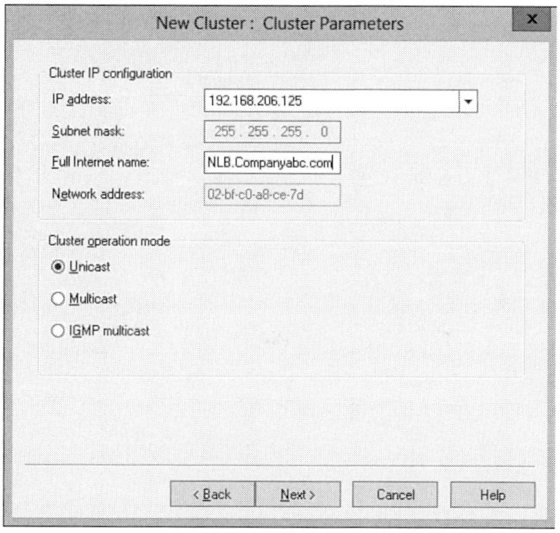

FIGURE 29.18 Specifying the DNS/Internet name associated with an NLB cluster IP address.

10. If multiple IP addresses were defined on the previous page, the IP address can be chosen from the IP address drop-down list, and the Internet name and cluster operation mode can be defined for each additional address. When all the IP addresses have had their properties defined, click Next to continue.

11. On the Port Rules page, a default rule is displayed that allows all traffic on all ports to be load balanced across the NLB cluster between the cluster IP address and the dedicated IP address of the local server's dedicated IP address. Select this rule and click the Remove button to delete it.

12. Click the Add button to create a new port rule.

13. When the Add/Edit Port Rule window opens, type in the starting and ending port range (for example, 80 and 80 for a single HTTP port rule), but do not close the window.

14. Under Protocols, select the TCP option button, but do not close the window.

15. In the Filtering Mode section, select Multiple Host, and select Single Affinity, but do not close the window.

16. Finally, review the settings, and click OK to create the port rule, as shown in Figure 29.19.

17. Back on the Port Rules page, click the Add button to create an additional port rule.

18. Specify the starting port as 0 and the ending port as 79, select Both for the protocol's configuration, select the Disable This Port Range Filtering mode, and click OK to create the rule.

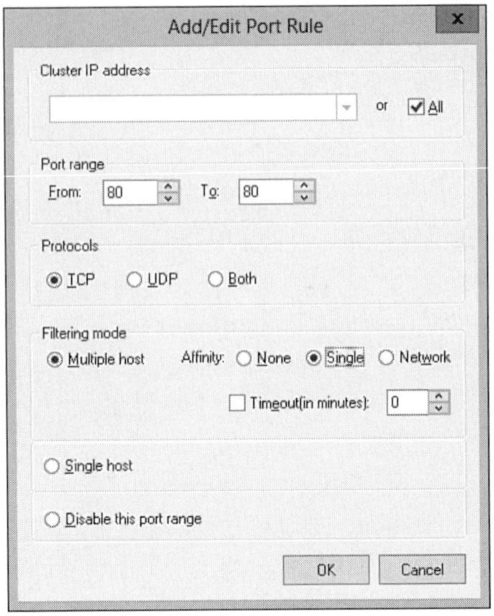

FIGURE 29.19 Defining a port rule for TCP port 80 with multiple hosts, single affinity.

19. Back in the Port Rules page, click the Add button to create a third port rule.
20. Specify the starting port as 81 and the ending port as 65535, select Both for the protocol's configuration, select the Disable This Port Range Filtering mode, and click OK to create the rule. Create another rule with a disabled port range of 0 to 79.
21. Back on the Port Rules page, review the list of port rules, and if the rules look correct, click Finish, as shown in Figure 29.20.

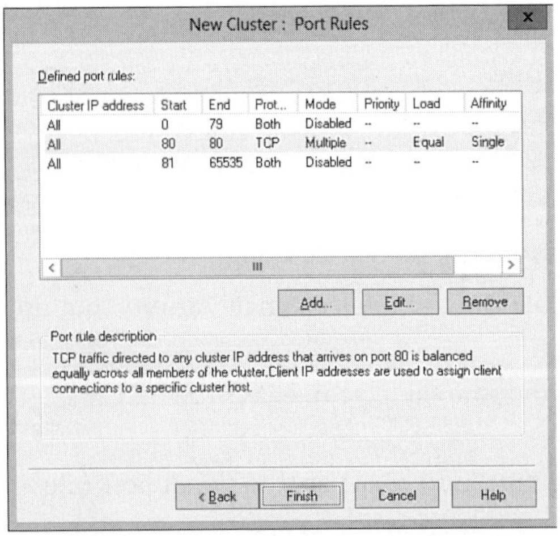

FIGURE 29.20 Reviewing the port rules that will allow only TCP port 80 for all clustered IP addresses.

22. Back in the Network Load Balancing Manager window, the cluster will be created and brought online. The cluster IP addresses are automatically added to the TCP properties of the designated network adapter.

Adding Additional Nodes to an Existing NLB Cluster

After an NLB cluster is created, additional nodes can be added to it. To add nodes to an existing cluster, follow these steps:

1. Open Network Load Balancing Manager on the original node and click the Cluster menu, and select Connect to Existing.
2. When the Connect page opens, type in the hostname of a cluster node in the cluster that will have nodes added to it. For this example, the hostname is NLBNODE1. Type in the server name and click Connect to retrieve a list of all NLB clusters running on the specified host. Select the desired cluster, and click Finish to connect to it.
3. Back in the Network Load Balancing Manager window, in the tree pane select and right-click the cluster, and select Add Host to Cluster.
4. When the Connect page opens, type in the hostname of the Windows Server 2012 system that will be added to the cluster, and click Connect.
5. After the system is connected, a list of all the available network adapters is shown. Select the desired adapter to use for the NLB cluster, and then click Next.
6. On the Host Parameters page, review the details of the page, and click Next to continue. The default settings should be sufficient unless the host ID needs to be changed or if multiple IP addresses are already bound to the adapter. Select the desired IP address to use for dedicated NLB cluster communication, and click Next to continue.
7. On the Port Rules page, the existing port rules for the cluster are listed. Unless this node will handle different traffic on this cluster, accept the defaults and click Finish.
8. The node will be added to the cluster, and if the node addition is successful, both nodes will be listed under the cluster with a green background and listed with a status of Converged, as shown in Figure 29.21.
9. Close the Network Load Balancing Manager and log off of the server.

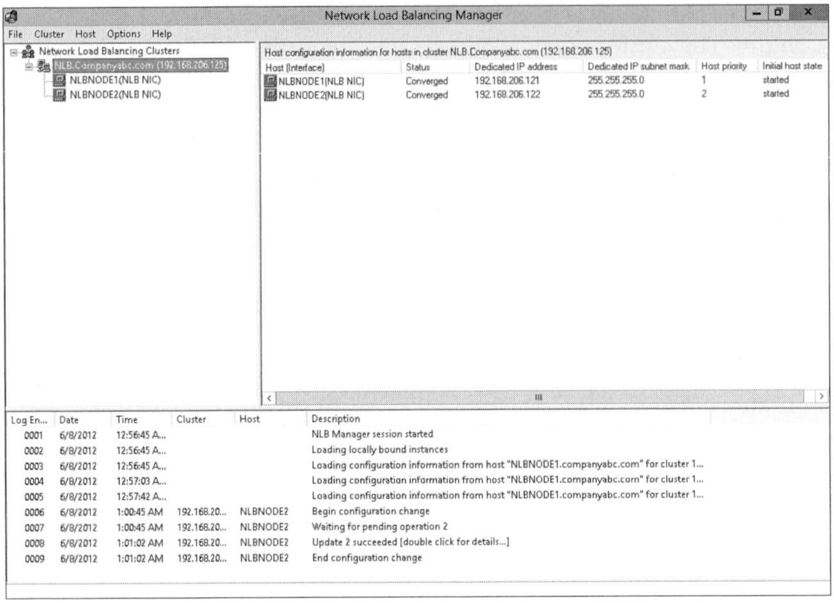

FIGURE 29.21 Verifying that all NLB cluster nodes are operating properly.

Managing NLB Clusters

An NLB cluster can be managed using the Network Load Balancing Manager from a local cluster node or from a remote machine with the Remote Administration tools installed. Network Load Balancing can also be managed using the command-line tool NLB.exe and by using some of the new Windows PowerShell commands included with Windows Server 2012. Using the NLB Manager, a node can be added, removed, or suspended from cluster operation to perform maintenance, including hardware or software updates. Because data is not replicated between cluster nodes, any data that is required by all nodes in the cluster either needs to be replicated to each node or the application needs to be configured to access data on a system that is not in the NLB cluster.

Backing Up and Restoring NLB Nodes

The procedure for backing up and restoring NLB nodes is no different than for standalone servers. A full system backup using Windows Server Backup or the organization's Windows Server 2012 approved backup software should be created before and after any major server or NLB cluster configuration changes are implemented. An NLB configuration can be restored when the system state of a particular node is restored. If a full node recovery is necessary, the system state and local disks should be restored using a full system restore.

For detailed backup and restore procedures, see Chapters 30 and 31.

Performing Maintenance on an NLB Cluster Node

To perform maintenance on an NLB cluster node, the administrator can temporarily stop the NLB service on the node in the cluster, perform the upgrade, and start it back up later. Stopping the cluster node without impacting user connections requires the use of the Drainstop option from the Network Load Balancing Manager. The Drainstop option informs the NLB cluster that the particular node will be stopped and no new connections should be directed toward this node. All existing connections will remain up and running, and when all the sessions are closed, the NLB service will be shut down on the designated node. After the maintenance has completed, the NLB service can be restarted on the NLB node, and client connections can be initiated. To perform maintenance on a cluster node, follow these steps:

1. Log on to each Windows Server 2012 system with an account that has local administrator rights.
2. Open Server Manager and from the Tools menu and select Network Load Balancing Manager.
3. When the Network Load Balancing Manager console opens, click the Cluster menu, select Connect to Existing, and type in the server name of one of the nodes that will remain online.
4. In the tree pane, expand the cluster to reveal all the nodes in the cluster.
5. Locate the node that will be taken offline for maintenance. Right-click the node, select Control Host, and click Drainstop, as shown in Figure 29.22.

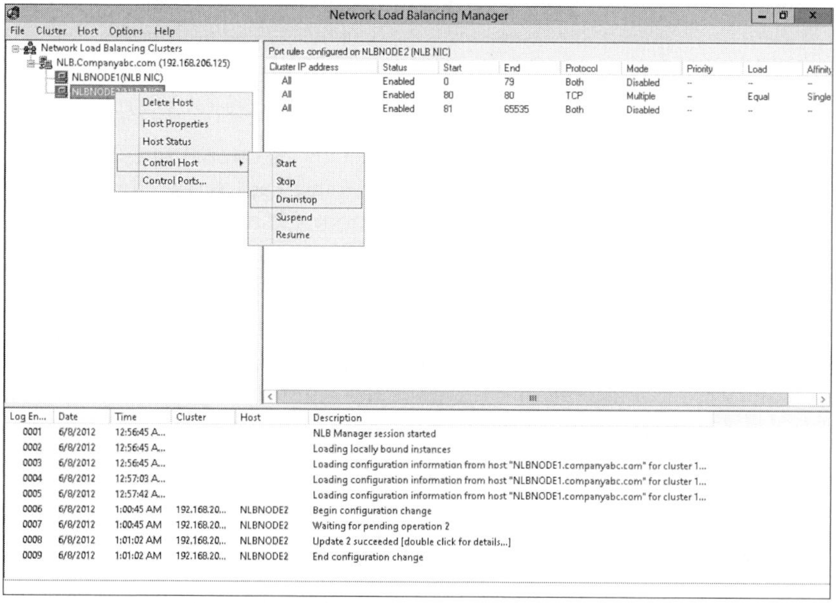

FIGURE 29.22 Taking an NLB cluster node offline using the Drainstop option.

6. After all connections are closed, the node will be highlighted in red, and the status will be changed to Stopped. Perform the necessary maintenance on the NLB cluster node.
7. After the maintenance has been performed, open NLB Manager, connect to the cluster, and expand the cluster to reveal the nodes.
8. Select the node that has been stopped, right-click the node, select Control Host, and click Start.
9. After the host starts up, it will have a green background and will immediately be ready to accept client connections.
10. Close the Network Load Balancing Manager and log off of the server.

To perform the drainstop using PowerShell, follow these steps:

1. Open Windows PowerShell from the taskbar.
2. To stop the NLB service on NLBNODE2, using drainstop as an example, type in the command **Stop-NlbClusterNode –Drain – Hostname "NLBNODE2"** and press Enter.
3. The PowerShell cmdlet will return the status of the command after the server has stopped.
4. To resume operation on this node, type in the command **Start-NlbClusterNode –Hostname "NLBNODE2"** and press Enter.
5. When completed, close the PowerShell window and log out of the server.

Network Teaming

Windows Server 2012 introduces built-in network teaming. This functionality enables administrators to configure multiple adapters in a single system to act as one, for the purpose of adding in redundancy at the network layer, without the need for any clustering technology. Teaming can however work with failover clustering and NLB if configured before the clustering technologies are configured. To create a new network team, follow these steps:

1. Log on to the desired server using a console connection and open Network Connections. Using remote session will disconnect the administrator when the team is created.
2. Identify and name the adapters that will be used as TEAM NIC 1 and TEAM NIC2. Leave IPv4 and IPv6 unconfigured.
3. Open Server Manager and in the tree pane select the Local Server link.
4. When the local server information is displayed, click the Disabled link to the right of Network Adapter Teaming in the center pane.

5. When the NIC Teaming window opens, in the lower-left TEAMS section click the Tasks menu and select New Team.

6. Type in a name for the team, such as **PRODUCTION**, check the boxes for the adapters that will be part of the team, and then click the OK, as shown in Figure 29.23.

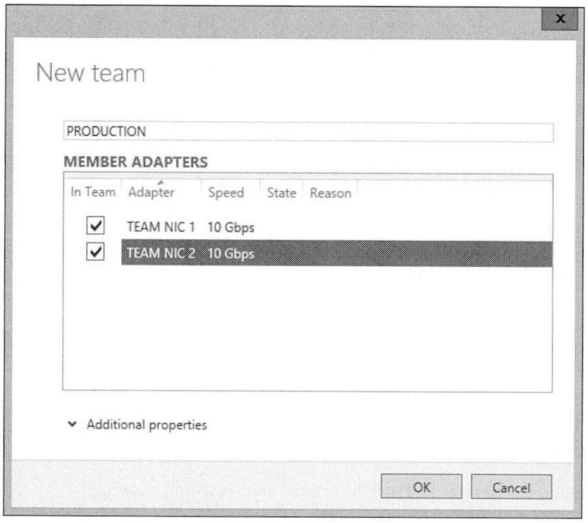

FIGURE 29.23 Naming the network team and selecting adapters.

7. After the team is created, close the NIC Teaming window and open Network Connections, select the new adapter, and configure the IPv4 and IPv6 IP address settings.

This completes the creation of a new network team.

Summary

Windows Server 2012 provides two very different clustering technologies that enable organizations to create system-level fault tolerance and provide high availability for mission-critical applications and services. Although failover clusters and NLB are each characteristically different and are best deployed on very different types of applications, between them they can increase fault tolerance for almost any service or application.

Best Practices

The following are best practices from this chapter:

- Purchase quality server, network hardware, and shared-storage devices and HBAs that are certified for Windows Server 2012 when deployed on failover clusters.

- If network teaming is desired, leverage the built-in Windows Server 2012 network team and configure the teams before failover or NLB clusters are created.
- Deploy cluster node operating systems on fault-tolerant disk arrays.
- Thoroughly understand the application that will be used before determining which clustering technology to use.
- Use Windows Server 2012 failover clusters to provide system-level fault tolerance for mission-critical applications, such as enterprise messaging, databases, file and print services, and other networking services.
- If iSCSI is used for shared storage, ensure that any network adapters used for iSCSI communication are excluded from cluster communication.
- Use NLB to provide connectivity to TCP/IP-based services, such as Remote Desktop Services, websites, VPN services, and SMTP gateways.
- Rename and clearly label all network adapters on each cluster node and configure static IPv4 and IPv6 addresses.
- Configure the appropriate power management settings for the system and network adapters on all cluster nodes.
- Configure the appropriate cluster quorum model that is right for the deployment and, hopefully, the recommended model.
- Use multiple network cards in each node so that one card can be dedicated to internal cluster communication (internal/heartbeat network) while the other can be used only for client connectivity and cluster communication.
- If failback is required, configure the failback schedule to allow failback only during nonpeak times or after-hours to reduce the chance of having a group failing back to a node during regular business hours.
- Thoroughly test failover and failback mechanisms.
- Be sure that a majority of the nodes remain running to keep the cluster in a working state if you're removing a node from a cluster that leverages the Node Majority Quorum model.
- Carefully consider backing up and restoring a cluster and do not deploy any clusters until a tested and documented backup and recovery plan exists.
- For NLB clusters, create a port rule that allows only specific ports to the clustered IP address and an additional rule blocking all other ports and ranges.

CHAPTER 30

Backing Up the Windows Server 2012 Environment

IN THIS CHAPTER

- Understanding Your Backup and Recovery Needs and Options
- Creating the Disaster Recovery Solution
- Documenting the Enterprise
- Developing a Backup Strategy
- Windows Server Backup Overview
- Managing Backups Using the Command-Line Utility wbadmin.exe and Windows PowerShell Cmdlets
- Backing Up Active Directory
- Backing up Windows Server 2012 Roles
- Volume Shadow Copy Service
- Extending Server Backup to the Enterprise with Data Protection Manager 2012

Windows Server 2012 is a very powerful and feature-rich operating system that can provide many organizations with the tools they require from their computer and network infrastructure. Some of the functions a Windows Server 2012 system can provide include centralized directory and authentication services, file and print services, web services, networking services, virtual private network (VPN) services and many more. Of course, before any new system, service, or application is deployed in an organization's computer and network infrastructure, the responsible parties should understand how to set up, optimize, administer, and properly back up and recover data and functionality in the event of a failure.

A valid backup and recovery plan should be created for any new server or system that will be deployed on a production network. Unfortunately, some organizations deploy systems without a tested backup and recovery plan, and as a result of this, when a critical business system unexpectedly fails or when disasters strike, it could result in data loss, lost employee productivity, and even loss or revenue.

This chapter provides IT decision makers and their technical staff with the information they require to start planning and implementing viable backup strategies for a Windows Server 2012 infrastructure.

Understanding Your Backup and Recovery Needs and Options

A key to creating a valuable backup and recovery plan is to have a clear understanding of how the computer and network infrastructure is configured as well as having an understanding of how the business operates and utilizes the infrastructure. This discovery process involves mapping out both the computer and network systems in place and also documenting and understanding the business services and processes that depend on the infrastructure. For example, an organization might fulfill orders and create quotes through a central application that sales reps can access from the field on their tablets. If this application is hosted on Windows Server Internet Information Services (IIS) or on remote desktop host systems, an offline server or an inability a server or an inability to access those systems in real time could directly impact business. This is just one example, but there are several different outage scenarios that can severely affect day-to-day business operations in any company. Understanding which systems and services are most important to the business can help IT staff set the order or prioritize which systems will be recovered first and where redundancy is most important.

Identifying the Different Services and Technologies

Each deployed role, role service, feature, or application hosted on a Windows Server 2012 system can be provide a key system function. Each of these roles and services should be clearly documented so that the IT group can better understand the complexity of the environment, for the purposes of developing and maintaining backup and recovery plans.

Identifying Single Points of Failure

A single point of failure is a device, application, or service on a computer and networking infrastructure that provides an exclusive function with no redundancy. A common single point of failure in smaller organizations is a network switch that provides the connectivity between all the servers, client workstations, firewalls, wireless access points, and routers on a network. Within a Windows Server 2012 Active Directory infrastructure as an example, Active Directory Domain Services (AD DS) inherently comes with its own set of single points of failure, with its Flexible Single Master Operations (FSMO) roles. These roles provide an exclusive function to the entire Active Directory forest or just a single domain and if the designated domain controller hosting that role fails, the FSMO roles become unavailable. Even though the FSMO roles are single points of failure, recovering a domain controller can be very simple if proper backup and recovery planning is performed. For more information about FSMO roles, see Chapter 7, "Active Directory Infrastructure."

Evaluating Different Disaster Scenarios

Before a backup and disaster recovery plan can be formulated, IT managers and administrators should meet with the business owners to discuss and decide on which types of failures or disasters should be planned for. This section of the chapter provides a high-level description of common disaster scenarios to consider. Of course, planning for every disaster scenario is nearly impossible or, more commonly, will exceed an organization's backup and recovery budget, but discussing each scenario and evaluating how the scenario can impact the business is necessary.

Physical Disaster

A physical disaster is anything that can keep employees or customers from reaching their desired office or store location. Examples include natural disasters such as floods, fires, earthquakes, hurricanes, or tornadoes that can destroy an office. A physical disaster can also be a physical limitation, such as a road closure or highway blockage caused by a car accident. When only physical access is limited or restricted, a remote-access solution could reestablish connectivity between users and the corporate network. See Chapter 24, "Server-to-Client Remote and Mobile Access," for more information in this area.

Power Outage or Rolling Blackouts

Power outages can occur unexpectedly at any time. Some power outages are caused by bad weather or other natural disasters, but other times they can be caused by high power consumption that causes system overloads or damaged power equipment. When power systems are overloaded, rolling blackouts may occur. A rolling blackout is when a power company shuts off power to certain power subscribers or areas of service, so that it maintains power to critical services, such as fire departments, police departments, hospitals, and traffic lights. The rolling part of rolling blackouts is that the blackout is managed; after a predetermined amount of the time, the power company shuts down a different power grid and restore power to a previously shutdown grid. Of course, during power outages, many businesses are unable to function because the core of their work is conducted on computers or even telephone systems that require power to function.

Network Outage

Organizations that share data and applications between multiple offices and require access to the Internet as part of their daily business operations are susceptible to network and Internet outages. These outages can cause loss of employee productivity and possibly loss of revenue. Network outages can affect just a single computer, the entire office, or multiple offices depending on the cause of the outage. IT staff must take network outages into consideration when creating the backup and recovery plans.

Hardware Failures

Hardware failures seem to be the most common disaster encountered and coincidentally are the most common type of problem organizations plan for. Server hardware failures include failed motherboards, processors, memory, network interface cards, network cables, fiber cables, disk and HBA controllers, power supplies, and, of course, the hard disks in the local server or in a storage-area network (SAN). Each of these failures can be dealt with differently, but to provide system- or server-level redundancy, critical systems should be deployed in a redundant clustered configuration, such as is provided with Windows Server 2012, Failover Clustering, and Network Load Balancing (NLB).

Hard Drive Failure

Hard drives are indeed the most common type of computer and network-related hardware failure organizations have to deal with. Windows Server 2012 supports hot-swappable hard drives and two types of disks: basic disks, which provide backward compatibility; and dynamic disks, which allow software-level disk arrays to be configured without a separate hardware-based disk array controller. Also, both basic and dynamic disks, when used as data disks, can be moved to other servers easily to provide data or disk capacity elsewhere if a system hardware failure occurs and the data on these disks needs to be made available as soon as possible. Windows Server 2012 also includes new storage services known as storage spaces, storage pools, and virtual disks. Virtual disks in storage pools can be made up of different disks deployed in a redundant or resilient configuration are more flexible in terms of how they can be utilized. Storage spaces is covered in Chapter 28, "File System Management and Fault Tolerance."

Software Corruption

Software corruption can occur at many different levels. Operating system files could be corrupted, antivirus software can interfere with the writing of a file or database causing corruption, or a new application or driver installation could overwrite a critical file leaving a system unstable or in a failed state. Also, more commonly found in today's networks, a security or system update conflicts with an existing application or service causing undesirable issues.

Prioritizing the Recovery

After all the computer services and applications used on a network are identified and you have decided which typical disaster scenarios will be considered in the backup and recovery plan, the next step is to organize or prioritize how to recover critical systems and restore services. The prioritization usually involves getting the most critical services up and running first, and this always requires networking services such as domain name system (DNS) and Dynamic Host Configuration Protocol (DHCP) as well as Active Directory domain controllers on many corporate networks that use Microsoft Windows servers and client operating systems.

Maintaining up-to-date backup and recovery plans requires following strict processes when changing an organization's computer and network infrastructure. With an up-to-date technology priority list, administrators can tackle the planning for the most important services first to ensure that if a disaster strikes sooner than later, the most important systems are always protected and recoverable.

Identifying Bare Minimum Services

The bare-minimum services are the fewest possible services and applications that must be up and running for business operations to continue. Only the top few services and applications in the technology prioritized list will become part of the bare-minimum services list. For example, a bare-minimum computer service for a retail outlet could be a server that runs the retail software package and manages the register and receipt printer. For a web-based company, it could be the web and e-commerce servers that process online orders.

Creating the Disaster Recovery Solution

When administrators understand what sorts of failures can occur and know which services and applications are most critical to their organization, they have gathered almost all the information necessary to create a preliminary high-level, disaster recovery solution. Many different pieces of information and several documents will be required even for the preliminary solutions. Some of the items required within the solution are listed in the following sections.

Disaster Recovery Solution Overview Document

The Disaster Recovery Solution Overview document is short narrative of the solution in action, including presentations with quality graphics / Microsoft Visio diagrams. This document first provides an executive summary that includes only high-level details to provide executives and management with enough information to understand what steps are being taken to provide business continuity in the event of a disaster. The remainder of the document should contain detailed information about the plan, including the following:

- Current computer and network infrastructure review
- Detailed history of the planning meetings and the information that was presented and discussed in those meetings
- The list of which disaster and outage scenarios will be mitigated by this plan, and which scenarios will not be addressed by this plan
- The list of the most critical applications, systems, and services for the organization and the potential impact to the business if these systems encounter a failure or are not available
- Description of the high-level solution, including how the proposed disaster recovery solution will enhance the organization by improving the reliability and recoverability
- Defined service-level agreements (SLAs) and recovery time objective (RTO) time estimates this solution provides to each failure and disaster scenario
- Associated computer and network hardware specifications, including initial purchasing and ongoing support and licensing costs
- Associated software specifications and licensing costs for initial purchase and ongoing support, licensing, and maintenance costs
- Additional wide-area network (WAN) or wireless link costs
- Additional outside services costs, including hosting services, data center lease costs, offsite disk and tape storage fees, consulting costs for the project, technical writing, document management and ongoing support or lease costs

- Estimated internal staffing resource assignment and utilization for the solution deployment as well as the ongoing utilization requirements to support the ongoing backup and recovery tasks
- The initial estimated project schedule and project milestones

Getting Disaster Recovery Solutions Approved

Prioritizing and identifying the bare-minimum services is not only the responsibility of the IT staff; these decisions belong to management, as well. The IT staff is responsible for identifying single points of failure, gathering the statistical information of application and service usage, and possibly also understanding how an outage can affect business operations.

Before the executives budget for an organization's disaster recovery plan, they should be presented with as much information as possible, so that they can make the most informed decision. As a general guideline, when presenting the preliminary disaster recovery solution, make sure to also do some preliminary planning for a lower-cost alternate plan highlighting different costs and differences in the solutions.

Getting the budget approved for a secondary disaster recovery solution is better than getting no budget for the preferred solution. The staff should always try to be very clear on the SLA for a chosen solution and to document or have a paper trail concerning all disaster recovery solutions that have been accepted or denied. If a failure that could have been planned for occurs but budget was denied, IT staff members or IT managers should make sure to have all their facts straight and documentation to prove it. In the end, regardless of who denied the budget and who chose which failure or disaster to plan for, IT staff will always take the blame, so always push to get the best plan approved.

Documenting the Enterprise

So far, in the backup and recovery preparation, a computer and network discovery has been performed, different failure scenarios have been considered, and the most critical services have been identified and prioritized. Now, it is time to start actually building the backup and disaster recovery plan that a qualified individual will use in the event of a failure. To begin creating the plan, the current computer and network infrastructure must be documented. You can find information about documenting a Windows Server 2012 system in Chapter 22, "Documenting a Windows Server 2012 Environment." Documentation should include the following:

- **Server configuration document**—This document details which services and applications each server provides, in addition to the network settings, software installed, and hardware specifications.
- **Server build document**—This document contains step-by-step instructions on how to build a Windows Server 2012 system for a specific role, such as domain controller or file server, including which software is required and hardware specifications.

This document also includes specific security configurations, hardware and software configurations, and other organizational server configuration standards.

- **Network diagrams**—Network diagrams should contain network configurations and the hardware included in the infrastructure and the WAN links.
- **Network device configuration**—These documents contain the configurations of the network devices, including the switches, firewall, and routers on the network.
- **SAN configuration**—Most medium and large-size organizations utilize one form of centralized storage or another. When storage devices are utilized, these device configurations should be documented so that they can be recovered in the event of a device issue.
- **Software documentation**—This document contains a list of all the software used in the organization, possibly including the licensing information and the storage location.
- **Service accounts and password document**—A master list of user accounts and network device usernames and passwords should be created and kept in a sealed envelope in a secured location (both onsite and offsite).
- **Hosted or cloud service documentation**—Most organizations today leverage cloud services for one application or another. Documenting how to manage the service, including account and contact information, is critical to IT operations and to backup and disaster recovery planning.
- **Contact and support documentation**—This document should contain all IT staff and vendor contact information required to support the infrastructure.

Developing a Backup Strategy

Determining not only what needs to be backed up, but also how the backups will be performed and stored, is an important task. Many organizations back up data to tape media and have that media shipped to offsite storage locations on a weekly basis. Windows Server 2012 Server Backup is built to support backup to local internal and externally connected disks and network shares for scheduled backups. Windows Server Backup does not natively support tape devices for backup. Windows Server Backup for Windows Server 2012 includes a new online backup option that organizations can leverage as part of Microsoft's cloud-based solutions. For organizations that want to leverage Windows Server Backup online options, tape backup solutions, or obtain enterprise-level backup, Microsoft System Center Data Protection Manager or a third-party backup suite is recommended.

Assigning Tasks and Designating Team Members

To make sure that Windows Server 2012 systems are getting backed up properly, IT staff should train and assign at least two IT staff members to monitor and manage backups when using Windows Server Backup. Windows Server 2012 systems, by default, allow users in the local Administrators or Backup Operators security groups to back up and restore data. On domain controllers, the domain-based security groups have these same rights on the Active Directory domain controllers in the respective domains.

Creating Regular Backup Procedures

Creating a regular backup procedure helps ensure that the entire enterprise is backed up consistently and properly. When a regular procedure or checklist is created, the assigned staff members will soon become accustomed to the procedure, and it will become second nature. If there is no documented procedure, certain items or systems might be overlooked or might not be backed up, which can turn out to be a major problem if a failure occurs. An example of a backup checklist or procedure could be as simple as configuring backups on Windows systems to run a full backup of a server every night, reviewing the backup status of each system every morning, regularly swapping backup managed disks, and rotating the disks to offsite disk and tape storage facilities. Additional steps in the backup checklists could include performing test restores of data and applications hosted on Windows Server 2012 systems.

Windows Server Backup Overview

Windows Server 2012 contains a built-in powerful backup program appropriately named Windows Server Backup. Windows Server Backup is installed as a system feature, and it enables administrators to back up and restore system, file, folder, and application data for Windows Server 2012 systems.

Windows Server Backup includes a graphical user interface (GUI) Microsoft Management Console (MMC) snap-in and a very functional command-line utility and several Windows PowerShell cmdlets.

Backup Storage Support and Media Management

Windows Server Backup enables administrators to back up to locally attached disks, network shares, and DVD writable media. Tape devices are not supported by Windows Server Backup, and to back up to DVD media, the system requires a local writable DVD drive.

Windows Server Backup handles all the media management itself. When leveraging local backup storage, it performs the labeling of the media and efficiently stores backup data by using block-level backups that only back up new and changed blocks. The backup on a single disk may contain several days' or weeks' worth of backups, depending on the disk size and the size of the backup datasets. Free space is also managed, and when additional space is required, the backup program deletes the oldest backup sets as required.

External Disks

Windows Server Backup supports backup data to be stored on locally attached disks and writable DVD media located in local writable DVD drives. Locally attached disks include internal disk drives, hot-swappable disk drives, and drives externally connected via USB 2.0 or IEEE 1394 interfaces. Also, SAN attached disks can be used as backup destinations.

Storing backups on SAN storage enables faster rotation or replication of backup disks volumes to other SAN storage without impacting Windows system performance.

CD/DVD Writer Drives

Windows Server 2012 contains many features that can take advantage of DVD writer drives. These include the Windows Server Backup feature to capture backups to DVD and Windows Deployment Services, which can be used to create boot, capture, and discover images on DVD media. With regard to Windows Server Backup and DVDs, a manual backup can be created to contain server volumes only. Backups of system state or applications cannot be stored on DVDs.

Remote Shared Folder and Folder on Local Volume

Shares on remote servers or folders on local volumes can be designated as backup targets for manual and scheduled backup jobs. If designating a remote shared folder, this allows an administrator to create a backup not stored on media physically mounted to the system, and also allows for the backup of multiple servers to be stored on a central server. When choosing to back up using a folder on a local volume, this removes the restriction of having to dedicate an entire volume for backup usage. However, when using remote shared folders and folders on local volumes, you need to be aware of a few things:

- The remote shared folder path, as defined by the Universal Naming Convention (UNC) path, cannot be changed; otherwise, the data will become unrecoverable unless a complete PC restore is initiated on a failed system and the new UNC is referenced.
- Only one copy of the backup can be stored within the folder, and each backup will perform a full overwrite backup.
- When a folder on a local volume is selected as a backup destination, the performance of that volume will be severely impacted during backup, which could cause poor system performance if any user data is stored and accessed on the same volume.

Tape Devices

Tape devices are not supported in Windows Server Backup. Administrators who want to back up data to tape will require Microsoft System Center Data Protection Manager or third-party backup applications or they will be forced to create manual backups to disk and then copy the data to tape drives.

Online Backup

Windows Server Backup on Windows Server 2012 now includes an online backup option. This option leverages a Windows Live account and sends backup data to Microsoft cloud-based services. This service only works for data drives so another backup method would be required for the system drive and system state, but it can prove to be very valuable for offsite data backup. For more information about the Windows Server Backup online option, refer to Microsoft documentation.

Backup Media Files

Windows Server Backup stores system backup data in a folder named WindowsImageBackup. Beneath this folder is subfolder named after the server that was backed up. Included in the server folder is a set of Extensible Markup Language (XML) files that detail the backup history, catalog, and system configuration details of the media. Also included in the server folder are one or more Virtual Hard Disk (VHD) files. The VHD files are close to exact duplicates of the backed-up server volumes.

The VHD file can quickly be added and viewed in a virtual machine, so protecting the backup folders is critical to server security.

Backup Options

Windows Server 2012 has made creating and managing backups simple within the Windows Server Backup interfaces. Using either the GUI-based console, the Wbadmin command-line utility, or through the Windows PowerShell cmdlets, backups can be run at the volume level, full system backup, or system state only; alternatively, individual files, folders, or applications can be backed up or excluded from a backup.

Manual Backup Options

Windows Server Backup allows for backups to be created on a recurring schedule or manually using the Backup Once option available in the Windows Server Backup console. Manual backups can be stored on local disks, burned to DVD media, or stored on remote shares. Manual backups on remote shares can be used for complete PC restore operations if the system to be recovered can access the network location during the restore operation.

Scheduled Backup Options

Scheduled backup operations allow administrators to create a backup that recurs, to add backup automation to a Windows Server 2012 system. Scheduled backups can be configured to run multiple times per day to provide additional layers of recoverability.

Windows Server Backup Console

The Windows Server Backup feature includes an MMC snap-in. You can perform most backup-related tasks using this console, including creating backups, reviewing backup history, and restoring data. The Windows Server Backup console can also be used to connect and manage backups on remote Windows Server 2012 systems with the Windows Server Backup feature installed.

Windows Backup Command-Line Utility

All editions of Windows Server 2012 include the Windows Server Backup command-line tool. The wbadmin.exe tool provides granular control of backup and recovery related tasks. Wbadmin enables administrators to start backups and recoveries of systems, get information, and configure new backup storage and scheduled backup policies.

Windows Server Backup PowerShell Cmdlets

Windows Server Backup for Windows Server 2012 includes many new and functional PowerShell cmdlets. Leveraging the cmdlets, as well as the Wbadmin tool, administrators can perform all the backup and restore functions without ever using the graphical interface. To get a list of the available cmdlets from a PowerShell window on a system that has the Windows Server Backup feature installed, enter the following command:

```
get-command -module WindowsServerBackup
```

Using Windows Server Backup

When an organization decides to use Windows Server Backup, the type of backup and the storage media for the backups must be determined. For example, if scheduled backups will be used, an organization must determine the correct storage destination for their Windows Server 2012 backups because each destination has its own set of locally attached disks that must be available and dedicated for the backup.

Installing Windows Server Backup

The easiest way to install the Windows Backup tools is to use the Add Roles and Features function within Server Manager or by installing it using Windows PowerShell. Upon installation, you get the backup feature as well as the console, command-line tools, and PowerShell cmdlets.

Installing Windows Server Backup Using Server Manager

If the Windows Server 2012 GUI is installed, you can install the Windows Server Backup feature using Server Manager. To install the Windows Server Backup feature, follow these steps:

1. Log on to the Windows Server 2012 system with an account with administrator privileges.
2. Open Server Manger and click the Add Roles and Features link.
3. Click Next on the Before You Begin page.
4. On the Select Installation Type page, select the Role-Based or Feature-Based Installation option and click Next.
5. On the Select Destination Server page, select the local server and click Next.
6. Click Next on the Select Server Roles page.
7. On the Select Features page, choose the Windows Server Backup feature and click Next.
8. On the Confirm Installation Selections page, review the summary, and click Install to continue.
9. On the Installation Progress page, review the results, and click Close to complete the installation.

Installing Windows Server Backup Using Windows PowerShell ServerManager Module

In many cases, administrators might choose to use the Windows PowerShell environment to manage a server and as a preference when installing roles, role services, or features. To install the Windows Server Backup feature using Windows PowerShell, follow these steps:

1. Log on to the Windows Server 2012 system with an account with administrator privileges.
2. Open Windows PowerShell from the taskbar.
3. Type the command **Add-WindowsFeature Windows-Server-Backup** and press Enter.
4. After the installation completes, the results will be displayed in the PowerShell Window. Type **exit** in the PowerShell window and press Enter.

Scheduling a Backup Using Windows Server Backup and Allocating Disks

After Windows Server Backup has been installed, no backups will be automatically scheduled. The fastest way to get a backup configured and define any dedicated disks for backups is to run the Backup Schedule Wizard. This wizard enables administrators to not only select and exclude which backup items will be contained within a backup, it also allows the administrator to configure a recurring backup schedule and allocate dedicated disks for scheduled backups. One thing to keep in mind is that if the configuration will support backing up to multiple dedicated disks, to provide some level of backup media rotation it is recommended that all the disks be available during the initial running of the wizard.

When dedicated disks will be used for Windows Server Backup jobs, these disks will be wiped out, reformatted, and from there on, assigned and managed by Windows Server Backup. The disk-allocation process creates a single NTFS-formatted volume that spans the entire disk and sets the disk volume label to include the server name, the date and time the disk is allocated, and the disk number for each disk. To create a full server scheduled backup and allocate disks, follow these steps:

1. Log on to the Windows Server 2012 system with an account with administrator privileges.
2. Ensure that the disks slated for dedicated backup usage are connected and configured as initialized and online. This can be performed using disk management in the computer management console or by using diskpart.exe from the PowerShell or command prompt.
3. Open Server Manager from the taskbar and click Windows Server Backup from the Server Manager Tools menu.
4. When Windows Server Backup opens, click Local Backup in the tree pane.

5. In the actions pane, click the Backup Schedule link to start the Backup Schedule Wizard. Selecting the Backup Schedule link is the only way multiple disks can be allocated to Windows Server Backup in one process.
6. Click Next on the Getting Started page.
7. On the Select Backup Configuration page, select the Full Server (Recommended) option, and click Next to continue.
8. On the Specify Backup Time page, select the time to run the scheduled backup from the Once a Day or the More Than Once a Day selections, and click Next to continue. Figure 30.1 details a backup that will run every day at 12:30 p.m. and 10:30 p.m.

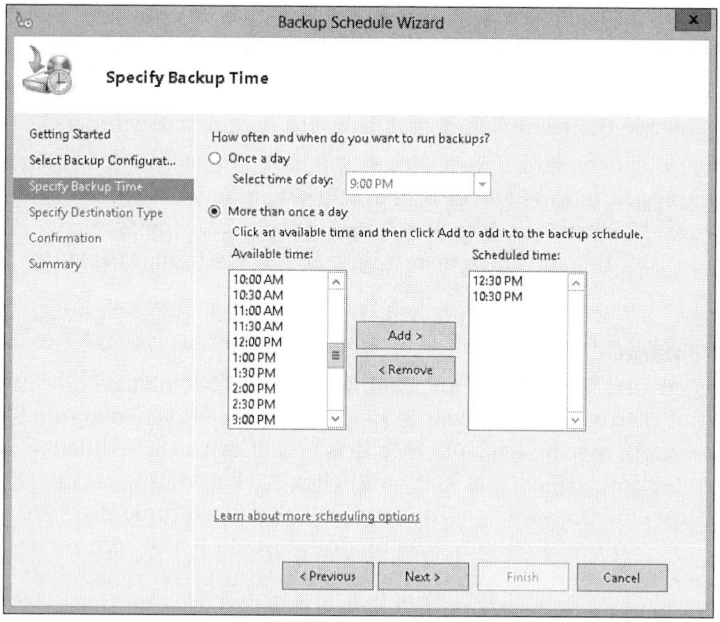

FIGURE 30.1 Setting the scheduled backup to run everyday at 12:30 p.m. and 10:30 p.m.

9. On the Specify Destination Type page, select the Back Up to a Hard Disk That Is Dedicated for Backups (Recommended) option and click Next.
10. Because we selected to use dedicated backup disks, the next page is the Select Destination Disk page. Click the Show All Available Disks button to select the desired disks.
11. In the Show All Available Disks window, check each of the disks that will be dedicated to the scheduled backup, and click OK to save the settings.

NOTE

When multiple disks are assigned to a single scheduled backup, any disk might be used, and that is not under the control of the administrator. If a disk is removed for offsite storage, the remaining disks are used for the next scheduled backup.

12. Back on the Select Destination Disk page, check all the disks that have been added, and click Next to continue.
13. A Windows Server Backup warning window opens requiring confirmation that the selected disks will be reformatted and used by Windows Server Backup exclusively; click Yes to assign the disks for backup.
14. On the Confirmation page, verify the settings, and click Finish to save the new scheduled backup and backup settings and to reformat and label each of the assigned disks.
15. On the Summary page, review the results, and click Close to complete the process.

Creating a scheduled backup using Windows Server Backup allows an administrator to automate the backup process, and with the backup and Volume Shadow Copy Service (VSS) managing the dedicated disks, the administrator only needs to verify that backups have been run successfully.

Manually Running a Scheduled Backup

After the scheduled backup is created for a server, an administrator can let the backup run as scheduled, or the backup can be run manually using the Backup Once link. To manually run a scheduled backup, simply use the Backup Once link and click the Scheduled Backup button on the Backup Options page. Click Next and click Backup on the confirmation page to start the backup. One important point to note is that if multiple disks are allocated to a scheduled backup, running a manual backup does not allow the administrator to select which disk to use. The only way to control which disk is used for scheduled backup is to either remove all the other allocated disks from the system or mark the disks as offline using Disk Management or Diskpart.exe.

Running a Backup to a Shared Network Folder

Windows Server Backup on Windows Server 2012 supports backups to a shared network folder. When a shared network folder is chosen as the backup destination, a system administrator can store full backups on alternate locations to allow for different recovery scenarios. Also, something important to consider is that if a dedicate disk or specific folder on a local volume is selected and is the only backup option, this offers no automated offsite backup. Using a shared network folder can enable offsite backup if the destination system is located in a remote datacenter or if that central server replicates its storage data offsite. To select a shared network folder as a backup destination for a manual backup as an example, follow these steps:

1. Log on to the Windows Server 2012 system with an account with administrator privileges.
2. Open Server Manager from the taskbar and click Windows Server Backup from the Server Manager Tools menu.
3. When Windows Server Backup opens, click Local Server in the tree pane.
4. In the actions pane, click the Backup Once link to start the Backup Once Wizard.
5. On the Backup Options page, select either the Scheduled Backup Options or the Different Options radial button and click Next.
6. On the Select Backup Configuration page, click the Full Server (Recommended) button, and click Next to continue.
7. On the Specify Destination Type page select Remote Shared Folder, and then click Next, as shown in Figure 30.2.

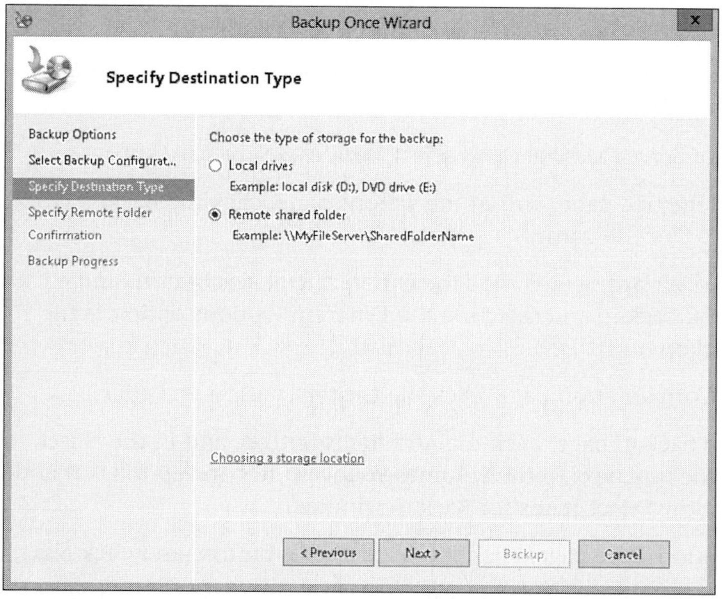

FIGURE 30.2 Selecting to store the backup on a remote shared folder.

8. On the Specify Remote Folder page, type in the UNC path of the remote server share, and click the Inherit Option button to leave the permissions on the folder the same as currently configured.
9. Click Next on the Specify Remote Folder page.

NOTE

Selecting a shared network folder will overwrite any previous backup in that folder for the particular server. Also, because it is an overwrite job, it will always run a full backup of the selection, and backups might take longer.

10. On the Confirmation page, review the settings, and then click Backup to start the manual backup.
11. On the Backup Progress page, you can view the progress in real time or click the Close button and track the progress in the tasks pane back in the Windows Server Backup console. Click Close when the backup completes.

Storing a Backup on DVD

On a Windows Server 2012 system with a local DVD writer drive, backups can be directed to a DVD for storage. Backups stored on DVD media can be used to back up and restore entire volumes only. To create a backup on DVD media, follow these steps:

1. Log on to the Windows Server 2012 system with an account with administrator privileges and open Server Manager.
2. Click the Tools menu of Server Manager and select Windows Server Backup.
3. Select Local Backup in the tree pane, and in the actions pane, click the Backup Once link to start the Backup Once Wizard.
4. When the Backup Once Wizard opens, click the Different Options button, and click Next. Running a manual backup and selecting the Different Options option is the only way to store a backup on DVD.
5. On the Select Backup Configuration page, click the Custom button and click Next.
6. On the Select items for backup page, click the Add Items button, and in the Select Items window, check the box next to the volumes you want to back up to DVD and click OK. Click Next in the Select Items for Backup window.
7. On the Specify Destination Type page, click the Local Drives button, and click Next.
8. On the Select Backup Destination page, select the DVD drive from the pull-down menu, check the Verify After Writing (Recommended) check box, and click Next.
9. On the Confirmation page, review the selections and click Backup to start the manual backup to DVD.
10. On the Backup Progress page, a shadow copy of the volumes is created first. After the shadow copy is created, a window opens prompting the administrator to insert a labeled DVD in the drive. Label the DVD with the name presented in the window, and then insert the blank DVD and click OK to continue.
11. If additional DVDs are required, label and place them in the drive as prompted.

12. Overall backup progress should be viewed in real time, and the window can be closed after the backup completes.

Managing Backups Using the Command-Line Utility Wbadmin.exe and Windows PowerShell Cmdlets

Windows Server 2012 systems running Server Core installations only contain the Windows Server Backup command-line and Windows PowerShell tools. For systems with the GUI installed, the Windows PowerShell cmdlets can also be used. The command-line backup tool used for this example is named wbadmin.exe and can be accessed using a command prompt window. The windows PowerShell cmdlets are accessed in the PowerShell windows. Both tools are very functional and can be used to perform most of the functions available in the GUI.

NOTE

A Windows Server 2012 system with the GUI installed can be used to manage the Windows Server Backup on a remote Server Core installation, if the graphics based backup tools are preferred.

The following sections detail a few common tasks you can accomplish using wbadmin.exe and the PowerShell cmdlets.

Viewing Backup History

To view the backup history of a system, follow these steps:

1. Log on to the Windows Server 2012 system with an account with administrator privileges and open a command window.
2. Type **wbadmin.exe Get Versions** and press Enter to list the backup history.

To perform the same task using Windows PowerShell, follow these steps:

1. Open a Windows PowerShell window and type **Get-WbBackupSet** and press Enter. If the cmdlet cannot be located, you might first need to add in the module by typing **import-module WindowsServerBackup** and pressing Enter.
2. To get a list of all WindowsServerBackup PowerShell cmdlets, type **get-command –module WindowsServerBackup** and press Enter.

Running a Manual System-State Backup to Remote Storage Using Wbadmin.exe and PowerShell

Using wbadmin.exe to run backups can be tedious. To understand each of the options available for a manual backup in a command prompt window, type **wbadmin.exe Start Backup /?** and press Enter. For this example, the data will be stored on the remote server share \\FileServer1\CentralBackup\NLBNODE2, and we will back up the Bare Metal Recovery item, referred to as the AllCritical option. This item includes all volumes in use by the system, including volumes that contain application and share data folders and the system state. For this example, the companyabc\administrator account will be used to connect to the remote share. To run the manual backup using the preceding criteria, follow these steps:

1. Log on to the Windows Server 2012 system with an account with administrator privileges and open a command prompt.
2. Type in the following command:

   ```
   wbadmin.exe Start Backup -Backuptarget:\\FileServer1\CentralBackup\
   NLBNODE2\ -SystemState -user:companyabc\administrator -
   password:My$3cretPW!
   ```

   Then, press Enter to start the backup.
3. The backup window will state that the network share cannot be securely protected. Press Y, and then press the Enter key to allow the backup to run to this network share.
4. The backup progress will be detailed in the command prompt window. After the backup completes, type **exit** to close the command prompt window.

To perform the previous backup task using Windows PowerShell we need to create a backup policy that includes the what will be backed up, the backup destination and the credentials we will use to connect to the backup destination. To run the backup, follow these steps:

1. Log on to the Windows Server 2012 system with an account with administrator privileges and open Windows PowerShell.
2. Type in **$BackupPolicy = New-WbPolicy** and press Enter.
3. Type in **$BackupCred = Get-Credential** and press Enter.
4. When a Windows dialog box opens, enter the username and password combination that will be used to connect to the network share and click OK to save the credentials and return back to the PowerShell window.
5. Back in the PowerShell window, type in **$NetShareBackup = New-WbBackupTarget –NetworkPath \\FileServer1\CentralBackup\NLBNODE2\ -Credential $BackupCred** and press Enter.
6. Type in the following:

   ```
   Add-WbBackupTarget -policy $BackupPolicy -Target $NetShareBackup
   ```

7. Then, press Enter. A warning message will be listed stating that the backup cannot be secured at this location, and the window will show the information related to the new backup target.

8. Type in **Add-WBSystemState –policy $BackupPolicy** and press Enter.
9. Type in **Start-WbBackup –policy $BackupPolicy** and press Enter. The backup should start, as shown in Figure 30.3

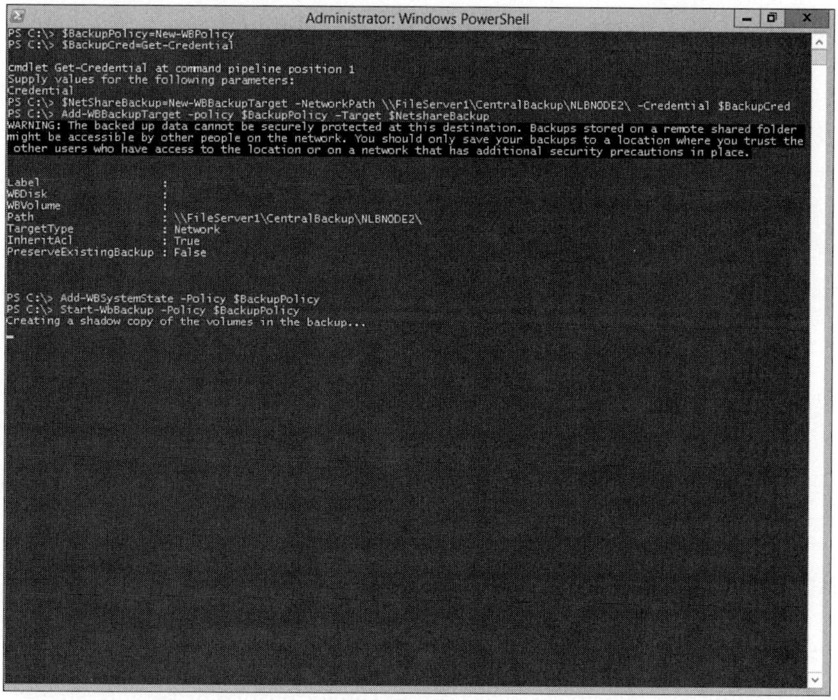

FIGURE 30.3 Running a manual backup to a network share using PowerShell.

Backing Up the System State Using the GUI

The system state of a Windows Server 2012 system contains, at a minimum, the system Registry, boot configuration files, and the COM+ class registration database. Backing up the system state creates a point-in-time backup that can be used to restore a server to a previous working state. Having a copy of the system state is essential if a server restore is necessary. A system-state backup is included in a full server backup, it is included in the Bare Metal Recovery selection, and it can also be backed up separately. To create a separate system-state backup using the GUI, follow these steps:

1. Log on to the Windows Server 2012 system with an account with administrator privileges and open Server Manager from the taskbar.
2. In Server Manager, click the Tools menu and select Windows Server Backup.
3. Click Backup Once in the actions pane.

4. On the Backup Options page, click the Different Options button, and then click Next to continue.
5. On the Select Backup Configuration page, click the Custom button, and then click Next to continue.
6. On the Select Items for Backup page, click the Add Items button. In the Select Items window, check System State check box, as shown in Figure 30.4, and then click OK.

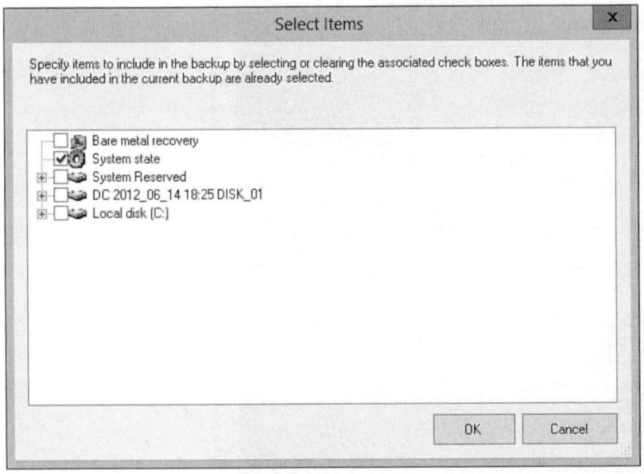

FIGURE 30.4 Selecting a System State only backup.

7. Back on the Select Items for Backup page, click Next to continue.
8. On the Specify Destination Type page, select either the local drive or Remote Shared Folder button and click Next.
9. On the Select Backup Destination page, select a local drive or the specify the path for the remote shared folder, and then click Next to continue.
10. On the Confirmation page review the selections, and then click Backup to continue.

Backing Up Active Directory

Active Directory domain controllers contain a copy of the database that stores all Active Directory-related information. This is stored by default on the C: drive, but to back it up properly administrators need to back up the domain controller's system state. Also critical to an Active Directory backup is the backup of the SYSVOL folder, which contains all of the Group Policy-related files and folders. To properly back up a domain controller, a full backup should be scheduled to run nightly or multiple times per day. In addition to scheduled backups, text file exports and securing the most important objects can assist with reliability and recovery efforts. If full backups cannot be performed daily, performing system-state backups would be sufficient for Active Directory recovery, but that would not be enough to recover the entire domain controller if a bigger issue is encountered.

Active Directory backup and restore tasks are required for the purposes of restoring a deleted object, reverting a configuration change, or to restore a database to a specific domain controller if disk or database corruption occurs.

Exporting Active Directory Object Data Using PowerShell

Windows Server 2012 includes many PowerShell cmdlets for managing Active Directory. To get all the Active Directory-related cmdlets, open a PowerShell window and enter **Get-Command –Module ActiveDirectory**.

Common Active Directory PowerShell cmdlets for reading or exporting data from Active Directory, creating objects, or updating object values are as follows:

- **Get-AdObject**—This cmdlet is used to read AD object data and return it to the screen for reading, exporting, or piping into another cmdlets as a variable value. Some other useful closely related functionality cmdlets include Get-AdUser, Get-ADComputer, Get-AdGroup, Get-AdGroupMember, and several more.
- **Set-AdObject**—This cmdlet enables administrators to update attribute values on specified Active Directory objects. Some other useful closely related functionality cmdlets include Set-AdUser, Set-ADComputer, Set-AdOrganizationalUnit, and several more.
- **Remove-ADObject**—This cmdlet can be used to delete an object or several objects from Active Directory, provided of course that Deletion Protection is not configured for the desired objects. Some other useful closely related functionality cmdlets include Remove-AdUser, Remove-ADGroupmember, Remove-AdOrganizationalUnit, and several more.
- **New-AdObject**—This cmdlet can be used to create new Active Directory objects. Some other useful closely related functionality cmdlets include New-AdUser, New-ADGroup, New-AdOrganizationalUnit, and several more.
- **Restore-AdObject**—This cmdlet can be used to restore an Active Directory object that has been previously deleted as long as the Active Directory Recycle Bin has been enabled before the object was deleted. You can find more information about this cmdlet in Chapter 31, "Recovering from a Disaster."

More AD cmdlets that can be used for common tasks include Unlock-AdAccount and Search-AdAccount. All in all, there are more than 130 Active Directory-related cmdlets included with Windows Server 2012 PowerShell. To perform a few basic Active Directory export tasks using PowerShell, follow these steps:

1. Log on to the Windows Server 2012 system with an account with domain administrator privileges and open Windows PowerShell from the taskbar.
2. Type in **Get-ADObject –Filter *** and press Enter. This will return all the Active Directory objects to the PowerShell window with a default list of attributes.

3. Type in **Get-ADObject –Filter * | Export-csv All-ADObjects.csv** and press Enter. This will return all the Active Directory objects and write the output to a CSV file instead of the window and will include a default list of attributes.

4. Type in **Get-ADObject –Filter * -Properties *| Export-csv All-ADObjects.csv** and press Enter. This will return all of the Active Directory objects and write the output to a CSV file, but this file will include all populated attributes for each object.

The previous command is similar to **ldifde –F allobjects.ldf**, which some administrators may have become accustomed to using to export Active Directory data to text files. For more granular exports, the following list provides a few more examples of Active Directory cmdlet commands that can be run in a PowerShell window with the Active Directory Module loaded:

- get-adobject -LdapFilter "(&(objectcategory=person)(objectclass=user))" -properties * |export-csv all-users.csv
- get-adobject –LdapFilter "(&(objectcategory=person)(objectclass=user))" -properties * |FT
- get-adobject -LdapFilter "(&(objectcategory=person)(objectclass=contact))" |export-csv all-contacts.csv
- get-adobject -LdapFilter "(&(objectcategory=computer)(objectclass=computer))" |export-csv all-computers.csv
- get-adobject -LdapFilter "(&(objectcategory=group)(objectclass=group))" |export-csv all-groups.csv

Accidental-Deletion Protection

A feature first released with the Windows Server 2008 Active Directory Users and Computers and Administrative Center consoles and included in the Windows Server 2012 edition is an option to protect an object from accidental deletion. Setting this option defines a Deny permission to object deletion, so the result is not new, just the simple way to protect the object. To protect an object from accidental deletion, follow these steps:

1. Log on to the Windows Server 2012 domain controller system with an account with domain administrator privileges and open Server Manager.
2. Click the Tools menu and select Active Directory Administrative Center.
3. In the tree pane, select the Users container link beneath the domain.
4. In the users pane in the center, locate the Administrator account, and double-click the user account to open the property pages.
5. Check the Protect from Accidental Deletion box, and click OK to apply the changes, as shown in Figure 30.5.

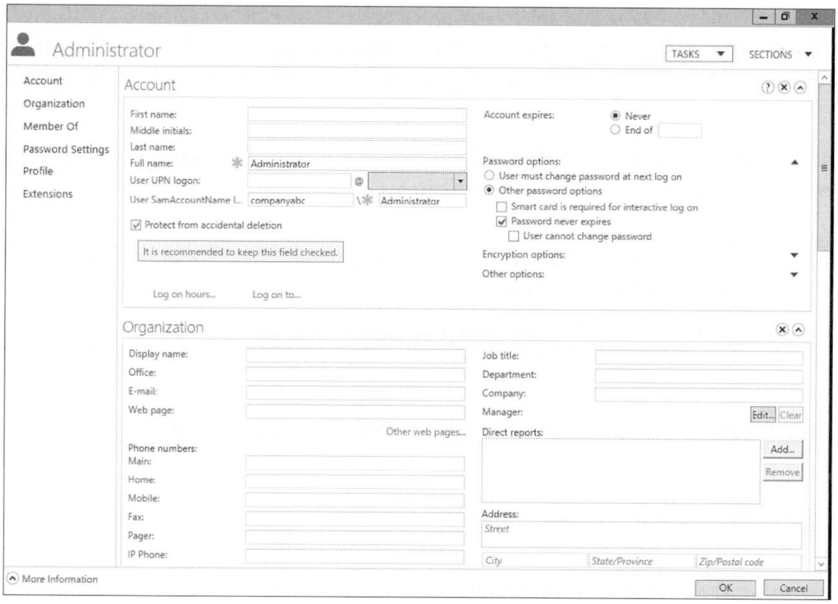

FIGURE 30.5 Enabling accidental-deletion protection on an Active Directory user account.

Using the Directory Services Restore Mode Password

When a Windows Server 2012 system is promoted to a domain controller, the Directory Services Restore Mode (DSRM) password is created. This password is used only when booting into DSRM. Restore mode is used when the Active Directory database is in need of maintenance or needs to be restored from backup. Many administrators have found themselves without the ability to log on to DSRM when necessary and have been forced to rebuild systems from scratch to restore the system-state data. Many hours can be saved if this password is stored in a safe place, where it can be accessed by the correct administrators.

Now with Windows Server 2012, if a full authoritative restore of the entire Active Directory database and SYSVOL folder is required, this can be performed using the Windows Server Backup GUI. If a single object or a container with objects within is accidentally deleted, it can be granularly restored by restoring a backed copy of the domain controller's system state and booting that domain controller into DSRM and performing an authoritative restore of the desired objects. There is an impact, however. When the domain controller is running DSRM, it is offline to domain requests. To avoid this, Windows Server 2012 has a new feature called the AD Recycle Bin, which allows for object recovery while the domain controller is running in normal mode. This is detailed in the next section.

Sometimes restores still require booting a domain controller into DSRM, and the DSRM password is required. To make sure this password is known, the password can be updated regularly on all domain controllers. The Restore mode password is server specific and created on each domain controller. If the password is forgotten, and the domain controller is still functional, it can be changed using the command-line tool NTDSutil.exe from the command prompt. To update the DSRM password on a domain controller named dc1.companyabc.com, follow these steps:

1. Log on to the Windows Server 2012 domain controller with an account with domain administrator privileges and open a command prompt or PowerShell window.
2. Type **NTDSutil.exe** and press Enter.
3. Type **Set DSRM Password** and press Enter.
4. Type **Reset Password on Server dc1.companyabc.com** and press Enter.
5. Type in the new DSRM password, and press Enter.
6. Type in the new DSRM password again for confirmation, and press Enter.
7. Repeat the previous three steps for any additional domain controllers that will have the DSRM password updated. To close out from NTDSutil.exe, type **quit**, press Enter, type **quit** again, and press Enter.
8. Back at the command prompt or PowerShell window, type **exit** to close the window.

Active Directory Recycle Bin

Windows Server 2012 Active Directory includes a feature that can be enabled called the Active Directory Recycle Bin. When enabled, this feature can allow for a deleted Active Directory object to be restored without having to restore the system state of a domain controller and boot to DSRM to perform a selective authoritative restore of that object. Enabling the Active Directory Recycle Bin requires that all domain controllers are running at least Windows Server 2008 R2 or Windows Server 2012. Also, the forest functional level must be set to Windows Server 2008 R2 or greater, and then functionality can be manually enabled. To enable the Active Directory Recycle Bin, follow these steps:

1. Log on to a Windows Server 2012 domain controller and open Active Directory Administrative Center (ADAC) from the Server Manager Tools menu.
2. In the ADAC window, right-click the domain in the tree pane and select properties. Verify that the Forest functional level is set to Windows Server 2008 R2 or Windows Server 2012. Click cancel to close the domain properties window.
3. If the Forest functional level is lower than Windows Server 2008 R2 or Windows Server 2012, in the tree pane right-click the domain and select Raise the forest functional level. In the Raise Forest functional level window select the desired level and click ok.
4. To enable the Active Directory Recycle bin, in the tree pane right-click the domain and select Enable Recycle Bin, as shown in Figure 30.6. Click OK in the confirmation pop-up window to enable the Active Directory recycle bin and press OK one more

time in the window that states to that the recycle bin is enabled and the ADAC window should be refresh to reflect the changes.

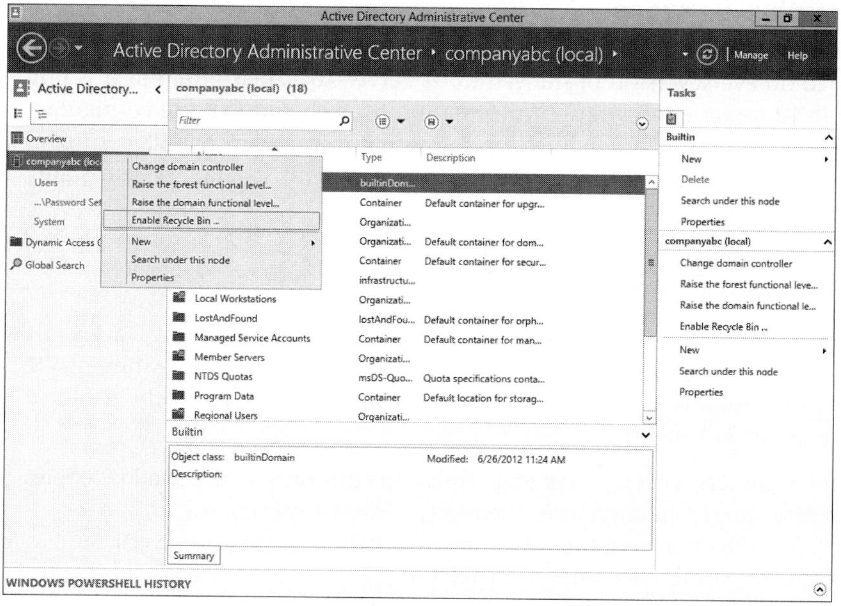

FIGURE 30.6 Enable the Active Directory Recycle Bin in ADAC.

Backing Up Windows Server 2012 Roles

Many Windows Server 2012 role services store configuration and status data in separate files or databases located in various locations on the boot volume. If a scheduled backup is configured to run a full backup or a bare metal recovery backup, this includes all boot, system, and data volumes used by the system as well as any application data and the system state necessary for a complete PC restore. A few services also provide alternative backup and restore options, and should be leveraged to provide additional recovery options in the event of a service failure, as opposed to a full system failure.

Distributed File System Backup

The Distributed File System (DFS) is a Windows Server 2012 service that improves file share availability by providing a single unified namespace to access shared folders hosted across different servers. When DFS domain namespaces are used, DFS folders can be configured to replicate with one another using the DFS Replication service. Domain namespace servers store the DFS folders, targets, and replication group configurations in Active Directory. When a standalone namespace is used, the configuration is stored in the namespace server's Registry. Backing up the system state of a standalone DFS server backs up the DFS configuration. For domain DFS namespaces, backing up the system state of a domain controller accomplishes this task. You can find more information about DFS in Chapter 28.

Internet Information Services

Internet Information Services (IIS) 7.5 is Windows Server 2012's web application and FTP server. It is included on every version of the Windows Server 2012 platform, but it is not installed by default. IIS stores configuration information for web and FTP site configurations and security in a set of XML files stored in the system root folder. The IIS configuration is automatically backed up with full system backups and with separate system-state backups.

Volume Shadow Copy Service

Window Server 2012 Volume Shadow Copy Service (VSS) provides some great features that can be used to enhance backup and recovery for Windows disks. One great feature of VSS is called Shadow Copies for Shared Volumes; it captures and stores copies of the files and folders at a specific point in time.

Administrators and end users with the correct permissions can browse the shadow copies based on the time and date of creation and essentially restore a specific folder, file, or entire volume without restoring from tape. The shadow copies are very space efficient because the first copy is a complete compressed version of the data on the volume, and subsequent copies store only the changes made since the last shadow copy was created.

Another great feature of the VSS is the tight integration it provides for third-party software vendors and to Windows Server Backup. VSS is used by all Windows Server 2012-compliant backup systems.

Enabling Shadow Copies for Shared Volumes

Enabling shadow copies on a volume can be very simple. Administrators have more options when it comes to recovering lost or deleted data and, in many cases, can entirely avoid restoring data to disk from a backup tape device or tape library. In addition, select users can be given the necessary rights to restore files that they've accidentally deleted.

The VSS is already installed and is automatically available on NTFS-formatted volumes. For best backup performance it is recommended to enable shadow copies on all volumes and reserve at least 10% of free space of that volume for shadow copies.

To enable and configure shadow copies, follow these steps:

1. Log on to the Windows Server 2012 system with an account with administrator privileges and open Server Manager.
2. From the Tools menu in Server Manager, select Computer Management.
3. In the tree pane, expand the Storage node, and select Disk Management.
4. In the tasks pane, scroll down to locate the desired disk and volume, right-click the volume, and select Properties.

5. Select the Shadow Copies tab; in the Select a Volume section, click the desired volume, and click the Enable button. A pop-up window will open stating that the default schedule and settings will be used. Click the Yes button. This will enable shadow copies with the default schedule and will create the initial shadow copy.
6. Select the next volume and click the Enable button and Yes in the pop-up window. Repeat for each volume as necessary.
7. To change the schedule, select the desired volume, and then click the Settings button.
8. The Settings page allows you to set the storage space limit for the volume and change the schedule. The default is usually set to 10% of the volume size.
9. Click the Schedule button and define the schedule. The defaults create a shadow copy at 7:00 a.m. and 12:00 p.m.
10. Click OK to close the Schedule window, and click OK again to close the Volume Shadow Copy Settings window.
11. After the shadow copies are created, click OK to close the Shadow Copies page, close the Server Manager, and log off of the server.

To learn how to recover lost or overwritten data using Shadow Copies for Shared Folders, see Chapter 31.

Extending Server Backup to the Enterprise with Data Protection Manager 2012

Windows Server 2012 includes a very powerful backup tool with Windows Server Backup. However, this built-in tool lacks many features when it comes to managing the backup of multiple servers and different applications. Microsoft System Center Data Protection Manager 2012 fills the gaps where Windows Server Backup comes up short. For example, Data Protection Manager 2012 includes support for tape backup and tape libraries, disk-to-disk-to-tape backup and cloud-based backup services provided by Microsoft online services and by third party Microsoft partners. Data Protection Manager also enables large organizations to back up locally and replicate backup sets across WAN links, without leveraging hosted backup services. For more information about Microsoft System Center Data Protection Manager 2012, refer to the Microsoft System Center website.

Summary

When it comes to disaster recovery planning and backing up Windows Server 2012 systems, you have many options to consider. Specialized utilities can be leveraged for specific backup tasks, but for complete server backup, the GUI, command line, and PowerShell cmdlets of Windows Server Backup take care of all the Windows Server 2012 role services requirements.

Best Practices

The following are best practices from this chapter:

- Make sure that disaster recovery planning includes considerations for the physical site, power, entire system failure, server component failure, and software corruption.
- Identify the different services and technologies, points of failure, and critical areas; then prioritize in order of importance.
- Make sure that the disaster recovery solution contains costs associated with additional hardware, complex configurations, and a service-level agreement estimating how long it will take to recover the service should a failure occur. Different options should also be presented.
- Document the server configuration for any environment, regardless of size, number of servers, or disaster recovery budget.
- Verify that any backup disks or remote server shares used to store backups are both physically secure and secured by NTFS and share permissions to reduce the risk of compromising or losing company data.
- Enable shadow copies on all Windows volumes and dedicate at least 10% of the volume size to shadow copies.
- To avoid performance issues on highly utilized systems that will be backed up with Windows Server Backup or Data Protection Manager, set the shadow copies' backup schedule to once a month, and only leave the default schedule for file servers with frequently changing user data.

CHAPTER 31

Recovering from a Disaster

IN THIS CHAPTER

When organizations need to recover data or restore business services and operations after a disruption in business operations, having a well-formulated and validated recovery plan is vital to success. This requires a disciplined process of creating and maintaining backup and recovery procedures and documentation, as well as periodically validating the recovery tasks by simulating different failure scenarios and recovering data and applications.

In addition to having a disaster recovery plan, many organizations—not just the organizations that are required by law—should also implement and follow a strict change management system to evaluate the benefits and risks associated with proposed changes to current business systems, services, applications, and operational processes.

This chapter, as a complement to Chapter 30, "Backing Up the Windows Server 2012 Environment," details how to recover a Windows Server 2012 environment using Windows Server Backup after a failure or disaster has occurred. In addition to system recovery, this chapter provides some best practices and ideas organizations should consider when planning how to support and restore operation to the computer and network infrastructure when system failures and disasters occur.

Ongoing Backup and Recovery Preparedness

Creating and documenting processes that detail how to properly back up and recover from a disaster is an essential step in a disaster recovery project. Equally important as creating these processes is periodically reviewing, validating, and updating the processes. Disaster recovery planning should not be considered a project for the current calendar year; instead, it should be considered an essential part of regular business operations and should have dedicated annual budget and assigned staff.

Each year, many businesses, business divisions, or departments update their computer and network infrastructure and change the way they provide services to their staff, vendors, and clients. In many of these cases, the responsible information technology staff, cross-departmental managers, executives, and employees are not involved or properly informed in advance of the execution or implementation of these changes. Computer and network infrastructure changes can have ripple effects throughout an entire organization during transition and during disaster and failure situations, so proper planning and approval of changes should always be performed and documented.

To reduce the risk of a change negatively impacting business operations, many organizations implement processes that require new projects and system changes to be submitted, evaluated, and either approved or rejected based on the information provided. Although this chapter does not focus or even really discuss project management, all organizations that utilize computer and network infrastructures should consider implementing a project management office and change-control committee to review and oversee organizational projects and infrastructure changes.

Project Management Office

Many organizations have introduced project management offices (PMOs) into their business operations. A PMO is used to provide somewhat of a project oversight committee to organizations that frequently operate several projects simultaneously. Organizations that utilize a proven project methodology can further extend this methodology to include workflow processes that include checkpoints with the PMO staff.

The role of the PMO can be different in almost every organization, but most include a few key functions. The role of the PMO usually involves reviewing proposed projects to determine how or if the project deliverables coincide with the organization's current or future business plans or strategies. PMO membership can also be very different among organizations. PMO membership can include departmental managers, directors or team leads, executive staff, employee advocates, and, in some cases, board members. Having the PMO staff represent views and insight from the different levels and departments of an organization enables the PMO to add value to any proposed project.

Having diverse staff included in the PMO staff enables the organization to evaluate and understand current and proposed projects and how these projects will positively or negatively affect the organization as a whole. General functions or roles a PMO can provide include the following:

- **High-level project visibility**—All proposed projects are presented to the PMO and if approved, the project is tracked by the PMO. This provides a single entity that is knowledgeable and informed about all ongoing and future projects in an organization and how they align to business and technical objectives.

- **Project sounding board**—When a new project is proposed or presented to the PMO, the project will be scrutinized and many questions will be asked. Some of these questions might not have been considered during the initial project design and planning phases. The PMO improves project quality by constantly reviewing and monitoring projects from when the project is proposed and during regular scheduled project status and PMO meetings.
- **Committee-based project approval or denial**—The PMO is informed of all the current and future projects as well as business direction and strategy and is the best-equipped group to decide on whether a project should be approved, denied, or postponed.
- **Enterprise project management**—The PMO tracks the status of all ongoing projects and upcoming projects, which enables the PMO to provide additional insight and direction with regard to internal resource utilization, vendor management for outsourced projects, and, of course, project budget and scheduling.

Change Control

Whereas a PMO improves project management and can provide the necessary checkpoints to verify that backup and recovery requirements are addressed within the new projects, an organization with a change-control system can ensure that any proposed changes have been carefully evaluated and scheduled before approval or change execution. Change control involves a submittal, review, and approval process for each change that typically includes the following information:

- **Change description**—Includes which systems will be changed, what the change is, and why it is proposed or required
- **Impact of the change**—Details if any systems or services will be unavailable during the execution of the change and who will be affected or impacted by the change
- **Change duration**—Details how long it will take to execute and complete the change and, if necessary, revert or roll back the change
- **Change schedule**—Includes the proposed date and time to execute the change
- **Change procedure**—Details how the change will be executed, including a detailed description; this usually also includes detailed steps or an accompanying document
- **Change rollback plan**—Details the steps necessary to recover or roll back the change in the event that the change causes undesirable results
- **Change owners**—Includes who will execute the change and is responsible for communicating the status and results of the change back to the change-control committee

A change-control committee, similar to a PMO, is made of up of managers, executives, and employee advocates who will review and determine if the change is approved, denied, or needs to be postponed. Proposed changes are submitted in advance. A day or two later, a change-control review meeting is held where each change is discussed by the change-control committee and the change owner and the change will be approved, denied, postponed, or closed, or more information will be requested.

During failure or disaster situations, going through the normal change-control process might not be an option due to the impact of the failure. During these situations, emergency change-request processes should be followed. An emergency change request usually involves getting the particular departmental manager and the responsible information technology manager, director, or CIO to sign off on the change before it is executed. In short, all changes need to be considered and approved, even in failure scenarios when time is of the essence. When an administrator is troubleshooting and trying to resolve a failure or trying to recover from a disaster, especially in a stressful situation, making changes without getting approval can lead to costly mistakes. Following the proper change-control and emergency change-control processes to inform and involve others, getting approval from management, and following documented processes will provide accountability and might even save the administrator's job.

Disaster Recovery Delegation of Responsibilities

At this point, the organization might have a documented and functional backup and recovery plan, a PMO, and a change-control committee, but the ownership and maintenance of disaster recovery operations is not yet defined or assigned. Disaster recovery roles, functions, or responsibilities might be wrapped up into an existing executive's or manager's duties, or a dedicated staff member might be required. Commonly, disaster recovery responsibilities are owned by the chief information officer, operations manager, chief information security officer, or a combination of these positions. Of course, responsibilities for different aspects of the overall disaster recovery plan are delegated to managers, departmental leads, and staff volunteers as necessary. An example of delegating disaster recovery responsibilities is contained in the following list:

- The chief information officer is responsible for disaster recovery planning and maintaining and executing disaster recovery-related tasks for the entire telecom, desktop and server computer infrastructure, network infrastructure, and all other electronic and fax-related communication.
- The manager of facilities or operations is responsible for planning alternate office locations and offsite storage of original or duplicates of all important paper documents, such as leases, contracts, insurance policies, stock certificates, and so on, to support disaster recovery operations to alternate sites or offices.
- The manager of human resources is responsible for creating and maintaining emergency contact numbers for the entire company, storing this information offsite, and communicating with employees to provide direction and information prior to disasters striking and during a disaster recovery operation.

The list of responsibilities can be very granular and extensive, and disaster recovery planning should not be taken lightly or put on the back burner. Although there are many aspects of disaster recovery planning, the remainder of this chapter focuses only on the disaster recovery responsibilities and tasks that should be assigned to qualified Windows administrators who need to support a Windows Server 2012 environment.

When Disasters Strike

When a failure occurs or disaster strikes is when not only having but also following a disaster recovery plan is most important. Having a procedure or checklist to follow allows all involved parties to be on the same page and understand what steps are being taken to rectify the situation. The following sections detail steps that can be followed to ensure that no time is wasted and that resources are not being led in the wrong direction.

Qualifying the Disaster or Failure

When a system failure occurs or is reported as failed, the information can come from a number of different sources and should be verified. The reported issue can be caused by user or operator error, network connectivity, or a problem with a specific user account configuration or status. A reported system failure should be verified as failed by performing the same steps reported by the reporting party.

If the system is, in fact, in a failed state, the impact of the failure should be noted, and this information should be escalated within the organization so that a formal recovery plan can be created. This can be known as qualifying the disaster or failure. An example of qualifying a failure includes a short description of the failure, the steps used to validate the failure, who is affected, how many end users are affected, which dependent applications or systems are affected, which branch offices are affected, and who is responsible for the maintenance and recovery of this system.

Validating Priorities

When a disaster strikes that affects an entire server room or office location, the priority of restoring systems and operations should already be determined. First and foremost are the core infrastructure systems, such as networking and power, followed by authentication systems, and the remaining core bare-minimum services. In the event of a failure that involves multiple systems (for example, a web server failure that supports 10 separate applications), the priority of recovery should be presented and approved by management. If each of these 10 applications takes 30 minutes to recover, it could be 5 hours before the system is fully functional, but if one particular application is critical to business operations, this application should be recovered first. Always perform checkpoints and verification to ensure that the priorities of the organization are in line with the recovery work that is being performed.

Synchronizing with Business Owners

Prioritizing the recovery of critical and bare-minimum business systems is part of disaster recovery planning. When a situation strikes that requires an entire data center or group of systems to be restored or recovered, the steps that will be followed need to be put back in front of the business owners. Remember that between the time a disaster recovery plan is created and the time the failure occurs, business priorities might have shifted and the business owners might be the only ones aware of this change. During a recovery situation, always take the time to stay calm and focused and communicate with the managers, executives, and business owners so that they can be informed of the progress. An informed business owner is less likely to stay in the server room or data center if he or she believes that recovery efforts are in good hands.

Communicating with Vendors and Staff

When a failure or a disaster strikes, communication is key. Regardless of whether customers, vendors, employees, or executives are affected, some level of communication is required or suggested. This is where the skills of an experienced manager, sales executive, technical consultant, and possibly even lawyers can be most valuable. Providing too much information, information that is too technical, or, worst of all, incorrect or no information is a common mistake technical staff frequently make. My recommendation to technical staff is to communicate only with your direct manager or his or her boss if you direct manager is unavailable. If the CEO or an end user asks for an update, try to defer to the manager as best you can so that focus can be kept on restoring services.

Assigning Tasks and Scheduling Resources

The situation is that we have a failure, we have an approved plan, we have communicated the situation, and we are ready to begin fixing the issue. The next step is to delegate the specific tasks to the qualified staff members for execution. As stated previously, hand off communication to a manager or spokesperson and only communicate through that person if possible. Determining who will restore a particular system is as important if not more important than assigning communication. Only certain technical staff members might be qualified to restore a system, so selecting the correct resource is essential.

When a serious failure has occurred, recovery efforts might require multiple technical resources onsite for an extended period of time. Furthermore, some dependencies might affect which systems can be restored, and, of course, the order or priority of restore will advance or delay the recovery of a system. Mapping out the extended recovery timeline and technical resource scheduling ensures that a technical resource is not onsite until their skills and time are required. Also, rotating technical resources after 6 to 8 hours of time helps to keep progress moving forward.

Recovering the Infrastructure

After the failure has been validated, the initial communications meetings have been held, restore tasks have been confirmed and possibly reprioritized, and recovery task assignment of resources has been completed, the recovery efforts can finally begin. Verify that each technical resource has all the documentation, phone numbers, software, and hardware they require to perform their task. Hold periodic checkpoint meetings, starting every 15 minutes and tapering off to every 30 or 60 minutes as recovery efforts continue.

Postmortem Meeting

After a system failure or disaster strikes, and the recovery has been completed, an organization should hold a meeting to review the entire process. The meeting might just be an event where individuals are recognized for their great work; however, the meeting will most likely involve reviewing what went wrong and identifying how the process could be improved in the future. A lot of interesting things will happen during disaster recovery situations—both unplanned and simulated—and this meeting can provide the catalyst for ongoing improvement of the processes and documentation.

Disaster Scenario Troubleshooting

This section of the chapter details the high-level steps that can be taken to recover from particular types of disaster scenarios, especially in Windows Server 2012 environments.

Network Outage

When an organization is faced with a network outage, the impact can affect a small set of users, an entire office, or the entire company. When a network outage occurs, the network administrators should perform the following tasks:

- Test the reported outage to verify if the issue is related to a wide-area network (WAN) connection between the organization and the Internet service provider (ISP), the router, a network switch, a firewall, a physical fiber or copper network connection or network port, or line power to any of the aforementioned devices.
- After the issue is isolated or, at least, the scope of the issue is understood, the network administrator should communicate the outage to the necessary managers or business owners and, as necessary, open communication to outside support vendors and ISP contacts to report the issue and create a trouble ticket. And no, this should not go out in email if the network is down.
- Create a logical action plan to resolve the issue and execute the plan.
- Create and distribute a summary of the cause and result of the issue and how it can be avoided in the future. Close the trouble ticket as required.

Physical Site Failure

In the event a physical site or office cannot be accessed, a number of business operations might be suspended. Planning how to mitigate issues related to physical site limitations can be extensive, but should include the considerations discussed in the following sections.

Physical Site Access Is Limited but Site Is Functional

This section lists a few considerations for a situation where the site or office cannot be accessed physically, but all systems are functional:

- Can the main and most critical phone lines be accessed or forwarded remotely?
- Is there a remote-access solution to allow employees with or without notebooks/laptop computers to connect to the organization's network and perform their work?
- Are any other business operations that require onsite access tied to a service-level agreement, such as responding to paper faxes or submitted customer support emails, phone calls, or custom applications?

Physical Site Is Offline and Inaccessible

This section lists a few considerations for a situation where the resources in a site are nonfunctional. This scenario assumes that the site resources cannot be accessed across the network or Internet, and the datacenter is offline with no chance of a quick recovery. When planning for a scenario such as this, the following items should be considered:

- Can all services be restored in an alternate capacity—or at least the most critical systems, such as the main phone lines, fax lines, devices, applications, system, and remote access services?
- If systems are cut over to an alternate location, what is the impact in performance, or what percentage of end-user load can the system support?
- If systems are cut over to an alternate location, will there be any data loss or will only some data be accessible?
- If the decision to cut over to the alternate location is made, how long will it take to cut over and restore the critical services?
- If the site outage is caused by power loss or network issues, how long of an outage should be sustained before deciding to cut over services to an alternate location?
- When the original system is restored, if possible, what will it take to failback or cut the systems back to the main location, and is there any data loss or synchronization of data involved?

These short lists merely break the surface when it comes to the planning of or dealing with a physical site outage, but, hopefully, they will spark some dialogue in the disaster recovery planning process to lead the organization to the solution that meets their needs and budget.

Server or System Failure

When a server or system failure occurs, administrators must decide on which recovery plan of action will be the most effective. Depending on the particular system, in some cases, it might be more efficient to build a new system and restore the functionality or data. In other cases, where rebuilding a system can take several hours, it might be more prudent to troubleshoot and repair the problem.

Application or Service Failure

If a Windows Server 2012 system is still operational but a particular application or service on the system is nonfunctional, in most cases troubleshooting and attempting repair or restoring the system to a previous backup state is the correct plan of action. The Windows Server 2012 event log is useful and it should be one of the first places an administrator looks to determine the cause of a validated issue. Following troubleshooting or recovery procedures for the particular application is the next logical step. For example, if an end user deleted a folder from a network share, the preferred recovery method might be to use shadow copy backups to restore the data instead of the Windows Server Backup.

For Windows services, using Server Manager to review the status of the role and role services assists administrators in identifying and isolating problems because the Server Manager tool displays a filtered representation of Event Viewer items and service state for each role installed on the system. Figure 31.1 details that the File and Storage Services role FILESERVER1 had logged and issue related to the role service.

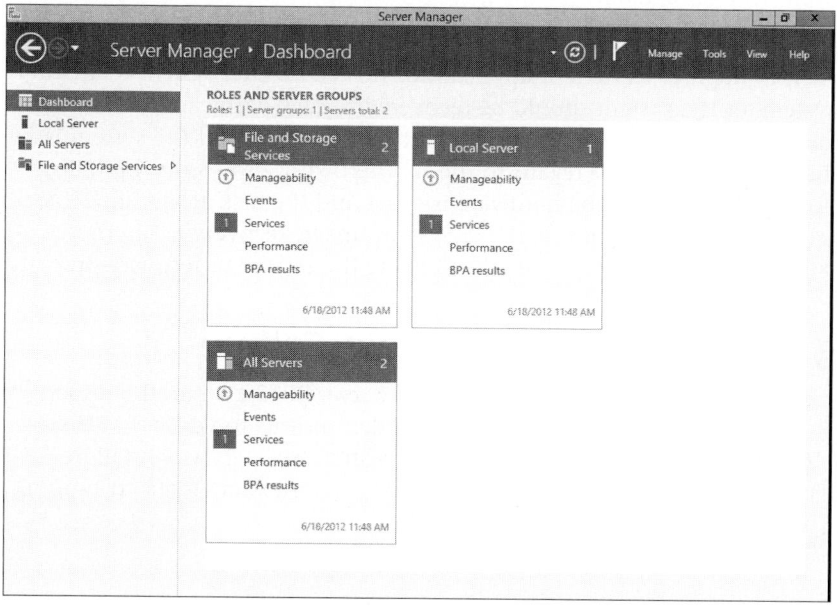

FIGURE 31.1 File and Storage Services role status.

Data Corruption or Loss

When a report has been logged that the data on a server is missing, is corrupted, or has been overwritten, Windows Server 2012 administrators have a few options to deal with this situation. Previous versions backed up with shadow copies can be used to restore selected files or folders, or Windows Server Backup can be used to restore the data. Using shadow copy backups, administrators and end users with the correct permissions can restore data right from the network. Using the restore features of Windows Server Backup, administrators can place the restored data back into the same folder by overwriting the existing data or placing a copy of the data with a different name based on the backup schedule date and time. For example, to restore a file named ClientProprosal.docx that was backed up on 6-10-2012 at 10:30 p.m., Windows Server Backup will restore the file as 2012-06-10 22-30 Copy of ClientProposal.docx.

Hardware Failure

When hardware failure occurs, a number of issues and symptoms might result. The most common issues related to hardware failures include system crashes, services or drivers stopping unexpectedly, frozen (hung) systems, and systems that are in a constant reboot cycle. When hardware is suspected as failed or failing on a Windows Server 2012 system, administrators should first review the event logs for any related system or application event warnings and errors. If nothing apparent is logged, hardware manufacturers usually provide several different diagnostic utilities that can be used to test and verify hardware configuration and functional state. Don't wait to call Microsoft and involve their professional support services department as they can be working in conjunction with your team to capture and review debugging data.

When a system is suspected of having hardware issues and it is a business-critical system, steps should be taken to migrate services or applications hosted on that system to an alternate production system, or the system should be recovered to new hardware. Windows Server 2012 can tolerate a System Image Recovery to alternate hardware if the system is an exact or close hardware match with regard to the motherboard, processors, hard disk controller, and network card. Even if the hardware is exact and the disk arrays, disk IDs, and volume or partition numbers do not match, a System Image Recovery to alternate hardware might fail if no additional steps are taken during the restore or recovery process.

Recovering from a Server or System Failure

When a failure or issue is reported regarding a Windows Server 2012 system, the responsible administrator should first perform the standard validation tests to verify that there is a real issue. The following sections include basic troubleshooting steps when failure reports are based around data or application access issues, network issues, data corruption, or recovery issues.

Access Issues

When end users report issues accessing a Windows Server 2012 system but the system is still online, this is categorized as an access issue. Administrators should start troubleshooting access issues by first verifying that the system can be accessed from the system console and then verify that it can be accessed across the network. After that is validated, the access issue should be tested to reveal whether the access issue is affecting everyone or just a set of users. Access issues can be system or network related, but they can also be related to security configurations on the network or local system firewall or application, share, or NTFS permissions. The following sections can be used to help troubleshoot access issues.

Network Access Troubleshooting

Troubleshooting access to a system that is network related can involve the networking group as well as the Windows Server 2012 system administrators. When networking issues are suspected, the protocol and system IP information should be noted before any tests are performed. Tests should be performed from the Windows system console to determine whether the system can access other devices on the local network and systems on neighboring networks located across a gateway or router. Tests should be performed using both the system domain name system (DNS) names as well as IP addresses and, if necessary, IPv6 addresses.

If the system can communicate out but users still cannot access the system, possible causes could be an incorrect IP subnet mask, default gateway or routing table, or firewall restrictions imposed locally or through group policy. Windows Firewall is enabled by default on Windows Server 2012 systems, and the firewall supports multiple firewall profiles simultaneously if multiple adapters are installed on the system. If a network is identified incorrectly as a public network instead of a private or domain network, depending on the firewall profile settings, this may undesirably restrict access. When administrators follow the proper procedures for installing roles and role services, during role installation, exceptions will be added to the firewall. Administrators can review the settings using the Windows Firewall applet from Control Panel, but to get very detailed firewall information, the Windows Firewall with Advanced Security console should be used. You can access this console through the Server Manager Tools menu.

Share and NTFS Permissions Troubleshooting

If network connectivity and firewall configurations check out, the next step in troubleshooting access issues is to validate the configured permissions to the affected application, service, or shared folder. For application access troubleshooting, see the section "Application Access Troubleshooting" and the application vendors' administration and troubleshooting guides. For Windows services and share folder permission troubleshooting, the Event Viewer can assist tremendously, especially if auditing is enabled. Auditing can be enabled within an Active Directory group policy on the Windows Server 2012 local computer policy, but auditing must also be enabled on the particular NTFS folder. For information about local and domain group policies, see Chapter 27, "Group Policy Management for Network Clients." To troubleshoot share and NTFS permissions, review the following sections.

Validating Share and NTFS Permissions

When you need to validate share and NTFS permissions, you can do so in several ways. The preferred method is to use the File and Storage Services node within Server Manager, as detailed in the following steps:

1. Log on to the Windows Server 2012 system with an account with administrator privileges and open Server Manager from the taskbar.
2. Click the File and Storage Services link in the tree pane on the left.
3. In the File and Storage Services section of Server Manager, click the Shares link and in the Shares pane, right-click the desired share, and select Properties.

4. Select the Permissions link on the left, and the window will display the NTFS permission and will summarize the share permissions.

5. Click the Customize Permissions button.

6. In the Advanced Security Settings window, select the permission tab for NTFS permissions, the Share tab for share permissions, and the Central Policy tab to review Dynamic Access Control settings for the shared folder, as shown in Figure 31.2.

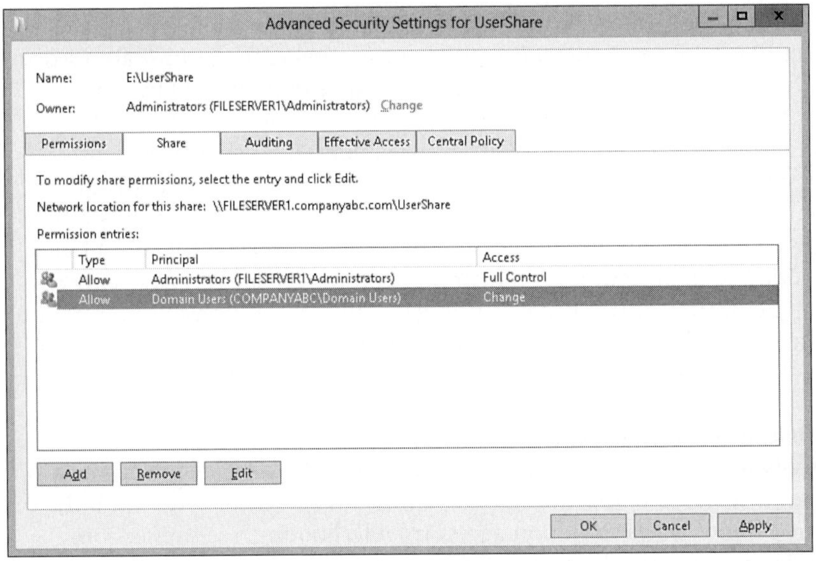

FIGURE 31.2 Reviewing shared folder permissions.

7. Close the Advanced Security Settings window, close the share properties window, and close Server Manager when done reviewing the settings.

Enabling Auditing for NTFS Folders

Enabling auditing on an NTFS folder can be a helpful aid in troubleshooting access to server folders. Enabling auditing for NTFS folders is a two-part configuration involving either Group Policy or local computer policy audit settings as well as configuring auditing on the folder itself. To enable auditing for a folder on a Windows Server 2012 system, follow these steps:

1. Log on to the Windows Server 2012 system with an account with administrator privileges and open Server Manager.

2. From the Server Manager tools menu, select Local Security Policy.

3. In the tree pane of the Local Security Policy window, double-click Local Policies, and double-click Audit Policy.

4. In the tasks pane, double-click Audit Object Access.
5. When the Audit Object Access window opens, check the Failure check box, and click OK, as shown in Figure 31.3.

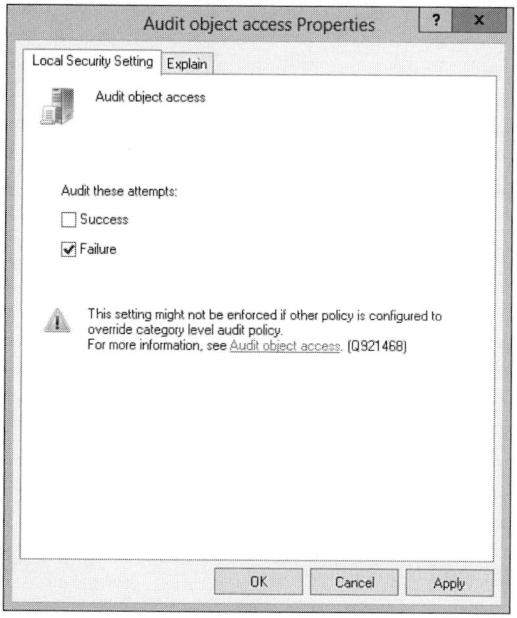

FIGURE 31.3 Enabling failure audit for object access.

6. Close the Local Security Policy window.
7. Back in Server Manager, click the File and Storage Services link in the tree pane on the left.
8. In the File and Storage Services section of Server Manager, click the Shares link and in the Shares pane, right-click the desired share, and select Properties.
9. Select the Permissions link on the left, and the window will display the NTFS permission and will summarize the share permissions.
10. Click the Customize Permissions button.
11. Select the Auditing tab and click the Add button to change the audit settings of the shared folder. In this particular example, we want to log failed attempts to access the folder, so we will use the Everyone group and enable All Failure Audits.
12. In the Audit Entry for the share window, click the Select a Principal link at the top of the window.
13. When the Select User, Computer, Service Account, or Group window opens, type in **Everyone** and click OK.

14. In the Auditing Entry for the share window, pull down the Type menu and select the Fail Audit option and check the Full Control Permissions check box. Click OK to apply the new audit settings, as shown in Figure 31.4.

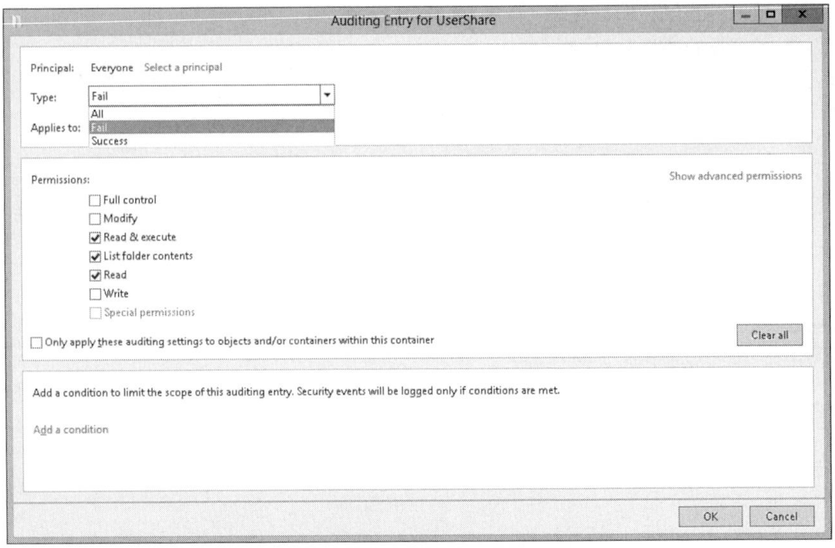

FIGURE 31.4 Configuring an audit entry for the shared NTFS folder.

15. In the Advanced Security Settings window, check the Replace All Existing Inheritable Auditing Entries check box, and then click OK.

16. Click OK to close the Advanced Security page, click OK to close the share property pages, and close Server Manager.

When a user then attempts to access the shared folder with the enabled audit settings and fails based on permissions, a failed audit entry will be logged on the server's Security event log.

Application Access Troubleshooting

If the issue revolves around an application running on a Windows Server 2012 system, troubleshooting the application according to the application administration guide is the recommended approach. Many applications can be configured to use authentication using Active Directory via Lightweight Directory Access Protocol (LDAP), Kerberos, or NTLM authentication. Also, applications might use custom application or database user accounts and might still require permissions via application pool identities and service accounts. Each application is different and should be treated as such. Specific troubleshooting guides and backup and recovery documentation should be created for applications before they are deployed on a network.

Data Corruption and File and Folder Recovery

When data is reported as corrupted or deleted, administrators have the option of restoring the data from backup using Windows Server Backup or from a previous version of that folder captured with shadow copies. When data has been mistakenly changed, overwritten, or deleted, the only options are to recover from shadow copies or from backup media as detailed in the following sections.

Recovering File and Folder Data Using Shadow Copies

To recover individual files and folders using previously created shadow copies, follow these steps:

1. Log on to a Windows Server 2012 system or a client system running Windows XP SP1 or greater and open Windows Explorer.
2. In the Windows Explorer window type **servername**\ and press Enter, where servername represents the NetBIOS or fully qualified domain name of the server hosting the file share. The share must already exist and be stored on a volume in which a shadow copy has already been created.
3. Right-click the folder beneath the share, or the share itself, that contains the file or folder that will be restored, and select Restore Previous Versions.
4. When the window opens, if necessary, select the Previous Versions tab, and select the desired previous version based on the date and click Open, as shown in Figure 31.5.

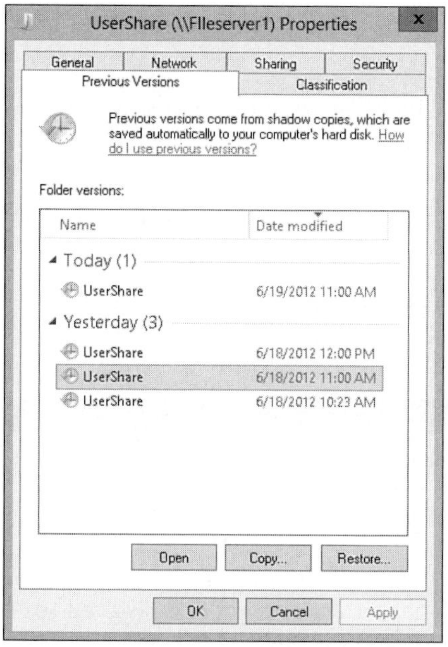

FIGURE 31.5 Selecting the desired previous version shadow copy for data restore.

5. After the previous version of the share or folder beneath the share is opened, displaying the contents, select a single file single folder or multiple items, right-click the selections, and choose Copy. This places the selected items in the Clipboard.
6. Close the previous version window and close the share or folder properties window.
7. Browse to the location where the data will be restored, right-click in an empty location, and choose Paste. Overwrite the file as desired or restore the data to an alternate location, and close all the windows when completed.

Recovering File and Folder Data Using Windows Server Backup

To recover individual files and folders using backup media created with Windows Server Backup, follow these steps:

1. Log on to the Windows Server 2012 system with an account with administrator privileges and open Server Manager from the taskbar.
2. From the Tools menu, select Windows Server Backup.
3. When the Windows Server Backup window opens, select Local Backup in the tree pane.
4. Click Recover from the actions pane.
5. On the Getting Started page, select either to restore data previously backed up from the local computer or a different computer. For this example, select This Server (Servername), and click Next to continue.
6. On the Select Backup Data page, select the date of the backup by selecting the correct month and click the particular day.
7. After the month and day are selected, if multiple backups were run in a single day, click the Time drop-down list arrow, and select the correct backup. Click Next to continue after the month, day, and time are selected.
8. On the Select Recovery Type page, select the Files and Folders option button, and click Next to continue.
9. On the Select Items to Recover page, expand the server node; select the disks, folders, and files to be restored; and click Next to continue.

NOTE

Unlike other backup utilities, Windows Server Backup does not contain check boxes to select items for recovery. To select an item or multiple items, simply click the item to highlight it and use the Shift or Ctrl keys to make multiple sections.

10. On the Specify Recovery Options page, specify whether the files will be restored to the original location or an alternate location. Do not click Next.

11. On the Specify Recovery Options page, if the restore will be placed in the original location, specify how to deal with existing files by choosing to either create copies in the same folder, overwrite the existing data with restore data or do not recover items that already exist. Also check or uncheck the check box to determine whether NTFS access control lists will also be restored with the data, as shown in Figure 31.6.

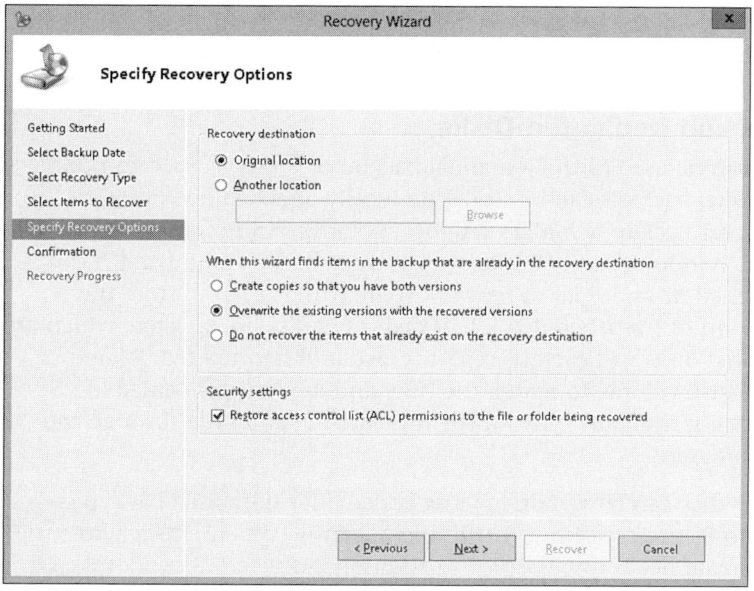

FIGURE 31.6 Selecting the desired recovery options.

12. On the Confirmation page, verify the restore selections and options. If everything is correct, click the Recover button to start the recovery process.

13. On the Recovery Progress page, verify the success of the recovery or troubleshoot the errors if the recovery fails.

14. Click Close to complete the recovery and close Windows Server Backup.

15. Browse to the location of the restore to verify the recovery and notice that there are two copies, the original and the restored, which is named after the date and time the backup was taken. When you have finished, log off of the server.

Managing and Accessing Windows Server Backup Media

Windows Server Backup for Windows Server 2012 can create backups of the entire system, specific volumes, system state, applications or granular folders or files. Windows Server Backup also supports the exclusion of individual files and folders within a configured backup job. Windows Server Backup can store backups on dedicated locally attached disk folders, dedicated backup disks or network shared folders. New for Windows Server 2012 there is also an online cloud based backup that can backup data volumes directly to the cloud with the use of a specific online backup agent.

Windows Server Backup can be configured to run a scheduled backup or a manual backup. Either can be run from the graphical user interface or the command-line utility, but the backup options, including where the backup can be stored and the recovery options available, are different.

Windows Server Backup Dedicated Disks

Windows Server Backup can be used to run a manual backup or it can be used to run a scheduled backup. Scheduled backups can be stored on locally attached disks that are dedicated to Windows Server Backup, a folder on a local volume or a network shared folder. When a scheduled Windows Server Backup job is created, the administrator can define which locally attached disks, folder or network share will be used to store the backups. During the creation of the scheduled job, if dedicated disk are selected, which are recommended, the allocated disks will each be repartitioned and reformatted. Windows Server Backup stamps the disk volume to match the time and date the scheduled job is created. By default, this disk is available only on the local system and only through the Windows Server Backup program.

A Windows Server Backup disk can have a drive letter added after the initial backup is created if the disk needs to be accessed from within the operating system, from across the network, or if the backup data needs to be copied to additional disks or network folders for offsite storage. Backups contained on a Windows Server Backup dedicated disk can be used to restore an entire system, an entire volume, a set of specified files and folders, or application data.

Network Shared Folders

When Windows Server Backup is configured to back up to a network shared folder, backup administrators need to consider a few things. First, the share and NTFS permissions should be configured so that only backup administrators and specific service accounts can access and read this data. Also, if this share contains data that will be replicated by a third-party provider, special permissions may need to added to support this. Another very important point to note about network shared folders for Windows Server Backup is that only the most recent copy of the backup will be stored, because each backup overwrites the previous. This is unlike backup to dedicated disks, which can store multiple versions and copies of a Windows Server 2012 system backup.

Windows Server Backup Volume Recovery

When an entire disk or disk volume has been corrupted and needs to be recovered, you can use Windows Server Backup to restore the volume. Local disks, local folder backups, and network shared folder backups can be used to restore an entire volume using Windows Server Backup. When an entire volume needs to be recovered, unless the volume contains system data, the volume can be restored using the Windows Server Backup program from within a running operating system. If the volume contains system folders, the restore needs to be restored using the Repair Your Computer option when booting the system using the Windows installation media.

Windows Server 2012 Data Volume Recovery

When a data volume on a Windows Server 2012 system has failed and needs to be restored using Windows Server Backup, follow these steps:

1. Log on to the Windows Server 2012 system with an account with administrator privileges and open Server Manager from the taskbar.
2. From the Tools menu, select Windows Server Backup.
3. When the Windows Server Backup window opens, select Local Backup in the tree pane.
4. Click Recover from the actions pane.
5. On the Getting Started page, select either to restore data previously backed up from the local computer or a different computer. For this example, select This Server (Servername), and click Next to continue.
6. On the Select Backup Data page, select the date of the backup by selecting the correct month and click the particular day.
7. After the month and day are selected, if multiple backups were run in a single day, click the Time drop-down list arrow, and select the correct backup. Click Next to continue after the month, day, and time are selected.
8. On the Select Recovery Type page, select the Volumes option button, and click Next to continue.
9. On the Select Volumes page, the window displays each of the volumes contained in the backup that was previously chosen. Check the box next to the desired volume that will be restored, and select the destination volume to which you will restore the backed-up volume. Figure 31.7 displays that the backed-up F: volume will be restored to the existing F: volume. Click Next to continue after the correct selections are made.
10. After clicking Next on the Select Volumes page, a window opens requesting confirmation that the data on the volumes will be lost by the recovery process; click Yes to continue with the volume recovery process.
11. On the Confirmation page, review the selections. If everything looks correct, click the Recover button to start the volume recovery.
12. On the Recovery Progress page, the recovery status of the volume will be displayed. After the recovery completes, review the results and click Close if the recovery was successful; otherwise, select the Errors tab to review the errors.

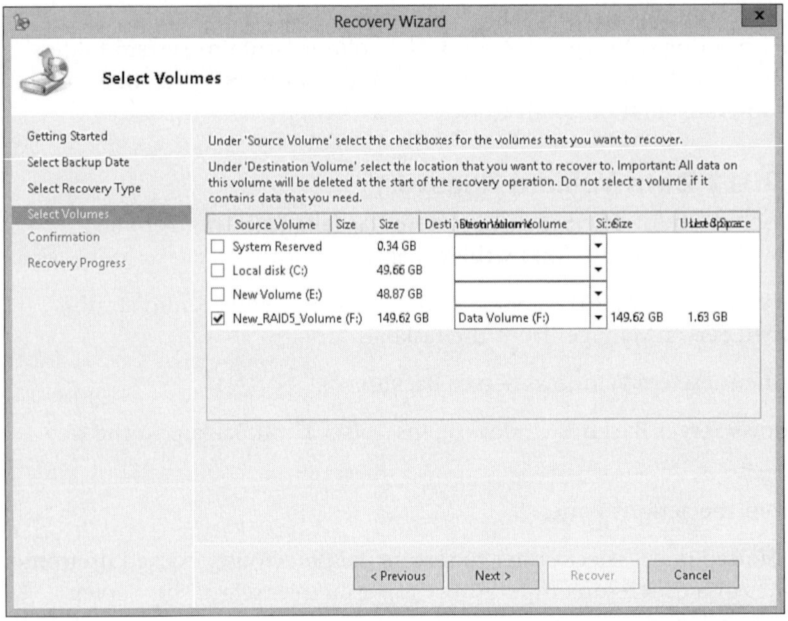

FIGURE 31.7 Selecting the source and destination volumes for volume recovery.

13. If the volume recovery was successful, the only additional step that might be required is to reboot the system if the data on the volume is shared or used by any applications or services. Reboot as required.

Windows Server 2012 System Volume Recovery

You cannot restore a system volume by using Windows Server Backup. System volumes can only be restored using the Windows installation recovery environment from the Windows installation media. System volumes should only be restored separately when the system volume is corrupted or failed but the system hardware has not changed and data disks remain intact. Any Windows disk that contains system volumes will be erased and restored as part of this process. If a single disk contains two volumes (the system volume and a separate data volume), the data volume will also be erased and restored by this process. To restore the system volume, follow these steps:

1. Boot your system using the Windows Server 2012 installation media. If necessary, configure the BIOS to allow booting from the CD/DVD drive and, if prompted, press a key to boot from the DVD.

2. When the Windows Setup interface opens, select the correct language, time, and keyboard settings, and click Next to continue.

3. On the next page, click the Repair Your Computer link located in the lower-left corner of the window.

4. On the Choose an Option page, select the Troubleshoot tile.

5. On the Advanced Options page, select System Image Recovery tile to continue.

6. On the System Image Recovery page, select to restore the Windows Server 2012 installation by clicking the tile.

7. A Re-Image Your Computer window will open and will display the option to restore the latest available system image by default, as shown in Figure 31.8.

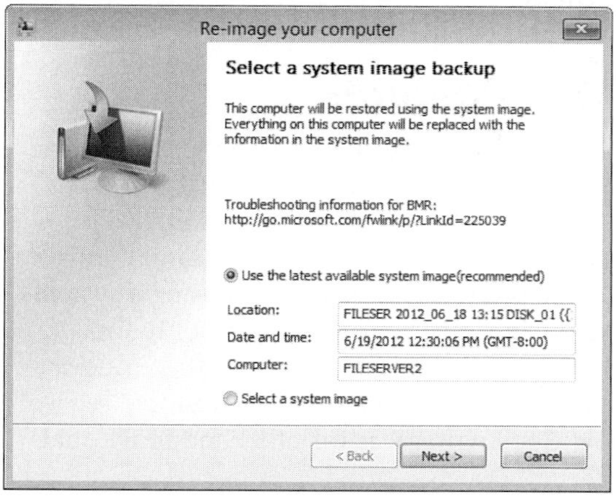

FIGURE 31.8 Selecting to restore the latest system image.

8. On the Choose Additional Restore Options page, the box labeled Only Restore System Drives will be checked and dimmed (grayed out). Do not make any other changes. Click Next to continue. This will leave any other disks intact, but any volumes that are hosted on the same disks that contain system volumes will be formatted, re-created, and restored as well.

9. The next page details the date and time of the backup that will be restored, the server that will be restored, and the volumes that are contained in this restore set. Review the information and click Finish to continue with the recovery of the system volumes.

10. A dialog box will appear stating that all drives selected will be restored with the data in the system image. Click Yes to approve this and continue.

    The recovery time frame will vary depending on the size of the system volume, the performance of the volume, and the restore disk or network share. After the recovery completes, the system will automatically reboot.

11. After the system reboots, log on and verify functionality. If everything is back up and running, run a full backup and log off.

Windows System Image Recovery

In the event of a complete system failure, it might be necessary to restore a Windows Server 2012 system in its entirety. If this is the case, perform the same steps as a system volume recovery, except on the Choose Additional Restore Options page, check the Format And Repartition Disks check box. This restores all the disks and also performs the disk partitioning, drive letter assignment, and mounted volume configuration. If different-size disks are provided, the restore partitions the disks based on the original size of the disk volumes only. Smaller disks will cause the restore to fail, but larger disks can easily be extended after the recovery completes successfully.

Recovering Role Services and Features

Each particular role on a Windows Server 2012 system can have very specific backup and recovery procedures. As a general rule, though, performing full backups using Windows 2012 Windows Server Backup will enable the restore of a system to a previous imaged version, including restoring all Windows Server roles, role services, features, and configuration to that previously backed-up state. Most role services can be restored using a system-state recovery; however, a system-state recovery cannot be restored in part; only the complete system state can be restored. Depending on the role, however, with Windows 2012, different application databases, such as the cluster database, can be restored separately as long as a compatible Volume Shadow Copy writer was installed and functional before the backup was taken.

Windows Server 2012 System-State Recovery

When operating systems become corrupt or unstable or a role service needs to be rolled back to a previously backed-up state, the quickest and easiest way to perform this task is to restore the system state. The system state can be backed up independently, but is also contained within a full server backup. To restore the System state on a member server from a previous backup, follow these steps:

1. Log on to the Windows Server 2012 system with an account with administrator privileges and open Server Manager from the taskbar.
2. From the Tools menu, select Windows Server Backup.
3. When the Windows Server Backup window opens, select Local Backup in the tree pane.
4. Click Recover from the actions pane.
5. On the Getting Started page, select either to restore data previously backed up from the local computer or a different computer. For this example, select This Server (Servername), and click Next to continue.

6. On the Select Backup Data page, select the date of the backup by selecting the correct month and click the particular day.
7. After the month and day are selected, if multiple backups were run in a single day, click the Time drop-down list arrow, and select the correct backup. Click Next to continue after the month, day, and time are selected.
8. On the Select Recovery Type page, select the System State option button, and click Next to continue.
9. On the Select Location for System State Recovery page, click the Original Location button and click Next to continue. If this system was a domain controller, more options will be available, but that is covered later in this chapter.
10. On the Confirmation page, review the section and then press Recover to start the process. Once the process starts a checkbox to Automatically reboot the server to complete the recovery process is presented and already checked by default.
11. After the system reboots, log on to the server to verify functionality. If the system is working properly, perform a full system backup.

Active Directory Recycle Bin Recovery

Let me start this section with a very clear statement: If you need to recover a deleted Active Directory object and the Active Directory Recycle Bin was not enabled before the object was deleted, skip this section and proceed to the following "Active Directory Authoritative Restore" section. If the Active Directory Recycle Bin feature was enabled before an Active Directory object was deleted, follow these steps to recover objects using the Active Directory Recycle Bin:

1. Log on to the Windows Server 2012 domain controller system with an account with domain administrator privileges and open Server Manager from the taskbar.
2. From the Tools menu of Server Manager, select Active Directory Administrative Center.
3. In the tree pane, click the domain to reveal each of the root-level organizational units and containers. Select the Deleted Objects container.
4. In the center pane, each of the deleted objects should be listed. Review or expand the Last Known Parent column. This is the location the object will be restored to by default.
5. If the last known parent is where the object should be restored to, right-click the object and select Restore, as shown in Figure 31.9. If the object should be restored elsewhere, right-click the object and select Restore To, and then select the desired container or organizational unit.

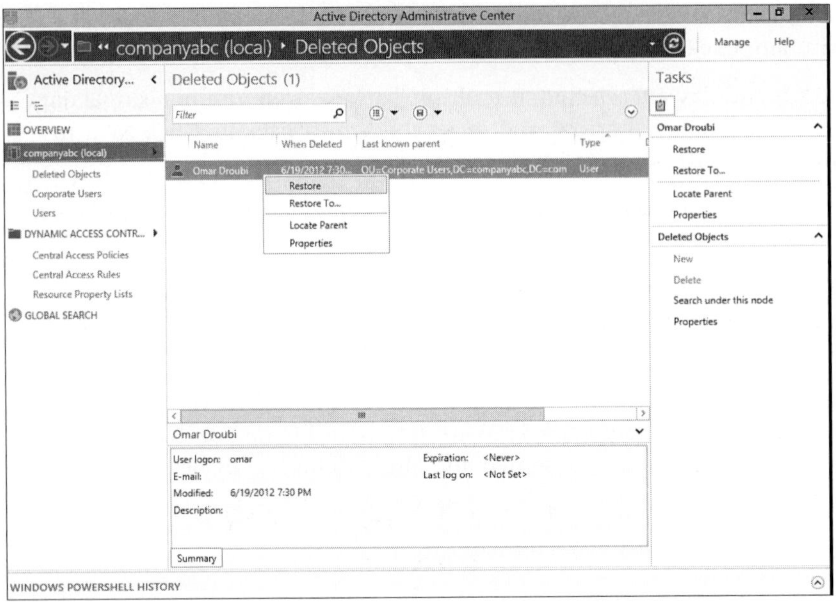

FIGURE 31.9 Restoring a deleted Active Directory user object from the AD Recycle Bin.

System-State Recovery for Domain Controllers

Performing a system-state recovery for a domain controller is similar to the recovery of a member server, but the domain controller will need to be booted into Directory Services Restore Mode (DSRM) before attempting the restore. Recovering the system state of a domain controller should only be performed if one or more of the following scenarios are encountered:

- A deleted object needs to be restored and the Active Directory Recycle Bin is not enabled, or was not enabled when the object was originally deleted.
- The Active Directory Domain Services service will not start or the Active Directory database on that domain controller is corrupted.
- The files, possibly including scripts or group policies, stored in the SYSVOL folder have been deleted or overwritten and need to be restored and replicated across the domain.

Before a domain controller can be booted into DSRM, the DSRM password is required. This password is configured when a system is promoted to a domain controller and is stored locally on each domain controller. The DSRM username is administrator with no domain designation, and the password can manually be changed on a working domain controller by using Ntdsutil. To restore the system state of a domain controller, follow these steps:

1. If the domain controller is still functional, log on to the Windows Server 2012 domain controller system with an account with domain administrator privileges.
2. Click the charms bar and select the Search option. In the Search pane, type in **MSConfig** and press Enter.
3. In the MSConfig.exe window (System Configuration Utility), select the Boot tab.
4. In the Boot Options section, check the Safe Boot check box, click the Active Directory Repair button, as shown in Figure 31.10, and then click OK.
5. The System Configuration utility will ask for a reboot, and if there are no additional tasks to perform, click the Restart button to boot the system into DSRM.

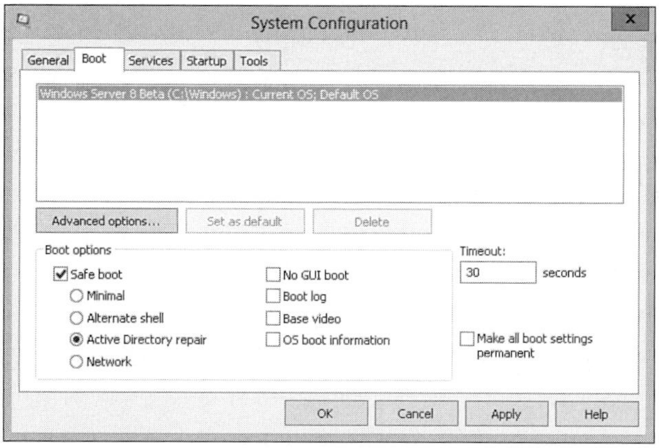

FIGURE 31.10 Using the System Configuration utility to boot a domain controller into Directory Services Restore Mode.

6. When the system completes a reboot, log on as administrator with the DSRM password. Make sure to specify the local server as the logon domain (for example, DC\administrator instead of companyabc\administrator).
7. Open Server Manager from the taskbar, and from the Tools menu select Windows Server Backup.
8. When the Windows Server Backup window opens, select Local Backup in the tree pane.
9. Click Recover from the actions pane.
10. On the Getting Started page, select either to restore data previously backed up from the local computer or a different computer. For this example, select This Server (Servername), and click Next to continue.
11. On the Select Backup Data page, select the date of the backup by selecting the correct month and click the particular day.

12. After the month and day are selected, if multiple backups were run in a single day, click the Time drop-down list arrow, and select the correct backup. Click Next to continue after the month, day, and time are selected.

13. On the Select Recovery Type page, click the System State button, and click Next to continue.

14. On the Select Location for System State Recovery page, click the Original Location button. Do not check the Perform an Authoritative Restore of Active Directory Files box unless the SYSVOL folder and contents will be marked as the definitive/authoritative copy and replicated to all other domain controllers. For our example, we will recover the system state but not mark the SYSVOL as an authoritative restore, as shown in Figure 30.11. Click Next to continue.

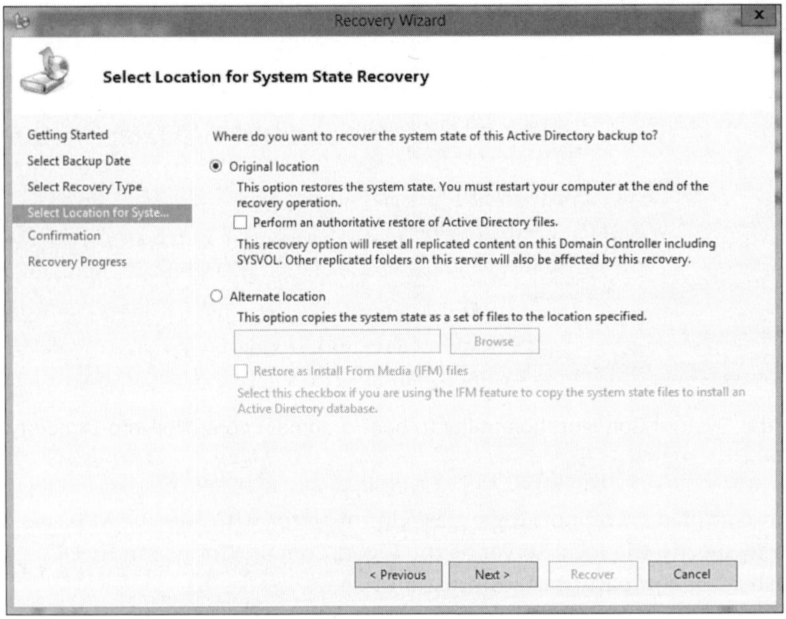

FIGURE 31.11 Restoring a domain controller system state without marking the SYSVOL data as authoritative.

15. A dialog box opens that states that this recovery option will cause the server to re-sychronize after recovery. Click OK to continue.

16. On the Confirmation page, verify that the system state is listed, and click Recover to start the system-state recovery of the domain controller.

17. A dialog box opens detailed that once the recovery is started it cannot be paused and a restart will be required to complete the recovery. Click Yes to start the recovery. System-state recovery can take a long time to complete, so be patient.

18. When the system-state restore completes, Windows Server Backup presents a dialog box with only a Restart button and no other option. Restart the server now.
19. When the server reboots, it reboots into DSRM again. Log on with the DSRM local username and password.
20. Once logged in, a wbadmin command prompt will open stating that the restore completed successfully. Close the command prompt window by pressing Enter.
21. Click the charms bar and select the Search option. In the Search pane, type in **MSConfig** and press Enter.
22. In the MSConfig.exe window (System Configuration Utility), select the Boot tab.
23. In the Boot Options section, uncheck the Safe Boot check box, and then click OK.
24. If an authoritative restore of Active Directory objects is not required, click the Restart button in the dialog box and allow the server to reboot normally. If an authoritative restore is required, click the Exit Without Restart button in the dialog box and perform the steps outlined in the following section, "Active Directory Authoritative Restore."

Active Directory Authoritative Restore

When Active Directory has been modified and needs to be restored to a previous state, and this rollback needs to be replicated to all domain controllers in the domain and possibly the forest, an authoritative restore of Active Directory is required. An authoritative restore of Active Directory can include the entire Active Directory database, a single object, or a container, such as an organizational unit, including all objects previously stored within the container. When performing an authoritative restore of a container or a single object within Active Directory, run the system state restore of a domain controller as previously outlined and after the first reboot continue with these steps:

1. Open a command prompt on the domain controller that is running in DSRM and has just completed a system-state recovery and a reboot.
2. In the command prompt window, type **Ntdsutil** and press Enter.
3. Type **Activate Instance NTDS** and press Enter.
4. Type in **Authoritative Restore** and press Enter.
5. To restore a single object, type **Restore Object** followed by the distinguished name of the previously deleted object. For example, to restore an object named Jamil Droubi in the Users container of the companyabc.com domain, type the following:

```
Restore Object "cn=Jamil Droubi,cn=users,
dc=companyabc,dc=com"
```

6. To restore a container or organizational unit and all objects beneath it, replace the "restore object" with "restore subtree," followed by the appropriate distinguished name.

7. After the appropriate command is typed in, press Enter. A window opens asking for confirmation of the authoritative restore; click the Yes button to complete the authoritative restore of the object or subtree.

8. The Ntdsutil tool displays the name of the text file that may contain any back-links for objects just restored. Note the name of the files and whether any back-links were contained in the restored objects.

9. Type **quit** and press Enter; type **quit** again to close out of the Ntdsutil tool. Type **exit** to close the command prompt window.

10. Open the charms bar and select the Settings icon and click the Power button.

11. Choose to restart the server and select Operating System Recovery(Planned) as the reason, and then click Continue to restart the server into normal operation.

12. After normal reboot, verify the authoritatively restored object replicates to all domain controllers, and then perform a full backup of the domain controller.

Restoring the SYSVOL Folder

When a domain controller system state is restored, the SYSVOL is also restored to the point in time the backup was taken. If the SYSVOL that has replicated across the domain needs to be rolled back, an authoritative restore of the SYSVOL, known previously as a primary restore of SYSVOL, must be performed. To perform an authoritative restore of the SYSVOL, restore the system state of a domain controller using Windows Server Backup, as outlined in the earlier in the "System-State Recovery for Domain Controllers" section, but on the Select Location for System State Recovery page, check the Perform an Authoritative Restore of Active Directory Files check box. Follow the steps to recover the system state of the domain controller, and then boot the domain controller normally. When the domain controller is returned to operation, the Active Directory database syncs with other domain controllers, but the SYSVOL of this particular domain controller is pushed out to all other domain controllers in the domain as the authoritative copy and overwrites the other copies. No other steps are required.

Restoring Group Policies

When group policies need to be restored, performing a restore of the SYSVOL as well as the Active Directory database is required. Group Policy object information is stored in a container in the domain naming context partition called the Group Policy Objects container, and the files are stored in the SYSVOL folder on each domain controller. The most effective way to back up and restore group policies is to use the backup and restore features built in to the Group Policy Management Console included with Windows Server 2012 Group Policy Management Tools. For detailed information about how to back up and recover group policies using the Group Policy Management Console, see Chapter 19, "Windows Server 2012 Group Policies and Policy Management."

Summary

This chapter covered many aspects Windows Server 2012 recovery. Administrators and IT managers responsible for disaster recovery tasks, including planning and execution, should test all plans regularly to ensure that in the event of a failure, the critical systems and most important data are backed up and can be recovered properly and efficiently.

Many technologies and solutions built in to Windows Server 2012 were covered in this chapter to provide you with useful recovery processes for Windows Server Backup or shadow copies to recover data and systems. Also covered were the tasks involved in creating the recovery plan, testing it, and making sure (through tested procedures) that what you think will happen in a recovery process actually can happen.

Best Practices

The following are best practices from this chapter:

- Document all backup and recovery procedures.
- Periodically test the restore procedures to verify accuracy and test the backup media to ensure that data can actually be recovered.
- Validate reported system failures before attempting to restore data or fix an issue.
- Allocate the appropriate hardware devices, including servers with enough processing power and disk space to accommodate the restored machines' resources.
- Store a copy of all disaster recovery documentation and copies of dedicated Windows Server Backup disks at secure offsite locations.
- Understand the dependencies of the applications and services to the operating system to choose whether to rebuild or restore from backup.
- Identify and document special restore requirements for each server.
- If an organization has not or cannot standardize on server hardware platforms or if systems will be used in production even when the hardware is at its end of life or the maintenance on a system has expired; consider moving critical physical systems to virtual servers.
- When planning for recovery scenarios, ensure that a proper chain of communication is established to allow the technical staff to focus on their tasks and not be inundated with requests for status updates.

CHAPTER 32

Optimizing Windows Server 2012 for Branch Office Communications

IN THIS CHAPTER

Today's organizations are likely to consist of many branch offices. On average, a branch office is a small office hosting fewer than 50 employees in a remote location. Typically, a branch office infrastructure is connected to the headquarters site, centralized data center, or hub site by means of a wide-area network (WAN) link.

For many organizations, maintaining branch offices generates significant operational costs and administrative challenges. Two scenarios exist when dealing with branch offices because of the high costs of securing high-speed links between the branch office and hub site. Either the organization implements server infrastructure at the branch office, or IT services are provided to the branch office from a centralized site such as the company headquarters.

By providing branch offices with their own infrastructure, productivity increases; however, operational and management costs typically rise. When providing services to a branch office from a centralized site, its productivity is reduced as all branch office users must obtain services over a slow and unreliable WAN link. If the WAN link becomes unavailable, productivity at the branch office can come to a halt until the WAN link is repaired. To address these and other branch office scenarios, Windows 2012 offers a number of new and enhanced features that provide improved support for the branch office environment.

Key Branch Office Features in Windows 2012

- **Read-only domain controllers**—Windows Server 2012 offers the functionality of having a read-only domain controller (RODC) in a branch office location. An RODC is an additional domain controller for an Active Directory domain that contains read-only partitions of the Active Directory database. RODCs are designed to be deployed in branch office environments with relatively few users, limited network bandwidth, and minimal local IT knowledge.
- **BitLocker Drive Encryption**—To further enhance the security of a server in a branch office location, Windows 2012 provides the BitLocker Drive Encryption option to encrypt the operating system and data volumes of a server. BitLocker Drive Encryption is particularly useful in a branch office where physical server security may be limited. BitLocker can be used in conjunction with a RODC to provide a high level of domain controller security for the branch office.
- **BranchCache**—Windows Server 2012 includes a number of updates to the BranchCache feature. BranchCache in Windows 2012 maintains a local cache of file, web, and application content in designated branch office locations. This allows clients in the branch office to access this cached content at local-area network (LAN) speeds, which provides improved performance for users and minimizes the use of WAN links.
- **Branch Office Direct Printing**—Windows Server 2012 includes a new feature known as Branch Office Direct Printing (BODP). BODP reduces the network bandwidth required for print jobs by allowing clients to print directly to a printer instead of a print queue on a server. BODP can be enabled for selected printers and does not require any additional user training to print using BODP.

Understanding Read-Only Domain Controllers

One of the key features for branch offices in Windows 2012 is a type of domain controller referred to as a read-only domain controller (RODC). The RODC hosts a copy of the Active Directory (AD) database like any other writable domain controller, but as its name implies, the contents replica of the domain database residing on the domain controller is read-only, and write operations are not supported. It is equally important to mention that the RODCs do not participate in Active Directory replication in the same fashion as writable domain controllers. The fundamental difference between RODC replication and the typical multimaster replication model between writable domain controllers is that RODC replication is unidirectional. This means all changes from a writable domain controller are propagated to the RODCs. As a result, the RODC receives changes, but does not participate in outbound replication with other domain controllers. This characteristic of RODCs provides an extra layer of security as any unauthorized data changes, especially changes made with the intent to hurt the organization, will not replicate out to other domain controllers. Unidirectional replication also reduces the workload of bridgehead servers in the hub site and the effort required to monitor replication.

Another new RODC functionality that improves security can be seen when replication takes place between a writable domain controller and an RODC. Here, user account information is replicated, but account passwords are not replicated. Security is maintained in this situation because the only password that resides on the RODC is the local administrator's password and Krbtgt accounts (the account used for Kerberos authentication). In essence, the read-only behavior of an RODC is similar to the NT 4.0 backup domain controller (BDC); however, with the NT 4.0 BDC, all user information was replicated from the primary domain controller (PDC), including passwords.

NOTE

If needed, it is also possible to configure credential caching of passwords for a specific user account to an RODC. Moreover, by default, security groups with high privileges such as domain administrators and enterprise administrators are configured to never allow their passwords to replicate to RODCs.

RODCs are most often used to provide Active Directory Domain Services (AD DS) to remote locations and branch offices where heightened security is essential, where Windows Active Directory administrators are lacking, and where the promise of physical security is practically nonexistent. In many cases, RODCs offer a practical headache-free solution for branch office environments that in the past had to endure solutions that always put them in compromising situations.

Branch Office Concerns and Dilemmas

The next section illustrates typical branch office concerns about having domain controllers onsite. This section makes it evident why the RODC is becoming popular if not extremely necessary for branch offices.

Lack of Physical Security at the Branch Office

Typically, branch office locations do not have the facilities to host a data center. For that reason, it is common to find domain controllers hiding in closets, tucked away in the kitchen next to the fridge, or even in a restroom. Therefore, branch offices lack physical security when it comes to storing domain controllers, which results in these servers being prime targets for thieves.

Domain Controllers Stolen from the Branch Office

With inadequate physical security in the branch offices, it was very common for domain controllers to be stolen. This posed a major security threat to organizations because domain controllers contain a copy of all the user accounts associated with the domain. Confidential items such as highly privileged administrator accounts, domain name system (DNS) records, and the Active Directory schema could fall into the hands of the wrong people in this situation.

Removing Domain Controllers from the Branch Office

Because of a lack of physical security and concerns over domain controller theft, branch offices were often configured to operate without a local domain controller. With no local domain controller, users were forced to authenticate over the WAN to a domain controller residing at their corporate headquarters or to the closest hub site. Although this configuration addressed a security issue, it also cultivated a new problem by making the branch office dependent on the WAN link for all authentication requests. If the WAN link between the branch office and hub site was unreliable or unavailable, users could not log on to the workstations at the branch office, or the amount of time required to log on was greatly increased. This resulted in a loss of productivity for users in the branch office or outages that resulted in downtime if the WAN link was severed. These types of outages commonly lasted for days.

Lack of Administration Role Separation at the Branch Office

In small branch offices, it is also very common for multiple server functions to be hosted on a single server to reduce costs. For example, a single server might provide domain controller, file, print, messaging, and other line-of-business (LOB) functionality. In such cases, it is necessary for the administrators of these applications to log on to the system to manage their applications. By granting administrators privileges to the domain controller, these individuals also received full access to the Active Directory domain, which is considered to be a major security risk.

Lack of IT Support Personnel at the Branch Office

It is very common for secretaries, receptionists, or even high-level personnel such as managers and directors without any prior knowledge of IT management or maintenance to manage servers in a branch office. Typically, these individuals get nominated or promoted to a branch office IT support role because a local IT administrator does not exist. Unfortunately, even when conducting basic administration tasks like restarting an unresponsive server, these individuals can inadvertently wreak havoc on the Active Directory domain when granted administrator privileges on a domain controller. In a Windows Server 2003 environment, there was little that could be done about this situation. You just had to be careful about who you promoted to the exclusive club of domain administrators.

Understanding When to Leverage RODCs

As you can see from the scenarios above, businesses are faced with numerous challenges regarding the use of domain controllers in branch offices. Because of the many features of RODCs, however, branch offices can now have domain controllers on site without compromising security.

The main benefits of running RODC in branch offices are associated with the following:

- Read-only AD DS
- Reduced replication workload over the network
- Credential caching

- Administrator role separation
- Read-Only DNS
- Read-Only SYSVOL

These features of RODCs, which are discussed in detail in the following sections, assist in alleviating concerns and dilemmas for organizations.

Read-Only AD DS

Poor physical security is typically the most common rationale for deploying an RODC at a branch office. A read-only copy of the domain controller provides fast and reliable authentication, while simultaneously protecting against data loss in the event the server is compromised or stolen. Because no changes can originate from an RODC, a malicious hacker or IT support personnel with little knowledge of Active Directory administration cannot make changes at the branch level. On a writable domain controller, not only can changes be made, but these changes would also propagate to all other domain controllers, eventually damaging or polluting the Active Directory domain and forest.

Reduced Replication Workload over the Network

As mentioned earlier, RODCs do not participate in Active Directory replication in the same fashion as writable domain controllers. Replication with RODC is one way, meaning all changes from a writable domain controller are propagated to the RODC. An RODC receives changes, but does not partake in or perform any outbound replication to other domain controllers. This results in the replication workload being minimized over the network because changes do not have to be pulled from an RODC and because Active Directory replication is unidirectional. Also reduced is the amount of time required to monitor replication, which is another plus for having an RODC.

Credential Caching

Credential caching with an RODC provides numerous security enhancements for a domain controller residing at a branch office. Take, for example, a new functionality in RODCs that increases security in the event an RODC is stolen. When replication transpires between a writable domain controller and an RODC, only a user's account information is replicated—not the user's password. Equally important, passwords are not stored on an RODC. In the event the RODC is stolen, the only accounts that can be hacked and compromised are the local administrator accounts and the RODC account, which is specific to the RODC server. These accounts are not considered to be highly privileged, nor do they have access authorization on the forest and domain. On the other hand, traditional writable domain controllers store both the user's account information and password on a domain controller, ultimately leaving users very vulnerable.

Because an RODC by default does not store user accounts or passwords locally, branch office users must authenticate against a writable domain controller in a hub site. This is often not practical for branch office users, especially if the WAN link between the sites is slow or unavailable. In this case, it is possible to configure password replication caching for specific branch office users on the branch office RODC. After the credentials are cached on the RODC, the domain controller will service users the next time they try to log on and every other time after that until the credentials change. Typically, a branch office only has a few users, so only a subset of an organization's users' accounts are cached on the RODC at the branch office, limiting the exposure of credentials in the event of a system breach.

To provide an additional level of security and at the same time reduce the amount of information exposed in the event an RODC is stolen, a domain administrator can use tools within Active Directory Users and Computers to delete the RODC from the Active Directory domain/forest and reset the passwords for user accounts cached on the RODC.

NOTE

By default, security groups with high privileges such as domain administrators and enterprise administrators are configured to never allow their passwords to replicate to RODCs.

Administrator Role Separation

Organizations are encouraged to use RODCs when there is a need to satisfy unique administrative requirements and to maintain administrator role separation and isolation. The use of an RODC is especially encouraged if the domain controller situated in a branch office hosts more than one server function or server role, such as a print server, messaging server, file server, and much more. The use of an RODC is also recommended when there are other applications installed on the domain controller. Traditionally, in this situation the administrator of these applications has privileges not only to the applications, but also to the entire Active Directory, which can pose a threat. With RODC, however, you can delegate permissions to local administrators, granting them rights to a particular server, roles, or LOB applications without ever granting them access to Active Directory or domain resources beyond the scope of the branch. As a result, the local administrator at the branch can perform his or her administrator work activities effectively without compromising the entire Active Directory environment.

Read-Only DNS

When using RODCs, it is possible to add the DNS role/service to the RODC. After the DNS service is added to an RODC, the RODC will replicate Active Directory-integrated DNS information such as DNS-related AD partitions, including both the ForestDNS and DomainDNS zones.

Running DNS on an RODC is very similar to running DNS on a writable domain controller. Users can query the local DNS server residing on the branch office RODC for A records and other DNS-related items such as Internet requests. However, unlike traditional writable domain controllers, DNS on RODC does not support dynamic updates. The DNS zone information is entirely read-only.

If a client wants to update their DNS A or PTR record in the local branch office, the RODC sends a DNS replicate-single-object change request to a writable domain controller running the traditional DNS service. The DNS change for the client occurs on the writable

DNS server and, eventually, the change is propagated back to the RODC via unidirectional Active Directory replication.

NOTE

It is a best practice to have clients in the branch office point to their local RODC DNS server for DNS lookups. This can be achieved via an Active Directory group policy or DNS lookup list based on Dynamic Host Configuration Protocol (DHCP).

Read-Only SYSVOL

In Windows Server 2008, it was still possible for changes to be made to the SYSVOL folder of an RODC. When changes were made to the contents of the SYSVOL folder, those changes persisted until being overwritten by the next DFS Replication (DFSR) cycle. In Windows Server 2012, Microsoft made changes to the RODC functionality such that the SYSVOL folder is now read-only on an RODC.

Installing a Read-Only Domain Controller

RODCs can be implemented on a full or core installation of Windows Server 2012. The installation can be performed in a standard or in a staged manner. Because RODCs are tailored toward branch office implementations where physical security and theft are a concern, it is a best practice to heighten security even further by installing an RODC on a Server Core installation. A Server Core installation minimizes surface attacks and provides the maximum amount of protection in the event of a system breach.

The upcoming sections include step-by-step procedures for installing an RODC on a full installation of Windows Server 2012, installing an RODC on a Windows Server 2012 Server Core installation, and performing a staged installation. Before launching into the procedures, however, let's examine the prerequisites associated with installing RODCs and understanding the limitations associated with using an RODC.

NOTE

The following steps assume an RODC install is being performed using Windows Server 2012.

Examining Prerequisite Tasks When Deploying an RODC

The following bullets list the items you should review and complete before installing RODCs:

- Active Directory running on Windows Server 2008 or Windows Server 2008 R2 must already exist in the environment.

- The forest and domain functional level must be running Windows Server 2003 or higher.

- The permissions on all the DNS application directory partitions in the forest must be updated to support RODCs by running the command **adprep /rodcprep** from the domain controller which hosts the Schema Master Flexible Single Master Operations (FSMO) role.
- A regular non-read-only (writable) domain controller must already exist within the Active Directory infrastructure.
- The RODC cannot be the first domain controller within the Active Directory infrastructure.
- If the DNS service will be configured on a Server Core installation, a non-read-only DNS server must be present within the domain.

Limitations Associated with Windows Server 2012 RODCs

In some situations, RODCs cannot be used. This is the case with bridgehead servers and operations master role holders as well as time source servers. For example, a Windows Server 2012 bridgehead server is responsible for managing Active Directory replication from a physical site. Because an RODC can only perform inbound unidirectional replication, it cannot be designated as a bridgehead server because these servers must support both inbound and outbound replication.

An RODC also cannot function as an FSMO role holder. Each FSMO role needs to write information to an Active Directory domain controller. For example, consider extending the Active Directory schema for Microsoft Exchange Server 2010. The new schema extensions would be written on a domain controller to support Exchange 2010. The schema extensions would fail on an RODC because the domain controller is not writable, which, of course, explains why an RODC cannot perform the FSMO role.

A final limitation to keep in mind is that by default RODCs cannot authenticate a smart card logon. This is because the enterprise read-only domain controller (ERODC) group is not defined in the domain controller certificate template by default. Because the ERODC is not associated with the default group defined in the template, the RODC is not automatically enrolled in the certificate process, which is a requirement for authenticating smart card logons. Unlike the limitations of RODCs stated in the previous two paragraphs, there is a way to work around this particular drawback so an RODC can authenticate a smart card logon. The following changes must be orchestrated in the certificate templates for an RODC to support smart card logons:

- ERODC group permissions for Enroll must be set to Allow on the Domain Controller certificate template.
- ERODC group permissions for Enroll and Autoenroll must be set to Allow on the Domain Controller Authentication and Directory E-Mail Replication certificate template.

- The Authenticated Users group permissions must be set to Allow Read on the Domain Controller Authentication and Directory E-Mail Replication certificate template.

Conducting an RODC Installation

As mentioned earlier, an RODC can be implemented on either a full installation of Windows Server 2012 or on a Windows Server 2012 Server Core installation. The upcoming sections include step-by-step instructions on installing an RODC for both types of scenarios.

Installing an RODC on a Full Installation of Windows Server 2012

Before installing an RODC within your Active Directory infrastructure, ensure the prerequisites are met and that you fully understand the circumstances under which the RODC should not be used or else you will jeopardize the success of your installation.

Now, let's look at how to install an RODC; this example assumes the base Windows Server 2012 system has already been installed and that the server has been joined to an Active Directory domain. The installation is very similar to a traditional domain controller installation, but a number of additional steps specific to the RODC also need to be completed. To conduct the installation with the Active Directory Domain Services Wizard, follow these steps:

1. Log on to the new branch office Windows Server 2012 system with an account that has domain administrative privileges.
2. On the Server Manager screen, click the Add Roles and Features link.
3. Review the information on the Before You Begin screen and click Next to continue.
4. On the Select Installation Type screen, select Role-Based or Feature-Based Installation and click Next.
5. Confirm that the branch office server is selected on the Select Destination Server screen, and then click Next to continue.
6. On the Add Server Roles screen, select the Active Directory Domain Services check box.
7. The Add Roles And Features Wizard will prompt you to install features that are required to manage AD DS. Click Add Features to add the required features, and then click Next to continue.
8. On the Select Features screen, click Next. The features that are required to manage AD DS have already been selected in the previous step.
9. The Active Directory Domain Services installation screen will appear. Click Next to continue.
10. Review your installation selections, and then click the Install button to install AD DS.

11. The Installation Progress screen will appear and display the status of the installation. When the text below the progress bar indicates that the installation has succeeded, click Close to close the window. Figure 32.1 shows the Installation Progress screen.

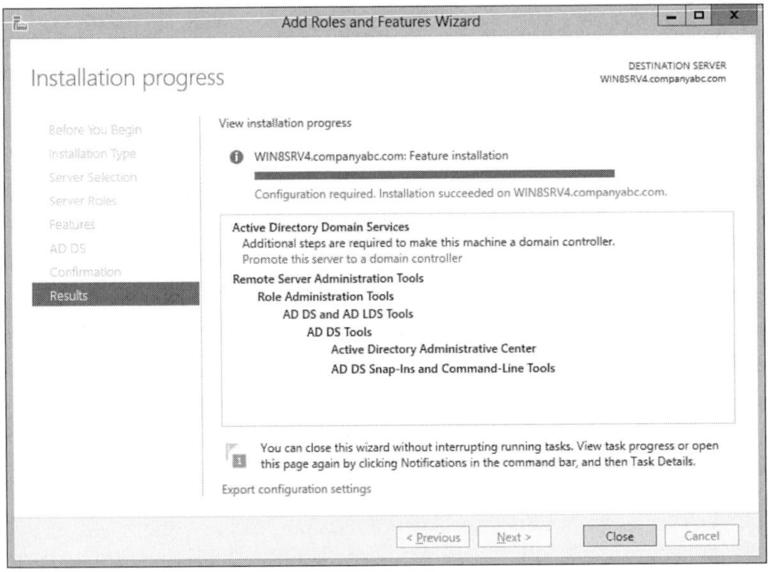

FIGURE 32.1 Installing AD DS.

12. When the Installation Progress screen is closed, the Server Manager screen displays a yellow triangle in the Notifications area in the upper-right corner, as shown in Figure 32.2. Click the yellow triangle to display the notification, and then click the link labeled Promote this server to a domain controller.

13. After you click the link in the notification, the Deployment Configuration screen will appear. Verify that the option to add a domain controller to an existing domain is selected, make sure that the domain information and credential are correct, and then click Next to continue.

14. On the Domain Controller Options screen, note that the Domain Naming System (DNS) server and Global Catalog (GC) options are selected by default. Check the Read Only Domain Controller (RODC) box, verify the AD site where the RODC will be installed, and enter a Directory Services Restore Mode password. The completed screen should look similar to Figure 32.3.

NOTE

For branch office deployments, it is a best practice to configure a RODC as a global catalog. However, it is important to note that certain directory-enabled applications (such as Microsoft Exchange) do not support RODCs as global catalog servers. If you plan to deploy an Exchange server in the branch office, it is a requirement to have a writable global catalog server in the same location as the Exchange server.

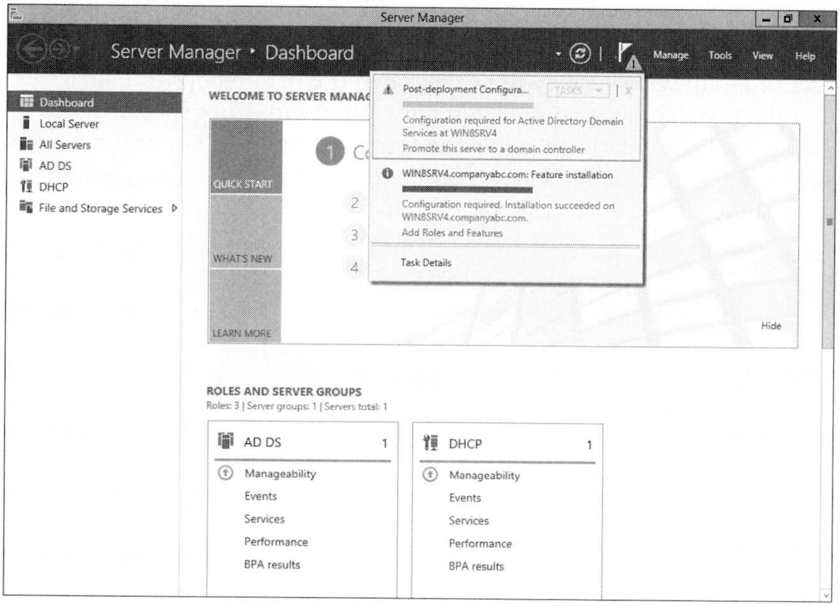

FIGURE 32.2 Post-deployment configuration notification in Server Manager.

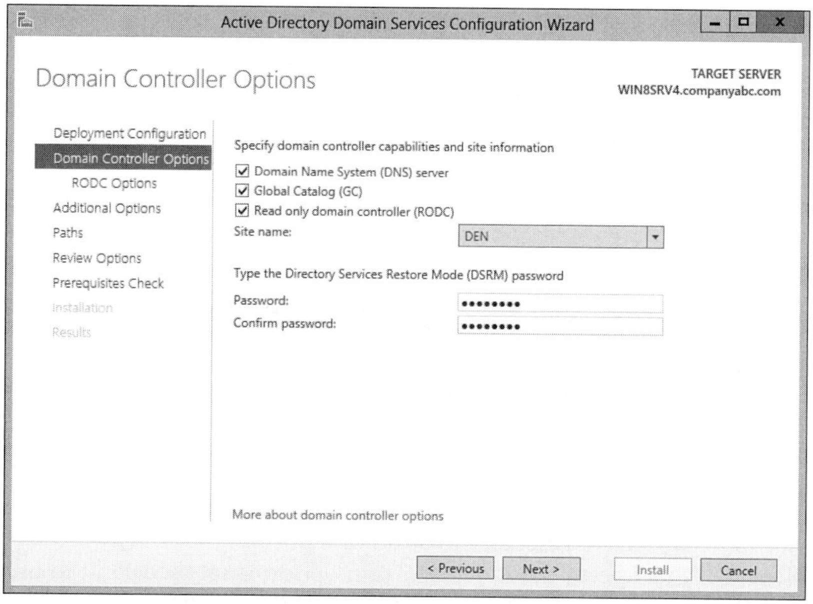

FIGURE 32.3 Domain controller configuration options.

15. The RODC Options screen will appear. The first item on this screen is an option to select the delegated administrator account, which can be an Active Directory user or group. The user or group you specify will be delegated the permissions to manage the RODC after the installation is complete. If a user or group is not specified, the Installation Wizard will automatically allow the Domain Admin or Enterprise Admin group to attach to the RODC. Enter a group on the RODC Options screen, and then click Next to continue. Figure 32.4 displays the completed RODC Options screen.

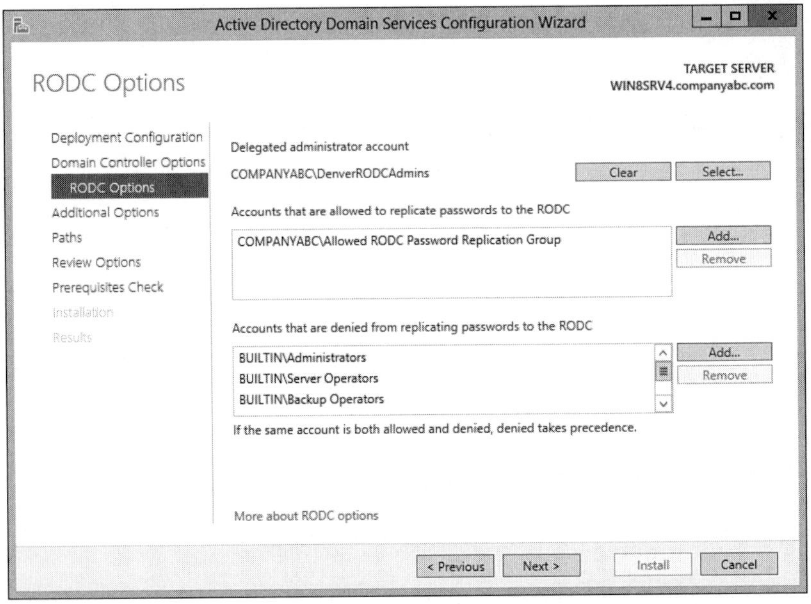

FIGURE 32.4 Specifying a group on the Delegation of RODC Installation and Administration page.

NOTE

For simplicity, it is a best practice to specify a group and add users to the group as needed. Each user associated with the group will have the opportunity to log on to the RODC and will have full control over the server.

16. On the Additional Options screen, you have the option to specify the Install From Media (IFM) path to install Active Directory (instead of replicating from a live domain controller). On this screen, the Replicate From option is set by default to use any domain controller to replicate Active Directory information, or you can select a specific domain controller from the drop-down list. When complete, click Next to continue.

NOTE

The Install From Media (IFM) option requires a specific path to be entered and does not allow you to browse to the path. The Verify button will confirm if the specified path contains valid IFM media. To be considered valid for Windows 2012, an IFM media set must be created using Windows Server Backup or ntdsutil.exe from another Windows 2012 computer. If the IFM media is password protected, Server Manager will prompt for the password during verification.

17. Enter the folder location of the database, log files, and SYSVOL files on the Location for Database, Log Files, and SYSVOL page, and then click Next to continue.

NOTE

For maximum performance and recoverability, it is a best practice to store the database and log files on separate volumes.

18. Review the selections on the Summary page, and then click Next to continue.
19. Server Manager will validate the prerequisites for the selected installation and display a results screen. Confirm that all prerequisite checks have been passed successfully, as shown in Figure 32.5, and then click Install to perform the installation.

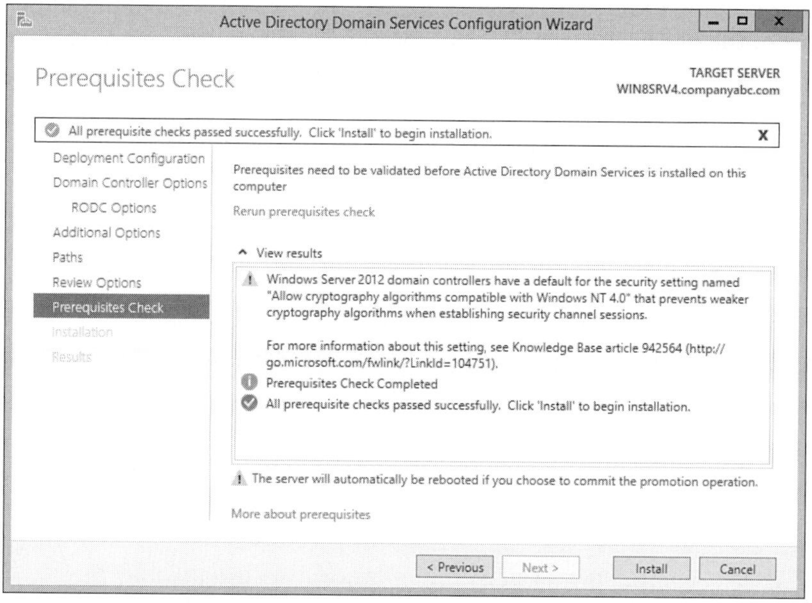

FIGURE 32.5 Verifying prerequisites for RODC installation.

20. At the conclusion of the installation, the server will be automatically restarted.

21. Once the server comes back up, the new AD DS role will be shown in Server Manager.

Installing an RODC on a Windows Server 2012 Server Core Installation

One of the most innovative security features of Windows Server 2012 is Windows Server Core, a scaled-down installation option that uses command-line prompts instead of graphical user interfaces (GUIs) to manage the server. Because a Server Core installation is able to provide a minimal environment by only installing a subset of the Windows Server 2012 binaries to support server roles, it is ideal for remote locations such as branch offices where only the bare essentials need to be installed.

Operating with a lean server has its benefits. Through Windows Server Core, a minimal environment is created that decreases the amount of maintenance and management an administrator is required to perform when running specific server roles such as Active Directory Domain Services. This comes in handy at branch offices as organizations don't typically want inexperienced administrators managing the branch office domain controller. Therefore, the reduced amount of administration is an advantage. In addition, by having a minimal environment, the attack surface for the server roles residing on the Server Core installation is also reduced. It is also worth mentioning that Server Core is in line with Microsoft's Trustworthy Computing initiative.

Unlike installing other Windows Server 2012 roles on a Server Core installation, installing AD DS—which is part of the RODC installation—on a Server Core installation of Windows Server 2012 requires an unattended answer file to first be created. The unattended answer file provides answers to questions that might be asked during the installation of an AD DS installation. After the unattended answer file is created, the next step is to run dcpromo from the RODC and reference the unattended answer file by using the following syntax at the command prompt: **dcpromo /unattend:<unattendfile>**. The role can also be installed remotely using Server Manager. However, using an unattended file is still useful in cases in which the deployment must happen on the DC or to facilitate deploying a large number of DCs.

NOTE

It is possible to create an unattended answer file by exporting settings on the Summary page when using the Active Directory Domain Services Installation Wizard. This answer file can be used for creating subsequent installations of Active Directory domain controllers on Server Core installations.

The following example depicts installing an RODC on a Server Core installation. The first step creates the unattended answer file based on settings included in Table 32.1. The second step conducts the dcpromo process on the Server Core installation by referencing the answer file created in the first step. This example assumes a Windows Server 2012 Server Core installation already exists at the branch office.

TABLE 32.1 Parameters and Values for Creating an Unattended Answer File

Parameter	Value
Site	DEN
Additional options	Read-only DC: Yes Global catalog: Yes DNS server: Yes
Update DNS delegation	No
Source DC	Any writable domain controller
Password Replication Policy	Allow: COMPANYABC1\Allowed RODC Password Replication Group Deny: BUILTIN\Administrators Deny: BUILTIN\Server Operators Deny: BUILTIN\Backup Operators Deny: BUILTIN\Account Operators Deny: COMPANYABC1\Denied RODC Password Replication Group
Delegation for RODC installation and administration	COMPANYABC1\DenverRODCAdmins
Active Directory file placement	Database folder: c:\Windows\NTDS Log file folder: c:\Windows\NTDS SYSVOL folder: c:\Windows\SYSVOL
DNS server settings	The DNS service will be installed on this computer. The DNS service will be configured on this computer. This computer will be configured to use this DNS server as its preferred DNS server.

Creating the Unattended Answer File Based on the Values in Table 32.1

1. First create an unattended answer file similar to the following example. The parameters and values found in this example have been summarized in Table 32.1.

```
; DCPROMO unattend file (automatically generated by dcpromo)
; Usage:
;   dcpromo.exe /unattend:C:\Temp\RODCAnswerFile.txt
;
;
[DCInstall]
; Read-Only Replica DC promotion
ReplicaOrNewDomain=ReadOnlyReplica
ReplicaDomainDNSName=companyabc1.com
ServerAdmin="COMPANYABC1\DenverRODCAdmins"
```

```
SiteName=DEN
InstallDNS=Yes
ConfirmGc=Yes
DNSDelegation=No
UserDomain=companyabc1.com
UserName=*
Password=*
DatabasePath=C:\Windows\NTDS
LogPath=C:\Windows\NTDS
SYSVOLPath=C:\Windows\SYSVOL
; Set SafeModeAdminPassword to the correct value prior to using the unattend
file
SafeModeAdminPassword=
; Run-time flags (optional)
; CriticalReplicationOnly=Yes
; RebootOnCompletion=Yes
TransferIMRoleIfNecessary=No
```

NOTE

This example represents the unattended answer file for the RODC installation, which also includes parameters and values for installing DNS, a global catalog, password replication policy, administrator delegation, Active Directory file placement, and DNS settings. Modify the values as needed.

NOTE

You might need to fill in password fields before using the unattended file. If you leave the values for Password or DNSDelegationPassword as *, you will be asked for credentials at runtime.

2. Save the unattended file and copy it to the Windows Server 2012 Server Core installation system that will be the new branch office RODC server.

Implementing the RODC on a Server Core Installation by Using an Unattended Answer File

Now that the unattended answer file is created, you must run the following syntax **dcpromo.exe /CreateDCAccount /unattend:"<Path to answer file>"** from a Server Core installation command prompt.

Performing a Staged RODC Installation

A staged approach can also be leveraged to install an RODC in a branch office. There are two steps to the new approach. Each step is described in the following list from a high-level perspective:

- The first step involves creating a computer account for the RODC in Active Directory. After the computer account is created, you must delegate its installation and management to a user at the branch office. The person being delegated does not require elevated privileged rights within the Active Directory forest like domain administrators or enterprise administrators.

- The next step requires branch office personnel to complete the RODC installation by attaching a server to the RODC account created in the previous step.

By delegating the installation of the RODC to a regular user account at the branch office, you eliminate the need to stage the RODC in a hub site and physically ship the server to the branch office. This was a common approach to configuring domain controllers for branch offices when using previous versions of Windows because administrators did not want to grant regular users at the branch office elevated administrative privileges to conduct the installation. In addition, if the domain controller was traditionally built at the branch office, using this new staged approach eliminates the need to ship media and product keys.

NOTE

Another alternative to performing a staged RODC installation is to have the branch office prepare a base installation of the Windows Server 2012 operating system. After this installation is complete and the server is on the network, a domain administrator from the hub site can use the Remote Desktop Protocol (RDP) and remotely perform the dcpromo process. This strategy also eliminates the need to use branch personnel in any facet of the domain controller installation process.

Complete the following steps to create an account for an RODC. You will be using the Active Directory Users and Computers interface in the first step of this staged approach.

1. On a writable Windows Server 2012 domain controller, invoke Active Directory Users and Computers by selecting it from the Administrative Tools.
2. In Active Directory Users and Computers, expand the domain tree, and then select the Domain Controllers Organizational Unit folder.
3. Right-click the Domain Controllers OU container, and then select Pre-Create Read-Only Domain Controller Account.
4. The Active Directory Domain Services Installation Wizard is invoked. Review the Welcome page, and then click Next to continue.
5. On the Network Credentials page, specify the account credentials that will be used to perform the installation. The options include either My Current Logged On Credentials or Alternate Credentials. Click Next to continue.
6. Enter a computer name for the RODC in the Computer Name text box located on the Specify the Computer Name page, and then click Next.

NOTE

This procedure creates a computer account in AD DS. The RODC computer name specified in this step should be the name of the server you plan on promoting to an RODC. As part of the prerequisite tasks and also to minimize server name conflicts, do not join the server you plan on using as an RODC to the domain. The server should reside in a workgroup.

7. On the Select a Site page, select a site for the new domain controller installation, and then click Next.
8. On the Additional Domain Controller Options page, select the additional options for the domain controller. Additional items could include a DNS server and a global catalog server. Also, notice that the RODC is selected automatically and cannot be unselected.

NOTE

In general, to minimize unnecessary WAN utilization, it is a best practice to also make the RODC a DNS server and a global catalog server.

9. On the Delegation of RODC Installation and Administration page, specify a user or group who will ultimately manage and attach the server to the RODC account being created. Do this by selecting Set and entering the desired user account or group. Click Next to continue.
10. Review the summary of the Active Directory installation, and click Next on the Summary page to finalize the inauguration of the RODC.
11. Click Finish to finalize the creation of the RODC account.

At this point, the RODC account has been created. The next step is to run the Active Directory Domain Services Installation Wizard on a server that will eventually become the RODC by leveraging the user or group the RODC installation was delegated to in the previous steps. To attach a server to an RODC account, follow these simple steps:

1. Using credentials with local administrative privileges, log on to the server that will be the RODC in the branch office.

NOTE

To reiterate, make sure this server is in a workgroup and not associated with the Active Directory domain.

2. Click Start, Run, type the command **dcpromo/ UseExistingAccount:Attach**, and then click OK.

NOTE

The Active Directory Domain Services binaries will be installed. After this is complete, the Active Directory Domain Services Installation Wizard will be invoked.

3. On the Welcome to the Active Directory Domain Services Installation Wizard page, click Next to attach the server to a corresponding domain controller account created in the previous steps.
4. On the Network Credentials page, first specify the name of the forest where the RODC installation will occur. Then click Set to specify the alternate account credentials that will be used to perform the installation. Provide the username and password of the IT support personnel at the branch office, which was delegated in the previous steps, and then click Next.

NOTE

If the source server computer account name deviates from the RODC name that was created in the previous step, the installation is sure to fail. The two account names must be identical.

5. On the Select Domain Controller page, the wizard will automatically link and match the server name to the account name of the RODC created in the previous step. Ensure the computer name, DC type, and domain and site information located in the Account Details section is correct. If it is, click Next to continue.
6. Validate the folder location for the Database, Logs Files, and SYSVOL folder, and then click Next.
7. Enter and confirm the password for the Directory Services Restore Mode administrator account, and click Next.
8. Review the summary of the Active Directory installation, and click Next on the Summary page to finalize the inauguration of the RODC.
9. Click Finish and restart the RODC system.

Using BitLocker with Windows Server 2012

Microsoft brings the third version of its enterprise class encryption system, BitLocker, to Windows Server 2012. Understanding encryption options for servers as well as clients is now a key responsibility of technology security staff. The enhancements and improvements added to the new version make BitLocker a key component in the server security toolkit for enterprises and IT departments.

Understanding BitLocker Drive Encryption in Windows 2012

Microsoft added Windows BitLocker Drive Encryption to Windows Server 2008 mostly as a result of organizations demanding protection not only for their operating systems in remote locations, but also for the vital data stored on the system volume, data volumes, and USB flash drives that were used in these locations. BitLocker Drive Encryption, commonly referred to as just BitLocker, is a software-based Full Disk Encryption (FDE) data-protection security feature included in all versions of Windows Server 2012. It is an optional component that must be installed if you choose to use it.

BitLocker increases data at rest protection for an operating system by merging two concepts together: encrypting a volume and guaranteeing the integrity of the operating system's boot components. The first component, drive encryption, safeguards data residing on the system volume and configured data volumes by preventing unauthorized users from compromising Windows system files encrypted with BitLocker. The second component provides integrity verifications of the early boot components, which essentially refers to components used during the startup process, by validating that the hard disk has not been tampered with or removed from its original server. Equally important, when you use BitLocker, confidential data on a protected server cannot be viewed even if the hard disks are transferred to another operating system. If these two conditions are met, only then will data on a BitLocker volume be accessible and the system allowed to boot.

If you have worked with previous versions of Windows Server, you will recognize immediately that BitLocker is a great addition to Windows Server 2012 because it protects all the data residing on a server's hard disks because everything written to the disk including the operating system is encrypted. In previous versions of Windows Server, encryption based on integration with integrity controls was not supported, which meant personal information could be compromised. In addition, with BitLocker now on the map, branch offices concerned over the physical security and theft of their domain controllers stand to benefit the greatest from leveraging BitLocker because this feature further bolsters security and ensures confidential data is not disclosed without authorization.

NOTE

Many professionals are posing questions as they wonder about the differences between BitLocker and Encrypting File System (EFS). Both technologies offer tools for encryption; however, BitLocker is intended to protect all personal and system files on a system and after it is enabled, it is transparent as well as automatic. EFS, on the other hand, encrypts individual files based on an administrator's judgment call.

Examining BitLocker's Drive Encryption

BitLocker was first introduced with the release of Windows Vista. Within the Windows Server 2012 family of operating systems, Microsoft has continued to improve BitLocker by adding new features (for example, support for data volumes, smart card certificates, data recovery agents, USB flash drives, and a new Remote Server Administration Tools [RSAT] BitLocker interface). By using BitLocker in conjunction with Windows Server 2012, an organization can enjoy a number of benefits:

- Network based unlock for BitLocker protected boot volumes with Windows 8 or Windows Server 2012.
- Prevention of unauthorized access to data at rest, which is located on Windows managed system volumes, data volumes, and USB flash drives.
- Support for integrity checking of early boot components using Trusted Platform Module (TPM) to ensure that a machine has not been tampered with and that encrypted materials are located on the original machine.
- Protection against cold boot attacks by requiring an interactive form of authentication (including a PIN or a USB key) in addition to the presence of the TPM hardware before a machine will boot or resume from hibernation.
- Support for escrow of BitLocker recovery materials in Active Directory.
- A streamlined recovery process, which can be delegated to non-domain administrators.
- Windows Server 2008 R2 and Windows 7 or later Windows versions automatically creates the necessary BitLocker disk partitions during installation.
- Support for BitLocker protection on USB flash drives. This feature is called BitLocker To Go.
- Lastly, support for Data Recovery Agent (DRA) so that authorized IT administrators will always have access to BitLocker protected volumes.

Understanding TPM

The term *Trusted Platform Module* (TPM) refers to both the name of a published specification by the Trusted Computing Group for a secure cryptoprocessor and the implementation of that specification in the form of a TPM chip. A TPM chip's main purpose is the secure generation of cryptographic keys, the protection of those keys, and the ability to act as a hardware pseudo-random number generator. In addition, a TPM chip can provide remote attestation and sealed storage. Remote attestation is a feature in which a hash key summary is created based on a machine's current hardware and software configuration. Typically, remote attestation is used by third-party applications such as BitLocker to ensure a machine's state has not been tampered with. Sealed storage is used to encrypt data such that it may only be decrypted once the TPM chip releases the appropriate decryption key. This release is only done by TPM chip once the required authenticator for that data has been provided. Lastly, a TPM chip can also be used to authenticate hardware devices.

In BitLocker, a TPM chip is used to protect the encryption keys and provide integrity authentication for a trusted boot pathway (that is, BIOS, boot sector, and so on). This type of TPM-supported protection is only performed when BitLocker is in either Transparent Operation mode or User Authentication mode. When in either of these modes, BitLocker uses the TPM chip to detect if there are unauthorized changes to the preboot environment (trusted boot pathway protection) such as the BIOS and Master Boot Record (MBR).

If unauthorized changes were made, BitLocker will then request that a recovery key be provided before the Volume Master Key can be decrypted and boot of the machine can continue.

NOTE

Because of how a TPM chip is used, it is often referred to as a *root of trust*.

Comprehending BitLocker's Drive Encryption Hardware Requirements

Configuring BitLocker Drive Encryption is not as simple as clicking through a few screens on a Windows Server 2012 wizard. A number of prerequisite steps must be fulfilled before BitLocker can be configured and implemented. Several of the requirements are applicable only when encrypting a boot or operating system volume.

Before you implement BitLocker Drive Encryption, make certain the following hardware requirements and prerequisites are met and understood:

- The system should have a Trusted Platform Module (TPM) version 1.2 or higher.
- A Trusted Computing Group (TCG)-compliant BIOS, which can also support USB devices during startup.
- If the system does not have TPM, a removable USB memory device can be used to store the encryption key.
- There must be a minimum of at least two partitions on the system. One partition is an active partition, referred to as the system partition, which is used by bootmgr to boot Windows. This partition should be at least 100MB and not be encrypted. The second partition, the primary partition, is where the Windows binaries are installed.
- All drives and partitions must be formatted with the NTFS file system.

NOTE

The TPM and BIOS requirements only come into play when you want to use the TPM as a root of trust for a machine's BitLocker configuration.

Understanding BitLocker Deployment Scenarios

Similar to an RODC, branch office domain controllers are great candidates for implementing BitLocker. BitLocker can be exploited at the branch office to protect against physical breaches or theft of a domain controller or hard drive, and it can secure data during shipment of a branch office domain controller from a hub site to a branch office location. BitLocker can also be used to protect against data theft using disk cloning by maintenance or outsourcing techniques.

Configuring BitLocker Drive Encryption on a Windows Server 2012 Branch Office Domain Controller

The following sections cover step-by-step procedures on how to implement BitLocker by first configuring the system partitions, installing the BitLocker feature, and then enabling BitLocker Drive Encryption. The enabling section includes steps for enabling BitLocker when using TPM hardware, when not using TPM hardware, and enabling BitLocker on additional volumes beyond the scope of the volume hosting the operating system. The final step-by-step procedures include how to utilize the BitLocker recovery password in the event of an issue and how to remove BitLocker after it has been installed and configured.

Installing the BitLocker Drive Encryption Feature

Now that the system partition has been configured, there are different ways to install BitLocker. Install it during the initial configuration through Server Manager or through a command prompt. The next sections illustrate how to execute both of these installations.

Installing BitLocker with Server Manager

To install the BitLocker feature on a Windows 2012 server using Server Manager, follow these steps:

1. Log on to the server with a privileged account and navigate to the Server Manager utility.
2. Click Manage in the upper-right corner and select Add Roles and Features.
3. On the Before You Begin page, click Next.
4. Select Role-Based or Feature-Based Installation and click Next.
5. Select the target server from the server pool and click Next.
6. On the Add Server Roles screen, click Next.
7. On the Add Server Features screen, check the BitLocker Drive Encryption box.
8. Confirm adding the required features for BitLocker Drive encryption by clicking Add Features.
9. Verify that the BitLocker Drive Encryption check box is selected, as shown in Figure 32.6, and then click Next.
10. On the Confirm Installation Selections page, review the roles, services, and features selected for installation, and then click Install to begin the installation process.
11. Ensure that the installation succeeded by reviewing the messages on the Installation Results page, and then click Close.
12. After the BitLocker Drive Encryption feature has completed installing, restart the system.

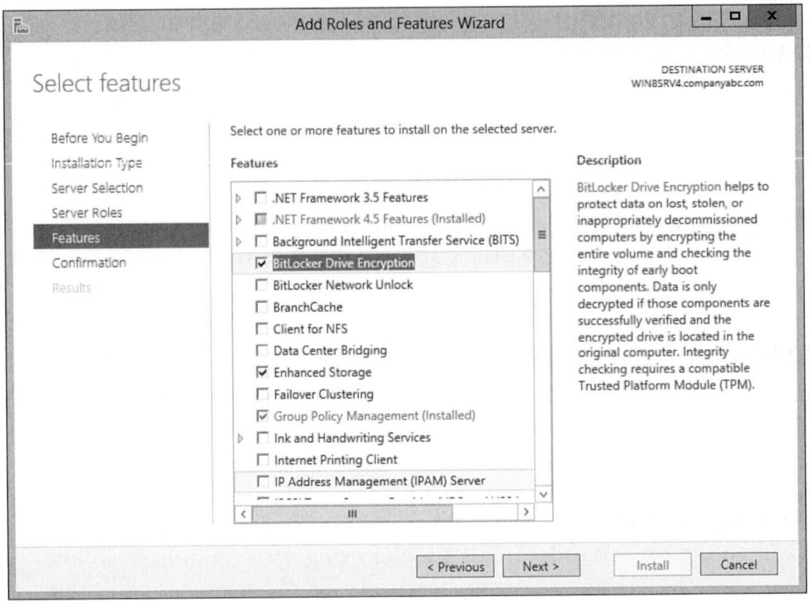

FIGURE 32.6 Selecting the BitLocker feature for installation.

Installing BitLocker via the Command Line

Another option for installing BitLocker is via the command line (PowerShell). To install the BitLocker feature using PowerShell, follow these steps:

1. From within a PowerShell console session, execute **Install-WindowsFeature BitLocker –IncludeAllSubFeature -IncludeManagementTools**.
2. After the BitLocker feature has finished installing, restart the system.

Configuring the System Partitions for BitLocker

As mentioned earlier, one of the prerequisite tasks when configuring an operating system for BitLocker is configuring a nonencrypted active partition, also referred to as a system partition. In Windows 2012, the necessary disk partitions are automatically created when Windows is installed.

Enabling BitLocker Drive Encryption

By default, BitLocker is configured to use a TPM. To recap, however, BitLocker's full functionality will not be enabled unless the system being used is compatible with the TPM chip and BIOS. This next section looks at how to enable BitLocker Drive Encryption with TPM. Microsoft recognizes that many laptops and computers do not have TPM chips (or are not TPM enabled). If you are in this situation, don't despair; you can still use BitLocker without a compatible TPM chip and BIOS. This section also covers how to enable BitLocker without TPM.

Enabling BitLocker Drive Encryption with TPM

The first step to enabling BitLocker with TPM is to turn on the TPM. Use the following steps to complete this task:

1. Go into the system's BIOS setup and set TPM Security to on.
2. Next, save the changes in the BIOS setup, and reboot the system.
3. Then, reenter the system's BIOS setup and activate the TPM.

After the TPM has been enabled, the next step is to enable BitLocker, as follows:

1. Launch the Trusted Platform Management Console by opening Windows PowerShell and entering the command **TPM.MSC**.
2. In the actions pane, click Prepare the TPM. This will clear the current TPM values and restart the computer.

NOTE

After preparing the TPM and restarting the machine, physical access to the server will be required to accept the BIOS TPM configuration change.

3. After accepting the BIOS TPM configuration change, the server will boot to the logon screen. Log on to the server and note that the Manage TPM Security Hardware Wizard will launch and begin taking ownership of the TPM.
4. Verify that the Manage TPM Security Hardware wizard displays the message TPM is ready, and then click the Remember My TPM Owner Password link to export the TPM owner password to a file. The administrator can save the BitLocker recovery password on a USB drive or to a folder on the system. In addition, the third option allows for printing of the password. Choose the desired storage location for saving the recovery password, and then click Save to save the password.
5. To turn on BitLocker for the OS volume of the RODC, open Control Panel and select the BitLocker Drive Encryption option.
6. Before BitLocker is configured, the BitLocker Drive Encryption status will show that BitLocker is off for the operating system volume, as shown in Figure 32.7. Click the Turn On BitLocker link to start the BitLocker Drive Encryption Wizard and begin the process of enabling BitLocker for the operating system volume.
7. The BitLocker Drive Encryption Wizard launches and performs a configuration check to verify that all system requirements for BitLocker have been met. When the configuration check is passed, you are prompted to create a password to unlock the drive. This should be a strong password that uses uppercase and lowercase letters, numbers, symbols and spaces. Enter the password twice and click Next to continue.

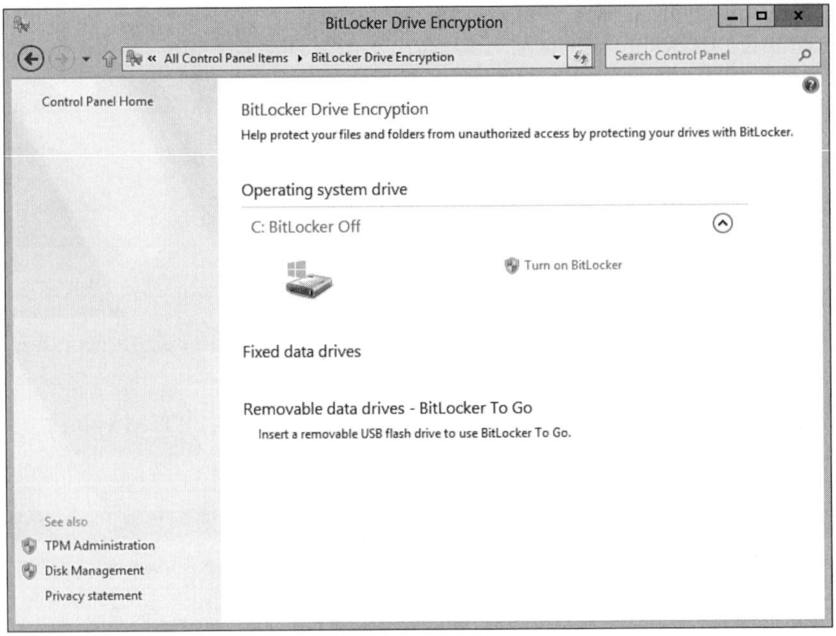

FIGURE 32.7 Turning on BitLocker for the operating system drive.

8. After a strong password has been created for the volume, the wizard generates a recovery key and prompts to save or print the recovery key. The recovery key can be printed or stored in a location outside of the volume that is being encrypted, such as a USB drive or a file share on a remote computer.

9. After the recovery key has been saved, the wizard prompts the user to select the encryption type for the drive. The available options are to Encrypt Used Disk Space Only or Encrypt Entire Drive. For volumes that have little or no data, the best practice is to use the Encrypt Used Disk Space Only option. For volumes that have data or have an operating system installed, the best practice is to select the Encrypt Entire Drive option. Select the appropriate option for your installation and click Next.

10. On the Are You Ready to Encrypt This Drive screen, verify that the Run BitLocker System Check box is checked. The system check guarantees that BitLocker can access and read the recovery and encryption keys before encrypting the volume.

11. After the system check is completed, the wizard restarts the computer to begin the encryption process. When the system reboots, The Encryption in Progress status bar appears. Restart the system when the encryption process is finalized.

NOTE

After the operating system volume has been encrypted, users are required to enter the password to boot into the operating system volume.

Enabling BitLocker Drive Encryption When TPM Is Not Available

If TPM hardware is not available on the system, BitLocker can be configured to leverage a USB key at startup. The following example configures a local group policy for the Group Policy object titled Enabling Advanced Startup Options: Control Panel Setup:

1. Click Start, Run, and then type **gpedit.msc**. Click OK, and the Local Group Policy Object Editor is invoked.
2. In the Local Group Policy Object Editor, expand Local Computer Policy, Computer Configuration, Administrative Templates, Windows Components, BitLocker Drive Encryption, and then select Operating System Drives.
3. In the right pane, double-click Require Additional Authentication at Startup.
4. Enable the BitLocker Group Policy settings by selecting the Enabled option, and then click OK, as displayed in Figure 32.8.
5. Apply the new Group Policy settings by typing **gpupdate.exe /force** at the command prompt.

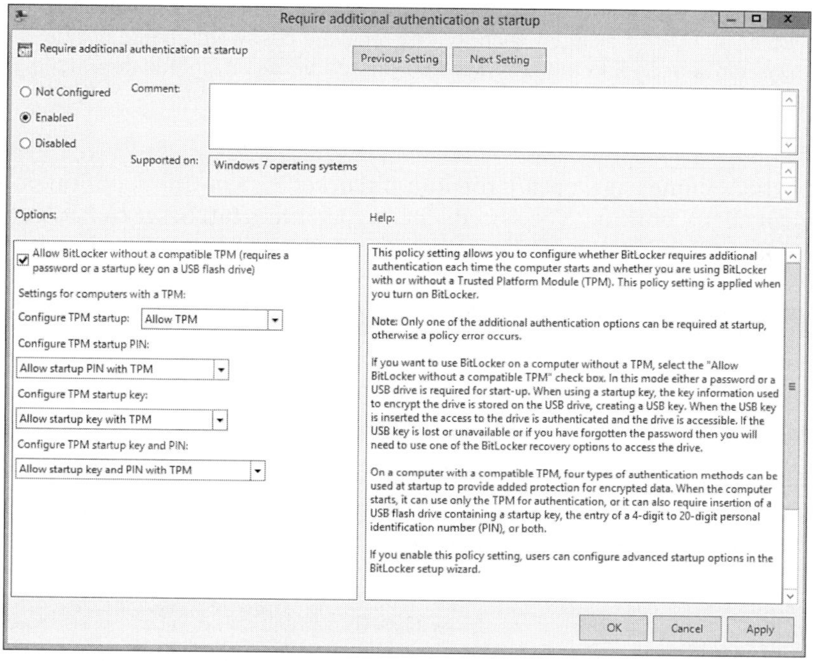

FIGURE 32.8 Enabling additional authentication options for BitLocker support.

BitLocker Drive Encryption utilizing a USB device can now be configured, as follows:

1. Click Start, Control Panel, and double-click BitLocker Drive Encryption.
2. Enable BitLocker Drive Encryption by clicking Turn On BitLocker on the BitLocker Drive Encryption page.

3. Review the message on the BitLocker Drive Encryption Platform Check page, and then click Continue with BitLocker Drive Encryption to start the BitLocker process.
4. If necessary, the installation prepares the system for BitLocker. Then, click Next.
5. Because a TPM does not exist in this example, select the option Require a Startup USB Key at Every Startup, and then click Next. You can find this option on the Set BitLocker Startup Preferences page.
6. Ensure a USB memory device has been inserted into the system. Then on the Save Your Startup Key page, specify the removable drive to which the startup key will be saved, and then click Save.
7. The Save the Recovery Password page is then invoked. The administrator can save the BitLocker recovery password on a USB drive or to a folder on the system. In addition, the third option allows for printing of the password. Choose the desired storage alternative for saving the recovery password, and then click Next to continue.

NOTE

It is a best practice to make additional copies of the recovery password and store them in a secure location like a vault. For maximum security, the recovery password should not be stored on the local system, nor should the password be printed on paper. In addition, do not store the recovery password and the startup key on the same media.

8. On the Encrypt the Volume page, ensure the Run BitLocker System Check option is enabled, and then click Continue. The system check guarantees BitLocker can access and read the recovery and encryption keys before encrypting the volume.

NOTE

Do not bypass the option to run a system check before encrypting the volume. Data loss can occur if there is an error reading the encryption or recovery key.

9. Insert the USB memory device containing the startup key into the system, and then click Restart Now. The Encryption in Progress status bar is displayed showing the completion status of the disk volume encryption.

NOTE

The USB device must be plugged in to the system every time the system starts to boot and gain access to the encrypted volume. If the USB device containing the startup key is lost or damaged, you must use the Recovery mode and provide the recovery key to start the system.

Enabling BitLocker Drive Encryption on Additional Data Volumes

In some situations, BitLocker Drive Encryption might be warranted not only on the volume containing the operating system files, but also on the data volumes. This is especially common with domain controllers in branch offices where a lack of physical security and theft are concerns.

When encrypting data volumes with BitLocker, the keys generated for the operating system volume are independent of the drive volume. However, encryption of a data volume is similar to the encryption process of the operating system volume.

Follow these steps to enable BitLocker Drive Encryption for server data volumes:

1. Click Start, Run, and then type **cmd**. Click OK to launch a command prompt.
2. From within the command prompt, type **manage-bde -on <volume>: -rp –rk <removable drive>:**.

NOTE

Replace the **<volume>** argument with the desired volume drive letter that you want to encrypt. In addition, replace the **<removable drive>** argument with the drive letter of a USB device. The USB device is utilized to store the recovery key.

The data volume must be unlocked each time the server is rebooted. This can be accomplished through a manual or automatic process. The syntax to manually unlock a data volume after every restart consists of the following two options:

- **manage-bde -unlock <volume>: -rp <recovery password>**
- **manage-bde -unlock <volume>: -rk U:\<recovery-key-filename>**

The first option uses the recovery password, whereas the second option takes advantage of passing the recovery key to decrypt the data volume. As mentioned in the previous paragraph, it is possible to enable automatic unlocking of a data volume by utilizing the following syntax at the command prompt:

```
manage-bde -autounlock -enable <volume>:
```

This command creates a recovery key and stores it on the operating system volume. The data volume is automatically unlocked after each system reboot.

Utilizing the BitLocker Recovery Password

You might at some point need to leverage the recovery password to gain access to a volume that is encrypted with BitLocker. This situation might occur when there is an error related to the TPM hardware, one of the boot files becomes corrupt or modified, or if TPM is unintentionally cleared or disabled. The following instructions outline the recovery steps:

1. Restart the system, and the BitLocker Drive Encryption console will come into view.
2. Insert the USB device containing the recovery password, and then press Esc. If the USB device is not available, bypass step 2 and proceed to step 3.

3. Press Enter. You will be prompted to enter the recovery password manually.
4. Type in the recovery password, press Enter, and then restart the system.

Scenarios for when the Recovery Password Is Required

BitLocker recovery must be performed in a number of different scenarios, including the following

- Changing or replacing the motherboard with a new TPM
- Changing the status of the TPM
- Updating the BIOS and or any other ROM on the motherboard
- Attempting to access a BitLocker-enabled drive on a different system
- Entering the wrong PIN information too many times
- Losing or damaging the USB startup key

Removing BitLocker Drive Encryption

The course of action for turning off BitLocker Drive Encryption is the same for both TPM-based hardware configurations and USB devices. When turning off BitLocker, two options exist. You can either remove BitLocker entirely and decrypt a volume or you can temporarily disable BitLocker so changes can still be made. The following steps depict the process for removing and disabling BitLocker:

1. Open Control Panel and double-click BitLocker Drive Encryption.
2. Turn off BitLocker Drive Encryption by clicking Turn Off BitLocker on the BitLocker Drive Encryption page.
3. The status of the decryption process can be monitored by clicking the notification area of the taskbar. A dialog box will appear with a progress bar indicating the percentage of decryption that has been completed.

BranchCache in Windows 2012

The modern branch office often needs to provide services to users who are "hoteling" or traveling between offices. These users may work out of one primary office but frequently travel to other branch offices. Hoteling users will need to have access to their files at their current work location, which could adversely impact the WAN performance if the user's files are located on a central server. Solutions such as Offline Files allow traveling users to synchronize their files to their laptop computer when they leave their primary office and resynchronize them when they return. However, because the user's offline files are a "point-in-time" copy of the live files on the central server, this type of solution can limit the user's ability to collaborate with other users in real time. Also, any technical issues that may occur with the Offline Files synchronization process can require IT intervention to correct, and may leave users unable to access their files or resynchronize their changes. Because businesses are often being forced to do more with fewer resources, these types of traveling user scenarios are becoming more common and need to be factored into the modern IT department's support requirements.

To address branch office scenarios such as the ones above, Windows 2012 offers a technology known as BranchCache. BranchCache was originally introduced in Windows 7 and Windows 2008 R2, and has been significantly improved in Windows 2012. BranchCache in Windows 2012 maintains a local cache of file, web and application content in designated branch office locations. This allows clients in the branch office to access this cached content at LAN speeds, which provides improved performance for users and minimizes the use of WAN links.

BranchCache is designed to include a number of specific roles for different computers that participate in a BranchCache topology. A computer can participate in a BranchCache topology as a content server, a hosted cache server, or a distributed cache client computer. In addition, BranchCache content servers can include application servers, web servers, and file servers. Table 32.2 describes these roles.

TABLE 32.2 BranchCache Server Roles

BranchCache Role	Role Details
Content server (application server)	BranchCache application content servers reside in a central location and deliver application content that is requested by clients.
Content server (file server)	BranchCache file content servers reside in a central location and deliver file server content that is requested by clients.
Content server (web server)	BranchCache web content servers reside in a central location and deliver web content that is requested by clients.
Hosted cache server	BranchCache hosted cache servers reside in a branch office location. Hosted cache servers store content that has been requested by clients. After the initial client request for content, the hosted cache server delivers the content from its cache directly to clients in the branch office.
Distributed cache client computer	BranchCache distributed cache client computers reside in a branch office location. Distributed cache client computers store content that has been requested by clients. After the initial client request for content, the distributed cache client computer delivers the content from its cache directly to clients in the branch office.

NOTE

Only content that is retrieved from a BranchCache-enabled content server (application, file, or web) will be cached by BranchCache. For example, if a user downloads a web page from an external web server, this content will not be included in the cache and will not be available to other users in the branch office. If a second user opens the same web page, the web page content will be downloaded directly from the external web server.

An important feature of BranchCache in Windows 2012 is that both servers and clients can cache content from remote locations and make that content available to other users in the branch office. This is especially useful for branch offices that do not have a local file server. Because data security is always a concern and client workstations are often physically unsecure when compared to servers in a datacenter, BranchCache encrypts its cached content to make it inaccessible to unauthorized users.

BranchCache in Windows 2012 can operate in two modes: distributed cache and hosted cache. In distributed cache mode, client computers are used to store the cached content and respond to requests. In hosted cache mode, the cached content is placed on one or more server computers, which are designated as hosted cache servers. Even though distributed cache mode and hosted cache mode can both be deployed in an enterprise, only one mode can be used for a given branch office. By default, client machines that support BranchCache operate in distributed cache mode. If a server that is configured in hosted cache mode is present in the branch office, the clients detect the hosted cache server and configure themselves to operate in hosted cache mode. Whether distributed cache or hosted cache mode is used in a given branch office, either mode allows the branch office to cache content from a central office (or a hosted cloud) to make the content available to users in the branch office.

In either BranchCache mode, when clients request content that is located in the cache, the clients download content information instead of the actual content from the cache. The content information is a calculated hash value that is created based on pieces of the original content. These content information hash values are then used by the client to locate the requested content in a cache in the local branch office. As new content is downloaded and stored in the cache, content information hashes are created for this new content so that branch office clients only need to request content from the central office once; all subsequent requests for the content are serviced by the local branch office cache. Figure 32.9 shows an example of a BranchCache topology that uses both distributed cache and hosted cache mode.

New Features in Windows 2012 BranchCache

Windows 2012 introduces a number of new features in BranchCache that provide improved performance, scalability, manageability, and availability, including the following:

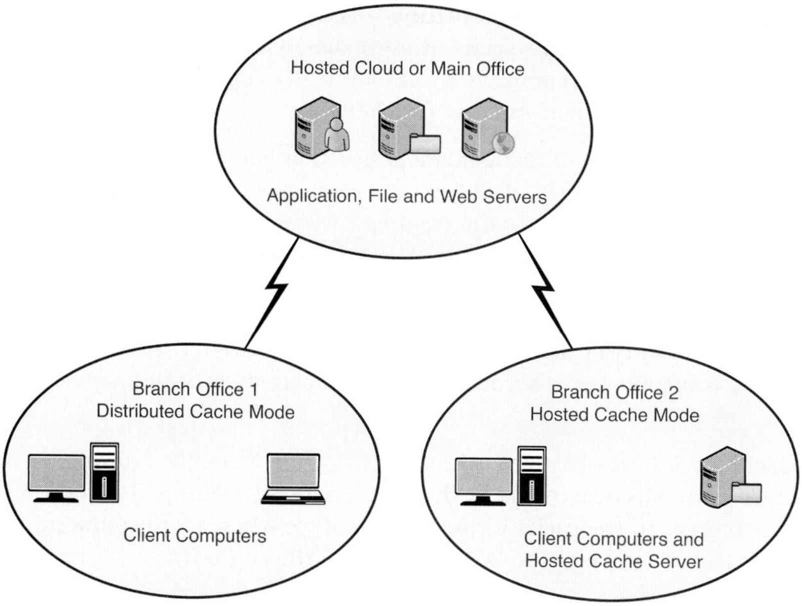

FIGURE 32.9 BranchCache topology utilizing distributed cache and hosted cache modes.

- **Scalability for office sizes and number of branch offices**—BranchCache in Windows 2012 can scale to provide access to cached content for branch offices of any size, including those branch offices without a local file server. In addition, there is no hard limit on the number of branch offices that can participate in a hosted cache topology.
- **Streamlined configuration requirements**—In Windows 2012, BranchCache settings can be configured through a single GPO with a minimal number of settings for the entire organization. This reduces the administrative overhead for branch office administration. In addition, Windows 2012 clients will search for a hosted cache server in their local site and will automatically configure themselves to operate in hosted cached mode when a hosted cache server is discovered.
- **Deduplication of data in the hosted cache.** On Windows 2012 servers, BranchCache automatically performs data deduplication for the hosted cache content.
- **Single instance storage for hosted cache content**—When duplicate data exists within files in the hosted cache, BranchCache stores only a single instance of the content, which reduces the amount of disk storage required.

- **Indexing of cached content is performed offline**—As soon as a BranchCache-enabled server has content stored in its cache, it immediately begins creating the content information hashes for this content, even before any clients have requested the data. This provides improved performance for clients.
- **Encryption of cached content**—All cached data is stored as encrypted by default. This helps to ensure that BranchCache data is secure even when stored on physically unsecure workstations, and also removes the need for a separate drive encryption process to protect the cached data. In addition, when deployed on Windows 2012 operating systems, BranchCache performs the encryption and decryption of the cached data transparently, with no requirement for client or server certificates. This is a significant improvement over BranchCache under Windows 7 / Windows 2008 R2, which requires a Transport Layer Security (TLS) certificate to encrypt and decrypt data.
- **Preloading of cached content**—BranchCache content can be preloaded onto a hosted cache server using physical media or through a network transfer. This ensures that the content is present in the cache in the branch office when clients request it, so the clients never need to traverse the WAN to retrieve the content.
- **BranchCache administration through PowerShell and WMI**—In Windows Server 2012, BranchCache supports scripting and remote management of content servers, hosted cache servers, and client computers.

Planning and Deploying BranchCache

Because BranchCache can operate in a number of different configurations, it is important to plan for the deployment of BranchCache in your organization. This section discusses the supported platforms for the BranchCache components, using Group Policy to configure BranchCache settings in the enterprise, installing and configuring the BranchCache hosted cache function in Windows 2012, verifying client settings for BranchCache, and preparing content for the hosted cache and importing packaged content into the cache.

BranchCache Supported Operating Systems

The BranchCache functions are supported on the following Windows operating systems:

- **BranchCache Content Server**—With two exceptions, Windows Server 2008 R2 and Windows Server 2012 are supported platforms for the BranchCache Content Server function. The BranchCache Content Server function is *not* supported on Windows 2008 R2 Server Core with Hyper-V (Enterprise or Datacenter).
- **BranchCache Hosted Cache Server**—Any edition of Windows Server 2012 is supported for the BranchCache hosted cache function. The following editions of Windows Server 2008 R2 can also support the hosted cache function:
    - Windows Server 2008 R2 (Enterprise or Datacenter)
    - Windows Server 2008 R2 with Hyper-V (Enterprise or Datacenter)
    - Windows Server 2008 R2 Server Core (Enterprise or Datacenter)

  - Windows Server 2008 R2 Server Core with Hyper-V (Enterprise or Datacenter)
  - Windows Server 2008 R2 for Itanium-Based Systems

- **BranchCache Distributed Cache Client Computer**—The Windows 7 Enterprise, Windows 7 Ultimate, and Windows 8 Client operating systems each support the BranchCache distributed cache function.

Configuring BranchCache Options Using Group Policy

Before deploying the server components to support BranchCache, it is recommended to create a Group Policy to automatically configure Windows 2012 clients to enable BranchCache and to perform automatic discovery of any hosted cache servers in their local site. In this configuration, if a hosted cache server cannot be located in the client's site, the client will configure itself to operate in distributed cache mode. If you are using BranchCache with Windows 2012 clients and servers, a single Group Policy can be used to assign the required settings for BranchCache and configure the required Windows Firewall exceptions to enable BranchCache communications.

To create a Group Policy to configure BranchCache, as described previously, follow these steps:

1. Expand Group Policy Management, expand the Forest and Domains nodes, and then expand the domain where you want to configure BranchCache.
2. The Group Policy that is created in this process can be linked either at the domain level or linked to a specific OU. In this example, the Group Policy will be linked to the domain so that it can automatically apply to all computers in the domain. Right-click the domain object and choose the option Create a GPO in this domain, and link it here...
3. For the name of the new GPO, enter **Enable BranchCache** and click OK. You will see a new Group Policy object appear at the domain level in the left pane of the console.
4. Right-click the Enable BranchCache GPO and choose Edit.
5. In the Group Policy Management Editor, expand Computer Configuration, Policies, Administrative Templates: Policy definitions (ADMX files) retrieved from the local machine, Network, BranchCache.
6. In the right pane, double-click the Turn On BranchCache policy, select the Enabled radio button and click OK.
7. Double-click the Set BranchCache Distributed Cache Mode policy, select the Enabled radio button, and click OK.
8. Double-click the Enable Automatic Hosted Cache Discovery by Service Connection Point policy, select the Enabled radio button, and click OK.
9. Next, we add settings to the EnableBranchCache GPO to enable BranchCache communications through Windows Firewall. In the Group Policy Management

Editor, expand Computer Configuration, Policies, Windows Settings, Security Settings, Windows Firewall with Advanced Security, Inbound Rules.

10. From the Action menu, select New Rule.

11. The New Inbound Rule Wizard will launch. Click the radio button next to Predefined, and then select BranchCache – Content Retrieval (Uses HTTP) from the drop-down menu. Click Next on the Predefined Rules screen. On the Action screen, verify that the radio button next to Allow the Connection is selected, and then click Finish to create the rule.

12. Back on the Inbound Rules node, from the Action menu, select New Rule.

13. The New Inbound Rule Wizard will launch. Click the radio button next to Predefined, then select BranchCache – Peer Discovery (WSD-In) from the drop-down menu. Click Next on the Predefined Rules screen. On the Action screen, verify that the radio button next to Allow the connection is selected, then click Finish to create the rule.

14. Close the Group Policy Management Editor.

15. Back in the Group Policy Management Console, select the Enable BranchCache GPO in the left pane and click the Settings tab in the center pane. Click the Show link under Computer Configuration, Administrative Templates. The result should look similar to Figure 32.10.

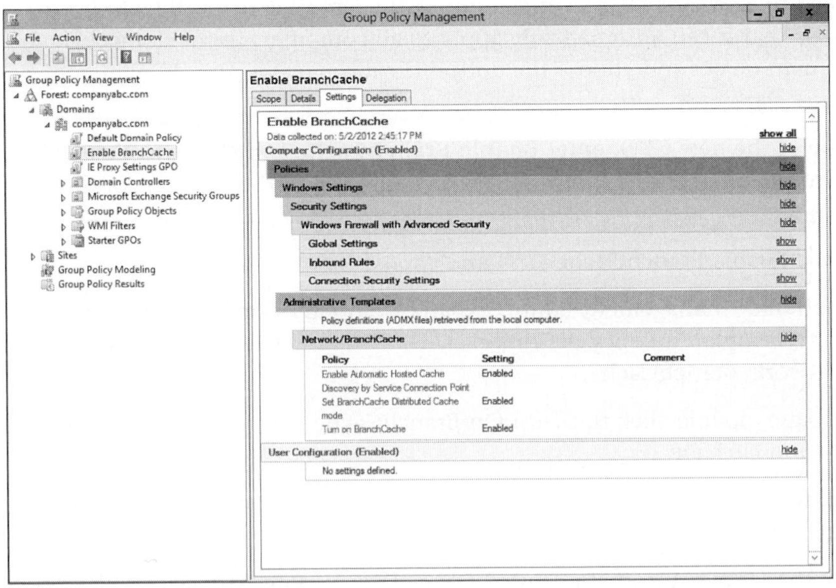

FIGURE 32.10 Group Policy Management Console displaying the BranchCache settings for the Enable BranchCache GPO.

Installing and Configuring the BranchCache Feature on Windows 2012

The installation and configuration of the BranchCache feature on Windows 2012 can be completed using Windows PowerShell. The following procedures describe how to install the BranchCache feature on a Windows 2012 server, enable hosted cache mode and register the service connection point, and verify the BranchCache configuration settings on the server.

1. Log on to the Windows 2012 server with a privileged account (for example, a member of the local Administrators group on the server).
2. Open the Server Manager application, click Tools and select Windows PowerShell (x86).
3. At the PowerShell command prompt, enter the command **Import-Module ServerManager**.
4. Next, enter the command **Add-WindowsFeature –name BranchCache**. This installs the BranchCache feature on the server. Please note that it may be necessary to restart the server after the BranchCache feature is installed.
5. Next, enter the command **Import-Module BranchCache**. This enables the BranchCache administrative cmdlets.
6. To enable hosted cache mode for the server and register the service connection point for BranchCache, enter the command **Enable-BCHostedServer -RegisterSCP**.
7. After the previous commands have been completed, enter the command **Get-BCStatus**. This displays the details of the BranchCache settings on the server. An example of the output of the PowerShell commands described earlier is shown in Figure 32.11. The highlighted areas show the status of the BranchCache service and the BranchCache mode that the server is using (hosted cache in this example).

NOTE

By default, file shares on a server with BranchCache installed are not automatically enabled for use with BranchCache. If you have installed the BranchCache and BranchCache for Network Files features on an existing file server and want to configure certain shares for use with BranchCache, right-click the share in Server Manager, click the Offline Settings button on the General tab, select the radio button labeled Only the Files and Programs That Users Specify Are Available Offline, check the Enable BranchCache check box, and then click OK.

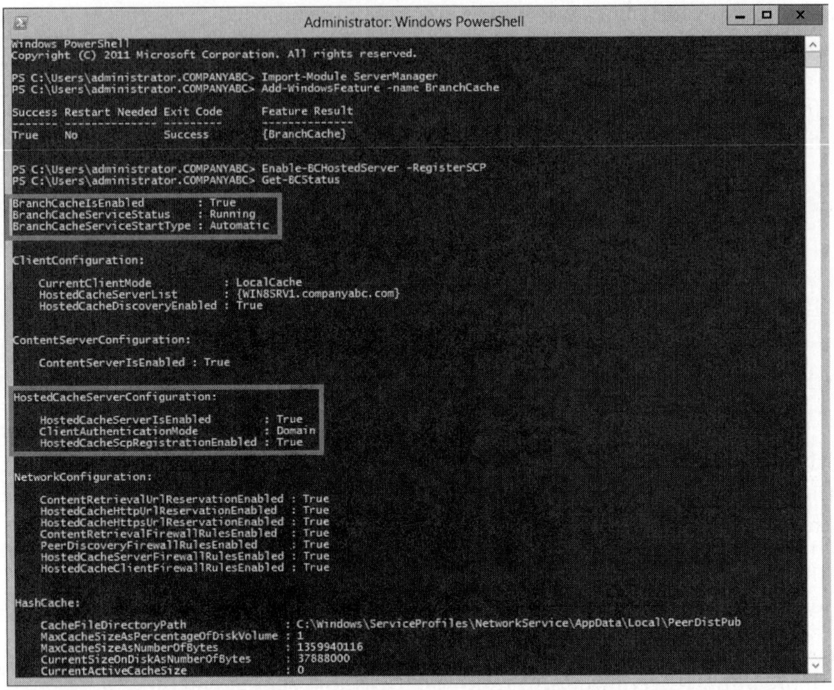

FIGURE 32.11 Enabling BranchCache and verifying configuration settings.

Verifying BranchCache Client Configuration Settings

After the Group Policy settings for BranchCache are in place, we can verify that clients are automatically receiving and applying these settings, as follows:

1. Log on to a Windows 7 or Windows 2012 workstation as a user who is a member of the local Administrators group and launch Windows PowerShell.
2. At the PowerShell prompt, enter the command **gpupdate /force**. This causes the workstation to refresh the list of Group Policies and reapply all settings, which will include the settings from the new Enable BranchCache GPO that was created and linked in an earlier step. This command should complete with the messages "Computer Policy update has completed successfully" and "User Policy update has completed successfully."
3. To ensure that the BranchCache service on the workstation is operating using the settings from the EnableBranchCache GPO, enter the command **net stop peerdistsvc**. Note that the BranchCache service on the client (peerdistsvc) may not be running at this point.
4. Next, enter the command **net start peerdistsvc**. This starts the BranchCache service on the client with the updated settings from the Enable BranchCache GPO.

5. Once the BranchCache service on the workstation has been restarted, enter the command **Get-BCStatus**. This displays the details of the BranchCache settings on the workstation. An example of the output of the PowerShell commands is shown in Figure 32.12. The highlighted area shows that the BranchCache service is operating in hosted cache mode and that the HostedCacheServerList property contains the names of two servers in the client's Active Directory site (WIN8SRV2.companyabc.com and WIN8SRV2A.companyabc.com in this example).

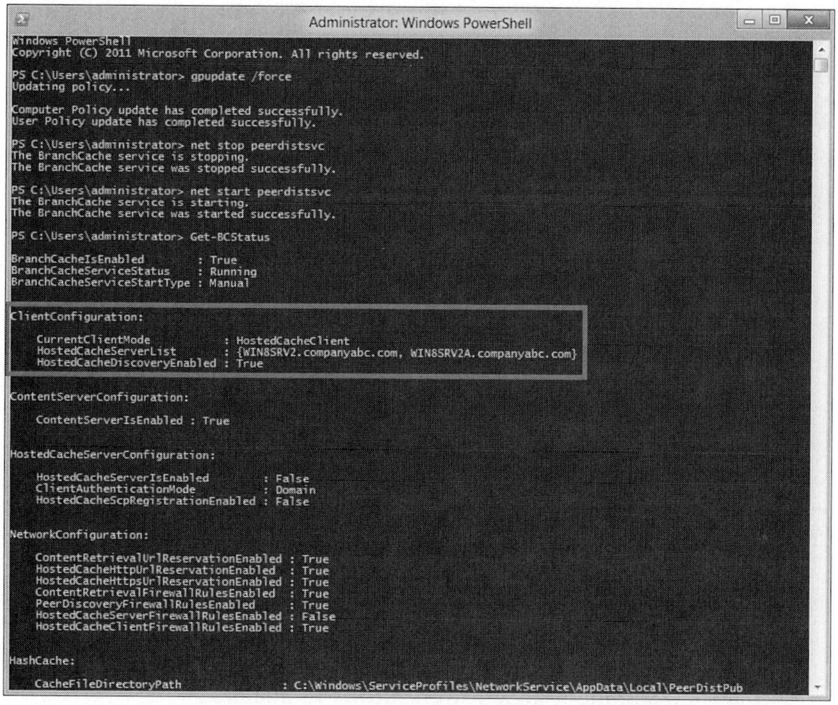

FIGURE 32.12 Refreshing Group Policy on a client and verifying BranchCache configuration settings.

NOTE

Although the BranchCache automatic discovery process for hosted cache servers within a client's Active Directory site is sufficient for most BranchCache implementations, it is also possible to manually configure a static list of hosted cache servers on a workstation. This can be done through Group Policy or by using the Enable-BCHostedClient cmdlet and specifying the **-ServerNames** parameter to designate the hosted cache servers that the client should use.

Preparing Content for the Hosted Cache

For clients to take advantage of the BranchCache improvements, content information hashes must be available for the files and folders which are stored in the cache. While the BranchCache content servers will generate the hash values for content that they store, it is also possible to generate a data package file which contains the files and their associated content information hashes. This data package file can then be imported into a hosted cache server, which will allow the content information hashes to be immediately available for BranchCache clients. The following procedures describe the steps to create a data package file and reference catalog from a file server for import on a remote hosted cache server.

NOTE

This series of examples uses file server data in the packaging process. The procedures for packaging data from a BranchCache enabled web server are very similar, and use the Publish-BCWebContent cmdlet instead of the Publish-BCFileContent cmdlet.

1. Using an account with local administrative privileges, log on to the server that contains the files and folders to be included in the data package. In this example, the content is located on the WIN8SRV2 server in the folder C:\ContentToPackage.
2. To use the PowerShell cmdlets to create a data package file for BranchCache, the BranchCache for Network Files feature must be installed on the source server. To check the status of this feature, launch Windows PowerShell and enter the command **Get-WindowsFeature FS-BranchCache**. This command is used to confirm that the BranchCache for Network Files feature is installed on the server and should return a list indicating that the FS-BranchCache feature has a status of Installed. If this feature is not installed, enter the command **Import-Module ServerManager** followed by the command **Add-WindowsFeature FS-BranchCache**. Once this command completes, run the command **Get-WindowsFeature FS-BranchCache** again and verify that the FS-BranchCache feature shows as Installed.
3. Change to the directory that contains the content that you want to package (for example, C:\ContentToPackage).
4. Enter the command **Publish-BCFileContent C:\ContentToPackage –StageData -Recurse**. (Replace the string C:\ContentToPackage with the name of the directory containing the content you are packaging.) This begins the process of publishing the content to BranchCache on the local server, as shown in Figure 32.13. Depending on the amount of data being packaged, this step may take some time to finish. The PowerShell command prompt returns when the publishing process is complete.
5. Once the content has been published to the cache, enter the command **Export-BCCachePackage –Destination C:\Temp –OutputReferenceFile C:\Temp**. (Replace the path C:\Temp with the directory where you want to store the exported data package and reference catalog.) This command creates two files in the designated export directory: PeerDistPackage.zip (the data package) and PeerDistPackage.pds (the reference catalog).

6. At this point, the data in the source folder has been packaged and cataloged and can be transferred to a remote server over the network or physical media (such as DVDs or portable hard drives). An example of the output of the previous PowerShell commands is shown in Figure 32.13.

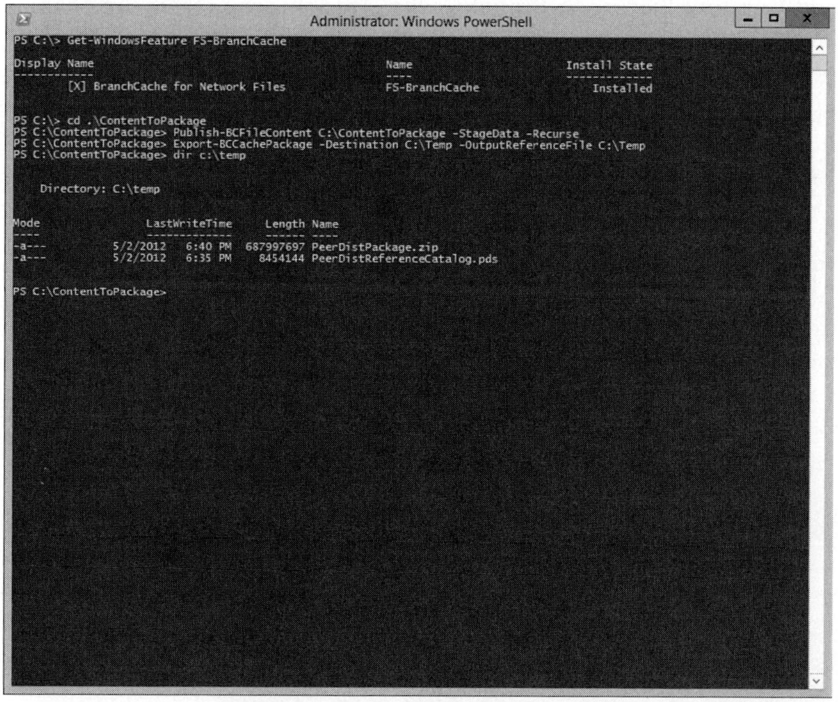

FIGURE 32.13 Publishing data to BranchCache and creating a data package file and reference catalog.

Importing Packaged Content into the Cache

After exporting a data package and reference catalog from an existing file server, the next step is to import the packaged data on a remote server so that it will be available for BranchCache clients.

1. Transfer the data package and reference catalog to the remote server that will import the packaged content. In this example, the remote server is named WIN8SRV3 and the packaged content has been transferred to the folder C:\ContentToImport.

2. Using an account with local administrative privileges, log on to the remote server that will import the packaged data.

3. To use the PowerShell cmdlets to import a data package file for BranchCache, the BranchCache for Network Files feature must be installed on the destination server. To check the status of this feature, launch Windows PowerShell and enter

the command **Get-WindowsFeature FS-BranchCache**. This command is used to confirm that the BranchCache for Network Files feature is installed on the server, and should return a list indicating that the FS-BranchCache feature has a status of Installed. If this feature shows a status of Available (meaning it is not currently installed), enter the command **Import-Module ServerManager** followed by the command **Add-WindowsFeature FS-BranchCache**. After this command completes, run the command **Get-WindowsFeature FS-BranchCache** again and verify that the FS-BranchCache feature shows as Installed.

4. Change to the directory which contains the content that you want to import (for example, C:\ContentToImport).

5. To import a data package file and reference catalog on a remote BranchCache hosted cache server, enter the command **Import-BCCachePackage –Path C:\ContentToImport\PeerDistPackage.zip**. (Replace the path in the example with the actual path to the data package file on the remote server.) This will begin the process of importing the packaged content into BranchCache on the remote server. The PowerShell command prompt will return when the import process is complete. Figure 32.14 shows an example of the output of the PowerShell commands.

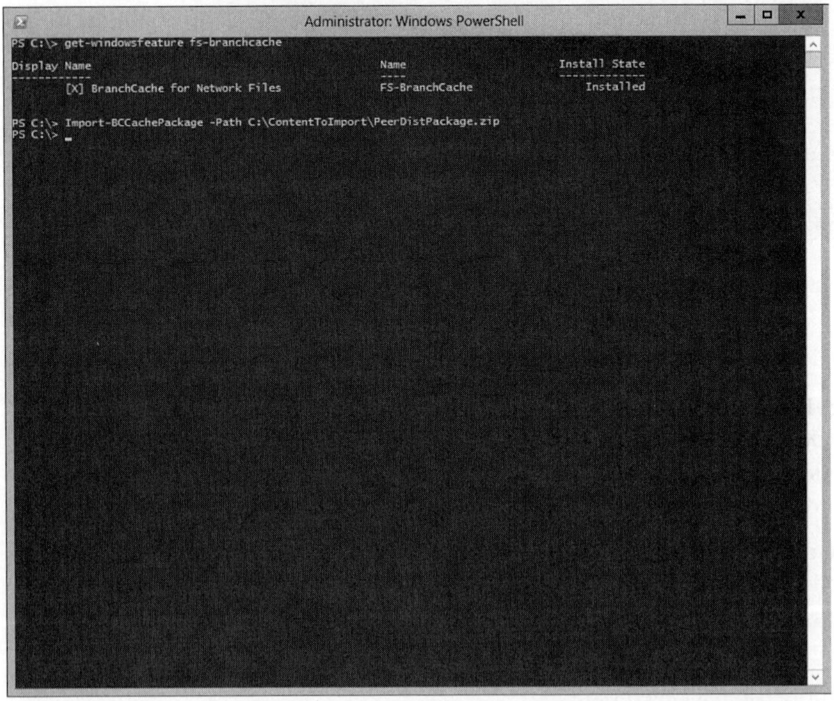

FIGURE 32.14 Importing packaged data to BranchCache on a remote server.

NOTE

If changes are made to the packaged data in the future (for example, adding a new folder), it is possible to create a new data package containing just the changed files and not the original content. This can be done by using the Publish-BCFileContent cmdlet with the **–ReferenceFile** parameter pointing to the directory containing the reference catalog file from the original packaging process.

Printing with Branch Office Direct Printing

An important new feature for branch offices in Windows Server 2012 is Branch Office Direct Printing, or BODP. BODP allows users to print directly to a print device instead of requiring that the print job traverse the WAN, which is a significant advantage for branch offices that do not have a local print server available. The following procedures describe the steps to set up the Print Server role on a Windows 2012 server, configure a print queue, configure a client to connect to the print queue, and enable BPOD for the print queue.

Configuring Windows 2012 for Branch Office Direct Printing

To configure the BPOD feature on a Windows 2012 server and Windows 8 client, execute the following:

1. Using an account with local administrative privileges, log on to the server that will host the Print Server role. In this example, the Print Server role will be installed on the WIN8SRV1 server.
2. Launch Windows PowerShell and enter the command **Add-WindowsFeature Print-Server**. This command is used to install the Print and Document Services feature on the server.
3. Enter the command **Add-WindowsFeature RSAT-Print-Services**. This command is used to install the Print and Document Services Tools feature on the server.
4. Identify the IP address of an available printer (for example, 10.1.0.100. At the Windows PowerShell prompt, enter the command **Add-PrinterPort –name Test –PrinterHostAddress "10.1.0.100"**. This command configures a printer port on the print server using the IP address of an available printer.
5. The next step in setting up the printer is to install a printer driver. For this example, we will use the Microsoft XPS Class Driver. At the PowerShell prompt, enter the command **Add-PrinterDriver –name "Microsoft XPS Class Driver"**. This command adds the Microsoft XPS Class printer driver to the server.
6. The final step in the initial printer configuration is to create and share a printer from the print server. From the PowerShell prompt, enter the command **Add-Printer –name "Microsoft XPS Printer" –DriverName "Microsoft XPS Class Driver" –Shared –ShareName "Microsoft XPS Printer" –PortName Test -Published**. This

command adds the printer to the server, designates the Microsoft XPS Class Driver as the printer driver, connects the printer to the port named Test, shares the printer out using the name Microsoft XPS Printer, and publishes the printer to Active Directory.

7. Log in to a Windows 2012 client machine. In this example, the client machine is called CLIENT1. On the Start screen, click PC Settings, and then click Devices and choose Add a Device. Click Microsoft XPS Printer on WIN8SRV1 to install the printer on the client machine.
8. On the CLIENT1 client machine, double-click Microsoft XPS Printer on WIN8SRV1 to open the client side print queue.
9. On the WIN8SRV1 server, open the Print Management Console, right-click Microsoft XPS Printer and select the Open Printer Queue option.
10. On the WIN8SRV1 server, select Printer in the queue window, and then click on Pause Printing to pause the queue.
11. On CLIENT1, select Printer in the queue window, and then select Properties.
12. On CLIENT1, click the Print Test Page button to send a test page to the Microsoft XPS Printer on WIN8SRV1.
13. Review the print queues on both WIN8SRV1 and CLIENT1. You will notice that the print job is still in both queues. On WIN8SRV1, uncheck the Pause Printing checkbox to resume printing. Notice that the print job finishes printing on the server side queue.
14. Next, we will enable Branch Office Direct Printing on the Microsoft XPS Printer on WIN8SRV1. On WIN8SRV1, right-click the Microsoft XPS Printer and select Enable Branch Office Direct Printing. Next, pause the print queue on WIN8SRV1 to prevent jobs in this queue from printing.
15. On CLIENT1, click the Print Test Page button to send a test page to the Microsoft XPS Printer on WIN8SRV1.
16. Check the print queues on the server and the client. Notice that the print job only displays in the print queue on the client and never appears in the print queue on the server.
17. On WIN8SRV1, uncheck the Pause Printing box to resume printing. Notice that the print job finishes printing from the client side queue. This illustrates the capabilities of Branch Office Direct Printing to remove the potential bottleneck of a remote print server queue from a branch office scenario.

Summary

Windows Server 2012 provides fundamental technologies that assist organizations in implementing solutions for their branch offices. When dealing with branch offices that lack physical security and IT personnel, it is a best practice for organizations to leverage technologies such as RODCs when deploying domain controllers at their remote locations. The BranchCache feature also offers significant benefits for users in branch offices, specifically increased performance for cached content and the flexibility of distributed cache and hosted cache mode. BranchCache also addresses traveling user scenarios by scaling to store copies of cached data in multiple branch office locations so that users always have access to the most current data regardless of where they are working. Finally, the introduction of the new Branch Office Direct Printing feature provides a great option for increased printing performance, especially in small branch offices with no local print server. By leveraging the features of Windows Server 2012, organizations can maintain the performance, availability, and productivity benefits of a local branch office server while avoiding the negative issues typically associated with branch office environments, including connectivity setbacks and management overhead.

Best Practices

The following are best practices from this chapter:

- Leverage RODCs when there is a lack of experienced IT support personnel supporting the domain controller at the branch office and to reduce replication workload between the branch office and hub site.
- Use RODCs at the branch office to maintain administrator role separation and isolation when the domain controller is hosting more than one application.
- Conduct a staged implementation of an RODC if there is a need to have a non-highly privileged administrator conduct the RODC installation at the branch office.
- Use BitLocker Drive Encryption to encrypt the volumes of an RODC to further enhance domain controller security.
- Review your existing branch office application, web, and file access bandwidth requirements and consider deploying BranchCache to reduce network bandwidth utilization and provide greater flexibility for traveling users.
- For smaller branch offices with no local print server, consider deploying Branch Office Direct Printing to improve performance and further reduce network bandwidth utilization.

CHAPTER 33
Logging and Debugging

IN THIS CHAPTER

- Using the Task Manager for Logging and Debugging
- Using Event Viewer for Logging and Debugging
- Performance and Resource Monitoring
- Setting Baseline Values
- Using the Debugging Tools Available in Windows Server 2012
- Task Scheduler
- Server Manager

Up to this point, this book has focused on planning, designing, implementing, and migrating to Windows Server 2012. This chapter turns your attention to the built-in management tools for monitoring, logging, debugging, and validating reliability, which help organizations identify and isolate problems in their networking environments.

Many of the tools identified in this chapter are similar to those used in earlier versions of Windows. However, as with most features of the Windows Server family of products, the features and functionality of the tools have been improved and expanded on in Windows Server 2012.

This chapter covers the Task Manager for logging and debugging issues, the Event Viewer for monitoring and troubleshooting system issues, Performance Monitor, the Best Practices Analyzer tool, the Task Scheduler for automation, and additional debugging tools available with Windows Server 2012.

Using the Task Manager for Logging and Debugging

The Task Manager is a familiar monitoring tool found in Windows Server 2012. Ultimately, the tool is very similar to the Task Manager included with earlier versions of Windows, such as Windows Server 2008 R2. It still provides an instant view of system resources, such as processor activity, process activity, memory usage, networking activity, user information, and resource consumption. However, there are some noticeable changes, focusing primarily on the usability and functionality of the toolset.

The Windows Server 2012 Task Manager is useful for an immediate view of key system operations. It comes in handy when a user notes slow response time, system problems, or other nondescript problems with the network. With just a quick glance at the Task Manager, you can see whether a server is using all available disk, processor, memory, or networking resources.

You can launch the Task Manager in three ways:

- **Method 1**—Right-click the taskbar and select Task Manager.
- **Method 2**—Press Ctrl+Shift+Esc.
- **Method 3**—Press Ctrl+Alt+Del and select Start Task Manager.

When the Task Manager loads, you will notice a new minimalist view, as shown in Figure 33.1.

TIP

From the minimalist view, you can select any nonresponding task and choose to End Task. To swap to full view, click More Details.

The following sections provide a closer look at how helpful the Task Manager components can be.

FIGURE 33.1 The Windows Task Manager, in the default minimalist view.

TIP

The More Details view includes Processes, Performance, Users, Details, and Services tabs.

Microsoft introduced us to Windows Task Manager with Windows NT 4.0. This version enabled you to run a process, list running processes, or kill a running process. Over the years, the enhancements grew to allow for prioritizing processes, setting affinity, seeing logged-on users, viewing services, and displaying various system utilization monitors.

With such augmentations, Windows Task Manager has matured into a central repository of key information. However, with hardware improvements along the way, Windows Task Manager was a site for sore eyes when it came to real-time charting. Looking at the Performance tab on a Windows Server 2008 Task Manager proves to be rather difficult when attempting to review details on a larger number of logical cores simultaneously. You are effectively staring at side-by-side tiny charts. Furthermore, no easy method exists for grabbing the processor ID.

Microsoft had three goals in mind with the Windows Server 2012 version of Task Manager:

- Optimize Task Manager for the most common scenario: using the Processes tab to kill processes based on utilization.
- Use modern information design to achieve functional goals: focusing on information provided and visualization to enhance functionality/usability.
- Do not remove functionality.

Monitoring Processes

The first tab on the Task Manager, in the detailed view, is the Processes tab. It provides a list of running processes, or image names, on the server. It also measures the performance in simple data format. This information includes CPU percent used and memory allocated to each process.

You can sort the processes by clicking the CPU or Memory column header. The processes are then sorted in order of usage. This way, you can tell which one is using the most of these resources and is slowing down performance of your server. You can terminate a process by selecting the process and clicking the End Task button.

The new heat map concept translates well in the CPU & Memory Utilization columns of the Processes tab, where darker orange colors indicate higher utilizations.

The Processes tab also comes with a few new features (all shown in Figure 33.2):

- Sorted classifications (designating processes as either Apps [generally safe to end task], Background processes, and Windows processes [generally not safe to end task]).
- Grouping (where processes are grouped under their parent process).
- Friendly names.
- You are just a right-click away from Search Online, which brings you to a Bing search results page on any item in question.

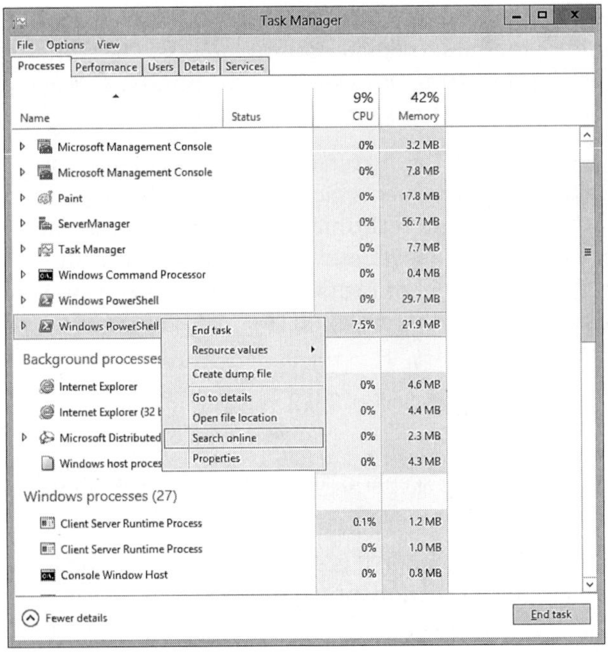

FIGURE 33.2 The Windows Task Manager, in the More Details view.

Monitoring Performance

The Performance tab enables you to view the CPU, memory, and Ethernet usage in graphical form. This information is especially useful when you need a quick view of a CPU or memory performance bottleneck.

One of the most noticeably functionally enhanced tabs in Windows Server 2012, the Performance tab, now includes dynamic graphs, showing additional details for CPU, memory, disk, and Ethernet utilization. As seen in Figure 33.3, selecting an item in the left frame (CPU for example) produces details on utilization, speed, processes, threads, handles, and uptime in a detailed frame on the right side.

First look at enhancements:

- ▶ Hovering over the heat map reveals the processor ID when the graph view is set to Logical Processors.
- ▶ Double-clicking the frame on the right, which hosts the charts, reduces Task Manager to a minimalist view (and double-clicking again reverts back to full view).

NOTE

Similar views, detailed frames, and minimalist views, similar to what is shown in Figure 33.4, are available for memory utilization and network throughput.

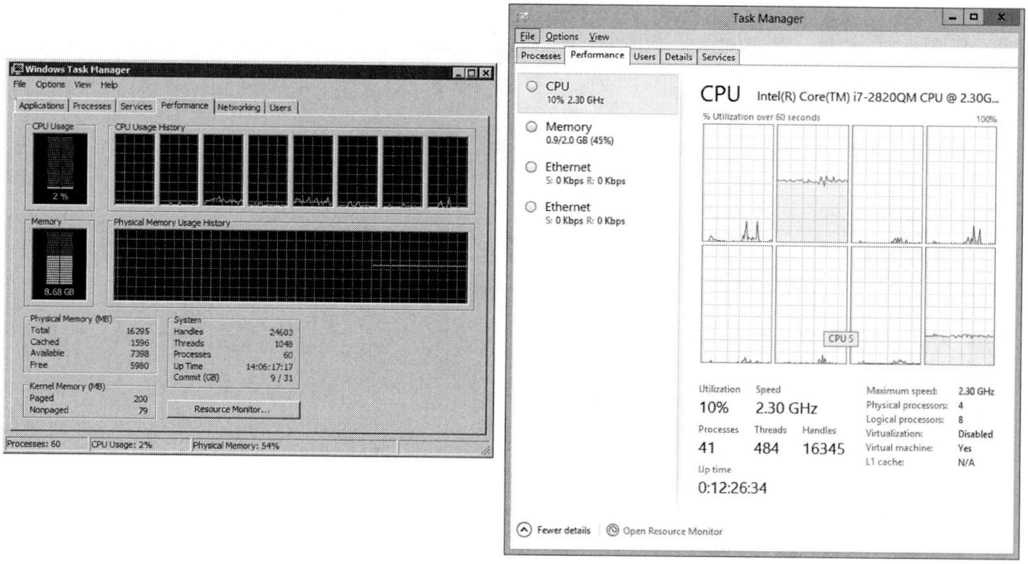

FIGURE 33.3 A side-by-side comparison of a Windows Server 2008 R2 (left) & Windows Server 2012 (right) Task Manager focused on the Performance tab. Systems shown have eight logical processors.

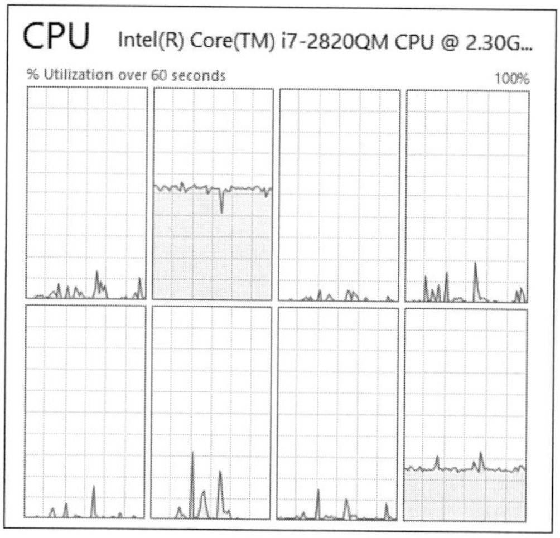

FIGURE 33.4 CPU utilization: minimalist view.

The color-shaded heat map has been touted for its ability to better scale and capture comparisons in real time. The idea is as simple as it is useful. Supporting 160 logical cores on one screen (16 across x 10 down) or up to 640 (with a scrollbar), the CPU utilization screen is the biggest obvious benefiter of this new feature. In Figure 33.5, courtesy of Microsoft, you see a comparison of a Windows Server 2008 Task Manager to a Windows

Server 2012 Task Manager on systems that have 160 logical processors. Whereas previously you would have up to 160 little graphs, you now have up to 160 little boxes with shades of blue. (The darker the color, the higher the utilization.)

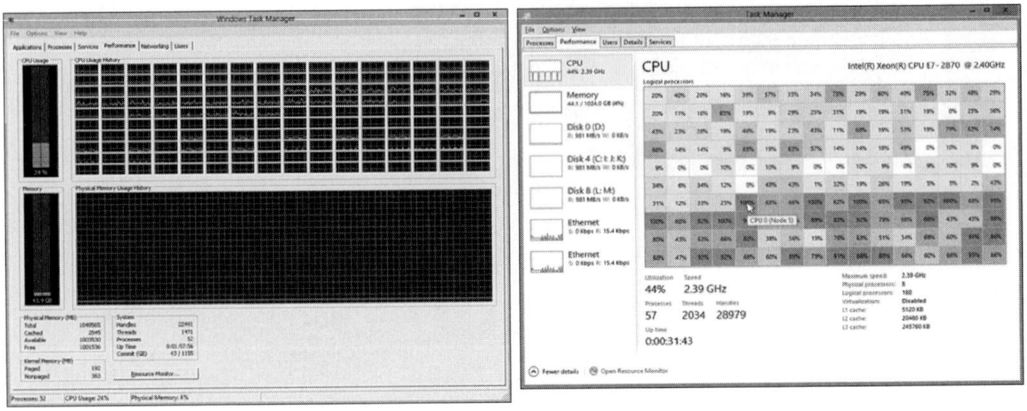

FIGURE 33.5 The Performance tab: graphs versus heat map.

Monitoring User Activity

Sorting tasks, under the owner, the Users tab enables you to disconnect a user or handle a specific task listed under a given user (end task, create a dump file, open file location, search online, or see the properties of a task). Each user, and each of that user's child tasks, is individually listed with CPU and memory utilization. There is also a right-click option on any given user that takes you directly to Manage User Accounts.

Monitoring Details

From the Details tab, shown in Figure 33.6, you can handle many of the requests available in earlier versions of Task Manager, including ending a task, ending a process tree, setting priority, setting affinity, creating a dump file, opening the file location, or going to the services.

- **Set Affinity**—Configuring threads to run on specific processors allows unused cores to be activated and clock speeds to be increased. Configuring threads to run on different processors may increase performance.
- **Search Online**—The Search Online option is again only a right-click away for a Bing search on the selected topic.
- **Analyze Wait Chain**—A feature previously available by opening Resource Monitor now finds itself present right within Task Manager. This tree view shows which processes are using or waiting to use a required resource that is being used by another process.

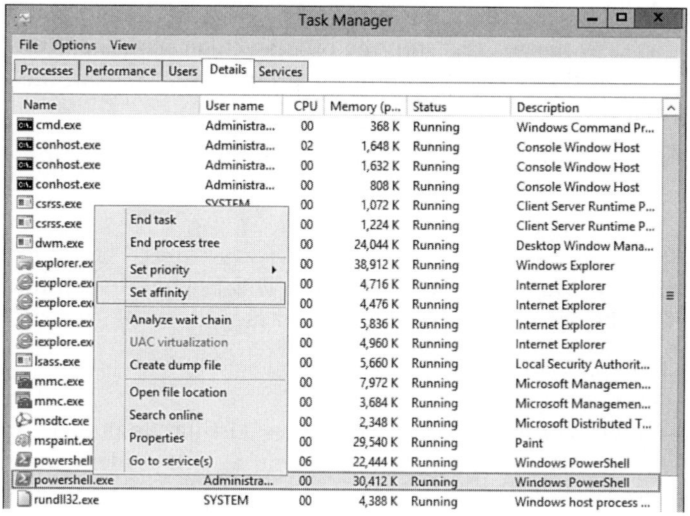

FIGURE 33.6 The Details tab.

Monitoring Services

For the most part unchanged from its predecessor, the Services tab continues to show the name, process ID (PID), description, status, and group of all services. This makes starting, stopping, or restarting an offending service feasible within one tool. You also have a link that takes you directly to the Services Microsoft Management Console (MMC), should you need to change startup type, change the service account, set recovery options, or study dependencies.

Related PowerShell Functionality

As discussed, Task Manager enables you to quickly see information about and interact with processes and tasks. Here are some ways to go about similar tasks with Windows PowerShell.

Get-Process

The Get-Process cmdlet returns running processes on the target computer (local or remote).

Description

The Get-Process cmdlet returns running processes on a local or remote computer.

A basic execution (without any parameters) of the command returns all the running processes on the local computer. You can also specify process using the name or PID. As with any PowerShell commands, you can pass a process object through the pipeline to Get-Process using the identity value.

By default, Get-Process returns a process object that has detailed information about the process and supports methods that let you start and stop the process. You can also use the parameters of Get-Process to get file version information for the program that runs in the process and to get the modules that the process loaded.

Examples

```
Get-Process *
```

What it does: This lists all running processes on a local computer. This is a quick snapshot of running processes that can easily be used on a remote computer as well.

```
Get-Process explorer.exe | get-member
```

What it does: This lists all the properties of the explorer.exe process. Listing the properties of an object provides detailed information about the component as well as identifying further operations that can be performed.

```
Get-Process * | ft name, workingset, basepriority, starttime, threads, cpu,
processoraffinity -auto
```

What it does: This returns a set of useful properties for all running processes on the local computer. Formatting the output using commands such as Format-Table, or ft, makes comparing relevant data and identifying patterns much easier.

TIP

The processor affinity value is calculated by adding the representative values for each core. In our sample system with eight CPUs, we have the following values: 1 for (Core0), 2 for (Core1), 4 for (Core2), 8 for (Core3), 16 for (Core4), 32 for (Core5), 64 for (Core6) and 128 for (Core7). For example, if cores 0 through 3 were selected, the representative values of 1, 2, 4 and 8 would be added to get the processor affinity value of 15.

Get-Service

The Get-Service cmdlet gets the services on a local or remote computer.

Description

The Get-Service cmdlet returns information about services on the local computer or on a remote computer. Services in various states including running and stopped services are returned.

You can direct Get-Service to get only particular services by specifying the service name or display name of the services, or you can pipe service objects to Get-Service.

Examples

```
Get-Service w32time -DependentServices
```

What it does: This lists services dependent on the windows Time service. An understanding of service boot order and dependencies can help troubleshoot boot issues.

```
Get-Service | Where {$_.Status -eq "Running"}
```

What it does: This lists the current running services on the local computer. A very useful way to quickly determine running services on the local or remote computer.

Start-Process and Stop-Process

Starts and stops one or more processes on the local computer.

Description

Starts or stops one or more processes on the local computer. To specify the process, enter a filename (executable or script file). You can use the parameters of the command to specify options, such as loading a user profile, starting the process in a new window, or using alternate credentials.

Examples

```
Start-Process temp.txt -Verb print
```

What it does: Starts Notepad (or other associated program) to open C:\Temp.txt and print it. A handy way to include simple application actions within a script.

```
Stop-Process -processname netlogon -force
Start-Process -processname netlogon
```

What it does: Restarts the Netlogon process without confirmation, a common maintenance task.

Using Event Viewer for Logging and Debugging

Event Viewer is the next tool to use when debugging, problem solving, or troubleshooting to resolve a problem with a Windows Server 2012 system. Event Viewer, as shown in Figure 33.7, is a built-in Windows Server 2012 tool completely rewritten based on an Extensible Markup Language (XML) infrastructure, which is used for gathering troubleshooting information and conducting diagnostics. Event Viewer was completely rewritten in Windows Server 2008, and many new features and functionality were introduced, including a new user interface and a home page, which includes an overview and summary of the system.

The upcoming sections focus on the basic elements of an event, including detailed sections covering the features and functionality.

Microsoft defines an event as any significant occurrence in the operating system or an application that requires tracking of the information. An event is not always negative. A successful logon to the network, a successful transfer of messages, or replication of data can also generate an event in Windows. It is important to sift through the events to determine which are informational events and which are critical events that require attention.

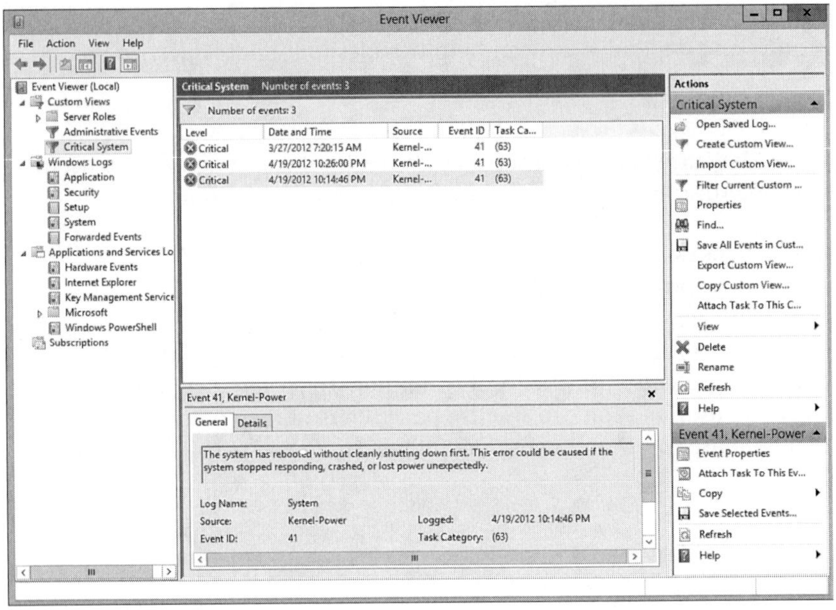

FIGURE 33.7 Event Viewer, including the Overview and Summary pane.

When server or application failures occur, Event Viewer is one of the first places to check for information. You can use Event Viewer to monitor, track, view, and audit security of your server and network. It is used to track information of both hardware and software contained in your server. The information provided in Event Viewer can be a good starting point to identify and track down the root cause of any system errors or problems.

Event Viewer can be accessed through the Server Manager. You can also launch Event Viewer by running the Microsoft Management Console (mmc.exe) and adding the snap-in or through a command line by running eventvwr.msc.

Each log has common properties associated with its events. The following bullets define these properties:

- **Level**—This property defines the severity of the event. An icon appears next to each type of event. It helps to quickly identify whether the event is informational, a warning, or an error.
- **Date and Time (Logged)**—This property indicates the date and time that the event occurred. You can sort events by date and time by clicking this column. This information is particularly helpful in tracing back an incident that occurred during a specific time period, such as a hardware upgrade before your server started experiencing problems.
- **Source**—This property identifies the source of the event, which can be an application, remote access, a service, and so on. The source is very useful in determining what caused the event.

- **Event ID**—Each event has an associated event ID, which is a numeral generated by the source and is unique to each type of event. You can use the event ID on the Microsoft Support website (www.microsoft.com/technet/) to find topics and solutions related to an event on your server.
- **Task Category**—This property determines the category of an event. Task Category examples from the Security log include Logon/Logoff, System, Object Access, and others.

Examining the Event Viewer User Interface

The interface for Event Viewer in Windows Server 2008 R2 has changed significantly from earlier versions, and those changes remain intact for Windows Server 2012. Although the information produced by logged events remains much the same, it's important to be familiar with the interface to take advantage of the features and functionality.

Administrators accustomed to using the latest Microsoft Management Console (MMC) 3.0 will notice similarities in the new look and feel of the Event Viewer user interface. The navigation tree on the left pane of the Event Viewer window lists the event logs available to view and also introduces new folders for creating custom event views and subscriptions from remote systems. The central details pane, located in the center of the console, displays relevant event information based on the folder selected in the navigation tree. The home page central details pane also includes a layout to bolster the administrator's experience by summarizing administrative events by date and criticality, providing log summaries and displaying recently viewed nodes. Finally, the tasks pane, located on the extreme right side of the window, contains context-sensitive actions depending on the focus in the Event Viewer snap-in.

The folders residing in the left pane of the Event Viewer are organized as follows:

- Custom Views
- Windows Logs
- Applications and Services Logs
- Subscriptions

The Custom Views Folder

Custom views are filters either created automatically by Windows Server 2012 when new server roles or applications such as Active Directory Certificate Services (AD CS) and Dynamic Host Configuration Protocol (DHCP) servers are added to the system or manually by administrators. It is important for administrators to have the ability to create filters that target only the events they are interested in viewing to quickly diagnose and remediate issues on the Windows Server 2012 system and infrastructure. By expanding the Custom Views folder in the Event Viewer navigation tree and right-clicking Administrative Events, selecting Properties, and clicking the Edit Filter button, you can see how information from the event log is parsed into a set of filtered events. The Custom View Properties

Filter tab is displayed in Figure 33.8. In the built-in Administrative Events custom views, all critical, error, and warning events are captured for all event logs. Instead of looking at the large number of informational logs captured by Windows Server 2012 and cycling through each Windows log, this filter gives the administrator a single place to go and quickly check for any potential problems contained on the system.

Also listed in the Custom View section of Event Viewer are predefined filters created by Windows Server 2012 when new roles are added to the system. These queries cannot be edited; however, they provide events related to all Windows Server 2012 roles and the logical grouping can be used to quickly drill down into issues affecting the performance of the system as it relates to specific server roles. Again, this is a way of helping an administrator find the information needed to identify and ultimately resolve server problems quickly and efficiently.

The filter was first introduced with Windows Server 2008. The Administrative Events filter groups all events associated with the system from an administrative perspective. By drilling down to the Administrative Events filter, an administrator can quickly decipher issues associated with all administrative events.

Creating a New Custom View

To create a new custom view in Event Viewer, right-click the Custom View folder and select Create Custom View. Alternatively, select Custom View from the Action menu. This results in the Custom View Properties box, as shown in Figure 33.8.

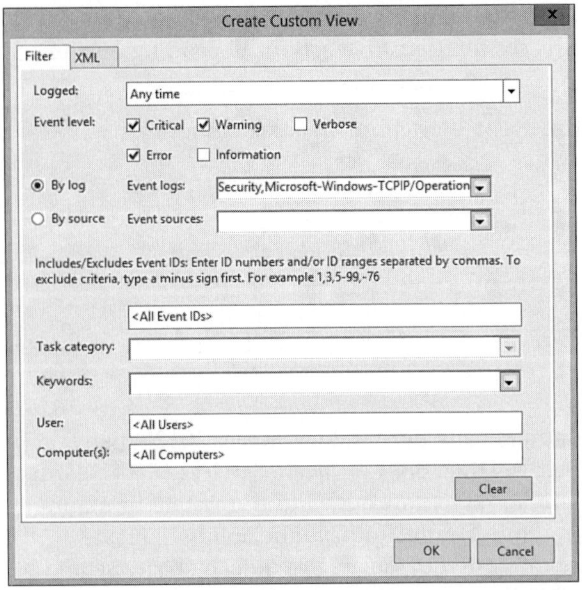

FIGURE 33.8 The Filter tab located in the Custom View Properties page.

First, decide whether you want to filter events based on date; if so, specify the date range by using the Logged drop-down list. Options include Any Time, Custom Range, and specific time intervals. The next step is to specify the event level criteria to include in the custom view. Options include Critical, Error, Warning, Information, and Verbose. After the event level settings are specified, the next area to focus on is the By Log and By Source sections. By leveraging the drop-down lists, specify the event log and event log sources to be included in this custom filter. To further refine the custom filter, enter specific event IDs, task categories, keywords, users, computers, and then click OK and save the filter by providing it a name, description, and the location of where to save the view.

TIP

Performance and memory consumption might be negatively affected if you have included too many events in the custom view.

After you define a custom view, you can export it as an XML file, which can then be imported into other systems. Filters can also be written or modified directly in XML; but keep in mind, after a filter has been modified using the XML tab, it can no longer be edited using the GUI described previously.

The Windows Logs Folder

The Windows Logs folder contains the traditional application, security, and system logs. Windows Server 2012 also includes two out-of-the-box logs, which can also be found under the Windows Logs folder: the Setup and Forwarded Events logs. The following is a brief description of the different types of Windows logs that are available:

- **Application log**—This log contains events based on applications or programs residing on the system.
- **Security log**—Depending on the auditing settings configured, the security log captures events specific to authentication and object access.
- **Setup log**—This log captures information tailored toward installation of applications, server roles, and features.
- **System log**—Events associated with Windows system components are logged to the system log. This might include driver errors or other components failing to load.
- **Forwarded Events log**—Because computers can experience the same issues, this feature consolidates and stores events captured from remote computers into a single log to facilitate problem isolation, identification, and remediation.

The Applications and Services Logs Folder

The Applications and Services Logs folder introduces a way to logically organize, present, and store events based on a specific Windows application, component, or service instead of capturing events that affect the whole system. An administrator can easily drill into a specific item such as DFS Replication or DNS Server and easily review those events without being bombarded or overwhelmed by all the other systemwide events.

These logs include four subtypes: Admin, Operational, Analytic, and Debug logs. The events found in Admin logs are geared toward end users, administrators, and support personnel. This log is very useful because it not only describes a problem, but also identifies ways to deal with the issues. Operational logs are also a benefit to systems administrators but they typically require more interpretation.

Analytic and Debug logs are more complex. Analytic logs trace an issue and often a high number of events are captured. Debug logs are primarily used by developers to debug applications. Both Analytic and Debug logs are hidden and disabled by default. To view them, right-click Applications and Services Logs, and then select View, Show Analytic and Debug Logs.

The Subscriptions Folder

The final folder in the Event Viewer console tree is called Subscriptions. Subscriptions is another feature included with the Windows Server 2012 Event Viewer. It allows remote computers to forward events; therefore, they can be viewed locally from a central system. For example, if you are experiencing issues between two Windows Server 2012 systems, diagnosing the problem becomes challenging because both systems typically log data to their respective event logs. In this case, it is possible to create a subscription on one of the servers to forward the event log data from the other server. Therefore, both system event logs can be reviewed from a central system.

Configuring Event Subscriptions

To configure event subscriptions between two systems, you must first prepare each source computer to send events to remote computers:

1. Log on to the source computer. Best practice is to log on with a domain account that has administrative permissions on the source computer.
2. Open a PowerShell console session and ensure Remote Management is enabled by executing the **Enable-PSRemoting** command.
3. Add the collector computer to the local administrators group of the source computer.
4. Log on to the collector computer following the steps outlined previously for the source system.
5. From an elevated command prompt, run **wecutil qc**.
6. If you intend to manage event delivery optimization options such as Minimize Bandwidth or Minimize Latency, also run **Enable-PSRemoting** on the collector computer.

After the collector and source computers are prepared, a subscription must be made identifying the events that will be pulled from the source computers. To create a new subscription, follow these steps:

1. On the collector computer, run Event Viewer with an account with administrative permissions.

2. Click the Subscriptions folder in the console tree and select Create Subscription or right-click and select the same command from the context menu.
3. In the Subscription Name box, type a name for the subscription.
4. In the Description box, enter an optional description.
5. In the Destination Log box, select the log file where collected events will be stored. By default, these events are stored in the forwarded events log in the Windows Logs folder of the console tree.
6. Click Select Computers to select the source computers that will be forwarding events. Add the appropriate domain computers, and then click OK.
7. Click Select Events and configure the event logs and types to collect. Click OK.
8. Click OK to create the subscription.

Conducting Additional Event Viewer Management Tasks

Now that you understand the functionality of each of the folders associated with the Event Viewer included with Windows Server 2012, it is beneficial to review the upcoming sections for additional management tasks associated with Event Viewer. These tasks include the following:

- Saving event logs
- Organizing data
- Viewing logs on remote servers
- Archiving events
- Customizing the event log
- Understanding the security log

Saving Event Logs

Event logs can be saved and viewed at a later time. You can save an event log by either right-clicking a specific log and choosing Save Events As or by picking individual events from within a log, right-clicking the selected events, and choosing Save Selected Items. Entire logs and selected events can also be saved by selecting the same command from the Actions pane. After being saved, these logs can be opened by right-clicking the appropriate log and selecting Open Saved Log or by clicking the same command in the Actions pane. After a log has been opened, it will be displayed in a new top-level folder called Saved Logs from within Event Viewer.

Organizing Data

Vast numbers of logs can be collected by Windows and displayed in the central pane of Event Viewer. New tools or enhancement to old ones make finding useful information much easier than in any other iteration of Event Viewer:

- **Sorting**—Events can be sorted in many ways, for example, by right-clicking the folder or Custom View icon and then selecting View, Sort By, or by selecting the column name on which to sort in the left pane or clicking the column to be sorted or the heading. Sorting is a quick way to find items at a very high level (for example, by time, source, or event ID). The features for finding and sorting data are more robust and well worth learning.
- **Selection and sorting of column headings**—Various columns can be added to or removed from any of the event logs. The order in which columns are displayed from left to right can be altered as well by selecting the column in the Select Column dialog box and clicking the up- or down-arrow button.
- **Grouping**—A way to view event log information is through the grouping function. By right-clicking on column headings, an administrator can opt to group the event log being viewed by any of the columns in view. By isolating events, desired and specific criteria trends can be spotted that can help in isolating issues and ultimately resolving problems.
- **Filtering**—As mentioned earlier, filtering, like grouping, provides a means to isolate and only display the data you want to see in Event Viewer. Filtering, however, gives the administrator many more options for determining which data should be displayed than grouping or sorting does. Filters can be defined based on any or all the event levels, log or source, event IDs, task category, keywords, or user or computers. After being created, filters can be exported for use on other systems.
- **Tasks**—By attaching tasks to events, logs, or custom views, administrators can bring some automation and notification into play when certain events occur. To create a task, simply right-click the custom view, built-in log, or specific event of your choice, and then right-click Attach a Task to This Custom View, Log, or Event. The Create a Basic Task Wizard then launches; on the first tab, just select a name and description for the task. Click Next to view the criteria that will trigger the task action. (This section cannot be edited and is populated based on the custom view, log, or task selected when the wizard is initiated.) Click Next and select Start a Program, Send an E-mail, or Display a Message as desired.

Viewing Logs on Remote Servers

You can use Event Viewer to view event logs on other computers on your network. To connect to another computer from the console tree, right-click Event Viewer (Local) and click Connect to Another Computer. Select Another Computer and then enter the name of the computer or browse to it and click OK. You must be logged on as an administrator or be a member of the Administrators group to view event logs on a remote computer. If you are not logged on with adequate permissions, you can select the Connect as Another User check box and set the credentials of an account that has proper permissions to view the logs on the remote computer.

Archiving Events

Occasionally, you might need to archive an event log. Archiving a log copies the contents of the log to a file. Archiving is useful in creating benchmark records for the baseline of a server or for storing a copy of the log so it can be viewed or accessed elsewhere. When an event log is archived, it is saved in one of four forms:

- **Comma-delimited text file (.csv)**—This format allows the information to be used in a program such as Microsoft Excel.
- **Text-file format (.txt)**—Information in this format can be used in a program such as a word processing program.
- **Log file (.evtx)**—This format allows the archived log to be viewed again in the Windows Server 2012 or Windows 8 Event Viewer. Note that the event log format is XML, which earlier versions of Windows, prior to Windows Server 2008 or Windows 7, cannot read.
- **XML (.xml)**—This format saves the event log in raw XML. XML is used throughout Event Viewer for filters, tasks, and logging.

The event description is saved in all archived logs. To archive, right-click the log to be archived and click Save Log File As. In the File Name field of the resulting property page, type in a name for the archived log file, choose a file type from the file format options of .csv, .txt, .evtx, or .xml, and then click Save.

NOTE

You must be a member of the Backup Operators group at the minimum to archive an event log.

Logs archived in the log-file format (.evtx) can be reopened using the Windows Server 2012 Event Viewer utility. Logs saved in log-file format retain the XML data for each event recorded. Event logs, by default, are stored on the server where the Event Viewer utility is being run. Data can, however, be archived to a remote server by simply providing a UNC path (such as \\servername\share\) when entering a filename.

Logs archived in comma-delimited (.csv) or text (.txt) format can be reopened in other programs such as Microsoft Word or Excel. These two formats do not retain the XML data or formatting.

Customizing the Event Log

The properties of an event log can be configured. In Event Viewer, the properties of a log are defined by general characteristics: log path, current size, date created, when last modified or accessed, maximum size, and what should be done when the maximum log size is reached.

To customize the event log, access the properties of the particular log by highlighting the log and selecting Action and then Properties. Alternatively, you can right-click the log and select Properties to display the General tab of the log's property page, as shown in Figure 33.9.

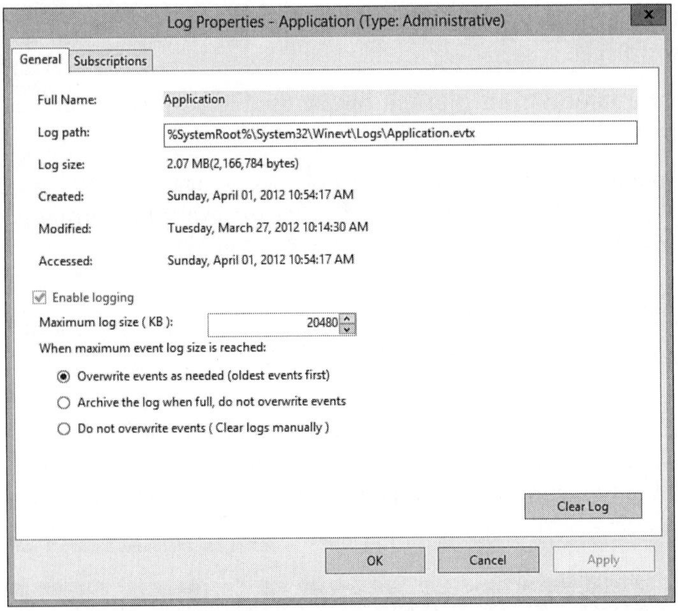

FIGURE 33.9 Selecting properties for the event log.

The Log Size section specifies the maximum size of the log and the subsequent actions to take when the maximum log size limit is reached. The three options are as follows:

- Overwrite Events as Needed (Oldest Events First)
- Archive the Log When Full, Do Not Overwrite Events
- Do Not Overwrite Events (Clear Logs Manually)

If you select the Do Not Overwrite Events option, Windows Server 2012 stops logging events when the log is full. Although Windows Server 2012 notifies you when the log is full, you need to monitor the log and manually clear the log periodically so that new events can be tracked and stored in the log file.

In addition, log file sizes must be specified in multiples of 64KB. If a value is not in multiples of 64KB, Event Viewer automatically sets the log file size to a multiple of 64KB.

When you need to clear the event log, click the Clear Log button in the lower right of the property page.

Understanding the Security Log

Effectively logging an accurate and wide range of security events in Event Viewer requires an understanding of auditing in Windows Server 2012. It is important to know events are not audited by default. You can enable auditing in the local security policy for a local server, the domain controller security policy for a domain controller machine, and the Active Directory (AD) Group Policy object (GPO) for a domain. Through auditing, you can track Windows Server 2012 security events. It is possible to request that an audit entry be written to the security event log whenever certain actions are carried out or an object such as a file or printer in AD is accessed. The audit entry shows the action carried out, the user responsible for the action, and the date and time of the action.

Related PowerShell Functionality

As discussed, one of the main functions of Event Viewer is to quickly see filtered Event Log entries. Here are some ways to go about similar tasks with Windows PowerShell.

Get-EventLog

The Get-EventLog cmdlet gets the events in an event log, or a list of the event logs, on the local or remote computers.

Description

The cmdlet returns events and event logs on the specified computer (local or remote). This is useful when scripting searches for specific event message or ID. Creating reports for recent event messages is also facilitated by this command.

The cmdlet parameters provide the ability to refine the returned result set using any proerty values. The EventLog cmdlets work only on classic event logs. To get events from applications and services event logs, you must use Get-WinEvent.

Examples

```
Get-EventLog Application -Message "*failed*"
```

What it does: Searches for the word *failed* in the message body of the Application Log entries and returns applicable event log entries.

```
Get-EventLog "Windows PowerShell" | Where-Object {$_.EventID -eq 403}
```

What it does: Returns event ID 403 PowerShell log entries.

```
Get-EventLog -LogName System -Newest 80 | ConvertTo-HTML | Out-File
C:\Reports\Events.htm
```

What it does: Returns 80 newest system log entries, converts to HTML and exports to C:\Reports\Event.htm

```
Get-EventLog -LogName Application -newest 500 | Group-Object -Property source
-NoElement
```

What it does: Returns 500 newest application log entries and sorts them by count of each unique source.

```
Get-EventLog -LogName System -newest 10000 | Where-Object { $_.EventID -like "200?"}
|
Format-Table TimeWritten, EventID, Message -auto
```

What it does: Returns events from the System event log that have an event ID between 2000 and 2009 and are in the 10,000 newest events in the log. Events are returned as a table with the indicated fields.

```
Get-EventLog Application -EntryType Error -After (Get-Date).AddDays(-1)
```

What it does: Return errors received in the past day in the application log.

Performance Monitoring

Performance is a basis for measuring how fast application and system tasks are completed on a computer, and reliability is a basis for measuring system operation. How reliable a system is will be based on whether it regularly operates at the level at which it was designed to perform. Based on these descriptions, it should be easy to recognize that performance and reliability monitoring are crucial aspects in the overall availability and health of a Windows Server 2012 infrastructure. To ensure maximum uptime, a well-thought-through process needs to be put in place to monitor, identify, diagnose, and analyze system performance. This process should invariably provide a means for quickly comparing system performances at varying instances in time and detecting and potentially preventing a catastrophic incident before it causes system downtime.

Performance Monitor, which is an MMC snap-in, provides a number of tools for administrators that enable them to conduct real-time system monitoring, examine system resources, collect performance data, and create performance reports from a single console. This tool is literally a combination of three legacy Windows Server monitoring tools: System Monitor, Performance Monitor, and Server Performance Advisor. However, new features and functionalities have been introduced to shake things up, including data collector sets, Resource view, scheduling, diagnostic reporting, and wizards and templates for creating logs. To launch the Performance Monitor MMC snap-in tool, select Server Manager or type **perfmon.msc** at a command prompt.

The Performance Monitor MMC snap-in consists the following elements:

- Overview screen
- Performance Monitor
- Data collector sets
- Report generation

The upcoming sections further explore these major elements of the Performance Monitoring tool.

Performance Monitor Overview

The first area of interest in the Performance Monitor snap-in is the Overview of Performance Monitor screen, also known as the Performance icon. It is displayed as the home page in the central details pane when the Performance Monitor tool is invoked.

The Overview of Performance Monitor screen presents holistic, real-time graphical illustrations of a Windows Server 2012 system's CPU usage, disk usage, network usage, and memory usage, as displayed in Figure 33.10.

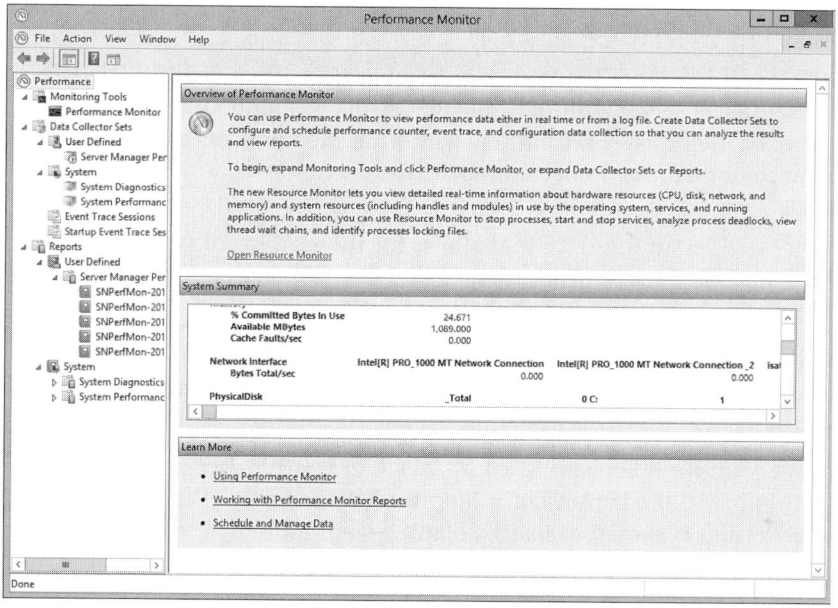

FIGURE 33.10 Viewing the Overview of Performance Monitor screen.

Additional process-level details can be viewed to better understand your system's current resource usage by reviewing subsections beneath each metric being displayed. For example, the Memory section includes % Committed Bytes in Use, Available Mbytes, and Cache Faults/sec.

The Overview of Performance Monitor screen is the first level of defense when there is a need to get a quick overview of a system's resources. If quick diagnosis of an issue cannot be achieved, an administrator should leverage the additional tools within Performance Monitor. These are covered in the upcoming sections.

Performance Monitor

First, defining some terms used in performance monitoring will help clarify the function of Performance Monitor and how it ties in to software and system functionality. The three components noted in Performance Monitor, data collector sets, and reports are as follows:

- **Object**—Components contained in a system are grouped into objects. Objects are grouped according to system functionality or by association within the system. Objects can represent logical entities such as memory or a physical mechanism such as a hard disk drive. The number of objects available in a system depends on the configuration. For example, if Microsoft Exchange Server is installed on a server, some objects pertaining to Exchange would be available.
- **Counter**—Counters are subsets of objects. Counters typically provide more detailed information for an object such as queue length or throughput for an object. The System Monitor can collect data through the counters and display it in either a graphical format or a text log format.
- **Instances**—If a server has more than one similar object, each one is considered an instance. For example, a server with multiple processors has individual counters for each instance of the processor. Counters with multiple instances also have an instance for the combined data collected for the instances.

Performance Monitor provides an interface that allows for the analysis of system data, research performance, and bottlenecks. Performance Monitor displays performance counter output in line graphs, histogram (bar chart), and report format.

The histogram and line graphs can be used to view multiple counters at the same time, as shown in Figure 33.11. However, each data point displays only a single value that is independent of its object. The Report view is better for displaying multiple values.

Accessing Performance Monitor is accomplished by selecting Performance Monitor from the Monitoring Tools folder in the Performance Monitor MMC snap-in. When a new Performance Monitor session is started, it loads a blank system monitor graph into the console with % Processor Time as the only counter defined.

Adding Counters with Performance Monitor

Before counters can be displayed, they have to be added. The counters can be added simply by using the menu bar. The Counter button on the toolbar includes Add, Delete, and Highlight. You can use the Add Counter button to display new counters. Use the Delete Counter button to remove unwanted counters from the display. The Highlight Counter button is helpful for highlighting a particular counter of interest; a counter can be highlighted with either a white or black color around the counter.

To add counters to Performance Monitor, follow these steps:

1. In the navigation tree of Performance Monitor, first expand Performance, Monitoring Tools, and then Performance Monitoring.
2. Either click the Add icon on the menu bar or right-click anywhere on the graph and select Add Counters.

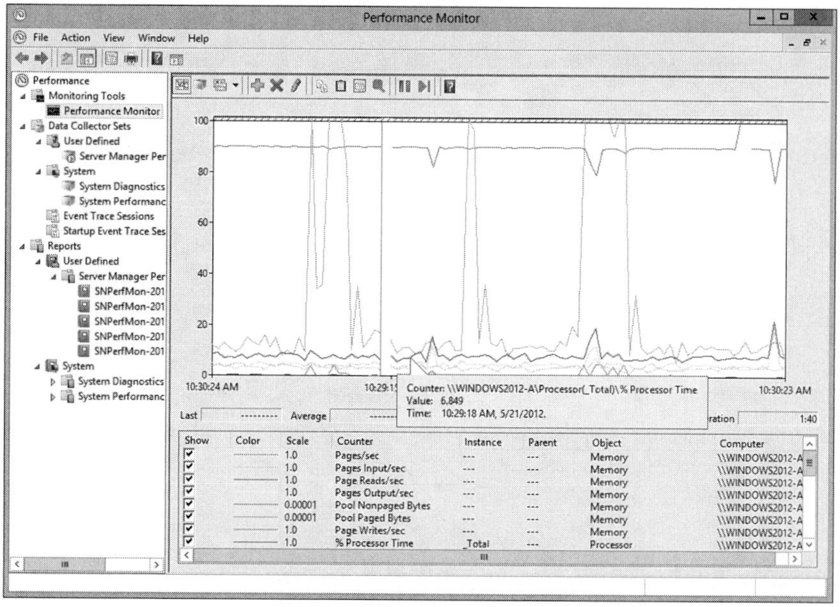

FIGURE 33.11 The graph view of Performance Monitor.

NOTE

Typical baseline counters include Memory - Pages/Sec, PhysicalDisk - Avg. Disk Queue Length, and Processor - % Processor Time.

3. The Add Counters dialog box is invoked, as shown in Figure 33.12. In the Available Counters section, select the desired counters, and then click the Add button.

NOTE

Windows Server 2012 includes a tremendous number of counters to choose from when conducting performance monitoring. It is challenging to fully explain what each counter offers in this section. If you are interested in finding out more about a counter, enable the Show Description option in the Add Counters dialog box and highlight a specific counter to obtain a detailed explanation of it.

4. Review the selected counters in the Added Counters section, and then click OK.

NOTE

When adding counters, it is possible to conduct remote monitoring by selecting counters from another system. To simplify things, it is also possible to search for instances of a counter and add a group of counters.

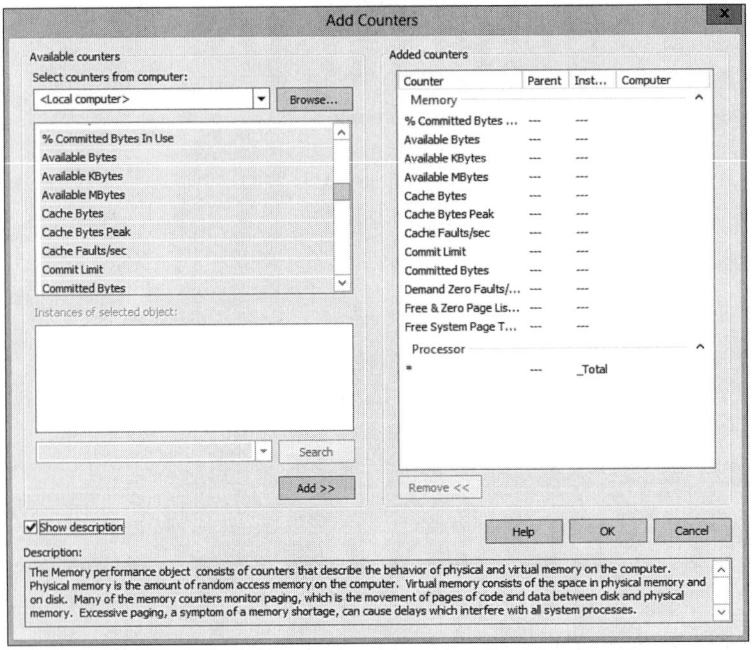

FIGURE 33.12 Adding counters to Performance Monitor.

Managing Performance Monitor Settings

While back on the Performance Monitor display, update displays by clicking the Clear Display button. Clicking the Freeze Display button or pressing Ctrl+F freezes displays, which suspends data collection. Data collection can be resumed by pressing Ctrl+F or clicking the Freeze Display button again. Click the Update Data button to display an updated data analysis.

It is also possible to export and import a display by using the Cut and Paste buttons. For example, a display can be saved to the Clipboard and then imported into another instance of Performance Monitor. This is commonly used to view or analyze system information about a different system, such as information from a production server.

The Properties page of Performance Monitor has five additional tabs of configuration: General, Source, Data, Graph, and Appearance. Generally, the Properties page provides access to settings that control the graph grid, color, style of display data, and so on. Data can be saved from the monitor in different ways. The easiest way to retain the display features is to save the control as an HTML file.

Performance Monitor enables you to also save log files in HTML or tab-separated (.tsv) format, which you can then analyze by using third-party tools. Alternatively, a tab-separated file can be imported into a spreadsheet or database application such as Excel or Microsoft Access. Windows Server 2012 also enables you to collect data in SQL database format. This is useful for performance analysis at an enterprise level rather than a per-server basis. Reports displayed in Excel can help you better understand the data and provide reports to management. As well as saving log files, you can save the results from Performance Monitor as an image. This is great when you need to obtain a point-in-time depiction of a performance graph.

Data Collector Sets

The Data Collector Sets subfolder is a vital feature available within the Performance Monitor snap-in. The purpose of a data collector set is to review or log system performance data. This is achievable through a single component that encompasses organized multiple data collection points. This information can then be analyzed to diagnose problems, correct system performance issues, or create baselines.

Performance counters, event trace data, and system configuration information are all data collector elements that can be captured and contained in a data collector set. Data collector sets can be based on a predefined template, from a data collector set that already exists, by creating it manually, with a wizard, or it can be user defined. Data collector sets can be exported and used for multiple systems, easing the administrative load involving the configuration of new systems producing more effective monitoring. Wizards facilitate the creation of data collector sets and enable an administrator to quickly create collections based on server roles or the type of information that is required.

NOTE

To create data collector sets, you must be a member of the Administrators group or logged on with an account that is a member of the Performance Log Users group.

Creating Data Collector Sets

You can create data collector sets manually from a template or from Performance Monitor. The following examples will help you understand the different methods for creating data collector sets.

To create a data collector set from Performance Monitor, follow these steps:

1. In the Performance Monitor console, navigate to Performance Monitor.
2. Add counters based on items you want to capture. For this example, the following counters were used: Memory - Pages/Sec, Physical Disk - Avg.Disk Queue Length, and Processor - % Processor Time.
3. After the counters are added, right-click Performance Monitor in the navigation tree, select New, and then select Data Collector Set. The Create New Data Collector Set Wizard is launched.
4. Enter a name for this new data collector set on the Create New Data Collector Set page, and then click Next.
5. On the next page, specify where you want the data to be saved. The default path is the %systemdrive%\PerfLogs\. Click Finish to save the current settings and exit or click Next to enter a user account to run as.

6. Click the Change button to enter a user for this dataset.
7. Select the option to Save and Close or Start This Data Collector Set Now, and then click Finish to complete the data collector set creation process.

You can configure the resulting data collector set to run immediately by right-clicking the new data collector set and selecting Start. You can view the properties of the data collector set by right-clicking and selecting Properties.

Data collector sets can be created, saved, or restored from templates. Many templates are built in and can be created using the Create New Data Collector Set Wizard in Windows Performance Monitor. This wizard is invoked by right-clicking the User Defined folder, the Event Trace Sessions folder, or the Startup Event Trace Sessions folder under Data Collector Sets and selecting New, Data Collector Set.

To create a data collector set from a template, follow these steps:

1. Expand the Data Collector Sets folder and then the User Defined subfolder in the Performance Monitor snap-in.
2. Right-click the User Defined subfolder and select New Data Collector Set to launch the Create New Data Collector Set Wizard.
3. Enter a name for this new data collector set, select the Create from a Template option, and then click Next.
4. On the next page, select the desired template to use, and then click Next.

NOTE

The Create New Data Collector Set Wizard offers four templates for creating Data Collector Sets: Basic, System Diagnostics, System Performance, and WDAC Diagnostics. Use the Basic template when you want create a basic data collector set. The System Diagnostics template generates a report detailing the status of local hardware resources, system response times, system information, and configuration data. The Systems Performance template is leveraged when you want to not only generate a report detailing the status of local hardware resources and system response times, but also processes on the local computers. In summary, the Basic template usually provides basic diagnostics, the Systems Diagnostics template is good for maximizing performance and streamlining system operations, the System Performance template is a good choice when you want to identify performance issues, and the WDAC Diagnostics template is used for performing analyzing WDAC components. Each of the templates can be edited after they have been created. In addition, it is possible to click the Browse button and import templates from other servers.

5. On the next page, specify where you want the data to be saved. The default path is the %systemdrive%\PerfLogs\. Click Finish to save the current settings and exit or click Next to enter a user account to run as.

6. Click the Change button to enter a user for this data collector set.
7. Select the option to Save and Close, Start This Data Collector Set Now, or Open Properties for This Data Collector Set, and then click Finish to complete the data collector set creation process.

Reports

The final folder in the Performance Monitor snap-in is Reports. The Reports folder provides diagnostic reports to support administrators in troubleshooting and diagnosing system performance problems including reliability. Reports are viewed in the central details pane of the Performance Monitor snap-in.

The reports are based on data collector sets that were previously defined by users or preconfigured and included with Windows Server 2012 Performance Monitor. The report console's features and functionality are very similar to those seen by means of the reports introduced with Server Performance Advisor in Windows Server 2003.

The Reports folder contains two subfolders: User Defined reports and System reports. The default System reports typically include reports relating to LAN diagnostics, system diagnostics, and system performance. Additional system reports are automatically generated depending on the server role installed on the Windows Server 2012 system. For example, an Active Directory Diagnostics system report is automatically included in the console when the AD DS server role is installed on the Windows Server 2012 system.

Creating a User-Defined Report

The first step in creating a user-defined report is creating a user-defined collector set and defining the parameters for a collection. After the user-defined collector set is created, data collection must be manually started or scheduled to run at a specific date. At this time, a report folder is automatically generated under the User Defined folder. After the report is created, you can review the contents by selecting it. When viewing reports, it is possible to expand specific items such as the report summary, diagnostic results, or CPU for additional information. This is shown in the System Performance Report in Figure 33.13.

Viewing Predefined System Reports

Another option for assessing system health and troubleshooting system anomalies is to leverage the predefined system reports. To view these system reports, follow these steps:

1. In the Performance Monitor navigation tree, expand the Data Collector Sets folder and then System.
2. Right-click one of the predefined data collector sets, such as System Diagnostics, and then click Start. This starts the data collection process.
3. Now expand the Reports folder, System, and then System Diagnostics.
4. Highlight the newly created report and review the contents of the report in the central details pane.

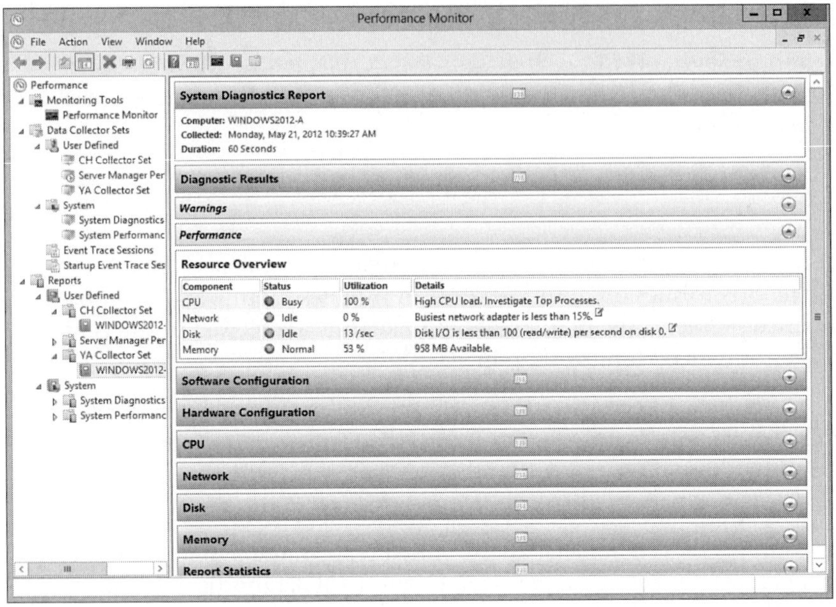

FIGURE 33.13 Viewing the System Performance Report.

NOTE

The report generates and appears when the data collection process is complete. The report is automatically tagged with the current date.

Resource Monitor

Resource Monitor's functionality remains unchanged from Windows Server 2008 R2, providing real-time data about the core components of your server: CPU, disk, network, and memory. This allows for monitoring health and performance, identifying utilization hogs, or making business decisions, including increasing or decreasing resources as needed, resuming or suspending activities, utilizing a server for additional roles, and setting up firewall rules based on network activities (see Figure 33.14).

- Resource Monitor can be invoked in any of the following ways:
- Clicking Open Resource Monitor within the Performance tab of Task Manager
- Clicking Resource Monitor from the Tools link within the new Server Manager
- Typing **ResMon** at the command prompt or in the Run window

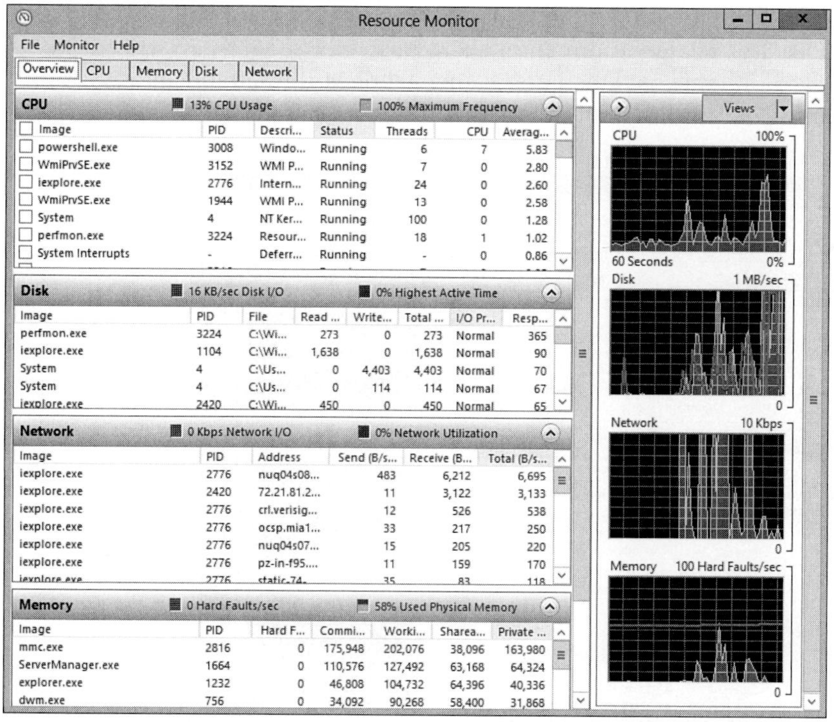

FIGURE 33.14 Windows 2012 Resource Monitor.

Overview Tab

The Overview tab hosts CPU, disk, network, and memory details and graphs. Of note is that not only is the current information shown, but maximum frequency (CPU) for the system overall and average CPU utilization for each process is listed. This allows for more a real-time, yet more relevant view of utilization.

TIP

To filter on a specific process or processes, simply choose the check mark in the Image column (under the CPU header). All Disk, network, and memory details will be limited to the selected processes. This option carries over to the other tabs.

Although not as complete as specific properties in Performance Manager, you can watch Resource Monitor before making changes to investigate the high-level, yet core impact experienced during or after the change.

Using the information in the Overview screen to identify a potential issue, you can then proceed to the related Tab for further analysis and troubleshooting.

CPU Tab

The CPU tab provides CPU-related information about processes, services, associated handles, and associated module sections. After taking a look at this tab in Figure 33.15, let's review the details behind each section and the information it provides.

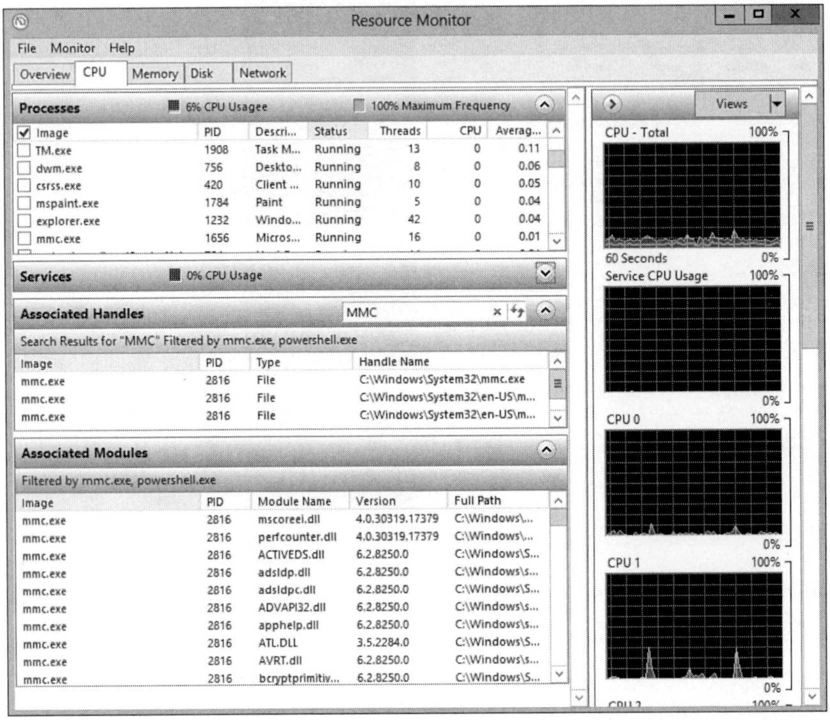

FIGURE 33.15 Resource Monitor: CPU tab.

Processes

This section lists any process actively running and consuming CPU resources.

> **TIP**
>
> In the Processes section, you can right-click and choose End Task.

- **Image**—*Filename*.exe of each process
- **PID**—Process ID of each associated process, which can be used to identify the process in Task Manager, other tools, or even the command line
- **Description**—The file description that can be found by checking the properties of the EXE

- **Status**—Shows whether a process is running or terminated
- **Threads**—Number of processor instances
- **CPU**—Current CPU utilization percent for a given process
- **Average CPU**—Average CPU utilization percent over 60 seconds for a given process

Services

This section lists any services actively running and consuming CPU resources.

TIP

In the Services section, you can right-click and choose Start/Stop/Restart Services.

- **Name**—Name of service
- **PID**—Process ID of each associated process, which can be used to identify the process in Task Manager, other tools, or even the command line
- **Description**—The service description
- **Status**—Shows whether a process is running or terminated
- **Group**—Group of Services running together
- **CPU**—Current CPU utilization percent for a given process
- **Average CPU**—Average CPU utilization percent over 60 seconds for a given process

Associated Handles

This section lists associated pointers to files, regkeys, directories, events, sections, and so on. When an application calls the appropriate API to create or open a resource, it is allocated a handle.

TIP

In the Search Handles box, type the name of the file/path to file and a list of processes with associated handles are listed.

Why is this information useful? With the type and handle name provided, you can check applications against handle leaks, paged pool, and so on. This information is also useful in determining when an item needs to be updated, but is seen as "in use."

Associated Modules

In this section, modules, including DLLs, sys files, and EXE files, are referenced and used by processes to perform a function:

- **Image**—Name of service
- **PID**—Process ID of each associated process, which can be used to identify the process in Task Manager, other tools, or even the command line
- **Module Name**—Name of the module used by a given process
- **Version**—The version number of the associated module
- **Full Path**—The full path to the module in use

Why is this information useful? With the version number, you can see the effects of a hotfix or other patch that intends to update a module. By sorting on Full Path, various processes can be identified as running the same module (DLL, for example).

Graphs

On the right, you see CPU-specific graphs:

- **CPU - Total**—Shows an overall utilization
- **Service CPU Usage**—Shows background processes' utilization
- **CPU 0 - CPU 7**—Shows utilization on a per core basis

Memory Tab

The Memory tab provides memory-related information about Processes and Physical Memory sections. After taking a look at this tab in Figure 33.16, let's review the details behind each section and the information it provides.

Processes

This section displays the following information about all running processes:

- **Image**—*Filename*.exe of each process
- **PID**—Process ID of each process, which can be used to identify the process in Task Manager, other tools, or even the command line
- **Hard Faults/sec**—Number of instances per second when information has be retrieve from disk based virtual memory rather than RAM
- **Commit (KB)**—Total amount of memory (physical and virtual) committed to a process
- **Working Set (KB)**—Total amount of physical memory (shareable and private) committed to a process
- **Shareable (KB)**—Total amount of physical memory committed to a process (shareable by another process)
- **Private (KB)**—Total amount of physical memory committed to a process (not shareable by another process)

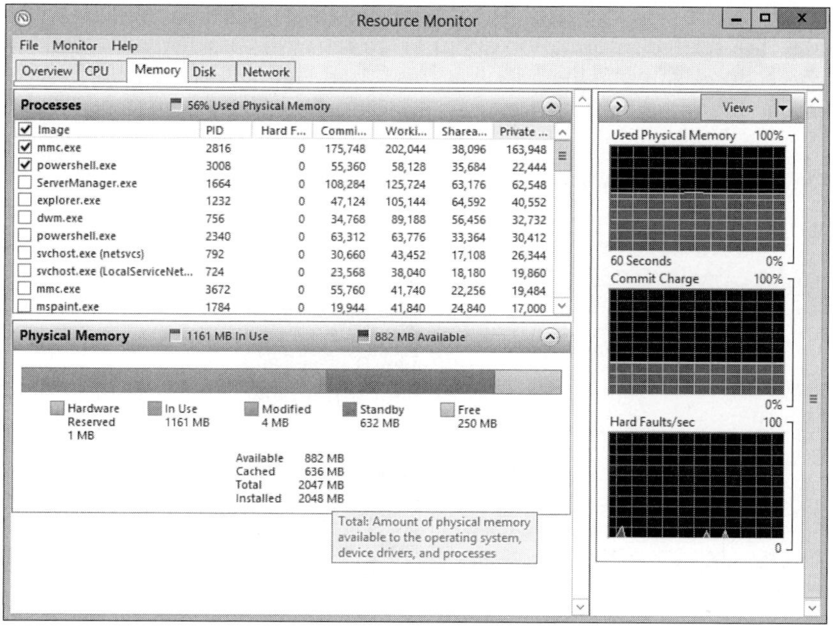

FIGURE 33.16 Resource Monitor: Memory Tab.

Physical Memory

A variety of system statistics about memory usage are displayed in this section:

- **Hardware Reserved**—Total memory reserved by various hardware devices on the server
- **In Use**—Total current physical memory used
- **Modified**—Modified pages that have not yet been released
- **Standby**—Cached data that is not actively in use, but readily available if called
- **Free**—Total physical memory that is available, but not in use, modified, or in standby
- **Available**—Total physical memory that is available, including in use, modified, or in standby
- **Cached**—Modified and standby combined

Why is this information useful? Persistent high numbers in the Hard Faults/sec column suggests a need for additional physical RAM. However, if the amount of cached memory is high, but the hard faults remain low, applications may very well be designed to cache a high percentage of free memory for better performance.

Disk Tab

The Disk tab provides disk-related information about Processes with Disk Activity, Disk Activity, and Storage sections. After taking a look at this tab in Figure 33.17, let's review the details behind each section and the information it provides.

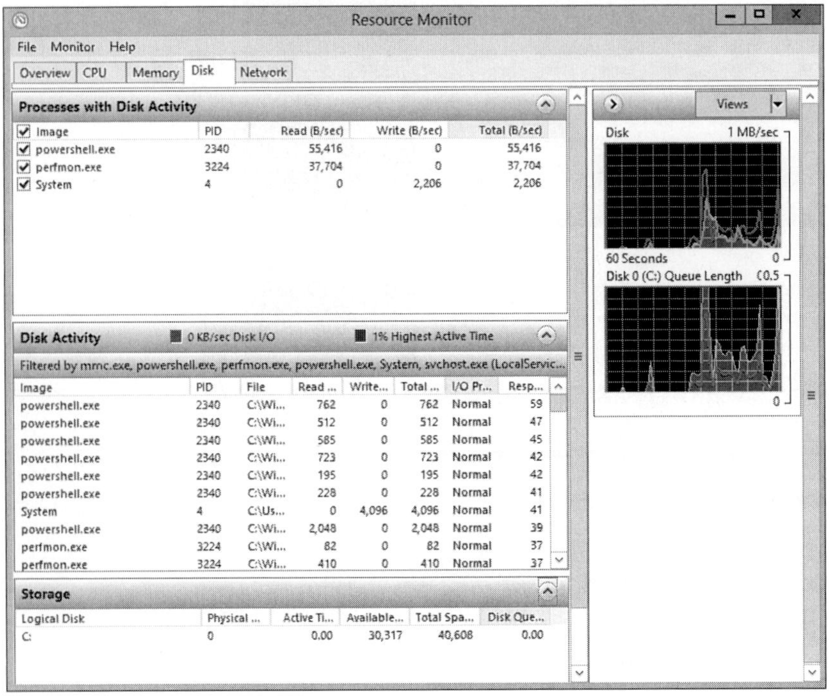

FIGURE 33.17 Resource Monitor: Disk tab.

Processes with Disk Activity

This section provides a list of processes that are currently running and showing disk resource usage:

- **Name**—Name of process
- **PID**—Process ID of each associated process, which can be used to identify the process in Task Manager, other tools, or even the command line
- **Read (B/sec)**—Average bytes/sec read by the process over the past 60 seconds
- **Write (B/sec)**—Average bytes/sec written by the process over the past 60 seconds
- **Total (B/sec)**—Read (B/sec) + Write (B/sec)

Why is this information useful? Look for applications/processes that generate a lot of disk activity and ensure that the activity is expected.

Disk Activity

This section provides a list of files, I/O priority, and response time per process:

- **Name**—Name of process
- **PID**—Process ID of each associated process, which can be used to identify the process in Task Manager, other tools, or even the command line
- **File**—Full path to file used by specified process
- **I/O Priority**—Priority of I/O for specified process
- **Response Time (ms)**—Disk response time in milliseconds

Why is this information useful? Look at the response times and ensure that the numbers are below 15ms for good responses; higher numbers mean degraded performance. I/O numbers may be indicate a need for disk changes or might indicate an effect of other issues such as CPU overutilization and request delays.

TIP

The following are expected response time examples (in milliseconds) based on disk type:

- 7200 RPM HD @ 13ms
- 10K RPM HD @ 8ms
- 15K RPM HD @ 7ms
- Solid state drive @ 0.2ms

Storage

This section displays the following information about each fixed disk:

- **Logical Disk**—The drive letter associated a given drive
- **Physical Disk**—The system number associated to a given drive
- **Active Time (%)**—Percentage of time that the disk is active
- **Available Space (MB)**—Available space for a given driven
- **Total Space (MB)**—Total size of given drive
- **Disk Queue Length**—Number of pending/waiting requests

Why is this information useful? High Active Time (over 75%) and/or High Disk Queue Length (one to two times the number of disks) may indicate a need for faster disk to support an I/O activity-hungry application.

Graphs

The right pane provides quick access to disk specific graphs, including the following:

- **Disk**—Transfer speeds between system and disk
- **Disk 0 (C:) Queue Length**—A series of graphs presenting queue length on a per disk basis

Network Tab

The Network tab provides network-related information about processes with Network Activity, Network Activity, TCP Connections and Listening Ports sections. After taking a look at this tab in Figure 33.18, let's review the details behind each section and the information it provides.

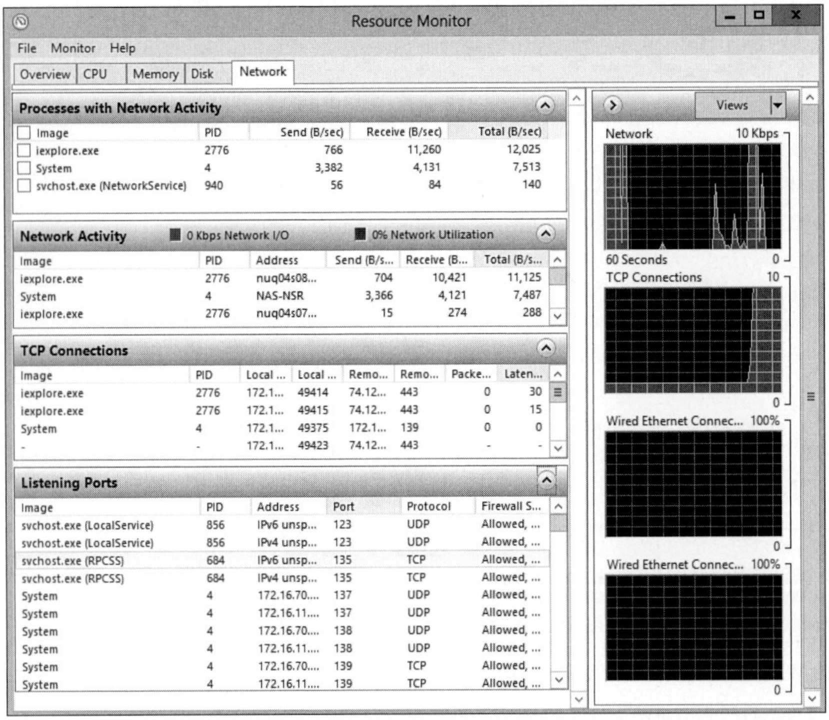

FIGURE 33.18 Resource Monitor: Network tab.

Processes with Network Activity and Network Activity

These sections provide useful information for running processes:

- **Image**—Name of process
- **PID**—Process ID of each associated process, which can be used to identify the process in Task Manager, other tools, or even the command line

- **Address (Network Activity section only)**—Name or IP address to which the process is connected
- **Send (B/sec)**—Average bytes/sec sent over the network by the process over the past 60 seconds
- **Receive (B/sec)**—Average bytes/sec received over the network by the process over the past 60 seconds
- **Total (B/sec)**—Send (B/sec) + Receive (B/sec)

TIP

Note the little graphs in the Network Activity section: Kbps Network I/O (Total I/O Activity on the Network) and % Network Utilization (Total Percentage Utilized). The graphs are extremely useful in that they provide the size of network activity and the percentage of network utilization. Even if high usage is anticipated, constant high utilization may indicate a bottleneck.

TCP Connections

This extremely useful section shows information about all open TCP connections and the process that opened the connection, information such as the following:

- **Image**—Name of process
- **PID**—Process ID of each associated process, which can be used to identify the process in Task Manager, other tools, or even the command line
- **Local Address**—Local address of the connection (one of the local NICs)
- **Local Port**—Local port of the connection (one of the local NICs)
- **Remote Address**—Remote address of the connection
- **Remote Port**—Remote port of the connection
- **Packet Loss (%)**—Percent of packets lost
- **Latency (ms)**—Round-trip latency measuring time it takes for a packet to travel

Why is this information useful? High packet loss or latency indicates performance issues that should be looked into, especially for live communication traffic such as VoIP.

Listening Ports

This section also has a very useful set of information, including the following:

- **Image**—Name of process
- **PID**—Process ID of each associated process, which can be used to identify the process in Task Manager, other tools, or even the command line

- **Address**—Listed here if an address is not specified for a given process
- **Protocol**—TCP (Transmission Control Protocol) or UDP (User Datagram Protocol)
- **Firewall Status**—Identifies whether traffic is *not* allowed or is restricted by Windows Firewall

Related PowerShell Functionality

As discussed, Resource Monitor provides lists and graphical representations of various counters. Here are some ways to go about similar tasks with PowerShell:

Get-Counter

The Get-Counter cmdlet returns performance counter data from a specified computer (local or remote).

Description

The cmdlet returns real-time performance counter data directly from the operating system's performance monitoring components. It can be used to get performance data from any computer as long as access and credentials are available. The command can specify the sample interval and can therefore be used to create a rudimentary monitoring tool for troubleshooting purposes.

Without parameters, the Get-Counter cmdlet returns counter data for a default set of system counters. The parameters can be used not only to direct the command to a specific computer but also to specify the required counters.

Examples

```
Get-Counter
```

What it does: Returns the values of a set of default counters on the local computer.

```
Get-Counter '\Memory\Available MBytes'
```

What it does: Returns the specified counter - current available memory in MB on the local computer.

```
Get-Counter "\\ABCDC1\Processor(_Total)\% Processor Time" -SampleInterval 10 -
MaxSamples 5
```

What it does: Returns the CPU utilization counter on the specified computer (local or remote) every 10 seconds until it has 5 returned values.

```
$diskreads = "\LogicalDisk(C:)\Disk Writes/sec"
$diskreads | get-counter -computer abcdc1, abcdc2 -maxsamples 10
```

What it does: Returns 10 samples of the Disk Writes/sec counter from the two listed servers.

Server Manager

Having looked at Task Manager, Event Viewer, Performance Monitor, command-line debugging tools, and various aspects of each, we have noted that it is 1) feasible to connect remotely with most tools, and 2) it is preferred to do so in the interest of reducing overhead. With this in mind, let's look at the new Dashboard-like Server Manager, which not only serves as a central repository to call many of our logging and debugging tools, but also allows us to do so remotely and collectively.

Server Manager has additional functions discussed in this book that can be used for the control and configuration of the enterprise, allowing manageability of grouped servers.

Server Manager can be installed on an administrator's desktop and utilized in the same manner as when used locally on a server:

- Add servers or custom groups
- Get status of servers, groups or roles
- Manage groups of servers simultaneously (adding/removing roles and features)

Server Manager opens up at logon (by default), can be called by typing **Server Manager** in the Metro start screen, or by entering **servermanager.exe** from the Run prompt or command prompt.

On opening, Server Manager loads to the Dashboard screen where you can see red item counts on manageability, events, service, performance, and BPA results for local servers or server group.

To best make use of the Dashboard, server groups should be composed of the servers you monitor, in groupings that make sense for your role.

To create a server group, click Manage in the top menu, and choose Create Server Group from the drop-down menu. The Create Server Group screen pops up. First, simply enter a name for the server group. Then, choose a server from the list already present under the Server Pool tab, by browsing Active Directory, by entering a name or IP address under the DNS tab, or by using a list of servers in a text file under the Import tab (or a combination of all four). In Figure 33.19, we're importing a text file of server names. Select any servers on the frame on the left that you want to add to the server group, and then click the arrow to bring them to the right frame. When you have a complete list of selected computers on the frame on the right, just click OK.

NOTE

The Import Wizard is intelligent enough to skip duplicate servers. Even though we listed NYCDM01 twice in our text file, only one was added to the selected computer list.

As shown on the frame on the left in Figure 33.19, we've created three examples: SQL Servers 2012 (based on role and functionality), Walnut Creek Servers (based on location and security), and YSA Servers (consisting of a couple of servers that serve as a back end to our YSA application).

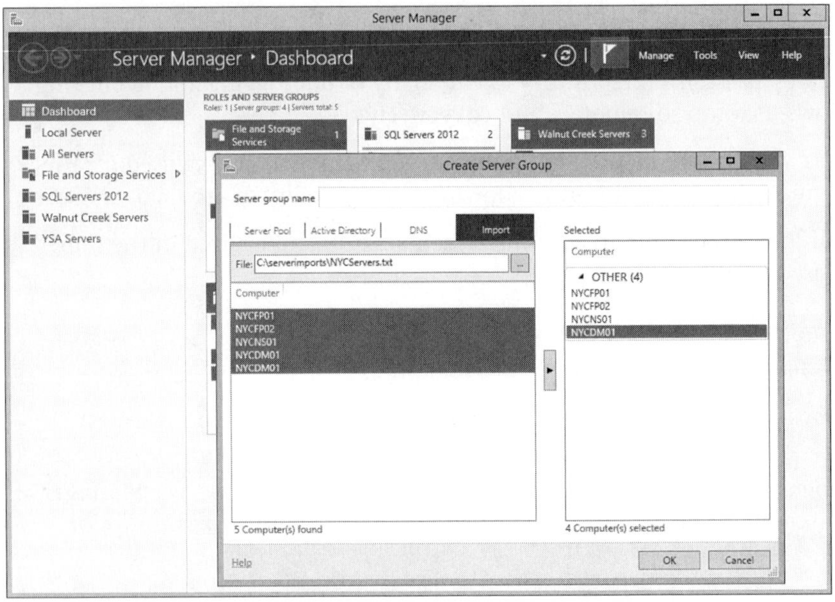

FIGURE 33.19 The new Server Manager in Windows Server 2012.

Clicking any of our server groups provides a centralized view, capturing Events, Services, Best Practices Analyzer results, Performance Alerts, and Roles & Features for the selected server in the group, as shown in Figure 33.20.

TIP

Right-clicking a server provides you several interactive options, including the ability to call Computer Manager, call PowerShell, or restart the server.

Clicking the Tasks drop-down menu above each section provides some configuration options. For example, the Performance Tasks menu shows Configure Performance Alerts, bringing the option to define performance alert thresholds.

The YSA Servers (consisting of a couple of servers that serve as a back end to our YSA application): The YSA application is CPU-use intensive, so while we leave the default alerting on both CPU and memory in place, we increased the alert level for CPU from the default 85% to 95%, as shown in Figure 33.21.

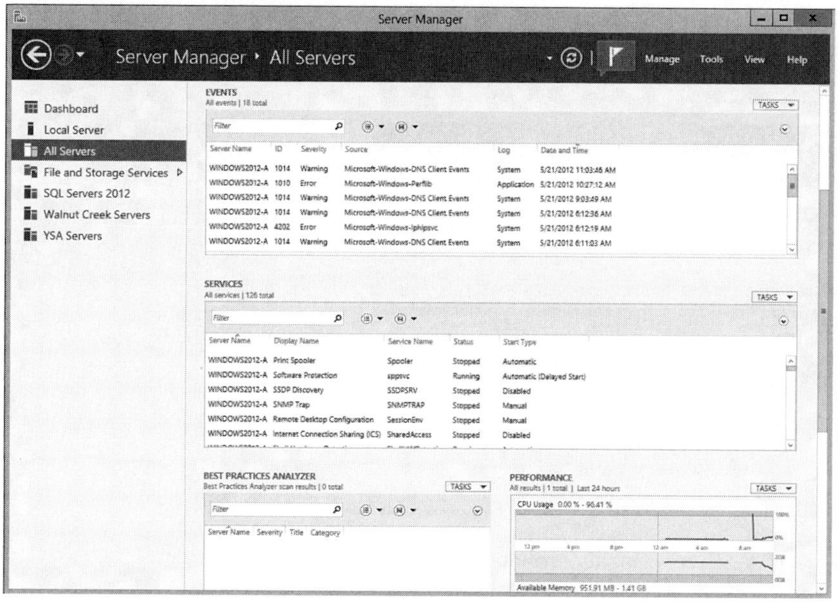

FIGURE 33.20 Server Manager, All Servers View.

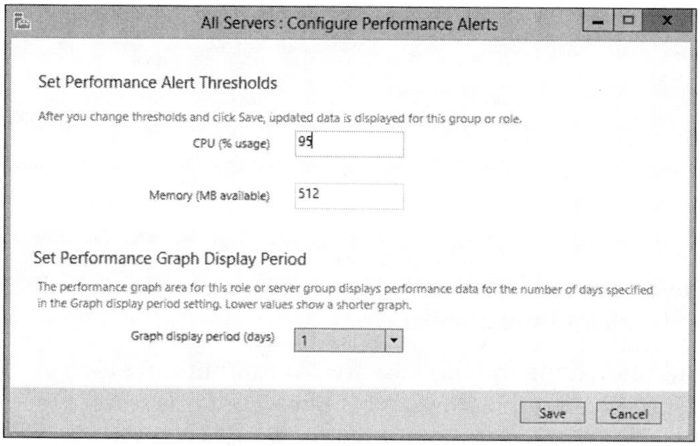

FIGURE 33.21 Configure performance alerts.

Dashboard View

Back in the top choice in the left frame (our Dashboard view, shown in Figure 33.22), we go on to view alerts and customize the alerts shown/counted for each server group.

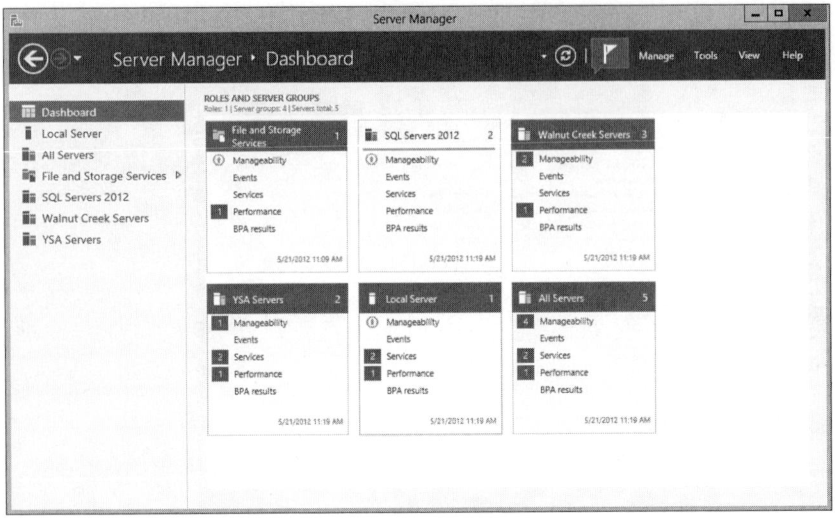

FIGURE 33.22 Server Manager > Dashboard View.

Some of the categories of alerts are as follows:

- Events alerts
- Manageability alerts
- Services alerts
- Performance alerts
- BPA results

Events Alerts

A noninteractive look at events on monitored services, this is a complement to Event Viewer and Subscriptions discussed earlier in this chapter.

SQL Servers 2012 (based on role and functionality): Because we have monitoring tools capturing additional details on these servers, our Dashboard is filtered for this server group to report on SQL-specific event IDs only within Events (for high-level support when a systems administrator is backing up our SQL administrator).

Clicking the word Events underneath the SQL Server 2012 Dashboard widget brings up the option to specify event IDs, as shown in Figure 33.23. Also, the current alerts, if any, are listed at the bottom of the screen.

Manageability Alerts

Manageability alerts cover the general inability to access and manage a remote server. Figure 33.24 shows the default filtered selections, which include missing components, unsupported operating systems, concerns with credentials, connectivity concerns, and unknown errors. These filters can be configured differently for each monitored server group.

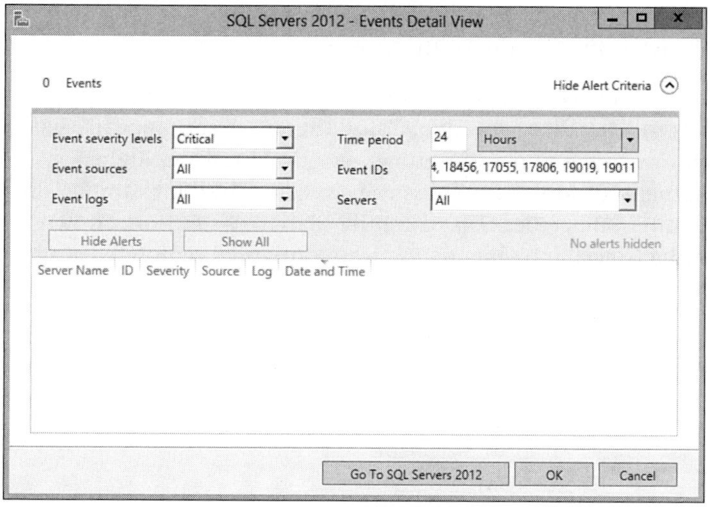

FIGURE 33.23 Filtering on Events Detail view.

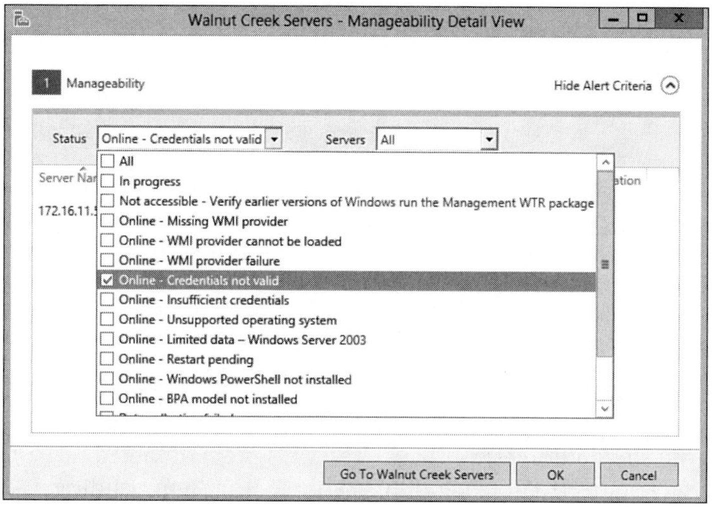

FIGURE 33.24 Filtering on Manageability Detail view.

Walnut Creek Servers (based on location and security): The dashboard is configured only to capture Credentials Not Valid status within Manageability. These servers are on a DMZ with intentional safeguards that prevent elevated permissions. The accounts used to manage the Walnut Creek Servers are used for specific connectivity through homegrown apps, which require user manual input. By monitoring the credentials, we can confirm that 1) the servers are online and 2) that the accounts are valid.

Clicking the word Manageability underneath the Walnut Creek Servers widget, we have the option to filter on specfic statuses, similar to what was shown in Figure 33.24. Also, the current alerts, if any, are listed at the bottom of the screen.

Looking at our SQL Servers 2012 Server Group, we see a red 2 next to Manageability Alerts. Clicking that 2 brings us to a detailed view explaining these alerts. It appears that we have invalid credentials on one server and an unknown error on another. Right-clicking an alert brings us to a menu of tools to address the concerns. In our example, one alert is addressed by providing alternate credentials using the Manage As option, shown in Figure 33.25; the other required a firewall change, which was configured remotely using the Windows PowerShell option.

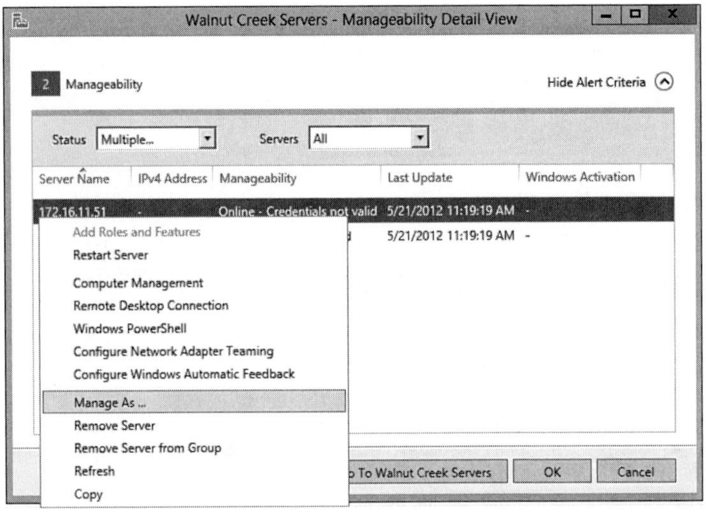

FIGURE 33.25 Manage As option.

Services Alerts

As its name implies, this section provides a look at the service status. This view can be filtered to show alerts for any combination of specific services, specific servers, specific startup types (automatic/delayed start, automatic, manual, restart, system, disabled, unknown), and/or specific service status (resume pending, start pending, stop pending, stopped, pause pending, or paused). By default, the Dashboard alerts on automatic/delayed start and automatic services only.

The Services Detail view also has the added functionality of directly interacting with a service, to start, stop, restart, pause or resume it, as desired, simply by right-clicking an alert and choosing to do so (see Figure 33.26).

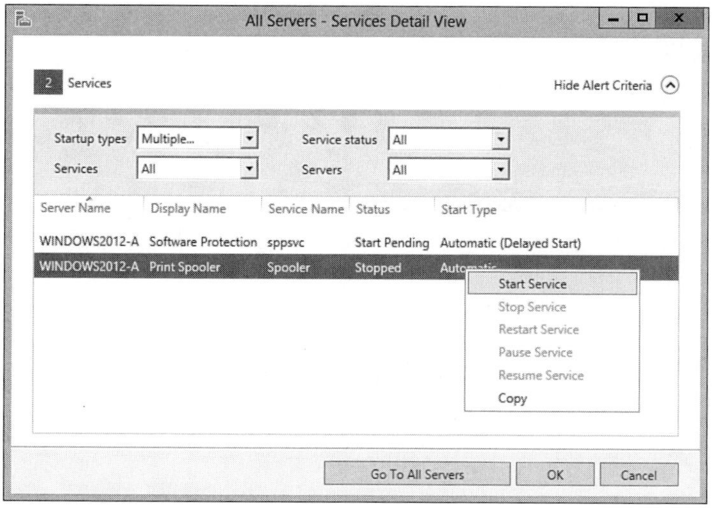

FIGURE 33.26 Filtering on Services Detail view.

Performance Alerts

This section raises alerts on the basis of CPU utilization (%) and Memory (MB available). As discussed earlier, default thresholds are 85% and 512MB. Filtering here allows you to monitor CPU, memory, or both (default). You also have the option to turn off performance alerts.

Clicking the word Performance underneath a given server group allows you to make these decisions. Also, the current alerts, if any, are listed at the bottom of the screen.

In Performance Detail view, you also have the option to right-click and choose View Details. This brings up the alert and a list of services at the bottom of the screen, each identified with PID and utilization, as shown in Figure 33.27.

BPA Results

These alerts display only if a Best Practices Analyzer (BPA) scan has been executed. The alerts are informational, warning, and error. Only errors are alerted on in the default filter.

NOTE

It is worth noting that a direct link exists within Server Manager to a number of tools. The Tools menu in the top menu includes shortcuts to Computer Manager, Event Viewer, Performance Monitor, Resource Monitor, Services, Task Scheduler, and PowerShell, as shown in Figure 33.28.

33

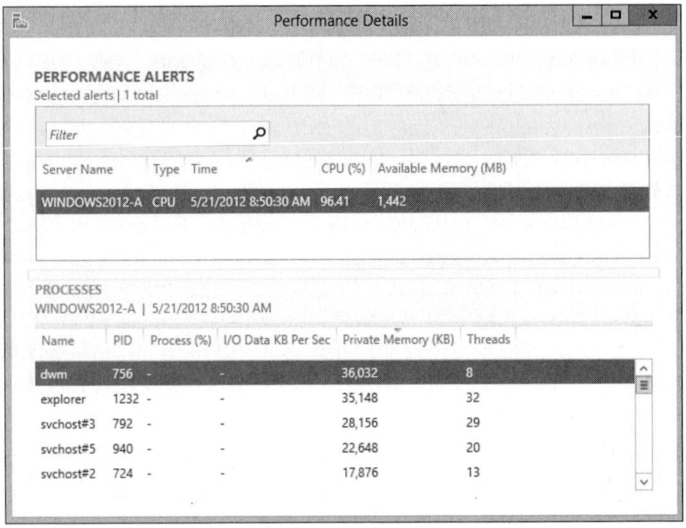

FIGURE 33.27 Performance Details view.

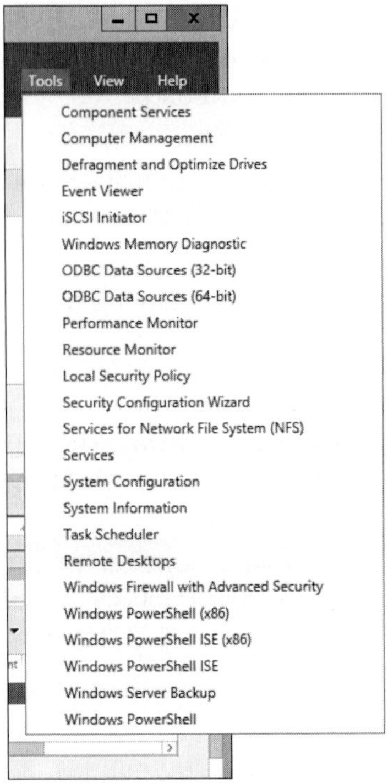

FIGURE 33.28 Server Manager links to other tools.

Setting Baseline Values

A baseline is a performance level that can be used as a starting point to compare against future network performance operations. When a server is first monitored, there is very little to compare the statistics against. After a baseline is created, information can be gathered at any time in the future and compared against the baseline. The difference between the current statistics and the baseline statistics is the variance caused by system load, application processing, or system performance contention.

To be able to set a baseline value, you need to gather a normal set of statistics on each system that will eventually be monitored or managed in the future. Baselines should be created for normal and stressed times. The workload on a machine at night when there are fewer users connected to it provides a poor baseline to compare real-time data in the middle of the day. Information sampled in the middle of the day should be compared with a baseline of information collected at around the same time of day during normal load prior to the sample comparison.

Creating baselines should be an ongoing process. If an application or a new service is added to a server, a new baseline should be created so that any future comparisons can be made with a baseline with the most current status of system performance.

Reducing Performance Monitoring Overhead

Performance monitoring uses system resources that can affect the performance of a system as well as affect the data being collected. To ensure that performance monitoring and analyzing do not affect the machines being monitored themselves, you need to decrease the impact of performance monitoring. Some steps can be taken to ensure that performance-monitoring overhead is kept to a minimum on the server being monitored to create as accurate of an analysis on a system as possible:

- Use a remote server to monitor the target server. Servers can actually be dedicated to monitoring several remote servers. Although this might also lead to an increase in network bandwidth, at least the monitoring and tracking of information do not drastically degrade CPU or disk I/O as if the monitoring tool were actually running on the server being monitored.
- Consider reducing the frequency of the data collection interval because more frequent collection can increase overhead on the server.
- Avoid using too many counters. Some counters are costly in terms of taxing a server for system resources and can increase system overhead. Monitoring several activities at one time also becomes difficult.
- Use logs instead of displaying graphs. The logs can then be imported into a database or report. Logs can be saved on hard disks not being monitored or analyzed.

Important Objects to Monitor

The numbers of system and application components, services, and threads to measure in Windows Server 2012 are so extensive that it is impossible to monitor thousands of processor, print queue, network, or storage usage statistics. Defining the roles a server plays in a network environment helps to narrow down what needs to be measured. Servers could be defined and categorized based on the function of the server, such as application server, file and print server, or services server such as DNS, domain controller, and so on.

Because servers perform different roles, and hence have different functions, it makes sense to monitor the essential performance objects. This helps prevent the server from being overwhelmed from the monitoring of unnecessary objects for measurement or analysis.

Overall, four major areas demand the most concern: memory, processor, disk subsystem, and network infrastructure. They all tie into any role the server plays.

The following list describes objects to monitor based on the roles played by the server:

- **Active Directory Domain Services**—Because the DC provides authentication, stores the Active Directory database, holds schema objects, and so on, it receives many requests. To be able to process all these requests, it uses up a lot of CPU resources, disks, memory, and network bandwidth. Consider monitoring memory, CPU, system, network segment, network interface, and protocol objects such as TCP, UDP, NBT, NetBIOS, and NetBEUI. Also worth monitoring are the Active Directory NTDS service and site server LDAP service objects. DNS and WINS also have applicable objects to be measured.
- **File and print server**—The print servers that process intensive graphics jobs can utilize extensive resources of system CPU cycles very quickly. The file server takes up a lot of storage space. Monitor the PrintQueue object to track print spooling data. Also monitor CPU, memory, network segment, and logical and physical disks for both file and print data collection.
- **Messaging collaboration server**—A messaging server such as an Exchange Server 2010 uses a lot of CPU, disk, and memory resources. Monitor memory collection, cache, processor, system, and logical and physical disks. Exchange objects are added to the list of objects after Exchange is installed, such as message queue length or name resolution response time.
- **Web server**—A web server is usually far less disk intensive and more dependent on processing performance or memory space to cache web pages and page requests. Consider monitoring the cache, network interface, processor, and memory usage.
- **Database server**—Database servers such as Microsoft SQL Server 2008 can use a lot of CPU and disk resources. Database servers can also use an extensive amount of memory to cache tables and data, so RAM usage and query response times should be monitored. Monitoring objects such as system, processor, logical disk, and physical disk is helpful for overall system performance operations.

Using the Debugging Tools Available in Windows Server 2012

Several useful tools are available in Windows Server 2012 for troubleshooting and diagnosing various problems, ranging from TCP/IP connection issues to verification and maintenance issues. These tools also make it much easier for IT professionals and administrators, allowing IT personnel to focus on business improvement tasks and functions, not on simply running specific tools in the networking environment.

Best Practices Analyzer Tools

Many years ago, Microsoft introduced Best Practices Analyzer (BPA) tools for server products such as SQL Server and Exchange. The tools enabled IT professionals to conduct a scan against a product to ensure it was configured based on industry best practices. For many years, IT professionals wanted a similar tool to scan their Windows infrastructure; however, one did not exist. Windows Server 2008 R2 introduced a BPA tool, which is included with all editions of Windows Server 2012 except for Server Core. When scanning server roles to find best-practice violations, the BPA tool measures a server role's compliance based on eight different rule categories. The rule categories are Security, Performance, Configuration, Policy, Operation, Predeployment, Postdeployment, and BPA Prerequisites. Compliance is measured based on three severity levels: Error, Warning, and Information. It is worth noting that only a select few server roles are supported with BPA.

NOTE

The Windows BPA tool should be run on a regular basis to alleviate incorrect configurations, poor performance, poor reliability, and security violations.

Follow these steps to launch the Best Practice Analyzer tool:

1. Open Server Manager from the taskbar.
2. From the left pane, select a server role view.
3. Scroll down to the Best Practice Analyzer section, and from the Tasks menu select Start BPA Scan.
4. From the Select Servers dialog, select the servers that should scanner for best practice configuration for the selected role.
5. When the scan is complete, review the results in the same Best Practices Analyzer section, as displayed in Figure 33.29. Each result is categorized as Information, Warning, or Error.

When using the GUI to run a BPA scan, it is possible to filter the scan results using a variety of criteria. The common filter tools of Server Manager are available for the BPA GUI and can be used to include or exclude specific categories and severities among other fields.

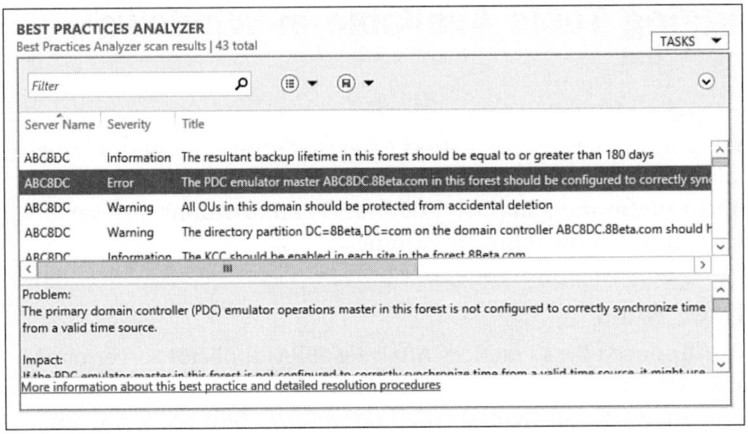

FIGURE 33.29 The Best Practices Analyzer Results screen.

TCP/IP Tools

TCP/IP forms the backbone of communication and transportation in Windows Server 2012. Before you can communicate between machines, TCP/IP must be configured.

In Windows Server 2012, TCP/IP is installed by default during the OS installation, which also makes it impossible to add or remove TCP/IP through the GUI.

If a TCP/IP connection fails, you need to determine the cause or point of failure. Windows Server 2012 includes some dependable and useful tools that can be used to troubleshoot connections and verify connectivity. The tools described in the following 10 subsections are very useful for debugging TCP/IP connectivity problems. Most of these tools have been updated to include switches for IPv4 and IPv6.

Ping

Ping means Packet Internet Groper. It is used to send an Internet Control Message Protocol (ICMP) echo request and echo reply to verify the availability of a local or remote machine. You can think of ping as a utility that sends a message to another machine asking, "Are you still there?" By default, in Windows Server 2012, ping sends out four ICMP packages and waits 1 second for responses back. However, the number of packages sent or time to wait for responses can be changed through the options available for ping.

Besides verifying the availability of a remote machine, ping can help determine a name-resolution problem.

To use ping, go to a command prompt and type **Ping *Targetname***. Different parameters can be used with ping. To display them, type **Ping /?** or **Ping** (without parameters).

The parameters for the **ping** command are as follows:

- **-4**—Specifies that IPv4 is used to ping. This parameter is not required to identify the target host with an IPv4 address. It is required only to identify the target host by name.

- **-6**—Specifies that IPv6 is used to ping. Just like **-4**, this parameter is not required to identify the target host with an IPv6 address. It is required only to identify the target host by name.
- **-a**—Resolves the IP address to the hostname. The hostname of the target machine is displayed if this command is successful.
- **-f**—Requests that echo back messages are sent with the Don't Fragment flag in packets. This parameter is available only in IPv4.
- **-i ttl**—Increases the timeout on slow connections. The parameter also sets the value of the Time to Live (TTL). The maximum value is 255.
- **-j HostList**—Routes packets using the host list, which is a series of IP addresses separated by spaces. The host can be separated by intermediate gateways (loose source route).
- **-k HostList**—Similar to **–j**, but hosts cannot be separated by intermediate gateways (strict source route).
- **-l size**—Specifies the length of packets in bytes. The default is 32. The maximum size is 65,527.
- **-n count**—Specifies the number of packets sent. The default is 4.
- **-r count**—Specifies the route of outgoing and incoming packets. It is possible to specify a count that is equal to or greater than the number of hops between the source and destination. The count can be between 1 and 9 only.
- **-R**—Specifies that the round-trip path is traced (available on IPv6 only).
- **-s count**—Sets the time stamp for the number of hops specified by count. The count must be between 1 and 4.
- **-S SrcAddr**—Specifies the source address to use (available on IPv6 only).
- **-t**—Specifies that ping should continue sending packets to the destination until interrupted. To stop and display statistics, press Ctrl+Break. To stop and quit ping, press Ctrl+C.
- **-v TOS**—Specifies the value of the type of service in the packet sent. The default is zero. TOS is specified as a decimal value between 0 and 255.
- **-w timeout**—Specifies the time in milliseconds for packet timeout. If a reply is not received within the timeout, the Request Timed Out error message is displayed. The default timeout is 4 seconds.
- **TargetName**—Specifies the hostname or IP address of the destination to ping.

NOTE

Some remote hosts can be configured to ignore ping traffic as a method of preventing acknowledgment as a security measure. Therefore, your inability to ping a server might not necessarily mean that the server is not operational, just that the server is not responding for some reason.

Tracert

Tracert is generally used to determine the route or path taken to a destination by sending ICMP packets with varying TTL values. Each router the packet meets on the way decreases the value of the TTL by at least one; invariably, the TTL is a hop count. The path is determined by checking the ICMP Time Exceeded messages returned by intermediate routers. Some routers do not return Time Exceeded messages for expired TTL values and are not captured by tracert. In such cases, asterisks are displayed for that hop.

To display the different parameters that can be used with tracert, open a command prompt and type **tracert** (without parameters) to display help or type **tracert** /?. The parameters associated with tracert are as follows:

- **-4**—Specifies that tracert.exe can use only IPv4 for the trace.
- **-6**—Specifies that tracert.exe can use only IPv6 for the trace.
- **-d**—Prevents resolution of IP addresses of routers to their hostname. This is particularly useful for speeding up results of tracert.
- **-h maximumHops**—Specifies the maximum number of hops to take before reaching the destination. The default is 30 hops.
- **-j HostList**—Specifies that packets use the loose source route option. Loose source routing allows successive intermediate destinations to be separated by one or multiple routers. The maximum number of addresses in the host list is nine. This parameter is useful only when tracing IPv4 addresses.
- **-R**—Sends packets to a destination in IPv6, using the destination as an intermediate destination and testing reverse route.
- **-S**—Specifies the source address to use. This parameter is useful only when tracing IPv6 addresses.
- **-w timeout**—Specifies the time in milliseconds to wait for each reply.

NOTE

Tracert is a good utility to determine the number of hops and the latency of communications between two points. Even if an organization has an extremely high-speed connection to the Internet, if the Internet is congested or if the route a packet must follow requires forwarding the information between several routers along the way, the performance and, ultimately, the latency (or delay in response between servers) will cause noticeable communications delays.

Pathping

Pathping is a route-tracing tool that combines both features of **ping** and **tracert** commands with some more information that neither of those two commands provides. Pathping is most ideal for a network with routers or multiple routes between the source and destination hosts. The **Pathping** command sends packets to each router on its way to a destination, and then gets results from each packet returned from the router. Because Pathping computes the loss of packets from each hop, you can easily determine which router is causing a problem in the network.

To display the parameters in Pathping, open a command prompt and type **Pathping /?**. The parameters for the **Pathping** command are as follows:

- **-4**—Specifies that tracert.exe can use only IPv4 for the trace.
- **-6**—Specifies that tracert.exe can use only IPv6 for the trace.
- **-g Host-list**—Allows hosts to be separated by intermediate gateways.
- **-h maximumHops**—Specifies the maximum number of hops before reaching the target. The default is 30 hops.
- **-i address**—Uses the specified source address.
- **-n**—Specifies that it is not necessary to resolve the address to the hostname.
- **-p period**—Specifies the number of seconds to wait between pings. The default is a quarter of a second.
- **-q num_queries**—Specifies the number of queries to each host along the route. The default is three.
- **-w timeout**—Specifies the timeout for each reply in milliseconds.

Ipconfig

Ipconfig displays all TCP/IP configuration values. It is of particular use on machines running DHCP. It is used to refresh DHCP settings and to determine which TCP/IP configuration values have been assigned by DHCP. If Ipconfig is used without parameters, it displays IP addresses, subnet masks, and gateways for each of the adapters on a machine. The adapters can be physical network adapters or logical adapters such as dial-up connections.

Some of the parameters for Ipconfig are as follows:

- **/all**—Displays all TCP/IP configuration values.
- **/displaydns**—Displays the contents of the DNS client resolver cache.
- **/flushdns**—Resets and flushes the contents of the DNS client resolver cache. This includes entries made dynamically.
- **/registerdns**—Sets manual dynamic registration for DNS names and IP addresses configured on a computer. This is particularly useful in troubleshooting DNS name registration or dynamic update problems between a DNS server and client.

- **/release[Adapter]**—Sends a DHCP release message to the DHCP server to discard DHCP-configured settings for adapters. This parameter is available only for DHCP-enabled clients. If no adapter is specified, IP address configuration is released for all adapters.
- **/renew[Adapter]**—Renews DHCP configuration for all adapters (if an adapter is not specified) and for a specific adapter if the Adapter parameter is included. This parameter is available only for DHCP-enabled clients.
- **/setclassid Adapter [classID]**—Configures the DHCP class ID for a specific adapter. You can configure the DHCP class ID for all adapters by using the wildcard (*) character in place of Adapter.
- **/showclassid Adapter**—Displays the DHCP class ID for a specific adapter.
- **/allcompartments**—Displays information about all compartments.
- **/allocmpartments /all**—Displays detailed information about all compartments.

NOTE

Ipconfig displays the assigned configuration for a system such as the default gateway, DNS servers, local IP address, subnet mask, and so on. When you're debugging network problems, you can use Ipconfig to validate that the proper TCP/IP settings have been set up for a system so that a server properly communicates on the network.

ARP

ARP stands for Address Resolution Protocol. ARP enables the display and modification of the ARP table on a local machine, which matches physical MAC addresses of machines to their corresponding IP addresses. ARP increases the speed of connection by eliminating the need to match MAC addresses with IP addresses for subsequent connections.

Some of the parameters for the **Arp** command are as follows:

- **-a[InetAddr] [-N IfaceAddr]**—Displays the ARP table for all adapters on a machine. Use **Arp –a** with the **InetAddr** (IP address) parameter to display the ARP cache entry for a specific IP address.
- **-dInetAddr [IfaceAddr]**—Deletes an entry with a specific IP address (**InetAddr**). Use the **IfaceAddr** parameter (IP address assigned to the interface) to delete an entry in a table for a specific interface. Use the wildcard character in place of **InetAddr** to delete all entries.
- **-g[InetAddr] [-N IfaceAddr]**—Similar to the **–a** parameter.
- **-sInetAddr EtherAddr [IfaceAddr]**—Adds a static entry to the ARP cache that resolves the IP address (**InetAddr**) to a physical address (**EtherAddr**). To add a static ARP cache entry to the table for a specific interface, use the IP address assigned to the interface (**IfaceAddr**).

Netstat

As its name implies, Netstat (or Network Statistics) is used to display protocol statistics for any active connections, monitor connections to a remote host, and monitor IP addresses or domain names of hosts with established connections.

The parameters for Netstat are as follows:

- **-a**—Displays all connections and listening ports by hostname.
- **-b**—Displays the executable involved in creating each connection.
- **-e**—Displays Ethernet packets and bytes to and from the host.
- **-n**—Displays address and port numbers without resolving the address to the hostname.
- **-o**—Displays TCP connections and includes the corresponding process ID (PID). Used in combination with **-a**, **-n**, and **-p**. Not available in previous Windows versions.
- **-p protocol**—Displays statistics based on the protocol specified. Protocols that can be specified are TCP, UDP, TCPv6, or UDPv6. It can be used with **-s** to display TCP, UDP, ICMP, IP, TCPv6, UDPv6, ICMPv6, or IPv6.
- **-s**—Displays statistics on a protocol-by-protocol basis. Can be used with the **-p** parameter to specify a set of protocols.
- **-t**—Displays the current connection offload state.
- **-r**—Displays the route table. Information displayed includes network destination, netmask, gateway, interface, and metric (number of hops).
- **[Parameter] Interval**—Displays the information at every interval specified. Interval is a numeral in seconds. Press Ctrl+C to stop the intervals.

Route

Route is particularly useful for troubleshooting incorrect static routes or for adding a route to a route table to temporarily bypass a problem gateway. Static routes can be used in place of implicit routes specified by a default gateway. Use Route to add static routes to forward packets going to a gateway specified by default to avoid loops, improve traffic time, and so on.

The parameters for Route are as follows:

- **-add**—Adds a route to a table. Use **–p** to make the route persistent for subsequent sessions.
- **-Delete**—Deletes a route from the table.
- **-Print**—Prints a route.
- **-change**—Modifies an existing route.
- **-destination**—Specifies the host address.

- **-gateway**—Specifies the address of gateway for Route.
- **IF interface**—Specifies the interface for the routing table to modify.
- **-mask Netmask**—Uses the subnet mask specified by **Netmask**. If **-mask** is not used, it defaults to 255.255.255.255.
- **-METRIC Metric**—Specifies the metric, or cost, for the route using the value **Metric**.
- **-f**—Clears the routing table of all gateway entries.
- **-p**—Used with **-add** to create a persistent route.

Nslookup

Nslookup is used to query DNS. You can think of Nslookup as a simple diagnostic client for DNS servers. It can operate in two modes: Interactive and Noninteractive. Use Noninteractive mode to look up a single piece of data. To look up more than one piece of data, use Interactive mode. To stop Interactive mode at any time, press Ctrl+B. To exit from the command, type **exit**. If Nslookup is used without any parameters, it uses the default DNS name server for lookup.

The parameters for Nslookup are as follows:

- **-ComputerToFind**—Looks up information for the specified **ComputerToFind**. By default, it uses the current default DNS name server.
- **-Server**—Specifies the server as the DNS name server.
- **-SubCommand**—Specifies one or more Nslookup subcommands as a command-line option. Type a question mark (?) to display a list of subcommands available.

DCDiag

The Domain Controller Diagnostic (DCDiag) tool analyzes the state of domain controllers and services in an Active Directory forest. It is installed when the Active Directory Domain Services (AD DS) role is added to a Windows Server 2012 installation. This is a great general-purpose test tool for checking the health of an Active Directory infrastructure.

Tests include domain controller connectivity, replication errors, permissions, proper roles, and connectivity, and other general Active Directory health checks. It can even run non-domain controller-specific tests, such as whether a server can be promoted to a domain controller (the dcpromo test), or register its records properly in DNS (RegisterInDNS test).

DCDiag is run on domain controllers exclusively, with the exception of the dcpromo and RegisterInDNS tests.

When run without any parameters, the tests will be run against the current domain controller. This runs all the key tests and is usually sufficient for most purposes.

The parameters for DCDiag are as follows:

- **/s:DomainController**—Uses the domain controller as the home server
- **/n:NamingContext**—Uses the specified naming context (NetBIOS, FQDN, or distinguished name) to test
- **/u:Domain\UserName /p:{*|Password|""}**—Uses the supplied credentials to run the tool
- **/a**—Tests all domain controllers in the site
- **/e**—Tests all domain controllers in the enterprise
- **/q**—Displays quiet output (errors only)
- **/v**—Displays verbose output
- **/I**—Ignores minor error messages
- **/fix**—Fixes minor problems
- **/f:LogFile**—Logs to the specified log file
- **/ferr:ErrorLogFile**—Logs errors to the specified log file
- **/c**—Comprehensively runs all tests
- **/test:TestName**—Runs the specified tests only
- **/skip:TestName**—Skips the specified tests

When specifying tests to run or to skip, nonskippable tests will still be run.

NOTE

DCDiag is automatically included on a Windows Server 2012 system when the Active Directory Domain Services role is added. Otherwise, on non-domain controllers, the utility can be added by adding the Remote Server Administration Tools feature in Server Manager.

Other Useful Troubleshooting Command-Line Tools

Driverquery

Displays a list of all installed device drivers and their properties.

Commonly used parameters of Driverquery are as follows:

- **/Computer**—Specifies the name (or IP address) of the target computer (without backslashes). The default is the local computer.
- **/UDomain \ User**—Runs the command with the account permissions of the user entered. The default is the currently logged-on user.

- **/P Password**—Specifies the password of the user account that is specified in the **/u** parameter.
- **/FO { TABLE | LIST | CSV }**—Specifies output format.
- **/NH**—Doesn't include column headers in the output.
- **/V**—Displays verbose driver information.
- **/SI**—Displays digital signature information for device drivers.

Eventcreate

Enables an administrator to create a custom event in a specified event log.

Commonly used parameters of Eventcreate are as follows:

- **/S Computer**—Specifies the name (or IP address) of the target computer (without backslashes). The default is the local computer.
- **/U Domain \ User**—Runs the command with the account permissions of the user entered. The default is the currently logged-on user.
- **/P Password**—Specifies the password of the user account that is specified in the **/u** parameter.
- **/L { APPLICATION | SYSTEM }**—Specifies the event log where the event will be created. Valid values are **APPLICATION** and **SYSTEM**.
- **/SO Source**—Specifies the event source.
- **/T { ERROR | WARNING | INFORMATION | SUCCESSAUDIT | FAILUREAUDIT }**—Specifies the type of event. Valid values are **ERROR**, **WARNING**, **INFORMATION**, **SUCCESSAUDIT**, and **FAILUREAUDIT**.
- **/ID EventID**—Specifies the event ID for the event.
- **/D Description**—Specifies the description for the event.

Fc

Compares two files and displays the differences between them.

Commonly used parameters of Fc are as follows:

- **/A**—Abbreviated output for a text file comparison. Only ranges of lines that are different are displayed.
- **/B**—Binary mode. The two files are compared byte by byte. This is the default mode for comparing files that have the following file extensions .exe, .com, .sys, .obj, .lib, or .bin.
- **/C**—Non-case-sensitive (ignores the case of letters).

- **/L**—ASCII (text) mode. Fc compares the files line by line and attempts to resynchronize the files after finding a mismatch. This is the default mode for all files except files with the following file extensions .exe, .com, .sys, .obj, .lib, or .bin.
- **/LBn**—Sets the limit of number of consecutive different lines. If the files have more than **n** consecutive differing lines, Fc cancels the comparison.
- **/N**—Displays the line numbers during an ASCII comparison.
- **/U**—Unicode mode.
- **[drive1 :][path1] filename1**—Specifies the first file you want to compare. This parameter is required.
- **[drive2 :][path2] filename2**—Specifies the second file you want to compare. This parameter is required.

Getmac

Returns the Media Access Control (MAC) address and list of network protocols associated with each address for all network cards in each computer, either locally or across a network. This command is especially useful to capture the MAC address of a remote computer.

Commonly used parameters of Getmac are as follows:

- **/S System**—Specifies the name (or IP address) of the target computer (without backslashes). The default is the local computer.
- **/U Domain\User**—Runs the command with the account permissions of the user entered. The default is the currently logged-on user.
- **/P Password**—Specifies the password of the user account that is specified in the **/u** parameter.
- **/FO { TABLE | LIST | CSV }**—Specifies output format.
- **/NH**—Doesn't include column headers in the output.
- **/V**—Displays verbose information.

Taskkill

Ends one or more tasks or processes. Processes can be killed by process ID or image name.

Commonly used parameters of Taskkill are as follows:

- **/S System**—Specifies the name (or IP address) of the target computer (without backslashes). The default is the local computer.
- **/U Domain\User**—Runs the command with the account permissions of the user entered. The default is the currently logged-on user.

- **/P Password**—Specifies the password of the user account that is specified in the **/u** parameter.
- **/FI FilterName**—Creates a filter for the query based on a variety of fields. All processes that meet the filter are terminated
- **/PID ProcessID**—Specifies the process ID of the process to be terminated.
- **/IM ImageName**—Specifies the image name of the process to be terminated. Use the wildcard (*) to specify all image names.
- **/F**—Forces the processes to be terminated. When specifying a remote computer, processes are always forcefully terminated.
- **/T**—Specifies to terminate all child processes along with the parent process (known as a tree kill).

Tasklist

Displays a list of applications and services with their PID for all tasks running on either a local or a remote computer.

Commonly used parameters of Tasklist are as follows:

- **/S System**—Specifies the name (or IP address) of the target computer (without backslashes). The default is the local computer.
- **/U Domain\User**—Runs the command with the account permissions of the user entered. The default is the currently logged-on user.
- **/P Password**—Specifies the password of the user account that is specified in the **/u** parameter.
- **/FO { TABLE | LIST | CSV }**—Specifies output format.
- **/NH**—Doesn't include column headers in the output.
- **/FI FilterName**—Creates a filter for the query based on a variety of fields.
- **/V**—Displays verbose task information in the output.

System Startup and Recovery

The System Startup and Recovery utility stores system startup, system failure, and debugging information. It also controls the behavior (what to do) when a system failure occurs.

To open System Startup and Recovery, launch Control Panel, select System and Security, select System, Advanced System Settings, click the Advanced tab in the Systems Settings dialog box, and then click Settings under Startup and Recovery to display a property page similar to the one shown in Figure 33.30.

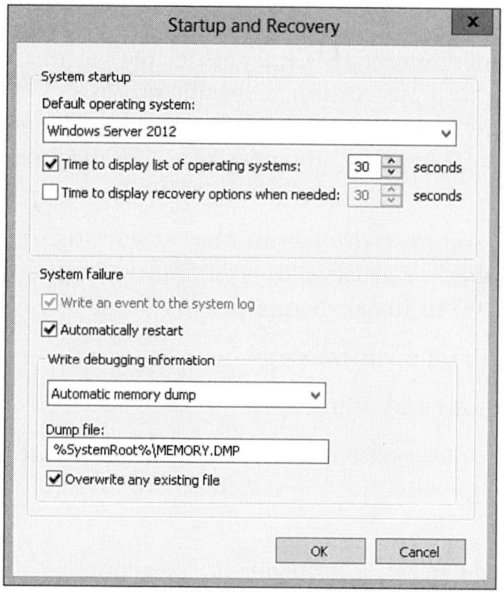

FIGURE 33.30 The Startup and Recovery page.

The Default Operating System field contains information that is displayed at startup. This information is typically the name of the operating system such as Windows Server 2012. You can edit this information using bcdedit from a command prompt. If the machine is dual-booted, there will be an entry for each operating system. The Time to Display List of Operating Systems option specifies the time the system takes to display the name of the operating system at startup. The default time is 30 seconds. This can be increased or reduced. The Time to Display Recovery Options When Needed is unchecked by default but can be selected and an interval in seconds entered.

You can set the action to be taken when system failure occurs in the System Failure section. There are two options. The first option is Write an Event to the System Log. This action is not editable in Windows Server 2012 because this action occurs by default every time a stop error occurs. The next option, Automatically Restart, reboots the system in the event of a system failure.

The Write Debugging Information section tells the system where to write debugging information when a system failure occurs. The options available include where the debugging information can be written to and the level of debugging information: Small Memory Dump (128KB), Kernel Memory Dump, Complete Memory Dump, or (None). The Write Debugging Information To option requires a paging file on the boot volume, which should be large enough to contain the select debugging option.

Windows Memory Diagnostics Tool

Many troubleshooting scenarios revolve around memory-related issues associated with a system. Typical memory issues can involve an errant application, a specific process consuming too much memory, or failing hardware such as bad RAM or the memory system on the motherboard. Thankfully, Windows Server 2012 includes a tool for diagnosing problems associated with system memory.

By using Windows Memory Diagnostics Tool, an administrator has another way to isolate root issues when a server is performing poorly, subject to crashes, or is exhibiting other abnormal behavior not caused by issues with the OS or installed applications.

To launch the Windows Memory Diagnostics Tool, follow these steps:

1. Save all work and close down open applications and utilities.
2. To invoke the tool, select Start by hovering your mouse at the bottom-left corner of the screen and type **Windows Memory Diagnostic** into the search box to display and then launch the program.
3. Select whether you want to Restart Now and Check for Problems or Check for Problems the Next Time I Start My Computer, as displayed in Figure 33.31.
4. When the system is rebooted, the Diagnostics tool automatically launches and conducts a Basic test by using default settings. Additional Test Mix options, Cache options, and Pass Count can be selected by pressing F1. The Test Mix options consist of Basic, Standard, and Extended. The Cache option includes Default, On, or Off. In addition, set the pass count value. The value represents the number of times the entire test mix will be repeated. Note a value of 0 represents infinitely. Press F10 to apply the settings and start the memory tests. Status is reported throughout the test indicating results.

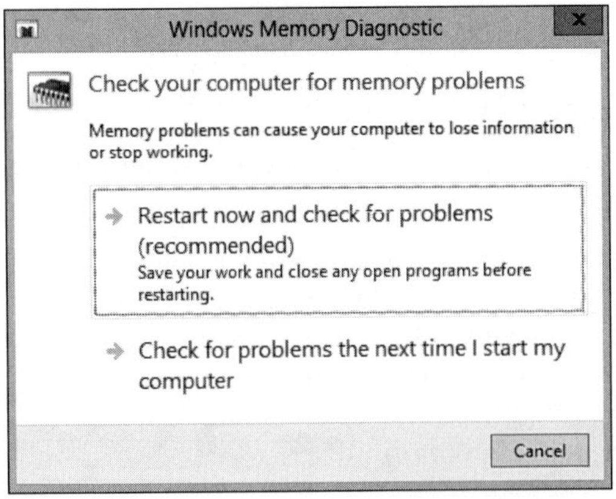

FIGURE 33.31 The options associated with running the Windows Memory Diagnostics Tool.

TIP

The Windows Memory Diagnostics Tool might not detect all the problems with the system RAM. Just because no errors are reported doesn't mean the RAM or even the motherboard is working properly. Typically, the manufacturer of the hardware device will have additional diagnostics utilities that enable an administrator to conduct a deeper analysis of the root problems at the hardware level.

Task Scheduler

The Task Scheduler in Windows Server 2008 R2 replaced the Scheduled Tasks tool that was literally unchanged since the release of Windows 98. The tool remains unchanged in Windows Server 2012. The main focal point of the tool is to assist administrators by automating tasks. In addition, by consolidating standard and recurring tasks into a central location, administrators gain insight into system functionality and control over their Windows Server 2012 infrastructure through automation. These things together assist administrators in the areas of logging and debugging.

One of the most compelling features of the Task Scheduler is that it fully integrates with Event Viewer. As such, a task can be triggered based on an event captured in the event log. This is a great feature because administrators can be automatically notified when a specific event transpires.

Understanding Task Scheduler

Scheduling tasks involves triggers and actions. A task runs once it is triggered. Tasks are initiated by triggers that are based on an event or time. Multiple triggers can be associated with a task as defined by an administrator. An action represents the work being performed as the task is being executed. Examples of actions include starting a program or sending an email. When a task is running multiple actions, up to 32 can be performed.

An additional functionality is task conditions. When a task is triggered, it will only run if specific defined conditions are met. Task conditions eliminate ambiguous situations by providing criteria-based functions. With these improvements to Task Scheduler functionality, it has become a very powerful and extensive development and activation tool for automating and assisting with troubleshooting tasks.

Windows Server 2012 Task Scheduler is accessed using the Tools menu in Server Manager. Figure 33.32 shows the user interface.

Tasks are created by selecting Create Basic Task, Create Task, or Import Task from the Actions pane in the Task Scheduler snap-in. When creating a task, you need to configure five tabs of options: Settings, Triggers, Actions, Conditions, and Additional Settings. The following subsections explain the options when creating tasks.

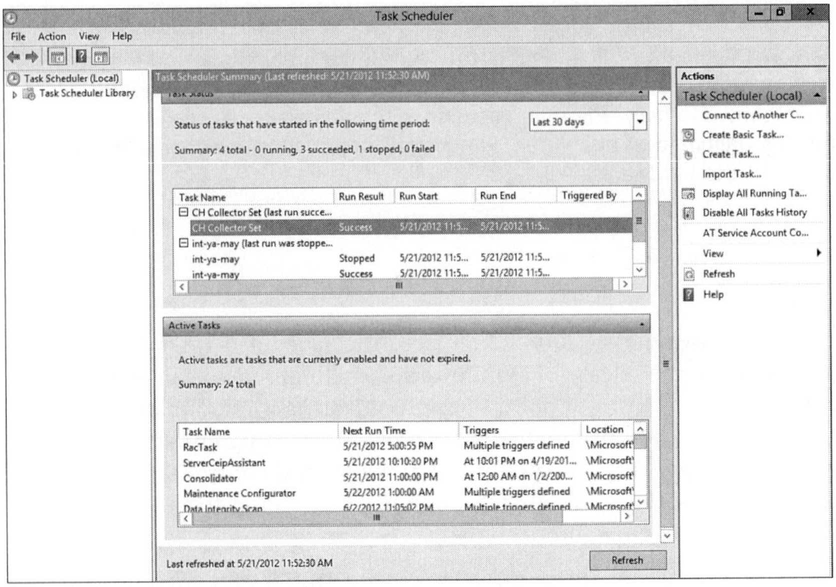

FIGURE 33.32 The Task Scheduler user interface.

Understanding Trigger Options and Settings

The first thing to consider when configuring a task is what triggers will cause the task to execute. Triggers can be based on time, events, or various system states. As noted earlier, each task can contain multiple triggers. With more than one trigger, the task will launch when any of the conditions in any of the triggers is met.

The following list describes the various trigger types and the settings that you can configure for each type:

- **On a Schedule**—Triggers for a schedule allow tasks to run on a specific date (one time), daily, weekly, or monthly. For recurring tasks, the start time can be configured along with reoccurring options to completely customize when the task will run.
- **At Log On**—Tasks scheduled to run when At Log On is set for any user or for a specific user or group of users.
- **At Startup**—There are no specific settings for tasks configured to run at startup. This type of trigger runs whenever the system starts and the only settings are the advanced ones, which are described later in the chapter.
- **On Idle**—The settings for tasks set to run when the computer is idle are set on the Conditions tab.
- **On an Event**—This trigger causes a task to run when specific events are created in an event log. You can choose either a basic event trigger or custom event settings. Basic settings fire based on a single event from a specific event log. You choose

which log contains the event, the publisher name, and the event ID. If you specify the custom event trigger settings, you can specify an XML event query or custom event filter to query for events that will fire the task.

NOTE

It is easier to create event-based triggers from within the event log unless you know exactly what events you want to trigger. See the section "Customizing the Event Log," earlier in this chapter, for a detailed explanation of how to create events from within the event log.

- **At Task Creation/Modification**—Tasks created with this trigger are fired as soon as they are created or whenever they are modified. The only settings for this trigger are the advanced settings as described in the next section, "Understanding the Advanced Settings Associated with Triggers."
- **On Connection to User Session**—The trigger fires when a user connects to the system using the Remote Desktop Connection program from another system and can be set to run when any user connects, or when a specific user or group connects to the server.
- **On Disconnect from User Session**—This trigger works the same as the On Connection to User Session; however, it fires when users disconnect from the server from a Remote Desktop Connection session. The trigger can be set to run for all users or a specific user or group.
- **On Workstation Lock**—The trigger fires when the workstation is locked. The settings for this trigger enable you to set it for all users or a specific user or group.
- **On Workstation Unlock**—This trigger fires when the workstation is unlocked. The settings for this trigger enable you to set it for all users or a specific user or group.

Understanding the Advanced Settings Associated with Triggers

Advanced settings exist when creating triggers. Familiarize yourself with these advanced settings to ensure trigger creation and the workflow process is fully optimized. The following bullets explain each of the advanced settings associated with triggers:

- **Delay Task for or Delay Task for Up To (Random Delay)**—Tasks can be delayed randomly so that they do not start immediately when the schedule triggers a task. For systems that might run the same tasks, this ensures there is some load balancing and that all systems do not run tasks at exactly the same time. Random delays can be set for 30 seconds, 1 minute, 30 minutes, 1 hour, 8 hours, or up to 1 day.
- **Repeat Task Every**—Tasks can also be set to repeat at regular intervals and for a set duration (for example, a task could be set to ping a particular system every minute for 1 day, write an event to the event log in the case of a failure, and email a distribution group to notify the IT team about the issue).

- **Stop Any Task If It Runs Longer Than**—Tasks can be stopped if they run past a defined amount of time and can be set to expire at a certain date and time.
- **Start and Expire**—Start and Expiration times can be set to synchronize across time zones to ensure tasks set to run on systems in multiple time zones start and stop at the same time.
- **Enabled**—Tasks can be enabled or disabled by checking or unchecking the enabled box.

Understanding the Actions Associated with a Task

As mentioned earlier, an action is the work conducted when a task runs. Tasks can have a single action or up to a maximum of 32 actions. The Actions tab of a task contains a list of actions associated with a particular task. An administrator can edit each action as follows:

- **Start a Program**—This action starts a program or script. In the Program/Script text box, type either the name of the program or script that should be run. Alternatively, the administrator can browse the application or script. If further command-line arguments are required, these can be specified in the Add Arguments (Optional) text box. In the Start In (Optional) text box, the working directory can be specified for the command line that executes the program or script. This path is either the path to the program or script or to the files that are used by the executable.
- **Send an E-mail**—This action sends an email when the task is triggered. In the Edit Action dialog box, you enter whom the email is from, whom it should be sent to, a subject, and any desired text. You must also enter a valid SMTP server.
- **Display a Message**—This action simply displays a message on the console of the system where the task is created. You can enter a title for the message as well as any text that should be displayed. This type of action only launches if the Run Only If User Is Logged On security option has been selected on the General tab of the Task Properties in the Create Task dialog box.

Understanding Conditions Associated with a Task

Conditions in conjunction with triggers determine whether the task will run. Tasks will not run if any condition associated with a given task is not fulfilled. The following list describes the types of conditions associated with a task:

- **Idle Conditions**—A trigger can be based on idle time of a computer. Idle time is checked by the Task Scheduler service every 15 minutes. Computers are idle if a screensaver is running. When a screensaver is not running, the computer is considered to be idle if for 15 minutes the CPU usage and disk input or output were at 0% for 90% of the overall time. In this situation, mouse or keyboard input should also be nil during this period of time. The Task Scheduler service only waits for user input to mark the end of an idle state.

- **Power Conditions**—Administrators can specify that tasks run only on computers operating on AC power. If administrators do not want a task to run when a computer is on battery power, a condition must be set to stop the task. Also, if the computer is off, a condition can be set to awaken the computer from a Sleep or Hibernate mode so that the task can run. Although this is unlikely in a server environment, it is still an option.
- **Network Conditions**—Administrators can choose to start a task only if a specified network connection is available. This setting is appropriate if the action requires access to a remote system or network.

NOTE

The Network Conditions do not support interoperability with Windows 2000 or XP.

Understanding Task Settings

The Settings tab of the Tasks Properties or Create Task dialog box offers settings that help you control how the task is run, restarted, stopped, or deleted, as follows:

- **Allow Task to Be Run on Demand**—If selected, this setting enables the administrator to manually start the task regardless of triggers or conditions by selecting the tasks and clicking Run in the Actions pane or right-clicking the task and selecting Run from the context menu.
- **Run Task as Soon as Possible After a Scheduled Start Is Missed**—If this option is selected, a task that has been scheduled to start at a specific time but did not run (for example, the computer was off or the scheduler service was busy) will be started, but only after 10 minutes has elapsed from the original start time.
- **If the Task Fails, Restart Every**—This setting controls what to do when a task does not run (for example, if a task fails to start a service due to an undetermined system problem). If this option is selected, an administrator can also configure the number of attempts that should be made to initiate the task.
- **If the Running Task Does Not End When Requested, Force It to Stop**—If a task does not respond to a request to stop, an administrator can set a condition to force it to stop.
- **Stop the Task If It Runs Longer Than**—If this item is checked, a limit on how long the task can run is enforced. As a result of this setting, a task might not be completed when it is stopped.
- **If the Task Is Not Scheduled to Run Again, Delete It After**—This selection helps the administrator keep the Task Scheduler MMC free from old tasks that might have been put in place to accomplish a specific action but are no longer needed or will never be repeated. Note that a trigger must contain an expiration task.

- **If the Task Is Already Running: Do Not Start a New Instance**—The task will not start a new instance if an instance of the task is already running.
- **If the Task Is Already Running: Run a New Instance in Parallel**—A new task will run in parallel if one instance is running and the triggers and conditions cause the task to be triggered again.
- **If the Task Is Already Running: Queue a New Instance**—A new task will queue, but it will not start until the first instance is complete and will not stop the instance that is already running.
- **If the Task Is Already Running: Stop the Existing Instance**—A new task is triggered and conditions specified in the task will first stop the current instance and then start a new instance of the task.

Viewing Task History

The History tab on the properties page for a task contains events filtered from the Operational events for the Task Scheduler in the Event Viewer and enables an administrator to see success and failures for any given task without having to review all task-related event information for a system or collection of systems.

NOTE

Although the Task Scheduler enables an administrator to create folders for organizing tasks and new tasks can be given meaningful names, after a folder or task is created, it cannot be renamed. Further, tasks cannot be moved from one folder to another. However, tasks can be exported and then imported into a new folder or another system.

Summary

Logging and debugging tools help administrators monitor, manage, and problem solve errors on a Windows Server 2012 system and infrastructure. Many of the tools used to identify system problems in a Windows Server 2012 environment have been improved from earlier versions of the applications in earlier releases of the Windows operating system. In addition, new tools have been introduced to enhance the administration logging and debugging experience. Key to problem solving is enabling logging and monitoring the logs to identify errors, research the errors, and perform system recovery based on problem resolution.

In addition to the tools and utilities that come with the Windows Server 2012 environment are resources such as the Microsoft TechNet database (http://www.microsoft.com/technet/). Between utility and tool improvements as well as online technical research databases, problem solving can be simplified in a Windows Server 2012 infrastructure.

Best Practices

The following are best practices from this chapter:

- Use the Task Manager to provide an instant view of system resources, such as processor activity, process activity, memory usage, and resource consumption.
- Use Event Viewer to check whether Windows Server 2012 is experiencing problems.
- To mitigate configuration issues, server roles should be scanned with the Best Practices Analyzer tool on a regular basis.
- Use filters, grouping, and sorting to help isolate and identify key events.
- Create custom filters to expedite problem identification and improve monitoring processes.
- Create alerts using triggers and actions to identify issues quickly.
- Archive security logs to a central location on your network and then review them periodically against local security logs.
- Use subscriptions to consolidate logs from multiple systems to ensure that problems are identified quickly.
- Set an auditing policy to shut down the server immediately when the security log is full. This prevents generated logs from being overwritten or old logs from being erased.
- Establish a process for monitoring and analyzing system performance to promote maximum uptime and to meet service-level agreements.
- Run Resource Monitor from a remote computer to monitor servers.
- Use logging when monitoring a larger number of servers.
- Establish performance baselines.
- Create logging jobs based on established baselines to ensure performance data is captured during times when the system is having resource issues and to facilitate altering for proactive system management.
- Create new baselines as applications or new services are added to a server.
- Consider reducing the frequency of data collection to reduce the amount of data that must be collected and analyzed.
- Use logs to capture performance data.
- Use the Memory Diagnostics Tool to facilitate hardware troubleshooting.
- Use Server Manager as a central console to monitor and address issues from a consolidated view, easily switching to other tools as needed.

CHAPTER 34

Capacity Analysis and Performance Optimization

IN THIS CHAPTER

- Defining Capacity Analysis
- Using Capacity-Analysis Tools
- Monitoring System Performance
- Optimizing Performance by Server Roles

Capacity analysis and performance optimization is a critical part of deploying or migrating to Windows Server 2012. Capacity analysis and performance optimization ensures that resources and applications are available, uptime is maximized, and systems scale well to meet the growing demands of business. The release of Windows Server 2012 includes some new and some refreshed tools to assist IT administrators and staff with properly assessing server capacity and performance—before and after Windows Server 2012 is deployed on the network. If you invest time in understanding and using these processes, you will spend less time troubleshooting or putting out fires, thus making your life less stressful and also reducing business costs.

Defining Capacity Analysis

The majority of capacity analysis is working to minimize unknown or immeasurable variables, such as the number of gigabytes or terabytes of storage the system will need in the next few months or years (to adequately size a system). The high number of unknown variables is largely because network environments, business policy, and people are constantly changing. As a result, capacity analysis is an art as much as it involves experience and insight.

If you have ever found yourself having to specify configuration requirements for a new server or having to estimate whether your configuration will have enough power to sustain various workloads now and in the foreseeable future, proper capacity analysis can help in the design and configuration. These capacity-analysis processes help weed out the unknowns and assist you while making decisions as accurately as possible. They do so by giving you a greater understanding of your Windows Server 2012 environment. You can then use this knowledge and understanding to reduce time and costs associated with supporting and designing an infrastructure. The result is that you gain more control over the environment, reduce maintenance and support costs, minimize firefighting, and make more efficient use of your time.

Business depends on network systems for a variety of different operations, such as performing transactions or providing security so that the business functions as efficiently as possible. Systems that are underutilized are probably wasting money and are of little value. Systems that are overworked or cannot handle workloads might prevent the business from completing tasks or transactions in a timely manner, cause a loss of opportunity, or keep the users from being productive. Either way, these systems are typically not providing as much benefit as they can to operating the business. To keep network systems well tuned for the given workloads, capacity analysis seeks a balance between the resources available and the workload required of the resources. The balance provides just the right amount of computing power for given and anticipated workloads.

This concept of balancing resources extends beyond the technical details of server configuration to include issues such as gauging the number of administrators that might be needed to maintain various systems in your environment. Many of these questions relate to capacity analysis, and the answers are not readily known because they cannot be predicted with complete accuracy.

To lessen the burden and dispel some of the mysteries of estimating resource requirements, capacity analysis provides the processes to guide you. These processes include vendor guidelines, industry benchmarks, analysis of present system resource utilization, and more. Through these processes, you'll gain as much understanding as possible of the network environment and step away from the compartmentalized or limited understanding of the systems. In turn, you'll also gain more control over the systems and increase your chances of successfully maintaining the reliability, serviceability, and availability of your system.

There is no set or formal way to start your capacity-analysis processes. However, a proven and effective means to begin to proactively manage your system is to first establish systemwide policies and procedures. Policies and procedures, discussed shortly, help shape service levels and users' expectations. After these policies and procedures are classified and defined, you can more easily start characterizing system workloads, which will help gauge acceptable baseline performance values.

The Benefits of Capacity Analysis and Performance Optimization

The benefits of capacity analysis and performance optimization are almost inconceivable. Capacity analysis helps define and gauge overall system health by establishing baseline performance values, and then the analysis provides valuable insight into where the system is heading. Continuous performance monitoring and optimization will ensure systems are stable and perform well, reducing support calls from end users, which, in turn, reduces costs to the organization and helps employees be more productive. It can be used to uncover both current and potential bottlenecks and can also reveal how changing management activities can affect performance today and tomorrow.

Another benefit of capacity analysis is that it can be applied to small environments and scale well into enterprise-level systems. The level of effort needed to initially drive the capacity-analysis processes will vary depending on the size of your environment, geography, and political divisions. With a little upfront effort, you'll save time, expense, and gain a wealth of knowledge and control over the network environment.

Establishing Policy and Metric Baselines

As mentioned earlier, it is recommended that you first begin defining policies and procedures regarding service levels and objectives. Because each environment varies in design, you can't create cookie-cutter policies—you need to tailor them to your particular business practices and to the environment. In addition, you should strive to set policies that set user expectations and, more important, help winnow out empirical data.

Essentially, policies and procedures define how the system is supposed to be used—establishing guidelines to help users understand that they cannot use the system in just any way they see fit. Many benefits are derived from these policies and procedures. For example, in an environment where policies and procedures are working successfully but where network performance becomes sluggish, it would be safe to assume that groups of people weren't playing a multiuser network game, that several individuals weren't sending enormous email attachments to everyone in the global address list, or that a rogue web or FTP server was not placed on the network.

The network environment is shaped by the business more so than the IT department. Therefore, it is equally important to gain an understanding of users' expectations and requirements through interviews, questionnaires, surveys, and more. Some examples of policies and procedures that you can implement in your environment pertaining to end users could be the following:

- Email message size, including attachments, cannot exceed 10MB.
- SQL Server databases settings are enforced with Policy Based Management.
- Beta software, freeware, and shareware can be installed only on test equipment (that is, not on client machines or servers in the production environment).
- Specify what software is allowed to run on a user's PC through centrally managed but flexible group policies.
- All computing resources are for business use only (in other words, no gaming or personal use of computers is allowed).
- Only business-related and approved applications are supported and allowed on the network.
- All home directories are limited in size (for example, 5GB) per user.

- Users can receive IT support by filling out the technical support web form or through the advertised help desk phone number.

Policies and procedures, however, aren't just for end users. They can also be established and applied to IT personnel. In this scenario, policies and procedures can serve as guidelines for technical issues, rules of engagement, or an internal set of rules to abide by. The following list provides some examples of policies and procedures that might be applied to the IT department:

- System backups must include system state data and should be completed by 5 a.m. each workday, and restores should be tested monthly for accuracy and disaster preparedness.
- Routine system maintenance should be performed only outside of normal business hours (for example, weekdays between 8 p.m. and 5 a.m. or on weekends).
- Basic technical support requests should be attended to within 2 business days.
- Priority technical support requests should be attended to within 4 hours of the request.
- Any planned downtime for servers should follow a change-control process and must be approved by the IT director at least one week in advance with a 5-day lead time provided to those impacted by the change.

Benchmark Baselines

If you've begun defining policies and procedures, you're already cutting down the number of immeasurable variables and amount of empirical data that challenge your decision-making process. The next step to prepare for capacity analysis is to begin gathering baseline performance values. The Microsoft Baseline Security Analyzer (MBSA) is one tool that performs a security compliance scan against a predefined baseline.

Baselines give you a starting point with which you can compare results. For the most part, determining baseline performance levels involves working with hard numbers that represent the health of a system. A few variables coincide with the statistical representations, however, such as workload characterization, vendor requirements or recommendations, industry-recognized benchmarks, and the data that you collect.

Workload Characterization

Workloads are defined by how processes or tasks are grouped, the resources they require, and the type of work being performed. Examples of how workloads can be characterized include departmental functions, time of day, the type of processing required (such as batch or real time), companywide functions (such as payroll), volume of work, and much more.

It is unlikely that each system in your environment is a separate entity that has its own workload characterization. Most, if not all, network environments have systems that depend on other systems or are even intertwined among different workloads. This makes workload characterization difficult at best.

So, why is workload characterization so important? Identifying system workloads allows you to determine the appropriate resource requirements for each of them. This way, you can properly plan the resources according to the performance levels the workloads expect and demand.

Benchmarks

Benchmarks are a means to measure the performance of a variety of products, including operating systems, nearly all computer components, and even entire systems. Many companies rely on benchmarks to gain competitive advantage because so many professionals rely on them to help determine what is appropriate for their network environment.

As you would suspect, sales and marketing departments all too often exploit the benchmark results to sway IT professionals over their way. For this reason, it is important to investigate the benchmark results and the companies or organizations that produced the results. Vendors, for the most part, are honest with the results, but it is always a good idea to check with other sources, especially if the results are suspicious. For example, if a vendor has supplied benchmarks for a particular product, check to ensure that the benchmarks are consistent with other benchmarks produced by third-party organizations (such as magazines, benchmark organizations, and in-house testing labs). If none are available, try to gain insight from other IT professionals or run benchmarks on the product yourself before implementing it in production.

Although some suspicion might arise from benchmarks because of the sales and marketing techniques, the real purpose of benchmarks is to point out the performance levels that you can expect when using the product. Benchmarks can be extremely beneficial for decision making, but they should not serve as your sole source for evaluating and measuring performance. Use the benchmark results only as a guideline or starting point when consulting benchmark results during capacity analysis. It is also recommended that you pay close attention to their interpretation.

Table 34.1 lists companies or organizations that provide benchmark statistics and benchmark-related information, and some also offer tools for evaluating product performance.

TABLE 34.1 Organizations That Provide Benchmarks

Company/Organization Name	Web Address
The Tolly Group	www.tollygroup.com
Transaction Processing Performance Council	www.tpc.org
LioNBRIDGE (VeriTest)	www.etestinglabs.com
Computer Measurement Group	www.cmg.org

Using Capacity-Analysis Tools

Analyzing system capacity and performance requires a handful of tools and the knowledge to use them properly to obtain valuable data. Windows Server 2012 includes several tools to assist with this initiative, and even more are available for download or purchase from Microsoft. In addition, several other companies have performance and capacity-analysis solutions available. Some of these tools can even forecast system capacity, depending on the amount of information they are given.

A number of sizing tools are available from various companies. A sizing tool takes data relative to the networking environment and returns recommended hardware configurations, usually in a Microsoft Excel spreadsheet or similar reporting application. One such tool is the Microsoft Assessment and Planning (MAP) Toolkit. This tool, available for download from Microsoft at http://technet.microsoft.com/en-us/solutionaccelerators/dd537566, assists you when planning your migration to Windows Server 2012 by creating an inventory of your current server infrastructure; therefore, you can determine hardware and device compatibility and Windows Server 2012 readiness.

Microsoft also offers free virtualization solution accelerators. For example, you can use the MAP Toolkit to accelerate your migration to Hyper-V on Windows Server 2012 by identifying underutilized servers within your infrastructure, which can be potential virtualization candidates.

Microsoft also offers several useful utilities that are either inherent to Windows Server 2012 or are sold as separate products. Some of these utilities are included with the operating system, such as Task Manager, Network Monitor, Performance Monitor, and the enhanced Event Viewer. Data that is collected from these applications can be exported to other applications, such as Excel or Microsoft Access, for inventory and analysis. Other Microsoft utilities like System Center Configuration Manager (SCCM) and System Center Operations Manager (OpsMgr) can also be used; however, they are sold separately.

Task Manager

The Windows Server 2012 Task Manager is similar to its Windows Server 2008 and Windows Server 2008 R2 predecessors in that it offers multifaceted functionality. You can view and monitor processor, memory, application, network, disk, services, user, and process-related information in real time for a given system. This utility is a well-known favorite among IT personnel and is great for getting a quick view of key system health indicators with the lowest performance overhead.

To begin using Task Manager, use any of the following methods:

- Press Ctrl+Shift+Esc (or Ctrl+Alt+End if connected through Remote Desktop).
- Right-click the taskbar and select Task Manager.
- Press Ctrl+Alt+Delete, and then click Task Manager.

When you start Task Manager, a screen similar to that shown in Figure 34.1 opens.

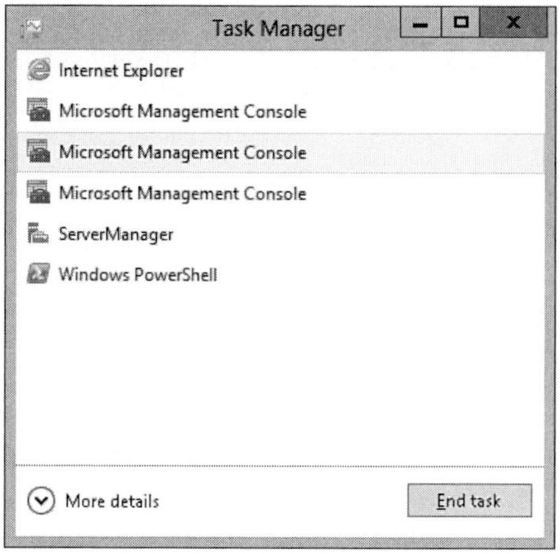

FIGURE 34.1 Summary view of Windows Server 2012 Task Manager.

The default view of Task Manager in Windows Server 2012 is the Summary view, which shows the list of running applications. You can end applications from this view.

The More Details button opens the more familiar Task Manager window, which contains the following five tabs:

- **Processes**—On this tab, you can find basic information about processes currently running on the system. Sorted by application processes and background processes, available data includes CPU and memory usage, process status, command line, and more.

NOTE

One welcome addition to the Windows Server 2012 version is a better identification of the program using commonly used processes, such as Microsoft Management Console or Services Host. Task Manager now identifies the specific application or service for each instance of the process, as shown in figure 34.2.

- **Performance**—This tab provides a lot of information about CPU utilization and configuration, memory usage and allocation and network utilization and configuration. This tab also includes a link to Resource Monitor a full features monitoring tool included in Windows Server 2012 and discussed in depth in this chapter.
- **Users**—This tab displays users who are currently logged on to the system and includes the option to disconnect users.
- **Details**—The Details tab presents detailed information about running processes in a view familiar from earlier versions of the Task Manager tool. The more in-depth information includes I/O information, session ID, memory pool data, and visibility and control into process affinity and priority.

- **Services**—A somewhat recent addition to Task Manager is the Services tab. With it, administrators can see what services are running and can start and stop services without having to load an additional console.

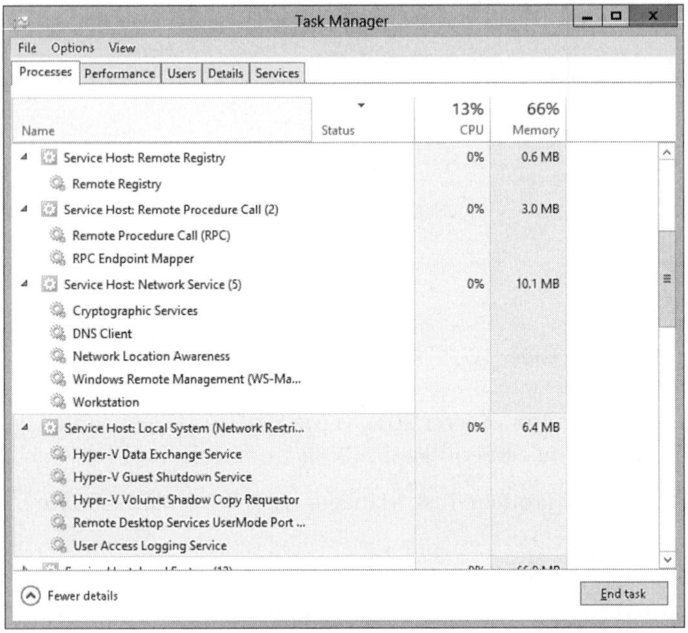

FIGURE 34.2 Improved process identification in Windows Server 2012 Task Manager.

As you can see, Task Manager presents a variety of valuable real-time performance information. This tool is particularly useful for determining what processes or applications are problematic and gives you an overall picture of system health with quick access to terminate applications and processes or identify potential bottlenecks.

There are limitations, however, which prevent it from becoming a useful tool for long-term or historical analysis. For example, Task Manager cannot store collected performance information for future analysis and viewing; it is capable of monitoring only certain aspects of the system's health, and the information that is displayed pertains only to the local machine. For these reasons alone, Task Manager is typically used for troubleshooting and only the most basic of capacity planning tasks.

Network Monitor

Network Monitor is a crucial tool that system administrators should have in their arsenal. Network Monitor, now in its third version, was overhauled to support the new networking changes that were introduced in Windows 2008 R2. Network Monitor 3.4 includes several enhancements for capturing network traffic and parsing the captured data for use in troubleshooting, capacity analysis, and performance tuning. The next few sections cover using Network Monitor to capture network traffic between two computers, on a wireless connection, over remote-access connections; how to analyze captured data; and how to parse captured data for analysis. You can download Network Monitor 3.4, shown in Figure 34.3, from Microsoft Download Center at www.microsoft.com/download/en/details.aspx?id=4865.

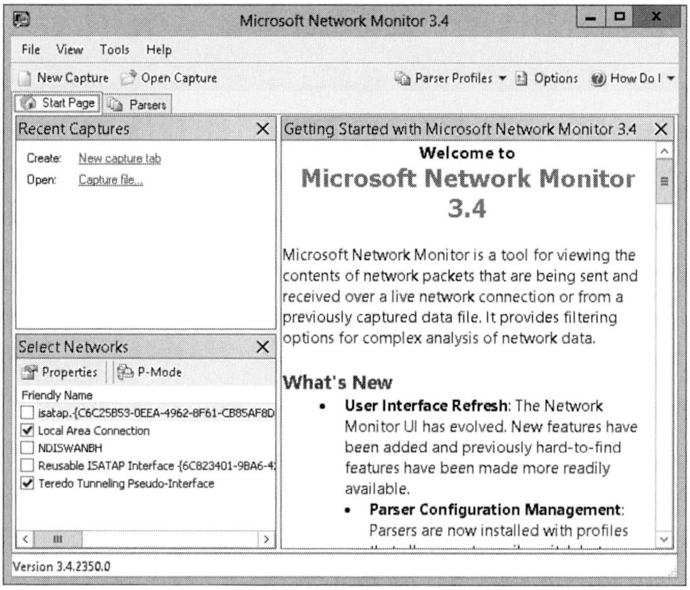

FIGURE 34.3 The Network Monitor 3.4 interface.

NOTE

The Network Monitor TechNet blog located at http://blogs.technet.com/netmon contains a wealth of information about Network Monitor and capturing and analyzing data.

NOTE

Network Monitor 3.4 is available in IA64, x64, and x86 versions and can run on Windows Server 2012, Windows Server 2008 R2, Windows Server 2008, Windows Server 2003 SP 2, Windows 8, Windows 7, Windows Vista SP1, and Windows XP SP3 systems.

What's in Network Monitor 3.4

Network Monitor 3.4 expands on the capabilities of the earlier versions of Network Monitor by including several more features and fixes for issues that were discovered in the 3.x versions. Network Monitor 3.4 is very flexible and can even stop a capture based on an event log entry in Event Viewer.

The features in Network Monitor 3.4 include the following:

- ▶ Support for Windows Server 2012, Hyper-V, Windows 8 and Windows 7
- ▶ The ability to capture WWAN and tunnel traffic on Window 7 and Windows 8 computers
- ▶ Support for both IPv4 and IPv6

Using Network Monitor 3.4

Before you can start using the advanced features of Network Monitor, analyzing captured data, and identifying potential issues and bottlenecks, a basic understanding of Network Monitor and how it works is necessary.

To capture network traffic, install Network Monitor 3.4 and follow these steps:

1. Run Network Monitor (Start, Microsoft Network Monitor 3.4).
2. Click the New Capture Tab link in the left pane.
3. Click the Start button or press F5 to start capturing traffic.

To apply filters to a captured stream of information, follow these steps:

- ▶ **To create a capture filter**—With the Capture tab selected, click the Capture Settings button or press F4. Click Load Filter, Standard Filters to select a preconfigured filter that will capture traffic relative to a specific item such as DNS, as shown in Figure 34.4.

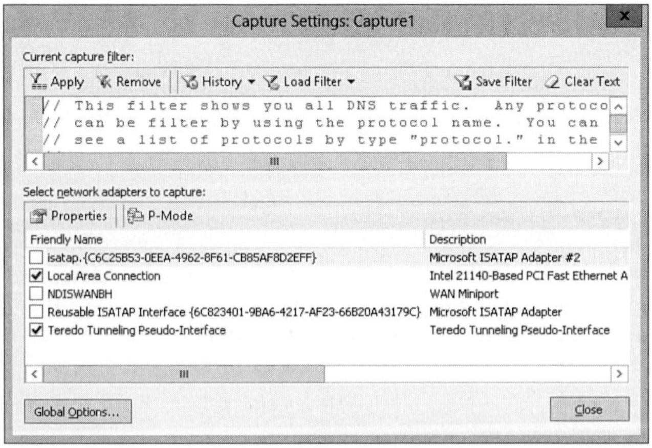

FIGURE 34.4 Configuring Capture Filters in Network Monitor.

- ▶ **To create a display filter**—From the Filter menu, click Display Filter, Load Filter, Standard Filters to select a preconfigured filter that will only display information relative to a specific item such as DNS from captured data.

- **To create a color filter**—From the Frames menu, select Color Rules. Click New to create a new rule, select Load Filter, Standard Filters to apply a color effect to specific items such as DNS.

After a capture or display filter has been added, it must be applied, as shown in Figure 34.5. Apply the filters:

- To apply a capture filter, open the capture settings and click the Apply button.
- To apply a display filter, select the Display Filter pane and click Apply Filter.

A color rule or display filter can be fine-tuned based on captured data. Hover the mouse over the desired value, right-click, and select Add Property to Color Rule or Display Filter. This action adds a filter condition for the property to equal the value of the selected frame, as shown in Figure 34.6.

To remove a filter, follow these steps:

- To remove a capture filter, open the capture settings and click the Remove button.
- To remove a display filter, select the Display Filter pane and click Remote.
- To remove a color rule, delete the rule from the Color Rules tab of the Options dialog.

NOTE

Removing a filter does not remove it from the filter list. It just removes it from being applied.

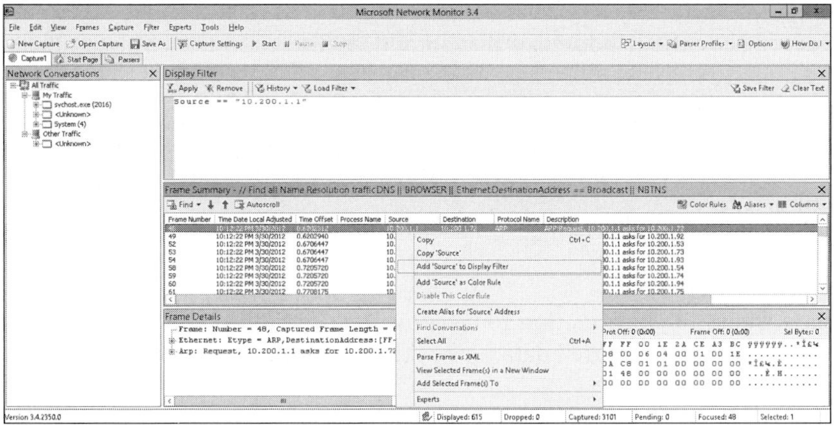

FIGURE 34.5 Choosing to add a value to display filter.

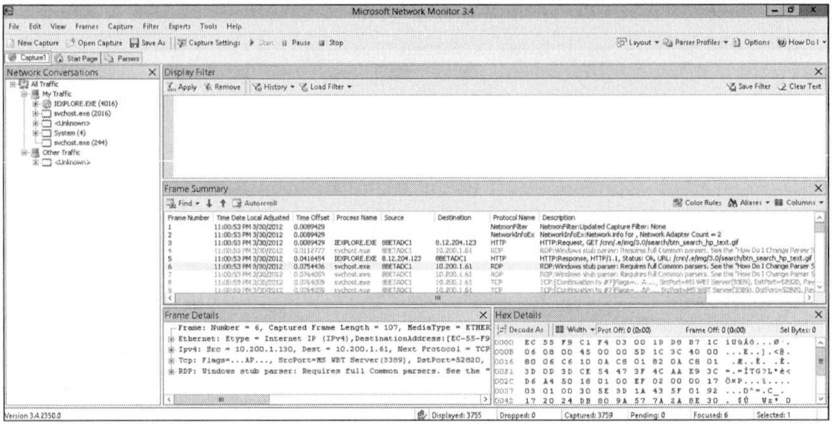

FIGURE 34.6 Sample capture with red highlighted data.

Capturing Network Traffic Between Computers

As outlined previously, Network Monitor enables you to capture wireless, remote, local area network (LAN), and wide area network (WAN) traffic using a remote agent. In some cases, network administrators want to diagnose or monitor a conversation between two computers. The steps necessary to monitor traffic between two different computers are outlined in the following list.

To capture network traffic between two different computers using IPv4 source and destination addresses, as shown in Figure 34.7, follow these steps:

1. In Network Monitor, click the New Capture button on the left.
2. Click the Capture Settings button. Click Load Filter, Standard Filters.
3. Select Addresses, and then IPv4 Addresses.
4. Edit the filter to specify the IP addresses that should be filtered in the Capture Filter window (for example, 192.168.0.100 and Any).
5. Click the Apply button in the Capture Filter pane, and then click Close.
6. Click the Start button on the main Network Monitor menu bar or press the F5 key to start the capture.

Parsing Captured Network Traffic Data

Parsing captured data allows the information to be converted into a format that is more legible to the naked eye. Parsing captured data makes analysis of the captured data easier—in fact, it's almost essential.

To modify parsing of captured data in Network Monitor, follow these steps:

1. With a capture running or loaded from a saved file, select the Parsers tab in Network Monitor, as shown in Figure 34.8.

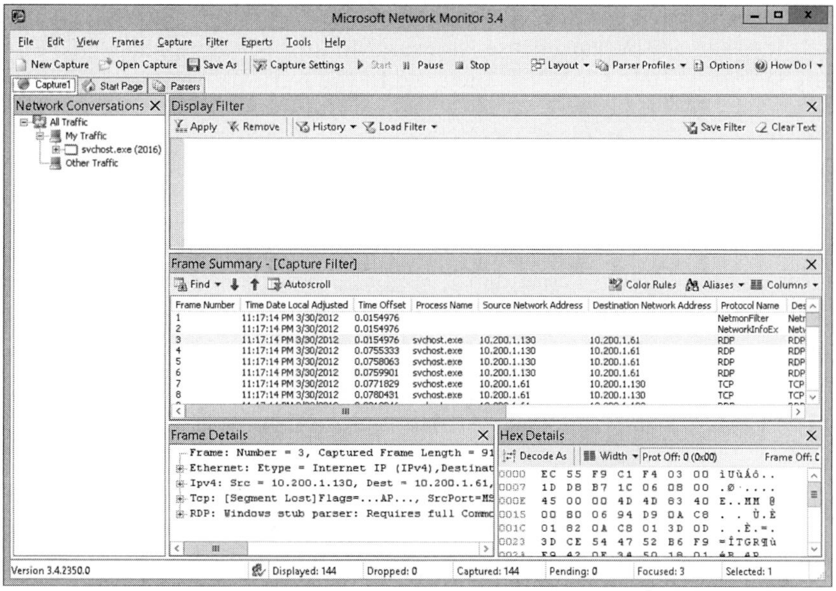

FIGURE 34.7 Network Monitor capture of network traffic between two IP addresses.

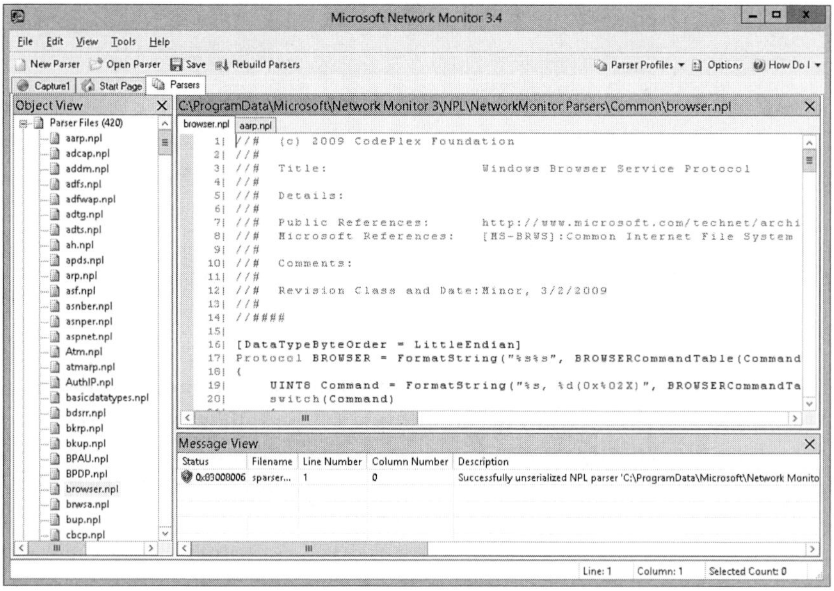

FIGURE 34.8 Parsers tab of Network Monitor.

2. Expand the appropriate parsing category and double-click the desired parser to load the parser code into the editor. Parsers use Network Monitor Parser Language (NPL), a simple-to-use language. Help for NPL is included in the Network Monitor Help file.

Windows Performance Monitor

The Performance Monitor in Windows Server 2012, shown in Figure 34.9, is structurally similar to Windows Server 2008 R2. The Performance Monitor is composed of three main components: monitoring tools such as Performance Monitor, data collector sets, and a reporting component. You can launch Performance Monitor from within the Windows Server 2012 Server Manager or from the Metro UI.

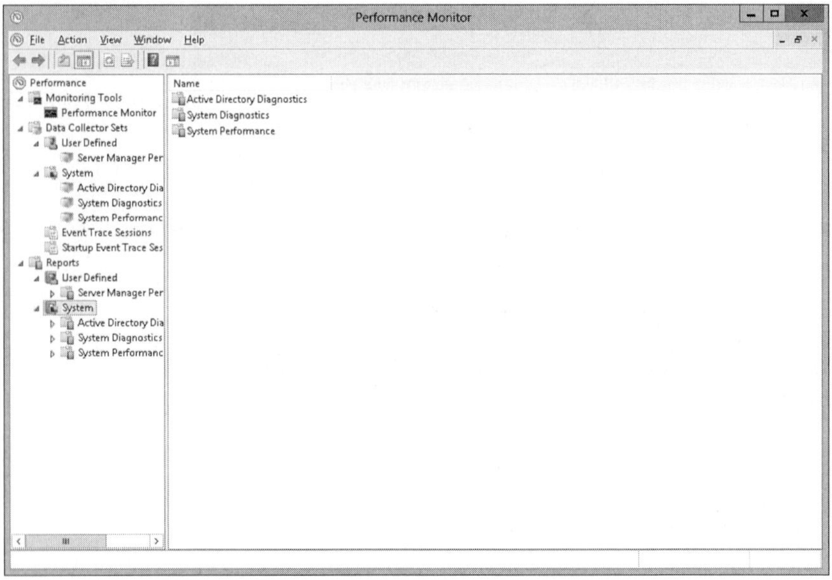

FIGURE 34.9 Performance Monitor in Windows 2012.

Using Performance Monitor, administrators can identify bottlenecks and pinpoint resource issues with applications, processes, or hardware. Monitoring of these items can help identify and resolve issues, plan for capacity changes, and help establish baselines for use in future analysis. Upon launching the Performance Monitor, a summary of system performance is displayed, showing current memory, disk, processor, and network loads.

Performance Monitor

Many IT professionals rely on the Performance Monitor because it is bundled with the operating system and it allows you to capture and monitor every measurable system object within Windows Server 2012. The tool requires little effort to learn. You can find and start the Performance Monitor by opening Server Manager, clicking Tools, and then selecting the Performance Monitor option. The Performance Monitor, shown in Figure 34.10, is by far the best utility provided in the operating system for capacity-analysis purposes. With this utility, you can analyze data from almost all aspects of the system, both in real time and historically. You can view this data analysis through charts, reports, and logs. The log format can be stored for use later so that you can scrutinize data from succinct periods of time.

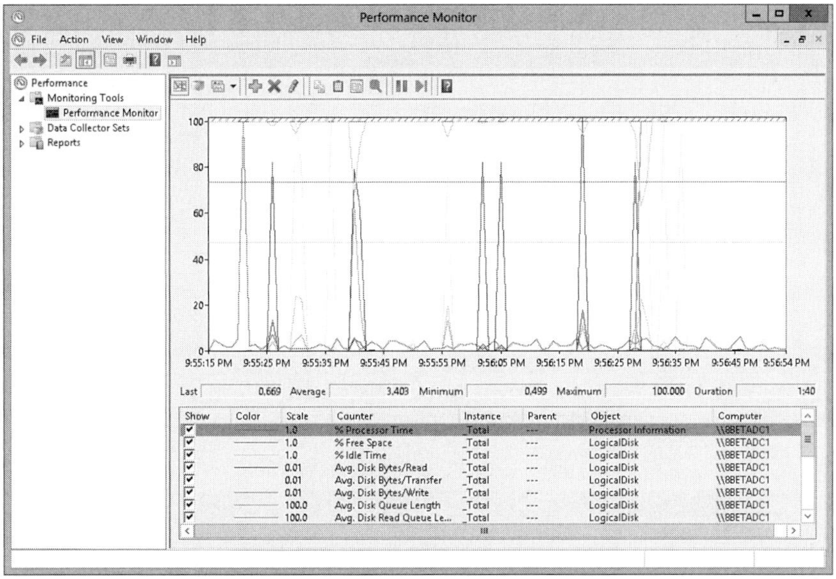

FIGURE 34.10 Performance Monitor real-time system monitoring.

Data Collector Sets

As mentioned previously, data collector sets are a collective grouping of items to be monitored. You can use one of the predefined sets or create your own to group together items that you want to monitor. Data collector sets are useful for several reasons. First, data collectors can be a common theme or a mix of items. For example, you could have one data collector set that monitors only memory or a data collector set that contains myriad items such as memory, disk usage, processor time, and more. Data collector sets can also be scheduled to run when needed. Figure 34.11 shows the Data Collector Sets section of the Performance Monitor.

Reports

As previously discussed, the Performance Monitor includes an updated reporting mechanism and several template performance and diagnostic reports for use. In addition, reports can also be created manually or generated from data collector sets. Three system reports are included for diagnosing and assessing system performance: Active Directory Diagnostics, System Diagnostics, and System Performance. The following steps outline the process to view a System Diagnostics report. Figure 34.12 shows a sample System Diagnostics report.

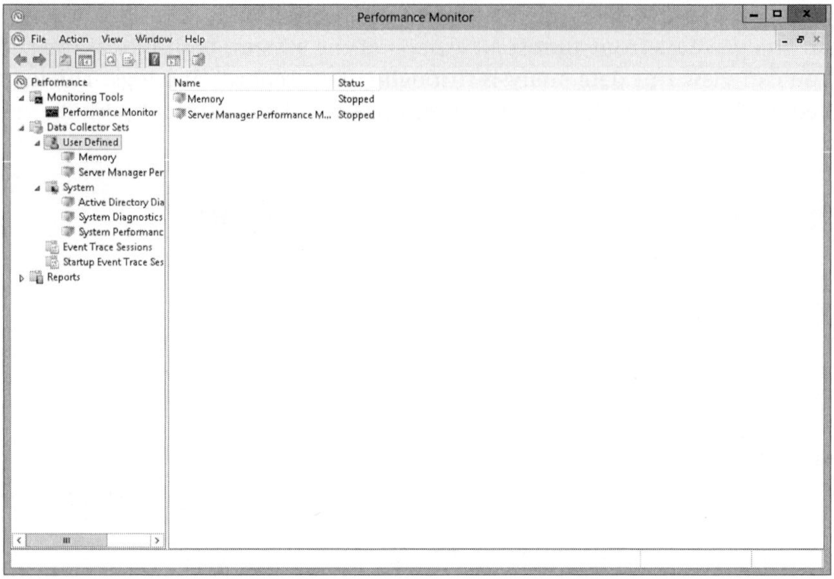

FIGURE 34.11 Data collector sets in Performance Monitor.

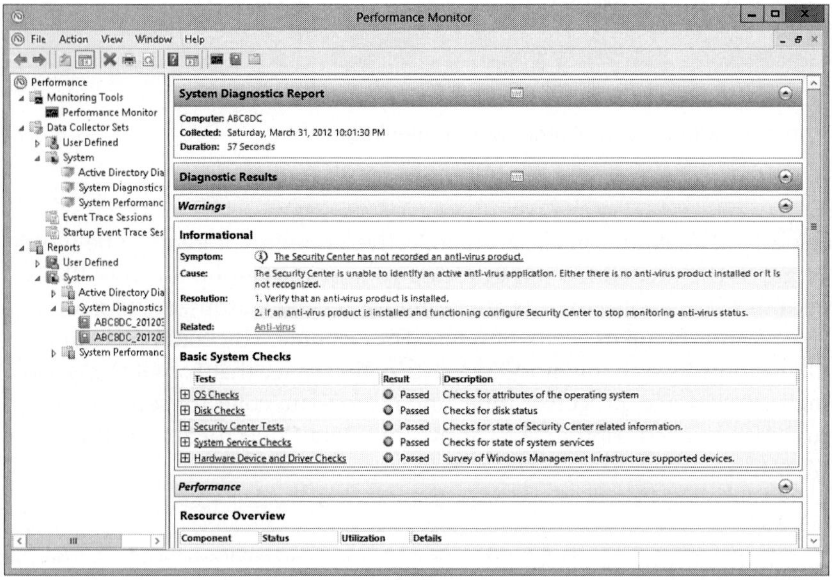

FIGURE 34.12 System Diagnostics report in Performance Monitor.

To create and view reports in Performance Monitor, follow these steps:

1. Expand Data Collector Sets and System in the console tree of Performance Monitor.
2. Right-click either the System Diagnostics or System Performance sets and select Start. Windows will begin collecting data for the report.
3. When you have collected enough data, right-click the collection set again, and select Stop.
4. Expand Reports, System and click the collection set you chose earlier. Double-click the report listed under that performance set.

The report will be compiled and displayed, as in Figure 34.12.

Other Microsoft Assessment and Planning Tools

Several other products and tools are available from Microsoft to assist with proper capacity analysis and performance monitoring. Some of these tools are available for purchase separately or can be downloaded for free. Selecting the right tool or product depends on the goal you are trying to accomplish. For example, you should use the Windows System Resource Manager (WSRM) if you want to implement thresholds for the amount of resources an application or process is allowed to consume, and System Center Operations Manager might be deployed if you want to be notified when critical processes behave abnormally on production servers.

Discussing each of these tools in depth is beyond the scope of this book; however, a basic understanding and overview of their purposes will help you make an informed decision when selecting the right technologies for analyzing system resources, availability, and performance.

Windows System Resource Manager

Windows System Resource Manager is officially listed as a deprecated tool in Windows Server 2012 but is still included in the feature set of Windows Server. Some of the functionality has been replaced with Hyper-V for virtual guest and WSRM will likely be removed from future versions but is still a useful tool. WSRM enables you to configure how processor and memory resources are allocated among applications, services, and processes. Having the ability to control these items at such a granular level can help ensure system stability, thus improving system availability and improving the user experience. Assigned thresholds to services, applications, and processes can prevent issues like high CPU consumption or heavy resource contention. System Resource Manager is installed as a feature via Server Manager. System Resource Manager can manage multiple items on the local system and remote computers. Figure 34.13 shows the System Resource Manager interface.

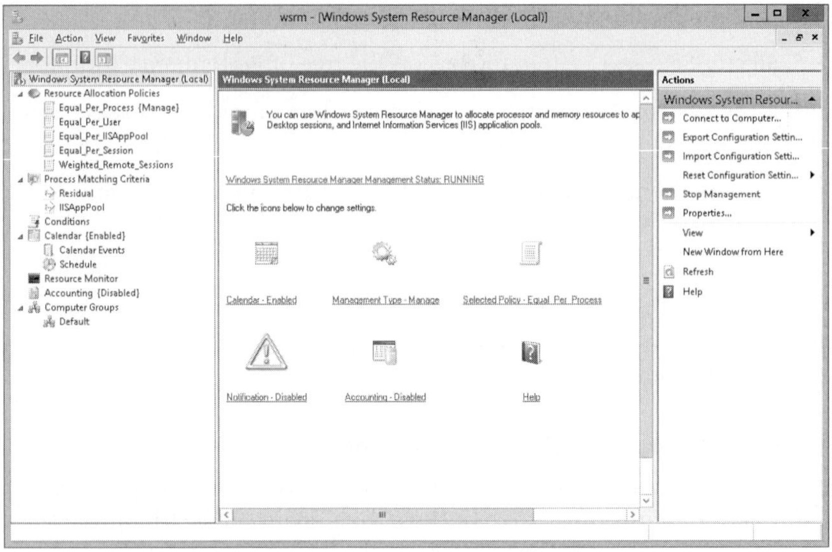

FIGURE 34.13 Windows System Resource Manager.

To install System Resource Manager, follow these steps:

1. Launch Server Manager from the task bar.
2. From the Manage menu, select Add Roles and Features.
3. Click Next twice to get to the server selection page.
4. Select the local server and click Next.
5. Click Next to maintain the current system roles
6. Scroll down and select Windows System Resource Manager.
7. Click Add Features to confirm the installation of the administration console.
8. Click Next.
9. Click Install to install the Windows System Resource Manager and required components.
10. Click Close when the installation completes.

NOTE

A warning appears in Server Manager if the Windows System Resource Manager service is not started. This service must be running to use Windows System Resource Manager.

The same process can be completed using PowerShell by executing the following commands in a PowerShell session that was started as administrator:

```
Import-Module ServerManager
Add-WindowsFeature WSRM
```

After WSRM is installed, you can start fine-tuning the Windows Server 2012 server's processes, services, applications, and other items to ensure CPU cycles and memory usage are allocated appropriately. WSRM provides administrators with a means of adjusting the system to meet the demands of those accessing it. WSRM can allocate CPU time and memory usage through the use of the included resource-allocation policies or a customized one. Observed system usage and data obtained from tools like Performance Monitor can be applied directly to WSRM policies. For example, if system monitoring reveals that a particular application is in high demand but the same server is busy providing other services, making the application sluggish, the WSRM can allocate enough resources to both items to ensure that neither the system nor the items being used are negatively impacted. It is very common for WSRM to be implemented in conjunction with SQL Server to improve sustainability in a consolidated environment. For example, if 10 WSRM-managed SQL Server instances exist, each instance can be granted 10% of the total processor. Each instance can use its entire share of the processor, but if nine instances are using less than their allocated processor resource, the remaining instance can use more processor resources. If demand for processor resources then increases on one of the other instances, WSRM returns the resources as needed.

Resource-allocation policies are used in WSRM to divide processor and memory usage among applications, services, processes, and users. Resource-allocation policies can be in effect at all times, or they can run on a scheduled basis. If certain events occur or the system behaves differently, WSRM can switch to a different policy to ensure system stability and availability. Resource-allocation policies can be exported and imported between Windows Server 2012 servers, and the policies can also contain exclusions when something doesn't require specific resource assignments.

When accounting is enabled in WSRM, administrators of the servers can review data collected to determine when and why resource-allocation policies were too restrictive or too loose. Accounting can also help identify problems with the items in the policy as well as peak access times. Administrators can use the information obtained by the accounting component of WSRM to make adjustments to the policies. WSRM resource-allocation policies can manage local and remote computers as well as Remote Desktop Services sessions.

WSRM comes packaged with five predefined policies. These templates provide administrators with a way to quickly allocate resources, leaving room for fine-tuning at a later time. The predefined resource-allocation policy templates are as follows:

- **Equal per Process**—Allocates resources equally among all running processes, preventing one process from consuming all available CPU and memory resources.
- **Equal per User**—Allocates resources equally among all users, preventing one user from consuming all available CPU and memory resources.

- **Equal per Session**—Allocates resources equally among all Remote Desktop Services sessions, preventing one session from consuming all available CPU and memory resources.
- **Equal per IIS Application Pool**—Allocates resources equally among all Internet Information Services (IIS) application pools, preventing one session from consuming all available CPU and memory resources.
- **Weighted Remote Sessions**—Controls priority for users who are remotely connected to the system.

NOTE

WSRM policies are only enforced when CPU usage climbs above 70%. The WSRM policies are never active on processes owned by the core operating system or any items in the exclusion list.

TIP

Memory limits should be applied in policies only when the application, service, or process is having issues or not allocating memory usage properly on its own.

A common task performed in WSRM is to create matching criteria rules. Matching criteria rules allow an administrator to define (or exclude) processes, services, or applications that should be monitored by WSRM. This definition is used later in the WSRM management process. To create a matching criteria rule, follow these steps:

1. Launch Windows System Resource Manager from the Tools menu in Server Manager and choose to Connect to the This Computer.
2. Right-click the Process Matching Criteria item in the WSRM console and select New Process Matching Criteria.
3. Enter a unique name for the matching criteria in the Criteria Name box at the top and click Add under the Rules section.
    - Enter the processes, services, or applications in the Included Files or Command Lines section of the Files or Command Lines tab.

    Or

    - Select the object type (Registered Services, Running Process, Application or IIS App-Pool) from the drop-down list, and click the Select button and select the object to include.
4. To exclude items from the policy, check the Excluded Files or Command Lines check box.

- Enter the processes, services, or applications in the Included Files or Command Lines section of the Files or Command Lines tab.

Or

- Select the object type (Registered Services, Running Process, Application or IIS App-Pool) from the drop-down list, and click the Select button and select the object to exclude.

5. Repeat the preceding steps to add all the exclusions and items that should be managed by or excluded from a WSRM policy.

Another task that is commonly performed is creating custom resource-allocation policies. Similar to "matching criteria rules" that look for specific process, service, and application criteria, the custom resource-allocation policy provides the administrator the ability to define how much of a resource should be allocated to a specific process, service, or application. As an example, if only 20% of the system processing should be allocated to a print process, the resource allocation would be defined to limit the allocation of resources to that process. To create a custom resource-allocation policy, follow these steps:

1. Launch Windows System Resource Manager from the Tools menu in Server Manager and choose to Connect to the This Computer.
2. Right-click the Resource Allocation Policies option in the WSRM console, and select New Resource Allocation Policy.
3. Provide a name for the policy, and click the Add button in the Allocate These Resources section.
4. On the General tab, select the Process Matching Criteria and specify the percentage of processor time that will apply.
5. On the Memory tab, specify the maximum committed memory and working set limits.
6. The Advanced tab allows you to select which processors the policy should be assigned to as well as suballocating processor resources. If you want to edit these parameters, make the changes and click OK.
7. Click OK when you have finished.

You can use the calendar component of WSRM to schedule policy enforcement on a regular basis and by one-time or recurring events. For example, policy enforcement might only be necessary during normal business hours. Calendar control is enabled by default and can be controlled by right-clicking the Calendar item in the WSRM console and selecting the Enable or Disable option. To create calendar items based on scheduled times, follow these steps:

1. Launch Windows System Resource Manager from the Tools menu in Server Manager and choose to Connect to the This Computer.

2. Expand the Calendar item in the WSRM console by clicking the right arrow.
3. Right-click the Schedule option and select New Schedule.
4. Enter a name and description for the schedule.
5. Double-click a time slot in the New Schedule window, specify the policy, start and stop times, and click OK.

Instead of creating a calendar item based on scheduled times, you can create the calendar item based on a specific triggered event. To create calendar items based on specific events, follow these steps:

1. Launch Windows System Resource Manager from the Tools menu in Server Manager and choose to Connect to the This Computer.
2. Expand the Calendar item in the WSRM console by clicking the right arrow.
3. Right-click the Calendar Event option, and select New One Time Event.
4. Enter a name for the event.
5. Select Policy Name or Schedule Name, and select the appropriate policy.
6. Specify a start and end date and time (not available if associated with a schedule) and click OK.

For calendar events that you want to trigger based on recurring events, you can create a rule for this to happen. To create recurring events, follow these steps:

1. Launch Windows System Resource Manager from the Tools menu in Server Manager and choose to Connect to the This Computer.
2. Expand the Calendar item in the WSRM console by clicking the right arrow.
3. Right-click the Calendar Event option, and select New Recurring Event.
4. Enter a name for the event.
5. Select Policy Name or Schedule Name, and select the appropriate policy.
6. Specify a start and end time and specify a recurrence schedule, such as every Monday (not available if associated with a schedule) and click OK.

One example of where WSRM is useful is when an administrator wants to allocate system resources to sessions or users who are active on a Windows Server 2012 Remote Desktop Services system. Configuring a WSRM policy for Remote Desktop Services can ensure the sessions will not behave erratically and system availability will be stabilized for all who use the Remote Desktop Session Host server. This is accomplished using the Equal per User or Equal per Session policy templates provided with WSRM. To allocate resources to a Windows Server 2012 Remote Desktop Services system, follow these steps:

1. Launch Windows System Resource Manager from the Tools menu in Server Manager and choose to Connect to the This Computer.
2. Expand the Resource Allocation Policies option in the WSRM console.
3. Right-click Equal_Per_Session or Equal_Per_User, and select Set as Managing Policy.
4. A dialog box opens indicating that the calendar function will be disabled. Click OK.
5. Click OK.

Assessment and Planning Solution Tool

As mentioned earlier in the chapter, the Microsoft Assessment and Planning Toolkit (MAP) provides a solution to IT personnel when faced with questions like "Which product should we buy or deploy?" or "Are we ready for Windows Server 2012?" Granted, there are multiple approaches to tackling questions like these; however, Microsoft has again developed a tool that will do most of the work for you. The Assessment and Planning Solution Tool inventories and assesses systems, hardware, and software and makes product and technology recommendations based on those results. The discovery and readiness tools included in the latest version of MAP include the following business scenarios: Windows Server 2012, Windows Server 2008 R2, Windows 7 and IE 9, Office 365, Microsoft Azure, SQL Server 2012, Office 2010, and more. You can download the Assessment and Planning Solution Tool from the Microsoft Download site at www.microsoft.com/downloads/.

System Center Operations Manager 2012

System Center Operations Manager (OpsMgr) 2012 has replaced its popular predecessor, SCOM 2007 R2. OpsMgr 2012 provides substantial improvements on earlier versions in availability, scalability, and monitoring of heterogeneous systems. OpsMgr is a mature comprehensive monitoring and reporting solution that reports on conditions related to services, system, and network performance, and alerts administrators when problems arise (for example, when critical services have failed to start, when CPU usage consistently stays above a designated threshold, or when excessive paging is observed by the OpsMgr agent). OpsMgr integrates directly with Active Directory, Windows Server 2012, and most other Microsoft technologies to provide an overall solution to help automate monitoring of critical systems and processes. OpsMgr uses management packs specific to the technology, such as the Windows Server 2012 baseline operating system, Exchange 2007/2010 or Internet Information Services (IIS), so little configuration is needed out of the box. You can find more information about OpsMgr 2012 in Chapter 23, "Integrating System Center Operations Manager 2012 with Windows Server 2012."

Third-Party Toolset

Without a doubt, many third-party utilities are excellent for capacity-analysis and performance-monitoring purposes. Most of them provide additional functionality not found in Windows Server 2012's Performance Monitor and other tools, but they have a cost and might have special requirements for deployment and integration into the organization's network. You might want to evaluate some third-party utilities to get a more thorough understanding of how they might offer more features than Microsoft solutions. Generally speaking, these utilities enhance the functionality that's inherent to Microsoft monitoring solutions, such as scheduling, an enhanced level of reporting functionality, superior storage capabilities, the ability to monitor non-Windows systems, or algorithms for future trend analysis. Table 34.2 lists some of these third-party tools.

TABLE 34.2 Third-Party Capacity-Planning and Monitoring Tools

Utility Name	Company	Website
AppManager Suite	NetIQ Corporation	www.netiq.com/products/am/default.asp
BMC ProactiveNet Performance Management	BMC Software	www.bmc.com/
HP Service Health Optimizer	HP	www8.hp.com/us/en/software/software-product.html?compURI=tcm:245-937079&pageTitle=service-health-optimizer
Longitude	Heroix	www.heroix.com/
NSM	CA	www.ca.com/

Although it might be true that most third-party capacity-analysis and performance-monitoring products might add more or different functionality to your capacity-analysis and performance-monitoring procedures or goals, there are still pros and cons to using them over the free tools included with Windows Server 2012 or other solutions available from Microsoft. The key is to decide what you need to adequately and efficiently perform capacity-analysis and performance-monitoring procedures in your environment. Taking the time to research and experiment with the different solutions available today, from Microsoft and others, will only benefit you in making an informed decision for managing your Windows Server 2012 environment.

Monitoring System Performance

Capacity analysis is not about how much information you can collect; it is about collecting the appropriate system health indicators and the right amount of information. Without a doubt, you can capture and monitor an overwhelming amount of information from performance counters. There are more than 1,000 counters, so you want to carefully choose what to monitor. Otherwise, you might collect so much information that the data will be hard to manage and difficult to decipher. Keep in mind that more is not necessarily better with regard to capacity analysis. This process is more about efficiency. Therefore, you need to tailor your capacity-analysis monitoring as accurately as possible to how the server is configured.

Every Windows Server 2012 server has a common set of resources that can affect performance, reliability, stability, and availability. For this reason, it is important that you monitor this common set of resources (namely CPU, memory, disk, and network utilization).

In addition to the common set of resources, the functions that the Windows Server 2012 server performs can influence what you should consider monitoring. So, for example, you would monitor certain aspects of system performance on file servers differently than you would for a domain controller running on Windows Server 2012 Active Directory Domain Services (AD DS). There are many functional roles (such as file and print sharing, application clustering, database functions, web server duties, domain controller roles, and more) that Windows Server 2012 can perform, and it is important to understand all those roles that pertain to each server system. By identifying these functions and monitoring them along with the common set of resources, you gain much greater control and understanding of the system.

The following sections go more in depth on what specific items you should monitor for the different components that constitute the common set of resources. It's important to realize, though, that there are several other items that should be considered when monitoring in addition to the ones described in this chapter. You should consider the following material a baseline of the minimum number of things to begin your capacity-analysis and performance-optimization procedures.

Key Elements to Monitor for Bottlenecks

As mentioned, four resources compose the common set of resources: memory and pagefile usage, processor, disk subsystem, and network subsystem. They are also the most common contributors to performance bottlenecks. A bottleneck can be defined in two ways. The most common perception of a bottleneck is that it is the slowest part of your system. It can either be hardware or software, but generally speaking, hardware is usually faster than software. When a resource is overburdened or just not equipped to handle higher workload capacities, the system might experience a slowdown in performance. For any system, the slowest component of the system is, by definition, considered the bottleneck. For example, a web server might be equipped with ample RAM, disk space, and a high-speed network interface card (NIC); but if the disk subsystem has older drives that are relatively slow, the web server might not be able to effectively handle requests. The bottleneck (that is, the antiquated disk subsystem) can drag the other resources down.

A less-common, but equally important, form of bottleneck is one where a system has significantly more RAM, processors, or other system resources than the application requires. In these cases, the system creates extremely large pagefiles, has to manage very large sets of disk or memory sets, but yet never uses the resources. When an application needs to access memory, processors, or disks, the system might be busy managing the idle resource, thus creating an unnecessary bottleneck caused by having too many resources allocated to a system. Thus, performance optimization means not having too few resources, but also means not having too many resources allocated to a system.

Monitoring System Memory and Pagefile Usage

Available system memory is usually the most common source for performance problems on a system. The reason is simply that incorrect amounts of memory are usually installed on a Windows Server 2012 system. Windows Server 2012 tends to consume a lot of memory. Fortunately, the easiest and most economical way to resolve the performance issue is to configure the system with additional memory. This can significantly boost performance and upgrade reliability.

There are many significant counters in the memory object that could help determine system memory requirements. Most network environments shouldn't need to consistently monitor every single counter to get accurate representations of performance. For long-term monitoring, two very important counters can give you a fairly accurate picture of memory pressure: Page Faults/sec and Pages/sec Memory. These two memory counters alone can indicate whether the system is properly configured and experiencing memory pressure. Table 34.3 describes the counters necessary to monitor memory and pagefile usage.

TABLE 34.3 Important Counters and Descriptions Related to Memory Behavior

Object	Counter	Description
Memory	Committed Bytes	Monitors how much memory (in bytes) has been allocated by the processes. As this number increases above available RAM, so does the size of the pagefile (because paging has increased).
Memory	Pages/sec	Displays the number of pages that are read from or written to the disk.
Memory	Pages Output/sec	Displays virtual memory pages written to the pagefile per second. Monitor this counter to identify paging as a bottleneck.
Memory	Page Faults/sec	Reports both soft and hard faults.
Process	Working Set, _Total	Displays the amount of virtual memory that is actually in use.
Paging file	%pagefile in use	Reports the percentage of the paging file that is actually in use. This counter is used to determine whether the Windows pagefile is a potential bottleneck. If this counter remains above 50% or 75% consistently, consider increasing the pagefile size or moving the pagefile to a different disk.

By default, the Memory tab in Resource Monitor, shown in Figure 34.14, provides a good high-level view of current memory activity. For more advanced monitoring of memory and pagefile activity, use the Performance Monitor snap-in.

Systems experience page faults when a process requires code or data that it cannot find in its working set. A working set is the amount of memory that is committed to a particular process. When this happens, the process has to retrieve the code or data in another part of physical memory (referred to as a soft fault) or, in the worst case, has to retrieve it from the disk subsystem (a hard fault). Systems today can handle a large number of soft faults without significant performance hits. However, because hard faults require disk subsystem access, they can cause the process to wait significantly, which can drag performance to a crawl. The difference between memory and disk subsystem access speeds is exponential even with the fastest solid state drives available. The Memory section of the Resource Monitor in Performance Monitor includes columns that display working sets and hard faults by default.

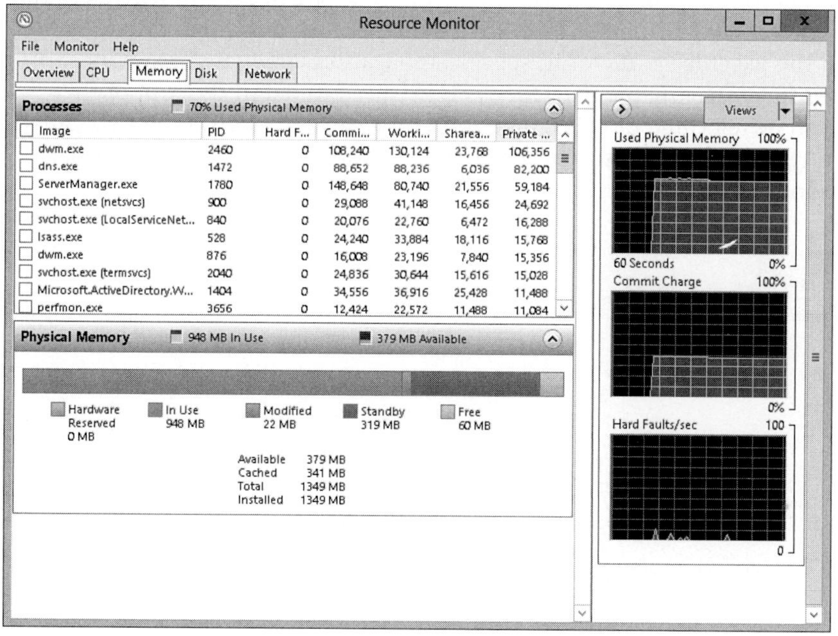

FIGURE 34.14 Memory section of the Resource Monitor.

The Page Faults/sec counter reports both soft and hard faults. It's not uncommon to see this counter displaying rather large numbers. Depending on the workload placed on the system, this counter can display several hundred faults per second. When it gets beyond several hundred page faults per second for long durations, you should begin checking other memory counters to identify whether a bottleneck exists.

Probably the most important memory counter is Pages/sec. It reveals the number of pages read from or written to disk and is, therefore, a direct representation of the number of hard page faults the system is experiencing. Microsoft recommends upgrading the amount of memory in systems that are seeing Pages/sec values consistently averaging above 5 pages per second. In actuality, you'll begin noticing slower performance when this value is consistently higher than 20. So, it's important to carefully watch this counter as it nudges higher than 10 pages per second.

NOTE

The Pages/sec counter is also particularly useful in determining whether a system is thrashing. *Thrashing* is a term used to describe systems experiencing more than 100 pages per second. Thrashing should never be allowed to occur on Windows Server 2012 systems because the reliance on the disk subsystem to resolve memory faults greatly affects how efficiently the system can sustain workloads.

System memory (RAM) is limited in size, and Windows supplements the use of RAM with virtual memory, which is not as limited. Windows will begin paging to disk when all RAM is being consumed, which, in turn, frees RAM for new applications and processes. Virtual memory resides in the pagefile.sys file or in specific application designated memory mapped files. The primary paging file, pagefile.sys is usually located in the root of the system drive and can be relocated or configured for performance reasons. Each disk can contain a pagefile. The location and size of the pagefile is configured under the Virtual Memory section, shown in Figure 34.15.

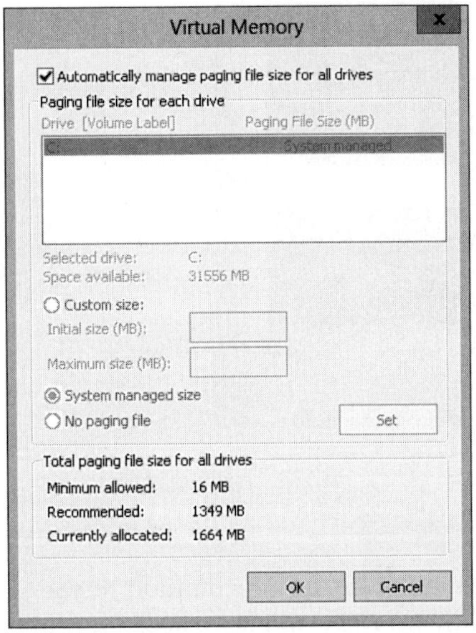

FIGURE 34.15 Virtual Memory configuration options.

To access the Performance Options window, follow these steps:

1. Open the metro UI and type Control Panel and launch the Control Panel from the search results.
2. Click the System and Security category and then the System control panel
3. Click the Advanced System Settings link on the left.

4. When the System Properties window opens, click the Settings button under the Performance section.
5. Select the Advanced tab.
6. Click Change under Virtual Memory.

TIP

Windows usually automatically handles and increases the size of pagefile.sys as needed; however, in some cases, you might want to increase performance and manage virtual memory settings yourself. Keeping the default pagefile on the system drive and adding a second pagefile to another hard disk can significantly improve performance.

Spanning virtual memory across multiple disks or simply placing the pagefile.sys on another, less-used disk will also allow Windows to run faster. Just ensure that the other disk is not slower than the disk pagefile.sys is currently on. The more physical memory a system has, the more virtual memory will be allocated.

Analyzing Processor Usage

Most often, the processor resource is the first one analyzed when system performance decreases noticeably. For capacity-analysis purposes, you should monitor two counters: % Processor Time and Interrupts/sec.

The % Processor Time counter indicates the percentage of overall processor utilization. If the system has more than one processor, an instance for each one is included along with a total (combined) value counter. If this counter averages a usage rate of 50% or greater for long durations, you should first consult other system counters to identify any processes that might be improperly using the processors or consider upgrading the processor or processors. Generally speaking, consistent utilization in the 50% range doesn't necessarily adversely affect how the system handles given workloads. When the average processor utilization spills over the 65% or higher range, performance might become intolerable. If you have multiple processors installed in the system, use the % Total Processor Time counter to determine the average usage of all processors.

The Interrupts/sec counter is also a good guide of processor health. It indicates the number of device interrupts that the processor (either hardware or software driven) is handling per second. Like the Page Faults/sec counter mentioned in the section "Monitoring System Memory and Pagefile Usage," this counter might display very high numbers (in the thousands) without significantly impacting how the system handles workloads.

Conditions that could indicate a processor bottleneck include the following:

- Average of % Processor Time is consistently over 60% to 70%. In addition, spikes that occur frequently at 90% or greater could also indicate a bottleneck even if the average drops below the 60% to 70% mark.

- Maximum of % Processor Time is consistently over 90%.
- Average of the System Performance Counter; Context Switches/second is consistently over 20,000.
- The System Performance Counter; Processor Queue Length is consistently greater than 2.

By default, the CPU tab in Resource Monitor, shown in Figure 34.16, provides a good high-level view of current processor activity. For more advanced monitoring of processors, use the Performance Monitor snap-in with the counters discussed previously.

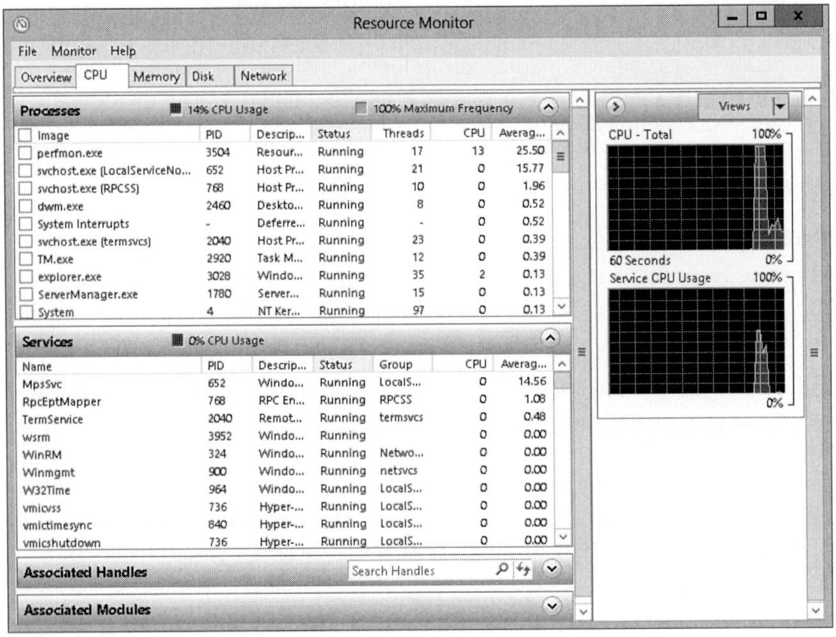

FIGURE 34.16 CPU section of the Resource Monitor.

Evaluating the Disk Subsystem

Hard disk drives and hard disk controllers are the two main components of the disk subsystem. The two objects that gauge hard disk performance are Physical and Logical Disk. Although the disk subsystem components are becoming more and more powerful, they are often a common bottleneck because their speeds are exponentially slower than other resources. The effects, though, can be minimal and maybe even unnoticeable, depending on the system configuration.

To support the Resource Monitor's Disk section, the physical and logical disk counters are enabled by default in Windows Server 2012. The Disk section in Resource Monitor, shown in Figure 34.17, provides a good high-level view of current physical and logical disk activity (combined). For more advanced monitoring of disk activity, use the Performance Monitor component with the desired counters found in the Physical Disk and Logical Disk sections.

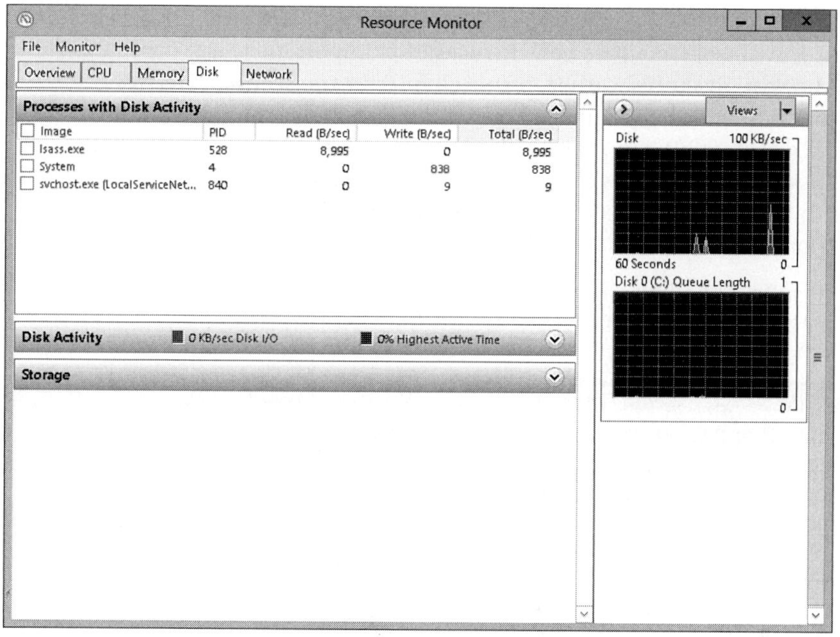

FIGURE 34.17 Disk section of the Resource Monitor.

Monitoring with the Physical and Logical Disk objects does come with a small price. Each object requires a little resource overhead when you use them for monitoring. As a result, you might want to keep them disabled unless you are going to use them for monitoring purposes.

So, what specific disk subsystem counters should be monitored? The most informative counters for the disk subsystem are % Disk Time and Avg. Disk Queue Length. The % Disk Time counter monitors the time that the selected physical or logical drive spends servicing read and write requests. The Avg. Disk Queue Length monitors the number of requests not yet serviced on the physical or logical drive. The Avg. Disk Queue length value is an interval average; it is a mathematical representation of the number of delays the drive is experiencing. If the delay is frequently greater than 2, the disks are not equipped to service the workload and delays in performance might occur.

Monitoring the Network Subsystem

The network subsystem is by far one of the most difficult subsystems to monitor because of the many different variables. The number of protocols used in the network, NICs, network-based applications, topologies, subnetting, and more play vital roles in the network, but they also add to its complexity when you're trying to determine bottlenecks. Each network environment has different variables; therefore, the counters that you'll want to monitor will vary.

The information that you'll want to gain from monitoring the network pertains to network activity and throughput. You can find this information with the Performance Monitor alone, but it will be difficult at best. Instead, it is important to use other tools, such as Network Monitor, discussed earlier in this chapter in the section "Network Monitor," in conjunction with Performance Monitor, to get the best representation of network performance as possible. You might also consider using third-party network-analysis tools such as network sniffers to ease monitoring and analysis efforts. Using these tools simultaneously can broaden the scope of monitoring and more accurately depict what is happening on the wire.

Because the TCP/IP suite is the underlying set of protocols for a Windows Server 2012 network subsystem, this discussion of capacity analysis focuses on this protocol.

NOTE

Windows Server 2012 and Windows 8 deliver enhancement to the existing quality of service (QoS) network traffic–shaping solution that is available in earlier versions. QoS uses Group Policy to shape and give priority to network traffic without recoding applications or making major changes to the network. Network traffic can be "shaped" based on the application sending the data, TCP/UDP addresses (source/destination), TCP or UDP protocols, and the ports used by TCP or UDP, or any combination thereof. You can find more information about QoS at Microsoft TechNet: http://technet.microsoft.com/en-us/network/bb530836.aspx.

Several different network performance objects relate to TCP/IP, including ICMP, IPv4, IPv6, Network Interface, TCPv4, UDPv6, and more. Other counters, such as FTP Server and WINS Server, are added after these services are installed. Because entire books are dedicated to optimizing TCP/IP, this section focuses on a few important counters that you should monitor for capacity-analysis purposes.

First, examining error counters, such as Network Interface: Packets Received Errors or Packets Outbound Errors, is extremely useful in determining whether traffic is easily traversing the network. The greater the number of errors indicates that packets must be present, causing more network traffic. If a high number of errors are persistent on the network, throughput will suffer. This can be caused by a bad NIC, unreliable links, and so on.

If network throughput appears to be slowing because of excessive traffic, keep a close watch on the traffic being generated from network-based services, such as the ones described in Table 34.4. Figure 34.18 shows these items being recorded in Performance Monitor.

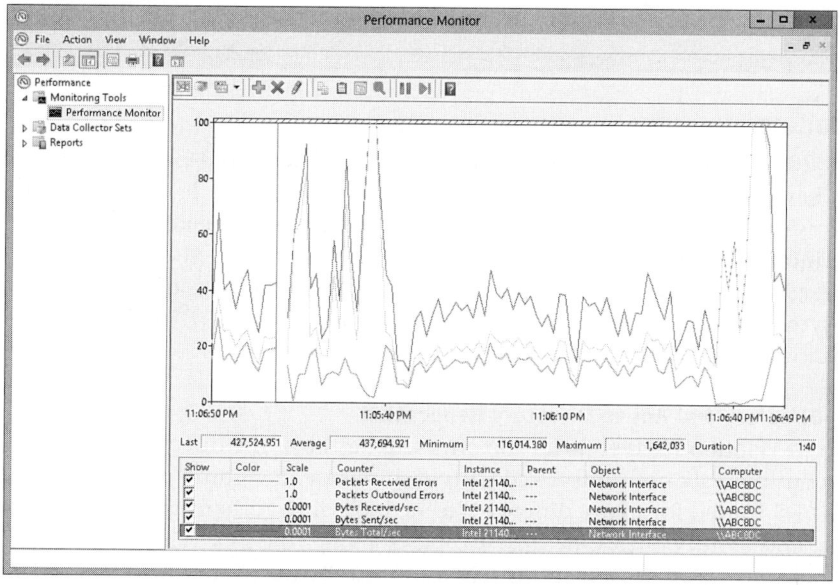

FIGURE 34.18 Network-based counters in Performance Monitor.

TABLE 34.4 Network-Based Service Counters Used to Monitor Network Traffic

Object	Counter	Description
Network Interface	Current Bandwidth	Displays used bandwidth for the selected network adapter
Server	Bytes Total/sec	Monitors the network traffic generated by the Server service
Redirector	Bytes Total/sec	Processes data bytes received for statistical calculations
NBT Connection	Bytes Total/sec	Monitors the network traffic generated by NetBIOS over TCP connections

Optimizing Performance by Server Roles

In addition to monitoring the common set of bottlenecks (memory, processor, disk subsystem, and network subsystem), the functional roles of the server influence what other counters you should monitor. The following sections outline some of the most common roles for Windows Server 2012 that require the use of additional performance counters for analyzing system behavior, establishing baselines, and ensuring system availability and scalability.

Microsoft also makes several other tools available that will analyze systems and recommend changes. Ensuring a system is properly configured to deliver services for the role it supports is essential before performance monitoring and capacity planning can be taken seriously.

Domain Controllers

A Windows Server 2012 domain controller (DC) houses Active Directory Domain Services (AD DS) and may have additional roles such as being responsible for one or more Operations Master (OM) roles (schema master, domain naming master, relative ID master, PDC emulator, or infrastructure master) or a Global Catalog (GC) server. Also, depending on the size and design of the system, a DC might serve many other functional roles, such as domain name system (DNS) or Dynamic Host Configuration Protocol (DHCP). In this section, AD, replication, and DNS monitoring are explored.

Monitoring Active Directory and Active Directory Replication

AD DS is the heart of Windows Server 2012 domains and has been the directory of choice for years. AD has continuously been improved with each release, including performance enhancements. AD DS is used for many different facets, including authentication, authorization, encryption, and group policies. Because AD plays a vital role in a Windows Server 2012 network environment and organizations rely on it heavily for communication and user management, it must perform its responsibilities as efficiently as possible. You can find more information about Windows Server 2012's AD in Chapter 4, "Active Directory Domain Services Primer." Each facet by itself can be optimized, but this section focuses on the Directory Services and Database objects. Organizations that take advantage of System Center Operations Manager can take advantage of the management pack available for Active Directory.

The Directory Services Performance Monitor object provides various AD performance indicators and statistics that are useful for determining AD's workload capacity. You can use many of these counters to determine current workloads and how these workloads can affect other system resources. This object has quite a few counters, so it's recommended to identify your specific monitoring needs in advance. The naming convention of many counters is used to group them by component, such as Lightweight Directory Access Protocol (LDAP), DRA (directory replication agent), DS, and Security Accounts Manager (SAM). With this combination of counters, you can review the status of every component of AD DS and determine whether the system is overloaded and whether AD performance is impacted.

Measuring AD DS replication performance is a complex process because of the many variables associated with replication, including the following:

- Intrasite versus intersite replication
- The compression being used (if any)
- Available bandwidth
- Inbound versus outbound replication traffic

Fortunately, there are performance counters for every possible AD replication scenario. These counters are located within the Directory Services object and are prefixed by the primary process that is responsible for AD DS replication: the DRA. Therefore, to monitor AD replication, you need to choose those counters beginning with *DRA*.

Like most other server products, AD DS uses a database, and its performance should also be monitored to provide an accurate reflection of AD DS performance. Understanding a domain controller's overall system resource usage and the performance of AD DS will help you align future upgrades and changes with capacity and performance needs. As companies continue to grow, it is essential that the systems be able to grow with them, especially with regard to something critical like AD DS. Many counters are available, and Table 34.5 describes some of the relevant counters necessary to monitor AD DS and the database. This is only a sample list, and additional counters might need to be added, depending on the desired outcome of the monitoring and specific AD DS functionality.

TABLE 34.5 Performance Counters Relative to AD DS Performance and Replication

Object	Counter	Description
Directory Services	DRA Inbound Full Sync Objects Remaining	Objects remaining before synchronization is marked complete.
Directory Services	DRA Inbound Object Updates Remaining in Packet	Objects remaining that need to be processed by the domain controller. Indicates delay in applying changes to the database.
Directory Services	DRA Pending Replication Synchronizations	Number of queued directory synchronizations remaining. Indicates replication backlog.
Directory Services	LDAP Client Sessions	Sessions generated from LDAP clients.
Directory Services	LDAP Searches/sec	Search queries performed by LDAP clients per second.
Directory Services	LDAP Writes/sec	Number of writes per second from LDAP clients.
Security Systemwide Statistics	Kerberos Authentications	Client authentication tickets passed to the domain controller per second.
Security Systemwide Statistics	NTLM Authentications	NTLM authentication requests served per second.
Database	Database Cache % Hit	Percentage of page requests for the database file that were fulfilled by the database cache without causing a file operation. If this percentage is low (85% or lower), you might consider adding more memory.
Database	Database Cache Size	Amount of system memory used by the database cache manager to hold commonly used information from the database to prevent file operations.

Monitoring DNS

The domain name system (DNS) has been the primary name-resolution mechanism in almost all networks, and this continues with Windows Server 2012. For more information about DNS, see Chapter 10, "Domain Name System, WINS, and DNSSEC." Numerous counters are available for monitoring various aspects of DNS in Windows Server 2012. The most important categories in terms of capacity analysis are name-resolution response times and workloads and replication performance.

The counters listed in Table 34.6 are used to compute name query traffic and the workload that the DNS server is servicing. These counters should be monitored along with the common set of bottlenecks to determine the system's health under various workload conditions. If users are noticing slower responses, you can compare the query workload usage growth with your performance information from memory, processor, disk subsystem, and network subsystem counters.

TABLE 34.6 Performance Counters to Monitor DNS

Counter	Description
Dynamic Update Received/sec	The average number of dynamic update requests received by the DNS server in each second
Recursive Queries/sec	The average number of recursive queries received by the DNS server in each second
Recursive Query Failure/sec	The average number of recursive query failures in each second
Secure Update Received/sec	The average number of secure update requests received by the DNS server in each second
TCP Query Received/sec	The average number of TCP queries received by the DNS server in each second
TCP Response Sent/sec	The average number of TCP responses sent by the DNS server in each second
Total Query Received/sec	The average number of queries received by the DNS server in each second
Total Response Sent/sec	The average number of responses sent by the DNS server in each second
UDP Query Received/sec	The average number of UDP queries received by the DNS server in each second
UDP Response Sent/sec	The average number of UDP responses sent by the DNS server in each second

Comparing results with other DNS servers in the environment can also help you to determine whether you should relinquish some of the name query responsibility to other DNS servers that are less busy.

Replication performance is another important aspect of DNS. Windows Server 2012 supports legacy DNS replication, also known as zone transfers, which populate information from the primary DNS to any secondary servers. There are two types of legacy DNS replication: incremental (propagating only changes to save bandwidth) and full (the entire zone file is replicated to secondary servers).

Asynchronous full zone transfers (AXFR) occur on the initial transfer, and then the incremental zone transfers (IXFR) are performed thereafter. The performance counters for both AXFR and IXFR (see Table 34.7) measure both the requests and successful transfers. It is important to note that if your network environment integrates DNS with non-Windows systems, it is recommended that those systems support IXFR.

NOTE

If your network environment is fully AD integrated, the counters listed in Table 34.7 will all be zero because AD-integrated DNS replicates with AD DS.

TABLE 34.7 DNS Zone Transfer Counters

Counter	Description
AXFR Request Received	Total number of full zone transfer requests received by the DNS service when operating as a master server for a zone
AXFR Request Sent	Total number of full zone transfer requests sent by the DNS service when operating as a secondary server for a zone
AXFR Response Received	Total number of full zone transfer requests received by the DNS service when operating as a secondary server for a zone
AXFR Success Received	Total number of full zone transfers received by the DNS service when operating as a secondary server for a zone
AXFR Success Sent	Total number of full zone transfers successfully sent by the DNS service when operating as a master server for a zone
IXFR Request Received	Total number of incremental zone transfer requests received by the master DNS server
IXFR Request Sent	Total number of incremental zone transfer requests sent by the secondary DNS server
IXFR Response Received	Total number of incremental zone transfer responses received by the secondary DNS server
IXFR Success Received	Total number of successful incremental zone transfers received by the secondary DNS server
IXFR Success Sent	Total number of successful incremental zone transfers sent by the master DNS server

Remote Desktop Services Server

Remote Desktop Services Server has its own performance objects for the Performance Monitor, still called the Terminal Services Session and Terminal Services objects. It provides resource statistics such as errors, cache activity, network traffic from Remote Desktop Server, and other session-specific activity. Many of these counters are similar to those found in the Process object. Some examples include % Privileged Time, % Processor Time, % User Time, Working Set, Working Set Peak, and so on.

NOTE

You can find a comprehensive list of all performance counters and descriptions relative to Remote Desktop Services at http://support.microsoft.com/kb/186536. You can find more information about Remote Desktop Services in Chapter 25, "Remote Desktop Services."

Three important areas to always monitor for Remote Desktop Session Host capacity analysis are the memory, processor, and application processes for each session. Application processes are by far the hardest to monitor and control because of the extreme variances in programmatic behavior. For example, all applications might be 32-bit, but some might not be certified to run on Windows Server 2012. You might also have in-house applications running on Remote Desktop Services that might be poorly designed or too resource intensive for the workloads they are performing.

Hyper-V Servers

Deployment of virtual servers and consolidation of hardware is becoming more and more prevalent in the business world. When multiple servers are running in a virtual environment on a single physical hardware platform using the Hyper-V role, performance monitoring and tuning become essential to maximize the density of the virtual systems. If three or four virtual servers are running on a system and the memory and processors are not allocated to the virtual guest session that could use the resources, virtual host resources are not being utilized efficiently. In addition to monitoring the common items of memory, disk, network, and CPU, dozens of counters provide information about the host and guest processes. Monitoring counters for guest sessions can be very valuable in determining whether specific guest sessions are monopolizing host resources. The categories that provide guest related counter are Hyper-V Dynamic Memory VM, Hyper-V Hypervisor Virtual Processor, Hyper-V Virtual IDE Controller and Hyper-V Virtual Network Adapter. Many of the counters in these categorize can be configured to measure a single guest session or the total of all guest sessions. For example, Figure 34.19 shows the available counters for the Hyper-V Virtual IDE Controller object. In addition to the counters, Hyper-V performance can also be monitored using Microsoft System Center Virtual Machine Manager and System Center Operations Manager, added when virtualization is running on the Windows Server 2012 host.

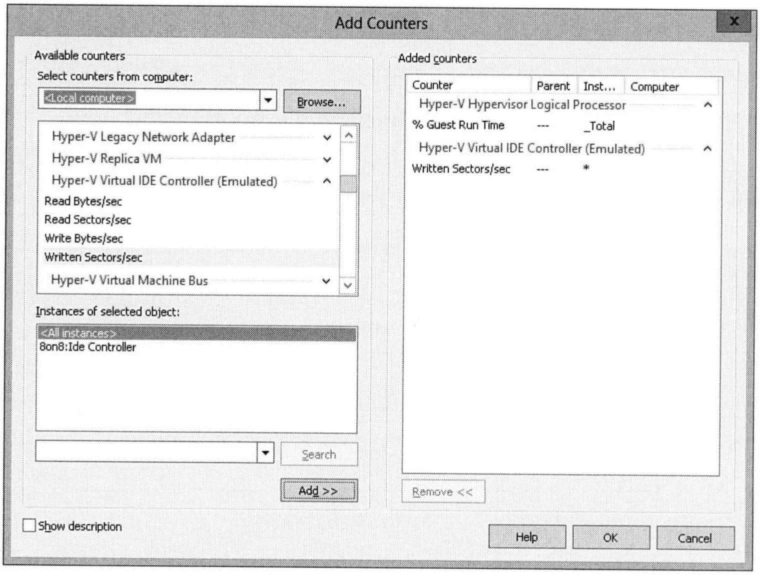

FIGURE 34.19 Performance Monitor IDE counters for virtualization.

Summary

Capacity planning and performance analysis are critical tasks in ensuring that systems are running efficiently and effectively in the network environment. Too much capacity being allocated to systems indicates resources are being wasted and not used efficiently, which in the long run can cause an organization to overspend in their IT budgets and not get the value out of IT spending. Too little capacity in production systems, and performance suffers in serving users, and this condition also creates a hardship on servers that can ultimately cause system failure.

By properly analyzing the operational functions of a network, a network administrator can consolidate servers or virtualize servers to gain more density in system resources, which can result in additional physical servers that can ultimately be used for other purposes, such as disaster recovery failover servers or cluster servers providing high availability of IT resources.

Although it is easy to get caught up in daily administration and firefighting, it is important to step back and begin capacity-analysis and performance-optimization processes and procedures. These processes and procedures can minimize the environment's complexity, help IT personnel gain control over the environment, assist in anticipating future resource requirements, and, ultimately, reduce costs and keep users of the network happy.

Best Practices

The following are best practices from this chapter:

- Spend time performing capacity analysis to save time troubleshooting and firefighting.
- Use capacity-analysis processes to help weed out the unknowns.
- Establish systemwide policies and procedures to begin to proactively manage your system.
- After establishing systemwide policies and procedures, start characterizing system workloads.
- Use performance metrics and other variables such as workload characterization, vendor requirements or recommendations, industry-recognized benchmarks, and the data that you collect to establish a baseline.
- Use the benchmark results only as a guideline or starting point.
- Use the Task Manager or the Resource Monitor in Performance Monitor to quickly view performance.
- Use the Performance Monitor to capture performance data on a regular basis.
- Consider using System Center Operations Manager or Microsoft products and third-party products to assist with performance monitoring, capacity and data analysis, and reporting.
- Carefully choose what to monitor so that the information doesn't become unwieldy.
- At a minimum, monitor the most common contributors to performance bottlenecks: memory and pagefile usage, processor, disk subsystem, and network subsystem.
- Identify and monitor server functions and roles along with the common set of resources.
- When monitoring specific roles like virtual servers or AD DS, include the common performance counters such as memory, CPU, disk, and network as well as counters specific to the role of the server.
- Examine network-related error counters.

CHAPTER 35

SharePoint 2010 Products

IN THIS CHAPTER

- History of SharePoint Technologies
- SharePoint Foundation 2010 Versus SharePoint Server 2010
- Identifying the Need for SharePoint 2010 Products
- Designing a SharePoint 2010 Farm
- Exploring a Basic SharePoint 2010 Site
- Lists and Libraries in SharePoint 2010
- Managing the Site Collection

The SharePoint 2010 family of products is well suited for organizations interested in exploring the collaboration and document management capabilities of the product line. SharePoint Server 2010 is the "v4" version of the product and therefore builds upon the previous version of the product with an updated architecture and a number of new features.

This chapter focuses on how SharePoint 2010 products can be used to extend the functionality of Windows Server 2012 so that it can function as a powerful document management and collaboration platform. SharePoint Server 2013 was not released at the time of the original shipment of Windows Server 2012, so the focus of this chapter is on the SharePoint 2010 release of the product.

This chapter introduces SharePoint Server 2010 features with a brief history of the evolution of the product, an introduction to the differences between the "free" version of the product (SharePoint Foundation 2010) and the version that needs to be purchased (SharePoint Server 2010), and then covers the building blocks provided by SharePoint (document libraries and lists). The discussion then turns to the management tools an administrator can use to manage sites, site collections, and the entire farm. This approach will help you understand how different groups of users benefit from the new and improved features of SharePoint 2010 products and the challenges involved with properly configuring the environment to meet user needs.

To learn more about the full range of features in the SharePoint product line, consider purchasing *Microsoft SharePoint 2010 Unleashed* (Sams Publishing, ISBN 978-0672333255).

History of SharePoint Technologies

Most readers have probably run into SharePoint in one incarnation or another, and may work with it on a daily basis. Even so, a brief review of the history of the product is helpful to understand the maturation process of the product line and differences between the SharePoint Foundation 2010 and the full SharePoint Server 2010 products.

SharePoint Origins

In 2001, Microsoft released SharePoint Portal Server 2001. The intent was to provide a customizable portal environment focused on collaboration, document management, and knowledge sharing. The product carried the "digital dashboard" web part technology a step further to provide an out-of-the-box solution. SharePoint Portal Server 2001 was the product that could link together the team-based websites that were springing up. SharePoint Team Services was a separate product that offered a subset of features of the "Portal" product.

Then, in the 2003 version of the SharePoint products, Microsoft developed and rebranded the products as Windows SharePoint Services, which served as the engine for the team collaboration environment. SharePoint Portal Server 2003 remained a separate server-based product. It built upon the Windows SharePoint Services technology platform and was intended as an enterprise solution for connecting internal and external sources of information. SharePoint Portal Server 2003 allowed the creation of portal "areas," searching across multiple sites, and enabled the integration of business applications into the portal.

These versions of SharePoint integrated closely with Microsoft Office 2003 products, making it easier for users to leverage SharePoint 2003 features without leaving the comfort of the Office 2003 applications. For example, users could create meeting and document workspaces directly from Office 2003 products. Most Office 2003 applications also included the Shared Workspace Task Pane, which allowed users to see information stored on the site if the document they were editing was opened.

When the SharePoint 2007 products were released, many organizations already had experience with the first and second iterations of the products, and were eagerly awaiting the "v3" products, knowing that the product was even more mature and that many new features had been added. The SharePoint 2007 family includes SharePoint Server 2007, and Windows SharePoint Services 3.0, and abandoned the often confusing term *Portal* from the product title. The v3 SharePoint products also continued the trend of close integration with Office products, and although they worked well with Office 2003 products, were optimized for use with Office 2007 products. Microsoft also broke out a key component from the server product, and made it available separately: SharePoint Server 2007 for Search. Microsoft also introduced a set of features that were only available when the Enterprise features were activated during or after the SharePoint Server 2007 installation process: primarily Excel Services, Business Data Catalog, and Web Based InfoPath forms.

SharePoint 2010 (v4) soon came about and offered yet another step in the evolution of the product line are retired the Shared Services Provider (SSP) component of Central Administration (a fact that caused much rejoicing) and instead implemented Service Applications in Central Administration. These compartmentalized the "plug-ins" to SharePoint into individual "service applications," which are essentially applications that can be individually managed, turned on and off, and fine-tuned. A number of the service applications are "cross-farm," as well, which enables these components to communicate and work across the boundaries of different SharePoint Server 2010 farms, which enhanced the scalability of the product. SharePoint 2010 products also now provided the familiar ribbon interface within the product, which increased the usability of the product. Most of the core features such as workflows, metadata, content types, search, and other tools were also enhanced, along with the scalability of the product in terms of file size and number of files that could be handled effectively. The "social" components of SharePoint also underwent a face lift, and "I like it" tags and comments could now easily be applied by users, and the personal My Sites could be used to track this level of activity with one's colleagues.

It is important to note that SharePoint 2010 represents the fourth version of the product and by far the most stable, scalable, and feature-rich product of the line. Companies in today's competitive environment appreciate this mature state of the product and are putting increasing faith in the product line. Specifically, this manifests as a willingness to build bigger farms, leverage more tools and features of the product line, and increasingly use SharePoint as a development foundation for line-of-business applications and solutions such as purchase order workflows, extranet collaboration sites that involve trusted partners, and feature-rich intranets that are heavily branded and customized.

Understanding the Need for SharePoint 2010 Products

Organizations have increasingly recognized the need for collaboration and document management products over the past decade, and most organizations have implemented one or more products to meet these needs. Overarching goals include enhancing productivity of the knowledge workers in the organization, managing documents for legal and business process reasons, providing better search capabilities, and exposing information to Internet and external users.

Most organizations have solutions in place that provide intranet solutions, or portals that often overlap with intranet functionality and features, but typically provide access to software services and applications. As the SharePoint product line matured and provided enhanced feature sets, security, and performance, many clients decided to replace one or more other technologies with SharePoint-based technologies.

Cost effectiveness was, and still is, a driving factor for SharePoint implementation. Microsoft has offered free versions of SharePoint products with each version. SharePoint Foundation is the free version of the SharePoint 2010 product line. These are commonly implemented to test-drive the features. SharePoint Foundation 2010 isn't technically free because the organization must still purchase the Windows Server operating system that houses the SharePoint Foundation sites and must purchase the SQL Server software and licenses if the full version of SQL Server is being used. SharePoint Foundation 2010 does not require the purchase of the SharePoint Server 2010 software, nor does it require that the organization pay for the client access licenses (CALs). Therefore, the implementation cost is lower than the full version of SharePoint Server 2010, and this has arguably been a key factor in the adoption of SharePoint software.

With this less-expensive option, organizations can test-drive the features of the SharePoint family at very low software costs, test migrations from other collaboration/intranet/portal/document management solutions, and determine whether their needs would be met. In many cases, this resulted in savings of tens of thousands of dollars over competing products.

Another driving factor was the close integration of SharePoint products with the Office product line, which a large percentage of organizations use. Their knowledge workers could easily publish documents to their SharePoint sites from their familiar applications like Word and Excel, and could "connect" to calendar or task data in SharePoint lists and libraries from their Outlook clients. Many competitor products sought to offer the same level of integration, but these were usually several steps behind in features and ease of use.

For organizations requiring the full set of features, they can later upgrade to SharePoint Server (whether Portal Server 2003, SharePoint Server 2007, or SharePoint Server 2010), and then need to purchase CALs for each user (internal or external) that would be accessing the SharePoint sites, or purchase the "unlimited" licenses for public use. Typically, enterprise-class SharePoint implementations use the full version of SQL Server and benefit from enhanced features, management tools, performance, and scalability.

Organizations that had been experimenting with SharePoint technologies gradually came to depend on them for managing large amounts of data and enhancing existing business processes, and as SharePoint dabblers evolved into power users, requests came up for features that SharePoint didn't provide out of the box. Fortunately, third-party companies quickly evolved to offer new, cutting-edge features, such as workflow tools, backup and archiving tools, governance and management tools, and many snap-in solutions. Microsoft also has offered separate tools to customize the SharePoint environment, starting with FrontPage 2003, which evolved into SharePoint Designer 2007 and now SharePoint Designer 2010. These allow customization of SharePoint pages and sites, are now available for free download, and are relatively easy to learn. More serious developers can also turn to the Visual Studio line of products for more advanced development needs.

SharePoint Foundation 2010 Versus SharePoint Server 2010

This fundamental question has caused many inquisitive IT personnel many hours of research: What exactly is the difference between SharePoint Foundation 2010 and SharePoint Server 2010? To answer this question, it is helpful to look at what the basic features of SharePoint Foundation are, and because SharePoint Server 2010 includes SharePoint Foundation 2010 as part of the installation, those features are all included in SharePoint Server 2010. However, the Server version of the product adds a large number of features to these base capabilities, a sampling of which are listed in this section. Although these features are not explored in depth in this chapter, they give examples of the features that make the Server version of the product appealing to organizations with more complex needs.

Basic Features of SharePoint Foundation 2010

The following list provides an overview of the standard features included in SharePoint Foundation, many of which are examined in more detail throughout this chapter. This very basic list ignores a number of features, but gives a basic summary:

- **Document libraries**—This basic component of a SharePoint site is designed to store and manage documents, and allows the administrator to add additional columns of data to the library (called metadata) as well as create custom views, track versions of the documents, and control access on a document level. Many other features are available in a document library, such as requiring checkout before a document can be edited or creating alerts that send email when certain conditions are met, such as a document changing. Other standard libraries include the picture library, slide library, and wiki page library.

NOTE

Metadata is data about data. So, for example, a Microsoft Word document has metadata associated with it, such as author, creation date, and modification date. SharePoint Foundation 2010 document libraries allow administrators to define other columns that can contain a wide variety of other information that is associated with a document.

- **Lists**—Another basic component of a SharePoint site, a list can take many forms, but is essentially data arranged in spreadsheet format that can be used to meet a nearly limitless array of needs. For example, standard lists include announcements, calendar, contacts, discussion boards, tasks, and surveys.
- **Web pages and web parts**—SharePoint web pages are key building blocks of SharePoint environments as they present data, tools, and web parts to the users of the environment that are rendered by the browser. Web parts are modular components that can be placed on pages and perform functions such as displaying data that resides in a document library or list, displaying data such as weather information or stock quotes. Users can create and customize new pages such as wiki pages, provide targeted content (often called dashboards) to specific users, and provide text and graphics for communications purposes.
- **Sites and workspaces**—Sites and workspaces are essentially groupings of lists, libraries, and SharePoint pages that provide a variety of features and functions to the users. For example, there might be a site for human resources or information technology, or a workspace that enables users to collaborate on a document or a workspace could be created for a specific event, such as a company quarterly meeting.

- **Site management tools**—These come in a variety of forms, including the browser-based page editing tools, site management tools, and site collection management tools. Basic tools for branding the site (changing colors and fonts) are provided, and you can turn on or off site features to control what tools users have access to. Organizations often allow "power users" access to these tools to distribute administration of the sites and reduce the impact on IT resources.
- **Central Administration tools**—These tools enable a SharePoint farm administrator to configure the server or servers to perform properly and to perform backups and restores of data. SharePoint service applications are also managed here, along with search settings, connectivity to Active Directory, and performance- and configuration-related changes can be made on many "levels" of the SharePoint structure. Microsoft also encourages the use of PowerShell tools by IT resources for more complex and repetitive tasks. IT typically retains control over these tools because they can affect the overall stability and performance of the whole SharePoint environment.
- **Business Data Connectivity Service**—Microsoft offers the Business Data Connectivity Service (BDCS) in SharePoint Foundation 2010, which enables SharePoint Server 2010 to connect to external sources of data, such as a web service, SQL Server database, or other relational databases while maintaining security in these sources. A number of dedicated web parts then enable SharePoint Foundation 2010 to display this data to form advanced dashboards.

This is only a partial list, and plenty more information is available online. For example, you can find plenty of additional information about SharePoint Foundation 2010 at http://sharepoint.microsoft.com/en-us/buy/pages/editions-comparison.aspx. It is also helpful to understand what the "full" version includes, which is covered from a high level in the next section.

Not Included in SharePoint Foundation 2010, but Included in SharePoint Server 2010

The SharePoint Server 2010 product includes SharePoint 2010 Foundation as part of the installation and so includes all of SharePoint Foundation features and then adds a host of additional features on top of these. Many IT administrators, departmental managers, and power users are curious about what is not included in SharePoint Foundation because they need to justify the cost of SharePoint Server 2010 to other decision makers and want to better understand what the more complete product includes. Keep in mind that there are two possible installations of SharePoint Server 2010: the Standard installation and the Enterprise installation.

An overview of the main features that require the purchase of SharePoint Server 2010 is provided in the following list:

- My Sites is available only in SharePoint Server 2010. If enabled, My Sites allows users to create their own site and customize personal information that can be shared with the organization and used to track their own activities in the SharePoint environment and the activities of their colleagues.

- User profiles are included in the SharePoint Server 2010 product. SharePoint Server 2010 connects to Active Directory (AD) and pulls in user information on a regular basis, which is then stored in the profiles database. Additional SharePoint-specific fields are added to this database creating a new database of user information that can be leveraged and customized in SharePoint Server 2010.
- The Secure Store service is provided with SharePoint Server 2010, and it provides a database that is used to store credentials that usually include user identities and passwords, but can be configured to contain other fields. These can then be used with some of the more advanced SharePoint features, such as Excel Services, Visio Services and PerformancePoint Services discussed later in this section.
- Content sources outside of the SharePoint content databases can be searched and indexed with SharePoint Server 2010 by creating search scopes. SharePoint Server 2010 can index file shares, websites, Exchange public folders, and other sources out of the box.
- Managed metadata allows the creation of centralized term sets in Central Administration that can then be referenced from any list or library in the SharePoint environment. With this tool, IT can provide "official" lists of terms (such as customer names, project names, product numbers) that can then be accessed via dialog boxes during document uploads or list item edits. Managed Metadata has become a vital tool for organizations wanting to create "taxonomies" for managing data stored in SharePoint.
- SharePoint Foundation 2010 is very limited in out-of-the-box workflows, offering only the three-state workflow, whereas SharePoint Server 2010 offers more flexibility with Approval, Collect Feedback, Collect Signatures, and Disposition Approval workflows.
- SharePoint Server 2010 Enterprise edition provides Access Services, which allows users to publish an Microsoft Access 2010 web database to a SharePoint site. This process moves all of the data to a SharePoint list, thus migrating the database to a centralized, controlled and secure environment.
- If browser-based forms are required, the Enterprise edition of SharePoint Server 2010 provides the tools needed to publish browser-based forms using InfoPath Forms Services. With the Enterprise edition, InfoPath is not required on end-user desktops to fill out forms.
- Excel Services are available only in SharePoint Server 2010 Enterprise edition. Through Excel Services, a Microsoft Excel 2007 or 2010 user can publish a spreadsheet, or portions of it, to a SharePoint Server 2010 document library so that it can be accessed via the Excel Web Access web part.
- PerformancePoint is only available in SharePoint Server 2010 Enterprise edition. PerformancePoint Services provides powerful tools to monitor and analyze business

activities by connecting to data sources and allowing the creation of powerful dashboards and scorecards.

- Visio Graphics Service is available only in SharePoint Server 2010 Enterprise edition. This allows users to view Visio diagrams in their browser without having Visio installed on their machines, as well as integrate diagrams into SharePoint applications and view workflow status with Visio graphical elements.

Identifying the Need for SharePoint 2010 Products

A number of organizational needs have spurred the adoption of SharePoint technologies. Many organizations see SharePoint technologies as the next evolution in document management and sharing, where the silo is more intelligent, controls access to (and use of) documents better, tracks usage information, and alerts users of certain conditions. The files stored in SharePoint can have data attached to them (metadata) to enhance management and categorization of the files. Workflows in lists and libraries can be kicked off automatically or started manually for a variety of business processes. The somewhat amorphous term *collaboration* can be enhanced with these tools, as can the ability to quickly create sites for smaller groups of users to share ideas, work on a document, or store data pertaining to a specific event. The most common requirements include the following:

- **A need for better document management than the file system can offer**—This includes document versioning, checkout and check-in features, adding metadata to documents, and better control of document access (by using groups and granular security). The high-level need is simply to make it easier for users to find the latest version of the document or documents they need to do their jobs, and, ultimately, to make them more efficient in those jobs.

- **Improved collaboration among users with a minimal learning curve**—Although almost everyone has a different definition of what collaboration is, a functional definition is a technology solution that allows users to interact efficiently with each other using software products to share documents and information in a user-friendly environment. With regard to SharePoint, this typically refers to document and meeting workspaces, site collections, discussion lists, integration of instant messaging and presence information, and integration with the Office suite of applications. Integration with Office applications is a key component: Most organizations do not want to force users to learn a new set of tools to collaborate more effectively because users generally resist such requirements.

- **A better intranet**—Although most companies have an intranet in place, common complaints are that it is too static, that it is not user friendly, and that every change has to go through IT or the "web guy." These complaints generally comes from a departmental manager, team lead, or project manager frustrated with their inability to publish information to a select group of users and regularly update resources their team needs to do their jobs.

- **A centralized way to search for information**—Instead of using the "word-of-mouth" search engine, there should be an engine in place that allows the user to quickly and efficiently find particular documents. The user can search for documents that contain certain words, documents created or modified during a certain time frame, documents authored by a specific person, or documents that meet other criteria, such as file type.
- **Creation of a portal**—Many definitions exist for the term *portal*, but a general definition is that a portal is a web-enabled environment that allows internal and, potentially, external users to access company intellectual resources and software applications. A portal typically extends standard intranet functionality by providing features such as single sign-on, powerful search tools, and access to other core company applications, such as help desk, human resources software, educational resources, and other corporate information and applications.

Customizing SharePoint 2010 Products to Organizational Needs

If the default functionality in SharePoint 2010 is not enough, or does not satisfy the specific business requirements of an organization, the product can easily be customized. Easily customizable or downloadable web parts can be "snapped-in" to a SharePoint 2010 site, without the need to understand HTML code. The more basic web parts allow the site designer or administrator to choose what information from document libraries and lists is displayed on the home page, or on web part pages. More complex web parts roll up or filter data, or provide data to other web parts (for example, the user's name or choices from a drop-down menu) to customize the data they present. Literally hundreds (if not thousands) of web parts can be purchased or downloaded that provide specific functionality, such as providing stock quote information, weather information, or connect to social media sites, or other sources of data.

Further enhancement of SharePoint 2010 sites can be accomplished using SharePoint Designer 2010, which is a free download from Microsoft and allows for a great deal of customization with relative ease and limited potential for damage to the environment. More advanced developers can use Visual Studio 2010 or other programming tools to produce custom code to work with SharePoint 2010. However, training is required to ensure that the code developed doesn't damage the environment.

Designing a SharePoint 2010 Farm

SharePoint 2010 products can be installed on Windows Server 2012, but the process is currently quite complex and requires several modifications to operate. In addition, organizations should validate supportability of SharePoint and third-party add-ins to SharePoint before putting any server into a production environment.

Microsoft may provide patches and updated to SharePoint Foundation 2010 and SharePoint Server 2010 to facilitate an easier installation process. It is, however, informative to review some of the requirements for SharePoint 2010 installations, to better understand the requirements for a test or production-level implementation. It is also reasonable to assume that requirements will be similar for SharePoint 2013 products when they become available.

Some organizations may choose to not adopt SharePoint 2013 products upon first release and prefer to implement SharePoint 2010 in their existing environment to stick with the more stable, and patched, previous version. In addition, many SharePoint 2010 environments have been heavily customized and it may make more sense to simply move existing SharePoint 2010 farms to the new Windows Server 2012 platform than to migrate the SharePoint 2010 configuration to SharePoint 2013.

Outlining SharePoint 2010 Requirements

SharePoint 2010 designs can range from single-server installations to multiple servers that make up a SharePoint farm, or even multiple farms that share different components and features. Basic server configurations may consist of "single server installations," which may meet the requirements of smaller organizations, whereas larger organizations typically configure multiserver environments, which include web servers, and application servers.

To make matters more complicated, SharePoint 2010 products can be installed on Windows Server 2008 and on Windows Server 2012 servers. As mentioned previously in this chapter, SharePoint 2010 products can use a variety of different versions of SQL Server products, too, further complicating the design process.

The following is a list of the Microsoft minimum recommendations for SharePoint 2010 products. It is important to note that this list indicates only the bare minimum necessary for support. In most cases, servers deployed for SharePoint 2010 should be more robust than the minimum requirements dictate.

Hardware Requirements

Planning for the appropriately sized servers is an art as well as a science. The process gets more complex when virtual servers are used as along with physical servers because the rules that apply to physical servers in terms of processors do not necessarily apply to virtual servers. However, Microsoft does publish specific recommendations for physical server specifications, and these are a good starting point when planning an implementation.

The following are the minimum hardware requirements as published by Microsoft for the implementation of SharePoint Server 2010. These apply to web servers, application servers, and single server installations:

- Server with a 64-bit processor and at least four cores.
- RAM capacity of 4GB minimum for developer or evaluation use, 8GB recommended for production use in a single server or multiple server farm.
- 80GB for system drive. It is also recommended to allocate sufficient space on a separate volume for the index files created by the search service.

The following are the minimum hardware requirements for the implementation of the database server with multiple servers in the farm:

- Server with a 64-bit processor and at least four cores for small deployments, or eight cores for medium deployments
- RAM capacity of 8GB minimum for small deployments and 16GB for medium deployments
- 80GB for system drive and sufficient storage space on other logical drives for SharePoint databases, and other SQL TempDBs and log files

Another common question revolves around the versions of Microsoft SQL Server that are compatible with SharePoint 2010 products, as well as limits to the sizes of the content databases that are supported by each. The following list describes the databases that can support SharePoint 2010 products:

- **Microsoft SQL Server 2012 64-bit edition**—No database size limit, except as specified by Microsoft best practices
- **Microsoft SQL Server 2008 R2 64-bit edition**—No database size limit, except as specified by Microsoft best practices
- **Microsoft SQL Server 2008 64-bit edition with Service Pack 1 (SP1) and Cumulative Update 2, or Cumulative Update 5 or a later Cumulative Update**—No database size limit, except as specified by Microsoft best practices
- **Microsoft SQL Server 2005 64-bit edition with SP3 and Cumulative Update 3**—No database size limit, except as specified by Microsoft best practices
- **SQL Server 2008 Express with SP1**—4GB database size limit
- **SQL Server 2008 R2 Express**—10GB database size limit

NOTE

Microsoft makes general recommendations on database size limits for SharePoint content databases (which store the documents, list items, and other information) but doesn't set hard limits for the "full" SQL Server products (SQL Server 2005, 2008, and 2012). For example, on TechNet (http://technet.microsoft.com/en-us/library/cc262787.aspx#ContentDB), it is stated that "we strongly recommended limiting the size of content databases to 200 GB, except when the circumstances in the following rows in this table apply." The document continues to clarify that if certain conditions are met, such as disk subsystem performance of 0.25 IOPs per GB, content databases of up to 4TB are supported. However, Microsoft is also careful to mention that for larger databases (that exceed 200GB) the native SharePoint backup tools may not meet backup and restore requirements. In essence, the general best practice is to limit the size of content databases to 200GB unless there are specific business requirements for larger databases.

Because this information can be confusing, a summary is helpful: If either SharePoint Foundation 2010 or SharePoint Server 2010 is connected to any of the supported full versions of SQL Server 2005, 2008, or 20120, no hard limits apply as to database sizes. It's only when SharePoint Foundation is installed with SQL Server Express that hard limits are enforced.

Browser Requirements

Clients access SharePoint pages and site through a web browser. Microsoft supports several different web browsers for use with SharePoint 2010 and classifies them as either Supported, Supported with Limitations, or Not Supported:

- Supported web browsers for SharePoint 2010 are
    - Internet Explorer 7 and later (32-bit)
    - Google Chrome (latest publically released version)
    - Mozilla Firefox (latest publically released version)
- Supported with Limitations web browsers for SharePoint 2010 are
    - Internet Explorer 7 and later (64-bit)
    - Apple Safari (latest publically released version)
- Not Supported web browsers for SharePoint 2010 are
    - Internet Explorer 6
    - Other browsers

It is important to understand what the "limitations" of the 64-bit Internet Explorer browsers are, as well as Apple Safari, since many organizations have deployed these versions. Some features in SharePoint 2010 require the use of ActiveX controls, many of which are only supported by 32-bit versions of Internet Explorer. Therefore, all non-32-bit browser will have the following limitations:

- Datasheet view
- Edit in Microsoft Office application
- File upload and copy
- Microsoft InfoPath 2010 integration
- Microsoft Visio 2010 diagram creation
- New Document

For additional information about browser support and limitations, as well as mobile browser support, see: http://technet.microsoft.com/en-us/library/cc288142.aspx.

Exploring a Basic SharePoint 2010 Site

When SharePoint 2010 is successfully installed on Windows Server 2012, an empty top-level site is created, as shown in Figure 35.1. Access this site by opening a browser on the server or from a workstation with access to the server and entering the URL you saw after completing the basic installation (typically the fully qualified domain name [FQDN] of the server). Enter the username and password of the account that was used to configure SharePoint 2010, and you should see a page identical to the one shown in Figure 35.1.

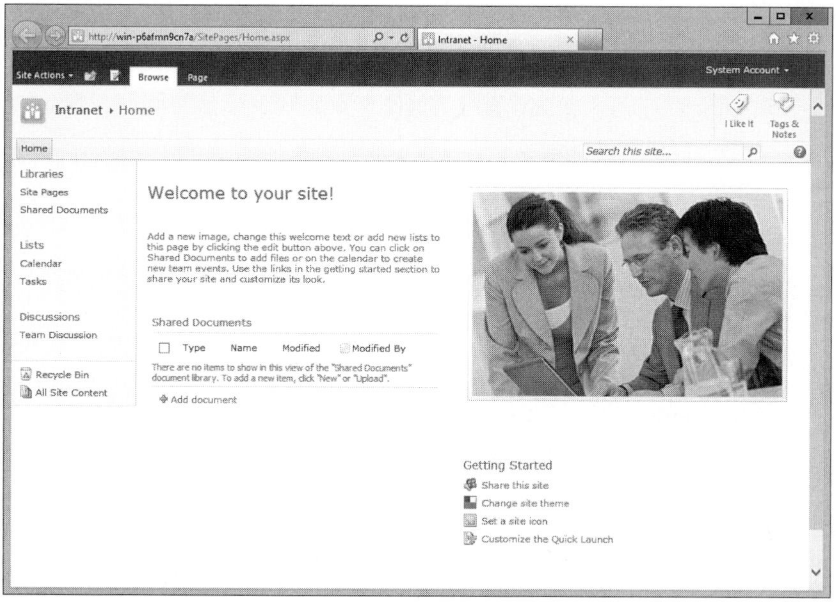

FIGURE 35.1 Default top-level site in SharePoint 2010.

The main components of this site are as follows:

- **Current user**—In the upper-right corner, the identity of the currently logged-on user is listed. Clicking this link opens a menu that gives options such as My Settings, My Profile, My Settings, Sign In as a Different User, and Sign Out.
- **I Like It**—Clicking on this icon tags the page in question so that it appears in your news feed on your My Site.
- **Tags and Notes**—Clicking this icon opens a window in which you can enter tags or keywords to help define the content being tagged as shown in Figure 35.2. The Note Board tab in this window can be used to add more detailed notes that will also appear in the Tags and Notes tab on your My Site.

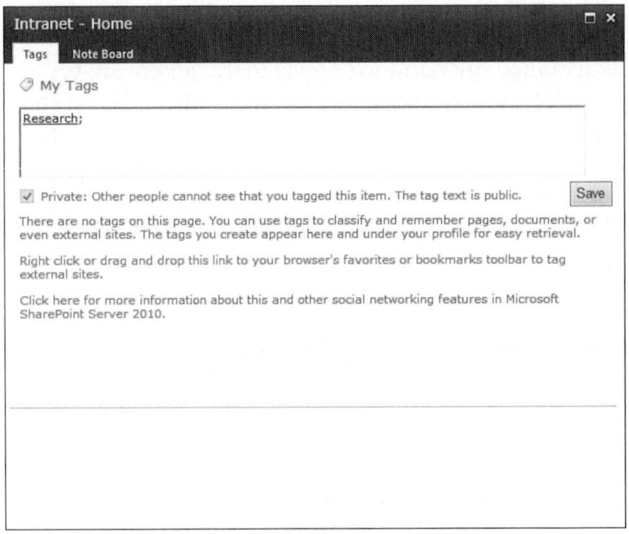
Intranet - Home
Tags
Note Board
My Tags
Research;
Private: Other people cannot see that you tagged this item. The tag text is public.
Save
There are no tags on this page. You can use tags to classify and remember pages, documents, or even external sites. The tags you create appear here and under your profile for easy retrieval.
Right click or drag and drop this link to your browser's favorites or bookmarks toolbar to tag external sites.
Click here for more information about this and other social networking features in Microsoft SharePoint Server 2010.

FIGURE 35.2 Tags & Notes window.

- **Help icon**—You can click the question mark icon to gain access to SharePoint 2010 Help and how-to information. This information is categorized into commonly accessed topics such as Getting Started with SharePoint Server, Libraries, Lists, Site and Page Creation, and other topics.
- **Search field**—The search field allows users to enter specific terms or combinations of terms, and then either press Enter or click the search icon. SharePoint indexes content stored on pages or in most standard document types uploaded to SharePoint to facilitate finding appropriate pages and documents.
- **Quick Launch area**—On the left side of the page is the Quick Launch area, which by default provides links to Libraries, Links, and Discussions as well as the Recycle Bin and View All Site Content.
- **Site actions**—The options displayed will vary based on the level of privileges the user has on the site. An administrator with Full Control privileges will see links for Edit Page, New Page, New Document Library, New Site, More Options, View All Site Content, Edit in SharePoint Designer, Site Permissions, and Site Settings.
- **Navigation, Edit icons, and Brose and Page tabs**—The Office ribbon has been incorporated as a standard component to SharePoint 2010 products, and provides quick access to different tool sets for users and administrators.
- **Web part zones**—To the right of the Quick Launch area are two web part zones that contain rich text, graphics, links, and a web part for the Shared Documents library. These web part zones can be used to customize the content that shows up on pages, as shown in Figure 35.3. where the Edit Page tool was selected from the Site Actions

drop-down menu. In Figure 35.3, the Insert tab is selected, and options such as Table, Picture, Link, Web Part, Existing List, and New List are available for insertion. The Format Text tab allows the insertion of rich text and the use of different text layout and markup styles.

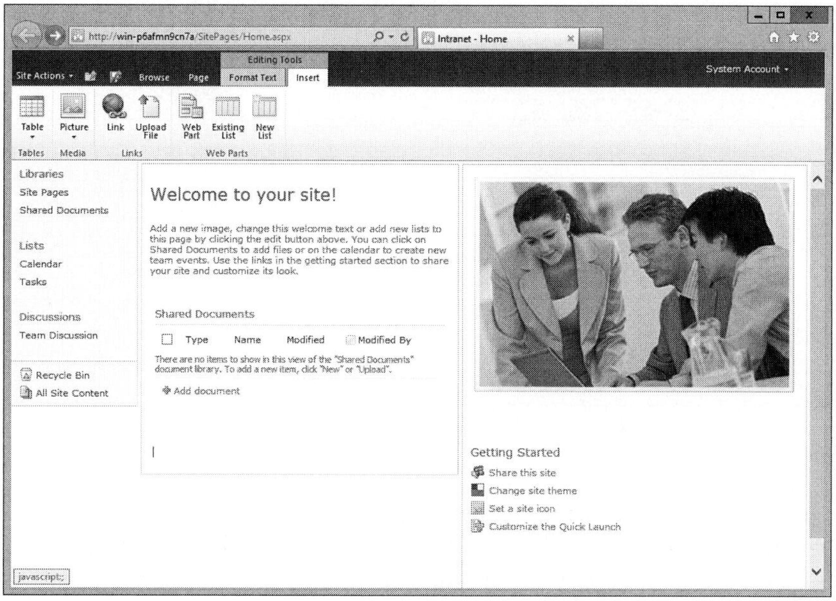

FIGURE 35.3 Editing a home page in SharePoint 2010.

When you click the View All Site Content link at the bottom of the Quick Launch area on the left side of the screen, the full contents of the current site that the logged-in user has access to will be revealed, as shown in Figure 35.4. The libraries, lists, and subsites, if any, are shown in this view. The Create button is also accessible here (assuming your account has permissions to create lists or sites), as is a button for Site Workflows. Site Workflows will show any workflows that are available for use on the site, as well as running and completed workflows.

This is a great place to check when visiting a new site to see which lists, libraries, and subsites are available for the current user to access.

As shown in Figure 35.4, the name of the list or library is shown, along with a description of the purpose and content of the list or library, how many items are stored in it, and the last modified date. With this information, it is easy to tell how active the site is, the number of documents or list items available, and the most recently modified list and libraries. Clicking the title of the list or library will open it so the contents can be viewed, and if your account has the appropriate privileges, you can add new items or modify existing.

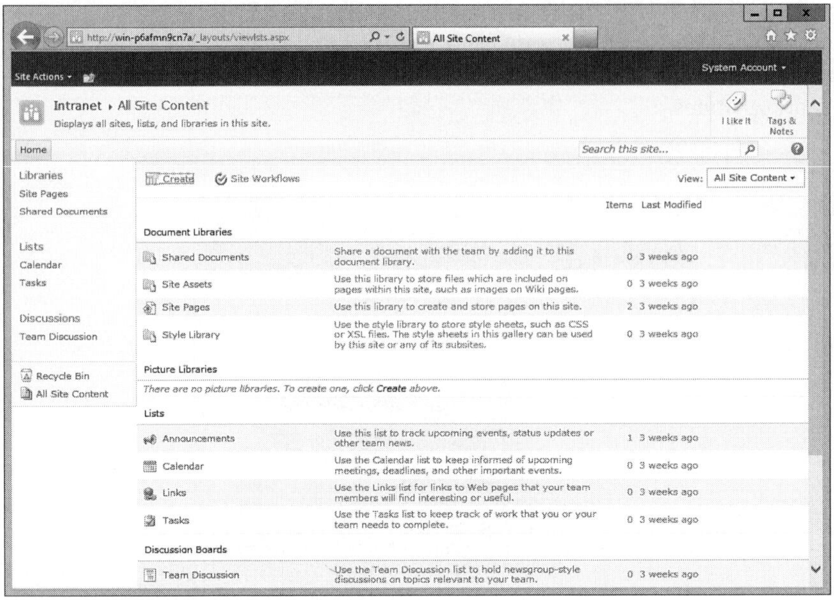

FIGURE 35.4 All Site Content page.

The Create link is provided for users with appropriate privileges on the site, and it gives access to the create.aspx page, as shown in Figure 35.5. The items that can be created are divided into the following groups: Libraries, Communications, Tracking, Custom Lists, and Pages and Sites. Note that the very last item under the Pages and Sites header is Sites and Workspaces, which allows you to pick a site or workspace template from the available templates.

Lists and Libraries in SharePoint 2010

Lists and libraries are two key components of the SharePoint 2010 environment. They allow users to manage documents by uploading them to libraries or to manage rows and columns of information in a list, which is similar to a spreadsheet in many ways. This section reviews the basic features of SharePoint 2010 document libraries and lists. As the name suggests, a document library is designed to store documents, and each document can have metadata attached to it. This metadata allows a visitor to the library to get a sense for when the document was added or modified, by whom, and to better understand the purpose or content of the document in question. A SharePoint 2010 list is essentially a "spreadsheet on steroids" and is designed to store data in much the same way as an Excel spreadsheet does. The following sections provide an overview of the capabilities of these two key components of SharePoint 2010.

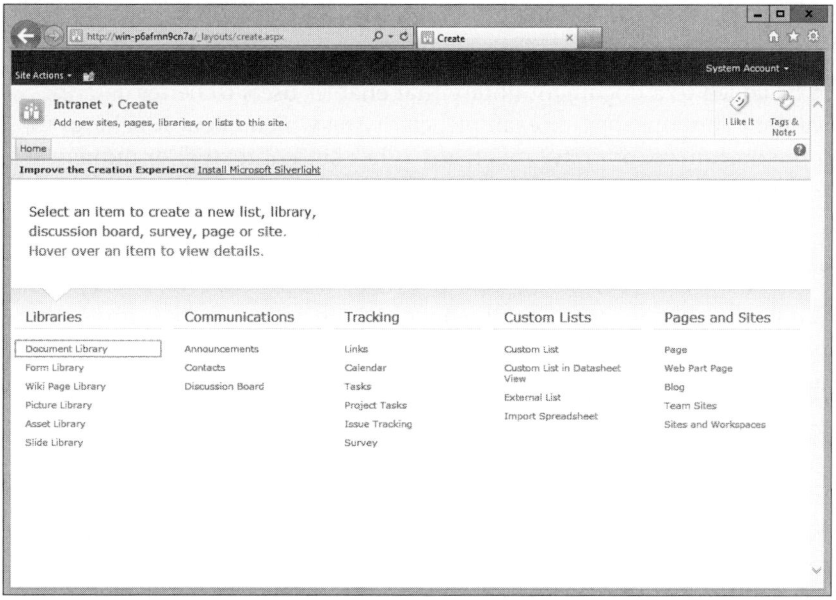

FIGURE 35.5 The Create page.

Libraries in SharePoint 2010

Many users wonder what the difference is between simply continuing to store their files in a file share on a network server, keeping them on their local hard drives to make sure they are close at hand, or emailing them to people when needed. SharePoint 2010 document libraries offer a variety of features that have proven to be useful to a wide range of users and projects and that empower the site administrators to customize the storage and collaborative features of the library and enhance user productivity. Some of the advantages provided by a SharePoint document library include the following:

- The administrator of a document library can customize who can add, modify, and delete documents in a document library, or just read them.
- Versioning can be turned on for a document library that keeps a complete copy of previous versions of the documents for reference or recovery purposes.
- Alerts can be set on a document within the library or for the entire library so the user receives an email notification if a document is modified, added, or deleted.
- Documents can be checked out, and the name of the person who has the document checked out can be listed in the library, so that other users can't modify the document and know who has it reserved.

- A template can be stored in the document library that can be used to create a new document in the library.
- Metadata can be added to a document library that enables users to better describe what the document contains, by, for example, clarifying which client it belongs to, key words in the document, or pretty much any other kind of textual or numerical information.
- Views can be created that group documents by certain criteria, sort them by any of the columns in the library, or only display documents that meet certain criteria.
- The library can be searched for text contained within the document, a feature often not available on a corporate network. In addition, the metadata associated with a document can be searched.
- If the organization decides on certain standards for the customization of a document library, it can create a template that can be used in other sites.

The following section walks through the main features of a document library. Other libraries are available, varying based on the version of SharePoint 2010 installed (SharePoint Foundation 2010 versus SharePoint 2010 Standard versus SharePoint 2010 Enterprise) as well as the site template used to create the site. Available libraries can include Form Libraries, Wiki Page Library, and Asset Library. The SharePoint administrator should familiarize herself with the full range of libraries available within the standard sites to determine which should be preconfigured for end-user use.

A Tour of a Document Library

To access a document library, a user first needs to have a level of privileges that allows access to the site that houses the library, and also have privileges to open the library. Figure 35.6 shows the default view of a document library.

Note that many of the features on this web page are similar to the home page of the site itself, including the look and feel of the home page and the Quick Launch area on the left side, but it now displays library-specific data in the main body of the page, where three documents are visible that were uploaded to this sample library. It is also important to note that the ribbon now displays a tab labeled Library Tools that includes two tabs: Documents and Library. These tabs will be reviewed in the following section, with attention paid to the most used tools and to some tools for those individuals interested in some of the more advanced features of SharePoint 2010.

In Figure 35.6, the view of the document shows the icon related to the file type of the documents, the Name of file uploaded, the Modified date (which is the date that SharePoint tracks, so in this case the time and date the file was uploaded to SharePoint), and Modified By information.

Following is an overview of several standard features offered to users of a document library from the Documents tab and the Library tab.

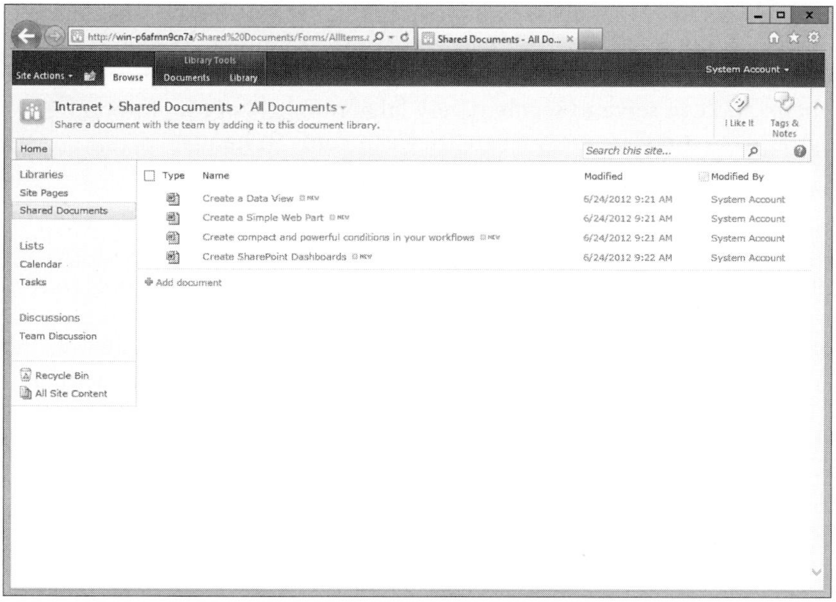

FIGURE 35.6 The default view of the document library.

Documents Tab Tools Overview

Figure 35.7 shows the Documents tab active in a SharePoint document library with an item selected by a user when the box to the left of the item was clicked. The drop-down menu is also shown which provides access to a subset of tools. This provides users with the option of selecting the item and using tools from the ribbon, or using the drop-down menu tools to access commonly used tools. An overview of the most used tools is as follows:

- **New tools**—In the New tools section of the ribbon, the New Document and Upload Document icons are provided. The New Document icon allows a user with the Add Items permission for lists and libraries to launch a template document that can be modified and saved by default back to the library or to create a new folder in the document library. Users without Add Items permissions will see the icon grayed out. The library administrator can modify or customize the template document if needed. The Upload Document icon offers the Upload Document option, and if the appropriate version of Office is installed, the Upload Multiple Documents option is provided. Only users with the Add Items permission for the library will see this menu on the toolbar. If a user chooses to Upload Multiple Documents, an interface allows multiple documents from within the same folder to be uploaded. Note that whole folders cannot be checked, nor can files from multiple folders be uploaded simultaneously. The New Folder icon allows the user to create folders within the library. A general best practice is to discourage the use of folders in

SharePoint libraries, and instead encourage the use of metadata columns, but many organizations retain the use of folders to make end users feel more "at home" in the SharePoint product. Folders within document libraries can have unique permissions assigned to them, and can serve to segment very large numbers of files into more manageable groups, so there are areas where they can come in handy.

- **Open & Checkout tools**—When one or more documents are selected, as shown in Figure 35.7, the Edit Document icon and other icons become active and usable on the Documents tab. The tools displayed differ depending on the privileges of the user in the library and the configuration of the library (in terms of what tools the administrator has configured to be active). For example, in Figure 35.7 the tools that become available once the document is checked on the Documents tab are Edit Document and Check Out. These are two key actions for end users working with a document library. Edit Document opens the appropriate Microsoft Office application and allows the user to then edit the document. The Check Out tool sets the document status to "checked out," and only that user can make changes to the document. An administrator can override a check out if needed. This ability to check out documents is a key component of a document management platform.

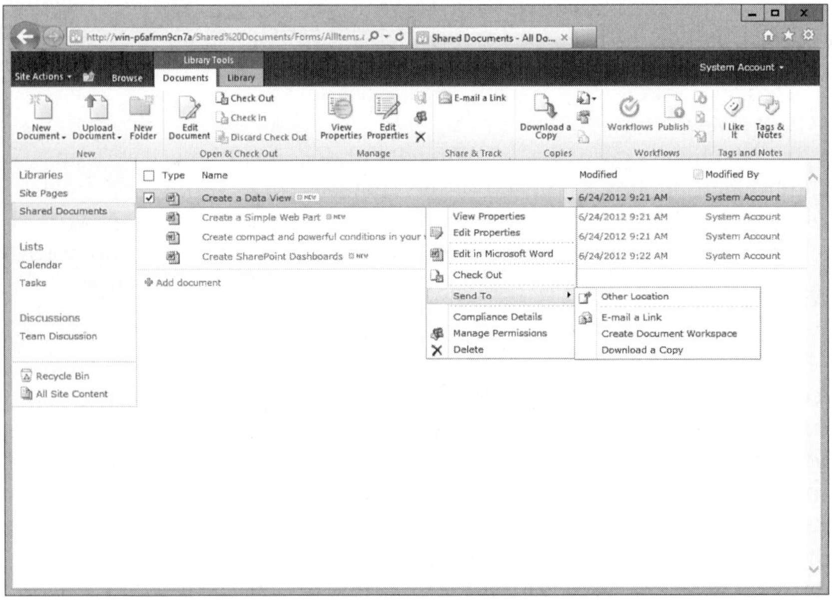

FIGURE 35.7 Documents Tab tools in a document library.

- **Manage tools**—These include the View Properties, Edit Properties, Version History, Document Permissions, and Delete icons. Properties of a document include the metadata about the item Name and Title, Created By, and Modified date and time as well as the account that performed the action.

- **Share & Track tool**—The E-mail a Link icon is provided here, enables allows the user to email a link to the specific item. This tool offers an alternative to attaching the item to an email and sending to other co-workers.
- **Copies tools**—The Download a Copy tool simply allows the user to download a copy of the document for editing purposes. This is especially useful when non-Microsoft documents (such as AutoCAD or Adobe files) are being stored in a SharePoint document library. The Send To icon allows the user to "publish" a copy of the document to another SharePoint location and keep a link to this copy, so that updates to this source document can be published to the other destination.
- **Workflows tools**—If workflows have been made available by the administrator, the end user can start a new workflow, publish or unpublish a major copy of the document, and approve or reject a document.
- **Tags and notes**—The I Like It and Tags & Notes icons allow the user to tag a document or multiple documents that are of interest or add specific descriptive terms to documents. These are key features in SharePoint 2010's "social networking" capabilities; any I Like It tags, or other tags and notes, are tracked from the user's My Site, and colleagues of that user can also see these tags and notes.

The SharePoint 2010 administrator should become familiar with these tools to ensure that training is provided to end users on the tools that are most important for them to use. It may be apparent already that there is a fairly large number of different tools and options available, which can be overwhelming to new users, especially if there aren't "tech savvy" or anxious to learn new technologies.

Compliance Details Tool Overview

Figure 35.8 shows the results on clicking Compliance Details on the drop-down menu. If a Retention Policy has been created and applies to the document, the details will be shown in this window. Likewise, if an exemption status, hold status, or record status has been applied to the document, it displays here. Because this example applies to a brand new default configuration, none of these features have been configured, but when used properly, these types of features allow SharePoint 2010 to function as an enterprise content management (ECM) system, rather than just a document repository. Note also in Figure 35.8 that there is a link to Generate Audit Log Report, which provides access to a number of reports that can be generated to display different activities on the site, including Content Modifications, Content Viewing, Deletion, Expiration and Dispositions, and Policy Modifications.

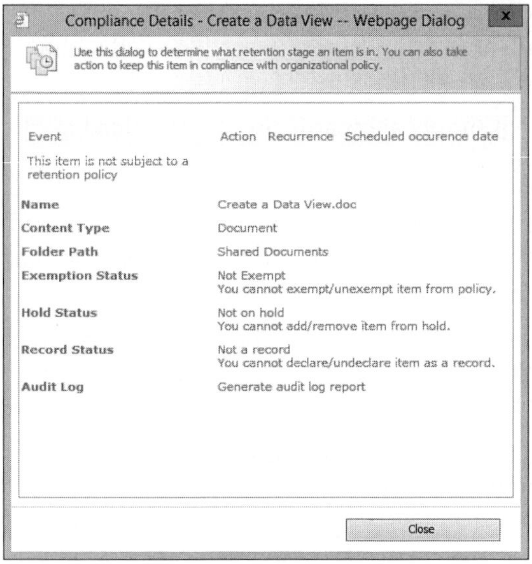

FIGURE 35.8 Compliance Details window.

Library Tab Tools Overview

As shown in Figure 35.9, the Library tab in the document library ribbon provides access to another set of tools. The tools on this tab are generally intended for administrators of the library, but a number can be used by individuals with Manage Lists permissions.

- **View Format tools**—Offers the Standard View and Datasheet View icons. It is important to note that different views for a list or library can be accessed from the Browse tab on the ribbon, by clicking the down arrow after the view name in the breadcrumb trail. The tools in the Manage Views section are used to create a modify views. The Datasheet view shows a gridlike view of the data, and is most useful when performing bulk edits in SharePoint lists.

- **Datasheet tools**—More useful in SharePoint lists than in SharePoint libraries, the New Row, Show Taskpane, Show Totals, and Refresh Data icons allow users to edit data cell by cell and perform functions such as Exporting to Excel or Access.

- **Manage Views tools**—Views are a very powerful tool in SharePoint lists and libraries and serve to differentiate these repositories from standard file share folders. Multiple views can be created to serve the needs of list and library users. Figure 35.10 shows the different types of views that can be created for a document library: Standard view, Calendar view, Datasheet view, Gantt View, and Custom view in SharePoint Designer. In a document library, the administrator may want to create a simplified view that is used in a web part on the home page to only show the document name and last modified date, and then sort the results to display the last modified document at the top. Or for a SharePoint list of products that the company produces, the administrator may create a view that groups items by category, allowing users to drill down by category to find specific items.

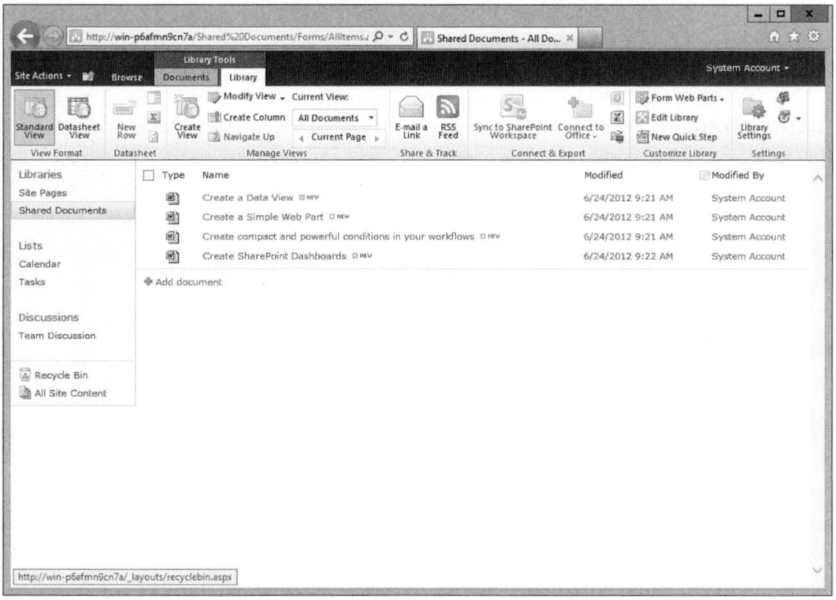

FIGURE 35.9 Library Tab tools.

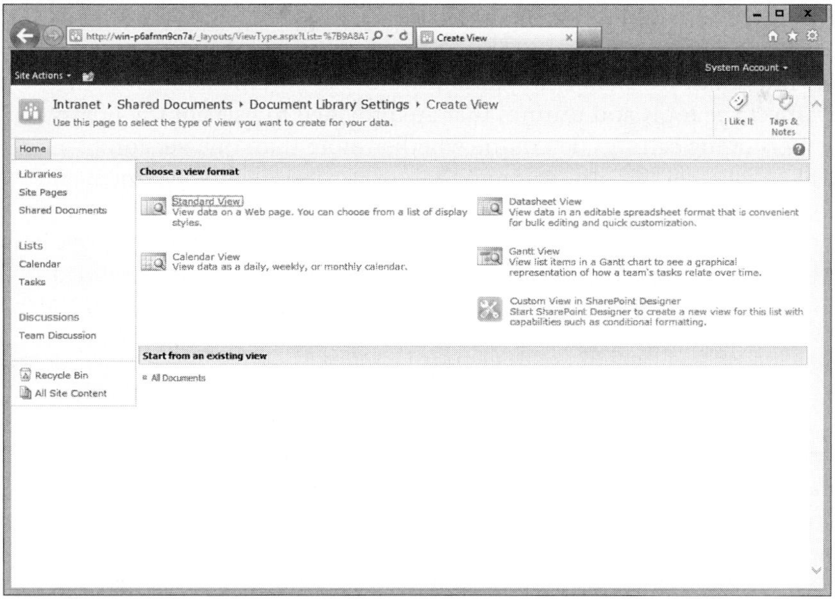

FIGURE 35.10 Create View page for a SharePoint document library.

- **Share & Track tools**—The E-mail a Link icon enables the user to send a hyperlink to the specific item, while the RSS Feed icon provides access to an RSS feed link that can be subscribed to.
- **Connect & Export tools**—These tools enable an end user to connect from different Microsoft Office applications to the content in the SharePoint list or library. For example, users can use the Sync to SharePoint Workspace icon to connect to the SharePoint Workspace application (assuming it's installed on their computer). Other Microsoft Office applications such as Outlook or Excel can be connected to, as well. These are also capabilities that differentiate SharePoint from a file share or competitive document management products. Many users see value in connecting SharePoint document libraries to an Outlook client so that they can sync documents to Outlook. Task lists and Calendars in SharePoint 2010 can also be synced to Outlook.
- **Customize Library tools**—These tools include Form Web Parts, Edit Library, and New Quick Step and allow significant modifications to be made to the library. The administrator can modify the forms that users access when entering information or properties for the list or library, the list or library itself via SharePoint Designer 2010, or create a Quick Step in SharePoint Designer 2010. These tasks should be ideally be performed by a trained developer because they can damage the capabilities of the list or library if used improperly.
- **Settings tools**—These include Library Settings, Library Permissions, and Workflow Settings. Figure 35.11 shows the Document Library Settings page, which is divided into General Settings, Permissions and Management, and Communications sections. These are also important for SharePoint administrators to become familiar with because they affect the tools and features that are provided to users of the library. For example, Versioning settings determine whether more than one version of a document will be retained, if both major and minor versions will be retained, and set limits for the number of major versions that will be retained, and for how many major versions draft versions will be retained. In addition, the administrator can determine whether documents must be checked out before they can be modified.

Summarizing the Challenges and Benefits of Document Libraries

As the previous sections summarized, many, many features and options are available in a document library. Although it takes only a few minutes to understand the basic processes of uploading and checking out documents, it can take many months of using and managing document libraries to master the more complex features (many of which, such as content types, aren't even presented in this section because of space constraints). Because document libraries are such a critical component of the SharePoint 2010 ecosystem, ample time should be given to testing them, exploring the different features, and coming up with some standards that meet the needs of the user community.

For example, an organization that has never used SharePoint 2010 before shouldn't immediately try to leverage all the advanced features of a document library, such as minor and major drafts, item-level security, RSS feeds, and complex columns (such as lookup or calculated columns). Instead, the organization should add one or two new columns to a document library that meet the needs of the user group (such as a column titled Client Name or Part Number), create a custom view, and then provide some training to the pilot users. The best ways to promote the adoption of SharePoint are to limit the complexity, add value to the users, and provide training.

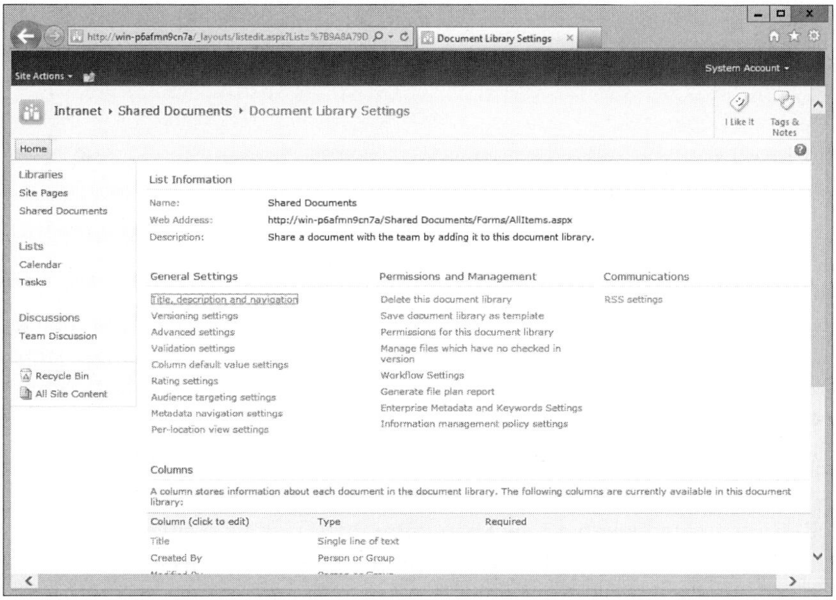

FIGURE 35.11 Settings page for a document library.

SharePoint 2010 Lists Demystified

Arguably just as important as document libraries, lists provide a huge range of tools to end users and administrators, project managers, customers, and partners. A list presents information in columns and rows, much as a spreadsheet does, and then provides special features suited to the purpose of the list. A number of people can work on a SharePoint 2010 list at the same time, facilitating collaboration much more easily than trying to share an Excel spreadsheet.

The standard lists available in SharePoint 2010 are as follows:

- Announcements list
- Contacts list
- Discussion board list
- Links list
- Calendar list

- Tasks list
- Project tasks list
- Issue tracking list
- Survey list
- Custom list
- Custom list in Datasheet view
- External list
- Import spreadsheet list

The tasks list will be reviewed to provide insight into the features and capabilities of a list.

Reviewing the Tasks List

Tasks lists are an essential management tool that facilitate day-to-day operations of a department, activities that need to be performed by a group, or specific, well-defined steps that need to take place in a project, such as a marketing, engineering, or IT project. Project managers are usually great people to involve in pilot testing of SharePoint 2010 configurations because tools such as the tasks lists are extremely helpful for managing projects of any size.

The default site collection created when a new SharePoint 2010 farm is configured will typically include a tasks list as a standard feature of the site. By default, this list does not have any items in it, so items will need to be added.

Figure 35.12 shows a New Item page for a tasks list. The fields are fairly self-explanatory, and, of course, new fields can be added if the existing fields don't provide enough granularity. The choices in drop-down menus—Priority and Status—can also be modified. The List tab provides the Connect to Outlook tool. If selected, this will ask the user if they want to Connect This SharePoint Task List to Outlook, and the tasks will then be displayed in an Outlook 2007 or 2010 tasks list. These tasks can be dragged and dropped to the user's own tasks list in Outlook 2007 or 2010. Figure 35.13 shows the results of creating a Gantt View after several items have been added to the list.

Custom Lists Provide a Blank Slate

If one of the template lists doesn't offer the right combination of elements, you can create one from scratch by selecting the Custom List or Custom List in Datasheet View option. This allows you to choose how many columns make up the list and determine what kind of data each column will contain, such as text, choices (a menu to choose from), numbers, currency, date and time, lookup (information already on the site), yes/no, person or group, hyperlink or picture, calculations based on other columns, external data or managed metadata (See Figure 35.14). With this combination of contents available and the capability to link to other data contained in the site from other lists, the range of lists that can be created can get quite complex and meet a variety of business requirements.

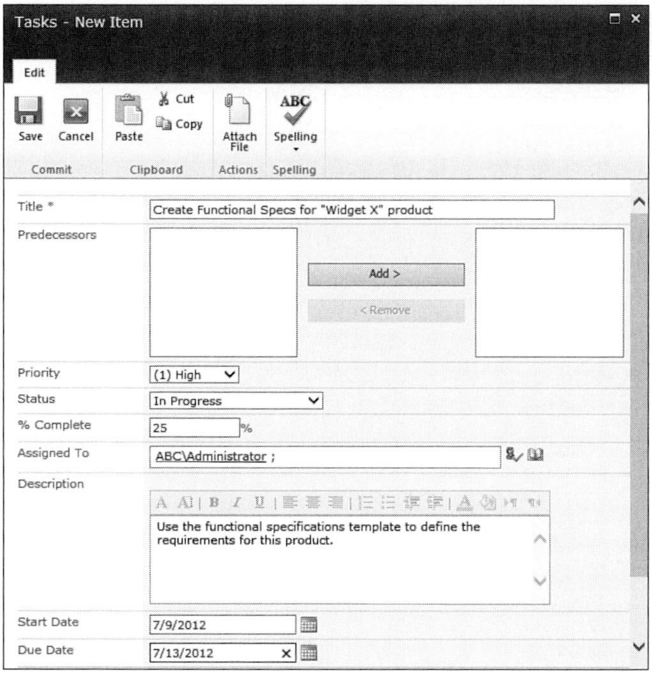

FIGURE 35.12 New Item page for a tasks list.

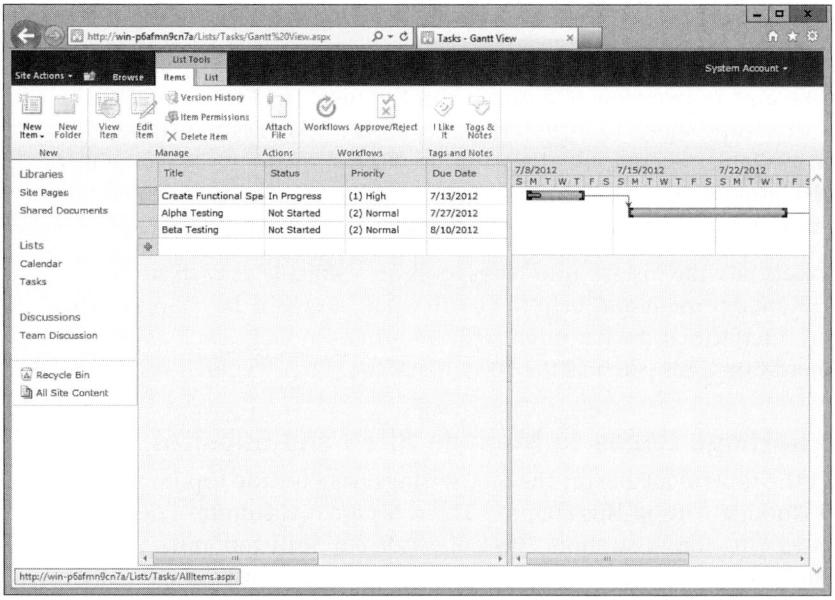

FIGURE 35.13 Gantt view of several items in a tasks list.

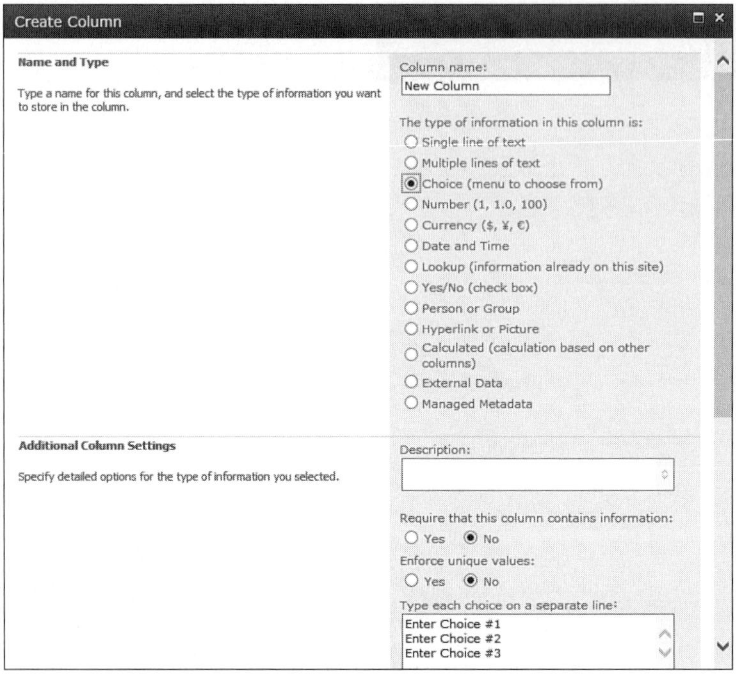

FIGURE 35.14 Creating a new column in a custom list.

Managing the Site Collection

The previous sections gave some insight into the different components of a site, including lists and libraries, and an overview of a number of the most used features of these components. This section provides an overview of the tools a SharePoint 2010 farm administrator have available. These tools allow him to control many of the elements of the SharePoint 2010 farm (which can consist of one server or a collection of servers), the collection of sites from the top-level site and subsites beneath the top-level site.

These different toolsets provide insight into what tools are available at each strata of the SharePoint 2010 environment and help to clarify what can easily be changed from within the different interfaces and what might require other products, such as SharePoint Designer or command-line tools (such as the stsadm.exe tool or PowerShell commandlets).

Using the Site Settings Pages to Manage Sites and Subsites

Figure 35.15 shows the tools available on the Site Settings page for the top-level site that we have been working with in this chapter. The tools are divided into Users and Permissions, Galleries, Site Administration, Site Collection Administration, Look and Feel, Site Actions, and Reporting Services. Once again, SharePoint 2010 presents a large number of tools that an administrator should become acquainted with before launching SharePoint for general usage.

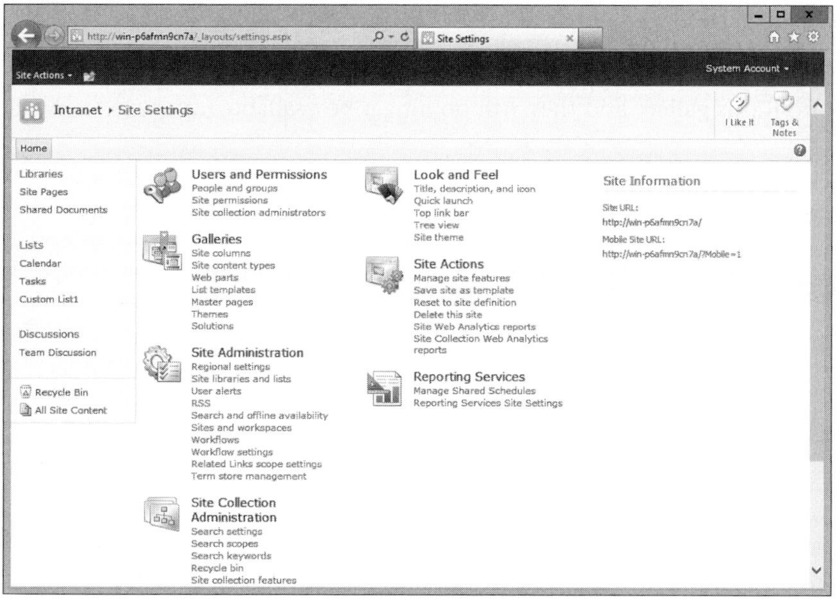

FIGURE 35.15 Site Settings page for a top-level site.

It is important to note that the tools that appear will vary based on the privileges of the account that is being used, and whether the Site Settings page was accessed from a top-level site in the site collection or from a lower-level subsite. For example, the Site Collection Administration Tools section, and the links provided in that section, is only available if the Site Settings page is accessed from the top-level site in the site collection.

The following list provides an overview of the different types of tools available for the administrator in Site Settings:

- **Users and Permissions**—The tools provide here (People and Groups, Site Permissions, and Site Collection Administrators) determine "who can do what" on the site. One of the most important decisions is which users or accounts will have site collection administration capabilities, so that should be determined during the design and configuration process. Then users or groups can be assigned to SharePoint default groups (Members, Visitors, and Owners groups) and the specific permissions granted to each group can be customized if needed. It is generally recommended to not modify the default permissions given to the Members, Visitors, and Owners groups because doing so can cause confusion later and may have unintended consequences. For example, these groups may be customized for the first site collection, but then not for the next site collection, resulting in confusion about which users are able to perform which tasks on the different site collections.
- **Galleries**—The Galleries provided (Site Columns, Site Content Types, Web Parts, List Templates, Master Pages, Themes, Solutions) allow the administrator to determine which of these items are provided to users of the site collection. For example, the

Web Parts gallery, shown in Figure 35.16, lists all the web parts available for use in the site collection. The administrator can remove web parts that he thinks might not be appropriate (for example, not appropriate for the site's proposed functionality as an intranet) from this gallery and they will no longer be available for use in that site collection.

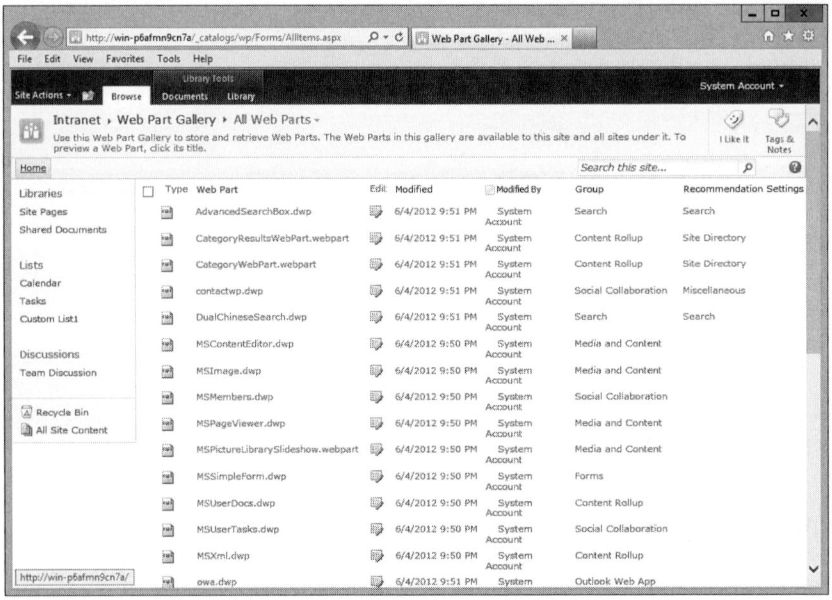

FIGURE 35.16 Web part gallery for a site collection.

- **Site Administration**—This section provides a number of tools, as shown in Figure 35.16, and provides access to a number of important settings for the current site in the site collection. These can be configured for each individual site in the site collection if needed, allowing for settings specific to the users of that site (for example, time zones). Following is a partial list of the settings that can be configured here:
  - **Regional Settings**—Time zone and calendar type.
  - **RSS**—Determines whether RSS feeds are allowed or not in the site collection.
  - **Search and Offline Availability**—Determines whether users can download items from this site to offline clients (such as SharePoint Workspace 2010).
  - **Workflow Settings**—Shows the workflows currently associated with the site collection, and allows the administrator to create new workflows for users of the site collection.
  - **Term Store Management**—Provides access to any managed metadata term stores that are available. Figure 35.17 shows an example where the administrator created a group in the Managed Metadata service application called ABC

Metadata and a term set called Subject Matter. This is a feature not available in SharePoint Foundation 2010, but is available in SharePoint 2010 Server products. The Managed Metadata feature is discussed more in the previous section titled "Not Included in SharePoint Foundation 2010, but Included in SharePoint Server 2010."

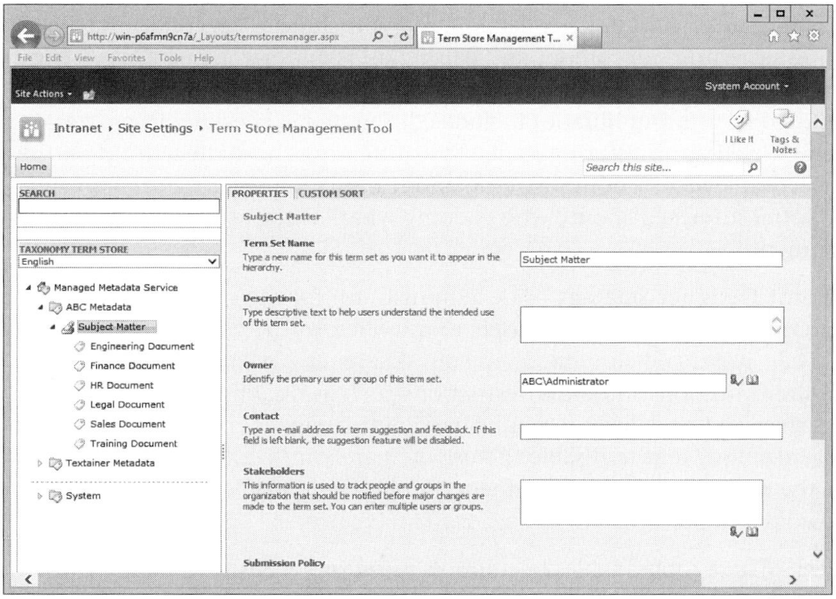

FIGURE 35.17 Term Store management tool.

- **Site Collection Administration**—This group of tools provides additional tools that apply to the entire site collection, and are only accessible from the top-level site of the site collection. Following is a partial list of the settings that can be configured here:

  - **Search Scopes**—Allows the administrator to define new search scopes the options for search scopes available in the drop-down list next to the search bar. Custom search scopes can make the search engine more user friendly if created properly. For example, a search scope could be created that is titled PDFs Only and would only show search results from documents with the .pdf extension.

  - **Recycle Bin**—The site collection Recycle Bin stores items that were deleted from the top-level site, or cleared from subsite Recycle Bins, and can be restored or emptied using this tool. This is helpful in case items were deleted accidentally from a subsite's Recycle Bin, because they can be restored at the top level.

  - **Site Collection Features**—This tool shows the SharePoint features that are installed and activated or deactivated for the site collection. A SharePoint feature is essentially an application that can provide functionality within the SharePoint user interface. For example, workflows in SharePoint 2010 are a feature, and will not be available within the site collection unless enabled in Site Collection Features. Typically, third-party software components are installed as features, as are custom applications created by software developers.

- **Site Collection Audit Settings**—SharePoint 2010 provides auditing tools that can be configured for the site collection. These include events on the site level, including searching site content and editing users and permissions, as well as at the list or library level. The events that can be audited on documents and items stored in lists and libraries include editing items, checking in or checking out items, deleting or restoring items. By configuring the audit settings on the site collection level, the administrator, and if needed, management as a whole, can be better informed about "who is doing what" within the SharePoint 2010 environment.

- **SharePoint Designer Settings**—The administrator for the site collection can also determine whether to allow users to use Microsoft SharePoint Designer 2010 to edit pages and content. SharePoint Designer 2010 use can be disabled for the site collection, and other restrictions such as disabling customizing master pages and page layouts using SharePoint Designer 2010. More conservative organizations tent to disable the use of SharePoint Designer 2010 to help ensure the stability of the environment and limit the freedom of trained and untrained developers.

- **Look and Feel**—These tools enable the administrator, or a website designer with the appropriate privileges, to customize the look and feel of the site (also typically called branding). These tools allow "safe" editing of the following: title, description and icon, Quick Launch, top link bar, tree view and site theme. They are, in fact, quite powerful, and Figure 35.18 shows the Site Theme page, where the administrator can choose a predesigned theme to apply to the site or tweak the color assigned to text or other page elements.

- **Site Actions**—These tools are specific to the site, rather than the site collection and allow the administrator to configure a number of areas specific to the site. For example, the Manage Site Features link shows the SharePoint Features that are installed and their status relative to the specific site as opposed to the SharePoint features that are applicable to the site collection as found in the Site Collection Administration section. Other Site Actions tools enable you to save the site as a site template, delete the site, or review Site Web Analytics Reports, an example of which is shown in Figure 35.19.

- **Reporting Services**—SharePoint 2010 products rely on SQL Server Reporting Services for many of the reports generated, and these tools allow the administrator to configure settings specific to report generation.

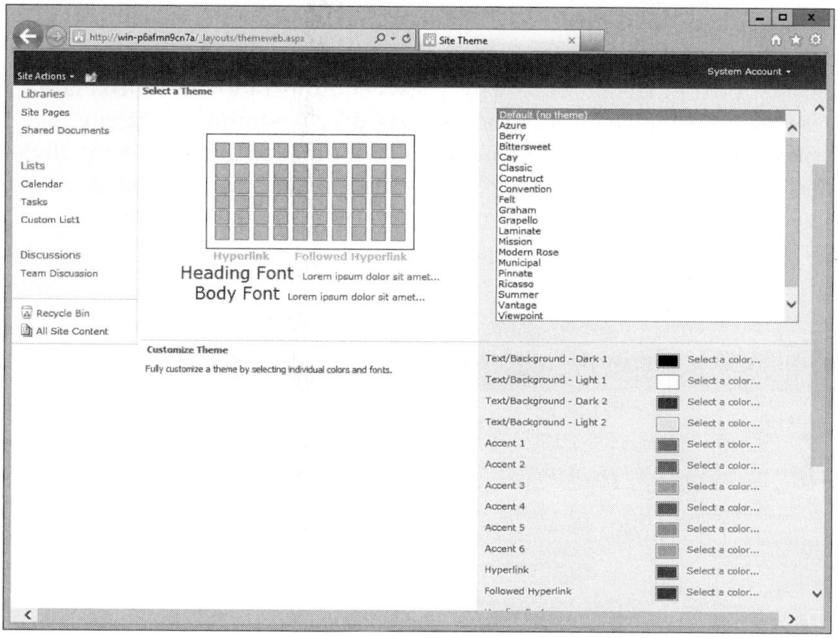

FIGURE 35.18 Site theme configuration page.

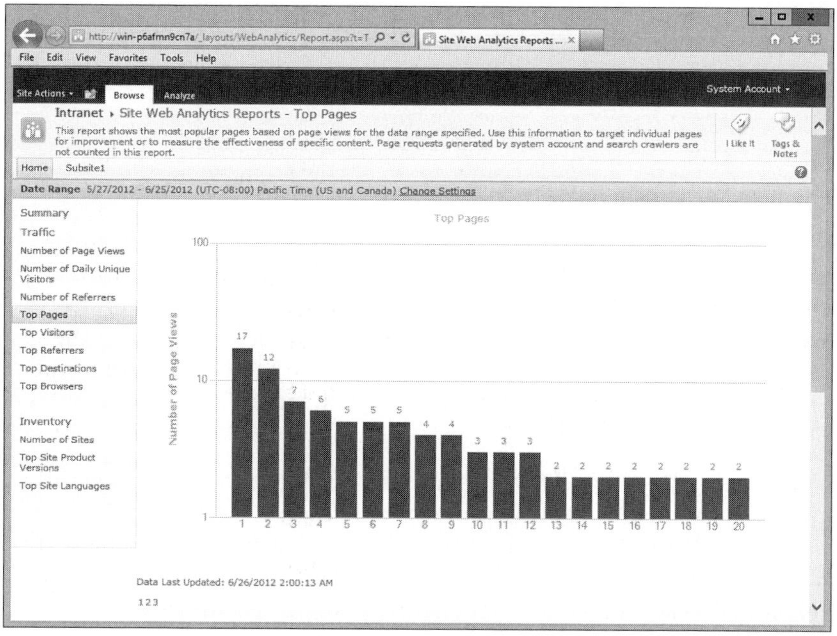

FIGURE 35.19 Sample Site Web Analytics Report.

Reviewing Central Administration Tools

SharePoint 2010 separates out key "farm administration tools" in the Central Administration site, as shown in Figure 35.20. This allows administration of central farm components to be separated completely from the tools needed to administer the site collection and subsites, allowing different strata of administrators for the SharePoint environment. For smaller environments (for example, a hundred users), this might seem to be overkill, but for larger organizations of many thousands of users, this structure becomes more advantageous.

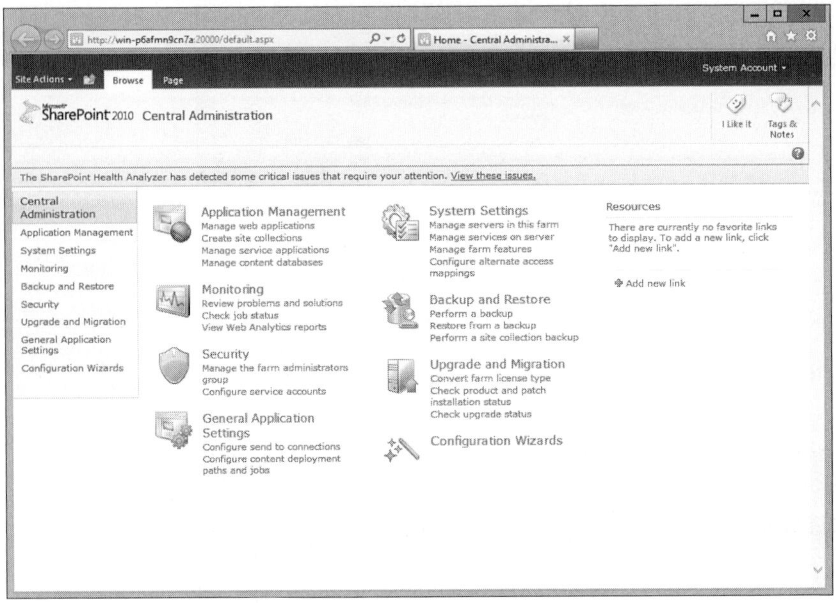

FIGURE 35.20 Central Administration home page.

The tools in Central Administration are divided into a number of sections, each with a handful of links. On this home page, only a subset of the total number of tools under each topic is shown. Clicking the topic in the Quick Launch to the left, or clicking the section header, reveals the full range of tools available under each topic. Space isn't available in this chapter to go over the capabilities of each in detail, but an overview is as follows:

- **Application Management**—This section provides access to tools that manage the primary components for the SharePoint farm: web applications, service applications, and content databases. New site collections can also be created from here. It is important to point out that SharePoint service applications can be managed individually in SharePoint 2010 as individual components. Figure 35.21 shows the Service Applications page in Central Administration. Most of these items can be managed, stopped and started, and configured individually.

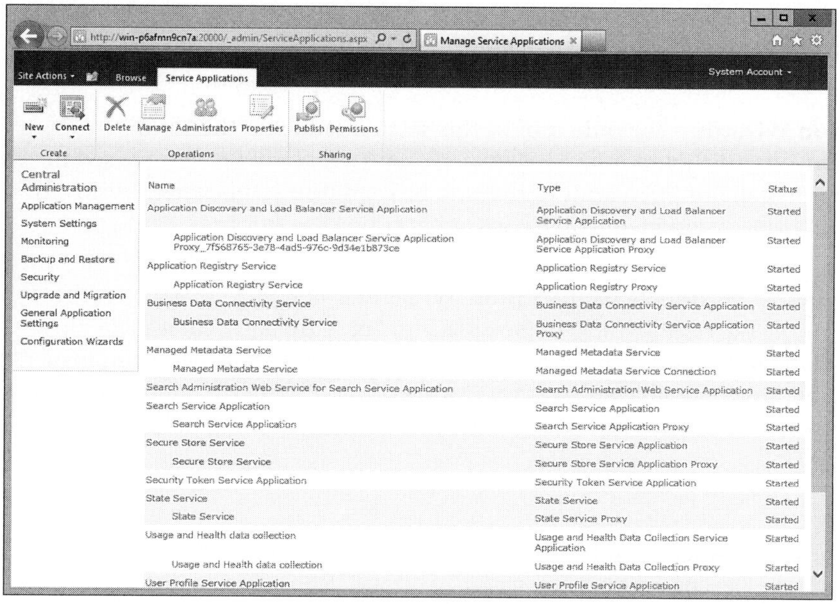

FIGURE 35.21 Service Applications page in Central Administration.

- **Monitoring**—Central Administration monitoring tools provide best-practices input on configuration errors or issues that it discovers. Access to Web Analytics Reports for specific web applications is also provided.
- **Security**—The tools in the Security section enable the administrator to determine which accounts have farm administration privileges and to configure and manage the service accounts that run the different services required to run the SharePoint farm. Additional tools not shown on the home page enable the administrator to determine the specific file types that are blocked by adding to or editing a default list.
- **General Application Settings**—Tools in this section include External Service Connections, Site Directory tools, SharePoint Designer usage control, Search tools, Reporting Services tools, and Content Deployment tools.
- **System Settings**—These tools include server management tools to manage the different servers in the farm and the services that run on each, as well as email settings (because SharePoint uses basic SMTP email tools to send alerts and receive emails to document libraries), and additional farm management tools. Some of these additional tools include managing farmwide SharePoint features and farmwide SharePoint solutions.
- **Backup and Restore**—SharePoint 2010 provide basic but functional backup and restore tools, and this section provides access to those tools. It should be noted that most organizations purchase more complete and flexible tools from third party software companies.

- **Upgrade and Migration**—These tools include tools to convert the farm license from SharePoint 2010 Standard to SharePoint 2010 Enterprise, to enable Enterprise features, check patch installation status, and review database status.
- **Configuration Wizards**—The only tool in this section launches the Farm Configuration Wizard should it be needed at a later date. Normally this is used to configure the SharePoint 2010 farm in the first place, but in some cases it needs to be revisited in some components or service applications haven't been configured.

A full mastery of these tools usually requires professional training or significant on-the-job experience with the different management tools and "moving parts" that make up a SharePoint 2010 farm. Most organizations seek professional assistance from technology service providers and professional training organizations to accelerate the process and help the organization ensure the SharePoint 2010 environment is functioning optimally.

Summary

SharePoint 2010 products range from the "free" SharePoint Foundation 2010 to the versions that need to be purchased on a per-server basis and licensed for each user: SharePoint Server 2010 Standard and SharePoint Server 2010 Enterprise. This chapter provided an overview of the history of the product line, and a number of areas in which the SharePoint 2010 product line provides valuable tools and capabilities to organizations all over the world. For example, SharePoint 2010 products provide extremely powerful and feature-rich solutions for document management and for web content management. A summary of these features was provided, which included document libraries in SharePoint 2010, task lists in SharePoint 2010, and an overview of some of the site management tools from the Site Settings page, and the farm management tools from Central Administration. The surface was really just "scratched" in each of these areas, because the SharePoint 2010 family offers such a range of tools that it requires much more than one chapter to provide a full overview.

Best Practices

The following are best practices from this chapter:

- SharePoint 2010 can run on Windows Server 2012, but the installation is complex and the supportability of the implementation and third-party add-ins should be validated. Many organizations may choose to implement the latest version of SharePoint 2013. However, some organizations will prefer to use the more tried-and-true version of SharePoint and so may choose to install SharePoint 2010 product.
- Although SharePoint 2010 products can work with the free version of SQL Server 2008, the Express edition, most organizations decide to use the full version of SQL Server 2008 or 2012 if SharePoint 2010 will be used extensively by the organization and will contain mission-critical data.

- SharePoint Foundation 2010 is well suited to lightweight use of the toolset, but it is important to understand its limitations when compared to the full SharePoint Server 2010 Standard and Enterprise products to avoid an inconvenient, and possibly expensive, upgrade in the future.
- Document libraries are building blocks of SharePoint 2010 sites and provide tools such as document versioning, check-in and checkout features, workflows, and custom views.
- Lists are similar to Excel spreadsheets in many ways, and offer capabilities such as calendaring, task management, discussion groups, and other types of functionality.
- SharePoint 2010 products offers different tiers of management tools for the administrators, including tools for managing lists and libraries, subsites, top-level sites, site collections, and the farm itself.
- It is important to understand the complexity of the product when designing a SharePoint implementation to ensure that it meets the needs of the user base without being overly complex to manage and possibly confuse the user community.

CHAPTER 36

Deploying and Using Windows Virtualization

IN THIS CHAPTER

- Understanding Microsoft's Virtualization Strategy
- Integration of Hypervisor Technology in Windows Server 2012
- Planning Your Implementation of Hyper-V
- Installing the Microsoft Hyper-V Role
- Becoming Familiar with the Hyper-V Administrative Console
- Installing a Guest Operating System Session
- Modifying Guest Session Configuration Settings
- Launching a Hyper-V Guest Session
- Using Snapshots of Guest Operating System Sessions
- Quick Migration and Live Migration

Hyper-V within Windows Server 2012 underwent a series of significant improvements, to where it now meets and exceeds the feature and function capabilities of what used to be the top virtualization technologies in the market. Hyper-V now supports 64 virtual CPUs and a terabyte of RAM per virtual machine, it has built-in host to host failover clustering, and can do site-to-site failover in an extremely efficient manner, all built on the base Windows Server 2012 operating system that network administrators know how to configure and operate. In just a few short years, Microsoft not only jumped into the virtual server marketplace, but has invested and expanded the capabilities of Hyper-V over the years, and now with Hyper-V in Windows Server 2012, has surpassed the competition in features, functions, and ease of implementation of core high availability, scalability, and disaster recovery technologies.

Understanding Microsoft's Virtualization Strategy

Server virtualization is the ability for a single system to host multiple guest operating system sessions, effectively taking advantage of the processing capabilities of a very powerful server. Just a couple years ago, most servers in datacenters were running under 5% to 10% processor utilization, meaning that there was significant excess capacity on the servers unused. By combining multiple servers running within a virtual server host operating system, organizations can now utilize more capacity of a server. Even with server virtualization, however, organizations are still only pushing their servers to 40% to 50% utilization, leaving more than half the capacity of the server unused.

The key to pushing capacity to 70% or 80% or more falls on the virtualization technology to better support redundancy, failover, capacity utilization, monitoring, and automated management. This is what Microsoft has added in Hyper-V in Windows Server 2012, along with even more enhanced monitoring and management from the System Center 2012 family of products it recently released (covered in Chapter 23, "Integrating Operations Manager 2012 with Windows Server 2012"). With the core technology improvements within Windows Server 2012 Hyper-V, organizations can safely push server utilization to higher limits, which includes the ability to built-in failover redundancy and capacity management for a more efficiently managed and maintained virtual server environment.

History of Windows Virtualization

Microsoft's position in the virtualization marketplace before the release of the last version of Windows Server (Windows Server 2008 R2) wasn't one where Microsoft particularly had a bad product. However, because Microsoft had only jumped into the server virtualization space just a couple years prior to the release of Windows 2008 R2, it was a relatively newcomer to server virtualization and so required more maturity in its product.

Acquisition of Virtual PC

Microsoft jumped into the virtualization marketplace through the acquisition of a company called Connectix in 2003. At the time of the acquisition, Virtual PC provided a virtual session of Windows on either a Windows system or on a Macintosh computer system. Virtual PC was used largely by organizations testing server software or performing demos of Windows systems on desktop and laptop systems—or in the case of Virtual PC for the Mac, the ability for a Macintosh user to run Windows on their Macintosh computer.

Microsoft later dropped the development of Virtual PC for the Mac; however, it continued to develop virtualization for Windows systems with the release of Virtual PC 2007. Virtual PC 2007 enabled users running Windows XP or Windows Vista to install, configure, and run virtual guest sessions of Windows or even non-Windows operating systems.

Microsoft Virtual Server

Virtual PC was targeted at operating under an operating system that was typically optimized for personal or individual applications, so Virtual PC did not scale for a datacenter wanting to run four, eight, or more sessions on a single system. At the time of the acquisition of Connectix, Connectix was in development of a virtual server solution that allowed for the operation of virtualization technologies on a Windows 2003 host server system.

Because a Windows Server 2003 system provided more RAM availability, supported multiple processors, and generally had more capacity and capabilities than a desktop client system, Microsoft Virtual Server provided organizations with more capabilities for server-based virtualization in a production environment.

Virtual Server 2005

Although the initial Virtual Server acquired through the Connectix acquisition provided basic server virtualization capabilities, it wasn't until Virtual Server 2005 that Microsoft had its first internally developed product. Virtual Server 2005 provided better support and integration into a Windows 2003 environment, better support for multiprocessor systems and systems with more RAM, and better integration and support with other Microsoft server products.

In just 2 years, Microsoft went from having no virtual server technologies to a second-generation virtual server product; however, even with Virtual Server 2005, Microsoft was still very far behind its competitors.

Virtual Server 2005 R2

Over the subsequent 2 years, Microsoft released two major updates to Virtual Server 2005 with the release of an R2 edition of the Virtual Server 2005 product and a service pack for the R2 edition. Virtual Server 2005 R2 Service Pack 1 provided the following capabilities:

- **Virtual Server host clustering**—This technology allowed an organization to cluster host systems to one another, thus allowing guest sessions to have higher redundancy and reliability.
- **x64 host support**—x64 host support meant that organizations had the capability to use the 64-bit version of Windows 2003 as the host operating system, thus providing better support for more memory and system capacity found in x64-bit systems. Guest operating systems, however, were still limited to x86 platforms.
- **Hardware-assisted virtualization**—New to processors released from Intel (Intel VT) and AMD (AMD-V) were processors that provided better distribution of processor resources to virtual guest sessions.
- **iSCSI support**—This technology allowed virtual guest sessions to connect to iSCSI storage systems, thus providing better storage management and storage access for the guest sessions running on a virtual server host.
- **Support for more than 16GB virtual disk sizes**—Virtual disk sizes were now able to reach 2TB in size, thus allowing organizations the ability to have guest sessions with extremely large storage capacity.

These capabilities—among other capabilities of the latest Virtual Server 2005 product—brought Microsoft a little closer to its competition in the area of server virtualization.

Hyper-V in Windows Server 2008 and Window Server 2008 R2

It really wasn't until the release of Windows Server 2008 just a few short years ago that Microsoft truly had a server virtualization offering. Microsoft knew it had to make significant investments in Hyper-V to be able to be taken seriously in the faster growing server virtualization marketplace, and with the release of Windows Server 2008 and Hyper-V, Microsoft finally had a contender. Over the subsequent 2 years, Microsoft released major updates to Hyper-V in its Windows Server 2008 R2 and Windows Server 2008 R2 SP1 updates.

Major enhancement in Hyper-V in the Windows Server 2008 family of operating systems include the following:

- **Support for 64-bit guest sessions**—This was critical, until Hyper-V, Microsoft would only support 32-bit guest sessions. By 2008, in a world where servers were 64-bit, Microsoft needed to support 64-bit guest sessions, and Hyper-V supported that capability!
- **Guest Sessions with up to 64GB memory**—With support for 64-bit server guest sessions, Microsoft had to support more than 16GB or 32GB of RAM memory, and with each subsequent release of Hyper-V, Microsoft expanded its support for more and more RAM in each guest session
- **Ability to support 4 virtual CPUs per virtual guest sessions**—With physical hardware supporting 8, 16, 32 core processors, Microsoft provided support for up to 4 virtual CPUs per virtual guest session, thus enabling scalability of the processing support within each guest session
- **Built-in Live Migration high availability**—As organizations were putting multiple server workloads onto a single physical server, if that physical server failed, an organization could lose several guest session systems simultaneously. Microsoft added Live Migration to Hyper-V in Windows Server 2008, thus enabling failover of a single guest session or multiple guest sessions from one Hyper-V host server to another Hyper-V host server with (typically) *no* interruption to the application or user's accessing the application. Live Migration enabled organizations to successfully fail over host-to-host servers and to have redundancy just in case a host server failed.

All of these capabilities finally got Microsoft into contention in the virtual server marketplace, and for small businesses and for relatively basic application workloads, Hyper-V was an excellent solution for organizations. Hyper-V was included in Windows Server licensing, it used a familiar Windows interface for administration and management, and it worked on any hardware platform that Windows Server 2008 / 2008 R2 worked on. It simply provided server virtualization without special hardware, configuration, or complexity. However, Hyper-V was still a step (or two) behind its biggest rival, VMware, in terms of core scalability, high availability, and functionality. With the release of Windows Server 2012, that now all changes as Microsoft has now met and exceeded the capabilities of VMware.

Integration of Hypervisor Technology in Windows Server 2012

To leap beyond its competition in the area of server virtualization, Microsoft had to make some significant changes to the operating system that hosted its next-generation virtual server technology. Starting with the original development of Hyper-V within Windows Server 2008, Microsoft took the opportunity to lay the foundation for the integrated server virtualization technology right within the core Windows Server operating system. The core technology, commonly known as the hypervisor, is effectively the layer within the host operating system that provides better support for guest operating systems sessions. As has been noted already in this chapter, Microsoft calls this hypervisor-based technology Hyper-V.

Prior to the inclusion of Hyper-V in Windows 2008 and Windows 2012, the virtualization "stack" sat on top of the host operating system and effectively required all guest operating systems to share system resources, such as network communications, video-processing capabilities, memory allocation, and system resources. In the event that the host operating system had a system failure of something like the host network adapter driver, all guest sessions would simultaneously fail to communicate on the network.

Technologies such as VMware ESX, Citrix XenServer, as well as Hyper-V leverage a hypervisor-based technology that allows the guest operating systems to effectively bypass the host operating system and communicate directly with system resources. In some instances, the hypervisor manages shared guest session resources, and in other cases guest sessions bypass the hypervisor and process requests directly to the hardware layer of the system. By providing better independence of systems communications, the hypervisor-supported environment provides organizations better scalability, better performance, and, ultimately, better reliability of the core virtual host environment.

Hyper-V is available right within the Windows Server 2012 Standard and Datacenter editions.

NOTE

Hyper-V in Windows Server 2012 is only supported on x64-bit systems that have hardware-assisted virtualization support. CPUs must support Intel VT or AMD-V option and Data Execution Protection (DEP). Also, these features must be enabled in the computer BIOS. Fortunately, almost all new servers purchased since late 2006 include these capabilities.

What's New in Windows Server 2012 Hyper-V

As mentioned, there are significant improvements in Hyper-V in Windows Server 2012 that finally makes Hyper-V not only a comparative contender in the server virtualiztion marketplace, but now a leader that has raised the bar on what virtual server technologies need to be and do for an organization. There are many long-awaited features and technologies built in to Hyper-V. These can be broken down into three major categories: increased host and guest session capacity, integrated high-availability technologies, and enhanced manageability.

Increased Host and Guest Session Capacity

Microsoft not only improved host and guest session capacity, it blew the roof off what it supports in terms of the amount of memory support within a virtual guest session, the number of virtual CPUs supported per guest session, among other core guest session capabilities. Table 36.1 compares Hyper-V in Windows Server 2012 with what was supported in Hyper-V in Windows Server 2008 R2 and what is supported in Microsoft's biggest competitor, VMware.

TABLE 36.1 Hyper-V Capacity Comparison

Capability	Hyper-V (Windows Server 2008 R2)	VMware ESXi 5.0 / vSphere 5.0 Enterprise Plus	Hyper-V (Windows Server 2012)
Logical processors (per host)	64	160 / 160	320
Physical memory (per host)	1TB	32GB / 2TB	4TB
Virtual CPUs per virtual guest session	4	8 / 32	64
Memory per guest session	64GB	32GB / 1TB	1TB
Active virtual guests per host	384	512 / 512	1,024
Maximum nodes in a cluster	16	NA / 32	64

Integrated High-Availability Technologies

Hyper-V in Windows Server 2012 also greatly improved high availability of Hyper-V host and guest sessions on everything from zero-downtime patching and updating of hosts and guest sessions as well as server-to-server and site-to-site failover. Specifically, the integrated technologies in Hyper-V for high availability include the following:

- **Live migration failover (no SAN required)**—Live migration is the ability to fail over a guest session from one Hyper-V host server to another without the end users connected to the guest session losing connectivity to their application. Introduced in Windows 2008 Hyper-V, Live Migration at that time required a storage-area network (SAN) as the shared storage for the guest session failover. This made Live Migration expensive and not as flexible for smaller businesses or sites of large organizations. With Hyper-V in Windows Server 2012, live migrations of guest sessions can now be done with just a basic Windows 2012 file server as the shared storage for the cluster failover. This is covered in the "Leveraging Hyper-V over SMB for Simple Guest Session Redundancy" section later in this chapter.

- **Zero downtime patching/updating**—Another challenge with server virtualization is the reliance of one host server managing several (sometimes a dozen or more) live guest sessions. When the host operating system has to be patched or updated, it required bringing down all the virtual guest sessions, or Live Migrating the guest sessions to other servers. With Windows Server 2012, Microsoft now includes Cluster Aware Updates (CAU), a feature that automatically updates a node of a cluster (like a Hyper-V cluster node) without interruption to end users by automatically failing the cluster node to another cluster node during the patching process. You can find more information about CAU in Chapter 29, "System-Level Fault Tolerance (Clustering / Network Load Balancing).

- **Integrated site-to-site replication**—As much as failover of guest sessions has been supported in Hyper-V since Windows Server 2008 Hyper-V, the ability to failover guest session between sites has not been a strength in Hyper-V. Now with Windows Server 2012 Hyper-V, Microsoft has included a technology called Hyper-V Replica that replicates virtual guest session data between sites so that in the event of a site failure, another site can come online with replicated copies of the guest session systems. You can find more about site-to-site replication in the section "Utilizing Hyper-V Replica for Site-to-Site Redundancy."

- **Built-in NIC teaming—**NIC teaming, effectively the ability to have multiple network adapters in a virtual server host system sharing network communications load, is nothing new in the industry, as hardware vendors like Hewlett-Packard, Dell, IBM have provided drivers and support for NIC teaming. The significance of NIC teaming in Windows Server 2012 is that it is now built-into the operating system. Now when network interface card (NIC) aggregation or NIC separation is configured on a Hyper-V host for performance/redundancy and a Hyper-V host server fails over to another host server, Windows Server 2012 Hyper-V understands the underlying networking operations to support the failover. No more finger pointing between vendors of drivers and functionality because the technology is now core to Windows Server 2012.

Enhanced Manageability

Core to consolidating physical servers to virtual guest sessions on a limited number of physical host servers is the ability to more easily manage and support the guest sessions. Without manageability, "server sprawl" exists, where it is so easy to spin up a server that organizations do so without realizing it. Eventually, the organization has a lot more servers than it needs, doesn't have an easy way to manage or administer the servers, and the organization spends more time managing the guest sessions than it did before with physical servers.

Key to Windows Server 2012 is its ability to more easily manage and support systems (physical and virtual). Key improvements in manageability include the following:

- **Server Manager console—**Windows Server 2012 Server Manager is a centralized server management console that enables an administrator to virtually see, organizationally group, and centrally manage systems, whether physical or virtual. By being able to see, manage, and administer groups of systems at a time, a simple configuration or a simple update can be done once to many systems simultaneously. Unlike other virtual server technologies that focus just on the ability to create more virtual guest sessions, Windows Server 2012 with Hyper-V provides not only a better way of spinning up guest sessions, but also a better way of managing the guest sessions. Server Manager and Windows systems management is covered in Chapter 18, "Windows Server 2012 Administration."
- **IP address mobility—**During a failover from one datacenter to another, one of the biggest challenges for organizations is the need to change IP addresses based on the subnet and configuration of network resources after the site failover. Windows Server 2012 enables you to make IP addresses, including Dynamic Host Configuration Protocol (DHCP)-issued addresses, portable between sites. Upon failover, address tables are automatically updated, and issued IP addresses are available in the

redundant datacenter for immediate operations with no need for IT to re-address systems in the surviving datacenter. You can find more information about IP address mobility in Chapter 11, "DHCP / IPv6 / IPAM."

- **BitLocker encryption of hosts and guests**—With virtual guest sessions spinning up virtually everywhere in an enterprise, even in small and remote sites, the need for better security of hosts and guest sessions becomes critical for the security of the enterprise. Windows Server 2012 supports BitLocker encryption of both host and guest sessions with the ability to encrypt local disk storage, encrypt failover cluster disks, and encrypt cluster shared volumes. This helps an organization better improve security of Hyper-V hosts and guests. You can find more about BitLocker encryption in Chapter 13, "Server-Level Security."

NOTE

Hyper-V provides the capability to host guest operating systems for Windows servers, client systems, and non-Windows systems, and additional tools and virtual host and guest session management can be enhanced with the use of Microsoft System Center 2012 Virtual Machine Manager (VMM).

VMM enables you to do physical-to-virtual image creation and virtual-to-virtual image copying and extends beyond just virtual guest and host management to also include the management of the "fabric" of a network. The fabric of a network includes the management of SANs, creation of virtual local-area networks (VLANs), and the automatic creation of entire two-tier and three-tier bundles of servers.

System Center 2012 is complementary to the management and administration of Hyper-V hosts. The entire System Center 2012 suite of products is covered in the Sams Publishing book *System Center 2012 Unleashed*, which addresses not only VMM for automating the process of spinning up guest session environments, but also covers Configuration Manager for patching and managing host servers and virtual guest sessions, Data Protection Manager for backing up hosts and guests, and the other components in the System Center family.

Microsoft Hyper-V Server as a Role in Windows Server 2012

Hyper-V is enabled as a server role just as Windows Server 2012 Remote Desktop Services, DNS Server, or Active Directory Domain Services are added to the server.

The installation of the Microsoft Hyper-V Server role is covered later in this chapter in the section "Installation of the Microsoft Hyper-V Server Role."

Planning Your Implementation of Hyper-V

For the organization that chooses to leverage the capabilities of Windows Server 2012 virtualization, a few moments should be spent to determine the proper size, capacity, and capabilities of the host server that would be used as the virtual server host system. Many server system applications get installed with little assessment as to resource requirements of the application itself, because most servers in a datacenter are running less than 10% server utilization, so there is plenty of excess server capacity to handle server workload capabilities.

With Hyper-V, however, because each guest session is a discretely running operating system, the installation of as few as three or four high-performance guest sessions could quickly bring a server to 60% or 70% of the server performance limits, and as much as you want host servers to be running at 60% to 80% utilization, balancing the server load and optimization utilization is key. So, the planning phase is an important step in a Hyper-V implementation.

Sizing Your Windows Server 2012 Server to Support Virtualization

The minimum requirements for server compatibility for Windows Server 2012 applies, but because server virtualization is the focus of this server system, the minimum Windows Server 2012 server requirements will not be sufficient to run Hyper-V virtualization.

In addition, although Windows Server 2012 supports up to 320 processor cores, 4TB of RAM, and 1,024 concurrently running virtual machines, the reality on the scaling of Windows virtualization comes down to the raw capabilities of network I/O that can be driven from a single host server. In many environments where a virtualized guest system has a relatively low system utilization and network traffic demand, a single host system could easily support a dozen, two dozen, or more guest sessions. In other environments where virtualized guest sessions have an extremely high system utilization, lots of disk I/O, and significant server network I/O, the organization might find that a single host server would maximize its capacity with as few as seven or eight guest sessions.

RAM for the Host Server

The rule of thumb for memory of a Windows Server 2012 server running Hyper-V is to have 2GB of RAM for the host server, plus enough memory for each guest session. Therefore, if a guest session needs to have 2GB of RAM, and there are three such guest sessions running on the host system, the host system should be configured with at least 8GB of RAM. If a guest session requires 8GB of memory and three of those systems are running on the system, the server should be configured with 24GB of memory to support the three guest sessions, plus at least 2GB of memory for the host system itself.

Processors for the Host Server

The host server itself in Windows Server 2012 virtualization has very little processor I/O requirements. In the virtualized environment, the processor demands of each guest session dictate how much processing capacity is needed for the server. If a guest session requires 2 cores to support the processing requirements of the application, and 7 guest sessions are running on the system, the server should have at least 15 cores available in the system. With quad-core processors, the system would need four physical processors. With dual-core processors, the system would need at least eight physical processors. Because Microsoft licenses Windows Server 2012 based on the number of physical processor sockets, the organization is best off getting a single quad-core system than two dual-core processors. Processor density is the balance between maximizing the most number of core processors in as few of sockets as possible.

With Windows Server 2012 virtualization, each host server can have up to 320 logical processors, so processing capacity can be distributed, either equally or as necessary to meet the performance demands of the organization. By sharing cores among several virtual machines that have low processing needs, an organization can more fully utilize their investment in hardware systems.

Disk Storage for the Host Server

A host server typically has the base Windows Server 2012 operating system running on the host system itself with additional guest sessions either sharing the same disk as the host session or the guest sessions virtual disks being stored on a SAN or some form of external storage.

Each guest session takes up at least 7GB of disk space. For guest sessions running databases or other storage-intensive configurations, the guest image can exceed 10GB, 20GB, or more. When planning disk storage for the virtual server system, plan to have enough disk space to support the host operating system files (typically about 7GB of actual files plus space for the pagefile) and then disk space available to support the guest sessions.

Running Other Services on the Hyper-V System

On a system running Hyper-V, typically an organization would not run other services on the host system, such as making the host server also a file and print server, making the host server a SharePoint server, or so on. Typically, a server running virtualization is already going to be a system that will maximize the memory, processor, and disk storage capabilities of the system. So, instead of impacting the performance of all the guest sessions by having a system-intensive application like SharePoint running on the host system, organizations choose to make servers running virtualization dedicated solely to the operation of virtualized guest sessions.

Of course, exceptions apply to this general recommendation. If a system will be used for demonstration purposes, frequently the host system is set up to run Active Directory Domain Services, DNS, DHCP, and other domain utility services. So, effectively, the host server is the Active Directory system. Then, the guest sessions are created to run things like Microsoft Exchange, SharePoint, or other applications in the guest sessions that connect back to the host for directory services.

Other organizations might choose to not make the host system the Active Directory server, but rather put the global catalog functions in yet another guest session and keep the host server dedicated to virtualization.

Planning for the Use of Snapshots on the Hyper-V System

A technology built in to Hyper-V is the concept of a snapshot. A snapshot uses the Microsoft Volume Shadow Copy Service (VSS) to make a duplicate copy of a file; however, in the case of virtualization, the file is the virtual server guest virtual disk.

The first time a snapshot is taken, the snapshot contains a compressed copy of the contents of RAM on the system along with a bitmap of the virtual disk image of the guest session. If the original guest image is 8GB in size, the snapshot will be significantly smaller in size; however, the server storage system still needs to have additional disk space to support both the original disk image, plus the amount of disk space needed for the contents of the snapshot image.

Subsequent snapshots can be taken of the same guest session. However, the way VSS works, each additional snapshot just identifies the bits that are different from the original snapshot, thus reducing the required disk space for those additional snapshots to be just the same as needed for the incremental difference from the original snapshot to the current snapshot. This difference might be just megabytes in size.

The use of snapshots in a Windows virtualization environment is covered in more detail later in this chapter in the section "Using Snapshots of Guest Operating System Sessions."

Installing the Microsoft Hyper-V Role

With the basic concepts of Windows virtualization covered so far in this chapter, and the background on sizing and planning for server capacity and storage, this section now focuses on the installation of the Microsoft Hyper-V Server role on a Windows Server 2012 system.

Installing Windows Server 2012 as the Host Operating System

The first step is to install Windows Server 2012 with Hyper-V as the host operating system. The step-by-step guidance to install the Windows operating system is covered in Chapter 3, "Installing Windows Server 2012 and Server Core." Typically, the installation of a Windows Server 2012 to run the Hyper-V role is a new clean server installation, so the "Installing a Clean Version of Windows Server 2012 Operating System" section in Chapter 3 is the section to follow to set up Windows Server 2012 for virtualization.

Running Server Manager to Add the Hyper-V Role

After the base image of Windows Server 2012 has been installed, some basic initial tasks should be completed, as noted in Chapter 3. The basic tasks are as follows:

1. Change the server name to be a name that you want the virtual server to be.
2. Configure the server to have a static IP address.
3. Join the server to an Active Directory domain (assuming the server will be part of a managed Active Directory environment with centralized administration).
4. Run Windows Update to confirm that all patches and updates have been installed and applied to the server.

After these basic tasks have been completed, the next step is to add the Hyper-V role to the server system. Do the following to add the server role to the system:

1. Make sure you are logged on to the server with local administrator or domain admin privileges.
2. Start the Server Manager console if it is not already running on the system.
3. Click Manage in the upper-right side of the console, and select Add Roles and Features, as shown in Figure 36.1.

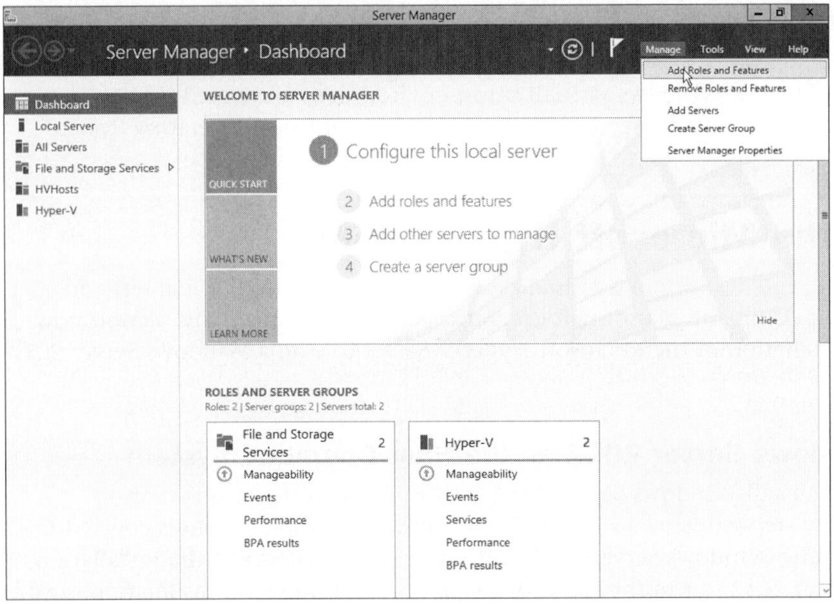

FIGURE 36.1 Adding a role to the Server Manager console.

4. After the Add Roles Wizard loads, click Next to continue past the Welcome screen.
5. On the Select installation type page, select Role-Based or Feature-Based Installation, and then Next
6. On the Select Destination Server page, chose Select a Server from the Server Pool, which should have highlighted the server you are on, and then click Next
7. On the Select Server Roles page, select the Hyper-V role, and then click Next.

NOTE

Hyper-V requires a supported version of hardware-assisted virtualization. Both Intel VT and AMD-V chipsets are supported by Hyper-V. In addition, virtualization must be enabled in the BIOS. Check your server documentation for details on how to enable this setting.

8. When prompted to Add Features that include the Remote Server Administration Tools and Hyper-V Management Tools, click Add Features, and then click Next
9. On the Select features page, just click Next, because you are not adding any new features beyond the Hyper-V role and features.
10. On the Hyper-V page, just click Next.
11. On the Create Virtual Switches page, select the LAN adapters you want to have shared with guest sessions. Click Next to continue.

NOTE

It is recommended that you reserve one network adapter for remote access to the host server. To reserve a network, do not select it to be used as a virtual network.

12. When prompted about whether you want to Allow This Server to Send and Receive Live Migrations of Virtual Machines, if you plan to use this machine for failover of guest sessions between hosts, check the check box, if not, leave it unchecked, and then click Next.

NOTE

If you choose not to select the send and receive live migration option at this time, it can be configured later from the Hyper-V Manager console (Actions, Hyper-V Settings, Live Migrations)

13. For the default stores, choose where you want the VHDX virtual server files and configuration files for the guest sessions stored by default, and then click Next.
14. On the Confirm Installation Selections page, review the selections made, and then click Install.

NOTE

On the Confirm Installation Selections page, checking the Restart the Destination Server Automatically if Required check box will reboot the server upon completion. This is usually preferred because the server will need to be rebooted; it might as well do it automatically upon completion.

15. After the server restarts, log on to the server with local administrator or domain admin privileges.
16. After logging on, the installation and configuration will continue for a few more moments. When complete, the Installation Results page will be displayed. Review the results on the page and confirm that the Windows Hyper-V role has been installed successfully. Click Close.

NOTE

The server's network configuration will change when virtual networking is installed. When network adapters are used in virtual networks, the physical network adapter becomes a Microsoft virtual switch and a new virtual network adapter will be created. By default, this virtual network adapter is shared between the host and the guest VMs.

Installing the Hyper-V Role Using PowerShell

Another option for installing the Hyper-V Server role is to using PowerShell. PowerShell is convenient in that with just a handful of line commands, a server is built, simplifying the installation process, and allowing organizations to more consistently build servers because the PowerShell installation script can be simply copy/pasted or run as a PS1 PowerShell script.

To install the Hyper-V role using PowerShell, do the following

1. From Server Manager, click the Tools option in the upper right of the console and choose Windows PowerShell to launch PowerShell.
2. In PowerShell, type **Install-WindowsFeature –Name Hyper-V –IncludeManagementTools**.

Becoming Familiar with the Hyper-V Administrative Console

After Hyper-V has been installed, the next step is to install guest images that will run on the virtual server. However, before jumping into the installation of guest images, here is a quick guide on navigating the Hyper-V administrative console and the virtual server settings available to be configured that apply to all guest sessions on the server.

Launching the Hyper-V Administrative Console

There are (at least) two ways to open the Hyper-V administrative console and access the server's configuration options. One way is to use the Server Manager console and launch the Hyper-V Manager from the Tools option, and the other option is to launch the Hyper-V Manager straight from the Administrative Tools of the host server.

NOTE

In earlier versions of Windows Server, the Server Manager provided the ability to run administrative functions from within the Server Manage console. With Windows 2012, the Server Manager allows systems to be centrally viewed and tools to be launched, but the actual administrative console for Hyper-V is the separate Hyper-V Manager tool.

To launch the Hyper-V Manager from within the Server Manager console, follow these steps:

1. Click Tools in the upper-right corner of Server Manager and choose Hyper-V Manager

2. Click the name of one of the virtual hosts, and then select one of the virtual machines listed to see details and actions available for the guest system. By default, the Hyper-V Manager will have the local virtual server system listed, as shown in Figure 36.2.

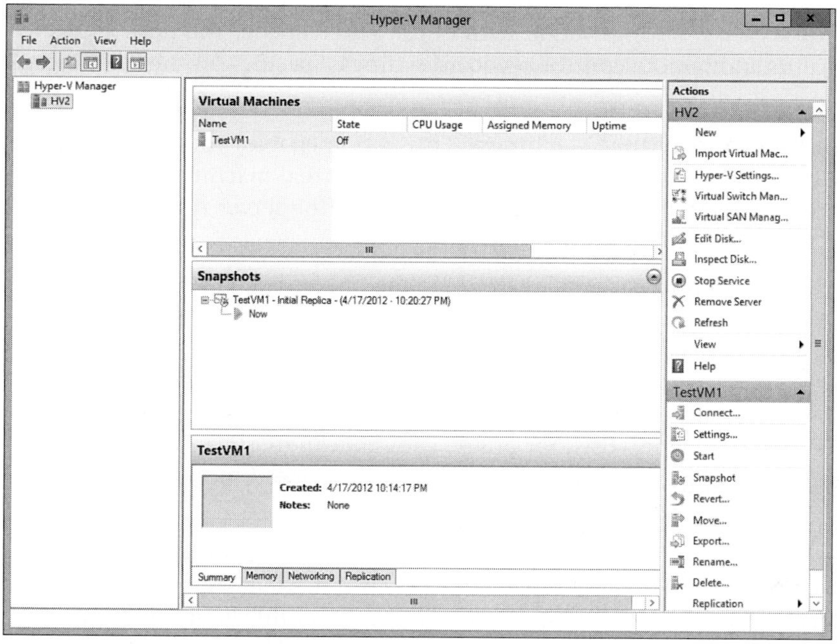

FIGURE 36.2 Hyper-V Manager.

Connecting to a Remote Hyper-V Host

If you want to administer or manage a remote Hyper-V host system, you can connect to that server using the Hyper-V Manager. To connect to a remote virtual server, follow these steps:

1. From within the Hyper-V Manager Console, click the Hyper-V Manager object in the left pane.

2. In the actions pane, click Connect to Server.

3. Select Another Computer and either enter in the name of the server and click OK, or click Browse to search Active Directory for the name of the Hyper-V server you want to remotely monitor and administer.

4. When the server appears in the Hyper-V Manager Console, click to select the server to see the actions available for administering and managing that server.

36

Navigating and Configuring Host Server Settings

Once in the Hyper-V Manager, there are host server settings you'd want to set, such as specifying where virtual guest session images are stored, networking configuration settings, and the like. When you click the virtual server system you want to administer, action settings become available. These action settings appear on the right side of the Hyper-V console.

Hyper-V Settings

When you select the Hyper-V Settings action item in the actions pane, you have access to configure default paths and remote control keyboard settings. Specifics on these settings are as follows:

- **Virtual Hard Disks and Virtual Machines**—This option enables you to set the drive path for the location where virtual hard disk files and virtual machine configuration files are stored. This might be on the local C: volume of the server system or could be stored on an external SAN or storage system.
- **Physical GPUs**—This option allows for the enabling of physical graphical processing units (GPUs) that are used for RemoteFX when the Hyper-V host server is used as a Remote Desktop Server (RDS) or for Virtual Desktop Infrastructure (VDI) guest sessions. If you are using the Hyper-V host for remote guest session access for client systems and want to improve video graphic rendering and processing, have a GPU video graphic card (frequently used for online gaming) can drastically improve the graphical experience of guest sessions connected to the Hyper-V host.
- **NUMA Spanning**—This option is enabled by default and allows for more virtual machines to run at the same time, but NUMA spanning does result in the decrease of performance of the virtual guest sessions. Non-Uniform Memory Architecture (NUMA) allocates memory per CPU in the system based on the architecture of the system motherboard. If the system motherboard has two CPU sockets each running a quad-core processor with eight memory sockets, four memory sockets are often allocated to each CPU, or effectively one memory socket per core processor. The relationship between core CPU and memory is allocated by the NUMA boundaries. Crossing the NUMA boundary by enabling NUMA spanning provides a broader distribution of guest sessions on a host system, although a slight performance degradation occurs as more guest sessions cross the NUMA boundaries during execution.
- **Live Migrations**—Enabling incoming and outgoing live migrations allows the Hyper-V host server to move guest sessions to and from other Hyper-V host servers. Live migrations are covered later in this chapter in the "Live Migrations" section.
- **Storage Migrations**—Storage migrations are the ability to move the VHDs of guest sessions from one host server to another as a method of redundancy. By default, a Hyper-V host can migrate two guest session VHDs at the same time. This number can be increased. Increasing the number impacts disk and LAN performance for other Hyper-V functions during the migration process.
- **Replication Configuration**—Enabling replication allows Hyper-V guest sessions to move between host server, typically across a wide-area network to a different

datacenter site. You can find more on Hyper-V replication in the section "Utilizing Hyper-V Replica for Site-to-site Redundancy."

- **Keyboard**—This option specifies where special Windows key combinations (for example, Alt+Tab and the Windows key) are sent. These keys can always be sent to the virtual machine, the host machine, or the virtual machine only when it is running in full screen.
- **Mouse Release Key**—By default, the key combination that releases the guest session so the administrator can gain keyboard control back to the host console is Ctrl+Alt+left arrow. The Remote Control/Release Key option allows for the selection of other key options.
- **Reset Check Boxes**—Selecting to reset this option returns Hyper-V confirmation messages and wizard pages back to default so that pages and messages are not hidden.

Virtual Switch Manager

By selecting the Virtual Switch Manager action item, you have access to configure the virtual network switches, as shown in Figure 36.3. Here is where you configure the LAN and WAN connections available for the guest sessions of the virtual server host.

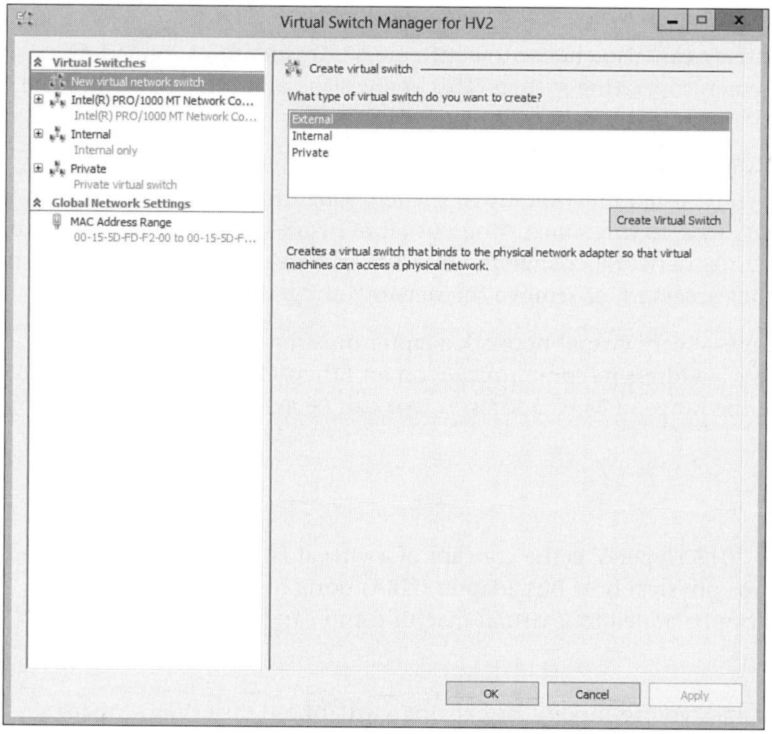

FIGURE 36.3 Virtual network switch management.

Configuration settings include the following:

- **Create Virtual Switch**—This configuration option allows for the addition of a new external, internal, or private network segment available to the guest sessions. An external network binds to the physical network so the virtual machines can access the physical network, just like any other host on the network. An internal network segment would be a connection that is solely within the virtual server system, where you might want to set up a VLAN so that the virtual server guests within a system can talk to each other and the host, but not with the physical network. A private network segment can only be used by the virtual machines that run on that host. They are completely isolated and cannot even communicate directly with the host server.

NOTE

The option to Allow Management Operating System to Share This Network Adapter in external networks (when checked) simplified communications where both network traffic from virtual guest sessions and Hyper-V management all goes across a single network adapter. However, by deselecting this option, you isolate the management operating system from communications between virtual machines and other computers on a physical network, thus improving security by separating Hyper-V management from normal Hyper-V communications traffic.

Here, the administrator can also choose to configure VLAN identification (VLAN ID) for the management operating system. This enables the administrator to tag the virtual network for a specified VLAN.

- **Virtual Switches**—If the system you are managing already has virtual networks configured, they will be listed individually in the left pane of the Virtual Network Manager dialog box. By selecting an existing virtual network switch, you can change the name of the virtual network; change the internal, private, or external connection that the network has access to; or remove the network altogether.
- **MAC Address Range**—Every virtual network adapter must have a unique Media Access Control (MAC) address to communicate on an Ethernet network. The administrator can define the range of MAC addresses that can be assigned dynamically to these adapters.

Virtual SAN Manager

New to Windows Server 2012 Hyper-V is the concept of a virtual Fibre Channel SAN. The Fibre Channel SAN groups physical host bus adapter (HBA) ports together so that virtual Fibre Channel adapters can be added to a virtual machine and can be connected to a SAN.

Edit Disk

The Edit Disk option enables you to modify an existing virtual hard disk (VHD) image. Specifically, the options are as follows:

- **Compact**—This option enables you to shrink a virtual hard disk to remove portions of the disk image file that are unused. This is commonly used when a disk image will be archived and stored and having the smallest disk image file possible is preferred.
- **Convert**—This option enables you to convert a virtual hard disk to VHD format (that support a 2TB VHD) or to VHDX (that supports up to 64TB VHDX). In addition, the VHD/VHDX can be set to a fixed size or dynamically expanding size disk
- **Expand**—This option enables you grow the size of a dynamic disk image. For example, you might have initially created the disk image to only be 8GB maximum in size, and now that you've added a lot of applications to the guest image, you are running out of space in the VHD file. By expanding the image file, you effectively have the ability to add more applications and data to the guest session without having to recreate the guest session all over again.
- **Merge**—This option allows you to merge changes stored in a differencing disk into the parent disk or another disk.
- **Shrink**—This option allows you to reduce the storage capacity of a virtual hard disk.

Inspect Disk

The Inspect Disk option in the Virtual Network Manager action item menu enables you to view the settings of an existing virtual image file. For the example shown in Figure 36.4, the disk image is currently 4MB in size, can dynamically grow up to the maximum limit of 127GB, and is located on the local hard drive in the directory C:\VMS1.

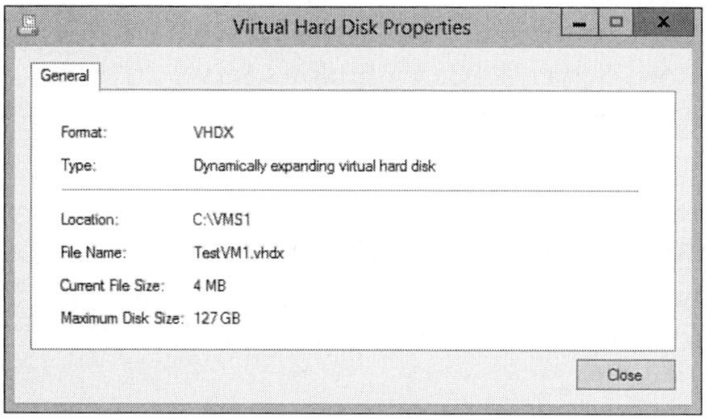

FIGURE 36.4 Virtual hard disk properties shown in the Inspect Disk option.

Stop Service

The Stop Service option in the Hyper-V Manager actions pane provides for the ability to stop the Hyper-V Virtual Machine Management on the Hyper-V host machine being managed. You might choose to stop the service if you needed to perform maintenance or begin the shutdown process of an administered system.

New Configuration Wizard

One of the options listed in the Hyper-V Manager actions pane (in fact, at the top of the Actions list) is a wizard that allows for the creation of new virtual machines, hard disks, and floppy disks. Configuration options are as follows:

- **New – Virtual Machine**—This option enables you to create a new virtual guest session. The whole purpose of running Windows virtualization is to run virtual guest sessions, and this option is the one that enables you to create new guest sessions.
- **New – Hard Disk**—This option enables you to create a new virtual hard disk (VHD/VHDX) images. When you create a new virtual machine in the first option, this includes creating a hard disk image for the operating system; however, some servers will need additional virtual hard disks. This wizard walks you through the configuration of a new virtual hard disk image.
- **New – Floppy Disk**—This option enables you to take an existing floppy disk and create a virtual floppy disk image from the physical disk. This might be used to create an image of a bootable floppy disk that would later be used in configuring or managing a guest image, or used to create a floppy disk image of a disk that has drivers or utilities on it that will be used in a virtual guest session.

Installing a Guest Operating System Session

One of the key tasks noted in the previous section is to begin the installation of a new guest operating system session. The guest operating system installation is wizard driven and enables the administrator to configure settings for the guest session, and to begin the installation of the guest operating system software itself. A guest session could be a server-based session running something like Windows Server 2008 or Windows Server 2012, a client-based session running Windows 8 or Windows 7, or a guest session running a non-Windows operating system.

Gathering the Components Needed for a Guest Session

When creating a guest operating system, the administrator needs to make sure they have all the components needed to begin the installation. The components needed are as follows:

- **Operating system media**—A copy of the operating system installation media is required for the installation of the guest image. The media could be either a DVD or an ISO image of the media disc itself.
- **License key**—During the installation of the operating system software, if you are normally prompted to enter in the license key for the operating system, you should have a copy of the license key available.

Other things you should do before starting to install a guest operating system on the virtual server system include the following:

- **Guest session configuration settings**—You will be prompted to answer several core guest session configuration setting options, such as how much RAM you want to allocate for the guest session, how much disk space you want to allocate for the guest image, and so on. Either jump ahead to the next section, "Beginning the Installation of the Guest Session," so that you can gather up the information you'll need to answer the questions you'll be asked, or be prepared to answer the questions during the installation process.
- **Host server readiness**—If you will be preplanning the answers to the questions that you'll be asked, make sure that the host system has enough RAM, disk space, and so on to support the addition of your guest session to the virtual server system. If your requirements exceed the physical capacity of the server, stop and add more resources (memory, disk space, and so on) to the server before beginning the installation of the guest operating system.

Beginning the Installation of the Guest Session

After you are ready to begin the installation of the guest operating system, launch the guest operating system Installation Wizard as follows:

1. From the actions pane, choose New, Virtual Machine. The New Virtual Machine Wizard will launch.
2. Click Next to continue past the initial Before You Begin screen.
3. Give your virtual machine a name that will be descriptive of the virtual guest session you are creating, such as **AD Global Catalog Server**, or **Exchange 2010 Client Access Server 1**, or **SharePoint Frontend**.
4. If you had set the default virtual machine folder location where guest images are stored, the new image for this virtual machine will be placed in a subfolder of that default folder. However, if you need to select a different location where the image files should be stored, click Store the Virtual Machine in a Different Location, and select Browse to choose an existing disk directory or to create a new directory where the image file for this guest session should be stored. Click Next to continue.
5. Enter in the amount of RAM you want to be allocated to this guest image (in megabytes), and then click Next.

NOTE

When assigning memory, you can chose the option Use Dynamic Memory for This Virtual Machine, which is a good option to choose in optimizing the memory in a server. Instead of randomly picking (typically more) memory than is needed for a guest session that may not be fully utilized, choosing dynamic memory allows you to configure a range of memory. If the additional memory is not needed, the guest session "gives back" the unused memory for other guest sessions to use.

6. Choose the network segment to which you want this guest image to be initially connected. This would be an external, internal, or private network segment created in the section "Virtual Switch Manager" earlier in this chapter. Click Next.

NOTE

You can also choose Not Connected during this virtual machine creation process and change the network segment option at a later date.

7. The next option, shown in Figure 36.5, enables you to create a new virtual hard disk or use an existing virtual hard disk for the guest image file. Creating a new virtual hard disk creates a VHDX disk image in the directory you choose. By default, a dynamic virtual disk image size setting is set to 127GB. The actual file itself will only be the size of the data in the image (potentially 4GB or 8GB to start, depending on the operating system) and will dynamically grow up to the size indicated in this setting. Alternately, you can choose an existing hard disk image you might have already created (including an older image you might have created in Windows Server 2008 Hyper-V), or you can choose to select a hard disk image later. Click Next to continue.

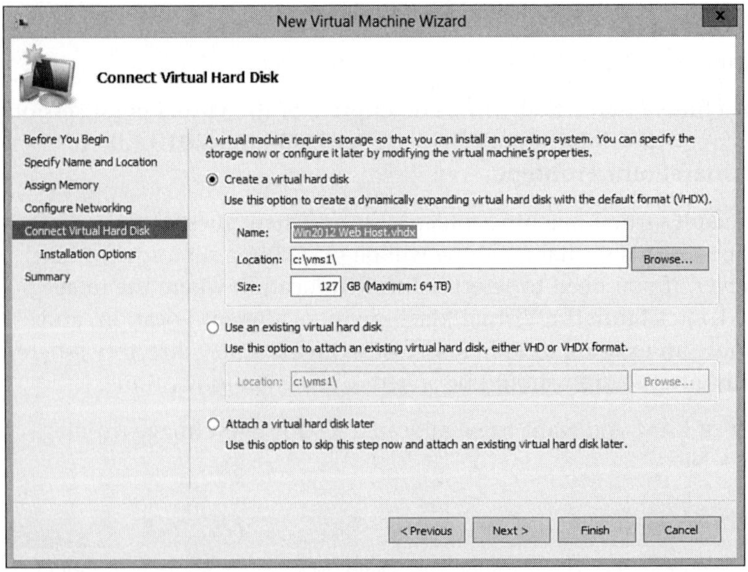

FIGURE 36.5 Connect virtual hard disk.

NOTE

Dynamic VHD performance in Windows Server 2012 has been greatly enhanced, essentially equaling that of fixed disks. This means you can now seriously consider using dynamic disks instead of fixed disks in production environments.

8. The next option, shown in Figure 36.6, allows for the installation of an operating system on the disk image you created in the previous step. You can choose to install an operating system at a later time, install an operating system from a bootable CD/DVD or ISO image file, install an operating system from a boot floppy disk image, or install an operating system from a network-based installation server (such as Windows Deployment Services). Typically, operating system source discs are on either a physical disc or ISO image file, and choosing a CD or DVD or an associated ISO image file will allow for the operating system to be installed on the guest image. Select your option, and then click Next to continue.

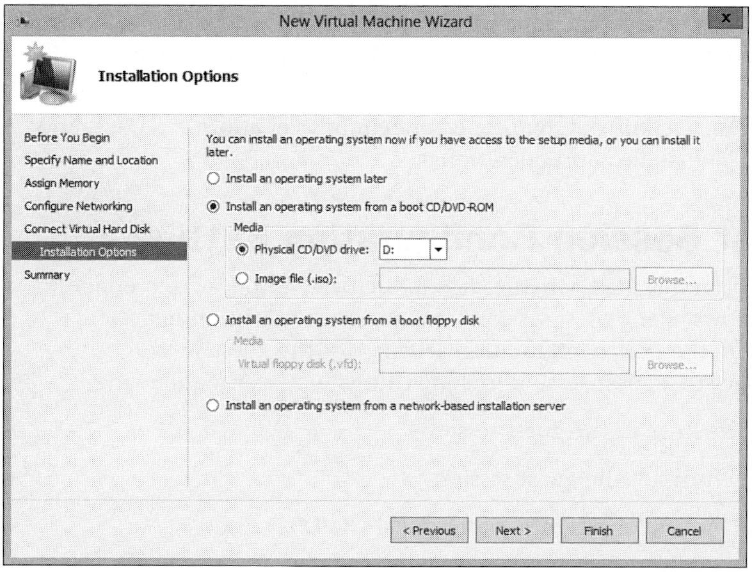

FIGURE 36.6 Selecting the operating system installation options.

9. Review the summary of the options you have selected and click Finish if the settings you've chosen are fine, or click Previous to go back and make changes. Click Finish to create the new virtual machine.

Completing the Installation of the Guest Session

When the new virtual machine is started, the guest operating system installation will proceed to install just like the process of installing the operating system on a physical system. Typically, at the end of an operating system installation, the guest session will restart and bring the session to a logon prompt. Log on to the guest operating system and configure the guest operating system as you would any other server system. This usually has you do things such as the following:

36

1. Change the system name to a name that you want the virtual server to be. For many versions of operating systems, you will be prompted to enter the name of the system during the installation process.
2. Configure the guest session with an appropriate IP address. This might be DHCP issued; however, if you are building a server system, a static IP address is typically recommended.
3. Join the system to an Active Directory domain (assuming the system will be part of a managed Active Directory Domain Services environment with centralized administration).
4. Download and apply the latest patches and updates on the guest session to confirm that all patches and updates have been installed and applied to the system.

The installation of the guest operating system typically requires yet another reboot, and the operating system will be installed and operational.

Modifying Guest Session Configuration Settings

After a guest session has been installed, whether it is a Microsoft Windows server guest session, a Microsoft Windows client guest session, or a guest session running a non-Windows operating system, the host configuration settings for the guest session can be changed. Common changes to a guest session include things such as the following:

- Adding or limiting the RAM of the guest session
- Changing network settings of the guest session
- Mounting a CD/DVD image or mounting a physical CD/DVD disc

Adding or Limiting the RAM of the Guest Session

A common configuration change that is made of a guest session is to increase or decrease the amount of memory allocated to the guest session. The default memory allocated to the system frequently is fine for a basic system configuration; however, with the addition of applications to the guest session, there might be a need to increase the memory. As long as the host server system has enough memory to allocate additional memory to the guest session, adding memory to a guest session is a very simple task.

To add memory to the guest session, follow these steps:

1. From the Hyper-V Manager, click to select the guest session for which you want to change the allocated memory.
2. Right-click the guest session name, and choose Settings.
3. Click Memory and enter in the amount of RAM you want allocated for this guest session (in megabytes).
4. Click OK when you are finished.

NOTE

You cannot change the allocated RAM on a running virtual guest session. The guest session must be shut down first, memory reallocated to the image, and then the guest image booted for the new memory allocation to take effect.

Changing Network Settings for the Guest Session

Another common configuration change made to a guest session is to change the network setting for the guest session. An administrator of a virtual server might choose to have each guest session connected directly to the network backbone with an external network, just as if the guest session had a network adapter connected to the backbone, or the network administrator might choose to set up an isolated (internal or private) network just for the guest sessions. The configuration of the internal, private, and external network segments that the administrator can configure the guest sessions to connect to is covered earlier in this chapter in the section "Virtual Switch Manager."

The common configuration methods of the virtual network configurations can be broken down into two groups, as follows:

- **Direct addressing**—The guest sessions can connect directly to the backbone of the network to which the virtual server host system is attached. In this instance, an administrator would configure an external connection in the Virtual Switch Manager and have an IP address on that external segment.
- **Isolated network**—If the administrator wants to keep the guest sessions isolated off of the network backbone, the administrator can set up either an internal or private connection in the Virtual Switch Manager and the guest sessions would have an IP address of a segment common to the other guest sessions on the host system. In this case, the virtual server acts as a network switch connecting the guest sessions together.

NOTE

To connect the internal network segment with the external network segment, a guest session can be configured as a router or gateway between the internal network and external network. This router system would have two virtual network adapters, one for each network.

To change the connected network used by a guest session adapter, follow these steps:

1. From the Hyper-V Manager console, click to select the guest session for which you want to change the network configuration.
2. Right-click the guest session name, and choose Settings.
3. Click the network adapter that requires reconfiguration. From the list in the Network field, select the desired network.
4. Click OK when you are finished.

Mounting a Physical CD/DVD Image or Mounting a CD/DVD Image File

When installing software on a guest session of a virtual server system, the administrator would either insert a CD or DVD into the drive of the physical server and access the disc from the guest session, or mount an ISO image file of the disc media.

To access a physical CD or DVD disc or to mount an image of a CD or DVD, follow these steps:

1. From the Hyper-V Manager console, click to select the guest session for which you want to provide access to the CD or DVD.
2. Right-click the guest session name, and choose Settings.
3. Click DVD Drive and choose Physical CD/DVD Drive if you want to mount a disc in the physical drive of the host system, or click Image File and browse for the ISO image file you want to mount as a disc image.
4. Click OK when you are finished.

Other Settings to Modify for a Guest Session Configuration

You can also change other settings for a guest session. These options can be modified by going into the Settings option of the guest session and making changes. These other settings include the following:

- **BIOS**—This setting allows for the selection of boot order on the guest machine to boot in an order that can include floppy, CD, IDE (disk), or network boot.
- **Processor**—Hyper-V provides the ability to allocate core processors to the guest image, so a guest image can have up to 32 virtual CPUs allocated for each session. In addition, resource control can be weighted between guest sessions by allocating system resource priority to key guest server sessions versus other guest sessions.

NOTE

Windows Server 2012 provides a processor compatibility check box to limit processor functionality for virtual machines that will be live migrated between dissimilar hosts. Live migration is discussed later in this chapter.

- **IDE Controller**—The guest session initially has a single virtual hard drive associated with it. Additional virtual hard drives can be added to a virtual guest session.
- **SCSI Controller**—A virtual SCSI controller can be associated with a virtual guest session as well providing different drive configuration options for the different drive configurations.
- **COM Ports**—Virtual communication ports such as COM1 or COM2 can be associated with specific named pipes for input and output of information.

Launching a Hyper-V Guest Session

After a Hyper-V guest session has been created, and the settings have been properly modified to meet the expected needs of the organization, the virtual guest session can now be launched and run. Decisions need to be made whether you want the guest session to automatically launch as soon as the host server is booted, or whether you want to manually launch a guest session. In addition, a decision needs to be made on the sequence in which guest sessions should be launched so that systems that are prerequisites to other sessions come up first. For example, you'd want a global catalog server session and DHCP server session to come up before an application server that logs on and authenticates to Active Directory comes online and needs to authenticate to Active Directory before the server service begins.

Automatically Launching a Guest Session

One option for launching and loading guest sessions is to have the guest session boot right after the physical host server completes the boot cycle. This is typically the preferred option if a guest session is core to the network infrastructure of a network (such as a domain controller or host server system) so that in the event of a physical server reboot, the virtual guest sessions boot up automatically as well. It would not be convenient to have to manually boot each virtual server session every time the physical server is rebooted.

The option for setting the startup option for a virtual session is in the configuration settings for each guest session.

To change the startup action, follow these steps:

1. From the Hyper-V Manager console, right-click the virtual machine for which you want to change the setup option, and select Settings.
2. In the Management section of the settings, click Automatic Start Action.
3. You are provided with three options, as shown in Figure 36.7, of what to do with this virtual guest session upon startup of the physical host server. Either click Nothing (which would require a manual boot of the guest session), click Automatically Start If It Was Running When the Service Stopped, or click Always Start This Virtual Machine Automatically. To set the virtual session to automatically start after the physical server comes up, choose the Always Start This Virtual Machine Automatically option.
4. Also on this setting is the ability to have an automatic start delay. This enables you to sequence the startup of virtual machines by having some VMs take longer to automatically start than others. If a server requires another system to start before it is started (such as an Exchange server requires a domain controller to start and be available before the Exchange server comes online), then delaying the start for that Exchange server guest session will improve the success of that Exchange server of starting as expected. Click OK to save these settings.

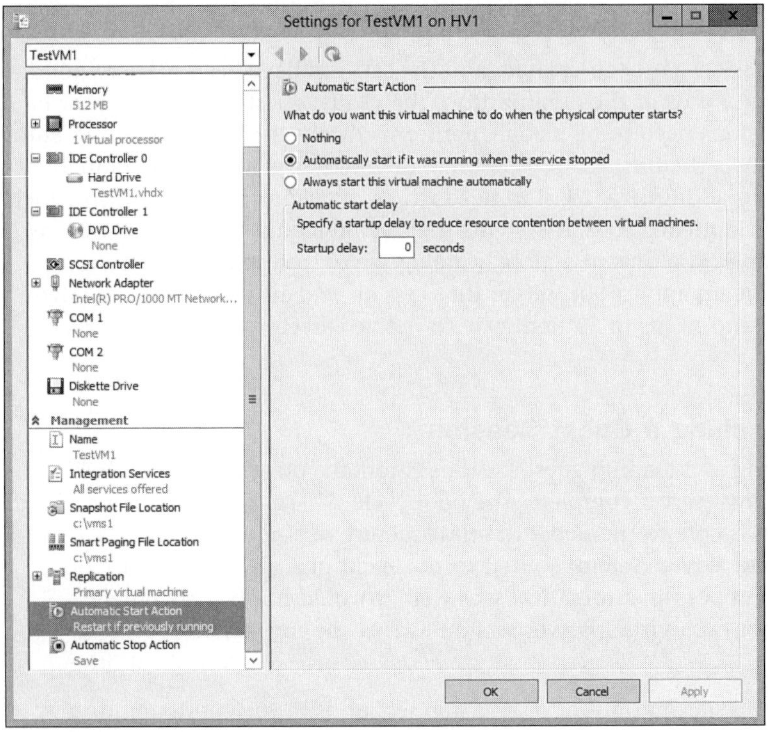

FIGURE 36.7 Automatic start actions.

Manually Launching a Guest Session

Another option for guest session startup is to not have a guest session automatically start after a physical server boots up. This is typically the preferred option if a guest session will be part of a demonstration or test server where the administrator of the system wants to control which guest sessions are automatically launched, and which sessions need to be manually launched. It would not be convenient to have a series of demo or test sessions automatically boot up every time the system is booted. The administrator of the system would typically want to choose to start these guest sessions.

To set the startup action to manually launch a guest session, follow these steps:

1. From the Hyper-V Manager console, right-click the virtual machine for which you want to change the setup option, and select Settings.

2. In the Management section of the settings, click Automatic Start Action.

3. When provided the three options of what to do with this virtual guest session upon startup of the physical server, either click Nothing (which would require a manual boot of the guest session), click Automatically Start If It Was Running when the Service Stopped, or click Always Start This Virtual Machine Automatically. Choose the Nothing option, and the session will need to be manually started.

Save State of a Guest Session

In Windows Server 2012 Hyper-V, there are two ways to save guest images: snapshots and a saved state. At any time, an administrator can right-click a guest session and choose Save. This Save function is similar to a Hibernate mode on a desktop client system. It saves the image state into a file with the option of bringing the saved state image file back to the state the image was in prior to being saved.

Using Snapshots of Guest Operating System Sessions

A highly versatile function in Windows Server 2012 Hyper-V is the option to create a snapshot of a guest session. A snapshot in Windows Hyper-V uses Microsoft Volume Shadow Copy Service (VSS) technology that captures an image of a file on a server; in this case, the file is the VHD image of the virtual server itself. At any point in time in the future, the snapshot can be used for recovery.

Snapshots for Image Rollback

One common use of a guest image snapshot is to roll back an image to a previous state. This is frequently done with guest images used for demonstration purposes, or test labs where a scenario is tested to see the results and compared with identical tests of other scenarios, or for the purpose of preparing for a software upgrade or migration.

In the case of a guest image used for demonstration purposes, a user might run through a demo of a software program where they add information, delete information, make software changes, or otherwise modify information in the software on the guest image. Rather than having to go back and delete the changes, or rebuilding the image from scratch to do the demo again, with a snapshot, the user can simply roll the image back to the snapshot that was available before the changes were made to the image.

Image rollback has been successfully used for training purposes where an employee runs through a process, then rolls back the image so they can run through the same process all over again repeating the process on the same base image but without previous installations or configurations.

In network infrastructures, a snapshot is helpful when an organization applies a patch or update to a server, or a software upgrade is performed and problems occur; the administrator can simply roll back the image to the point prior to the start of the upgrade or migration.

Snapshots for Guest Session Server Fault Tolerance

Snapshots are commonly used in business environments for the purpose of fault tolerance or disaster recovery. A well-timed snapshot right before a system failure can help an organization roll back their server to the point right before the server failed or problem occurred. Instead of waiting hours to restore a server from tape, the activation of a snapshot image is nothing more than choosing the snapshot and selecting to start the guest image. When the guest image starts up, it is in the state that the image was at the time the snapshot was created.

Creating a Snapshot of a Guest Image

Snapshots are very easy to create. To create a snapshot, follow these steps:

1. From the Hyper-V Manager console, click to select the guest session for which you want to create a snapshot.
2. Right-click the guest session name, and choose Snapshot. A snapshot of the image will immediately be taken of the guest image and the snapshot will show up in the Snapshots pane, as shown in Figure 36.8.

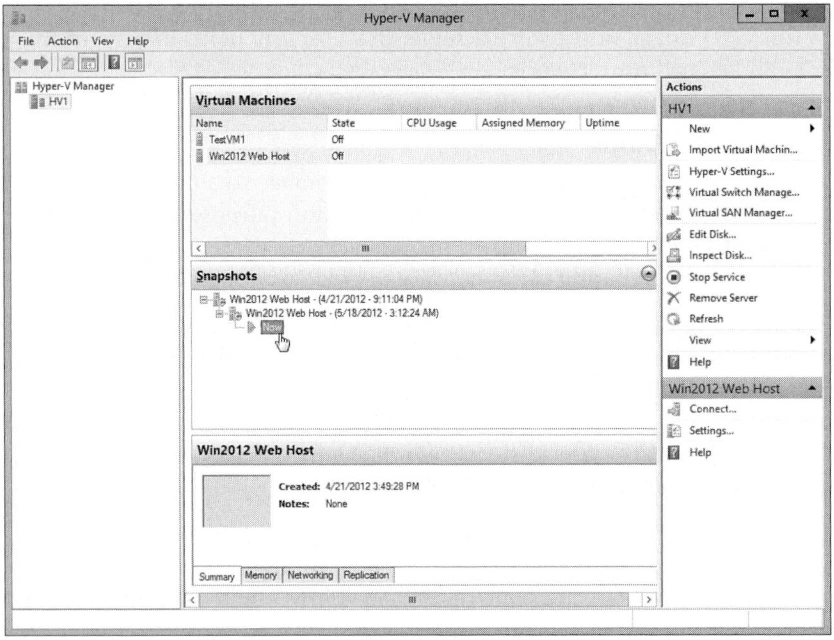

FIGURE 36.8 Snapshot of a running Hyper-V guest session.

Rolling Back a Guest Image to a Previous Snapshot Image

The term used in Windows Server 2012 Hyper-V to roll back an image is called *applying* a snapshot to an existing image. When an image is rolled back, the image that is currently running has the snapshot information applied to the image, thus bringing the image back to an earlier configuration state. To apply a snapshot, follow these steps:

1. From the Hyper-V Manager console, click the snapshot to which you want to revert the running guest image.

2. Right-click the snapshot image and choose Apply. The configuration state of the image will immediately be reverted to the state of the image when the snapshot was taken.

NOTE

By default, the name of the snapshot image takes on the date and time the image was created. For example, if the virtual machine is called Windows 2012 IIS, an image taken on September 2, 2012 at 9:42 p.m. shows up as Windows 2012 IIS - (9/2/2012 - 9:42:22 PM). Snapshots can be renamed to something more meaningful, if desired, such as Clean Build with All Patches.

Reverting a Snapshot Session

When working with snapshots, if you snapshot a session, the revert action can be used on the virtual machine to revert the guest session's state to the last created or applied snapshot. All changes since the last creation or application of a snapshot will be discarded.

Quick Migration and Live Migration

There are two forms of automated migration provided by Windows Server 2012 Hyper-V: quick migration and live migration. These migration processes can be used to increase service availability for planned and unplanned downtime.

Although both technologies achieve the same thing—moving virtual servers between Hyper-V hosts—they use different methods and mechanisms to achieve it. Both require at least two Hyper-V host servers in a cluster, attached to the shared storage system. The shared storage can be a traditional SAN over iSCSI or Fibre Channel, and with Windows Server 2012 clustering, shared storage can now be simply a Server Message Block (SMB) file share.

Quick Migration

The Quick Migration function provides a way to quickly move a virtual machine from one host server to another with a small amount of downtime.

In a quick migration, the guest virtual machine is suspended on one host and resumed on another host. This operation happens in the time it takes to transfer the active memory of the virtual machine over the network from the first host to the second host. For a host with 8GB of RAM, this might take about two minutes using a gigabit iSCSI connection.

Quick migration was the fastest migration available for Windows Server 2008 Hyper-V. Microsoft made considerable investments in Hyper-V migration technologies, trying to reduce the time required to migrate virtual machines between Hyper-V hosts. The result was the Live Migration feature, which has the same hardware requirements as Quick Migration, but with a near instantaneous failover time.

Live Migration

Since the release of Hyper-V v1 with Windows Server 2008, a highly requested functionality by organizations is the ability to migrate running virtual machines between hosts, with no downtime. VMware's VMotion has been able to do this for some time. With Windows Server 2008 R2 Hyper-V, doing live migrations between hosts was now done natively with Hyper-V for no extra cost. This made it a compelling reason to move to Hyper-V.

Live Migration uses failover clustering. The quorum model used for the cluster depended on the number of Hyper-V nodes in the cluster. In this example, we will use two Hyper-V nodes in a Node and Disk Majority Cluster configuration. There will be one shared storage LUN used as the cluster quorum disk and another used as the Cluster Shared Volume (CSV) disk, described later in this chapter. For more details on clustering, see Chapter 29.

NOTE

If there is only one shared storage LUN available to the nodes when the cluster is formed, Windows will allocate that LUN as the cluster quorum disk and it will not be available to be used as a CSV disk.

This section describes how to use Hyper-V Live Migration to move virtual machines between clustered Hyper-V hosts.

Configuring the Cluster Quorum Witness Disk

Live migration with shared storage requires a Windows Server 2012 cluster configured to use shared storage. Typically, these are LUNs provisioned on an iSCSI or Fibre Channel SAN. One LUN will be used as the witness disk for quorum and another will be used as a CSV to store the virtual machine images. The CSV will be configured later in this chapter.

The LUN for the shared witness quorum disk must be configured before the cluster is formed, so that cluster manager can configure the cluster properly. Connect this LUN via iSCSI or Fibre Channel to both nodes you will use for the cluster. The disk must be initialized and formatted with an NTFS file format prior to cluster use. When properly configured, both nodes share the same online Basic disk and can access the disk at the same time.

IMPORTANT

The Windows cluster service always uses the first shared disk as the cluster quorum disk. Provision this disk first on each node.

Now that the shared storage witness disk has been configured, we can move on to installing the Windows cluster.

Installing the Failover Clustering Feature

Before a failover clustering can be deployed, the necessary feature must be installed on each Hyper-V host. To install the Failover Clustering feature, follow these steps:

1. Log on to each of the Windows Server 2012 Cluster nodes with an account with administrator privileges.
2. From Server Manager, click the upper-right Manager, and select Add Roles and Features
3. In the Before you being option, click Next to continue
4. On the Select installation type page, select Role-Based or Feature-Based Installation, and then click Next.
5. On the Select Destination Server page, chose Select a Server from the Server Pool, which should have highlighted the server you are on, and then click Next.
6. On the Select Server Roles page, just click Next (not selecting any new roles).
7. When prompted to add features, select Failover Clustering (and when prompted to add features that are required for Failover Clustering, click Add Features), and then click Next.
8. On the Confirm Installation Selections page, click install to install Failover Clustering to this server

NOTE

On the Confirm Installation Selections page, click Restart the Destination Server Automatically If Required so that the server will reboot after installation of the Failover Clustering feature.

9. When the installation completes, click Close to close the information screen.

Running the Validate a Configuration Wizard

Failover Cluster Manager is used to administer the Failover Clustering feature. After the feature is installed, run the Validate a Configuration Wizard from the Tasks pane of the Failover Cluster Manager console. All nodes should be up and running when the wizard is run. To run the Validate a Configuration Wizard, follow these steps:

1. Log on to one of the Windows Server 2012 cluster nodes with an account with administrator privileges over all nodes in the cluster.
2. From Server Manager, select Tools in the upper-right side of the consultant, and select Failover Cluster Manager.
3. When the Failover Cluster Manager console opens, click the Validate Configuration link in the actions pane.

4. When the Validate a Configuration Wizard opens, click Next on the Before You Begin page.

5. On the Select Servers or a Cluster page, enter the name of a cluster node, and click the Add button. Repeat this process until all nodes are added to the list, as shown in Figure 36.9, and then click Next to continue.

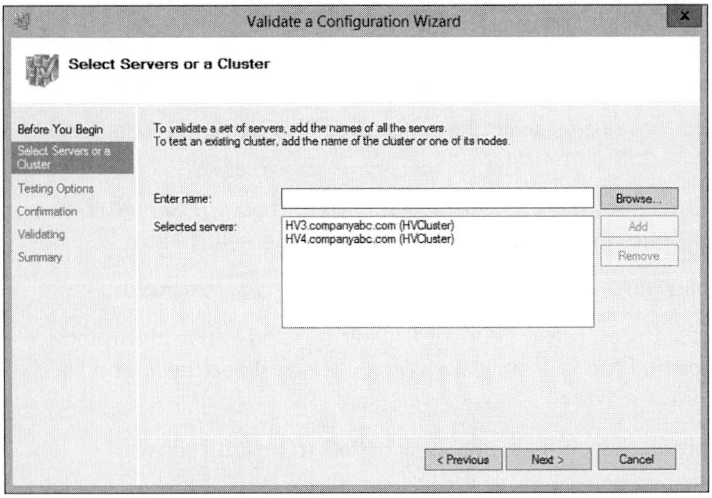

FIGURE 36.9 Adding the servers to be validated by the Validate a Configuration Wizard.

6. On the Testing Options page, read the details that explain the requirements for all tests to pass to be supported by Microsoft. Select the Run All Tests (Recommended) option button, and click Next to continue.

7. On the Confirmation page, review the list of servers that will be tested and the list of tests that will be performed, and then click Next to begin testing the servers.

NOTE

For years, administrators have complained that the Validate a Configuration Wizard window is too small. In Windows Server 2012, administrators can resize the window by dragging the lower-right corner. This is not obvious, but try it; it works!

8. When the tests complete, the Summary page displays the results, and if the tests pass, click Finish to complete the Validate a Configuration Wizard. If the tests failed, click the View Report button to review the details and determine which test failed and why the test failed.

Even if the Validate a Configuration Wizard does not pass every test, depending on the test, creating a cluster might still be possible. After the Validation a Configuration Wizard is completed successfully, the cluster can be created.

Creating a Node and Disk Majority Cluster

When the failover cluster is first created, all nodes in the cluster should be up and running. To create the failover cluster, follow these steps:

1. Log on to one of the Windows Server 2012 cluster nodes with an account with administrator privileges over all nodes in the cluster.
2. From Server Manager, click Tools in the upper-right corner of the console and choose Failover Cluster Manager.
3. When the Failover Cluster Manager console opens, click the Create a Cluster link in the actions pane.
4. When the Create Cluster Wizard opens, click Next on the Before You Begin page.
5. On the Select Servers page, enter the name of each cluster node, and click the Add button. When all the nodes are listed, click Next to continue.
6. On the Validation Warning page, select No. I Do Not Require. The validation test can be run after the configuration is complete. Click Next to continue.
7. On the Access Point for Administering the Cluster page, type in the name of the cluster, complete the IPv4 address (if DHCP services are not available), and click Next, as shown in Figure 36.10. The name you choose for the cluster will become a cluster computer account in Active Directory.

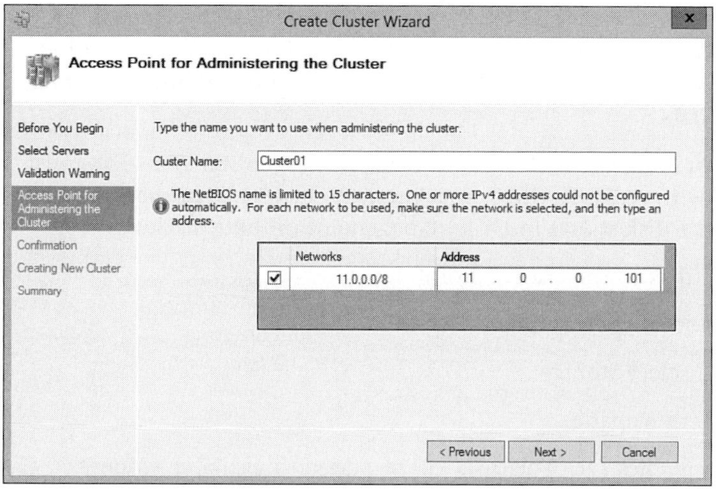

FIGURE 36.10 Defining the network name and IPv4 address for the failover cluster.

8. On the Confirmation page, review the settings, and then click Next to create the cluster.

9. On the Summary page, review the results of the cluster creation process, and click Finish to return to the Failover Cluster Manager console. If there are any errors, you can click the View Report button to reveal the detailed cluster creation report.
10. Back in the Failover Cluster Manager console, select the cluster name in the tree pane. In the Tasks pane, review the configuration of the cluster.
11. In the tree pane, select and expand Nodes to list all the cluster nodes.
12. Select Storage and review the cluster storage in the Tasks pane. The shared storage disk will be listed as the witness disk in quorum. This disk is used to maintain quorum.
13. Expand Networks in the tree pane to review the list of networks. Select each network and review the names of the adapters in each network.
14. Click Validate Configuration in the actions pane to start an automated review of the cluster configuration. See the previous section, "Running the Validate a Configuration Wizard," for more details. Keep in mind that Microsoft support for the cluster will require a successful execution of the validation process.

Adding Additional Shared Storage

At this point, we have a Node and Disk Majority cluster using a shared witness disk to maintain quorum. We can now add the shared storage that will be used as a Cluster Shared Volume.

Another LUN must be provisioned for the CSV to hold the virtual machine images used in live migration. This LUN may be a new unpartitioned volume or one that already contains virtual machine images and data.

Connect this LUN via iSCSI or Fibre Channel to both nodes in the cluster. The disk must be initialized and formatted with an NTFS file format prior to cluster use in the cluster. When properly configured, the disk shows in Disk Management on both nodes.

Next, we add the new shared disk to the cluster, as follows:

1. On one of the cluster nodes, open Failover Cluster Manager.
2. Expand the Cluster and select Storage.
3. Click Add Disk in the actions pane.
4. Select the disk to add and click OK. The disk will be added to available storage.

Configuring Hyper-V over SMB

Hyper-V over SMB is new with Windows Server 2012 and enables organizations to do clustering and failover of Hyper-V guests without a SAN. Hyper-V over SMB simply uses a Windows 2012 file share as the shared storage that Hyper-V users for live migration. With

Hyper-V over SMB, any node can host the virtual machine and any node can access the VHD on the SMB share, so virtual machine and disk ownership can move freely across cluster nodes.

NOTE

While Hyper-V over SMB is merely connected to a file share, the file share must be on a Windows Server 2012 server set up as a SMB share. A traditional Windows share (on Windows 2003 or Windows 2008) conceptually is the exact same thing, but Windows 2012 SMB provides a higher transport and transfer of data between the Windows 2012 SMB file server and the Hyper-V host that is needed for Hyper-V over SMB.

To enable and configure Hyper-V over SMB, you must first create an SMB share on a server. On a Windows Server 2012 with adequate storage space that will be used for the SMB share, add the File Services role to the system, as follows:

1. Make sure you are logged on to the server with local administrator or domain admin privileges.
2. Start the Server Manager console if it is not already running on the system.
3. Click Manage in the upper-right side of the console, and select Add Roles and Features.
4. After the Add Roles Wizard loads, click Next to continue past the Welcome screen.
5. On the Select Installation Type page, select Role-Based or Feature-Based Installation, and then click Next
6. On the Select Destination Server page, chose Select a Server from the Server Pool, which should have highlighted the server you are on, and then click Next
7. On the Select Server Roles page, select the File Services role, and then click Next.
8. On the Select Features page, because you are not adding any new features beyond the File Services role and features, just click Next.
9. On the Confirm Installation Selections page, review the selections made, and then click Install.

NOTE

On the Confirm Installation Selections page, selecting the Restart the Destination Server Automatically If Required check box will reboot the server upon completion. This is usually preferred; because the server will need to be rebooted, it might as well do it automatically upon completion.

10. After the server restarts, log on to the server with local administrator or domain admin privileges.

Once the file services role has been installed on the server that'll serve as the SMB share host, create an SMB share that will be accessible by the Hyper-V cluster host servers. To create a share, follow these steps:

1. Make sure you are logged on to the server with local administrator or domain admin privileges.
2. Start the Server Manager console if it is not already running on the system.
3. Click File and Storage Services.
4. Click Shares.
5. Click To Create a File Share, Start the New Share Wizard.
6. When prompted to select the profile for this share, choose SMB Share – Basic, and then click Next
7. In the Select the Server and Path for This Share section, choose the storage location where you plan to share (such as Share Location C:, or custom path e:\share, or the like), and then click Next
8. When prompted to specify the share name, give it a name that makes sense for this share, such as **HyperVShare**, and then click Next.
9. Choose whether you want to enable access based enumeration, Allow caching of share, or encrypt data access. (These items are usually left unchecked for Hyper-V shares because it is anticipated the access to this shared server will be protected and relatively limited. However, if this shared server and the Hyper-V hosts are in a semi-unsecured branch location or the like, encrypting data access may be of interest.) Click Next.
10. For your Specify Permissions to Control Access options, the defaults are usually adequate. However, with the assumption that the access from Hyper-V to this shared server will only be done by the Hyper-V host systems, customizing permissions to only allow the Hyper-V hosts to access the share will tighten security. The key is if you tighten security for the initial two or three cluster hosts you are providing access. If you add more servers, you'll need to make sure to modify the permission rights of the additional servers for continued access of the cluster. Make changes as necessary, and click Next to continue.
11. Review the settings and click Create to continue.

After the share has been created, go to each of the nodes of the cluster to validate you have access to the SMB share you just created. A simple test is as follows:

1. On each of the Windows cluster nodes, open Windows Explorer (the yellow folder thing at the bottom of the screen).
2. Enter the Universal Naming Convention (UNC) for the file share (which is \\server name\share name). In my example shown in Figure 36.11, it is \\file\smbshare\.

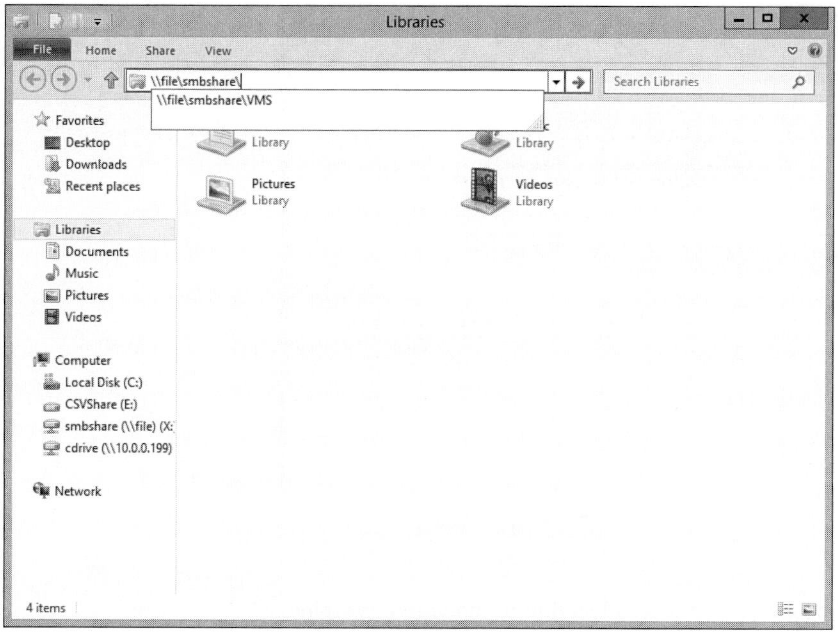

FIGURE 36.11 Verifying access to SMB share.

With successful access to the SMB share, you can now proceed to create a clustered Hyper-V virtual guest session.

Deploying New Virtual Machines on a Hyper-V Failover Cluster

After the desired cluster configuration and storage access is achieved, the cluster is ready for the deploying of virtual machines:

1. On one of the cluster nodes, open Failover Cluster Manager.
2. Expand the cluster and select Roles.
3. Now that Cluster Storage Volumes have been configured, the Virtual Machines application is available in the actions pane. Click Virtual Machines, New Virtual Machine, and then select the cluster node on which to deploy the virtual machine. (If you are unsure, just choose the first cluster node shown.) Then click OK.
4. The New Virtual Machine Wizard will launch. Click Next at the Before You Begin screen.
5. Provide a name for the new virtual machine and check the Store the Virtual Machine in a Different Location check box. Enter the path to the SMB share you just created (in my case, it is \\file\smbshare\vms), similar to what is shown in Figure 36.12, and then click Next.

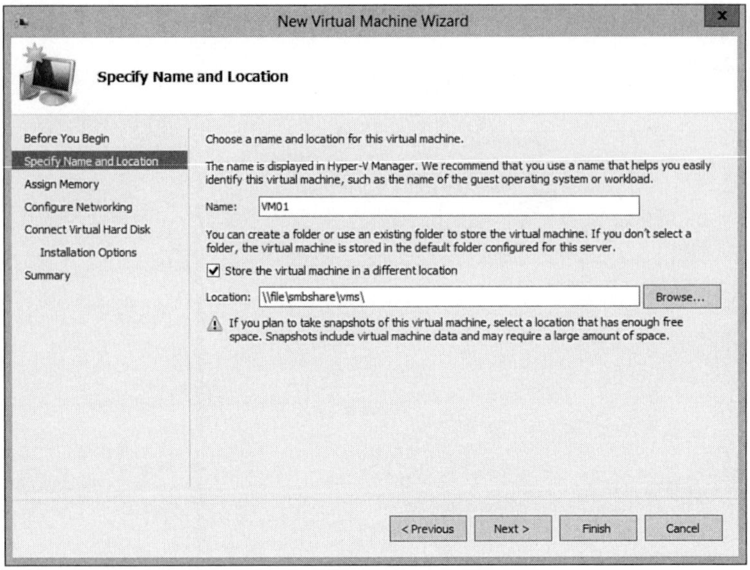

FIGURE 36.12 Specify the name and location of the virtual machine.

NOTE

It is recommended on Hyper-V servers using Live Migration to change the default location to store virtual machines to the CSV path. This is configured in Hyper-V Settings of the Hyper-V Manager console, as described earlier in this chapter.

6. Assign the desired amount of memory for the new virtual machine and click Next.
7. Select the virtual network, or choose Not Connected to configure it later. Click Next.
8. Create a new virtual hard disk in the SMB share folder or select an existing VHD, and click Next.

NOTE

Both the virtual machine configuration file and its associated VHD files must reside in the CSV folder location for Live Migration to work.

9. Select how you will install the operating system for the new virtual machine, either using a boot CD-DVD ROM, ISO image, floppy disk, or from a network-based installation server, and click Next.
10. Review the summary of the options you have selected and click Finish if the settings you've chosen are fine, or click Previous to go back and make changes.

11. Click Finish to create the new virtual machine. After the virtual machine is saved to the CSV path, the High Availability Wizard configures the virtual machine for use in live migration. Click View Report to review the step the High Availability Wizard used to configure the virtual machine for live migration.

NOTE

It is normal for the High Availability Wizard to report a warning if the operating system for the virtual machine will be installed from the host's physical CD/DVD-ROM, an ISO file, or a floppy drive. This is because the drive or file used for installation is not in a location available to the cluster. Most of the time, this does not matter, but it can be overcome if needed by installing the operating system from an ISO located on the CSV location.

12. Click Finish to complete the configuration of the new virtual machine.
13. Change the virtual machine settings, if desired, to increase the number of virtual processors, change the drive configuration, and so on.
14. Right-click the virtual machine in Failover Cluster Manager and select Start Virtual Machines to start the virtual machine and install the operating system.

Once the operating system is installed, you can use Live Migration to move the cluster from one node to another.

Deploying Existing Virtual Machines on Failover Clusters

If the storage provisioned as a shared storage in the cluster contains existing virtual machine images, these can be made highly available. You can also copy any virtual hard disk to the shared storage volume and make it highly available, as follows:

1. On one of the cluster nodes, open Failover Cluster Manager.
2. Expand the cluster and select Roles.
3. Right-click Roles and select Configure Role. This opens the High Availability Wizard.
4. Click Next on the Before You Begin page.
5. On the Select Role page, click Virtual Machine and click Next.
6. Select the virtual machines to be made highly available, as shown in Figure 36.13, and click Next.
7. Review the Summary page in the wizard and click Finish.
8. Select the virtual machine in the Roles pane and click Start to start the virtual machine.

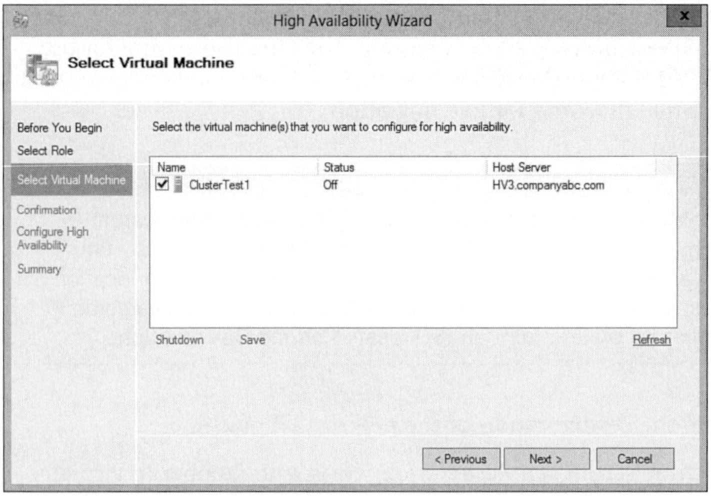

FIGURE 36.13 Selecting the virtual machine for high availability.

Performing a Live Migration

The virtual machine runs on one of the cluster nodes, known as the owner. When a live migration is performed, multiple steps are performed. These steps can be broken down into three stages: preflight migration, virtual machine transfer, and final transfer/startup of the virtual machine.

The first step in live migration occurs on the source node (where the virtual machine is currently running) and the target node (where the virtual machine will be moved) to ensure that migration can, in fact, occur successfully.

The detailed steps of a live migration are as follows:

1. Identify the source and destination machines.
2. Establish a network connection between the two nodes.
3. The preflight stage begins. Check whether the various resources available are compatible between the source and destination nodes:
   - Are the processors using similar architecture? (For example, a virtual machine running on an AMD node cannot be moved to an Intel node, and vice versa.)
   - Are there a sufficient number of CPU cores available on the destination?
   - Is there sufficient RAM available on the destination?
   - Is there sufficient access to required shared resources (VHD, network, and so on)?

- Is there sufficient access to physical device resources that must remain associated with the virtual machine after migration (CD drives, DVDs, and LUNs or offline disks)?

 Migration cannot occur if there are any problems in the preflight stage. If there are, the virtual machine will remain on the source node and processing ends here. If preflight is successful, migration can occur and the virtual machine transfer continues.

4. The virtual machine state (inactive memory pages) moves to the target node to reduce the active virtual machine footprint as much as possible. All that remains on the source node is a small memory working set of the virtual machine.

 The virtual machine configuration and device information are transferred to the destination node and the worker process is created. Then, the virtual machine memory is transferred to the destination while the virtual machine is still running. The cluster service intercepts memory writes and tracks actions that occur during the migration. This page will be retransmitted later. Up to this point, the virtual machine technically remains on the source node.

5. What remains of the virtual machine is briefly paused on the source node. The virtual machine working set is then transferred to the destination host, storage access is moved to the destination host, and the virtual machine is reset on the destination host.

The only downtime on the virtual machine occurs in the last step, and this outage is usually much less than most network applications are designed to tolerate. For example, an administrator can be accessing the virtual machine via Remote Desktop while it is being live migrated and will not experience an outage. Or a virtual machine could be streaming video to multiple hosts, live migrated to another node, and the end users don't know the difference.

Use the following steps to perform a live migration between two cluster nodes:

1. On one of the cluster nodes, open Failover Cluster Manager.
2. Expand the Cluster and select Roles.
3. Select the virtual machine to live migrate.
4. Click Move, Live Migration, and either let the Failover Cluster Manager choose the Best Possible Node or manually select Select Node and choose your preferred destination for the guest session. The virtual machine will migrate to the selected node using the process described previously.

NOTE

If there are processor differences between the source and destination node, Live Migration will display a warning that the CPU capabilities do not match. To perform a live migration, you must shut down the virtual machine and edit the settings of the processor to Migrate to a Physical Computer with a Different Processor Version.

Performing a Quick Migration

To perform a quick migration, the same process is followed, the difference is that during the quick migration the memory state of the guest session is not moved real time. The guest session is effectively hibernated and saved to disk, and then the guest session is restarted on another node. Quick migrations have 20 seconds to 2 to 3 minutes of downtime during the cutover process. If an application migrates across in a live migration without any performance problems caused by network bandwidth or disk performance, it is better to just do a live migration as the end state is the same. If you want to perform a quick migration, follow these steps:

1. On one of the cluster nodes, open Failover Cluster Manager.
2. Expand the Cluster and select Roles.
3. Select the virtual machine to quick migrate.
4. Click Move, Quick Migration, and either let the Failover Cluster Manager choose the Best Possible Node or manually select Select Node and choose your preferred destination for the guest session. The virtual machine will migrate to the selected node using the process described previously.

NOTE

The same processor differential for a Quick Migration exists as in a live migration in that if there are processor differences between the source and destination node, Quick Migration will display a warning that the CPU capabilities do not match. To perform a quick migration, you must shut down the virtual machine and edit the settings of the processor to Migrate to a Physical Computer with a Different Processor Version.

Utilizing Hyper-V Replica for Site-to-Site Redundancy

New to Windows 2012 Hyper-V is the ability to do a Hyper-V replica from one Hyper-V host server to another. A Hyper-V replica trickles changes of Hyper-V guest sessions from one host to another so that if the primary (source) Hyper-V fails or needs to be brought offline, the secondary (destination) Hyper-V guest session can be brought online. Unlike a live migration where there are two hosts and one VHDX virtual guest session file, in Hyper-V replicas, there are two hosts and two VHDX virtual guest session files, and information replicates from source to destination.

Hyper-V Replica is a great solution for a cross-datacenter environment in two separate locations, effectively "disaster recovery" of Hyper-V guests. In the event that Site A fails, Site B can come online with the guest session. However, before getting too excited about making Hyper-V Replica the sole high-availability (local) and disaster recovery (remote) replicated solution, do note that Hyper-V Replica's replicate every 5 minutes, which is a nonchangeable configuration state. While changed state of the VHDX files is tracked, logged, and queued up to be sent to the destination server continuously, the actual transfer is queued up and batch sent.

In addition, Hyper-V replicas can only go from one server to a target server (one to one relationship), a Hyper-V replica cannot go one to many, or daisy chained from one server to another server to yet another server. For a high-availability and disaster recovery solution, an organization can set up a live migration cluster within a datacenter for high availability and near zero downtime, and then secondarily set up Hyper-V replica between sites for disaster recovery; that is a supported configuration.

The key to Hyper-V Replica is that it is included right in the box with Hyper-V. It does not require anything fancy to replica (no need for SANs, no need for Fibre Channel, no need for third-party plug-ins). You take any Windows 2012 Hyper-V host server, select a Hyper-V guest session, and choose to replicate that guest session to another Hyper-V host server and the pairing relationship happens, and the guest session data is replicated between the two servers.

Initial Hyper-V Replica Configuration

To be able to support Hyper-V Replica, the destination server needs to be configured to accept the replication of the source server Hyper-V guest session. And if you configure the destination server for configuration, you might as well configure the source server so that you can replica the guest session back to the primary server as part of the failback process. The configuration on a destination server is as follows:

1. On a Windows Server 2012 Hyper-V host server that you want to configure as a destination for replication, open the Hyper-V Manager console.
2. Expand the Hyper-V Manager navigation on the left pane, and click the Hyper-V host you want to configure as a destination server.
3. On the actions pane on the right, click Hyper-V Settings.
4. Click Replication Configuration and select Enable This Computer as a Replica Server.
5. Choose either Kerberos (HTTP) or certificate-based (HTTPS) authentication. Kerberos is the easiest to configure; because it is all done through Windows and Active Directory, no special configuration settings need to be done. However, certificate-based authentication (HTTPS) is more secure because the data is sent over the network encrypted. In addition, if you plan to replicate guest sessions on Hyper-V hosts that are not part of an Active Domain (that is, Hyper-V hosts that might be in a DMZ unsecure leg of a network, or a Hyper-V host that is being hosted in

a datacenter by a third-party cloud provider, or the like), then doing the certificate-based authentication is required for certificate exchange. If you choose Use Certificate-Based Authentication (HTTP), you are prompted to select the certificate in the Trusted Root certificate store of the local (destination server) you can currently configuring.

6. One the same Hyper-V Settings page, choose to allow replication from any authenticated server (and specify the directory on the local (destination) server where you want the guest images from the primary (source) server to be replicated to). In addition, you can choose to allow replication from the specified servers and choose servers you allow to receive replicated guest sessions from. The configuration will look similar to Figure 36.14. Click OK

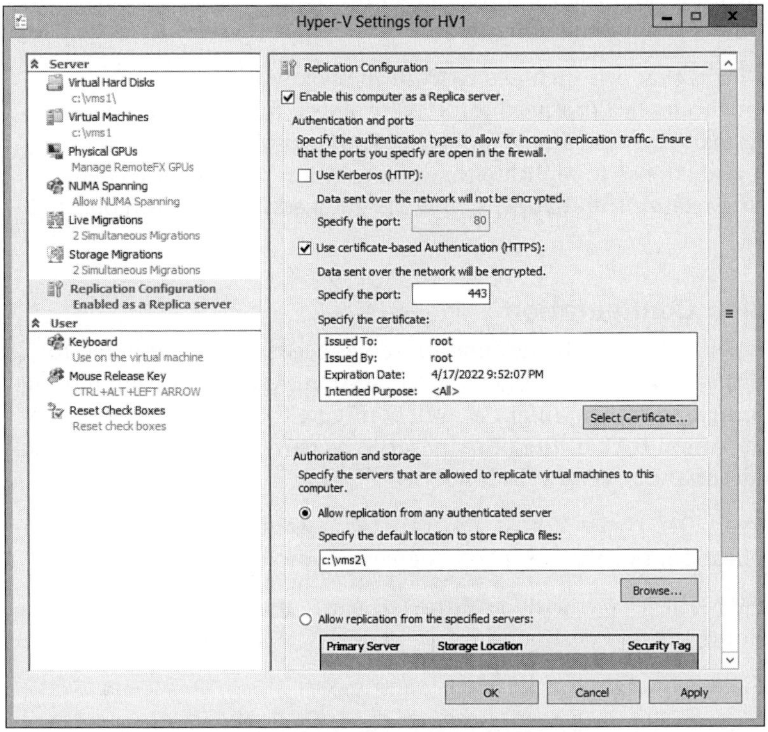

FIGURE 36.14 Hyper-V replication configuration settings.

Repeat this configuration on all Hyper-V host servers you intend to be destination servers for Hyper-V Replica.

Initiating a Guest Session to Replicate to Another Host Server

With the source and destination servers configured from the previous section, "Initial Hyper-V Replica Configuration," to initiate the guest session replication from one host server to another on the source server, follow these steps:

1. From within the Hyper-V Manager console, right-click the Virtual Machine in the Hyper-V Manager and choose Enable Replication.
2. In the Before you Begin section, click Next.
3. In the Specify Replica Server section, click Browse and choose your server, and then click Next.
4. If you get a "The specified Replica server is not configured to receive replication from this server" error, click Configure Server. Otherwise, if you followed the previous section steps already, skip to step 8.
5. In the Hyper-V settings under Replication Configuration, click Enable This Computer as a Replica Server.
6. For authentication and ports, choose either HTTP or HTTPS (prefer HTTPS as it encrypts the communications), choose to Allow Replication from Any Authenticated Server, and choose the directory where you want the VMs stored, and then click OK.
7. For Specify Connection Parameters, the Replica server should already be showing port 443. Choose Use Certificate-Based Authentication (choose the root CA), choose to Compress the data that is transmitted over the network, and then click Next.
8. For Choose Replication VHDs, choose the virtual hard disks you want to replicate (unselect those you do not want to replicate) and click Next.
9. For Configure Recovery History, choose either Only the Latest Recovery Point or choose Additional Recovery Points (and then choose 1 to 15 recovery points). The Latest Recovery Point option only keeps 1 replica. Many times organizations choose to replicate every 2 to 4 hours. If so, choose Replicate Incremental VSS Copy Every 1, 2, 4, or 12 hours as you see fit, and for additional recovery points, keep 4 or 6 recovery points so that you have a day of recovery points available in case of corruption or a problem. Click Next.
10. For Choose Initial Replication Method, choose Send Initial Copy over the Network, Send Initial Copy Using External Media, Use an Existing Virtual Machine on the Replica Server as the Initial Copy. Many organizations in testing just replicate over the network, which could take 2 hours to 2 days to replicate dependent on the size of the guest session and the available bandwidth between host servers. Alternatively, exporting an initial copy of the guest session to a USB drive and shipping the drive can save days of replication (especially if several guest sessions are involved). Choose to Start Replication Immediately or choose a time to start, and then click Next.
11. Review the summary and click Finish.

Checking Hyper-V Replication Health

To determine whether Hyper-V replication is working properly and the health of the replica, follow these steps:

1. In Hyper-V Manager, usually on the source server where your primary guest session resides, right-click the guest session and choose Replication, View Replication Health

2. View the Replication Health summary similar to what is shown in Figure 36.15. Key factors to view are the replication health, the replication state, and any pending replication. If there are errors, the errors are noted as well as an opportunity to click View Events (which opens event logging on the source server that'll provide more information).

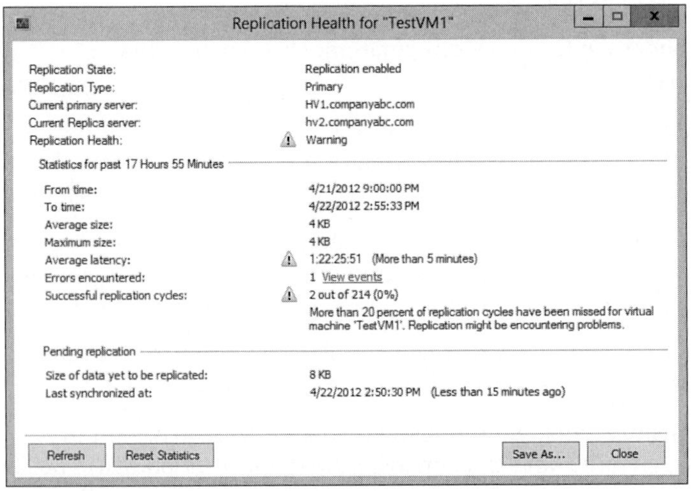

FIGURE 36.15 Replication health.

NOTE

If replication is working properly, the replication state will show Replication Enabled. Successful replication cycles will show several successful replications, and pending replication will be minutes of information (not days or information queued up still pending replication).

Planned Failover from Source to Destination Hyper-V Replica

To fail over a guest session to another site, a *planned failover*, follow these steps:

1. In the Hyper-V Manager console on the source server, right-click the guest session that you want to fail over to the destination server and choose Replication, Planned Failover.

2. Review the prerequisites for a planned failover, as shown in Figure 36.16. Pre-requisites include shutting down the source server. Click Fail Over to initiate the failover process.

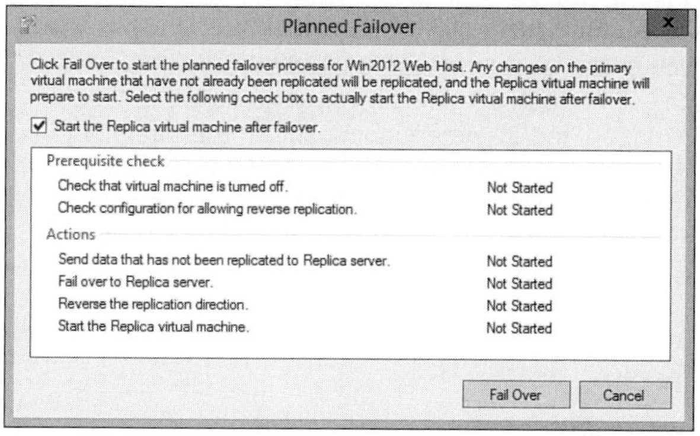

FIGURE 36.16 Planned failover of a Hyper-V replica.

The guest session will fail over from primary server to destination server and still start up as soon as the session fails over.

Unplanned Failover to Destination Hyper-V Replica

In the event of a failure event where the source server is nonresponsive, or the site is nonresponsive, and the organization needs to fail over to the destination server, follow these steps:

1. In the Hyper-V Manager console on the destination server, right-click the guest session that you want to fail over to the destination server and choose Replication, Failover.

2. A warning appears that notes that data may be lost because the last replication data has not transferred. Review the warning, as shown in Figure 36.17. Click Fail Over to initiate the failover process.

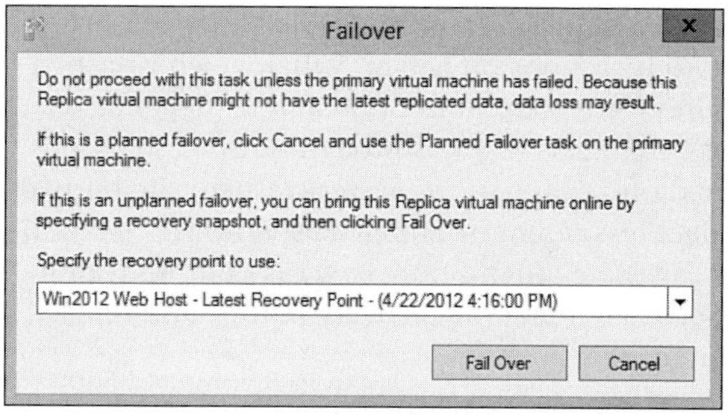

FIGURE 36.17 Initiating failover in an unplanned state.

NOTE

In an unplanned failover, the latest replica of the source server is used as the initial state of the recovered server. Some data will be lost, specifically any data from the last snapshot. Validate the state of lost information and its potential impact on the integrity of the system. For traditional file servers, relatively static web servers, and systems that have minimal replication, the loss of data will likely not be a problem for the organization. However, for SQL database servers, transaction servers, messaging servers, and systems where data integrity is highly critical, the use of Hyper-V replication for those instances needs to be considered.

Options in Hyper-V Replication Failover

In a Hyper-V replication failure state, you have several different options. Depending on the state of the replication, it is critical to understand the impact. Review these options carefully before proceeding with one or another state, because data loss will occur. It is best to test the assumed process in a lab before initiating a failover and failover recovery so that it is clear what the results will be and what data may potentially be lost in the process.

Assuming a guest session on Server A was replicating to Server B, and the connection between the two servers failed (WAN break, Internet connection failure, either Server A or Server B rebooted or temporarily went down), when the servers are back up and running and connection state has resumed, *if* Server A was not failed over to Server B, the administrator can simply go to Server A (the source server), right-click Replication, and choose Resume Replication. Replication then picks up where it left off, continuing to replicate from Server A to Server B. It might take some time for replication to catch up and for Server B to have a full updated set of data if Server A continued to operate for a long period of time while users continued to access Server A as normal. But no data would have been lost, and once Server B catches up for replication, it'll be available to be a failover destination target server.

In the situation where Server A failed for some period of time and Server B was manually brought online as a forced failover, then *all* transactions on Server A that weren't flushed to Server B would have been lost. This might be a few minutes of data; it all depends on the replication timing and how long it was before Server B was brought online. In the situation where Server A will never be turned on again (that is, server crashed, site burned down, site will never be recoverable), the data loss might be better than nothing. Server B can be brought online and operational. In this state, once a new server is built up (call it Server C), replication can be removed on Server B, including recovery points, and replication from Server B to Server C can be initiated.

If Server A failed for some period of time and Server B was manually brought online as a forced failover, and Server B came online temporarily, but the organization wants to just go back to Server A and resume replication, the administrator can Cancel Failover on Server B and the Resume Replication on Server A. Any data that was temporarily written to Server B will be lost. Server A will resume replication.

If Server A is failed over to Server B, and Server B is forced to be the main server, data written to Server A that didn't make it over to Server B in a replication cycle is invalid and lost. Server B would run for a period of time, and when Server A comes back online, Server A can be set to Remove Replication, and then on Server B, replication can be set to Reverse Replication. This will cause Server B to replicate to Server A, effectively overwriting what was on Server A with whatever is new in Server B.

Hyper-V replication is very powerful and provides an "in-the-box" solution for site-to-site failover and recovery. As with any high availability or disaster recovery solution, knowing exactly how it performs and testing the process is critical so that information is not accidentally lost when a process is initiated that deletes data that might otherwise be recoverable at a later date.

NOTE

When replicating between source and destination servers, one way to improve replication performance and eliminate unnecessary changes from source to destination servers is to exclude the pagefile.sys from replication. The pagefile is the size of memory of the server, which could be 8GB or 16GB or more in size. The pagefile changes as the contents of the server memory changes. But when it comes to real data in site-to-site failover, the pagefile is unnecessary for replication. Unfortunately there is no way to individually eliminate the pagefile from replication, so the way to eliminate the pagefile is to create a separate VHD, place the pagefile on that VHD, and replicate the VHD that has just the Windows, applications, and data, not the pagefile.

Summary

Microsoft Hyper-V has come a long way in just a few short years, and even further since Windows Server 2008 was released. With Windows Server 2012, virtualization provides organizations with a way to consolidate server applications onto a fewer number of virtual server systems and provide enterprise-level high availability and fault tolerance. Key to the release of Windows Server 2012, Hyper-V is the ability to perform live migrations without a SAN, reducing failover times from minutes to nearly instantaneous. This technology competes directly with other competitors, such as VMware, head-to-head, but at a much lower cost.

Hyper-V in Windows Server 2012 enables you to host Windows server, Windows client, and non-Windows guest sessions and consolidate dozens of physical servers into a single virtual server system. By adding additional virtual server systems to an enterprise, an organization can drastically reduce the number of physical servers it has, plus provide a method of implementing server redundancy, clustering, and disaster recovery without the need to double the number of physical servers the organization requires to provide better computing services to the organization.

Best Practices

The following are best practices from this chapter:

- Plan for the number of virtual guest sessions you plan to have on a server to properly size the host system with respect to memory, processor, and disk requirements.
- Have the installation media and license keys needed for the installation of the guest operating system handy when you are about to install the guest operating system session.
- Apply all patches and updates on guest sessions soon after installing the guest operating system, just as you would for the installation of updates on physical systems.
- For Microsoft Windows guest sessions, install the Windows add-in components to improve the use and operation of the guest session.
- After installing the guest session and its associated applications, confirm whether the memory of the guest session is enough, and adjust the memory of the guest session accordingly to optimize the performance of the guest session.
- Allocate enough disk space to perform snapshots of images so that the disk subsystem can handle both the required guest image and the associated snapshots of the guest session.
- Consider using snapshots before applying major patches, updates, or upgrades to an image session to allow for a rollback to the original image.
- Consider Live Migration rather than Quick Migration to quickly migrate virtual servers between hosts with little to zero downtime.
- Ensure that the hardware used in Live Migration is on the Windows Server 2012 compatibility list and is using the same Intel or AMD platform.
- Use Cluster Shared Volumes for Hyper-V live migration clusters and consider using the new Hyper-V over SMB replication for lower-cost (non-SAN required) failovers.
- Configure Windows Failover Cluster before adding shared storage, which will be provisioned as CSVs.
- For Live Migration nodes, change the default location to store virtual machines to either a Cluster Shared Volume path or a SMB share path that is accessible by all Hyper-V cluster nodes.
- Ensure that both the virtual machine configuration file and its associated VHD files reside in the CSV folder location for live migration virtual machines.
- Use Hyper-V replication for site-to-site replication of Hyper-V guest sessions for improved site redundancy.
- Test Hyper-V replication for failover and failback scenarios in a test environment before performing the replication in a live production environment on live data so that the results are clear and understandable before initiating any failover, re-replication, reverse replication, or the like.

Index

Numbers

A

B

C

D

E

F

G

H

I

K

L

M

N

O

P

Q

R

S

T

U

V

W

X

Z

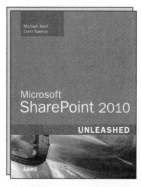

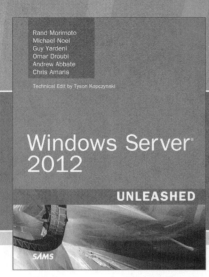